NEW PERSPECTIVES ON

# Microsoft® Office 2013

## FIRST COURSE

# NEW PERSPECTIVES ON
# Microsoft® Office 2013

## FIRST COURSE

**Ann Shaffer**
**Patrick Carey**
**Kathleen T. Finnegan**
**Katherine T. Pinard**
**Roy Ageloff**

**Lisa Ruffolo**
**Robin M. Romer**
**Joseph J. Adamski**
**June Jamrich Parsons**
**Dan Oja**

**Sharon Scollard**
Mohawk College

**Carol A. DesJardins**
St. Clair County Community College

**S. Scott Zimmerman**
Brigham Young University

**Beverly B. Zimmerman**
Brigham Young University

CENGAGE
Learning·

Australia • Brazil • Japan • Korea • Mexico • Singapore • Spain • United Kingdom • United States

**New Perspectives on Microsoft Office 2013, First Course**

Director of Development: Marah Bellegarde

Executive Editor: Donna Gridley

Associate Acquisitions Editor: Amanda Lyons

Product Development Manager: Leigh Hefferon

Senior Product Manager: Kathy Finnegan

Product Manager: Julia Leroux-Lindsey

Developmental Editors: Kim T. M. Crowley, Robin M. Romer, Mary Pat Shaffer, Sasha Vodnik

Editorial Assistant: Melissa Stehler

Brand Manager: Elinor Gregory

Market Development Managers: Kristie Clark, Gretchen Swann

Senior Content Project Manager: Jennifer Goguen McGrail

Composition: GEX Publishing Services

Art Director: GEX Publishing Services

Text Designer: Althea Chen

Cover Art: ©Michael Adendorff/Flickr Open/Getty Images

Copyeditors: Suzanne Huizenga, Michael Beckett

Proofreader: Lisa Weidenfeld

Indexer: Alexandra Nickerson

For product information and technology assistance, contact us at **Cengage Learning Customer & Sales Support, 1-800-354-9706**

For permission to use material from this text or product, submit all requests online at **www.cengage.com/permissions**
Further permissions questions can be emailed to **permissionrequest@cengage.com**

Some of the product names and company names used in this book have been used for identification purposes only and may be trademarks or registered trademarks of their respective manufacturers and sellers.

Microsoft and the Office logo are either registered trademarks or trademarks of Microsoft Corporation in the United States and/or other countries. Cengage Learning is an independent entity from the Microsoft Corporation, and not affiliated with Microsoft in any manner.

Disclaimer: Any fictional data related to persons or companies or URLs used throughout this book is intended for instructional purposes only. At the time this book was printed, any such data was fictional and not belonging to any real persons or companies.

Library of Congress Control Number: 2013937406

ISBN-13: 978-1-285-16764-0

ISBN-10: 1-285-16764-3

**Cengage Learning**
200 First Stamford Place, 4th Floor
Stamford, CT 06902
USA

Cengage Learning is a leading provider of customized learning solutions with office locations around the globe, including Singapore, the United Kingdom, Australia, Mexico, Brazil, and Japan. Locate your local office at: **www.cengage.com/global**

Cengage Learning products are represented in Canada by Nelson Education, Ltd.

For your course and learning solutions, visit **www.cengage.com**

Purchase any of our products at your local college store or at our preferred online store **www.cengagebrain.com**

ProSkills Icons © 2014 Cengage Learning.

Printed in the United States of America
1 2 3 4 5 6 7 19 18 17 16 15 14 13

# Preface

The New Perspectives Series' critical-thinking, problem-solving approach is the ideal way to prepare students to transcend point-and-click skills and take advantage of all that Microsoft Office 2013 has to offer.

In developing the New Perspectives Series, our goal was to create books that give students the software concepts and practical skills they need to succeed beyond the classroom. We've updated our proven case-based pedagogy with more practical content to make learning skills more meaningful to students.

With the New Perspectives Series, students understand *why* they are learning *what* they are learning, and are fully prepared to apply their skills to real-life situations.

## About This Book

This book provides thorough coverage of Microsoft Office 2013, and includes the following:
- Detailed, hands-on instruction of Microsoft Word, Excel, Access, and PowerPoint, as well as integration among the four applications
- Coverage of essential computer concepts, Windows 8 basics, file management, and Internet Explorer
- Exploration of exciting new features in Microsoft Office 2013, including Read Mode and the enhanced DESIGN tab in Word, Flash Fill and the Quick Analysis tool in Excel, the updated Backstage view in Access, and theme variants and the improved Presenter view in PowerPoint
- Introduction to cloud computing

*New for this edition!*
- Each tutorial has been updated with new case scenarios throughout, which provide a rich and realistic context for students to apply the concepts and skills presented.
- A new Troubleshoot type of Case Problem, in which certain steps of the exercise require students to identify and correct errors—which are intentionally placed in the files students work with—promotes problem solving and critical thinking.
- The new Capstone Projects appendix provides eight comprehensive projects, two for each application (Word, Excel, Access, and PowerPoint), that cover the major skills and concepts presented in the text, giving instructors more opportunities for assessing how well their students can apply what they have learned to new situations.

## System Requirements

This book assumes a typical installation of Microsoft Office 2013 and Microsoft Windows 8. (You can also complete the material in this text using another version of Windows 8, or using Windows 7. You may see only minor differences in how some windows look.) The browser used for any steps that require a browser is Internet Explorer 10.

# The New Perspectives Approach

### Context
Each tutorial begins with a problem presented in a "real-world" case that is meaningful to students. The case sets the scene to help students understand what they will do in the tutorial.

### Hands-on Approach
Each tutorial is divided into manageable sessions that combine reading and hands-on, step-by-step work. Colorful screenshots help guide students through the steps. **Trouble?** tips anticipate common mistakes or problems to help students stay on track and continue with the tutorial.

**VISUAL OVERVIEW**

### Visual Overviews
Each session begins with a Visual Overview, a two-page spread that includes colorful, enlarged screenshots with numerous callouts and key term definitions, giving students a comprehensive preview of the topics covered in the session, as well as a handy study guide.

**PROSKILLS**

### ProSkills Boxes and Exercises
ProSkills boxes provide guidance for how to use the software in real-world, professional situations, and related ProSkills exercises integrate the technology skills students learn with one or more of the following soft skills: decision making, problem solving, teamwork, verbal communication, and written communication.

**KEY STEP**

### Key Steps
Important steps are highlighted in yellow with attached margin notes to help students pay close attention to completing the steps correctly and avoid time-consuming rework.

**INSIGHT**

### InSight Boxes
InSight boxes offer expert advice and best practices to help students achieve a deeper understanding of the concepts behind the software features and skills.

**TIP**

### Margin Tips
Margin Tips provide helpful hints and shortcuts for more efficient use of the software. The Tips appear in the margin at key points throughout each tutorial, giving students extra information when and where they need it.

**REVIEW**

**APPLY**

### Assessment
Retention is a key component to learning. At the end of each session, a series of Quick Check questions helps students test their understanding of the material before moving on. Engaging end-of-tutorial Review Assignments and Case Problems have always been a hallmark feature of the New Perspectives Series. Colorful bars and headings identify the type of exercise, making it easy to understand both the goal and level of challenge a particular assignment holds.

**REFERENCE**

**TASK REFERENCE**

**GLOSSARY/INDEX**

### Reference
Within each tutorial, Reference boxes appear before a set of steps to provide a succinct summary and preview of how to perform a task. In addition, a complete Task Reference at the back of the book provides quick access to information on how to carry out common tasks. Finally, each book includes a combination Glossary/Index to promote easy reference of material.

# Our Complete System of Instruction

BRIEF

INTRODUCTORY

COMPREHENSIVE

### Coverage To Meet Your Needs

Whether you're looking for just a small amount of coverage or enough to fill a semester-long class, we can provide you with a textbook that meets your needs.

- Brief books typically cover the essential skills in just 2 to 4 tutorials.
- Introductory books build and expand on those skills and contain an average of 5 to 8 tutorials.
- Comprehensive books are great for a full-semester class, and contain 9 to 12+ tutorials.

So if the book you're holding does not provide the right amount of coverage for you, there's probably another offering available. Go to our Web site or contact your Cengage Learning sales representative to find out what else we offer.

COURSECASTS

### CourseCasts – Learning on the Go. Always available...always relevant.

Want to keep up with the latest technology trends relevant to you? Visit http://coursecasts. course.com to find a library of weekly updated podcasts, CourseCasts, and download them to your mp3 player.

Ken Baldauf, host of CourseCasts, is a faculty member of the Florida State University Computer Science Department where he is responsible for teaching technology classes to thousands of FSU students each year. Ken is an expert in the latest technology trends; he gathers and sorts through the most pertinent news and information for CourseCasts so your students can spend their time enjoying technology, rather than trying to figure it out. Open or close your lecture with a discussion based on the latest CourseCast.

Visit us at http://coursecasts.course.com to learn on the go!

### Instructor Resources

We offer more than just a book. We have all the tools you need to enhance your lectures, check students' work, and generate exams in a new, easier-to-use and completely revised package. This book's Instructor's Manual, ExamView testbank, PowerPoint presentations, data files, solution files, figure files, and a sample syllabus are all available on a single CD-ROM or for downloading at http://www.cengage.com.

### SAM: Skills Assessment Manager

Get your students workplace-ready with SAM, the premier proficiency-based assessment and training solution for Microsoft Office! SAM's active, hands-on environment helps students master computer skills and concepts that are essential to academic and career success.

Skill-based assessments, interactive trainings, business-centric projects, and comprehensive remediation engage students in mastering the latest Microsoft Office programs on their own, allowing instructors to spend class time teaching. SAM's efficient course setup and robust grading features provide faculty with consistency across sections. Fully interactive MindTap Readers integrate market-leading Cengage Learning content with SAM, creating a comprehensive online student learning environment.

# Acknowledgments

The entire New Perspectives team would like to extend its sincere thanks to the New Perspectives Office 2013 advisory board members and textbook reviewers listed below. We are extremely grateful to all of them for their contributions in the development of this text. Their valuable insights and excellent feedback helped us to shape this text, ensuring that it will meet the needs of instructors and students both in the classroom and beyond. Thank you all!

## New Perspectives Office 2013 Advisory Board

Brian Ameling, Limestone College
Lynn Baldwin, Madison Area Technical College
Earl Belcher, Sinclair Community College
Lydia Bell, Rasmussen College
Melisa Bryant, Forsyth Technical Institute
Kathleen Bent, Cape Cod Community College
Jennifer Day, Sinclair Community College
Mackinzee Escamilla, South Plains College
Hazel Freeman, University of Alabama
Sherrie Geitgey, Northwest State Community College
Jean Graham, Rasmussen College
Judy Grotefendt, Kilgore College
Dana Hooper, University of Alabama
Ralph Hooper, University of Alabama
Rahndy Jadinak, Rasmussen College
Beata Jones, Texas Christian University
Jamie Kretsch, Monmouth University
Jackie Lamoureux, Central New Mexico Community College

Diane Larson, Indiana University Northwest
Judy Matteson, Oakland Community College
Karen Miller, Hohokus Hackensack School
Don Naff, Charter College
Barb Neuwerth, Southeast Community College
Kathy Niebur, Dakota County Technical College
Karen O'Connor, Cerro Coso Community College
Nathan Plitzuweit, Rasmussen College
Anastasia Rashtchian, Rasmussen College
Gail Schroeder, Northwest Wisconsin Technical College
Susan Taylor, Highline Community College
Valerie Thompson, West Kentucky Community and Technical College
Terri Tiedeman, Southeast Community College
Joseph Torok, Bryant & Stratton College

## Textbook Reviewers

John Bojonny, Brown Mackie College
Cliff Brozo, Monroe College
Rollie Cox, Madison Area Technical College
Will Demeré, Michigan State University
Peggy Foreman, Texas State University
Deborah Franklin, Bryant & Stratton College
Maryann Gallant, Curry College
Debi Griggs, Bellevue College
Jennifer Gwizdala, Rasmussen College
Martha Huggins, Pitt Community College

Bill Hutchinson, Charter College
Diane Kosharek, Madison Area Technical College
Steve Luzier, Fortis Institute
Paul Smith, Brown Mackie College
Kerrie Specker, Rio Salado College
Bradley West, Sinclair Community College
Christine Yero, Madison Area Technical College

# BRIEF CONTENTS

# TABLE OF CONTENTS

## EXCEL TUTORIALS

**Tutorial 1 Getting Started with Excel**
*Creating a Customer Order Report* . . . . . . . . . . . . **EX 1**

# INTEGRATING WORD, EXCEL, ACCESS, AND POWERPOINT
*Creating Documents for a Green Initiative Plan. .* **INT 1**

# APPENDIX A INTRODUCTION TO CLOUD COMPUTING
*Sharing Files and Collaborating with Others
Online* . . . . . . . . . . . . . . . . . . . . . . . . . . . . . . . **APP A1**

# Essential Computer Concepts

## Learning About the Components of Computer Systems

## Case | *The Farmer's Wife*

Ten years ago, Elizabeth and Scott MacDonald started The Farmer's Wife, a fruit and vegetable stand in Oquossoc, Maine. Their business quickly grew to include flowers, gourmet foods, home-baked goods, wines, and seasonal items, including holiday decorations. Elizabeth and Scott have spent so much time building their business that they haven't had time to research and purchase an updated computer system. They need to buy a computer soon because several of their suppliers are switching to all-electronic ordering systems. Also, customers who visit the area in the summer have begun asking if The Farmer's Wife has a website from which they could order. Elizabeth and Scott ask you to research and recommend a computer system that fits their needs. They want a system that will grow with their business, but they have a limited budget to start (approximately $1500). They ask you to help them decide what to buy.

In this tutorial, you will learn about computers and their components. You will learn how data is represented, processed, and stored. You will examine input and output devices, how information is transmitted between computers, and ways to secure that information. Finally, you will learn about system and application software, and cloud computing.

**STARTING DATA FILES**

There are no starting Data Files needed for this tutorial.

# Visual Overview:

The monitor, keyboard, and mouse are **peripheral devices**, which are hardware components that are not part of the CPU or motherboard.

The motherboard, CPU, hard disk, and cards that expand the capabilities of the motherboard are inside the tower in a desktop computer or in the monitor in an all-in-one computer.

**Output** is the results of the computer processing input. The **monitor** is the device that displays the output from a computer.

**Input** is data or instructions you type into the computer. The **keyboard** is the most frequently used input device.

**Pointing devices** control the **pointer**, which is a small arrow or other symbol displayed on the monitor that you use to select commands and manipulate text or graphics. The most popular pointing device for a desktop computer is a **mouse**.

Our award-winning computers offer strong performance at a reasonable price. MicroPlus computers feature superior engineering, starting with a processor and a motherboard designed specifically to take advantage of the latest technological advancements. Of course, you are covered by our one-year parts and labor warranty.*

2015
BEST
TECH
!

COMPUTER
CHOICE
TOP
AWARD

QUALITY
PICK
2015

All credit cards welcome. Call 1-800-555-0000 today!

*ON-SITE SERVICE AVAILABLE FOR HARDWARE ONLY AND MAY NOT BE AVAILABLE IN CERTAIN REMOTE AREAS. SHIPPING AND HANDLING EXTRA. RETURNS ACCEPTED; CALL FOR AN RMA NUMBER (SEE YOUR INVOICE FOR DETAILS). ALL RETURNS MUST BE IN ORIGINAL BOX WITH ALL MATERIALS. DEFECTIVE PRODUCTS REPAIRED AT THE DISCRETION OF MICROPLUS. PRICES AND AVAILABILITY SUBJECT TO CHANGE WITHOUT NOTICE.

# Computer Advertisement

This desktop PC is powerful enough to meet your most demanding computing needs.

> The **central processing unit (CPU)** or **processor** is mounted on the motherboard and is responsible for executing instructions to process data.

> **Specifications** are the technical details about each component.

## SPECIFICATIONS

Processor: Dual-core 2nd generation Intel© Core™ i3-2130 (3MB cache, 3.4GHz)

Memory: 4GB DDR3 SDRAM (expandable to 16 GB)

> **Memory** is a set of storage locations on the motherboard.

Graphics: Integrated graphics processor

Hard drive: 1TB SATA

> A **hard disk drive** (also called a **hard drive** or a **hard disk**) is the most common magnetic storage device.

Monitor: MicroPlus 20-inch LED monitor with built-in speakers

Keyboard: MicroPlus USB ergonomic keyboard

Mouse: Wireless optical mouse

DVD/CD drive: Dual layer 16X DVD +/-RW drive

> A **DVD** is an optical storage device that can store 4.7 GB of data in a single layer on one side of the device and up to 17.1 GB of data in dual layers on both sides. A **CD** is an optical storage device that can store up to 700 MB in a single layer on one side.

Network card: Integrated 10/100/1000 Ethernet

Operating system: Microsoft Windows 8, 64-bit

USB ports: 6 USB ports

Speakers: Built into monitor

> A **port** is an opening on a computer connected to a card or to an appropriate place on the motherboard into which you can plug a connector. A **USB (Universal Serial Bus) port** is a high-speed port that allows multiple connections at the same port.

Video: HDMI, DVI, and VGA ports

Digital media card reader: 6-in-1 (Secure Digital, Secure Digital High Capacity, SDXC, Memory Stick, Memory Stick PRO, and MultiMediaCard)

Printer (not shown): Wireless MicroPlus PhotoPlus color inket printer and scanner

Installed software: 90-day trial of Microsoft Office 2013 and 30-day trial of Norton AntiVirus

> **HDMI (high-definition multimedia interface) ports** transmit video and audio digitally, **DVI (digital video interface) ports** transmit video digitally, and **VGA (video graphics array) ports** transmit analog video.

# What Is a Computer?

Computers are essential tools in almost all kinds of activity in virtually every type of business. A **computer** is an electronic device that accepts information and instructions from a user, manipulates the information according to the instructions, displays the information in some way, and stores the information for retrieval later. It is a versatile tool with the potential to perform many different tasks. Computers and prices are constantly changing, but most of today's computers are well suited to running a small business.

**PROSKILLS**

### Decision Making: Why Learn Basic Computer Concepts?

Although it's not necessary to become an expert in computers before purchasing one, it is a good idea to familiarize yourself with terminology and gain a basic understanding of how computers work before you spend your hard-earned money. Understanding the functions and capabilities of each system component helps you to make informed decisions so that you can purchase a system that will fulfill your needs within your budget.

**Personal computers** (**PCs**) are computers typically used by one person in a home or an office. A PC is used for general computing tasks such as word processing, manipulating numbers, working with photographs or graphics, exchanging email, and accessing the Internet. Figure 1 shows three types of personal computers.

| Figure 1 | Personal computers |

Desktop computer

Laptop                                                            Netbook

© iStockphoto/Alex Slobodkin, © Yulia Nikulyasha Nikitina/Shutterstock.com, © iStockphoto/teamtime

There are several types of PCs. **Desktop computers** are designed to sit on a desk and run on power from an electrical outlet. The computer in the advertisement shown in the Visual Overview is a desktop computer. **All-in-one computers** are desktop computers, but the motherboard and CPU are part of the monitor instead of in a separate tower. **Laptops** (also referred to as **notebooks**) are small, lightweight, and designed for portability. They can run on power supplied by an electrical outlet or on battery power. **Netbooks** are laptops that are smaller than typical laptop computers and usually less powerful, but have a longer battery life than laptops.

**Tablets** are a type of personal computer also designed for portability, but they are typically thinner than laptops or netbooks because they do not have a keyboard, and they have a touchscreen. A **touchscreen** is a display that, while showing you information, allows you to touch it with your finger or a **stylus**—a pen-like device used to interact with touchscreens—to input commands. Tablets vary widely in the tasks they can do. Some can do everything netbooks can do; others are more limited. Figure 2 shows two brands of tablets. Hybrids of laptops and tablets, sometimes called **convertibles**, also exist; these are essentially laptops that have a touchscreen. These hybrids are often used in doctor's offices and hospitals.

---

**Figure 2**      Tablets

Apple iPad

Google Nexus

© iStockphoto/mozcann, © iStockphoto/Petar Chernaev

The prices for desktop computers, laptops, netbooks, and tablets range widely from as low as $300 to as much as several thousand dollars for high-end machines. Many computer users spend between $500 and $1000 when purchasing a new PC.

**Mobile devices** are small computers that are designed to fit in the palm of your hand, run on batteries, and usually have more limited capabilities than PCs. One of the most common types of mobile devices is a smartphone like those shown in Figure 3.

---

**Figure 3**      Smartphones

© iStockphoto/Gergana Valcheva, © iStockphoto/Torian Dixon

A **smartphone** is used to make and receive phone calls; maintain an address book, electronic appointment book, calculator, and notepad; send email; connect to the Internet; play music; take photos or video; and even perform some of the same functions as a PC, such as word processing. The price of smartphones varies widely. In addition, to use all the capabilities of a smartphone, you need a contract with a cell phone company and must pay a monthly fee for access to its phone network and to the Internet.

Many small and large businesses use PCs extensively. But some businesses, government agencies, and other institutions also use larger and faster types of computers, such as midrange computers, mainframes, and supercomputers. **Mainframe computers** are typically used by larger businesses and government agencies to centrally store, process, and manage large amounts of data. The price of a mainframe computer varies widely, from several hundred thousand dollars to close to a million dollars. A **midrange computer** (sometimes called a **minicomputer**) is a computer somewhere between a PC and a mainframe in both size and power. Multiple computers can access midrange servers at one time.

The largest and fastest computers, called **supercomputers**, were first developed for high-volume computing tasks such as weather prediction. Supercomputers, like the one owned by NASA shown in Figure 4, are also used by large corporations and government agencies when the tremendous volume of data would seriously delay processing on a mainframe computer. Supercomputers can cost millions of dollars. However, a supercomputer's processing speed is so much faster than that of PCs and mainframes that the investment is worthwhile for agencies that need it.

| Figure 4 | Supercomputer |
| --- | --- |

Courtesy of NASA

Your initial recommendation to Elizabeth and Scott will be for them to purchase a desktop PC because most daily tasks can be performed very efficiently using one, and it will not require a large initial investment. They also might want to consider getting a laptop or tablet if they think they will be working in locations other than the store.

INSIGHT

## Converging Technologies

Every year, the lines between the types of computers are getting more blurry. Mobile devices such as smartphones are more powerful than the first laptops were, and today's desktop PCs are more powerful than the mainframe computers of a few decades ago. Tablets, which are available in several sizes and with varying capabilities, can be considered mobile devices rather than PCs. As new technologies are developed, consumers will need fewer and fewer devices to accomplish their tasks.

A computer has both hardware and software. **Hardware** is the physical components of a computer. **Software** is the intangible components of a computer system, particularly **programs**, or **applications**, which are the lists of instructions the computer needs to perform a specific task. You can use word-processing software to type memos, letters, and reports. You can use accounting software to maintain information about what customers owe you, display a graph showing the timing of customer payments, or keep track of your personal finances.

The advertisement shown in the Visual Overview includes several specifications describing the computer system shown.

# Processing Hardware

The hardware and software of a computer work together to process data and commands. **Processing** is modifying data and executing commands. **Commands** are instructions to the computer on how to process the data. For example, you issue a command in the word-processing program to instruct the computer to center the title in a report.

Processing tasks occur on the **motherboard**, which contains the processing hardware—the computer's major electronic components—and is located inside the computer. The motherboard is a **circuit board**, which is a rigid piece of insulating material with **circuits**, or electrical paths, on it that control specific functions. See Figure 5.

**Figure 5**    Motherboard

Courtesy of Intel Corporation

The CPU consists of transistors and electronic circuits on a silicon **chip**, which is an integrated circuit embedded in semiconductor material that is mounted on the motherboard and is responsible for executing instructions to process data. Figure 6 shows a CPU for a PC.

| Figure 6 | CPU for a PC |

Courtesy of Intel

Most PCs have a 64-bit processor, which means they can process 64 bits at a time. Some older PCs have 32-bit processors. A **dual-core processor**, which has two processors on a single chip, can process information up to twice as fast as a **single-core processor**, which has one processor on the chip. Likewise, a **quad-core processor**, with four processors on a chip, processes information up to four times faster than a single-core processor.

**Cards** (sometimes called **expansion cards**) are removable circuit boards that are inserted into electrical connectors on the motherboard called **slots** (sometimes called **expansion slots**) to expand the capabilities of the motherboard. A sound card, for example, translates the digital audio information from the computer into analog sounds that the human ear can hear. To display graphics, a computer must have a **graphics processor** (sometimes called a **built-in graphics card**) or a **graphics card**, also called a **video display adapter** or **video card**. The graphics processor or card controls the signals the computer sends to the monitor. For speakers to work, a sound card must be installed on the motherboard. The sound card converts sounds so that they can be broadcast through speakers.

## Input Devices

You use an **input device**, such as a keyboard or a mouse, to input data and issue commands. The computer can also receive input from a storage device. In Figure 7, the top keyboard is a standard keyboard. The bottom keyboard in Figure 7 is **ergonomic**, which means that it has been designed to fit the natural placement of your hands and should reduce the risk of repetitive motion injuries. Many keyboards, like the ones shown, have additional keys programmed as shortcut keys to commonly used functions.

| Figure 7 | Keyboards |
|---|---|

© Creativa/Shutterstock.com, © Petr Malyshev/Shutterstock.com

When you use a pointing device to move the pointer on the screen and then click, you are providing input by issuing an instruction. The most common pointing device is a mouse, shown on the left in Figure 8. To move the pointer using a mouse, you slide the entire mouse around on your desk. To select items on the screen or execute an instruction, you point to something and then click a button on the mouse. A mouse usually has a **scroll wheel** that you roll to scroll the page on the screen and that also might function as a button. A **trackball**, such as the one shown in the middle in Figure 8, is similar to a mouse except that you control the movement of the pointer by moving only the ball. Notebook computers are usually equipped with a touchpad, as shown on the right in Figure 8. A **touchpad** is a touch-sensitive device on which you drag your finger to control the pointer. The buttons are located below the touchpad. When you use a touchscreen, there is no pointer. Instead, you tap or swipe your finger across the screen to input commands or scroll. If you do not have a touchscreen, you can use an external touchpad to use the same commands as with a touchscreen.

| Figure 8 | Personal computer pointing devices |
|---|---|

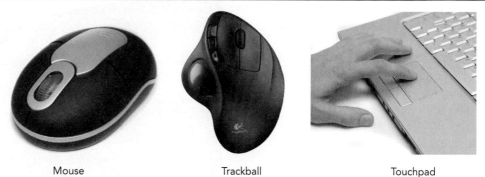

Mouse          Trackball          Touchpad

© NIKSPHOTO dot COM/Shutterstock.com, Courtesy of Logitech, © INSAGO/Shutterstock.com

A **scanner** transfers the content on a piece of paper into memory. When you place a piece of paper on the glass, a beam of light moves across the glass, similar to a photocopier, and the images or words on the paper are stored as digital information. You can scan a document or a photo and save it as an image file, or you can scan a document and have the text "read" by the scanner and saved in a document file for editing later.

Microphones are another type of input device. You can use them to record sound for certain types of files, or, if you have voice-recognition software, you can use them to input data and commands.

Web cams are included with many computers. With a **web cam**, you can send pictures and video of yourself to others. You can also use a web cam to talk to others using a video phone service that connects over the Internet, such as Skype.

The input devices that come with the system advertised in the Visual Overview are a mouse, an ergonomic keyboard, and a scanner that is built into the printer.

### Understanding Assistive Devices

People with physical impairments or disabilities can use computers because of technology that makes computers accessible. For example, people who cannot use their arms or hands instead can use foot, head, or eye movements to control the pointer. People with poor vision can use keyboards with large keys for input, screen enlargers to enlarge the type and images on the monitor, or screen readers to read the content on the screen aloud. Computers have even been developed that can be controlled by a person's thoughts—that is, the brain's electromagnetic waves.

# Output Devices

**Output devices** store or show you output. The most common devices for displaying output are monitors and printers. The monitor shown in Figure 9 is a **flat panel monitor** or a **flat screen monitor**. Some flat panel monitors use **LCD** (**liquid crystal display**) technology, which creates the image you see on the screen by manipulating light within a layer of liquid crystal. This is the same technology used in digital watches or the time display on a microwave oven. LCD monitors require a backlight. Flat-panel monitors labeled as **LED** (**light emitting diode**) monitors use LEDs to provide the backlight. LED backlighting is more energy efficient than ordinary backlighting.

**Figure 9**    Flat panel monitor

© iStockphoto/Alex Slobodkin

**Screen size** is the diagonal measurement from one corner of the screen to the other (not including the plastic housing). Desktop monitors range from 18 to 32 inches. Most monitors on laptops are approximately 15 or 17 inches.

Monitor screens are divided into a matrix of small dots called **pixels**. The number of pixels the monitor displays is the **screen resolution**, which is expressed as horizontal and vertical measurements, such as 1366x768, 1600x900, or 1920x1200. The higher these numbers are, the smaller the objects appear because more objects can fit on the screen at once.

**TIP**

The viewing angle is not always given in computer ads.

The horizontal **viewing angle** indicates how far to the side you can be and still see the images on the screen clearly, and the vertical viewing angle indicates how far above or below the monitor you can be. It is measured in degrees up to 180. The higher the number, the wider the viewing angle. If the measurement is written as a fraction in the manufacturer's description of a monitor, the top number is the horizontal viewing angle and the bottom is the vertical viewing angle.

The monitor included with the computer advertised in the Visual Overview is a 20-inch flat panel LED monitor.

A **printer** produces a paper copy of the text or graphics processed by the computer. Printed computer output is called **hard copy** because it is more tangible than the electronic version found in the computer or on the monitor.

**Laser printers**, such as the one shown on the left in Figure 10, use the same technology as a photocopier to create a temporary image on paper and then spray it with a powdery substance called **toner**. The speed of laser printers is measured in **pages per minute** (**ppm**). Laser printers are a popular choice for businesses because they produce high-quality output quickly and efficiently.

---

**Figure 10** ▶ **Printers**

Laser printer

Inkjet printer

© Ihor Pasternak/Shutterstock.com, Courtesy of Epson America Inc.

**Inkjet printers**, such as the one shown on the right in Figure 10, spray ink onto paper. The quality of the inkjet output is comparable to a laser printer's output. The speed of inkjet printers is also measured in pages per minute. Although inkjet printers and ink cartridges are less expensive than laser printers and toner cartridges, the ink for inkjet printers needs to be replaced far more often than the toner for laser printers. Inkjet printers are popular for home use. Most inkjet printers are called "all-in-one" because they include a scanner, a photocopier, and fax capabilities.

Another type of printer is the dot matrix printer. **Dot matrix printers** transfer ink to the paper by striking a ribbon with pins. Dot matrix printers are most often used to print a large number of pages fairly quickly, or multipage, continuous forms such as payroll checks. The speed of dot matrix printers is measured in **characters per second** (**cps**).

**Speakers** allow you to hear sounds from the computer. Speakers can be separate peripheral devices attached to the computer, or they can be built into the computer or monitor.

In the computer advertised in the Visual Overview, speakers are built into the monitor. It also includes a color inkjet printer, although it is not shown. Elizabeth and Scott might want to consider upgrading to a color laser printer that will enable them to print high-quality correspondence, advertisements, and brochures.

# Connecting Peripheral Devices

An external peripheral device connects to the computer either via a cable from the device to the computer or wirelessly. If you are using a cable, the cable connects to the computer in a port. Personal computers can have several types of ports. See Figure 11. Ports are connected to cards or to appropriate places on the motherboard.

| Figure 11 | Ports on a desktop PC |

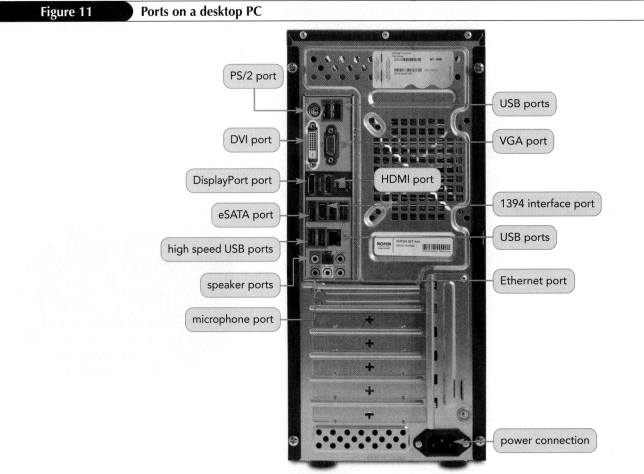

© Quiet PC LLP

Monitors are connected to computers through display ports. Common types of display ports used to transmit digital video are HDMI, DVI, and DisplayPort. VGA ports are used to transmit analog video. Speakers and a microphone connect to a computer via ports on the sound card. A keyboard and a mouse connect via **PS/2 ports** or USB ports. A wireless keyboard or mouse often connects via a special connector that plugs into a USB port. Printers also connect via a USB port.

**Ethernet ports** allow data to be transmitted at high speeds. You can connect to another computer, a LAN, a **modem** (a device that connects your computer to a standard telephone jack or to a cable connection), or sometimes directly to the Internet using an Ethernet port.

USB ports are high-speed ports that are not dedicated to any particular peripheral device. Any device that has a **USB connector**, such as the one shown in Figure 12, can connect to a USB port. Any USB device can use any USB port interchangeably and in any order. For most USB devices, power is supplied via the port, so there is no need for extra power cables. USB ports are either 1.0, 2.0, or 3.0, with 3.0 able to transmit data the fastest. The computer shown in the advertisement in the Visual Overview has six USB ports—two of them are on the front of the computer and the others are on the back. Two other types of ports that provide high-speed data transfer are 1394 and eSATA ports.

| Figure 12 | USB connector |

© Ramon Espelt Photography/Shutterstock.com

# Data Representation

**Data** refers to the words, numbers, figures, sounds, and graphics that describe people, events, things, and ideas. To a computer, the characters used in human language, such as the characters in a word-processed document, are meaningless because the computer is an electronic device. Like a light bulb, the computer must interpret every signal as either "on" or "off." To do this, a computer represents every piece of data as distinct or separate numbers; specifically, it represents "on" with a 1 and "off" with a 0. Each of these numbers, called **binary digits**, or **bits**, is the smallest piece of data a computer can process. Each character you type is represented by 8 bits. For example, the 8 bits that represent the number 0 are 00000000, with all eight bits "off" or set to 0.

A series of eight bits is called a **byte**. Processing capacity, storage capacity, and file sizes are all measured in bytes. A **kilobyte** (**KB** or simply **K**) is 1024 bytes, or approximately one thousand bytes; a **megabyte** (**MB**) is 1,048,576 bytes, or about one million bytes; a **gigabyte** (**GB**) is 1,073,741,824 bytes, or about one billion bytes; a **terabyte** (**TB**) is 1024 GB, or approximately one trillion bytes; and a **petabyte** (**PB**) is approximately 1000 terabytes.

# Memory

A computer has several types of memory. **Random access memory** (**RAM**), which consists of chips on cards that plug into the motherboard, temporarily holds programs and data while the computer is on and allows the computer to access that information randomly; in other words, RAM doesn't need to access data in the same sequence in which it was stored. For example, when you write a report, the CPU temporarily copies the word-processing program into RAM so that the CPU can quickly access the instructions you need as you type and format the report. The characters you type are also stored in RAM. RAM is **volatile memory** or **temporary memory** because it constantly changes while the computer is on and clears when the computer is turned off. Most PCs use **DDR SDRAM**, which stands for "double data rate synchronous dynamic random access memory." RAM is measured in gigabytes (GB).

**Cache memory**, sometimes called **RAM cache** or **CPU cache**, is a special, high-speed memory chip on the motherboard or CPU. Because the computer can access cache memory more quickly than RAM, frequently and recently accessed data and commands are stored there instead of in RAM.

The computer advertised in the Visual Overview has 4 GB of RAM and 3 MB of cache memory. Next to the RAM specification, the note "expandable to 16 GB" indicates that you can add more RAM to this computer.

**Read-only memory** (**ROM**) is a chip on the motherboard prerecorded with instructions the computer uses to check its components to ensure they are working, and to activate the software that provides the computer's basic functionality when you turn it on. This set of instructions, called the **BIOS** (basic input/output system), tells the computer to initialize the motherboard, how to recognize devices connected to the computer, and to start the boot process. The **boot process** is the set of events that occurs between the moment you turn on the computer and the moment you can begin to use the computer. This is why turning on the computer is sometimes called booting up. ROM never changes and remains intact when the computer is turned off; therefore, it is called **nonvolatile memory** or **permanent memory**.

**Complementary metal oxide semiconductor** (**CMOS**, pronounced "SEE-moss") **memory** is a chip installed on the motherboard that is activated during the boot process and identifies where essential software is stored. A small rechargeable battery powers CMOS so its contents are saved when the computer is turned off. Unlike ROM, which cannot be changed, CMOS changes every time you add or remove hardware; therefore, CMOS is often referred to as **semipermanent memory**. CMOS stores the date and time because it retains its contents when the computer is turned off.

**INSIGHT**

*Upgrading RAM*

One of the easiest ways to make your computer run faster is to add more RAM. The more RAM a computer has, the more instructions and data it can store. You can often add more RAM to a computer by installing additional memory cards on the motherboard. Currently, you can buy cards that contain from 512 MB to 16 GB of RAM, and usually you can add more than one card. Check your computer's specifications to see what size RAM cards fit the slots on your motherboard.

# Storage Media

Because RAM retains data only while the computer is powered on, your computer must have a more permanent storage option. **Storage** is where the data you create and the instructions you use remain when you are not using them. All data and instructions are stored as files. A **file** is a named collection of stored data. An **executable file** contains the instructions that tell a computer how to perform a specific task; for instance, the files used when the computer starts are executable. A **data file** is created by a user; for instance, a report you write with a word-processing program can be saved as a data file. As Figure 13 shows, a storage device receives data from RAM and stores it on a storage medium, such as a hard disk drive or a USB drive, CD, or DVD. Later, the data can be read and sent back to RAM to use again. The information stored in RAM can be retrieved more quickly than information that is stored permanently.

**Figure 13** Storage and RAM

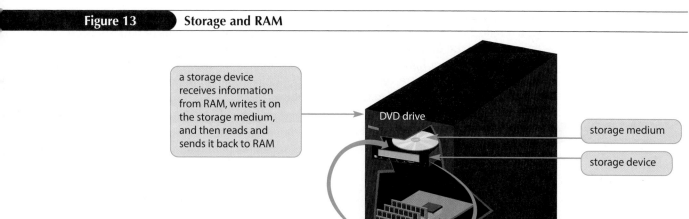

a storage device receives information from RAM, writes it on the storage medium, and then reads and sends it back to RAM

DVD drive

storage medium

storage device

RAM

© 2014 Cengage Learning

**Magnetic storage media** store data as magnetized particles on a surface. Before data is stored on magnetic media, the particles in the magnetic surface of the disk are scattered in random patterns. The read-write heads above the disk magnetize the particles to represent data.

Figure 14 shows a hard disk, a common magnetic storage device. It contains several magnetic oxide-covered metal platters that are usually sealed in a case inside the computer. The hard disk described in the ad in the Visual Overview has a capacity of 1 TB. Although this might seem like a high number, a computer fully loaded with typical software can easily use 18 to 20 GB of space, and disks fill up surprisingly quickly as you add data and multimedia files (pictures, music, and video).

**Figure 14** Inside a hard disk drive

© iStockphoto/Tyler Boyes

**Optical storage devices**, such as CDs and DVDs, are polycarbonate discs coated with a reflective metal on which data is recorded as a trail of tiny pits or dark spots on the surface of the disc. The data that these pits or spots represent can then be "read" with a beam of laser light. Figure 15 shows how data is stored on optical media. Optical storage media are very durable but not indestructible. Take care not to scratch the disc surface or expose it to high temperatures.

**Figure 15**    **How data is stored on an optical disc**

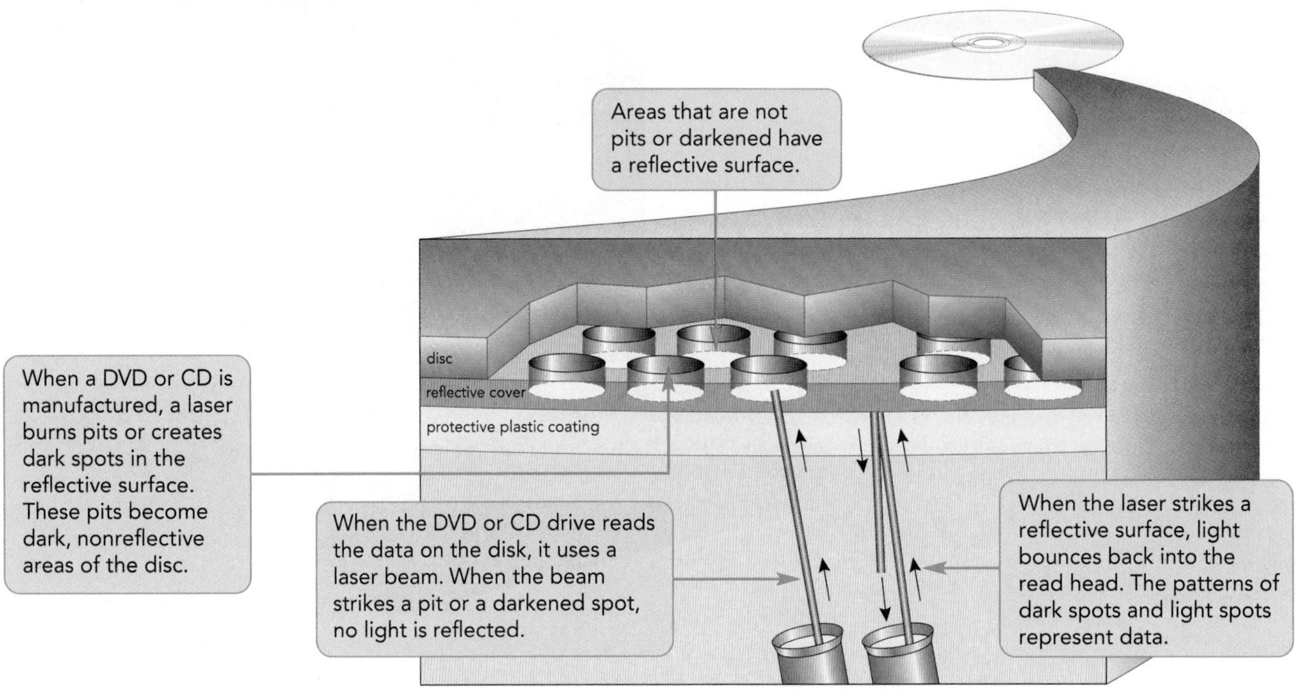

Areas that are not pits or darkened have a reflective surface.

disc
reflective cover
protective plastic coating

When a DVD or CD is manufactured, a laser burns pits or creates dark spots in the reflective surface. These pits become dark, nonreflective areas of the disc.

When the DVD or CD drive reads the data on the disk, it uses a laser beam. When the beam strikes a pit or a darkened spot, no light is reflected.

When the laser strikes a reflective surface, light bounces back into the read head. The patterns of dark spots and light spots represent data.

© 2014 Cengage Learning

To store data on a CD, you need to record it on a **CD-R** (**compact disc recordable**) or **CD-RW** (**compact disc rewritable**) disc. CDs that you buy with software or music already on them are **CD-ROMs** (**compact disc read-only memory**)—you can read from them, but you cannot record additional data onto them.

On a CD-R, after the data is recorded and finalized, you cannot erase or modify it. In contrast, you can re-record a CD-RW. Recordable DVD drives are also available. As with CDs, you can buy a DVD to which you can record only once, or a rewritable DVD to which you can record and then re-record data. Recordable DVDs come in two formats—**DVD-R** and **DVD+R**. Likewise, re-recordable DVDs come in two formats—**DVD-RW** and **DVD+RW**. DVD drives on most computers are capable of reading from and writing to both -RW and +RW DVDs and CDs, as well as DVDs with two layers. **BD-R** are Blu-ray discs that you can record to once, and **BD-RE** are Blu-ray discs that you can record to multiple times. You need a Blu-ray drive to use Blu-ray discs.

The data transfer rate of CD and DVD drives is measured in **kilobytes per second** (**Kbps**). The original CD drives transferred data at about 150 Kbps, but newer CD drives can transfer data at 7200 Kbps and DVD drives can transfer data at 21,640 Kbps. CD and DVD drives are typically classified as a multiple of the speed of the original drives. For CDs, this means 1X is the original speed (150 Kbps), 2X is twice the original speed (300 Kbps), 4X is four times the original speed (600 Kbps), and so on. The 1X speed for DVD drives is 1350 Kbps, so 2X is 2700 Kbps, and 16X is 21,600 Kbps.

Although CDs and DVDs are the same physical size, the amount of data they can store is very different. Refer to the Visual Overview for more information about the storage capacities of CDs and DVDs. A single-sided, single-layer DVD capable of storing 4.7 GB of data has more than enough storage capacity for an entire feature-length film—up to 9 hours of video or 30 hours of CD-quality audio. **Blu-ray discs**, which are used for storing high-definition video, store up to 500 GB of data on up to 20 layers.

The computer shown in the ad in the Visual Overview includes a 16X recordable/ rewritable DVD drive. It supports both the -RW and +RW formats.

**Flash memory** (also called **solid state storage**) is similar to ROM except that it can be written to more than once. **Flash memory cards**, like the one shown in Figure 16, are small, portable cards encased in hard plastic to which data can be written and rewritten. They are used in digital cameras, mobile devices, video game controllers, and other devices. The computer shown in the Visual Overview comes with a card reader so that you can insert flash memory cards and copy their contents to the hard drive.

| Figure 16 | Flash memory card |

Courtesy of Kingston Technology Company, Inc.

A popular type of flash memory is a **USB flash storage device**, also called a **USB drive** or a **flash drive**. See Figure 17. USB drives for PCs are available in a wide range of sizes from 1 to 128 GB of data. They are popular for use as a secondary or backup storage device for data typically stored on a hard disk drive. USB drives plug directly into the PC; the computer recognizes the device as another disk drive.

| Figure 17 | USB flash storage device |

Courtesy of Kingston Technology Company, Inc.

You'll recommend that Elizabeth and Scott purchase a computer with a DVD drive that can record DVDs. You'll also recommend at least a 1 TB hard drive and at least 4 GB of RAM.

# Networks

A **network** connects one computer to other computers and peripheral devices, enabling you to share data and resources with others. Each computer that is part of the network must have a **network adapter** to create a communications connection between the computer and the network. In wired connections, a cable is used to connect the network adapter port to the network. **Network software** establishes the communications protocols that will be observed on the network and controlling the "traffic flow" as data travels throughout the network.

Some networks have one or more computers called **servers** that act as the central storage location for programs and provide mass storage for most of the data used on the network. A network consisting of computers dependent on a server is called a **client/server network**. The dependent computers are the **clients**. These computers are dependent on the server because it contains most of the data and software. When a network does not have a server, all the computers are essentially equal, and programs and data are distributed among them. This is called a **peer-to-peer network**. A **router** connects devices on a network so all the devices can access network components. Figure 18 illustrates a typical network configuration.

| Figure 18 | Typical network configuration |
|---|---|

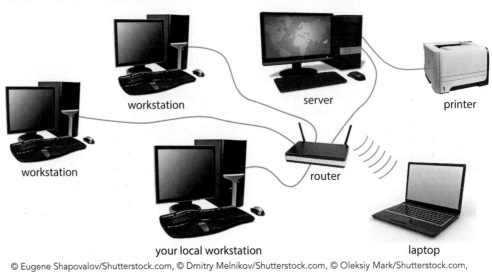

workstation

server

printer

workstation

router

your local workstation

laptop

© Eugene Shapovalov/Shutterstock.com, © Dmitry Melnikov/Shutterstock.com, © Oleksiy Mark/Shutterstock.com, © Maxx-Studio/Shutterstock.com, © Ihor Pasternak/Shutterstock.com, © 2014 Cengage Learning

In a **local area network** (**LAN**), computers and peripheral devices are located relatively close to each other, generally in the same building. A **wide area network** (**WAN**) consists of multiple LANs connected together. The Internet is the largest example of a WAN. In a **wireless local area network** (**WLAN**), computers and peripherals use high-frequency radio waves instead of wires to connect in a network. A **personal area network** (**PAN**) is a network that allows two or more devices located close to each other to communicate or to connect a device to the Internet.

# Data Communications

The transmission of data from a computer to a peripheral device or from one computer to another is called **data communications**. The four essential components of data communications are a sender, a receiver, a channel, and a protocol. The computer that originates the message is the **sender**. The message is sent over some type of **channel**, such as telephone or coaxial cable, a microwave or radio signal, or optical fibers. The computer or device at the message's destination is called the **receiver**. The rules that establish an orderly transfer of data between the sender and the receiver are **protocols**.

Data can be transmitted via a wired or wireless connection. To transmit data via a wired connection, you need to connect a cable to a port on the computer and connect the other end to another computer or peripheral device. To transmit data wirelessly, the appropriate hardware must be built into or attached to a computer.

Two common ways to transmit data wirelessly over short distances are **Bluetooth** and **Certified Wireless USB**, which both use short-range radio waves to connect one device to another. The devices must each have a Bluetooth or Wireless USB transmitter. The two devices must be approximately 30 feet from each other, although a new version of Bluetooth allows the devices to be up to 200 feet from each other. Other wireless technologies that are becoming more widely used for transmitting over short distances are **ultra wideband** (**UWB**), **WirelessHD** (**WiHD**), and **TransferJet**.

**Wi-Fi** (short for wireless fidelity) is a standard radio frequency established by the Institute of Electrical and Electronics Engineers (IEEE) that allows you to transmit data wirelessly over medium-range distances. The distance and speed at which data transfers varies depending on the hardware and the Wi-Fi version. The distance can range from 100 to 900 feet. Wi-Fi is the standard used to connect to the Internet at Wi-Fi hotspots, such as a public library, an airport, a college campus, or another public spot such as Starbucks or McDonald's.

WiMAX (short for **Worldwide Interoperability for Microwave Access**), another standard defined by the IEEE, allows computer users to connect over many miles. A WiMAX tower sends signals to a WiMAX receiver built or plugged into a computer. WiMAX towers can communicate with each other or with a company that provides connections to the Internet.

**3G** and **4G** describe the standards used by cell phone companies to transmit data. Exactly what is used to transmit data depends on the type of network and the phone in use. Some cell phones use mobile WiMAX to provide access to their 4G networks. A newer wireless standard used by some cell phone companies to deliver access to their 4G networks is **LTE (long-term evolution)**. To access 3G and 4G networks, you need to have a contract with a cell phone provider, such as AT&T, Verizon, or Sprint, and a smartphone, tablet, or other device that can access the network.

# The Internet

The **Internet** is the largest network in the world. People use the Internet to send **email**, messages sent from one user's computer to another user's computer. The **World Wide Web**, or simply the **web**, is a huge collection of information stored on network servers around the world. The information is stored as a type of file called a **webpage**, which can include text, graphics, sound, animation, and video. A collection of webpages is a **website**. A **hyperlink**, or **link**, is text, a graphic, or another object on a webpage programmed to connect to another webpage or file on any web server in the world. A **web browser** is software that you use to navigate the web. Figure 19 shows a webpage on the Library of Congress website.

| Figure 19 | Webpage on the World Wide Web |

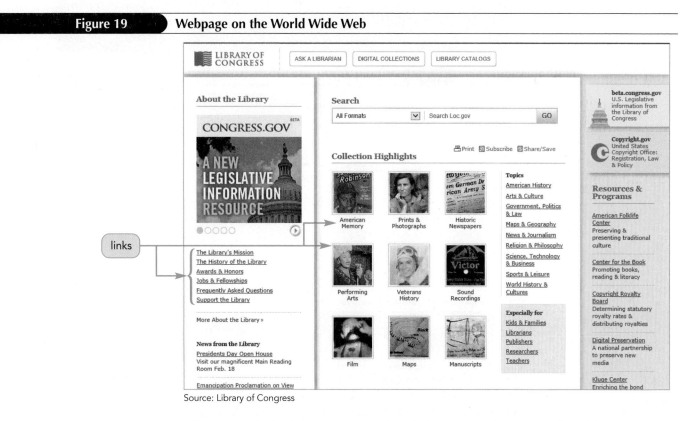

Source: Library of Congress

To connect to the Internet, you need a wireless connection or a modem. Most computers come with a built-in network and wireless adapters, and a modem to connect to phone lines. To use a high-speed connection over phone lines, such as **DSL (digital subscriber line)**, or over a cable connection, you need to purchase an external DSL or cable modem. High-speed connections are often called **broadband connections**.

A broadband connection will enable Elizabeth and Scott to connect to suppliers at other locations without waiting an undue amount of time to send and receive data. You decide to include the benefits of Internet and web access in your recommendation to Elizabeth and Scott. Specifically, you plan to convince them that they could sell their products over the Internet.

# Security Threats on Your Computer

After a computer is connected to a network, it is essential to protect the computer against possible threats from people intent on stealing information or causing malicious damage. **Malware** is a broad term that describes any program that is intended to cause harm or convey information to others without the owner's permission. One type of malware is a **virus**, which instructs your computer to perform annoying or destructive activities, such as erasing or damaging data and programs on your hard disk. Worms and Trojan horses are specific types of viruses. **Antivirus software**, sometimes referred to as **virus-protection software**, searches executable files for the sequences of characters that might cause harm, and disinfects the files by erasing or disabling those commands. Figure 20 shows the dialog box that appears when you use Trend Micro's free antivirus program on its website to scan your computer for potential threats. The computer advertised in the Visual Overview comes with a 30-day trial version of antivirus software.

| Figure 20 | Antivirus scan in progress |

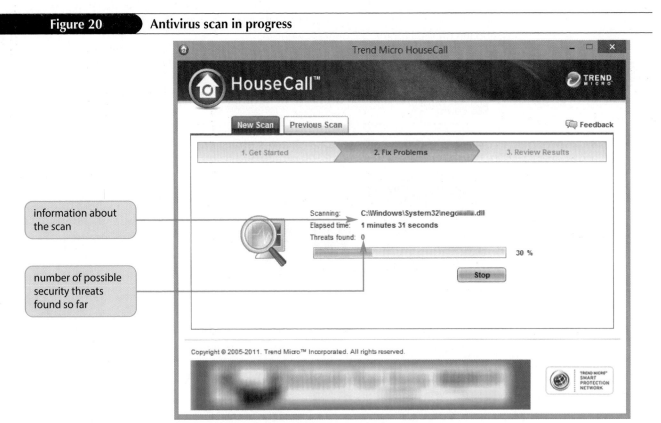

Source: Trend Micro Incorporated

Some software programs contain other programs called **spyware** that track a computer user's Internet usage and send this data back to the company or person who created it. Most often, this is done without the computer user's permission or knowledge. **Anti-spyware software** can detect these programs and delete them. **Adware** is software installed along with another program, usually with the user's permission, that generates advertising revenue for the program's creator by displaying targeted ads to the program's user.

Malware on one computer sometimes tries to access another computer without the owner's permission. A **firewall**, which can be either hardware (usually built into a router) or software, prevents this from happening.

Another way criminals try to gain access to personal information stored on computers connected to the Internet is to trick people into visiting a spoofed website. A **spoofed site** is a website set up to look exactly like another website, such as a bank's website. The spoofed site attempts to convince customers of the real site to enter personal information, such as credit card numbers, Social Security numbers, and passwords, so that the thief collecting the information can use it to steal the customer's money or identity.

One way criminals get people to visit spoofed sites is by **phishing**, which is the practice of sending email messages to customers or potential customers of a legitimate website asking them to click a link in the email message. The link leads to a spoofed site where the user is asked to "verify" personal information. If you receive a message like this, never click the link in the message. Instead, use a web browser to visit the organization's website.

**INSIGHT**

### Protecting Information with Passwords

You can protect data on your computer by using passwords. When you set up accounts on your computer for multiple users, consider requiring that users sign in with a username and password before they can use the computer. This is known as **logging in** or **logging on**. You can also protect individual files on your computer so that people who try to open or alter a file need to type the password before they are allowed access to the file. Many websites require a username and password to access the information stored on it. To prevent anyone from guessing your passwords, you should always create and use strong passwords. A **strong password** consists of at least eight characters of upper- and lowercase letters and numbers. Avoid using common personal information, such as birthdays and addresses, in your password.

# Computer Software

Software can be divided into two major categories—system software and application software. **System software** helps the computer carry out its basic operating tasks. **Application software** helps the user carry out a variety of specific tasks.

## System Software

System software manages the fundamental operations of your computer, such as loading programs and data into memory, executing programs, saving data to disks, displaying information on the monitor, and transmitting data through a port to a peripheral device. There are four types of system software—operating systems, utilities, device drivers, and programming languages. An **operating system** performs the following tasks:

- Controls the flow of input and output
- Allocates hardware resources, such as memory and processing time, so programs run properly; this allows computers to **multitask**—start and run more than one program at a time, such as producing a document in your word-processing program while you check your email
- Manages files on your storage devices so that you can open and save them
- Maintains security, such as requiring a username and password to use the computer
- Guards against and detects equipment failure by checking electronic circuits periodically, and then notifying the user if there is a problem by displaying a warning message on the screen

**Utilities** augment the operating system by taking over some of its responsibility for allocating hardware resources. Many utilities come with the operating system, but some independent software developers offer utilities for sale separately. **Device drivers** are computer programs that handle the transmission protocol between a computer and its peripherals by establishing communication between a computer and a device. When you add a device to an existing computer, part of its installation includes adding its device driver to the computer's configuration. **Programming languages** are software that a programmer uses to write computer instructions. Some examples of popular programming languages are BASIC, Visual Basic, C, C++, C#, Java, and Delphi.

Microsoft Windows, used on many PCs, and the Mac OS, used exclusively on Apple computers, are referred to as **operating environments** because they provide a **graphical user interface** (**GUI**, pronounced "goo-ey") that acts as a liaison between the user and all of the computer's hardware and software. In addition to the operating system, Windows and the Mac OS also include utilities, device drivers, and some application programs that perform common tasks. Figure 21 shows the Start screen for Microsoft Windows 8.

| Figure 21 | Windows 8 Start screen |

Windows 8, the newest version of the Windows operating system, requires a computer with at least a 1 GHz processor, 1 GB of RAM for the 32-bit version or 2 GB of RAM for the 64-bit version, a DirectX 9 graphics processor, and 16 GB of available space on the hard disk for the 32-bit version or 20 GB for the 64-bit version. Keep in mind that these are the minimum recommendations.

## Application Software

The primary factor in choosing specifications for a computer you purchase is the software you will be using. Application software enables you to perform specific computer tasks, such as document production, spreadsheet calculations, and database management.

**Document production software** includes word-processing software, desktop publishing software, email editors, and web authoring software. All of these production tools have a variety of features that assist you in writing and formatting documents, including changing the style of type or adding color and design elements. Most offer tools to help you avoid typographical and spelling errors, as shown in the document in Figure 22. The document in the figure was created in Microsoft Word 2013, the word-processing program included with Microsoft Office 2013. Many programs also provide grammar-checking and thesaurus tools to improve your writing by offering suggestions and alternatives.

**Figure 22**    **Document with a misspelled word**

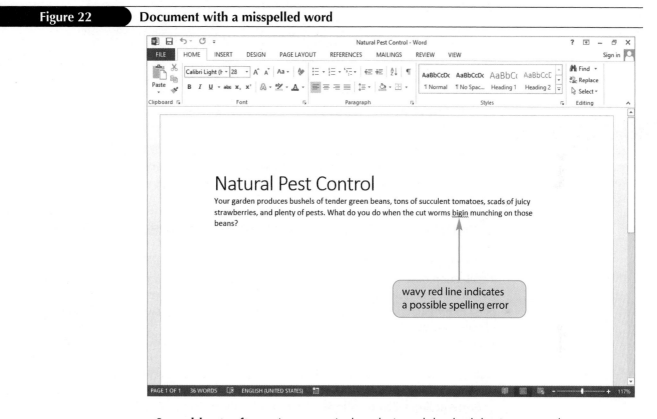

**Spreadsheet software** is a numerical analysis tool that both businesses and individuals use extensively. Spreadsheet software creates a **worksheet** composed of a grid of columns and rows. Each column is lettered, and each row is numbered. The intersection of a column and a row is a **cell**. You type numbers into the cells, and then create mathematical formulas in other cells that perform calculations using these numbers. With the appropriate data and formulas, you can use an electronic spreadsheet to prepare financial reports, analyze investment portfolios, calculate amortization tables, examine alternative bid proposals, and project income, as well as perform many other tasks involved in making informed business decisions. You can also use spreadsheet software to produce graphs and reports based upon the data. A worksheet created in Microsoft Excel 2013, which is included with Microsoft Office 2013, is shown in Figure 23 and includes a simple calculation and a chart that represents the data in the spreadsheet.

| Figure 23 | Worksheet with numerical data and a graph |

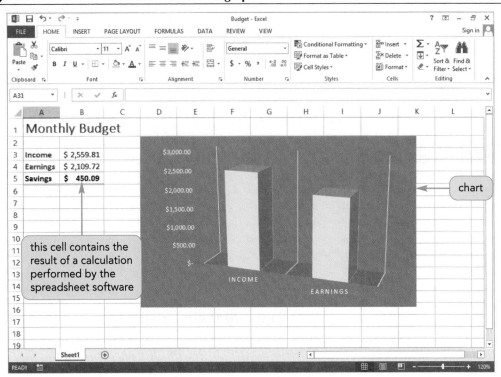

Database management software lets you collect and manage data. A **database** is a collection of related data stored on one or more computers organized in a uniform format. An example of a database is an address book or a contacts list that contains one tab for each person, and appearing on each tab is the person's name, address, phone number, email address, and birthdate. You can extract specific information from a database, such as a list of all the people in the database who have a birthday in July, and create reports to list the data in many ways. Microsoft Access 2013, which comes with some versions of Microsoft Office 2013, is an example of database management software.

**Presentation software** allows you to display or project text, graphics, video, and other information to a group; print them for quick reference; or transmit them to remote computers. Figure 24 shows a slide from a presentation created in Microsoft PowerPoint 2013, which is part of the suite of programs included with Microsoft Office 2013.

**Figure 24**    Slide in Microsoft PowerPoint 2013

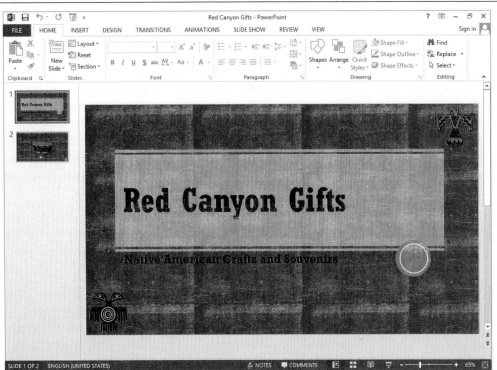

Information management software allows people to keep track of their schedules, appointments, contacts, and to-do lists. Some information software allows you to synchronize information between a handheld device such as a smartphone and a desktop or notebook computer. Microsoft Outlook 2013, the information manager and email software that comes with Microsoft Office, is shown in Figure 25.

**Figure 25**    Microsoft Outlook 2013 program window

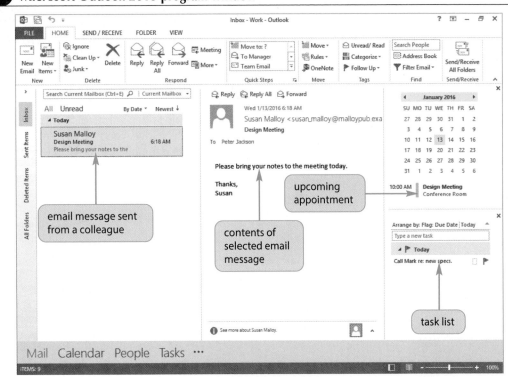

In addition to the application software included with Microsoft Office 2013, there are many other useful types of application software:

- **Photo editing software**, such as Adobe Photoshop and Picasa, allows you to edit and manipulate digital photos.
- **Video editing software**, such as Windows Movie Maker and Adobe Premiere, allows you to edit video by clipping it, adding captions and a soundtrack, or rearranging clips.
- **Graphics software**, such as Microsoft Paint and Adobe Illustrator CS6, allows you to create illustrations, diagrams, graphs, and charts.
- **Website creation and management software**, such as Adobe Dreamweaver, allows you to create and manage websites.
- **Multimedia authoring software**, such as Adobe Director, allows you to record digital sound files, video files, and animations that can be included in presentations and other documents.
- **Accounting software**, such as Intuit's Quicken, helps individuals and businesses input and track income and expenses, and create and track budgets.

Refer back to the Visual Overview. The computer in the ad includes Microsoft Windows 8 and a trial version of Microsoft Office 2013, as well as a trial version of Norton AntiVirus. Many computer systems are available with both the operating system and software installed, such as Microsoft Office. You should, however, examine the features of the software that is included, and research other available options.

# Computing in the Cloud

**Cloud computing** means that data, applications, and even resources are stored on servers accessed over the Internet rather than on users' computers, and you access only what you need when you need it. Many individuals and companies are moving toward "the cloud" for at least some of their needs. For example, some companies provide space and computing power to developers for a fee. Individuals might subscribe to a backup service such as Carbonite or Mozy so that their data is automatically backed up on a computer at the physical location of those companies.

Microsoft Office WebApps and Google Docs provide both free and paid versions of various applications that you access by logging in to their websites. In addition, if you purchase a subscription to Office 365 instead of buying Office 2013, you get access to Office on Demand, which is the cloud-based version of Microsoft Office. With Office on Demand, you can sign in to your account from any computer running Windows 7 or Windows 8 and use Office applications stored on Microsoft's server.

In addition to using services over the Internet, many people store files on servers accessed over the Internet. For example, SkyDrive is space on Microsoft servers where you can store files in public or private folders, or in folders that you make available to only people you specify. To access SkyDrive, you need a free Microsoft account. Figure 26 shows a user's SkyDrive. Many other companies offer storage space for file on their servers as well, such as Dropbox and Box.

**Figure 26**    SkyDrive start page

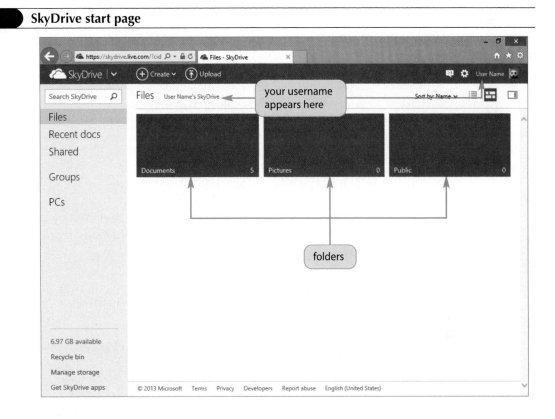

# Putting It All Together

Your recommendation for Scott and Elizabeth will include a PC with 4 GB of RAM, a 1 TB hard drive, and at least a 2.90 GHz processor, as well as document production, spreadsheet, and database management software, such as Microsoft Word, Excel, and Access. You want them to also add photo editing software; but because several free programs, such as Windows Photo Gallery, will probably suit their needs, they don't need to purchase that now. In addition, you will recommend that they purchase accounting software specifically designed for small businesses, such as Sage 50 Pro Accounting or QuickBooks. You will also recommend that they consider buying a high-speed modem and a router. The router will provide firewall protection now, and will enable them to easily set up a network when they expand their computer system. To complete their system, you will recommend that they purchase a 20-inch LED monitor and a color laser printer.

## Review Questions

1. Which of the following would not be considered a PC?
   a. tablet PC
   b. desktop
   c. mainframe
   d. notebook

2. The intangible components of a computer system, including the programs, are called:
   a. software
   b. peripherals
   c. hardware
   d. price

3. To display graphics, a computer needs a monitor and a(n):
   a. expansion port
   b. network card (NIC)
   c. sound card
   d. graphics card or processor

4. What part of the computer is responsible for executing instructions to process information?
   a. peripheral device
   b. processor
   c. card
   d. motherboard

5. Keyboards, monitors, and printers are all examples of which of the following?
   a. input devices
   b. output devices
   c. software
   d. peripheral devices

6. Which of the following is a pointing device that allows you to control the pointer by moving the entire device around on a surface?
   a. mouse
   b. trackball
   c. touchpad
   d. touchscreen

7. What do you call each 1 or 0 used in the representation of computer data?
   a. a bit
   b. a byte
   c. a pixel
   d. a point

8. What is a gigabyte?
   a. 10,000 kilobytes
   b. about a billion bits
   c. about a billion bytes
   d. one-half of a petabyte

9. The transmission protocol between a computer and its peripheral devices is handled by a:
   a. sender
   b. driver
   c. card
   d. channel

10. What are high-speed connections to the Internet often called?
    a. cables
    b. wireless connections
    c. broadband connections
    d. Wi-Fi

11. Which of the following temporarily stores data and programs while you are using them?
    a. peripherals
    b. RAM
    c. ROM
    d. the hard disk

12. When you turn the computer on, which of the following permanently stores the set of instructions that the computer uses to activate the software that controls the processing function?
    a. cache
    b. RAM
    c. ROM
    d. the hard disk

13. What do you call a named collection of data stored on a disk?
    a. a file
    b. a pixel
    c. a protocol
    d. the operating system

14. Which of the following is not a permanent storage medium?
    a. hard disk
    b. cache
    c. optical disk
    d. DVD

15. Which of the following prevents unauthorized access to a computer by another computer?
    a. DNS server
    b. firewall
    c. antivirus software
    d. spyware

16. Which of the following is not a function of an operating system?
    a. allocates system resources
    b. controls basic input and output
    c. carries out a specific task for the user
    d. manages storage space

17. Which of the following is system software?
    a. Microsoft Excel
    b. Microsoft Paint
    c. Microsoft Windows
    d. Microsoft Word

18. What are the technical details about each hardware component called?

19. What is processing?

20. What is a removable circuit board that is inserted into slots on the motherboard to expand the capabilities of the motherboard?

21. What is a display that while showing you the output, allows you to touch it with your finger or a stylus to input commands?

22. What is a printed copy of computer output called?

23. What is similar to ROM except that it changes every time you add or remove hardware?

24. What is magnetic storage media that is usually sealed in a case inside the computer?

25. What must each computer that is part of the network have installed in order to connect it to the network?

26. What is a computer on a network that acts as the central storage location for programs and data used on the network called?

27. What is a program that tracks a user's Internet usage without the user's permission?

28. What is software that a programmer uses to write computer instructions?

29. What is the term that describes starting and running more than one program at a time?

30. What is the term that describes data, applications, and resources being stored on servers rather than on users' computers?

# ☑ Decision Making

## Identify Your Needs Before Purchasing a Computer and Software

In order to effectively evaluate a potential course of action, data and information must be gathered. First, consider the tasks you want to accomplish. Do you want to surf the web and use email? Do you need to do financial calculations? Do you need to create complex documents with a lot of formatting and graphics, or only plain text documents? Do you plan to play games online? Decide what types of software you can use to complete these tasks.

Next, think about the peripheral devices you will be using. Usually you don't need to worry about choosing which ports to include on your computer. However, if you will be attaching many peripheral devices that connect to the computer via a USB cable, you might want to consider the number of USB ports included. You might also want to make sure the computer has ports for flash memory cards.

You also need to consider your monitor. Will you be working on a single document at a time, or will you have multiple windows open simultaneously that you will need to reference? Do you plan to use your computer to watch DVDs or streaming video over the Internet? Determine the smallest size monitor you would like. (You might need to adjust this expectation later if your total price exceeds your budget.)

Finally, think about your printer needs. Remember that many printers also function as a scanner or a copier, and some printers print exceptionally high quality photos. In addition, if your computer doesn't have a card reader (to read flash memory cards), you might want to get a printer that has one.

## Organize Your Data

After collecting the relevant information, you need to organize it so that you can objectively make your decision. In this case, list your needs in one column, list the type of software that will fulfill those needs in another column, and list the brand of software in a third column. Then decide which operating system you want—if you are buying a PC, usually you will want to buy the latest version of the Windows operating system. Find the system requirements for the software and operating system you want. You will need a computer that meets at least those requirements. However, because the system requirements listed are usually the minimum, it's a good idea to buy a computer with components that exceed these minimum requirements so that your computer doesn't run too slowly.

### Research Buying a New Personal Computer

You are buying a new desktop computer. You want the computer to run Microsoft Office 2013, and you want to make sure you are protected against security threats. You would like a large LED monitor and you need a printer. However, you have a limited budget, and can spend no more than $800 for everything (all hardware and software).

**Note:** Please be sure not to include any personal information of a sensitive nature in the documents you create to submit to your instructor. Later, you can update the documents with such information for your personal use.

To help you organize your information, use the table shown in Figure 27.

| Figure 27 | Systems requirements table |
|---|---|

| | Your Requirements | Computer Retailer #1 | Computer Retailer #2 | Computer Retailer #3 |
|---|---|---|---|---|
| Windows 8 | | | | |
| Microsoft Office (version of Office 2013 or Office 365) | | | | |
| Brand of computer | | | | |
| Processor (brand and speed) | | | | |
| RAM (amount) | | | | |
| Hard disk (size) | | | | |
| Monitor (type and size) | | | | |
| Printer (type and speed) | | | | |
| Speakers | | | | |
| Antivirus software | | | | |
| Firewall (software or router with built-in firewall) | | | | |
| System price | | | | |
| Additional costs | | | | |
| Total price | | | | |

© 2014 Cengage Learning

1. Decide which version and edition of Windows you want to use. Enter this information in the Your Requirements column of the table. Go to www.microsoft.com and search the Microsoft website for information about the available editions of Windows.
2. Research the hardware requirements for running the edition of Windows you selected.
3. Decide which edition of Office you want—a version of Office 2013 or Office 365—and enter it in the first column of the table. Search the Microsoft website to find a description of the software included with each edition of Office, and then search for the hardware requirements for running the edition that you chose. If necessary, change the hardware requirements in the table.
4. Research the cost of your new computer system. To begin, visit local stores, look at advertisements, or search the web for computer system retailers. Most computer retailers sell complete systems that come with all the necessary hardware, an operating system, and additional software already installed. Consider visiting a small, local computer store that has the capability to custom-build a system for you. In the Computer Retailer #1 column of the table, fill in the specifications for the system you chose. If any item listed as a minimum requirement is not included with the system you chose, find the cost of adding that item and enter the price in the table. Repeat this process with systems from two other retailers, entering the specifications in the Computer Retailer #2 and Computer Retailer #3 columns.
5. If the system you chose does not come with a printer, add a color inkjet printer priced within your budget.
6. If the system you chose does not come with antivirus software, search the web for the cost, if any, of an antivirus software package. Make sure you look up reviews of the package you choose. Decide whether to purchase this software or download free software, and enter this cost in the table.

7. If you decide you need a router with a built-in firewall, search the web for the price of one. Enter this information in the table.

8. Total the costs you entered in the table for the various items. Is the total cost $800 or less? If not, revisit some of the items. Can you get a less expensive printer? Do you need to downgrade to a less expensive monitor? Likewise, if you are under budget, upgrade a part of your system. For example, if the system you chose meets only the minimum requirements for running Windows and Office, consider upgrading the processor or adding more RAM. Or perhaps you can afford to upgrade the monitor to a larger one. Reevaluate your choices if necessary and try to get your total cost close to $800.

## OBJECTIVES

- Start and turn off Windows 8
- Describe how to use Windows 8 with a touchscreen device
- Tour the Start screen and the desktop
- Start Windows 8 and desktop applications
- Switch between applications and close them
- Identify and use the controls in windows and dialog boxes
- Get help with Windows 8 tasks

# Exploring the Basics of Windows 8

*Investigating the Windows 8 Operating System*

## Case | *Behind the Scenes*

Behind the Scenes is a small but growing temporary employment agency in St. Louis, Missouri. The agency specializes in training and providing virtual assistants, high-quality support staff that work from home to perform office tasks and projects for clients. As the training manager at Behind the Scenes, Emma Garcia coordinates staff training sessions on a wide range of professional and computer skills.

Emma recently hired you as her assistant. She has asked you to lead the upcoming training sessions on the fundamentals of the Microsoft Windows 8 operating system. As you prepare for the sessions, she offers to help you identify the topics you should cover and the skills you should demonstrate while focusing on the new features in Windows 8.

In this tutorial, you will start Windows 8 and practice some fundamental computer skills. You will tour the Start screen, start applications, and then explore the desktop. You will also work with windows and their tools, use the Windows 8 Help system, and turn off Windows 8.

## STARTING DATA FILES

There are no starting Data Files needed for this tutorial.

# Visual Overview:

The four corners of the Start screen are **hot corners**; point to one to display objects for interacting with Windows.

The **user icon** identifies the current user and provides access to your account settings.

The **Start screen** appears after you sign in to Windows; you use it to start applications.

Click the Desktop tile to display the Windows 8 desktop.

The name you use to sign in to Windows appears next to the user icon.

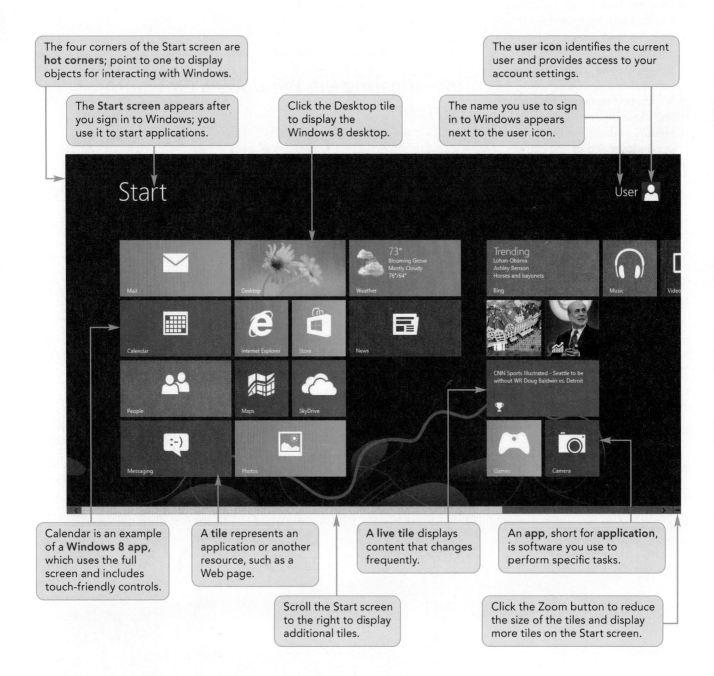

Calendar is an example of a **Windows 8 app**, which uses the full screen and includes touch-friendly controls.

A **tile** represents an application or another resource, such as a Web page.

A **live tile** displays content that changes frequently.

An **app**, short for **application**, is software you use to perform specific tasks.

Scroll the Start screen to the right to display additional tiles.

Click the Zoom button to reduce the size of the tiles and display more tiles on the Start screen.

# Windows 8 Start Screen & Desktop

The **Recycle Bin** holds deleted items until you remove them permanently.

The **desktop** is your work area for running many productivity applications and applications designed for previous versions of Windows.

This graphic is part of a **theme**, a set of coordinated desktop backgrounds, window colors, sounds, and screen savers.

Recycle Bin

Two applications are **pinned** to the taskbar, which means their buttons always appear on the left side of the taskbar.

7:20 PM
10/24/2016

The **taskbar** contains icons and buttons that give you quick access to common tools and running applications.

An **icon** is a small picture that represents a resource on your computer.

The **notification area** displays icons corresponding to services Windows provides, such as an Internet connection.

The **Date/time control** is an element that shows the current date and time and lets you set the clock.

# Introducing Windows 8

The **operating system** is software that manages and coordinates activities on the computer and helps the computer perform essential tasks, such as displaying information on the screen and saving data on disks. Your computer uses the **Microsoft Windows 8** operating system—**Windows 8** for short. Windows is the name of the operating system, and 8 indicates the version you are using.

Computers can run two types of software—system software and applications. **System software** is the software that runs a computer, including the operating system. An application (abbreviated as "app") is the software you use most directly to perform tasks such as writing a screenplay or viewing a webpage. In general, a computer runs system software to perform computer tasks, and you run applications to carry out your work or personal tasks. On Windows 8, you can run applications created specifically for the Windows 8 operating system and for earlier versions of Windows, such as Windows 7. With both versions of Windows, you can use more than one application at a time and switch seamlessly from one application to another to perform your work effectively.

Windows 8 is designed to run on computers that use a touchscreen, such as tablets, those that use a keyboard and mouse, such as a desktop computer, and those that use a touchpad, such as a laptop. A **touchscreen** is a display that lets you touch areas of the screen to interact with software. See Figure 1.

| Figure 1 | Windows 8 on different types of computers |

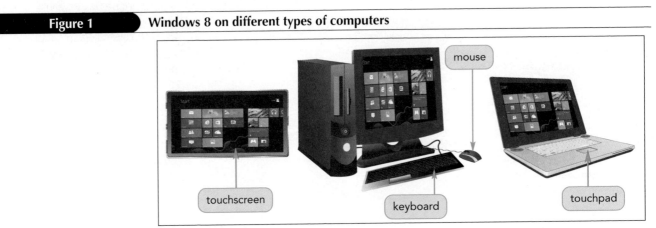

© 2014 Cengage Learning

## Using Windows 8 with Pointing Devices

As shown in the Visual Overview, when you work with Windows 8, you interact with objects such as tiles and icons to start applications, provide information to Windows, and perform other computer tasks. If you are using a laptop or desktop computer, you most likely use a **pointing device** to interact with the objects on the screen. Pointing devices come in many shapes and sizes. The most common one is called a **mouse**, so this book uses that term. If you are using a different pointing device, such as a trackball or touchpad, substitute that device whenever you see the term "mouse."

You use a mouse to move the pointer over locations and objects on the screen, or to **point** to them. The **pointer** is an on-screen object, often shaped like an arrow, though it changes shape depending on its location on the screen and the tasks you are performing. As you move the mouse on a surface, such as a table top, the pointer moves in a corresponding direction.

You also use the mouse to interact with specific objects on the screen. For example, you can use the mouse to click an object. **Clicking** refers to pressing a mouse button and immediately releasing it. Clicking sends a signal to your computer that you want to perform an action with the object you click. In Windows 8, you perform most actions with the left mouse button. If a step instructs you to click an on-screen object, such as a Start screen tile, position the pointer on that object and click the left mouse button. Another common mouse action is **double-clicking**, which means to click the left mouse button twice in quick succession. You can also press and release the right button on a mouse, which is called **right-clicking**. (If your mouse has only one button, you right-click by pressing the right side of the button.) Finally, you can point to an object, press and hold down the mouse button, and then move the mouse, which is called **dragging** the object.

## Using Windows 8 with Touchscreen Devices

If you are using a computer with a touchscreen, such as a tablet, you use your fingertips to interact with on-screen objects. The movements you make as you touch the screen with your fingertips are called **gestures**. The six basic gestures are tap, press, swipe, slide or drag, pinch, and rotate. For example, instead of clicking a tile on the Start screen, you tap the tile, which means you use your fingertip to touch the item briefly. Figure 2 illustrates the six gestures you use with touchscreen devices.

**Figure 2**    **Gestures used with touchscreen devices**

| Touch Gesture | Description | Illustration |
|---|---|---|
| Tap | Touch an item with a fingertip | 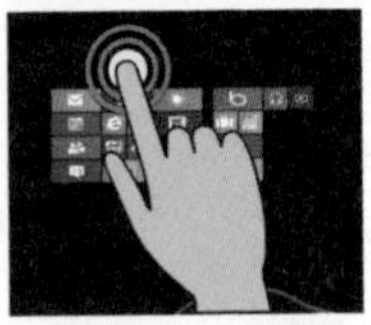 Tap to start an application or select an object |
| Press | Touch and hold an item |  Press and hold to learn |
| Swipe | Drag a fingertip across the screen and then release | 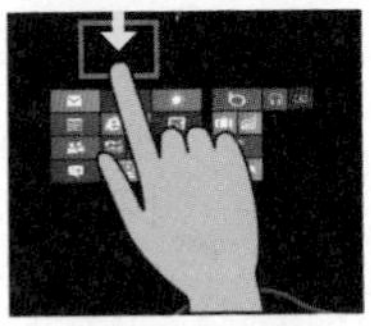 Swipe to display commands |
| Slide or drag | Drag a fingertip across the screen without releasing | 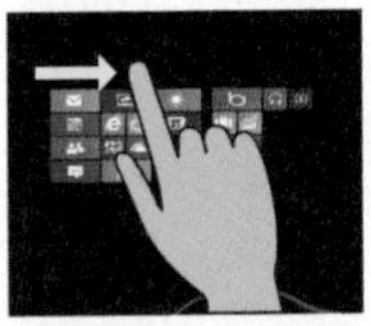 Slide to scroll the screen or move an object |
| Pinch | Touch the screen with two fingers and then drag your fingertips toward each other to zoom out, or drag your fingertips away from each other to zoom in | 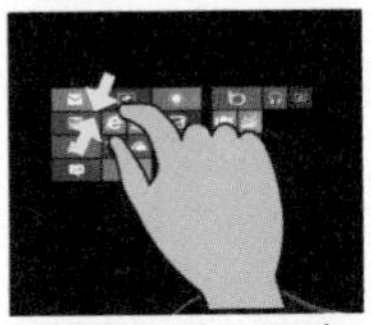 Pinch and stretch to zoom |
| Rotate | Touch the screen with two fingers and then drag either clockwise or counterclockwise |  Turn to rotate |

© 2014 Cengage Learning

Many elements of Windows 8 are designed with touchscreen users in mind. For example, the Start screen includes large tiles instead of small icons because tiles are easier to tap. However, you are not required to use a touchscreen with Windows 8. In fact, this book assumes that you are using a computer with a keyboard and a mouse.

## INSIGHT

### The Windows 8 User Interface

The part of the operating system you use when you work with a computer is called the **user interface (UI)**. The UI includes everything that lets you interact with the computer, including the layout of the screen and the controls that the operating system provides so you can make selections and change settings. (**Controls** are graphical or textual objects you use to work with the operating system and applications.) On the Start screen, the Windows 8 UI uses a design that emphasizes large, clear graphical icons to identify screen objects. When you use a Windows 8 app, the focus is on the content, so the screen is not cluttered with tools and controls. The Windows 8 UI also uses animation and fluid motions to respond to your actions and selections, which make the system seem livelier than a collection of static objects. To take advantage of wide screens, multiple monitors, and touch-screen devices, the Windows 8 UI is more horizontally oriented than previous versions of Windows. For example, you scroll right and left to access content currently out of view.

# Starting Windows 8

**TIP**

If you have a Microsoft account, you can use the username and password for that account to sign in to Windows 8. However, this tutorial assumes you are not signed in to a Microsoft account.

Windows 8 starts automatically when you turn on your computer. After completing some necessary startup tasks, Windows 8 might display a **lock screen**, which includes a picture, the date, and the time. You clear the lock screen to display the Welcome screen, which lists all the users for the computer. Before you start working with Windows 8, you might also need to click your **username** (a unique name that identifies you to Windows 8) and type a **password** (a confidential series of characters). After you provide this information, the Windows 8 Start screen appears, as shown in the Visual Overview.

## PROSKILLS

### Decision Making: Selecting a User Account Type

In order to use Windows 8, you must have a user account. A **user account** identifies you to the computer. You access your user account by selecting your username and typing your password, if required. You can create additional user accounts at any time. If you share a computer with other people, your user account allows you to keep your work and settings separate from the other users. When you create your user account, you must choose from one of the following types of accounts:

- Microsoft account—This is a user account that is associated with Microsoft's **SkyDrive**, a Microsoft server on the Internet on which you can store files and access some Microsoft programs. If you have a user account on more than one computer running Windows 8, you can access your applications, preferences, and other settings. In addition, you can use some Windows 8 applications only if you are signed in with a Microsoft account, including the Store app, which lets you add new applications to your computer, and the Music app, which you use to purchase songs and albums. You sign in to a Microsoft account using an email address. Any email address can be associated with a Microsoft account, and that email address then becomes the username for that account. You can also set up a Microsoft account when you create your user account in Windows 8.
- Local account—When you sign in with a local account, you are signed in to Windows 8 but you are not automatically connected to SkyDrive. This type of account accesses resources on your computer in the same way user accounts worked in earlier versions of Windows. You can, however, create a separate account on Microsoft SkyDrive to access SkyDrive features.

Make sure you understand the differences between these two types of user accounts so you can decide which one is the best type for you and your work habits.

To begin preparing for the Windows 8 training session you will deliver, Emma asks you to start Windows 8.

**To start Windows 8:**

1. Turn on your computer. After a moment, Windows 8 starts and displays the Welcome screen.

   **Trouble?** If you are asked to select an operating system, do not take action. Windows 8 should start automatically after a designated number of seconds. If it does not, ask your instructor or technical support person for help.

   **Trouble?** If a lock screen appears before the Welcome screen does, press any key to clear the lock screen.

2. If the Welcome screen is displayed for more than a few seconds, click your username, type your password, and then press the **Enter** key.

   The Windows 8 Start screen appears, as shown in the Visual Overview. Your screen might look different.

   **Trouble?** If your username does not appear on the Welcome screen, ask your instructor or technical support person for further assistance.

   **Trouble?** If a blank screen or an animated design replaces the Start screen, your computer might be set to use a **screen saver**, a program that causes a monitor to go blank or to display an animated design after a specified amount of idle time. Press any key or move your mouse to restore the Start screen.

   **Trouble?** If your computer is using a screen resolution other than 1366 x 768, the figures shown in this tutorial might not match exactly what you see in Windows 8 as you work through the steps. Take the screen resolution difference into account as you compare your screen to the figures.

# Touring the Start Screen

The screen that appears after you sign in to Windows 8 is called the Start screen because you start working on your computer from this screen. The Start screen includes multicolored rectangles called tiles, which represent applications and other resources your computer can access. See Figure 3.

**Figure 3**   **Tiles on the Start screen**

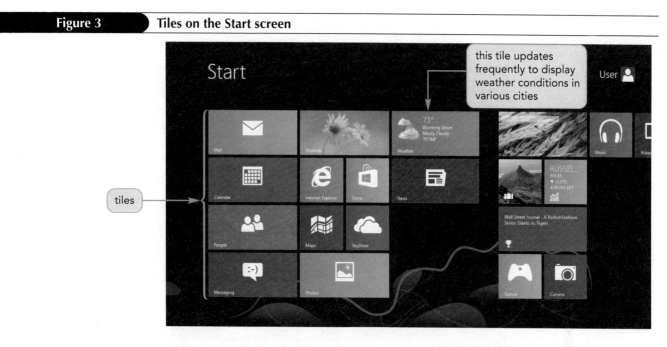

Some tiles display changing pictures or text that previews the contents of the tile. A tile that displays updated content is called a live tile. For example, the Weather tile is a live tile that displays current weather conditions in cities around the world. You click the Weather live tile to open the Weather app, a Windows 8 app that lets you check the current and forecasted weather in various locations.

The first time you start Windows 8, the computer uses **default settings**, which are preset by the operating system. The default Start screen you see after you first install Windows 8, for example, displays a number of tiles, including those for Internet Explorer (an application you use to access the Internet), Weather, and Photos. However, Microsoft designed Windows 8 so that you can easily change the appearance of the Start screen. You can, for example, move and add tiles and change the background color.

Emma suggests that during your class, you introduce Behind the Scenes employees to the Start screen by showing them how to scroll in case some tiles are out of view.

### To scroll the Start screen:

**TIP**

Make sure you position the pointer on the very edge of the Start screen. You might also need to press and hold the mouse button as you scroll.

1. Use the mouse to point to the **right edge** of the Start screen. The screen scrolls to display additional tiles or those not shown on the main Start screen. See Figure 4.

   **Trouble?** If a bar of buttons appears on the right side of the screen, you pointed to the upper-right or lower-right corner. Point to the middle of the right edge of the screen to scroll.

   **Trouble?** If the screen does not scroll, your Start screen might not contain additional or half-shown tiles.

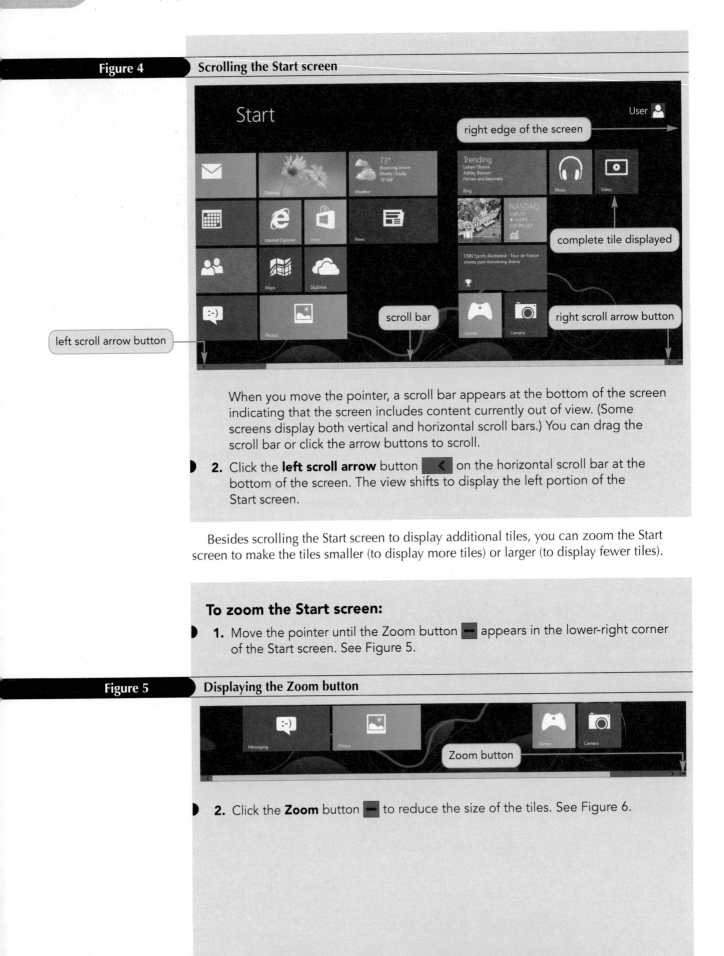

**Figure 4**  Scrolling the Start screen

When you move the pointer, a scroll bar appears at the bottom of the screen indicating that the screen includes content currently out of view. (Some screens display both vertical and horizontal scroll bars.) You can drag the scroll bar or click the arrow buttons to scroll.

▶ **2.** Click the **left scroll arrow** button ◄ on the horizontal scroll bar at the bottom of the screen. The view shifts to display the left portion of the Start screen.

Besides scrolling the Start screen to display additional tiles, you can zoom the Start screen to make the tiles smaller (to display more tiles) or larger (to display fewer tiles).

**To zoom the Start screen:**

▶ **1.** Move the pointer until the Zoom button ▬ appears in the lower-right corner of the Start screen. See Figure 5.

**Figure 5**  Displaying the Zoom button

▶ **2.** Click the **Zoom** button ▬ to reduce the size of the tiles. See Figure 6.

| Figure 6 | Zooming the Start screen |

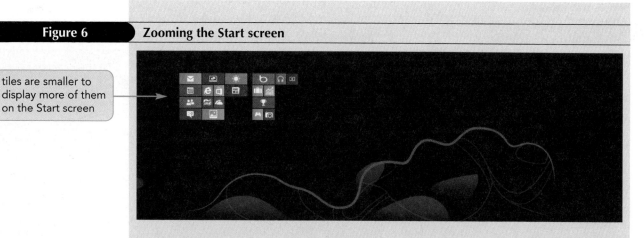

tiles are smaller to display more of them on the Start screen

**3.** Click a blank area on the Start screen to return the tiles to their original size.

When you moved the pointer to the Zoom button to click it, a bar appeared on the right edge of the Start screen. This is called the **Charms bar**, and it contains buttons, also called **charms**, for interacting with Windows 8. The Charms bar appears when you point to the upper-right or lower-right corner of the screen. These locations are two of the four hot corners Windows 8 provides for mouse users. When you point to the Charms bar, it appears with a black background, indicating it is the **active object**. You can interact with active objects by clicking them. For example, when you click some charms, such as the Settings charm, a menu opens. A **menu** is a list, or group, of commands, and a **menu command** is an item on the list that you can click to perform a task. The **Settings menu** lets you access options and information for your current task and your system. Emma suggests you use the Settings charm on the Charms bar to open the Settings menu.

### To open the Settings menu:

**1.** Point to the upper-right corner of the screen to display the Charms bar.

**2.** Point to the **Charms bar** to display it with a black background, indicating it is active. See Figure 7. When you activate the Charms bar, a status box appears on the screen displaying the date and time. It might also display other status information, such as the strength of your network connection or battery level.

TIP

You can also press and hold the Windows key and then press the C key to display the Charms bar.

| Figure 7 | Active Charms bar |
|---|---|

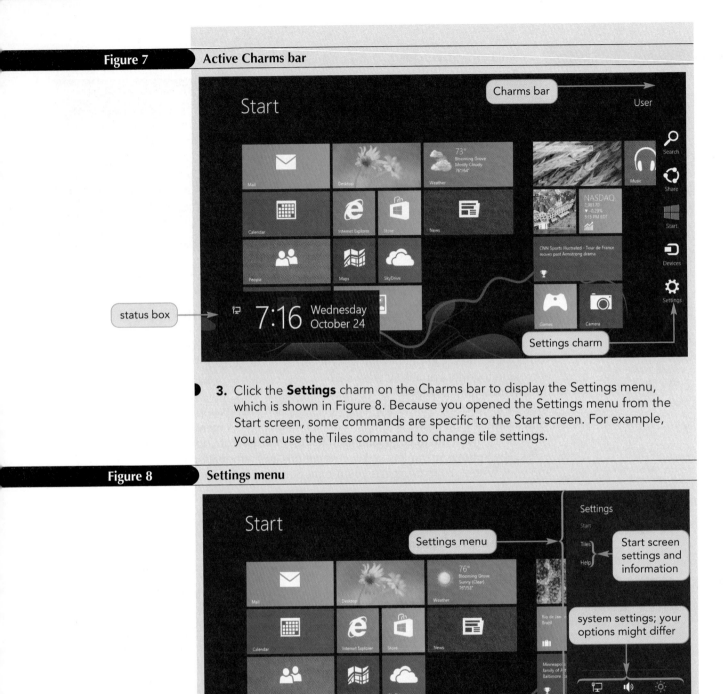

3. Click the **Settings** charm on the Charms bar to display the Settings menu, which is shown in Figure 8. Because you opened the Settings menu from the Start screen, some commands are specific to the Start screen. For example, you can use the Tiles command to change tile settings.

| Figure 8 | Settings menu |
|---|---|

4. Click a blank area on the Start screen to close the Settings menu.

# Starting Applications

Windows 8 runs two types of applications. Windows 8 applications, as the name suggests, are designed to use the Windows 8 interface and work with touchscreen devices. They are often called apps. When you start a Windows 8 application, it takes up the entire screen and provides an uncluttered workspace for performing tasks. You can also use Windows 8 to run **desktop applications**, programs that open and run on the desktop, which is shown in the Visual Overview. For example, WordPad is a desktop application you use to create basic word-processing documents.

**REFERENCE**

### Starting an Application

- Click the application's tile on the Start screen.

*or*

- Right-click a blank area on the Start screen, click the All apps button on the Apps bar at the bottom of the screen, and then click the application on the Apps screen.

*or*

- On the Start screen, type the name of the application until the application appears in the search results on the Apps screen.
- Click the application in the search results.

The easiest way to start an application is to click its tile on the Start screen. Emma suggests you use this technique to start the Weather app.

**To start the Weather app from the Start screen:**

1. Click the **Weather** tile on the Start screen to start the Weather app.

   **Trouble?** If a message appears asking if you want to allow Weather to use your location, click the Block button.

2. If an Enter Location box appears, type **St** to display a list of location names that start with "St," and then click **St Louis, Missouri, United States** in the list to display weather information for that location. See Figure 9. Your weather information will differ.

   **Trouble?** If an Enter Location box does not appear after you click the Weather tile, your Weather app is set to use a specific location and shows the weather for that location. Continue to Step 3.

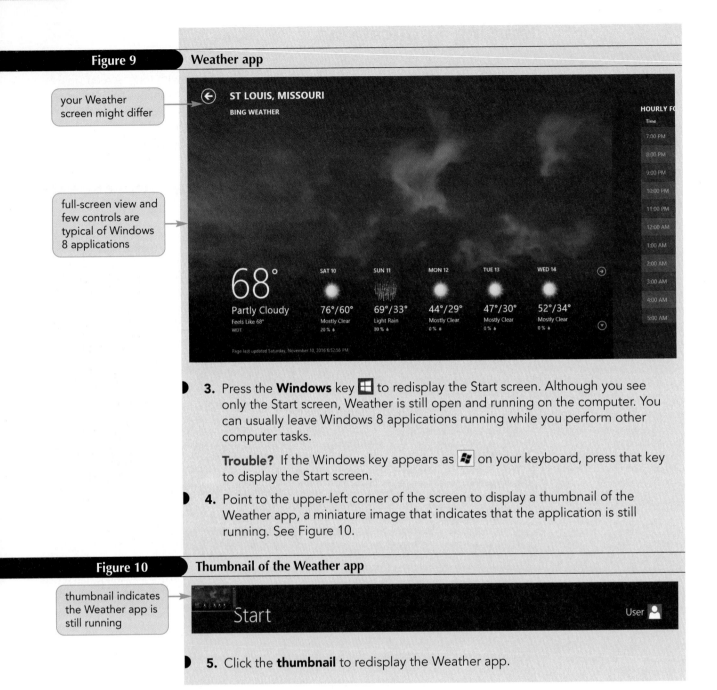

**Figure 9**    Weather app

your Weather screen might differ

full-screen view and few controls are typical of Windows 8 applications

ST LOUIS, MISSOURI

BING WEATHER

HOURLY FO

Time

7:00 PM

8:00 PM

9:00 PM

10:00 PM

11:00 PM

12:00 AM

1:00 AM

2:00 AM

3:00 AM

4:00 AM

5:00 AM

68°

Partly Cloudy
Feels Like 68°
WDT

SAT 10
76°/60°
Mostly Clear
20 % ♦

SUN 11
69°/33°
Light Rain
80 % ♦

MON 12
44°/29°
Mostly Clear
0 % ♦

TUE 13
47°/30°
Mostly Clear
0 % ♦

WED 14
52°/34°
Mostly Clear
0 % ♦

Page last updated Saturday, November 10, 2016 6:52:56 PM

3. Press the **Windows** key ⊞ to redisplay the Start screen. Although you see only the Start screen, Weather is still open and running on the computer. You can usually leave Windows 8 applications running while you perform other computer tasks.

   **Trouble?** If the Windows key appears as ⊞ on your keyboard, press that key to display the Start screen.

4. Point to the upper-left corner of the screen to display a thumbnail of the Weather app, a miniature image that indicates that the application is still running. See Figure 10.

**Figure 10**    Thumbnail of the Weather app

thumbnail indicates the Weather app is still running

Start                                                    User 👤

5. Click the **thumbnail** to redisplay the Weather app.

## Using the Apps Screen to Start an Application

If an application's tile does not appear on the Start screen, you can open the application using the **Apps screen**, which lists all the applications installed on your computer. One way to display the Apps screen is to right-click a blank area of the Start screen to display the **Apps bar**, which includes buttons related to your current task, and then click the All apps button.

Emma wants you to demonstrate how to use more than one technique to start applications, so you will use the Apps screen to start Reader, a Windows 8 application that does not appear on the Start screen by default. Reader lets you view and navigate **PDF documents**, which are files in the Portable Document Format that usually include text and graphics and are readable on most computer systems. First, you must return to the Start screen so you can display the Apps bar with the All apps button.

### To start the Reader app from the Apps screen:

1. Press the **Windows** key 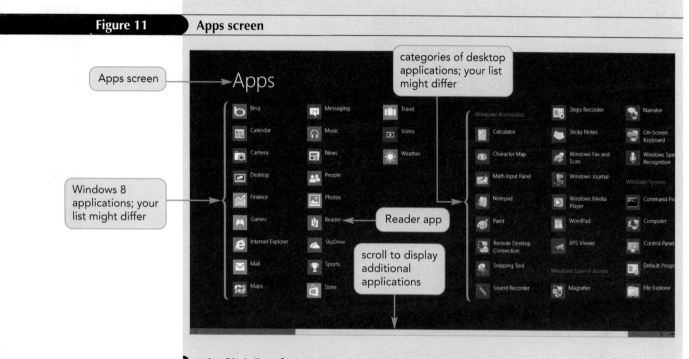 to display the Start screen.

2. Right-click a blank area on the Start screen to display the Apps bar at the bottom of the screen.

3. Click the **All apps** button on the right side of the Apps bar to display the Apps screen. See Figure 11. The Apps screen lists Windows 8 applications on the left and categories of desktop applications on the right.

| Figure 11 | Apps screen |
|---|---|

Apps screen

Apps

categories of desktop applications; your list might differ

Windows 8 applications; your list might differ

| Bing | Messaging | Travel | Windows Accessories | Steps Recorder | Narrator |
| Calendar | Music | Video | Calculator | Sticky Notes | On-Screen Keyboard |
| Camera | News | Weather | Character Map | Windows Fax and Scan | Windows Speech Recognition |
| Desktop | People | | Math Input Panel | Windows Journal | Windows System |
| Finance | Photos | | Notepad | Windows Media Player | Command Pr |
| Games | Reader | Reader app | Paint | WordPad | Computer |
| Internet Explorer | SkyDrive | | Remote Desktop Connection | XPS Viewer | Control Panel |
| Mail | Sports | scroll to display additional applications | Snipping Tool | Windows Ease of Access | Default Progr |
| Maps | Store | | Sound Recorder | Magnifier | File Explorer |

4. Click **Reader** to start the Reader app. A PDF document opens in Reader explaining how to edit PDF files using Microsoft Word.

   **Trouble?** You might have a different PDF document that opens in Reader, or no document will open at all and you will see the Recent screen for Reader. This is not a problem.

Windows 8 applications start and run as full-screen programs so you can focus on your task and the content on the screen. Occasionally, you need to refer to information in one application while you are working in another application. For example, you might want to keep the Weather app open so you can check the weather while you are reading a document in the Reader app. If you are using a high screen resolution (at least 1366 × 768), you can **snap** an app, which means you display a Windows 8 application on the left or right side of the screen and leave it open as you work in another Windows 8 application. You can snap only Windows 8 applications, not desktop applications.

**TIP**

You can right-click other objects on the Start screen and the desktop to view a shortcut menu of commands associated with that object.

If a Windows 8 application appears on the screen, you snap it by dragging it to the left or right. If the application is open and running but does not appear on the screen, you can display its thumbnail, and then right-click the thumbnail to open a **shortcut menu**, which lists actions you can take with the application. The thumbnail shortcut menu includes commands for snapping the application to the left or right side of the screen.

### To snap the Weather app:

1. Point to the upper-left hot corner to display the Weather thumbnail.

2. Right-click the **Weather** thumbnail, and then click **Snap left** on the shortcut menu to snap the Weather app to the left side of the screen while the Reader app is open on the right. See Figure 12.

**Figure 12**    **Weather app snapped on the left**

Weather app

drag this bar to the left edge of the screen to unsnap the Weather app

Reader app; your Reader app might show different content

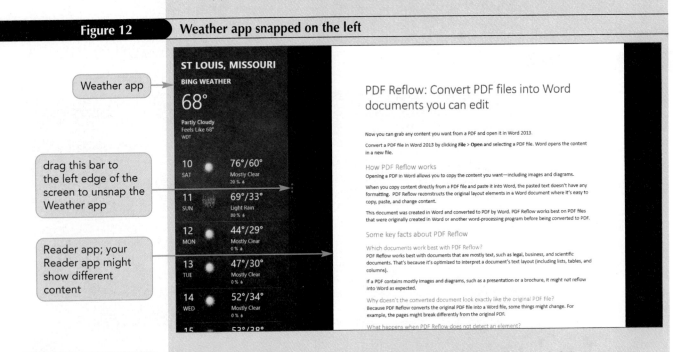

TIP

You can also drag the bar between the applications to adjust the amount of screen space devoted to each one.

3. Drag the **bar** between the two applications to the left edge of the screen to unsnap the Weather app. Both Reader and Weather are still running, but the Weather app is no longer snapped to the screen.

## Using the Search Menu to Start an Application

Besides using the Apps screen to start Windows 8 applications, you can also use it to start desktop applications. When you first install Windows 8, the Apps screen lists so many applications that you need to scroll to the right at least once to display all of them. As you add other applications to your computer, you might need to scroll a few more times to find the application you want to start. Instead of scrolling the Apps screen, you can use the **Search menu** as a time-saving shortcut for starting applications. You open the Search menu from the Charms bar. When you do, it appears on top of the Apps screen by default. See Figure 13.

| Figure 13 | Apps screen and Search menu |

use the Search menu to search for applications, settings, and files

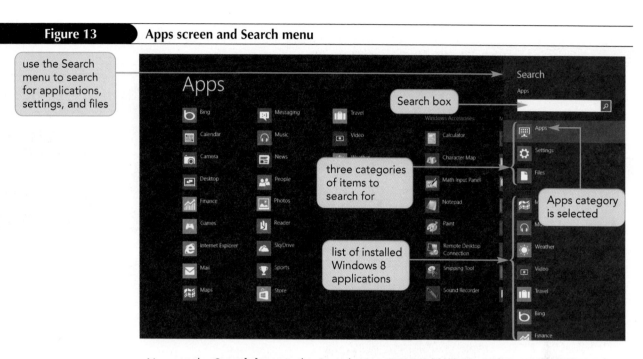

You use the **Search box** on the Search menu to quickly find anything stored on your computer including applications, documents, pictures, music, videos, and settings. Below the Search box, the Search menu lists three major categories of items you can search for—Apps, Settings, and Files. The Apps category is selected by default. Below the category list on the Search menu is a list of Windows 8 applications installed on your computer. To search for an application, click in the Search box and start typing the name of the application. As you type, the Apps screen displays the search results—applications containing words beginning with that text in their names. Another way to search for an application is to type some or all of the application name on the Start screen. (You don't need to click a particular part of the screen or open a box first.) When you start typing, the Search menu opens on the Apps screen and the text you typed appears in the Search box. The Apps screen displays the search results, which are the applications whose names start with the text in the Search box. You then click the application in the search results to start the application.

If you want to search for settings, you enter the text relating to the setting you are searching for, and then click Settings in the category list. Searching for files works the same way—in the Search box, type the text related to the file you are looking for, and then click Files in the category list.

Emma suggests you use the Search menu to locate and start the WordPad desktop application, which Behind the Scenes employees can use to write and open text documents.

**To start WordPad:**

**TIP**

You can also display the Charms bar and then click the Search charm to open the Search menu.

1. Press the **Windows** key ⊞ to display the Start screen.

2. On the Start screen, type **wordp** to display the Search menu with "wordp" inserted in the Search box. The Apps screen lists the search results, which include the WordPad application. See Figure 14.

**Figure 14** WordPad in the search results

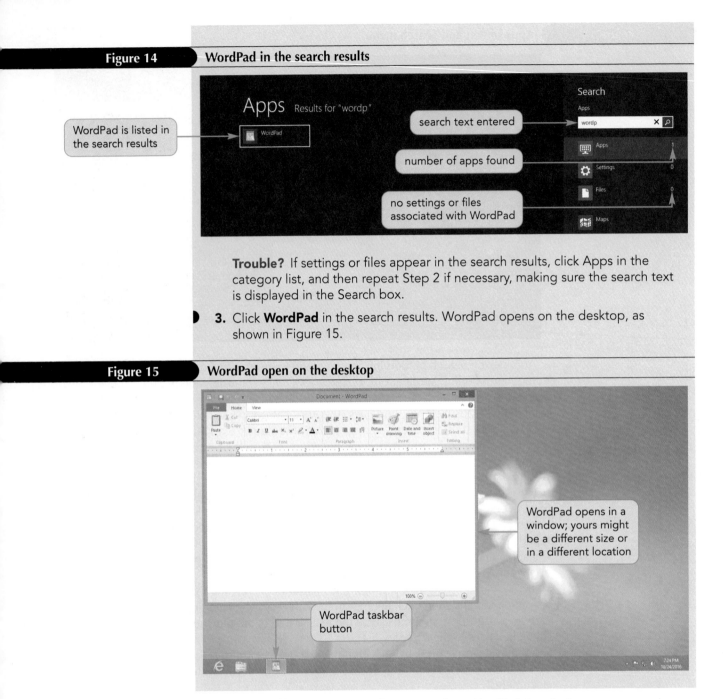

WordPad is listed in the search results

Apps Results for "wordp"

WordPad

search text entered

number of apps found

no settings or files associated with WordPad

Search

Apps

wordp

Apps 1

Settings 0

Files 0

Maps

**Trouble?** If settings or files appear in the search results, click Apps in the category list, and then repeat Step 2 if necessary, making sure the search text is displayed in the Search box.

3. Click **WordPad** in the search results. WordPad opens on the desktop, as shown in Figure 15.

**Figure 15** WordPad open on the desktop

WordPad opens in a window; yours might be a different size or in a different location

WordPad taskbar button

When you open a desktop application such as WordPad, its **window**—a rectangular work area that contains tools for performing tasks in the application—is displayed on the desktop and a taskbar button for WordPad appears on the taskbar. You use **taskbar buttons** to identify and work with open desktop applications.

## Manipulating Windows

After you open a window, you can manipulate it to display as much or as little information as you need. In most windows, three buttons appear on the right side of the title bar. See Figure 16. The first button is the Minimize button, which you can use to **minimize** a window, or hide it so that only its button is visible on the taskbar. Depending on the status of the window, the middle button either maximizes the window or restores it to a predefined size. **Maximizing** means to enlarge a window so that it fills the entire screen. The last button is the Close button, which closes the window.

| Figure 16 | Window buttons |
| --- | --- |

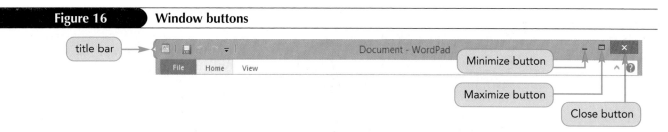

To make sure Behind the Scenes employees know how to manipulate windows, Emma suggests you show them how to use the WordPad taskbar button and the buttons on the WordPad title bar.

**To manipulate the WordPad window:**

1. Click the **Minimize** button ▬ on the WordPad title bar to minimize the WordPad window. The WordPad window shrinks so that only the WordPad button is visible on the taskbar. With the WordPad window hidden, you can view the entire desktop.

2. Click the **WordPad** button 📄 on the taskbar to redisplay the WordPad window.

3. Click the **Maximize** button ☐ on the WordPad title bar to maximize the WordPad window.

   **Trouble?** If the window is already maximized, it fills the entire screen and the Maximize button ☐ doesn't appear. Instead, you see the Restore Down button ❐. Skip Step 3.

4. Click the **Restore Down** button ❐ on the title bar to make the WordPad window smaller than the entire screen. After a window is restored, the Restore Down button ❐ changes to the Maximize button ☐.

You can also manipulate windows by moving and resizing them. To move a window, you drag the window by its title bar. You also drag to resize a window. When you point to an edge or a corner of a window, the pointer changes to a resize pointer, which is a double-headed arrow, similar to ⤡. You can use the resize pointer to drag an edge or a corner of the window and change the size of the window. If a window is maximized, you must click the Restore Down button before you can move or resize the window.

**To move and resize the WordPad window:**

1. Position the mouse pointer on the title bar of the WordPad window.

2. Press and hold the mouse button, and then move the pointer up or down a little to drag the window. The window moves as you move the pointer.

3. Drag the window to the middle of the desktop so it does not cover any part of the Recycle Bin icon that appears on the desktop, and then release the mouse button. The WordPad window remains in the new location.

   **Trouble?** If the WordPad window becomes maximized when you drag it, click the Restore Down button ❐ before performing Step 4.

**4.** Point to the lower-right corner of the WordPad window until the ⬉ pointer appears, and then drag down and to the right to enlarge the window.

**5.** Drag up and to the left until the window is about its original size.

In addition to the window manipulation buttons, the WordPad window contains other tools common in desktop applications.

# Using Tools in Desktop Applications

In a desktop application, you use controls to manipulate the application window and perform your work in the application. Many desktop applications organize controls in two places—ribbons and dialog boxes.

## Using the Ribbon

Many desktop applications use a **ribbon** to consolidate the application's features and commands. The ribbon is located at the top of a desktop application window, immediately below the title bar, and is organized into tabs. Each **tab** contains commands that perform a variety of related tasks. For example, the **Home tab** has commands for tasks you perform frequently, such as changing the appearance of a document. You use the commands on the **View tab** to change your view of the WordPad window. You use the commands on the **File tab** to work with WordPad documents, such as to save or print them.

To select a command and perform an action, you click a button or another type of control on the ribbon. Controls for related actions are organized on a tab in **groups**. For example, on the Home tab in the Font group, you click the Bold button to enter bold text in a WordPad document. If a button displays only an icon and not the button name, you can point to the button to display a **ScreenTip**, which is text that identifies the name or purpose of the button.

Figure 17 shows examples of the types of controls on the ribbon.

| Figure 17 | Examples of ribbon controls |
| --- | --- |

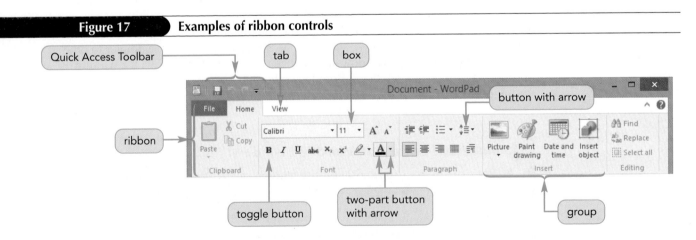

If a button includes an arrow, you click the button to display a menu of related commands. To use a box, you click the box and type an entry, such as numbers or other text, or you click the arrow button to select an item from the list. A toggle button is like a switch; you click the button to turn on or apply a setting, and then click the button again to turn off the setting. When a toggle button is turned on, it is highlighted. To use a two-part button with an arrow, you first point to the button. If an arrow is displayed on a separate part of the button, click the arrow to display a menu of commands. Click the button itself to apply the current selection.

Most desktop applications, including WordPad, include a **Quick Access Toolbar**, which is a row of buttons on the title bar that let you perform common tasks such as saving your work and undoing an action. You can display the name of each button on the Quick Access Toolbar in a ScreenTip by pointing to the button, just as you do for buttons on the ribbon.

Emma mentions that the WordPad application displays the controls you are likely to see in most desktop application windows, including the ribbon, which might be unfamiliar to Behind the Scenes employees. She suggests that you identify the controls on the WordPad ribbon and in WordPad dialog boxes during your first training session.

### To use buttons on the WordPad ribbon and the Quick Access Toolbar:

1. On the Home tab, in the Font group, click the **Bold** button $\boxed{B}$. Now any text you type will appear as bold text.

2. Type your full name in the WordPad window. See Figure 18.

| Figure 18 | Bold text in the WordPad window |

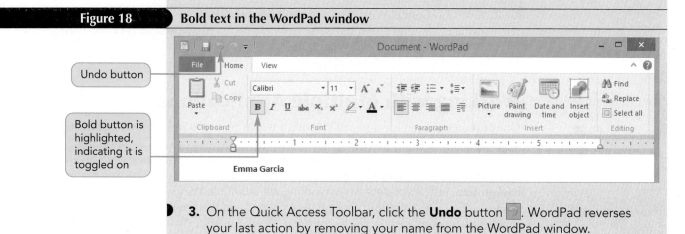

Undo button

Bold button is highlighted, indicating it is toggled on

Emma Garcia

3. On the Quick Access Toolbar, click the **Undo** button. WordPad reverses your last action by removing your name from the WordPad window.

## Using Dialog Boxes

A **dialog box** is a special kind of window in which you enter or choose settings for performing a task. Dialog boxes can include tabs, option buttons, check boxes, and other controls to collect information about how you want to perform the task. Emma says a good way to learn how dialog box controls work is to open a typical WordPad dialog box, such as the Print dialog box, which you use to print a document.

### To work with a typical Windows 8 dialog box:

1. On the ribbon, click the **File** tab, and then click **Print** on the menu to open the Print dialog box. See Figure 19.

**Figure 19**    **Print dialog box**

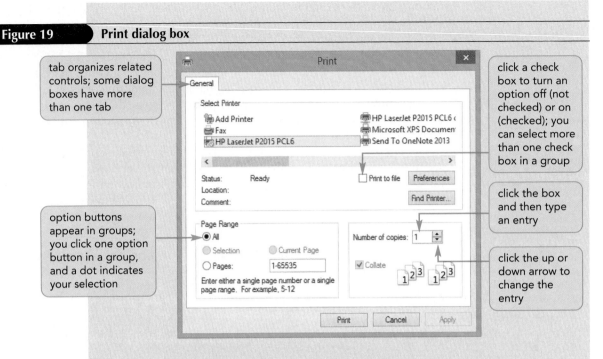

tab organizes related controls; some dialog boxes have more than one tab

click a check box to turn an option off (not checked) or on (checked); you can select more than one check box in a group

click the box and then type an entry

option buttons appear in groups; you click one option button in a group, and a dot indicates your selection

click the up or down arrow to change the entry

2. Click the **Cancel** button to close the Print dialog box. If you were ready to print a document with the settings you specified, you would click the Print button instead of the Cancel button.

# Working with Multiple Applications

One of the most useful features of Windows 8 is its ability to run multiple applications at the same time. This feature, known as **multitasking**, allows you to work on more than one task at a time and to switch quickly between open applications. When an application is open but not being used to complete tasks, it is said to be running in the **background**. Just as you saw when working with multiple Windows 8 apps on the Start screen, you can run multiple desktop applications and then switch from one to another so you can work efficiently. To demonstrate, Emma suggests that you open the Recycle Bin so that two applications are running on the desktop. (The Recycle Bin is part of an application that lets you explore the contents of your computer.)

### To open the Recycle Bin on the desktop:

1. Point to the **Recycle Bin** icon on the desktop, and then double-click the **Recycle Bin** icon by pressing the left mouse button twice quickly. The Recycle Bin window opens on top of the WordPad window, as shown in Figure 20.

Figure 20    **Recycle Bin and WordPad open on the desktop**

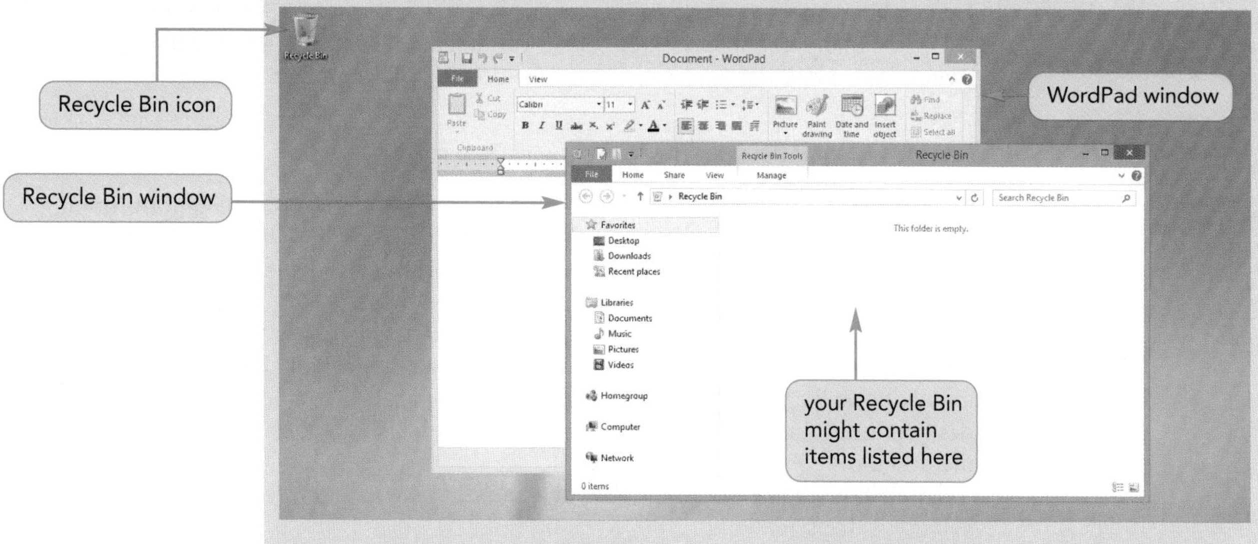

Recycle Bin icon

Recycle Bin window

WordPad window

your Recycle Bin might contain items listed here

**Trouble?** If the Recycle Bin window does not open and you see only the Recycle Bin name highlighted below the icon, you double-clicked too slowly. Double-click the icon again more quickly.

**Trouble?** If the Recycle Bin window opens as a maximized window, click the Restore Down button 🗗 so the window does not fill the screen.

2. If necessary, drag the Recycle Bin window to a location on the desktop that allows you to see both it and the WordPad window open on the desktop.

Now that two application windows are open, Emma wants you to demonstrate how to switch from one to the other.

## Switching Between Desktop Applications

When two or more applications are open and their windows are displayed on the desktop, only one can be the **active window**, which is the application window in which you are currently working. When a window is active, any keystroke or command you select applies only to that window. The active window appears on top of all other open windows, and its title bar and window borders are blue; the title bar and window border of all other open windows are gray. Right now, the Recycle Bin is the active window. To switch to the WordPad window, you can click its button on the taskbar or you can click in the window itself. If you minimize an active window, it is no longer active, and the window directly under it becomes the active window.

### To switch between the Recycle Bin and WordPad:

1. Click the **WordPad** button 🖼 on the taskbar. The WordPad window now appears on top of the Recycle Bin window, and the color of its title bar and borders changes to blue, indicating that WordPad is the active window.

2. Click any part of the Recycle Bin window to make it the active window.

3. Click the **Minimize** button ➖ on the Recycle Bin title bar to minimize the Recycle Bin window and make WordPad the active window.

In addition to the Recycle Bin and WordPad, recall that two Windows 8 apps are also running in the background—Weather and Reader. Although Weather and Reader are running right now, neither one is visible from the desktop. Only desktop applications have buttons on the taskbar, so you cannot use the taskbar to switch to a running Windows 8 app from the desktop. Next, you'll learn how to use a different technique to switch from a desktop application to a Windows 8 app running in the background.

## Switching Between Windows 8 Applications

You use the **Switch List** to display thumbnails of the Windows 8 applications running in the background, and then select the one you want to work with. You can display the Switch List from the Start screen, while working with a Windows 8 app, or from the desktop by using the upper-left hot corner on the screen.

When you display the Switch List from the Start screen or a Windows 8 application, it displays one thumbnail for the desktop. Although the Switch List includes thumbnails for Windows 8 applications only, not desktop applications, Windows 8 treats the desktop as a Windows 8 application, so the Switch List includes a thumbnail for the desktop.

Emma encourages you to use the Switch List to switch between the running Windows 8 applications.

### To switch between Windows 8 applications:

1. Point to the upper-left hot corner of the desktop to display a thumbnail of the Reader app, and then move the pointer down along the left edge of the screen to display the Switch List. See Figure 21.

| Figure 21 | Switch List displayed on the desktop |

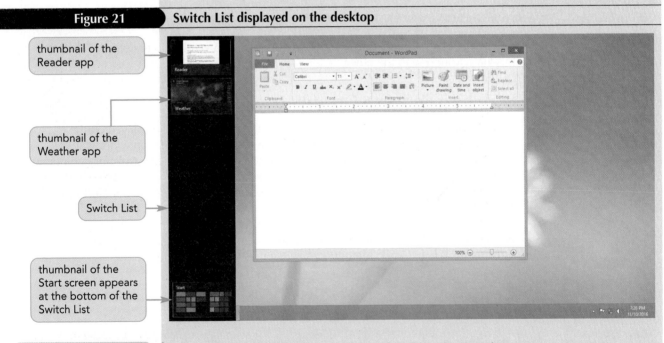

thumbnail of the Reader app

thumbnail of the Weather app

Switch List

thumbnail of the Start screen appears at the bottom of the Switch List

TIP

You can also click the thumbnail that appears when you point to the upper-left hot corner to start the associated application without displaying the Switch List.

2. Click the **Weather** thumbnail to switch to the Weather app.

3. Point to the upper-left hot corner of the screen to display a thumbnail, and then move the pointer down along the left edge of the screen to display the Switch List, which now includes a thumbnail for the desktop.

4. Click the **Reader** thumbnail to switch to the Reader app.

If you want to switch from the Start screen or a Windows 8 application to an inactive desktop application using the Switch List, you must click the Desktop thumbnail in the Switch List, and then activate the application's window on the desktop. A simpler way is to use a keyboard shortcut.

## Using Keyboard Shortcuts

Windows 8 provides many keyboard shortcuts for streamlining your work. A **keyboard shortcut** is one or more keys you press on the keyboard to perform an action. The keyboard shortcut for switching to any type of running application is Alt+Tab. To use this keyboard shortcut, you press and hold the Alt key and then press the Tab key to display thumbnails of all running applications. Continue pressing the Alt key as you press the Tab key to select a thumbnail, and then release the Alt key to make that application active.

You can use the Alt+Tab keyboard shortcut to switch to any running application, such as from a Windows 8 application to an inactive desktop application. Right now, the Recycle Bin is inactive on the desktop. Emma wants you to show Behind the Scenes employees how to use the Alt+Tab keyboard shortcut to switch to the inactive Recycle Bin window.

### To use the Alt+Tab keyboard shortcut:

1. Press and hold the **Alt** key, and then press the **Tab** key to display thumbnails of the running applications, including Windows 8 and desktop applications. See Figure 22.

**Figure 22** Thumbnails of running applications

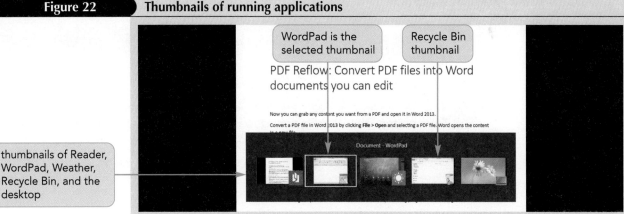

thumbnails of Reader, WordPad, Weather, Recycle Bin, and the desktop

WordPad is the selected thumbnail

Recycle Bin thumbnail

2. While holding down the Alt key, press the **Tab** key as many times as necessary to select the Recycle Bin thumbnail, and then release the Alt key. You return to the desktop, where the Recycle Bin is no longer minimized but is now the active window.

Emma says you don't need to demonstrate any other skills with WordPad and the Recycle Bin. When you're finished working with an application, you can close it.

# Closing Applications

When you finish working with applications, you can close them to keep the desktop and the Switch List free of clutter, and to allow your computer to run more efficiently. To close a desktop application, you close its window. To close a Windows 8 application, you can use a shortcut menu or drag the application off the screen. You can also use a keyboard shortcut to close either type of application.

## Closing Desktop Applications

When you are finished working in a desktop application, you can close it. One way to close an application is to use the Close button on the window's title bar. Another way is to right-click the application window's taskbar button to display a shortcut menu that includes a command to close the window. The advantage of using the shortcut menu is that it lets you close active or inactive windows, even if they are minimized.

Emma suggests that you show Behind the Scenes employees two ways to close a desktop application. You'll start by using a shortcut menu to close the inactive WordPad window.

### To close desktop applications:

▶ **1.** Right-click the **WordPad** button 🖼 on the taskbar. The shortcut menu for the WordPad taskbar button opens. See Figure 23.

| Figure 23 | Taskbar button shortcut menu |

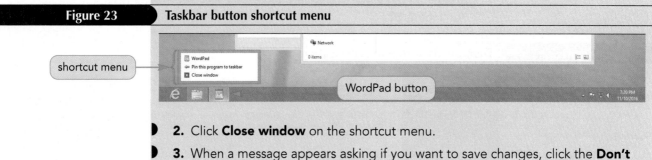

shortcut menu

WordPad button

▶ **2.** Click **Close window** on the shortcut menu.

▶ **3.** When a message appears asking if you want to save changes, click the **Don't Save** button. The WordPad window closes and its button no longer appears on the taskbar.

▶ **4.** Click the **Close** button ❌ in the title bar of the Recycle Bin window to close the application.

Now the WordPad and Recycle Bin windows are closed and only the desktop is displayed on the screen.

## Closing Windows 8 Applications

**TIP**

You can also point to the top of a Windows 8 application until a hand pointer appears, drag the application down until it shrinks to a thumbnail, and then continue dragging to the bottom of the screen to close the application.

As you've seen, Windows 8 applications do not include a control such as a Close button that you can use to close the application. Instead, you close a Windows 8 application using its thumbnail when it appears on its own in the upper-left corner of the screen, or when it appears in the Switch List. You right-click the thumbnail and then click Close on the shortcut menu to close the application. You can also use the Alt+F4 keyboard shortcut to close any application. To do so, you press the Alt and F4 keys at the same time when the application is displayed on the screen.

To demonstrate how to close Windows 8 applications, Emma suggests that you use the shortcut menu and the keyboard shortcut to close the open Windows 8 applications.

**To close Windows 8 applications:**

▶ **1.** Point to the upper-left hot corner, and then click the **Reader** thumbnail to display the Reader app.

▶ **2.** Press the **Alt+F4** keys to close the Reader app and return to the Start screen.

▶ **3.** Point to the upper-left hot corner, and then move the mouse down to display the Switch List.

▶ **4.** Right-click the **Weather** thumbnail, and then click **Close** on the shortcut menu to close the Weather app.

▶ **5.** Click a blank area on the Start screen to close the Switch List.

Before you finish working with Windows 8, you should show Behind the Scenes employees how to get help when they need it.

# Getting Help

Windows 8 **Help and Support** provides on-screen information about Windows 8 and its applications. Help and Support gives you access to Help files stored on your computer as well as Help information stored on the Microsoft website. If you are not connected to the web, you have access to only the Help files stored on your computer.

**To start Windows 8 Help and Support:**

▶ **1.** On the Start screen, type **help** to display the Apps screen and Search menu, with "help" inserted in the Search box.

▶ **2.** Click **Help and Support** in the search results to open the Windows Help and Support window on the desktop. By default, this window displays the Help home page when you start Help and Support.

▶ **3.** Click the **Maximize** button ◻ to maximize the Windows Help and Support window. See Figure 24. The contents of the home page differ depending on whether you are connected to the Internet.

**Trouble?** If the Help and Support window does not display the home page, click the Help home link near the top of the window.

**Figure 24**    **Windows Help and Support window**

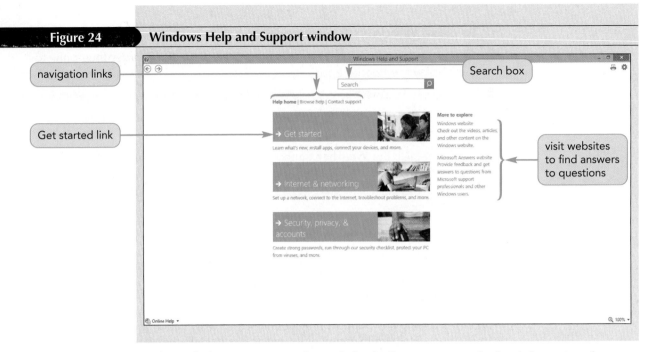

The Help home page provides tools for finding answers and other information about Windows 8. You can click links on the page to view information about popular topics, browse for a specific topic, or search to find an answer to a Windows 8 question.

## Viewing the Get Started Topics

Windows Help and Support includes instructions on the basics of using Windows 8. You can learn more about these basic topics by using the Get started link on the Windows Help and Support home page.

### To view Get started topics:

▶ 1. Click the **Get started** link. A list of topics related to using Windows 8 appears in the Windows Help and Support window.

▶ 2. Click the **Mouse and keyboard: What's new** topic. An article explaining how to use the mouse and keyboard appears.

▶ 3. Scroll down to the bottom of the page, and then click the **Get to know Windows** link. A page opens describing the new features in Windows 8.

▶ 4. Click the **Back** button ⊙ at the top of the window to return to the previous page you visited, which is the Mouse and keyboard page, and then click the **Back** button ⊙ to return to the Get started page.

## Selecting a Topic from the Browse Help List

The Browse help list organizes the information in Windows Help and Support into topics and categories. You can click a link to display the titles of related categories, and then click a topic in a specific category to get help with a particular task or feature. For example, you can use the Browse help list to learn more about personalizing your computer.

### To find a Help topic using the Browse help list:

▶ **1.** Click the **Browse help** link. A list of Windows Help topics appears in the Windows Help and Support window.

▶ **2.** Click the **Personalization** topic to display a list of topics divided by categories related to personalizing your computer.

▶ **3.** In the Customize your PC category, click the **Adding apps, websites, and more to Start** topic. The Windows Help and Support window displays information about that topic.

▶ **4.** Scroll down to review the information on this page, and then scroll up to return to the top of the page.

## Searching the Help Pages

If you can't find the topic you need by clicking a link or browsing topics, or if you want to quickly find Help pages related to a particular topic, you can use the Search box. Suppose you want to know how to exit Windows 8, but you don't know if Windows refers to this as exiting, quitting, closing, or shutting down. Emma suggests you can search the Help pages to find just the right topic.

### To search the Help pages for information on exiting Windows 8:

▶ **1.** Click the **Help home** link to return to the home page.

▶ **2.** Click the **Search** box, type **shut down**, and then press the **Enter** key. A list of Help pages containing the words "shut down" appears in the Windows Help and Support window. See Figure 25. (Your results might differ.)

**Figure 25**     Search Help results

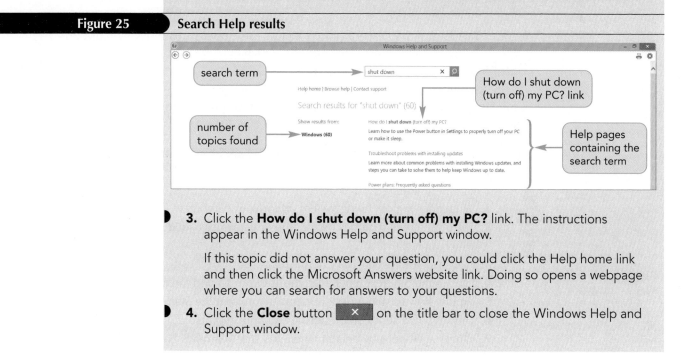

▶ **3.** Click the **How do I shut down (turn off) my PC?** link. The instructions appear in the Windows Help and Support window.

If this topic did not answer your question, you could click the Help home link and then click the Microsoft Answers website link. Doing so opens a webpage where you can search for answers to your questions.

▶ **4.** Click the **Close** button [ × ] on the title bar to close the Windows Help and Support window.

Now that you know how Windows 8 Help works, Emma reminds you to use it when you need to perform a new task or want a reminder about how to complete a procedure.

# Turning Off Windows 8

When you're finished working in Windows 8, you should always turn it off properly. Doing so saves energy, preserves your data and settings, and makes sure your computer starts quickly the next time you use it.

You turn off Windows 8 using the Power button on the Settings menu. First, you use the Charms bar to display the Settings menu, and then you click the Power button to display a menu, which includes the Shut down option. Click Shut down to have Windows close all open programs, including Windows itself, and then completely turn off your computer.

The Power button menu might also include the Sleep option, which instructs Windows to save your work and then turn down the power to your monitor and computer, a condition called **sleep**. A light on the outside of your computer case blinks or changes color to indicate that the computer is sleeping. Because Windows saves your work, you do not need to close your programs or files before your computer goes to sleep. To wake a computer, you typically press the hardware power button on your computer case. Some computer manufacturers might set the computer to wake when you press a key or move the mouse. After you wake a computer, the screen looks exactly as it did when you put your computer to sleep.

> **TIP**
>
> Shutting down does not automatically save your work, so be sure to save your files before selecting the Shut down or Restart option.

### To turn off Windows 8:

1. Point to the upper-right hot corner on the desktop to display the Charms bar, and then click the **Settings** charm to display the Settings menu.

2. Click the **Power** button, and then click **Shut down**. Windows 8 turns off the computer.

   **Trouble?** If the Power button displays the Update and shut down option instead of Shut down, click Update and shut down.

In this tutorial, you started Windows 8 and toured the Start screen and the desktop. You also worked with Windows 8 apps and desktop applications, and learned how to get help when you need it. Finally you learned how to turn off Windows 8.

## REVIEW

### Quick Check

1. What does the operating system do for your computer?
2. The Start screen includes multicolored rectangles called _____, which represent _____.
3. How can you display the Charms bar?
4. Explain the difference between the Start screen and the desktop.
5. Explain how to start a desktop application from the Start screen.
6. The keyboard shortcut for closing an application is _____.
7. What page opens by default when you start Windows Help and Support?
8. What option saves your work before turning off your computer?

**PRACTICE**

## Review Assignments

**There are no Data Files needed for the Review Assignments.**

The day before your first Windows 8 training session for Behind the Scenes employees, Emma Garcia offers to observe your tour of the operating system and help you fine-tune your lesson. You'll start working on the Start screen, with no applications open. Complete the following steps, recording your answers to any questions according to your instructor's preferences:

1. Start Windows 8 and sign in, if necessary.
2. Use the mouse to scroll the Start screen. How many full tiles appear on the screen when you scroll?
3. Zoom the Start screen to reduce the size of the tiles. How many tiles appear on the screen now?
4. Display the desktop. List the major parts of the desktop, including any icons.
5. Start WordPad. Identify each object on the taskbar (not including the notification area). Minimize the WordPad window.
6. Open the Recycle Bin window and then maximize it. How do you know that the Recycle Bin window is active?
7. Redisplay the WordPad window. Which window is active now? How can you tell?
8. Start the Weather app, and then display the Switch List. Which thumbnails are displayed in the Switch List?
9. Display the Start screen, and then start the Reader app. How did you start the Reader app?
10. If possible, snap the Weather app to the left side of the screen, and then unsnap it. Explain how to snap a Windows 8 application to the left side of the screen and then unsnap it.
11. Use a keyboard shortcut to close the Reader app and then the Weather app. Which keyboard shortcut did you use?
12. Use a keyboard shortcut to switch back to the desktop. Which keyboard shortcut did you use?
13. Minimize the WordPad window. In the Recycle Bin window, click the Home tab. Which buttons are active (not gray)? Use any button on the Home tab to open a dialog box. What dialog box did you open? What do you think this dialog box is used for? Click the Cancel button to close the dialog box, and then close the Recycle Bin window.
14. Close the WordPad window from the taskbar. What command did you use?
15. Open Windows Help and Support. Use any link on the home page to learn something new about Windows 8. What did you learn? How did you find this topic?
16. Close Help and Support.
17. Turn off Windows 8 by using the Sleep option, shutting down, or signing out.

**CHALLENGE**

## Case Problem 1

**There are no Data Files needed for this Case Problem.**

*Up and Running*   Up and Running is a computer support firm located in major electronics stores throughout the Midwest. Ken Mathias is the manager of a store in Red Wing, Minnesota. He hired you to work with customers in their homes or businesses. You are preparing for a visit to a customer who is new to Windows 8 and wants to learn about the applications installed on his computer. Complete the following steps:

1. Start Windows 8 and sign in, if necessary.
2. Examine the tiles on the Start screen and use one to start an application that plays music or videos. Which application did you start?
3. Search for an application installed on your computer related to photos. What application did you find?
4. Start the application you found in Step 3. Is it a Windows 8 application or a desktop application? How can you tell?

5. Search for an application installed on your computer that lets you perform calculations. What application did you find?

6. Start the application you found in Step 5. Is it a Windows 8 application or a desktop application? How can you tell?

✦ Explore  7. Use the Search menu to find settings related to music. (*Hint*: After you use the Search menu to search for "music," click the Settings category on the Search menu.) How many settings did you find?

8. Use the Apps screen to start the Paint application. Describe how you started this application.

✦ Explore  9. Point to the buttons in the Paint window until you find one that displays a "Paint Help (F1)" ScreenTip. Click this button, and then describe what happens.

10. Close all open Windows 8 applications only. Describe how you closed the applications.

11. Use Windows Help and Support to find and read about topics that describe two Windows features that make your PC more secure. Which two features did you read about?

12. Close all open windows.

## Case Problem 2

**RESEARCH**

**There are no Data Files needed for this Case Problem.**

*Home Care Therapy*    After earning their certifications as physical and occupational therapists, Josh Cohen and Deborah Whiting decided to start a service called Home Care Therapy for people who need physical or occupational therapy in their homes. They have been using Windows 8 on laptops to schedule client appointments and track client progress, but recently purchased tablet computers to use when they are working with clients face to face. They hired you as a consultant to help them use and maintain their computers. Because Josh and Deborah learned to use Windows 8 on laptop computers, they anticipate that they might have trouble adapting to tablets. Josh asks you to research the skills and techniques they need to use Windows 8 on a tablet. Complete the following:

1. In Windows Help and Support, find information about how to perform the following tasks on a tablet computer:
   * Display the Charms bar.
   * Scroll the Start screen.
   * Zoom the Start screen.
   * Display the desktop.
   * Display app settings, such as Save and Edit.

2. Use the Windows website link to visit the Microsoft website to obtain more information about Windows 8 on a tablet computer. Watch a video that showcases Windows 8 touch features. Then, describe how to rearrange tiles on the Start screen.

3. Choose a topic that describes how to browse the web, and then watch the related video. Explain what's new and different in Internet Explorer for touchscreen devices.

4. Write one to two paragraphs for Josh and Deborah explaining the basics of using Windows 8 on a tablet with a touchscreen.

## OBJECTIVES

- Explore the differences between Windows 7 and Windows 8
- Plan the organization of files and folders
- Use File Explorer to view and manage libraries, folders, and files
- Open and save files
- Create folders
- Copy and move files and folders
- Compress and extract files

# Managing Your Files

*Organizing Files and Folders with Windows 8*

## Case | *Savvy Traveler*

After spending a summer traveling in Italy, Matt Marino started Savvy Traveler, a travel company that organizes small tours in Europe. To market his company, Matt created flyers, brochures, webpages, and other materials that describe the tours he offers. Matt uses the Savvy Traveler office computer to locate and store photos, illustrations, and text documents he can include in his marketing materials. He recently hired you to help manage the office. To keep Matt connected to the office while traveling, he just purchased a new laptop computer running Windows 8. He is familiar with Windows 7, so he needs an overview explaining how Windows 8 is different. Matt asks you to train him on using Windows 8 to organize his files and folders. Although he has only a few files, he knows it's a good idea to set up a logical organization now so he can find his work later as he stores more files and folders on the computer.

In this tutorial, you'll explore the differences between Windows 7 and Windows 8, especially those related to file management tools. You'll also work with Matt to devise a plan for managing his files. You'll learn how Windows 8 organizes files and folders, and then create files and folders yourself and organize them on Matt's computer. You'll also use techniques to display the information you need in folder windows, and explore options for working with compressed files.

## STARTING DATA FILES

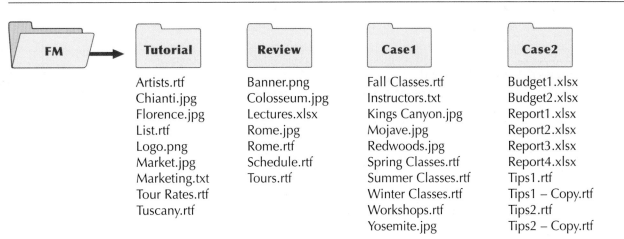

| FM → Tutorial | Review | Case1 | Case2 |
|---|---|---|---|
| Artists.rtf | Banner.png | Fall Classes.rtf | Budget1.xlsx |
| Chianti.jpg | Colosseum.jpg | Instructors.txt | Budget2.xlsx |
| Florence.jpg | Lectures.xlsx | Kings Canyon.jpg | Report1.xlsx |
| List.rtf | Rome.jpg | Mojave.jpg | Report2.xlsx |
| Logo.png | Rome.rtf | Redwoods.jpg | Report3.xlsx |
| Market.jpg | Schedule.rtf | Spring Classes.rtf | Report4.xlsx |
| Marketing.txt | Tours.rtf | Summer Classes.rtf | Tips1.rtf |
| Tour Rates.rtf | | Winter Classes.rtf | Tips1 – Copy.rtf |
| Tuscany.rtf | | Workshops.rtf | Tips2.rtf |
| | | Yosemite.jpg | Tips2 – Copy.rtf |

# Visual Overview:

You use the Change your view button to change the size of the icons in the window.

In Windows 7, you use **Windows Explorer** to navigate the contents of your computer.

Use the arrow buttons in the Address bar to navigate to other locations on your computer.

The **file path** is a notation that indicates a file's location on your computer.

Use the Search box to search for files in the current folder.

The Windows Explorer **toolbar** provides buttons for completing tasks.

Windows Explorer includes a **navigation pane**, which displays icons and links to resources and locations on your computer.

By default, Windows Explorer includes the **Details pane** at the bottom of the window, which displays the properties of the selected object.

Windows provides **libraries** so you can organize files by category—documents, music, pictures, and video.

A thumbnail image previews the file contents for certain types of files.

The zipped folder icon indicates a **compressed folder**, which stores files so they take up less disk space.

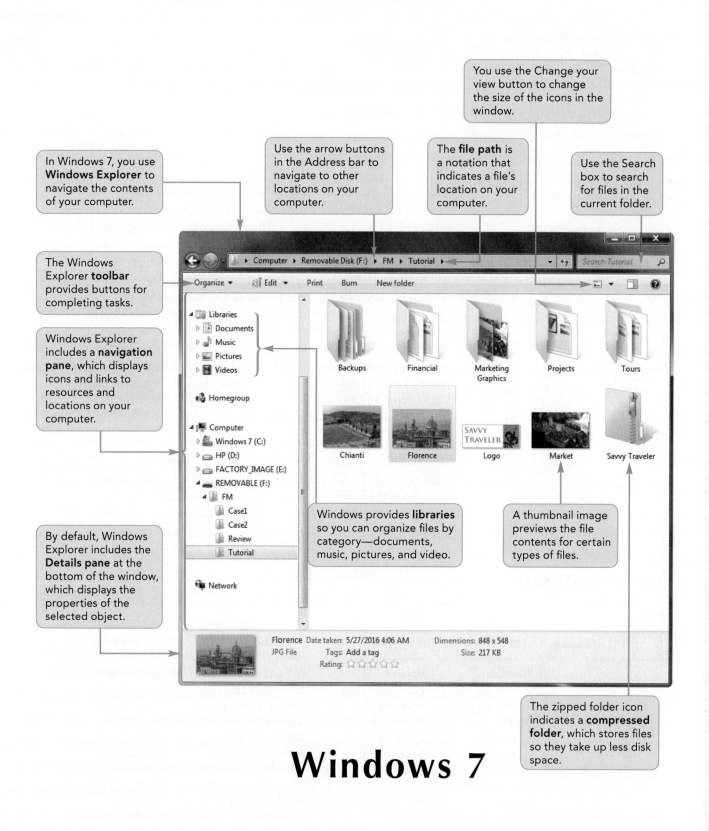

# Windows 7

# Comparing Windows 7 & Windows 8

The **View tab** on the ribbon contains options for specifying how the information displays in File Explorer.

Windows provides **libraries** so you can organize files by category—documents, music, pictures, and videos.

The **Quick Access toolbar** contains buttons for viewing properties and creating a folder.

Use the arrow buttons in the Address bar to navigate to other locations on your computer.

The **file path** in the Address bar shows a file's location on your computer.

In Windows 8, you use **File Explorer** to navigate the contents of your computer.

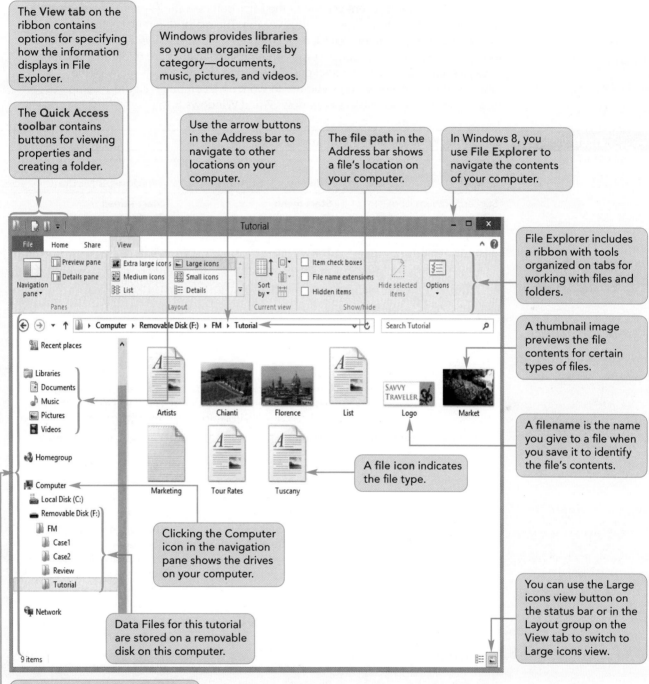

File Explorer includes a ribbon with tools organized on tabs for working with files and folders.

A thumbnail image previews the file contents for certain types of files.

A **filename** is the name you give to a file when you save it to identify the file's contents.

A file icon indicates the file type.

Clicking the Computer icon in the navigation pane shows the drives on your computer.

You can use the Large icons view button on the status bar or in the Layout group on the View tab to switch to Large icons view.

Data Files for this tutorial are stored on a removable disk on this computer.

File Explorer includes a **navigation** pane, which displays icons and links to resources and locations on your computer.

# Windows 8

# Exploring the Differences Between Windows 7 and Windows 8

Windows 8, the most recent version of the Microsoft operating system, is significantly different from Windows 7, the previous version. The major difference is that Windows 8 is designed for touchscreen computers such as tablets and laptops with touch-activated displays, though it runs on computers with more traditional pointing devices such as a mouse or a trackpad. This design change affects many of the fundamental Windows features you use to work on a computer. Figure 1 compares how to perform typical tasks in Windows 7 and Windows 8.

| Figure 1 | Comparing Windows 7 and Windows 8 | |
|---|---|---|

| Task | Windows 7 Method | Windows 8 Method |
|---|---|---|
| Start applications (sometimes called apps) | **Start menu** Open the Start menu by clicking the Start button. | **Start screen** The Start screen appears when you start Windows. |
| Access applications, documents, settings, and other resources | **Start menu** Use the Start menu, All Programs list, and Search box. | **Charms bar** The Charms bar appears when you point to the upper-right or lower-right corner of the screen, and displays buttons, called charms, for interacting with Windows 8 and accessing applications. |
| Select objects and commands | **Icons** Icons are small and detailed, designed for interaction with mechanical pointing devices. | **Icons and tiles** Icons and tiles are large and simplified, designed for interaction with your fingertips. |
| Open and work in applications | **Desktop** Applications all use a single desktop interface featuring windows and dialog boxes. | **Windows 8 and desktop** Applications use one of two interfaces: the Windows 8 interface (featuring tiles and a full-screen layout) or the desktop. |
| Display content out of view | **Vertical scrolling** Applications allow more vertical scrolling than horizontal scrolling. | **Horizontal scrolling** The Start screen and applications allow more horizontal scrolling than vertical scrolling to take advantage of wide-screen monitors. |
| Store files | **Physical storage devices** Windows primarily provides access to disks physically connected to the computer. | **Cloud storage locations** A Microsoft user account provides access to information stored online. |
| Enter text | **Physical keyboard** Type on the keyboard attached to the computer. | **On-screen keyboard** If your computer does not have a physical keyboard, type using the on-screen keyboard. |

© 2014 Cengage Learning

Although Windows 7 introduced a few gestures for touchscreen users, Windows 8 expands the use of gestures and interactions. In Windows 8, you can use touch gestures to do nearly everything you can do with a pointing device. Figure 2 lists common Windows 8 interactions and their touch and mouse equivalents.

| Figure 2 | Windows 8 touch and mouse interactions |

| Interaction | Touch Gesture | Mouse Action |
|---|---|---|
| Display a ScreenTip, text that identifies the name or purpose of the button | Touch and hold (or press) an object such as a button. | Point to an object such as a button. |
| Display an Apps bar, which displays options related to the current task and access to the Apps screen | Swipe from the top or bottom of the screen toward the center. | Right-click the bottom edge of the screen. |
| Display the Charms bar | Swipe from the right edge of the screen toward the center. | Point to the upper-right or lower-right corner of the screen. |
| Display thumbnails of open apps (the Switch List) | Swipe from the left edge of the screen toward the center. | Point to the upper-left corner of the screen, and then drag the pointer down. |
| Drag an object | Press and then drag. | Click, hold, and then drag. |
| Scroll the Start screen | Swipe from the right edge of the screen to the left. | Click the scroll arrows, or drag the scroll bar. |
| Select an object or perform an action such as starting an app | Tap the object. | Click the object. |
| Zoom | Pinch two fingers to zoom out or move the fingers apart to zoom in. | Click the Zoom button. |

© 2014 Cengage Learning

Despite the substantial differences between how you interact with Windows 7 and Windows 8, the steps you follow to perform work in either operating system are the same. In a typical computer session, you start an application and open a **file**, often referred to as a document, which is a collection of data that has a name and is stored on a computer. You view, add, or change the file contents, and then save and close the file. You can complete all of these steps using Windows 7 or Windows 8. Because most of your work involves files, you need to understand how to save and organize files so you can easily find and open them when necessary.

# Organizing Files and Folders

Knowing how to save, locate, and organize computer files makes you more productive when you are working with a computer. After you create a file, you can open it, edit its contents, print the file, and save it again—usually using the same application you used to create the file. You organize files by storing them in folders. A **folder** is a container for files. You need to organize files and folders so that you can find them easily and work efficiently.

A file cabinet is a common metaphor for computer file organization. As shown in Figure 3, a computer is like a file cabinet that has two or more drawers—each drawer is a storage device, or **disk**. Each disk contains folders that hold files. To make it easy to retrieve files, you arrange them logically into folders. For example, one folder might contain financial data, another might contain your creative work, and another could contain information you're gathering for an upcoming vacation.

**Figure 3**    **Computer as a file cabinet**

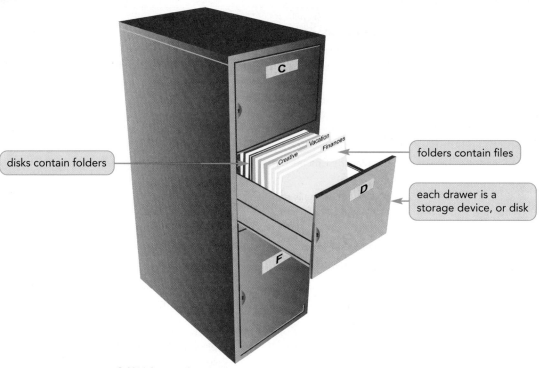

disks contain folders

folders contain files

each drawer is a storage device, or disk

© 2014 Cengage Learning

A computer can store folders and files on different types of disks, ranging from removable media—such as **USB drives** (also called USB flash drives) and digital video discs (DVDs)—to **hard disks**, or fixed disks, which are permanently housed in a computer. Hard disks are the most popular type of computer storage because they provide an economical way to store many gigabytes of data. (A **gigabyte**, or **GB**, is about 1 billion bytes, with each byte roughly equivalent to a character of data.)

To have your computer access a removable disk, you must insert the disk into a **drive**, which is a device that can retrieve and sometimes record data on a disk. A computer's hard disk is already contained in a drive inside the computer, so you don't need to insert it each time you use the computer.

A computer distinguishes one drive from another by assigning each a drive letter. The hard disk is assigned to drive C. The remaining drives can have any other letters, but are usually assigned in the order that the drives were installed on the computer—so your USB drive might be drive D or drive F.

## Understanding How to Organize Files and Folders

Windows stores thousands of files in many folders on the hard disk of your computer. These are system files that Windows needs to display the Start screen and desktop, use drives, and perform other operating system tasks. To keep the system stable and to find files quickly, Windows organizes the folders and files in a hierarchy, or **file system**. At the top of the hierarchy, Windows stores folders and important files that it needs when you turn on the computer. This location is called the **root directory** and is usually drive C (the hard disk). As Figure 4 shows, the root directory contains all the other folders and files on the computer. The figure also shows that folders can contain other folders. An effectively organized computer contains a few folders in the root directory, and those folders contain other folders, also called **subfolders**.

| Figure 4 | Organizing folders and files on a hard disk |
| --- | --- |

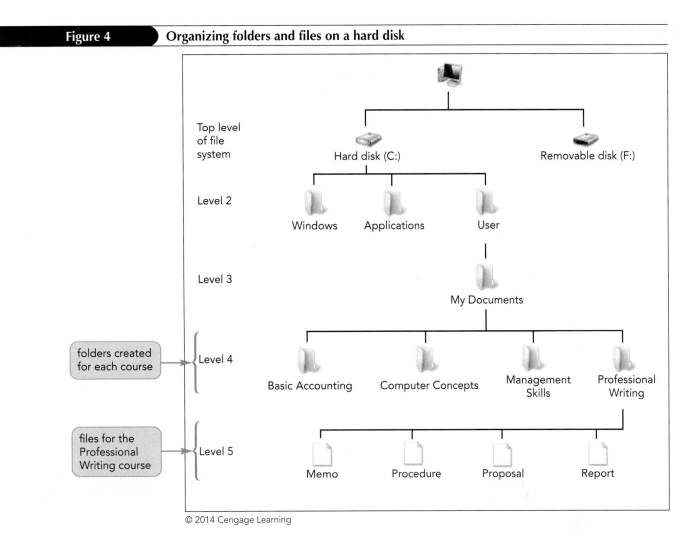

© 2014 Cengage Learning

The root directory is the top level of the hard disk and is for system files and folders only. You should not store your own work in the root directory because your files could interfere with Windows or an application. (If you are working in a computer lab, you might not be allowed to access the root directory.)

Do not delete or move any files or folders from the root directory of the hard disk; doing so could disrupt the system so that you can't start or run the computer. In fact, you should not reorganize or change any folder that contains installed software because Windows 8 expects to find the files for specific applications within certain folders. In Figure 4, folders containing software are stored at Level 2 of the file system. If you reorganize or change these folders, Windows 8 can't locate and start the applications stored in those folders. Likewise, you should not make changes to the folder (usually named Windows) that contains the Windows 8 operating system.

Level 2 of the file system also includes a folder for your user account, such as the User folder. This folder contains all of your system settings, preferences, and other user account information. It also contains subfolders, such as the My Documents folder, for your personal files. The folders in Level 3 of the file system are designed to contain subfolders for your personal files. You can create as many subfolders at Level 4 of the file system as you need to store other folders and files and keep them organized.

Figure 4 shows how you could organize your files on a hard disk if you were taking a full semester of business classes. To duplicate this organization, you would open the main folder for your documents, such as My Documents, create four folders— one each for the Basic Accounting, Computer Concepts, Management Skills, and Professional Writing courses—and then store the writing assignments you complete in the Professional Writing folder.

If you store your files on removable media, such as a USB drive, you can use a simpler organization because you do not have to account for system files. In general, the larger the storage medium, the more levels of folders you should use because large media can store more files and, therefore, need better organization. For example, if you were organizing your files on a 12 GB USB drive, you could create folders in the top level of the USB drive for each general category of documents you store—one each for Courses, Creative, Financials, and Vacation. The Courses folder could then include one folder for each course (Basic Accounting, Computer Concepts, Management Skills, and Professional Writing), and each of those folders could contain the appropriate files.

PROSKILLS

### Decision Making: Determining Where to Store Files

When you create and save files on your computer's hard disk, you should store them in subfolders. The top level of the hard disk is off-limits for your files because they could interfere with system files. If you are working on your own computer, store your files within the My Documents folder in the Documents library, which is where many applications save your files by default. When you use a computer on the job, your employer might assign a main folder to you for storing your work. In either case, if you simply store all your files in one folder, you will soon have trouble finding the files you want. Instead, you should create subfolders within a main folder to separate files in a way that makes sense for you.

Even if you store most of your files on removable media, such as USB drives, you still need to organize those files into folders and subfolders. Before you start creating folders, whether on a hard disk or removable disk, you need to plan the organization you will use. Following your plan increases your efficiency because you don't have to pause and decide which folder to use when you save your files. A file organization plan also makes you more productive in your computer work—the next time you need a particular file, you'll know where to find it.

## Exploring Files and Folders

As shown in the Visual Overview, you use File Explorer in Windows 8 to explore the files and folders on your computer. File Explorer displays the contents of your computer by using icons to represent drives, folders, and files. When you open File Explorer, it shows the contents of the Windows built-in libraries by default. Windows provides these libraries so you can organize files by category—documents, music, pictures, and video. A library can display these categories of files together, no matter where the files are actually stored. For example, you might keep some music files in a folder named Albums on your hard disk. You might also keep music files in a Songs folder on a USB drive. Although the Albums and Songs folders are physically stored in different locations, you can set up the Music library to display both folders in the same File Explorer window. You can then search and arrange the files as a single collection to quickly find the music you want to open and play. In this way, you use libraries to organize your files into categories so you can easily locate and work with files.

The File Explorer window is divided into two sections, called panes. The left pane is the navigation pane, which contains icons and links to locations on your computer. The right pane displays the contents of the location selected in the navigation pane. If the navigation pane showed all the contents on your computer at once, it could be a very long list. Instead, you open drives and folders only when you want to see what they contain. For example, to display the hierarchy of the folders and other locations on your computer, you select the Computer icon in the navigation pane, and then select the icon for a drive, such as Local Disk (C:) or Removable Disk (F:). You can then open and explore folders on that drive.

If a folder contains undisplayed subfolders, an expand icon appears to the left of the folder icon. (The same is true for drives.) To view the folders contained in an object, you click the expand icon. A collapse icon then appears next to the folder icon; click the collapse icon to hide the folder's subfolders. To view the files contained in a folder, you click the folder icon, and the files appear in the right pane. See Figure 5.

**Figure 5**    **Viewing files in File Explorer**

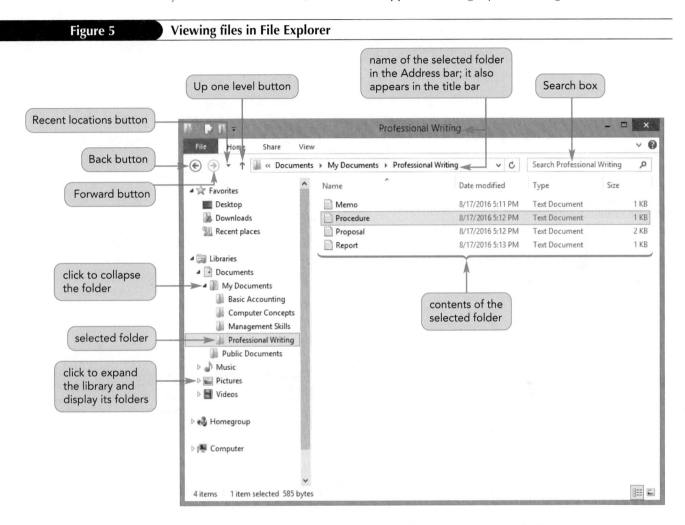

Using the navigation pane helps you explore your computer and orients you to your current location. As you move, copy, delete, and perform other tasks with the files and folders in the right pane of File Explorer, you can refer to the navigation pane to see how your changes affect the overall organization of the selected location.

In addition to using the navigation pane, you can explore your computer in File Explorer using the following navigation techniques:

- Opening drives and folders in the right pane—To view the contents of a drive or folder, double-click the drive or folder icon in the right pane of File Explorer.
- Using the Address bar—You can use the Address bar to navigate to a different folder. The Address bar displays the file path for your current folder. (Recall that a file path shows the location of a folder or file.) Click a folder name such as My Documents in the Address bar to navigate to that folder, or click an arrow button to navigate to a different location in the folder's hierarchy.
- Clicking the Back, Forward, Recent locations, and Up to buttons—Use the Back, Forward, and Recent locations buttons to navigate to other folders you have already opened. Use the Up to button to navigate up to the folder containing the current folder.
- Using the Search box—To find a file or folder stored in the current folder or its subfolders, type a word or phrase in the Search box. The search begins as soon as you

start typing. Windows finds files based on text in the filename, text within the file, and other properties of the file.

You'll practice using some of these navigation techniques later in the tutorial. Right now, you'll show Matt how to open File Explorer. Your computer should be turned on and displaying the Start screen.

### To open File Explorer:

▶ **1.** On the Start screen, click the **Desktop** tile to display the desktop.

▶ **2.** On the taskbar, click the **File Explorer** button [icon]. The File Explorer window opens, displaying the contents of the default libraries.

▶ **3.** In the Libraries section of the navigation pane, click the **expand** icon [▷] next to the Documents icon. The folders in the Documents library appear in the navigation pane; see Figure 6. The contents of your computer will differ.

| Figure 6 | Viewing the contents of the Documents library |

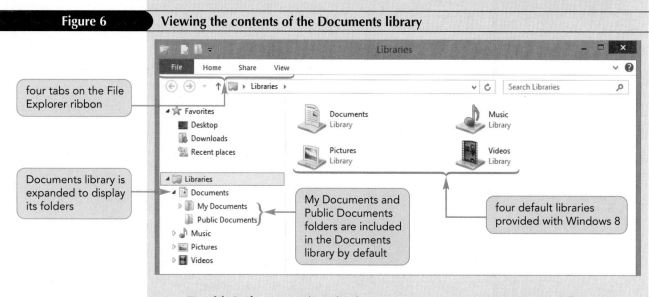

four tabs on the File Explorer ribbon

Documents library is expanded to display its folders

My Documents and Public Documents folders are included in the Documents library by default

four default libraries provided with Windows 8

**Trouble?** If your window displays icons in a size or arrangement different from the one shown in the figure, you can still explore files and folders. The same is true for all the figures in this tutorial.

▶ **4.** In the navigation pane, click the **My Documents** folder to display its contents in the right pane.

**TIP**

When you are working in the navigation pane, you only need to click a folder to open it; you do not need to double-click it.

As Figure 6 shows, the File Explorer window includes a ribbon, which is collapsed by default so it displays only tab names, such as File, Home, Share, and View. The Visual Overview shows the expanded ribbon, which displays the options for the selected tab. You'll work with the ribbon and learn how to expand it later in the tutorial.

### Navigating to Your Data Files

To navigate to the files you want, it helps to know the file path because the file path tells you exactly where the file is stored in the hierarchy of drives and folders on your computer. For example, Matt has a file named "Logo," which contains an image of the company's logo. If Matt stored the Logo file in a folder named "Marketing" and saved that folder in a folder named "Savvy Traveler" on drive F (a USB drive) on his computer, the Address bar would show the following file path for the Logo file:

**Computer ▸ Removable Disk (F:) ▸ Savvy Traveler ▸ Marketing ▸ Logo.png**

This path has five parts, with each part separated by an arrow button:

- Computer—The main container for the file, such as "Computer" or "Network"
- Removable Disk (F:)—The drive name, including the drive letter followed by a colon, which indicates a drive rather than a folder
- Savvy Traveler—The top-level folder on drive F
- Marketing—A subfolder in the Savvy Traveler folder
- Logo.png—The name of the file

Although File Explorer uses arrow buttons to separate locations in a file path, printed documents use backslashes ( \ ). For example, if you read an instruction to open the Logo file in the Savvy Traveler\Marketing folder on your USB drive, you know you must navigate to the USB drive attached to your computer, open the Savvy Traveler folder, and then open the Marketing folder to find the Logo file.

File Explorer displays the file path in the Address bar so you can keep track of your current location as you navigate between drives and folders. You can use File Explorer to navigate to the Data Files you need for this tutorial. Before you perform the following steps, you should know where you stored your Data Files, such as on a USB drive. The following steps assume that drive is Removable Disk (F:), a USB drive. If necessary, substitute the appropriate drive on your system when you perform the steps.

### To navigate to your Data Files:

▶ **1.** Make sure your computer can access your Data Files for this tutorial. For example, if you are using a USB drive, insert the drive into the USB port.

   **Trouble?** If you don't have the starting Data Files, you need to get them before you can proceed. Your instructor will either give you the Data Files or ask you to obtain them from a specified location (such as a network drive). If you have any questions about the Data Files, see your instructor or technical support person for assistance.

▶ **2.** In the navigation pane of File Explorer, click the **expand** icon ▷ next to the Computer icon to display the drives on your computer, if necessary.

▶ **3.** Click the **expand** icon ▷ next to the drive containing your Data Files, such as Removable Disk (F:). A list of the folders on that drive appears below the drive name.

▶ **4.** If the list of folders does not include the FM folder, continue clicking the **expand** icon ▷ to navigate to the folder that contains the FM folder.

▶ **5.** Click the **expand** icon ▷ next to the FM folder to expand the folder, and then click the **FM** folder so that its contents appear in the navigation pane and in the right pane of the folder window. The FM folder contains the Case1, Case2, Review, and Tutorial folders, as shown in Figure 7. The other folders on your computer might vary.

**Figure 7**    **Navigating to the FM folder**

**Figure 7**    **Navigating to the FM folder**

- file path displayed in the Address bar
- the name of the selected folder appears in the File Explorer title bar
- contents of the FM folder; your Date modified information might differ
- your Data Files might be stored on a different drive
- selected FM folder is expanded in the navigation pane
- Tutorial folder

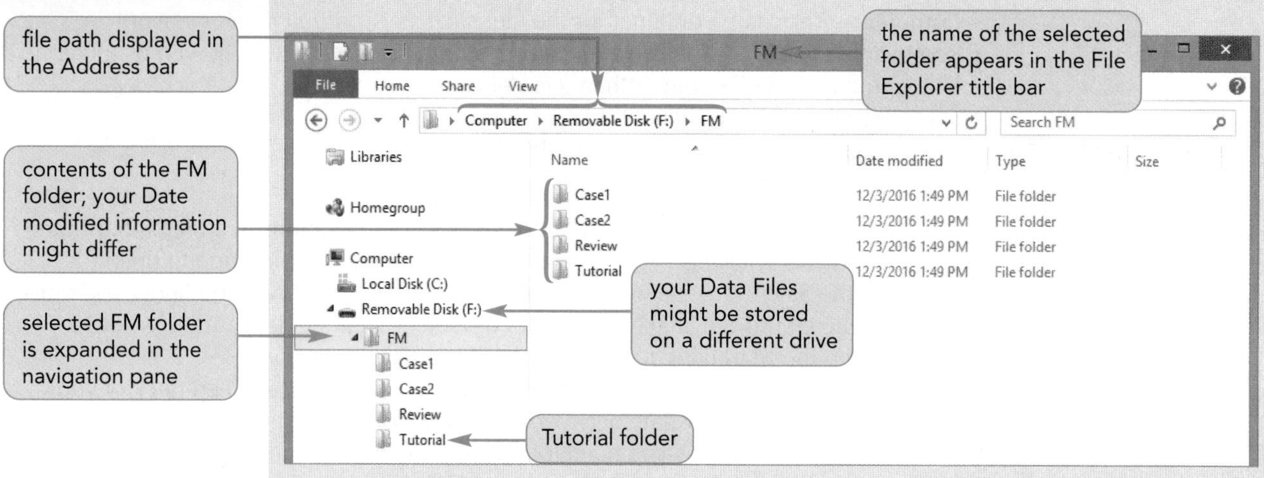

**6.** In the navigation pane, click the **Tutorial** folder. The files it contains appear in the right pane.

You can change the appearance of the File Explorer window to suit your preferences. You'll do so next so you can see more details about folders and files.

## Changing the View

File Explorer provides eight ways to view the contents of a folder: Extra large icons, Large icons, Medium icons, Small icons, List, Details, Tiles, and Content. For example, the files in the Tutorial folder are currently displayed in Details view, which is the default view for all folders except those stored in the Pictures library. Details view displays a small icon to identify each file's type and lists file details in columns, such as the date the file was last modified, the file type, and the size of the file. Although only Details view lists the file details, you can see these details in any other view by pointing to a file to display a ScreenTip.

To change the view of File Explorer to any of the eight views, you use the View tab on the ribbon. To switch to Details view or Large icons view, you can use the view buttons on the status bar.

**REFERENCE**

*Changing the View in File Explorer*

- Click a view button on the status bar.

*or*

- Click the View tab on the ribbon.
- In the Layout group, click the view option; or click the More button, if necessary, and then click a view option.

You'll show Matt how to change the view of the Tutorial folder in the File Explorer window.

## To change the view of the Tutorial folder in File Explorer:

▶ **1.** On the ribbon, click the **View** tab.

▶ **2.** In the Layout group, click **Medium icons**. The files appear in Medium icons view in File Explorer. See Figure 8.

---

| Figure 8 | Files in the Tutorial folder in Medium icons view |

View tab on the ribbon

Expand the Ribbon button

icons are displayed in Medium icons view

thumbnail image previews the file contents for certain file types

file icon identifies the file type; your icons might be different

Tutorial folder is selected in the navigation pane

Details view button

9 items

Photos courtesy of Lisa Ruffolo

Because the icons used to identify types of files depend on the applications installed on your computer, the file icons that appear in your window might be different.

▶ **3.** On the status bar, click the **Large icons view** button. The window shows the files with large icons and no file details.

When you clicked the View tab in the previous steps, the ribbon expanded so you could select an option and then collapsed after you clicked the Medium icons option. You can keep the ribbon expanded in the File Explorer window so you can easily access all of its options. You'll show Matt how to expand the ribbon and then use the View tab to switch to Details view.

## To expand the ribbon in File Explorer:

▶ **1.** Click the **Expand the Ribbon** button to expand the ribbon. The Expand the Ribbon button changes to the Minimize the Ribbon button, which you could click if you wanted to collapse the ribbon.

▶ **2.** On the View tab, in the Layout group, click **Details**. The window shows the files with small icons and lists the file details.

No matter which view you use, you can sort the file list by the name of the files or another detail, such as size, type, or date. When you **sort** files, you list them in ascending order (A to Z, 0 to 9, or earliest to latest date) or descending order (Z to A, 9 to 0, or latest to earliest date) by a file detail. If you're viewing music files, you can sort by details such as contributing artists or album title; and if you're viewing picture files, you can sort by details such as date taken or size. Sorting can help you find a particular file in a long file listing. For example, suppose you want to work on a document that you know you edited on June 4, 2016, but you can't remember the name of the file. You can sort the file list by date modified to find the file you want.

When you are working in Details view in File Explorer, you sort by clicking a column heading that appears at the top of the file list. In other views, you use the View tab on the ribbon to sort. In the Current view group, click the Sort by button, and then click a file detail.

**TIP**

To sort by a file detail that does not appear as a column heading, right-click any column heading and then select a file detail.

### To sort the file list by date modified:

▶ **1.** At the top of the file list, click the **Date modified** column heading button. The down arrow that appears above the label of the Date modified button indicates that the files are sorted in descending (newest to oldest) order by the date the file was modified. At the top of the list is the List file, which was modified on June 18, 2016.

    **Trouble?** If your folder window does not contain a Date modified column, right-click any column heading, click Date modified on the shortcut menu, and then repeat Step 1.

▶ **2.** Click the **Date modified** column heading button again. The up arrow on the Date modified button indicates that the sort order is reversed, with the files listed in ascending (oldest to newest) order.

▶ **3.** Click the **Name** column heading button to sort the files in alphabetical order by name. The Artists file is now listed first.

Now that Matt is comfortable working in File Explorer, you're ready to show him how to manage his files and folders.

## Managing Files and Folders

As discussed earlier, you manage your personal files and folders by storing them according to a logical organization so that they are easy to find later. You can organize files as you create, edit, and save them, or you can do so later by creating folders, if necessary, and then moving and copying files into the folders.

To create a file-organization plan for Matt's files, you can review Figure 8 and look for files that logically belong together. In the Tutorial folder, Chianti, Florence, Logo, and Market are all graphics files that Matt uses for marketing and sales. He created the Artists and Tuscany files to describe Italian tours. The Marketing and Tour Rates files relate to business finances. Matt thinks the List file contains a task list for completing a project, but he isn't sure of its contents. He does recall creating the file using WordPad.

If the List file does contain a project task list, you can organize the files by creating four folders—one for graphics, one for tours, another for the financial files, and a fourth folder for projects. When you create a folder, you give it a name, preferably one that describes its contents. A folder name can have up to 255 characters, and any character is allowed, except / \ : * ? " < > and |. Considering these conventions, you could create four folders to contain Matt's files, as follows:

- Marketing Graphics folder—Chianti, Florence, Logo, and Market files
- Tours folder—Artists and Tuscany files
- Financial folder—Marketing and Tour Rates files
- Projects folder—List file

Before you start creating folders according to this plan, you need to verify the contents of the List file. You can do so by opening the file.

## Opening a File

**TIP**

To select the default application for opening a file, right-click the file in File Explorer, point to Open with, and then click Choose default application. Click an application in the list that opens, and then click OK.

You can open a file from a running application or from File Explorer. To open a file in a running application, you select the application's Open command to access the Open dialog box, which you use to navigate to the file you want, select the file, and then open it. In the Open dialog box, you use the same tools that are available in File Explorer to navigate to the file you want to open. If the application you want to use is not running, you can open a file by double-clicking it in the right pane of File Explorer. The file usually opens in the application that you used to create or edit it.

Occasionally, File Explorer will open the file in an application other than the one you want to use to work with the file. For example, double-clicking a digital picture file usually opens the picture in a picture viewer application. If you want to edit the picture, you must open the file in a graphics editing application. When you need to specify an application to open a file, you can right-click the file, point to Open with on the shortcut menu, and then click the name of the application that you want to use.

Matt says that he might want to edit the List file to add another task. You'll show him how to use File Explorer to open the file in WordPad, which he used to create the file, and then edit it.

### To open and edit the List file:

▶ 1. In the right pane of File Explorer, right-click the **List** file, and then point to **Open with** on the shortcut menu to display a list of applications that can open the file. See Figure 9.

**Trouble?** If a list does not appear when you point to Open with on the shortcut menu, click Open with to display a window asking how you want to open this file.

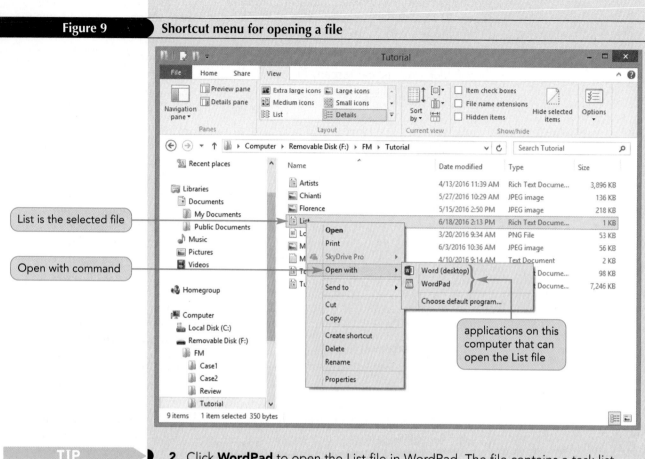

**Figure 9    Shortcut menu for opening a file**

List is the selected file

Open with command

applications on this computer that can open the List file

**TIP**

In File Explorer, you can also double-click a file to open it in the default application for that file type.

2. Click **WordPad** to open the List file in WordPad. The file contains a task list for the marketing project, which includes three items.

   **Trouble?** If you had to click Open with instead of pointing to it, in the window that asks how you want to open this file, click Keep using WordPad.

3. Press the **Ctrl+End** keys to move the insertion point to the end of the document, press the **Enter** key if necessary to start a new line, and then type **4. Review the Tours in Italy webpage.**

Now that you've added text to the List file, you need to save it to preserve the changes you made.

## Saving a File

As you are creating or editing a file, you should save it frequently so you don't lose your work. When you save a file, you need to decide what name to use for the file and where to store it. Most applications provide a default location for saving a file, which makes it easy to find the file again later. However, you can select a different location depending on where you want to store the file.

Besides a storage location, every file must have a filename, which provides important information about the file, including its contents and purpose. A filename such as Italian Tours.docx has the following three parts:

- Main part of the filename—When you save a file, you need to provide only the main part of the filename, such as "Italian Tours."
- Dot—The dot ( . ) separates the main part of the filename from the extension.
- Extension—The **extension** includes the three or four characters that follow the dot in the filename and identify the file's type.

Similar to folder names, the main part of a filename can have up to 255 characters. This gives you plenty of room to name your file accurately enough so that you'll recognize the contents of the file just by looking at the filename. You can use spaces and certain punctuation symbols in your filenames. However, filenames cannot contain the symbols / \ : * ? " < > or | because these characters have special meanings in Windows 8.

Windows and other software add the dot and the extension to a filename, though File Explorer does not display them by default. Instead, File Explorer shows the file icon associated with the extension or a thumbnail for some types of files, such as graphics. For example, in a file named Italian Tours.docx, the docx extension identifies the file as one created in Microsoft Word, a word-processing application. File Explorer displays this file using a Microsoft Word icon and the main part of its filename. For a file named Italian Tours.png, the png extension identifies the file as one created in a graphics application such as Paint. In Details view or List view, File Explorer displays this file using a Paint icon and the main part of its filename. In other views, File Explorer does not use an icon, but displays the file contents in a thumbnail. File Explorer treats the Italian Tours.docx and Italian Tours.png files differently because their extensions distinguish them as different types of files, even though the main parts of their filenames are identical.

When you save a new file, you use the Save As dialog box to provide a filename and select a location for the file. You can create a folder for the new file at the same time you save the file. When you edit a file you saved previously, you can use the application's Save command to save your changes to the file, keeping the same name and location. If you want to save the edited file with a different name or in a different location, however, you need to use the Save As dialog box to specify the new name or location.

As with the Open dialog box, you specify the file location in the Save As dialog box using the same navigation techniques and tools that are available in File Explorer. You might need to click the Browse Folders button to expand the Save As dialog box so it displays these tools. In addition, the Save As dialog box always includes a File name box where you specify a filename.

## INSIGHT

### Saving Files on SkyDrive

Some Windows 8 applications, such as Microsoft Office, include SkyDrive as a location for saving and opening files. **SkyDrive** is a Microsoft service that provides up to 7 GB of online storage space for your files at no charge. You can purchase additional space if you need it. For example, if you create a document in Microsoft Word, your SkyDrive appears as a location for saving the document. (Your SkyDrive appears with your username, such as Matt's SkyDrive.) If you have a Microsoft account, you can select a folder on your SkyDrive to save the document online. (If you don't have a Microsoft account, you can sign up for one by visiting the SkyDrive website.) Because the file is stored online, it takes up no storage space on your computer and is available from any computer with an Internet connection. You access the document by opening it in Word or by visiting the SkyDrive website, and then signing in to your Microsoft account. To share the document with other people, you can send them a link to the document via email. They can use the link to access the document even if they do not have a Microsoft account.

One reason that Matt had trouble remembering the contents of the List file is that "List" is not a descriptive name. A better name for this file is Task List. You will save this document in the Tutorial subfolder of the FM folder provided with your Data Files. You will also use the Save As dialog box to specify a new name for the file as you save it.

## To save the List file with a new name:

▶ 1. On the ribbon in the WordPad window, click the **File** tab to display commands for working with files.

▶ 2. Click **Save as** to open the Save As dialog box, as shown in Figure 10. The Tutorial folder is selected as the storage location for this file because you opened the file from this folder.

**Figure 10**    Saving a file using the Save As dialog box

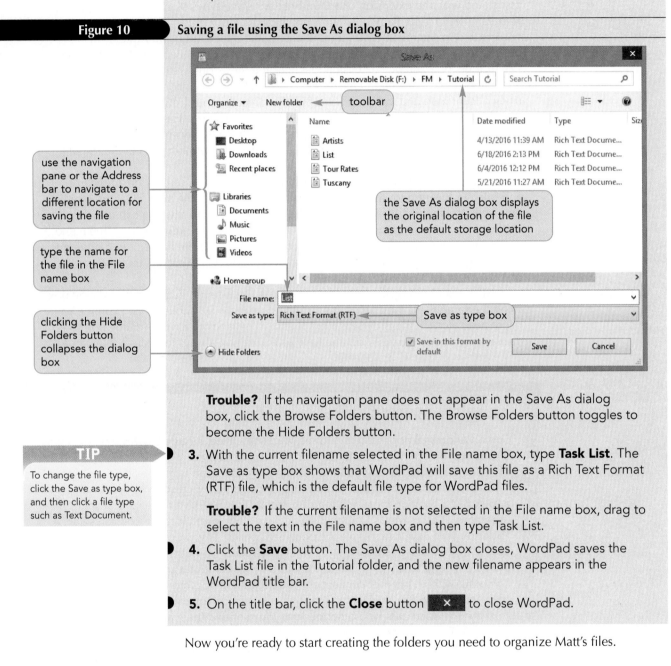

use the navigation pane or the Address bar to navigate to a different location for saving the file

the Save As dialog box displays the original location of the file as the default storage location

type the name for the file in the File name box

clicking the Hide Folders button collapses the dialog box

Save as type box

**Trouble?** If the navigation pane does not appear in the Save As dialog box, click the Browse Folders button. The Browse Folders button toggles to become the Hide Folders button.

**TIP**

To change the file type, click the Save as type box, and then click a file type such as Text Document.

▶ 3. With the current filename selected in the File name box, type **Task List**. The Save as type box shows that WordPad will save this file as a Rich Text Format (RTF) file, which is the default file type for WordPad files.

**Trouble?** If the current filename is not selected in the File name box, drag to select the text in the File name box and then type Task List.

▶ 4. Click the **Save** button. The Save As dialog box closes, WordPad saves the Task List file in the Tutorial folder, and the new filename appears in the WordPad title bar.

▶ 5. On the title bar, click the **Close** button ![X] to close WordPad.

Now you're ready to start creating the folders you need to organize Matt's files.

# Creating Folders

You originally proposed creating four new folders for Matt's files: Marketing Graphics, Tours, Financial, and Projects. Matt asks you to create these folders now. After that, you'll move his files to the appropriate folders. You create folders in File Explorer using one of three methods: using the New folder button in the New group on the Home tab; using the New folder button on the Quick Access Toolbar; or right-clicking to display a shortcut menu that includes the New command.

## Guidelines for Creating Folders

Consider the following guidelines as you create folders:

- Keep folder names short yet descriptive of the folder's contents. Long folder names can be more difficult to display in their entirety in folder windows, so use names that are short but clear. Choose names that will be meaningful later, such as project names or course numbers.
- Create subfolders to organize files. If a file list in File Explorer is so long that you must scroll the window, you should probably organize those files into subfolders.
- Develop standards for naming folders. Use a consistent naming scheme that is clear to you, such as one that uses a project name as the name of the main folder, and includes step numbers in each subfolder name (for example, 1-Outline, 2-First Draft, 3-Final Draft, and so on).

In the following steps, you will create the four folders for Matt in your Tutorial folder. Because it is easier to work with files using large file icons, you'll switch to Large icons view first.

## To create the folders:

▶ 1. On the status bar in the File Explorer window, click the **Large icons view** button ▣ to switch to Large icons view.

▶ 2. Click the **Home** tab to display the Home tab on the ribbon.

▶ 3. In the New group, click the **New folder** button. A folder icon with the label "New folder" appears in the right pane of the File Explorer window. See Figure 11.

| Figure 11 | Creating a new folder in the Tutorial folder |

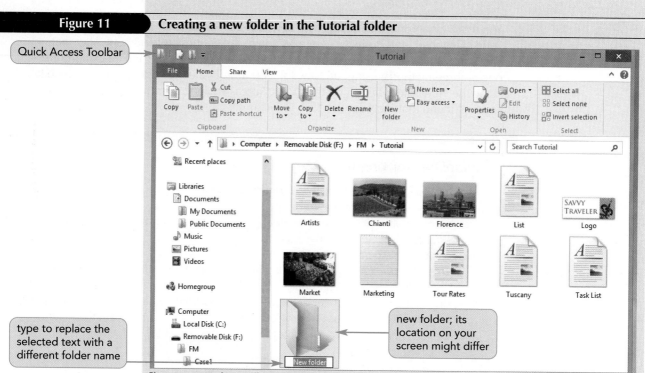

Photos courtesy of Lisa Ruffolo

> **Trouble?** If the "New folder" name is not selected, right-click the new folder, click Rename on the shortcut menu, and then continue with Step 4.

Windows uses "New folder" as a placeholder, and selects the text so that you can replace it immediately by typing a new name. You do not need to press the Backspace or Delete key to delete the text.

4. Type **Marketing Graphics** as the folder name, and then press the **Enter** key. The new folder is named Marketing Graphics and is the selected item in the right pane. To create a second folder, you can use a shortcut menu.

5. In the right pane, right-click a blank area, point to **New** on the shortcut menu, and then click **Folder**. A folder icon appears in the right pane with the "New folder" text selected.

6. Type **Tours** as the name of the new folder, and then press the **Enter** key. To create the third folder, you can use the Quick Access Toolbar.

7. On the Quick Access Toolbar, click the **New folder** button ⬚, type **Financial**, and then press the **Enter** key to create and name the folder.

8. Create a new folder in the Tutorial folder named **Projects**.

After creating four folders, you're ready to organize Matt's files by moving them into the appropriate folders.

## Moving and Copying Files and Folders

You can either move or copy a file from its current location to a new location. **Moving** a file removes it from its current location and places it in a new location that you specify. **Copying** a file places a duplicate version of the file in a new location that you specify, while leaving the original file intact in its current location. You can also move and copy folders. When you do, you move or copy all the files contained in the folder. (You'll practice copying folders in a Case Problem at the end of this tutorial.)

In File Explorer, you can move and copy files by using the Move to or Copy to buttons in the Organize group on the Home tab; using the Copy and Cut commands on a file's shortcut menu; or using keyboard shortcuts. When you copy or move files using these methods, you are using the **Clipboard**, a temporary storage area for files and information that you copy or move from one location to place in another.

You can also move files by dragging the files in the File Explorer window. You will now organize Matt's files by moving them to the appropriate folders you have created. You'll start by moving the Marketing file to the Financial folder by dragging the file.

### To move the Marketing file by dragging it:

▶ **1.** In File Explorer, point to the **Marketing** file in the right pane, and then press and hold the mouse button.

▶ **2.** While still pressing the mouse button, drag the **Marketing** file to the **Financial** folder. See Figure 12.

| Figure 12 | Dragging a file to move it to a folder |

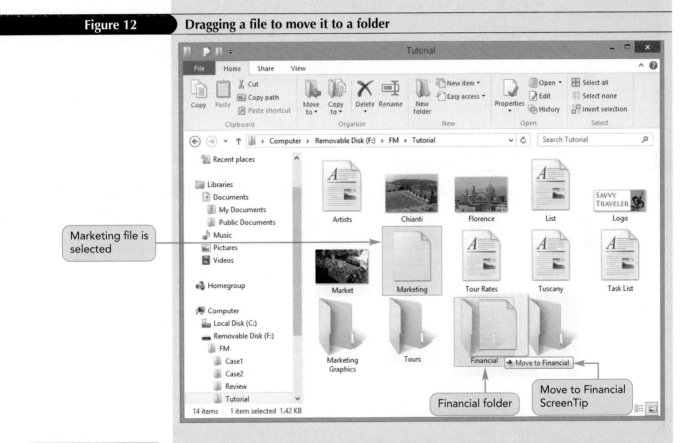

▶ **3.** When the Move to Financial ScreenTip appears, release the mouse button. The Marketing file is removed from the main Tutorial folder and stored in the Financial subfolder.

**Trouble?** If you released the mouse button before the Move to Financial ScreenTip appeared, press the Ctrl+Z keys to undo the move, and then repeat Steps 1–3.

**Trouble?** If you moved the Market file instead of the Marketing file, press the Ctrl+Z keys to undo the move, and then repeat Steps 1–3.

▶ **4.** In the right pane, double-click the **Financial** folder to verify that it contains the Marketing file.

**TIP**

If you drag a file or folder to a location on a different drive, the file is copied, not moved, to preserve the file in its original location.

**Trouble?** If the Marketing file does not appear in the Financial folder, you probably moved it to a different folder. Press the Ctrl+Z keys to undo the move, and then repeat Steps 1–3.

▶ **5.** Click the **Back** button ⊖ on the Address bar to return to the Tutorial folder.

You'll move the remaining files into the folders using the Clipboard.

## To move files using the Clipboard:

▶ **1.** Right-click the **Artists** file, and then click **Cut** on the shortcut menu. Although the file icon still appears selected in the right pane of File Explorer, Windows removes the Artists file from the Tutorial folder and stores it on the Clipboard.

▶ **2.** In the right pane, right-click the **Tours** folder, and then click **Paste** on the shortcut menu. Windows pastes the Artists file from the Clipboard to the Tours folder. The Artists file icon no longer appears in the File Explorer window, which is currently displaying the contents of the Tutorial folder.

▶ **3.** In the navigation pane, click the **expand** icon ▷ next to the Tutorial folder, if necessary, to display its contents, and then click the **Tours** folder to view its contents in the right pane. The Tours folder now contains the Artists file. See Figure 13.

**Figure 13**    **Artists file in its new location**

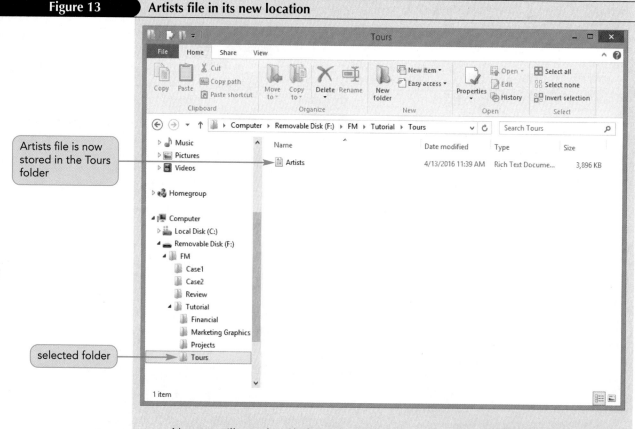

Artists file is now stored in the Tours folder

selected folder

Next, you'll use the Clipboard again to move the Tuscany file from the Tutorial folder to the Tours folder. But this time, you'll access the Clipboard using the ribbon.

▶ **4.** On the Address bar, point to the **Up to** button ⬆ to display its ScreenTip (Up to "Tutorial"), click the **Up to** button ⬆ to return to the Tutorial folder, and then click the **Tuscany** file to select it.

▶ **5.** On the Home tab, in the Clipboard group, click the **Cut** button to remove the Tuscany file from the Tutorial folder and temporarily store it on the Clipboard.

▶ **6.** In the Address bar, click the **arrow** button ▶ to the right of "Tutorial" to display a list of subfolders in the Tutorial folder, and then click **Tours** to display the contents of the Tours folder in File Explorer.

▶ **7.** In the Clipboard group, click the **Paste** button to paste the Tuscany file in the Tours folder. The Tours folder now contains the Artists and Tuscany files.

Finally, you'll move the Task List file from the Tutorial folder to the Projects folder using the Move to button in the Organize group on the Home tab. This button and the Copy to button are ideal when you want to move or copy files without leaving the current folder. When you select a file and then click the Move to or Copy to button, a list of locations appears, including all of the Windows libraries and one or more folders you open frequently. You can click a location in the list to move the selected file to that library or folder. You can also select the Choose location option to open the Move Items or Copy Items dialog box, and then select a location for the file, which you'll do in the following steps.

### To move the Task List file using the Move to button:

▶ **1.** In the Address bar, click **Tutorial** to return to the Tutorial folder, and then click the **Task List** file to select it.

▶ **2.** On the Home tab, in the Organize group, click the **Move to** button to display a list of locations to which you can move the selected file. The Projects folder is not included on this list because you haven't opened it yet.

▶ **3.** Click **Choose location** to open the Move Items dialog box. See Figure 14.

| Figure 14 | Move Items dialog box |
|---|---|

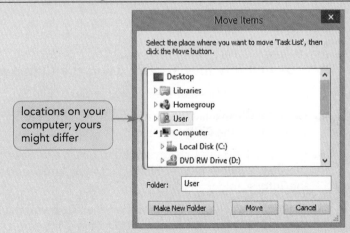

locations on your computer; yours might differ

▶ **4.** If necessary, scroll the list of locations, and then click the **expand** icon ▷ next to the drive containing your Data Files, such as Removable Disk (F:).

▶ **5.** Navigate to the FM ▸ Tutorial folder, and then click the **Projects** folder to select it.

▶ **6.** Click the **Move** button to close the dialog box and move the Task List file to the Projects folder.

▶ **7.** Open the Projects folder to confirm that it contains the Task List file.

One way to save steps when moving or copying multiple files or folders is to select all the files and folders you want to move or copy, and then work with them as a group. You can use several techniques to select multiple files or folders at the same time, which are described in Figure 15.

**Figure 15**    **Selecting multiple files or folders**

| Items to Select in the Right Pane of File Explorer | Method |
|---|---|
| Files or folders listed together | Click the first item, press and hold the Shift key, click the last item, and then release the Shift key.<br><br>*or*<br><br>Drag the pointer to create a selection box around all the items you want to include. |
| Files or folders not listed together | Press and hold the Ctrl key, click each item you want to select, and then release the Ctrl key. |
| All files and folders | On the Home tab, in the Select group, click the Select all button. |
| **Items to Deselect in the Right Pane of File Explorer** | **Method** |
| Single file or folder in a selected group | Press and hold the Ctrl key, click each item you want to remove from the selection, and then release the Ctrl key. |
| All selected files and folders | Click a blank area of the File Explorer window. |

© 2014 Cengage Learning

Next, you'll copy the four graphics files from the Tutorial folder to the Marketing Graphics folder using the Clipboard. To do this efficiently, you will select multiple files at once.

### To copy multiple files at once using the Clipboard:

▶ **1.** Display the contents of the Tutorial folder in File Explorer.

▶ **2.** Click the **Chianti** file, press and hold the **Shift** key, click the **Market** file, and then release the **Shift** key.

▶ **3.** Press and hold the **Ctrl** key, click the **List** file to deselect it, and then release the **Ctrl** key. Four files—Chianti, Florence, Logo, and Market—are selected in the Tutorial folder window.

▶ **4.** Right-click a selected file, and then click **Copy** on the shortcut menu. Windows copies the selected files to the Clipboard.

▶ **5.** Right-click the **Marketing Graphics** folder, and then click **Paste** on the shortcut menu.

▶ **6.** Open the **Marketing Graphics** folder to verify it contains the four files you copied, and then return to the Tutorial folder.

> **7.** Right-click the **Tour Rates** file, and then click **Copy** on the shortcut menu.

> **8.** In the right pane, double-click the **Financial** folder to open it, right-click a blank area of the right pane, and then click **Paste** on the shortcut menu.

## Duplicating Your Folder Organization

If you work on two computers, such as one computer at an office or school and another computer at home, you can duplicate the folders you use on both computers to simplify the process of transferring files from one computer to another. For example, if you have four folders in your My Documents folder on your work computer, create these same four folders on a USB drive and in the My Documents folder of your home computer. If you change a file on the hard disk of your home computer, you can copy the most recent version of the file to the corresponding folder on your USB drive so the file is available when you are at work. You also then have a **backup**, or duplicate copy, of important files. Having a backup of your files is invaluable if your computer has a fatal error.

All the files that originally appeared in the Tutorial folder are now stored in appropriate subfolders. You can streamline the organization of the Tutorial folder by deleting the duplicate files you no longer need.

## Deleting Files and Folders

You should periodically delete files and folders you no longer need so that your main folders and disks don't get cluttered. In File Explorer, you delete a file or folder by deleting its icon. When you delete a file from a hard disk, Windows 8 removes the file from the folder but stores the file contents in the Recycle Bin. The Recycle Bin is an area on your hard disk that holds deleted files until you remove them permanently. When you delete a folder from the hard disk, the folder and all of its files are stored in the Recycle Bin. If you change your mind and want to retrieve a deleted file or folder, you can double-click the Recycle Bin on the desktop, right-click the file or folder you want to retrieve, and then click Restore. However, after you empty the Recycle Bin, you can no longer recover the files it contained.

Because you copied the Chianti, Florence, Logo, Market, and Tour Rates files to the subfolders in the Tutorial folder, you can safely delete the original files. You can also delete the List file because you no longer need it. You can delete a file or folder using various methods, including using a shortcut menu or selecting one or more files and then pressing the Delete key.

### To delete files in the Tutorial folder:

> **1.** Display the Tutorial folder in the File Explorer window.

> **2.** In the right pane, click **Chianti**, press and hold the **Shift** key, click **Tour Rates**, and then release the **Shift** key. All files in the Tutorial folder are now selected. None of the subfolders should be selected.

> **3.** Right-click the selected files, and then click **Delete** on the shortcut menu. A message box appears, asking if you're sure you want to permanently delete these files.

> **4.** Click the **Yes** button to confirm that you want to delete the files.

## Renaming Files

After creating and naming a file or folder, you might realize that a different name would be more meaningful or descriptive. You can easily rename a file or folder by using the Rename command on the file's shortcut menu.

Now that you've organized Matt's files into folders, he reviews your work and notes that the Artists file was originally created to store text specifically about Florentine painters and sculptors. You can rename that file to give it a more descriptive filename.

**To rename the Artists file:**

1. In the right pane of the File Explorer window, double-click the **Tours** folder to display its contents.

2. Right-click the **Artists** file, and then click **Rename** on the shortcut menu. The filename is highlighted and a box appears around it.

3. Type **Florentine Artists**, and then press the **Enter** key. The file now appears with the new name.

    **Trouble?** If you make a mistake while typing and you haven't pressed the Enter key yet, press the Backspace key until you delete the mistake and then complete Step 3. If you've already pressed the Enter key, repeat Steps 2 and 3 to rename the file again.

    **Trouble?** If your computer is set to display filename extensions, a message might appear asking if you are sure you want to change the filename extension. Click the No button, and then repeat Steps 2 and 3.

# Working with Compressed Files

You compress a file or a folder of files so it occupies less space on the disk. It can be useful to compress files before transferring them from one location to another, such as from your hard disk to a removable disk or vice versa, or from one computer to another via email. You can then transfer the files more quickly. Also, if you or your email contacts can send and receive files only up to a certain size, compressing large files might make them small enough to send and receive. Compare two folders—a folder named Photos that contains files totaling about 8.6 MB, and a compressed folder containing the same files but requiring only 6.5 MB of disk space. In this case, the compressed files use about 25 percent less disk space than the uncompressed files.

You can compress one or more files in File Explorer using the Zip button, which is located in the Send group on the Share tab of the ribbon. Windows stores the compressed files in a special type of folder called an **archive**, or a compressed folder. File Explorer uses an icon of a folder with a zipper to represent a compressed folder. To compress additional files or folders, you drag them into the compressed folder. You can open a file directly from a compressed folder, although you cannot modify the file. To edit and save a compressed file, you must extract it first. When you **extract** a file, you create an uncompressed copy of the file in a folder you specify. The original file remains in the compressed folder.

Matt suggests that you compress the files and folders in the Tutorial folder so that you can more quickly transfer them to another location.

## To compress the folders and files in the Tutorial folder:

**TIP**

Another way to compress files is to select the files, right-click the selection, point to Send to on the shortcut menu, and then click Compressed (zipped) folder.

1. In File Explorer, navigate to the Tutorial folder, and then select all the folders in the Tutorial folder.

2. Click the **Share** tab on the ribbon.

3. In the Send group, click the **Zip** button. After a few moments, a new compressed folder appears in the Tutorial window with the filename selected. By default, File Explorer uses the name of the first selected item as the name of the compressed folder. You'll replace the name with a more descriptive one.

4. Type **Savvy Traveler**, and then press the **Enter** key to rename the compressed folder. See Figure 16.

| Figure 16 | Compressing files and folders |
| --- | --- |

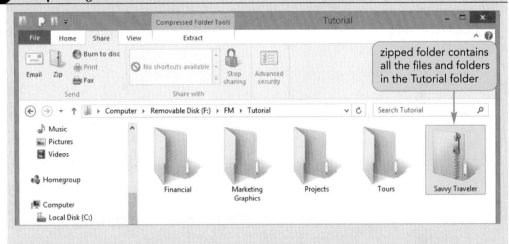

5. Double-click the **Savvy Traveler** compressed folder to open it, open the **Tours** folder, and then note the size of the compressed Tuscany file, which is 1,815 KB.

6. Navigate back to the Tutorial folder.

You can move and copy the files and folders from an opened compressed folder to other locations, although you cannot rename the files. More often, you extract all of the files from the compressed folder to a new location that you specify, preserving the files in their original folders as appropriate.

## To extract the compressed files:

1. Click the **Savvy Traveler** compressed folder to select it, and then click the **Compressed Folder Tools Extract** tab on the ribbon.

2. In the Extract all group, click the **Extract all** button. The Extract Compressed (Zipped) Folders Wizard starts and opens the Select a Destination and Extract Files dialog box.

3. Press the **End** key to deselect the path in the box and move the insertion point to the end of the path, press the **Backspace** key as many times as necessary to delete the Savvy Traveler text, and then type **Backups**. The final three parts of the path in the box should be \FM\Tutorial\Backups. See Figure 17.

**Figure 17**    Extracting files from a compressed folder

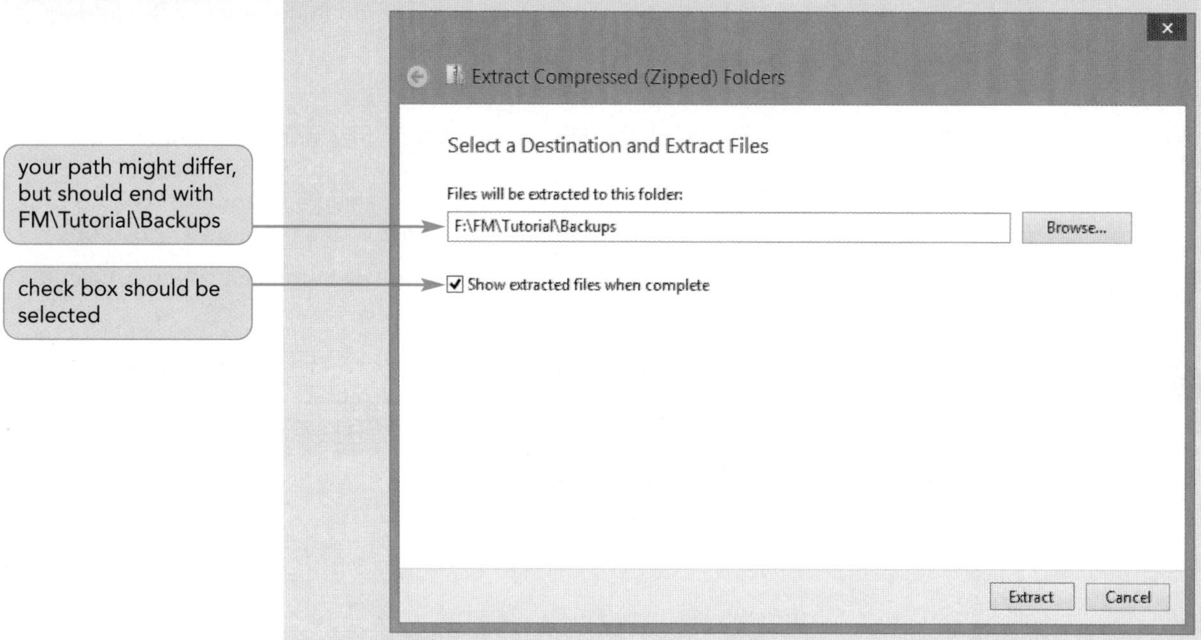

your path might differ, but should end with FM\Tutorial\Backups

check box should be selected

Extract Compressed (Zipped) Folders

Select a Destination and Extract Files

Files will be extracted to this folder:

F:\FM\Tutorial\Backups    Browse...

☑ Show extracted files when complete

Extract    Cancel

**4.** Make sure the Show extracted files when complete check box is checked, and then click the **Extract** button. Windows extracts the files and then opens the Backups folder, showing the Financial, Marketing Graphics, Projects, and Tours folders.

**5.** Open each folder to make sure it contains the files you worked with in this tutorial. When you open the Tours folder, note the uncompressed size of the Tuscany file, which is about four times as large as its compressed version.

**6.** Close all open windows.

In this tutorial, you examined the purpose of organizing files and folders, and you planned and created an organization for a set of related files and folders. You also explored your computer using File Explorer and learned how to navigate to your Data Files using the navigation pane. You used File Explorer to manage files and folders by opening and saving files; creating folders; and selecting, moving, and copying files. You also renamed and deleted files according to your organization plan. Finally, you compressed and extracted files.

**REVIEW**

## Quick Check

1. You organize files by storing them in _____.

2. What is the purpose of the Address bar in File Explorer?

3. A filename _____ identifies the file's type and indicates the application that created the file.

4. Explain how to use File Explorer to navigate to a file in the following location: E: ▸ Courses ▸ Computer Basics ▸ Operating Systems.txt.

5. One way to move files and folders is to use the _____, a temporary storage area for files and information that you copied or moved from one place and plan to use somewhere else.

6. What happens if you click the first file in a folder window, press the Shift key, click the last file, and then release the Shift key?

7. When you delete a file from a hard disk, Windows removes the file from the folder but stores the file contents in the _____.

8. Describe how to compress a file or folder.

9. What are the benefits of compressing files and folders?

PRACTICE

## Review Assignments

**Data Files needed for the Review Assignments: Banner.png, Colosseum.jpg, Lectures.xlsx, Rome.jpg, Rome.rtf, Schedule.rtf, Tours.rtf**

Matt has saved a few files from his old computer to a removable disk. He gives you these files in a single, unorganized folder, and asks you to organize them logically into subfolders. To do this, you will need to devise a plan for managing the files, and then create the subfolders you need. Next, you will rename, copy, move, and delete files, and then perform other management tasks to make it easy for Matt to work with these files and folders. Complete the following steps:

1. Use File Explorer to navigate to and open the FM ▶ Review folder provided with your Data Files. Examine the seven files in this folder and consider the best way to organize the files.

2. Open the **Rome** text file in WordPad, and then add the following tip to the end of the document: **Dine on the Italian schedule, with the main meal in the middle of the day.**

3. Save the document as **Rome Dining Tips** in the Review folder. Close the WordPad window.

4. In the Review folder, create three folders: **Business**, **Destinations**, and **Supplements**.

5. To organize the files into the correct folders, complete the following steps:
   - Move the Banner and Schedule files from the Review folder to the Business folder.
   - Move the Colosseum and Rome JPEG image files and the Rome Dining Tips and Tours text files to the Destinations folder.
   - Copy the Lectures file to the Supplements folder.

6. Copy the Tours file in the Destinations folder to the Business folder.

7. Rename the Schedule file in the Business folder as **2016 Schedule**. Rename the Lectures file in the Supplements folder as **On-site Lectures**.

8. Delete the Lectures file and the Rome text file from the Review folder.

9. Create a compressed (zipped) folder in the Review folder named **Rome** that contains all the files and folders in the Review folder.

10. Extract the contents of the Rome compressed folder to a new folder named **Rome Backups** in the Review folder. (*Hint:* The file path will end with \FM\Review\Rome Backups.)

11. Close the File Explorer window.

APPLY

## Case Problem 1

**See the Starting Data Files section at the beginning of this tutorial for the list of Data Files needed for this Case Problem.**

***Bay Shore Arts Center***    Casey Sullivan started the Bay Shore Arts Center in Monterey, California, to provide workshops and courses on art and photography. Attracting students from the San Francisco and San José areas, Casey's business has grown and she now holds classes five days a week. She recently started a course on fine art landscape photography, which has quickly become her most popular offering. Casey hired you to help her design new classes and manage other parts of her growing business, including maintaining electronic business files and communications. Your first task is to organize the files on her new Windows 8 computer. Complete the following steps:

1. Open File Explorer. In the FM ▸ Case1 folder provided with your Data Files, create three folders: **Classes**, **Landscapes**, and **Management**.
2. Move the Fall Classes, Spring Classes, Summer Classes, and Winter Classes files from the Case1 folder to the Classes folder.
3. Rename the four files in the Classes folder by deleting the word "Classes" from each filename.
4. Move the four JPEG image files from the Case1 folder to the Landscapes folder.
5. Copy the remaining two files to the Management folder.
6. Copy the Workshops file to the Classes folder.
7. Delete the Instructors and Workshops files from the Case1 folder.
8. Make a copy of the Landscapes folder in the Case1 folder. The name of the duplicate folder appears as Landscapes – Copy. Rename the Landscapes – Copy folder as **California Photos**.
9. Copy the Workshops file from the Classes folder to the California Photos folder. Rename this file **California Workshops**.
10. Compress the graphics files in the California Photos folder in a new compressed folder named **Photos**.
11. Move the compressed Photos folder to the Case1 folder.
12. Close File Explorer.

**TROUBLESHOOT**

## Case Problem 2

**See the Starting Data Files section at the beginning of this tutorial for the list of Data Files needed for this Case Problem.**

*Charlotte Area Business Incubator*    Antoine Jackson is the director of the Charlotte Area Business Incubator, a service run by the University of North Carolina in Charlotte to consult with new and struggling small businesses. You work as an intern at the business incubator and spend part of your time organizing client files. Since Antoine started using Windows 8, he has been having trouble finding files on his computer. He sometimes creates duplicates of files and then doesn't know which copy is the most current. Complete the following steps:

1. Navigate to the FM ▸ Case2 folder provided with your Data Files, and then examine the files in this folder. Based on the filenames and file types, begin to create an organization plan for the files.

⚙ **Troubleshoot** 2. Open the Tips1 and the Tips1 – Copy files and consider the problem these files could cause. Close the files and then fix the problem, renaming one or more files as necessary to reflect the contents.

⚙ **Troubleshoot** 3. Open the Tips2 and the Tips2 – Copy files and compare their contents. Change the filenames to clarify the purpose and contents of the files.

4. Complete the organization plan for Antoine's files. In the FM ▸ Case2 folder, create the subfolders you need according to your plan.

5. Move the files in the Case2 folder to the subfolders you created. When you finish, the Case2 folder should contain at least two subfolders containing files.

6. Rename the spreadsheet files in each subfolder according to the following descriptions.
   - Budget1: **Website budget**
   - Budget2: **Marketing budget**
   - Report1: **Travel expense report**
   - Report2: **Project expense report**
   - Report3: **Balance sheet**
   - Report4: **Event budget**

⚙ **Troubleshoot** 7. Make sure all files have descriptive names that accurately reflect their contents.

⚙ **Troubleshoot** 8. Based on the work you did in Steps 6 and 7, move files as necessary to improve the file organization.

9. Close File Explorer.

# Internet Basics and Information Literacy

*Conducting Research on Energy Conservation*

## Case | *Hinsdale University*

Martha Weiss is a graduate student studying environmental engineering at Hinsdale University. She is writing a paper on how large corporations in different industries are using natural resources, and ways that these organizations can improve their energy efficiency and use natural resources more effectively. She has gathered information in many areas related to energy, sustainability, and the environment, including upgrading computer systems to reduce energy consumption, making company facilities more energy-smart, using recycled resources whenever practical such as using recycled water from the city's waste center in the cooling systems, and using renewable energy resources such as wind, solar, and hydropower.

Now, Martha wants to feature a few case studies highlighting the efforts large companies like Microsoft Corporation are making to reduce their carbon footprint, which is the amount of greenhouse gases, such as carbon dioxide, that are released into the atmosphere during activities like air travel and commuting. She wants to find the most current information for her case studies, so she plans to use the Internet for her research. Martha recently bought a new computer running Windows 8 and Internet Explorer 10. She is not familiar with Internet Explorer 10, so she asks for your help in conducting her research.

## STARTING DATA FILES

There are no starting Data Files needed for this tutorial.

# Visual Overview:

The Internet Explorer app opens from the Start screen. Internet Explorer is a **web browser**, a program that locates, retrieves, and displays webpages.

Most webpages have a **search box** that allows you to enter **keywords**, which are specific words and phrases that describe a topic of interest. You then click the search button and the browser displays a list of pages pertaining to your topic.

**Tabs** are used to open multiple webpages simultaneously in one browser window.

The Tabs bar appears at the top of the browser when you right-click the window.

The New Tab button opens a tab for displaying another webpage.

A **webpage** is a document created with a special programming language that displays in a web browser.

In the Internet Explorer app, the navigation bar appears at the bottom of the browser when you right-click the window.

A **hyperlink** (or **link**) is text or a graphic that, when clicked, connects to and displays another part of the webpage or a different webpage.

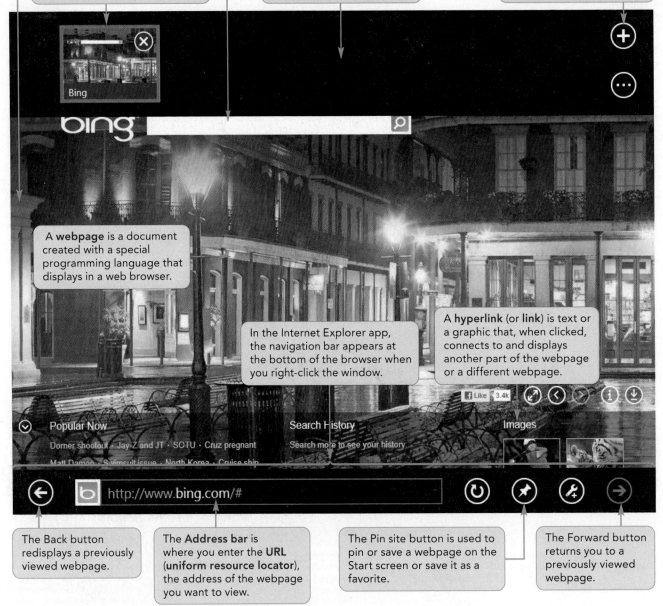

The Back button redisplays a previously viewed webpage.

The **Address bar** is where you enter the **URL** (**uniform resource locator**), the address of the webpage you want to view.

The Pin site button is used to pin or save a webpage on the Start screen or save it as a favorite.

The Forward button returns you to a previously viewed webpage.

# Internet Explorer App

# Microsoft Internet Explorer 10

The Back button redisplays a previously viewed webpage. The Forward button returns you to a previously viewed webpage.

The Internet Explorer desktop application opens from the desktop. Internet Explorer is a **web browser**, a program that locates, retrieves, and displays webpages.

The **Address bar** is where you enter the **URL (Uniform Resource Locator)**, the address of the webpage you want to view.

**Tabs** are used to open multiple webpages simultaneously in one browser window.

The New Tab button opens a tab for displaying another webpage.

http://www.bing.com/#

Bing

IMAGES VIDEOS MAPS NEWS SEARCH HISTORY MORE | MSN | HOTMAIL

Sign in ▾     0 of 5

bing

The Favorites button opens the **Favorites Center**, which has tools for saving favorite webpages and viewing a history list of previously visited webpages.

A **webpage** is a document created with a special programming language that displays in a web browser. The **home page** is the webpage that appears when the browser starts. The main page of a website is also called the home page.

Like  3.4k

Popular Now    Dorner shootout · Jay-Z and JT · SOTU · Cruz pregnant · Matt Damon

©2013 Microsoft  |  Privacy and Cookies  |  Legal  |  Advertise  |  About our ads  |  Help  |  Feedback

9:39 PM
4/2/2016

The Internet Explorer button on the taskbar opens the Internet Explorer desktop application.

Most webpages have a **search box** that allows you to enter **keywords**, which are specific words and phrases that describe a topic of interest. You then click the search button and the browser displays a list of pages pertaining to your topic.

A **hyperlink** (or **link**) is text or a graphic that, when clicked, connects and displays another part of the webpage or a different webpage.

# Internet Explorer Desktop Application

# Understanding the Internet and the World Wide Web

The **web** (short for **World Wide Web**) is a collection of electronic documents or files—called webpages—that are available through the Internet. The **Internet** is a worldwide collection of computer networks that allows people to communicate and exchange information. Webpages are stored on **web servers**, which are computers connected to the Internet that manage the display of the webpages. A collection of related webpages is called a **website**. Webpages are connected by hyperlinks, or links, which you click to move from one webpage to another.

You use a web browser to access, retrieve, and display webpages from a computer that is connected to the Internet. Common browsers include Microsoft Internet Explorer, Mozilla Firefox, Google Chrome, Apple Safari, and Opera. Internet Explorer 10, the current version of Microsoft's web browser, provides all the tools you need to communicate, access, and share information on the web. As shown in the Visual Overview, Internet Explorer is available in two versions—the Internet Explorer app that opens from the Start screen, and the Internet Explorer application that opens from the desktop. Both versions perform the same basic functions, but you access them differently.

INSIGHT

### Connecting to the Internet

To access information on the web, you must use a computer that is connected to the Internet. Common Internet connections include cable, DSL, dial-up, and wireless networks. A **wireless** network uses radio frequency signals to transmit data between computers and devices, such as routers, that are physically connected to a network. Home connections require an account with an **Internet service provider (ISP)**, a company that provides Internet access by connecting your computer to one of its servers via a telephone or cable modem. When you are logged on to your ISP account, you use a web browser to access, retrieve, and display webpages.

Martha can use either version of Internet Explorer to conduct her research into Microsoft's initiatives to reduce its carbon footprint. First, she needs your help to become familiar with the features of Internet Explorer and basic browsing skills. You will begin by starting the Internet Explorer app and visiting a website.

## Starting the Internet Explorer App

The Internet Explorer app hides the browser interface so that the focus is on the webpage content. Because the tools are hidden until you need them, the Internet Explorer app is a good choice for casual browsing or looking up information quickly. When you start Internet Explorer, the home page set for your browser appears in the browser window.

**To start the Internet Explorer app:**

▶ 1. On the Start screen, click the **Internet Explorer** tile. The home page appears and fills the screen. Refer back to the Visual Overview at the beginning of this tutorial. The home page on your screen might be different, or you might not see any home page at all.

**Trouble?** If a message bar appears at the bottom of the screen, indicating that Internet Explorer blocked content with security certificate errors, you can click the Show content button to display blocked content, click the Close button to hide the message bar, or do nothing and leave the message displayed. You will need to make this decision each time this message appears.

2. Compare the tools in the navigation bar at the bottom of your screen to the Visual Overview at the beginning of this tutorial.

## Entering a URL in the Address Bar

A Uniform Resource Locator (URL) identifies where a webpage is located on the Internet. For example, the URL for the Microsoft home page is http://www.microsoft.com/en-us/default.aspx. A URL consists of the following four parts:

- The first part of the URL, *http://*, is the **protocol**, which is a set of rules that computers use to exchange files. Hypertext Transfer Protocol (HTTP) and File Transfer Protocol (FTP) are two of the most common protocols used on the Internet. In this example, *http://* is the protocol.

**TIP**

Generally, organizations use URLs that include their name, making it easier to find their site.

- The second part of the URL, www.microsoft.com, specifies the location of the web server. The prefix is often *www*, indicating the server is a web server, but it can be something else or omitted entirely. The next part provides a unique name for the website, and the last part identifies the type of website. In this example, *microsoft* is the unique name and *.com* indicates that it is a commercial enterprise. Other categories include .edu (educational institutions), .gov (government agencies), .mil (U.S. military units or agencies), .net (network service providers or resources), .org (organizations, usually not-for-profit), and .biz (businesses).
- The third portion of the URL, */en-us/* in this example, provides the path for the folder in which the webpage file is located.
- The last part of the URL, *default.aspx*, is the filename of the webpage.

### INSIGHT

### IP Addresses and Domain Names

The web server address corresponds to an Internet Protocol (IP) address. An **IP address** is a unique number consisting of four sets of numbers from 0 to 255, separated by periods (such as 216.35.148.4), that identifies the server or computer connected to the Internet. Because IP addresses can be difficult to remember, web addresses use a **domain name**, which is a unique string of letters and/or numbers that are easy to remember, such as *microsoft.com* in the previous example. Some URLs include a filename after the domain name. If a URL does not include a filename, many web browsers will load the file that contains the website's home page—for example, index.htm or default.aspx.

To display a specific webpage, you can enter its URL in the Address bar. As you type, the names or URLs of other webpages you have visited that start with the same characters appear in a list above the Address bar. URLs are not case sensitive, so you can type them in all lowercase letters even though some longer URLs use a mix of uppercase and lowercase letters to distinguish the different words in the address.

You will begin your research into Microsoft's environmental sustainable business practices by visiting the Microsoft website. You can type the URL for the website into the Address bar of the Internet Explorer app.

### To visit the Microsoft website by entering its URL:

1. Click in the **Address bar** to select the URL of the currently displayed webpage. The navigation bar expands, and it might show tiles for webpages you visited recently or have saved as favorites.

2. Type **http://www.microsoft.com**. As you type, URLs of other websites you have visited that begin with the same letters you are typing appear above the Address bar.

3. Press the **Enter** key. The home page of the Microsoft website appears in the browser window. See Figure 1. The content you see might differ because webpages are dynamic and their content is updated frequently.

| Figure 1 | Microsoft's home page in the Internet Explorer app |

a Microsoft link appears in the upper-left corner of each page on the site and links back to this home page

navigation bar of links to other webpages on the site

search box used to enter keywords for searching for a topic on this website

Find a Microsoft Store near you

Products    Downloads    Security    Support    Store

more, do more

Explore

URL in the Address bar

Discover

For home    For work

http://clk.atdmt.com/MRT/go/431101865/direct/01/

http://www.microsoft.com/en-us/default.aspx

**Trouble?** If a message bar appears at the bottom of the screen, indicating that Internet Explorer blocked content with security certificate errors, click the Close button to hide the message bar.

Although there are millions of websites that are designed for a multitude of purposes and audiences, most websites are organized similarly. The home page provides basic information about the individual or organization and includes a navigation bar with links to other pages of information. The number of additional pages depends on how much information the person or organization wants to share. Common pages include a Contact page that contains information about how to get in touch with the company; an About page that contains information about the company such as its history, mission, and staff; and a Products or Services page that contains information about the items the company sells or the services it provides. Depending on the amount of information that is included, each top-level page could be linked to additional pages with more details or related information. In addition, each page usually includes a link to return to the site's home page.

### Information Bar Messages

Webpages are designed for different audiences and purposes. Some pages contain elements that require the Internet Explorer desktop application. Others might have blocked content for security purposes. If an issue arises when you try to load a webpage, a message bar with details about the issue appears near the bottom of the browser window. It includes buttons for resolving the issue, such as showing blocked content, opening a page in the desktop application, ignoring the issue for the current site, and closing the information bar without making a change. You can also do nothing and just leave the message bar displayed. You'll need to decide on a course of action whenever you see a message bar.

## Clicking Links

Each time you click a link, a new webpage appears in the browser window, replacing the previous page. Likewise, the URL in the Address box changes to correspond to the new webpage.

You can use links to navigate the site and locate information. The Microsoft home page has many links to a variety of resources. The navigation bar includes links to the following categories—Products, Downloads, Security, Support, and Store. In addition, you can use other links on the page to find a Microsoft store near you, to visit other Microsoft sites, and to get information about Microsoft products.

Martha is interested in finding basic information about Microsoft Corporation to use in her case study. You will begin to navigate the site to find out more about Microsoft.

**TIP**

To scroll the page, move the pointer to the right edge of the screen to display the scroll bar, and then click and drag the scroll bar to see more of the webpage.

### To use links to navigate webpages on the Microsoft site:

1. On the Microsoft home page, scroll down to the bottom of the page. A list of links appears.

2. In the About list, point to the **Microsoft** link, as shown in Figure 2. The pointer changes to 🖑 and a ScreenTip lists the URL of the page that the link will open.

| Figure 2 | Links on a webpage |

Follow us

Facebook
Twitter
News Center

STATE OF THE UNION

Bing turns SOTU into a national dialog
Feb. 11, ███ - Bing.com to host largest interactive State of the Union experience in history.

**Other Microsoft sites**

Windows
Office
Surface
Windows Phone
Xbox
Skype
Bing
Microsoft Store

**Downloads**

Download Center
Windows downloads
Office downloads

**Support**

Support home
Knowledge base

**Security**

Security home
Microsoft Security Essentials

**About**

Microsoft     ← pointer over a link
Careers
Company News
Investor relations
Site map

**Popular resources**

Windows RT
PC and Laptops
Tablet and Computers
Windows Phone smartphones
Windows Phone apps and games
Microsoft computer security
Malware removal tool
Microsoft Dynamics CRM Online

Microsoft

United States - English

http://www.microsoft.com/about/en/us/default.aspx   ← ScreenTip shows link's URL     Contact us    Privacy & Cookies    Terms of use    Trademarks    © 2013 Microsoft

> **3.** Click the **Microsoft** link. The About Microsoft page loads. It includes some information about the company, such as its mission, company information, corporate citizenship, and customer and partner experience, as well as a variety of links to additional information.
>
> **Trouble?** If a message bar appears above the Address bar indicating the site uses add-ons that require Internet Explorer on the desktop, click the Close button.
>
> **4.** Click the **Company Information** link to open the corresponding webpage, and then read the information that appears.
>
> **5.** Click the **Our Businesses** link to load Microsoft's Business page, and then read the information about the various business divisions at Microsoft.

## Moving Between Viewed Pages

In Internet Explorer, you can move back and forth between the different webpages you have viewed during a browsing session. As shown in the Visual Overview, the Back button appears to the left of the navigation bar and the Forward button appears to the right of the navigation bar in the Internet Explorer app. Clicking the Back button redisplays the previous webpage you visited. You can continue backward through the visited pages until you reach the first page that opened when you started Internet Explorer. Once you navigate back a page, the Forward button becomes available so you can return to the more recent pages you visited. In the Internet Explorer app, you can also click the arrow buttons that appear when you move the pointer to the left or right side of the screen to move between the pages you have viewed.

You will go back to a previous page.

### To navigate between visited pages:

▶ **1.** If the navigation bar is hidden, right-click the webpage to redisplay it. The Tabs bar also opens at the top of the window.

▶ **2.** On the left side of the navigation bar, click the **Back** button ⬅. The Company Information page reappears in the browser window.

▶ **3.** Move the pointer to the left side of the webpage. An arrow button appears.

▶ **4.** Click the **Back arrow** button ◀. The About Microsoft page reappears in the browser window.

▶ **5.** Point to the right side of the webpage, and then click the **Forward arrow** button ▶. The Company Information page reappears.

The web provides a vast amount of information. As you can see from visiting the Microsoft website, some information can be easy to find by going directly to a known website and using the navigation tools provided on the site to locate specific information—in this case, basic information about Microsoft Corporation and its business divisions. You also could have used the search box on the Microsoft website to enter keywords to search for more specific information on the site, such as the company's mission statement.

Sometimes information you are looking for on the web might be more difficult to track down. In those instances, when the information could be available on a variety of websites or it isn't related to a specific person or organization that has a website, you will need to search the web to find the sites that have the relevant information. To do that, you can use a search engine.

## Understanding Search Engines

If you don't know the URL of the site you want to visit or which site contains the information you want, you can use a **search engine** to locate webpages related to the keywords you enter. Popular search engines include Google, Bing, and Yahoo!

Search engines use a program called a spider or bot to compile databases of webpages that are indexed by keywords. When you enter keywords in a search engine, it searches its database to find webpages that include those keywords, and shows the results as a list of links to those webpages. Because each search engine creates its own database, collecting different information or different levels of detail, the results delivered by each search engine can be different.

Each search engine has its own website. From the search engine's home page, you can enter keywords for your topic in a search box and then click the search button or press the Enter key to conduct the search. The results page that appears includes a list of links to pages that contain your search words. The links are arranged in descending order by relevancy—the pages that seem more related to your search term appear at the top of the list. Other webpages at the search engine site let you search for images, videos, news, and so forth.

Because search engines are the most effective way to locate information on the web, the Address bar in Internet Explorer also provides access to a search engine. Instead of entering a URL, you can enter keywords that relate to your search topic in the Address bar, and then press the Enter key. The search engine's results page, which contains links to other webpages, appears—the same as if you entered the keywords in the search box on the search engine site's home page. Although the default search engine for Internet Explorer is Bing, you can change this to another search engine if you prefer.

**INSIGHT**

## Other Web Search Tools

Although search engines are a great place to start your research, there are other, more specialized search tools that can be useful. Some of these search tools are:

- **Metasearch engines** explore multiple search engines and show the combined results, which include a list of links to webpages that match your keywords. Some common metasearch engines are www.dogpile.com and www.webcrawler.com.
- The **deep web** (also called the **invisible web**) refers to information that is stored in databases rather than on webpages. Most search engines do not include deep web resources in their results. To find these resources, you usually have to search a specific website, such as infomine.ucr.edu, www.lii.org, and www.wolframalpha.com.
- **Web directories** list websites organized by categories. These directories are compiled by people, so the results can be more refined than those generated by search engines. If you want general information on a topic, you might find better results with a web directory.
- **Blogs**, short for web logs, are personal commentaries that present the writer's opinion, but they can also provide innovative ideas or breaking news. Bloggers sometimes include links to other resources to support their views, providing additional resources for you to review about your topic. You can search for blogs with a blog search engine, such as technorati.com and Google Blog Search at www.google.com/blogsearch.

While visiting the Microsoft website, you did not see information on how Microsoft is working to reduce its carbon footprint. To help Martha find the information for her case study, you need to broaden your search by using a search engine to locate more resources on this topic.

# Finding Information on the Web

Organizations and individuals use the web for a variety of reasons. Businesses use websites to sell or advertise their products, and to communicate information to customers or employees. Individuals use the web to find a wide variety of information, to communicate and share information with others, and to purchase products and services. Because so much information is available, you need a way to sift through and find the information that is relevant to your needs. To do this, you first must develop a search strategy.

## Formulating a Search Strategy

When you are looking for information on the web, it is important to figure out exactly what you want to find and how to find it before you start. This means developing a search strategy so you can find the information you need efficiently and effectively. Otherwise, you will find a lot of information, but not necessarily the information you need or want. Before beginning your search, develop a search strategy by doing the following:

- **Identify your topic.** You want to pinpoint the main concept, subject, or issue that you want to research. You can do this by formulating a question. For example, Martha might formulate the question "What are Microsoft's sustainable business practices?" or "How is Microsoft reducing its carbon footprint?"
- **List keywords that represent your topic.** Keywords should be specific words and phrases that are connected to your main topic, such as unique words, names, abbreviations, or organizations associated with your topic. At this point, you should jot down any keywords you think might be relevant. For Martha's research, keywords might include "Microsoft," "carbon footprint," "sustainable," and "environment."

**TIP**

Keywords are not case sensitive. Typing "microsoft" will have the same effect as typing "Microsoft."

- **Refine your keywords list.** Once you have a list of potential keywords, you need to review them to determine which are most relevant, identify synonyms that might provide better results, and consider if the keywords provide a complete representation of your topic. Add, remove, and modify the list as needed. You want to use keywords that are most likely to be on the webpages you want to find. For example, Martha might refine her list to the keywords "Microsoft" and "carbon footprint."
- **Develop your search query.** A **search query** is the translation of your original question into a form that a search engine can understand. A search query is built from the keywords you identified as most related to your topic. Be descriptive and specific, and combine keywords to pare the search results to the most relevant. The more descriptive and complete your search query is, the better and more accurate the results. For example, Martha might find that "carbon footprint" will return many results, as will "Microsoft." But, "Microsoft carbon footprint" will return fewer but more specific results.
- **Refine your search query.** As you review the initial results from your search query, you might not find the exact information you were looking for. However, you might discover related information that will help you refine your search query. For example, you might find additional keywords you could add to your query to locate more specific information related to your topic. Conversely, you might need to remove a keyword because it's leading to incorrect or misleading results. Likewise, you might need to change some of the keywords to synonyms to obtain better results. You might need to adjust your search query several times to refine the results to locate the specific information you wanted to find.

You will use a search engine to implement Martha's search strategy for finding information on how Microsoft is reducing its carbon footprint. When conducting more in-depth research on the web, it is often more efficient to use the Internet Explorer desktop application. Because you are working on the desktop, you can use other desktop applications to compile your research as you go. For example, you might want to use Microsoft WordPad to record some of the information you gathered and to begin outlining a report.

# Starting the Internet Explorer Desktop Application

The Internet Explorer desktop application functions similarly to the Internet Explorer app; however, the Address bar and navigation bar appear at the top of the browser window and remain displayed. Having these tools easily and consistently available will be helpful as you conduct your research. You will start the Internet Explorer desktop application now.

**To start the Internet Explorer desktop application:**

1. Return to the **Start** screen, and then click the **Desktop** tile. The Desktop application opens.

2. On the taskbar, click the **Internet Explorer** button 🄯. The Internet Explorer desktop application opens, as shown in the Visual Overview at the beginning of this tutorial. Your home page might differ.

   **Trouble?** If a message bar appears at the bottom of the screen, indicating that Internet Explorer blocked content with security certificate errors, click the Close button in the upper-right corner of the message bar to hide the message bar.

As stated earlier, you can use the Address bar to access a search engine, or you can go directly to a search engine's home page to access all of its features and functionality. Either way, the search results appear in the browser window. At the top of the results page, the search box shows the current search words. You can enter new keywords to start a new search at any time. The number of results indicates the number of **hits**, which are pages containing content that matches your search words. Hits are generally organized in order of relevancy. The first line contains a link with a headline of the page, the second line shows the URL, and the next lines display a more detailed summary or description of what you will find on the page. Also, website owners can purchase a paid placement, or ad, to get a hit to appear in the first page of search results that include a specific keyword—even if it is not the most relevant. Ads appear in the right column of the page and sometimes at the top of the page.

You will use the Bing search engine to implement Martha's search strategy for finding details on how Microsoft is working to reduce its carbon footprint.

### To use the Bing search engine from the Address bar:

▶ **1.** Click in the Address bar to select the URL of your home page, type **microsoft carbon footprint** as the search query, and then press the **Enter** key. The search query is sent to Bing. After a moment, the search results appear in the browser window. See Figure 3.

| Figure 3 | Search results in Bing |
|---|---|

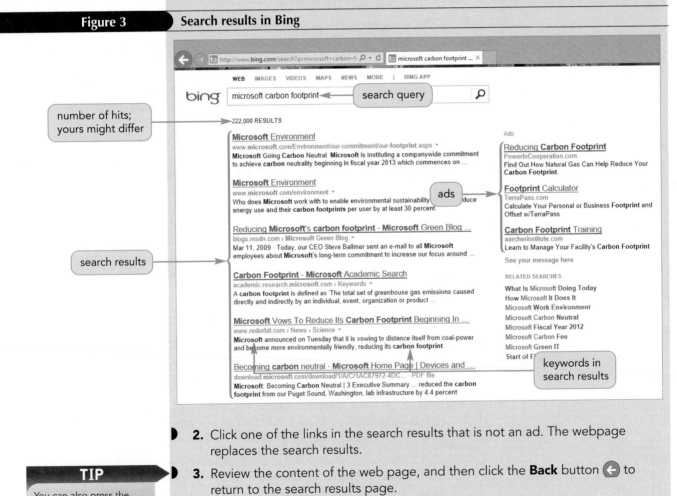

▶ **2.** Click one of the links in the search results that is not an ad. The webpage replaces the search results.

▶ **3.** Review the content of the web page, and then click the **Back** button ⬅ to return to the search results page.

**TIP**

You can also press the Backspace key to return to a previously viewed page.

You should review the links that appear in the search results, looking for ones that seem to have the information most related to the topic you are researching. The description following each search result highlights the keywords from your search, giving you some indication of how relevant that search result might be to your topic.

It is also a good idea to conduct your search using multiple search engines. Different search engines can return different results depending on which part of the web the search engine's spider accesses. Also, each search engine uses a unique ranking system when listing search results. Tabbed browsing can make it convenient to compare search results from multiple search engines.

## Using Page Tabs

**Tabbed browsing** displays multiple webpages in the same browser window. With tabbed browsing, you can open a tab for each webpage you visit that you might want to return to quickly. Opening multiple pages in tabs lets you easily compare the content of different pages, or follow a pathway of information without losing your starting point.

When multiple pages are open in different tabs, the tab with the Close Tab button is the active tab. You click a tab to display that page. You can close a tab for a webpage that no longer interests you by clicking its Close Tab button.

When you point to the Internet Explorer button on the taskbar, **thumbnail** images (which are miniature pictures) of all open tabs are displayed. You can click a thumbnail to display its related page in the browser. You can also close a tab by pointing to the thumbnail and then clicking the Close button that appears in the upper-right corner of the thumbnail.

**REFERENCE**

### Opening Tabs for Browsing

- Click the New Tab button, which appears to the right of the open tabs.
- In the Address box, enter the URL for the webpage you want to visit, and then press the Enter key.

*or*

- Press and hold the Ctrl key as you click a link on a webpage to open a new webpage in a new tab.
- Right-click a link on a webpage, and then on the shortcut menu, click Open in new tab.

You will open a new tab so that you can perform the same search with a different search engine–Google.

### To open, switch between, and close page tabs in the Internet Explorer desktop application:

1. To the right of the open page tab, point to the **New Tab** button ☐. The New Tab button changes to ☐.
2. Click ☐. A new tab opens with the insertion point blinking in the Address bar. The tab displays links to sites that you have recently or regularly visited, and you can click a link to open one of the sites in the tab. See Figure 4.

| Figure 4 | Tabbed browsing |

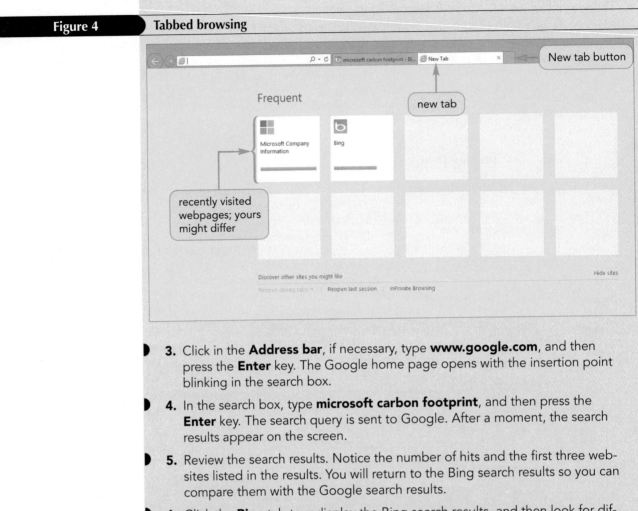

3. Click in the **Address bar**, if necessary, type **www.google.com**, and then press the **Enter** key. The Google home page opens with the insertion point blinking in the search box.

4. In the search box, type **microsoft carbon footprint**, and then press the **Enter** key. The search query is sent to Google. After a moment, the search results appear on the screen.

5. Review the search results. Notice the number of hits and the first three websites listed in the results. You will return to the Bing search results so you can compare them with the Google search results.

6. Click the **Bing** tab to redisplay the Bing search results, and then look for differences in the search results. For example, the number of hits on Bing will differ from the number of hits on Google, and the list of results might have different hits at the top, or the same hits but in a different order.

   You will open pages from the search results in different tabs so you can leave the search results open in the original tab.

7. Press and hold the **Ctrl** key as you click a promising link in the Bing search results, and then release the **Ctrl** key. The linked webpage opens in a new tab, but the Bing search results tab remains active.

8. In the Bing search results, right-click the link for another page with promising information, and then click **Open in new tab** on the shortcut menu. The page opens in another tab.

9. Point to the **Google** tab. A Close Tab button ⊠ appears in the upper-right corner of the tab. You don't need these search results any longer, so you can close the page.

10. Click the **Close Tab** button ⊠. The page with the Google search results closes, leaving the other tabs available.

The Internet Explorer app also offers tabbed browsing. As described in the Visual Overview, the tabs don't appear until you right-click in the browser window, which displays the Tabs bar at the top of the screen and the navigation bar at the bottom of the screen. From the Tabs bar, you can create new tabs by clicking the New Tabs button, switch between open tabs by clicking each page tab, and closing tabs by clicking the Close Tab button.

## Using the History List

**TIP**

The suggestions that appear when you start typing a URL in the Address bar are based on the History list.

The **History list** tracks the webpages you visit over a certain time period, not just during one browsing session. The History list contains the URLs for the websites and pages that you have visited using both versions of Internet Explorer; however, you can only access the complete History list from the desktop application. By default, the entries in the History list are organized into date folders (Today, Yesterday, Two Weeks ago, and so on). Each date folder contains a folder for every website you visited. Within each site folder, the webpages you visited appear in alphabetical order.

You will use the History list to open the Microsoft home page you viewed earlier in the Internet Explorer app.

### To use the History list:

1. In the upper-right corner of the window, click the **View favorites, feeds, and history** button 🌟. The Favorites Center opens on the right side of the screen.

2. Click the **History** tab. The list of visited sites is displayed by date.

   **Trouble?** If the History list is not organized by date, you need to change the setting. Click the View by button just below the History tab, and then click View By Date.

3. Click **Today**. The Today list expands so you can see a list of the sites you viewed today.

4. Click the **microsoft** folder to display the pages you viewed at the Microsoft site today. See Figure 5.

**Figure 5**    History list

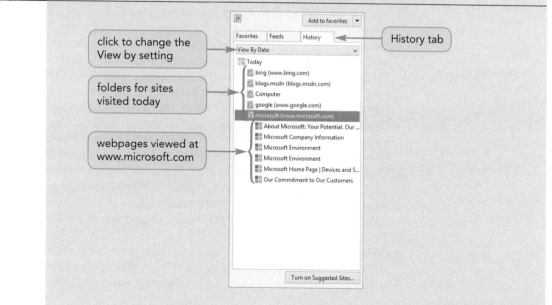

**5.** Click **Microsoft Home Page | Devices and Services** to open the same Microsoft home page you viewed in the Internet Explorer app.

Now that you have implemented your search strategy, you need to determine if the results meet your needs.

# Evaluating the Search Results

You should review and evaluate all of the information you find on the web to identify its author, source, and accuracy, and to evaluate the usefulness of the information. The cost of publishing on the web is low, and anyone who has access to a computer connected to the Internet can publish content. The content of webpages is not regulated or verified. Although information can be and is updated regularly, there is plenty of outdated information on the web. As you gather facts, be sure to read the information you find to determine whether it is relevant, useful, accurate, balanced, and objective. The following list provides the basic steps for evaluating your search results:

- **Identify the author.** Determine who wrote the information and check whether the author has the credentials or expertise to write about the topic. Some credentials to consider are the author's background, education, professional experience, and affiliations. Often, the site includes a link to more information about the author—either on the site or at the author's site.
- **Check for objectivity/bias.** Think about the author's purpose for writing—conveying information, persuading others, creating controversy, and so forth. Determine whether the information is fact, opinion, or speculation. Consider whether other viewpoints might provide differing or conflicting information. One way to determine bias is to read articles from a variety of different sources and compare the information they present. Sources can include periodicals (magazines, newspapers, and other publications), blogs (websites on which people post commentaries and readers respond), wikis (websites that many people contribute to and edit but whose content is not necessarily validated for accuracy), online references (dictionaries, thesauri, encyclopedias, atlases, quotations, and grammar checkers), government sites, business sites, and personal sites.
- **Verify currency.** Try to find out when the information was last updated. Consider whether timeliness affects the reliability of the information. Most webpages include a last revision date somewhere on the page (usually at the top or the bottom).
- **Assess accuracy.** Evaluate the content for correctness—take note of glaring errors, misspellings, or other sloppy errors. Confirm the information with a second source, like you would with other research materials. On the web, the same information might appear in multiple places; but when you dig deeper, you might find that everyone is repeating the same information from a single source.
- **Determine validity.** Look at the source of the site to determine whether this is a trustworthy information resource. Consider who owns the website on which you found the information—a recognized, legitimate publication or an individual. Check whether the website has a stated goal that might influence how it presents information or what information it presents. From the About and Contact pages, you can check out the site's history, read mission or vision statements, and find the address and details about key staff. You can also search the web to find reviews of the source.
- **Consider relevancy.** As a final step, you need to consider whether the information you find is relevant to your topic. You will encounter a lot of interesting information as you go, and it's easy to get lost in tangential information.

Based on your evaluation, you can determine whether the information is useful. For example, Figure 6 shows how Martha evaluated one webpage from the search results. Although this webpage provides information on her topic, given her evaluation, she might want to continue looking for more information.

| **Figure 6** | **Webpage evaluated for usefulness to search topic** |
| --- | --- |

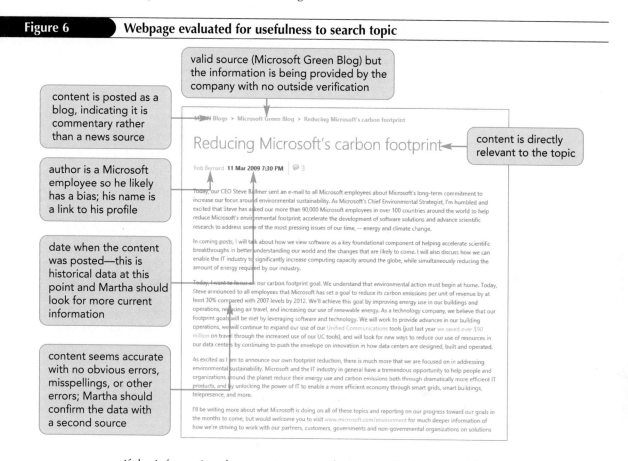

If the information does meet your needs, Internet Explorer provides several ways to save the information so you can access it later as you compile your research results.

## Saving Webpages as Favorites

Web addresses can be very long and, as a result, difficult to remember. In Internet Explorer, you can save the URL of a website as a favorite in the **Favorites list**, a feature that you can use to store and organize a list of webpages you want to revisit.

You can save a webpage as a favorite from both versions of Internet Explorer. From the Internet Explorer desktop application, you open the Favorites Center, and then click the Add to favorites button. The Add a Favorite dialog box opens, allowing you to specify a name for the favorite and select a folder in which to save the favorite in the Favorites list. Using folders to organize your Favorites list makes it easier to find a favorite when you need it. From the Internet Explorer app, you click the Pin site button in the navigation bar, and then click Add to favorites. The page is added to the Favorites list using the title of the webpage.

Martha will want to refer back to the Microsoft home page as she completes her case study. You will save the Microsoft home page as a favorite.

## To save the Microsoft home page as a favorite:

1. With the Microsoft home page displayed in the browser window, click the **View favorites, feeds, and history** button 🌟.

2. At the top of the Favorites Center, click the **Add to favorites** button. The Add a Favorite dialog box opens. You can change the name used for the favorite and the folder in which it is stored from this dialog box. See Figure 7.

**Figure 7    Add a Favorite dialog box**

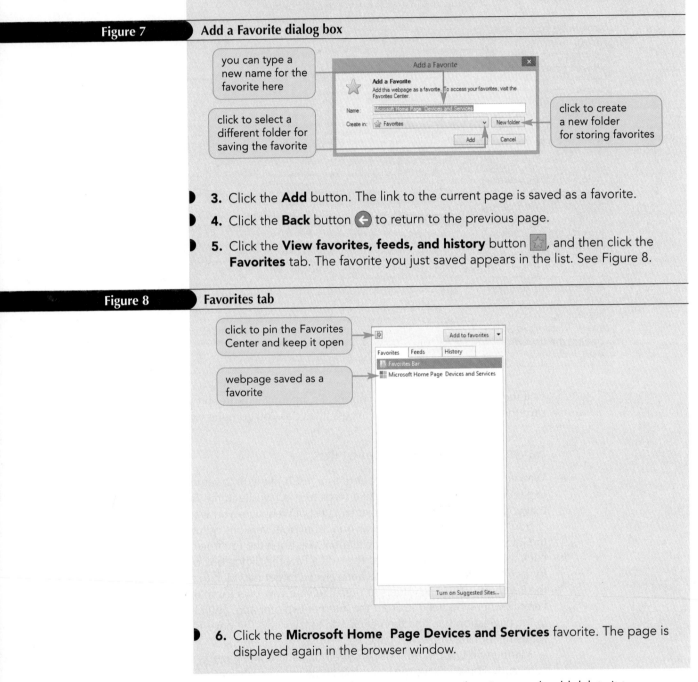

you can type a new name for the favorite here

click to select a different folder for saving the favorite

click to create a new folder for storing favorites

3. Click the **Add** button. The link to the current page is saved as a favorite.

4. Click the **Back** button ⬅ to return to the previous page.

5. Click the **View favorites, feeds, and history** button 🌟, and then click the **Favorites** tab. The favorite you just saved appears in the list. See Figure 8.

**Figure 8    Favorites tab**

click to pin the Favorites Center and keep it open

webpage saved as a favorite

6. Click the **Microsoft Home Page Devices and Services** favorite. The page is displayed again in the browser window.

When you no longer need to save a page as a favorite, you should delete it to keep your Favorites list current and streamlined. You will delete the Microsoft home page favorite.

### To delete the Microsoft home page favorite:

▶ 1. Click the **View favorites, feeds, and history** button 🌟.

▶ 2. On the Favorites tab, right-click the **Microsoft Home Page  Devices and Services** favorite. A shortcut menu opens with options for working with favorites.

▶ 3. On the shortcut menu, click **Delete**. The Microsoft Home Page Devices and Services favorite is deleted from the Favorites Center.

## Pinning Webpages

You can pin a page to the taskbar so you can open the webpage directly from the desktop without first starting Internet Explorer. To pin a webpage to the taskbar, drag the tab of the webpage from the Internet Explorer window to the taskbar, and then release the mouse button when the ScreenTip "Pin to Taskbar" appears. The button on the taskbar is a shortcut to the webpage. When you click the button for the pinned page, the page opens in a new browser window.

You can also pin a page to the right side of the Start screen. In the Internet Explorer desktop application, click the Tools button, and then click Add site to Start Screen. A dialog box opens asking you to confirm the name and URL for the tile. In the Internet Explorer app, you pin a page to the Start screen by clicking the Pin site button on the navigation bar, and then clicking Pin to Start. A dialog box opens so you can change the name that will appear on the tile.

You will pin the Microsoft home page to the Start screen for Martha.

### To pin the Microsoft home page to the Start screen:

▶ 1. Click the **Tools** button ⚙ to open the Tools menu, and then click **Add site to Start Screen**. A dialog box opens in which you can confirm the name for the tile and the URL for the website. See Figure 9.

| Figure 9 | Dialog box to pin site to Start screen |
| --- | --- |

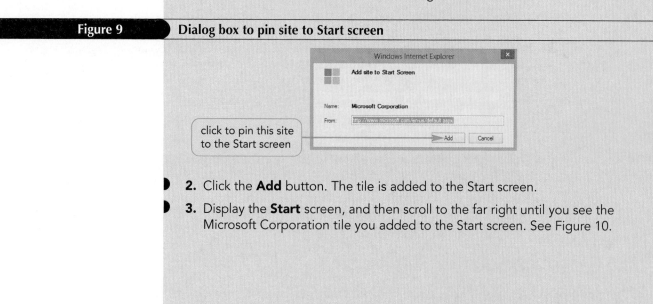

click to pin this site to the Start screen

▶ 2. Click the **Add** button. The tile is added to the Start screen.

▶ 3. Display the **Start** screen, and then scroll to the far right until you see the Microsoft Corporation tile you added to the Start screen. See Figure 10.

**Figure 10**    **Tile for pinned site on the Start screen**

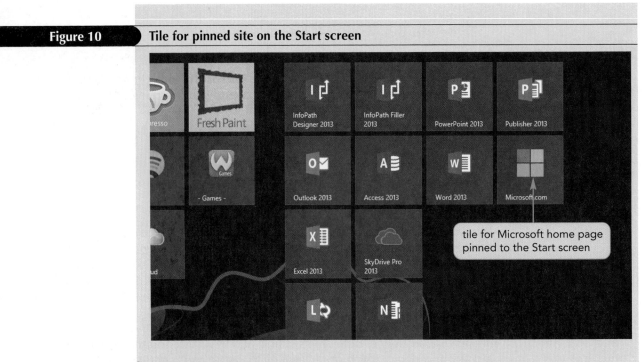

tile for Microsoft home page pinned to the Start screen

▶ **4.** Click the **Microsoft.com** tile. The Microsoft home page opens in the Internet Explorer desktop application in a new browser window.

▶ **5.** Click the **Close Tab** button ☒ to close the tab and the browser window displaying the Microsoft home page. The other browser window remains open.

As with favorites, you should delete the tiles for pinned pages you no longer need to avoid unwanted clutter on your Start screen. You unpin a page directly from the Start screen. You will unpin the tile for the Microsoft home page from the Start screen.

### To unpin the tile for the Microsoft home page:

▶ **1.** Display the **Start** screen, and then scroll to the far right until you see the Microsoft.com tile you added to the Start screen.

▶ **2.** Right-click the **Microsoft.com** tile. On the navigation bar at the bottom of the screen, you have options to unpin the page from the Start screen, pin the page to the taskbar, or open the file location.

▶ **3.** Click the **Unpin from Start** button. The Microsoft.com tile is removed from the Start screen.

Before Martha compiles and uses information in her case study on Microsoft's efforts to reduce its carbon footprint, she needs to understand the rules of copyright and fair use. This knowledge will help her determine what information she can use for her own purposes and how to properly cite its source.

# Using the Information You Find

The content you find on the web is a form of **intellectual property**, which includes all creations of the human mind, such as original ideas and creative works presented in a form that can be shared or that others can recreate, emulate, or manufacture. On a webpage, intellectual property includes the text, images, and videos on the page, as well as the design of the page itself. Intellectual property as a tangible expression of an idea is protected just like other tangible forms of property, such as houses and cars. Each country has its own rules and laws governing intellectual property rights and protection. In the United States, intellectual property is protected through patents, trademarks, trade secrets, and copyrights.

A **copyright** is a protection granted by law to the author or creator of an original work who creates a tangible expression of that work or creation. Creations that can be copyrighted include virtually all forms of artistic or intellectual expression, such as books, music, artwork, audio and video recordings, architectural drawings, choreographic works, product packaging, and computer software. The tangible form of the work can be words, numbers, notes, sounds, pictures, and so forth. A collection of facts can be copyrighted, but only if the collection is arranged, coordinated, or selected in a way that causes the resulting work to rise to the level of an original work. Copyright protection exists whether the work is published or unpublished.

The copyright is in effect for the length of time specified in the copyright law and gives the author or creator the exclusive right to reproduce, adapt, distribute, publicly perform, publicly display, or sell the work. In the United States, under the 1976 Copyright Act, works created after 1977 are protected for the life of the author (or the last surviving author in the case of a "joint work" with multiple authors) plus another 70 years. Works made for hire and anonymous or pseudonymous works are protected for 95 years from the date of publication or 120 years from the date of creation, whichever is earlier. The copyright holder can transfer, license, sell, donate, or leave the copyright to his or her heirs. Works created before 1978 are protected under the 1909 Copyright Act and have more complex and variable terms of copyright.

## Determining Fair Use

U.S. copyright law allows people to use portions of copyrighted works without obtaining permission from the copyright holder if that use is a fair use. Section 107 of the 1976 Copyright Act lists criticism, comment, news reporting, teaching, scholarship, and research as examples of uses that may be eligible for fair use. However, the circumstances surrounding a particular use determine whether that use is considered fair. Keep in mind that the legal definition of fair use is intentionally broad and can be difficult to interpret. As a result, many disputes about whether a use is fair have landed in court. Courts generally consider the following four factors when determining fair use:

- **The purpose and character of the new work**—This factor considers such issues as whether the use adds something new to the body of knowledge and arts or just reproduces the work, and whether the use is commercial or for nonprofit educational purposes.

- **The nature of the copyrighted work**—In general, more creative works have stronger protection than factual works. Keep in mind that an unpublished work has the same copyright protections for fair use as a published work.
- **The amount and substantiality of the portion used in relation to the copyrighted work as a whole** (in other words, how much of the copyrighted work was used)—The less work that is used, the more likely it falls under fair use. However, using even a small amount of the work can be copyright infringement if it is the heart of the work.
- **The effect of the use on the potential market, or value, of the copyrighted work**—For example, does the use of the copyrighted material hurt the market for the original work, and does it impair or limit the ability of the copyright owner to earn income or otherwise benefit from the work?

Again, no hard-and-fast rule determines fair use. If you are unsure whether your use is indeed fair use, the safest course of action is to contact the copyright owner and ask for permission to use the work.

## Identifying Works in the Public Domain

Once the term of the copyright has expired, the work moves into the **public domain**, which means that anyone is free to copy the work without requesting permission from the last copyright holder. Older literary works, such as *A Tale of Two Cities* by Charles Dickens, which was published in 1859, are in the public domain and can be reproduced freely. Songs or musical works published earlier than 1922, such as the *Star-Spangled Banner,* written by Francis Scott Key in 1814, are also in the public domain in the United States. However, if a publisher creates a new print edition of the public domain literary work or an orchestra makes an audio recording of the public domain musical work, the book or performance is a separate work that can be copyrighted and protected under current copyright laws.

Authors or creators can place their work into the public domain voluntarily at any time. For example, some websites provide graphics files that visitors can use free of charge. You can include public domain content on a webpage, in a paper, or in any other form of creative expression. However, you should still acknowledge the source of the public domain material and not represent the work as your own, which is plagiarism.

## Avoiding Plagiarism

The web makes it very easy to copy someone else's work. If you use someone else's work, whether the work is in the public domain or protected by copyright, you must cite the source of the material. Failure to cite the source of material that you use is called **plagiarism**. Claiming someone else's work as your own is a serious legal violation that can lead to a failing grade, being expelled from school, being fired from a job, or being subjected to a hefty fine or prosecution.

Plagiarism can be as simple as including a sentence or two from someone else's work without using quotation marks or attribution. It can be as blatant as duplicating substantial parts of someone else's work and claiming them as your own. It can be more subtle, such as paraphrasing someone else's content without the proper citation of the source. Another form of plagiarism is when students purchase essays, term papers, and even theses or dissertations from commercial services and then pass them off as their own.

To ensure that you don't unintentionally plagiarize someone else's work, be sure to properly reference the sources of works that you use. Keep in mind that just including a source citation is not enough if you plan to use the finished product commercially. You must also obtain the copyright holder's permission if you want to use the work in a way that falls outside of fair use.

**TIP**

For more information about current U.S. copyright law, you can visit the United States Copyright Office website at www.copyright.gov.

## Documenting Web Resources

To avoid charges of plagiarism, all works you reference—whether they are protected by copyright, in the public domain, or considered fair use—need to be documented. This gives proper credit to the original authors as well as provides readers with the information they need to find and review the works you used.

However, documentation can become a challenge when you are referencing a webpage. Because the web is a dynamic medium, the content of any given page can change in an instant. Also, its URL can change or disappear from day to day. Unlike published books and journals, which have a physical existence, a webpage exists only in an HTML document on a web server computer. If the file's name or location changes, or if the web server is disconnected from the Internet, the page is no longer accessible.

For academic research, the two most widely followed standards for citations are those of the American Psychological Association (APA) and the Modern Language Association (MLA). The APA and MLA formats for webpage citations are similar. Figure 11 shows both APA and MLA citations for a specific webpage, and how the citation information is obtained from the webpage.

**Figure 11**    **Webpage citations**

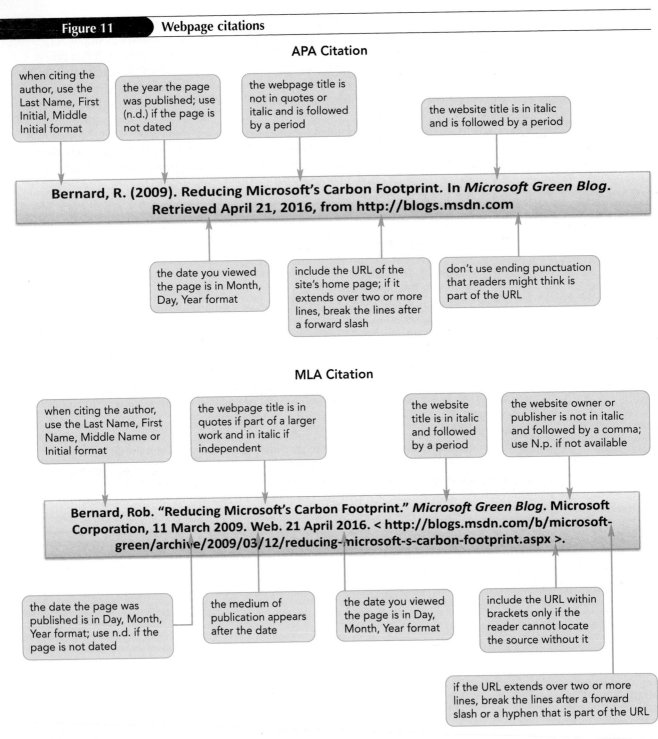

### APA Citation

when citing the author, use the Last Name, First Initial, Middle Initial format

the year the page was published; use (n.d.) if the page is not dated

the webpage title is not in quotes or italic and is followed by a period

the website title is in italic and is followed by a period

**Bernard, R. (2009). Reducing Microsoft's Carbon Footprint. In _Microsoft Green Blog_. Retrieved April 21, 2016, from http://blogs.msdn.com**

the date you viewed the page is in Month, Day, Year format

include the URL of the site's home page; if it extends over two or more lines, break the lines after a forward slash

don't use ending punctuation that readers might think is part of the URL

### MLA Citation

when citing the author, use the Last Name, First Name, Middle Name or Initial format

the webpage title is in quotes if part of a larger work and in italic if independent

the website title is in italic and followed by a period

the website owner or publisher is not in italic and followed by a comma; use N.p. if not available

**Bernard, Rob. "Reducing Microsoft's Carbon Footprint." _Microsoft Green Blog_. Microsoft Corporation, 11 March 2009. Web. 21 April 2016. < http://blogs.msdn.com/b/microsoft-green/archive/2009/03/12/reducing-microsoft-s-carbon-footprint.aspx >.**

the date the page was published is in Day, Month, Year format; use n.d. if the page is not dated

the medium of publication appears after the date

the date you viewed the page is in Day, Month, Year format

include the URL within brackets only if the reader cannot locate the source without it

if the URL extends over two or more lines, break the lines after a forward slash or a hyphen that is part of the URL

Be aware, however, that both the APA and MLA standards change from time to time. Consult these organizations' websites as well as the APA and MLA style guides for the latest rules and updates to these styles before using them. Also, always check to see if your instructor or editor (for work you are submitting for publication) has established other guidelines.

## Printing a Webpage

The web is a dynamic medium, so pages can be removed or changed without warning. When doing research, you might want to print or save copies of pages that you have used during your research to document the information.

**INSIGHT**

### Printing Webpages

Webpages are not necessarily designed with printing in mind. Before you print a webpage, it is a good idea to preview it to ensure that the text and graphics fit well on the page. If necessary, you can change the settings to adjust the webpage to fit better on the paper. In both versions of Internet Explorer, you can change the orientation from portrait to landscape to better accommodate the text and graphics on the page. The Internet Explorer desktop application provides more options, including changing the print size to shrink the webpage to fit onto a certain number of pages and adjusting the margins.

Also, many webpages provide a link to a separate printer-friendly version of the page. This option controls what is printed, including only essential information and ensuring that it will print in an appropriate format.

The Print dialog box lets you review the print settings and select a different printer, the pages to print, and the number of copies. It is a good idea to preview the page before you print so that you can see how it will fit on the page. The Print Preview window lets you change the page orientation between portrait (where the page is taller than it is wide) and landscape (where the page is wider than it is tall), and change the print size to force the content to fit on a specific number of pages.

You will preview and print one of the pages with promising information that you reviewed.

### To preview and print a webpage:

1. Return to the Internet Explorer desktop application.
2. Display one of the pages you opened.
3. Click the **Tools** button ⚙, point to **Print** on the menu, and then click **Print preview** on the submenu. The Print Preview window opens. See Figure 12.

**TIP**

To open the Print dialog box without displaying the Print Preview window, click the Tools button, point to Print, and then click Print.

**Figure 12**      **Print Preview window**

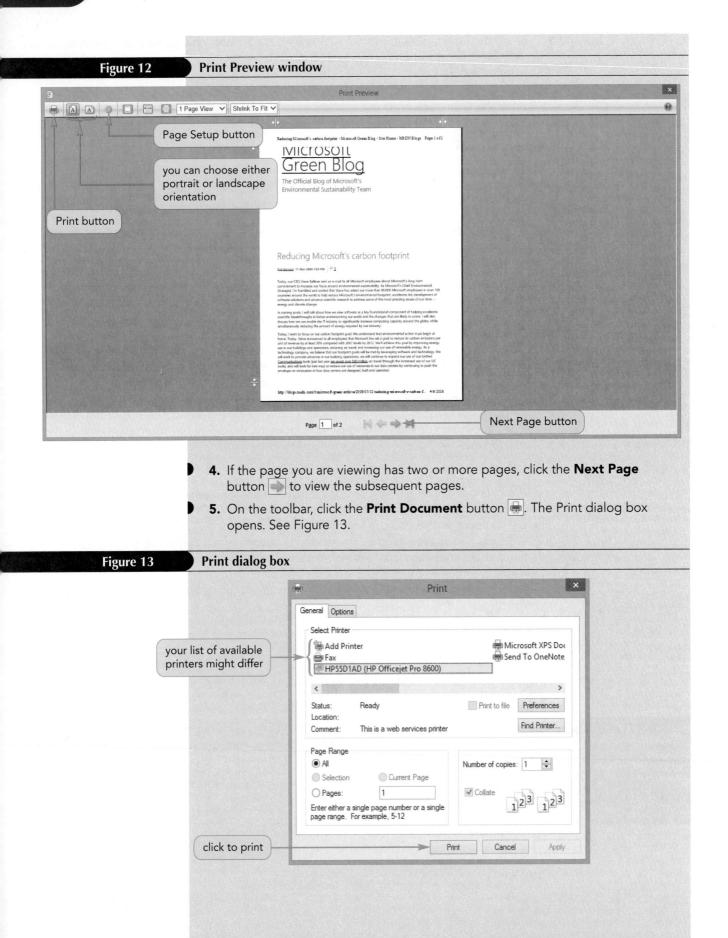

Page Setup button

you can choose either portrait or landscape orientation

Print button

Next Page button

4. If the page you are viewing has two or more pages, click the **Next Page** button 🖶 to view the subsequent pages.

5. On the toolbar, click the **Print Document** button 🖶. The Print dialog box opens. See Figure 13.

**Figure 13**      **Print dialog box**

your list of available printers might differ

click to print

▶ **6.** In the Select Printer section, click the printer you want to use, if necessary.

▶ **7.** If you are instructed to print, click the **Print** button. Otherwise, click the **Cancel** button.

▶ **8.** In the title bar of the Print Preview window, click the **Close** button [ × ].

## Saving a Webpage

Saving a webpage is a good option if you want to keep a version of a webpage with the content it contained when you accessed it, but you don't want to use the resources to print. You have several options for saving a webpage, depending on what portion of the webpage you want to save. The "Webpage, complete (*.htm,*.html)" option in the Save Webpage dialog box saves the entire webpage, including its graphics and other elements that make up the page. This option creates a folder with all of the site's related files, including page elements, such as images and sounds. The "Web Archive, single file (*.mht)" option saves a "picture" of the current webpage, without any of the page elements. The two other options—"Webpage, HTML only (*.htm,*.html)" and "Text File (*.txt)"—let you save just the HTML code or the text from the webpage, respectively, without saving the graphics, frames, or styles on the webpage.

Martha asks you to save the page you found for future reference.

### To save the webpage:

▶ **1.** Click the **Tools** button [⚙], point to **File** on the menu, and then click **Save as** on the submenu. The Save Webpage dialog box opens. See Figure 14.

**Figure 14**    **Save Webpage dialog box**

specify the location for saving the file

File name: Reducing Microsoft's carbon footprint - Microsoft Green Blog - Site Home - MSDN Blogs_aspx

Save as type: Web Archive, single file (*.mht)    Save button

Encoding: Unicode (UTF-8)    Save    Cancel

Save as type button

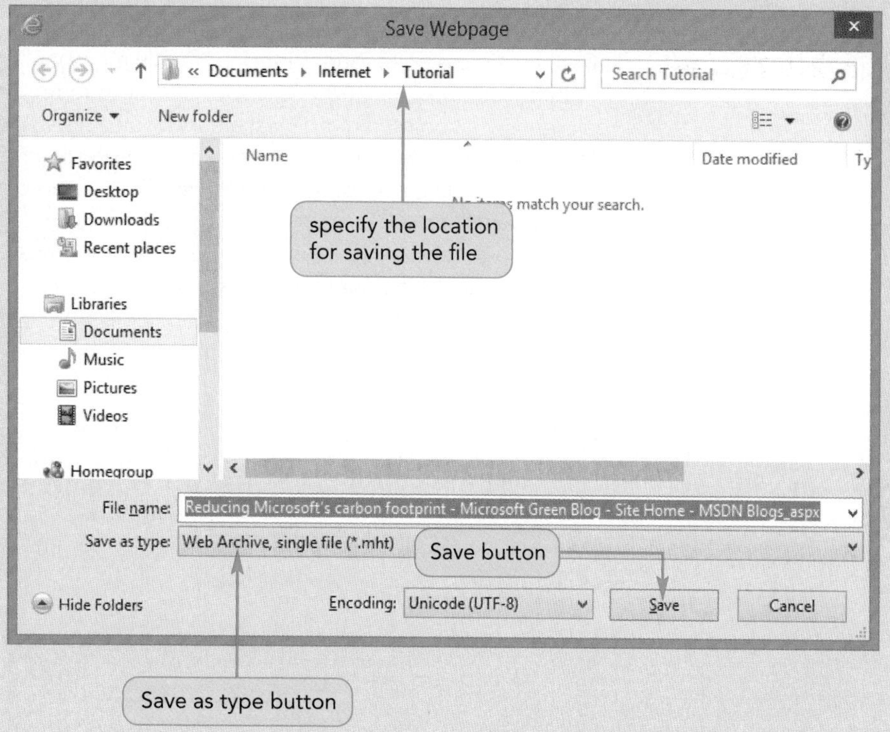

2. Navigate to the location where you are saving your files.

3. If necessary, click the **Save as type** button, and then click **Webpage, complete (*.htm,*.html)**. You can leave the default filename.

4. Click the **Save** button. After a few moments, a folder with all of the files needed for the webpage is saved in the location you specified.

Martha will keep the saved webpage on file with the rest of her research.

## PROSKILLS

### Written Communication: Organizing Your Research

Research is the first step toward conveying information and facts in a written report. When you summarize your research results, how you organize the information and write the report is just as important as the quality of the research that you have done. If you do an excellent job gathering the facts, be sure to deliver a report that is clear and easy to understand. This ensures that your audience benefits from your hard work and gets the information it needs. A lack of clarity can introduce noise into the communication and prevent readers from getting the message you intend to convey.

As you research a topic, be sure to take accurate notes about what you learn. Remember to include complete information about your sources so you can cite them as needed in your report. After you finish your research, you should organize your notes into a logical order so that you can present the information clearly and logically. This is also a good way to check whether you need to locate additional information.

As you begin writing, make sure it is apparent why you are writing in the first place. Are you writing to inform, to entertain, or to express your opinion? When writing a factual report, your opinions are not relevant and should not be included. Next, determine the appropriate writing style—formal or informal. If you are writing for a professor or supervisor, you usually use a more formal tone than you would in a casual email to a colleague, friend, or family member.

When you have finished your report, be sure to read it carefully, keeping the recipient's viewpoint in mind. Make sure your points are clear and are presented in a logical order. Also, check your spelling and grammar, and correct any errors that you find. However, do not rely only on spelling and grammar checkers because they do not always find all errors. You might find it helpful to read what you have written out loud to determine whether your intended message and tone are coming through clearly. As a final step, you could ask a friend or colleague to read your final report and provide feedback.

Martha feels comfortable continuing to use Internet Explorer to research Microsoft's methods for reducing its carbon footprint. She is confident she can find relevant information, and that she can compile and document her sources appropriately.

## Quick Check

REVIEW

1. How do you open the two versions of Internet Explorer 10?
2. What are the two functions of the Address bar?
3. What are the basic steps for developing a search strategy?
4. Why should you conduct a search using multiple search engines?
5. Why would you want to use tabbed browsing?
6. What is the difference between the History list and the Favorites list?
7. Why should you review and evaluate information you find on the web?
8. What is plagiarism and how can you avoid it?

## Review Assignments

**There are no Data Files needed for the Review Assignments.**

Martha wants to gather information about how another large company is reducing its impact on the environment. Sprint, with 40,000 employees, provides another good case study. Martha has already gathered information on some of the programs that Sprint has implemented, including moving toward renewable energy sources, reducing its electricity use, reducing its use of paper, and collecting customer phones for reuse and recycling. Now Martha wants to research how the company is reducing its greenhouse gas emissions. Complete the following:

1. Start the Internet Explorer app, and then visit the Sprint website by entering its URL **www.sprint.com** in the Address bar.
2. Click links on the page to navigate the site, looking for basic information about Sprint.
3. Formulate a search strategy for finding the information Martha wants to gather for her case study.
4. Start the Internet Explorer desktop application, and then use the Address bar to implement the search strategy you developed.
5. Open a new tab, visit the website for a different search engine (such as Google, Bing, or Yahoo!), and then implement the same search strategy using that search engine.
6. Compare the results of the two search engines, and then open three promising pages on new tabs.
7. Evaluate one of the pages you opened to determine whether it is relevant, useful, accurate, balanced, and objective.
8. Preview and then print the page you evaluated. Record your evaluation notes on the printout.
9. Include a complete citation for the webpage on the printout.
10. Save the webpage using its default name as a Web Archive, single file in the location specified by your instructor.

## Case Problem 1

**There are no Data Files needed for this Case Problem.**

***Chicken Coops***    Mable Chong is planning to raise chickens in her backyard so she can enjoy fresh eggs. She has already researched the local regulations, how to care for chickens, and the pros and cons of different types of chickens. Before she purchases the chicks, she needs to build a chicken coop. She plans to have four chicks. She asks you to research the backyard coops and find one that will meet her needs and be simple to build. Complete the following steps:

1. Formulate a search strategy for finding the information Mable wants to gather about chicken coops.
2. Start Internet Explorer, and then implement the search strategy you developed using the default search engine.
3. On a new tab, repeat the search strategy using a different search engine.
4. Compare the results of the two search engines, and then open three promising pages on new tabs.
5. Evaluate the pages you opened to find one that is relevant, useful, accurate, balanced, and objective.
6. Preview and then print the page you evaluated. Record your evaluation notes on the printout.
7. Include a complete citation for the webpage on the printout.
8. Save the webpage using its default name as a Web Archive, single file in the location specified by your instructor.

**RESEARCH**

## Case Problem 2

**There are no Data Files needed for this Case Problem.**

*Great Espresso*    Ira Moss is planning to open Great Espresso, a coffee cart that will provide top-quality espresso and coffee drinks as well as some pastries and cookies. He has all of his business licenses in place, has purchased most of his equipment and supplies, and has set up orders with local bakeries for the snacks. The last thing he needs to do is determine what kind of coffee grinder he should purchase. He knows that there are blade grinders and burr grinders, and he asks you to research the differences between them. He also asks you to recommend a type of grinder and suggest two different models that he might purchase. Complete the following steps:

1. Formulate a search strategy for finding the information Ira wants to gather about coffee grinders.
2. Start Internet Explorer, and then implement the search strategy you developed. Repeat your strategy on a different search engine.
3. Open as many pages as needed to find information about the differences between the two grinders.
4. Start WordPad, and then record the information you found. Be sure to document your sources.
5. Evaluate the pages you opened to find one that is relevant, useful, accurate, balanced, and objective.
6. Preview and then print the page you evaluated. Record your evaluation notes on the printout.
7. Include a complete citation for the webpage on the printout.
8. Save the webpage using its default name as a Web Archive, single file in the location specified by your instructor.

## OBJECTIVES

**Session 1.1**
- Create and save a document
- Enter text and correct errors as you type
- Use AutoComplete and AutoCorrect
- Select text and move the insertion point
- Undo and redo actions
- Adjust paragraph spacing, line spacing, and margins
- Preview and print a document
- Create an envelope

**Session 1.2**
- Open an existing document
- Use the Spelling and Grammar task panes
- Change page orientation, font, font color, and font size
- Apply text effects and align text
- Copy formatting with the Format Painter
- Insert a paragraph border and shading
- Delete, insert, and edit a photo
- Use Word Help

# Creating and Editing a Document

*Writing a Business Letter and Formatting a Flyer*

## Case | *Sandy Hill Portrait Studio*

Sandy Hill Portrait Studio in Baltimore, Maryland, specializes in wedding photography and family portraits. It also offers weekend and evening classes for new and experienced photographers. The sales manager, Tim Bartolutti, has asked you to create a cover letter to accompany a set of prints that he needs to send to a client, and an envelope for sending a class schedule to another client. He also wants your help creating a flyer announcing a class that focuses on photographing pets.

You will create the letter and flyer using **Microsoft Office Word 2013** (or simply **Word**), a word-processing program. You'll start by opening Word and saving a new document. Then you'll type the text of the cover letter and print it. In the process of entering the text, you'll learn several ways to correct typing errors and how to adjust paragraph and line spacing. When you create the envelope, you'll learn how to save it as part of a document for later use. As you work on the flyer, you will learn how to open an existing document, change the way text is laid out on the page, format text, and insert and resize a photo. Finally, you'll learn how to use Word's Help system.

## STARTING DATA FILES

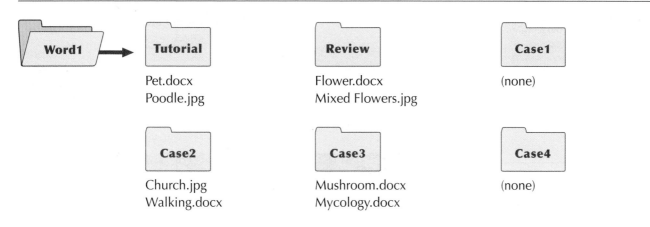

| Word1 → | Tutorial | Review | Case1 |
| --- | --- | --- | --- |
| | Pet.docx<br>Poodle.jpg | Flower.docx<br>Mixed Flowers.jpg | (none) |

| | Case2 | Case3 | Case4 |
| --- | --- | --- | --- |
| | Church.jpg<br>Walking.docx | Mushroom.docx<br>Mycology.docx | (none) |

# Session 1.1 Visual Overview:

The **Quick Access Toolbar** is a collection of buttons that provides one-click access to commonly used commands, such as Save, Undo, and Repeat.

Each **tab** includes commands related to particular activities or tasks. The HOME tab includes options for formatting and editing text.

The **title bar** displays the name of the open file and the program.

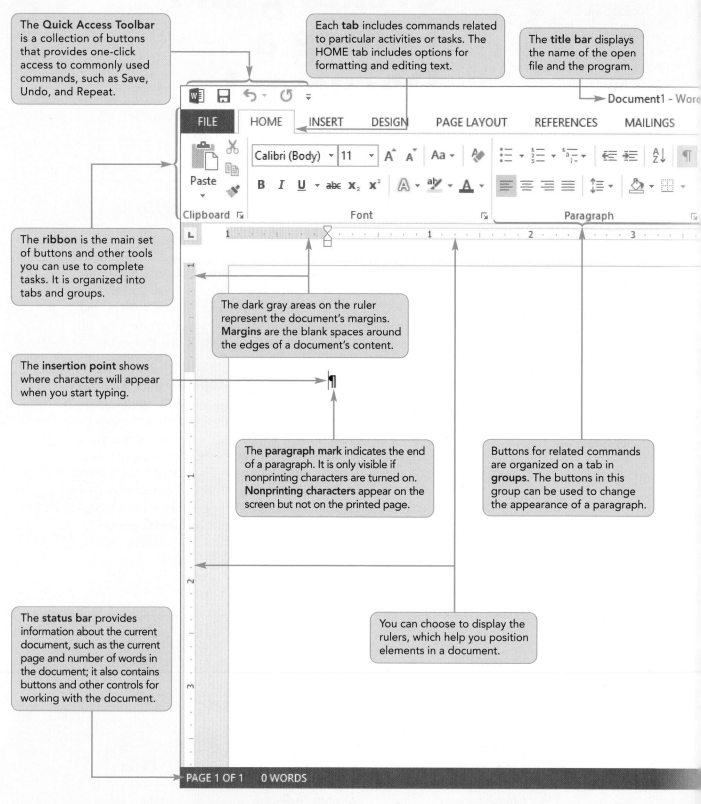

The **ribbon** is the main set of buttons and other tools you can use to complete tasks. It is organized into tabs and groups.

The dark gray areas on the ruler represent the document's margins. **Margins** are the blank spaces around the edges of a document's content.

The **insertion point** shows where characters will appear when you start typing.

The **paragraph mark** indicates the end of a paragraph. It is only visible if nonprinting characters are turned on. **Nonprinting characters** appear on the screen but not on the printed page.

Buttons for related commands are organized on a tab in **groups**. The buttons in this group can be used to change the appearance of a paragraph.

The **status bar** provides information about the current document, such as the current page and number of words in the document; it also contains buttons and other controls for working with the document.

You can choose to display the rulers, which help you position elements in a document.

# The Word Window

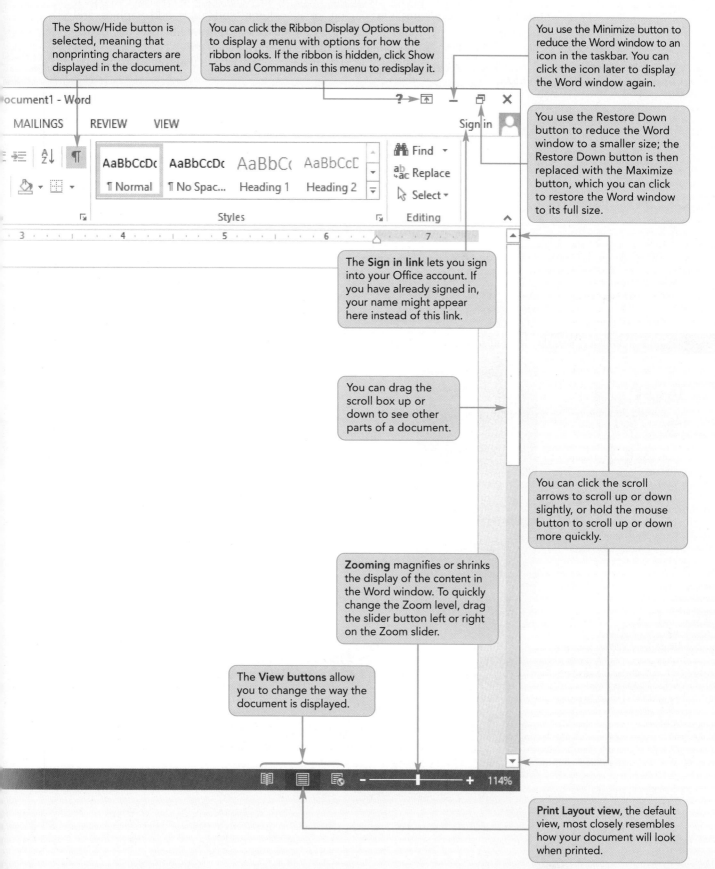

The Show/Hide button is selected, meaning that nonprinting characters are displayed in the document.

You can click the Ribbon Display Options button to display a menu with options for how the ribbon looks. If the ribbon is hidden, click Show Tabs and Commands in this menu to redisplay it.

You use the Minimize button to reduce the Word window to an icon in the taskbar. You can click the icon later to display the Word window again.

You use the Restore Down button to reduce the Word window to a smaller size; the Restore Down button is then replaced with the Maximize button, which you can click to restore the Word window to its full size.

The **Sign in link** lets you sign into your Office account. If you have already signed in, your name might appear here instead of this link.

You can drag the scroll box up or down to see other parts of a document.

You can click the scroll arrows to scroll up or down slightly, or hold the mouse button to scroll up or down more quickly.

**Zooming** magnifies or shrinks the display of the content in the Word window. To quickly change the Zoom level, drag the slider button left or right on the Zoom slider.

The **View buttons** allow you to change the way the document is displayed.

**Print Layout view**, the default view, most closely resembles how your document will look when printed.

# Starting Word

With Word, you can quickly create polished, professional documents. You can type a document, adjust margins and spacing, create columns and tables, add graphics, and then easily make revisions and corrections. In this session, you will create one of the most common types of documents—a block style business letter.

To begin creating the letter, you first need to start Word and then set up the Word window.

## To start Microsoft Word:

▶ **1.** Display the Windows Start screen, if necessary.

**Using Windows 7?** To complete Step 1, click the Start button on the taskbar.

▶ **2.** Click the **Word 2013** tile.

Word starts and displays the Recent screen in Backstage view, with template options for new documents on the right. A list of recently opened documents might appear on the left. **Backstage view** provides access to various screens with commands that allow you to manage files and Word options. See Figure 1-1.

| Figure 1-1 | Recent screen in Backstage view |
| --- | --- |

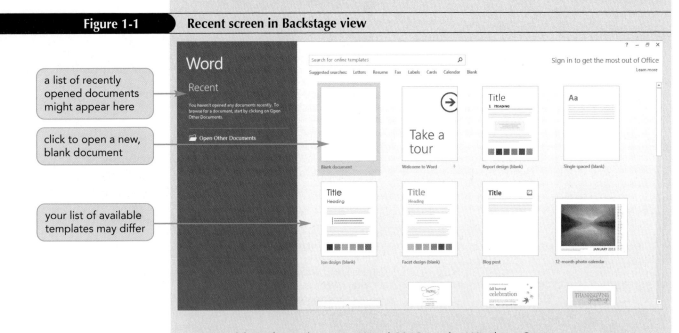

a list of recently opened documents might appear here

click to open a new, blank document

your list of available templates may differ

**Trouble?** If you don't see Word 2013 on the Windows Start screen, type Word 2013 to display the Apps screen with the Word 2013 tile highlighted, and then click the tile. If you still can't find Word 2013, ask your instructor or technical support person for help.

**Using Windows 7?** To complete Step 2, point to All Programs on the Start menu, click Microsoft Office 2013, and then click Word 2013.

> **3.** Click **Blank document**. The Word window opens, with the ribbon displayed.
>
> **Trouble?** If you don't see the ribbon, click the Ribbon Display Options button 🔲, as shown in the Session 1.1 Visual Overview, and then click Show Tabs and Commands.
>
> Don't be concerned if your Word window doesn't match the Session 1.1 Visual Overview exactly. You'll have a chance to adjust its appearance shortly.

## Working in Touch Mode

You can interact with the Word screen using a mouse, or, if you have a touch screen, you can work in Touch Mode, using a finger instead of the mouse pointer. In **Touch Mode**, extra space around the buttons on the ribbon allows your finger to tap the specific button you need. The figures in this text show the screen with Mouse Mode on, but it's helpful to learn how to switch back and forth between Touch Mode and Mouse Mode.

**Note:** The following steps assume that you are using a mouse. If you are instead using a touch device, please read these steps but don't complete them so that you remain working in Touch Mode.

> **To switch between Touch and Mouse Mode:**
>
> **1.** On the Quick Access Toolbar, click the **Customize Quick Access Toolbar** button 🔽 to open the menu. The Touch/Mouse Mode command near the bottom of the menu does not have a checkmark next to it, indicating that it is currently not selected.
>
> **Trouble?** If the Touch/Mouse Mode command has a checkmark next to it, press the Esc key to close the menu, and then skip to Step 3.
>
> **2.** On the menu, click **Touch/Mouse Mode**. The menu closes, and the Touch/Mouse Mode button 🖑 appears on the Quick Access Toolbar.
>
> **3.** On the Quick Access Toolbar, click the **Touch/Mouse Mode** button 🖑. A menu opens with two options—Mouse and Touch. The icon next to Mouse is shaded blue to indicate it is selected.
>
> **Trouble?** If the icon next to Touch is shaded blue, press the Esc key to close the menu and skip to Step 5.
>
> **4.** On the menu, click **Touch**. The menu closes, and the ribbon increases in height so that there is more space around each button on the ribbon. See Figure 1-2.

| **Figure 1-2** | Word window in Touch Mode |

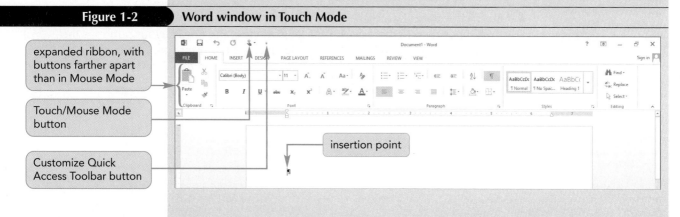

expanded ribbon, with buttons farther apart than in Mouse Mode

Touch/Mouse Mode button

Customize Quick Access Toolbar button

insertion point

**Trouble?** If you are working with a touch screen and want to use Touch Mode, skip Steps 5 and 6.

▶ **5.** On the Quick Access Toolbar, click the **Touch/Mouse Mode** button 👆, and then click **Mouse**. The ribbon changes back to its Mouse Mode appearance, as shown in the Session 1-1 Visual Overview.

▶ **6.** On the Quick Access Toolbar, click the **Customize Quick Access Toolbar** button ▾, and then click **Touch/Mouse Mode** to deselect it. The Touch/Mouse Mode button is removed from the Quick Access Toolbar.

# Setting Up the Word Window

Before you start using Word, you should make sure you can locate and identify the different elements of the Word window, as shown in the Session 1.1 Visual Overview. In the following steps, you'll make sure your screen matches the Visual Overview.

**To set up your Word window to match the figures in this book:**

▶ **1.** If the Word window does not fill the entire screen, click the **Maximize** button ▢ in the upper-right corner of the Word window.

The insertion point on your computer should be positioned about an inch from the top of the document, as shown in Figure 1-2, with the top margin visible.

**Trouble?** If the insertion point appears at the top of the document, with no white space above it, position the mouse pointer between the top of the document and the horizontal ruler, until it changes to ⬍, double-click, and then scroll up to top of the document.

▶ **2.** On the ribbon, click the **VIEW** tab. The ribbon changes to display options for changing the appearance of the Word window.

▶ **3.** In the Show group, click the **Ruler** check box to insert a checkmark, if necessary. If the rulers were not displayed, they are displayed now.

Next, you'll change the Zoom level to a setting that ensures that your Word window will match the figures in this book. To increase or decrease the screen's magnification, you could drag the slider button on the Zoom slider in the lower-right corner of the Word window. But to choose a specific Zoom level, it's easier to use the Zoom dialog box.

**TIP**

Changing the Zoom level affects only the way the document is displayed on the screen; it does not affect the document itself.

▶ **4.** In the Zoom group, click the **Zoom** button to open the Zoom dialog box. Double-click the **Percent** box to select the current zoom percentage, type **120**, and then click the **OK** button to close the Zoom dialog box.

▶ **5.** On the status bar, click the **Print Layout** button 📄 to select it, if necessary. As shown in the Session 1.1 Visual Overview, the Print Layout button is the middle of the three View buttons located on the right side of the status bar. The Print Layout button in the Views group on the View tab is also now selected.

Before typing a document, you should make sure nonprinting characters are displayed. Nonprinting characters provide a visual representation of details you might otherwise miss. For example, the (¶) character marks the end of a paragraph, and the (•) character marks the space between words.

### To verify that nonprinting characters are displayed:

1. On the ribbon, click the **HOME** tab.

2. In the blank Word document, look for the paragraph mark (¶) in the first line of the document, just to the right of the blinking insertion point.

   **Trouble?** If you don't see the paragraph mark, click the Show/Hide ¶ button ¶ in the Paragraph group.

   In the Paragraph group, the Show/Hide ¶ button should be highlighted in blue, indicating that it is selected, and the paragraph mark (¶) should appear in the first line of the document, just to the right of the insertion point.

## Saving a Document

Before you begin working on a document, you should save it with a new name. When you use the Save button on the Quick Access Toolbar to save a document for the first time, Word displays the Save As screen in Backstage view. In the Save As screen, you can select the location where you want to store your document. After that, when you click the Save button, Word saves your document to the same location you specified earlier, and with the same name.

### To save the document:

1. On the Quick Access Toolbar, click the **Save** button 🖫. Word switches to the Save As screen in Backstage view, as shown in Figure 1-3.

**Figure 1-3** | **Save As screen in Backstage view**

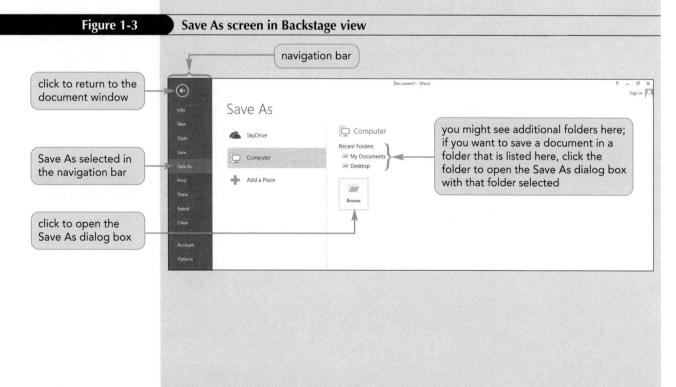

Because a document is now open, more commands are available in Backstage view than when you started Word. The **navigation bar** on the left contains commands for working with the open document and for changing settings that control how Word works.

2. Click **Computer**, if necessary, and then click the **Browse** button. The Save As dialog box opens.

   **Trouble?** If your instructor wants you to save your files to your SkyDrive account, click SkyDrive, log in to your account, if necessary, and then click the Browse button.

3. Navigate to the location specified by your instructor. The default filename, "Doc1," appears in the File name box. You will change that to something more descriptive. See Figure 1-4.

| Figure 1-4 | Save As dialog box |
| --- | --- |

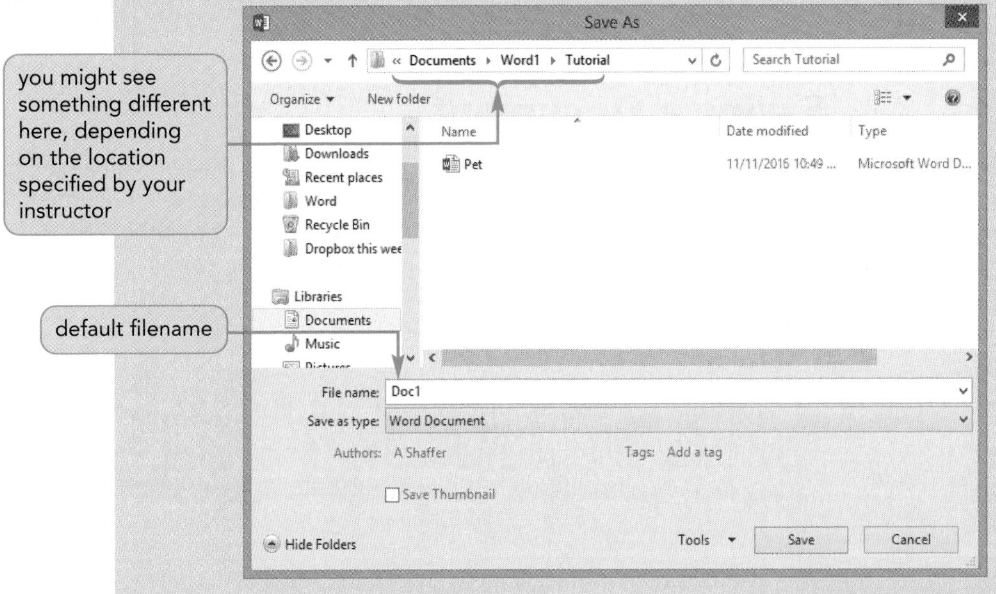

you might see something different here, depending on the location specified by your instructor

default filename

4. Click the File name box, and then type **Robbins Letter**. The text you type replaces the selected text in the File name box.

5. Click the **Save** button. The file is saved, the dialog box and Backstage view close, and the document window appears again, with the new filename in the title bar.

Now that you have saved the document, you can begin typing the letter. Tim has asked you to type a block style letter to accompany a set of family portraits that will be sent to Sonia Robbins, a regular client. Figure 1-5 shows the block style letter you will create in this tutorial.

**Figure 1-5**     Completed block style letter

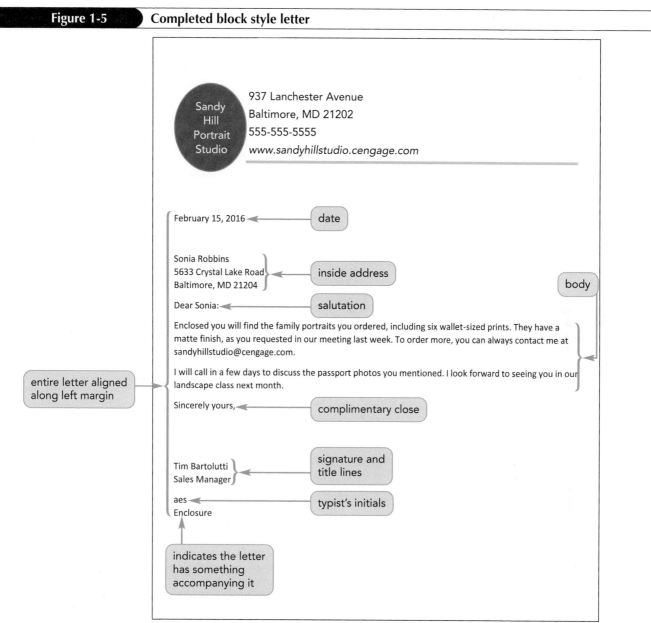

© 2014 Cengage Learning

## Written Communication: Creating a Business Letter

Several styles are considered acceptable for business letters. The main differences among the styles have to do with how parts of the letter are indented from the left margin. In the block style, which you will use in this tutorial, each line of text starts at the left margin. In other words, nothing is indented. Another style is to indent the first line of each paragraph. The choice of style is largely a matter of personal preference, or it can be determined by the standards used in a particular business or organization. To further enhance your skills in writing business correspondence, you should consult an authoritative book on business writing that provides guidelines for creating a variety of business documents, such as *Business Communication: Process & Product*, by Mary Ellen Guffey.

# Entering Text

The letters you type in a Word document appear at the current location of the blinking insertion point.

## Inserting a Date with AutoComplete

The first item in a block style business letter is the date. Tim plans to send the letter to Sonia on February 15, so you need to insert that date into the document. To do so, you can take advantage of **AutoComplete**, a Word feature that automatically inserts dates and other regularly used items for you. In this case, you can type the first few characters of the month and let Word insert the rest.

**To insert the date:**

▶ **1.** Type **Febr** (the first four letters of February). A ScreenTip appears above the letters, as shown in Figure 1-6, suggesting "February" as the complete word.

| Figure 1-6 | AutoComplete suggestion |
| --- | --- |

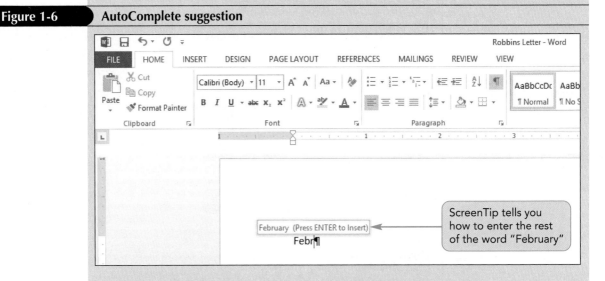

A **ScreenTip** is a box with descriptive text about an object or button you are pointing to.

If you wanted to type something other than "February," you could continue typing to complete the word. You want to accept the AutoComplete suggestion.

▶ **2.** Press the **Enter** key. The rest of the word "February" is inserted in the document. Note that AutoComplete works for long month names like February but not shorter ones like May, because "Ma" could be the beginning of many words besides "May."

▶ **3.** Press the **spacebar,** type **15, 2016** and then press the **Enter** key twice, leaving a blank paragraph between the date and the line where you will begin typing the inside address, which contains the recipient's name and address. Notice the nonprinting character (•) after the word "February" and before the number "15," which indicates a space. Word inserts this nonprinting character every time you press the spacebar.

**Trouble?** If February happens to be the current month, you will see a second AutoComplete suggestion displaying the current date after you press the spacebar. To ignore that AutoComplete suggestion, continue typing the rest of the date as instructed in Step 3.

## Continuing to Type the Block Style Letter

In a block style business letter, the inside address appears below the date, with one blank paragraph in between. Some style guides recommend including even more space between the date and the inside address. But in the short letter you are typing, more space would make the document look out of balance.

### To insert the inside address:

1. Type the following information, pressing the **Enter** key after each item:

   **Sonia Robbins**

   **5633 Crystal Lake Road**

   **Baltimore, MD 21204**

   Remember to press the Enter key after you type the zip code. Your screen should look like Figure 1-7. Don't be concerned if the lines of the inside address seem too far apart. You'll use the default spacing for now, and then adjust it after you finish typing the letter.

**Figure 1-7**  **Letter with inside address**

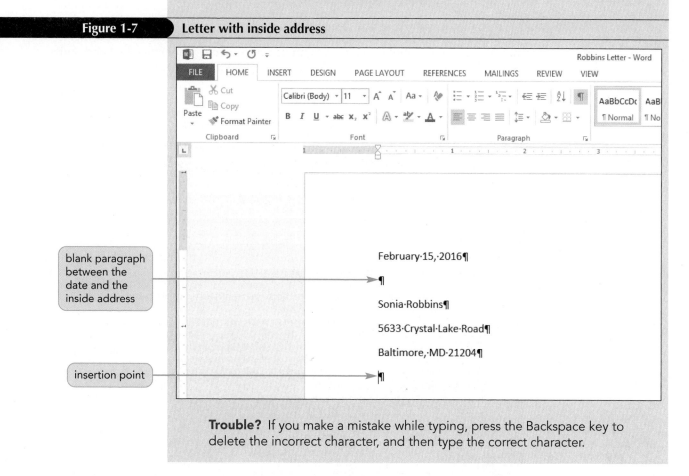

blank paragraph between the date and the inside address

insertion point

**Trouble?** If you make a mistake while typing, press the Backspace key to delete the incorrect character, and then type the correct character.

Now you can move on to the salutation and the body of the letter. As you type the body of the letter, notice that Word automatically moves the insertion point to a new line when the current line is full.

### To type the salutation and the body of the letter:

1. Type **Dear Sonia:** and then press the **Enter** key to start a new paragraph for the body of the letter.

2. Type the following sentence, including the period: **Enclosed you will find the family portraits you ordered, including six wallet-sized prints.**

3. Press the **spacebar**. Note that you should only include one space between sentences.

4. Type the following sentence, including the period: **They have a matte finish, as you requested in our conversation last week.**

5. On the Quick Access Toolbar, click the **Save** button 🖫. Word saves the document as Robbins Letter to the same location you specified earlier.

The next sentence you need to type includes Tim's email address.

## Typing a Hyperlink

When you type an email address and then press the spacebar or the Enter key, Word converts it to a hyperlink, with blue font and an underline. A **hyperlink** is text or a graphic you can click to jump to another file or to somewhere else in the same file. The two most common types of hyperlinks are: 1) an email hyperlink, which you can click to open an email message to the recipient specified by the hyperlink; and 2) a web hyperlink, which opens a webpage in a browser. Hyperlinks are useful in documents that you plan to distribute via email. In printed documents, where blue font and underlines can be distracting, you'll usually want to convert a hyperlink back to regular text.

### To add a sentence containing an email address:

1. Press the **spacebar**, and then type the following sentence, including the period: **To order more, you can always contact me at sandyhillstudio@cengage.com.**

2. Press the **Enter** key. Word converts the email address to a hyperlink, with blue font and an underline.

3. Position the mouse pointer over the hyperlink. A ScreenTip appears, indicating that you could press and hold the Ctrl key and then click the link to follow it—that is, to open an email message addressed to Sandy Hill Portrait Studio.

4. With the mouse pointer positioned over the hyperlink, right-click—that is, press the right mouse button. A shortcut menu opens with commands related to working with hyperlinks.

   You can right-click many items in the Word window to display a **shortcut menu** with commands related to the item you right-clicked. The **Mini toolbar** also appears when you right-click or select text, giving you easy access to the buttons and settings most often used when formatting text. See Figure 1-8.

**Figure 1-8**    Shortcut menu

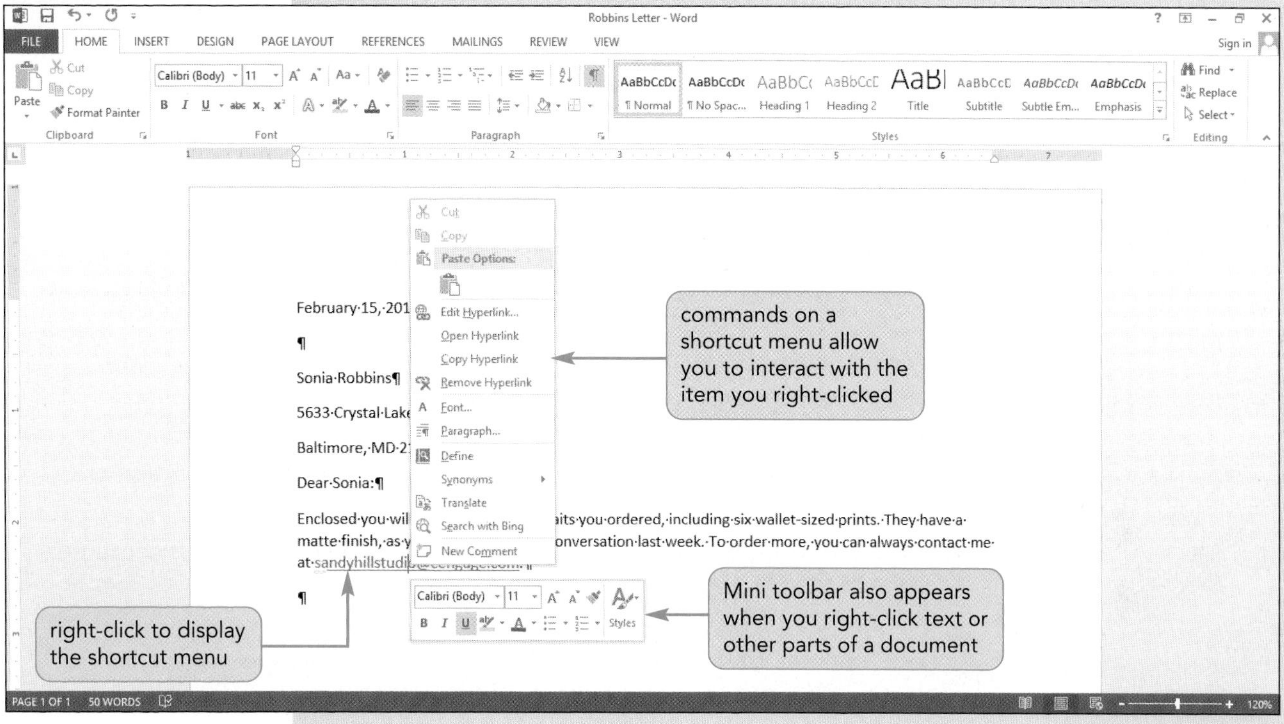

commands on a shortcut menu allow you to interact with the item you right-clicked

right-click to display the shortcut menu

Mini toolbar also appears when you right-click text or other parts of a document

**5.** Click **Remove Hyperlink** in the shortcut menu. The shortcut menu and the Mini toolbar are no longer visible. The email address is now formatted in black, like the rest of the document text.

**6.** On the Quick Access Toolbar, click the **Save** button 🖫.

# Using the Undo and Redo Buttons

To undo (or reverse) the last thing you did in a document, click the Undo button on the Quick Access Toolbar. To restore your original change, click the Redo button, which reverses the action of the Undo button (or redoes the undo). To undo more than your last action, you can continue to click the Undo button, or you can click the Undo button arrow on the Quick Access Toolbar to open a list of your most recent actions. When you click an action in the list, Word undoes every action in the list up to and including the action you clicked.

Tim asks you to change the word "conversation" to "meeting" in the second-to-last sentence you typed. You'll make the change now. If Tim decides he doesn't like it after all, you can always undo it. To delete a character, space, or blank paragraph to the right of the insertion point, you use the Delete key; or to delete an entire word, you can use the Ctrl+Delete key combination. To delete a character, space, or blank paragraph to the left of the insertion point, you use the Backspace key; or to delete an entire word, you can use the Ctrl+Backspace key combination.

### To change the word "conversation":

**1.** Press the ↑ key once and then press the → key as necessary to move the insertion point to the left of the "c" in the word "conversation."

> **2.** Press and hold the **Ctrl** key, and then press the **Delete** key to delete the word "conversation."

> **3.** Type **meeting** as a replacement, and then press the **spacebar**.
>
> After reviewing the sentence, Tim decides he prefers the original wording, so you'll undo the change.

> **4.** On the Quick Access Toolbar, click the **Undo** button ↶. The word "meeting" is removed from the sentence.

> **5.** Click the **Undo** button ↶ again to restore the word "conversation."
>
> Tim decides that he does want to use "meeting" after all. Instead of retyping it, you'll redo the undo.

> **6.** On the Quick Access Toolbar, click the **Redo** button ↷ twice. The word "meeting" replaces "conversation" in the document, so that the phrase reads "…in our meeting last week."
>
> You can also press the Ctrl+Z keys to execute the Undo command, and press the Ctrl+Y keys to execute the Redo command.

> **7.** Press and hold the **Ctrl** key, and then press the **End** key to move the insertion point to the blank paragraph at the end of the document.

> **8.** On the Quick Access Toolbar, click the **Save** button 💾. Word saves your letter with the same name and to the same location you specified earlier.

In the previous steps, you used the arrow keys and a key combination to move the insertion point to specific locations in the document. For your reference, Figure 1-9 summarizes the most common keystrokes for moving the insertion point in a document.

**Figure 1-9**    **Keystrokes for moving the insertion point**

| To Move the Insertion Point | Press |
| --- | --- |
| Left or right one character at a time | ← or → |
| Up or down one line at a time | ↑ or ↓ |
| Left or right one word at a time | Ctrl+← or Ctrl+→ |
| Up or down one paragraph at a time | Ctrl+↑ or Ctrl+↓ |
| To the beginning or to the end of the current line | Home or End |
| To the beginning or to the end of the document | Ctrl+Home or Ctrl+End |
| To the previous screen or to the next screen | Page Up or Page Down |
| To the top or to the bottom of the document window | Alt+Ctrl+Page Up or Alt+Ctrl+Page Down |

© 2014 Cengage Learning

# Correcting Errors as You Type

As you have seen, you can use the Backspace or Delete keys to remove an error, and then you can type a correction. In many cases, however, Word's AutoCorrect feature will do the work for you. Among other things, **AutoCorrect** automatically corrects common typing errors, such as typing "adn" instead of "and." For example, you might have noticed AutoCorrect at work if you forgot to capitalize the first letter in a sentence as you typed the letter. After you type this kind of error, AutoCorrect automatically corrects it when you press the spacebar, the Tab key, or the Enter key.

Word draws your attention to other potential errors by marking them with wavy underlines. If you type a word that doesn't match the correct spelling in Word's dictionary, or if a word is not in the dictionary at all, a wavy red line appears beneath it. A wavy red underline also appears if you mistakenly type the same word twice in a row. Misused words (for example, "your" instead of "you're") are underlined with a wavy blue line. Likewise, punctuation errors, problems with possessives and plurals, and grammatical errors are marked with a wavy blue underline.

You'll see how this works as you continue typing the letter and make some intentional typing errors.

### To learn more about correcting errors as you type:

1. Type the following sentence, including the errors shown here: **i will call in a few few days to disuss teh pasport photos you mentioned.**

   As you type, AutoCorrect changes the lowercase "i" at the beginning of the sentence to uppercase. It also changes "teh" to "the" and "pasport" to "passport." The spelling error "disuss" and the second "few" are marked with wavy red underlines. You will correct these errors after you finish typing the rest of the paragraph.

2. Press the **spacebar**, and then type the following sentence, including the extra period and the other errors: **I look forward too seeing you in our landscape class next month..** The word "too" is underlined with a wavy blue line, indicating a misused word. The sentence also contains a punctuation error, but Word won't identify it until you start a new sentence or press the Enter key to begin a new paragraph.

3. Press the **Enter** key to begin a new paragraph. As shown in Figure 1-10, the two periods at the end of the sentence are now underlined in blue.

**Figure 1-10    Errors marked in the document**

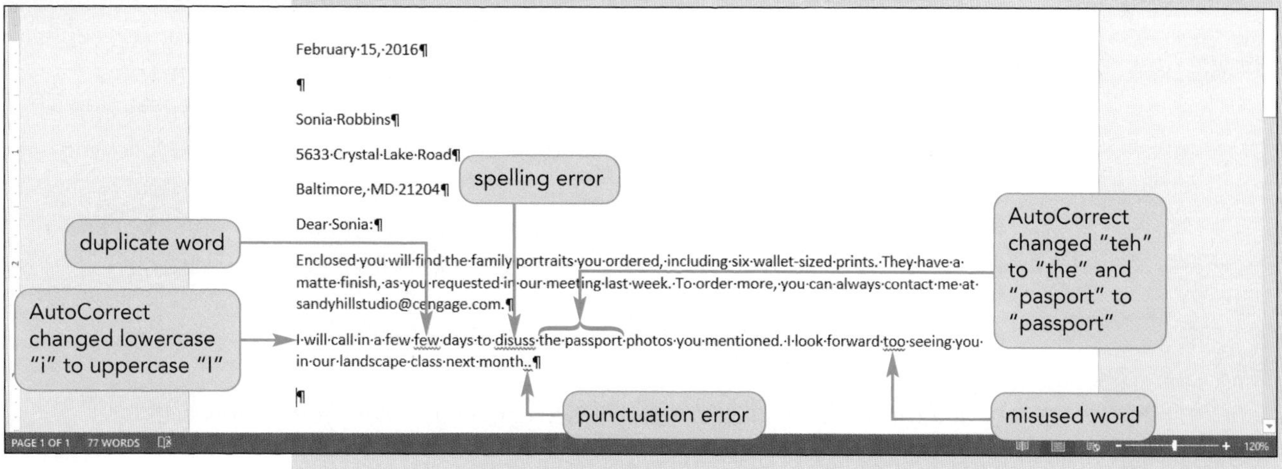

To correct an error marked with a wavy underline, you can right-click the error, and then click a replacement in the shortcut menu. If you don't see the correct word in the shortcut menu, click anywhere in the document to close the menu, and then type the correction yourself. You can also bypass the shortcut menu entirely, and simply delete the error and type a correction.

## To correct the spelling and grammar errors:

▶ **1.** Right-click **disuss** to display the shortcut menu shown in Figure 1-11.

**Figure 1-11**    **Shortcut menu with suggested spellings**

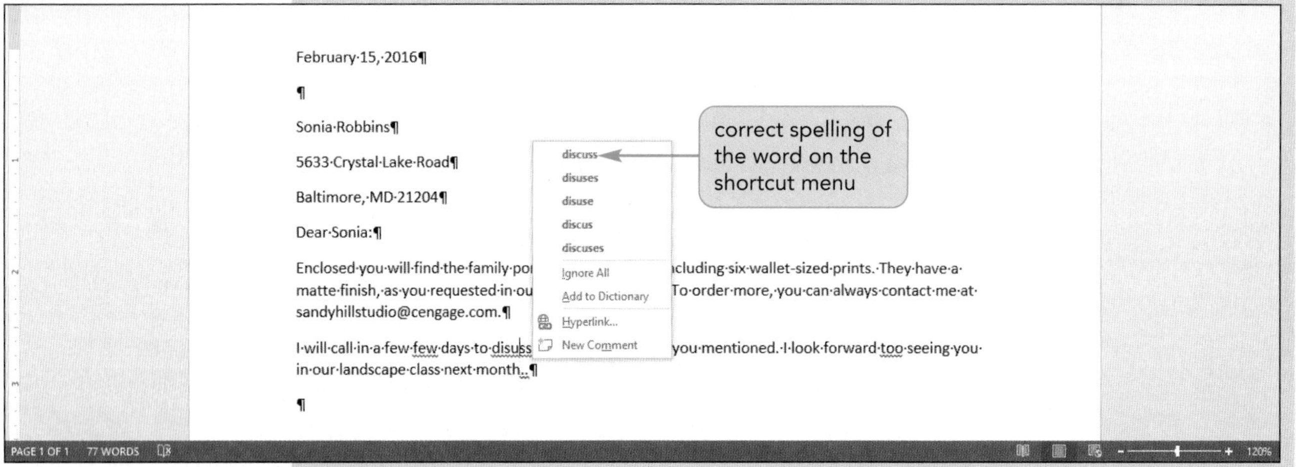

February·15,·2016¶

¶

Sonia·Robbins¶

5633·Crystal·Lake·Road¶

Baltimore,·MD·21204¶

Dear·Sonia:¶

correct spelling of
the word on the
shortcut menu

discuss
disuses
disuse
discus
discuses
Ignore All
Add to Dictionary
Hyperlink...
New Comment

Enclosed·you·will·find·the·family·po[...]cluding·six·wallet-sized·prints.·They·have·a·
matte·finish,·as·you·requested·in·ou[...]To·order·more,·you·can·always·contact·me·at·
sandyhillstudio@cengage.com.¶

I·will·call·in·a·few·few·days·to·disuss[...]you·mentioned.·I·look·forward·too·seeing·you·
in·our·landscape·class·next·month...¶

¶

PAGE 1 OF 1    77 WORDS                                                                                  120%

**Trouble?** If you see a shortcut menu other than the one shown in Figure 1-11, you didn't right-click exactly on the word "disuss." Press the Esc key to close the menu, and then repeat Step 1.

▶ **2.** On the shortcut menu, click **discuss**. The correct word is inserted into the sentence, and the shortcut menu closes. You could use a shortcut menu to remove the second instance of "few," but in the next step you'll try a different method—selecting the word and deleting it.

**TIP**

To deselect highlighted text, click anywhere in the document.

▶ **3.** Double-click anywhere in the underlined word **few**. The word and the space following it are highlighted in gray, indicating that they are selected. The Mini toolbar is also visible, but you can ignore it.

**Trouble?** If the entire paragraph is selected, you triple-clicked the word by mistake. Click anywhere in the document to deselect it, and then repeat Step 3.

▶ **4.** Press the **Delete** key. The second instance of "few" and the space following it are deleted from the sentence.

▶ **5.** Use the shortcut menu to replace the underlined word "too" with "to," and then click to the right of the second period after "month" and press the **Backspace** key to delete it.

▶ **6.** On the Quick Access Toolbar, click the **Save** button 🖫.

You can see how quick and easy it is to correct common typing errors with AutoCorrect and the wavy red and blue underlines, especially in a short document that you are typing yourself. If you are working on a longer document or a document typed by someone else, you'll also want to have Word check the entire document for errors. You'll learn how to do this in Session 1.2.

Next, you'll finish typing the letter.

## To finish typing the letter:

1. Press the **Ctrl+End** keys. The insertion point moves to the end of the document.

2. Type **Sincerely yours,** (including the comma).

3. Press the **Enter** key three times to leave space for the signature.

4. Type **Tim Bartolutti** and then press the **Enter** key. Because Tim's last name is not in Word's dictionary, a wavy red line appears below it. You can ignore this for now.

**TIP**

You only need to include your initials in a letter if you are typing it for someone else.

5. Type your first, middle, and last initials in lowercase, and then press the **Enter** key. AutoCorrect wrongly assumes your first initial is the first letter of a new sentence, and changes it to uppercase.

6. On the Quick Access Toolbar, click the **Undo** button ⤺. Word reverses the change, replacing the uppercase initial with a lowercase one.

7. Type **Enclosure**. At this point, your screen should look similar to Figure 1-12. Notice that as you continue to add lines to the letter, the top part of the letter scrolls off the screen. For example, in Figure 1-12, you can no longer see the date.

**Figure 1-12**    **Robbins Letter**

top part of the document has scrolled off the screen →

Sonia·Robbins¶

5633·Crystal·Lake·Road¶

Baltimore,·MD·21204¶

Dear·Sonia:¶

Enclosed·you·will·find·the·family·portraits·you·ordered,·including·six·wallet-sized·prints.·They·have·a· matte·finish,·as·you·requested·in·our·meeting·last·week.·To·order·more,·you·can·always·contact·me·at· sandyhillstudio@cengage.com.¶

I·will·call·in·a·few·days·to·discuss·the·passport·photos·you·mentioned.·I·look·forward·to·seeing·you·in·our· landscape·class·next·month.¶

Sincerely·yours,¶

space for the signature →    ¶

¶

Tim·Bartolutti¶

your lowercase initials should appear here →    aes¶

Enclosure¶

PAGE 1 OF 1    82 WORDS    120%

8. Save the document.

Now that you have finished typing the letter, you need to proofread it.

## Proofreading a Document

After you finish typing a document, you need to proofread it carefully from start to finish. Part of proofreading a document in Word is removing all wavy underlines, either by correcting the text or by telling Word to ignore the underlined text because it isn't really an error. For example, Tim's last name is marked as an error, when in fact it is spelled correctly. You need to tell Word to ignore "Bartolutti" wherever it occurs in the letter. You need to do the same for your initials.

### To proofread and correct the remaining marked errors in the letter:

▶ **1.** Right-click **Bartolutti**. A shortcut menu opens.

▶ **2.** On the shortcut menu, click **Ignore All** to indicate that Word should ignore the word "Bartolutti" each time it occurs in this document. (The Ignore All option can be particularly helpful in a longer document.) The wavy red underline disappears from below Tim's last name. If your initials do not form a word, a red wavy underline appears beneath them; otherwise, a blue wavy underline appears there.

▶ **3.** If you see a wavy red underline below your initials, right-click your initials. On the shortcut menu, click **Ignore All** to remove the red wavy underline. If you didn't see a wavy blue underline below your initials before, you should see one now.

▶ **4.** Right-click your initials again. On the shortcut menu, click **Ignore Once** to remove the blue underline.

▶ **5.** Read the entire letter to proofread it for typing errors. Correct any errors using the techniques you have just learned.

▶ **6.** Save the document.

The text of the letter is finished. Now you need to think about how it looks—that is, you need to think about the document's **formatting**. First, you need to adjust the spacing in the inside address.

# Adjusting Paragraph and Line Spacing

When typing a letter, you might need to adjust two types of spacing—paragraph spacing and line spacing. **Paragraph spacing** is the space that appears directly above and below a paragraph. In Word, any text that ends with a paragraph mark symbol (¶) is a paragraph. So, a **paragraph** can be a group of words that is many lines long, a single word, or even a blank line, in which case you see a paragraph mark alone on a single line. Paragraph spacing is measured in points; a **point** is 1/72 of an inch. The default setting for paragraph spacing in Word is 0 points before each paragraph and 8 points after each paragraph. When laying out a complicated document, resist the temptation to simply press the Enter key to insert extra space between paragraphs. Changing the paragraph spacing gives you much more control over the final result.

**Line spacing** is the space between lines of text within a paragraph. Word offers a number of preset line spacing options. The 1.0 setting, which is often called **single-spacing**, allows the least amount of space between lines. All other line spacing options are measured as multiples of 1.0 spacing. For example, 2.0 spacing (sometimes called **double-spacing**) allows for twice the space of single-spacing. The default line spacing setting is 1.08, which allows a little more space between lines than 1.0 spacing.

Now consider the line and paragraph spacing in the Robbins letter. The three lines of the inside address are too far apart. That's because each line of the inside address is actually a separate paragraph. Word inserted the default 8 points of paragraph spacing after each of these separate paragraphs. See Figure 1-13.

| Figure 1-13 | Line and paragraph spacing in the letter to Sonia Robbins |

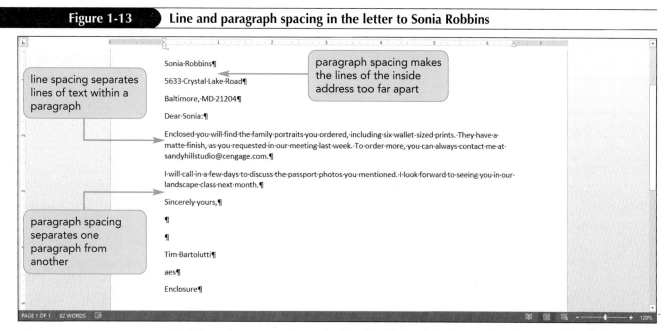

line spacing separates lines of text within a paragraph

paragraph spacing makes the lines of the inside address too far apart

paragraph spacing separates one paragraph from another

> Sonia·Robbins¶
> 5633·Crystal·Lake·Road¶
> Baltimore,·MD·21204¶
> Dear·Sonia:¶
> Enclosed·you·will·find·the·family·portraits·you·ordered,·including·six·wallet-sized·prints.·They·have·a·matte·finish,·as·you·requested·in·our·meeting·last·week.·To·order·more,·you·can·always·contact·me·at·sandyhillstudio@cengage.com.¶
> I·will·call·in·a·few·days·to·discuss·the·passport·photos·you·mentioned.·I·look·forward·to·seeing·you·in·our·landscape·class·next·month.¶
> Sincerely·yours,¶
> ¶
> ¶
> Tim·Bartolutti¶
> aes¶
> Enclosure¶

PAGE 1 OF 1    82 WORDS          120%

To follow the conventions of a block style business letter, the three paragraphs that make up the inside address should have the same spacing as the lines of text within a single paragraph—that is, they need to be closer together. You can accomplish this by removing the 8 points of paragraph spacing after the first two paragraphs in the inside address. To conform to the block style business letter format, you also need to close up the spacing between your initials and the word "Enclosure" at the end of the letter.

To adjust paragraph and line spacing in Word, you use the Line and Paragraph Spacing button in the Paragraph group on the HOME tab. Clicking this button displays a menu of preset line spacing options (1.0, 1.15, 2.0, and so on). The menu also includes two paragraph spacing options, which allow you to add 12 points before a paragraph or remove the default 8 points of space after a paragraph.

Next you'll adjust the paragraph spacing in the inside address and after your initials. In the process, you'll also learn some techniques for selecting text in a document.

## To adjust the paragraph spacing in the inside address and after your initials:

1. Move the pointer to the white space just to the left of "Sonia Robbins" until it changes to a right-facing arrow.

2. Click the mouse button. The entire name, including the paragraph symbol after it, is selected.

3. Press and hold the mouse button, drag the pointer down to select the next paragraph of the inside address as well, and then release the mouse button.

   The name and street address are selected as well as the paragraph marks at the end of each paragraph. You did not select the paragraph containing the city, state, and zip code because you do not need to change its paragraph spacing. See Figure 1-14.

**TIP**

The white space in the left margin is sometimes referred to as the selection bar because you click it to select text.

**Figure 1-14    Inside address selected**

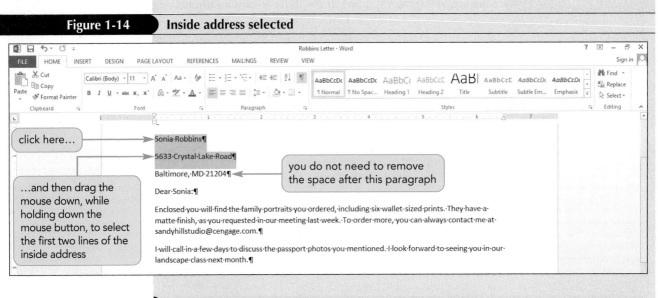

4. Make sure the HOME tab is selected on the ribbon.

5. In the Paragraph group on the HOME tab, click the **Line and Paragraph Spacing** button 📄▾. A menu of line spacing options appears, with two paragraph spacing options at the bottom. See Figure 1-15. At the moment, you are only interested in the paragraph spacing options. Your goal is to remove the default 8 points of space after the first two paragraphs in the inside address.

**Figure 1-15    Line and paragraph spacing options**

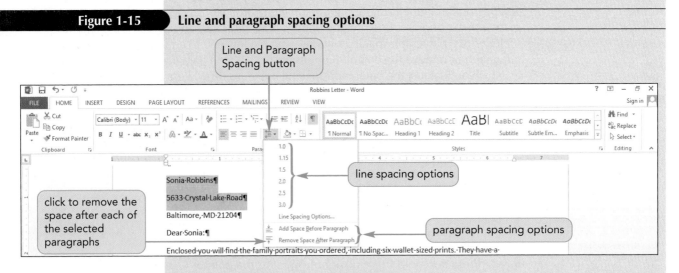

6. Click **Remove Space After Paragraph**. The menu closes, and the paragraphs are now closer together.

7. Double-click your initials to select them and the paragraph symbol after them.

8. In the Paragraph group, click the **Line and Paragraph Spacing** button 📄▾, click **Remove Space After Paragraph**, and then click anywhere in the document to deselect your initials.

Another way to compress lines of text is to press the Shift+Enter keys at the end of a line. This inserts a **manual line break**, also called a **soft return**, which moves the insertion point to a new line without starting a new paragraph. You will use this technique now as you add Tim's title below his name in the signature line.

**To use a manual line break to move the insertion point to a new line without starting a new paragraph:**

▶ **1.** Click to the right of the "i" in "Bartolutti."

▶ **2.** Press the **Shift+Enter** keys. Word inserts a small arrow symbol ↵ , indicating a manual line break, and the insertion point moves to the line below Tim's name.

▶ **3.** Type **Sales Manager**. Tim's title now appears directly below his name with no intervening paragraph spacing, just like the lines of the inside address.

▶ **4.** Save the document.

**INSIGHT**

*Understanding Spacing Between Paragraphs*

When discussing the correct format for letters, many business style guides talk about single-spacing and double-spacing between paragraphs. In these style guides, to single-space between paragraphs means to press the Enter key once after each paragraph. Likewise, to double-space between paragraphs means to press the Enter key twice after each paragraph. With the default paragraph spacing in Word 2013, however, you only need to press the Enter key once after a paragraph. The space Word adds after a paragraph is not quite the equivalent of double-spacing, but it is enough to make it easy to see where one paragraph ends and another begins. Keep this in mind if you're accustomed to pressing the Enter key twice; otherwise, you could end up with more space than you want between paragraphs.

As you corrected line and paragraph spacing in the previous set of steps, you used the mouse to select text. Word provides multiple ways to select, or highlight, text as you work. Figure 1-16 summarizes these methods and explains when to use them most effectively.

| Figure 1-16 | Methods for selecting text |

| To Select | Mouse | Keyboard | Mouse and Keyboard |
|---|---|---|---|
| A word | Double-click the word | Move the insertion point to the beginning of the word, press and hold Ctrl+Shift, and then press → | |
| A line | Click in the white space to the left of the line | Move the insertion point to the beginning of the line, press and hold Shift, and then press ↓ | |
| A sentence | Click at the beginning of the sentence, then drag the pointer until the sentence is selected | | Press and hold Ctrl, then click any location within the sentence |
| Multiple lines | Click and drag in the white space to the left of the lines | Move the insertion point to the beginning of the first line, press and hold Shift, and then press ↓ until all the lines are selected | |
| A paragraph | Double-click in the white space to the left of the paragraph, or triple-click at any location within the paragraph | Move the insertion point to the beginning of the paragraph, press and hold Ctrl+Shift, and then press ↓ | |
| Multiple paragraphs | Click in the white space to the left of the first paragraph you want to select, and then drag to select the remaining paragraphs | Move the insertion point to the beginning of the first paragraph, press and hold Ctrl+Shift, and then press ↓ until all the paragraphs are selected | |
| An entire document | Triple-click in the white space to the left of the document text | Press Ctrl+A | Press and hold Ctrl, and click in the white space to the left of the document text |
| A block of text | Click at the beginning of the block, then drag the pointer until the entire block is selected | | Click at the beginning of the block, press and hold Shift, and then click at the end of the block |
| Nonadjacent blocks of text | | | Press and hold Ctrl, then drag the mouse pointer to select multiple blocks of nonadjacent text |

© 2014 Cengage Learning

# Adjusting the Margins

Another important aspect of document formatting is the amount of margin space between the document text and the edge of the page. You can check the document's margins by changing the Zoom level to display the entire page.

## To change the Zoom level to display the entire page:

**1.** On the ribbon, click the **VIEW** tab.

**2.** In the Zoom group, click the **One Page** button. The entire document is now visible in the Word window. See Figure 1-17.

**Figure 1-17** **Document zoomed to show entire page**

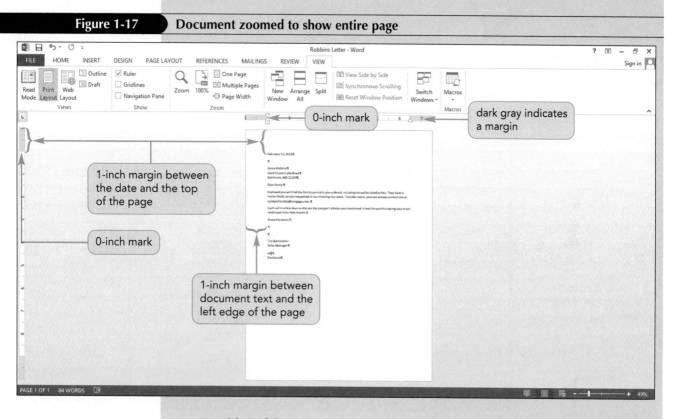

**Trouble?** If the wavy blue underline reappears under your initials, you can ignore it.

On the rulers, the margins appear dark gray. By default, Word documents include 1-inch margins on all sides of the document. By looking at the vertical ruler, you can see that the date in the letter, the first line in the document, is located 1 inch from the top of the page. Likewise, the horizontal ruler indicates the document text begins 1 inch from the left edge of the page.

Reading the measurements on the rulers can be tricky at first. On the horizontal ruler, the 0-inch mark is like the origin on a number line. You measure from the 0-inch mark to the left or to the right. On the vertical ruler, you measure up or down from the 0-inch mark.

Tim plans to print the letter on Sandy Hill Portrait Studio letterhead, which includes a graphic and the company's address. To allow more blank space for the letterhead, and to move the text down so it doesn't look so crowded at the top of the page, you need to increase the top margin. The settings for changing the page margins are located on the PAGE LAYOUT tab on the ribbon.

## To change the page margins:

**1.** On the ribbon, click the **PAGE LAYOUT** tab. The PAGE LAYOUT tab displays options for adjusting the layout of your document.

**2.** In the Page Setup group, click the **Margins** button. The Margins gallery opens, as shown in Figure 1-18.

**Figure 1-18** **Margins gallery**

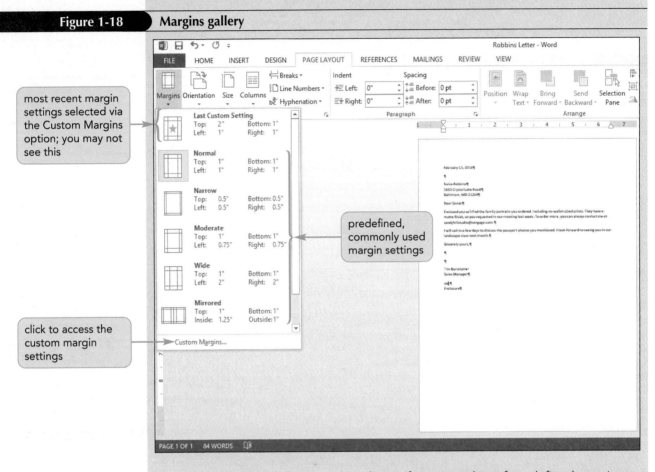

most recent margin settings selected via the Custom Margins option; you may not see this

predefined, commonly used margin settings

click to access the custom margin settings

In the Margins gallery, you can choose from a number of predefined margin options, or you can click the Custom Margins command to select your own settings. After you create custom margin settings, the most recent set appears as an option at the top of the menu. For the Robbins letter, you will create custom margins.

**3.** Click **Custom Margins**. The Page Setup dialog box opens with the Margins tab displayed. The default margin settings are displayed in the boxes at the top of the Margins tab. The top margin of 1" is already selected, ready for you to type a new margin setting.

**4.** In the Top box in the Margins section, type **2.5**. You do not need to type an inch mark ("). See Figure 1-19.

**Figure 1-19**     **Creating custom margins in the Page Setup dialog box**

enter a Top margin of 2.5

allows you to make this new margin setting the default for all new Word documents

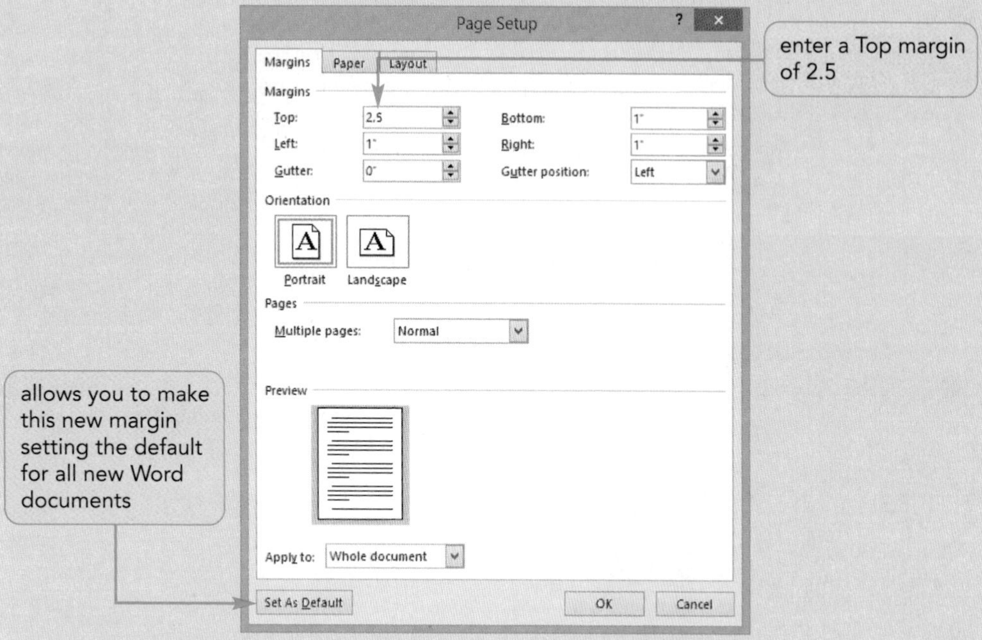

> **5.** Click the **OK** button. The text of the letter is now lower on the page. The page looks less crowded, with room for the company's letterhead.
>
> **6.** Change the Zoom level back to **120%**, and then save the document.

For most documents, the Word default of 1-inch margins is fine. In some professional settings, however, you might need to use a particular custom margin setting for all your documents. In that case, define the custom margins using the Margins tab in the Page Setup dialog box, and then click the Set As Default button to make your settings the default for all new documents. Keep in mind that most printers can't print to the edge of the page; if you select custom margins that are too narrow for your printer's specifications, Word alerts you to change your margin settings.

# Previewing and Printing a Document

To make sure the document is ready to print, and to avoid wasting paper and time, you should first review it in Backstage view to make sure it will look right when printed. Like the One Page zoom setting you used earlier, the Print option in Backstage view displays a full-page preview of the document, allowing you to see how it will fit on the printed page. However, you cannot actually edit this preview. It simply provides one last opportunity to look at the document before printing.

### To preview the document:

> **1.** Proofread the document one last time and correct any remaining errors.
>
> **2.** Click the **FILE** tab to display Backstage view.
>
> **3.** In the navigation bar, click **Print**.

The Print screen displays a full-page version of your document, showing how the letter will fit on the printed page. The Print settings to the left of the preview allow you to control a variety of print options. For example, you can change the number of copies from the default setting of "1." The 1 Page Per Sheet button opens a menu where you can choose to print multiple pages on a single sheet of paper, or to scale the printed page to a particular paper size. You can also use the navigation controls at the bottom of the screen to display other pages in a document. See Figure 1-20.

**Figure 1-20**     **Print settings in Backstage view**

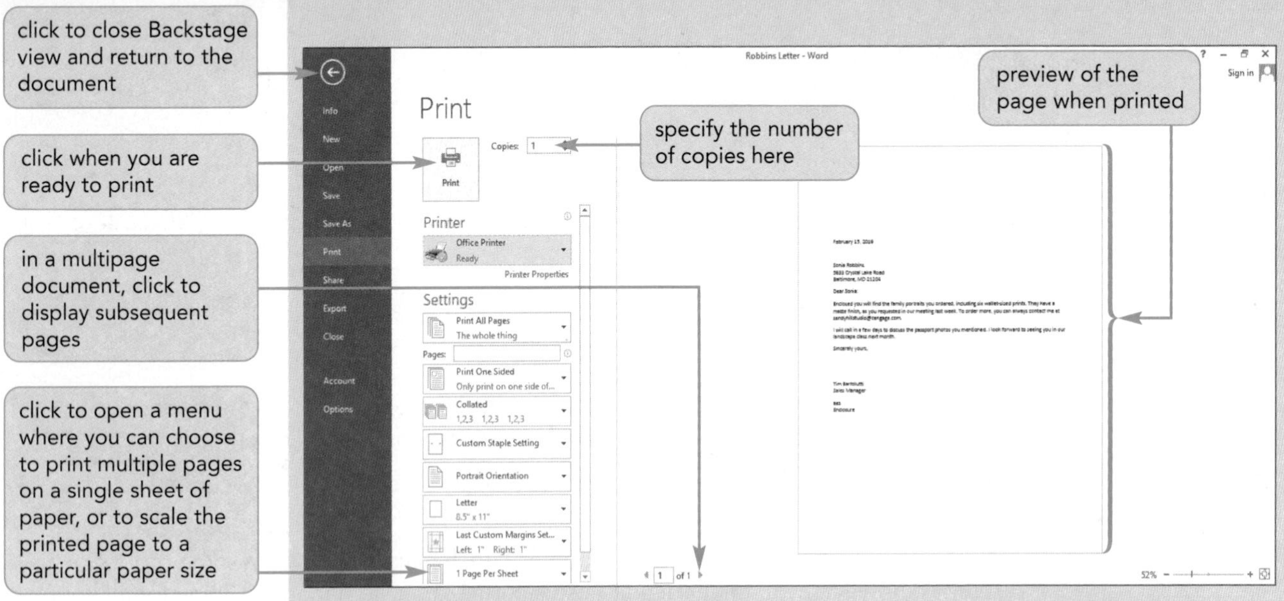

click to close Backstage view and return to the document

click when you are ready to print

in a multipage document, click to display subsequent pages

click to open a menu where you can choose to print multiple pages on a single sheet of paper, or to scale the printed page to a particular paper size

specify the number of copies here

preview of the page when printed

4. Review your document and make sure its overall layout matches that of the document in Figure 1-20. If you notice a problem with paragraph breaks or spacing, click the **Back** button at the top of the navigation bar to return to the document, make any necessary changes, and then start again at Step 2.

At this point, you can print the document or you can leave Backstage view and return to the document in Print Layout view. In the following steps, you should only print the document if your instructor asks you to. If you will be printing the document, make sure your printer is turned on and contains paper.

**To leave Backstage view or to print the document:**

1. Click the **Back** button at the top of the navigation bar to leave Backstage view and return to the document in Print Layout view, or click the **Print** button. Backstage view closes, and the letter prints if you clicked the Print button.

2. Click the **FILE** tab, and then click **Close** in the navigation bar to close the document without closing Word.

Next, Tim asks you to create an envelope he can use to send a class schedule to another client.

# Creating an Envelope

Before you can create the envelope, you need to open a new, blank document. To create a new document, you can start with a blank document—as you did with the letter to Sonia Robbins—or you can start with one that already contains formatting and generic text commonly used in a variety of professional documents, such as a fax cover sheet or a memo. These preformatted files are called **templates**. You could use a template to create a formatted envelope, but first you'll learn how to create one on your own in a new, blank document. You'll have a chance to try out a template in the Case Problems at the end of this tutorial.

## To create a new document for the envelope:

1. Click the **FILE** tab, and then click **New** in the navigation bar. The New screen is similar to the one you saw when you first started Word, with a blank document in the upper-left corner, along with a variety of templates. See Figure 1-21.

| Figure 1-21 | New options in Backstage view |
| --- | --- |

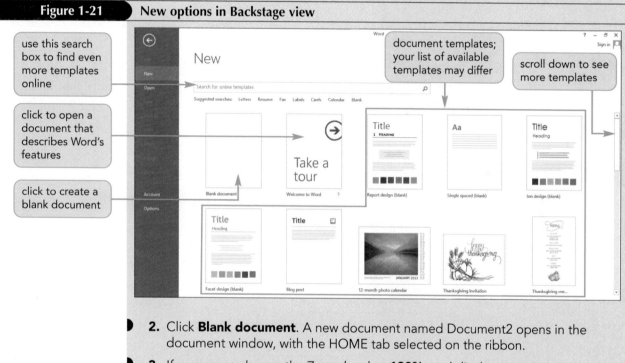

2. Click **Blank document**. A new document named Document2 opens in the document window, with the HOME tab selected on the ribbon.

3. If necessary, change the Zoom level to **120%**, and display nonprinting characters and the rulers.

4. Save the new document as **Keating Envelope** in the location specified by your instructor.

## To create the envelope:

1. On the ribbon, click the **MAILINGS** tab. The ribbon changes to display the various Mailings options.

2. In the Create group, click the **Envelopes** button. The Envelopes and Labels dialog box opens, with the Envelopes tab displayed. The insertion point appears in the Delivery address box, ready for you to type the recipient's address. Depending on how your computer is set up, and whether you are working on your own computer or a school computer, you might see an address in the Return address box.

3. In the Delivery address box, type the following address, pressing the Enter key to start each new line:

   **Lakeisha Keating**

   **2245 Farley Lane**

   **Baltimore, MD 21206**

   Because Tim will be using the studio's printed envelopes, you don't need to print a return address on this envelope.

4. Click the **Omit** check box to insert a checkmark, if necessary.

   At this point, if you had a printer stocked with envelopes, you could click the Print button to print the envelope. To save an envelope for printing later, you need to add it to the document. Your Envelopes and Labels dialog box should match the one in Figure 1-22.

**Figure 1-22**  **Envelopes and Labels dialog box**

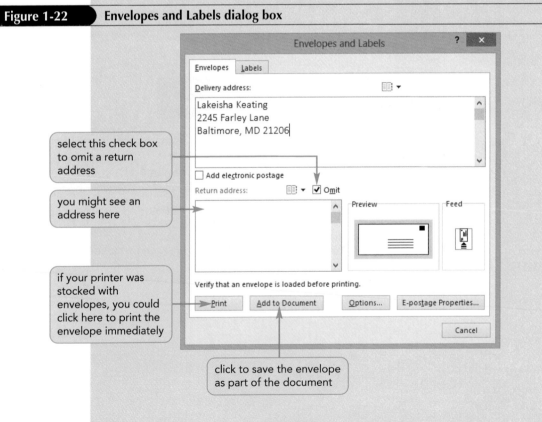

5. Click the **Add to Document** button. The dialog box closes, and you return to the document window. The envelope is inserted at the top of your document, with 1.0 line spacing. The double line with the words "Section Break (Next Page)" is related to how the envelope is formatted, and will not be visible when you print the envelope. The envelope will print in the standard business envelope format.

6. Save the document. Tim will print the envelope later, so you can close the document now.

7. Click the **FILE** tab and then click **Close** in the navigation bar. The document closes, but Word remains open.

## INSIGHT

### Creating Documents with Templates

Microsoft offers predesigned templates for all kinds of documents, including calendars, reports, and thank you cards. You can use the scroll bar on the right of the New screen (shown earlier in Figure 1-21) to scroll down to see more templates, or you can use the Search for online templates box in the New screen to search among hundreds of other options available at Office.com. When you open a template, you actually open a new document containing the formatting and text stored in the template, leaving the original template untouched. A typical template includes placeholder text that you replace with your own information.

Templates allow you to create stylish, professional-looking documents quickly and easily. To use them effectively, however, you need to be knowledgeable about Word and its many options for manipulating text, graphics, and page layouts. Otherwise, the complicated formatting of some Word templates can be more frustrating than helpful. As you become a more experienced Word user, you'll learn how to create your own templates.

You're finished creating the cover letter and the envelope. In the next session, you will modify a flyer that announces an upcoming class by formatting the text and adding a photo.

## REVIEW

### Session 1.1 Quick Check

1. In a block style letter, does each line of text start at the left or right margin?
2. What do you call the recipient's address, which appears below the date in a block style letter?
3. Explain how to use a hyperlink in a Word document to open a new email message.
4. Explain how to display nonprinting characters.
5. Define the term "paragraph spacing."
6. How does Word indicate a potential spelling error?

# Session 1.2 Visual Overview:

Alignment buttons control the text's **alignment**—that is, the way it lines up between the left and right margins. Here, the Center button is selected because the text containing the insertion point is center-aligned.

You can click the Clear All Formatting button to restore selected text to the default font, font size, and color.

Clicking the Format Painter button displays the Format Painter pointer, which you can use to copy formatting from the selected text to other text in the document.

The Font group on the HOME tab includes the Font box and the Font size box for setting the text's font and the font size, respectively. A **font** is a set of characters that uses the same typeface.

You click the Shading button arrow to apply a colored background to a selected paragraph.

This document has a landscape orientation, meaning it is wider than it is tall.

You can insert a photo or another type of picture in a document by using the **Pictures button** located on the INSERT tab of the ribbon. After you insert a photo or another picture, you can format it with a style that adds a border or a shadow, or changes its shape.

Pet Flyer - Word

FILE    HOME    INSERT    DESIGN    PAGE LAYOUT    REFERENCES    MAILINGS

Arial    22

Paste

Clipboard    Font    Paragraph

Do you want the perfect portrait of your furry fren

Learn how the pet pros do it at Sandy Hill Port

Beginning·Pet·Photography¶

Tuesdays,·March·1·-·April·4·from·7·to·8·p.m

Contact·Tim·Bartolutti·at·sandyhillstudio@cengage.com·to·

PAGE 1 OF 1    1 OF 44 WORDS

The boldface and blue font color applied to this text are examples of formatting that you would use sparingly to draw attention to a specific part of a document.

# Formatting a Document

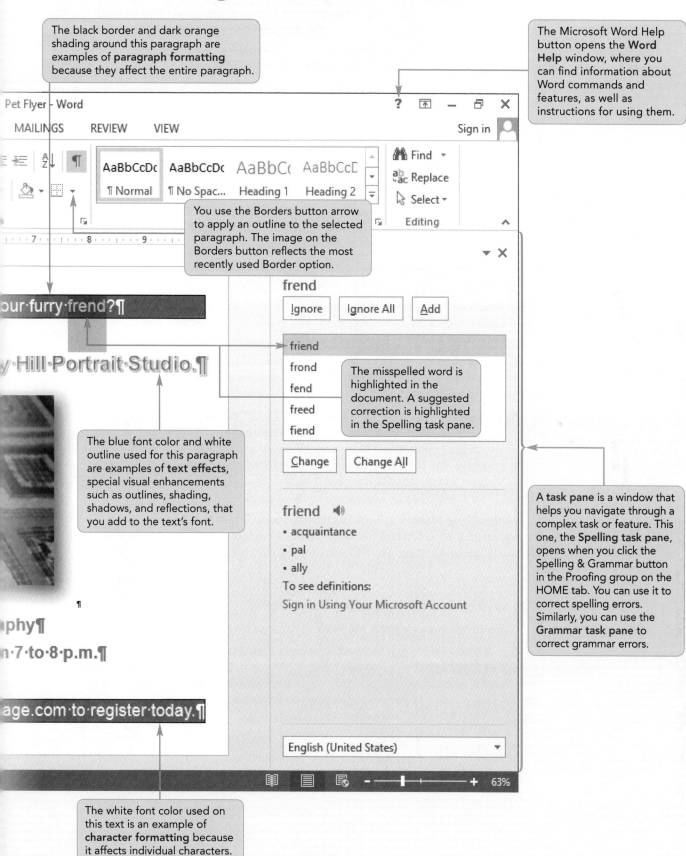

The black border and dark orange shading around this paragraph are examples of **paragraph formatting** because they affect the entire paragraph.

The Microsoft Word Help button opens the **Word Help** window, where you can find information about Word commands and features, as well as instructions for using them.

You use the Borders button arrow to apply an outline to the selected paragraph. The image on the Borders button reflects the most recently used Border option.

The misspelled word is highlighted in the document. A suggested correction is highlighted in the Spelling task pane.

The blue font color and white outline used for this paragraph are examples of **text effects**, special visual enhancements such as outlines, shading, shadows, and reflections, that you add to the text's font.

A task pane is a window that helps you navigate through a complex task or feature. This one, the **Spelling task pane**, opens when you click the Spelling & Grammar button in the Proofing group on the HOME tab. You can use it to correct spelling errors. Similarly, you can use the Grammar task pane to correct grammar errors.

The white font color used on this text is an example of **character formatting** because it affects individual characters.

# Opening an Existing Document

In this session, you'll complete a flyer announcing a pet photography class. Tim has already typed the text of the flyer, inserted a photo into it, and saved it as a Word document. He would like you to check the document for spelling and grammar errors, format the flyer to make it eye-catching and easy to read, and then replace the current photo with a new one. You'll start by opening the document.

**To open the flyer document:**

 1. On the ribbon, click the **FILE** tab to open Backstage view, and then verify that **Open** is selected in the navigation bar. On the left side of the Open screen is a list of places you can go to locate other documents, and on the right is a list of recently opened documents.

    **Trouble?** If you closed Word at the end of the previous session, start Word now, click Open Other Documents at the bottom of the navigation bar in Backstage view, and then begin with Step 2.

 2. Click **Computer**, and then click the **Browse** button. The Open dialog box opens.

    **Trouble?** If your instructor asked you to store your files to your SkyDrive account, click SkyDrive, log in to your account, if necessary, and then click the Browse button.

 3. Navigate to the Word1 ▸ Tutorial folder included with your Data Files, click **Pet**, and then click the **Open** button. The document opens with the insertion point blinking in the first line of the document.

    **Trouble?** If you don't have the starting Data Files, you need to get them before you can proceed. Your instructor will either give you the Data Files or ask you to obtain them from a specified location (such as a network drive). If you have any questions about the Data Files, see your instructor or technical support person for assistance.

Before making changes to Tim's document, you will save it with a new name. Saving the document with a different filename creates a copy of the file and leaves the original file unchanged in case you want to work through the tutorial again.

**To save the document with a new name:**

 1. On the ribbon, click the **FILE** tab.

 2. In the navigation bar in Backstage view, click **Save As**. Save the document as **Pet Flyer** in the location specified by your instructor. Backstage view closes, and the document window appears again with the new filename in the title bar. The original Pet document closes, remaining unchanged.

**PROSKILLS**

*Decision Making: Creating Effective Documents*

Before you create a new document or revise an existing document, take a moment to think about your audience. Ask yourself these questions:

- Who is your audience?
- What do they know?
- What do they need to know?
- How can the document you are creating change your audience's behavior or opinions?

Every decision you make about your document should be based on your answers to these questions. To take a simple example, if you are creating a flyer to announce an upcoming seminar on college financial aid, your audience would be students and their parents. They probably all know what the term "financial aid" means, so you don't need to explain that in your flyer. Instead, you can focus on telling them what they need to know—the date, time, and location of the seminar. The behavior you want to affect, in this case, is whether or not your audience will show up for the seminar. By making the flyer professional looking and easy to read, you increase the chance that they will.

You might find it more challenging to answer these questions about your audience when creating more complicated documents, such as corporate reports. But the focus remains the same—connecting with the audience. As you are deciding what information to include in your document, remember that the goal of a professional document is to convey the information as effectively as possible to your target audience.

Before revising a document for someone else, it's a good idea to familiarize yourself with its overall structure.

**To review the document:**

1. Verify that the document is displayed in Print Layout view and that nonprinting characters are displayed. For now, you can ignore the wavy underlines that appear in the document.

2. Change the Zoom level to **120%**, if necessary.

   At this point, the document is very simple. By the time you are finished, it will look like the document shown in the Session 1.2 Visual Overview, with the spelling and grammar errors corrected. Figure 1-23 summarizes the tasks you will perform.

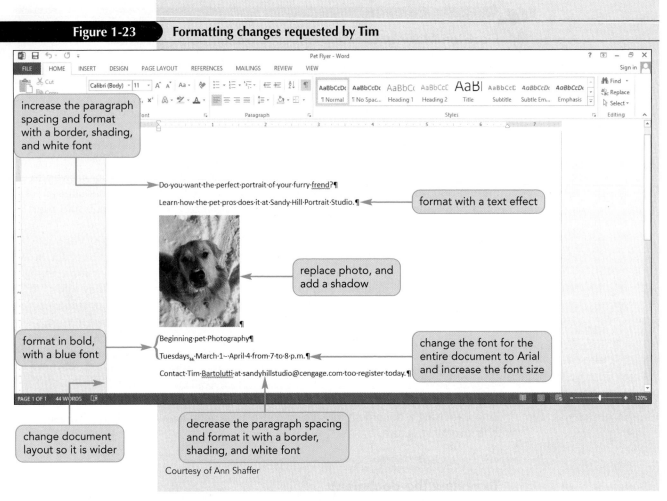

**Figure 1-23** **Formatting changes requested by Tim**

increase the paragraph spacing and format with a border, shading, and white font

Do·you·want·the·perfect·portrait·of·your·furry·frend?¶

Learn·how·the·pet·pros·does·it·at·Sandy·Hill·Portrait·Studio.¶ ← format with a text effect

replace photo, and add a shadow

format in bold, with a blue font

Beginning·pet·Photography¶

Tuesdays,·March·1···April·4·from·7·to·8·p.m.¶ ← change the font for the entire document to Arial and increase the font size

Contact·Tim·Bartolutti·at·sandyhillstudio@cengage.com·too·register·today.¶

change document layout so it is wider

decrease the paragraph spacing and format it with a border, shading, and white font

Courtesy of Ann Shaffer

You will start by correcting the spelling and grammar errors.

# Using the Spelling and Grammar Task Panes

As you learned in Tutorial 1, Word marks possible spelling and grammatical errors with wavy underlines as you type so you can quickly go back and correct those errors. A more thorough way of checking the spelling in a document is to use the Spelling and Grammar task panes to check a document word by word for a variety of errors. You can customize the spelling and grammar settings to add or ignore certain types of errors.

Tim asks you to use the Spelling and Grammar task panes to check the flyer for mistakes. Before you do, you'll configure the grammar settings to look for subject/verb agreement, in addition to other types of errors.

### To customize the grammar settings:

1. On the ribbon, click the **FILE** tab, and then click **Options** in the navigation bar. The Word Options dialog box opens. You can use this dialog box to change a variety of settings related to how Word looks and works.

2. In the left pane, click **Proofing**, and then, in the "When correcting spelling and grammar in Word" section, click the **Settings** button. The Grammar Settings dialog box opens.

3. If necessary, scroll down in the Grammar Settings dialog box to display all the check boxes under "Grammar," and then click the **Subject-verb agreement** check box to insert a checkmark. See Figure 1-24.

**Figure 1-24**    **Grammar Settings dialog box**

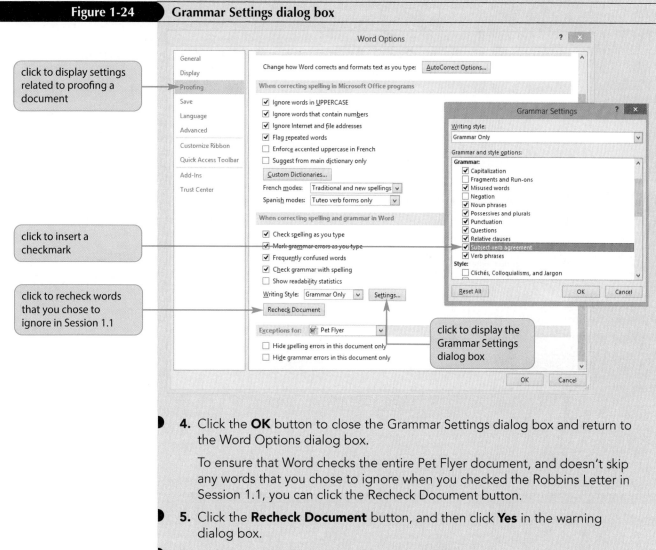

click to display settings related to proofing a document

click to insert a checkmark

click to recheck words that you chose to ignore in Session 1.1

click to display the Grammar Settings dialog box

4. Click the **OK** button to close the Grammar Settings dialog box and return to the Word Options dialog box.

To ensure that Word checks the entire Pet Flyer document, and doesn't skip any words that you chose to ignore when you checked the Robbins Letter in Session 1.1, you can click the Recheck Document button.

5. Click the **Recheck Document** button, and then click **Yes** in the warning dialog box.

6. In the Word Options dialog box, click the **OK** button to close the dialog box.

You return to the Pet Flyer document, where three errors are now marked with wavy blue underlines. The two new errors are related to subject-verb agreement. You should also see two words marked with wavy red underlines, including Tim's last name in the final paragraph.

Now you are ready to check the document's spelling and grammar. All errors marked with red underlines are considered spelling errors, while all errors marked with blue underlines are considered grammatical errors.

### To check the Pet Flyer document for spelling and grammatical errors:

1. Press the **Ctrl+Home** keys, if necessary, to move the insertion point to the beginning of the document, to the left of the "D" in "Do." By placing the insertion point at the beginning of the document, you ensure that Word will check the entire document from start to finish without having to go back and check an earlier part.

2. On the ribbon, click the **REVIEW** tab. The ribbon changes to display reviewing options.

3. In the Proofing group, click the **Spelling & Grammar** button.

   The Spelling task pane opens on the right side of the Word window, with the word "frend" listed as a possible spelling error. The same word is highlighted in gray in the document. In the task pane's list of possible corrections, the correctly spelled word "friend" is highlighted in light blue. See Figure 1-25.

**Figure 1-25** Spelling task pane

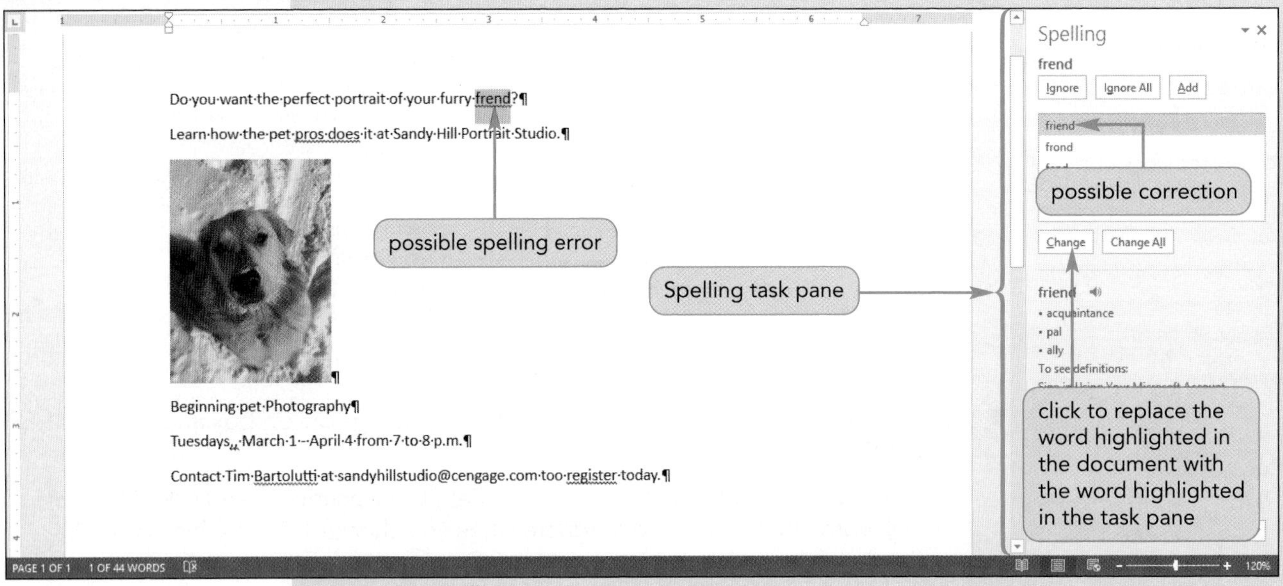

Courtesy of Ann Shaffer

4. In the task pane, click the **Change** button. The misspelled word "frend" is replaced with "friend."

   Next, Word highlights the entire second sentence, indicating another possible error. The Spelling task pane changes to the Grammar task pane, and the information at the bottom of the task pane explains that the error is related to subject-verb agreement.

5. Verify that "pros do" is selected in the Grammar task pane, and then click the **Change** button. The second to last paragraph of text is now highlighted in the document. The explanation at the bottom of the task pane indicates that the error is related to punctuation.

6. Verify that the comma is selected in the Grammar task pane, and then click the **Change** button.

   Tim's last name is now highlighted in the document, and the Grammar task pane changes to the Spelling task pane. Although the Spelling task pane doesn't recognize "Bartolutti" as a word, it is spelled correctly, so you can ignore it.

▶ **7.** Click the **Ignore** button in the Spelling task pane.

The last paragraph in the document is highlighted, and the Grammar task pane indicates a possible subject-verb agreement problem related to the word "register." However, the real problem is the word "too," just before "register." It should be replaced with "to." You can fix this problem by typing directly in the document.

▶ **8.** In the document, click to the right of the word "too," delete the second letter "o," and then click the **Resume** button in the task pane. The task pane closes and a dialog box opens indicating that the spelling and grammar check is complete.

▶ **9.** Click the **OK** button to close the dialog box.

Finally, you'll restore the grammar settings to their original configuration.

▶ **10.** Click the **FILE** tab, and then click **Options**.

▶ **11.** In the Word Options dialog box, click **Proofing**, and then click the **Settings** button.

▶ **12.** Scroll down, and then click the **Subject-verb agreement** check box to remove the checkmark.

▶ **13.** Click the **OK** button to close the Grammar Settings dialog box, and then click the **OK** button to close the Word Options dialog box.

**PROSKILLS**

*Written Communication: Proofreading Your Document*

Although the Spelling and Grammar task panes are useful tools, they won't always catch every error in a document, and they sometimes flag "errors" that are actually correct. This means there is no substitute for careful proofreading. Always take the time to read through your document to check for errors the Spelling and Grammar task panes might have missed. Keep in mind that the Spelling and Grammar task panes cannot pinpoint inaccurate phrases or poorly chosen words. You'll have to find those yourself. To produce a professional document, you must read it carefully several times. It's a good idea to ask one or two other people to read your documents as well; they might catch something you missed.

You still need to proofread the Pet Flyer document. You'll do that next.

**To proofread the Pet Flyer document:**

▶ **1.** Review the document text for any remaining errors. In the third paragraph of text, change the lowercase "p" in "pet" to an uppercase "P."

▶ **2.** In the last line of text, replace "Tim Bartolutti" with your first and last name, and then save the document. Including your name in the document will make it easier for you to find your copy later if you print it on a shared printer.

Now you're ready to begin formatting the document. You will start by turning the page so it is wider than it is tall. In other words, you will change the document's **orientation**.

# Changing Page Orientation

**Portrait orientation**, with the page taller than it is wide, is the default page orientation for Word documents because it is the orientation most commonly used for letters, reports, and other formal documents. However, Tim wants you to format the pet flyer in **landscape orientation**—that is, with the page turned so it is wider than it is tall to better accommodate the photo. You can accomplish this task by using the Orientation button located on the PAGE LAYOUT tab on the ribbon. After you change the page orientation, you will select narrower margins so you can maximize the amount of color on the page.

## To change the page orientation:

1. Change the document zoom setting to **One Page** so that you can see the entire document.

2. On the ribbon, click the **PAGE LAYOUT** tab. The ribbon changes to display options for formatting the overall layout of text and images in the document.

3. In the Page Setup group, click the **Orientation** button, and then click **Landscape** on the menu. The document changes to landscape orientation.

4. In the Page Setup group, click the **Margins** button, and then click the **Narrow** option on the menu. The margins shrink from 1 inch to .5 inch on all four sides. See Figure 1-26.

| Figure 1-26 | Document in landscape orientation with narrow margins |
|---|---|

click to select either portrait or landscape orientation

margins are now .5 inch, instead of the default 1 inch

Courtesy of Ann Shaffer

# Changing the Font and Font Size

Tim typed the document in the default font size, 11 point, and the default font, Calibri, but he would like to switch to the Arial font instead. Also, he wants to increase the size of all five paragraphs of the document text. To apply these changes, you start by selecting the text you want to format. Then you select the options you want in the Font group on the HOME tab.

### To change the font and font size:

1. On the ribbon, click the HOME tab.

2. Change the document Zoom level to **120%**.

3. To verify that the insertion point is located at the beginning of the document, press the **Ctrl+HOME** keys.

4. Press and hold the **Shift** key, and then click to the right of the second paragraph marker, at the end of the second paragraph of text. The first two paragraphs of text are selected, as shown in Figure 1-27.

**Figure 1-27** Selected text, with default font displayed in Font box

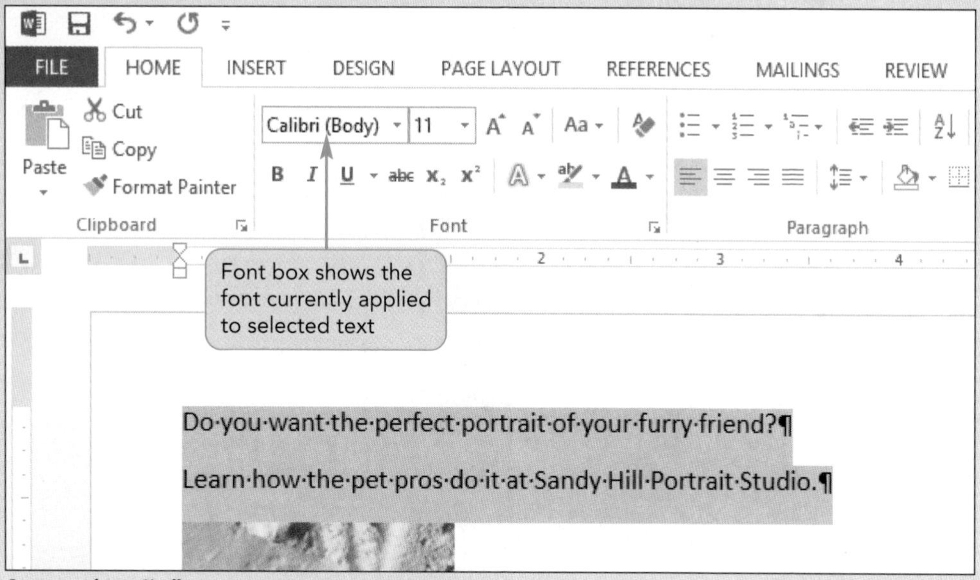

Courtesy of Ann Shaffer

The Font box in the Font group displays the name of the font applied to the selected text, which in this case is Calibri. The word "Body" next to the font name indicates that the Calibri font is intended for formatting body text. **Body text** is ordinary text, as opposed to titles or headings.

5. In the Font group on the HOME tab, click the **Font** arrow. A list of available fonts appears, with Calibri Light and Calibri at the top of the list. Calibri is highlighted in blue, indicating that this font is currently applied to the selected text. The word "Headings" next to the font name "Calibri Light" indicates that Calibri Light is intended for formatting headings.

Below Calibri Light and Calibri, you might see a list of fonts that have been used recently on your computer, followed by a complete alphabetical list of all available fonts. (You won't see the list of recently used fonts if you just installed Word.) You need to scroll the list to see all the available fonts. Each name in the list is formatted with the relevant font. For example, the name "Arial" appears in the Arial font. See Figure 1-28.

**Figure 1-28** Font list

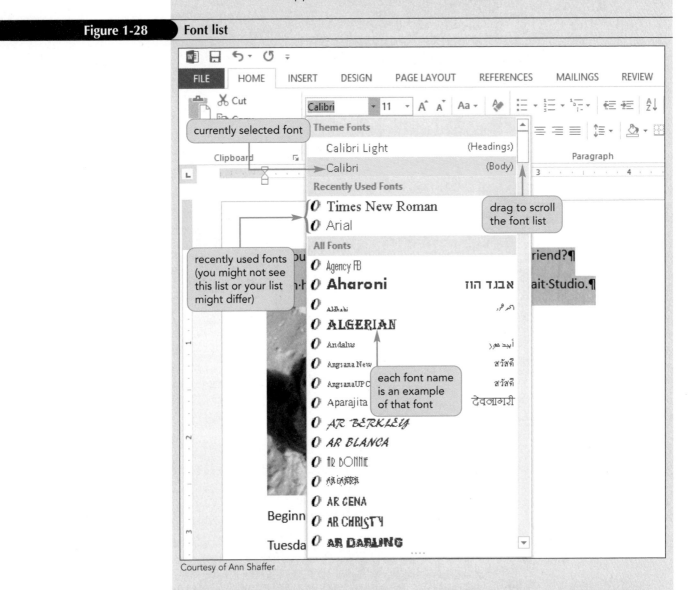

Courtesy of Ann Shaffer

▶ **6.** Without clicking, move the pointer over a dramatic-looking font in the font list, such as Algerian or Arial Black, and then move the pointer over another font.

The selected text in the document changes to show a Live Preview of the font the pointer is resting on. **Live Preview** shows the results that would occur in your document if you clicked the option you are pointing to.

▶ **7.** When you are finished reviewing the Font list, click **Arial**. The Font menu closes, and the selected text is formatted in Arial.

Next, you will make the text more eye-catching by increasing the font size. The Font Size box currently displays the number "11," indicating that the selected text is formatted in 11-point font.

8. Verify that the two paragraphs are still selected, and then click the **Font Size** arrow in the Font group to display a menu of font sizes. As with the Font menu, you can move the pointer over options in the Font Size menu to see a Live Preview of that option.

9. On the Font Size menu, click **22**. The selected text increases significantly in size and the Font Size menu closes.

10. Select the three paragraphs of text below the photo, format them in the Arial font, and then increase the paragraphs' font size to 22 points.

11. Click a blank area of the document to deselect the text, and then save the document.

**TIP**

To restore selected text to its default appearance, click the Clear All Formatting button in the Font group on the HOME tab.

Tim examines the flyer and decides he would like to apply more character formatting, which affects the appearance of individual characters, in the middle three paragraphs. After that, you can turn your attention to paragraph formatting, which affects the appearance of the entire paragraph.

# Applying Text Effects, Font Colors, and Font Styles

To really make text stand out, you can use text effects. You access these options by clicking the Text Effects button in the Font group on the HOME tab. Keep in mind that text effects can be very dramatic. For formal, professional documents, you probably only need to use **bold** or *italic* to make a word or paragraph stand out.

Tim suggests applying text effects to the second paragraph.

### To apply text effects to the second paragraph:

1. Scroll up, if necessary, to display the beginning of the document, and then click in the selection bar to the left of the second paragraph. The entire second paragraph is selected.

2. In the Font group on the HOME tab, click the **Text Effects and Typography** button A ⏷.

   A gallery of text effects appears. Options that allow you to fine-tune a particular text effect, perhaps by changing the color or adding an even more pronounced shadow, are listed below the gallery. A **gallery** is a menu or grid that shows a visual representation of the options available when you click a button.

3. In the middle of the bottom row of the gallery, place the pointer over the blue letter "A." This displays a ScreenTip with the text effect's full name, which is "Fill - Blue, Accent 1, Outline - Background 1, Hard Shadow - Accent 1." A Live Preview of the effect appears in the document. See Figure 1-29.

**Figure 1-29**    **Live Preview of a text effect**

Courtesy of Ann Shaffer

▶  **4.** In the bottom row of the gallery, click the blue letter "A." The text effect is applied to the selected paragraph and the Text Effects gallery closes. The second paragraph is formatted in blue, as shown in the Session 1.2 Visual Overview. The Bold button in the Font group is now highlighted because bold formatting is part of this text effect.

Next, to make the text stand out a bit more, you'll increase the font size. This time, instead of using the Font Size button, you'll use a different method.

▶  **5.** In the Font group, click the **Increase Font Size** button A˄. The font size increases from 22 points to 24 points.

▶  **6.** Click the **Increase Font Size** button A˄ again. The font size increases to 26 points. If you need to decrease the font size of selected text, you can use the Decrease Font Size button.

   Tim asks you to emphasize the third and fourth paragraphs by adding bold and a blue font color.

**To apply a font color and bold:**

▶  **1.** Select the third and fourth paragraphs of text, which contain the class name as well as the dates and times.

▶  **2.** In the Font group on the Home tab, click the **Font Color button arrow** A˅. A gallery of font colors appears. Black is the default font color and appears at the top of the Font Color gallery, with the word "Automatic" next to it.

   The options in the Theme Colors section of the menu are complementary colors that work well when used together in a document. The options in the Standard Colors section are more limited. For more advanced color options, you could use the More Colors or Gradient options. Tim prefers a simple blue.

   **Trouble?** If the class name turned red, you clicked the Font Color button A instead of the arrow next to it. On the Quick Access Toolbar, click the Undo button ⟲, and then repeat Step 2.

3. In the Theme Colors section, place the mouse pointer over the square that's second from the right in the top row. A ScreenTip with the color's name, "Blue, Accent 5," appears. A Live Preview of the color appears in the document, where the text you selected in Step 1 now appears formatted in blue. See Figure 1-30.

| Figure 1-30 | Font Color gallery showing a Live Preview |

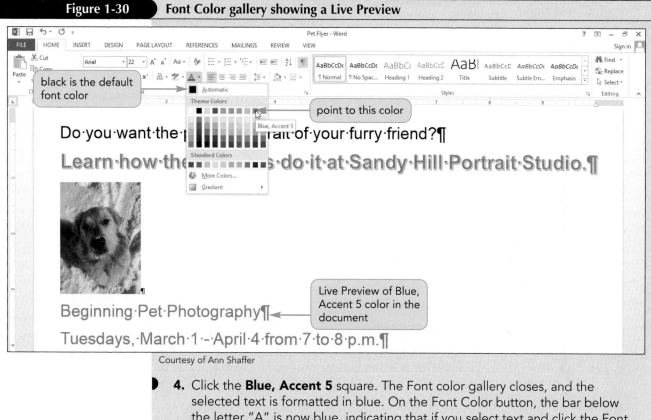

Courtesy of Ann Shaffer

4. Click the **Blue, Accent 5** square. The Font color gallery closes, and the selected text is formatted in blue. On the Font Color button, the bar below the letter "A" is now blue, indicating that if you select text and click the Font Color button, the text will automatically change to blue.

5. In the Font group, click the **Bold** button B. The selected text is now formatted in bold, with thicker, darker lettering.

**TIP**

You can use other buttons in the Font group on the HOME tab to apply other character attributes, such as underline, italic, or superscript.

Next, you will complete some paragraph formatting, starting with paragraph alignment.

## Aligning Text

Alignment refers to how text and graphics line up between the page margins. By default, Word aligns text along the left margin, with the text along the right margin **ragged**, or uneven. This is called **left alignment**. With **right alignment**, the text is aligned along the right margin and is ragged along the left margin. With **center alignment**, text is centered between the left and right margins and is ragged along both the left and right margins. With **justified alignment**, full lines of text are spaced between both the left and the right margins, and no text is ragged. Text in newspaper columns is often justified. See Figure 1-31.

| Figure 1-31 | Varieties of text alignment |

**left alignment**

The term "alignment" refers to the way a paragraph lines up between the margins. The term "alignment" refers to the way a paragraph lines up between the margins.

**right alignment**

The term "alignment" refers to the way a paragraph lines up between the margins. The term "alignment" refers to the way a paragraph lines up between the margins.

**center alignment**

The term "alignment" refers to the way a paragraph lines up between the margins.

**justified alignment**

The term "alignment" refers to the way a paragraph lines up between the margins. The term "alignment" refers to the way a paragraph lines up between the margins.

© 2014 Cengage Learning

The Paragraph group on the HOME tab includes a button for each of the four major types of alignment described in Figure 1-31: the Align Left button, the Center button, the Align Right button, and the Justify button. To align a single paragraph, click anywhere in that paragraph, and then click the appropriate alignment button. To align multiple paragraphs, select the paragraphs first, and then click an alignment button.

You need to center all the text in the flyer now. You can center the photo at the same time.

**To center-align the text:**

Use the Ctrl+A keys to select the entire document, instead of dragging the mouse pointer. It's easy to miss part of the document when you drag the mouse pointer.

1. Press the **Ctrl+A** keys to select the entire document, and make sure the HOME tab is still selected.

2. In the Paragraph group, click the **Center** button ☰, and then click a blank area of the document to deselect the selected paragraphs. The text and photo are now centered on the page, similar to the centered text shown earlier in the Session 1.2 Visual Overview.

3. Save the document.

# Adding a Paragraph Border and Shading

A **paragraph border** is an outline that appears around one or more paragraphs in a document. You can choose to apply only a partial border—for example, a bottom border that appears as an underline under the last line of text in the paragraph—or an entire box around a paragraph. You can select different colors and line weights for the border as well, making it more prominent or less prominent as needed. You apply paragraph borders using the Borders button in the Paragraph group on the HOME tab. **Shading** is background color that you can apply to one or more paragraphs and can be used in conjunction with a border for a more defined effect. You apply shading using the Shading button in the Paragraph group on the HOME tab.

Now you will apply a border and shading to the first paragraph, as shown earlier in the Session 1.2 Visual Overview. Then you will use the Format Painter to copy this formatting to the last paragraph in the document.

### To add shading and a paragraph border:

▶ **1.** Select the first paragraph. Be sure to select the paragraph mark at the end of the paragraph.

▶ **2.** On the HOME tab, in the Paragraph group, click the **Borders button arrow** ⊞ ▾. A gallery of border options appears, as shown in Figure 1-32. To apply a complete outline around the selected text, you use the Outside Borders option.

**Figure 1-32** | **Border gallery**

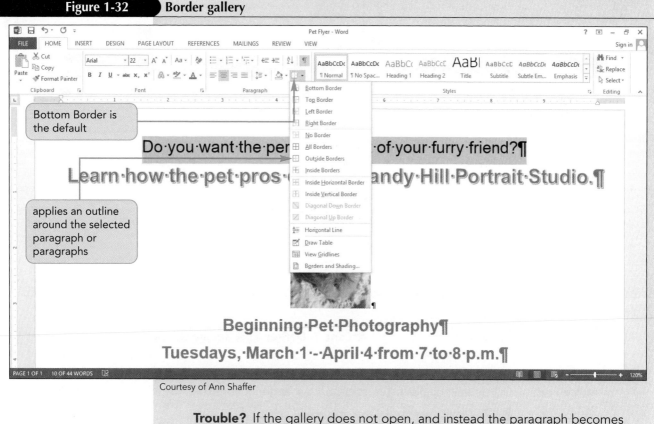

Courtesy of Ann Shaffer

**Trouble?** If the gallery does not open, and instead the paragraph becomes underlined with a single underline, you clicked the Borders button ⊞ instead of the arrow next to it. On the Quick Access Toolbar, click the Undo button ↺, and then repeat Step 2.

3.  In the Border gallery, click **Outside Borders**. The menu closes and a black border appears around the selected paragraph, spanning the width of the page. In the Paragraph group, the Borders button ⊞ changes to show the Outside Borders option.

    **Trouble?** If the border around the first paragraph doesn't extend all the way to the left and right margins, and instead only encloses the text, you didn't select the paragraph mark as directed in Step 1. Click the Undo button ⟳ repeatedly to remove the border, and begin again with Step 1.

4.  In the Paragraph group, click the **Shading button arrow** ⬛▾. A gallery of shading options opens, divided into Theme Colors and Standard Colors. You will use a shade of orange in the sixth column from the left.

5.  In the second row from the bottom in the Theme Colors section, move the pointer over the square in the sixth column from the left to display a ScreenTip that reads "Orange, Accent 2, Darker 25%." A Live Preview of the color appears in the document. See Figure 1-33.

**Figure 1-33**    **Shading gallery with a Live Preview displayed**

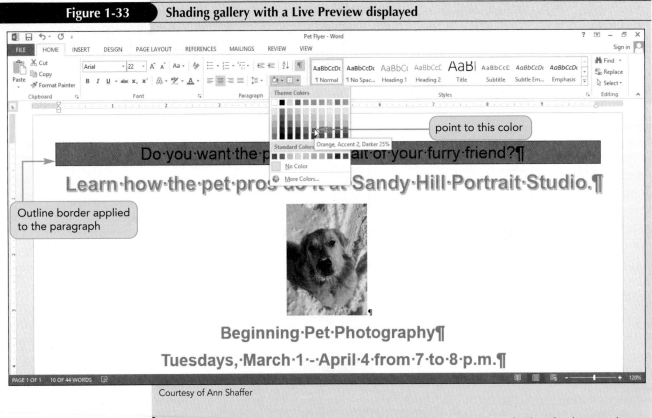

Courtesy of Ann Shaffer

6.  Click the **Orange, Accent 2, Darker 25%** square to apply the shading to the selected text.

    On a dark background like the one you just applied, a white font creates a striking effect. Tim asks you to change the font color for this paragraph to white.

7.  Make sure the HOME tab is still selected.

8.  In the Font group, click the **Font Color button arrow** 🅰▾ to open the Font Color gallery, and then click the **white** square in the top row of the Theme Colors. The Font Color gallery closes and the paragraph is now formatted with white font.

**9.** Click a blank area of the document to deselect the text, review the change, and then save the document. See Figure 1-34.

| Figure 1-34 | Paragraph formatted with dark orange shading, a black border, and white font |

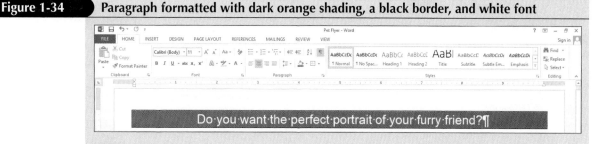

To add balance to the flyer, Tim suggests formatting the last paragraph in the document with the same shading, border, and font color as the first paragraph. You'll do that next.

# Copying Formatting with the Format Painter

You could select the last paragraph and then apply the border, shading, and font color one step at a time. But it's easier to copy all the formatting from the first paragraph to the last paragraph using the Format Painter button in the Clipboard group on the HOME tab.

### Using the Format Painter

- Select the text whose formatting you want to copy.
- On the HOME tab, in the Clipboard group, click the Format Painter button; or to copy formatting to multiple sections of nonadjacent text, double-click the Format Painter button.
- The mouse pointer changes to the Format Painter pointer, the I-beam pointer with a paintbrush.
- Click the words you want to format, or drag to select and format entire paragraphs.
- When you are finished formatting the text, click the Format Painter button again to turn off the Format Painter.

You'll use the Format Painter now.

### To use the Format Painter:

**1.** Change the document Zoom level to **One Page** so you can easily see both the first and last paragraphs.

**2.** Select the first paragraph, which is formatted with the dark orange shading, the border, and the white font color.

**3.** On the ribbon, click the HOME tab.

**4.** In the Clipboard group, click the **Format Painter** button to activate, or turn on, the Format Painter.

**5.** Move the pointer over the document. The pointer changes to the Format Painter pointer when you move the mouse pointer near an item that can be formatted. See Figure 1-35.

**Figure 1-35** **Format Painter**

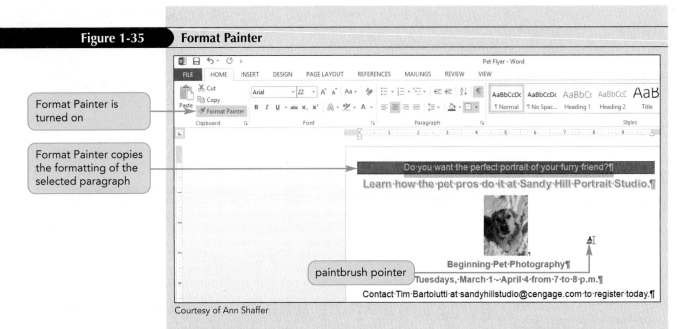

Format Painter is turned on

Format Painter copies the formatting of the selected paragraph

paintbrush pointer

Courtesy of Ann Shaffer

6. Click and drag the Format Painter pointer ▒Ī to select the last paragraph in the document. The paragraph is now formatted with dark orange shading, a black border, and white font. The mouse pointer returns to its original I-beam shape Ī.

   **Trouble?** If the text in the newly formatted paragraph wrapped to a second line, replace your full name with your first name, or, if necessary, use only your initials so the paragraph is only one line long.

7. Click anywhere in the document to deselect the text, review the change, and then save the document.

You're almost finished working on the document's paragraph formatting. Your last step is to increase the paragraph spacing below the first paragraph and above the last paragraph. This will give the shaded text even more weight on the page. To complete this task, you will use the settings on the PAGE LAYOUT tab, which offer more options than the Line and Paragraph Spacing button on the HOME tab.

**To increase the paragraph spacing below the first paragraph and above the last paragraph:**

1. Click anywhere in the first paragraph, and then click the **PAGE LAYOUT** tab. On this tab, the Paragraph group contains settings that control paragraph spacing. Currently, the paragraph spacing for the first paragraph is set to the default 0 points before the paragraph and 8 points after.

2. In the Paragraph group, click the **After** box to select the current setting, type **42**, and then press the **Enter** key. The added space causes the second paragraph to move down 42 points.

3. Click anywhere in the last paragraph.

4. On the PAGE LAYOUT tab, in the Paragraph group, click the **Before** box to select the current setting, type **42**, and then press the **Enter** key. The added space causes the last paragraph to move down 42 points.

*Formatting Professional Documents*

In more formal documents, use color and special effects sparingly. The goal of letters, reports, and many other types of documents is to convey important information, not to dazzle the reader with fancy fonts and colors. Such elements only serve to distract the reader from your main point. In formal documents, it's a good idea to limit the number of colors to two and to stick with left alignment for text. In a document like the flyer you're currently working on, you have a little more leeway because the goal of the document is to attract attention. However, you still want it to look professional.

Finally, Tim wants you to replace the photo of the golden retriever with one that will look better in the document's new landscape orientation. You'll replace the photo, and then you'll resize it so the flyer fills the entire page.

# Working with Pictures

A **picture** is a photo or another type of image that you insert into a document. To work with a picture, you first need to select it. Once a picture is selected, a contextual tab— the PICTURE TOOLS FORMAT tab—appears on the ribbon, with options for editing the picture and adding effects such as a border, a shadow, a reflection, or a new shape. A **contextual tab** appears on the ribbon only when an object is selected. It contains commands related to the selected object so you can manipulate, edit, and format the selected object. You can also use the mouse to resize or move a selected picture. To insert a new picture, you use the Pictures button in the Illustrations group on the INSERT tab.

**To delete the current photo and insert a new one:**

▶  **1.** Click the photo to select it.

The squares, called **handles**, around the edge of the photo indicate the photo is selected. The Layout Options button, to the right of the photo, gives you access to options that control how the document text flows around the photo. You don't need to worry about these options now. Finally, note that the PICTURE TOOLS FORMAT tab appeared on the ribbon when you selected the photo. See Figure 1-36.

**Figure 1-36** | Selected photo

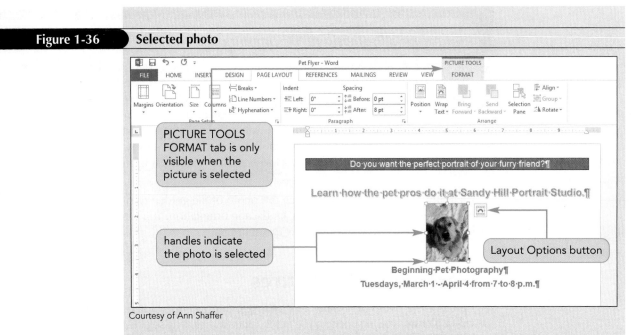

Courtesy of Ann Shaffer

**2.** Press the **Delete** key. The photo is deleted from the document. The insertion point blinks next to the paragraph symbol. You will insert the new photo in that paragraph.

**3.** On the ribbon, click the **INSERT** tab. The ribbon changes to display the Insert options.

**4.** In the Illustrations group, click the **Pictures** button. The Insert Picture dialog box opens.

**5.** Navigate to the Word1 ▸ Tutorial folder included with your Data Files, and then click **Poodle** to select the file. The name of the selected file appears in the File name box.

**6.** Click the **Insert** button to close the Insert Picture dialog box and insert the photo. An image of a black poodle appears in the document, below the text. The photo is selected, as indicated by the handles that appear on its border.

Now you need to enlarge the photo to fit the available space on the page. You could do so by clicking one of the picture's corner handles, holding down the mouse button, and then dragging the handle to resize the picture. But using the Shape Height and Shape Width boxes on the PICTURE TOOLS FORMAT tab gives you more precise results.

**To resize the photo:**

**1.** Make sure the PICTURE TOOLS FORMAT tab is still selected on the ribbon.

**2.** In the Size group on the far right edge of the ribbon, locate the Shape Height box, which tells you that the height of the selected picture is currently 2.46". The Shape Width box tells you that the width of the picture is 3.69". As you'll see in the next step, when you change one of these measurements, the other changes accordingly, keeping the overall shape of the picture the same. See Figure 1-37.

**Figure 1-37**     **Shape Height and Shape Width boxes**

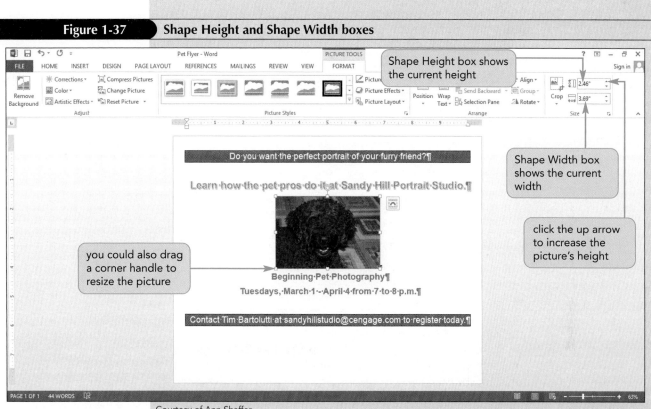

Courtesy of Ann Shaffer

▶ **3.** Click the **up arrow** in the Shape Height box in the Size group. The photo increases in size slightly. The measurement in the Shape Height box increases to 2.5" and the measurement in the Shape Width box increases to 3.75".

▶ **4.** Click the **up arrow** in the Shape Height box repeatedly until the picture is 3.3" tall and 4.95" wide.

Finally, to make the photo more noticeable, you can add a **picture style**, which is a collection of formatting options, such as a frame, a rounded shape, and a shadow. You can apply a picture style to a selected picture by clicking the style you want in the Picture Styles gallery on the PICTURE TOOLS FORMAT tab. In the following steps, you'll start by displaying the gallery.

### To add a style to the photo:

▶ **1.** Make sure the PICTURE TOOLS FORMAT tab is still selected on the ribbon.

▶ **2.** In the Picture Styles group, click the **More** button to the right of the Picture Styles gallery to open the gallery and display more picture styles. Some of the picture styles simply add a border, while others change the picture's shape. Other styles combine these options with effects such as a shadow or a reflection.

▶ **3.** Place the mouse pointer over various styles to observe the Live Previews in the document, and then place the mouse pointer over the Drop Shadow Rectangle style, which is the middle style in the top row. See Figure 1-38.

**Figure 1-38** Previewing a picture style

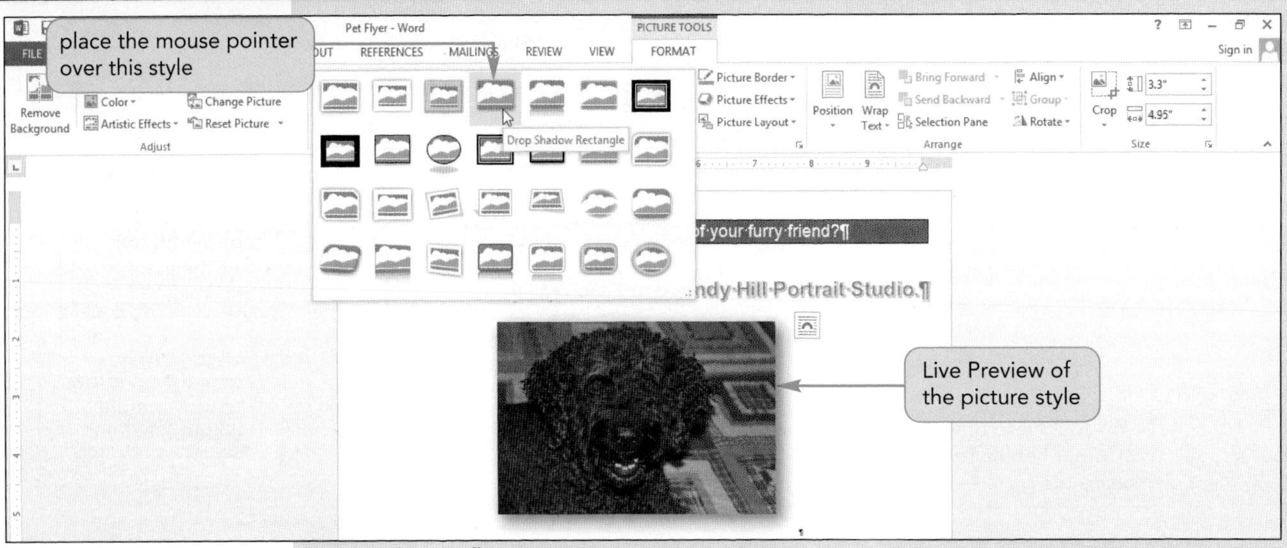

Courtesy of Ann Shaffer

**TIP**

To return a picture to its original appearance, click the Reset Picture button in the Adjust group on the PICTURE TOOLS FORMAT tab.

4. In the gallery, click the **Drop Shadow Rectangle** style to apply it to the photo and close the gallery. The photo is formatted with a shadow on the bottom and right sides, as shown earlier in the Session 1.2 Visual Overview.

5. Click anywhere outside the photo to deselect it, and then, save the document.

6. Click the **FILE** tab, and then click **Close** in the navigation bar to close the document without closing Word.

**INSIGHT**

### Working with Inline Pictures

By default, when you insert a picture in a document, it is treated as an inline object, which means its position changes in the document as you add or delete text. Also, because it is an inline object, you can align the picture just as you would align text, using the alignment buttons in the Paragraph group on the HOME tab. Essentially, you can treat an inline picture as just another paragraph.

When you become a more advanced Word user, you'll learn how to wrap text around a picture so that the text flows around the picture—with the picture maintaining its position on the page no matter how much text you add to or delete from the document. The alignment buttons don't work on pictures that have text wrapped around them. Instead, you can drag the picture to the desired position on the page.

The flyer is complete and ready for Tim to print later. Because Tim is considering creating a promotional brochure that would include numerous photographs, he asks you to look up information about other ways to format a picture. You can do that using Word's Help system.

# Getting Help

To get the most out of Help, your computer must be connected to the Internet so it can access the reference information stored at Office.com.

### To look up information in Help:

**TIP**

You can also open the Word Help window by pressing the F1 key.

1.  Verify that your computer is connected to the Internet, and then, on the title bar, click the **Microsoft Word Help** button ?. The Word Help window opens, with its Home page displayed. You might see the topics shown in Figure 1-39, or you might see other topics. You can click the various options in the Word Help window to browse among topics, or you can use the Search online help box to look up information on a particular topic.

**Figure 1-39**  | Word Help window

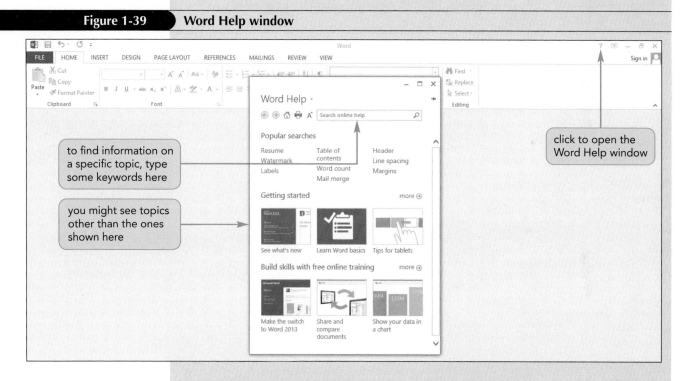

2.  Click in the **Search online help** box, type **format picture**, and then press the **Enter** key. The Word Help window displays a list of articles related to inserting pictures in a document.

3.  Click the first topic listed, and then read the article to see if it contains any information about formatting pictures that might be useful to Tim. Note that to print information about a topic, you can click the Print button near the top of the Word Help window.

4.  When are you finished reading the article, click the **Back** button ⊖ near the top of the Word Help window to return to the previous list of topics.

5.  Click the **Home** button 🏠 to return to the Home page.

6.  Click the **Close** button ✖ in the upper-right corner to close the Word Help window.

Word Help is a great way to learn more about Word's many features. Articles on basic skills provide step-by-step guides for completing tasks, while more elaborate, online tutorials walk you through more complicated tasks. Be sure to take some time on your own to explore Word Help so you can find the information you want when you need it.

**REVIEW**

### Session 1.2 Quick Check

1. Explain how to open the Spelling and Grammar task panes.
2. What is the default page orientation for Word documents?
3. What is the default font size?
4. Explain how to use the Format Painter button.
5. What button do you use to insert a photo in a document?
6. Explain how to open the Help window.

ASSESS

## SAM Projects

Put your skills into practice with SAM Projects! SAM Projects for this tutorial can be found online. If you have a SAM account, go to www.cengage.com/sam2013 to download the most recent Project Instructions and Start Files.

PRACTICE

## Review Assignments

**Data Files needed for the Review Assignments: Flower.docx, Mixed Flowers.jpg**

Tim asks you to write a cover letter to accompany a wedding photography contract. After that, he wants you to create an envelope for the letter, and to format a flyer announcing a class about photographing flowers. Change the Zoom level as necessary while you are working. Complete the following steps:

1. Open a new, blank document and then save the document as **Sommer Letter** in the location specified by your instructor.
2. Type the date **February 16, 2016** using AutoComplete for "February."
3. Press the Enter key twice, and then type the following inside address, using the default paragraph spacing and pressing the Enter key once after each line:
   **Kiley Sommer**
   **2355 Greenwillow Drive**
   **Baltimore, MD 21204**
4. Type **Dear Ms. Sommer:** as the salutation, press the Enter key, and then type the following as the body of the letter:
   **Enclosed you will find the contract summarizing our plans for your wedding. Please return your signed copy to me by next Monday, along with the down payment specified in the contract.**
   **As you'll see, the second page of the contract lists the specific shots we've already agreed on. For more ideas about possible group shots, please see our website at www.sandyhillstudio. cengage.com. Of course, the photographer will be taking candid shots throughout the day.**
5. Press the Enter key, type **Sincerely yours,** as the complimentary closing, press the Enter key three times, type **Tim Bartolutti** as the signature line, insert a manual line break, and type **Sales Manager** as his title.
6. Press the Enter key, type your initials, insert a manual line break, and then use the Undo button to make your initials all lowercase, if necessary.
7. Type **Enclosure** and save the document.
8. Scroll to the beginning of the document and proofread your work. Remove any wavy underlines by using a shortcut menu or by typing a correction yourself. Remove the hyperlink formatting from the web address.
9. Remove the paragraph spacing from the first two lines of the inside address.
10. Change the top margin to 2.75 inches. Leave the other margins at their default settings.
11. Save your changes to the letter, preview it, print it if your instructor asks you to, and then close it.
12. Create a new, blank document, and then create an envelope. Use Kiley Sommer's address (from Step 3) as the delivery address. Use your school's name and address for the return address. Add the envelope to the document. If you are asked if you want to save the return address as the new return address, click No.

13. Save the document as **Sommer Envelope** in the location specified by your instructor, and then close the document.

14. Open the file **Flower**, located in the Word1 ▸ Review folder included with your Data Files, and then check your screen to make sure your settings match those in the tutorial.

15. Save the document as **Flower Flyer** in the location specified by your instructor.

16. Configure the grammar settings to check for subject-verb agreement errors, and then use the Spelling and Grammar task panes to correct any errors marked with wavy underlines. When you are finished, return the grammar settings to their original configuration.

17. Proofread the document and correct any other errors. Be sure to change "gardens" to "garden's" in the first paragraph.

18. Change the page orientation to Landscape and the margins to Narrow.

19. Format the document text in 22-point Times New Roman font.

20. Center the text and the photo.

21. Format the first paragraph with an outside border, and then add green shading, using the Green, Accent 6, Darker 25% color in the Theme Colors section of the Shading gallery. Format the paragraph text in white.

22. Format the last paragraph in the document using the same formatting you applied to the first paragraph.

23. Increase the paragraph spacing after the first paragraph to 42 points. Increase the paragraph spacing before the last paragraph in the document to 42 points.

24. Format the second paragraph with the Fill - Orange, Accent 2, Outline - Accent 2 text effect. Increase the paragraph's font size to 26 points.

25. Format the third and fourth paragraphs (containing the class name, date, and time) in green, using the Green, Accent 6, Darker 50% font color, and then add bold and italic.

26. Delete the photo and replace it with the **Mixed Flowers.jpg** photo, located in the Word1 ▸ Review folder included with your Data Files.

27. Resize the new photo so that it is 3.8" tall, and then add the Soft Edge Rectangle style in the Pictures Styles gallery.

28. Save your changes to the flyer, preview it, and then close it.

29. Start Word Help and look up the topic "work with pictures." Read the article, return to the Help home page, and then close Help.

## Case Problem 1

**There are no Data Files needed for this Case Problem.**

*Prairie Public Health Consultants*   You are a program administrator at Prairie Public Health Consultants. Over the past few months, you have collected handwritten surveys from high school students about their exercise habits. Now you need to send the surveys to the researcher in charge of compiling the data. Create a cover letter to accompany the surveys by completing the following steps. Because your office is currently out of letterhead, you'll start the letter by typing a return address. As you type the letter, remember to include the appropriate number of blank paragraphs between the various parts of the letter. Complete the following steps:

1. Open a new, blank document, and then save the document as **Prairie Letter** in the location specified by your instructor. If necessary, change the Zoom level to 120%.

APPLY

2. Type the following return address, using the default paragraph spacing, and replacing [Your Name] with your first and last names:

   **[Your Name]**

   **Prairie Public Health Consultants**

   **6833 Erickson Lane**

   **Des Moines, IA 50301**

3. Type **November 7, 2016** as the date, leaving a blank paragraph between the last line of the return address and the date.

4. Type the following inside address, using the default paragraph spacing and leaving the appropriate number of blank paragraphs after the date:

   **Dr. Anna Witinski**

   **4643 University Circle**

   **Ames, IA 50010**

5. Type **Dear Dr. Witinski:** as the salutation.

6. To begin the body of the letter, type the following paragraph:

   **Enclosed please find the surveys I have collected so far. I hope to have another 200 for you in a week, but I thought you would like to get started on these now. After you've had a chance to review the surveys, please call or email me with your answers to these questions:**

7. Add the following questions as separate paragraphs, using the default paragraph spacing:

   **Do you need help tabulating the survey responses?**

   **Should we consider expanding the survey to additional schools?**

   **Should we rephrase any of the survey questions?**

8. Insert a new paragraph before the second question, and then add the following as the new second question in the list:

   **Have you hired a student to help you with your analysis?**

9. Insert a new paragraph after the last question, and then type the complimentary closing **Sincerely,** (including the comma).

10. Leave the appropriate amount of space for your signature, type your full name, insert a manual line break, and then type **Program Administrator**.

11. Type **Enclosure** in the appropriate place.

12. Use the Spelling and Grammar task panes to correct any errors. Instruct the Spelling task pane to ignore the recipient's name.

13. Italicize the four paragraphs containing the questions.

14. Remove the paragraph spacing from the first three lines of the return address. Do the same for the first two paragraphs of the inside address.

15. Center the four paragraphs containing the return address, format them in 16-point font, and then add the Fill - Black, Text 1, Shadow text effect.

16. Save the document, preview it, and then close it.

17. Create a new, blank document, and create an envelope. Use Dr. Witinski's address (from Step 4) as the delivery address. Use the return address shown in Step 2. Add the envelope to the document. If you are asked if you want to save the return address as the new return address, click No.

18. Save the document as **Witinski Envelope** in the location specified by your instructor, and then close the document.

**CREATE**

## Case Problem 2

**Data Files needed for this Case Problem: Church.jpg, Walking.docx**

*Walking Tours of Old San Juan*   You work as the guest services coordinator at Hotel Azul, a luxury resort hotel in San Juan, Puerto Rico. You need to create a flyer promoting a daily walking tour of Old San Juan, the historic Colonial section of Puerto Rico's capital city. Complete the following steps:

1. Open the file **Walking** located in the Word1 ▸ Case2 folder included with your Data Files, and then save the document as **Walking Tour Flyer** in the location specified by your instructor.

2. In the document, replace "Student Name" with your first and last names.

3. Use the Spelling and Grammar task panes to correct any errors, including problems with subject-verb agreement. Instruct the Spelling task pane to ignore the Spanish church names, as well as your name if Word marks it with a wavy underline.

4. Change the page margins to Narrow.

5. Complete the flyer as shown in Figure 1-40. Use the file **Church.jpg** located in the Word1 ▸ Case2 folder included with your Data Files. Use the default line spacing and paragraph spacing unless otherwise specified in Figure 1-40.

**Figure 1-40**   **Formatted Walking Tour flyer**

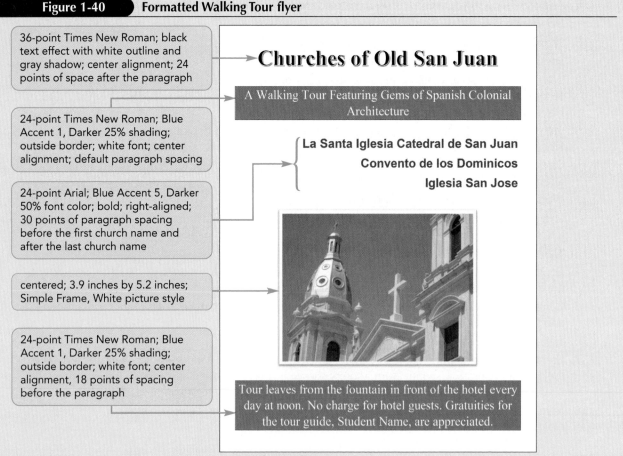

36-point Times New Roman; black text effect with white outline and gray shadow; center alignment; 24 points of space after the paragraph

24-point Times New Roman; Blue Accent 1, Darker 25% shading; outside border; white font; center alignment; default paragraph spacing

24-point Arial; Blue Accent 5, Darker 50% font color; bold; right-aligned; 30 points of paragraph spacing before the first church name and after the last church name

centered; 3.9 inches by 5.2 inches; Simple Frame, White picture style

24-point Times New Roman; Blue Accent 1, Darker 25% shading; outside border; white font; center alignment, 18 points of spacing before the paragraph

**Churches of Old San Juan**

A Walking Tour Featuring Gems of Spanish Colonial Architecture

La Santa Iglesia Catedral de San Juan
Convento de los Dominicos
Iglesia San Jose

Tour leaves from the fountain in front of the hotel every day at noon. No charge for hotel guests. Gratuities for the tour guide, Student Name, are appreciated.

Courtesy of Ann Shaffer

6. Save the document, preview it, and then close it.

**TROUBLESHOOT**

## Case Problem 3

**Data Files needed for this Case Problem: Mushroom.docx, Mycology.docx**

*Green Valley Arborists*   You work as the office manager for Green Valley Arborists, a tree care service in Billings, Montana. One of the company's arborists noticed a bright orange fungus growing on a tree stump in a client's backyard. She has started writing a letter to a mycologist at the local community college to ask if he can identify the fungus. The letter is almost finished, but the arborist needs help correcting errors and formatting the text to match the block style. The photo itself is stored in a separate document. The arborist mistakenly applied a picture style to the photo that is inappropriate for professional correspondence. She asks you to remove the picture style and then format the page. Complete the following steps:

1. Open the file **Mycology** located in the Word1 ▸ Case3 folder included with your Data Files, and then save the document as **Mycology Letter** in the location specified by your instructor.

2. Use the Spelling and Grammar task panes to correct any errors, including subject-verb errors. When you are finished, return the Grammar settings to their original configuration.

⚙ **Troubleshoot** 3. Make any necessary changes to ensure that the letter matches the formatting of a block style business letter, including the appropriate paragraph spacing. Keep in mind that the letter will include an enclosure. Include your initials where appropriate.

⚙ **Troubleshoot** 4. The letterhead for Green Valley Arborists requires a top margin of 2.5 inches. Determine if the layout of the letter will work with the letterhead, make any necessary changes, and then save the letter.

5. Save the document and preview it.

6. With the letter still open, create an envelope. Use the delivery address taken from the letter, but edit the delivery address. Click the Omit check box to deselect it (if necessary), and then, for the return address, type your school's name and address. Add the envelope to the document. If you are asked if you want to save the return address as the new default return address, answer No.

7. Save the document, preview it, and then close it.

8. Open the file **Mushroom** located in the Word1 ▸ Case3 folder included with your Data Files, and then save the document as **Mushroom Photo** in the location specified by your instructor.

⚙ **Troubleshoot** 9. Reset the picture to its original appearance, before the arborist mistakenly added the style with the reflection.

⚙ **Troubleshoot** 10. Modify the page layout and adjust the size of the photo so the photo fills as much of the page as possible without overlapping the page margins.

11. Save the document, preview it, and then close it.

**CHALLENGE**

## Case Problem 4

There are no Data Files needed for this Case Problem.

*Hapsburg Interior Design*    As a design assistant at Hapsburg Interior Design, you are responsible for distributing manufacturer samples throughout the office so the firm's designers can stay up to date on newly available paint colors, wallpaper patterns, and fabrics. Along with each sample, you need to include an explanatory memo. Complete the following steps:

⊕ **Explore** 1. Open a new document—but instead of selecting the Blank document option, search for a memo template online. In the list of search results, click the Memo (Simple design) template, and then click the Create button. A memo template opens in the Word window. Above the memo template is the Document Properties panel, where you could enter information about the document that might be useful later. You don't need the panel for this project, so you can ignore it, as well as any entries in the text boxes in the panel.

2. Save the document as **Samples Memo** in the location specified by your instructor. If you see a dialog box indicating that the document will be upgraded to the newest file format, click the OK button. Note that of the hundreds of templates available online, only a small portion have been created in the most recent version of Word, so you will often see this dialog box when working with templates.

⊕ **Explore** 3. In the document, click the text "[Company name]." The placeholder text appears in a box with gray highlighting. The box containing the highlighted text (with the small rectangle attached) is called a document control. You can enter text in a document control just as you enter text in a dialog box. Type **Hapsburg Interior Design**, and then press the Tab key. The "[Recipient names]" placeholder text now appears in a document control next to the word "To." (*Hint*: As you work on the memo in the following steps, keep in mind that if you accidentally double-click the word "memo" at the top of the document, you will access the header portion of the document, which is normally closed to editing. In that case, press the Esc key to return to the main document.)

4. Type **All Designers** and then press the Tab key twice. A document control is now visible to the right of the word "From." Depending on how your computer is set up, you might see your name or another name here, or the document control might be empty. Delete the name, if necessary, and then type your first and last names.

⊕ **Explore** 5. Continue using the Tab key to edit the remaining document controls as indicated below. If you press the Tab key too many times and accidentally skip a document control, you can click the document control to select it.

   - In the CC: document control, delete the placeholder text.
   - In the Date document control, click the down arrow, and then click the current date in the calendar.
   - In the Re: document control, type **Rowley Fabrics**.
   - In the Comments document control, type **Here are the latest offerings from Rowley Fabrics. After you have reviewed the collection, please write your initials at the bottom of this memo and pass the collection on to another designer. If you are the last of the group to review the samples, please return them to my desk. Thank you.**

6. Use the Spelling and Grammar task panes to correct any underlined errors, and then proofread the document to look for any additional errors.

7. Save the document, preview it, and then close it.

# Navigating and Formatting a Document

*Editing an Academic Document According to MLA Style*

## OBJECTIVES

### Session 2.1
- Read, reply to, delete, and add comments
- Create bulleted and numbered lists
- Move text using drag and drop
- Cut and paste text
- Copy and paste text
- Navigate through a document using the Navigation pane
- Find and replace text
- Format text with styles
- Apply a theme to a document

### Session 2.2
- Review the MLA style for research papers
- Indent paragraphs
- Insert and modify page numbers
- Create citations
- Create and update a bibliography
- Modify a source

## Case | *Rivas-Garcia College*

Kaya Cho, a student at Rivas-Garcia College, works part-time in the college's Media Studies department. She has written a handout describing the requirements for a Media Studies major, and asks you to help her finish it. The text of the handout needs some reorganization and other editing. It also needs formatting so the finished document looks professional and is easy to read.

Kaya is also taking a Media Studies class this semester, and is writing a research paper on the history of newspapers. To complete the paper, she needs to follow a set of very specific formatting and style guidelines for academic documents.

Kaya has asked you to help her edit these two very different documents. In Session 2.1, you will review and respond to some comments in the handout, and then revise and format that document. In Session 2.2, you will review the MLA style for research papers, and then format Kaya's research paper to match the MLA specifications.

## STARTING DATA FILES

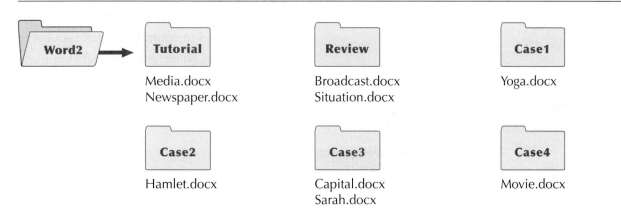

Word2 → Tutorial
Media.docx
Newspaper.docx

Review
Broadcast.docx
Situation.docx

Case1
Yoga.docx

Case2
Hamlet.docx

Case3
Capital.docx
Sarah.docx

Case4
Movie.docx

# Session 2.1 Visual Overview:

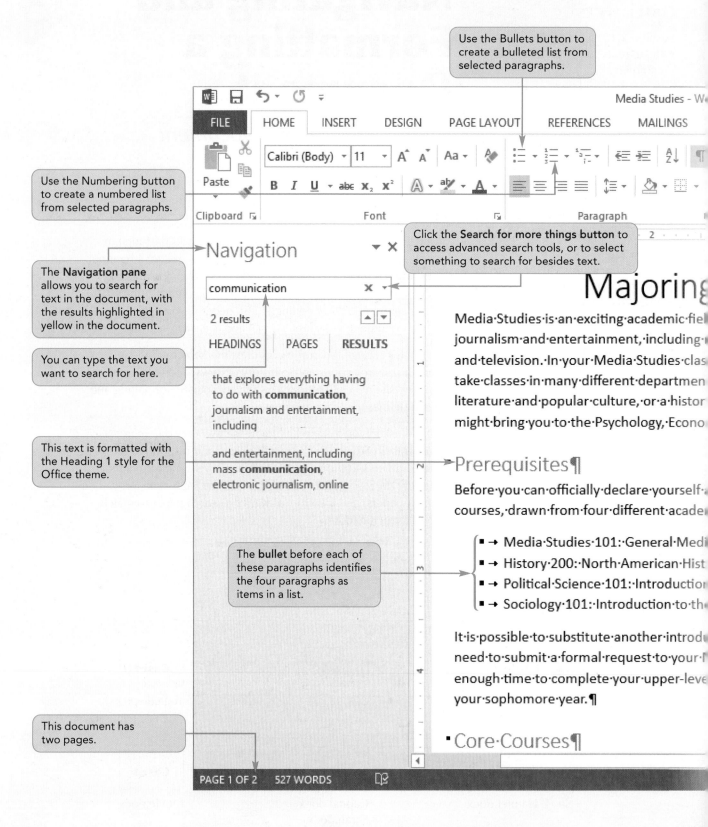

Use the Bullets button to create a bulleted list from selected paragraphs.

Use the Numbering button to create a numbered list from selected paragraphs.

Click the **Search for more things button** to access advanced search tools, or to select something to search for besides text.

The **Navigation pane** allows you to search for text in the document, with the results highlighted in yellow in the document.

You can type the text you want to search for here.

This text is formatted with the Heading 1 style for the Office theme.

The **bullet** before each of these paragraphs identifies the four paragraphs as items in a list.

This document has two pages.

Media Studies - W

FILE    HOME    INSERT    DESIGN    PAGE LAYOUT    REFERENCES    MAILINGS

Calibri (Body)    11

Paste

Clipboard    Font    Paragraph

Navigation

communication    ✕

2 results

HEADINGS    PAGES    **RESULTS**

that explores everything having to do with **communication**, journalism and entertainment, including

and entertainment, including mass **communication**, electronic journalism, online

# Majoring

Media·Studies·is·an·exciting·academic·fiel
journalism·and·entertainment,·including·
and·television.·In·your·Media·Studies·clas
take·classes·in·many·different·departmen
literature·and·popular·culture,·or·a·histor
might·bring·you·to·the·Psychology,·Econo

Prerequisites¶

Before·you·can·officially·declare·yourself·
courses,·drawn·from·four·different·acade

■ → Media·Studies·101:·General·Medi
■ → History·200:·North·American·Hist
■ → Political·Science·101:·Introductio
■ → Sociology·101:·Introduction·to·the

It·is·possible·to·substitute·another·introd
need·to·submit·a·formal·request·to·your·
enough·time·to·complete·your·upper-leve
your·sophomore·year.¶

Core·Courses¶

PAGE 1 OF 2    527 WORDS

# Working with Lists and Styles

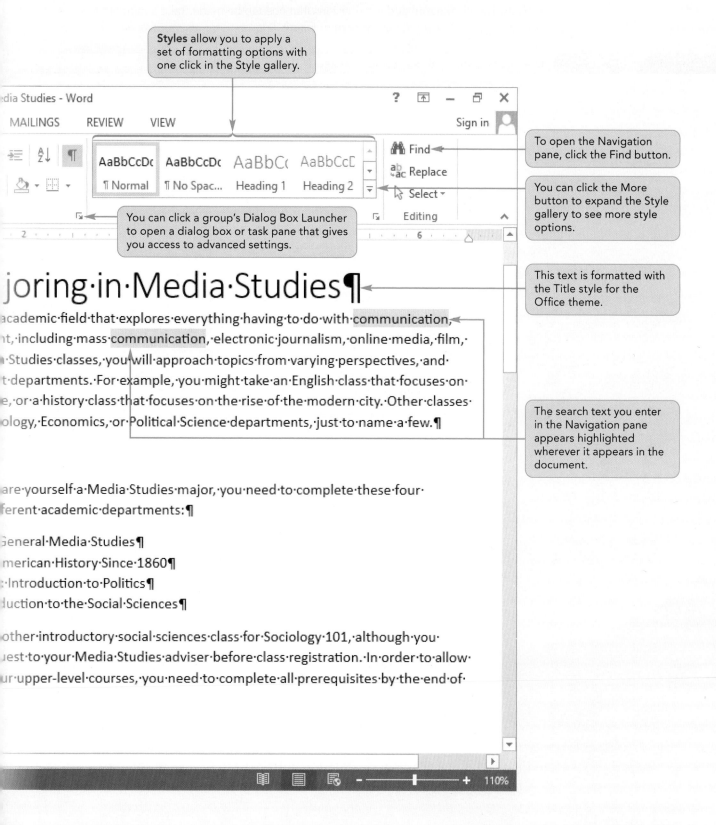

**Styles** allow you to apply a set of formatting options with one click in the Style gallery.

To open the Navigation pane, click the Find button.

You can click the More button to expand the Style gallery to see more style options.

You can click a group's Dialog Box Launcher to open a dialog box or task pane that gives you access to advanced settings.

This text is formatted with the Title style for the Office theme.

The search text you enter in the Navigation pane appears highlighted wherever it appears in the document.

# Reviewing the Document

Before revising a document for someone else, it's a good idea to familiarize yourself with its overall structure and the revisions that need to be made. Take a moment to review Kaya's notes, which are shown in Figure 2-1.

**Figure 2-1**   **Draft of handout with Kaya's notes (page 1)**

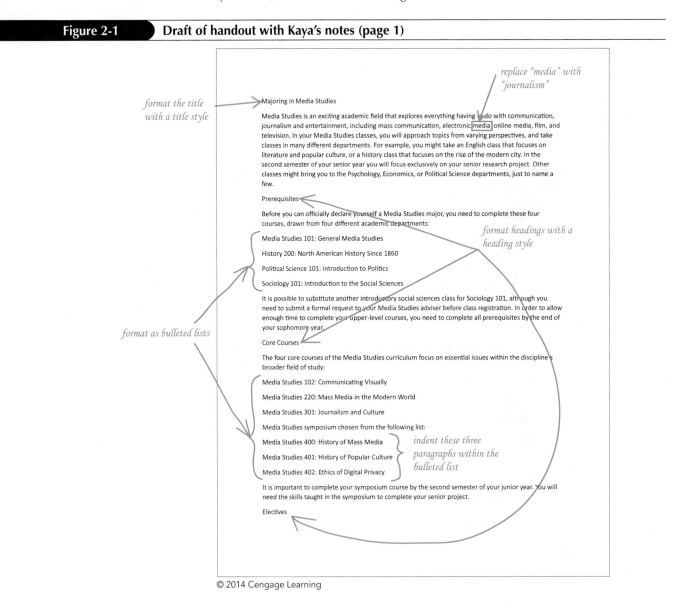

© 2014 Cengage Learning

| Figure 2-1 | Draft of handout with Kaya's notes (page 2) |

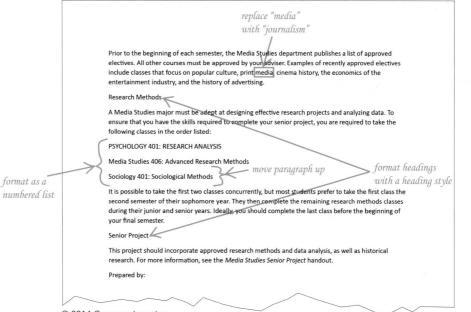

© 2014 Cengage Learning

Kaya also included additional guidance in some comments she added to the document file. A **comment** is like an electronic sticky note attached to a word, phrase, or paragraph in a document. Comments appear in the margin, along with the name of the person who added them. Within a single document, you can add new comments, reply to existing comments, and delete comments.

You will open the document now, save it with a new name, and then review Kaya's comments in Word.

## To open and rename the document:

1. Open the document named **Media** located in the Word2 ▶ Tutorial folder included with your Data Files.

2. Save the document as **Media Studies** in the location specified by your instructor.

3. Verify that the document is displayed in Print Layout view, that the zoom is set to **120%**, and that the rulers and nonprinting characters are displayed.

4. On the ribbon, click the **REVIEW** tab to display the tools used for working with comments. Comments can be displayed in several different ways, so your first step is to make sure the comments in the Media Studies document are displayed to match the figures in this book—using Simple Markup view.

5. In the Tracking group, click the **Display for Review** arrow, and then click **Simple Markup** to select it, if necessary. At this point, you might see comment icons to the right of the document text, or you might see the full text of each comment.

6. In the Comments group, click the **Show Comments** button several times to practice displaying and hiding the comments, and then, when you are finished, make sure the Show Comments button is selected so the full text of each comment is displayed.

**7.** At the bottom of the Word window, drag the horizontal scroll bar all the way to the right so you can read the full text of each comment. See Figure 2-2. Note that the comments on your screen might be a different color than the ones shown in the figure.

**Figure 2-2** **Comments displayed in the document**

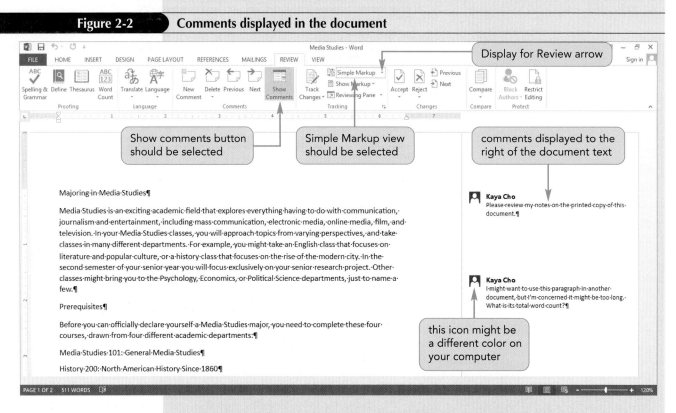

Note that when working on a small monitor, it can be helpful to switch the document Zoom level to Page Width, in which case Word automatically reduces the width of the document to accommodate the comments on the right.

**8.** Read the document, including the comments. The handout includes the title "Majoring in Media Studies" at the top, as well as headings (such as "Prerequisites" and "Core Courses") that divide the document into parts. Right now the headings are hard to spot because they don't look different from the surrounding text. Kaya used the default font size, 11-point, and the default font, Calibri (Body), for all the text in the document. Note, too, that the document includes some short paragraphs that would work better as bulleted or numbered lists.

**9.** Scroll down until you can see the first line on page 2, which begins "Prior to the beginning of each semester...." and then click anywhere in that sentence. The message "PAGE 2 OF 2" in the status bar, in the lower-left corner of the Word window, tells you that the insertion point is currently located on page 2 of the two-page document. The shaded space between the first and second pages of the document indicates a page break. To hide the top and bottom margins in a document, as well as the space between pages, you can double-click the shaded space between any two pages.

**10.** Position the mouse pointer over the shaded space between page 1 and page 2 until the pointer changes to 🔼, and then double-click. The shaded space disappears. Instead, the two pages are now separated by a gray, horizontal line.

**Trouble?** If the HEADER & FOOTER TOOLS DESIGN tab appears on the ribbon, you double-clicked the top or bottom of one of the pages, instead of in the space between them. Click the Close Header and Footer button on the DESIGN tab, and then repeat Step 10.

▶ **11.** Use the ↕ pointer to double-click the gray horizontal line between pages 1 and 2. The shaded space between the two pages is redisplayed.

# Working with Comments

Now that you are familiar with the Media Studies document, you can review and respond to Kaya's comments. The Comment group on the REVIEW tab includes helpful tools for working with comments.

**REFERENCE**

*Working with Comments*

- On the ribbon, click the REVIEW tab.
- To display comments in an easy-to-read view, in the Tracking group, click the Display for Review button, and then click Simple Markup.
- To see the text of each comment in Simple Markup view, click the Show Comments button in the Comments group.
- To move the insertion point to the next or previous comment in the document, click the Next button or the Previous button in the Comments group.
- To delete a comment, click anywhere in the comment, and then click the Delete button in the Comments group.
- To delete all the comments in a document, click the Delete button arrow in the Comments group, and then click Delete All Comments in Document.
- To add a new comment, select the document text you want to comment on, click the New Comment button in the Comments group, and then type the comment text.
- To reply to a comment, click the Reply button to the right of the comment, and then type your reply.
- To indicate that a comment or an individual reply to a comment is no longer a concern, right-click the comment or reply, and then click Mark Comment Done in the shortcut menu. To mark a comment and all of the replies attached to it as done, right-click the original comment and then click Mark Comment Done.

**To review and respond to the comments in the document:**

▶ **1.** Press the **Ctrl+Home** keys to move the insertion point to the beginning of the document.

▶ **2.** On the REVIEW tab, in the Comments group, click the **Next** button. The first comment now has an outline, indicating that it is selected. See Figure 2-3.

In the document, the word "Majoring" is highlighted. A line connects the comment to the word "Majoring," indicating that the comment is attached to that word. Because Kaya created the comment, her name appears at the beginning of the comment, followed by the date on which she created it. The insertion point blinks at the beginning of the comment, and is ready for you to edit the comment if you want.

| Figure 2-3 | Comment attached to document text |

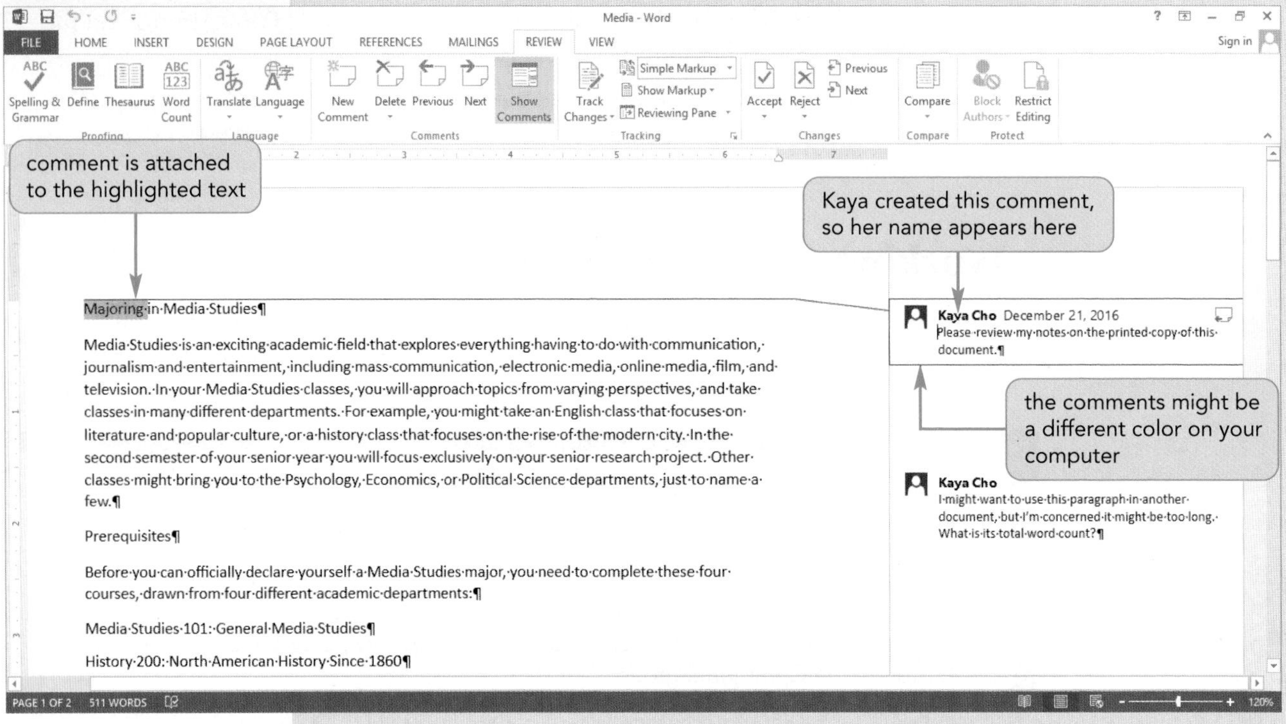

**3.** Read the comment, and then in the Comments group, click the **Next** button to select the next comment. According to this comment, Kaya wants to know the total word count of the paragraph the comment is attached to. You can get this information by selecting the entire paragraph and locating the word count in the status bar.

**4.** Triple-click anywhere in the second paragraph of the document (which begins "Media studies is an exciting academic field…") to select the paragraph. In the status bar, the message "110 of 511" tells you that 110 of the document's 511 words are currently selected. So the answer to Kaya's question is 110.

**5.** Point to the second comment to select it again, click the **Reply** button 🔲, and then type **110**. Your reply appears below Kaya's original comment.

**Trouble?** If you do not see the Reply button in the comment box, drag the horizontal scroll bar at the bottom of the Word window to the right until you can see it.

The name that appears in your reply comment is taken from the User name box in the General tab of the Word Options dialog box. If your name is the username for your computer, your name appears attached to the comment. If you are working on a shared computer at school, or on a computer owned by someone else, another name will appear in the comment.

You can quickly open the General tab of the Word Options dialog box by clicking the Dialog Box Launcher in the Tracking group on the REVIEW tab, and then clicking Change User Name. From there, you can change the username and the initials associated with your copy of Word. However, there is no need to change these settings for this tutorial, and you should never change them on a shared computer at school unless specifically instructed to do so by your instructor.

6. In the Comments group, click the **Next** button to move the insertion point to the next comment, which asks you to insert your name after "Prepared by:" at the end of the document.

7. Click after the colon in "Prepared by:", press the **spacebar**, and then type your first and last name. To indicate that you have complied with Kaya's request by adding your name, you could right-click the comment, and then click Mark Comment Done. However, in this case, you'll simply delete the comment. Kaya also asks you to delete the first comment in the document.

8. Click anywhere in the final comment, and then in the Comments group, click the **Delete** button.

9. In the Comments group, click the **Previous** button three times to select the comment at the beginning of the document, and then click the **Delete** button to delete the comment.

As you reviewed the document, you might have noticed that, on page 2, one of the class names in the Research Methods section appears in all uppercase letters. This is probably just a typing mistake. You can correct it, and then add a comment that points out the change to Kaya.

### To correct the mistake and add a comment:

1. Scroll down to page 2, and then select the fourth paragraph on the page, which contains the text "PSYCHOLOGY 401: RESEARCH ANALYSIS."

2. On the ribbon, click the **HOME** tab.

3. In the Font group, click the **Change Case** button Aa ▾ , and then click **Capitalize Each Word**. The text changes to read "Psychology 401: Research Analysis."

4. Verify that the paragraph is still selected, and then click the **REVIEW** tab on the ribbon.

5. In the Comments group, click the **New Comment** button. A new comment appears, with the insertion point ready for you to begin typing.

6. In the new comment, type **I assumed you didn't want this all uppercase, so I changed it.** and then save the document.

   You can now hide the text of the comments because you are finished working with them.

7. In the Comments group, click the **Show Comments** button. You now see a comment icon in the document margin rather than on the right side of the Word screen. A comment icon alerts you to the presence of a comment without taking up all the space required to display the comment text. You can click a comment icon to read a particular comment without displaying the text of all the comments.

8. Click the comment icon 🗨 . The comment icon is highlighted, and the full comment is displayed, as shown in Figure 2-4.

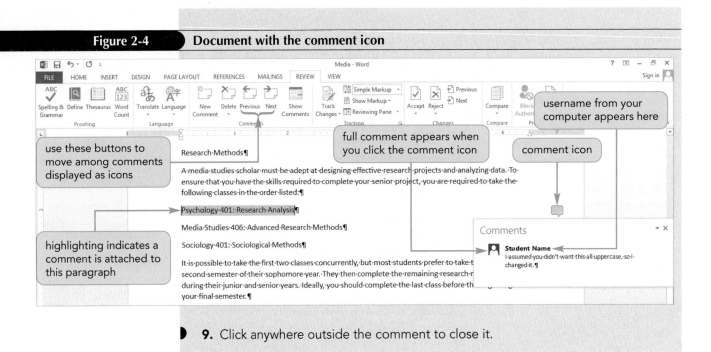

**Figure 2-4** **Document with the comment icon**

9. Click anywhere outside the comment to close it.

# Creating Bulleted and Numbered Lists

A **bulleted list** is a group of related paragraphs with a black circle or other character to the left of each paragraph. For a group of related paragraphs that have a particular order (such as steps in a procedure), you can use consecutive numbers instead of bullets to create a **numbered list**. If you insert a new paragraph, delete a paragraph, or reorder the paragraphs in a numbered list, Word adjusts the numbers to make sure they remain consecutive.

**PROSKILLS**

### Written Communication: Organizing Information in Lists

Bulleted and numbered lists are both great ways to draw the reader's attention to information. But it's important to know how to use them. Use numbers when your list contains items that are arranged by priority in a specific order. For example, in a document reviewing the procedure for performing CPR, it makes sense to use numbers for the sequential steps. Use bullets when the items in the list are of equal importance, or when they can be accomplished in any order. For example, in a resume, you could use bullets for a list of professional certifications.

To add bullets to a series of paragraphs, you use the Bullets button in the Paragraph group on the HOME tab. To create a numbered list, you use the Numbering button in the Paragraph group instead. Both the Bullets button and the Numbering button have arrows you can click to open a gallery of bullet or numbering styles.

Kaya asks you to format the list of prerequisites on page 1 as a bulleted list. She also asks you to format the list of core courses on page 1 as a separate bulleted list. Finally, you need to format the list of research methods classes on page 2 as a numbered list.

## To apply bullets to paragraphs:

1. Scroll up until you see the paragraphs containing the list of prerequisites, which begins with "Media Studies 101: General Media Studies," and then select this paragraph and the three that follow it.

2. On the ribbon, click the **HOME** tab.

3. In the Paragraph group, click the **Bullets** button ☰. Black circles appear as bullets before each item in the list. Also, the bulleted list is indented and the paragraph spacing between the items is reduced.

   After reviewing the default, round bullet in the document, Kaya decides she would prefer square bullets.

4. In the Paragraph group, click the **Bullets button arrow** ☰ ▾. A gallery of bullet styles opens. See Figure 2-5.

### TIP

The Bullets button is a toggle button which means you can click it to add or remove bullets from selected text.

**Figure 2-5    Bullets gallery**

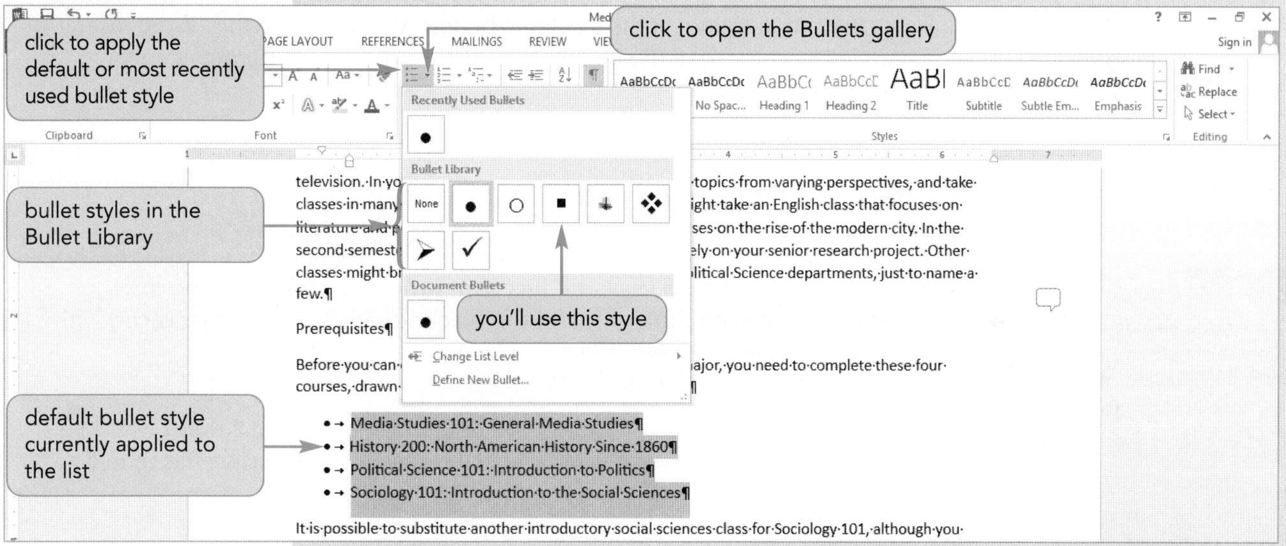

The Recently Used Bullets section appears at the top of the gallery of bullet styles; it displays the bullet styles that have been used since you started Word, which, in this case, is just the round black bullet style that was applied by default when you clicked the Bullets button. The **Bullet Library**, which offers a variety of bullet styles, is shown below the Recently Used Bullets. To create your own bullets from a picture file or from a set of predesigned symbols including diamonds, hearts, or Greek letters, click Define New Bullet, and then click the Symbol button or the Picture button in the Define New Bullet dialog box.

5. Move the mouse pointer over the bullet styles in the Bullet Library to see a Live Preview of the bullet styles in the document. Kaya prefers the black square style.

6. In the Bullet Library, click the **black square**. The round bullets are replaced with square bullets.

Next, you need to format the list of core courses on page 1 with square bullets. When you first start Word, the Bullets button applies the default, round bullets you saw earlier. But after you select a new bullet style, the Bullets button applies the last bullet style you used. So, to add square bullets to the decorating styles list, you just have to select the list and click the Bullets button.

### To add bullets to the list of core courses:

▶ **1.** Scroll down in the document and select the paragraphs listing the core courses, starting with "Media Studies 102: Communicating Visually" and ending with "Media Studies 402: Ethics of Digital Privacy."

▶ **2.** In the Paragraph group, click the **Bullets** button ▤. The list is now formatted with square black bullets.

The list is finished except for one issue. A Media Studies major only needs to take one of the last three classes in the list, but that's not clear because of the way the list is currently formatted. To clarify this information, you can use the Increase Indent button in the Paragraph group to indent the last three bullets. When you do this, Word inserts a different style bullet to make the indented paragraphs visually subordinate to the bulleted paragraphs above.

### To indent the last three bullets:

▶ **1.** In the list of core courses, select the last three paragraphs.

**TIP**

To remove the indent from selected text, click the Decrease Indent button in the Paragraph group.

▶ **2.** In the Paragraph group, click the **Increase Indent** button ▤. The three paragraphs move to the right, and the black square bullets are replaced with open circle bullets.

Next, you will format the list of research methods classes on page 2. Kaya wants you to format this information as a numbered list because the classes must be taken in a specific order.

### To apply numbers to the list of research methods classes:

▶ **1.** Scroll down to page 2 until you see the "Psychology 401: Research Analysis" paragraph. You added a comment to this paragraph earlier, but that will have no effect on the process of creating the numbered list.

▶ **2.** Select the three paragraphs containing the list of research methods classes, starting with "Psychology 401: Research Analysis" and ending with "Sociology 401: Sociological Methods."

▶ **3.** In the Paragraph group, click the **Numbering** button ▤. Consecutive numbers appear in front of each item in the list. See Figure 2-6.

Figure 2-6    **Numbered list**

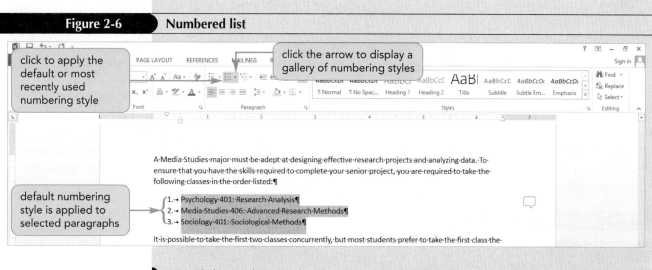

**Figure 2-6**  Numbered list

click to apply the default or most recently used numbering style

click the arrow to display a gallery of numbering styles

default numbering style is applied to selected paragraphs

**4.** Click anywhere in the document to deselect the numbered list, and then save the document.

As with the Bullets button arrow, you can click the Numbering button arrow and then select from a library of numbering styles. You can also indent paragraphs in a numbered list to create an outline, in which case the indented paragraphs will be preceded by lowercase letters instead of numbers. To apply a different list style to the outline (for example, with Roman numerals and uppercase letters), select the list, click the Multilevel List button in the Paragraph group, and then click a multilevel list style.

# Moving Text in a Document

One of the most useful features of a word-processing program is the ability to move text easily. For example, Kaya wants to reorder the information in the numbered list. You could do this by deleting a paragraph and then retyping it at a new location. However, it's easier to select and then move the text. Word provides several ways to move text—drag and drop, cut and paste, and copy and paste.

## Dragging and Dropping Text

To move text with **drag and drop**, you select the text you want to move, press and hold the mouse button while you drag the selected text to a new location, and then release the mouse button.

In the numbered list you just created, Kaya wants you to move the paragraph that reads "Sociology 401 Sociological Methods" up so it is the first item in the list.

**To move text using drag and drop:**

**1.** Select the third paragraph in the numbered list, "Sociology 401: Sociological Methods," being sure to include the paragraph marker at the end. The number 3 remains unselected because it's not actually part of the paragraph text.

**2.** Position the pointer over the selected text. The pointer changes to a left-facing arrow.

▶ **3.** Press and hold the mouse button until the drag-and-drop pointer ⬚ appears. A dark black insertion point appears within the selected text.

▶ **4.** Without releasing the mouse button, drag the pointer to the beginning of the list until the insertion point is positioned to the left of the "P" in "Psychology 401: Research Analysis." Use the insertion point, rather than the mouse pointer, to guide the text to its new location. See Figure 2-7.

**Trouble?** If the numbers in the numbered list appear highlighted in gray, you moved the mouse pointer too close to the numbers. Ignore the highlighting and position the insertion point just to the left of the "P" in "Psychology 401: Research Analysis."

**Figure 2-7**    **Moving text with the drag-and-drop pointer**

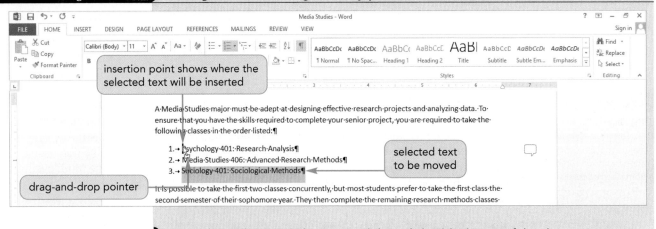

▶ **5.** Release the mouse button, and then click a blank area of the document to deselect the text. The text "Sociology 401: Sociological Methods" is now the first item in the list, and the remaining paragraphs have been renumbered as paragraphs 2 and 3. See Figure 2-8.

**Figure 2-8**    **Text in new location**

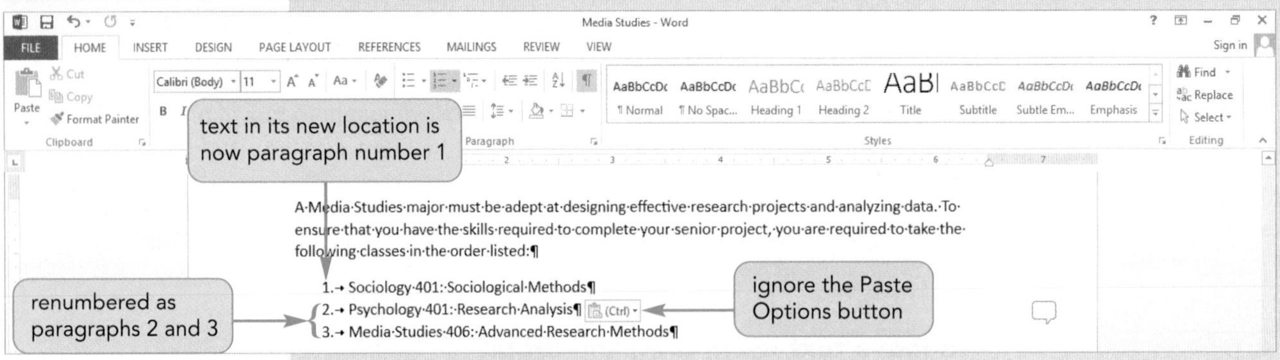

The Paste Options button appears near the newly inserted text, providing access to more advanced options related to pasting text. You don't need to use the Paste Options button right now; it will disappear when you start performing another task.

**Trouble?** If the selected text moves to the wrong location, click the Undo button 🔄 on the Quick Access Toolbar, and then repeat Steps 2 through 5.

▶ **6.** Save the document.

Dragging and dropping works well when you are moving text a short distance. When you are moving text from one page to another, it's easier to cut, copy, and paste text using the Clipboard.

## Cutting or Copying and Pasting Text Using the Clipboard

The **Office Clipboard** is a temporary storage area on your computer that holds objects such as text or graphics until you need them. To **cut** means to remove text or another item from a document and place it on the Clipboard. Once you've cut something, you can paste it somewhere else. To **copy** means to copy a selected item to the Clipboard, leaving the item in its original location. To **paste** means to insert a copy of whatever is on the Clipboard into the document, at the insertion point. When you paste an item from the Clipboard into a document, the item remains on the Clipboard so you can paste it again somewhere else if you want. The buttons for cutting, copying, and pasting are located in the Clipboard group on the HOME tab.

By default, Word pastes text in a new location in a document with the same formatting it had in its old location. To select other ways to paste text, you can use the Paste Options button, which appears next to newly pasted text, or the Paste button arrow in the Clipboard group. Both buttons display a menu of paste options. Two particularly useful paste options are Merge Formatting, which combines the formatting of the copied text with the formatting of the text in the new location, and Keep Text Only, which inserts the text using the formatting of the surrounding text in the new location.

When you need to keep track of multiple pieces of cut or copied text, it's helpful to open the **Clipboard task pane**, which displays the contents of the Clipboard. You open the Clipboard task pane by clicking the Dialog Box Launcher in the Clipboard group on the HOME tab. When the Clipboard task pane is displayed, the Clipboard can store up to 24 text items. When the Clipboard task pane is *not* displayed, the Clipboard can hold only the most recently copied item.

Kaya would like to move the second-to-last sentence under the heading "Majoring in Media Studies" on page 1. You'll use cut and paste to move this sentence to a new location.

**To move text using cut and paste:**

▶ **1.** Make sure the HOME tab is selected on the ribbon.

▶ **2.** Scroll up until you can see the second paragraph in the document, just below the heading "Majoring in Media Studies."

▶ **3.** Press and hold the **Ctrl** key, and then click anywhere in the sentence near the end of the second paragraph, which begins "In the second semester of your senior year...." The entire sentence and the space following it are selected.

4. In the Clipboard group, click the **Cut** button. The selected text is removed from the document and copied to the Clipboard.

5. Scroll down to page 2, and then click at the beginning of the second-to-last paragraph in the document, just to the left of the "T" in "This project should...."

6. In the Clipboard group, click the **Paste** button. The sentence and the space following it are displayed in the new location. The Paste Options button appears near the newly inserted sentence.

   **Trouble?** If a menu opens below the Paste button, you clicked the Paste button arrow instead of the Paste button. Press the Esc key to close the menu, and then repeat Step 6, taking care not to click the arrow below the Paste button.

7. Save the document.

Kaya explains that she'll be using some text from the Media Studies document as the basis for another department handout. She asks you to copy that information and paste it into a new document. You can do this using the Clipboard task pane.

### To copy text to paste into a new document:

1. In the Clipboard group, click the **Dialog Box Launcher**. The Clipboard task pane opens on the left side of the document window, as shown in Figure 2-9.

**Figure 2-9**    **Clipboard task pane**

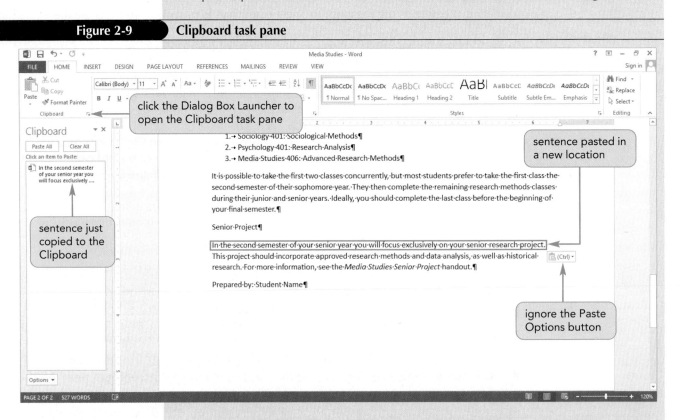

Notice the Clipboard contains the sentence you copied in the last set of steps, although you can only see the first part of the sentence. You'll copy the last two sentences in the current paragraph for use in Kaya's other document.

2. Select the text **This project should incorporate approved research methods and data analysis, as well as historical research. For more information, see the *Media Studies Senior Project* handout.** Do not select the paragraph mark.

3. In the Clipboard group, click the **Copy** button. The first few words of the text appear at the top of the Clipboard task pane, but in fact the entire two sentences are now stored on the Clipboard.

4. Click anywhere in the document to deselect the text, scroll up, if necessary, and then locate the first sentence on page 2.

5. Press and hold the **Ctrl** key, and then click anywhere in the first sentence on page 2, which begins "A Media Studies major must be adept...." The sentence and the space following it are selected.

6. In the Clipboard group, click the **Copy** button. The first part of the sentence appears at the top of the Clipboard task pane, as shown in Figure 2-10.

**Figure 2-10**    Items in the Clipboard task pane

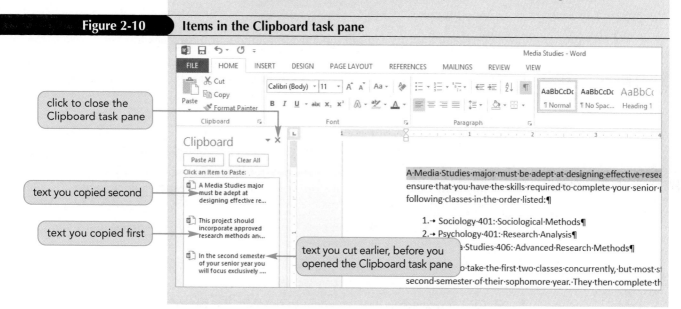

click to close the Clipboard task pane

text you copied second

text you copied first

text you cut earlier, before you opened the Clipboard task pane

Now you can use the Clipboard task pane to insert the copied text into a new document.

### To insert the copied text into a new document:

1. Open a new, blank document. If necessary, open the Clipboard task pane.

2. In the Clipboard task pane, click the second item in the list of copied items, which begins "This project should incorporate...." The text is inserted in the document and the "*Media Studies Senior Project*" title retains its italic formatting.

   Kaya doesn't want to keep the italic formatting in the newly pasted text. You can remove this formatting by using the Paste Options button, which is visible just below the pasted text.

3. Click the **Paste Options** button [ (Ctrl) ] in the document. The Paste Options menu opens, as shown in Figure 2-11.

**Figure 2-11**   **Paste Options menu**

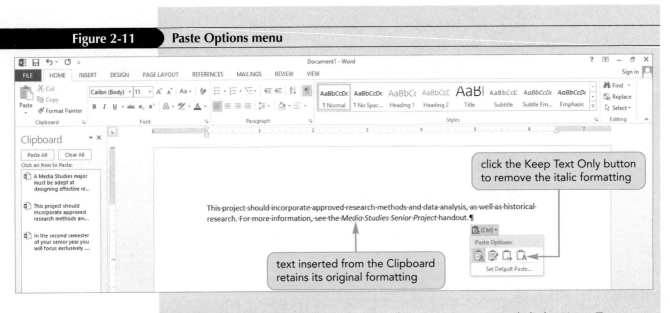

click the Keep Text Only button
to remove the italic formatting

This·project·should·incorporate·approved·research·methods·and·data·analysis,·as·well·as·historical·
research.·For·more·information,·see·the·*Media·Studies·Senior·Project*·handout.¶

text inserted from the Clipboard
retains its original formatting

To paste the text without the italic formatting, you can click the Keep Text Only button.

4. Click the **Keep Text Only** button. Word removes the italic formatting from "Media Studies Senior Project."

5. Press the **Enter** key to start a new paragraph, and then click the first item in the Clipboard task pane, which begins "A Media Studies major must be adept...." The text is inserted as the second paragraph in the document.

6. Save the document as **New Handout** in the location specified by your instructor, and then close it. You return to the Media Studies document, where the Clipboard task pane is still open.

7. In the Clipboard task pane, click the **Clear All** button. The copied items are removed from the Clipboard.

8. In the Clipboard task pane, click the **Close** button. The Clipboard task pane closes.

9. Click anywhere in the document to deselect the paragraph, and then save the document.

# Using the Navigation Pane

The Navigation pane simplifies the process of moving through a document page by page. You can also use the Navigation pane to locate a particular word or phrase. You start by typing the text you're searching for—the **search text**—in the Search box at the top of the Navigation pane. As shown in the Session 2.1 Visual Overview, Word highlights every instance of the search text in the document. At the same time, a list of the **search results** appears in the Navigation pane. You can click a search result to go immediately to that location in the document.

To become familiar with the Navigation pane, you'll use it to navigate through the Media Studies document page by page. You'll start by moving the insertion point to the beginning of the document.

### To navigate through the document page by page:

1. Press the **Ctrl+Home** keys to move the insertion point to the beginning of the document, making sure the HOME tab is still selected on the ribbon.

2. In the Editing group, click the **Find** button. The Navigation pane opens on the left side of the Word window.

   In the Search document box at the top, you can type the text you want to find. The three links below the Search document box—HEADINGS, PAGES, and RESULTS—allow you to navigate through the document in different ways. As you become a more experienced Word user, you'll learn how to use the HEADINGS link; for now, you'll ignore it. To move quickly among the pages of a document, you can use the PAGES link.

3. In the Navigation pane, click the **PAGES** link. The Navigation pane displays thumbnail icons of the document's two pages, as shown in Figure 2-12. You can click a page in the Navigation pane to display that page in the document window.

| Figure 2-12 | Document pages displayed in the Navigation pane |
| --- | --- |

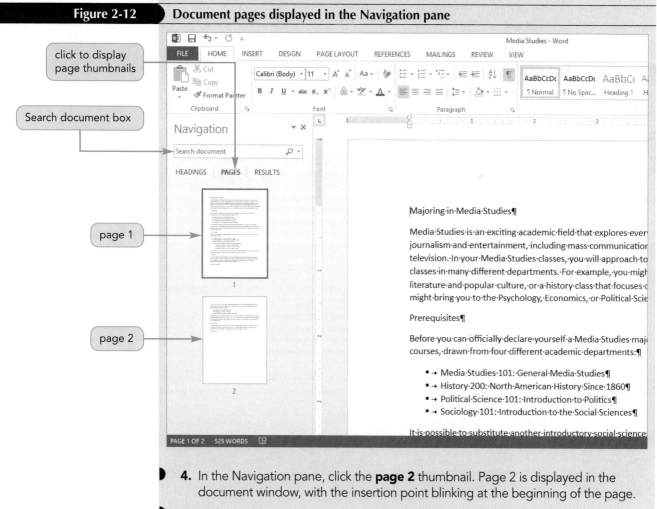

4. In the Navigation pane, click the **page 2** thumbnail. Page 2 is displayed in the document window, with the insertion point blinking at the beginning of the page.

5. In the Navigation pane, click the **page 1** thumbnail to move the insertion point back to the beginning of the document.

Kaya thinks she might have mistakenly used the word "media" when she actually meant to use "journalism" in certain parts of the document. She asks you to use the Navigation pane to find all instances of "media."

### To search for the word "media" in the document:

▶ **1.** In the Navigation pane, click the **RESULTS** link, click the **Search document** box, and then type **media**. You do not have to press the Enter key.

Every instance of the word "media" is highlighted in yellow in the document. The yellow highlight is only temporary; it will disappear as soon as you begin to perform any other task in the document. A full list of the 24 search results is displayed in the Navigation pane. Some of the search results contain the word "Media" (with an uppercase "M") while others contain the word "media" (with a lowercase "m"). To narrow the search results, you need to tell Word to match the case of the search text.

▶ **2.** In the Navigation pane, click the **Search for more things** button ▼. This displays a two-part menu. In the bottom part, you can select other items to search for, such as graphics or tables. The top part provides more advanced search tools. See Figure 2-13.

**Figure 2-13**     **Navigation pane with Search for more things menu**

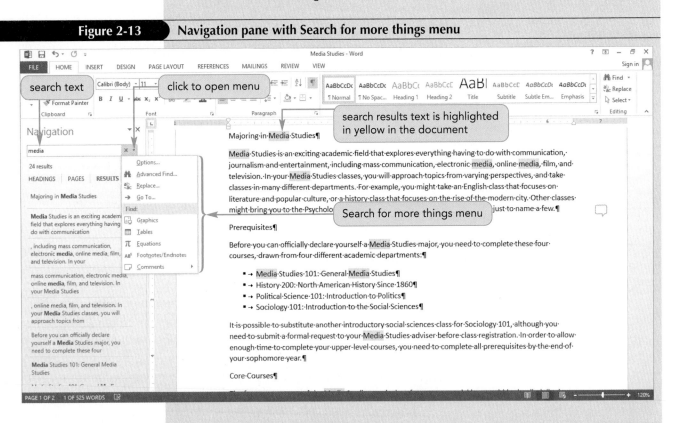

▶ **3.** At the top of the Search for more things menu, click **Options** to open the Find Options dialog box.

The check boxes in this dialog box allow you to fine-tune your search. For example, to ensure that Word finds the search text only when it appears as a separate word, and not when it appears as part of another word, you could select the Find whole words only check box. Right now, you are only concerned with making sure the search results have the same case as the search text.

4. Click the **Match case** check box to select it, and then click the **OK** button to close the Find Options dialog box. Now you can search the document again.

5. Press the **Ctrl+Home** keys to move the insertion point to the beginning of the document, click the **Search document** box in the Navigation pane, and then type **media**. This time, there are only three search results in the Navigation pane, and they all start with a lowercase "m."

To move among the search results, you can use the up and down arrows in the Navigation pane.

6. In the Navigation pane, click the **down arrow** button ⬇. Word selects the first instance of "media" in the Navigation pane, as indicated by a blue outline. Also, in the document, the first instance has a gray selection highlight over the yellow highlight. See Figure 2-14.

**Figure 2-14** **Navigation pane with the first search result selected**

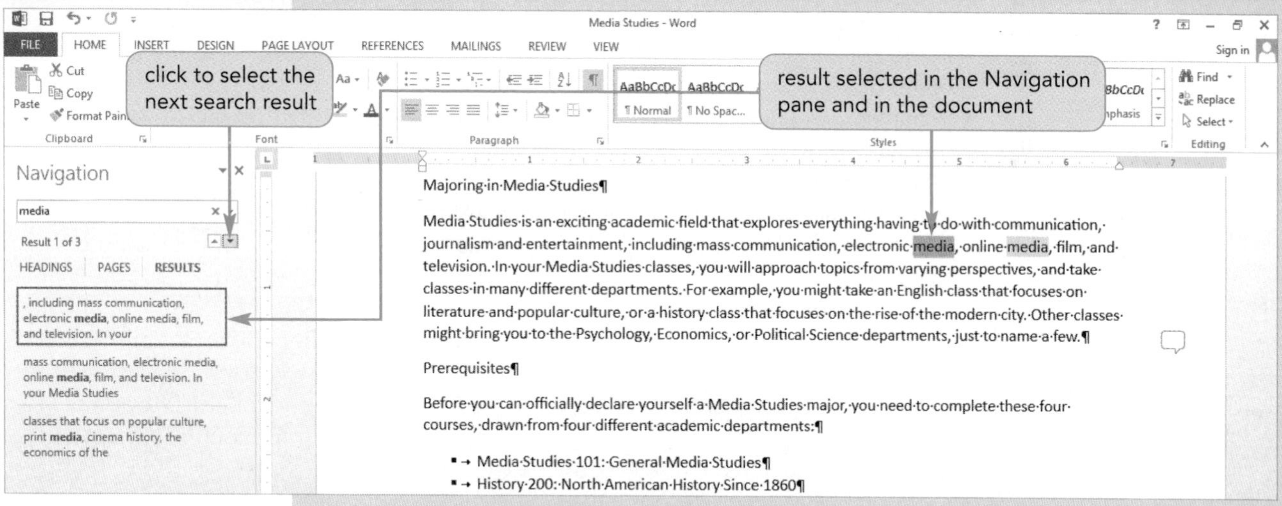

**Trouble?** If the second instance of "media" is selected in the Navigation pane, then you pressed the Enter key after typing "media" in Step 5. Click the up arrow button ⬆ to select the first instance.

7. In the Navigation pane, click the **down arrow** button ⬇. Word selects the second instance of "media" in the document and in the Navigation pane.

8. Click the **down arrow** button ⬇ again to select the third search result, in the paragraph after "Electives," and then click the **up arrow** button ⬆ to select the second search result again.

You can also select a search result in the document by clicking a search result in the Navigation pane.

9. In the Navigation pane, click the third search result, which begins "classes that focus on popular culture...." The third search result is selected in the document and in the Navigation pane.

After reviewing the search results, Kaya decides she would like to replace two of the three instances of "media" with the word "journalism." You can do that by using the Find and Replace dialog box.

# Finding and Replacing Text

To open the Find and Replace dialog box from the Navigation pane, click the Find more things button, and then click Replace. This opens the **Find and Replace dialog box**, with the Replace tab displayed by default. The Replace tab provides options for finding a specific word or phrase in the document and replacing it with another word or phrase. To use the Replace tab, type the search text in the Find what box, and then type the text you want to substitute in the Replace with box. You can also click the More button on the Replace tab to display the Search Options section, which includes the same options you saw earlier in the Find Options dialog box, including the Find whole words only check box and the Match case check box.

After you have typed the search text and selected any search options, you can click the Find Next button to select the first occurrence of the search text; you can then decide whether or not to substitute the search text with the replacement text.

**REFERENCE**

### Finding and Replacing Text

- Press the Ctrl+Home keys to move the insertion point to the beginning of the document.
- In the Editing group on the HOME tab, click the Replace button; or, in the Navigation pane, click the Search for more things button, and then click Replace.
- In the Find and Replace dialog box, click the More button, if necessary, to expand the dialog box and display the Search Options section of the Replace tab.
- In the Find what box, type the search text.
- In the Replace with box, type the replacement text.
- Select the appropriate check boxes in the Search Options section of the dialog box to narrow your search.
- Click the Find Next button.
- Click the Replace button to substitute the found text with the replacement text and find the next occurrence.
- Click the Replace All button to substitute all occurrences of the found text with the replacement text without reviewing each occurrence. Use this option only if you are absolutely certain that the results will be what you expect.

You'll use the Find and Replace dialog box now to replace two instances of "media" with "journalism."

## To replace two instances of "media" with "journalism":

1. Press the **Ctrl+Home** keys to move the insertion point to the beginning of the document.

2. In the Navigation pane, click the **Search for more things** button ▼ to open the menu, and then click **Replace**. The Find and Replace dialog box opens with the Replace tab on top.

   The search text you entered earlier in the Navigation pane, "media," appears in the Find what box. If you hadn't already conducted a search, you would need to type your search text now. Because you selected the Match case check box earlier in the Find Options dialog box, "Match Case" appears below the Find what box.

3. In the lower-left corner of the dialog box, click the **More** button to display the search options. Because you selected the Match case check box earlier in the Find Options dialog box, it is selected here.

   **Trouble?** If you see the Less button instead of the More button, the search options are already displayed.

4. Click the **Replace with** box, and then type **journalism**.

5. Click the **Find Next** button. Word highlights the first instance of "media" in the document. See Figure 2-15.

| Figure 2-15 | Find and Replace dialog box |
| --- | --- |

6. Click the **Replace** button. Word replaces "media" with "journalism," so the text reads "electronic journalism." Then, Word selects the next instance of "media," which happens to be in the same sentence. Kaya does not want to replace this instance, so you can find the next one.

7. Click the **Find Next** button. Word selects the last instance of "media," located in the sentence just before the "Research Methods" heading.

> **8.** Click the **Replace** button. Word makes the substitution, so the text reads "print journalism," and then displays a message box telling you that Word has finished searching the document.
>
> **9.** Click the **OK** button to close the message box, and then in the Find and Replace dialog box, click the **Close** button.

You are finished with the Navigation pane, so you can close it. But first you need to restore the search options to their original settings. It's a good practice to restore the original search settings so that future searches are not affected by any settings that might not apply.

**To restore the search options to their original settings:**

> **1.** In the Navigation pane, open the Find Options dialog box, deselect the Match case check box, and then click the **OK** button to close the Find Options dialog box.
>
> **2.** Click the **Close** button ☒ in the upper-right corner of the Navigation pane.
>
> **3.** Save the document.

**INSIGHT**

### Searching for Formatting

You can search for formatting just as you can search for text. For example, you might want to check a document to look for text formatted in bold and the Arial font. To search for formatting from within the Navigation pane, click the Search for more things button to display the menu, and then click Advanced Find. The Find and Replace dialog box opens with the Find tab displayed. Click the More button, if necessary, to display the Search Options section of the Find tab. Click the Format button at the bottom of the Search Options section, click the category of formatting you want to look for (such as Font or Paragraph), and then select the formatting you want to find.

You can look for formatting that occurs only on specific text, or you can look for formatting that occurs anywhere in a document. If you're looking for text formatted in a certain way (such as all instances of "Media Studies" that are bold), enter the text in the Find what box and then specify the formatting you're looking for. To find formatting on any text in a document, leave the Find what box empty, and then specify the formatting. Use the Find Next button to move through the document, from one instance of the specified formatting to another.

You can follow the same basic steps on the Replace tab to replace one type of formatting with another. First, click the Find what box and select the desired formatting. Then click the Replace with box and select the desired formatting. If you want, type search text and replacement text in the appropriate boxes. Then proceed as with any Find and Replace operation.

Now that the text in the Media Studies document is final, you will turn your attention to styles and themes, which affect the look of the entire document.

# Working with Styles

A style is a set of formatting options that you can apply by clicking an icon in the Style gallery on the HOME tab. Each style is designed for a particular use. For example, the Title style is intended for formatting the title at the beginning of a document.

All the text you type into a document has a style applied to it. By default, text is formatted in the Normal style, which applies 11-point Calibri font, left alignment, 1.08 line spacing, and a small amount of extra space between paragraphs. In other words, the Normal style applies the default formatting you learned about when you first began typing a Word document.

Note that some styles apply **paragraph-level formatting**—that is, they are set up to format an entire paragraph, including the paragraph and line spacing. The Normal, Heading, and Title styles all apply paragraph-level formatting. Other styles apply **character-level formatting**—that is, they are set up to format only individual characters or words (for example, emphasizing a phrase by adding italic formatting and changing the font color).

One row of the Style gallery is always visible on the HOME tab. To display the entire Style gallery, click the More button in the Styles group. After you begin applying styles in a document, the visible row of the Style gallery changes to show the most recently used styles.

You are ready to use the Style gallery to format the document title.

### To display the entire Style gallery and then format the document title with a style:

1. Press the **Ctrl+Home** keys to move the insertion point to the beginning of the document, if necessary.

2. Make sure the HOME tab is still selected and locate the More button in the Styles group, as shown earlier in the Session 2.1 Visual Overview.

3. In the Styles group, click the **More** button. The Style gallery opens, displaying a total of 16 styles arranged in two rows, as shown in Figure 2-16. If your screen is set at a lower resolution than the screenshots in this book, the Style gallery on your screen might contain more than two rows.

**Figure 2-16**   Displaying the Style gallery

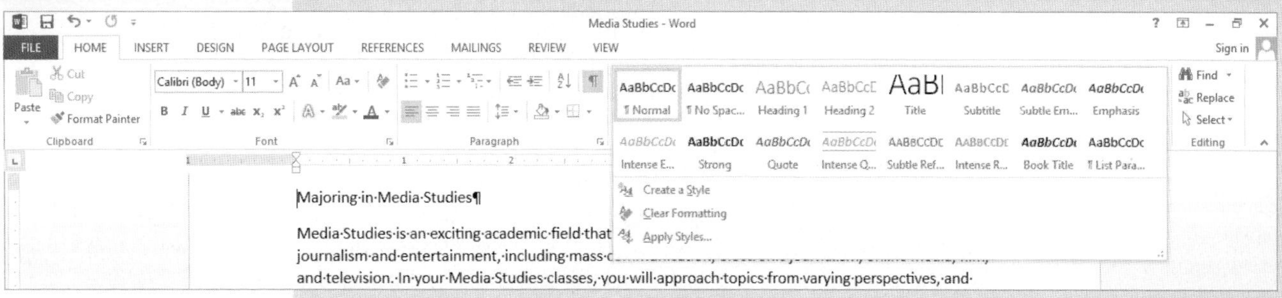

You don't actually need any of the styles in the bottom row now, so you can close the Style gallery.

4. Press the **Esc** key to close the Style gallery.

> **5.** Click anywhere in the first paragraph, "Majoring in Media Studies," and then point to (but don't click) the **Title** style, which is the fifth style from the left in the top row of the gallery. The ScreenTip "Title" is displayed, and a Live Preview of the style appears in the paragraph containing the insertion point, as shown in Figure 2-17. The Title style changes the font to 28-point Calibri Light.

**Figure 2-17**   **Title style in the Style gallery**

Live Preview of the Title style

Majoring·in·Media·Studies¶

Media·Studies·is·an·exciting·academic·field·that·explores·everything·having·to·do·with·communication,·

Title style

> **6.** Click the **Title** style. The style is applied to the paragraph. To finish the title, you need to center it.

> **7.** In the Paragraph group, click the **Center** button ☰. The title is centered in the document.

Next, you will format the document headings using the heading styles, which have different levels. The highest level, Heading 1, is used for the major headings in a document, and it applies the most noticeable formatting with a larger font than the other heading styles. (In heading styles, the highest, or most important, level has the lowest number.) The Heading 2 style is used for headings that are subordinate to the highest level headings; it applies slightly less dramatic formatting than the Heading 1 style.

The Media Studies handout only has one level of headings, so you will only apply the Heading 1 style.

### To format text with the Heading 1 style:

> **1.** Click anywhere in the "Prerequisites" paragraph.

> **2.** On the HOME tab, in the Style gallery, click the **Heading 1** style. The paragraph is now formatted in blue, 16-point Calibri Light. The Heading 1 style also inserts some paragraph space above the heading.

**TIP**

On most computers, you can press the F4 key to repeat your most recent action.

> **3.** Scroll down, click anywhere in the "Core Courses" paragraph, and then click the **Heading 1** style in the Style gallery.

> **4.** Repeat Step 3 to apply the Heading 1 style to the "Electives" paragraph, the "Research Methods" paragraph and the "Senior Project" paragraph. When you are finished, scroll up to the beginning of the document to review the new formatting. See Figure 2-18.

| Figure 2-18 | Document with Title and Heading 1 styles |

Title style → Majoring·in·Media·Studies¶

Media·Studies·is·an·exciting·academic·field·that·explores·everything·having·to·do·with·communication,· journalism·and·entertainment,·including·mass·communication,·electronic·journalism,·online·media,·film,· and·television.·In·your·Media·Studies·classes,·you·will·approach·topics·from·varying·perspectives,·and· take·classes·in·many·different·departments.·For·example,·you·might·take·an·English·class·that·focuses·on· literature·and·popular·culture,·or·a·history·class·that·focuses·on·the·rise·of·the·modern·city.·Other·classes· might·bring·you·to·the·Psychology,·Economics,·or·Political·Science·departments,·just·to·name·a·few.¶

Heading 1 style → Prerequisites¶

Before·you·can·officially·declare·yourself·a·Media·Studies·major,·you·need·to·complete·these·four·

## INSIGHT

### Understanding the Benefits of Heading Styles

By default, the Style gallery offers 16 styles, each designed for a specific purpose. As you gain more experience with Word, you will learn how to use a wider array of styles. You'll also learn how to create your own styles. Styles allow you to change a document's formatting in an instant. But the benefits of heading styles go far beyond attractive formatting. Heading styles allow you to reorganize a document or generate a table of contents with a click of the mouse. Also, the heading styles are set up to keep a heading and the body text that follows it together, so a heading is never separated from its body text by a page break. Each Word document includes nine levels of heading styles, although only the Heading 1 and Heading 2 styles are available by default in the Style gallery. Whenever you use the lowest heading style in the Style gallery, the next-lowest level is added to the Style gallery. For example, after you use the Heading 2 style, the Heading 3 style appears in the Styles group in the Style gallery.

After you format a document with a variety of styles, you can alter the look of the document by changing the document's theme.

## Working with Themes

A **theme** is a coordinated collection of fonts, colors, and other visual effects designed to give a document a cohesive, polished look. A variety of themes are installed with Word, with more available online at Office.com. When you open a new blank document in Word, the Office theme is applied by default. To change a document's theme, you click the Themes button, which is located in the Document Formatting group on the DESIGN tab, and then click the theme you want. Pointing to the Themes button displays a ScreenTip that tells you what theme is currently applied to the document.

When applying color to a document, you usually have the option of selecting a color from a palette of colors designed to match the current theme, or from a palette of standard colors. For instance, recall that the colors in the Font Color gallery are divided into Theme Colors and Standard Colors. When you select a Standard Color, such as Dark Red, that color remains the same no matter which theme you apply to the document. But when you click one of the Theme Colors, you are essentially telling Word to use the color located in that particular spot on the Theme Colors palette. Then, if you change the document's theme later, Word substitutes a color from the same location on the Theme Colors palette. This ensures that all the colors in a document are drawn from a group of colors coordinated to look good together. So as a rule, if you are going to use multiple colors in a document (perhaps for paragraph shading and font color), it's a good idea to stick with the Theme Colors.

A similar substitution takes place with fonts when you change the theme. However, to understand how this works, you need to understand the difference between headings and body text. Kaya's document includes the headings "Prerequisites," "Core Courses," "Electives," "Research Methods," and "Senior Project"—all of which you have formatted with the Heading1 style. The title of the document, "Majoring in Media Studies," is now formatted with the Title style, which is also a type of heading style. Everything else in the Media Studies document is body text.

To ensure that your documents have a harmonious look, each theme assigns a font for headings and a font for body text. Typically, in a given theme, the same font is used for both headings and body text, but not always. In the Office theme, for instance, they are slightly different; the heading font is Calibri Light, and the body font is Calibri. These two fonts appear at the top of the Font list as "Calibri Light (Headings)" and "Calibri (Body)" when you click the Font box arrow in the Font group on the HOME tab. When you begin typing text in a new document with the Office theme, the text is formatted as body text with the Calibri font by default.

When applying a font to selected text, you can choose one of the two theme fonts at the top of the Font list, or you can choose one of the other fonts in the Font list. If you choose one of the other fonts and then change the document theme, that font remains the same. But if you use one of the theme fonts and then change the document theme, Word substitutes the appropriate font from the new theme. When you paste text into a document that has a different theme, Word applies the theme fonts and colors of the new document. To retain the original formatting, use the Keep Source Formatting option in the Paste Options menu.

Figure 2-19 compares elements of the default Office theme with the Integral theme. The Integral theme was chosen for this example because, like the Office theme, its heading and body fonts are different.

Figure 2-19  **Comparing the Office theme to the Integral theme**

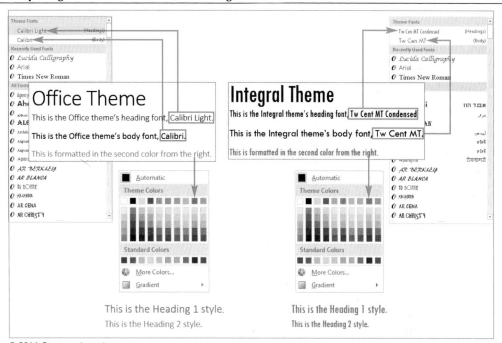

© 2014 Cengage Learning

Each document theme is designed to convey a specific look and feel. The Office theme is designed to be appropriate for standard business documents. Other themes are designed to give documents a flashier look. Because Kaya has not yet selected a new theme, the Office theme is currently applied to the Media Studies document. However, she thinks the Facet theme might be more appropriate for the Media Studies document. She asks you to apply it now.

**To change the document's theme:**

1. If necessary, press the **Ctrl+Home** keys to move the insertion point to the beginning of the document. With the title and first heading visible, you will more easily see what happens when you change the document's theme.

2. On the ribbon, click the **DESIGN** tab.

3. In the Document Formatting group, point to the **Themes** button. A ScreenTip appears containing the text "Current: Office Theme" as well as general information about themes.

4. In the Document Formatting group, click the **Themes** button. The Themes gallery opens. See Figure 2-20.

**Figure 2-20** Themes gallery displayed

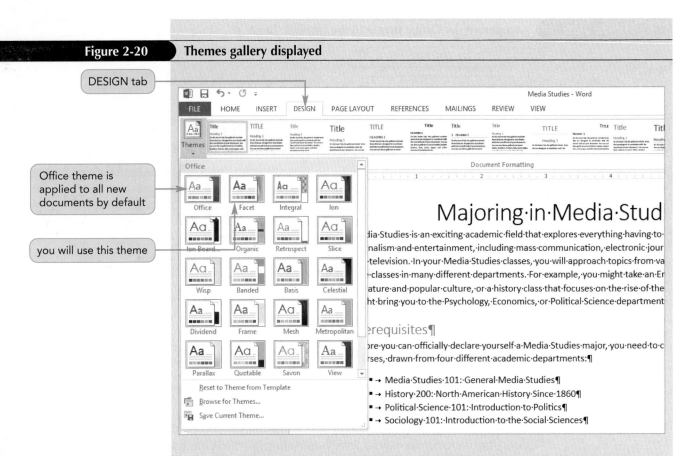

5. Move the mouse pointer (without clicking it) over the various themes in the gallery to see a Live Preview of each theme in the document. The heading and body fonts as well as the heading colors change to reflect the fonts associated with the various themes.

6. In the Themes gallery, click the **Facet** theme. The text in the Media Studies document changes to the body and heading fonts of the Facet theme, with the headings formatted in green. To see exactly what the Facet theme fonts are, you can point to the Fonts button in the Document Formatting group.

7. In the Document Formatting group, point to the **Fonts** button. A ScreenTip appears, listing the currently selected theme (Facet), the heading font (Trebuchet MS), and the body font (Trebuchet MS). See Figure 2-21.

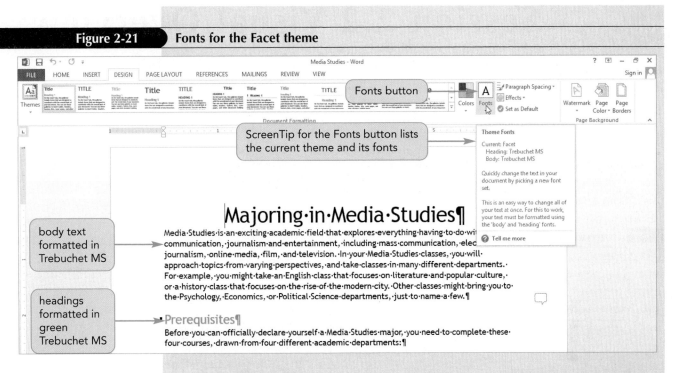

**Figure 2-21** **Fonts for the Facet theme**

**Trouble?** If a menu appears, you clicked the Fonts button instead of pointing to it. Press the Esc key, and then repeat Step 7.

8. Save your changes and then close the document.

Kaya's Media Studies document is ready to be handed in to her supervisor. The use of styles, bulleted and numbered lists, and a new theme gives the document a professional look appropriate for use in a department handout.

## Session 2.1 Quick Check

**REVIEW**

1. Explain how to display comments to the right of the document text in Simple Markup view.
2. What term refers to the process of using the mouse to drag text to a new location?
3. How can you ensure that the Navigation pane will find "ZIP code" instead of "zip code"?
4. What is a style?
5. What style is applied to all text in a new document by default?
6. Explain the relationship between a document's theme and styles.

# Session 2.2 Visual Overview:

Use an easy-to-read font, such as the default Calibri, set to 12 point.

An MLA-style research paper does not require a separate title page; instead, type your name, your instructor's name, the course number, and the date in the upper-left corner of the first page.

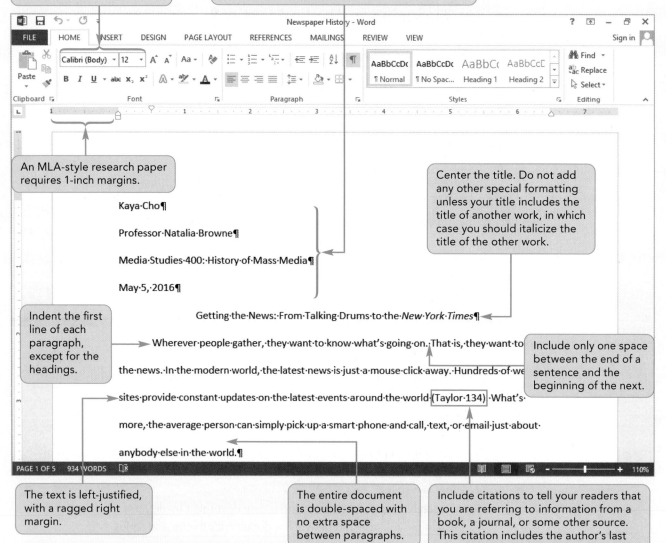

An MLA-style research paper requires 1-inch margins.

Center the title. Do not add any other special formatting unless your title includes the title of another work, in which case you should italicize the title of the other work.

Kaya·Cho¶

Professor·Natalia·Browne¶

Media·Studies·400:·History·of·Mass·Media¶

May·5,·2016¶

Getting·the·News:·From·Talking·Drums·to·the·*New·York·Times*¶

Indent the first line of each paragraph, except for the headings.

Wherever·people·gather,·they·want·to·know·what's·going·on.·That·is,·they·want·to

the·news.·In·the·modern·world,·the·latest·news·is·just·a·mouse·click·away.·Hundreds·of·we

Include only one space between the end of a sentence and the beginning of the next.

sites·provide·constant·updates·on·the·latest·events·around·the·world.·(Taylor·134)·What's·

more,·the·average·person·can·simply·pick·up·a·smart·phone·and·call,·text,·or·email·just·about·

anybody·else·in·the·world.¶

PAGE 1 OF 5    934 WORDS

The text is left-justified, with a ragged right margin.

The entire document is double-spaced with no extra space between paragraphs.

Include citations to tell your readers that you are referring to information from a book, a journal, or some other source. This citation includes the author's last name and the page number.

# MLA Formatting Guidelines

The REFERENCES tab includes options that help you create a research paper.

In the Style box, specify the style of research paper you are creating. For college research papers, the MLA style is commonly used.

After you create all the citations, click the Bibliography button to create a list of all the sources mentioned in your citations. This list is known as a **bibliography** or, in the MLA style, a **works cited list**.

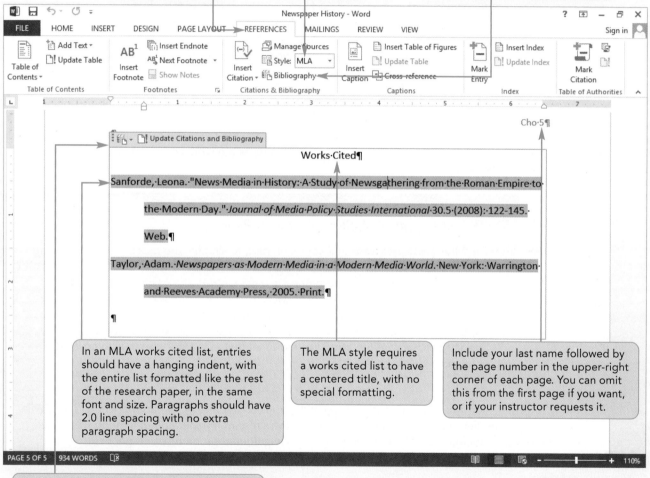

In an MLA works cited list, entries should have a hanging indent, with the entire list formatted like the rest of the research paper, in the same font and size. Paragraphs should have 2.0 line spacing with no extra paragraph spacing.

The MLA style requires a works cited list to have a centered title, with no special formatting.

Include your last name followed by the page number in the upper-right corner of each page. You can omit this from the first page if you want, or if your instructor requests it.

Word inserts a bibliography, or works cited list, contained in a special feature, known as a **content control**, used to display information that is inserted automatically and that may need to be updated later. You can use the buttons in the content control tab to make changes to material inside the content control.

# Reviewing the MLA Style

A **style guide** is a set of rules that describe the preferred format and style for a certain type of writing. People in different fields use different style guides, with each style guide designed to suit the needs of a specific discipline. For example, journalists commonly use the *Associated Press Stylebook*, which focuses on the concise writing style common in magazines and newspapers. In the world of academics, style guides emphasize the proper way to create **citations**, which are formal references to the work of others. Researchers in the social and behavioral sciences use the **American Psychological Association (APA) style**, which is designed to help readers scan an article quickly for key points and emphasizes the date of publication in citations. Other scientific and technical fields have their own specialized style guides.

In the humanities, the **Modern Language Association (MLA) style** is widely used. This is the style Kaya has used for her research paper. She followed the guidelines specified in the *MLA Handbook for Writers of Research Papers*, published by the Modern Language Association of America. These guidelines focus on specifications for formatting a research document and citing the sources used in research conducted for a paper. The major formatting features of an MLA-style research paper are illustrated in the Session 2.2 Visual Overview. Compared to style guides for technical fields, the MLA style is very flexible, making it easy to include citations without disrupting the natural flow of the writing. MLA-style citations of other writers' works take the form of a brief parenthetical entry, with a complete reference to each item included in the alphabetized bibliography, also known as the works cited list, at the end of the research paper.

**INSIGHT**

### Formatting an MLA-Style Research Paper

The MLA guidelines were developed, in part, to simplify the process of transforming a manuscript into a journal article or a chapter of a book. The style calls for minimal formatting; the simpler the formatting in a manuscript, the easier it is to turn the text into a published document. The MLA guidelines were also designed to ensure consistency in documents, so that all research papers look alike. Therefore, you should apply no special formatting to the text in an MLA-style research paper. Headings should be formatted like the other text in the document, with no bold or heading styles.

Kaya has started writing a research paper on the history of newspapers for her Media Studies class. You'll open the draft of Kaya's research paper and determine what needs to be done to make it meet the MLA style guidelines for a research paper.

### To open the document and review it for MLA style:

▶ 1. Open the document named **Newspaper** located in the Word2 ▶ Tutorial folder included with your Data Files, and then save the document as **Newspaper History** in the location specified by your instructor.

▶ 2. Verify that the document is displayed in Print Layout view, and that the rulers and nonprinting characters are displayed. Make sure the Zoom level is set to **120%**.

3. Review the document to familiarize yourself with its structure. First, notice the parts of the document that already match the MLA style. Kaya included a block of information in the upper-left corner of the first page, giving her name, her instructor's name, the course name, and the date. The title at the top of the first page also meets the MLA guidelines in that it is centered and does not have any special formatting except for "*New York Times*," which is italicized because it is the name of a newspaper. The headings ("Early News Media," "Merchant Newsletters," "Modern American Newspapers," and "Looking to the Future") have no special formatting; but unlike the title, they are left-aligned. Finally, the body text is left-aligned with a ragged right margin, and the entire document is formatted in the same font, Calibri, which is easy to read.

What needs to be changed in order to make Kaya's paper consistent with the MLA style? Currently, the entire document is formatted using the default settings, which are the Normal style for the Office theme. To transform the document into an MLA-style research paper, you need to complete the checklist shown in Figure 2-22.

| **Figure 2-22** | Checklist for formatting a default Word document to match the MLA style |
| --- | --- |

✓ Double-space the entire document.

✓ Remove paragraph spacing from the entire document.

✓ Increase the font size for the entire document to 12 points.

✓ Indent the first line of each body paragraph .5 inch from the left margin.

✓ Add the page number (preceded by your last name) in the upper-right corner of each page. If you prefer, you can omit this from the first page.

© 2014 Cengage Learning

You'll take care of the first three items in the checklist now.

### To begin applying MLA formatting to the document:

1. Press the **Ctrl+A** keys to select the entire document.

2. Make sure the HOME tab is selected on the ribbon.

3. In the Paragraph group, click the **Line and Paragraph Spacing** button ⌷▾, and then click **2.0**.

4. Click the **Line and Spacing** button ⌷▾ again, and then click **Remove Space After Paragraph**. The entire document is now double-spaced, with no paragraph spacing, and the entire document is still selected.

5. In the Font group, click the **Font Size** arrow, and then click **12**. The entire document is formatted in 12-point font.

6. Click anywhere in the document to deselect the text.

7. In the first paragraph of the document, replace Kaya's name with your first and last name, and then save the document.

Now you need to indent the first line of each body paragraph.

# Indenting a Paragraph

Word offers a number of options for indenting a paragraph. You can move an entire paragraph to the right, or you can create specialized indents, such as a **hanging indent**, where all lines except the first line of the paragraph are indented from the left margin. As you saw in the Session 2.2 Visual Overview, all the body paragraphs (that is, all the paragraphs except the information in the upper-left corner of the first page, the title, and the headings) have a first-line indent in MLA research papers. Figure 2-23 shows some examples of other common paragraph indents.

**Figure 2-23**    **Common paragraph indents**

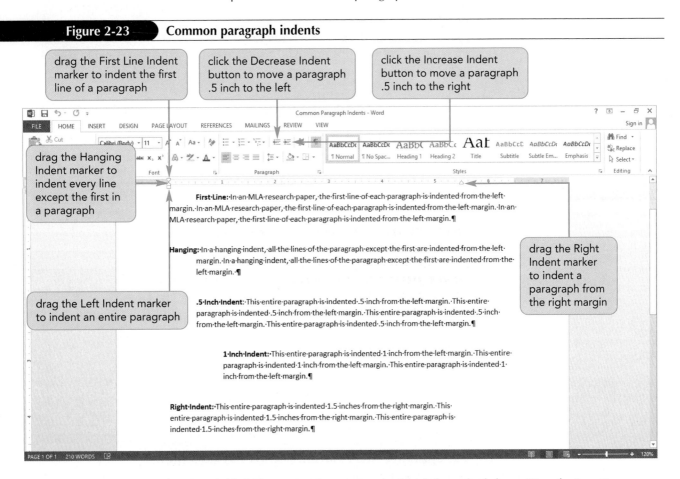

To quickly indent an entire paragraph .5 inch from the left, position the insertion point in the paragraph you want to indent and then click the Increase Indent button in the Paragraph group on the HOME tab. You can continue to indent the paragraph in increments of .5 inch by repeatedly clicking the Increase Indent button. To move an indented paragraph back to the left .5 inch, click the Decrease Indent button.

To create first line, hanging, or right indents, you can use the indent markers on the ruler. First, click in the paragraph you want to indent, or select multiple paragraphs. Then drag the appropriate indent marker to the left or right on the horizontal ruler. The indent markers are small and can be hard to see. As shown in Figure 2-23, the **First Line Indent marker** looks like the top half of an hourglass; the **Hanging Indent marker** looks like the bottom half. The rectangle below the Hanging Indent marker is the **Left Indent marker**. The **Right Indent Marker** looks just like the Hanging Indent marker except that it is located on the far-right side of the horizontal ruler.

Note that when you indent an entire paragraph using the Increase Indent button, the three indent markers, shown stacked on top of one another in Figure 2-23, move as a unit along with the paragraphs you are indenting.

In Kaya's paper, you will indent the first lines of the body paragraphs .5 inch from the left margin, as specified by the MLA style.

## To indent the first line of each paragraph:

1. On the first page of the document, just below the title, click anywhere in the first main paragraph, which begins "Wherever people gather...."

2. On the horizontal ruler, position the mouse pointer over the First Line Indent marker ▽. When you see the ScreenTip that reads "First Line Indent," you know the mouse is positioned correctly.

3. Press and hold the mouse button as you drag the **First Line Indent** marker ▽ to the right, to the .5-inch mark on the horizontal ruler. As you drag, a vertical guide line appears over the document, and the first line of the paragraph moves right. See Figure 2-24.

| Figure 2-24 | Dragging the First Line Indent marker |

First Line Indent marker

.5-inch mark

as you drag the indent marker, a guide line appears and the first line of the paragraph moves right

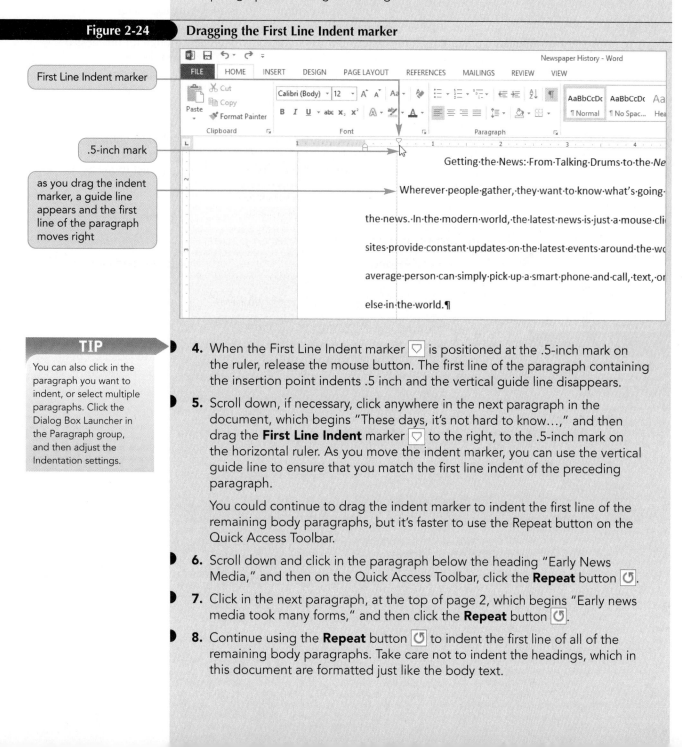

4. When the First Line Indent marker ▽ is positioned at the .5-inch mark on the ruler, release the mouse button. The first line of the paragraph containing the insertion point indents .5 inch and the vertical guide line disappears.

5. Scroll down, if necessary, click anywhere in the next paragraph in the document, which begins "These days, it's not hard to know...," and then drag the **First Line Indent** marker ▽ to the right, to the .5-inch mark on the horizontal ruler. As you move the indent marker, you can use the vertical guide line to ensure that you match the first line indent of the preceding paragraph.

    You could continue to drag the indent marker to indent the first line of the remaining body paragraphs, but it's faster to use the Repeat button on the Quick Access Toolbar.

6. Scroll down and click in the paragraph below the heading "Early News Media," and then on the Quick Access Toolbar, click the **Repeat** button ↻.

7. Click in the next paragraph, at the top of page 2, which begins "Early news media took many forms," and then click the **Repeat** button ↻.

8. Continue using the **Repeat** button ↻ to indent the first line of all of the remaining body paragraphs. Take care not to indent the headings, which in this document are formatted just like the body text.

▶ **9.** Scroll to the top of the document, verify that you have correctly indented the first line of each body paragraph, and then save the document.

Next, you need to insert page numbers.

# Inserting and Modifying Page Numbers

When you insert page numbers in a document, you don't have to type a page number on each page. Instead, you insert a **page number field**, which is an instruction that tells Word to insert a page number on each page, no matter how many pages you eventually add to the document. Word inserts page number fields above the top margin, in the blank area known as the **header**, or below the bottom margin, in the area known as the **footer**. You can also insert page numbers in the side margins, although for business or academic documents, it's customary to place them in the header or footer.

After you insert a page number field, Word switches to Header and Footer view. In this view, you can add your name or other text next to the page number field, or use the HEADER & FOOTER TOOLS DESIGN tab to change various settings related to headers and footers.

The MLA style requires a page number preceded by the student's last name in the upper-right corner of each page. If you prefer (or if your instructor requests it), you can omit the page number from the first page by selecting the Different First Page check box on the DESIGN tab.

## To add page numbers to the research paper:

▶ **1.** Press the **Ctrl+Home** keys to move the insertion point to the beginning of the document.

▶ **2.** On the ribbon, click the **INSERT** tab. The ribbon changes to display the Insert options, including options for inserting page numbers.

▶ **3.** In the Header & Footer group, click the **Page Number** button to open the Page Number menu. Here you can choose where you want to position the page numbers in your document—at the top of the page, at the bottom of the page, in the side margins, or at the current location of the insertion point.

▶ **4.** Point to **Top of Page**. A gallery of page number styles opens. You can scroll the list to review the many styles of page numbers. Because the MLA style calls for a simple page number in the upper-right corner, you will use the Plain Number 3 style. See Figure 2-25.

**TIP**

To remove page numbers from a document, click the Remove Page Numbers command on the Page Number menu.

**Figure 2-25**    **Gallery of page number styles**

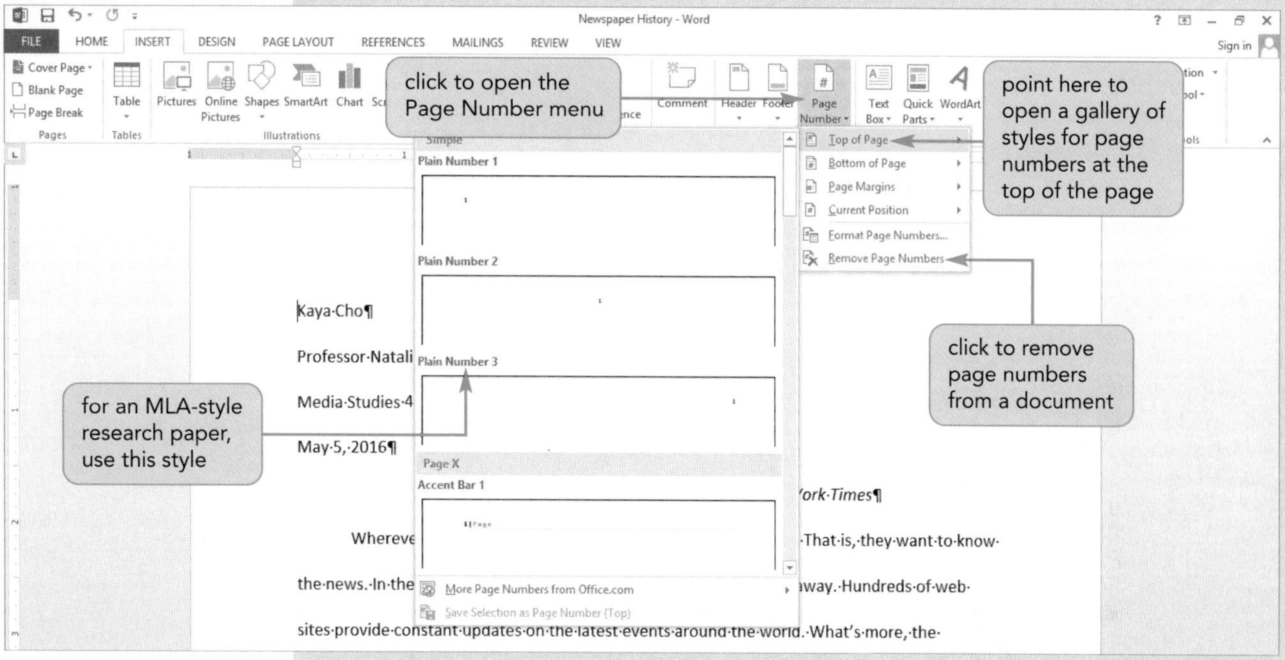

5. In the gallery, click the **Plain Number 3** style. The Word window switches to Header and Footer view, with the page number for the first page in the upper-right corner. The page number has a gray background, indicating that it is actually a page number field and not simply a number that you typed.

The HEADER & FOOTER TOOLS DESIGN tab is displayed on the ribbon, giving you access to a variety of formatting options. The insertion point blinks to the left of the page number field, ready for you to add text to the header if you wish. Note that in Header and Footer view, you can only type in the header or footer areas. The text in the main document area is a lighter shade of gray, indicating that it cannot be edited in this view.

6. Type your last name, and then press the **spacebar**. If you see a wavy red line below your last name, right-click your name, and then click **Ignore** on the Shortcut menu. See Figure 2-26.

**Figure 2-26** Last name inserted next to the page number field

- when selected, this check box removes the page number field and your last name from the first page
- your last name appears here
- Cho·1¶
- page number field
- text in the main document is light gray, indicating that it is not available for editing

Header

Kaya·Cho¶

Professor·Natalia·Browne¶

Media·Studies·400:·History·of·Mass·Media¶

May·5,·2016¶

Getting·the·News:·From·Talking·Drums·to·the·*New·York·Times*¶

Wherever·people·gather,·they·want·to·know·what's·going·on.·That·is,·they·want·to·know· the·news.·In·the·modern·world,·the·latest·news·is·just·a·mouse·click·away.·Hundreds·of·web-

---

7. Scroll down and observe the page number (with your last name) at the top of pages 2, 3, and 4. As you can see, whatever you insert in the header on one page appears on every page of the document by default.

8. Press the **Ctrl+Home** keys to return to the header on the first page.

9. On the HEADER & FOOTER TOOLS DESIGN tab, in the Options group, click the **Different First Page** check box to insert a check. The page number field and your last name are removed from the first page header. The insertion point blinks at the header's left margin in case you want to insert something else for the first page header. In this case, you don't.

10. In the Close group, click the **Close Header and Footer** button. You return to Print Layout view, and the HEADER & FOOTER TOOLS DESIGN tab is no longer displayed on the ribbon.

11. Scroll down to review your last name and the page number in the headers for pages 2, 3, and 4. In Print Layout view, the text in the header is light gray, indicating that it is not currently available for editing.

**TIP**

After you insert page numbers, you can reopen Header and Footer view by double-clicking a page number in Print Layout view.

You have finished all the tasks related to formatting the MLA-style research paper. Now Kaya wants your help with creating the essential parts of any research paper—the citations and the bibliography.

# Creating Citations and a Bibliography

A bibliography (or, as it is called in the MLA style, the works cited list) is an alphabetical list of all the books, magazine articles, websites, movies, and other works referred to in a research paper. The items listed in a bibliography are known as **sources**. The entry for each source includes information such as the author, the title of the work, the publication date, and the publisher.

Within the research paper itself, you include a parenthetical reference, or citation, every time you quote or refer to a source. Every source included in your citations then has a corresponding entry in the works cited list. A citation should include enough information to identify the quote or referenced material so the reader can easily locate the source in the accompanying works cited list. The exact form for a citation varies depending on the style guide you are using and the type of material you are referencing.

Some style guides are very rigid about the form and location of citations, but the MLA style offers quite a bit of flexibility. Typically, though, you insert an MLA citation at the end of a sentence in which you quote or refer to material from a source. For books or journals, the citation itself usually includes the author's last name and a page number. However, if the sentence containing the citation already includes the author's name, you only need to include the page number in the citation. Figure 2-27 provides some sample MLA citations for books and journals. For detailed guidelines, you can consult the *MLA Handbook for Writers of Research Papers, Seventh Edition,* which includes many examples.

| Figure 2-27 | MLA guidelines for citing a book or journal |

| Citation Rule | Example |
| --- | --- |
| If the sentence includes the author's name, the citation should only include the page number. | Peterson compares the opening scene of the movie to a scene from Shakespeare (188). |
| If the sentence does not include the author's name, the citation should include the author's name and the page number. | The opening scene of the movie has been compared to a scene from Shakespeare (Peterson 188). |

© 2014 Cengage Learning

Word greatly simplifies the process of creating citations and a bibliography. You specify the style you want to use, and then Word takes care of setting up the citation and the works cited list appropriately. Every time you create a citation for a new source, Word prompts you to enter the information needed to create the corresponding entry in the works cited list. If you don't have all of your source information available, Word also allows you to insert a temporary, placeholder citation, which you can replace later with a complete citation. When you are finished creating your citations, Word generates the bibliography automatically. Note that placeholder citations are not included in the bibliography.

PROSKILLS

*Written Communication: Acknowledging Your Sources*

A research paper is a means for you to explore the available information about a subject and then present this information, along with your own understanding of the subject, in an organized and interesting way. Acknowledging all the sources of the information presented in your research paper is essential. If you fail to do this, you might be subject to charges of plagiarism, or trying to pass off someone else's thoughts as your own. Plagiarism is an extremely serious accusation for which you could suffer academic consequences ranging from failing an assignment to being expelled from school.

To ensure that you don't forget to cite a source, you should be careful about creating citations in your document as you type. It's very easy to forget to go back and cite all your sources correctly after you've finished typing a research paper. Failing to cite a source could lead to accusations of plagiarism and all the consequences that entails. If you don't have the complete information about a source, you should at least insert a placeholder citation. But take care to go back later and substitute complete citations for any placeholders.

## Creating Citations

Before you create citations, you need to select the style you want to use, which in the case of Kaya's paper is the MLA style. Then, to insert a citation, you click the Insert Citation button in the Citations & Bibliography group on the REFERENCES tab. If you are citing a source for the first time, Word prompts you to enter all the information required for the source's entry in the bibliography or works cited list. If you are citing an existing source, you simply select the source from the Insert Citation menu.

By default, an MLA citation includes only the author's name in parentheses. However, you can use the Edit Citation dialog box to add a page number. You can also use the Edit Citation dialog box to remove, or suppress, the author's name, so only the page number appears in the citation. However, in an MLA citation, Word will replace the suppressed author name with the title of the source, so you need to suppress the title as well, by selecting the Title check box in the Edit Citation dialog box.

**REFERENCE**

*Creating Citations*

- On the ribbon, click the REFERENCES tab. In the Citations & Bibliography group, click the Style button arrow, and then select the style you want.
- Click in the document where you want to insert the citation. Typically, a citation goes at the end of a sentence, before the ending punctuation.
- To add a citation for a new source, click the Insert Citation button in the Citations & Bibliography group, click Add New Source, enter information in the Create Source dialog box, and then click the OK button.
- To add a citation for an existing source, click the Insert Citation button, and then click the source.
- To add a placeholder citation, click the Insert Citation button, click Add New Placeholder, and then, in the content control, type placeholder text, such as the author's last name, that will serve as a reminder about which source you need to cite. Note that a placeholder citation cannot contain any spaces.
- To add a page number to a citation, click the citation in the document, click the Citation Options button, click Edit Citation, type the page number, and then click the OK button.
- To display only the page number in a citation, click the citation in the document, click the Citation Options button, and then click Edit Citation. In the Edit Citation dialog box, select the Author and Title check boxes to suppress this information, and then click the OK button.

So far, Kaya has referenced information from two different sources in her research paper. You'll select a style and then begin adding the appropriate citations.

**To select a style for the citation and bibliography:**

1. On the ribbon, click the **REFERENCES** tab. The ribbon changes to display references options.

2. In the Citations & Bibliography group, click the **Style button arrow**, and then click **MLA Seventh Edition** if it is not already selected.

3. Press the **Ctrl+F** keys to open the Navigation pane.

4. Use the Navigation pane to find the phrase "As at least one historian has observed," which appears on page 1, and then click in the document at the end of that sentence (between the end of the word "medium" and the closing period).

5. Close the Navigation pane, and then click the **REFERENCES** tab on the ribbon, if necessary. You need to add a citation that informs the reader that historian Adam Taylor made the observation described in the sentence. See Figure 2-28.

**Figure 2-28**    MLA style selected and insertion point positioned for new citation

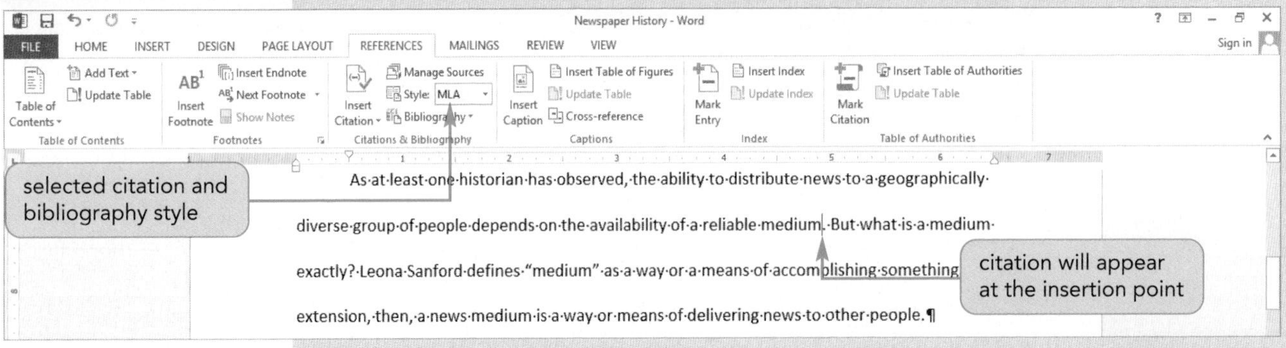

selected citation and bibliography style

As·at·least·one·historian·has·observed,·the·ability·to·distribute·news·to·a·geographically·

diverse·group·of·people·depends·on·the·availability·of·a·reliable·medium. But·what·is·a·medium·

exactly?·Leona·Sanford·defines·"medium"·as·a·way·or·a·means·of·accomplishing·something

citation will appear at the insertion point

extension,·then,·a·news·medium·is·a·way·or·means·of·delivering·news·to·other·people.¶

6. In the Citations & Bibliography group, click the **Insert Citation** button to open the menu. At this point, you could click Add New Placeholder on the menu to insert a temporary, placeholder citation. However, because you have all the necessary source information, you can go ahead and create a complete citation.

7. On the menu, click **Add New Source**. The Create Source dialog box opens, ready for you to add the information required to create a bibliography entry for Adam Taylor's book.

8. If necessary, click the **Type of Source** arrow, scroll up or down in the list, and then click **Book**.

**TIP**

When entering information in a dialog box, you can press the Tab key to move the insertion point from one box to another.

9. In the Author box, type **Adam Taylor**.

10. Click in the **Title** box, and then type **Newspapers as Modern Media in a Modern Media World**.

11. Click in the **Year** box, and then type **2005**. This is the year the book was published. Next, you need to enter the name and location of the publisher.

12. Click the **City** box, type **New York**, click the **Publisher** box, and then type **Warrington and Reeves Academy Press**.

Finally, you need to indicate the medium used to publish the book. In this case, Kaya used a printed copy, so the medium is "Print." For books or journals published online, the correct medium would be "Web."

13. Click the **Medium** box, and then type **Print**. See Figure 2-29.

**Figure 2-29**    Create Source dialog box with information for the first source

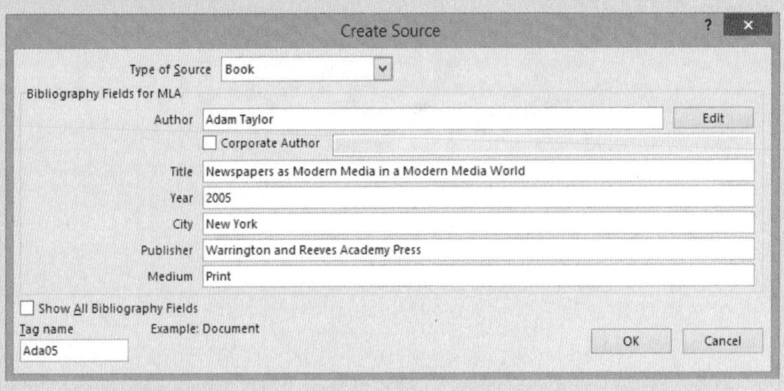

**14.** Click the **OK** button. Word inserts the parenthetical "(Taylor)" at the end of the sentence in the document.

Although the citation looks like ordinary text, it is actually contained inside a content control, a special feature used to display information that is inserted automatically and that may need to be updated later. You can only see the content control itself when it is selected. When it is unselected, you simply see the citation. In the next set of steps, you will select the content control, and then edit the citation to add a page number.

### To edit the citation:

**TIP**

To delete a citation, click the citation to display the content control, click the tab on the left side of the content control, and then press the Delete key.

**1.** In the document, click the citation **(Taylor)**. The citation appears in a content control, which is a box with a tab on the left and an arrow button on the right. The arrow button is called the Citation Options button.

**2.** Click the **Citation Options** button ⬚. A menu of options related to editing a citation opens, as shown in Figure 2-30. To edit the information about the source, you click Edit Source. To change the information that is displayed in the citation itself, you use the Edit Citation option.

| Figure 2-30 | Citation Options menu |
|---|---|

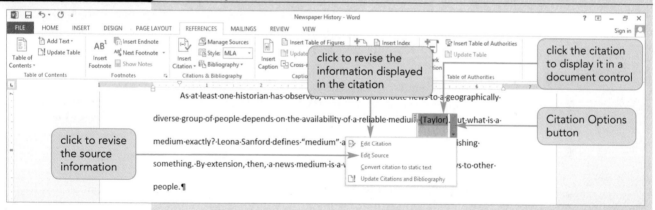

| Figure 2-31 | Edit Citation dialog box |
|---|---|

**3.** On the Citation Options menu, click **Edit Citation**. The Edit Citation dialog box opens, as shown in Figure 2-31.

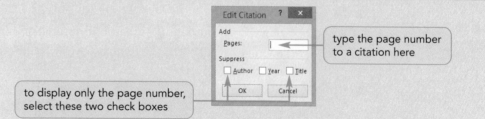

To add a page number for the citation, you type the page number in the Pages box. If you want to display only the page number in the citation (which would be necessary if you already mentioned the author's name in the same sentence in the text), then you would also select the Author and Title check boxes in this dialog box to suppress this information.

  ▶   **4.** Type **45** to insert the page number in the Pages box, click the **OK** button to close the dialog box, and then click anywhere in the document outside the citation content control. The revised citation now reads "(Taylor 45)."

Next, you will add two more citations, both for the same journal article.

### To insert two more citations:

  ▶   **1.** Click at the end of the second-to-last sentence of the current paragraph (which begins "Leona Sanford defines…"), between the word "something" and the period. This sentence mentions historian Leona Sanford; you need to add a citation to one of her journal articles.

  ▶   **2.** In the Citations & Bibliography group, click the **Insert Citation** button to open the Insert Citation menu. Notice that Adam Taylor's book is now listed as a source on this menu. You could click Taylor's book on the menu to add a citation to it, but right now you need to add a new source.

  ▶   **3.** Click **Add New Source** to open the Create Source dialog box, click the **Type of Source** arrow, and then click **Journal Article**.

The Create Source dialog box displays the boxes, or fields, appropriate for a journal article. The information required to cite a journal article differs from the information you entered earlier for the citation for the Taylor book. For journal articles, you are prompted to enter the page numbers for the entire article. If you want to display a particular page number in the citation, you can add it later.

By default, Word displays boxes, or fields, for the information most commonly included in a bibliography. In this case, you also want to include the volume and issue numbers for Leona Sanford's article, so you need to display more fields.

  ▶   **4.** In the Create Source dialog box, click the **Show All Bibliography Fields** check box to select this option. The Create Source dialog box expands to allow you to enter more detailed information. Red asterisks highlight the fields that are recommended, but these recommended fields don't necessarily apply to every source.

  ▶   **5.** Enter the following information, scrolling down to display the necessary boxes:

Author: **Leona Sanford**

Title: **News Media in History: A Study of Newsgathering from the Roman Empire to the Modern Day**

Journal Name: **Journal of Media Policy Studies International**

Year: **2008**

Pages: **122–145**

Volume: **30**

Issue: **5**

Medium: **Web**

When you are finished, your Create Source dialog box should look like the one shown in Figure 2-32.

**Figure 2-32**    Create Source dialog box with information for the journal article

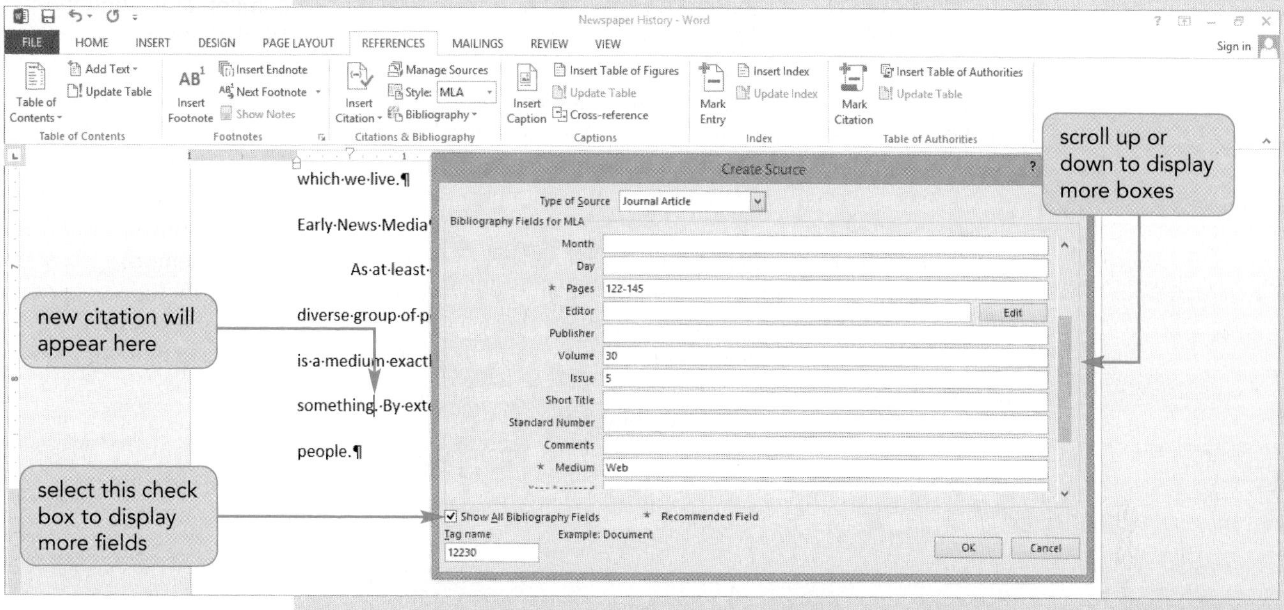

new citation will appear here

select this check box to display more fields

scroll up or down to display more boxes

6. Click the **OK** button. The Create Source dialog box closes, and the citation "(Sanford)" is inserted in the text. Because the sentence containing the citation already includes the author's name, you will edit the citation to include the page number and suppress the author's name.

7. Click the **(Sanford)** citation to display the content control, click the **Citation Options** button , and then click **Edit Citation** to open the Edit Citation dialog box.

8. In the Pages box, type **142**, and then click the **Author** and **Title** check boxes to select them. You need to suppress both the author's name and the title because otherwise Word will replace the suppressed author name with the title. When using the MLA style, you don't ever have to suppress the year because the year is never included as part of an MLA citation. When working in other styles, however, you might need to suppress the year.

9. Click the **OK** button to close the Edit Citation dialog box, and then click anywhere outside the content control to deselect it. The end of the sentence now reads "...accomplishing something (142)."

10. Use the Navigation pane to find the sentence that begins "Throughout history..." on the second page. Click at the end of the sentence, to the left of the period after "news," and then close the Navigation pane.

11. On the REFERENCES tab, in the Citations & Bibliography group, click the **Insert Citation** button, and then click the **Sanford, Leona** source at the top of the menu. You want the citation to refer to the entire article instead of just one page, so you will not edit the citation to add a specific page number.

12. Save the document.

You have entered the source information for two sources.

## Generating a Bibliography

Once you have created a citation for a source in a document, you can generate a bibliography. When you do, Word scans all the citations in the document, collecting the source information for each citation, and then it creates a list of information for each unique source. The format of the entries in the bibliography will reflect the style you specified when you created your first citation, which in this case is the MLA style. The bibliography itself is a **field**, similar to the page number field you inserted earlier in this session. In other words, it is really an instruction that tells Word to display the source information for all the citations in the document. Because it is a field and not actual text, you can update the bibliography later to reflect any new citations you might add.

You can choose to insert a bibliography as a field directly in the document, or you can insert a bibliography enclosed within a content control that also includes the heading "Bibliography" or "Works Cited." Inserting a bibliography enclosed in a content control is best because the content control includes a useful button that you can use to update your bibliography if you make changes to the sources.

In the MLA style, the bibliography (or works cited list) starts on a new page. So your first step is to insert a manual page break. A **manual page break** is one you insert at a specific location; it doesn't matter if the previous page is full or not. To insert a manual page break, use the Page Break button in the Pages group on the INSERT tab.

### To insert a manual page break:

1. Press the **Ctrl+End** keys to move the insertion point to the end of the document.

2. On the ribbon, click the **INSERT** tab.

**TIP**

Use the Blank Page button to insert a new, blank page in the middle of a document.

3. In the Pages group, click the **Page Break** button. Word inserts a new, blank page at the end of the document, with the insertion point blinking at the top. Note that you could also use the Ctrl+Enter keyboard shortcut to insert a manual page break.

4. Scroll up to see the dotted line with the words "Page Break" at the bottom of the text on page 4. See Figure 2-33.

**Figure 2-33**     **Manual page break inserted into the document**

this type of arrangement will allow newspapers to thrive, or if the current trend of newspaper closures will continue.¶

page break → ⸻Page Break⸻ ¶

Now you can insert the bibliography on the new page 5.

## To insert the bibliography:

1. Scroll down so you can see the insertion point at the top of page 5.

2. On the ribbon, click the **REFERENCES** tab.

3. In the Citations & Bibliography group, click the **Bibliography** button. The Bibliography menu opens, displaying three styles with preformatted headings—"Bibliography," "References," and "Works Cited." The Insert Bibliography command at the bottom inserts a bibliography without a preformatted heading. See Figure 2-34.

**Figure 2-34**    **Bibliography menu**

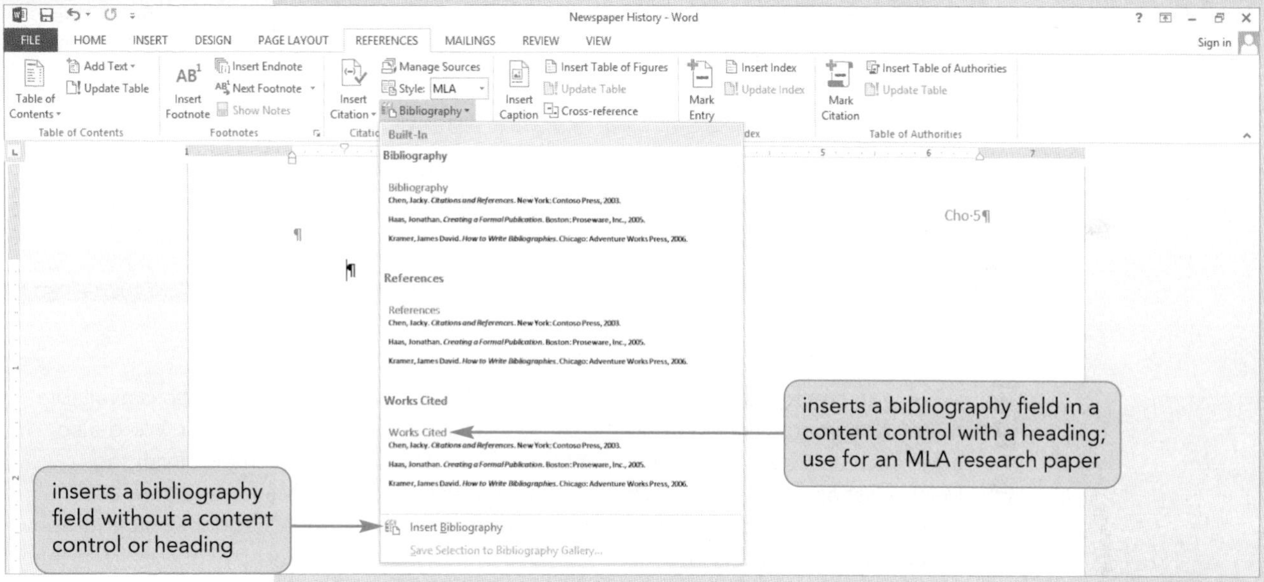

inserts a bibliography field without a content control or heading

inserts a bibliography field in a content control with a heading; use for an MLA research paper

4. Click **Works Cited**. Word inserts the bibliography, with two entries, below the "Works Cited" heading.

   The bibliography text is formatted in Calibri, the default font for the Office theme. The "Works Cited" heading is formatted with the Heading 1 style. To see the content control that contains the bibliography, you need to select it.

5. Click anywhere in the bibliography. Inside the content control, the bibliography is highlighted in gray, indicating that it is a field and not regular text. The content control containing the bibliography is also now visible in the form of a rectangular border and a tab with two buttons. See Figure 2-35.

**Figure 2-35** **Bibliography displayed in a content control**

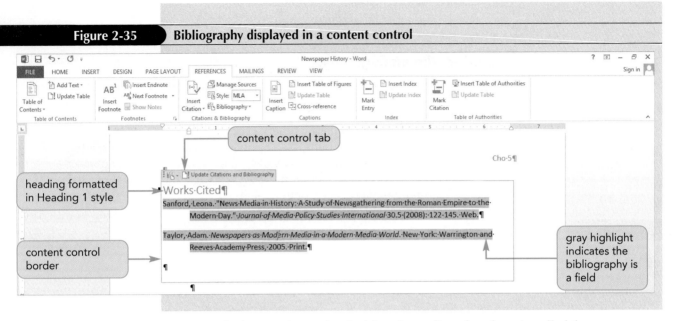

As Kaya looks over the works cited list, she realizes that she misspelled the last name of one of the authors. You'll correct the error now, and then update the bibliography.

## Modifying an Existing Source

To modify information about a source, you click a citation to that source in the document, click the Citation Options button on the content control, and then click Edit Source. After you are finished editing the source, Word prompts you to update the master list and the source information in the current document. In almost all cases, you should click Yes to ensure that the source information is correct in all the places it is stored on your computer.

### To edit a source in the research paper:

1. Click in the blank paragraph below the bibliography content control to deselect the bibliography.

2. Scroll up to display the last paragraph on page 2, and then click the **(Sanford)** citation you entered earlier in the first line of the paragraph. The content control appears around the citation.

▶ **3.** Click the **Citation Options** button ⬚, and then click **Edit Source**. The Edit Source dialog box opens. Note that Word displays the author's last name first in the Author box, just as it would appear in a bibliography.

▶ **4.** Click the **Author** box, and then add an "e" to the last name "Sanford" to change it to "Sanforde."

▶ **5.** Click the **OK** button. A message dialog box opens, asking if you want to update the master source list and the current document.

▶ **6.** Click the **Yes** button, and then click anywhere on the second page to deselect the citation content control. The revised author name in the citation now reads "Sanforde."

▶ **7.** Scroll up to the last paragraph on page 1, locate "Sanford" in the last paragraph on the page, and then change "Sanford" to "Sanforde."

▶ **8.** Save the document.

You've edited the document text and the citation to include the correct spelling of "Sanforde," but now you need to update the bibliography to correct the spelling.

## Updating and Finalizing a Bibliography

The bibliography does not automatically change to reflect edits you make to existing citations or to show new citations. To incorporate the latest information stored in the citations, you need to update the bibliography. To update a bibliography in a content control, click the bibliography, and then, in the content control tab, click Update Citations and Bibliography. To update a bibliography field that is not contained in a content control, right-click the bibliography, and then click Update Field on the shortcut menu.

**To update the bibliography:**

▶ **1.** Scroll down to page 5 and click anywhere in the works cited list to display the content control.

▶ **2.** In the content control tab, click **Update Citations and Bibliography**. The works cited list is updated, with "Sanford" changed to "Sanforde" in the first entry.

Kaya still has a fair amount of work to do on her research paper. After she finishes writing it and adding all the citations, she will update the bibliography again to include all her cited sources. At that point, you might think the bibliography would be finished. However, a few steps remain to ensure that the works cited list matches the MLA style. To finalize Kaya's works cited list to match the MLA style, you need to make the changes shown in Figure 2-36.

| Figure 2-36 | Steps for finalizing a bibliography to match MLA guidelines for a Works Cited list |

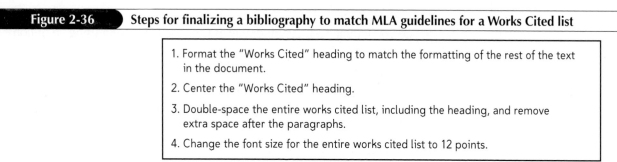

1. Format the "Works Cited" heading to match the formatting of the rest of the text in the document.

2. Center the "Works Cited" heading.

3. Double-space the entire works cited list, including the heading, and remove extra space after the paragraphs.

4. Change the font size for the entire works cited list to 12 points.

### To format the bibliography as an MLA style works cited list:

1. Click in the **Works Cited** heading, and then click the **HOME** tab on the ribbon.

2. In the Styles group, click the **Normal** style. The "Works Cited" heading is now formatted in Calibri body font like the rest of the document. The MLA style for a works cited list requires this heading to be centered.

3. In the Paragraph group, click the **Center** button ▤.

4. Select the entire works cited list, including the heading. Change the font size to **12** points, change the line spacing to **2.0**, and then remove the paragraph spacing after each paragraph.

5. Click below the content control to deselect the works cited list, and then review your work. See Figure 2-37.

**Figure 2-37** MLA-style Works Cited list

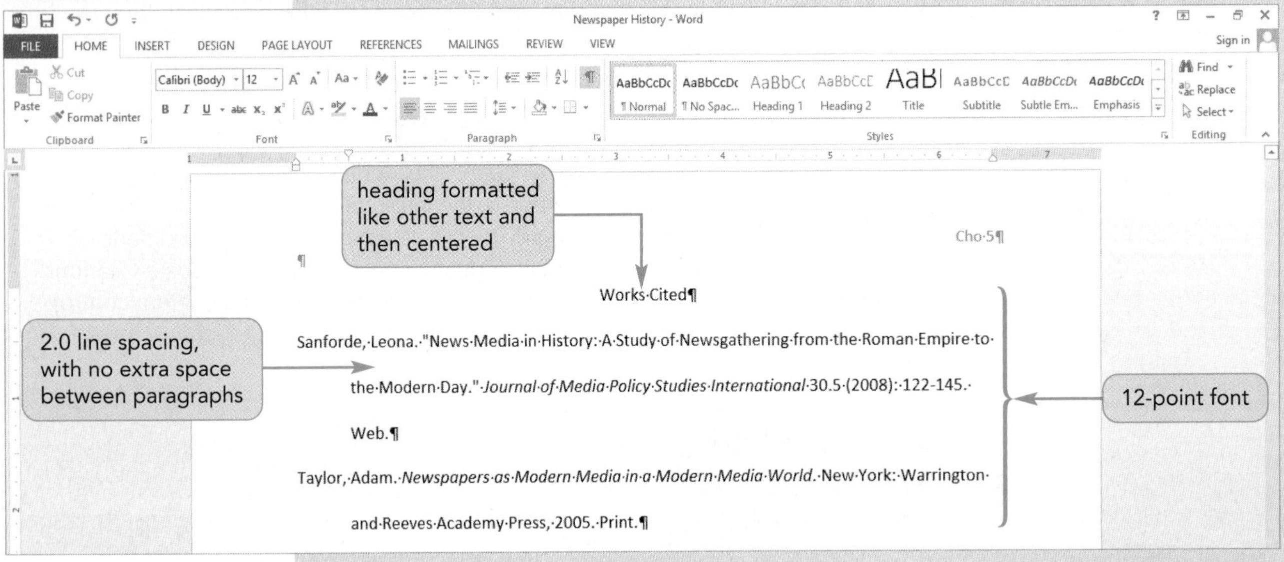

6. Save the document and close it.

Kaya's research paper now meets the MLA style guidelines.

## Session 2.2 Quick Check

1. List the five tasks you need to perform to make a default Word document match the MLA style.

2. How do you indent a paragraph one inch from the left margin using an option on the ribbon?

3. Explain how to remove a page number from the first page of a document.

4. What is a bibliography called according to the MLA style?

5. Explain how to create a citation for a new source.

6. Explain how to edit a citation to display only the page number.

**SAM Projects**

Put your skills into practice with SAM Projects! SAM Projects for this tutorial can be found online. If you have a SAM account, go to www.cengage.com/sam2013 to download the most recent Project Instructions and Start Files.

## Review Assignments

**Data Files needed for the Review Assignments: Broadcast.docx, Situation.docx**

Because the Media Studies document turned out so well, Kaya has been asked to help a student assistant in the Journalism department create a handout describing the classes required for a major in Broadcast Journalism. Kaya asks you to help her revise and format the document. She also asks you to create a document listing the prerequisites and core courses. Finally, as part of her Media Studies class, Kaya is working on a research paper on the history of situation comedy. She asks you to help her format the paper according to the MLA style, and to create some citations and a bibliography. She has inserted the uppercase word "CITATION" wherever she needs to insert a citation. Complete the following steps:

1. Open the file **Broadcast** located in the Word2 ▸ Review folder included with your Data Files, and then save the document as **Broadcast Journalism** in the location specified by your instructor.
2. Read the first comment, which provides an overview of the changes you will be making to the document in the following steps. Perform the task described in the second comment, and then delete both comments.
3. On page 2, in the second paragraph, revise the name of the first public speaking class so that only the first letter of each word is capitalized. Attach a comment to this paragraph that explains the change.
4. On page 2, move the "Senior Project" heading up to position it before the paragraph that begins "This project should incorporate…."
5. Replace the first instance of "journalism" with "media," being sure to match the case.
6. On page 1, format the list of four prerequisite classes as a bulleted list with square bullets. Do the same for the list of core courses, and then indent the three symposium names so they are formatted with an open circle bullet.
7. At the top of page 2, format the list of three public speaking classes as a numbered list, using the "1), 2), 3)" numbering style.
8. In the numbered list, move paragraph 3 ("Broadcast Journalism 220: Video Reporting") up to make it paragraph 2.
9. Format the title "Majoring in Broadcast Journalism" using the Title style. Format the following headings with the Heading 1 style: "Prerequisites," "Core Courses," "Electives," "Public Speaking," and "Senior Project."
10. Change the document theme to the Integral theme.
11. Display the Clipboard task pane. Copy the bulleted list of prerequisites to the Clipboard, and then copy the heading "Prerequisites" to the Clipboard. To ensure that you copy the heading formatting, be sure to select the paragraph mark after "Prerequisites" before you click the Copy button.
12. Open a new, blank document, and then save the document as **Prerequisite List** in the location specified by your instructor.
13. At the beginning of the document, paste the heading "Prerequisites," and then, from the Paste Options menu, apply the Keep Source Formatting option. Below the heading, paste the list of prerequisites, which begins with the text "Journalism 101…."

14. At the end of the document, insert a new paragraph, and then type **Prepared by:** followed by your first and last names.

15. Save the Prerequisite List document and close it.

16. In the Broadcast Journalism document, clear the contents of the Clipboard task pane, close the Clipboard task pane, save the document, and then close it.

17. Open the file **Situation** located in the Word2 ▸ Review folder included with your Data Files.

18. Save the document as **Situation Comedy** in the location specified by your instructor.

19. In the first paragraph, replace Kaya's name with your own.

20. Adjust the font size, line spacing, paragraph spacing, and paragraph indents to match the MLA style.

21. Insert your last name and a page number on every page except the first.

22. If necessary, select MLA Seventh Edition as the citations and bibliography style.

23. Use the Navigation pane to highlight all instances of the uppercase word "CITATION." Keep the Navigation pane open so you can continue to use it to find the locations where you need to insert citations in Steps 24–28.

24. Delete the first instance of "CITATION" and the space before it, and then create a new source with the following information:

    Type of Source: **Book**

    Author: **Cecile Webster**

    Title: **The Comedy of Situations: A History in Words and Pictures**

    Year: **2008**

    City: **Boston**

    Publisher: **Boston Valley Press**

    Medium: **Print**

25. Edit the citation to add **203** as the page number. Display only the page number in the citation.

26. Delete the second instance of "CITATION" and the space before it, and then create a new source with the following information:

    Type of Source: **Journal Article**

    Author: **Oliver Bernault**

    Title: **How Slapstick Conquered the World**

    Journal Name: **Pacific Film Quarterly: Criticism and Comment**

    Year: **2011**

    Pages: **68–91**

    Volume: **11**

    Issue: **2**

    Medium: **Web**

27. Edit the citation to add "80" as the page number.

28. Delete the third instance of "CITATION" and the space before it, and then insert a citation for the book by Cecile Webster.

29. At the end of the document, start a new page and insert a bibliography in a content control with the heading "Works Cited."

30. In the second source you created, add an "e" to change the last name "Bernault" to "Bernaulte," and then update the bibliography.

31. Finalize the bibliography to create an MLA-style Works Cited list.

32. Save the **Situation Comedy** document and close it.

33. Close any other open documents.

## Case Problem 1

**APPLY**

Data File needed for this Case Problem: Yoga.docx

*Green Willow Yoga Studio and Spa*    Karl Boccio, the manager of Green Willow Yoga Studio and Spa, created a flyer to inform clients of the studio's move to a new location. The flyer also lists classes for the summer session and explains the registration process. It's your job to format the flyer to make it look professional and easy to read. Karl included comments in the document explaining what he wants you to do. Complete the following steps:

1. Open the file **Yoga** located in the Word2 ▸ Case1 folder included with your Data Files, and then save the file as **Yoga Flyer** in the location specified by your instructor.

2. Format the document as directed in the comments. After you complete a task, delete the relevant comment. Respond "Yes" to the comment asking if twenty is the correct number of years. When you are finished with the formatting, the comment with the question and the comment with your reply should be the only remaining comments.

3. Move the third bulleted item (which begins "Yoga for Relaxation...") up to make it the first bulleted item in the list.

4. Change the theme to the Ion theme, and then attach a comment to the title listing the heading and body fonts applied by the Ion theme.

5. Save the document and then close it.

## Case Problem 2

**APPLY**

Data File needed for this Case Problem: Hamlet.docx

*South Valley Community College*    Jaleel Reynolds is a student at South Valley Community College. He's working on a research paper about Shakespeare's tragic masterpiece, *Hamlet*. The research paper is only partly finished, with notes in brackets indicating the material Jaleel still plans to write. He also inserted the uppercase word "CITATION" wherever he needs to insert a citation. Jaleel asks you to help him format this early draft to match the MLA style. He also asks you to help him create some citations and a first attempt at a bibliography. He will update the bibliography later, after he finishes writing the research paper. Complete the following steps:

1. Open the file **Hamlet** located in the Word2 ▸ Case2 folder included with your Data Files, and then save the document as **Hamlet Paper** in the location specified by your instructor.

2. In the first paragraph, replace "Jaleel Reynolds" with your name, and then adjust the font size, line spacing, paragraph spacing, and paragraph indents to match the MLA style.

3. Insert your last name and a page number in the upper-right corner of every page except the first page in the document.

4. If necessary, select MLA Seventh Edition as the citations and bibliography style.

5. Use the Navigation pane to find three instances of the uppercase word "CITATION."

6. Delete the first instance of "CITATION" and the space before it, and then create a new source with the following information:

    Type of Source: **Book**

    Author: **Andre Kahn**

    Title: **Tragic Drama in a Tragic Age**

    Year: **2000**

    City: **Chicago**

    Publisher: **Houghton University Press**

    Medium: **Print**

7. Edit the citation to add **127** as the page number.

8. Delete the second instance of "CITATION" and the space before it, and then create a new source with the following information:

   Type of Source: **Sound Recording**

   Performer: **Avery Pohlman**

   Title: **Live From New York's Golden Arch Theater**

   Production Company: **Prescott**

   Year: **1995**

   Medium: **CD**

   City: **New York**

9. Edit the citation to suppress the Author and the Year, so that it displays only the title.

10. Delete the third instance of "CITATION" and the space before it, and then insert a second reference to the book by Andre Kahn.

11. Edit the citation to add **35** as the page number.

12. At the end of the document, start a new page, and then insert a bibliography with the preformatted heading "Works Cited."

13. Edit the first source you created, changing the last name from "Kahn" to **Klann.**

14. Update the bibliography so it shows the revised name "Klann."

15. Finalize the bibliography so that it matches the MLA style.

16. Save the Hamlet Paper document and close it.

## Case Problem 3

**CREATE**

**Data Files needed for this Case Problem: Capital.docx, Sarah.docx**

*Sports Training*    Sarah Vang has more than a decade of experience as an athletic trainer in several different settings. After moving to a new city, she is looking for a job as a trainer in a hospital. She has asked you to edit and format her resume. As part of the application process, she will have to upload her resume to the hospitals' employee recruitment websites. Because these sites typically request a simple page design, Sarah plans to rely primarily on heading styles and bullets to organize her information. When the resume is complete, she wants you to remove any color applied by the heading styles. She also needs help formatting a document she created for a public health organization for which she volunteers. Complete the following steps:

1. Open the file **Sarah** located in the Word2 ▸ Case3 folder included with your Data Files, and then save the file as **Sarah Resume** in the location specified by your instructor.

2. Read the comment included in the document, and then perform the task it specifies.

3. Respond to the comment with the response **I think that's a good choice for the theme.**, and then mark Sarah's comment as done.

4. Replace all occurrences of "Mesacrest" with **Mesa Crest**.

5. Format the resume as shown in Figure 2-38. To ensure that the resume fits on one page, pay special attention to the paragraph spacing settings specified in Figure 2-38.

**Figure 2-38**    Formatting for Sarah Vang's resume

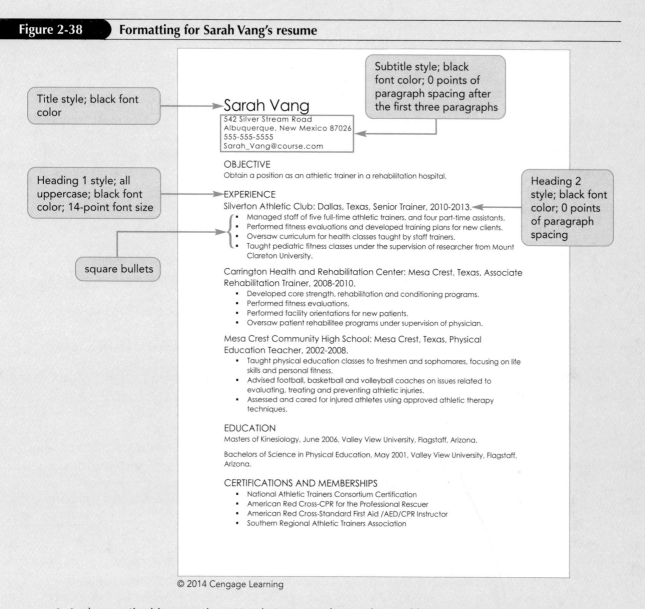

© 2014 Cengage Learning

6. In the email address, replace "Sarah_Vang" with your first and last names, separated by an underscore, and then save the document and close it.

7. Open the file **Capital** located in the Word2 ▶ Case4 folder included with your Data Files, and then save the file as **Capital Campaign** in the location specified by your instructor. Search for the text "Your Name", and then replace it with your first and last names.

8. Select the three paragraphs below your name, and then decrease the indent for the selected paragraphs so that they align at the left margin. Create a .5-inch hanging indent for the selected paragraphs instead.

9. Change the document theme to Ion, and then add a comment to the first word in the document that reads "I changed the theme to Ion."

10. Use the Advanced Find dialog box to search for bold formatting. Remove the bold formatting from the fourth bold element in the document, and then add a comment to that element that reads "I assumed bold here was a mistake, so I removed it."

11. Save and close the document.

**CHALLENGE**

## Case Problem 4

Data File needed for this Case Problem: Movie.docx

***Winona College***   Tristan Giroux is a student at Winona College. She's working on a research paper about disaster movies for Film Studies 105, taught by Professor Douglas Fischer. The research paper is only partly finished, but before she does more work on it, she asks you to help format this early draft to match the MLA style. She also asks you to help her create some citations, add a placeholder citation, and manage her sources. Complete the following steps:

1. Open the file **Movie** located in the Word2 ▸ Case4 folder included with your Data Files, and then save the document as **Movie Paper** in the location specified by your instructor.

2. Revise the paper to match the MLA style, seventh edition. Instead of Tristan's name, use your own. Also, use the current date.

3. Locate the sentences in which the authors Dana Someya and Peter Williams are mentioned. At the end of the appropriate sentence, add a citation for page 135 in the following book and one for page 152 in the following journal article:

    Someya, Dana. *Society and Disaster in the Silent Era: A Modern Analysis.* New York: Movie House Academy Press, 1997. Print.

    Williams, Peter. "Romance in the Shadow of Disaster." *New England Journal of Cinema Studies* (2012): 133–155. Web.

4. At the end of the second-to-last sentence in the document, insert a placeholder citation that reads "Candela." At the end of the last sentence in the document, insert a placeholder citation that reads "Goldman."

✦ **Explore** 5. Use Word Help to look up the topic "Create a bibliography," and then, within that article, read the sections titled "Find a source" and "Edit a citation placeholder."

✦ **Explore** 6. Open the Source Manager, and search for the name "Someya." From within the Current List in the Source Manager, edit the Dana Someya citation to delete "Society and" from the title, so that the title begins "Disaster in the Silent Era…." Click Yes when asked if you want to update the source in both lists. When you are finished, delete "Someya" from the Search box to redisplay all the sources in both lists.

✦ **Explore** 7. From within the Source Manager, copy a source not included in the current document from the Master List to the Current List. Examine the sources in the Current List and note the checkmarks next to the two sources for which you have already created citations, and the question marks next to the placeholder sources. Sources in the Current list that are not actually cited in the text have no symbol next to them in the Current List. For example, if you copied a source from the Master List into your Current List, that source has no symbol next to it in the Current List.

8. Close the Source Manager, create a bibliography in the MLA style, and note which works appear in it.

✦ **Explore** 9. Open the Source Manager, and then edit the Goldman placeholder source to include the following information about a journal article:

    Goldman, Simon. "Attack of the Killer Disaster Movie." *Cinema International Journal* (2009): 72–89. Web.

10. Update the bibliography.

✦ **Explore** 11. Open Internet Explorer and use the Web to research the difference between a works cited list and a works consulted list. If necessary, open the Source Manager, and then delete any uncited sources from the Current List to ensure that your document contains a true works cited list, as specified by the MLA style, and not a works consulted list. (Tristan will create a full citation for the "Candela" placeholder later.)

12. Update the bibliography, finalize it so it matches the MLA style, save the document and close it.

TUTORIAL 3

## OBJECTIVES

### Session 3.1
- Review document headings in the Navigation pane
- Reorganize document text using the Navigation pane
- Collapse and expand body text in a document
- Create and edit a table
- Sort rows in a table
- Modify a table's structure
- Format a table

### Session 3.2
- Set tab stops
- Turn on automatic hyphenation
- Create footnotes and endnotes
- Divide a document into sections
- Create a SmartArt graphic
- Create headers and footers
- Insert a cover page
- Change the document's theme
- Review a document in Read Mode

# Creating Tables and a Multipage Report

*Writing a Recommendation*

## Case | Orchard Street Art Center

Katherine Hua is the facilities director for Orchard Street Art Center, a nonprofit organization that provides performance, rehearsal, and classroom space for arts organizations in St. Louis, Missouri. The center's facilities include a 300-seat indoor theater, a 200-seat outdoor theater, public terraces and lobbies, five classrooms, 20 rehearsal rooms, and several offices. Katherine hopes to improve the wireless network that serves the center's staff and patrons through a process known as a wireless site survey. She has written a multiple-page report for the center's board of directors summarizing basic information about wireless site surveys. She has asked you to finish formatting the report. Katherine also needs your help with adding a table and a diagram to the end of the report.

In this tutorial, you'll use the Navigation pane to review the document headings and reorganize the document. You will also insert a table, modify it by changing the structure and formatting, set tab stops, create footnotes and endnotes, hyphenate the document, and insert a section break. In addition, you'll create a SmartArt graphic and add headers and footers. Finally, you will insert a cover page and review the document in Read Mode.

## STARTING DATA FILES

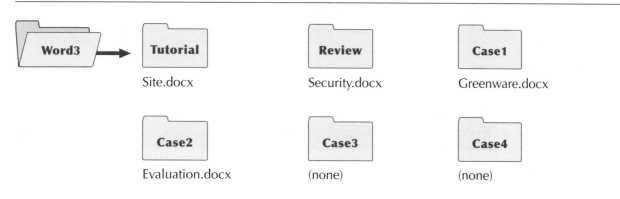

| Word3 → Tutorial | Review | Case1 |
|---|---|---|
| Site.docx | Security.docx | Greenware.docx |

| Case2 | Case3 | Case4 |
|---|---|---|
| Evaluation.docx | (none) | (none) |

Microsoft product screenshots used with permission from Microsoft Corporation.

# Session 3.1 Visual Overview:

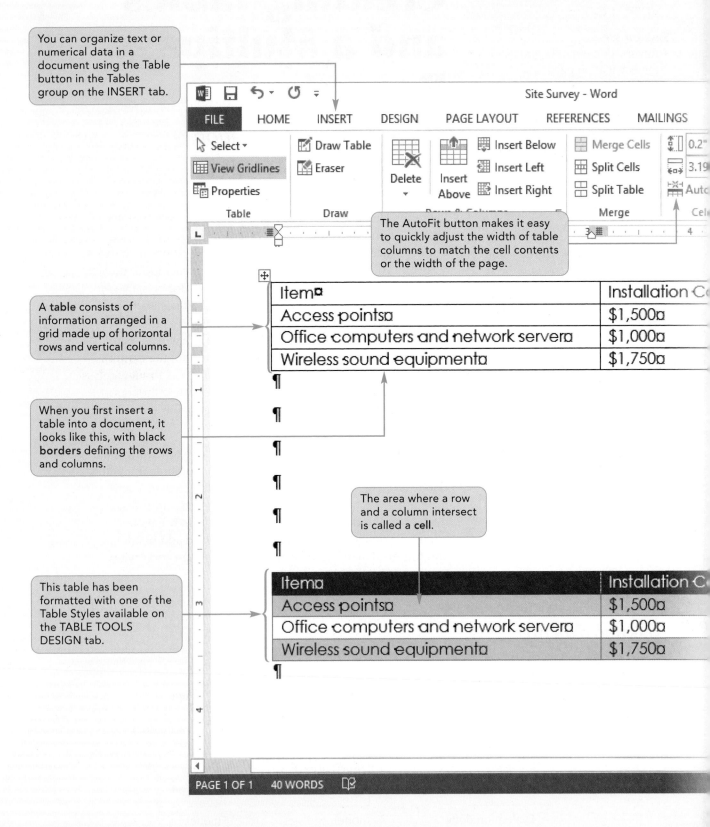

You can organize text or numerical data in a document using the Table button in the Tables group on the INSERT tab.

The AutoFit button makes it easy to quickly adjust the width of table columns to match the cell contents or the width of the page.

A **table** consists of information arranged in a grid made up of horizontal rows and vertical columns.

When you first insert a table into a document, it looks like this, with black **borders** defining the rows and columns.

The area where a row and a column intersect is called a **cell**.

This table has been formatted with one of the Table Styles available on the TABLE TOOLS DESIGN tab.

# Organizing Information in Tables

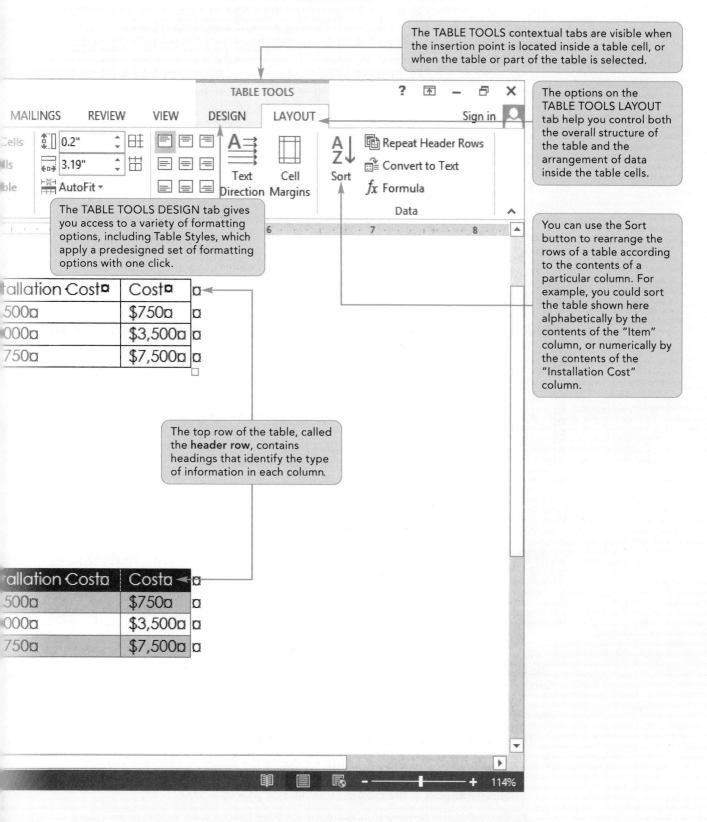

The TABLE TOOLS contextual tabs are visible when the insertion point is located inside a table cell, or when the table or part of the table is selected.

The options on the TABLE TOOLS LAYOUT tab help you control both the overall structure of the table and the arrangement of data inside the table cells.

The TABLE TOOLS DESIGN tab gives you access to a variety of formatting options, including Table Styles, which apply a predesigned set of formatting options with one click.

You can use the Sort button to rearrange the rows of a table according to the contents of a particular column. For example, you could sort the table shown here alphabetically by the contents of the "Item" column, or numerically by the contents of the "Installation Cost" column.

The top row of the table, called the **header row**, contains headings that identify the type of information in each column.

# Working with Headings in the Navigation Pane

When used in combination with the Navigation pane, Word's heading styles make it easier to navigate through a long document and to reorganize a document. You start by formatting the document headings with heading styles, displaying the Navigation pane, and then clicking the Headings link. This displays a hierarchy of all the headings in the document, allowing you to see, at a glance, an outline of the document headings.

Paragraphs formatted with the Heading 1 style are considered the highest level headings and are aligned at the left margin of the Navigation pane. Paragraphs formatted with the Heading 2 style are considered **subordinate** to Heading 1 paragraphs, and are indented slightly to the right below the Heading 1 paragraphs. Subordinate headings are often referred to as **subheadings**. Each successive level of heading styles (Heading 3, Heading 4, and so on) is indented farther to the right. To simplify your view of the document outline in the Navigation pane, you can choose to hide lower-level headings from view, leaving only the major headings visible.

From within the Navigation pane, you can **promote** a subordinate heading to the next level up in the heading hierarchy. For example, you can promote a Heading 2 paragraph to a Heading 1 paragraph. You can also do the opposite—that is, you can **demote** a heading to a subordinate level. You can also click and drag a heading in the Navigation pane to a new location in the document's outline. When you do so, any subheadings—along with their subordinate body text—move to the new location in the document.

**REFERENCE**

### Working with Headings in the Navigation Pane

- Format the document headings using Word's heading styles.
- On the ribbon, click the HOME tab.
- In the Editing group, click the Find button, or press the Ctrl+F keys, to display the Navigation pane.
- In the Navigation pane, click the HEADINGS link to display a list of the document headings, and then click a heading to display that heading in the document window.
- In the Navigation pane, click a heading, and then drag it up or down in the list of headings to move that heading and the body text below it to a new location in the document.
- In the Navigation pane, right-click a heading, and then click Promote to promote the heading to the next-highest level. To demote a heading, right-click it, and then click Demote.
- To hide subheadings in the Navigation pane, click the Collapse arrow next to the higher level heading above them. To redisplay the subheadings, click the Expand arrow next to the higher level heading.

Katherine saved the draft of her report as a Word document named Site. You will use the Navigation pane to review the outline of Katherine's report and make some changes to its organization.

### To review the document headings in the Navigation pane:

1. Open the document named **Site** located in the Word3 ▸ Tutorial folder included with your Data Files, and then save the file with the name **Site Survey Report** in the location specified by your instructor.

2. Verify that the document is displayed in Print Layout view, and that the rulers and nonprinting characters are displayed.

3. Make sure the Zoom level is set to **120%**, and that the HOME tab is selected on the ribbon.

4. Press the **Ctrl+F** keys. The Navigation pane opens to the left of the document.

5. In the Navigation pane, click the **HEADINGS** link. The document headings are displayed in the Navigation pane, as shown in Figure 3-1. The blue highlighted heading ("Summary") indicates which part of the document currently contains the insertion point.

Figure 3-1    **Headings displayed in the Navigation pane**

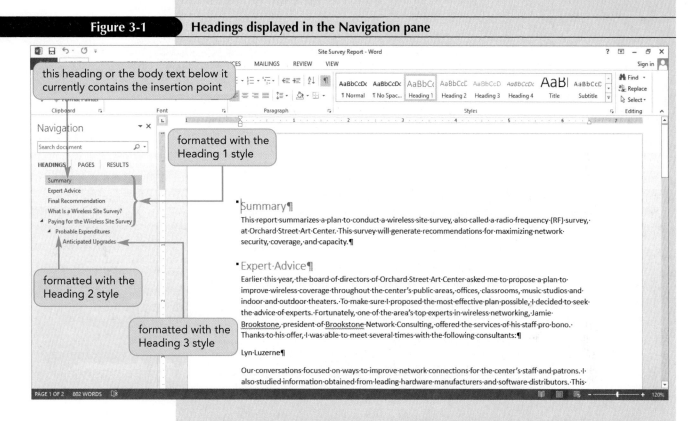

6. In the Navigation pane, click the **What Is a Wireless Site Survey?** heading. Word displays the heading in the document window, with the insertion point at the beginning of the heading. "The What Is a Wireless Site Survey?" heading is highlighted in blue in the Navigation pane.

7. In the Navigation pane, click the **Paying for the Wireless Site Survey** heading. Word displays the heading in the document window. In the Navigation pane, you can see that there are subheadings below this heading.

8. In the Navigation pane, click the **Collapse** arrow ◢ next to the "Paying for the Wireless Site Survey" heading. The subheadings below this heading are no longer visible in the Navigation pane. This has no effect on the text in the actual document. See Figure 3-2.

Figure 3-2 | Heading 2 and Heading 3 text hidden in Navigation pane

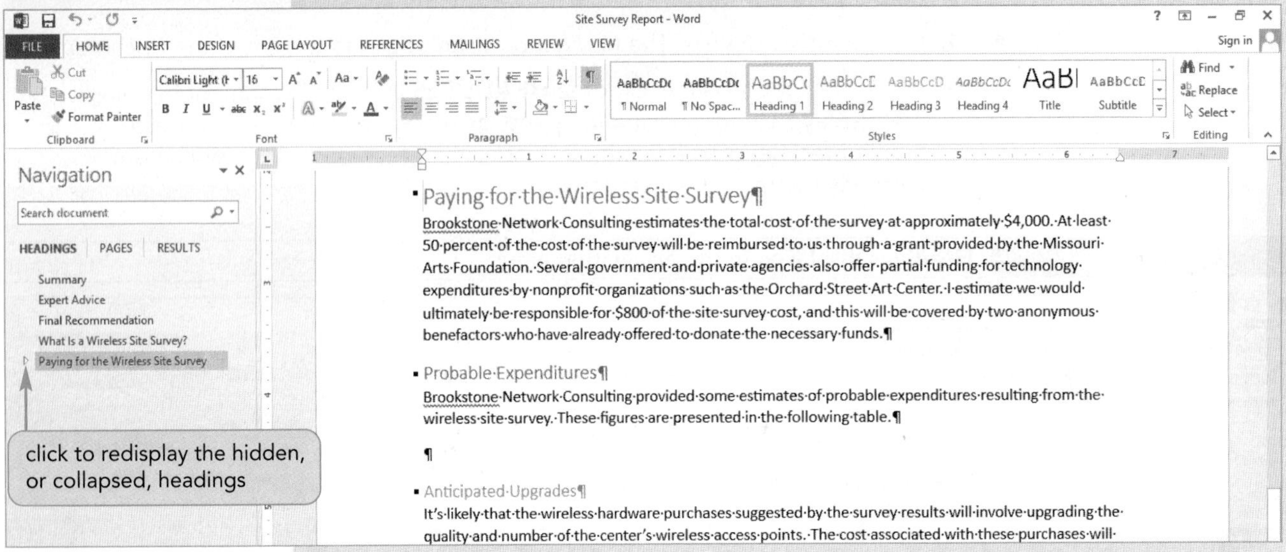

Navigation

Search document

HEADINGS | PAGES | RESULTS

Summary
Expert Advice
Final Recommendation
What Is a Wireless Site Survey?
Paying for the Wireless Site Survey

**click to redisplay the hidden, or collapsed, headings**

- **Paying·for·the·Wireless·Site·Survey¶**
Brookstone·Network·Consulting·estimates·the·total·cost·of·the·survey·at·approximately·$4,000.·At·least· 50·percent·of·the·cost·of·the·survey·will·be·reimbursed·to·us·through·a·grant·provided·by·the·Missouri· Arts·Foundation.·Several·government·and·private·agencies·also·offer·partial·funding·for·technology· expenditures·by·nonprofit·organizations·such·as·the·Orchard·Street·Art·Center.·I·estimate·we·would· ultimately·be·responsible·for·$800·of·the·site·survey·cost,·and·this·will·be·covered·by·two·anonymous· benefactors·who·have·already·offered·to·donate·the·necessary·funds.¶

- **Probable·Expenditures¶**
Brookstone·Network·Consulting·provided·some·estimates·of·probable·expenditures·resulting·from·the· wireless·site·survey.·These·figures·are·presented·in·the·following·table.¶

¶

- **Anticipated·Upgrades¶**
It's·likely·that·the·wireless·hardware·purchases·suggested·by·the·survey·results·will·involve·upgrading·the· quality·and·number·of·the·center's·wireless·access·points.·The·cost·associated·with·these·purchases·will·

**9.** In the Navigation pane, click the **Expand** arrow ▷ next to the "Paying for the Wireless Site Survey" heading. The subheadings are again visible in the Navigation pane.

Now that you have had a chance to review the report, you need to make a few organizational changes. Katherine wants to promote the Heading 3 text "Anticipated Upgrades" to Heading 2 text. Then she wants to move the "Anticipated Upgrades" heading and its body text up, so it precedes the "Probable Expenditures" section.

### To use the Navigation pane to reorganize text in the document:

**1.** In the Navigation pane, right-click the **Anticipated Upgrades** heading to display the shortcut menu.

**2.** Click **Promote**. The heading moves to the left in the Navigation pane, aligning below the "Probable Expenditures" heading. In the document window, the text is now formatted with the Heading 2 style, with its slightly larger font.

**3.** In the Navigation pane, click and drag the **Anticipated Upgrades** heading up. As you drag the heading, the pointer changes to ⬚, and a blue guideline is displayed. You can use the guideline to position the heading in its new location.

**4.** Position the guideline directly below the "Paying for the Wireless Site Survey" heading, as shown in Figure 3-3.

**Figure 3-3** — Moving a heading in the Navigation pane

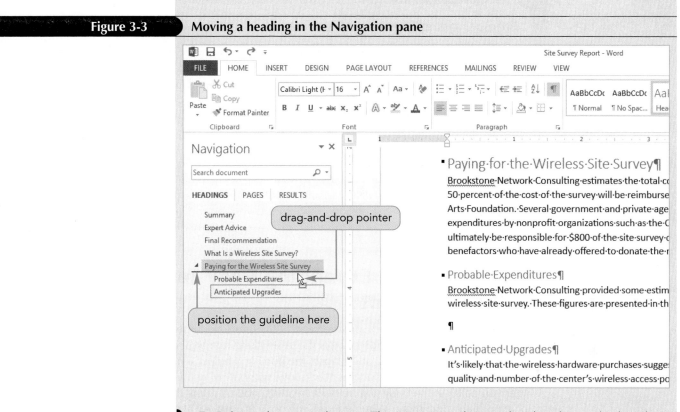

5. Release the mouse button. The "Anticipated Upgrades" heading is displayed in its new position in the Navigation pane, as the second-to-last heading in the outline. The heading and its body text are displayed in their new location in the document, before the "Probable Expenditures" heading. See Figure 3-4.

**Figure 3-4** — Heading and body text in new location

It's likely that the wireless hardware purchases suggested by the survey results will involve upgrading the quality and number of the center's wireless access points. The cost associated with these purchases will be relatively small. Also, the surveyor will probably recommend upgrading our network server, several office computers, and some sound equipment in the indoor theater. The cost of these improvements will of course be significant, but will immediately result in improved network connectivity and greatly enhanced network security.¶

Probable Expenditures¶

Brookstone Network Consulting provided some estimates of probable expenditures resulting from the wireless site survey. These figures are presented in the following table.¶

6. Click anywhere in the document to deselect the text, and then save the document.

Katherine also wants you to move the "Final Recommendation" heading and its accompanying body text. You'll do that in the next section, using a different method.

## Promoting and Demoting Headings

When you promote or demote a heading, Word applies the next higher or lower level heading style to the heading paragraph. You could accomplish the same thing by using the Style gallery to apply the next higher or lower level heading style, but it's easy to lose track of the overall organization of the document that way. By promoting and demoting headings from within the Navigation pane, you ensure that the overall document outline is right in front of you as you work.

You can also use Outline view to display, promote, and demote headings, and to reorganize a document. Turn on Outline view by clicking the VIEW tab, and then clicking the Outline button in the Views group to display the OUTLINING tab on the ribbon. To hide the OUTLINING tab and return to Print Layout view, click the Close Outline View button on the ribbon or the Print Layout button in the status bar.

# Collapsing and Expanding Body Text in the Document

The Navigation pane gives you an overview of the entire document, and dragging headings within the Navigation pane is the best way to reorganize a document. However, you can also hide, or collapse, the body text below a heading in a document. You do this from within the document window, without using the Navigation pane. After you collapse the body text below a heading, you can drag the heading to a new location in the document. When you do, the body text moves along with the heading, just as if you had dragged the heading in the Navigation pane. You'll use this technique now to move the "Final Recommendation" heading and its body text.

**To collapse and move a heading in the document:**

▶ **1.** In the Navigation pane, click the **Final Recommendation** heading to display it in the document window.

▶ **2.** In the document window, place the mouse pointer over the **Final Recommendation** heading to display the gray Collapse button ◢ to the left of the heading.

▶ **3.** Point to the gray **Collapse** button ◢ until it turns blue, and then click the **Collapse** button ◢. The body text below the "Final Recommendation" heading is now hidden. The Collapse button is replaced with an Expand button.

▶ **4.** Collapse the body text below the "What Is a Wireless Site Survey?" heading. The body text below that heading is no longer visible. Collapsing body text can be helpful when you want to hide details in a document temporarily, so you can focus on a particular part. See Figure 3-5.

| **Figure 3-5** | **Body text collapsed in the document** |

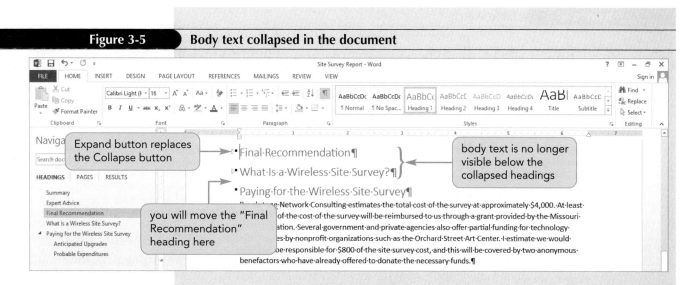

**5.** Select the **Final Recommendation** heading.

**6.** Click and drag the heading down. As you drag, a dark black insertion point moves along with the mouse pointer.

**7.** Position the dark black insertion point to the left of the "P" in the "Paying for the Wireless Site Survey" heading, and then release the mouse button. The "Final Recommendation" heading and its body text move to the new location, before the "Paying for the Wireless Site Survey" heading.

Finally, you need to expand the body text below the two collapsed headings.

**8.** Click anywhere in the document to deselect the text.

**9.** Point to the **Expand** button ▷ to the left of the "Final Recommendation" heading until it turns blue, and then click the **Expand** button ▶ to redisplay the body text below the heading.

**10.** Point to the **Expand** button ▷ to the left of the "What Is a Wireless Site Survey?" heading until it turns blue, and then click the **Expand** button ▶ to redisplay the body text below the heading.

**11.** Save the document.

The document is now organized the way Katherine wants it. Next, you need to create a table summarizing her data on probable expenditures.

# Inserting a Blank Table

**TIP**

The terms "table," "field," and "record" are also used to discuss information stored in database programs, such as Microsoft Access.

A table is a useful way to present information that is organized into categories, or **fields**. For example, you could use a table to organize contact information for a list of clients. For each client, you could include information in the following fields: first name, last name, street address, city, state, and zip code. The complete set of information about a particular client is called a **record**. In a typical table, each column is a separate field, and each row is a record. A header row at the top contains the names of each field.

The sketch in Figure 3-6 shows what Katherine wants the table in her report to look like.

**Figure 3-6**    Table sketch

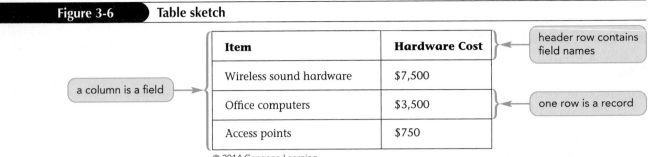

© 2014 Cengage Learning

Katherine's table includes two columns, or fields—"Item" and "Hardware Cost." The header row contains the names of these two fields. The three rows below contain the records.

Creating a table in Word is a three-step process. First, you use the Table button on the INSERT tab to insert a blank table structure. Then you enter information into the table. Finally, you format the table to make it easy to read.

Before you begin creating the table, you'll insert a page break before the "Probable Expenditures" heading. This will move the heading and its body text to a new page, with plenty of room below for the new table. As a general rule, you should not use page breaks to position a particular part of a document at the top of a page. If you add or remove text from the document later, you might forget that you inserted a manual page break, and you might end up with a document layout you didn't expect. By default, Word heading styles are set up to ensure that a heading always appears on the same page as the body text paragraph below it, so you'll never need to insert a page break just to move a heading to the same page as its body text. However, in this case, a page break is appropriate because you need the "Probable Expenditures" heading to appear at the top of a page with room for the table below.

### To insert a page break and insert a blank table:

1. In the Navigation pane, click **Probable Expenditures** to display the heading in the document, with the insertion point to the left of the "P" in "Probable."

2. Close the Navigation pane, and then press the **Ctrl+Enter** keys to insert a page break. The "Probable Expenditures" heading and the body text following it move to a new, third page.

3. Scroll to position the "Probable Expenditures" heading at the top of the Word window, and then press the **Ctrl+End** keys to move the insertion point to the blank paragraph at the end of the document.

4. On the ribbon, click the **INSERT** tab.

5. In the Tables group, click the **Table** button. A table grid opens, with a menu at the bottom.

6. Use the mouse pointer to point to the upper-left cell of the grid, and then move the mouse pointer down and across the grid to highlight **two columns** and **four rows**. (The outline of a cell turns orange when it is highlighted.) As you move the pointer across the grid, Word indicates the size of the table (columns by rows) at the top of the grid. A Live Preview of the table structure is displayed in the document. See Figure 3-7.

**TIP**

You can use the Quick Tables option to choose from preformatted tables that contain placeholder text.

**Figure 3-7**   Inserting a blank table

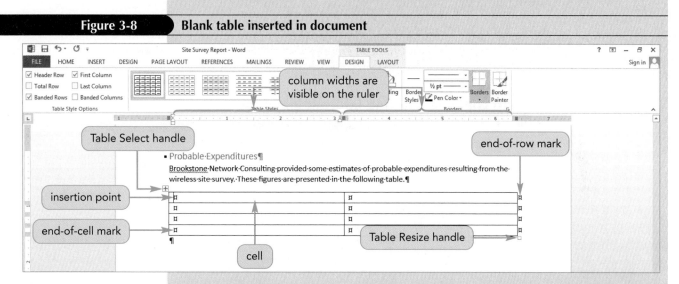

**7.** When the table size is 2×4, click the lower-right cell in the block of selected cells. An empty table consisting of two columns and four rows is inserted in the document, with the insertion point in the upper-left cell. See Figure 3-8.

**Figure 3-8**   Blank table inserted in document

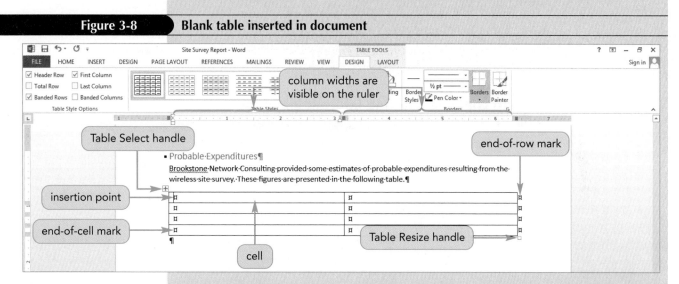

The two columns are of equal width. Because nonprinting characters are displayed in the document, each cell contains an end-of-cell mark, and each row contains an end-of-row mark, which are important for selecting parts of a table. The Table Select handle ⊞ is displayed at the table's upper-left corner. You can click the Table Select handle ⊞ to select the entire table, or you can drag it to move the table. You can drag the Table Resize handle ☐, which is displayed at the lower-right corner, to change the size of the table. The TABLE TOOLS DESIGN and LAYOUT contextual tabs appear on the ribbon.

**Trouble?** If you inserted a table with the wrong number of rows or columns, click the Undo button ↺ on the Quick Access Toolbar to remove the table, and then repeat Steps 4 through 7.

The blank table is ready for you to begin entering information.

# Entering Data in a Table

You can enter data in a table by moving the insertion point to a cell and typing. If the data takes up more than one line in the cell, Word automatically wraps the text to the next line and increases the height of that row. To move the insertion point to another cell in the table, you can click in that cell, use the arrow keys, or use the Tab key.

## To enter information in the header row of the table:

▶ **1.** Verify that the insertion point is located in the upper-left cell.

▶ **2.** Type **Item**. As you type, the end-of-cell mark moves right to accommodate the text.

▶ **3.** Press the **Tab** key to move the insertion point to the next cell to the right.

   **Trouble?** If Word created a new paragraph in the first cell rather than moving the insertion point to the second cell, you pressed the Enter key instead of the Tab key. Press the Backspace key to remove the paragraph mark, and then press the Tab key to move to the second cell in the first row.

▶ **4.** Type **Hardware Cost** and then press the **Tab** key to move to the first cell in the second row.

You have finished entering the header row—the row that identifies the information in each column. Now you can enter the information about the various expenditures.

## To continue entering information in the table:

▶ **1.** Type **wireless sound hardware** and then press the **Tab** key to move to the second cell in the second row. Notice that the "w" in "wireless" is capitalized, even though you typed it in lowercase. By default, AutoCorrect capitalizes the first letter in a cell entry.

▶ **2.** Type **$7,500** and then press the **Tab** key to move the insertion point to the first cell in the third row.

▶ **3.** Enter the following information in the bottom two rows, pressing the **Tab** key to move from cell to cell:

   **Office computers**; $3,500

   **Access points**; $750

At this point, the table consists of a header row and three records. Katherine realizes that she needs to add one more row to the table. You can add a new row to the bottom of a table by pressing the Tab key when the insertion point is in the rightmost cell in the bottom row.

## To add a row to the table:

▶ **1.** Verify that the insertion point is in the lower-right cell (which contains the value "$750") and then press the **Tab** key. A new, blank row is added to the bottom of the table.

▶ **2.** Type **Network server**, press the **Tab** key, and then type **$2,200**. When you are finished, your table should look like the one shown in Figure 3-9.

| Figure 3-9 | Table with all data entered |

**Trouble?** If a new row is added to the bottom of your table, you pressed the Tab key after entering "$2,200". Click the Undo button ⤺ on the Quick Access Toolbar to remove the extra row from the table.

The table you've just created presents information about expenditures in an easy-to-read format. To make it even easier to read, you can format the header row in bold so it stands out from the rest of the table. To do that, you need to first select the header row.

## Selecting Part of a Table

When selecting part of a table, you need to make sure you select the end-of-cell mark in a cell or the end-of-row mark at the end of a row. If you don't, the formatting changes you make next might not have the effect you expect. The foolproof way to select part of a table is to click in the cell, row, or column you want to select; click the Select button on the TABLE TOOLS LAYOUT contextual tab; and then click the appropriate command—Select Cell, Select Column, or Select Row. (You can also click Select Table to select the entire table.) To select a row, you can also click in the left margin next to the row. Similarly, you can click just above a column to select it. After you've selected an entire row, column, or cell, you can drag the mouse to select adjacent rows, columns, or cells.

Note that in the following steps, you'll position the mouse pointer until it takes on a particular shape so that you can then perform the task associated with that type of pointer. Pointer shapes are especially important when working with tables and graphics; in many cases, you can't perform a task until the pointer is the right shape. It takes some patience to get accustomed to positioning the pointer until it takes on the correct shape, but with practice you'll grow to rely on the pointer shapes as a quick visual cue to the options currently available to you.

### To select and format the header row:

1. Position the mouse pointer in the selection bar, to the left of the header row. The pointer changes to a right-facing arrow ⌐.

2. Click the mouse button. The entire header row, including the end-of-cell mark in each cell and the end-of-row mark, is selected. See Figure 3-10.

| Figure 3-10 | Header row selected |

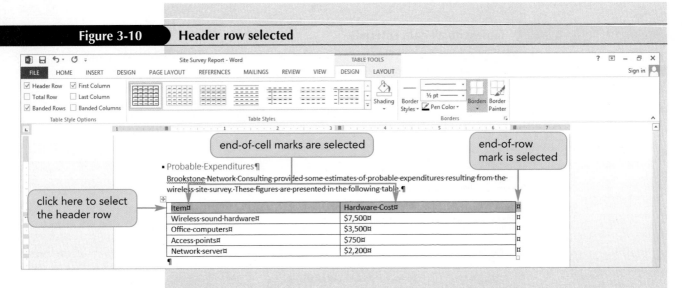

3. Press the **Ctrl+B** keys to apply bold to the text in the header row. You can also use the formatting options on the HOME tab to format selected text in a table, including adding italics, changing the font, aligning text within cells, or applying a style.

4. Click anywhere in the table to deselect the header row, and then save the document.

### Formatting a Multipage Table

In some documents, you might have a long table that extends across multiple pages. To make a multipage table easier to read, you can format the table header row to appear at the top of every page. To do so, click in the header row, click the TABLE TOOLS LAYOUT tab, and then click the Properties button in the Table group. In the Table Properties dialog box, click the Row tab, and then select the "Repeat as header row at the top of each page" check box.

Now that you have created a very basic table, you can sort the information in it and improve its appearance.

# Sorting Rows in a Table

The term **sort** refers to the process of rearranging information in alphabetical, numerical, or chronological order. You can sort a series of paragraphs, including the contents of a bulleted list, or you can sort the rows of a table.

When you sort a table, you arrange the rows based on the contents of one of the columns. For example, you could sort the table you just created based on the contents of the "Item" column—either in ascending alphabetical order (from *A* to *Z*) or in descending alphabetical order (from *Z* to *A*). Alternatively, you could sort the table based on the contents of the "Hardware Cost" column—either in ascending numerical order (lowest to highest) or in descending numerical order (highest to lowest).

Clicking the Sort button in the Data group on the TABLE TOOLS LAYOUT tab opens the Sort dialog box, which provides a number of options for fine-tuning the sort, including options for sorting a table by the contents of more than one column. This is useful if, for example, you want to organize the table rows by last name, and then by first name within each last name. By default, Word assumes your table includes a header row that should remain at the top of the table—excluded from the sort.

**REFERENCE**

### Sorting the Rows of a Table

- Click anywhere within the table.
- On the ribbon, click the TABLE TOOLS LAYOUT tab.
- In the Data group, click the Sort button.
- In the Sort dialog box, click the Sort by arrow, and then select the header for the column you want to sort by.
- In the Type box located to the right of the Sort by box, select the type of information stored in the column you want to sort by; you can choose Text, Number, or Date.
- To sort in alphabetical, chronological, or numerical order, verify that the Ascending option button is selected. To sort in reverse order, click the Descending option button.
- To sort by a second column, click the Then by arrow, and then click a column header. If necessary, specify the type of information stored in the Then by column, and the sort order.
- At the bottom of the Sort dialog box, make sure the Header row option button is selected. This indicates that the table includes a header row that should not be included in the sort.
- Click the OK button.

Katherine would like you to sort the contents of the table in ascending numerical order based on the contents of the "Hardware Cost" column.

### To sort the information in the table:

**1.** Make sure the insertion point is located somewhere in the table.

**2.** On the ribbon, click the **TABLE TOOLS LAYOUT** tab.

**3.** In the Data group, click the **Sort** button. The Sort dialog box opens. Take a moment to review its default settings. The leftmost column in the table, the "Item" column, is selected in the Sort by box, indicating the sort will be based on the contents in this column. Because the "Item" column contains text, "Text" is selected in the Type box. The Ascending option button is selected by default, indicating that Word will sort the contents of the "Item" column from A to Z. The Header row option button is selected in the lower-left corner of the dialog box, ensuring the header row will not be included in the sort. You want to sort the column by the contents of the "Hardware Cost" column, so you need to change the Sort by setting.

**4.** Click the **Sort by** button arrow, and then click **Hardware Cost**. Because the "Hardware Cost" column contains numbers, the Type box now displays "Number". The Ascending button is still selected, indicating that Word will sort the numbers in the "Hardware Cost" column from lowest to highest. See Figure 3-11.

| Figure 3-11 | Sort dialog box |
| --- | --- |

type of data in the "Hardware Cost" column

sort based on the contents of the "Hardware Cost" column

header row will be excluded from the sort

sort order

**5.** Click the **OK** button to close the Sort dialog box, and then click anywhere in the table to deselect it. Rows 2 through 5 are now arranged numerically, according to the numbers in the "Hardware Cost" column, with the "Wireless sound hardware" row at the bottom. See Figure 3-12.

| Figure 3-12 | Table after being sorted |
| --- | --- |

header row remains at the top

- Probable·Expenditures¶
Brookstone·Network·Consulting·provided·some·estimates·of·probable·expenditures·resulting·from·the·wireless·site·survey.·These·figures·are·presented·in·the·following·table.¶

| Item¤ | Hardware·Cost¤ | ¤ |
| --- | --- | --- |
| Access·points¤ | $750¤ | |
| Network·server¤ | $2,200¤ | |
| Office·computers¤ | $3,500¤ | |
| Wireless·sound·hardware¤ | $7,500¤ | |

¶

contents of the table are sorted in numerical order by cost

**6.** Save the document.

Katherine decides that the table should also include the installation cost for each item. She asks you to insert an "Installation Cost" column.

# Inserting Rows and Columns in a Table

To add a column to a table, you can use the tools in the Rows & Columns group on the TABLE TOOLS LAYOUT tab, or you can use the Add Column button in the document window. To use the Add Column button, make sure the insertion point is located somewhere within the table. When you position the mouse pointer at the top of the table, pointing to the border between two columns, the Add Column button appears. When you click that button, a new column is inserted between the two existing columns.

## To insert a column in the table:

1. Verify that the insertion point is located anywhere in the table.

2. Position the mouse pointer at the top of the table, so that it points to the border between the two columns. The Add Column button ⊕ appears at the top of the border. A blue guideline shows where the new column will be inserted. See Figure 3-13.

**Figure 3-13** **Inserting a column**

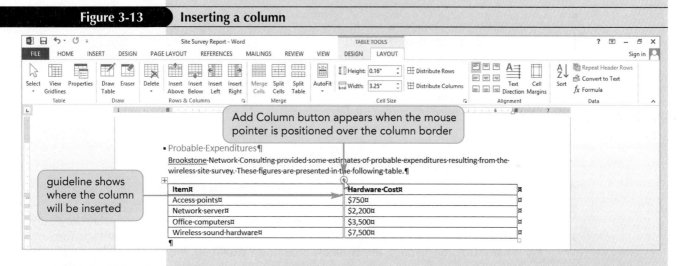

3. Click the **Add Column** button ⊕. A new, blank column is inserted between the "Item" and "Hardware Cost" columns. The three columns in the table are narrower than the original two columns, but the overall width of the table remains the same.

4. Click in the top cell of the new column, and then enter the following header and data. Use the ↓ key to move the insertion point down through the column.

**Installation Cost**

**$1,500**

**$850**

**$1,000**

**$1,750**

Your table should now look like the one in Figure 3-14.

**TIP**

You can also use the buttons in the Rows & Columns group on the TABLE TOOLS LAYOUT tab to insert a column or row.

| Figure 3-14 | New "Installation Cost" column |
| --- | --- |

Because you selected the entire header row when you formatted the original headers in bold, the newly inserted header, "Installation Cost," is also formatted in bold.

Katherine just learned that the costs listed for office computers actually cover both office computers and the network server. Therefore, she would like you to delete the "Network server" row from the table.

# Deleting Rows and Columns

When you consider deleting a row, you need to be clear about whether you want to delete the *contents* of the row, or the contents and the *structure* of the row. You can delete the contents of a row by selecting the row and pressing the Delete key. This removes the information from the row but leaves the row structure intact. The same is true for deleting the contents of an individual cell, a column, or the entire table. To delete the structure of a row, a column, or the entire table—including its contents—you select the row (or column or the entire table) and then use the Delete button in the Rows & Columns group, or on the Mini toolbar. To delete multiple rows or columns, start by selecting all the rows or columns you want to delete.

Before you delete the Network server row, you need to edit the contents in the last cell in the first column to indicate that the items in that row are for office computers and a server.

### To delete the Network server row:

▶ **1.** In the cell containing the text "Office computers," click to the right of the "s," press the **spacebar**, and then type **and network server**. The cell now reads "Office computers and network server." Part of the text wraps to a second line within the cell. Next, you can delete the Network server row, which is no longer necessary.

▶ **2.** Click in the selection bar to the left of the **Network server** row. The row is selected, with the Mini toolbar displayed on top of the selected row.

> **3.** On the Mini toolbar, click the **Delete** button. The Delete menu opens, displaying options for deleting cells, columns, rows, or the entire table. See Figure 3-15.

**Figure 3-15**    **Deleting a row**

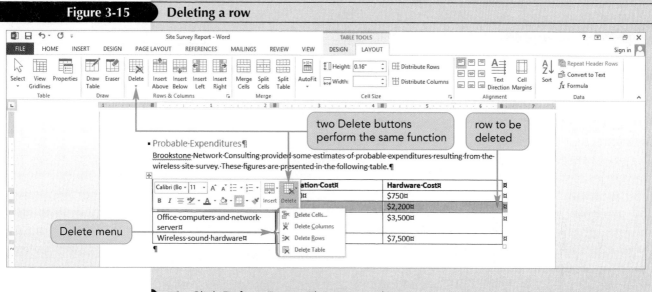

> **4.** Click **Delete Rows**. The "Network server" row is removed from the table, and the Mini toolbar disappears.

> **5.** Save your work.

The table now contains all the information Katherine wants to include. Next, you'll adjust the widths of the three columns.

# Changing Column Widths

Columns that are too wide for the material they contain can make a table hard to read. You can change a column's width by dragging the column's right border to a new position. Or, if you prefer, you can double-click a column border to make the column width adjust automatically to accommodate the widest entry in the column. To adjust the width of all the columns to match their widest entries, click anywhere in the table, click the AutoFit button in the Cell Size group on the TABLE TOOLS LAYOUT tab, and then click AutoFit Contents. To adjust the width of the entire table to span the width of the page, click the AutoFit Contents button and then click AutoFit Window.

You'll adjust the columns in Katherine's table by double-clicking the right column border. You need to start by making sure that no part of the table is selected. Otherwise, when you double-click the border, only the width of the selected part of the table will change.

When resizing a column, be sure that no part of the table is selected. Otherwise, you'll resize just the selected part.

### To change the width of the columns in the table:

▶ **1.** Verify that no part of the table is selected, and then position the mouse pointer over the right border of the "Installation Cost" column until the pointer changes to +‖+. See Figure 3-16.

| Figure 3-16 | Adjusting the column width |
| --- | --- |

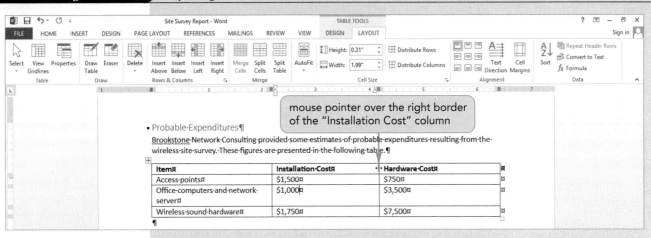

mouse pointer over the right border of the "Installation Cost" column

• Probable·Expenditures¶

Brookstone·Network·Consulting·provided·some·estimates·of·probable·expenditures·resulting·from·the· wireless·site·survey.·These·figures·are·presented·in·the·following·table.¶

| Item¤ | Installation·Cost¤ | • Hardware·Cost¤ | ¤ |
| --- | --- | --- | --- |
| Access·points¤ | $1,500¤ | $750¤ | ¤ |
| Office·computers·and·network· server¤ | $1,000¤ | $3,500¤ | ¤ |
| Wireless·sound·hardware¤ | $1,750¤ | $7,500¤ | ¤ |

¶

**TIP**

To change the height of a row, position the mouse pointer over the bottom row border and drag the border up or down.

▶ **2.** Double-click the mouse button. The right column border moves left so that the "Installation Cost" column is just wide enough to accommodate the widest entry in the column.

▶ **3.** Verify that no part of the table is selected, and that the insertion point is located in any cell in the table.

▶ **4.** Make sure the TABLE TOOLS LAYOUT tab is selected on the ribbon.

▶ **5.** In the Cell Size group, click the **AutoFit** button, and then click **AutoFit Contents**. All of the table columns adjust so that each is just wide enough to accommodate its widest entry. The text "Office computers and network server" in the lower-left cell no longer wraps to a second line.

To finish the table, you will add some formatting to improve the table's appearance.

## Formatting Tables with Styles

To adjust a table's appearance, you can use any of the formatting options available on the HOME tab. To change a table's appearance more dramatically, you can use table styles, which allow you to apply a collection of formatting options, including shading, color, borders, and other design elements, with a single click.

By default, a table is formatted with the Table Grid style, which includes only black borders between the rows and columns, no paragraph spacing, no shading, and the default black font color. You can select a more colorful table style from the Table Styles group on the TABLE TOOLS DESIGN tab. Whatever table style you choose, you'll give your document a more polished look if you use the same style consistently in all the tables in a single document.

Some table styles format rows in alternating colors, called **banded rows**, while others format the columns in alternating colors, called **banded columns**. You can choose a style that includes different formatting for the header row than for the rest of the table. Or, if the first column in your table is a header column—that is, if it contains headers identifying the type of information in each row—you can choose a style that instead applies different formatting to the first column.

### Formatting a Table with a Table Style

- Click in the table you want to format.
- On the ribbon, click the TABLE TOOLS DESIGN tab.
- In the Table Styles group, click the More button to display the Table Styles gallery.
- Position the mouse pointer over a style in the Table Styles gallery to see a Live Preview of the table style in the document.
- In the Table Styles gallery, click the style you want.
- To apply or remove style elements (such as special formatting for the header row, banded rows, or banded columns), select or deselect check boxes as necessary in the Table Style Options group.

Katherine wants to use a table style that emphasizes the header row with special formatting, does not include column borders, and uses color to separate the rows.

### To apply a table style to the Probable Expenditures table:

1. Click anywhere in the table, and then scroll to position the table at the very bottom of the Word window. This will make it easier to see the Live Preview in the next few steps.

2. On the ribbon, click the **TABLE TOOLS DESIGN** tab. In the Table Styles group, the plain Table Grid style is highlighted, indicating that it is the table's current style.

3. In the Table Styles group, click the **More** button. The Table Styles gallery opens. The default Table Grid style now appears under the heading "Plain Tables." The more elaborate styles appear below, in the "Grid Tables" section of the gallery.

4. Use the gallery's vertical scroll bar to view the complete collection of table styles. When you are finished, scroll up until you can see the "Grid Tables" heading again.

5. Move the mouse pointer over the style located in the fourth row of the Grid Tables section, second column from the right. See Figure 3-17.

**Figure 3-17**  Table Styles gallery

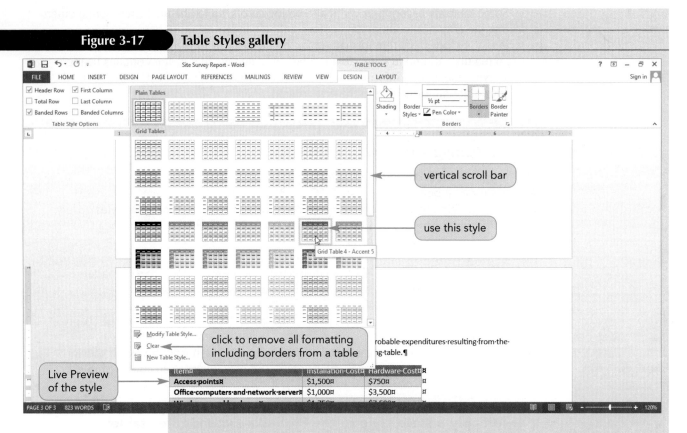

A ScreenTip displays the style's name, "Grid Table 4 - Accent 5." The style consists of a dark blue heading row, with alternating rows of light blue and white below. A Live Preview of the style is visible in the document.

▶ **6.** Click the **Grid Table 4 - Accent 5** style. The Table Styles gallery closes.

▶ **7.** Scroll to position the table at the top of the Word window, so you can review it more easily. The table's header row is formatted with dark blue shading and white text. The rows below appear in alternating colors of light blue and white.

The only problem with the newly formatted table is that the text in the first column is formatted in bold. In tables where the first column contains headers, bold would be appropriate—but this isn't the case with Katherine's table. You'll fix this by deselecting the First Column check box in the Table Style Options group.

### To remove the bold formatting from the first column:

▶ **1.** In the Table Style Options group, click the **First Column** check box to deselect this option. The bold formatting is removed from the entries in the Item column. Note that the Header Row check box is selected. This indicates that the table's header row is emphasized with special formatting (dark blue shading with white text). The Banded Rows check box is also selected because the table is formatted with banded rows of blue and white. Figure 3-18 shows the finished table.

| Figure 3-18 | Completed table |

checkmark has been removed

should be selected

first column text is no longer formatted in bold

| Item¤ | Installation·Cost¤ | Hardware·Cost¤ | ¤ |
| Access·points¤ | $1,500¤ | $750¤ | ¤ |
| Office·computers·and·network·server¤ | $1,000¤ | $3,500¤ | ¤ |
| Wireless·sound·hardware¤ | $1,750¤ | $7,500¤ | ¤ |

**2.** Save the document.

After you apply a table style, it's helpful to know how to remove it in case you want to start over from scratch. The Clear option on the menu below the Table styles gallery removes the current style from a table, including the borders between cells. When a table has no borders, the rows and columns are defined by **gridlines**, which are useful as guidelines but do not appear when you print the table.

In the following steps, you'll experiment with clearing the table's style, displaying and hiding the gridlines, and removing the table's borders.

### To experiment with table styles, gridlines, and borders:

**1.** In the Table Styles group, click the **More** button, and then click **Clear** in the menu below the gallery. Next, you need to make sure the table gridlines are displayed.

**2.** On the ribbon, click the **TABLE TOOLS LAYOUT** tab.

**3.** In the View group, click the **View Gridlines** button, if necessary, to select it. The table now looks much simpler, with no shading or font colors. Instead of the table borders, dotted gridlines separate the rows and columns. The text in the table is spaced farther apart because removing the table style restored the default paragraph and line spacing of the Normal style. The bold formatting that you applied earlier, which is not part of a table style, is visible again.

It is helpful to clear a table's style and view only the gridlines if you want to use a table to lay out text and graphics on a page, but you want no visible indication of the table itself. You'll have a chance to try this technique in the Case Problems at the end of this tutorial.

Another option is to remove only the table borders, leaving the rest of the table style applied to the table. To do this, you have to select the entire table. But first you need to undo the style change.

**4.** On the Quick Access Toolbar, click the **Undo** button to restore the Grid Table 4 - Accent 5 style, so that your table looks like the one in Figure 3-18.

**5.** In the upper-left corner of the table, click the **Table Select** handle to select the entire table, and then click the **TABLE TOOLS DESIGN** tab.

6. In the Borders group, click the **Borders button arrow** to open the Borders gallery, click **No Borders**, and then click anywhere in the table to deselect it. The borders are removed from the table, leaving only the nonprinting gridlines to separate the rows and columns. To add borders of any color to specific parts of a table, you can use the Border Painter.

7. In the Borders group, click the **Border Painter** button, and then click the **Pen Color** button to open the Pen Color gallery.

8. In the Pen Color gallery, click the **Orange, Accent 2** square in the sixth column of the first row of the gallery.

9. Use the Border Painter pointer 🖊 to click any gridline in the table. An orange border is added to the cell where you clicked.

10. Continue experimenting with the Border Painter pointer, and then press the **Esc** key to turn off the Border Painter pointer when you are finished.

11. Reapply the Grid Table 4 - Accent 5 table style to make your table match the one shown earlier in Figure 3-18.

12. Save the document and then close it.

**PROSKILLS**

### Problem Solving: Fine-Tuning Table Styles

After you apply a table style to a table, you might like the look of the table but find that it no longer effectively conveys your information or is not quite as easy to read. To solve this problem, you might be inclined to go back to the Table Styles gallery to find another style that might work better. Another method to correct problems with a table style is to identify the table elements with problematic formatting, and then manually make formatting adjustments to only those elements using the options on the TABLE TOOLS DESIGN tab. For example, you can change the thickness and color of the table borders using the options in the Borders group, and you can add shading using the Shading button in the Table Styles group. Also, if you don't like the appearance of table styles in your document, consider changing the document's theme and previewing the table styles again. The table styles have a different appearance in each theme. When applying table styles, remember there are many options for attractively formatting the table without compromising the information being conveyed.

In the next session, you'll complete the rest of the report by organizing information using tab stops, creating footnotes and endnotes, dividing the document into sections, inserting headers and footers, and finally inserting a cover page.

**REVIEW**

## Session 3.1 Quick Check

1. What must you do before you can display document headings in the Navigation pane?
2. Explain how to insert a table in a document.
3. After you enter data in the last cell in the last row in a table, how can you insert a new row?
4. Explain how to insert a new column in a table.
5. What button do you use to sort a table?
6. To adjust the width of a table's column to fit its widest entry, would you use the AutoFit Contents option or the AutoFit Window option?
7. How can you adjust a table style so that the first column in the table is formatted like all the others?

# Session 3.2 Visual Overview:

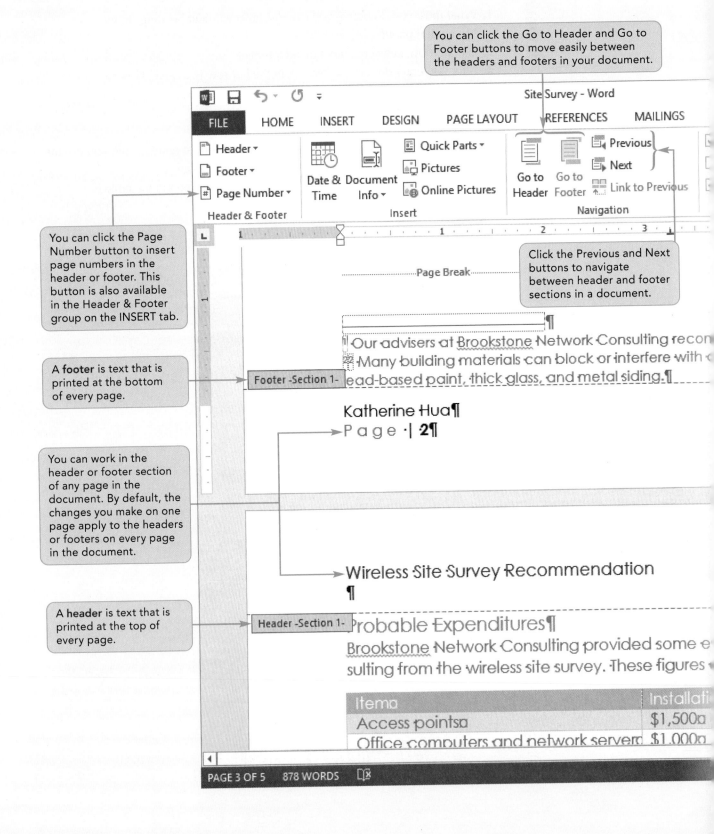

You can click the Go to Header and Go to Footer buttons to move easily between the headers and footers in your document.

You can click the Page Number button to insert page numbers in the header or footer. This button is also available in the Header & Footer group on the INSERT tab.

Click the Previous and Next buttons to navigate between header and footer sections in a document.

A **footer** is text that is printed at the bottom of every page.

You can work in the header or footer section of any page in the document. By default, the changes you make on one page apply to the headers or footers on every page in the document.

A **header** is text that is printed at the top of every page.

# Working with Headers and Footers

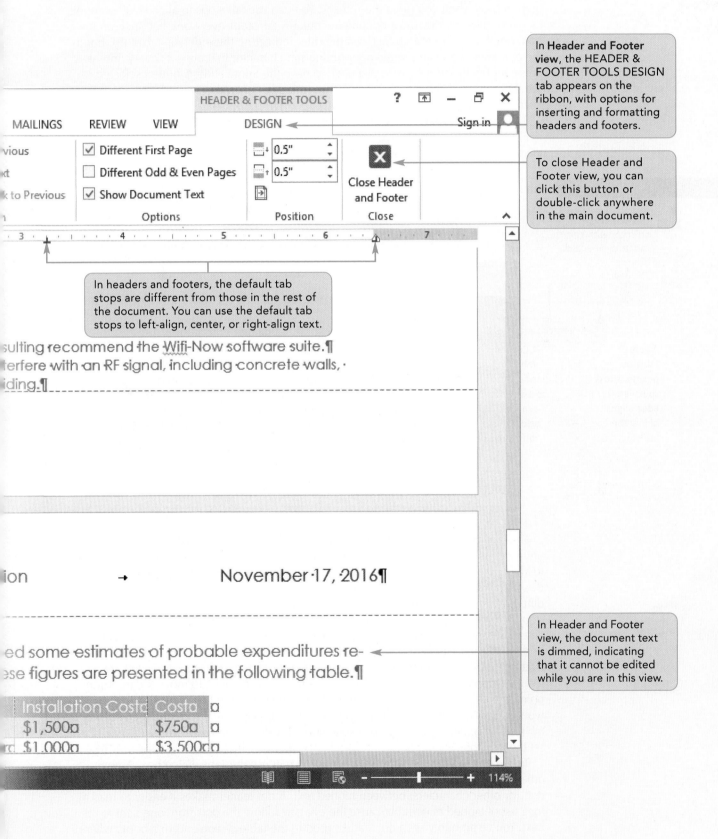

In **Header and Footer view**, the HEADER & FOOTER TOOLS DESIGN tab appears on the ribbon, with options for inserting and formatting headers and footers.

To close Header and Footer view, you can click this button or double-click anywhere in the main document.

In headers and footers, the default tab stops are different from those in the rest of the document. You can use the default tab stops to left-align, center, or right-align text.

In Header and Footer view, the document text is dimmed, indicating that it cannot be edited while you are in this view.

HEADER & FOOTER TOOLS

MAILINGS    REVIEW    VIEW    DESIGN    Sign in

☑ Different First Page         0.5"
☐ Different Odd & Even Pages  0.5"
☑ Show Document Text

Close Header and Footer

Options              Position          Close

sulting recommend the Wifi-Now software suite.¶
terfere with an RF signal, including concrete walls, ·
iding.¶

ion          →          November ·17, ·2016¶

ed some estimates of probable expenditures re-
se figures are presented in the following table.¶

| Installation Cost | Cost |  |
|---|---|---|
| $1,500 | $750 |  |
| $1,000 | $3,500 |  |

114%

# Setting Tab Stops

A **tab stop** (often called a **tab**) is a location on the horizontal ruler where the insertion point moves when you press the Tab key. You can use tab stops to align small amounts of text or data. By default, a document contains tab stops every one-half inch on the horizontal ruler. There's no mark on the ruler indicating these default tab stops, but in the document you can see the nonprinting Tab character that appears every time you press the Tab key. (Of course, you need to have the Show/Hide ¶ button selected to see these nonprinting characters.) A nonprinting tab character is just like any other character you type; you can delete it by pressing the Backspace key or the Delete key.

The five major types of tab stops are Left, Center, Right, Decimal, and Bar, as shown in Figure 3-19. The default tab stops on the ruler are all left tab stops because that is the tab style you'll probably use most often.

**Figure 3-19**    Tab stop alignment styles

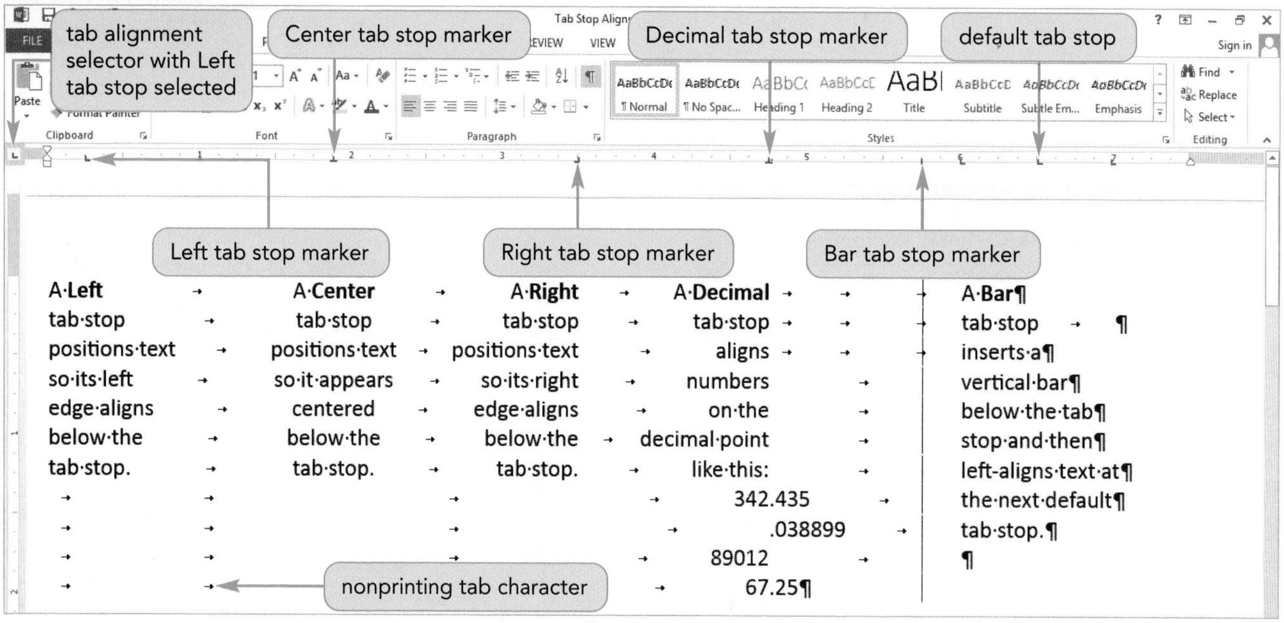

You can use tab stops a few different ways. The simplest is to press the Tab key until the insertion point is aligned where you want it, and then type the text you want to align. Each time you press the Tab key, the insertion point moves right to the next default tab stop, with the left edge of the text aligning below the tab stop. To use a different type of tab stop, or to use a tab stop at a location other than the default tab stop locations (every half-inch on the ruler), first select an alignment style from the tab alignment selector, located at the left end of the horizontal ruler, and then click the horizontal ruler where you want to insert the tab stop. This process is called setting a tab stop. When you set a new tab stop, all of the default tab stops to its left are removed. This means you have to press the Tab key only once to move the insertion point to the newly created tab stop. To set a new tab stop in text you have already typed, select the text including the nonprinting tab stop characters, and then set the tab stop by selecting an alignment style and clicking on the ruler where you want to set the tab stop.

To create more complicated tab stops, you can use the Tabs dialog box. Among other things, the Tabs dialog box allows you to insert a **dot leader**, which is a row of dots (or other characters) between tabbed text. A dot leader makes it easier to read a long list of tabbed material because the eye can follow the dots from one item to the next. You've probably seen dot leaders used in the table of contents in a book, where the dots separate the chapter titles from the page numbers.

To create a left tab stop with a dot leader, click the Dialog Box Launcher in the Paragraph group on the HOME tab, click the Indents and Spacing tab, if necessary, and then click the Tabs button at the bottom of the dialog box. In the Tab stop position box in the Tabs dialog box, type the location on the ruler where you want to insert the tab. For example, to insert a tab stop at the 4-inch mark, type 4. Verify that the Left option button is selected in the Alignment section, and then, in the Leader section, click the option button for the type of leader you want. Click the Set button and then click the OK button.

### Setting, Moving, and Clearing Tab Stops

- To set a tab stop, click the tab alignment selector on the horizontal ruler until the appropriate tab stop alignment style is displayed, and then click the horizontal ruler where you want to position the tab stop.
- To move a tab stop, drag it to a new location on the ruler. If you have already typed text that is aligned by the tab stop, select the text before dragging the tab stop to a new location.
- To clear a tab stop, drag it off the ruler.

In the Site Survey Report document you have been working on, you need to type the list of consultants and their titles. You can use tab stops to quickly format this small amount of information in two columns. As you type, you'll discover whether Word's default tab stops are appropriate for this document or whether you need to set a new tab stop. Before you get started working with tabs, you'll take a moment to explore Word's Resume Reading feature.

### To enter the list of consultants using tabs:

1. Open the **Site Survey Report** document. The document opens with the "Summary" heading at the top of the Word window. In the lower-right corner, a "Welcome back!" message is displayed briefly, and is then replaced with the Resume Reading button ▨.

2. Point to the **Resume Reading** button ▨ to expand its "Welcome back!" message. See Figure 3-20.

| Figure 3-20 | "Welcome back!" message displayed in reopened document |
|---|---|

indoor·and·outdoor·theaters.·To·make·sure·I·proposed·the·most·effective·plan·possible,·I·decided·to·seek·the·advice·of·experts.·Fortunately,·one·of·the·area's·top·experts·in·wireless·networking,·Jamie·Brookstone,·president·of·Brookstone·Network·Consulting,·offered·the·services·of·his·staff·pro·bono.·Thanks·to·his·offer,·I·was·able·to·meet·several·times·with·the·foll

click to display the part of the document you were working on before

Welcome back!
Pick up where you left off:
Probable Expenditures
8 minutes ago

Lyn·Luzerne¶

Our·conversations·focused·on·ways·to·improve·network·connect
also·studied·information·obtained·from·leading·hardware·manufacturers·and·software·distributors.·This·

PAGE 1 OF 3    823 WORDS

3. Click the **Welcome back!** message. The document window scrolls down to display the table, which you were working on just before you closed the document.

4. Scroll up to display the "Expert Advice" heading on page 1.

5. Confirm that the ruler and nonprinting characters are displayed, and that the document is displayed in Print Layout view, zoomed to 120%.

6. Click to the right of the last "e" in "Lyn Luzerne."

> **7.** Press the **Tab** key. An arrow-shaped tab character appears, and the insertion point moves to the first tab stop after the last "e" in "Luzerne." This tab stop is the default tab located at the 1-inch mark on the horizontal ruler. See Figure 3-21.

| Figure 3-21 | Tab character |
|---|---|

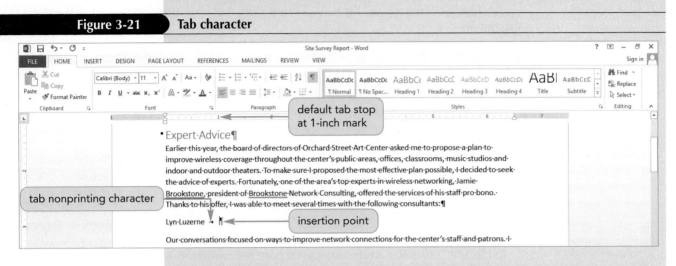

> **8.** Type **Associate Engineer**, and then press the **Enter** key to move the insertion point to the next line.

> **9.** Type **Dean Armstrong**, and then press the **Tab** key. The insertion point moves to the next available tab stop, this time located at the 1.5-inch mark on the rule.

> **10.** Type **Senior Engineer**, and then press the **Enter** key to move to the next line. Notice that Dean Armstrong's title does not align with Lyn Luzerne's title on the line above it. You'll fix this after you type the last name in the list.

> **11.** Type **Suzanne J. Sheffield-Harper**, press the **Tab** key, and then type **Project Manager**. See Figure 3-22.

| Figure 3-22 | List of consultants |
|---|---|

The list of names and titles is not aligned properly. You can fix this by inserting a new tab stop.

### To add a new tab stop to the horizontal ruler:

1. Make sure the HOME tab is displayed on the ribbon, and then select the list of consultants and their titles.

2. On the horizontal ruler, click at the 2.5-inch mark. Because the current tab stop alignment style is Left tab, Word inserts a left tab stop at that location. Remember that when you set a new tab stop, all the default tab stops to its left are removed. The column of titles shifts to the new tab stop. See Figure 3-23.

**Figure 3-23**    **Titles aligned at new tab stop**

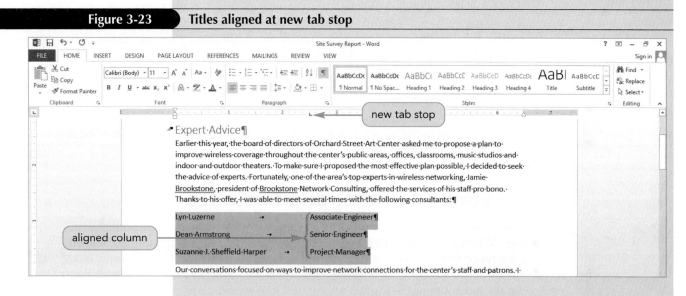

To complete the list, you need to remove the paragraph spacing after the first two paragraphs in the list, so the list looks like it's all one paragraph. You can quickly reduce paragraph and line spacing to 0 points by clicking the No Spacing style in the Styles group. In this case, you want to reduce only the paragraph spacing to 0 points, so you'll use the Line and Paragraph Spacing button instead.

3. Select the first two paragraphs in the list, which contain the names and titles for Lyn and Dean.

4. In the Paragraph group, click the **Line and Paragraph Spacing** button, and then click **Remove Space After Paragraph**.

5. Click anywhere in the document to deselect the list, and then save your work.

*Decision Making: Choosing Between Tabs and Tables*

When you have information that you want to align in columns in your document, you need to decide whether to use tabs or tables. Whatever you do, don't try to align columns of data by adding extra spaces with the spacebar. Although the text might seem precisely aligned on the screen, it probably won't be aligned when you print the document. Furthermore, if you edit the text, the spaces you inserted to align your columns will be affected by your edits; they get moved just like regular text, ruining your alignment.

So what is the most efficient way to align text in columns? It depends. Inserting tabs works well for aligning small amounts of information in just a few columns and rows, such as two columns with three rows, but tabs become cumbersome when you need to organize a lot of data over multiple columns and rows. In this case, using a table to organize columns of information is better. Unlike with tabbed columns of data, it's easy to add data to tables by inserting columns. You might also choose tables over tab stops when you want to take advantage of the formatting options available with table styles. As mentioned earlier, if you don't want the table structure itself to be visible in the document, you can clear its table style and then hide its gridlines.

Katherine would like to add two footnotes that provide further information about topics discussed in her report. You will do that next.

# Creating Footnotes and Endnotes

A **footnote** is an explanatory comment or reference that appears at the bottom of a page. When you create a footnote, Word inserts a small, superscript number (called a **reference marker**) in the text. The term **superscript** means that the number is raised slightly above the line of text. Word then inserts the same number in the page's bottom margin and positions the insertion point next to it so you can type the text of the footnote. **Endnotes** are similar, except that the text of an endnote appears at the end of a section or, in the case of a document without sections, at the end of the document. (You'll learn about dividing a document into sections later in this tutorial.) By default, the reference marker for an endnote is a lowercase Roman numeral.

Word automatically manages the reference markers for you, keeping them sequential from the beginning of the document to the end, no matter how many times you add, delete, or move footnotes or endnotes. For example, if you move a paragraph containing footnote 4 so that it falls before the paragraph containing footnote 1, Word renumbers all the footnotes in the document to keep them sequential.

*Inserting a Footnote or an Endnote*

- Click the location in the document where you want to insert a footnote or an endnote.
- On the ribbon, click the REFERENCES tab.
- In the Footnotes group, click the Insert Footnote button or the Insert Endnote button.
- Type the text of the footnote in the bottom margin of the page, or type the text of the endnote at the end of the document.
- When you are finished typing the text of a footnote or an endnote, click in the body of the document to continue working on the document.

Katherine asks you to insert a footnote that explains the phrase "barriers to RF signal propagation."

## To add a footnote to the report:

1. Use the Navigation pane to find the phrase "barriers to RF signal propagation" near the bottom of page 1, and then click to the right of the period after "propagation."

2. Close the Navigation pane.

3. On the ribbon, click the **REFERENCES** tab.

4. In the Footnotes group, click the **Insert Footnote** button. A superscript "1" is inserted to the right of the period after "propagation." Word also inserts the number "1" in the bottom margin below a separator line. The insertion point is now located next to the number in the bottom margin, ready for you to type the text of the footnote.

5. Type **Many building materials can block or interfere with an RF signal, including concrete walls, lead-based paint, thick glass, and metal siding.** See Figure 3-24.

| Figure 3-24 | Inserting a footnote |
| --- | --- |

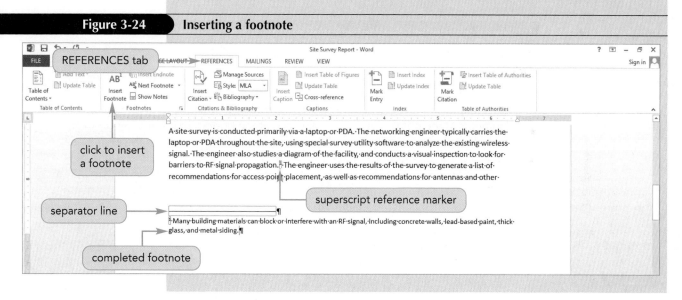

Now, Katherine would like you to insert a second footnote.

## To insert a second footnote:

1. In the third line of the same paragraph, click at the end of the second sentence to position the insertion point to the right of the period after "signal."

2. In the Footnotes group, click the **Insert Footnote** button, and then type **Our advisers at Brookstone Network Consulting recommend the Wifi-Now software suite.** Because this footnote is placed earlier in the document than the one you just created, Word inserts a superscript "1" for this footnote, and then renumbers the other footnote as "2." See Figure 3-25.

**Figure 3-25** | **Inserting a second footnote**

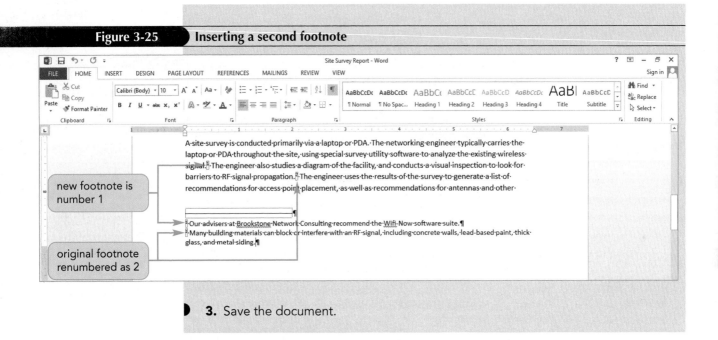

**3.** Save the document.

INSIGHT

## Understanding Endnotes, Footnotes, and Citations

It's easy to confuse footnotes with endnotes, and endnotes with citations. Remember, a footnote appears at the bottom, or foot, of a page, and always on the same page as its reference marker. You might have one footnote at the bottom of page 3, three footnotes at the bottom of page 5, and one at the bottom of page 6. By contrast, an endnote appears at the end of the document or section, with all the endnotes compiled into a single list. Both endnotes and footnotes can contain any kind of information you think might be useful to your readers. Citations, however, are only used to list specific information about a book or other source you refer to or quote from in the document. A citation typically appears in parentheses at the end of the sentence containing information from the source you are citing, and the sources for all of the document's citations are listed in a bibliography, or a list of works cited, at the end of the document.

Now you're ready to address some other issues with the document. First, Katherine has noticed that the right edges of most of the paragraphs in the document are uneven, and she'd like you to try to smooth them out. You'll correct this problem in the next section.

# Hyphenating a Document

By default, hyphenation is turned off in Word documents. That means if you are in the middle of typing a word and you reach the end of a line, Word moves the entire word to the next line instead of inserting a hyphen and breaking the word into two parts. This can result in ragged text on the right margin. To ensure a smoother right margin, you can turn on automatic hyphenation—in which case, any word that ends within the last .25 inch of a line will be hyphenated.

**To turn on automatic hyphenation in the document:**

1. Review the paragraph above the footnotes on page 1. The text on the right side of this paragraph is uneven. Keeping an eye on this paragraph will help you see the benefits of hyphenation.

2. On the ribbon, click the **PAGE LAYOUT** tab.

3. In the Page Setup group, click the **Hyphenation** button to open the Hyphenation menu, and then click **Automatic**. The Hyphenation menu closes. Throughout the document, the text layout shifts to account for the insertion of hyphens in words that break near the end of a line. For example, in the last paragraph on page 1, the word "recommendations" is now hyphenated. See Figure 3-26.

| Figure 3-26 | Hyphenated document |

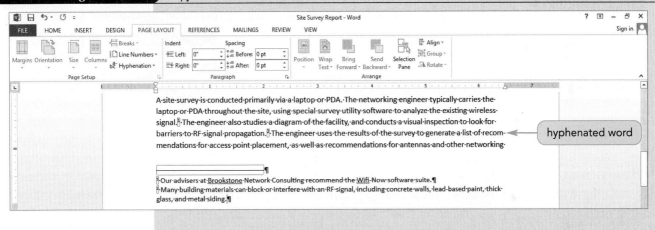

4. Save the document.

Katherine plans to post a handout on the bulletin board at the art center to help inform the staff about the upcoming site survey, and she wants to include a sample handout in the report. Before you can add the sample of the handout, you need to divide the document into sections.

# Formatting a Document into Sections

A **section** is a part of a document that can have its own page orientation, margins, headers, footers, and so on. In other words, each section is like a document within a document. To divide a document into sections, you insert a **section break**. You can select from a few different kinds of section breaks. One of the most useful is a Next page section break, which inserts a page break and starts the new section on the next page. Another commonly used kind of section break, a Continuous section break, starts the section at the location of the insertion point without changing the page flow. To insert a section break, you click the Breaks button in the Page Setup group on the PAGE LAYOUT tab and then select the type of section break you want to insert.

Katherine wants to format the handout in landscape orientation, but the report is currently formatted in portrait orientation. To format part of a document in an orientation different from the rest of the document, you need to divide the document into sections.

### To insert a section break below the table:

1. Press the **Ctrl+End** keys to move the insertion point to the end of the document, just below the table.

2. In the Page Setup group, click the **Breaks** button. The Breaks gallery opens, as shown in Figure 3-27.

**Figure 3-27**   Breaks gallery

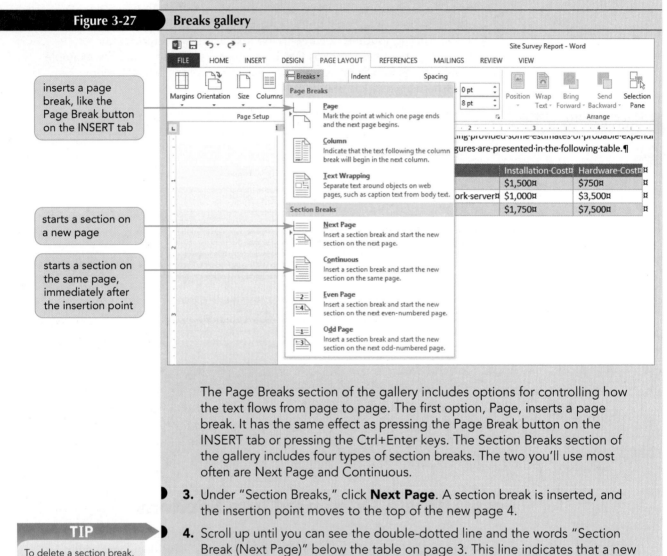

inserts a page break, like the Page Break button on the INSERT tab

starts a section on a new page

starts a section on the same page, immediately after the insertion point

The Page Breaks section of the gallery includes options for controlling how the text flows from page to page. The first option, Page, inserts a page break. It has the same effect as pressing the Page Break button on the INSERT tab or pressing the Ctrl+Enter keys. The Section Breaks section of the gallery includes four types of section breaks. The two you'll use most often are Next Page and Continuous.

3. Under "Section Breaks," click **Next Page**. A section break is inserted, and the insertion point moves to the top of the new page 4.

4. Scroll up until you can see the double-dotted line and the words "Section Break (Next Page)" below the table on page 3. This line indicates that a new section begins on the next page.

5. Save the document.

**TIP**

To delete a section break, click to the left of the line representing the break, and then press the Delete key.

You've created a new page that is a separate section from the rest of the report. The sections are numbered consecutively. The first part of the document is section 1, and the new page is section 2. Now you can format section 2 in landscape orientation without affecting the rest of the document.

**To format section 2 in landscape orientation:**

1. Scroll down and verify that the insertion point is positioned at the top of the new page 4.

2. Change the Zoom level to **30%** so you can see all four pages of the document displayed side-by-side.

3. On the ribbon, click the **PAGE LAYOUT** tab.

4. In the Page Setup group, click the **Orientation** button, and then click **Landscape**. Section 2, which consists solely of page 4, changes to landscape orientation, as shown in Figure 3-28. Section 1, which consists of pages 1–3, remains in portrait orientation.

**Figure 3-28**  **Page 4 formatted in landscape orientation**

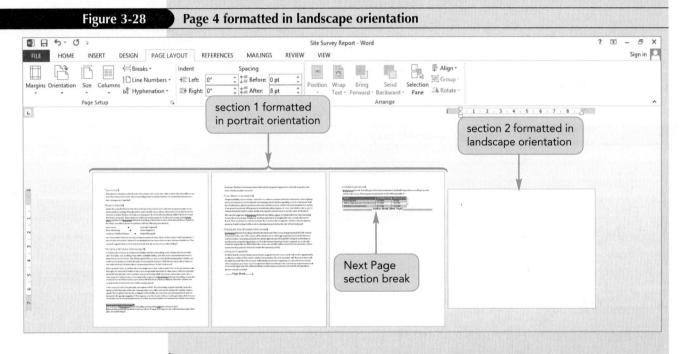

5. Change the Zoom level back to **120%**, and then save the document.

Page 4 is now formatted in landscape orientation, ready for you to create Katherine's handout, which will consist of a graphic that shows the benefits of a site survey. You'll use Word's SmartArt feature to create the graphic.

# Creating SmartArt

A **SmartArt** graphic is a diagram of shapes, such as circles, squares, or arrows. A well-designed SmartArt graphic can illustrate concepts that might otherwise require several paragraphs of explanation. To create a SmartArt graphic, you switch to the INSERT tab and then, in the Illustrations group, click the SmartArt button. This opens the Choose a SmartArt Graphic dialog box, where you can select from eight categories of graphics, including graphics designed to illustrate relationships, processes, and hierarchies. Within each category, you can choose from numerous designs. Once inserted into your document, a SmartArt graphic contains placeholder text that you replace with your own text. When a SmartArt graphic is selected, the SMARTART TOOLS DESIGN AND FORMAT tabs appear on the ribbon.

## To create a SmartArt graphic:

▶ **1.** Verify that the insertion point is located at the top of page 4, which is blank.

▶ **2.** On the ribbon, click the **INSERT** tab.

▶ **3.** In the Illustrations group, click the **SmartArt** button. The Choose a SmartArt Graphic dialog box opens, with categories of SmartArt graphics in the left panel. The middle panel displays the graphics associated with the category currently selected in the left panel. The right panel displays a larger image of the graphic that is currently selected in the middle panel, along with an explanation of the graphic's purpose. By default, All is selected in the left panel.

▶ **4.** Explore the Choose a SmartArt Graphic dialog box by selecting categories in the left panel and viewing the graphics displayed in the middle panel.

▶ **5.** In the left panel, click **Relationship**, and then scroll down in the middle panel and click the **Converging Radial** graphic (in the first column, seventh row from the top), which shows three rectangles with arrows pointing to a circle. In the right panel, you see an explanation of the Converging Radial graphic. See Figure 3-29.

| Figure 3-29 | Selecting a SmartArt graphic |
| --- | --- |

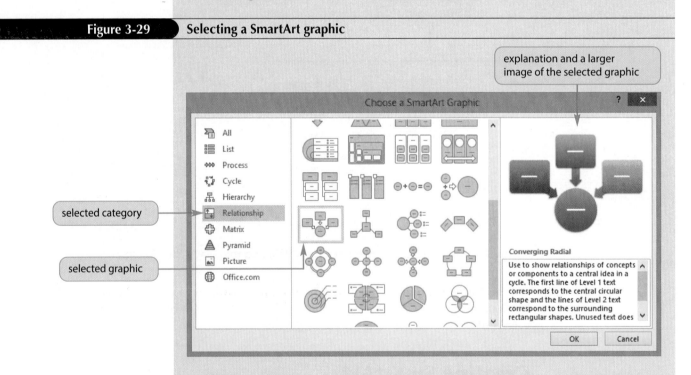

explanation and a larger image of the selected graphic

selected category

selected graphic

▶ **6.** Click the **OK** button. The Converging Radial graphic, with placeholder text, is inserted at the top of page 4. The graphic is surrounded by a rectangular border, indicating that it is selected. The SMARTART TOOLS contextual tabs appear on the ribbon. To the left or right of the graphic, you also see the Text pane, a small window with a title bar that contains the text "Type your text here." See Figure 3-30.

| Figure 3-30 | SmartArt graphic with Text pane displayed |

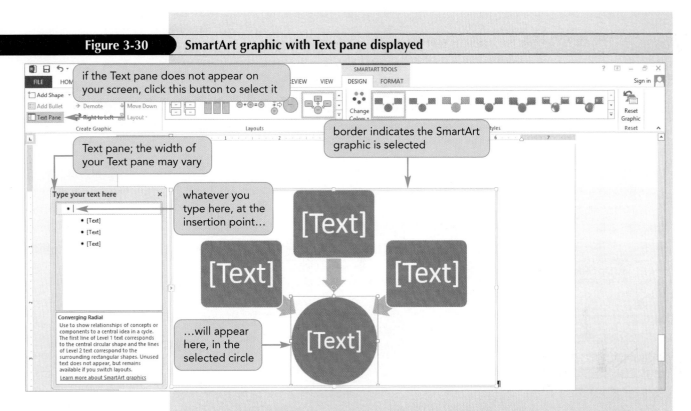

**Trouble?** If you do *not* see the Text pane, click the Text Pane button in the Create Graphic group on the SMARTART TOOLS DESIGN tab to select it.

The insertion point is blinking next to the first bullet in the Text pane, which is selected with an orange rectangle. The circle at the bottom of the SmartArt graphic is also selected, as indicated by the border with handles. At this point, anything you type next to the selected bullet in the Text pane will also appear in the selected circle in the SmartArt graphic.

**Trouble?** If you see the Text pane but the first bullet is not selected as shown in Figure 3-30, click next to the first bullet in the Text pane to select it.

Now you are ready to add text to the graphic.

### To add text to the SmartArt graphic:

1. Type **Better Wireless Network**. The new text is displayed in the Text pane and in the circle in the SmartArt graphic. Now you need to insert text in the three rectangles.

2. Press the ↓ key to move the insertion point down to the next placeholder bullet in the Text pane, and then type **Site Survey**. The new text is displayed in the Text pane and in the blue rectangle on the left. See Figure 3-31.

**Figure 3-31**   New text in Text pane and in SmartArt graphic

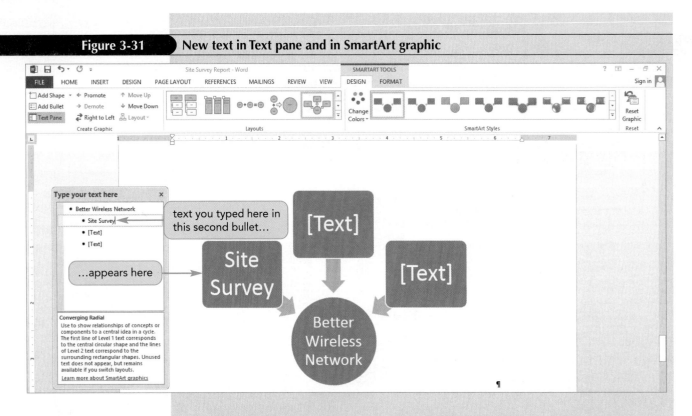

3. Press the ↓ key to move the insertion point down to the next placeholder bullet in the Text pane, and then type **Network Upgrades**. The new text appears in the middle rectangle and in the Text pane. You don't need the third rectangle, so you'll delete it.

4. Press the ↓ key to move the insertion point down to the next placeholder bullet in the Text pane, and then press the **Backspace** key. The rectangle on the right is deleted from the SmartArt graphic. The two remaining rectangles and the circle enlarge and shift position.

5. Make sure the SMARTART TOOLS DESIGN tab is still selected on the ribbon.

6. In the Create Graphic group, click the **Text Pane** button to deselect it. The Text pane closes.

7. Click in the white area inside the SmartArt border.

Next, you need to resize the SmartArt graphic so it fills the page.

**TIP**

To add a shape to a SmartArt graphic, click a shape in the SmartArt graphic, click the Add Shape arrow in the Create Graphic group on the DESIGN tab, and then click a placement option.

### To adjust the size of the SmartArt graphic:

1. Zoom out so you can see the entire page. As you can see on the ruler, the SmartArt is currently six inches wide. You could drag the SmartArt border to resize it, just as you can with any graphic, but you will get more precise results using the Size button on the SMARTART TOOLS FORMAT tab.

2. On the ribbon, click the **SMARTART TOOLS FORMAT** tab.

**3.** On the right side of the SMARTART TOOLS FORMAT tab, click the **Size** button to display the Height and Width boxes.

**4.** Click the **Height** box, type **6.5**, click the **Width** box, type **9**, and then press the **Enter** key. The SmartArt graphic resizes, so that it is now 9 inches wide and 6.5 inches high, taking up most of the page. See Figure 3-32.

**Figure 3-32**    **Resized SmartArt**

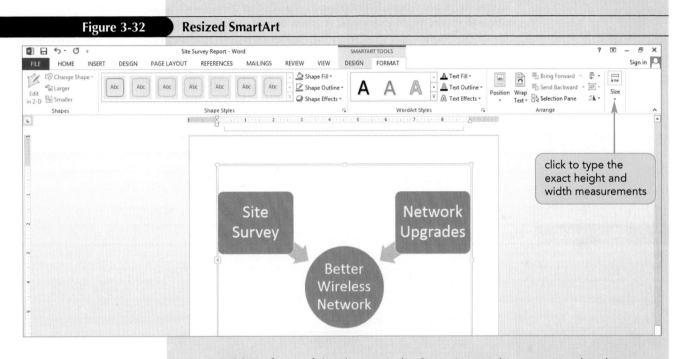

**Trouble?** If one of the shapes in the SmartArt graphic was resized, rather than the entire SmartArt graphic, the insertion point was located within the shape rather than in the white space. On the Quick Access Toolbar, click the Undo button 🔄, click in the white area inside the SmartArt border, and then repeat Steps 3 and 4.

**5.** Click outside the SmartArt border to deselect it, and then review the graphic centered on the page.

Next, you need to insert a header at the top of each page in the report and a footer at the bottom of each page in the report.

# Adding Headers and Footers

The first step to working with headers and footers is to open Header and Footer view. You can do that in three ways: (1) insert a page number using the Page Number button in the Header & Footer group on the INSERT tab; (2) double-click in the header area (in a page's top margin) or in the footer area (in a page's bottom margin); or (3) click the Header button or the Footer button on the INSERT tab.

By default, Word assumes that when you add something to the header or footer on any page of a document, you want the same text to appear on every page of the document. To create a different header or footer for the first page, you select the Different First Page check box in the Options group on the HEADER & FOOTER TOOLS DESIGN tab. When a document is divided into sections, like the Site Survey Report document, you can create a different header or footer for each section.

For a simple header or footer, double-click the header or footer area, and then type the text you want directly in the header or footer area, formatting the text as you would any other text in a document. To choose from a selection of predesigned header or footer styles, use the Header and Footer buttons on the HEADER & FOOTER TOOLS DESIGN tab (or on the INSERT tab). These buttons open galleries that you can use to select from a number of header and footer styles, some of which include page numbers and graphic elements such as horizontal lines or shaded boxes.

Some styles also include document controls that are similar to the kinds of controls that you might encounter in a dialog box. Any information that you enter in a document control is displayed in the header or footer as ordinary text, but it is also stored in the Word file so that Word can easily reuse it in other parts of the document. For example, later in this tutorial you will create a cover page for the report. Word's predefined cover pages include document controls similar to those found in headers and footers. So if you use a document control to enter the document title in the header, the same document title will show up on the cover page; there's no need to retype it.

In the following steps, you'll create a footer for the whole document (sections 1 and 2) that includes the page number and your name. As shown in Katherine's plan in Figure 3-33, you'll also create a header for section 1 only (pages 1 through 3) that includes the document title and the date. You'll leave the header area for section 2 blank.

| Figure 3-33 | Plan for headers and footers in Katherine's report |

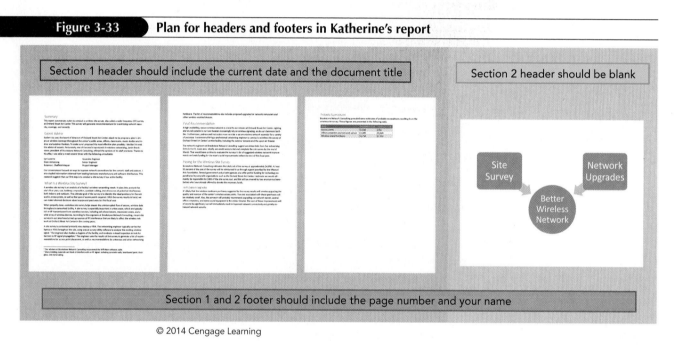

© 2014 Cengage Learning

First you will create the footer on page 1, so you can see how the footer fits below the footnotes at the bottom of the page.

### To create a footer for the entire document:

1. Change the Zoom level to **120%**, and then scroll up until you can see the bottom of page 1 and the top of page 2.

2. Double-click in the white space below the footnotes on page 1. The document switches to Header and Footer view. The HEADER & FOOTER TOOLS DESIGN tab is displayed on the ribbon. The insertion point is positioned on the left side of the footer area, ready for you to begin typing. The label "Footer -Section 1-" tells you that the insertion point is located in the footer for section 1. The document text (including the footnotes) is gray,

indicating that you cannot edit it in Header and Footer view. The header area for section 1 is also visible on top of page 2. The default footer tab stops (which are different from the default tab stops in the main document) are visible on the ruler. See Figure 3-34.

**Figure 3-34**    **Creating a footer**

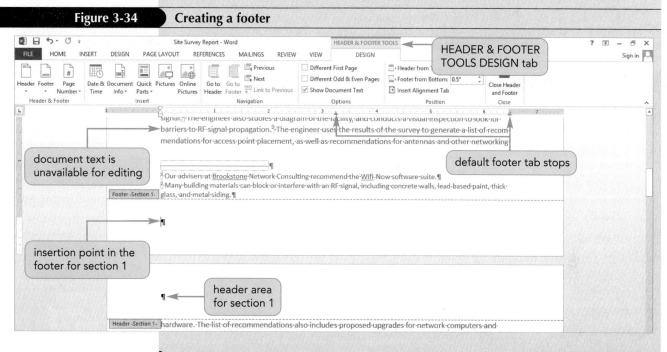

document text is unavailable for editing

default footer tab stops

insertion point in the footer for section 1

header area for section 1

HEADER & FOOTER TOOLS DESIGN tab

3. Type your first and last name, and then press the **Enter** key. The insertion point moves to the second line in the footer, aligned along the left margin. This is where you will insert the page number.

4. In the Header & Footer group, click the **Page Number** button. The Page Number menu opens. Because the insertion point is already located where you want to insert the page number, you'll use the Current Position option.

5. Point to **Current Position**. A gallery of page number styles opens. Katherine wants to use the Accent Bar 2 style.

6. Click the **Accent Bar 2** style (the third style from the top). The word "Page," a vertical bar, and the page number are inserted in the footer.

   Next, you'll check to make sure that the footer you just created for section 1 also appears in section 2. To move between headers or footers in separate sections, you can use the buttons in the Navigation group on the HEADER & FOOTER TOOLS DESIGN tab.

7. In the Navigation group, click the **Next** button. Word displays the footer for the next section in the document—that is, the footer for section 2, which appears at the bottom of page 4. The label at the top of the footer area reads "Footer -Section 2-" and it contains the same text (your name and the page number) in this footer as in section 1. Word assumes, by default, that when you type text in one footer, you want it to appear in all the footers in the document.

**TIP**

To change the numbering style or to specify a number to use as the first page number, click the Page Number button in the Header & Footer group, and then click Format Page Numbers.

Now you need to create a header for section 1. Katherine does not want to include a header in section 2 because it would distract attention from the SmartArt graphic. So you will first separate the header for section 1 from the header for section 2.

### To separate the headers for section 1 and section 2:

1. Verify that the insertion point is located in the section 2 footer area at the bottom of page 4, and that the HEADER & FOOTER TOOLS DESIGN tab is selected on the ribbon. To switch from the footer to the header in the current section, you can use the Go to Header button in the Navigation group.

2. In the Navigation group, click the **Go to Header** button. The insertion point moves to the section 2 header at the top of page 4. See Figure 3-35.

---

Figure 3-35    **Section 2 header is currently the same as the previous header, in section 1**

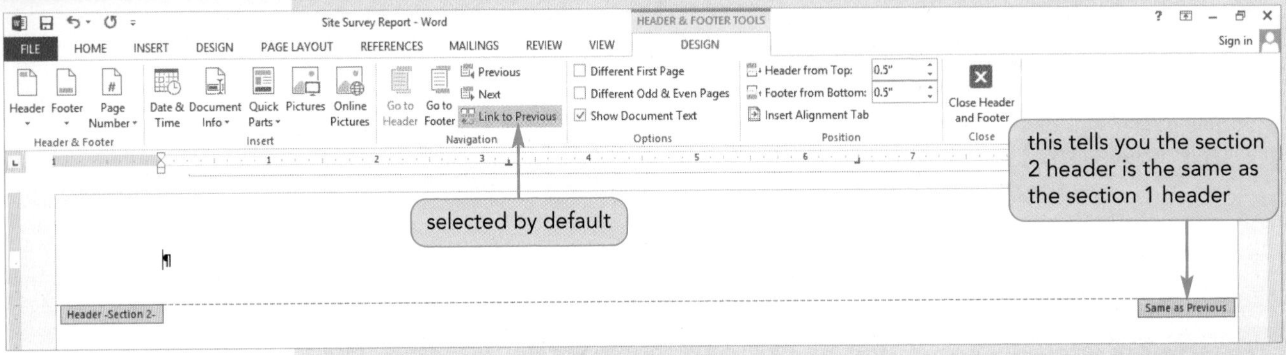

selected by default

this tells you the section 2 header is the same as the section 1 header

Header -Section 2-

Same as Previous

---

Notice that in the Navigation group, the Link to Previous button is selected. In the header area in the document window, the gray tab on the right side of the header border contains the message "Same as Previous," indicating that the section 2 header is set up to display the same text as the header in the previous section, which is section 1. To make the section 2 header a separate entity, you need to break the link between the section 1 and section 2 headers.

**TIP**

When you create a header for a section, it doesn't matter what page you're working on as long as the insertion point is located in a header in that section.

3. In the Navigation group, click the **Link to Previous** button to deselect it. The Same as Previous tab is removed from the right side of the section 2 header border.

4. In the Navigation group, click the **Previous** button. The insertion point moves up to the nearest header in the previous section, which is the section 1 header at the top of page 3. The label "Header -Section 1-" identifies this as a section 1 header.

5. In the Header & Footer group, click the **Header** button. A gallery of header styles opens.

6. Scroll down and review the various header styles, and then click the **Grid** style (eighth style from the top). The placeholder text "[Document title]" is aligned at the left margin. The placeholder text "[Date]" is aligned at the right margin.

7. Click the **[Document title]** placeholder text. The placeholder text is now selected within a document control. See Figure 3-36.

**Figure 3-36** — Adding a header to section 1

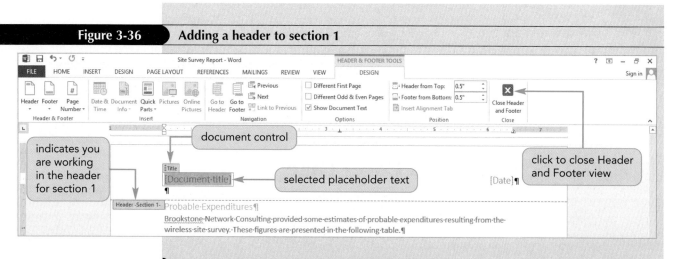

indicates you are working in the header for section 1

document control

selected placeholder text

click to close Header and Footer view

8. Type **Wireless Site Survey Recommendation**. The text you just typed is displayed in the document control instead of the placeholder text. Next, you need to add the date. The header style you selected includes a date picker document control, which allows you to select the date from a calendar.

9. Click the **[Date]** placeholder text to display an arrow in the document control, and then click the arrow. A calendar for the current month appears, as shown in Figure 3-37. In the calendar, the current date is outlined in dark blue.

**Figure 3-37** — Adding a date to the section 1 header

click the placeholder text to display the arrow…

…then click the arrow to display the calendar

click to display an earlier month

Wireless·Site·Survey·Recommendation

Header -Section 1-   Probable·Expenditures¶

Brookstone
wireless·si

current date is highlighted; your current date will be different

probable·expenditures
g·table.¶

November, 2016
Su Mo Tu We Th Fr Sa
30 31  1  2  3  4  5
 6  7  8  9 10 11 12
13 14 15 16 17 18 19
20 21 22 23 24 25 26
27 28 29 30  1  2  3
 4  5  6  7  8  9 10
Today

| Item¤ | Installation·Cost¤ | Hardware·Cost¤ | ¤ |
|---|---|---|---|
| Access·points¤ | $1,500¤ | $750¤ | ¤ |
| Office·computers·and·network·server¤ | $1,000¤ | $3,500¤ | ¤ |
| Wireless·sound·hardware¤ | $1,750¤ | $7,500¤ | ¤ |

Section Break (Next Page)

click to display a later month

10. Click the current date. The current date, including the year, is inserted in the document control.

11. Scroll up slightly and click anywhere in the Section 1 footer (on the preceding page) to deselect the date document control. You are finished creating the header and footer for Katherine's report, so you can close Header and Footer view and return to Print Layout view.

12. In the Close group, click the **Close Header and Footer** button, or double-click anywhere in the main document, and then save your work.

> **13.** Change the Zoom level to **30%** so you can see all four pages of the document, including the header at the top of pages 1–3 and the footer at the bottom of pages 1–4. Take a moment to compare your completed headers and footers with Katherine's plan for the headers and footers shown earlier in Figure 3-33.

Finally, you need to insert a cover page for the report.

# Inserting a Cover Page

A document's cover page typically includes the title and the name of the author. Some people also include a summary of the report on the cover page, which is commonly referred to as an abstract. In addition, you might include the date, the name and possibly the logo of your company or organization, and a subtitle. A cover page should not include the document header or footer.

To insert a preformatted cover page at the beginning of the document, you use the Cover Page button on the INSERT tab. You can choose from a variety of cover page styles, all of which include document controls in which you can enter the document title, the document's author, the date, and so on. These document controls are linked to any other document controls in the document. For example, you already entered "Wireless Site Survey Recommendation" into a document control in the header of Katherine's report. So if you use a cover page that contains a similar document control, "Wireless Site Survey Recommendation" will be displayed on the cover page automatically. Note that document controls sometimes display information entered when either Word or Windows was originally installed on your computer. If your computer has multiple user accounts, the information displayed in some document controls might reflect the information for the current user. In any case, you can easily edit the contents of a document control.

## To insert a cover page at the beginning of the report:

> **1.** Verify that the document is still zoomed so that you can see all four pages, and then press the **Ctrl+Home** keys. The insertion point moves to the beginning of the document.

> **2.** On the ribbon, click the **INSERT** tab.

> **3.** In the Pages group, click the **Cover Page** button. A gallery of cover page styles opens.
>
> Notice that the names of the cover page styles match the names of the preformatted header styles you saw earlier. For example, the list includes a Grid cover page, which is designed to match the Grid header used in this document. To give a document a uniform look, it's helpful to use elements with the same style throughout.

> **4.** Scroll down the gallery to see the cover page styles, and then locate the Grid cover page style.

> **5.** Click the **Grid** cover page style. The new cover page is inserted at the beginning of the document.

> **6.** Change the Zoom level to **120%**, and then scroll down to display the report title in the middle of the cover page. The only difference between the title "Wireless Site Survey Recommendation" here and the title you entered in the document header is that here the title is displayed in all uppercase. The cover page also includes document controls for a subtitle and an abstract. See Figure 3-38.

**TIP**

To delete a cover page that you inserted from the Cover Page gallery, click the Cover Page button in the Pages group, and then click Remove Current Cover Page.

Figure 3-38   Newly inserted cover page

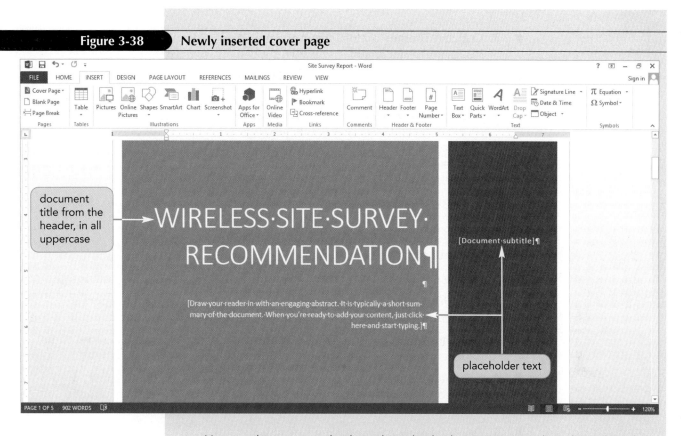

You need to type a subtitle in the subtitle document control on the right side of the page.

**7.** Click the **[Document subtitle]** placeholder text, and then type **Orchard Street Art Center**. Next, you will remove the abstract document control because you do not need an abstract for this report.

**8.** Below the document title, right-click the placeholder text that begins **[Draw your reader in...** to display the shortcut menu, and then click **Remove Content Control**. The content control is removed from the cover page.

**9.** Save the document.

# Changing the Theme

The report now contains several formatting elements that are controlled by the document's theme, so changing the theme will affect the document's overall appearance. Katherine suggests that you apply a different theme to the document.

### To change the document's theme:

**1.** Change the Zoom level to **40%** so you can see the first four pages side-by-side, with part of the fifth page visible on the bottom.

**2.** On the ribbon, click the **DESIGN** tab.

▶ **3.** Click the **Themes** button, select any theme you want, and then review the results in the document.

▶ **4.** Apply three or four more different themes of your choice and review the results of each in the document.

▶ **5.** Click the **Retrospect** theme, and then save the document. The cover page is now orange and olive green, the headings as well as the header and footer text are orange, and the table is formatted with an olive green header row and gray shading.

Your work on the report is finished. You should preview the report before closing it.

**To preview the report:**

▶ **1.** On the ribbon, click the **FILE** tab.

▶ **2.** In the navigation bar, click the **Print** tab. The cover page of the report is displayed in the document preview in the right pane.

▶ **3.** Examine the document preview, using the arrow buttons at the bottom of the pane to display each page.

▶ **4.** If you need to make any changes to the report, return to Print Layout view, edit the document, preview the document again, and then save the document.

▶ **5.** Display the document in Print Layout view.

▶ **6.** Change the Zoom level back to **120%**, and then press the **Ctrl+Home** keys to make sure the insertion point is located on the first page.

# Reviewing a Document in Read Mode

The members of the board of directors might choose to print the report, but some might prefer to read it on their computers instead. In that case, they can take advantage of **Read Mode**, a document view designed to make reading on a screen as easy as possible. Unlike Print Layout view, which mimics the look of the printed page with its margins and page breaks, Read Mode focuses on the document's content. Read Mode displays as much content as possible on the screen at a time, with buttons that allow you to display more. Note that you can't edit text in Read Mode. To do that, you need to switch back to Page Layout view.

**To display the Site Survey document in Read Mode:**

▶ **1.** In the status bar, click the **Read Mode** button 📖. The document switches to Read Mode, with a reduced version of the cover page on the left and the first part of the document text on the right. On the left edge of the status bar, the message "SCREENS 1-2 OF 8" explains that you are currently viewing the first two screens out of a total of 8.

  **Trouble?** If your status bar indicates that you have a different number of screens, change the Zoom level as needed so that the document is split into 8 screens.

The title page on the left is screen 1. The text on the right is screen 2. To display more of the document, you can click the arrow button on the right. See Figure 3-39.

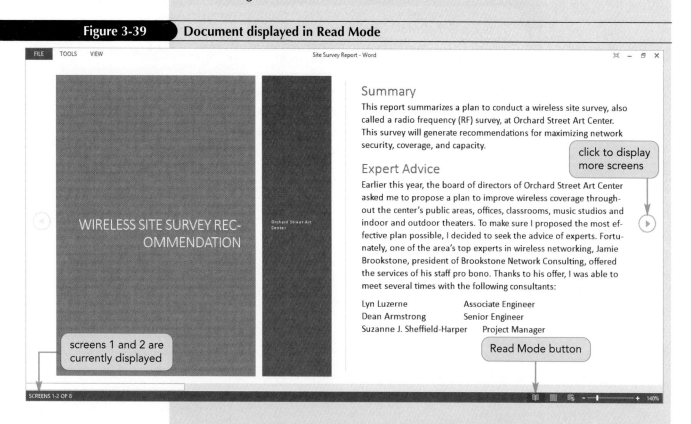

2. Click the **right arrow** button ⊙ on the right to display screens 3 and 4. A left arrow button now appears on the left side of the screen. You could click it to move back to the previous screens.

3. Click the **right arrow** button ⊙ to display screens 5 and 6, and then click the **right arrow** button ⊙ again to display the final two screens. To zoom in on the SmartArt graphic, you can double-click it.

4. Double-click the SmartArt graphic. An object zoom window opens, with the SmartArt graphic displayed. You can display an object zoom window like this for any graphic.

5. In the upper-right corner of the object zoom window, click the **magnifying glass** button ⊕ to zoom in on the SmartArt graphic even more.

6. Click the **magnifying glass** button ⊖ to return to the previous zoom level.

7. Click anywhere outside the object zoom window to return to screens 7 and 8 in Read Mode.

8. Click the **left arrow** button ⊙ on the left as necessary to return to screens 1 and 2, and then click the **Print Layout** button ▤ in the status bar to return to Page Layout view.

9. Close the document.

You now have a draft of the Site Survey Report document, including a cover page, the report text, a nicely formatted table, and the SmartArt graphic (in landscape orientation).

**REVIEW**

## Session 3.2 Quick Check

1. Where are the default tab stops located on the horizontal ruler?
2. What tab do you click to begin creating a footnote?
3. Explain how to configure Word to hyphenate a document automatically.
4. Explain how to create separate headers for a document with two sections.
5. List three ways to switch from Page Layout view to Header and Footer view.
6. Explain how to make a graphic easier to view in Read Mode.

### SAM Projects

Put your skills into practice with SAM Projects! SAM Projects for this tutorial can be found online. If you have a SAM account, go to www.cengage.com/sam2013 to download the most recent Project Instructions and Start Files.

**PRACTICE**

## Review Assignments

**Data File needed for the Review Assignments: Security.docx**

The wireless site survey has been completed, and the Orchard Street Art Center has upgraded its network. Now, Katherine Hua is organizing a series of network security training classes for the art center staff. She has begun working on a report for the board that outlines basic information about the training. You need to format the report, add a table at the end containing a preliminary schedule, and create a sample graphic that Katherine could use in a handout announcing the training. Complete the following steps:

1. Open the file **Security** located in the Word3 ▸ Review folder included with your Data Files, and then save it as **Security Training Report** in the location specified by your instructor.
2. Promote the "Training Schedule" and "Level 1 Equipment Needs" headings from Heading 2 text to Heading 1 text, and then move the "Level 1 Equipment Needs" heading and its body text up above the "Training Schedule" heading.
3. Insert a page break before the "Training Schedule" heading. Insert a blank paragraph at the end of the new page 2, and then insert a table using the information shown in Figure 3-40. Format the header row in bold.

**Figure 3-40**    Information for training schedule table

| Date | Topic |
| --- | --- |
| April 21 | Applications |
| March 16 | User account permissions |
| April 28 | Firewall procedures |
| April 6 | Wireless devices |
| March 3 | Password security |

© 2014 Cengage Learning

4. Sort the table by the contents of the "Date" column in ascending order.
5. In the appropriate location in the table, insert a new row for a **User privacy** class on **March 23**.
6. Delete the "Applications" row from the table.
7. Modify the widths of both columns to accommodate the widest entry in each.
8. Apply the Grid Table 4 - Accent 2 style to the table.
9. On page 1, replace the text "[instructor names]" with a tabbed list of instructors and their specialties, using the following information: **Jackie Fuhrman-Dunaway, Wireless security; Marcolo Jimenez, Multimedia wireless security; Surila Jin, Web privacy; Elizabeth Lawson, User support**. Insert a tab after each name, and don't include any punctuation in the list.
10. Use a left tab stop to align the instructors' specialities 2.5 inches from the left margin, and then adjust the list's paragraph spacing so it appears to be a single paragraph.

11. Locate the first sentence below the "Level 1 Equipment Needs" heading. At the end of that sentence, insert a footnote that reads **Some board members mentioned the possibility of holding classes in the concert hall, but the instructors prefer the smaller lecture hall, where microphones are unnecessary**.

12. Hyphenate the document using the default settings.

13. After the training schedule table on page 2, insert a section break that starts a new, third page, and then format the new page in landscape orientation. Insert a SmartArt graphic that illustrates the advantages of computer classes. Use the Equation graphic from the Process category, and, from left to right, include the following text in the SmartArt diagram: **User Education**, **Good Network Management**, and **Secure Wireless Network**. Do not include any punctuation in the SmartArt. Size the SmartArt graphic to fill the page.

14. Create a footer for sections 1 and 2 that aligns your first and last names at the left margin. Insert the page number, without any design elements and without the word "Page," below your name.

15. Separate the section 1 header from the section 2 header, and then create a header for section 1 using the Retrospect header style. Enter **SECURITY TRAINING** as the document title, and select the current date. Note that the document title will be displayed in all uppercase no matter how you type it.

16. Insert a cover page using the Retrospect style. If you typed the document title in all uppercase in the header, it will be displayed in all uppercase here. If you used a mix of uppercase and lowercase in the header, you'll see a mix here. Revise the document title as necessary to make it all uppercase, and then add the following subtitle: **A REPORT FOR THE ORCHARD STREET ART CENTER BOARD OF DIRECTORS**. Enter your name in the Author document control (you might have to replace a default name inserted by Word), and then delete the Company Name and Company Address document controls.

17. Change the document theme to Integral, save and preview the report, and then close it.

## Case Problem 1

**Data File needed for this Case Problem: Greenware.docx**

**Greenware Consortium**    You are the assistant business manager of Greenware Consortium, a professional organization for LEED contractors in Seattle, Washington and the surrounding area. LEED, which is short for Leadership in Energy and Environmental Design, is a certification system designed to encourage environmentally friendly building construction and maintenance. Contractors join the Greenware Consortium to make professional contacts with like-minded vendors and customers. You have been asked to help prepare an annual report for the board of directors. The current draft is not complete, but it contains enough for you to get started. Complete the following steps:

1. Open the file **Greenware** located in the Word3 ▶ Case1 folder included with your Data Files, and then save it as **Greenware Report** in the location specified by your instructor.

2. Adjust the heading levels so that the "Greenware Faire" and "Green Tech Fest" headings are formatted with the Heading 2 style.

3. Move the "Membership Forecast" heading and its body text down to the end of the report.

4. Format the Board of Directors list using a left tab stop with a dot leader at the 2.2-inch mark. (*Hint*: Use the Dialog Box Launcher in the Paragraph group on the PAGE LAYOUT tab to open the Paragraph dialog box, and then click the Tabs button at the bottom of the Indents and Spacing tab to open the Tabs dialog box.)

5. At the end of the first paragraph below the "Going Green Walking Tours" heading, insert the following footnote: **The Going Green walking tours are sponsored by the Seattle Public Works Department in association with the Seattle Green for Life Foundation**.

6. Locate the "Purpose" heading on page 1. At the end of the body text below that heading, insert the following footnote: **We recently signed a ten-year contract renewal with our website host, NetMind Solutions**.

7. Insert a page break that moves the "Membership Forecast" heading to the top of a new page, and then, below the body text on the new page, insert a table consisting of three columns and four rows.

8. In the table, enter the information shown in Figure 3-41. Format the column headings in bold.

**Figure 3-41**    **Information for membership forecast table**

| Membership Type | 2016 | Projected 2017 |
|---|---|---|
| Contractor | 260 | 285 |
| Vendor | 543 | 670 |
| Building Owner/Operator | 350 | 400 |

© 2014 Cengage Learning

9. Sort the table in ascending order by membership type.

10. In the appropriate location in the table, insert a row for a **Student/Apprentice** membership type, with **250** members in 2016, and **300** projected members in 2017.

11. Adjust the column widths so each column accommodates the widest entry.

12. Format the table using the Grid Table 4 - Accent 1 table style without banded rows or a first column.

13. Hyphenate the document using the default settings.

14. Insert a Blank footer, and then type your name to replace the selected placeholder text in the footer's left margin. In the right margin, insert a page number using the Accent Bar 3 style. (*Hint:* Press the Tab key twice to move the insertion point to the right margin before inserting the page number, and then insert the page number at the current location.)

15. Insert a cover page using the Sideline style. Enter the company name, **Greenware Consortium**, and the title, **Annual Report**, in the appropriate document controls. In the subtitle document control, enter **Prepared by [Your Name]** (but replace "[Your Name]" with your first and last names). Delete the Author document control, which might contain a default name inserted by Word, and then insert the current date in the Date document control.

16. Change the document theme to Ion.

17. Save, preview, and then close the document.

## Case Problem 2

Data File needed for this Case Problem: Evaluation.docx

*Customer Evaluation Report*    Academy Art Tours specializes in European tours emphasizing art and architecture. After managing this year's Masters of Architecture tour, Lisa Marisca has begun writing a report summarizing the customer evaluation forms. She asks you to review her incomplete draft and fix some problems. Complete the following steps:

1. Open the file named **Evaluation** located in the Word3 ▶ Case2 folder included with your Data Files, and then save it as **Evaluation Report** in the location specified by your instructor.

⚙ Troubleshoot 2. Adjust the document so that the following are true:

- The heading "Problems Acquiring Updated Passports," its body text, and the SmartArt graphic appear on the last page in landscape orientation, with the rest of the report in portrait orientation.

- In section 1, the heading "Summary" is displayed at the top of page 2.

- The document header contains your first and last names but not a content control for the document title.

- Neither the header nor the footer is displayed on page 1.

- The footer is not displayed on the last page of the document. (*Hint:* After you break the link between sections, you'll need to delete the contents of the footer in one section.)

⚙ Troubleshoot 3. On pages 2 and 3, promote headings as necessary so all the headings are on the same level.

TROUBLESHOOT

4. Increase the paragraph spacing before the first paragraph, "Masters of Architecture," on page 1 as much as necessary so that the paragraph is located at about the 2-inch mark on the vertical ruler. When you're finished, the text should be centered vertically on the page, so it looks like a cover page.

⚙ **Troubleshoot** 5. On page 2, remove any extra rows and columns in the table, and sort the information in a logical way. When you are finished, format it with a style that applies green (Accent 6) shading to the header row, with banded rows below, and remove any bold formatting as necessary.

6. Add a fourth shape to the SmartArt Graphic with the text **Submit completed form, photo, and fee to post office clerk**. Resize the graphic to fill the white space below the document text.

7. Save the document, review it in Read Mode, preview it, and then close it.

## Case Problem 3

**CREATE**

**There are no Data Files needed for this Case Problem.**

**"Aiden Eats" Blog and Newsletter**   Aiden Malloy publishes his reviews of Minneapolis restaurants both in his blog, Aiden Eats, and in a printed newsletter of the same name. These publications have become so popular that Aiden has decided to try selling advertising space in both venues to local businesses. A colleague has just emailed him a list of potential advertisers. Aiden asks you to create and format a table containing the list of advertisers. When you're finished with that project, you'll create a table detailing some of his recent expenses. Complete the following steps:

1. Open a new, blank document, and then save it as **Advertiser Table** in the location specified by your instructor.

2. Create the table shown in Figure 3-42.

**Figure 3-42**   **Advertiser table**

| Business | Contact | Phone |
|---|---|---|
| Allenton Knife Sharpening | Peter Allenton | 555-5555 |
| Bizmark Restaurant Supply | Nolan Everdeen | 555-5555 |
| Spices Boutique | Sigrid Larson | 555-5555 |
| WestMark Kitchen Design | Sheryl Wu | 555-5555 |

© 2014 Cengage Learning

For the table style, start with the Grid Table 4 - Accent 1 table style, and then make any necessary changes. Use the Blue, Accent 1 color for the borders. The final table should be about 6.5 inches wide and 2.5 inches tall, as measured on the horizontal and vertical rulers. (*Hint:* Remember that you can drag the Table Resize handle to increase the table's overall size.)

3. Replace "Peter Allenton" with your first and last names.

4. Save, preview, and then close the Advertiser Table document.

5. Open a new, blank document, and then save it as **Expense Table** in the location specified by your instructor.

6. Create the table shown in Figure 3-43.

Figure 3-43     Expense table

| Restaurant | Date | Expense |
|---|---|---|
| Beverly Coffee and Bake Shoppe | 2/3/16 | $13.50 |
| Vietnam Noodle House | 2/10/16 | $23.00 |
| The Everett Club | 2/23/16 | $45.50 |
| | Total | $82.00 |

© 2014 Cengage Learning

For the table style, start with the Grid Table 4 - Accent 1 table style, and then make any necessary changes. Use the Blue, Accent 1 color for the borders. Note that in the bottom row, you'll need to merge two cells and right-align text within the new, merged cell.

7. For the total, use a formula instead of simply typing the amount. (*Hint:* Click in the cell where you want to insert a formula to sum the values, click the TABLE TOOLS LAYOUT tab, and then click the Formula button in the Data group to open the Formula dialog box, and then click the OK button.)

8. Save, preview, and then close the Expense Table document.

CHALLENGE

## Case Problem 4

There are no Data Files needed for this Case Problem.

***Friends of Triangle Beach***   Kate Chomsky coordinates volunteers who monitor and protect native plant species on Triangle Beach, a nature preserve on the eastern coast of Florida. She needs a flyer to hand out at an upcoming neighborhood festival, where she hopes to recruit more volunteers. You can use Word's table features to lay out the flyer as shown in Kate's sketch in Figure 3-44. At the very end, you'll remove the table borders.

Figure 3-44     Sketch for Triangle Beach flyer

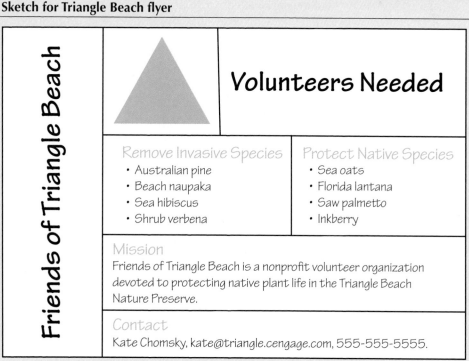

© 2014 Cengage Learning

Complete the following steps:

1. Open a new, blank document, and then save it as **Triangle Beach** in the location specified by your instructor.

2. Change the document's orientation to landscape.

⊕ **Explore** 3. Use the Table button on the INSERT tab, to access the Insert Table menu, and then click Draw Table at the bottom of the menu to activate the Draw Table pointer (which looks like a pencil). Click in the upper-left corner of the document (near the paragraph mark), and, using the rulers as guides, drag down and to the right to draw a rectangle that is 9 inches wide and 6 inches high. After you draw the rectangle, you can adjust its height and width using the Height and Width boxes in the Cell Size group on the TABLE TOOLS LAYOUT tab, if necessary. (*Hint:* If the Draw Table pointer disappears after you change the table's height and width, you can turn it back on by clicking the Draw Table button in the Draw group on the TABLE TOOLS LAYOUT tab.)

⊕ **Explore** 4. Use the Draw Table pointer to draw the columns and rows shown in Figure 3-44. For example, to draw the column border for the "Friends of Triangle Beach" column, click the top of the rectangle at the point where you want the right column border to be located, and then drag down to the bottom of the rectangle. Use the same technique to draw rows. (*Hint:* To delete a border, click the Eraser button in the Draw group on the TABLE TOOLS LAYOUT tab, click anywhere on the border you want to erase, and then click the Eraser button again to turn it off.)

5. When you are finished drawing the table, press the Esc key to turn off the Draw Table pointer.

⊕ **Explore** 6. In the left column, type the text **Friends of Triangle Beach**. With the pointer still in that cell, click the TABLE TOOLS LAYOUT tab, and then in the Alignment group, click the Text Direction button twice to position the text vertically so that it reads from bottom to top. Using the formatting options on the HOME tab, format the text in 36-point font. Use the Align Center button in the Alignment group to center the text in the cell. (*Hint:* You will probably have to adjust and readjust the row and column borders throughout these steps until all the elements of the table are positioned properly.)

7. Type the remaining text as shown in Figure 3-44. Replace "Kate Chomsky" with your own name, remove the hyperlink formatting from the email address, and format it in bold. Change the font size for "Volunteers Needed" to 36 points, and center align the text in that cell. Use the Heading 1 style for the following text—"Remove Invasive Species," "Protect Native Species," "Mission," and "Contact." Change the font size for this text to 20 points. For the remaining text, use the Normal style, and then change the font size to 16 points. If the table expands to two pages, drag a row border up slightly to reduce the row's height. Repeat as necessary until the table fits on one page.

⊕ **Explore** 8. On the INSERT tab, use the Shapes button in the Illustrations group to draw the Isosceles Triangle shape, similar to the way you drew the table rectangle, by dragging the pointer. Draw the triangle in the blank cell in the top row. If the triangle isn't centered neatly in the cell, click the Undo button and try again until you draw a triangle that has the same proportions as the one in Figure 3-44. Until you change the theme in the next step, the triangle will be blue.

9. Change the document theme to Facet.

10. Remove the table borders. When you are finished, your flyer should match the table shown in Figure 3-44, but without the table borders.

11. Save your work, preview the document, and then close it.

# Enhancing Page Layout and Design

*Creating a Newsletter*

## OBJECTIVES

**Session 4.1**
- Use continuous section break for page layout
- Format text in columns
- Insert symbols and special characters
- Distinguish between inline and floating objects
- Wrap text around an object
- Insert and format text boxes
- Insert drop caps

**Session 4.2**
- Create and modify WordArt
- Insert and crop a picture
- Add clip art to a document
- Rotate and adjust a picture
- Remove a photo's background
- Balance columns
- Add a page border
- Save a document as a PDF
- Open a PDF in Word

## Case | *Williamson Health Care*

Estefan Silva is a public outreach specialist at Williamson Health Care, a health maintenance organization located in Carson City, Nevada. He has written the text of a newsletter describing an upcoming series of wellness classes. Now he needs you to transform the text into an eye-catching publication with a headline, photos, drop caps, and other desktop publishing elements. Estefan's budget doesn't allow him to hire a professional graphic designer to create the document using desktop publishing software. But there's no need for that because you can do the work for him using Word's formatting, graphics, and page layout tools. After you finish the newsletter, Estefan wants you to save the newsletter as a PDF so he can email it to the printing company. You also need to make some edits to a document that is currently available only as a PDF.

## STARTING DATA FILES

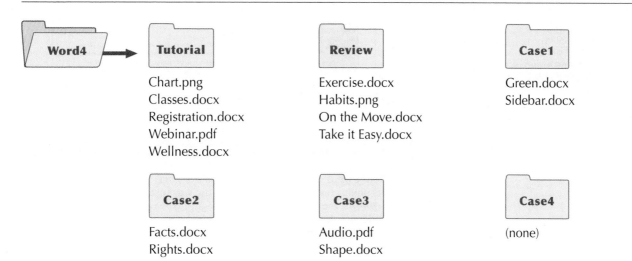

**Word4** → **Tutorial**

Chart.png
Classes.docx
Registration.docx
Webinar.pdf
Wellness.docx

**Review**

Exercise.docx
Habits.png
On the Move.docx
Take it Easy.docx

**Case1**

Green.docx
Sidebar.docx

**Case2**

Facts.docx
Rights.docx

**Case3**

Audio.pdf
Shape.docx

**Case4**

(none)

# Session 4.1 Visual Overview:

**Desktop publishing** is the process of preparing commercial-quality printed material, such as the newsletter shown here, using a personal computer. Using Word, you can create documents that have elements of desktop publishing, such as special font treatments, graphics, and page layout options, as well as design elements such as page borders.

This specially formatted text is an example of **WordArt**, which is created using the WordArt button in the Text group on the INSERT tab.

These are examples of text boxes, which are like mini documents within a document.

This photo and the drawing of the woman in a yoga pose under a tree (on the next page) are examples of clip art from Office.com. **Clip art** consists of premade electronic illustrations, photographs, and other graphics. Audio and video clip art are also available.

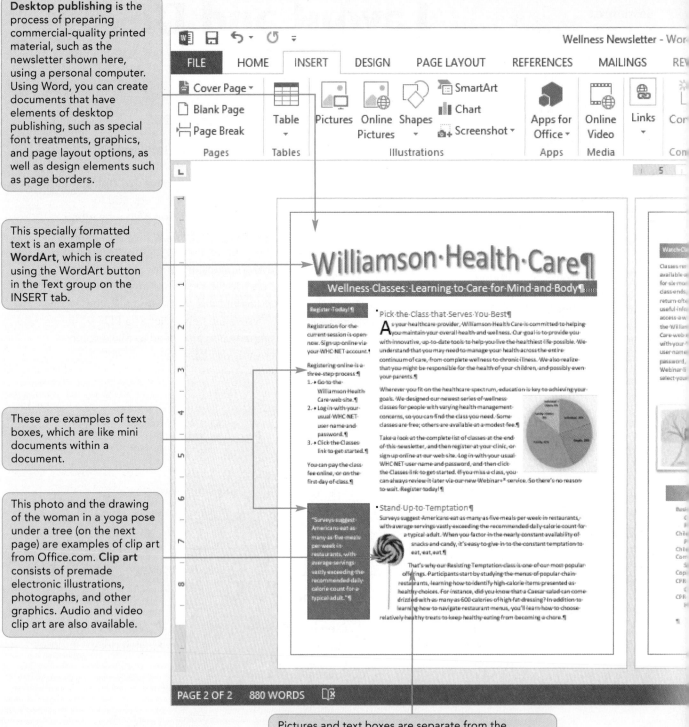

Pictures and text boxes are separate from the document text; you need to adjust the way text flows, or **wraps**, around them. Here, the Tight text wrap option is used to make text flow as closely as possible around the shape of the lollipop.

# Elements of Desktop Publishing

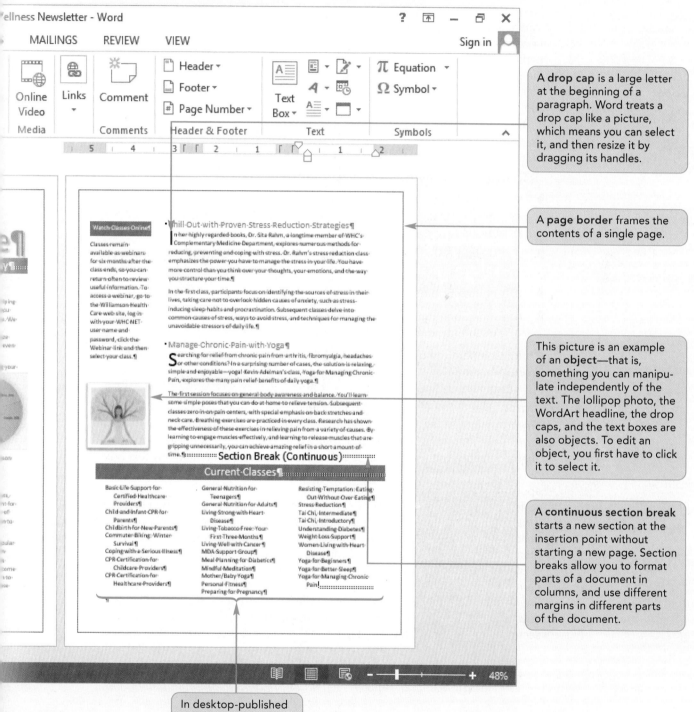

A **drop cap** is a large letter at the beginning of a paragraph. Word treats a drop cap like a picture, which means you can select it, and then resize it by dragging its handles.

A **page border** frames the contents of a single page.

This picture is an example of an **object**—that is, something you can manipulate independently of the text. The lollipop photo, the WordArt headline, the drop caps, and the text boxes are also objects. To edit an object, you first have to click it to select it.

A **continuous section break** starts a new section at the insertion point without starting a new page. Section breaks allow you to format parts of a document in columns, and use different margins in different parts of the document.

In desktop-published documents, text is sometimes arranged in two or more **columns**.

# Using Continuous Section Breaks to Enhance Page Layout

Newsletters and other desktop-published documents often incorporate multiple section breaks, with the various sections formatted with different margins, page orientations, column settings, and other page layout options. Continuous section breaks, which start a new section without starting a new page, are especially useful when creating a newsletter because they allow you to apply different page layout settings to different parts of a single page. To create the newsletter shown in the Session 4.1 Visual Overview, the first step is to insert a series of section breaks that will allow you to use different margins for different parts of the document. Section breaks will also allow you to format some of the text in multiple columns.

You'll start by opening and reviewing the document.

## To open and review the document:

1. Open the document **Wellness** from the Word4 ▸ Tutorial folder included with your Data Files, and then save it as **Wellness Newsletter** in the location specified by your instructor.

2. Display nonprinting characters and the rulers, and switch to Print Layout view, if necessary.

3. On the ribbon, click the **VIEW** tab.

4. In the Zoom group, click **Multiple Pages** so you can see both pages of the document side-by-side.

5. Compare the document to the completed newsletter shown in the Session 4.1 Visual Overview.

The document is formatted with the Office theme, using the default margins. The first paragraph is formatted with the Title style, and the remaining headings are formatted either with the Heading 1 style, or with blue paragraph shading, center alignment, and white font color. The document doesn't yet contain any text boxes or other desktop publishing elements. The list of classes at the end of the document appears as a standard, single column of text.

To make room for the text boxes, you need to change the left margin to 2.5 inches for all of the text between the "Wellness Classes: Learning to Care for Mind and Body" heading and the "Current Classes" heading. To accomplish this, you'll insert a section break after the "Wellness Classes: Learning to Care for Mind and Body" heading and another one before the "Current Classes" heading. You'll eventually format the list of current classes, at the end of the document, in three columns. To accomplish that, you need to insert a third section break after the "Current Classes" heading. Because you don't want any of the section breaks to start new pages, you will use continuous sections breaks for all three. See Figure 4-1.

**Figure 4-1**     Wellness Newsletter document before adding section breaks

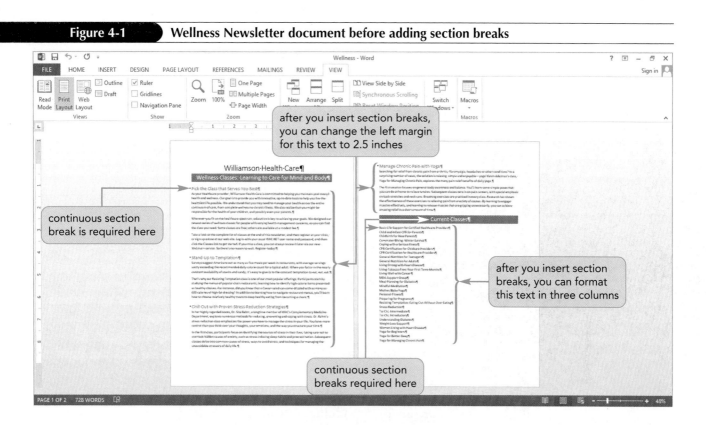

## To insert continuous section breaks in the document:

1. Change the Zoom level to **120%**.

2. In the document, click at the beginning of the third paragraph, which contains the heading "Pick the Class that Serves You Best."

3. On the ribbon, click the **PAGE LAYOUT** tab.

4. In the Page Setup group, click the **Breaks** button, and then click **Continuous**. A short dotted line, indicating a continuous section break, appears in the blue shading at the end of the preceding paragraph. If the paragraph text were shorter, you would see a longer line with the words "Section Break (Continuous)." You'll be able to see the section break text more clearly when you insert the next one.

5. Scroll down to page 2, click at the beginning of the shaded paragraph "Current Classes," and then insert a continuous section break. A dotted line with the words "Section Break (Continuous)" appears at the end of the preceding paragraph.

6. Click at the beginning of the next paragraph, which contains the first class title "Basic Life Support for Certified Healthcare Providers," and then insert a continuous section break. A dotted line with the words "Section Break (Continuous)" appears in the blue shading at the end of the preceding paragraph.

Now that you have created sections within the Wellness Newsletter document, you can format the individual sections as if they were separate documents. In the following steps, you'll format the first and third sections by changing their left and right margins to .75 inch. Then, you'll format the second section by changing its left margin to 2.5 inches.

## To set custom margins for sections 1, 2, and 3:

1. Press the **Ctrl+Home** keys to position the insertion point in section 1.

2. In the Page Setup group, click the **Margins** button, and then click **Custom Margins** to open the Page Setup dialog box.

3. Change the Left and Right margin settings to **.75** inch, and then click the **OK** button. The blue shading expands slightly on both sides of the paragraph.

4. On page 1, click anywhere in the heading "Pick the Class that Serves You Best" to position the insertion point in section 2.

5. In the Page Setup group, click the **Margins** button, and then click **Custom Margins** to open the Page Setup dialog box.

6. Change the Left margin setting to **2.5** inches, and then click the **OK** button. The text in section 2 shifts to the right, and the document text flows to a third page. Throughout this tutorial, as you add and resize various elements, the text will occasionally expand from two pages to three or four. But by the time you are finished, the newsletter will consist of only two pages.

7. Scroll down to page 2, click in the shaded heading "Current Classes" to position the insertion point in section 3, and then change the Left and Right margin settings to **.75** inch.

8. On the ribbon, click the **VIEW** tab.

9. In the Zoom group, click **Multiple Pages** so you can see all three pages of the document side-by-side. See Figure 4-2.

| Figure 4-2 | Sections 1, 2, and 3 with new margins |

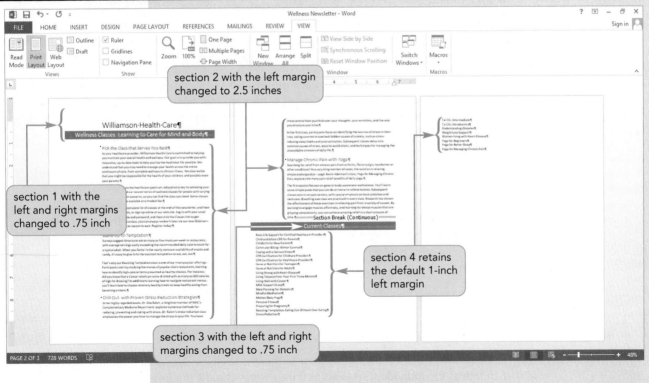

10. Save the document.

In addition to allowing you to format parts of a document with different margins, section breaks allow you to format part of a document in columns. You'll add some columns to section 4 next.

# Formatting Text in Columns

**TIP**

When working with large amounts of text formatted in columns, it's helpful to hyphenate the document to avoid excessive white space caused by short lines.

Text meant for quick reading is often laid out in columns, with text flowing down one column, continuing at the top of the next column, flowing down that column, and so forth. To get started, click the Columns button in the Page Setup group on the PAGE LAYOUT tab, and then click the number of columns you want in the Columns gallery. For more advanced column options, you can use the More Columns command to open the Columns dialog box. In this dialog box, you can adjust the column widths and the space between columns, and choose to format either the entire document in columns or just the section that contains the insertion point.

As shown in the Session 4.1 Visual Overview, Estefan wants section 4 of the newsletter document, which consists of the class list, to be formatted in three columns.

## To format section 4 in three columns:

1. Click anywhere in the list of classes at the end of the document to position the insertion point in section 4.

2. On the ribbon, click the **PAGE LAYOUT** tab.

3. In the Page Setup group, click the **Columns** button to display the Columns gallery. At this point, you could simply click Three to format section 4 in three columns of equal width. However, it's helpful to take a look at the columns dialog box so you can get familiar with some more advanced column options.

4. Click **More Columns** to open the Columns dialog box, and then in the Presets section, click **Three**. See Figure 4-3.

**Figure 4-3**    Columns dialog box

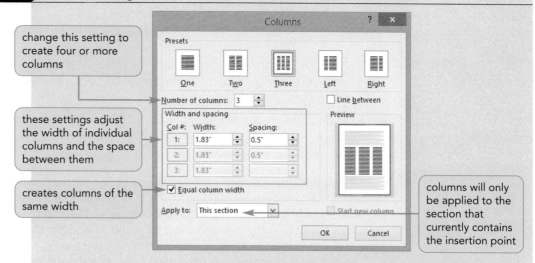

change this setting to create four or more columns

these settings adjust the width of individual columns and the space between them

creates columns of the same width

columns will only be applied to the section that currently contains the insertion point

To format text in four or more columns, you can change the setting in the Number of columns box instead of selecting an option in the Presets section. By default, the Apply to box, in the lower-left corner, displays "This section," indicating that the three-column format will be applied only to the current section. To apply columns to the entire document, you could click the Apply to arrow and then click Whole document. To change the width of the individual columns or the spacing between the columns, you can use the settings in the Width and spacing section of the Columns dialog box.

5. Click the **OK** button. Section 4 is now formatted in three columns of the default width. See Figure 4-4.

**Figure 4-4**   **Section 4 formatted in three columns**

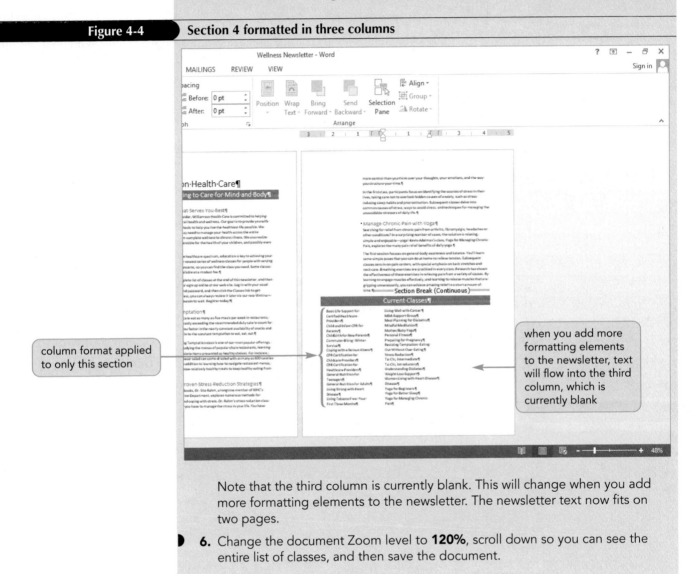

column format applied to only this section

when you add more formatting elements to the newsletter, text will flow into the third column, which is currently blank

Note that the third column is currently blank. This will change when you add more formatting elements to the newsletter. The newsletter text now fits on two pages.

6. Change the document Zoom level to **120%**, scroll down so you can see the entire list of classes, and then save the document.

Keep in mind that you can restore a document or a section to its original format by formatting it as one column. You can also adjust paragraph indents within columns, just as you would in normal text. In fact, Estefan would like you to format the columns in section 4 with hanging indents so that it's easier to read the class titles that take up more than one line.

To indent the class names, you first need to select the three columns of text. Selecting columns of text by dragging the mouse can be tricky. It's easier to use the Shift+click method instead.

### To format the columns in section 4 with hanging indents:

1. Make sure the **PAGE LAYOUT** tab is selected on the ribbon.

2. Click at the beginning of the first class name ("Basic Life Support for Certified Healthcare Providers"), press and hold the **Shift** key, and then click at the end of the last class name ("Yoga for Managing Chronic Pain"). The entire list of classes is selected.

3. In the Paragraph group, click the **Dialog Box Launcher** to open the Paragraph dialog box with the Indents and Spacing tab displayed.

4. In the Indentation section, click the **Special** arrow, click **Hanging**, and then change the By setting to **0.2"**.

5. Click the **OK** button to close the Paragraph dialog box, and then click anywhere in the list to deselect it. The class list is now formatted with a hanging indent, so the second line of each paragraph is indented .2 inches. See Figure 4-5.

| Figure 4-5 | Text formatted in columns with hanging indent |

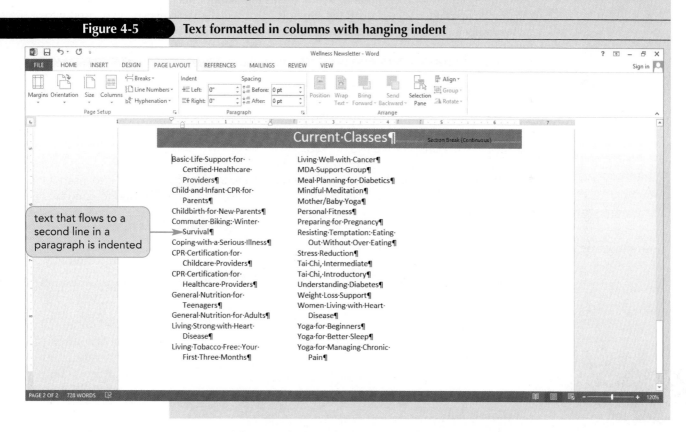

# Inserting Symbols and Special Characters

When creating documents in Word, you can change some of the characters available on the standard keyboard into special characters or symbols called **typographic characters**. Word's AutoCorrect feature automatically converts some standard characters into typographic characters as you type. In some cases, you need to press the spacebar and type more characters before Word inserts the appropriate typographic character. If Word inserts a typographic character that you don't want, you can click the Undo button to revert to the characters you originally typed. See Figure 4-6.

**Figure 4-6** Common typographic characters

| To insert this symbol or character | Type | Word converts to |
| --- | --- | --- |
| Em dash | word--word | word—word |
| Smiley face | :) | ☺ |
| Copyright symbol | (c) | © |
| Trademark symbol | (tm) | TM |
| Registered trademark symbol | (r) | ® |
| Fractions | 1/2, 1/4 | ½, ¼ |
| Arrows | <-- or --> | ← or → |

© 2014 Cengage Learning

Most of the typographic characters in Figure 4-6 can also be inserted using the Symbol button on the INSERT tab, which opens a gallery of commonly used symbols, and the More Symbols command, which opens the Symbol dialog box. The Symbol dialog box provides access to all the symbols and special characters you can insert into a Word document.

**REFERENCE**

### Inserting Symbols and Special Characters from the Symbol Dialog Box

- Move the insertion point to the location in the document where you want to insert a particular symbol or special character.
- On the ribbon, click the INSERT tab.
- In the Symbols group, click the Symbol button.
- If you see the symbol or character you want in the Symbol gallery, click it to insert it in the document. For a more extensive set of choices, click More Symbols to open the Symbol dialog box.
- In the Symbol dialog box, locate the symbol or character you want on either the Symbols tab or the Special Characters tab.
- Click the symbol or special character you want, click the Insert button, and then click the Close button.

Estefan forgot to include a registered trademark symbol (®) after "Webinar+" on page 1. He asks you to add one now. After you do, you'll explore the Symbol dialog box.

### To insert the registered trademark symbol and explore the Symbol dialog box:

1. Use the Navigation pane to find the term **Webinar+** in the document, and then close the Navigation pane.

2. Click to the right of the plus sign to position the insertion point between the plus sign and the space that follows it.

3. Type **(r)**. AutoCorrect converts the "r" in parentheses into the superscript ® symbol.

   If you don't know which characters to type to insert a symbol or special character, you can review the AutoCorrect replacements in the AutoCorrect: English (United States) dialog box.

**4.** On the ribbon, click the **FILE** tab.

**5.** In the navigation bar, click **Options** to open the Word Options dialog box.

**6.** In the left pane, click **Proofing**, and then click the **AutoCorrect Options** button. The AutoCorrect: English (United States) dialog box opens, with the AutoCorrect tab displayed.

**7.** Review the table at the bottom of the AutoCorrect tab. The column on the left shows the characters you can type, and the column on the right shows what AutoCorrect inserts as a replacement. See Figure 4-7.

---

**Figure 4-7**    **AutoCorrect: English (United States) dialog box**

when you type the characters shown in this column…

…Word inserts the typographic characters shown in this column

---

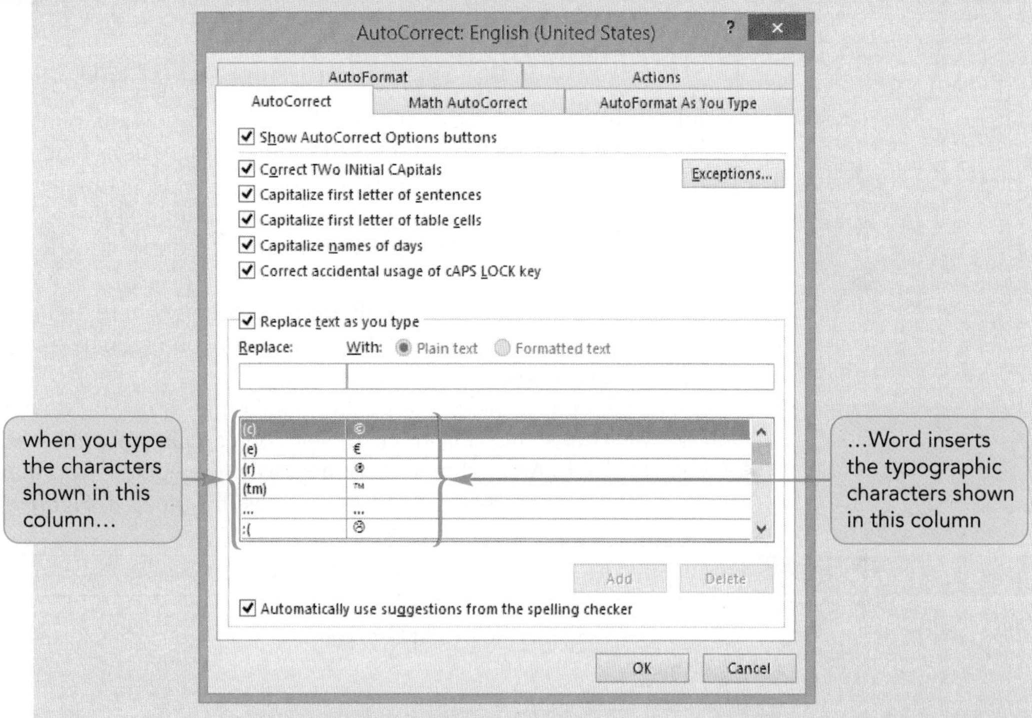

**8.** Scroll down to review the AutoCorrect replacements, click the **Cancel** button to close the AutoCorrect: English (United States) dialog box, and then click the **Cancel** button to close the Word Options dialog box.

Now you can explore the Symbol dialog box, which offers another way to insert symbols and special characters.

**9.** On the ribbon, click the **INSERT** tab.

**10.** In the Symbols group, click the **Symbol** button, and then click **More Symbols**. The Symbol dialog box opens with the Symbols tab displayed.

**11.** Scroll down the gallery of symbols on the Symbols tab to review the many symbols you can insert into a document. To insert one, you would click it, and then click the Insert button.

**12.** Click the **Special Characters** tab. The characters available on this tab are often used in desktop publishing. Notice the shortcut keys that you can use to insert many of the special characters.

**13.** Click the **Cancel** button to close the Symbol dialog box.

# Introduction to Working with Objects

An object is something that you can manipulate independently of the document text. In desktop publishing, you use objects to illustrate the document or to enhance the page layout. To complete the newsletter for Estefan, you'll need to add some text boxes, drop caps, and pictures. These are all examples of objects in Word.

## Inserting Graphic Objects

Objects used for illustration purposes or to enhance the page layout are sometimes called **graphic objects**, or simply **graphics**. The INSERT tab is the starting point for adding graphics to a document. After you insert a graphic object, you typically need to adjust its position on the page. Your ability to control the position of an object depends on whether it is an inline object or a floating object.

## Distinguishing Between Inline and Floating Objects

An **inline object** behaves as if it were text. Like an individual letter, it has a specific location within a line of text, and its position changes as you add or delete text. You can align an inline object just as you would align text, using the alignment buttons in the Paragraph group on the HOME tab. However, inline objects are difficult to work with because every time you add or remove paragraphs of text, the object moves to a new position.

In contrast, you can position a **floating object** anywhere on the page, with the text flowing, or wrapping, around it. Unlike an inline object, which has a specific position in a line of text, a floating object has a more fluid connection to the document text. It is attached, or **anchored**, to an entire paragraph—so if you delete that paragraph, you will also delete the object. However, you can also move the object independently of that paragraph. An anchor symbol next to an object tells you that the object is a floating object rather than an inline object, as illustrated in Figure 4-8.

| Figure 4-8 | Inline objects compared to floating objects |
|---|---|

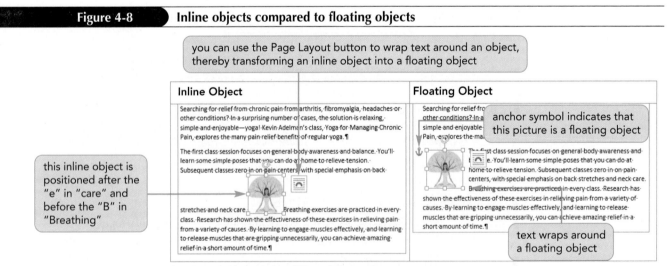

Image used with permission of Microsoft Corporation

You'll typically want to transform all inline objects into floating objects because floating objects are far more flexible.

# Wrapping Text Around an Object

To transform an inline object into a floating object, you apply a **text wrapping setting** to it. First, click the object to select it, click the Layout Options button next to the object, and then click an option in the Layout Options gallery. For example, you can select Square text wrapping to make the text follow a square outline as it flows around the object, or you can select Tight text wrapping to make the text follow the shape of the object more exactly. Figure 4-9 describes the different types of wrapping.

**Figure 4-9** | **Text wrapping options in the Layout Options gallery**

| Menu Icon | Type of Wrapping | Description |
|---|---|---|
| | Square | Text flows in a square outline around the object, regardless of the shape of the object; by default, Square text wrapping is applied to preformatted text boxes inserted via the Text Box button on the INSERT tab. |
| | Tight | Text follows the exact outline of the object; if you want the text to flow around an object, this is usually the best option. |
| | Through | Text flows through the object, filling up any open areas; this type is similar to Tight text wrapping. |
| | Top and Bottom | Text stops above the object and then starts again below the object. |
| | Behind Text | The object is layered behind the text, with the text flowing over it. |
| | In Front of Text | The object is layered in front of the text, with the text flowing behind it; if you want to position an object in white space next to the text, this option gives you the greatest control over its exact position. By default, In Front of Text wrapping is applied to any shapes inserted via the Shapes button in the Illustrations group on the INSERT tab. |

© 2014 Cengage Learning

Most graphic objects, including photos and SmartArt, are inline by default. All text boxes and shapes are floating by default. Objects that are inserted as floating objects by default have a specific text wrapping setting assigned to them, but you can change the default setting to any text wrapping setting you want.

**INSIGHT**

*Displaying Gridlines*

When formatting a complicated document like a newsletter, you'll often have to adjust the position of objects on the page until everything looks the way you want. To make it easier to see the relative position of objects, you can display the document's gridlines. These vertical and horizontal lines are not actually part of the document. They are simply guidelines you can use when positioning text and objects on the page. By default, when gridlines are displayed, objects align with, or **snap to**, the nearest intersection of a horizontal and vertical line. The figures in this tutorial do not show gridlines because they would make the figures difficult to read. However, you will have a chance to experiment with gridlines in the Case Problems at the end of this tutorial. To display gridlines, click the VIEW tab on the ribbon, and then click the Gridlines check box to insert a check.

# Inserting Text Boxes

You can choose to add a preformatted text box to a document, or you can create your own text box from scratch and adjust its appearance. To insert a preformatted text box, you use the Text Box button in the Text group. Text boxes inserted this way include placeholder text that you can replace with your own text. Preformatted text boxes come with preset font and paragraph options that are designed to match the text box's overall look. However, you can change the appearance of the text in the text box by using the options on the HOME tab, just as you would for ordinary text. The text box, as a whole, is designed to match the document's current theme. You could alter its appearance by using the Shape Styles options on the DRAWING TOOLS FORMAT tab, but there's typically no reason to do so.

Because the preformatted text boxes are so professional looking, they are usually a better choice than creating your own. However, if you want a very simple text box, you can use the Shapes button in the Illustrations group to draw a text box. After you draw the text box, you can adjust its appearance by using the Shape Styles options on the DRAWING TOOLS FORMAT tab. You can type any text you want inside the text box at the insertion point. When you are finished, you can format the text using the options on the HOME tab.

REFERENCE

### Inserting a Text Box

- To insert a preformatted, rectangular text box, click in the document where you want to insert the text box.
- On the ribbon, click the INSERT tab.
- In the Text group, click the Text Box button to open the Text Box gallery, and then click a text box style to select it.
- In the text box in the document, delete the placeholder text, type the text you want to include, and then format the text using the options on the HOME tab.

or

- To insert and format your own rectangular text box, click the INSERT tab on the ribbon.
- In the Text group, click the Shapes button to open the Shapes gallery, and then click Text Box.
- In the document, position the pointer where you want to insert the text box, press and hold the mouse button, and then drag the pointer to draw the text box.
- In the text box, type the text you want to include, and then format the text using the options on the HOME tab.
- Format the text box using the options in the Shape Styles group on the DRAWING TOOLS FORMAT tab.

## Inserting a Preformatted Text Box

Estefan's newsletter requires three text boxes. You need to insert the first text box on page 1, to the left of the "Pick the Class that Serves You Best" heading. For this text box, you'll insert one that is preformatted to work as a sidebar. A **sidebar** is a text box designed to look good positioned to the side of the main document text. A sidebar is typically used to draw attention to important information.

### To insert a preformatted text box in the document:

1. Scroll up to the top of page 1, and then click anywhere in the "Pick the Class that Serves You Best" heading.

2. Change the Zoom level to **Multiple Pages** so you can see both pages of the document.

3. On the ribbon, click the **INSERT** tab.

4. In the Text group, click the **Text Box** button to display the Text Box gallery, and then use the scroll bar to scroll down the gallery to locate the Ion Sidebar 1 text box.

5. Click **Ion Sidebar 1**. The text box is inserted in the left margin of page 1. See Figure 4-10.

| Figure 4-10 | Text box inserted on page 1 |
| --- | --- |

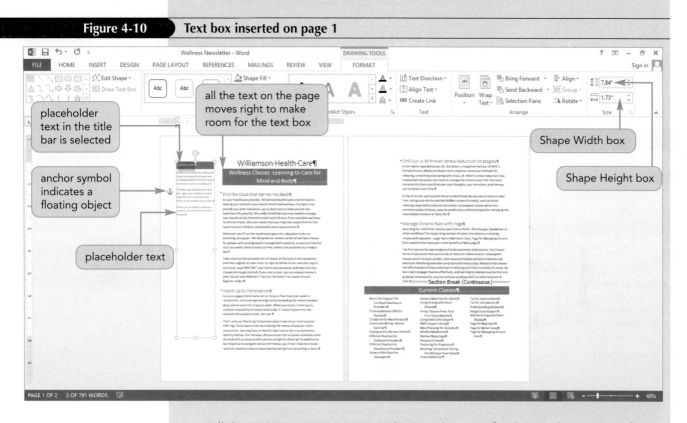

All the text on page 1 moves right to make room for the text box. Later, after you resize and move the text box, the first two paragraphs will resume their original positions, centered at the top of the page. The anchor symbol next to the text box tells you it is a floating object.

The text box consists of a blue title bar at the top that contains placeholder text, with additional placeholder text below the title bar. The dotted outline with handles indicates the borders of the text box. When you first insert a text box, the placeholder text in the title bar is selected, ready for you to type your own title. In this case, however, before you add any text, you'll resize and reposition the text box.

6. On the ribbon, click the **DRAWING TOOLS FORMAT** tab, if necessary.

7. In the Size group, click the **Shape Height** box, type **4.3**, click the **Shape Width** box, type **1.5**, and then press the **Enter** key. The text box is now shorter and narrower.

8. Change the Zoom level to **120%**.

   Next, you need to drag the text box down below the first two paragraphs. Currently, only the placeholder text in the text box title bar is selected. Before you can move it, you need to select the entire text box.

9. Position the pointer somewhere over the text box border until the pointer changes to ⌖.

10. Click the text box border to select the entire text box. The text box border changes from dotted to solid, and the Layout Options button appears to the right of the text box.

11. Position the pointer ⌖ over the text box's title bar, press and hold the mouse button, and then drag the text box down so that the top of the text box aligns with the first line of text below the "Pick the Class that Serves You Best" heading. The left edge of the text box should align with the left edge of the blue shaded heading "Wellness Classes: Learning to Care for Mind and Body." The anchor symbol remains in its original position, next to the shaded paragraph.

12. When you are sure the text box is positioned correctly, release the mouse button. See Figure 4-11.

| Figure 4-11 | Resized and repositioned text box |
| --- | --- |

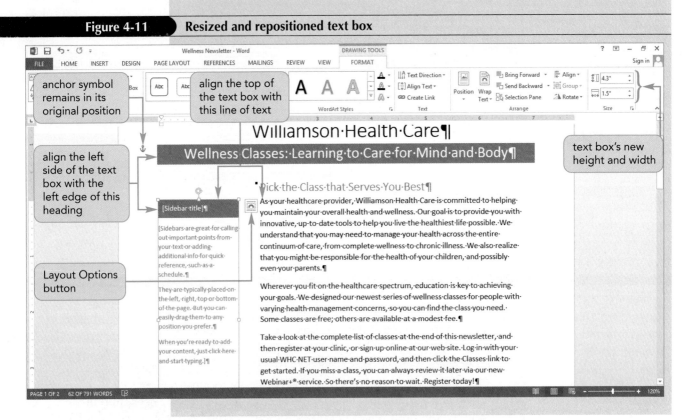

After you insert a text box or other object, you usually need to adjust its relationship to the surrounding text; that is, you need to adjust its text wrapping setting.

## Changing the Text Wrapping Setting for the Text Box

A preformatted text box inserted via the Text box button on the INSERT tab is, by default, a floating object formatted with Square text wrapping. You will verify whether this is true when you open the Layout Options gallery in the following steps. Then you'll select the In Front of Text option instead to gain more control over the exact position of the text box on the page.

**To open the Layout Options gallery and change the wrapping option:**

1. Change the Zoom level to **One Page** so you can see the text box's position relative to the text on page 1.

2. Click the **Layout Options** button. The Layout Options gallery opens with the Square option selected. See Figure 4-12.

**Figure 4-12** Square text wrapping currently applied to text box

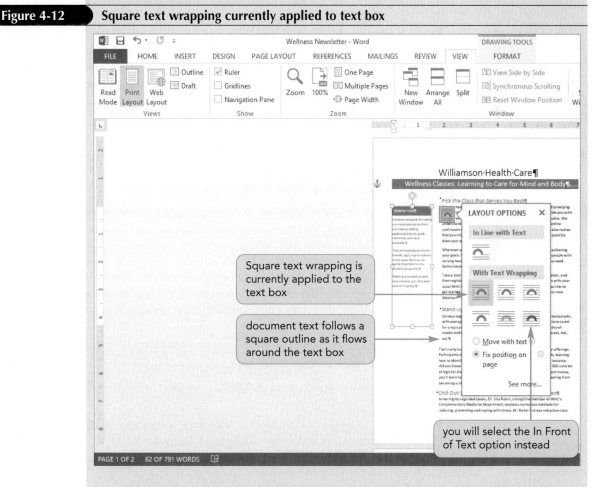

Square text wrapping is currently applied to the text box

document text follows a square outline as it flows around the text box

you will select the In Front of Text option instead

Square text wrapping is currently applied to the text box. You can see evidence of Square text wrapping where the document text flows around the lower-right corner of the text box. You'll have a chance to see some more dramatic examples of text wrapping later in this tutorial, but it's important to be able to identify subtle examples of it.

**Trouble?** If the Layout Options button is not visible, click the text box border to select the entire text box and display the Layout Options button.

▶ **3.** Click any of the other options in the Layout Options gallery and observe how the document text and the text box shift position. Continue exploring the Layout Options gallery, trying out several of the options.

▶ **4.** Click the **In Front of Text** option 🔲 and then click the **Close** button ✖ in the upper-right corner of the Layout Options gallery to close the gallery. The document text shifts so that it now flows directly down the left margin, without wrapping around the text box.

Your next formatting task is to make sure the text box is assigned a fixed position on the page. You could check this setting on the Layout Options button, but you'll use the Wrap Text button in the Arrange group instead.

▶ **5.** On the ribbon, click the **DRAWING TOOLS FORMAT** tab.

▶ **6.** In the Arrange group, click the **Wrap Text** button. The Wrap Text menu gives you access to all the options in the Layout Options gallery, plus some more advanced settings.

▶ **7.** Verify that Fix Position on Page has a checkmark next to it. To avoid having graphic objects move around unexpectedly on the page as you add or delete other elements, it's a good idea to check this setting either in the Wrap Text menu or in the Layout Options menu for every graphic object.

▶ **8.** Click anywhere in the document to close the gallery, and then save the document.

## Adding Text to a Text Box

Now that the text box is positioned where you want it, with the correct text wrapping, you can add text to it. In some documents, text boxes are used to present new information, while others highlight a quote from the main document. A direct quote from a document formatted in a text box is known as a **pull quote**. To create a pull quote text box, you can copy the text from the main document, and then paste it into the text box. You can also simply type text in a text box. Finally, you can insert text from another Word document by using the Object button arrow on the INSERT tab.

**TIP**

If you want to work on a document's layout before you've finished writing the text, you can insert placeholder text by inserting a new paragraph, typing =lorem() and then pressing the Enter key.

### To insert text in the text box:

▶ **1.** Change the Zoom level to **120%**, and then scroll as necessary so you can see the entire text box.

▶ **2.** In the text box's title bar, click the placeholder text **[Sidebar title]** to select it, if necessary, and then type **Register Today!**

▶ **3.** Click the placeholder text below the title bar to select it. See Figure 4-13.

Figure 4-13    Text box with placeholder text selected

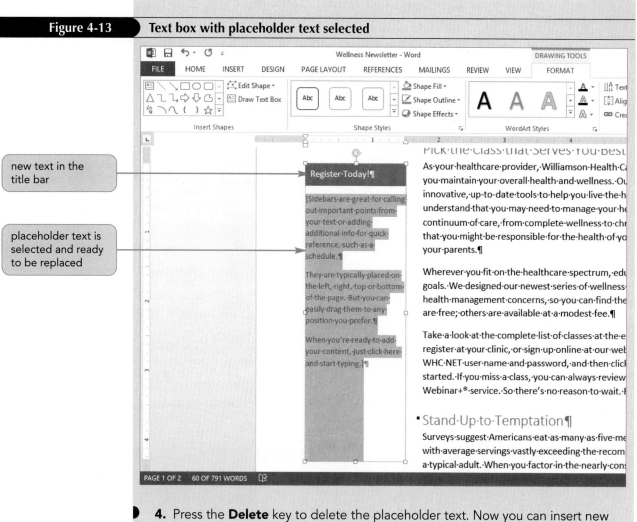

new text in the title bar

placeholder text is selected and ready to be replaced

4.  Press the **Delete** key to delete the placeholder text. Now you can insert new text from another Word document.

5.  On the ribbon, click the **INSERT** tab.

6.  In the Text group, click the **Object button arrow** to open the Object menu, and then click **Text from File**. The Insert File dialog box opens. Selecting a Word document to insert is just like selecting a document in the Open dialog box.

7.  Navigate to the Word4 ▸ Tutorial folder included with your Data Files, click **Registration** to select the file, and then click the **Insert** button. The registration information contained in the Registration document is inserted directly into the text box. The inserted text was formatted in 9-point Calibri in the Registration document, and it retains that formatting when you paste it into the Wellness Newsletter document. To make the text easier to read, you'll increase the font size to 11 points.

8.  With the insertion point located in the last paragraph in the text box (which is blank), press the **Backspace** key to delete the blank paragraph, and then click and drag the mouse pointer to select all the text in the text box, including the title in the shaded title box.

9.  On the ribbon, click the **HOME** tab.

10.  In the Font group, click the **Font Size** arrow, and then click **11**. The size of the text in the text box increases to 11 points. See Figure 4-14.

| Figure 4-14 | Registration information inserted in text box |
| --- | --- |

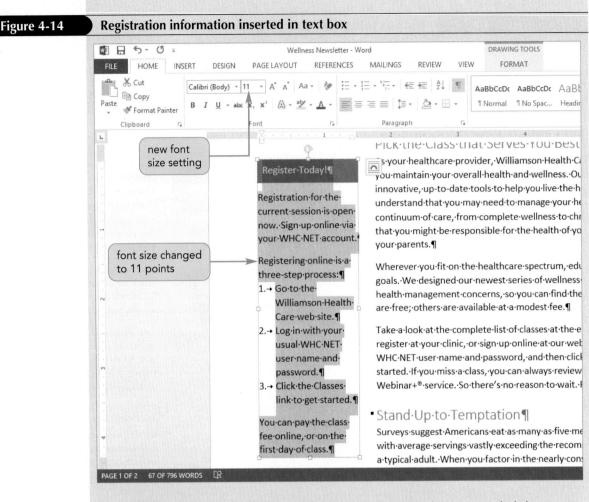

**Trouble?** Don't be concerned if the text in your text box wraps slightly differently from the text shown in Figure 4-14. The same fonts can vary slightly from one computer to another, causing slight differences in the way text wraps within and around text boxes.

▶ **11.** Click anywhere outside the text box to deselect it, and then save the document.

The first text box is complete. Now you need to add one more on page 1, and another on page 2. Estefan wants the second text box on page 1 to have a different look from the first one, so he asks you to use the Shapes button to draw a text box.

## Drawing and Formatting a Text Box Using the Shapes Menu

A text box is considered a shape, just like the other shapes you can insert via the Shapes button on the INSERT tab. This is true whether you insert a text box via the Text Box button or via the Shapes button. While text boxes are typically rectangular, you can actually turn any shape into a text box. Start by using the Shapes button to draw a shape of your choice, and then, with the shape selected, type any text you want. You won't see an insertion point inside the shape, but you can still type text inside it and then format it. You can format the shape itself by using the Shape Styles options on the DRAWING TOOLS FORMAT tab.

### To draw and format a text box:

▶ **1.** Scroll down to display the bottom half of page 1.

▶ **2.** On the ribbon, click the **INSERT** tab.

▶ **3.** In the Illustrations group, click the **Shapes** button to display the Shapes gallery. See Figure 4-15.

| **Figure 4-15** | **Shapes gallery** |

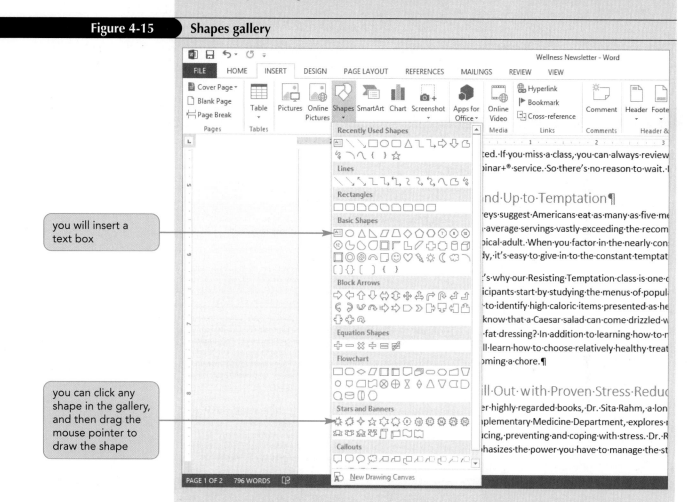

you will insert a text box

you can click any shape in the gallery, and then drag the mouse pointer to draw the shape

At this point, you could click any shape in the gallery, and then drag the pointer in the document to draw that shape. Then, after you finish drawing the shape, you could start typing in the selected shape to insert text.

▶ **4.** In the Basic Shapes section of the Shapes gallery, click the **Text Box** icon. The gallery closes and the mouse pointer turns to a black cross ✛.

▶ **5.** Position the pointer in the blank area in the left margin at about the 6-inch mark (according to the vertical ruler), and then click and drag down and to the right to draw a text box approximately **1.5** inches wide and **2.5** inches tall. When you are satisfied with the text box, release the mouse button.

Don't be concerned about the text box's exact dimensions or position on the page. For now, just make sure it fits in the blank space to the left of the last two paragraphs on the page.

The new text box is selected, with handles on its border and the insertion point blinking inside. The Layout Options button is visible and the text box's anchor symbol is positioned to the left of the paragraph below the heading "Stand Up to Temptation." By default, a shape is always anchored to the nearest paragraph that begins above the shape's top border. It doesn't matter where the insertion point is located.

6. Use the Shape Height and Shape Width boxes on the DRAWING TOOLS FORMAT tab to set the height to **2.7** inches and the width to **1.5** inches.

7. Drag the text box as necessary to align its bottom border with the last line of text on the page, and its left border with the left edge of the text box above. See Figure 4-16.

**Figure 4-16**      **Text box created using the Shapes button**

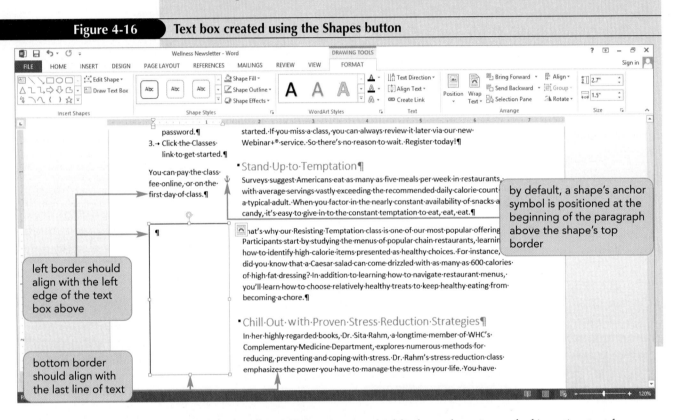

Now you need to add some text to the blank text box. Instead of inserting text from another Word document, you will copy a sentence from the newsletter and paste it into the text box to create a pull quote. After you add the text, you'll format the text box to make it match the one shown earlier in the Session 4.1 Visual Overview.

### To copy text from the newsletter and paste it into the text box:

1. Select the first sentence after the heading "Stand Up to Temptation," which begins "Surveys suggest…," and then press the **Ctrl+C** keys to copy it to the Office Clipboard.

2. Click in the blank text box, and then press the **Ctrl+V** keys to paste the copied sentence into the text box. The newly inserted sentence is formatted in 11-point Calibri, just as it was in the main document.

**3.** Add quotation marks at the beginning and end of the sentence, so it's clear the text box is a pull quote. Your next task is to center the sentence between the top and bottom borders of the text box. Then you'll add some color.

**4.** On the ribbon, click the **DRAWING TOOLS FORMAT** tab, if necessary.

**TIP**

You can use the Text Direction button in the Text group to rotate text within a text box.

**5.** In the Text group, click the **Align Text** button to display the Align text menu, and then click **Middle**. The text is now centered between the top and bottom borders of the text box. Next, you'll change the text's font color and add a background color.

**6.** In the Shape Styles group, click the **More** button to display the Shape Styles gallery. Like the text styles you have used to format text, shape styles allow you to apply a collection of formatting options, including font color and shading, with one click.

**7.** Move the mouse pointer over the various options in the Shape Styles gallery and observe the Live Previews in the document. When you are finished, position the mouse pointer over the Colored Fill - Blue, Accent 5, style, which is a dark blue box, the second from the right in the second row. See Figure 4-17.

**Figure 4-17**  **Shape Styles gallery**

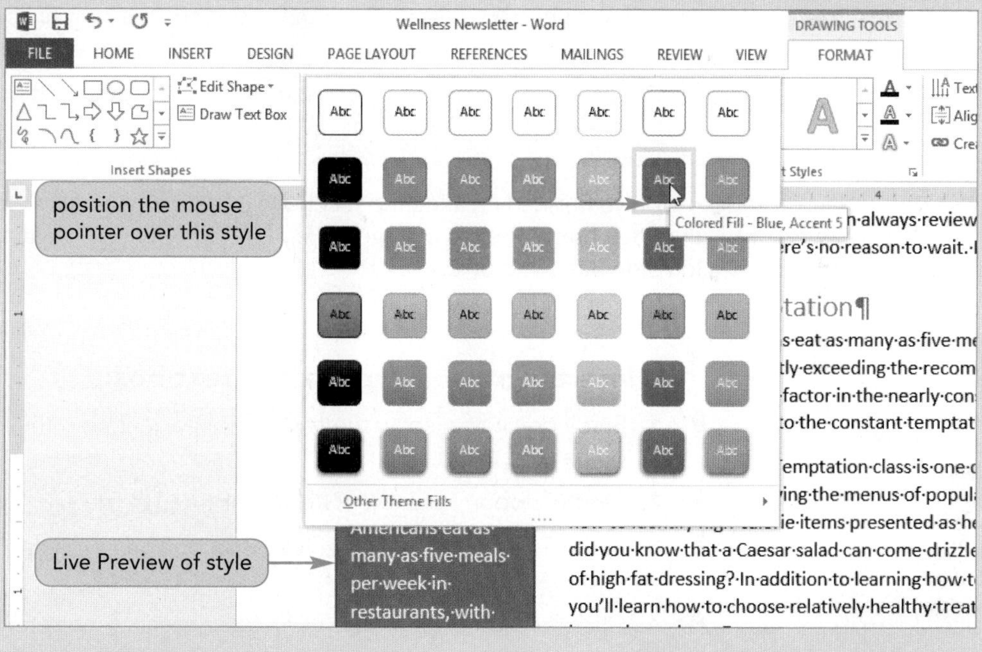

**8.** In the Shape Styles gallery, click the **Colored Fill - Blue, Accent 5** style. The style is applied to the text box, and the Shape Styles gallery closes.

**Trouble?** Don't be concerned if the text in your text box wraps slightly differently from the text shown in Figure 4-17. The same fonts can vary slightly from one computer to another, causing slight differences in the way text wraps within and around text boxes.

Now, you need to make sure the text box is located in a fixed position on the page. In the following steps, you'll also experiment with making some changes involving the text box's anchor symbol. It's important to understand the role the anchor symbol plays in the document's overall layout.

### To fix the text box's position on the page and experiment with the anchor symbol:

▶ 1. Verify that the text box is still selected, with the DRAWING TOOLS FORMAT tab displayed on the ribbon.

▶ 2. In the Arrange group, click the **Wrap Text** button. A checkmark appears next to Move with Text because that is the default setting for shapes.

▶ 3. Click **Fix Position on Page** to add a checkmark and close the Wrap Text menu. This setting helps ensure that the text box will remain in its position on page 1, even if you add text above the paragraph it is anchored to. However, if you add so much text that the paragraph moves to page 2, then the text box will also move to page 2, but it will be positioned in the same location on the page that it occupied on page 1—that is, in the bottom, lower-left corner.

   If you select the entire paragraph to which the text box is anchored, you will also select the text box, as you'll see in the next step.

▶ 4. Triple-click the paragraph below the "Stand Up to Temptation" heading. The entire paragraph and the text box are selected. If you pressed the Delete key at this point, you would delete the paragraph of text and the text box. If you ever need to delete a paragraph but not the graphic object that is anchored to it, you should first drag the anchor to a different paragraph.

▶ 5. Click anywhere in the document to deselect the text and the text box, and then save the document.

You've finished creating the second text box on page 1. Estefan wants you to add a third text box at the top of page 2. For this text box, you'll again use the preformatted Ion Side Bar 1 text box.

### To insert another preformatted text box:

▶ 1. Scroll down to display the top half of page 2, and then click in the first line on page 2.

▶ 2. On the ribbon, click the **INSERT** tab.

▶ 3. In the Text group, click the **Text Box** button to display the menu, scroll down, and then click **Ion Sidebar 1**.

▶ 4. Click the border of the text box to select the entire text box and display the Layout Options button.

▶ 5. Click the **Layout Options** button 🖾, click the **In Front of Text** 🖾 option, verify that the Fix position on page button is selected, and then close the Layout Options gallery.

▶ 6. Drag the text box left to center it in the blank space to the left of the document text, with the top of the text box aligned with the first line of text on page 2.

▶ 7. Change the text box's height to **3.5** inches and the width to **1.5** inches.

▶ 8. In the title bar, replace the placeholder text with **Watch Classes Online**.

▶ 9. In the main text box, click the placeholder text to select it, and then press the **Delete** key.

▶ **10.** On the ribbon, click the **INSERT** tab.

▶ **11.** In the Text group, click the **Object button arrow**, and then click **Text from File**.

▶ **12.** Navigate to the Word4 ▶ Tutorial folder, if necessary, and then insert the document named **Classes**.

▶ **13.** Delete the extra paragraph at the end of the text box, increase the font size for the text to **11** points, and then make sure your text box is positioned like the one shown in Figure 4-18.

| Figure 4-18 | Completed text box on page 2 |
|---|---|

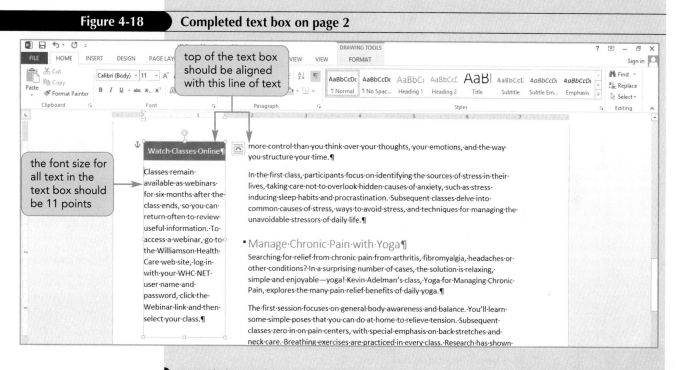

▶ **14.** Click anywhere in the document to deselect the text box, and then save the document.

### Linking Text Boxes

If you have a large amount of text that you want to place in different locations in a document, with the text continuing from one text box to another, you can use linked text boxes. For example, in a newsletter, you might have an article that starts in a text box on page 3 of the newsletter and continues in a text box on page 4. To flow the text automatically from one text box to a second, blank text box, click the first text box to select it (this text box should already contain some text). Next, on the ribbon, click the DRAWING TOOLS FORMAT tab, click the Create Link button in the Text group, and then click the empty text box. The text boxes are now linked. You can resize the first text box without worrying about how much text fits in the box. The text that no longer fits in the first text box is moved to the second text box. Note that you'll find it easier to link text boxes if you use simple text boxes without title bars.

To make the main document text look more polished, you will add some drop caps.

# Inserting Drop Caps

As you saw in the Session 4.1 Visual Overview, a drop cap is a graphic that replaces the first letter of a paragraph. Drop caps are commonly used in newspapers, magazines, and newsletters to draw the reader's attention to the beginning of an article. You can place a drop cap in the margin or next to the paragraph, or you can have the text of the paragraph wrap around the drop cap. By default, a drop cap extends down three lines, but you can change that setting in the Drop Cap dialog box.

Estefan asks you to create a drop cap for some of the paragraphs that follow the headings. He wants the drop cap to extend two lines into the paragraph, with the text wrapping around it.

**To insert drop caps in the newsletter:**

1. Scroll up to page 1, and then click anywhere in the paragraph below the "Pick the Class that Serves You Best" heading.

2. On the ribbon, click the **INSERT** tab.

3. In the Text group, click the **Drop Cap** button. The Drop Cap gallery opens.

4. Move the mouse pointer over the **Dropped** option and then the **In margin** option, and observe the Live Preview of the two types of drop caps in the document. The default settings applied by these two options are fine for most documents. Clicking Drop Cap Options, at the bottom of the menu, allows you to select more detailed settings. In this case, Estefan wants to make the drop cap smaller than the default. Instead of extending down through three lines of text, he wants the drop cap to extend only two lines.

5. Click **Drop Cap Options**. The Drop Cap dialog box opens.

6. Click the **Dropped** icon, click the **Lines to drop** box, and then change the setting to **2**. See Figure 4-19.

**Figure 4-19**    Drop Cap dialog box

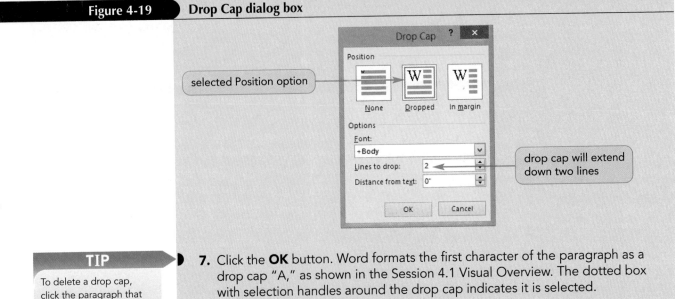

7. Click the **OK** button. Word formats the first character of the paragraph as a drop cap "A," as shown in the Session 4.1 Visual Overview. The dotted box with selection handles around the drop cap indicates it is selected.

**TIP**

To delete a drop cap, click the paragraph that contains it, open the Drop Cap dialog box and then click None.

**8.** Near the bottom of page 1, insert a similar drop cap in the paragraph following the "Chill Out with Proven Stress Reduction Strategies" heading. You skipped the paragraph following the "Stand Up to Temptation" heading because you'll eventually insert a graphic there. Including a drop cap there would make the paragraph look too cluttered.

**9.** On page 2, insert a similar drop cap in the paragraph following the "Manage Chronic Pain with Yoga" heading.

**10.** Click anywhere in the text to deselect the drop cap, and then save your work.

**PROSKILLS**

## Written Communication: Writing for a Newsletter

Clip art, WordArt, and other design elements can make a newsletter very appealing to readers. They can also be a lot of fun to create and edit. But don't let the design elements in your desktop-published documents distract you from the most important aspect of any document—clear, effective writing. Because the newsletter format feels less formal than a report or letter, some writers are tempted to use a casual, familiar tone. If you are creating a newsletter for friends or family, that's fine. But in most other settings—especially in a business or academic setting—you should strive for a professional tone, similar to what you find in a typical newspaper. Avoid jokes; you can never be certain that what amuses you will also amuse all your readers. Worse, you risk unintentionally offending your readers. Also, space is typically at a premium in any printed document, so you don't want to waste space on anything unessential. Finally, keep in mind that the best writing in the world will be wasted in a newsletter that is overburdened with too many design elements. You don't have to use every element covered in this tutorial in a single document. Instead, use just enough to attract the reader's attention to the page, and then let the text speak for itself.

**REVIEW**

## Session 4.1 Quick Check

1. Explain how to format a document in two columns of the default width.
2. Explain how to insert the ® symbol in a document.
3. What symbol tells you that an object is a floating object?
4. How do you convert an inline object to a floating object?
5. Which text wrapping option gives you the greatest control over an object's exact position, and is also the default text wrapping applied to shapes inserted via the Shapes button?
6. Explain how to insert a preformatted text box designed to match the current theme.

# Session 4.2 Visual Overview:

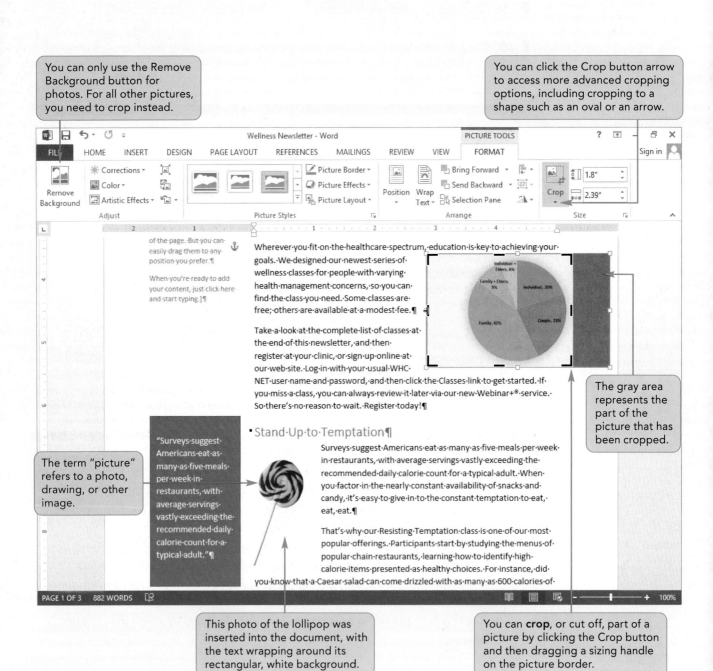

You can only use the Remove Background button for photos. For all other pictures, you need to crop instead.

You can click the Crop button arrow to access more advanced cropping options, including cropping to a shape such as an oval or an arrow.

The gray area represents the part of the picture that has been cropped.

The term "picture" refers to a photo, drawing, or other image.

This photo of the lollipop was inserted into the document, with the text wrapping around its rectangular, white background.

You can **crop**, or cut off, part of a picture by clicking the Crop button and then dragging a sizing handle on the picture border.

# Editing Pictures

Clicking the Remove Background button in the Adjust group on the PICTURE TOOLS FORMAT tab displays the BACKGROUND REMOVAL tab, with tools for removing a photo's background.

The photo of the lollipop is displayed here with its background removed, which allows the text to wrap around the shape of the lollipop itself.

You can use these buttons to mark areas in the photo that you want to keep, and to mark areas that you want to remove along with the rest of the photo background.

The pink area is the part of the photo that Word considers to be the background.

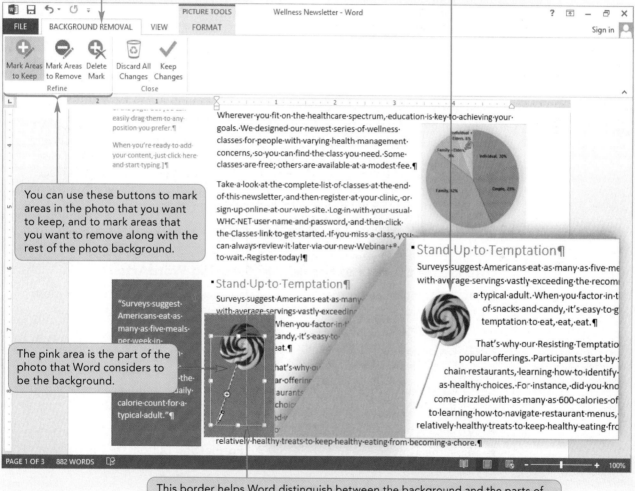

This border helps Word distinguish between the background and the parts of the image you want to keep. Any area of the image outside the border will be automatically excluded. In this case, part of the lollipop spiral lies outside the border, so Word considers it part of the background. To fix that, you can drag one of the border handles to expand the border until the entire lollipop spiral is inside the border.

# Formatting Text with WordArt

To create special text elements such as a newspaper headline, you can use decorative text known as WordArt. Essentially, WordArt is text in a text box that is formatted with a text effect. Before you move on to learning about WordArt, it's helpful to review the formatting options available with text effects.

To begin applying a text effect, you select the text you want to format. Then you can choose from several preformatted text effects via the Text Effects and Typography button in the Font group on the HOME tab. You can also modify a text effect by choosing from the options on the Text Effects and Typography menu. For example, you can add a shadow or a glow effect. You can also change the **outline color** of the characters—that is, the exterior color of the characters—and you can change the style of the outline by making it thicker or breaking it into dashes, for example. To change the character's **fill color**—that is, the interior color of the characters—you just select a different font color via the Font Color button in the Font group, just as you would with ordinary text.

All of these text effect options are available with WordArt. However, the fact that WordArt is in a text box allows you to add some additional effects. You can add rounded, or **beveled**, edges to the letters in WordArt, format the text in 3-D, and transform the text into waves, circles, and other shapes. You can also rotate WordArt text so it stretches vertically on the page. In addition, because WordArt is in a text box, you can use page layout and text wrap settings to place it anywhere you want on a page, with text wrapped around it.

To start creating WordArt, you can select text you want to transform into WordArt, and then click the WordArt button in the Text group on the INSERT tab. Alternatively, you can start by clicking the WordArt button without selecting text first. In that case, Word inserts a text box with placeholder WordArt text, which you can then replace with something new. In the following steps, you'll select the first paragraph and format it as WordArt to create the newsletter title that Estefan wants.

### To create the title of the newsletter using WordArt:

1. If you took a break after the last session, make sure the Wellness Newsletter is open and zoomed to 120%, with the rulers and nonprinting characters displayed.

2. On page 1, select the entire paragraph containing the "Williamson Health Care" heading, including the paragraph mark.

   To avoid unexpected results, you should start by clearing any formatting from the text you want to format as WordArt, so you'll do that next.

3. On the ribbon, click the **HOME** tab.

4. In the Font group, click the **Clear All Formatting** button ![icon]. The paragraph reverts to the Normal style. Now you can convert the text to WordArt.

5. On the ribbon, click the **INSERT** tab.

6. In the Text group, click the **WordArt** button. The WordArt gallery opens.

7. Position the mouse pointer over the WordArt style that is second from the left in the top row. A ScreenTip describes some elements of this WordArt style—"Fill - Blue, Accent 1, Shadow." See Figure 4-20.

Be sure to select the paragraph mark so the page layout in your newsletter matches the figures.

**Figure 4-20**     **WordArt gallery**

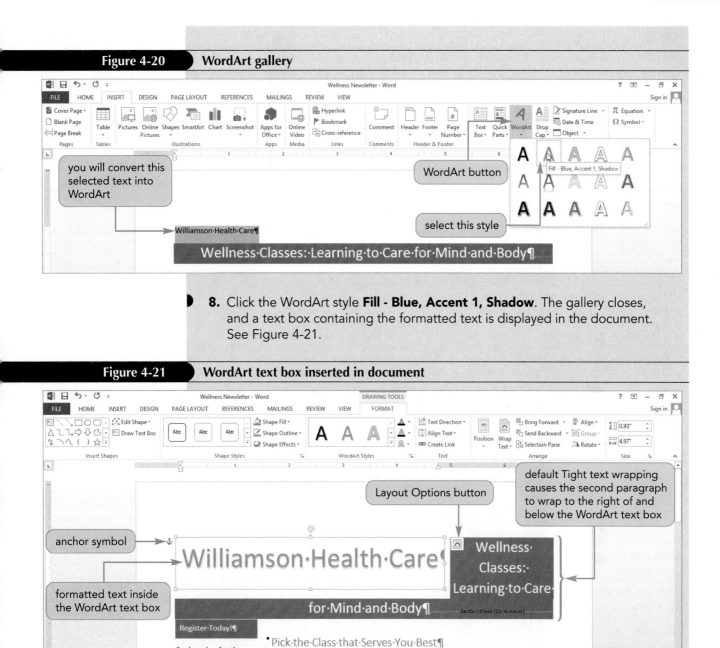

8. Click the WordArt style **Fill - Blue, Accent 1, Shadow**. The gallery closes, and a text box containing the formatted text is displayed in the document. See Figure 4-21.

**Figure 4-21**     **WordArt text box inserted in document**

Because the WordArt text box is formatted with Tight text wrapping by default, the shaded paragraph "Wellness Classes: Learning to Care for Mind and Body" wraps to the right of and below the WordArt text box. The DRAWING TOOLS FORMAT tab appears as the active tab on the ribbon, displaying a variety of tools that you can use to edit the WordArt. Before you change the look of the WordArt, you need to fix its position on the page and change its text wrap setting.

9. Make sure the **DRAWING TOOLS FORMAT** tab is selected on the ribbon.

10. In the Arrange group, click the **Wrap Text** button to open the Wrap Text menu, click **Fix Position on Page** to insert a checkmark, and then close the Wrap Text menu.

▶ **11.** Click the **Wrap Text** button again, and then click **Top and Bottom**. The Wrap Text menu closes, and the shaded paragraph moves down below the WordArt text box.

▶ **12.** Save the document.

Now that the document text is wrapped below the WordArt text box, you can modify the WordArt in several ways.

## Modifying WordArt

Your first task is to resize the WordArt. When resizing WordArt, you need to consider both the font size of the text and the size of the text box that contains the WordArt. You change the font size for WordArt text just as you would for ordinary text—by selecting it and then choosing a new font size using the Font size box in the Font group on the HOME tab. If you choose a large font for a headline, you might also need to resize the text box to ensure that the resized text appears on a single line. Estefan is happy with the font size of the new WordArt headline, so you only need to adjust the size of the text box so it spans the width of the page. The larger text box will then make it possible for you to add some more effects.

**To resize the WordArt text box and add some effects:**

▶ **1.** Make sure the **DRAWING TOOLS FORMAT** tab is selected on the ribbon.

▶ **2.** Change the width of the text box to **7** inches. The text box height should remain at the default .93 inches.

By default, the text is centered within the text box, which is what Estefan wants. Note, however, that you could use the alignment buttons on the HOME tab to align the text any way you wanted within the text box borders. You could also increase the text's font size so that it expands to span the full width of the text box. Instead, you will take advantage of the larger text box to apply a transform effect, which will expand and change the overall shape of the WordArt text. Then you'll make some additional modifications.

▶ **3.** Make sure the WordArt text box is selected.

▶ **4.** In the WordArt Styles group, click the **Text Effects** button A ▾ to display the Text Effects gallery, and then point to **Transform**. The Transform menu displays options for changing the WordArt's shape.

▶ **5.** Move the mouse pointer over the options in the Transform menu and observe the Live Previews in the WordArt text box. Note that you can always remove a transform effect that has been previously applied by clicking the option in the No Transform section, at the top of the gallery. When you are finished, position the mouse pointer over the Chevron Up effect. See Figure 4-22.

**Figure 4-22** | Applying a Transform text effect

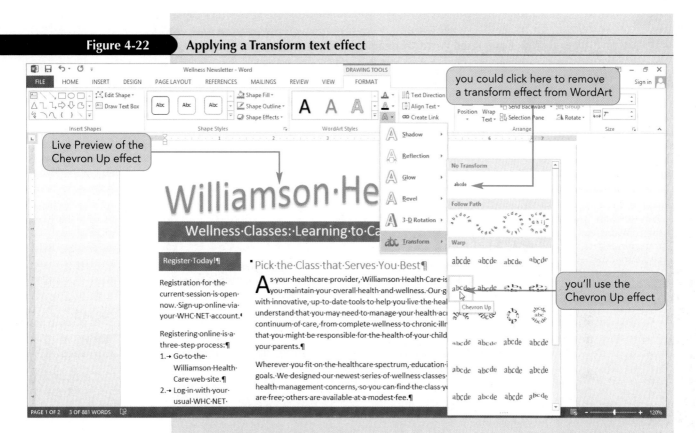

**Trouble?** If you don't see the Live Preview of the transform effect, that's okay. Continue with these steps.

6. Click the **Chevron Up** effect. The Transform menu closes, and the effect is applied to the WordArt. Now you will make some additional changes using the options in the WordArt Styles group. You'll start by changing the fill color.

7. In the WordArt Styles group, click the **Text Fill button arrow** to display the Text Fill color gallery.

8. In the Theme Colors section of the gallery, click the square that is second from the right in the top row to select the **Blue, Accent 5** color. The Text Fill gallery closes, and the WordArt is formatted in a shade of blue that matches the shading in the paragraph below. Next, you'll add a shadow to make the headline more dramatic.

9. In the WordArt Styles group, click the **Text Effects** button to display the Text Effects menu, and then point to **Shadow** to display the Shadow gallery. This menu is divided into several sections.

10. In the Outer section, point to the top-left option to display a ScreenTip that reads "Offset Diagonal Bottom Right."

11. Click the **Offset Diagonal Bottom Right** shadow style. A shadow is added to the WordArt text. See Figure 4-23.

**Figure 4-23**  **Completed WordArt headline**

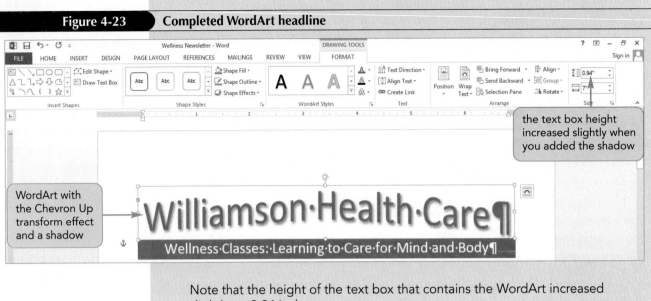

Figure 4-23    Completed WordArt headline

Note that the height of the text box that contains the WordArt increased slightly, to 0.94 inches.

**12.** Click a blank area of the document to deselect the WordArt, and then save the document.

The WordArt headline is complete. Your next job is to add some pictures to the newsletter.

## Working with Pictures

In Word, a picture is a photo, drawing, or other image. Although you can copy and paste pictures into a document from other documents, you'll typically insert pictures via either the Pictures button or the Online Pictures button, both of which are located in the Illustrations group on the INSERT tab. You use the Pictures button to insert a picture from a file stored on your computer. You use the Online Pictures button to insert clip art. A variety of clip art is available for Office users from the Office.com Website. As you saw in the Session 4.1 Visual Overview, the final version of the Wellness Newsletter document will contain two pieces of clip art—a photograph of a lollipop and a drawing of a woman doing yoga. The newsletter will also contain a picture of a chart, which Estefan's coworker created earlier and saved as a separate file.

After you insert a picture into a document, it functions as an object that you can move, resize, wrap text around, and edit in other ways using the appropriate contextual tab on the ribbon. In general, the skills you used when modifying text boxes apply to pictures as well.

*Written Communication: Understanding Copyright Laws*

The ownership of all forms of media, including text, line drawings, photographs, and video, is governed by copyright laws. You should assume that anything you find on the web is owned by someone who has a right to control its use. It's your responsibility to make sure you understand copyright laws and to abide by them. The U.S. Copyright Office maintains a Frequently Asked Questions page that should answer any questions you might have: www.copyright.gov/help/faq.

Generally, copyright laws allow a student to reuse a photo, drawing, or other item for educational purposes, on a one-time basis, without getting permission from the owner. However, to avoid charges of plagiarism, you need to acknowledge the source of the item in your work. You don't ever want to be accused of presenting someone else's work as your own. Businesses face much more stringent copyright restrictions. To reuse any material, you must request permission from the owner, and you will often need to pay a fee.

All the images on Office.com are available for use in your Word documents, as long as you don't use them for commercial purposes. To determine the copyright holder for a particular Office.com image, use a browser to go to Office.com, search for the image, and then click the image. If no copyright holder is listed, you should assume the image is owned by Microsoft and cannot be used for commercial purposes. Images owned by other sources, such as Shutterstock, are probably available for purchase, but it's up to you to contact the copyright holder and make the necessary arrangements.

## Inserting and Cropping a Picture

You can use the Chart button in the Illustrations group on the INSERT tab to enter data into a data sheet and then create a chart that illustrates the data. However, the chart Estefan wants to insert in the newsletter was created by a coworker using a different program, and then saved as a PNG file named Chart.png. That means you can insert the chart as a picture using the Pictures button in the Illustrations group.

Estefan asks you to insert the chart picture on page 1.

### To insert the chart picture on page 1:

1. On page 1, click at the end of the first paragraph below the "Pick the Class that Serves You Best" heading to position the insertion point between "…your parents." and the paragraph mark. Normally, there's no need to be so precise about where you click before inserting a picture, but doing so here will ensure that your results match the results described in these steps exactly.

2. On the ribbon, click the **INSERT** tab.

3. In the Illustrations group, click the **Pictures** button to open the Insert Pictures dialog box.

4. Navigate to the Word4 ▸ Tutorial folder included with your Data Files, and then insert the picture file named **Chart.png**. The chart picture is inserted in the document as an inline object. It is selected, and the PICTURE TOOLS FORMAT tab is displayed on the ribbon.

5. Scroll down if necessary so you can see the entire chart.

The chart is wider than it needs to be and would look better as a square. So you'll need to cut off, or crop, part of it. In addition to the ability to crop part of a picture, Word offers several more advanced cropping options. The one you'll probably use most often is cropping to a shape, which means trimming the edges of a picture so it fits into a star, an oval, an arrow, or another shape. You can also crop to a specific ratio of height to width.

Whatever method you use, once you crop a picture, the part you cropped is hidden from view. However, it remains a part of the picture in case you change your mind and want to restore the cropped picture to its original form.

Before you crop off the sides of the chart, you'll try cropping it to a specific shape.

**To crop the chart picture:**

▶ **1.** In the Size group, click the **Crop button arrow** to display the Crop menu, and then click **Crop to Shape**. A gallery of shapes is displayed, similar to the gallery you saw in Figure 4-15.

▶ **2.** In the Basic Shapes section of the gallery, click the **Lightning Bolt** shape ⬡ (third row down, sixth from the right). The chart picture takes on the shape of a lightning bolt, with everything outside the lightning bolt shape cropped off.

Obviously, this isn't a useful option for the chart, but cropping to shapes can be very effective with photos in informal documents such as party invitations or posters, especially if you then use the Behind Text wrapping option, so that the document text flows over the photo.

▶ **3.** Press the **Ctrl+Z** keys to undo the cropping.

▶ **4.** In the Size group, click the **Crop** button (not the Crop button arrow). Dark black sizing handles appear around the picture borders.

▶ **5.** Position the pointer directly over the middle sizing handle on the right border. The pointer changes to ├.

▶ **6.** Press and hold down the mouse button. The pointer changes to +.

▶ **7.** Drag the pointer toward the left until the chart border aligns with the 3.75-inch mark on the horizontal ruler, as shown in Figure 4-24.

| Figure 4-24 | Cropping a picture |
| --- | --- |

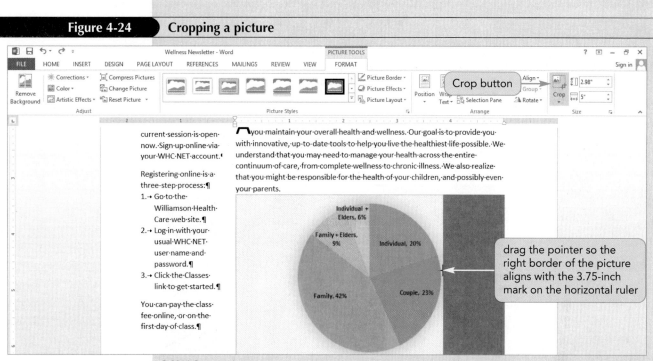

© 2014 Cengage Learning

**8.** When the chart looks like the one shown in Figure 4-24, release the mouse button. The right portion of the chart picture is no longer visible. The original border remains, indicating that the cropped portion is still saved as part of the picture in case you want to undo the cropping.

**9.** Drag the middle handle on the left border to the right until the left border aligns with the 2-inch mark on the horizontal ruler.

The chart now takes up much less space, but it's not exactly a square. To ensure a specific ratio, you can crop the picture by changing its **aspect ratio**—that is, the ratio of width to height. You'll try that next. But first, you'll restore the picture to its original state.

**10.** In the Adjust group, click the **Reset Picture button arrow** to display the Reset Picture menu, and then click **Reset Picture & Size**. The chart picture returns to its original state.

**11.** In the Size group, click the **Crop button arrow**, and then point to **Aspect Ratio** to display the Aspect Ratio menu, which lists various ratios of width to height. A square has a 1-to-1 ratio of width to height.

**12.** Under "Square," click **1:1**. The chart is cropped to a square shape. See Figure 4-25.

**TIP**

If you aren't sure what formatting has been applied to a picture, and you want to start over, use the Reset Picture button.

**Figure 4-25**   **Chart cropped to a 1:1 aspect ratio**

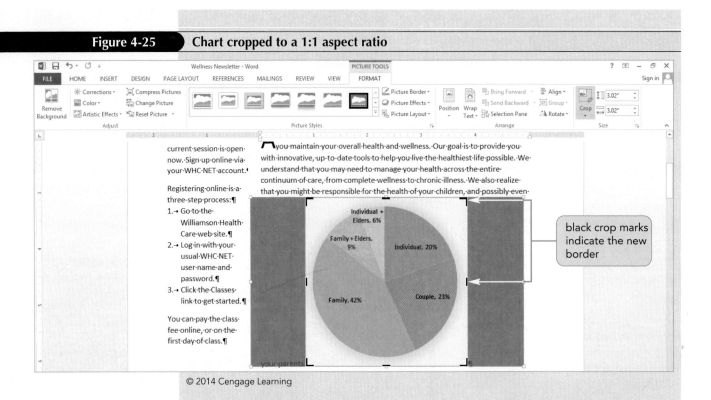

© 2014 Cengage Learning

▶ **13.** Click anywhere outside the chart to deselect it and complete the cropping procedure.

Next, you need to change the chart from an inline object to a floating object by wrapping text around it. You also need to position it on the page. You can complete both of these tasks at the same time by using the Position button in the Arrange group.

**To change the chart's position and wrapping:**

▶ **1.** Change the Zoom level to **One Page**, and then click the chart to select it.

▶ **2.** On the ribbon, click the **PICTURE TOOLS FORMAT** tab.

▶ **3.** In the Arrange group, click the **Position** button to display the Position gallery. You can click an icon in the "With Text Wrapping" section to move the selected picture to one of nine preset positions on the page. As with any gallery, you can see a Live Preview of the options before you actually select one.

**TIP**

When you select an option in the Position gallery, Fix Position on Page is also selected on the Wrap Text menu by default.

▶ **4.** Move the mouse pointer over the various icons and observe the changing Live Preview in the document, with the chart picture moving to different locations on the page and the text wrapping around it.

▶ **5.** Point to the icon in the middle row on the far right side to display a ScreenTip that reads "Position in Middle Right with Square Text Wrapping," and then click the **Position in Middle Right with Square Text Wrapping** icon. The chart picture moves to the middle of the page along the right margin. By default, it is formatted with Tight text wrapping, so the text wraps to its left, following its square outline.

Your final step is to resize the chart picture to make it a bit smaller.

**6.** In the Size group, click the **Shape Height** box, type **1.8**, and then press the **Enter** key. The settings in both the Shape Height and Shape Width boxes change to 1.8 inches. For most types of graphics, the aspect ratio is locked, meaning that when you change one dimension, the other changes to match. In this case, because the aspect ratio of the chart is 1:1, when you changed the height to 1.8 inches, the width also changed to 1.8 inches, ensuring that the chart retained its square shape.

**7.** Click anywhere outside the chart picture to deselect it, and then save the document.

## INSIGHT

### Aligning Graphic Objects and Using the Selection Task Pane

The steps in this tutorial provide precise directions about where to position graphic objects in the document. However, when you are creating a document on your own, you might find it helpful to use the Align button in the Arrange group on the PICTURE TOOLS FORMAT tab to align objects relative to the margin or the edge of the page. Aligning a graphic relative to the margin, rather than the edge of the page, is usually the best choice because it ensures that you don't accidentally position a graphic outside the page margins, causing the graphic to get cut off when the page is printed.

After you choose whether to align to the page or margin, you can open the Align menu again and choose an alignment option. For example, you can align the top of an object at the top of the page, or align the bottom of an object at the bottom of the page. You can also choose to have Word distribute multiple objects evenly on the page. To do this, it's helpful to open the Selection task pane first by clicking the PAGE LAYOUT tab and then clicking Selection Pane. Press and hold the Ctrl key, and then in the Selection task pane, click the objects you want to select. After the objects are selected, there's no need to switch back to the PICTURE TOOLS FORMAT tab. Instead, you can take advantage of the Align button in the Arrange group on the PAGE LAYOUT tab to open the Align menu, where you can then click Distribute Horizontally or Distribute Vertically.

The chart picture is finished. Next, Estefan asks you to insert the lollipop clip art near the bottom of page 1.

## Searching for and Inserting Clip Art

The first step in using clip art is finding the clip art you want. Most clip art websites include a search box where you can type some descriptive keywords to help you narrow the selection down to a smaller range. To find clip art on Office.com, you can type your keywords in the search box in the Insert Pictures window.

**To search for clip art and insert it in the Wellness Newsletter document:**

**1.** Zoom in so you can read the document text at the bottom of page 1, and then click at the end of the first paragraph below the "Stand Up to Temptation" heading to position the insertion point between "...eat, eat." and the paragraph mark.

**2.** Change the Zoom level to **Multiple Pages** so you can see the entire document.

**3.** On the ribbon, click the **INSERT** tab.

**4.** In the Illustrations group, click the **Online Pictures** button to display the Insert Pictures window. See Figure 4-26.

**Figure 4-26** Insert Pictures window

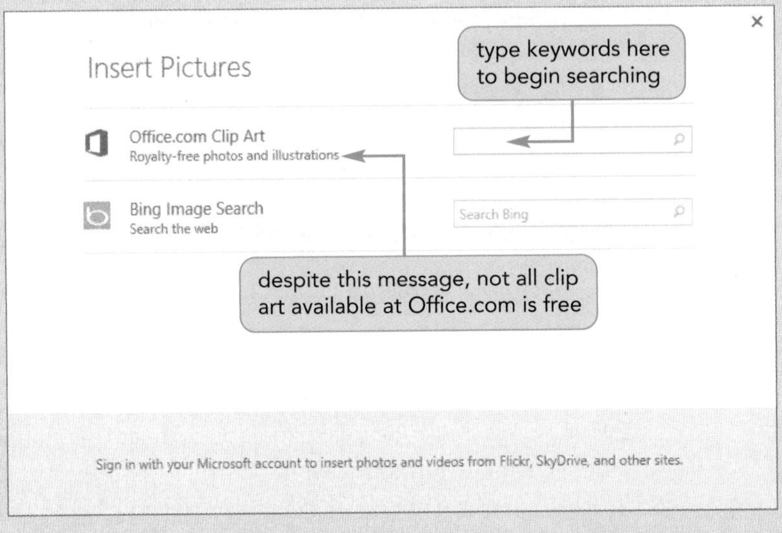

Here you can choose to search for clip art at Office.com, or you can use Microsoft's Bing search engine to search the entire web. Note that, despite the label "Royalty-free photos and illustrations" below the "Office.com Clip Art" heading, not all of the clip art available on Office.com is available for free. Some of it is offered by companies, such as Shutterstock, that require you to pay a fee.

**5.** In the search box to the right of "Office.com Clip Art," type **striped lollipop** and then press the **Enter** key. An image of a red and white striped lollipop appears in the search results window.

**TIP**

A pixel is the smallest possible element in a graphic image.

**6.** Click the red and white lollipop image to select it. Once selected, its border changes to blue. In the lower-left corner of the window, you see all the keywords associated with the picture ("Striped lollipop sucker") and its size in pixels (604 × 1024). See Figure 4-27.

**Figure 4-27** Selected clip art photo

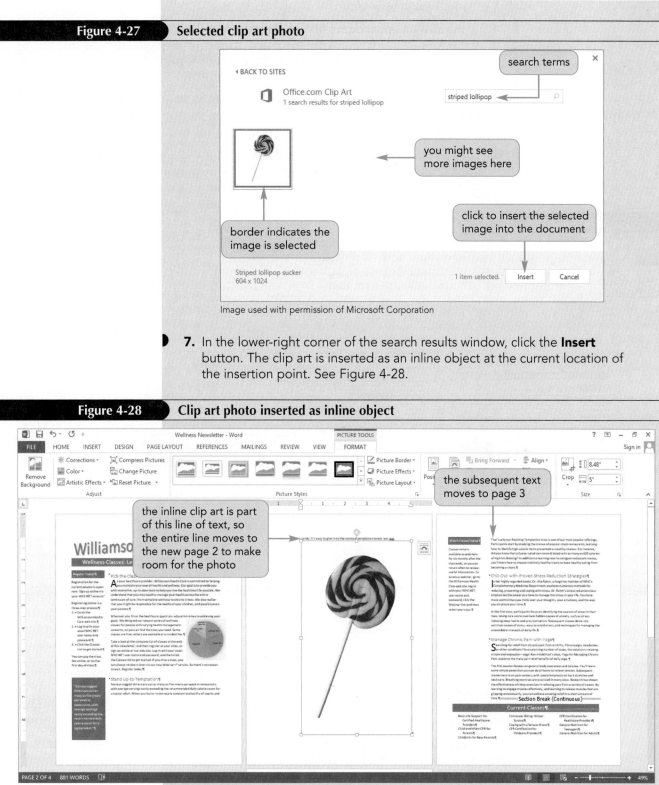

Image used with permission of Microsoft Corporation

7. In the lower-right corner of the search results window, click the **Insert** button. The clip art is inserted as an inline object at the current location of the insertion point. See Figure 4-28.

**Figure 4-28** Clip art photo inserted as inline object

© 2014 Cengage Learning; Image used with permission of Microsoft Corporation

Because the photo is too large to fit on page 1, the line of text that contains the insertion point jumps to page 2, with the photo displayed below the text. The rest of the document text starts on page 3 and flows to page 4. The clip art photo is selected, as indicated by its border with handles. The PICTURE TOOLS FORMAT tab is displayed on the ribbon. Now you can reduce the photo's size, wrap text around it, and position it on the page.

8.  In the Size group, click the **Shape Height** box, type **2**, and then press the **Enter** key. To maintain the photo's preset aspect ratio, Word changes the photo's width to 1.18 inches. Some of the text from page 3 moves up to fill the space below the smaller photo on page 2.

9.  In the Arrange group, click the **Wrap Text** button, and then click **Tight**. The photo, which is now a floating object, moves to the top of page 1, with text wrapping to its right.

10. Drag the photo down to position it so the first line of the paragraph under "Stand Up to Temptation" wraps above it. See Figure 4-29. The anchor symbol for the photo is not visible because it's covered by the blue text box.

**Figure 4-29** Resized clip art photo as a floating object

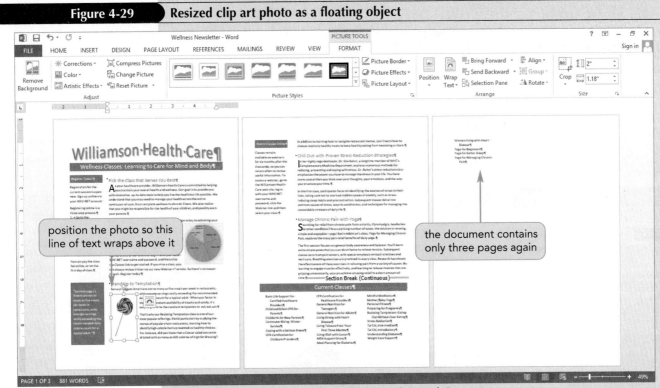

© 2014 Cengage Learning; Image used with permission of Microsoft Corporation

**Trouble?** Don't be concerned if you can't get the text to wrap around the lollipop photo exactly as shown in Figure 4-29.

11. Click the **Layout Options** button 🖼, click **Fix position on page**, and then close the Layout Options menu.

Estefan likes the photo, but he asks you to make a few changes. First, he wants you to rotate the lollipop to the left to position it vertically on the page. Also, Estefan wants the text to wrap around the curved shape of the lollipop itself, instead of around its rectangular outline. To accomplish that, you need to remove the photo's background.

## Rotating a Picture

You can quickly rotate a picture by dragging the Rotation handle that appears on the photo's border when the photo is selected. To access some preset rotation options, you can click the Rotate button in the Arrange group to open the Rotate menu. To quickly rotate a picture 90 degrees, click Rotate Right 90° or Rotate Left 90° in the Rotate menu. You can also flip a picture, as if the picture were printed on both sides of a card and you wanted to turn the card over. To do this, click Flip Vertical or Flip Horizontal in the Rotate menu.

Estefan only wants to rotate the lollipop picture slightly. You can do that by dragging the Rotation handle.

### To rotate the clip art photo:

1. Change the document Zoom level to **120%**, and then scroll down so you can see the bottom half of page 1.

2. Click the lollipop picture, if necessary, to select it, and then position the mouse pointer over the circular rotation handle above the middle of the photo's top border. The mouse pointer changes to ⟳.

3. Drag the mouse pointer down and to the left, until the lollipop rotates to a vertical position. See Figure 4-30.

**Figure 4-30    Dragging the Rotation handle**

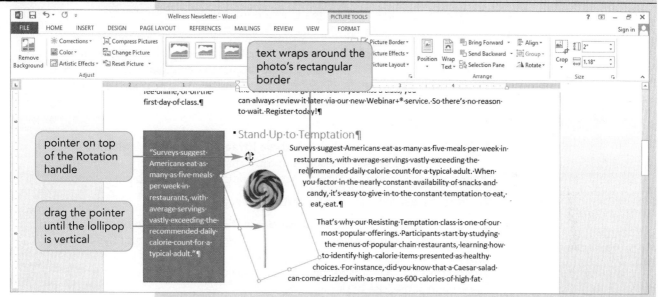

Image used with permission of Microsoft Corporation

Don't be concerned if the text wrapping around your rotated picture looks different from the text wrapping in Figure 4-30.

4. Release the mouse button. The lollipop is displayed in the new, rotated position, with the text wrapped around the photo's tilted, rectangular border.

5. Save the document.

You're almost finished editing the lollipop photo. Your last task is to remove its background so the text wraps around the shape of the lollipop itself. But before you remove the background from the lollipop photo, you'll explore the options in the Adjust group.

## Adjusting a Picture

The Adjust group on the PICTURE TOOLS FORMAT tab provides several tools for adjusting a picture's overall look. Some, such as the Remove Background button, only work for photos. Others, such as the Color button, provide some options that work only for photos and some that work for both photos and line drawings. You'll explore some of these options in the following steps.

**To try out some options in the Adjust group:**

▶ 1. Make sure that the lollipop photo is still selected, and that the **PICTURE TOOLS FORMAT** tab is selected on the ribbon.

▶ 2. In the Adjust group, click the **Corrections** button, and then move the mouse pointer over the various options in the Corrections gallery and observe the Live Preview in the document. You can use the Corrections gallery to sharpen or soften a photo's focus, or to adjust the brightness of a photo or line drawing.

▶ 3. Press the **Esc** key to close the Corrections gallery.

▶ 4. In the Adjust group, click the **Color** button, and then move the mouse pointer over the options in the Color gallery and observe the Live Preview in the document. For photos, you can adjust the color saturation and tone. For photos and line drawings, you can use the Recolor options to completely change the picture's colors.

▶ 5. Press the **Esc** key to close the Color gallery.

▶ 6. In the Adjust group, click the **Artistic Effects** button, and then move the mouse pointer over the options in the Artistic Effects gallery and observe the Live Preview in the document. Artistic Effects can only be used on photos.

▶ 7. Press the **Esc** key to close the Artistic Effects gallery.

▶ 8. In the Adjust group, click the **Compress Pictures** button to open the Compress Pictures dialog box. In the Target output portion of the dialog box, you can select the option that reflects the purpose of your document. Compressing pictures reduces the file size of the Word document, but can result in some loss of detail.

▶ 9. Click the **Cancel** button to close the Compress Pictures dialog box.

Now you are ready to remove the white background from the lollipop photo.

## Removing a Photo's Background

Removing a photo's background can be tricky, especially if you are working on a photo with a background that is not clearly differentiated from the foreground image. For example, you might find it difficult to remove a white, snowy background from a photo of an equally white snowman. You start by clicking the Remove Background button in the Adjust group, and then making changes to help Word distinguish between the background that you want to exclude and the image you want to keep.

**REFERENCE**

### Removing a Photo's Background

- Select the photo, and then on the PICTURE TOOLS FORMAT tab, in the Adjust group, click the Remove Background button.
- Drag the handles on the border as necessary to include any parts of the photo that have been incorrectly marked for removal.
- To mark areas to keep, click the Mark Areas to Keep button in the Refine group on the BACKGROUND REMOVAL tab, and then use the drawing pointer to select areas of the photo to keep.
- To mark areas to remove, click the Mark Areas to Remove button in the Refine group on the BACKGROUND REMOVAL tab, and then use the drawing pointer to select areas of the photo to remove.
- Click the Keep Changes button in the Close group.

You'll start by zooming in so you can clearly see the photo as you edit it.

### To remove the white background from the lollipop photo:

1. On the Zoom slider, drag the **slider button** to change the Zoom level to **180%**, and then scroll as necessary to display the selected lollipop photo.

2. In the Adjust group, click the **Remove Background** button. See Figure 4-31.

**Figure 4-31**    Removing the background of a photo

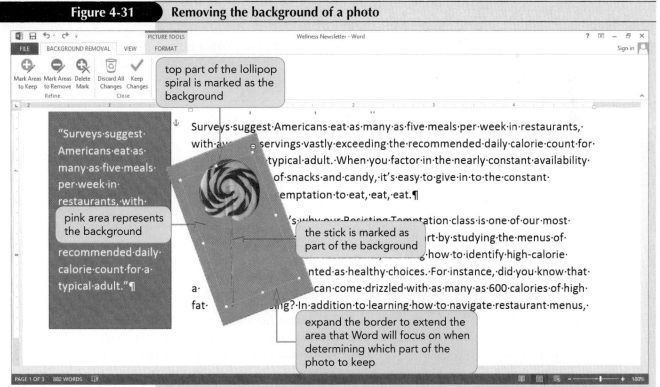

Image used with permission of Microsoft Corporation

The part of the photo that Word considers to be the background turns pink, and the BACKGROUND REMOVAL tab appears on the ribbon. A blue border with white handles surrounds the lollipop. The blue border helps Word narrow the area of focus as it tries to distinguish between the background and the parts of the image you want to keep. Word will automatically remove any part of the image outside the blue border when you click the Keep Changes button.

**Trouble?** If you don't see the blue border with the white handles, click the Mark Areas to Remove button in the Refine group on the BACKGROUND REMOVAL tab, and then click in the pink background, in the upper-right corner of the picture. This will insert a small white circle with a negative sign inside it, which you can ignore. The blue border with the white handles should now be displayed.

Notice that the lollipop stick is pink, indicating that Word considers it to be part of the background. The same might also be true for a small section at the top of the lollipop spiral, although this can vary from one computer to another. To ensure that Word keeps the entire lollipop spiral, you need to expand the blue border with the white handles. Then you can make additional adjustments using the tools on the BACKGROUND REMOVAL tab.

3. If necessary, drag the square handle in the upper-right corner of the blue border up slightly until the border contains the entire red and white lollipop spiral. The entire red and white spiral should now be visible in its original colors, with no pink shading, indicating that Word no longer considers any part of the spiral to be part of the background. The only problem is that Word still considers the lollipop stick part of the background. You can fix that problem by marking the stick as an area to keep.

4. On the BACKGROUND REMOVAL tab, click the **Mark Areas to Keep** button in the Refine group, and then move the drawing pointer 𝄃 over the lollipop. You can use this pointer to draw a line on the lollipop stick.

5. Position the mouse pointer at the top of the stick, and then press and hold the mouse button down as you drag the pointer down to the bottom of the stick. The pointer changes to a white arrow, and a dotted line appears as you drag the pointer. See Figure 4-32.

| Figure 4-32 | Marking an area to keep |
| --- | --- |

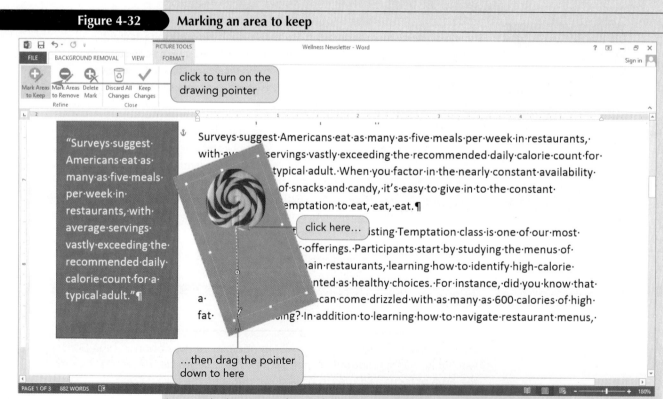

Image used with permission of Microsoft Corporation

**6.** Release the mouse button. A plus sign in a white circle appears on the dotted line, indicating that you have marked that part of the photo as an area to keep. The stick now appears in its original color, without pink shading. Now you will accept the changes you made to the photo.

**Trouble?** If Word uncovers a line of white from the background rather than the lollipop stick, you didn't draw the line precisely down the middle of the stick. Use the Undo button to reverse the change, and then begin again with Step 4.

**7.** In the Close group, click the **Keep Changes** button. The background is removed from the photo, leaving only the image of the lollipop. Now the text wrapping follows the curved shape of the lollipop, just as Estefan requested. Depending on exactly where you positioned the lollipop, some of the text might now wrap to the left of the lollipop stick.

**8.** Change the Zoom level to **100%** so that you can see the entire lollipop, as well as the top of page 2, and then drag the lollipop as necessary so the text wraps similarly to the text shown in Figure 4-33.

| Figure 4-33 | Lollipop with background removed |
| --- | --- |

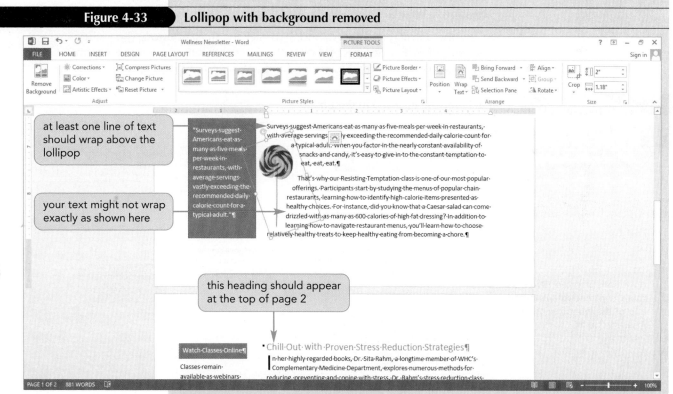

Image used with permission of Microsoft Corporation

Don't be concerned if you can't get the text wrapping to match exactly. The most important thing is that when you are finished, the "Chill Out with Proven Stress Reduction Strategies" heading should be positioned at the top of page 2. Also, at least one line of text should wrap above the lollipop.

**9.** Click outside the picture to deselect it, and then save the document.

You're finished with your work on the lollipop photo. Now Estefan asks you to add one more piece of clip art—the yoga drawing on page 3.

## Inserting and Editing a Clip Art Drawing

You can insert the clip art drawing the same way you inserted the clip art photo—by clicking the Online Pictures button in the Illustrations group on the INSERT tab and then typing some keywords. In the following steps, after you insert the yoga drawing, you'll add a picture style to it from the Picture Styles gallery.

### To insert and add a style to the yoga clip art drawing:

▶ 1. Change the Zoom level to **120%**, and then scroll to display the middle of page 2. You'll insert the yoga drawing in the blank space below the text box.

▶ 2. Click at the end of the paragraph below the "Manage Chronic Pain with Yoga" heading to position the insertion point between "…daily yoga." and the paragraph mark.

▶ 3. On the ribbon, click the **INSERT** tab.

▶ 4. In the Illustrations group, click the **Online Pictures** button, type **yoga under tree** in the Office.com Clip Art search box, and then press the **Enter** key. The drawing of the woman in a yoga pose under a tree, shown earlier in the Session 4.1 Visual Overview, is displayed in the search results window.

▶ 5. Click the drawing to select it, and then click the **Insert** button. The picture is inserted as an inline object below the line containing the insertion point because there is not enough room for it at the end of that line. See Figure 4-34.

**Figure 4-34**  **Clip art drawing inserted in document**

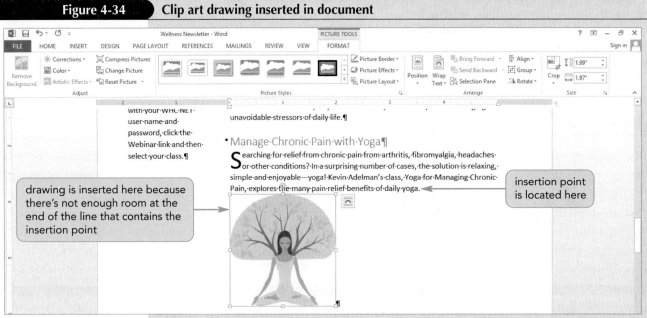

Image used with permission of Microsoft Corporation

Next, you need to resize the drawing, apply a picture style, wrap text around it, and then position it on the page.

6. In the Size group, click the **Shape Height** box, type **1.4**, and then press the **Enter** key. To maintain the picture's preset aspect ratio, the width automatically adjusts to 1.39 inches. The picture moves up to the preceding line because it's now small enough to fit.

7. In the Arrange group, click the **Wrap Text** button to open the Wrap Text menu. The In line with Text option is selected. Because the picture is still an inline picture, the Move with Text and Fix Position on Page options are grayed out, indicating that they are not available.

8. Click **In Front of Text** to select it and close the Wrap Text menu.

9. Click the **Wrap Text** button again, and then click **Fix Position on Page**. The yoga picture appears layered on top of the document text. Keep in mind that even though you selected Fix Position on Page, the picture is not stuck in one place. You can drag it anywhere you want. The point of the Fix Position on Page setting is that it prevents the picture from moving unexpectedly as you make changes to other parts of the document.

**TIP**

To add a simple border without adding a style, click the Picture Border button, and then click a color in the color gallery.

10. In the Picture Styles group, click the **Simple Frame, White** style, which is the first style in the visible row of the Picture Styles gallery. A frame and a shadow are applied to the yoga drawing.

11. Drag the picture to center it in the white space below the text box in the margin, deselect it, and then save the document. See Figure 4-35.

**Figure 4-35**    **Resized yoga picture with picture style**

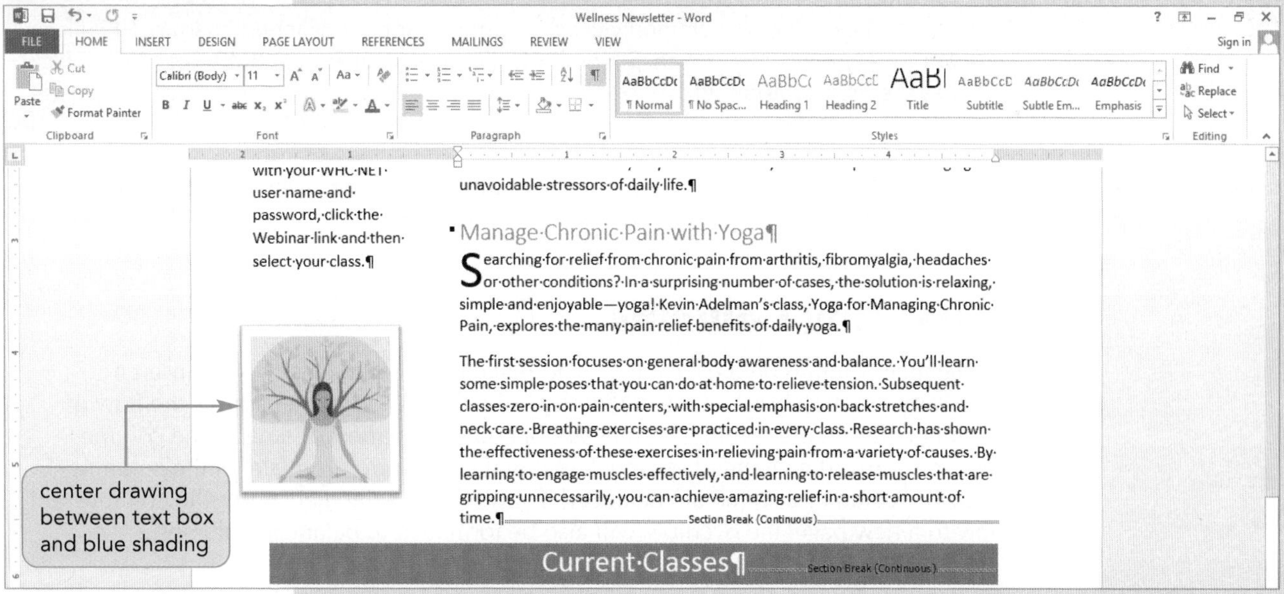

center drawing between text box and blue shading

Image used with permission of Microsoft Corporation

**INSIGHT**

*Working with Digital Picture Files*

Digital picture files come in two main types—vector graphics and raster graphics. A vector graphics file stores an image as a mathematical formula, which means you can increase or decrease the size of the image as much as you want without affecting its overall quality. Vector graphics are often used for line drawings and, because they tend to be small, are widely used on the web. File types for vector graphics are often proprietary, which means they only work in specific graphics programs. In Word, you will sometimes encounter files with the .wmf file extension, which is short for Windows Metafiles. A .wmf file is a type of vector graphics file created specifically for Windows.

In most cases, though, you'll work with raster graphics, also known as bitmap graphics. A **bitmap** is a grid of square colored dots, called **pixels**, that form a picture. A bitmap graphic, then, is essentially a collection of pixels. The most common types of bitmap files are:

- BMP—These files, which have the .bmp file extension, tend to be very large, so it's best to resave them in a different format before using them in a Word document.
- GIF—These files are suitable for most types of simple line art, without complicated colors. A GIF file is compressed, so it doesn't take up much room on your computer. A GIF file has the file extension .gif.
- JPEG—These files are suitable for photographs and drawings. Files stored using the JPEG format are even more compressed than GIF files. A JPEG file has the file extension .jpg. If conserving file storage space is a priority, use JPEG graphics for your document.
- PNG—These files are similar to GIF files, but suitable for art containing a wider array of colors.
- TIFF—These files are commonly used for photographs or scanned images. TIFF files are usually much larger than GIF or JPEG files, but smaller than BMP files. A TIFF file has the file extension .tif.

Now that you are finished arranging the graphics in the newsletter, you need to make sure the columns are more or less the same length.

# Balancing Columns

To **balance** columns on a page—that is, to make them equal length—you insert a continuous section break at the end of the last column. Word then adjusts the flow of content between the columns so they are of equal or near-equal length. The columns remain balanced no matter how much material you remove from any of the columns later. The columns also remain balanced if you add material that causes the columns to flow to a new page; the overflow will also be formatted in balanced columns.

**To balance the columns:**

▶ **1.** Press the **Ctrl+End** keys to move the insertion point to the end of the document, if necessary.

▶ **2.** Insert a continuous section break. See Figure 4-36.

**Figure 4-36**     **Newsletter with balanced columns**

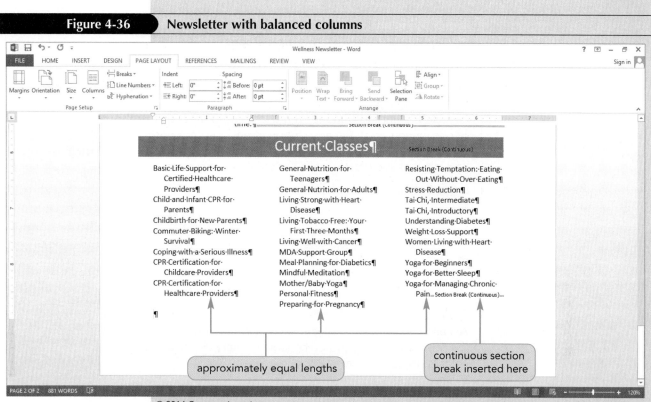

© 2014 Cengage Learning

Word balances the text between the three columns, moving some text from the bottom of the left column to the middle column, and from the middle column to the right column, so the three columns are approximately the same length.

Note that you can also adjust the length of a column by inserting a column break using the Breaks button in the Page Setup group on the PAGE LAYOUT tab. A column break moves all the text and graphics following it to the next column. Column breaks are useful when you have a multipage document formatted in three or more columns, with only enough text on the last page to fill some of the columns. In that case, balancing columns on the last page won't work. Instead, you can use a column break to distribute an equal amount of text over all the columns on the page. However, as with page breaks, you need to be careful with column breaks because it's easy to forget that you inserted them. Then, if you add or remove text from the document, or change it in some other significant way, you might end up with a page layout you didn't expect.

# Inserting a Border Around a Page

The newsletter is almost finished. Your last task is to add a border around both pages. The default style for a page border is a simple black line that forms a box around each page in the document. However, you can choose more elaborate options, including a dotted line, double lines, and, for informal documents, a border of graphical elements such as stars or trees. In this case, Estefan prefers the default line style, but he wants it to be blue.

## To insert a border around both pages of the newsletter:

1. Change the Zoom level to **Multiple Pages**.

2. On the ribbon, click the **DESIGN** tab.

3. In the Page Background group, click the **Page Borders** button. The Borders and Shading dialog box opens with the Page Border tab displayed. You can use the Setting options on the left side of this tab to specify the type of border you want. Because a document does not normally have a page border, the default setting is None. The Box setting is the most professional and least distracting choice, so you'll select that next.

> Be sure to select the Box setting before you select other options for the border. Otherwise, when you click OK, your document won't have a page border, and you'll have to start over.

4. In the Setting section, click the **Box** setting.

   At this point, you could scroll the Style box and select a line style for the border, such as a dotted line, but Estefan prefers the default style—a simple line. He's also happy with the default width of 1/2 pt. For very informal documents, you could click the Art arrow and select a predesigned border consisting of stars or other graphical elements. However, the only change Estefan wants to make is to change the border color to blue.

5. Click the **Color** arrow to open the Color gallery, and then click the **Blue, Accent 5** square, which is the second square from the right in the top row of the Theme Colors section. The Color gallery closes and the Blue, Accent 5 color is displayed in the Color box. See Figure 4-37.

| Figure 4-37 | Adding a border to the newsletter |
|---|---|

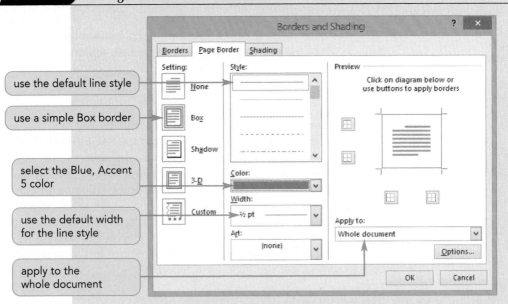

6. In the lower-right corner of the Borders and Shading dialog box, click the **Options** button. The Border and Shading Options dialog box opens.

   By default, the border is positioned 24 points from the edges of the page. If you plan to print your document on an older printer, it is sometimes necessary to change the Measure from setting to Text, so that the border is positioned relative to the outside edge of the text rather than the edge of the page. Alternatively, you can increase the settings in the Top, Bottom, Left, and Right boxes to move the border closer to the text. For most modern printers, however, the default settings are fine.

▶ **7.** In the Border and Shading Options dialog box, click the **Cancel** button, and then click the **OK** button in the Borders and Shading dialog box. The newsletter now has a simple, blue border, as shown earlier in the Session 4.1 Visual Overview.

▶ **8.** Save the document. Finally, to get a better sense of how the document will look when printed, it's a good idea to review it with nonprinting characters turned off.

▶ **9.** On the ribbon, click the **HOME** tab.

▶ **10.** In the Paragraph group, click the **Show/Hide** button to turn off nonprinting characters. Notice that the WordArt headline increases slightly in size to take up the space formerly occupied by the nonprinting paragraph mark.

▶ **11.** Change the Zoom level to **120%**, and then scroll to display page 2.

▶ **12.** On page 2, in the first line below the heading, replace "Dr. Sita Rahm" with your first and last name, and then save the document.

Estefan plans to have the newsletter printed by a local printing company. Betsy, his contact at the printing company, has asked him to email her the newsletter as a PDF.

## Saving a Document as a PDF

A **PDF**, or **Portable Document Format file**, contains an image showing exactly how a document will look when printed. Because a PDF can be opened on any computer, saving a document as a PDF is a good way to ensure that it can be read by anyone. This is especially useful when you need to email a document to people who might not have Word installed on their computers. All PDFs have a file extension of .pdf. By default, PDFs open in Adobe Acrobat Reader, a free program installed on most computers for reading PDFs, or in Adobe Acrobat, a PDF-editing program available for purchase from Adobe.

### To save the Wellness Newsletter document as a PDF:

▶ **1.** On the ribbon, click the **FILE** tab to display Backstage view.

▶ **2.** In the navigation bar, click **Export** to display the Export screen with Create PDF/XPS Document selected.

▶ **3.** Click the **Create PDF/XPS Document** button. The Publish as PDF or XPS dialog box opens.

▶ **4.** If necessary, navigate to the location specified by your instructor for saving your files, and then verify that "Wellness Newsletter" appears in the File name box. Below the Save as type box, the "Open file after publishing" check box is selected. By default, the "Standard (publishing online and printing)" button is selected. This generates a PDF suitable for printing. If you plan to distribute a PDF only via email or over the web, you should select the "Minimum size (publishing online)" button instead. See Figure 4-38.

**TIP**

To save a document as a PDF and attach it to an email message in Outlook, click the FILE tab, click Share in the navigation bar, click Email, and then click Send as PDF.

**Figure 4-38**

**Figure 4-38**   **Publish as PDF or XPS dialog box**

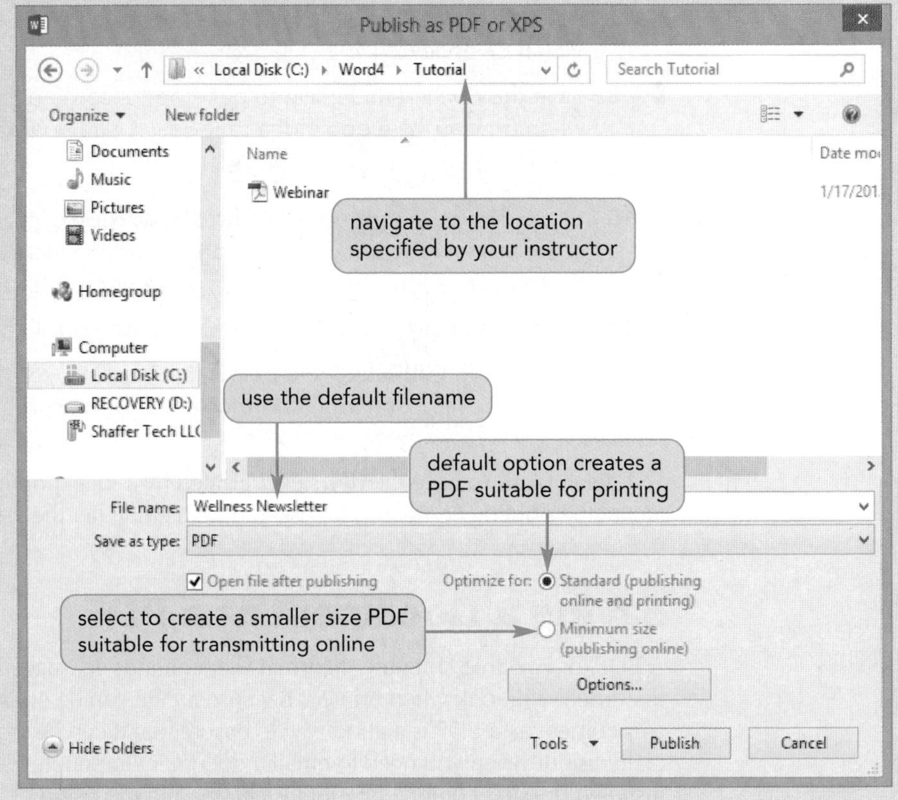

5. Click the **Publish** button. The Publish as PDF or XPS dialog box closes, and, after a pause, either Adobe Acrobat Reader or Adobe Acrobat opens with the Wellness Newsletter PDF displayed.

   **Trouble?** If the Wellness Newsletter PDF does not open, your computer might not have Acrobat Reader or Acrobat installed. In that case, skip Step 6.

6. Scroll down and review the PDF, and then close Adobe Acrobat Reader or Adobe Acrobat.

7. In Word, close the Wellness Newsletter document, but keep Word running.

In addition to saving a Word document as a PDF, you can convert a PDF to a Word document.

# Converting a PDF to a Word Document

You may sometimes need to use text from a PDF in your own Word documents. Before you can do this, of course, you need to make sure you have permission to do so. Assuming you do, you can open the PDF in Acrobat or Acrobat Reader, drag the mouse pointer to select the text you want to copy, press the Ctrl+C keys, return to your Word document, and then press the Ctrl+V keys to paste the text into your document. If you need to reuse or edit the entire contents of a PDF, it's easier to convert it to a Word document. This is a very useful option with PDFs that consist mostly of text. For more complicated PDFs, such as the Wellness Newsletter.pdf file you just created, the results are less predictable.

Estefan has a PDF containing some text about the Webinar+ service. He asks you to open it in Word and make some minor edits before converting it back to a PDF.

### To open the Webinar PDF in Word:

▶ **1.** On the ribbon, click the **FILE** tab to display Backstage view.

▶ **2.** In the navigation bar, click **Open**, if necessary, to display the Open screen, and then navigate to the Word4 ▶ Tutorial folder included with your Data Files.

▶ **3.** If necessary, click the arrow to the right of the File name box, and then click **All Files**.

▶ **4.** In the file list, click **Webinar**, click the **Open** button, and then, if you see a dialog box explaining that Word is about to convert a PDF to a Word document, click the **OK** button. The PDF opens as a Word document, with the name "Webinar" in the title bar. At this point, the Webinar.docx file is a temporary file stored in the temporary folder on your computer. If you want to retain a copy of the document, you need to save it.

▶ **5.** Save the document as **Webinar Revised** in the location specified by your instructor.

▶ **6.** Turn on nonprinting characters, set the Zoom level to **120%**, and then review the document, which consists of a WordArt headline and two paragraphs formatted in italic. If you see some extra spaces at the end of the paragraphs, they were added during the conversion from a PDF to a Word document. In a more complicated document, you might see graphics overlaid on top of text, or columns broken across multiple pages.

▶ **7.** Delete any extra spaces, remove the italic formatting from both paragraphs, and then save the document. You are finished editing the document, so now you can convert it back to a PDF.

▶ **8.** On the ribbon, click the **FILE** tab to display Backstage view.

▶ **9.** In the navigation bar, click **Export**.

▶ **10.** Click the **Create PDF/XPS Document** button.

▶ **11.** If necessary, navigate to the location specified by your instructor for saving your files, verify that "Webinar Revised" appears in the File name box, and then click the **Publish** button.

▶ **12.** Review the PDF in Acrobat or Acrobat Reader, close Acrobat or Acrobat Reader, and then close the Webinar Revised document in Word.

## REVIEW

### Session 4.2 Quick Check

1. What is WordArt?
2. Name five types of bitmap files.
3. Is all the clip art offered by Office.com available for free, with no copyright restrictions?
4. When cropping a picture, how can you maintain a specific ratio of width to height?
5. How do you rotate a picture?
6. Explain how to balance columns in a document.
7. What is a PDF?

**ASSESS**

## SAM Projects

Put your skills into practice with SAM Projects! SAM Projects for this tutorial can be found online. If you have a SAM account, go to www.cengage.com/sam2013 to download the most recent Project Instructions and Start Files.

**PRACTICE**

## Review Assignments

**Data Files needed for the Review Assignments: Exercise.docx, Habits.png, On the Move.docx, Take it Easy.docx**

Estefan is working on another newsletter. This one provides information about the benefits of exercise and good nutrition, and includes a list of exercise and nutrition classes. He has already written the text, and he asks you to transform it into a professional-looking newsletter. He also asks you to save the newsletter as a PDF so he can email it to the printer, and to edit some text currently available only as a PDF. The finished newsletter should match the one shown in Figure 4-39.

| Figure 4-39 | Completed Exercise Newsletter document |

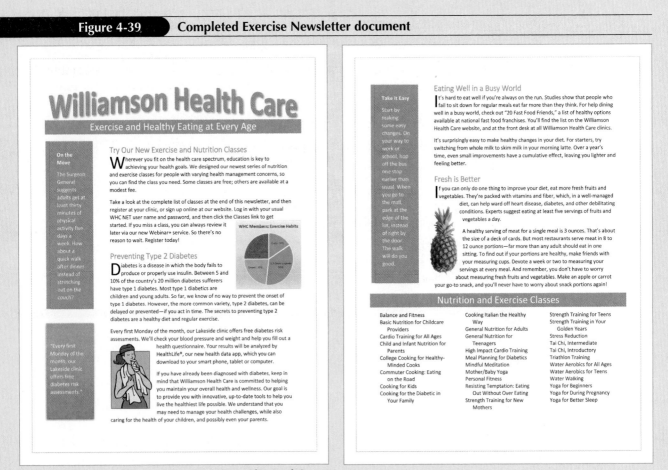

Complete the following steps:

1. Open the file **Exercise** from the Word4 ► Review folder included with your Data Files, and then save the document as **Exercise Newsletter** in the location specified by your instructor.

2. Insert continuous section breaks in the following locations:
   - On page 1, at the beginning of the "Try Our New Exercise and Nutrition Classes" heading, to the left of the "T" in "Try"
   - On page 2, at the beginning of the shaded heading "Nutrition and Exercise Classes," to the left of the "N" in "Nutrition"
   - On page 2, at the beginning of the first class name, to the left of the "B" in "Balance"

3. In sections 1 and 3, change the left and right margins to .75 inches. In section 2, change the left margin to 2.5 inches.

4. Format section 4 in three columns of equal width, and then format the entire list of class names with a 0.2-inch hanging indent.

5. Search for the term **HealthLife**, and then add the ® symbol to the right of the final "e."

6. On page 1, click anywhere in the "Try Our New Exercise and Nutrition Classes" heading, and then insert a preformatted text box using the Retrospect Sidebar option.

7. Change the text wrapping setting for the text box to In Front of Text. Change the height of the text box to 4.4 inches and its width to 1.2 inches, and then drag it left to position it in the white space in the left margin, with its top edge aligned with the first line of text below the "Try Our New Exercise and Nutrition Classes" heading. The left border of the text box should align with the left edge of the shaded paragraph above. Verify that the text box's position is fixed on the page, but note that its placement will shift slightly as you add other elements to the newsletter.

8. Delete all the placeholder text in the text box, and then insert the text of the Word document **On the Move**, which is located in the Word4 ► Review folder included with your Data Files. Delete any extra paragraph marks at the end of the text, if necessary.

9. On the INSERT tab, use the Shapes button to draw a rectangular text box that roughly fills the blank space in the lower-left margin of page 1. When you are finished, adjust the height and width as necessary to make the text box 2.5 inches tall and 1.3 inches wide.

10. Make sure the text wrap setting for the text box is set to In Front of Text, and that the text box has a fixed position on the page. Drag the text box's anchor up next to the "Preventing Type-2 Diabetes" heading to keep the text box from moving to page 2 later, when you add a graphic to page 1.

11. On page 1, in the second paragraph below the "Preventing Type 2 Diabetes" heading, select the first sentence (which begins "Every first Monday…"), and then copy it to the Office Clipboard.

12. Paste the copied sentence into the text box at the bottom of page 1, and then add quotation marks at the beginning and end.

13. Use the Align Text button to align the text in the middle of the text box, and then apply the Intense Effect - Orange, Accent 2 shape style (the orange style option in the bottom row of the Shape Styles gallery).

14. On page 2, click in the first paragraph, and then insert a preformatted text box using the Retrospect Sidebar option.

15. Change the text wrapping setting for the text box to In Front of Text. Change the height of the text box to 5.2 inches and its width to 1.2 inches, and then drag it left to position it in the white space in the left margin, with its top edge aligned with the first line of text. Verify that its position is fixed on the page. Don't be concerned that it overlaps the shaded paragraph below. This will change as you add more elements to the newsletter.

16. Delete all the placeholder text in the text box, and then insert the text of the Word document **Take it Easy**, which is located in the Word4 ► Review folder included with your Data Files. Delete any extra paragraph marks at the end of the text, if necessary.

17. After each of the four headings formatted with orange font, insert a drop cap that drops two lines.

18. On page 1, select the entire first paragraph, "Williamson Health Care," including the paragraph mark. Clear the formatting from the paragraph, and then format the text as WordArt, using the Fill - Orange, Accent 2, Outline - Accent 2 style.

19. Use the Position button to place the WordArt in the top center of the document, with square text wrapping, and make sure the WordArt has a fixed position on the page.

20. Change the text box width to 7 inches and retain the default height of .87 inches.

21. Apply the Chevron Up transform text effect, change the text fill to Orange, Accent 2 (the orange square in the top row of the Theme Colors section), and then add a shadow using the Offset Diagonal Bottom Right style (the first option in the top row of the Outer section).

22. Click at the end of the paragraph below the "Try Our New Exercise and Nutrition Classes" heading, and then insert the picture file named **Habits.png** from the Word4 ▸ Review folder included with your Data Files.

23. Practice cropping the chart to a shape, and then try cropping it by dragging the cropping handles. Use the Reset Picture button as necessary to restore the picture to its original appearance. When you are finished, crop the picture using a square aspect ratio, and then change its height and width to 1.8 inches. Use the Position button to place the chart picture in the middle of the right side of page 1 with square text wrapping.

24. On page 1, click at the end of the second paragraph below the "Preventing Type 2 Diabetes" heading, and then insert a clip art picture from Office.com that shows a woman in a pink headband, with a yellow towel around her neck, drinking from a water bottle, as shown in Figure 4-39. Search for the clip art using the keywords **exercising with water**.

25. Apply Square text wrapping, change the picture's height to 1.7 inches, retain the default width of 1.13 inches, and position the picture as shown in Figure 4-39. When the picture is properly positioned, the heading "Eating Well in a Busy World" should be positioned at the top of page 2, as shown in Figure 4-39.

26. On page 2, click at the end of the first paragraph below the "Fresh is Better" heading, and then insert a clip art photo from Office.com that shows a pineapple with green leaves, as shown in Figure 4-39. Search for the clip art using the keywords **pineapple photo**. When displayed in the search results, the photo will have a light blue background, with the pineapple tilted on its side.

27. Change the photo's width to 2 inches and retain the default height of 1.34 inches. Apply Tight text wrapping, fix its position on the page, and then remove the photo's background.

28. Rotate the photo so the pineapple is positioned vertically, with the leaves on top, and then drag the photo to position it as shown in Figure 4-39.

29. Balance the columns at the bottom of page 2.

30. Insert a simple box outline of the default style and width for the entire document. For the border color, use Blue, Accent 1 (the fifth square from the left in the top row of the Theme Colors).

31. In the top text box on page 1, replace "The surgeon general" with your first and last name. If you can't fit your entire name on the first two lines of the text box, use your first initial and your last name. Make any additional adjustments necessary to ensure that your newsletter matches the one shown in Figure 4-39.

32. Save the document, and then save it again as a PDF named **Exercise Newsletter.pdf** in the location specified by your instructor. Wait for the PDF to open, review it, and then close the program in which it opened. Close the **Exercise Newsletter.docx** document, but leave Word open.

33. In Word, open the **Exercise Newsletter.pdf** file, save it as a Word document named **Exercise Newsletter from PDF.docx**, review its appearance, note the problems with the formatting that you would have to correct if you actually wanted to use this new DOCX file, and then close it.

## Case Problem 1

**Data Files needed for this Case Problem: Green.docx, Sidebar.docx**

***Green Commission, Morelos, Arizona***     Clarice Stephan is the coordinator for the Green
Commission in Morelos, Arizona, a citizen committee charged with encouraging environmentally
friendly practices such as recycling, LEED construction, and water conservation. She has written the
text of the commission's bimonthly newsletter. Now she needs your help to finish it. The newsletter
must fit on one page so the commission's recycling guidelines can be printed on the other side. The
finished newsletter should match the one shown in Figure 4-40.

**Figure 4-40** ▸ **Completed Green Newsletter document**

# Recycle, Reuse, Renew
# Green Commission Updates

### Recycling Review

Each household is entitled
to one recycling bin. You
can recycle an unlimited
amount of materials, with
no extra fee for materials
that exceed the limit of
your household's recycling
bin. Please place extra
materials in a clean box
that is clearly labeled
"Recycling," and place it
next to your bin.

See the complete
recycling guidelines on
the other side of this
newsletter.

### Morelos Receives $5000 Recycling Grant

We're extremely happy to announce that the Morelos Green
Commission has been awarded a $5000 Change It Up grant
from the Arizona Department of Public Works. The money will pay
for new recycling bins at all city parks. Many thanks go to Suzette
Orleans, who spent many hours completing the grant application,
along with James Suarez and Leah Chang.

The recycling bins will be installed at the end of the summer. The
Department of Sanitation will be responsible for
emptying them twice a week during the summer,
and once a week the rest of the year. The Morelos
High School Honor Society has offered to clean the
bins once a month as part of their student volunteer
program.

### Hazardous Waste Collection

The next city-wide hazardous waste collection is scheduled for
the week of July 15. Sanitation workers will retrieve the items from
the curb next to your trash bins on your usual trash pickup day.
Please keep all hazardous waste items indoors until the morning of
your scheduled trash pickup. For a list of all accepted items, go to
the City of Morelos web site, and click Hazardous Waste Pickup.

Many household hazardous wastes can be recycled cleanly and
effectively by recycling professionals. Aren't sure what's considered
hazardous waste? The labels of most products will provide helpful
clues. Look for the following words: caution, warning, toxic,
pesticide, keep away from children, flammable, and warning.
Acceptable materials include antifreeze, brake fluid, kerosene, oil-
based paint, furniture polish, pesticides, herbicides, household
batteries, pool chemicals and fertilizers.

### Winners of the Citizen Green Award

| | | | |
|---|---|---|---|
| Kendra Ann Ramirez-Beech | Aralee Erbe | Marcos Jeschke | Harriet Soles |
| Michael Paul Bernault | Henry Douglas | Jaques Lambeau | Micah Schwerz |
| Beatrice Cai | Jose Caruccio | Maria Morelo-Jimenez | Alyssa Tonette |
| Emma Comerez | Sophie Carrucio | Elizabeth Juarez | Pamela Twist-Chamberlain |
| Jonathan Carnala | Krista Dennis | Mario Mondre | Roberto Oriel |
| Laydra Carole | Seamus Van Buren | Helena Pentakota Roys | |
| Samuel Butler | Jacqueline Fey-Esperanza | Maximillian Del Rio | |
| | Haiyan Jiang | | |

Complete the following steps:

1. Open the file **Green** located in the Word4 ▸ Case1 folder included with your Data Files, and then save it as **Green Newsletter** in the location specified by your instructor.

2. Change the document margins to Narrow, and then, where indicated in the document, insert continuous section breaks. Remember to delete each instance of the highlighted text "[INSERT SECTION BREAK]" before you insert a section break.

3. In section 2, change the left margin to 3 inches, and then format section 4 in four columns, with a 0.3-inch hanging indent.

4. Format the second paragraph in the document ("Green Commission Updates") as WordArt, using the Gradient Fill - Dark Green, Accent 1, Reflection style (second from the left in the middle row of the WordArt gallery). Change the text box height to 0.7 inches and the width to 7 inches. If necessary, drag the WordArt text box to center it between the left and right margins.

5. Insert drop caps that drop two lines in the first paragraph after the "Morelos Receives $5000 Recycling Grant" heading, and in the first paragraph after the "Hazardous Waste Collection" heading.

6. Click in the fourth paragraph in the document (the one with the drop cap "W"), and then insert a preformatted text box using the Ion Sidebar 1 option. Change the text wrapping setting for the text box to In Front of Text, and then change its height to 3 inches and its width to 2 inches.

7. Drag the text box down, and then align its top border with the "Morelos Receives $5000 Recycling Grant" heading.

8. Delete the title placeholder text in the text box, and type **Recycling Review**. In the main text box, delete the placeholder text and insert the text of the Word document **Sidebar** from the Word4 ▸ Case1 folder included with your Data Files. Change the font size for all the text in the text box, including the title, to 11 points.

9. In the blank space below the "Recycling Review" text box, draw a rectangular text box. When you are finished, adjust the height and width to make the text box 1.3 inches tall and 2 inches wide. Apply the Moderate Effect - Blue, Accent 2 shape style (third from the left in the second row from the bottom), and then position the text box as shown in Figure 4-40, leaving room for the recycling bin graphic you will add later.

10. In the text box, type **See the complete recycling guidelines on the other side of this newsletter**. Align the text in the middle of the text box, and then use the Center button to center the text between the text box's left and right borders.

11. At the end of the fifth paragraph (which begins "The recycling bins will be…"), insert a clip art picture from Office.com that shows a boy in an orange shirt and blue pants placing a tan bag in a green recycling bin. Search for the clip art using the keywords **boy putting trash in recycling**. Crop the picture to an oval shape, apply Tight text wrapping, fix its position on the page, and then change its height to 1 inch. Drag the picture to position it so the first line in the fifth paragraph wraps above it, as shown in Figure 4-40.

12. At the end of the first paragraph below the "Hazardous Waste Collection" heading, insert a clip art picture from Office.com that shows a green recycling bin. Search for the clip art using the keywords **recycling symbol on bin**. Change the picture's height to 1.3 inches, apply In Front of Text text wrapping, add the Center Shadow Rectangle picture style (second from right in the second row of the Picture Styles gallery), and then position the picture in the left margin, centered between the two text boxes, with a fixed position on the page, as shown in Figure 4-40.

13. Add a box page border using a line style with a thick exterior line and a thinner interior line, in the default width, and in the same color as the font for the "Morelos Receives $5000 Recycling Grant" heading.

14. In the last paragraph, replace "Roberto Oriel" with your first and last names.

15. Make any adjustments necessary so that your newsletter matches the one shown in Figure 4-40, and then save the document.

16. Save the document as a PDF named **Green Newsletter** in the location specified by your instructor. Review the PDF and then close the program in which it opened.

17. In Word, open the PDF named **Green Newsletter.pdf**, save it as **Green Newsletter from PDF.docx**, review its contents, note the corrections you would have to make if you actually wanted to use this document, and then close it.

APPLY

## Case Problem 2

**Data Files needed for this Case Problem: Facts.docx, Rights.jpg**

***Alexander Hamilton High School*** Paula McQuiddy teaches American history at Alexander Hamilton High School in Ruby Falls, Wisconsin. She has decided to create a series of handouts about important historical documents. Each handout will contain the text of the historical document, with red and blue accent colors, along with a picture of the American flag and a text box with essential facts about the document. Paula has asked you to help her complete her first handout, which is about the Bill of Rights. You will create the handout shown in Figure 4-41.

| Figure 4-41 | Completed Bill of Rights handout |
|---|---|

© 2014 Cengage Learning; Image used with permission of Microsoft Corporation

Complete the following steps:

1. Open the file **Rights** located in the Word4 ► Case2 folder included with your Data Files, and then save it as **Bill of Rights** in the location specified by your instructor.

2. Display the document gridlines.

3. Change the document margins to Narrow, change the theme to Facet, and format all the heading text using the Dark Blue font color in the Standard Colors section of the Font Color gallery.

4. At the top of the document, add the text **The Bill of Rights** as a new paragraph, and then format it as WordArt, using the Gradient Fill - Red, Accent 1, Reflection style (the second from the left in the middle row). Add Top and Bottom text wrapping, and then fix the text box's position on the page. If the position of the WordArt shifts, drag it back up to the top of the page. Change its height to 1.3 inches and its width to 7 inches. Apply the Square transform text effect (the first effect in the top row of the Warp section). Remove the reflection effect. Drag the WordArt as necessary to center it at the top of the page. The top edge of the text box should align with the top gridline.

5. At the end of the paragraph below the WordArt, insert a clip art photo of the American flag from Office.com. Search for the clip art using the keywords **waving American flag hanging on a pole**.

6. Apply Tight text wrapping to the photo, change the height to 2 inches, remove the photo's background, and then position it along the left margin, so the first two lines of regular text wrap above it, as shown in Figure 4-41.

7. Format the list of amendments in two columns. Use column breaks to format the amendments as shown in Figure 4-41, with Amendment IV at the top of the second column on page 1, and Amendment VIII at the top of the second column on page 2.

8. At the end of the last paragraph on page 2, insert a preformatted text box using the Grid Sidebar style. Apply In Front of Text text wrapping, and then change the height to 5.3 inches and the width to 7 inches. Position the text box at the bottom of page 2, centered in the white space, with a fixed position on the page.

9. Delete the placeholder text in the text box, and then insert the text of the Word document named **Facts** from the Word4 ▸ Case2 folder included with your Data Files. If necessary, delete any extra paragraph marks.

10. Add a box page border, using the default style, in the default width, and in the same color as the headings with the amendment numbers.

11. Make any adjustments necessary so that your newsletter matches the one shown in Figure 4-41, and then hide the gridlines.

12. At the end of the text box on page 2, insert a new, bulleted paragraph, remove the bullet formatting, right-align the paragraph, and then insert the text **Prepared by Student Name**, with your first and last names replacing the text "Student Name." Save the document.

13. Save the document as a PDF named **Bill of Rights.pdf** in the location specified by your instructor. Review the PDF in Acrobat or Acrobat Reader.

14. From within Acrobat or Acrobat Reader, use the appropriate keyboard shortcut to copy the bulleted paragraphs in the blue text box, open a new, blank Word document, and then paste the copied text into it. In a new bulleted list at the end of the document, list three differences between the formatting of the bulleted list in the current document and in the Bill of Rights.pdf file. Format the new paragraphs in red so they are easy to spot.

15. Save the Word document as **Facts from PDF** in the location specified by your instructor and then close it. Close Acrobat or Acrobat Reader.

## Case Problem 3

**Data Files needed for this Case Problem: Audio.pdf, Shape.docx**

*Shape Crafter 3D Printing* You have recently been hired as an assistant in the Human Resources department at Shape Crafter 3D Printing in Indianapolis, Indiana. Your supervisor explains that while working on the company's monthly newsletter, he left his laptop briefly unattended. His young daughter took advantage of the opportunity to make some unwelcome changes to his Word document. You've offered to troubleshoot the document and format the newsletter to look like the one shown in Figure 4-42. Your second task is to open a PDF containing a newsletter announcing a new program for employees, and edit the text to remove any irregularities that occurred in the conversion from a PDF to a Word document.

**TROUBLESHOOT**

**Figure 4-42**    **Completed Shape Crafter newsletter**

change the left margin to 1.75 inches

change the WordArt text direction setting to Rotate all text 270°; change its height to 9.94 inches and its width to 1.3 inches; and then change the font size to 72 points

for the border, use the Dark Red, Accent 1 color and the default line style and width

find this image at Office.com by searching for "tennis ball sitting next to a tennis racquet"

square text box shape with 1.5-inch sides; use the Light 1 Outline, Colored Fill - Dark Red, Accent 1 shape style

use the Blue - Gray, Accent color 5 Dark option in the Recolor section of the Color gallery

for the headings' shading, use the Dark Red, Accent 1 color; switch to white font

text is hyphenated

change spacing between columns to 0.2"

square text box shape with 1.25-inch sides

## Shape Crafter News

### CTO Tonella Desantes Honored

Chief Technology Officer, **Tonella Desantes**, ...

... achievements but also her community service. She began her career as an accountant at First Light Systems in Milwaukee, where she helped design and implement technical audits and became its first chief quality officer. She joined Shape Crafter 3D Printing in 2001 and was named CTO in 2006.

A valued member of many civic organizations, Desantes serves on the board of directors of the Foundation for Public Schools, the Prairieland Community Restoration Association, and the Wayton University Alumni Association. She was one of the founders and charter members of the governing board of The Phoenix House, a local community organization that helps unemployed single mothers re-enter the job market.

### Tennis Team Wins Third Place

Are you surprised to learn that Shape Crafter 3D Printing fields a prize-winning tennis team? Many participants in the Seventh Annual Indian Tennis Association's Executive Team Championships were. Not only did Shape Crafter 3D Printing field a team, but it finished third behind teams from Cottingham Investments (First Place) and Bryerly Pharmaceuticals (Second Place). On the other hand, tennis aficionados throughout the state wouldn't have been surprised at all with Shape Crafter 3D Printing's success. After all, playing for the Shape Crafter

3D Print... the ma... who als... sota Sta... The four-person team boasts two other tennis pros, **Maya Lapata**, who is Director of Internal Auditing at Shape Crafter 3D Printing and who finished fifth last year in the U.S. Women's Senior Invitational held in New York City, and **Juan Carlos Rica**, ...

"Are you surprised to learn that Shape Crafter 3D Printing fields a prize-winning tennis team?"

...mer tennis pro at Earlham Wood Country Club. Way to go, team!

### Take a Chance on Getting Away

First prize is a trip to the gorgeous San Juan Islands in Puget Sound. The San Juan Islands consist of three main islands—Orcas, Lopez, and San Juan. They are famous for stunning

scenery, great biking and hiking, and miles of quiet beaches. Visitors to San Juan Island will find quaint and historic fishing villages, and, if they're lucky, spot some of the magnificent orca whales that frequent the western side of the island. Orcas Island, with its many galleries, is the perfect destination for art and pottery lovers. Lopez attract thousands of bikers and ...

The raffle winner will receive round-trip air fare for two, one week accommodation at the Blackberry Bed and Breakfast on Orcas Island, and free daily passes for the San Juan Islands ferry, which travels to all three islands.

Don't forget to buy your ticket for the Get-Away Raffle.

© 2014 Cengage Learning; Photos courtesy of Ann Shaffer

Complete the following steps:

1. Open the file **Shape** located in the Word4 ▸ Case3 folder included with your Data Files, and then save it as **Shape Crafter Newsletter** in the location specified by your instructor.

⚙ **Troubleshoot** 2. Revise the document to match the newsletter shown in Figure 4-42. Start by fixing the border, changing the left margin, and resetting the pictures. Keep in mind that you can use the Selection Task Pane to select a picture, and remember to crop the photos so they match the ones shown in Figure 4-42. Also, you'll need to flip two of the pictures horizontally. You should be able to size the pictures appropriately by looking at their sizes relative to the text in Figure 4-42.

⚙ **Troubleshoot** 3. In the Arrange group, use the Selection task pane and the Align Objects button to align the photo of Tonella Desantes and the tennis racquet with the left margin. Also, align the two text boxes with the right margin.

4. Replace the double hyphens with an em dash.

5. In the middle of the second column, replace "Juan Carlos Rica" with your first and last names.

⚙ **Troubleshoot** 6. Make any adjustments necessary so that your newsletter matches the one shown in Figure 4-42. You might need to drag the WordArt text box left slightly to keep all the text on one page. Save the document.

7. Save the document as a PDF named **Shape Crafter Newsletter.pdf** in the location specified by your instructor. Review the PDF in Acrobat or Acrobat Reader, and then close Acrobat or Acrobat Reader.

8. Open the PDF **Audio.pdf** located in the Word4 ▶ Case3 folder included with your Data Files, and then save it as a Word document named **Audio Download Program** in the location specified by your instructor.

⚙ **Troubleshoot** 9. Edit the text to remove the picture, the WordArt, and the shaded text. Format the blue headings using the Heading 1 style, and then remove any extra spaces and paragraph breaks. Make any other edits necessary so that the text is formatted with consistent paragraph and line spacing throughout.

10. Save the document, and then close it. Close any other open documents.

## Case Problem 4

**CREATE**

**There are no Data Files needed for this Case Problem.**

*Glenfield Graphic Design*    You are an intern at Glenfield Graphic Design, a firm that specializes in designing fund-raising materials, including newsletters, for nonprofit organizations. As part of your training, your supervisor asks you to review examples of newsletter designs on the web, and then re-create the design of one of those newsletters in a Word document. Instead of writing the complete text of a newsletter, you can use placeholder text. Complete the following steps:

1. Open a new, blank document, and then save it as **Newsletter Design** in the location specified by your instructor.

2. Open your browser and search online for images of sample newsletters by searching for the keywords **newsletter image**. Review at least a dozen images of newsletters before picking a style that you want to re-create in a Word document. The style you choose should contain at least two pictures. Keep the image of the newsletter you select visible in your browser so you can return to it for reference as you work.

3. In your Word document, create the first page of the newsletter. To generate text that you can use to fill the page, type **=lorem()** and then press the Enter key.

4. Add at least two pictures to the newsletter, using clip art from Office.com. Rotate or flip pictures and remove the background from photos as necessary to make them work in the newsletter layout.

5. Make any other changes necessary so that the layout and style of your document match the newsletter example that you found online.

6. Somewhere in the document, attach a comment that reads **I used the following webpage as a model for this newsletter design:**, and then include the URL for the newsletter image you used as a model. To copy a URL from a browser window, click the URL in the browser's Address box, and then press the Ctrl+C keys.

7. Save the document, close it, and then close your browser.

# Written Communication

## Writing Clear and Effective Business Documents

Whether it's a simple email message sent to a group, a memo to provide information on an upcoming event, or a press release introducing a new product to the market, the quality of your written communication tells the world how prepared, informed, and detail-oriented you are. When searching for a job, the ability to write clearly and effectively is essential. After all, your first contact with a company is often a cover letter and resume. For a prospective employer, these documents provide the first indicators of the kind of employee you might be. To make the best possible impression, follow these important rules in all types of business communication.

## Rule One: Identify Your Audience

Who will read your document? What do they already know about your subject? For starters, you can assume your audience is made up of busy people who will only take the time to read what is important and relevant to them. They don't want to be entertained. They just want to read the information as quickly as possible. In the case of a resume and cover letter, your audience is typically one or more professional people who don't know you. Therefore, the goal of your resume and cover letter should be to introduce yourself quickly and efficiently.

## Rule Two: Do Your Research

Provide all the information the reader will need to make a decision or take action. Be absolutely certain that the facts you present are correct. Don't assume that something is true just because a friend told you it was, or because you read it online. Verify all your facts using reputable sources. Remember, your goal as a writer is to make the reader trust you. Nothing alienates a reader faster than errors or misleading statements. When applying for a job, make sure you are knowledgeable about the company so that you can mention relevant and accurate details in your cover letter.

## Rule Three: State Your Purpose

At the beginning of the document, explain why you are writing. The reader shouldn't have to wonder. Are you writing to inform, or do you want action to be taken? Do you hope to change a belief or simply state your position? In a cover letter accompanying your resume, state clearly that you are writing to apply for a job, and then explain exactly what job you are applying for. That might sound obvious, but many job applicants forget about directness in their efforts to come across as clever or interesting. This only hurts their chances because prospective employers typically have many cover letters to read, with no time to spare for sorting through irrelevant information.

## Rule Four: Write Succinctly

Use as few words as possible. Don't indulge in long, complicated words and sentences because you think they make you sound smart. The most intelligent writing is usually short and to the point. Keep in mind that hiring a new employee is a very time-consuming process. In small companies, people in charge of hiring often have to do it while performing their regular duties. Thus, the more succinct your resume and cover letter, the greater the chances that a potential employer will actually read both documents.

## Rule Five: Use the Right Tone

Be professional and courteous. In the case of writing to a prospective employer, don't make the mistake of being overly friendly because it might indicate to the reader that you are not taking the job application process seriously.

# Rule Six: Revise, Revise, Revise

After you finish a document, set it aside for a while, and then proofread it when it's no longer fresh in your mind. Even a small grammar or punctuation error can cause a potential employer to set aside your resume in favor of a more polished one with no errors. Remember, the best writers in the world seek out readers who can provide constructive suggestions, so consider having a friend or colleague read it and provide feedback. If someone points out an unclear passage, make every attempt to improve it.

Following these basic rules will help to ensure that you develop strong, professional written communication skills.

## Create a Resume and Cover Letter

You've seen how Microsoft Word 2013 allows you to create polished, professional-looking documents in a variety of business settings. The word-processing skills you've learned will be useful to you in many areas of your life. For example, you could create a Word table to keep track of a guest list for a wedding, or you could use Word's desktop publishing features to create a flyer promoting a garage sale or a concert for a friend's band. In the following exercise, you'll create a table summarizing information about prospective employers, and then you'll use that information to create a resume and a cover letter.

**Note:** Please be sure *not* to include any personal information of a sensitive nature in the documents you create to be submitted to your instructor for this exercise. Later on, you can update the documents with such information for your own personal use.

1. Pick a career field that interests you, and then go online and look up information about four companies or organizations in that field for which you would like to work.
2. Create a table that summarizes your research. Your table should include one column with information about how to apply for a job. Does the company require you to email your resume and cover letter as PDFs, to submit them as Word documents via a website, to paste them into a form on a website, or to mail printed copies? The process of applying for a job can vary widely from one company to another—and from one industry to another—so make sure you clearly explain the process for each company in your table and include any relevant website addresses. Include three columns in your table with general information that would be useful for you in a job interview. For example, you might include a "Most Important Product" column and a "Facts About Company Founder" column. Create a complete record for each company, and then sort the table alphabetically by company name.
3. Create a resume that you could use to apply for jobs at the four companies you researched. To ensure that your resume is suitable for your chosen field, search the web for sample resumes in your field. Find a resume design that you like, and then adapt the design for your resume. Your goal should be to create the most elegant, professional-looking resume you can, using advanced page layout options as necessary. For example, you could use a table to organize the page layout.
4. After creating your resume, proofread it for any errors, and then revise it for proper tone and clear and succinct content. If possible, ask a classmate or a family member to read it and provide constructive feedback.
5. Create a copy of your resume, and then revise this new version to use the simplest possible formatting. This time, your goal should be to create a resume that you could easily paste into a form on a website.
6. Create a cover letter to accompany your resume. Make sure that your letter clearly states your purpose, and that the letter is formatted correctly and written succinctly. When reviewing your cover letter and revising it, make sure your writing is professional and uses an appropriate tone.
7. Review all your documents carefully in Print Preview, make any necessary changes, and then save the documents.
8. Save your two resumes and your cover letter as PDFs.

# Getting Started with Excel

*Creating a Customer Order Report*

## OBJECTIVES

**Session 1.1**
- Open and close a workbook
- Navigate through a workbook and worksheet
- Select cells and ranges
- Plan and create a workbook
- Insert, rename, and move worksheets
- Enter text, dates, and numbers
- Undo and redo actions
- Resize columns and rows

**Session 1.2**
- Enter formulas and the SUM and COUNT functions
- Copy and paste formulas
- Move or copy cells and ranges
- Insert and delete rows, columns, and ranges
- Create patterned text with Flash Fill
- Add cell borders and change font size
- Change worksheet views
- Prepare a workbook for printing
- Save a workbook with a new filename

## Case | *Sparrow & Pond*

Sally Hughes is part owner of Sparrow & Pond, a small bookstore in Hudson, New Hampshire. Among her many tasks is to purchase new books from publishers. She also purchases rare and first edition books from online auctions as well as local library, estate, and garage sales.

Sally needs to quickly track sales data, compile customer profiles, and generate financial reports. She can perform all of these tasks with **Microsoft Excel 2013** (or **Excel**), an application used to enter, analyze, and present quantitative data. Sally asks you to use Excel to record a recent book order from a regular Sparrow & Pond customer.

## STARTING DATA FILES

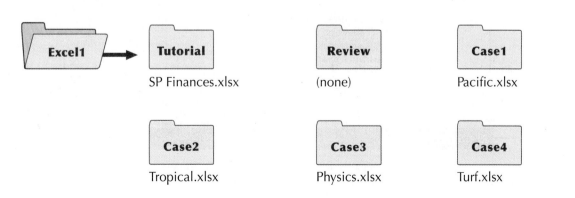

| Excel1 | | | |
|---|---|---|---|
| **Tutorial** | **Review** | **Case1** | |
| SP Finances.xlsx | (none) | Pacific.xlsx | |
| **Case2** | **Case3** | **Case4** | |
| Tropical.xlsx | Physics.xlsx | Turf.xlsx | |

# Session 1.1 Visual Overview:

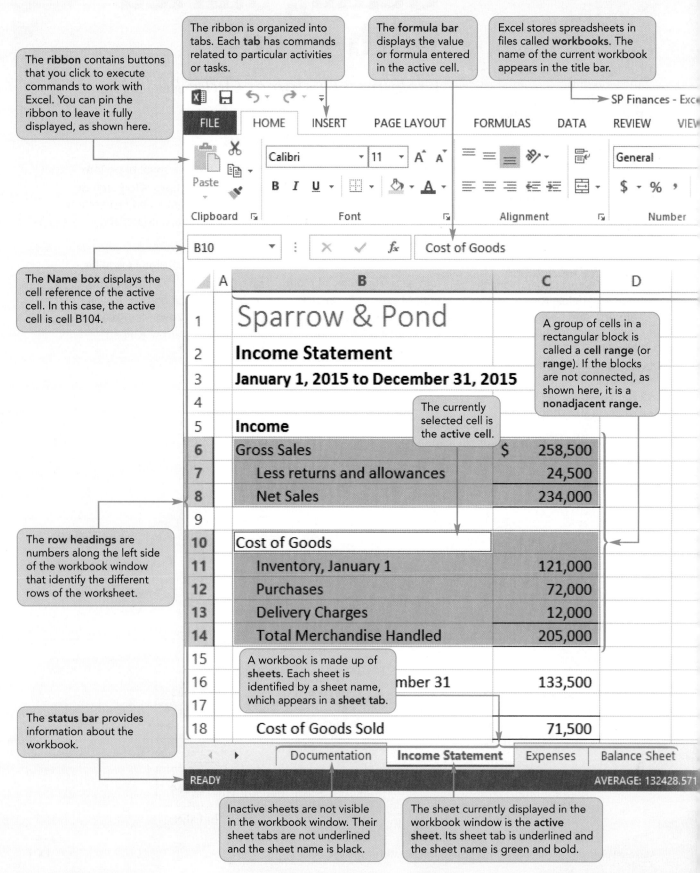

The **ribbon** is organized into tabs. Each **tab** has commands related to particular activities or tasks.

The **formula bar** displays the value or formula entered in the active cell.

Excel stores spreadsheets in files called **workbooks**. The name of the current workbook appears in the title bar.

The **ribbon** contains buttons that you click to execute commands to work with Excel. You can pin the ribbon to leave it fully displayed, as shown here.

SP Finances - Exc

The **Name box** displays the cell reference of the active cell. In this case, the active cell is cell B104.

A group of cells in a rectangular block is called a **cell range** (or **range**). If the blocks are not connected, as shown here, it is a **nonadjacent range**.

The currently selected cell is the **active cell**.

The **row headings** are numbers along the left side of the workbook window that identify the different rows of the worksheet.

A workbook is made up of **sheets**. Each sheet is identified by a sheet name, which appears in a **sheet tab**.

The **status bar** provides information about the workbook.

Inactive sheets are not visible in the workbook window. Their sheet tabs are not underlined and the sheet name is black.

The sheet currently displayed in the workbook window is the **active sheet**. Its sheet tab is underlined and the sheet name is green and bold.

# The Excel Window

The Ribbon Display Options button is used to display all, part, or none of the ribbon.

The Restore Down button returns a window to its previous size. If the Maximize button appears, it expands the window to fill the screen.

The Minimize button hides a window so that only its program button is visible on the taskbar.

P Finances - Excel

EVIEW     VIEW

Sign in

General

$ ▾ % ,  ←.0 .00
         .00 →.0

Number

Conditional Formatting ▾
Format as Table ▾
Cell Styles ▾

Styles

Insert ▾
Delete ▾
Format ▾

Σ ▾
↓ ▾
◆ ▾

Sort &
Filter ▾

Find &
Select ▾

Buttons for related commands are organized on a tab in groups.

D     E     F     G     H     I     J

The column headings are letters along the top of the workbook window that identify the different columns in the worksheet.

Each intersection of a row and a column is a cell. Each cell contains a separate value.

The contents of a worksheet are laid out in a grid of rows and columns in the workbook window.

ance Sheet     ...     ⊕

AGE: 132428.5714     COUNT: 15     SUM: 927000          ⊞  📃  📖     —  |  +   120%

The Zoom controls increase or decrease the magnification of the worksheet content. These tutorials show worksheets zoomed to 120%.

# Introducing Excel and Spreadsheets

A **spreadsheet** is a grouping of text and numbers in a rectangular grid or table. Spreadsheets are often used in business for budgeting, inventory management, and financial reporting because they unite text, numbers, and charts within one document. They can also be employed for personal use for planning a personal budget, tracking expenses, or creating a list of personal items. The advantage of an electronic spreadsheet is that the content can be easily edited and updated to reflect changing financial conditions.

### To start Excel:

▶ **1.** Display the Windows Start screen, if necessary.

   **Using Windows 7?** To complete Step 1, click the Start button on the taskbar.

▶ **2.** Click the **Excel 2013** tile. Excel starts and displays the Recent screen in Backstage view. **Backstage view** provides access to various screens with commands that allow you to manage files and Excel options. On the left is a list of recently opened workbooks. On the right are options for creating new workbooks. See Figure 1-1.

| Figure 1-1 | Recent screen in Backstage view |
| --- | --- |

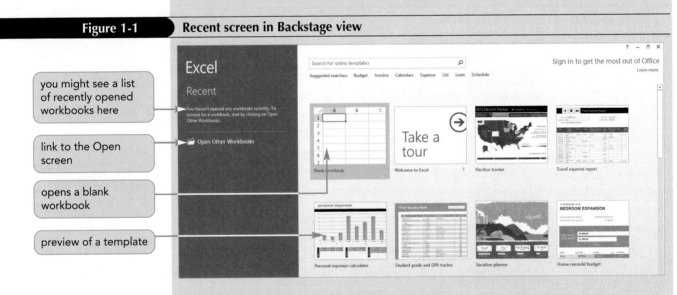

- you might see a list of recently opened workbooks here
- link to the Open screen
- opens a blank workbook
- preview of a template

**Trouble?** If you don't see the Excel 2013 tile on your Start screen, type Excel to display the Apps screen with the Excel 2013 tile highlighted, and then click the tile.

**Using Windows 7?** To complete Step 2, point to All Programs on the Start menu, click Microsoft Office 2013, and then click Excel 2013.

## Opening an Existing Workbook

Excel documents are called workbooks. From the Recent screen in Backstage view, you can open a blank workbook, open an existing workbook, or create a new workbook based on a template. A **template** is a preformatted workbook with many design features and some content already filled in. Templates can speed up the process of creating a workbook because much of the work in designing the appearance of the workbook and entering its data and formulas is already done for you.

Sally created an Excel workbook that contains several worksheets describing the current financial status of Sparrow & Pond. You will open that workbook now.

## To open Sally's workbook:

1. In the navigation bar on the Recent screen, click the **Open Other Workbooks** link. The Open screen is displayed and provides access to different locations where you might store files. The Recent Workbooks list shows the workbooks that were most recently opened on your computer.

2. Click **Computer**. The list of recently opened workbooks is replaced with a list of recently accessed folders on your computer and a Browse button.

   **Trouble?** If you are storing your files on your SkyDrive, click SkyDrive, and then log in if necessary.

3. Click the **Browse** button. The Open dialog box appears.

4. Navigate to the **Excel1 ▸ Tutorial** folder included with your Data Files.

   **Trouble?** If you don't have the starting Data Files, you need to get them before you can proceed. Your instructor will either give you the Data Files or ask you to obtain them from a specified location (such as a network drive). If you have any questions about the Data Files, see your instructor or technical support person for assistance.

5. Click **SP Finances** in the file list to select it.

6. Click the **Open** button. The SP Finances workbook opens in Excel.

   **Trouble?** If you don't see the full ribbon as shown in the Session 1.1 Visual Overview, the ribbon may be partially or fully hidden. To pin the ribbon so that the tabs and groups are fully displayed and remain visible, click the Ribbon Display Options button, and then click Show Tabs and Commands.

7. If the Excel window doesn't fill the screen, click the **Maximize** button in the upper-right corner of the title bar. See Figure 1-2.

**Figure 1-2    SP Finances workbook**

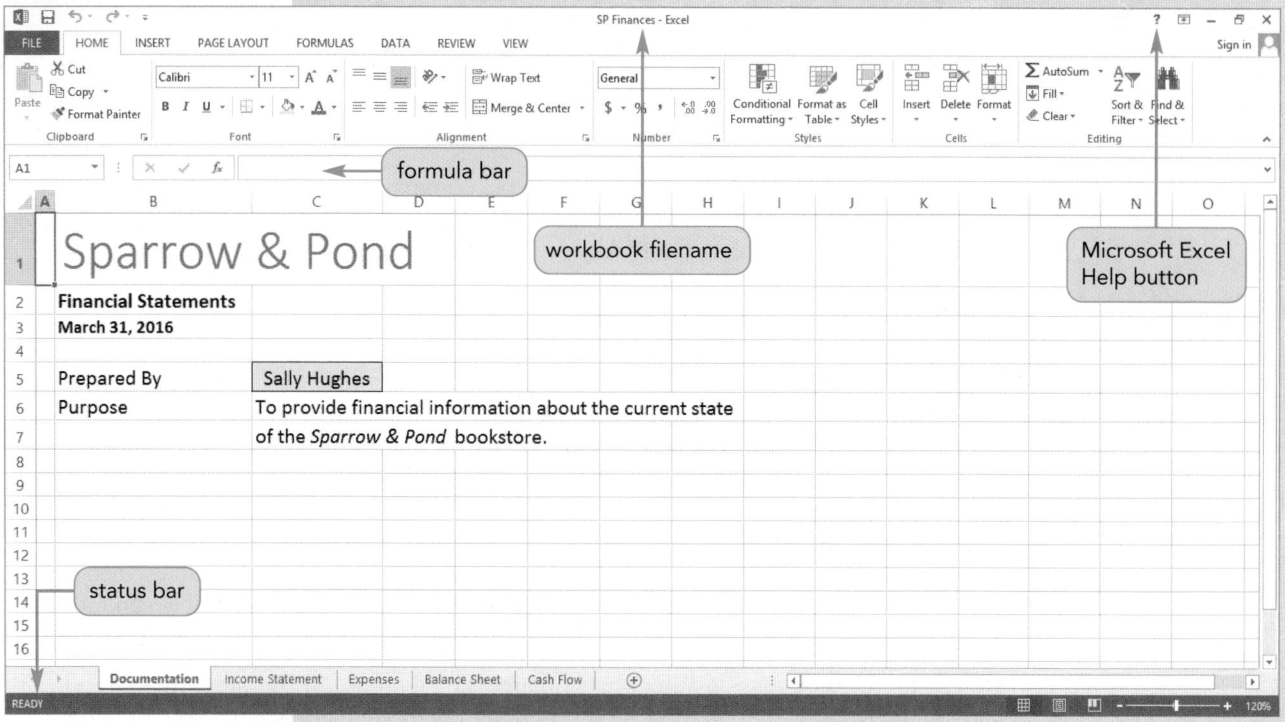

## Using Keyboard Shortcuts to Work Faster

Keyboard shortcuts can help you work faster and more efficiently because you can keep your hands on the keyboard. A **keyboard shortcut** is a key or combination of keys that you press to access a feature or perform a command. Excel provides keyboard shortcuts for many commonly used commands. For example, Ctrl+S is the keyboard shortcut for the Save command, which means you hold down the Ctrl key while you press the S key to save the workbook. (Note that the plus sign is not pressed; it is used to indicate that an additional key is pressed.) When available, a keyboard shortcut is listed next to the command's name in a ScreenTip. A **ScreenTip** is a box with descriptive text about a command that appears when you point to a button on the ribbon. Figure 1-3 lists some of the keyboard shortcuts commonly used in Excel. The tutorials in this text show the corresponding keyboard shortcuts for accomplishing an action when available.

**Figure 1-3** | **Excel keyboard shortcuts**

| Press | To | Press | To |
|-------|----|-------|----|
| Alt | Display the Key Tips for the commands and tools on the ribbon | Ctrl+V | Paste content that was cut or copied |
| Ctrl+A | Select all objects in a range | Ctrl+W | Close the current workbook |
| Ctrl+C | Copy the selected object(s) | Ctrl+X | Cut the selected object(s) |
| Ctrl+G | Go to a location in the workbook | Ctrl+Y | Repeat the last command |
| Ctrl+N | Open a new blank workbook | Ctrl+Z | Undo the last command |
| Ctrl+O | Open a saved workbook file | F1 | Display the Excel Help window |
| Ctrl+P | Print the current workbook | F5 | Go to a location in the workbook |
| Ctrl+S | Save the current workbook | F12 | Save the current workbook with a new name or to a new location |

© 2014 Cengage Learning

You can also use the keyboard to quickly select commands on the ribbon. First, you press the Alt key to display the **Key Tips**, which are labels that appear over each tab and command on the ribbon. Then, you press the key or keys indicated to access the corresponding tab, command, or button while your hands remain on the keyboard.

## Getting Help

If you are unsure about the function of an Excel command or you want information about how to accomplish a particular task, you can use the Help system. To access Excel Help, you either press the F1 key or click the Microsoft Excel Help button in the title bar of the Excel window or dialog boxes. From the Excel Help window, you can search for a specific topic or click a topic in a category.

## Using Excel 2013 in Touch Mode

In Office 2013, you can work with a mouse or, if you have a touchscreen, you can work in Touch Mode. In **Touch Mode**, the ribbon increases in height, the buttons are bigger, and more space appears around each button so you can more easily use your finger or a stylus to tap the button you need. As you work with Excel on a touchscreen, you tap objects instead of clicking them. Note that the figures in these tutorials show the screen with Mouse Mode on, but it's helpful to learn how to switch back and forth between Touch Mode and Mouse Mode. You'll switch to Touch Mode and then back to Mouse Mode now.

**Note:** The following steps assume that you are using a mouse. If you are instead using a touch device, please read these steps but don't complete them, so that you remain working in Touch Mode.

## To switch between Touch Mode and Mouse Mode:

▶ **1.** On the Quick Access Toolbar, click the **Customize Quick Access Toolbar** button ⬇. A menu opens listing buttons you can add to the Quick Access Toolbar as well as other options for customizing the toolbar.

   **Trouble?** If the Touch/Mouse Mode command on the menu has a checkmark next to it, press the Esc key to close the menu, and then skip Step 2.

▶ **2.** Click **Touch/Mouse Mode**. The Quick Access Toolbar now contains the Touch/Mouse Mode button 👆, which you can use to switch between Mouse Mode, the default display, and Touch Mode.

▶ **3.** On the Quick Access Toolbar, click the **Touch/Mouse Mode** button 👆. A menu opens listing Mouse and Touch, and the icon next to Mouse is shaded to indicate it is selected.

   **Trouble?** If the icon next to Touch is shaded, press the Esc key to close the menu and skip Step 4.

▶ **4.** Click **Touch**. The display switches to Touch Mode with more space between the commands and buttons on the ribbon. See Figure 1-4.

| Figure 1-4 | Ribbon displayed in Touch Mode |
| --- | --- |

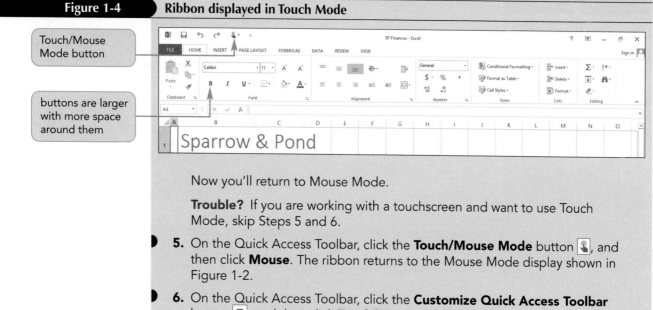

Touch/Mouse Mode button

buttons are larger with more space around them

Now you'll return to Mouse Mode.

   **Trouble?** If you are working with a touchscreen and want to use Touch Mode, skip Steps 5 and 6.

▶ **5.** On the Quick Access Toolbar, click the **Touch/Mouse Mode** button 👆, and then click **Mouse**. The ribbon returns to the Mouse Mode display shown in Figure 1-2.

▶ **6.** On the Quick Access Toolbar, click the **Customize Quick Access Toolbar** button ⬇, and then click **Touch/Mouse Mode** to deselect it. The Touch/Mouse Mode button is removed from the Quick Access Toolbar.

# Exploring a Workbook

Workbooks are organized into separate pages called sheets. Excel supports two types of sheets: worksheets and chart sheets. A worksheet contains a grid of rows and columns into which you can enter text, numbers, dates, and formulas, and display charts. A **chart sheet** contains a chart that provides a visual representation of worksheet data. The contents of a workbook are shown in the workbook window.

## Changing the Active Sheet

The sheets in a workbook are identified in the sheet tabs at the bottom of the workbook window. The SP Finances workbook includes five sheets labeled Documentation, Income Statement, Expenses, Balance Sheet, and Cash Flow. The sheet currently displayed in the workbook window is the active sheet, which in this case is the Documentation sheet. To make a different sheet active and visible, you click its sheet tab. You can tell which sheet is active because its name appears in bold green.

If a workbook includes so many sheets that not all of the sheet tabs can be displayed at the same time in the workbook window, you can use the sheet tab scrolling buttons to scroll through the list of tabs. Scrolling the sheet tabs does not change the active sheet; it only changes which sheet tabs are visible.

You will view the different sheets in the SP Finances workbook.

### To change the active sheet:

▶ **1.** Click the **Income Statement** sheet tab. The Income Statement worksheet becomes the active sheet, and its name is in bold green type. See Figure 1-5.

| Figure 1-5 | Income Statement worksheet |

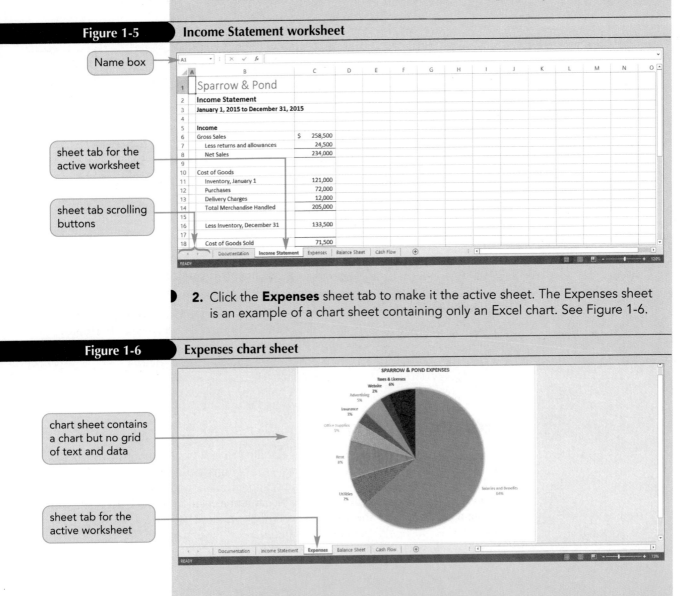

**2.** Click the **Expenses** sheet tab to make it the active sheet. The Expenses sheet is an example of a chart sheet containing only an Excel chart. See Figure 1-6.

| Figure 1-6 | Expenses chart sheet |

**TIP**

You can move to the previous or next sheet in the workbook by pressing the Ctrl+PgUp or Ctrl+PgDn keys.

▶ **3.** Click the **Balance Sheet** sheet tab to make it the active sheet. Note that this sheet contains a chart embedded into the grid of data values. A worksheet can contain data values, charts, pictures, and other design elements.

▶ **4.** Click the **Cash Flow** sheet tab. The worksheet with information about the company's cash flow is now active.

▶ **5.** Click the **Income Statement** sheet tab to make the Income Statement worksheet the active sheet.

## Navigating Within a Worksheet

The worksheet is organized into individual cells. Each cell is identified by a **cell reference**, which is based on the cell's column and row location. For example, in Figure 1-5, the company name, Sparrow & Pond, is in cell B1, which is the intersection of column B and row 1. The column letter always appears before the row number in any cell reference. The cell that is currently selected in the worksheet is referred to as the active cell. The active cell is highlighted with a thick green border, its cell reference appears in the Name box, and the corresponding column and row headings are highlighted. The active cell in Figure 1-5 is cell A1.

Row numbers range from 1 to 1,048,576, and column labels are letters in alphabetical order. The first 26 column headings range from A to Z. After Z, the next column headings are labeled AA, AB, AC, and so forth. Excel allows a maximum of 16,384 columns in a worksheet (the last column has the heading XFD). This means that you can create large worksheets whose content extends well beyond what is visible in the workbook window.

To move different parts of the worksheet into view, you can use the horizontal and vertical scroll bars located at the bottom and right edges of the workbook window, respectively. A scroll bar has arrow buttons that you can click to shift the worksheet one column or row in the specified direction, and a scroll box that you can drag to shift the worksheet in the direction you drag.

You will scroll the active worksheet so you can review the rest of the Sparrow & Pond income statement.

### To scroll through the Income Statement worksheet:

▶ **1.** On the vertical scroll bar, click the down arrow button ▼ to scroll down the Income Statement worksheet until you see cell C36, which displays the company's net income value of $4,600.

▶ **2.** On the horizontal scroll bar, click the right arrow button ▶ three times. The worksheet scrolls three columns to the right, moving columns A through C out of view.

▶ **3.** On the horizontal scroll bar, drag the scroll box to the left until you see column A.

▶ **4.** On the vertical scroll bar, drag the scroll box up until you see the top of the worksheet and cell A1.

Scrolling the worksheet does not change the location of the active cell. Although the active cell might shift out of view, you can always see the location of the active cell in the Name box. To make a different cell active, you can either click a new cell or use the keyboard to move between cells, as described in Figure 1-7.

**Figure 1-7**    Excel navigation keys

| Press | To move the active cell |
|---|---|
| ↑ ↓ ← → | Up, down, left, or right one cell |
| Home | To column A of the current row |
| Ctrl+Home | To cell A1 |
| Ctrl+End | To the last cell in the worksheet that contains data |
| Enter | Down one row or to the start of the next row of data |
| Shift+Enter | Up one row |
| Tab | One column to the right |
| Shift+Tab | One column to the left |
| PgUp, PgDn | Up or down one screen |
| Ctrl+PgUp, Ctrl+PgDn | To the previous or next sheet in the workbook |

© 2014 Cengage Learning

You will use both your mouse and your keyboard to change the location of the active cell in the Income Statement worksheet.

**To change the active cell:**

1. Move your pointer over cell **B5**, and then click the mouse button. The active cell moves from cell A1 to cell B5. A green border appears around cell B5, the column heading for column B and the row heading for row 5 are both highlighted, and the cell reference in the Name box changes from A1 to B5.

2. Press the → key. The active cell moves one cell to the right to cell C5.

3. Press the **PgDn** key. The active cell moves down one full screen.

4. Press the **PgUp** key. The active cell moves up one full screen, returning to cell C5.

5. Press the **Ctrl+Home** keys. The active cell returns to the first cell in the worksheet, cell A1.

The mouse and keyboard provide quick ways to navigate the active worksheet. For larger worksheets that span several screens, you can move directly to a specific cell using the Go To command or by typing a cell reference in the Name box. You will try both of these methods.

**To use the Go To dialog box and the Name box:**

1. On the HOME tab, in the Editing group, click the **Find & Select** button, and then click **Go To** on the menu that opens (or press the **F5** key). The Go To dialog box opens.

2. Type **C36** in the Reference box. See Figure 1-8.

Figure 1-8    Go To dialog box

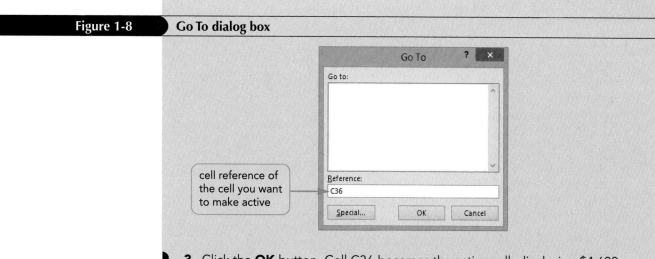

cell reference of the cell you want to make active

**3.** Click the **OK** button. Cell C36 becomes the active cell, displaying $4,600, which is Sparrow & Pond's net income for the year. Because cell C36 is the active cell, its cell reference appears in the Name box.

**4.** Click in the Name box, type **A1**, and then press the **Enter** key. Cell A1 is again the active cell.

## Selecting a Cell Range

Many tasks in Excel require you to work with a group of cells. You can use your mouse or keyboard to select those cells. A group of cells in a rectangular block is called a cell range (or simply a range). Each range is identified with a **range reference** that includes the cell reference of the upper-left cell of the rectangular block and the cell reference of the lower-right cell separated by a colon. For example, the range reference A1:G5 refers to all of the cells in the rectangular block from cell A1 through cell G5.

As with individual cells, you can select cell ranges using your mouse, the keyboard, or commands. You will select a range in the Income Statement worksheet.

**To select a cell range:**

**1.** Click cell **B5** to select it, and without releasing the mouse button, drag down to cell **C8**.

**2.** Release the mouse button. The range B5:C8 is selected. See Figure 1-9. The selected cells are highlighted and surrounded by a green border. The first cell you selected in the range, cell B5, is the active cell in the worksheet. The active cell in a selected range is white. The Quick Analysis button appears, providing options for working with the range; you will use this button in another tutorial.

Figure 1-9          Range B5:C8 selected

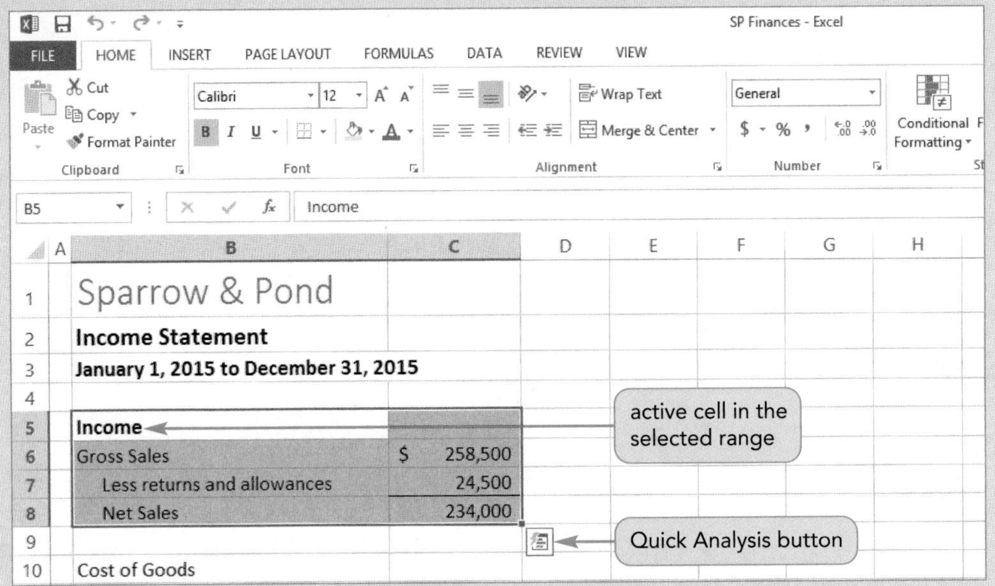

3. Click cell **A1** to deselect the range.

A nonadjacent range is a collection of separate ranges. The range reference for a nonadjacent range includes the range reference to each range separated by a semicolon. For example, the range reference A1:G5;A10:G15 includes two ranges—the first range is the rectangular block of cells from cell A1 to cell G5, and the second range is the rectangular block of cells from cell A10 to cell G15.

You will select a nonadjacent range in the Income Statement worksheet.

### To select a nonadjacent range in the Income Statement worksheet:

1. Click cell **B5**, hold down the **Shift** key as you click cell **C8**, and then release the **Shift** key to select the range B5:C8.

2. Hold down the **Ctrl** key as you select the range **B10:C14**, and then release the **Ctrl** key. The two separate blocks of cells in the nonadjacent range B5:C8;B10:C14 are selected. See Figure 1-10.

| Figure 1-10 | Nonadjacent range B5:C8;B10:C14 selected |

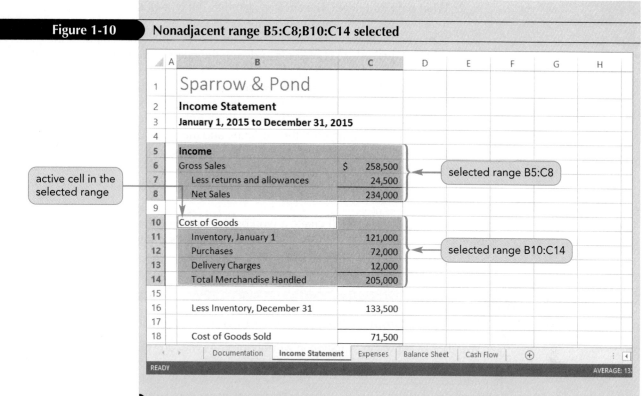

active cell in the selected range

selected range B5:C8

selected range B10:C14

3. Click cell **A1** to deselect the range.

# Closing a Workbook

When you close a workbook, a dialog box might open, asking whether you want to save the workbook. If you have made changes that you want to keep, you should save the workbook. You have finished reviewing the SP Finances workbook, so you will close it. You will not save the workbook because you want the original version to remain unchanged.

### To close the SP Finances workbook:

1. On the ribbon, click the **FILE** tab to display Backstage view, and then click **Close** in the navigation bar (or press the **Ctrl+W** keys).

2. If a dialog box opens asking whether you want to save your changes to the workbook, click the **Don't Save** button. The workbook closes without saving any changes. Excel remains opens, ready for you to create or open another workbook.

# Planning a Workbook

Before you begin creating a new workbook, you should develop a plan. You can do this by using a **planning analysis sheet**, which includes the following questions that help you think about the workbook's purpose and how to achieve your desired results:

1. **What problems do I want to solve?** The answer identifies the goal or purpose of the workbook. For example, Sally needs an easy way to record customer orders and analyze details from these orders.

2.  **What data do I need?** The answer identifies the type of data that you need to collect and enter into the workbook. For example, Sally needs customer contact information, an order ID number, the date the order shipped, the shipping method, a list of books ordered, the quantity of each book ordered, and the price of each book.
3.  **What calculations do I need to enter?** The answer identifies the formulas you need to apply to the data you have collected and entered. For example, Sally needs to calculate the charge for each book ordered, the number of books ordered, the shipping cost, the sales tax, and the total cost of the order.
4.  **What form should my solution take?** The answer describes the appearance of the workbook content and how it should be presented to others. For example, Sally wants the information stored in a single worksheet that is easy to read and prints clearly.

Based on Sally's plan, you will create a workbook containing the details of a recent customer order. Sally will use this workbook as a model for future workbooks detailing other customer orders.

**PROSKILLS**

### Written Communication: Creating Effective Workbooks

Workbooks convey information in written form. As with any type of writing, the final product creates an impression and provides an indicator of your interest, knowledge, and attention to detail. To create the best impression, all workbooks—especially those you intend to share with others such as coworkers and clients—should be well planned, well organized, and well written.

A well-designed workbook should clearly identify its overall goal and present information in an organized format. The data it includes—both the entered values and the calculated values—should be accurate. The process of developing an effective workbook includes the following steps:

*   Determine the workbook's purpose, content, and organization before you start.
*   Create a list of the sheets used in the workbook, noting each sheet's purpose.
*   Insert a documentation sheet that describes the workbook's purpose and organization. Include the name of the workbook author, the date the workbook was created, and any additional information that will help others to track the workbook to its source.
*   Enter all of the data in the workbook. Add labels to indicate what the values represent and, if possible, where they originated so others can view the source of your data.
*   Enter formulas for calculated items rather than entering the calculated values into the workbook. For more complicated calculations, provide documentation explaining them.
*   Test the workbook with a variety of values; edit the data and formulas to correct errors.
*   Save the workbook and create a backup copy when the project is completed. Print the workbook's contents if you need to provide a hard-copy version to others or for your files.
*   Maintain a history of your workbook as it goes through different versions, so that you and others can quickly see how the workbook has changed during revisions.

By including clearly written documentation, explanatory text, a logical organization, and accurate data and formulas, you will create effective workbooks that others can use easily.

# Creating a New Workbook

You create new workbooks from the New screen in Backstage view. Similar to the Recent screen that opened when you started Excel, the New screen include templates for a variety of workbook types. You can see a preview of what the different workbooks will look like. You will create a new workbook from the Blank workbook template, in which you can add all of the content and design Sally wants for the Sparrow & Pond customer order worksheet.

### To start a new, blank workbook:

**TIP**

You can also create a new, blank workbook by pressing the Ctrl+N keys.

► 1. On the ribbon, click the **FILE** tab to display Backstage view.

► 2. Click **New** in the navigation bar to display the New screen, which includes access to templates for a variety of workbooks.

► 3. Click the **Blank workbook** tile. A blank workbook opens. See Figure 1-11.

**Figure 1-11** | **Blank workbook**

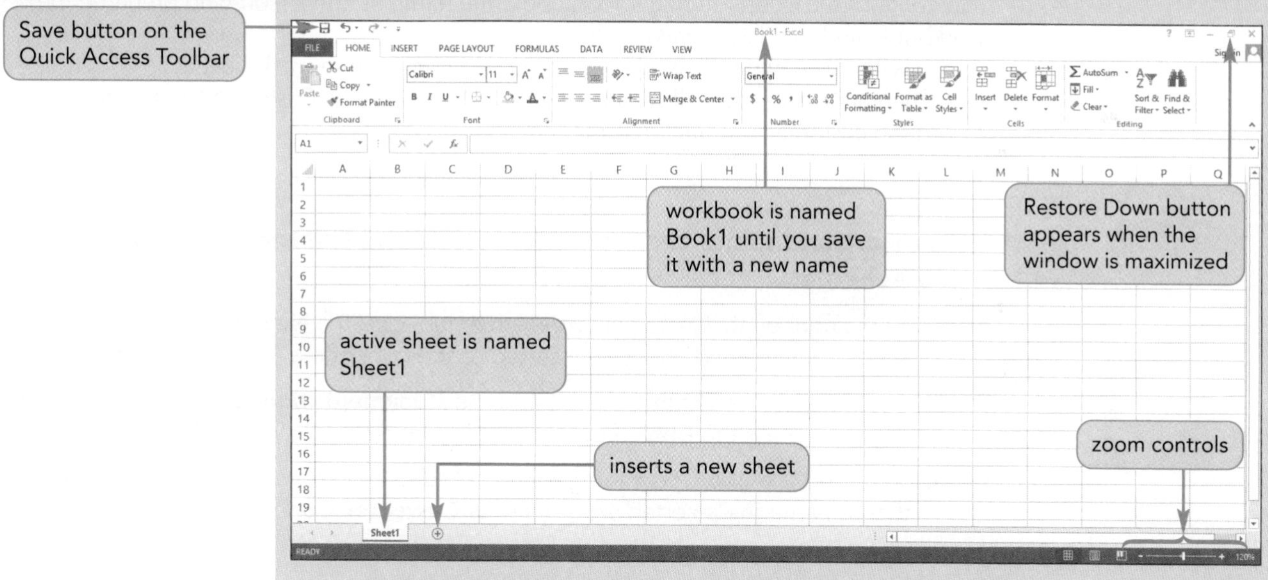

Save button on the Quick Access Toolbar

workbook is named Book1 until you save it with a new name

Restore Down button appears when the window is maximized

active sheet is named Sheet1

inserts a new sheet

zoom controls

In these tutorials, the workbook window is zoomed to 120% for better readability. If you want to zoom your workbook window to match the figures, complete Step 4. If you prefer to work in the default zoom of 100% or at another zoom level, read but do not complete Step 4; you might see more or less of the worksheet on your screen, but this will not affect your work in the tutorials.

► 4. If you want your workbook window zoomed to 120% to match the figures, click the **Zoom In** button ➕ on the status bar twice to increase the zoom level to 120%. The 120% magnification increases the size of each cell, but reduces the number of worksheet cells visible in the workbook window.

The name of the active workbook, Book1, appears in the title bar. If you open multiple blank workbooks, they are named Book1, Book2, Book3, and so forth until you save them with a more descriptive name.

## Renaming and Inserting Worksheets

Blank workbooks open with a single blank sheet named Sheet1. You can give sheets more descriptive and meaningful names. This is a good practice so that you and others can easily tell what a sheet contains. Sheet names cannot exceed 31 characters, but they can contain blank spaces and include upper- and lowercase letters.

Because Sheet1 is not a very descriptive name, Sally wants you to rename the worksheet as Customer Order.

### To rename the Sheet1 worksheet:

▶ **1.** Double-click the **Sheet1** tab. The Sheet1 label in the tab is selected.

▶ **2.** Type **Customer Order** as the new name, and then press the **Enter** key. The width of the sheet tab expands to fit the longer sheet name.

Many workbooks include multiple sheets so that data can be organized in logical groups. A common business practice is to include a worksheet named Documentation that contains a description of the workbook, the name of the person who prepared the workbook, and the date it was created.

You will create two new worksheets. You will rename one worksheet as Documentation and you will rename the other worksheet as Customer Contact to record the customer's contact information.

### To insert and name the Documentation and Customer Contact worksheets:

▶ **1.** To the right of the Customer Order sheet tab, click the **New sheet** button ⊕. A new sheet named Sheet2 is inserted to the right of the Customer Order sheet.

▶ **2.** Double-click the **Sheet2** sheet tab, type **Documentation** as the new name, and then press the **Enter** key. The second worksheet is renamed.

▶ **3.** To the right of the Documentation sheet, click the **New sheet** button ⊕, and then rename the inserted worksheet as **Customer Contact**.

## Moving Worksheets

A good practice is to place the most important sheets at the beginning of the workbook (the leftmost sheet tabs) and less important sheets at the end (the rightmost sheet tabs). To change the placement of sheets in a workbook, you drag them by their sheet tabs to the new location.

Sally wants you to move the Documentation worksheet to the front of the workbook, so that it appears before the Customer Order sheet.

**TIP**

To copy a sheet, hold down the Ctrl key as you drag and drop its sheet tab.

### To move the Documentation worksheet:

▶ **1.** Point to the **Documentation** sheet tab.

▶ **2.** Press and hold the mouse button. The pointer changes to ▷, and a small arrow appears in the upper-left corner of the tab.

▶ **3.** Drag to the left until the small arrow appears in the upper-left corner of the Customer Order sheet tab, and then release the mouse button. The Documentation worksheet is now the first sheet in the workbook.

## Deleting Worksheets

In some workbooks, you will want to delete an existing sheet. The easiest way to delete a sheet is by using a **shortcut menu**, which is a list of commands related to a selection that opens when you click the right mouse button. Sally asks you to include the customer's contact information on the Customer Order worksheet so all of the information is on one sheet.

**To delete the Customer Contact worksheet from the workbook:**

▶ **1.** Right-click the **Customer Contact** sheet tab. A shortcut menu opens.

▶ **2.** Click **Delete**. The Customer Contact worksheet is removed from the workbook.

## Saving a Workbook

As you modify a workbook, you should save it regularly—every 10 minutes or so is a good practice. The first time you save a workbook, the Save As dialog box opens so you can name the file and choose where to save it. You can save the workbook on your computer or network, or to your account on SkyDrive.

**To save your workbook for the first time:**

▶ **1.** On the Quick Access Toolbar, click the **Save** button 🖫 (or press the **Ctrl+S** keys). The Save As screen in Backstage view opens.

▶ **2.** Click **Computer** in the Places list, and then click the **Browse** button. The Save As dialog box opens.

   **Trouble?** If your instructor wants you to save your files to your SkyDrive account, click SkyDrive, and then log in to your account, if necessary.

▶ **3.** Navigate to the location specified by your instructor.

▶ **4.** In the File name box, select **Book1** (the suggested name) if it is not already selected, and then type **SP Customer Order**.

▶ **5.** Verify that **Excel Workbook** appears in the Save as type box.

▶ **6.** Click the **Save** button. The workbook is saved, the dialog box closes, and the workbook window reappears with the new filename in the title bar.

As you modify the workbook, you will need to resave the file. Because you already saved the workbook with a filename, the next time you save, the Save command saves the changes you made to the workbook without opening the Save As dialog box.

# Entering Text, Dates, and Numbers

Workbook content is entered into worksheet cells. Those cells can contain text, numbers, or dates and times. **Text data** is any combination of letters, numbers, and symbols. Text data is often referred to as a **text string** because it contains a series, or string, of text characters. **Numeric data** is any number that can be used in a mathematical calculation. **Date** and **time data** are commonly recognized formats for date and time values. For example, Excel interprets the cell entry April 15, 2016 as a date and not as text. New data is placed into the active cell of the current worksheet. As you enter data, the entry appears in both the active cell and the formula bar. By default, text is left-aligned in cells, and numbers, dates, and times are right-aligned.

# Entering Text

Text is often used in worksheets to label other data and to identify areas of a sheet. Sally wants you to enter some of the information from the planning analysis sheet into the Documentation sheet.

## To enter the text for the Documentation sheet:

1. Press the **Ctrl+Home** keys to make sure cell A1 is the active cell on the Documentation sheet.

2. Type **Sparrow and Pond** in cell A1. As you type, the text appears in cell A1 and in the formula bar.

3. Press the **Enter** key twice. The text is entered into cell A1 and the active cell moves down two rows to cell A3.

4. Type **Author** in cell A3, and then press the **Tab** key. The text is entered and the active cell moves one column to the right to cell B3.

5. Type your name in cell B3, and then press the **Enter** key. The text is entered and the active cell moves one cell down and to the left to cell A4.

6. Type **Date** in cell A4, and then press the **Tab** key. The text is entered and the active cell moves one column to the right to cell B4, where you would enter the date you created the worksheet. For now, you will leave the cell for the date blank.

7. Click cell **A5** to make it the active cell, type **Purpose** in the cell, and then press the **Tab** key. The active cell moves one column to the right to cell B5.

8. Type **To record customer book orders**. in cell B5, and then press the **Enter** key. Figure 1-12 shows the text entered in the Documentation sheet.

| Figure 1-12 | Documentation sheet |
| --- | --- |

text overflows into the empty cell to the right

your name appears here

The text you entered in cell A1 is so long that it appears to overflow into cell B1. The same is true for the text you entered in cells B3 and B5. Any text you enter in a cell that doesn't fit within that cell will cover the adjacent cells to the right as long as they are empty. If the adjacent cells contain data, only the text that fits into the cell is displayed. The rest of the text entry is hidden from view. The text itself is not affected. The complete text is still entered in the cell; it is just not displayed. (You will learn how to display all text in a cell in the next session.)

## Undoing and Redoing an Action

As you enter data in a workbook, you might need to undo a previous action. Excel maintains a list of the actions you performed in the workbook during the current session, so you can undo most of your actions. You can use the Undo button on the Quick Access Toolbar or press the Ctrl+Z keys to reverse your most recent actions one at a time. If you want to undo more than one action, you can click the Undo button arrow and then select the earliest action you want to undo—all of the actions after the earliest action you selected are also undone.

You will undo the most recent change you made to the Documentation sheet—the text you entered into cell B5. Then you will enter more descriptive and accurate description of the worksheet's purpose.

### To undo the text entry in cell B5:

▶ **1.** On the Quick Access Toolbar, click the **Undo** button ↺ (or press the **Ctrl+Z** keys). The last action is reversed, removing the text you entered in cell B5.

▶ **2.** In cell B5, type **To record book orders from a Sparrow & Pond customer.** and then press the **Enter** key.

If you want to restore actions you have undone, you can redo them. To redo one action at a time, you can click the Redo button ↻ on the Quick Access Toolbar or press the Ctrl+Y keys. To redo multiple actions at once, you can click the Redo button arrow and then click the earliest action you want to redo. After you undo or redo an action, Excel continues the action list starting from any new changes you make to the workbook.

## Editing Cell Content

As you work, you might find mistakes you need to correct or entries that you want to change. If you want to replace all of the content in a cell, you simply select the cell and then type the new entry to overwrite the previous entry. However, if you need to replace only part of a cell's content, you can work in **Edit mode**. To switch to Edit mode, you double-click the cell. A blinking insertion point indicates where the new content you type will be inserted. In the cell or formula bar, the pointer changes to an I-beam, which you can use to select text in the cell. Anything you type replaces the selected content.

You need to edit the text in cell A1 to Sparrow & Pond. You will switch to Edit mode to correct the text.

### To edit the text in cell A1:

▶ **1.** Double-click cell **A1** to select the cell and switch to Edit mode. A blinking insertion point appears within the text of cell A1. The status bar displays EDIT instead of READY to indicate that the cell is in Edit mode.

▶ **2.** Press the arrow keys to move the insertion point directly to the right of the word "and" in the company name.

▶ **3.** Press the **Backspace** key three times to delete the word "and."

▶ **4.** Type **&** to enter the new text, and then press the **Enter** key. The cell text changes to Sparrow & Pond. See Figure 1-13.

**Figure 1-13**     **Revised Documentation sheet**

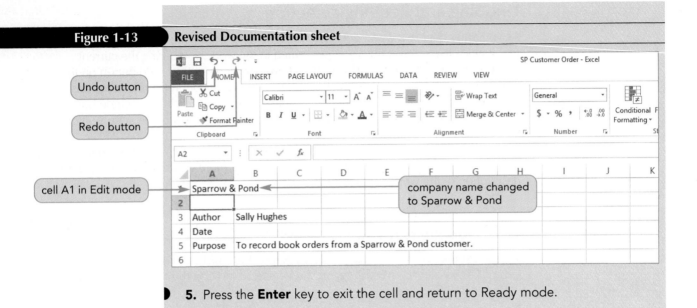

5. Press the **Enter** key to exit the cell and return to Ready mode.

## Understanding AutoComplete

As you type text in the active cell, Excel tries to anticipate the remaining characters by displaying text that begins with the same letters as a previous entry in the same column. This feature, known as **AutoComplete**, helps make entering repetitive text easier. To accept the suggested text, press the Tab or Enter key. To override the suggested text, continue to type the text you want to enter in the cell. AutoComplete does not work with dates or numbers, or when a blank cell is between the previous entry and the text you are typing.

Next, you will enter the contact information for Tobias Gregson, a customer who recently placed an order with Sparrow & Pond. You will enter the contact information on the Customer Order worksheet.

**To enter Tobias Gregson's contact information:**

1. Click the **Customer Order** sheet tab to make it the active sheet.

2. In cell A1, type **Customer Order** as the worksheet title, and then press the **Enter** key twice. The worksheet title is entered in cell A1, and the active cell is cell A3.

3. Type **Ship To** in cell A3, and then press the **Enter** key. The label is entered in the cell, and the active cell is now cell A4.

4. In the range A4:A10, enter the following labels, pressing the **Enter** key after each entry and ignoring any AutoComplete suggestions: **First Name**, **Last Name**, **Address**, **City**, **State**, **Postal Code**, and **Phone**.

5. Click cell **B4** to make that cell the active cell.

**6.** In the range B4:B10, enter the following contact information, pressing the **Enter** key after each entry and ignoring any AutoComplete suggestions: **Tobias, Gregson, 412 Apple Grove St., Nashua, NH, 03061**, and **(603) 555-4128**. See Figure 1-14.

| Figure 1-14 | Text entered in the Customer Order worksheet |

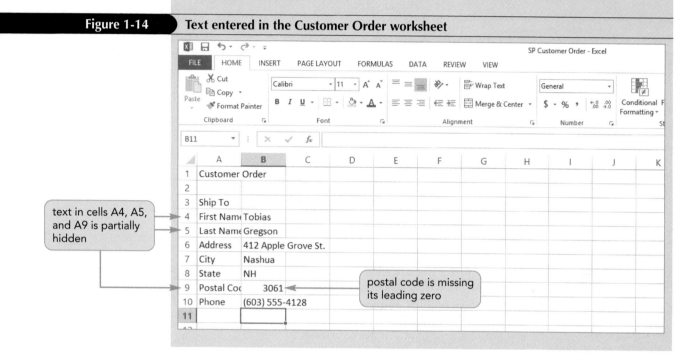

text in cells A4, A5, and A9 is partially hidden

postal code is missing its leading zero

## Displaying Numbers as Text

When you type numbers in the active cell, Excel treats the entry as a number and ignores any leading zero. For example, in cell B9, the first digit of the postal code 03061 is missing; Excel displays 3061 because the numbers 3061 and 03061 have the same value. To specify that a number entry should be considered text and all digits should be displayed, you include an apostrophe (') before the numbers.

You will make this change in cell B9 so that Excel treats the postal code as text and displays all of the digits you type.

### To enter the postal code as text:

**1.** Click cell **B9** to select it. Notice that the postal code is right-aligned in the cell, unlike the other text entries, which are left-aligned—another indication that the entry is being treated as a number.

**2.** Type **'03061** in cell B9, and then press the **Enter** key. The text 03061 appears in cell B9 and is left-aligned in the cell, matching all of the other text entries. See Figure 1-15.

| Figure 1-15 | Number displayed as text |

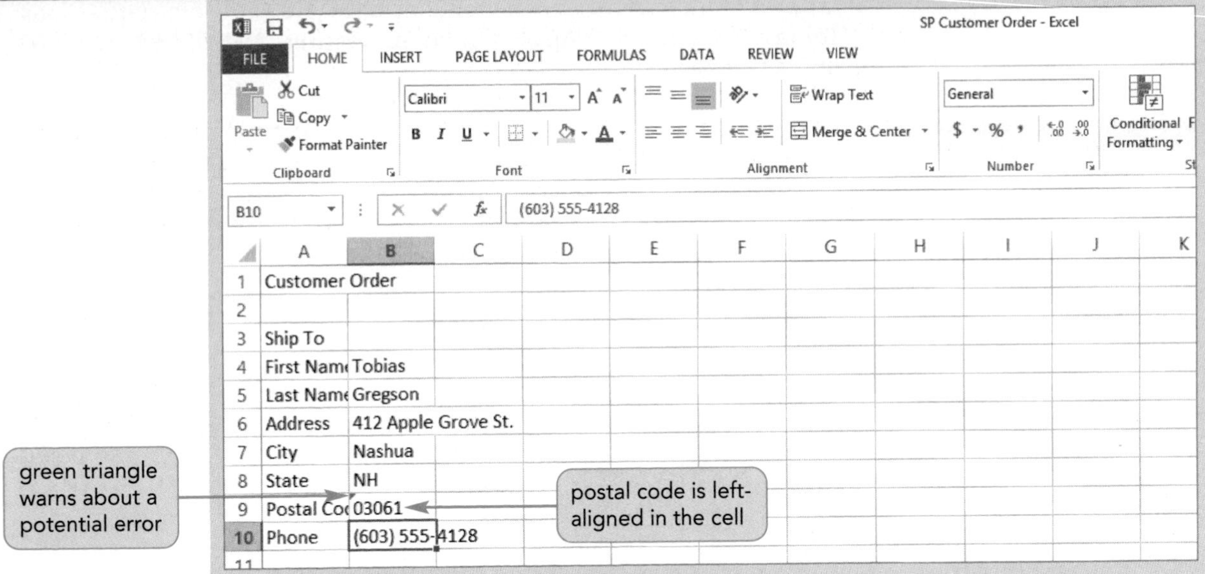

green triangle warns about a potential error

postal code is left-aligned in the cell

TIP

To remove a green triangle, click the cell, click the yellow caution icon that appears to the left of the cell, and then click Ignore Error.

Notice that a green triangle appears in the upper-left corner of cell B9. Excel uses green triangles to flag potential errors in cells. In this case, it is simply a warning that you entered a number as a text string. Because this is intentional, you do not have to edit the cell to fix the "error." Green triangles appear only in the workbook window and not in any printouts of the worksheet.

## Entering Dates

You can enter dates in any of the standard date formats. For example, all of the following entries are recognized by Excel as the same date:

- 4/6/2016
- 4/6/16
- 4-6-2016
- April 6, 2016
- 6-Apr-16

Even though you enter a date as text, Excel stores the date as a number equal to the number of days between the specified date and January 0, 1900. Times are also entered as text and stored as fractions of a 24-hour day. For example, the date and time April 4, 2016 @ 6:00 PM is stored by Excel as 42,464.75. Dates and times are stored as numbers so that Excel can easily perform date and time calculations, such as determining the elapsed time between one date and another.

Based on the default date format your computer uses, Excel might alter the format of a date after you type it. For example, if you enter the date 4/6/16 into the active cell, Excel might display the date with the four-digit year value, 4/6/2016; if you enter the text April 6, 2016, Excel might convert the date format to 6-Apr-16. Changing the date or time format does not affect the underlying date or time value.

**INSIGHT**

### International Date Formats

As business transactions become more international in scope, you may need to adopt international standards for expressing dates, times, and currency values in your workbooks. For example, a worksheet cell might contain 06/05/16. This format could represent any of the following dates: the 5th of June, 2016; the 6th of May, 2016; and the 16th of May, 2006.

The date depends on which country the workbook has been designed for. You can avoid this problem by entering the full date, as in June 5, 2016. However, this might not work with documents written in foreign languages, such as Japanese, that use different character symbols.

To solve this problem, many international businesses adopt ISO (International Organization for Standardization) dates in the format *yyyy-mm-dd*, where *yyyy* is the four-digit year value, *mm* is the two-digit month value, and *dd* is the two-digit day value. So, a date such as June 5, 2016 is entered as 2016/06/05. If you choose to use this international date format, make sure that people using your workbook understand this format so they do not misinterpret the dates. You can include information about the date format in the Documentation sheet.

For the SP Customer Order workbook, you will enter dates in the format *mm/dd/yyyy,* where *mm* is the 2-digit month number, *dd* is the 2-digit day number, and *yyyy* is the 4-digit year number.

### To enter the current date into the Documentation sheet:

1. Click the **Documentation** sheet tab to make the Documentation sheet the active worksheet.

2. Click cell **B4** to make it active, type the current date in the *mm/dd/yyyy* format, and then press the **Enter** key. The date is entered in the cell.

   **Trouble?** Depending on your system configuration, Excel might change the date to the date format *dd-mmm-yy*. This difference will not affect your work.

3. Make the **Customer Order** worksheet the active sheet.

The next part of the Customer Order worksheet will list the books the customer purchased from Sparrow & Pond. As shown in Figure 1-16, the list includes identifying information about each book, its price, and the quantity ordered.

**Figure 1-16     Book order from Tobias Gregson**

| ISBN | CATEGORY | BINDING | TITLE | AUTHOR(S) | PRICE | QTY |
|------|----------|---------|-------|-----------|-------|-----|
| 0-374-25385-4 | Used | Hardcover | Samurai William: The Englishman Who Opened Japan | Milton, Giles | $5.95 | 2 |
| 4-889-96213-1 | New | Softcover | Floral Origami Globes | Fuse, Tomoko | $24.95 | 3 |
| 0-500-27062-7 | New | Hardcover | Tao Magic: The Secret Language of Diagrams and Calligraphy | Legeza, Laszlo | $8.95 | 1 |
| 0-785-82169-4 | Used | Hardcover | The Holy Grail | Morgan, Giles | $3.75 | 1 |
| 0-854-56516-7 | New | Softcover | Murder on the Links | Christie, Agatha | $7.50 | 2 |

© 2014 Cengage Learning

You will enter the first five columns of the book order into the worksheet.

### To enter the first part of the book order:

1. In the Customer Order worksheet, click cell **A12** to make it the active cell, type **ISBN** as the column label, and then press the **Tab** key to move to cell B12.

2. In the range B12:E12, type the following labels, pressing the **Tab** key to move to the next cell: **CATEGORY**, **BINDING**, **TITLE**, and **AUTHOR(S)**.

3. Press the **Enter** key to go to the next row of the worksheet, making cell A13 the active cell.

4. In the range A13:E17, enter the ISBN, category, binding, title, and author text for the five books listed in Figure 1-16, pressing the **Tab** key to move from one cell to the next, and pressing the **Enter** key to move to a new row. See Figure 1-17. The text in some cells will be partially hidden; you will fix that problem shortly.

| Figure 1-17 | Tobias Gregson's partial book order |
| --- | --- |

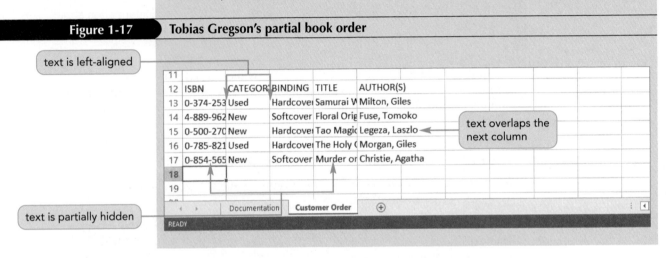

## Entering Numbers

In Excel, numbers can be integers such as 378, decimals such as 1.95, or negatives such as −5.2. In the case of currency and percentages, you can include the currency symbol and percent sign when you enter the value. Excel treats a currency value such as $87.25 as the number 87.25, and a percentage such as 95% as the decimal 0.95. Much like dates, currency and percentages are formatted in a convenient way for you to read, but only the number is stored within the cell. This makes it easier to perform calculations with currency and percentage values.

You will complete the information for Tobias Gregson's order by entering the price for each title and the quantity of each title he ordered.

### To enter the price and quantity of books ordered:

1. In the range F12:G12, enter **PRICE** and **QTY** as the labels.

2. In cell F13, enter **$5.95** as the price of the first book. The book price is stored as a number but displayed with the $ symbol.

3. In cell G13, enter **2** as the quantity of books ordered.

4. In the range F14:G17, enter the remaining prices and quantities shown in Figure 1-16. See Figure 1-18.

| Figure 1-18 | **Price and quantity data** |
| --- | --- |

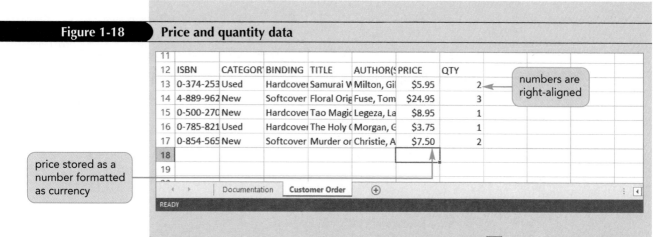

price stored as a number formatted as currency

numbers are right-aligned

5. On the Quick Access Toolbar, click the **Save** button 🖫 (or press the **Ctrl+S** keys) to save the workbook.

# Resizing Columns and Rows

Much of the information in the Customer Order worksheet is difficult to read because of the hidden text. You can make the cell content easier to read by changing the size of the columns and rows in the worksheet.

## Changing Column Widths

Column widths are expressed as the number of characters the column can contain. The default column width is 8.43 standard-sized characters. In general, this means that you can type eight characters in a cell; any additional text is hidden or overlaps the adjacent cell. Column widths are also expressed in terms of pixels. A **pixel** is a single point on a computer monitor or printout. A column width of 8.43 characters is equivalent to 64 pixels.

You will increase the width of column A so that the contact information labels in cells A4 and A5 and the ISBN numbers in the range A13:A17 are completely displayed.

**To increase the width of column A:**

1. Move the pointer over the right border of the column A heading until the pointer changes to ↔.

2. Click and drag to the right until the width of the column heading reaches **15** characters, but do not release the mouse button. The ScreenTip that appears as you resize the column shows the new column width in characters and in pixels.

**3.** Release the mouse button. The width of column A expands to 15 characters, and all of the text within that column is visible within the cells. See Figure 1-19.

| Figure 1-19 | Width of column A increased |
|---|---|

ScreenTip shows the column width in characters and pixels

pointer for resizing the column

text in column A fits within the cells

| | A | B | C | D | E | F | G | H | I | J |
|---|---|---|---|---|---|---|---|---|---|---|
| F18 | | | | | | | | | | |
| | | Width: 15.00 (110 pixels) | | | | | | | | |
| 1 | Customer Order | | | | | | | | | |
| 2 | | | | | | | | | | |
| 3 | Ship To | | | | | | | | | |
| 4 | First Name | Tobias | | | | | | | | |
| 5 | Last Name | Gregson | | | | | | | | |
| 6 | Address | 412 Apple Grove St. | | | | | | | | |
| 7 | City | Nashua | | | | | | | | |
| 8 | State | NH | | | | | | | | |
| 9 | Postal Code | 03061 | | | | | | | | |
| 10 | Phone | (603) 555-4128 | | | | | | | | |
| 11 | | | | | | | | | | |
| 12 | ISBN | CATEGOR| BINDING | TITLE | AUTHOR(S | PRICE | QTY | | | |
| 13 | 0-374-25385-4 | Used | Hardcove| Samurai W | Milton, Gi | $5.95 | 2 | | | |
| 14 | 4-889-96213-1 | New | Softcover | Floral Orig | Fuse, Tom | $24.95 | 3 | | | |
| 15 | 0-500-27062-7 | New | Hardcove| Tao Magic | Legeza, La | $8.95 | 1 | | | |
| 16 | 0-785-82169-4 | Used | Hardcove| The Holy ( | Morgan, G | $3.75 | 1 | | | |
| 17 | 0-854-56516-7 | New | Softcover | Murder or | Christie, A | $7.50 | 2 | | | |
| 18 | | | | | | | | | | |
| 19 | | | | | | | | | | |

Documentation    **Customer Order**    +

READY

You will increase the widths of columns B and C to 18 characters so that their complete entries are visible. Rather than resizing each column separately, you can select both columns and adjust their widths at the same time.

### To increase the widths of columns B and C:

**TIP**

To select multiple columns, you can also click and drag the pointer over multiple column headings.

**1.** Click the **column B** heading. The entire column is selected.

**2.** Hold down the **Ctrl** key, click the **column C** heading, and then release the **Ctrl** key. Both columns B and C are selected.

**3.** Move the pointer to the right border of the column C heading until the pointer changes to ✛.

**4.** Drag to the right until the column width changes to **18** characters, and then release the mouse button. Both column widths increase to 18 characters and display all of the entered text.

The book titles in column D are partially hidden. You will increase the width of this column to 30 characters. Rather than using your mouse, you can set the column width using the Format command on the HOME tab. The Format command gives you precise control over setting column widths and row heights.

## To set the width of column D with the Format command:

▶ **1.** Click the **column D** heading. The entire column is selected.

▶ **2.** On the HOME tab, in the Cells group, click the **Format** button, and then click **Column Width**. The Column Width dialog box opens.

▶ **3.** Type **30** in the Column width box to specify the new column width.

▶ **4.** Click the **OK** button. The width of column D changes to 30 characters.

▶ **5.** Change the width of column E to **15** characters.

▶ **6.** Click cell **A1**. The revised column widths are shown in Figure 1-20.

| Figure 1-20 | Resized columns |
|---|---|

| | A | B | C | D | E | F | G |
|---|---|---|---|---|---|---|---|
| 1 | Customer Order | | | | | | |
| 2 | | | | | | | |
| 3 | Ship To | | | | | | |
| 4 | First Name | Tobias | | | | | |
| 5 | Last Name | Gregson | | | | | |
| 6 | Address | 412 Apple Grove St. | | | | | |
| 7 | City | Nashua | | | | | |
| 8 | State | NH | | | | | |
| 9 | Postal Code | 03061 | | | | | |
| 10 | Phone | (603) 555-4128 | | | | | |
| 11 | | | | | | | |
| 12 | ISBN | CATEGORY | BINDING | TITLE | AUTHOR(S) | PRICE | QTY |
| 13 | 0-374-25385-4 | Used | Hardcover | Samurai William: The Englishman V | Milton, Giles | $5.95 | 2 |
| 14 | 4-889-96213-1 | New | Softcover | Floral Origami Globes | Fuse, Tomoko | $24.95 | 3 |
| 15 | 0-500-27062-7 | New | Hardcover | Tao Magic: The Secret Language of | Legeza, Laszlo | $8.95 | 1 |
| 16 | 0-785-82169-4 | Used | Hardcover | The Holy Grail | Morgan, Giles | $3.75 | 1 |
| 17 | 0-854-56516-7 | New | Softcover | Murder on the Links | Christie, Agatha | $7.50 | 2 |
| 18 | | | | | | | |
| 19 | | | | | | | |

Callouts: **18 characters in each column** · **30 characters** · **15 characters** · **15 characters**

Sheet tabs: Documentation | Customer Order | (+)

READY

Even with the width of column D increased, some of the book titles still don't fit within the allotted space. Instead of manually changing the column width to display all of the text, you can autofit the column. **AutoFit** changes the column width or row height to display the longest or tallest entry within the column or row. You autofit a column or a row by double-clicking the right border of the column heading or the bottom border of the row heading.

## To autofit the contents of column D:

▶ **1.** Move the pointer over the right border of column D until the pointer changes to ✛.

▶ **2.** Double-click the right border of the column D heading. The width of column D increases to about 54 characters so that the longest book title is completely visible.

## Wrapping Text Within a Cell

Sometimes, resizing a column width to display all of the text entered in the cells makes the worksheet more difficult to read. This is the case with column D in the Customer Order worksheet. Another way to display long text entries is to wrap text to a new line when it extends beyond the column width. When text wraps within a cell, the row height increases so that all of the text within the cell is displayed.

You will resize column D, and then wrap the text entries in the column.

**To wrap text in column D:**

1. Resize the width of column D to **30** characters.

2. Select the range **D13:D17**. These cells include the titles that extend beyond the new cell width.

3. On the HOME tab, in the Alignment group, click the **Wrap Text** button. The Wrap Text button is toggled on, and text in the selected cells that exceeds the column width wraps to a new line.

4. Click cell **A12** to make it the active cell. See Figure 1-21.

| Figure 1-21 | Text wrapped within cells |
|---|---|

If you want to create a new line within a cell, press the Alt+Enter keys to move the insertion point to the next line within the cell. Whatever you type next will appear on the new line in the cell.

## Changing Row Heights

The height of a row is measured in points or pixels. A **point** is approximately 1/72 of an inch. The default row height is 15 points or 20 pixels. Row heights are set in the same way as column widths. You can drag the bottom border of the row heading to a new row height, specify a row height using the Format command, or autofit the row's height to match its content.

Sanjit wants you add more space above the labels in the book list by resizing row 12.

### To increase the height of row 12:

1. Move the pointer over the bottom border of the row 12 heading until the pointer changes to ✛.

2. Drag the bottom border down until the height of the row is equal to **30** points (or **40** pixels), and then release the mouse button. The height of row 12 is set to 30 points.

3. Press the **Ctrl+S** keys to save the workbook.

You have entered most of the data for Tobias Gregson's order at Sparrow & Pond. In the next session, you will calculate the total charge for the order and print the worksheet.

## REVIEW

### Session 1.1 Quick Check

1. What are the two types of sheets used in a workbook?
2. What is the cell reference for the cell located in the fourth column and third row of a worksheet?
3. What is the range reference for the block of cells B10 through C15?
4. What is the reference for the nonadjacent block of cells B10 through C15 and cells B20 through D25?
5. What keyboard shortcut changes the active cell to cell A1?
6. What is text data?
7. Cell A4 contains *May 3, 2016*; why doesn't Excel consider this entry a text string?
8. How do you resize a column or row?

# Session 1.2 Visual Overview:

The **font size** refers to how big the text is.

You use the PAGE LAYOUT tab to change how the worksheet will appear on the printed page.

SP Customer Order - E

| FILE | HOME | INSERT | PAGE LAYOUT | FORMULAS | DATA | REVIEW | VIEW |

Calibri    11    A A

B  I  U

Currency

$ - % ,

Clipboard    Font    Alignment    Number

In Excel, every formula begins with an equal sign (=).

I23    =G23*H23

When the active cell contains a formula, the formula appears in the formula bar but the result of the formula appears in the cell.

|  | A | B | C | D | E |
|---|---|---|---|---|---|
| 9 | Ship To | | | | |
| 10 | First Name | Tobias | | | |
| 11 | Last Name | Gregson | | | |
| 12 | Address | 412 Apple Grove St. | | | |
| 13 | City | Nashua | | | |
| 14 | State | NH | | | |
| 15 | Postal Code | 03061 | | | |
| 16 | Phone | (603) 555-4128 | | | |
| 17 | | | | | |
| 18 | BOOK ID | ISBN | CATEGORY | BINDING | TITLE |
| 19 | 25385-Used | 0-374-25385-4 | Used | Hardcover | Samurai William: Who Opened Japa |
| 20 | 96213-New | 4-889-96213-1 | New | Softcover | Floral Origami Glo |
| 21 | 01089-Used | 0-151-01089-7 | Used | Hardcover | Pops: A Life of Lou |
| 22 | 27062-New | 0-500-27062-7 | New | Hardcover | Tao Magic: The Se Diagrams and Calli |
| 23 | 56516-New | 0-854-56516-7 | New | Softcover | Murder on the Lin |
| 24 | | | | | |
| 25 | | | | | |
| 26 | | | | | |
| 27 | | | | | |
| 28 | | | | | |

The gridlines that surround cells appear on the worksheet as a guide; they do not print.

Documentation    **Customer Order**    +

READY

A **border** is a line you can add along an edge of a cell. Borders are used to improve the readability of data.

# Formulas and Functions

**AutoSum** quickly inserts functions to sum, average, or count values in a range, or find the minimum or maximum value in a range.

Customer Order - Excel

? ⊞ — ⊡ ✕

PREVIEW    VIEW

Sign in

Currency

Conditional Formatting ▾
Format as Table ▾
Cell Styles ▾

Insert ▾
Delete ▾
Format ▾

Σ ▾
↓ ▾
◆ ▾

Sort & Filter ▾
Find & Select ▾

$ ▾ % ,   .0 .00
         .00 →.0

**Number**        **Styles**        **Cells**        **Editing**

A **function** is a named operation that replaces the action of an arithmetic expression.

=G19*H19
=G20*H20
=G21*H21

A **formula** is an expression that calculates a value. These formulas multiply values in different cells.

The **SUM** function adds the values in the specified range.

| E | F | G | H | I |
|---|---|---|---|---|
| | | | Sales Tax | 5% |
| E | AUTHOR(S) | PRICE | QTY | CHARGE |
| Samurai William: The Englishman | | | | |
| Who Opened Japan | Milton, Giles | $5.95 | 2 | $11.90 |
| Unusual Origami Globes | Fuse, Tomoko | $24.95 | 3 | $74.85 |
| Pops: A Life of Louis Armstrong | Teachout, Terry | $11.95 | 2 | $23.90 |
| Brush Magic: The Secret Language of | | | | |
| Grams and Calligraphy | Legeza, Laszlo | $8.95 | 1 | $8.95 |
| Murder on the Links | Christie, Agatha | $7.50 | 2 | $15.00 |

=SUM(I19:I23)
=I17*I25
15.3
=SUM(I25:I27)

| | | | Subtotal | $134.60 |
|---|---|---|---|---|
| | | | Tax | $6.73 |
| | | | Handling | $15.30 |
| | | | TOTAL | $156.63 |

**Page Break Preview** shows the location of page breaks in the printed sheet.

◀    ▶

⊞  ▤  ▥    —  ⬤  +    100%

**Normal view** shows the contents of the active sheet in the workbook window.

**Page Layout view** shows how the sheet will appear when printed.

# Adding Formulas to a Worksheet

So far you have entered text, numbers, and dates in the worksheet. However, the main reason for using Excel is to display values calculated from data. For example, Sally wants the workbook to calculate the number of books the customer ordered and how much revenue the order will generate. Such calculations are added to a worksheet using formulas and functions.

## Entering a Formula

A formula is an expression that returns a value. In most cases, this is a number—though it could also be text or a date. In Excel, every formula begins with an equal sign (=) followed by an expression describing the operation that returns the value. If you don't begin the formula with the equal sign, Excel assumes that you are entering text and will not treat the cell contents as a formula.

A formula is written using **operators** that combine different values, resulting in a single value that is then displayed in the cell. The most common operators are **arithmetic operators** that perform addition, subtraction, multiplication, division, and exponentiation. For example, the following formula adds 5 and 7, returning a value of 12:

=5+7

Most Excel formulas contain references to cells rather than specific values. This allows you to change the values used in the calculation without having to modify the formula itself. For example, the following formula returns the result of adding the values stored in cells A1 and B2:

=A1+B2

If the value 5 is stored in cell A1 and the value 7 is stored in cell B2, this formula would also return a value of 12. If you later changed the value in cell A1 to 10, the formula would return a value of 17. Figure 1-22 describes the different arithmetic operators and provides examples of formulas.

**Figure 1-22** — **Arithmetic operators**

| Operation | Arithmetic Operator | Example | Description |
|---|---|---|---|
| Addition | + | =B1+B2+B3 | Adds the values in cells B1, B2, and B3 |
| Subtraction | − | =C9−B2 | Subtracts the value in cell B2 from the value in cell C9 |
| Multiplication | * | =C9*B9 | Multiplies the values in cells C9 and B9 |
| Division | / | =C9/B9 | Divides the value in cell C9 by the value in cell B9 |
| Exponentiation | ^ | =B5^3 | Raises the value of cell B5 to the third power |

© 2014 Cengage Learning

If a formula contains more than one arithmetic operator, Excel performs the calculation using the same order of operations you might have already seen in math classes. The **order of operations** is a set of predefined rules used to determine the sequence in which operators are applied in a calculation. Excel first calculates the value of any operation within parentheses, then it applies exponentiation (^), multiplication (*), and division (/), and finally it performs addition (+) and subtraction (−). For example, the following formula returns the value 23 because multiplying 4 by 5 takes precedence over adding 3:

=3+4*5

If a formula contains two or more operators with the same level of priority, the operators are applied in order from left to right. In the following formula, Excel first multiplies 4 by 10 and then divides that result by 8 to return the value 5:

=4*10/8

When parentheses are used, the value inside them is calculated first. In the following formula, Excel calculates (3+4) first, and then multiplies that result by 5 to return the value 35:

=(3+4)*5

Figure 1-23 shows how slight changes in a formula affect the order of operations and the result of the formula.

**Figure 1-23**        Order of operations applied to Excel formulas

| Formula | Application of the Order of Operations | Result |
|---|---|---|
| =50+10*5 | 10*5 calculated first and then 50 is added | 100 |
| =(50+10)*5 | (50+10) calculated first and then 60 is multiplied by 5 | 300 |
| =50/10–5 | 50/10 calculated first and then 5 is subtracted | 0 |
| =50/(10–5) | (10–5) calculated first and then 50 is divided by that value | 10 |
| =50/10*5 | Two operators at same precedence level, so the calculation is done left to right in the expression | 25 |
| =50/(10*5) | (10*5) is calculated first and then 50 is divided by that value | 1 |

© 2014 Cengage Learning

Sally wants the Customer Order worksheet to include the total amount charged for each book. The charge is equal to the number of books ordered multiplied by the book's price. You already entered this information in columns F and G. Now you will enter a formula to calculate the charge for books ordered in column H.

**To enter the formula to calculate the charge for the first book order:**

1. Make cell **H12** the active cell, type **CHARGE** as the column label, and then press the **Enter** key. The label text is entered in cell H12, and cell H13 is now the active cell.

2. Type **=F13*G13** (the price of the book multiplied by the quantity of books ordered). As you type the formula, a list of Excel function names appears in a ScreenTip, which provides a quick method for entering functions. The list will close when you complete the formula. You will learn more about Excel functions shortly. Also, as you type each cell reference, Excel color codes the cell reference with the cell. See Figure 1-24.

| Figure 1-24 | Formula being entered in a cell |
| --- | --- |

formula displayed in the formula bar

formula in cell H13 multiplies the values in cells F13 and G13

cell references are color coded

**3.** Press the **Enter** key. The formula is entered in cell H13, which displays the value $11.90. The result is displayed as currency because cell F13, which is referenced in the formula, contains a currency value.

**4.** Click cell **H13** to make it the active cell. The cell displays the result of the formula, and the formula bar displays the formula you entered.

For the first book, you entered the formula by typing each cell reference in the expression. You can also insert a cell reference by clicking the cell as you type the formula. This technique reduces the possibility of error caused by typing an incorrect cell reference. You will use this method to enter the formula to calculate the charge for the second book.

## To enter the cell references in the formula using the mouse:

**1.** Click cell **H14** to make it the active cell.

Be sure to type = as the first part of the entry; otherwise, Excel will not interpret the entry as a formula.

**2.** Type =. The equal sign indicates that you are entering a formula. Any cell you click from now on inserts the cell reference of the selected cell into the formula until you complete the formula by pressing the Enter or Tab key.

**3.** Click cell **F14**. The cell reference is inserted into the formula in the formula bar. At this point, any cell you click changes the cell reference used in the formula. The cell reference isn't locked until you type an operator.

**4.** Type * to enter the multiplication operator. The cell reference for cell F14 is locked in the formula, and the next cell you click will be inserted after the operator.

**5.** Click cell **G14** to enter its cell reference in the formula. The formula is complete.

**6.** Press the **Enter** key. Cell H14 displays the value $74.85, which is the total charge for the second book.

## Copying and Pasting Formulas

Sometimes you will need to repeat the same formula throughout a worksheet. Rather than retyping the formula, you can copy a formula from one cell and paste it into another cell. When you copy a formula, Excel places the formula into the **Clipboard**, which is a temporary storage location for text and graphics. When you paste, Excel takes the formula from the Clipboard and inserts it into the selected cell or range. Excel adjusts the cell references in the formula to reflect the formula's new location in the worksheet. This occurs because you usually want to copy the actions of a formula rather than the specific value the formula generates. In this case, the formula's action is to multiply the price of the book by the quantity. By copying and pasting the formula, you can quickly repeat that action for every book listed in the worksheet.

You will copy the formula you entered in cell H14 to the range H15:H17 to calculate the charges on the remaining three books in Tobias Gregson's order. By copying and pasting the formula, you will save time and avoid potential mistakes from retyping the formula.

### To copy and paste the formula:

1. Click cell **H14** to select the cell that contains the formula you want to copy.

2. On the HOME tab, in the Clipboard group, click the **Copy** button (or press the **Ctrl+C** keys). Excel copies the formula to the Clipboard.

3. Select the range **H15:H17**. You want to paste the formula into these cells.

4. In the Clipboard group, click the **Paste** button (or press the **Ctrl+V** keys). Excel pastes the formula into the selected cells, adjusting each formula so that the total charges calculated for the books are based on the corresponding values within each row. A button appears below the selected range, providing options for pasting formulas and values. See Figure 1-25.

| Figure 1-25 | Copied and pasted formula |

button provides more options for pasting formulas and values

formula pasted into the selected cells

▶ **5.** Click cell **H15** and verify that the formula =F15*G15 appears in the formula bar. The formula was updated to reflect the cell references in the corresponding row.

▶ **6.** Click the other cells in column H and verify that the corresponding formulas are entered in those cells.

# Simplifying Formulas with Functions

In addition to cell references and operators, formulas can also contain functions. A function is a named operation that replaces the arithmetic expression in a formula. Functions are used to simplify long or complex formulas. For example, to add the values from cells A1 through A10, you could enter the following long formula:

=A1+A2+A3+A4+A5+A6+A7+A8+A9+A10

Or, you could use the SUM function to calculate the sum of those cell values by entering the following formula:

=SUM(A1:A10)

In both instances, Excel adds the values in cells A1 through A10, but the SUM function is faster and simpler to enter and less prone to a typing error. You should always use a function, if one is available, in place of a long, complex formula. Excel supports more than 300 different functions from the fields of finance, business, science, and engineering. Excel provides functions that work with numbers, text, and dates.

## Introducing Function Syntax

Every function follows a set of rules, or **syntax**, which specifies how the function should be written. The general syntax of all Excel functions is

FUNCTION (argument1, argument2, …)

where *FUNCTION* is the function name, and *argument1*, *argument2*, and so forth are values used by that function. For example, the SUM function shown above uses a single argument, A1:A10, which is the range reference of the cells whose values will be added. Some functions do not require any arguments and are entered as *FUNCTION()*. Functions without arguments still require the opening and closing parentheses, but do not include a value within the parentheses.

## Entering Functions with AutoSum

A fast and convenient way to enter commonly used functions is with AutoSum. The AutoSum button includes options to insert the SUM, AVERAGE, COUNT, MIN, and MAX functions to generate the following:

- Sum of the values in the specified range
- Average value in the specified range
- Total count of numeric values in the specified range
- Minimum value in the specified range
- Maximum value in the specified range

After you select one of the AutoSum options, Excel determines the most appropriate range from the available data and enters it as the function's argument. You should always verify that the range included in the AutoSum function matches the range that you want to use.

You will use AutoSum to enter the SUM function to add the total charges for Tobias Gregson's order.

### To use AutoSum to enter the SUM function:

▶ **1.** Click cell **G18** to make it the active cell, type **Subtotal** as the label, and then press the **Tab** key to make cell H18 the active cell.

▶ **2.** On the HOME tab, in the Editing group, click the **AutoSum button arrow**. The button's menu opens and displays five common summary functions: Sum, Average, Count Numbers, Max (for maximum), and Min (for minimum).

**TIP**

You can quickly insert the SUM function by pressing the Alt+= keys.

▶ **3.** Click **Sum** to enter the SUM function. The formula =SUM(H13:H17) is entered in cell H18. The cells involved in calculating the sum are selected and highlighted on the worksheet so you can quickly confirm that Excel selected the most appropriate range from the available data. A ScreenTip appears below the formula describing the function's syntax. See Figure 1-26.

**Figure 1-26**  **SUM function being entered with the AutoSum button**

- AutoSum button arrow
- formula appears in the formula bar → =SUM(H13:H17)
- cells used in the function are highlighted
- SUM function adds the values in the selected range
- ScreenTip shows the syntax of the SUM function
- range reference

| | A | B | C | E | F | G | H | I | J | K |
|---|---|---|---|---|---|---|---|---|---|---|
| 8 | State | NH | | | | | | | | |
| 9 | Postal Code | 03061 | | | | | | | | |
| 10 | Phone | (603) 555-4128 | | | | | | | | |
| 11 | | | | | | | | | | |
| 12 | ISBN | CATEGORY | BINDING | TITLE | AUTHOR(S) | PRICE | QTY | CHARGE | | |
| 13 | 0-374-25385-4 | Used | Hardcover | Samurai William: The Englishman Who Opened Japan | Milton, Giles | $5.95 | 2 | $11.90 | | |
| 14 | 4-889-96213-1 | New | Softcover | Floral Origami Globes | Fuse, Tomoko | $24.95 | 3 | $74.85 | | |
| 15 | 0-500-27062-7 | New | Hardcover | Tao Magic: The Secret Language of Diagrams and Calligraphy | Legeza, Laszlo | $8.95 | 1 | $8.95 | | |
| 16 | 0-785-82169-4 | Used | Hardcover | The Holy Grail | Morgan, Giles | $3.75 | 1 | $3.75 | | |
| 17 | 0-854-56516-7 | New | Softcover | Murder on the Links | Christie, Agatha | $7.50 | 2 | $15.00 | | |
| 18 | | | | | | Subtotal | =SUM(H13:H17) | | | |
| 19 | | | | | | | SUM(number1, [number2], ...) | | | |
| 20 | | | | | | | | | | |
| 21 | | | | | | | | | | |
| 22 | | | | | | | | | | |
| 23 | | | | | | | | | | |

▶ **4.** Press the **Enter** key to accept the formula. The subtotal of the book charges returned by the SUM function is $114.45.

AutoSum makes entering a commonly used formula such as the SUM function fast and easy. However, AutoSum can determine the appropriate range reference to include only when the function is adjacent to the cells containing the values you want to summarize. If you need to use a function elsewhere in the worksheet, you will have to select the range reference to include or type the function yourself.

Each sale made by Sparrow & Pond is subject to a 5 percent sales tax and a $15.30 handling fee. You will add these to the Customer Order worksheet so you can calculate the total charge for the order.

## To add the sales tax and handling fee to the worksheet:

▶ **1.** Click cell **G11**, type **Sales Tax** as the label, and then press the **Tab** key to make cell H11 the active cell.

▶ **2.** In cell H11, type **5%** as the sales tax rate, and then press the **Enter** key. The sales tax rate is entered in the cell, and can be used in other calculations. The value is displayed with the % symbol, but is stored as the equivalent decimal value 0.05.

▶ **3.** Click cell **G19** to make it the active cell, type **Tax** as the label, and then press the **Tab** key to make cell H19 the active cell.

▶ **4.** Type **=H11*H18** as the formula to calculate the sales tax on the book order, and then press the **Enter** key. The formula multiples the sales tax value in cell H11 by the order subtotal value in cell H18. The value $5.72 is displayed in cell H19, which is 5 percent of the book order subtotal of $114.45.

▶ **5.** In cell G20, type **Handling** as the label, and then press the **Tab** key to make cell H20 the active cell. You will enter the handling fee in this cell.

▶ **6.** Type **$15.30** as the handling fee, and then press the **Enter** key.

The last part of the customer order is to calculate the total cost by adding the subtotal, the tax, and the handling fee. Rather than using AutoSum, you will type the SUM function so you can enter the correct range reference for the function. You can type the range reference or select the range in the worksheet. Remember, that you must type parentheses around the range reference.

## To calculate the total order cost:

▶ **1.** In cell G21, type **TOTAL** as the label, and then press the **Tab** key.

▶ **2.** Type **=SUM(** in cell H21 to enter the function name and the opening parenthesis. As you begin to type the function, a ScreenTip lists the names of all functions that start with *S*.

Make sure the cell reference in the function matches the range you want to calculate.

▶ **3.** Type **H18:H20** to specify the range reference of the cells you want to add. The cells referenced in the function are selected and highlighted on the worksheet so you can quickly confirm that you entered the correct range reference.

**4.** Type **)** to complete the function, and then press the **Enter** key. The value of the SUM function appears in cell H21, indicating that the total charge for the order is $135.47. See Figure 1-27.

| Figure 1-27 | Total charge for the customer order |

The SUM function makes it simple to quickly add the values in a group of cells.

*Problem Solving: Writing Effective Formulas*

You can use formulas to quickly perform calculations and solve problems. First, identify the problem you need to solve. Then, gather the data needed to solve the problem. Finally, create accurate and effective formulas that use the data to answer or resolve the problem. Follow these guidelines:

- **Keep formulas simple.** Use functions in place of long, complex formulas whenever possible. For example, use the SUM function instead of entering a formula that adds individual cells, which makes it easier to confirm that the formula is making an accurate calculation as it provides answers needed to evaluate the problem.
- **Do not hide data values within formulas.** The worksheet displays formula results, not the actual formula. For example, to calculate a 5 percent interest rate on a currency value in cell A5, you could enter the formula =0.05*A5. However, this doesn't show how the value is calculated. A better approach places the value 0.05 in a cell accompanied by a descriptive label and uses the cell reference in the formula. If you place 0.05 in cell A6, the formula =A6*A5 would calculate the interest value. Other people can then easily see the interest rate as well as the resulting interest, ensuring that the formula is solving the right problem.
- **Break up formulas to show intermediate results.** When a worksheet contains complex computations, other people can more easily comprehend how the formula results are calculated when different parts of the formula are distinguished. For example, the formula =SUM(A1:A10)/SUM(B1:B10) calculates the ratio of two sums, but hides the two sum values. Instead, enter each SUM function in a separate cell, such as cells A11 and B11, and use the formula =A11/B11 to calculate the ratio. Other people can see both sums and the value of their ratio in the worksheet and better understand the final result, which makes it more likely that the best problem resolution will be selected.
- **Test formulas with simple values.** Use values you can calculate in your head to confirm that your formula works as intended. For example, using 1s or 10s as the input values lets you easily figure out the answer and verify the formula.

Finding a solution to a problem requires accurate data and analysis. With workbooks, this means using formulas that are easy to understand, clearly show the data being used in the calculations, and demonstrate how the results are calculated. Only then can you be confident that you are choosing the best problem resolution.

# Modifying a Worksheet

As you develop a worksheet, you might need to modify its content and structure to create a more logical organization. Some ways you can modify a worksheet include moving cells and ranges, inserting rows and columns, deleting rows and columns, and inserting and deleting cells.

## Moving and Copying a Cell or Range

One way to move a cell or range is to select it, position the pointer over the bottom border of the selection, drag the selection to a new location, and then release the mouse button. This technique is called **drag and drop** because you are dragging the range and dropping it in a new location. If the drop location is not visible, drag the selection to the edge of the workbook window to scroll the worksheet, and then drop the selection.

You can also use the drag-and-drop technique to copy cells by pressing the Ctrl key as you drag the selected range to its new location. A copy of the original range is placed in the new location without removing the original range from the worksheet.

## Moving or Copying a Cell or Range

- Select the cell or range you want to move or copy.
- Move the pointer over the border of the selection until the pointer changes shape.
- To move the range, click the border and drag the selection to a new location (or to copy the range, hold down the Ctrl key and drag the selection to a new location).

*or*

- Select the cell or range you want to move or copy.
- On the HOME tab, in the Clipboard group, click the Cut or Copy button (or right-click the selection, and then click Cut or Copy on the shortcut menu, or press the Ctrl+X or Ctrl+C keys).
- Select the cell or the upper-left cell of the range where you want to paste the content.
- In the Clipboard group, click the Paste button (or right-click the selection and then click Paste on the shortcut menu, or press the Ctrl+V keys).

Sally wants the subtotal, tax, handling, and total values in the range G18:H21 moved down one row to the range G19:H22 to provide more space from the book orders. You will use the drag-and-drop method to move the range.

### To drag and drop the range G18:H21:

1. Select the range **G18:H21**. These are the cells you want to move.

2. Move the pointer over the bottom border of the selected range so that the pointer changes to ⇖.

3. Press and hold the mouse button to change the pointer to ⇗, and then drag the selection down one row. Do not release the mouse button. A ScreenTip appears, indicating that the new range of the selected cells will be G19:H22. A darker border also appears around the new range. See Figure 1-28.

| Figure 1-28 | Range G18:H21 being moved to range G19:H22 |
| --- | --- |

4. Make sure the ScreenTip displays the range **G19:H22**, and then release the mouse button. The selected cells move to their new location.

Some people find dragging and dropping a difficult and awkward way to move a selection, particularly if the selected range is large or needs to move a long distance in the worksheet. In those situations, it is often more efficient to cut or copy and paste the cell contents. Cutting moves the selected content, whereas copying duplicates the selected content. Pasting places the selected content in the new location.

Sally wants the worksheet to include a summary of the customer order starting in row 3. You will cut the customer contact information and the book listing from range A3:A22 and paste it into range A9:H23, freeing up space for the order information.

**To cut and paste the customer contact information and book listing:**

▶ **1.** Click cell **A3** to select it.

▶ **2.** Press the **Ctrl+Shift+End** keys to extend the selection to the last cell in the lower-right corner of the worksheet (cell H22).

▶ **3.** On the HOME tab, in the Clipboard group, click the **Cut** button (or press the **Ctrl+X** keys). The range is surrounded by a moving border, indicating that it has been cut.

▶ **4.** Click cell **A9** to select it. This is the upper-left corner of the range where you want to paste the range that you cut.

▶ **5.** In the Clipboard group, click the **Paste** button (or press the **Ctrl+V** keys). The range A3:H22 is pasted into the range A9:H28. All of the formulas in the moved range were automatically updated to reflect their new locations.

## Using the COUNT Function

Sometimes you will want to know how many unique items are included in a range, such as the number of different books in the customer order. To calculate that value, you use the COUNT function, which has the syntax

```
=COUNT(range)
```

where *range* is the range of cells containing numeric values to be counted. Note that any cell in the range containing a non-numeric value is not counted in the final tally.

You will include the count of the number of different books for the order in the summary information. The summary will also display the order ID (a unique number assigned by Sparrow & Pond to the order), the shipping date, and the type of delivery (overnight, two-day, or standard) in the freed-up space at the top of the worksheet. In addition, Sally wants the total charge for the order to be displayed with the order summary so she does not have to scroll to the bottom of the worksheet to find that value.

**To add the order summary:**

▶ **1.** Click cell **A3**, type **Order ID** as the label, press the **Tab** key, type **14123** in cell B3, and then press the **Enter** key. The order ID is entered, and cell A4 is the active cell.

▶ **2.** Type **Shipping Date** as the label in cell A4, press the **Tab** key, type **4/3/2016** in cell B4, and then press the **Enter** key. The shipping date is entered, and cell A5 is the active cell.

▶ **3.** Type **Delivery** as the label in cell A5, press the **Tab** key, type **Overnight** in cell B5, and then press the **Enter** key. The delivery type is entered, and cell A6 is the active cell.

▶ **4.** Type **Items Ordered** as the label in cell A6, and then press the **Tab** key. Cell B6 is the active cell. You will enter the COUNT function to determine the number of different books ordered.

▶ **5.** In cell B6, type **=COUNT(** to begin the function.

6. With the insertion point still blinking in cell B6, select the range **G19:G23**. The range reference is entered as the argument for the COUNT function.

7. Type **)** to complete the function, and then press the **Enter** key. Cell B6 displays the value 5, indicating that five items were ordered by Tobias Gregson. Cell A7 is the active cell.

8. Type **Total Charge** as the label in cell A7, and then press the **Tab** key to make cell B7 the active cell.

9. Type **=** to start the formula, and then click cell **H28** to enter its cell reference in the formula in cell B7. The formula =H28 tells Excel to display the contents of cell H28 in the current cell.

10. Press the **Enter** key to complete the formula. See Figure 1-29.

**Figure 1-29    Customer order summary**

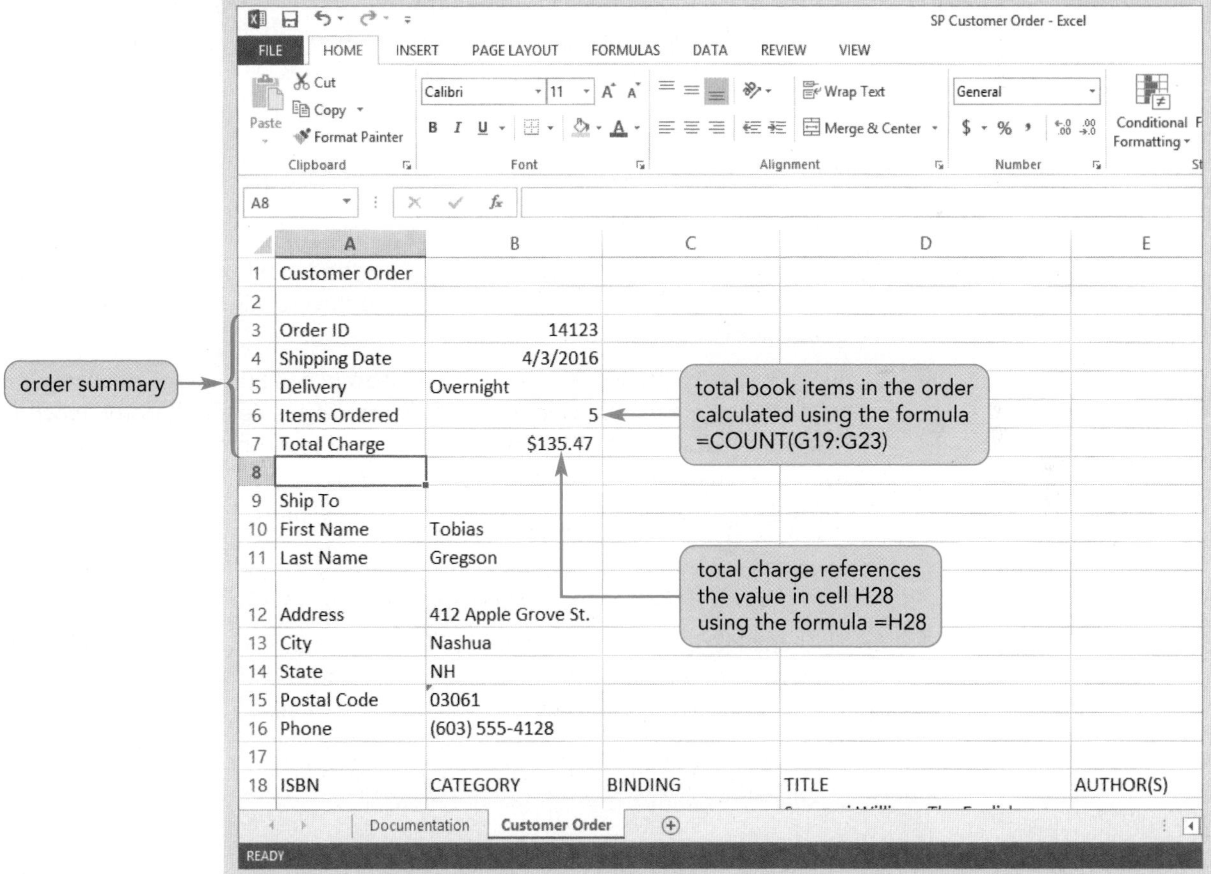

## Inserting a Column or Row

You can insert a new column or row anywhere within a worksheet. When you insert a new column, the existing columns are shifted to the right and the new column has the same width as the column directly to its left. When you insert a new row, the existing rows are shifted down and the new row has the same height as the row above it. Because inserting a new row or column moves the location of the other cells in the worksheet, any cell references in a formula or function are updated to reflect the new layout.

*Inserting or Deleting a Column or Row*

**To insert a column or row:**
- Select the column(s) or row(s) where you want to insert the new column(s) or row(s). Excel will insert the same number of columns or rows as you select to the *left* of the selected columns or *above* the selected rows.
- On the HOME tab, in the Cells group, click the Insert button (or right-click a column or row heading or selected column and row headings, and then click Insert on the shortcut menu; or press the Ctrl+Shift+= keys).

**To delete a column or row:**
- Select the column(s) or row(s) you want to delete.
- On the HOME tab, in the Cells group, click the Delete button (or right-click a column or row heading or selected column and row headings, and then click Delete on the shortcut menu; or press the Ctrl+– keys).

Tobias Gregson's order is missing an item. You need to insert a row directly below *Floral Origami Globes* in which to enter the additional book.

### To insert a new row for the missing book order:

1. Click the **row 21** heading to select the entire row.

2. On the HOME tab, in the Cells group, click the **Insert** button (or press the **Ctrl+Shift+=** keys). A new row is inserted below row 20 and becomes the new row 21.

3. Enter **0-151-01089-7** in cell A21, enter **Used** in cell B21, enter **Hardcover** in cell C21, enter **Pops: A Life of Louis Armstrong** in cell D21, enter **Teachout, Terry** in cell E21, enter **$11.95** in cell F21, and then enter **2** in cell G21.

4. Click cell **H20** to select the cell with the formula for calculating the book charge, and then press the **Ctrl+C** keys to copy the formula in that cell.

5. Click cell **H21** to select the cell where you want to insert the formula, and then press the **Ctrl+V** keys to paste the formula into the cell.

6. Click cell **H26**. The formula in this cell is now =SUM(H19:H24); the range reference was updated to reflect the inserted row. Also, the tax amount increased to $6.92 based on the new subtotal value of $138.35, and the total charge increased to $160.57 because of the added book order. See Figure 1-30. Also, the result of the COUNT function in cell B6 increased to 6 to reflect the item added to the book order.

**TIP**

You can insert multiple columns or rows by selecting that number of column or row headings, and then clicking the Insert button or pressing the Ctrl+Shift+= keys.

| Figure 1-30 | New row inserted |
| --- | --- |

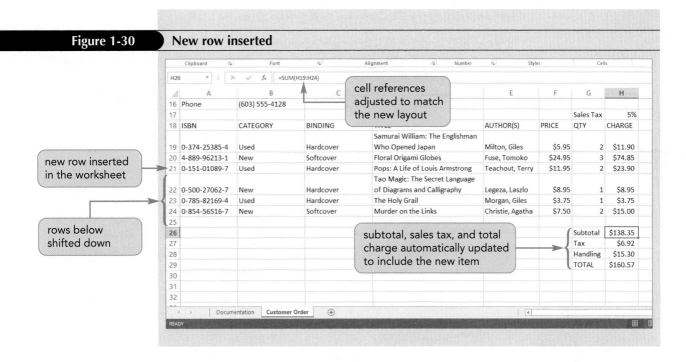

## Deleting a Row or Column

You can delete rows or columns from a worksheet. **Deleting** removes the data from the row or column as well as the row or column itself. The rows below the deleted row shift up to fill the vacated space. Likewise, the columns to the right of the deleted column shift left to fill the vacated space. Also, all cell references in the worksheet are adjusted to reflect the change. You click the Delete button in the Cells group on the HOME tab to delete selected rows or columns.

Deleting a column or row is not the same as clearing a column or row. **Clearing** removes the data from the selected row or column but leaves the blank row or column in the worksheet. You press the Delete key to clear the contents of the selected row or column, which leaves the worksheet structure unchanged.

Tobias Gregson did not order *The Holy Grail* by Giles Morgan, so that book needs to be removed from the order. You will delete the row containing that book.

### To delete the *The Holy Grail* row from the book order:

▶  1. Click the **row 23** heading to select the entire row.

▶  2. On the HOME tab, in the Cells group, click the **Delete** button (or press the **Ctrl+−** keys). Row 23 is deleted, and the rows below it shift up to fill the space.

All of the cell references in the worksheet are again updated automatically to reflect the impact of deleting row 23. The subtotal value in cell H25 now returns a value of $134.60 based on the sum of the cells in the range H19:H23. The sales tax amount in cell H26 decreases to $6.73. The total cost of the order decreases to $156.63. Also, the result of the COUNT function in cell B6 decreases to 5 to reflect the item deleted from the book order. As you can see, one of the great advantages of using Excel is that it modifies the formulas to reflect the additions and deletions you make to the worksheet.

## Inserting and Deleting a Range

You can also insert or delete ranges within a worksheet. When you use the Insert button to insert a range of cells, the existing cells shift down when the selected range is wider than it is long, and they shift right when the selected range is longer than it is wide, as shown in Figure 1-31. When you use the Insert Cells command, you specify whether the existing cells shift right or down, or whether to insert an entire row or column into the new range.

| Figure 1-31 | Cells being inserted in a worksheet |
| --- | --- |

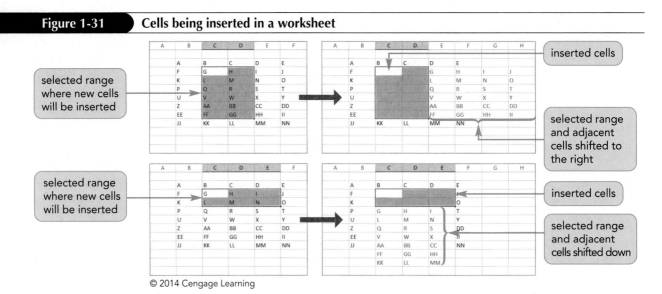

© 2014 Cengage Learning

The process works in reverse when you delete a range. As with deleting a row or column, the cells adjacent to the deleted range either move up or left to fill in the space vacated by the deleted cells. The Delete Cells command lets you specify whether you want to shift the adjacent cells left or up, or whether you want to delete the entire column or row.

When you insert or delete a range, cells that shift to a new location adopt the width of the columns they move into. As a result, you might need to resize columns and rows in the worksheet.

**REFERENCE**

### Inserting or Deleting a Range

- Select a range that matches the range you want to insert or delete.
- On the HOME tab, in the Cells group, click the Insert button or the Delete button.

*or*

- Select the range that matches the range you want to insert or delete.
- On the HOME tab, in the Cells group, click the Insert button arrow and then click Insert Cells, or click the Delete button arrow and then click Delete Cells (or right-click the selected range, and then click Insert or Delete on the shortcut menu).
- Click the option button for the direction to shift the cells, columns, or rows.
- Click the OK button.

Sally wants you to insert cells in the book list that will contain the Sparrow & Pond book ID for each book. You will insert these new cells into the range A17:A28, shifting the adjacent cells to the right.

## To insert a range in the book list:

1. Select the range **A17:A28**. You want to insert cells in this range.

2. On the HOME tab, in the Cells group, click the **Insert button arrow**. A menu of insert options appears.

3. Click **Insert Cells**. The Insert dialog box opens.

4. Verify that the **Shift cells right** option button is selected.

5. Click the **OK** button. New cells are inserted into the selected range, and the adjacent cells move to the right. The cell contents do not fit well in the columns and rows they shifted into, so you will resize the columns and rows.

6. Resize columns C and D to **12** characters, resize column E to **30** characters, and then resize column F to **15** characters. The text is easier to read in the resized columns.

7. Select the row **19** through row **23** headings.

**TIP**

You can also autofit by double-clicking the bottom border of row 23.

8. In the Cells group, click the **Format** button, and then click **AutoFit Row Height**. The selected rows autofit to their contents.

9. Click cell **A18**, type **BOOK ID** as the label, and then press the **Enter** key. See Figure 1-32.

| Figure 1-32 | Range added to the worksheet |
| --- | --- |

Why did you insert cells in the range A17:A28 even though the book ID values will be entered only in the range A18:A23? You did this to retain the layout of the page design. Selecting the additional rows ensures that the sales tax and summary values still line up with the QTY and CHARGE columns. Whenever you insert a new range, be sure to consider its impact on the layout of the entire worksheet.

## INSIGHT

### Hiding and Unhiding Rows, Columns, and Worksheets

Workbooks can become long and complicated, filled with formulas and data that are important for performing calculations but are of little interest to readers. In those situations, you can simplify these workbooks for readers by **hiding** rows, columns, and even worksheets. Although the contents of hidden cells cannot be seen, the data in those cells is still available for use in formulas and functions throughout the workbook.

Hiding a row or column essentially decreases that row height or column width to 0 pixels. To a hide a row or column, select the row or column heading, click the Format button in the Cells group on the HOME tab, point to Hide & Unhide on the menu that appears, and then click Hide Rows or Hide Columns. The border of the row or column heading is doubled to mark the location of hidden rows or columns.

A worksheet often is hidden when the entire worksheet contains data that is not of interest to the reader and is better summarized elsewhere in the document. To hide a worksheet, make that worksheet active, click the Format button in the Cells group on the HOME tab, point to Hide & Unhide, and then click Hide Sheet.

**Unhiding** redisplays the hidden content in the workbook. To unhide a row or column, click in a cell below the hidden row or to the right of the hidden column, click the Format button, point to Hide & Unhide, and then click Unhide Rows or Unhide Columns. To unhide a worksheet, click the Format button, point to Hide & Unhide, and then click Unhide Sheet. The Unhide dialog box opens. Click the sheet you want to unhide, and then click the OK button. The hidden content is redisplayed in the workbook.

Although hiding data can make a worksheet and workbook easier to read, be sure never to hide information that is important to the reader.

Sally wants you to add one more piece of data to the worksheet—a book ID that is used by Sparrow & Pond to identify each book in stock. You will use Flash Fill to create the book IDs.

## Using Flash Fill

**Flash Fill** enters text based on patterns it finds in the data. As shown in Figure 1-33, Flash Fill generates customer names from the first and last names stored in the adjacent columns in the worksheet. To enter the rest of the names, you press the Enter key; to continue typing the names yourself, you press the Esc key.

**Figure 1-33** Entering text with Flash Fill

|   | A | B | C | D | E |
|---|---|---|---|---|---|
| 1 | First | M.I. | Last | Full Name | |
| 2 | Tobias | A. | Gregson | Tobias Gregson | you enter the full name twice to begin the pattern |
| 3 | Maria | R. | Sanchez | Maria Sanchez | |
| 4 | Andrew | T. | Lewis | Andrew Lewis | |
| 5 | Brett | K. | Carls | Brett Carls | Flash Fill generates the remaining full names based on the pattern in the first two cells |
| 6 | Carmen | A. | Hzu | Carmen Hzu | |
| 7 | Karen | M. | Schultz | Karen Schultz | |
| 8 | Howard | P. | Gary | Howard Gary | |
| 9 | Natalia | N. | Shapiro | Natalia Shapiro | |
| 10 | Paul | O. | Douglas | Paul Douglas | |
| 11 | | | | | |

Flash Fill works best when the pattern is clearly recognized from the values in the data. Be sure to enter the data pattern in the column or row right next to the related data. The data used to generate the pattern must be in a rectangular grid and cannot have blank columns or rows. Also, Flash Fill enters text, not formulas. If you edit or replace an entry originally used by Flash Fill, the content generated by Flash Fill will not be updated.

The Sparrow & Pond book ID combines five digits of the book's ISBN and its category (used or new). For example, *Floral Origami Globes* has the ISBN 4-889-96213-1 and is new, so its book ID is 96213-New. The book IDs follow a consistent and logical pattern. Rather than typing every book ID, you will use Flash Fill to enter the book IDs into the worksheet.

**To enter the book IDs using Flash Fill:**

▶ **1.** Make sure that cell **A19** is the active cell.

▶ **2.** Type **25385-Used** as the ID for the first book in the list, and then press the **Enter** key.

▶ **3.** Type **9** in cell A20. As soon as you start typing, Flash Fill generates the remaining entries in the column based on the pattern you entered. See Figure 1-34.

| Figure 1-34 | Book IDs generated by Flash Fill |

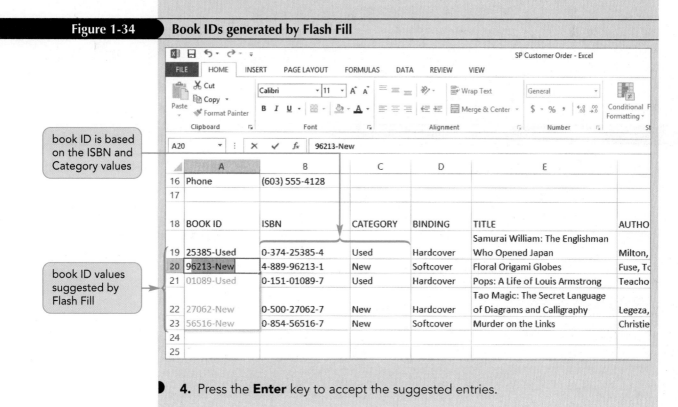

▶ **4.** Press the **Enter** key to accept the suggested entries.

# Formatting a Worksheet

**Formatting** changes a workbook's appearance to make the content of a worksheet easier to read. Two common formatting changes are adding borders to cells and changing the font size of text.

## Adding Cell Borders

Sometimes you want to include lines along the edges of cells to enhance the readability of rows and columns of data. You can do this by adding borders to the left, top, right, or bottom edge of a cell or range. You can also specify the thickness of and the number of lines in the border. This is especially helpful when a worksheet is printed because the gridlines that surround the cells are not printed by default; they appear on the worksheet only as a guide.

Sally wants add borders around the cells that contain content in the Customer Order worksheet to make the content easier to read.

### To add borders around the worksheet cells:

1. Select the range **A3:B7**. You will add borders around all of the cells in the selected range.

2. On the HOME tab, in the Font group, click the **Borders button arrow** ▦ ▾, and then click **All Borders**. Borders are added around each cell in the range. The Borders button changes to reflect the last selected border option, which in this case is All Borders. The name of the selected border option appears in the button's ScreenTip.

3. Select the nonadjacent range **A9:B16;H17:I17**. You will add borders around each cell in the selected range.

4. In the Font group, click the **All Borders** button ▦ to add borders to all of the cells in the selected range.

5. Click cell **A17** to deselect the cells. See Figure 1-35.

**Figure 1-35**    **Borders added to selected cells**

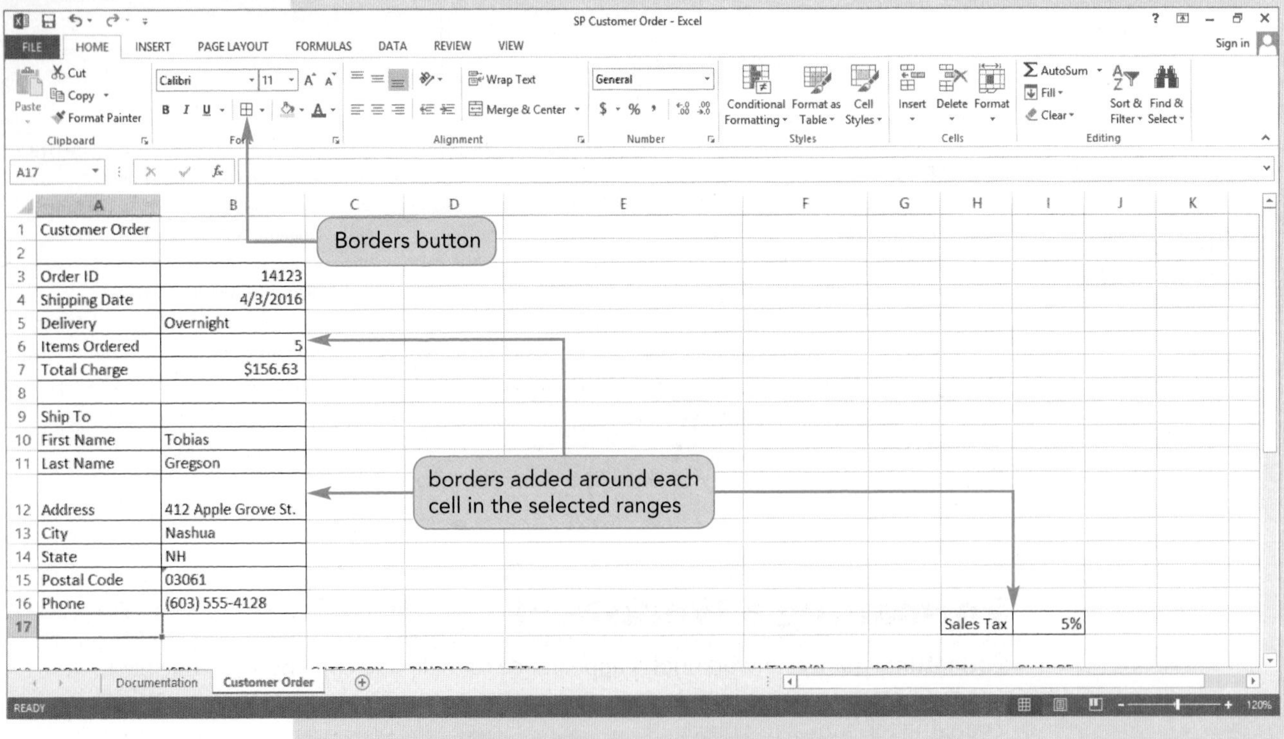

6. Select the nonadjacent range **A18:I23;H25:I28**, and then click the **All Borders** button ▦ to add borders to all of the cells in the selected range.

## Changing the Font Size

Changing the size of text in a sheet provides a way to identify different parts of a worksheet, such as distinguishing a title or section heading from data. The size of the text is referred to as the font size and is measured in points. The default font size for worksheets is 11 points, but it can be made larger or smaller as needed. You can resize text in selected cells using the Font Size button in the Font group on the HOME tab. You can also use the Increase Font Size and Decrease Font Size buttons to resize cell content to the next higher or lower standard font size.

Sally wants you to increase the size of the worksheet title to 26 points to make it stand out more.

### To change the font size of the worksheet title:

1. Click cell **A1** to select it. The worksheet title is in this cell.

2. On the HOME tab, in the Font group, click the **Font Size button arrow** to display a list of font sizes, and then click **28**. The worksheet title changes to 28 points. See Figure 1-36.

Figure 1-36    **Font size of cell content increased**

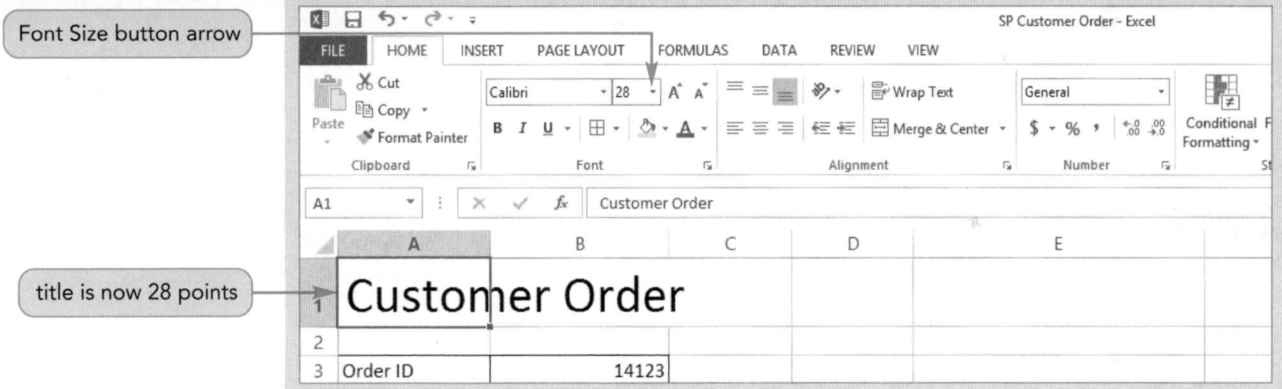

Font Size button arrow

title is now 28 points

3. Press the **Ctrl+S** keys to save the workbook.

# Printing a Workbook

Now that you have finished the workbook, Sally wants you to print a copy of the book order. Before you print a workbook, you should preview it to ensure that it will print correctly.

## Changing Worksheet Views

You can view a worksheet in three ways. Normal view, which you have been using throughout this tutorial, shows the contents of the worksheet. Page Layout view shows how the worksheet will appear when printed. Page Break Preview displays the location of the different page breaks within the worksheet. This is useful when a worksheet will span several printed pages and you need to control what content appears on each page.

Sally wants you to see how the Customer Order worksheet will appear on printed pages. You will do this by switching between views.

### To switch the Customer Order worksheet to different views:

1. Click the **Page Layout** button 🔲 on the status bar. The page layout of the worksheet appears in the workbook window.

2. Drag the **Zoom slider** to reduce the zoom level to 50%. The reduced magnification makes it clear that the worksheet will spread over two pages when printed. See Figure 1-37.

| Figure 1-37 | Worksheet in Page Layout view |

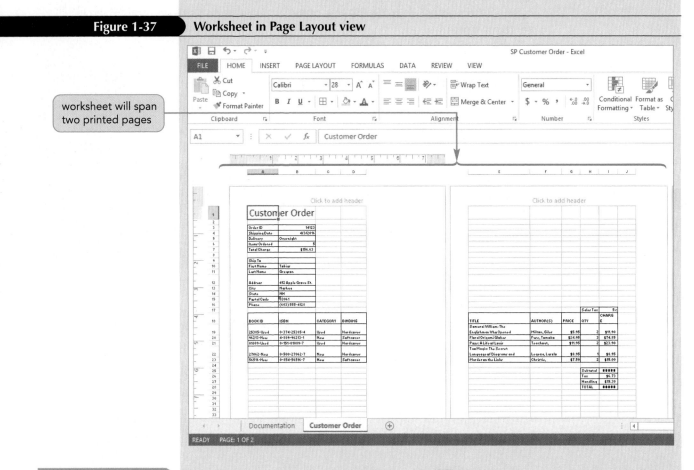

worksheet will span two printed pages

TIP

You can relocate a page break by dragging the dotted blue border in the Page Break Preview window.

3. Click the **Page Break Preview** button 🔲 on the status bar. The view switches to Page Break Preview, which shows only those parts of the current worksheet that will print. A dotted blue border separates one page from another.

4. Zoom the worksheet to **70%** so that you can more easily read the contents of the worksheet. See Figure 1-38.

**Figure 1-38**   **Worksheet in Page Break Preview**

page 1 of the printout

page 2 of the printout

| | A | B | C | D | E | F | G | H | I | J | K | L | M |
|---|---|---|---|---|---|---|---|---|---|---|---|---|---|
| | | | | | Customer Order | | | | | | | | |
| 1 | Customer Order | | | | | | | | | | | | |
| 2 | | | | | | | | | | | | | |
| 3 | Order ID | | 14123 | | | | | | | | | | |
| 4 | Shipping Date | | 4/3/2016 | | | | | | | | | | |
| 5 | Delivery | Overnight | | | | | | | | | | | |
| 6 | Items Ordered | | 5 | | | | | | | | | | |
| 7 | Total Charge | | $156.63 | | | | | | | | | | |
| 8 | | | | | | | | | | | | | |
| 9 | Ship To | | | | | | | | | | | | |
| 10 | First Name | Tobias | | | | | | | | | | | |
| 11 | Last Name | Gregson | | | | | | | | | | | |
| 12 | Address | 412 Apple Grove St. | | | | | | | | | | | |
| 13 | City | Nashua | | | | | | | | | | | |
| 14 | State | NH | | | | | | | | | | | |
| 15 | Postal Code | 03061 | | | | | | | | | | | |
| 16 | Phone | (603) 555-4128 | | | | | | | | | | | |
| 17 | | | | | | | | Sales Tax | 5% | | | | |
| 18 | BOOK ID | ISBN | CATEGORY | BINDING | TITLE | AUTHOR(S) | PRICE | QTY | CHARGE | | | | |
| 19 | 25385-Used | 0-374-25385-4 | Used | Hardcover | Samurai William: The Englishman Who Opened | Milton, Giles | $5.95 | 2 | $11.90 | | | | |
| 20 | 96213-New | 4-889-96213-1 | New | Softcover | Floral Origami Globes | Fuse, Tomoko | $24.95 | 3 | $74.85 | | | | |
| 21 | 01089-Used | 0-151-01089-7 | Used | Hardcover | Pops: A Life of Louis Armstrong | Teachout, | $11.95 | 2 | $23.90 | | | | |
| 22 | 27062-New | 0-500-27062-7 | New | Hardcover | Tao Magic: The Secret Language of Diagrams and | Legeza, Laszlo | $8.95 | 1 | $8.95 | | | | |
| 23 | 56516-New | 0-854-56516-7 | New | Softcover | Murder on the Links | Christie, | $7.50 | 2 | $15.00 | | | | |
| 24 | | | | | | | | | | | | | |
| 25 | | | | | | | | Subtotal | $134.60 | | | | |
| 26 | | | | | | | | Tax | $6.73 | | | | |
| 27 | | | | | | | | Handling | $15.30 | | | | |
| 28 | | | | | | | | TOTAL | $156.63 | | | | |

Documentation   Customer Order

READY

▶ **5.** Click the **Normal** button on the status bar. The worksheet returns to Normal view. A dotted black line indicates where the page break will occur.

## Changing the Page Orientation

Page orientation specifies in which direction content is printed on the page. In **portrait orientation**, the page is taller than it is wide. In **landscape orientation**, the page is wider than it is tall. By default, Excel displays pages in portrait orientation. Changing the page orientation affects only the active sheet.

As you saw in Page Layout view and Page Break Preview, the Customer Order worksheet will print on two pages—columns A through D will print on the first page, and columns E through I will print on the second page, although the columns that print on each page may differ slightly depending on the printer. Sally wants the entire worksheet to print on a single page, so you'll change the page orientation from portrait to landscape.

**To change the page orientation of the Customer Order worksheet:**

▶ **1.** On the ribbon, click the **PAGE LAYOUT** tab. The tab includes options for changing how the worksheet is arranged.

▶ **2.** In the Page Setup group, click the **Orientation** button, and then click **Landscape**. The worksheet switches to landscape orientation.

▶ **3.** Click the **Page Layout** button on the status bar to switch to Page Layout view. The worksheet will still print on two pages.

## Setting the Scaling Options

You change the size of the worksheet on the printed page by **scaling** it. You can scale the width or the height of the printout so that all of the columns or all of the rows fit on a single page. You can also scale the printout to fit the entire worksheet (both columns and rows) on a single page. If the worksheet is too large to fit on one page, you can scale the print to fit on the number of pages you select. You can also scale the worksheet to a percentage of its size. For example, scaling a worksheet to 50% reduces the size of the sheet by half when it is sent to the printer. When scaling a printout, make sure that the worksheet is still readable after shrinking. Scaling affects only the active worksheet, so you can scale each worksheet to best fit its contents.

Sally asks you to scale the printout so that all of the Customer Order worksheet fits on one page in landscape orientation.

### To scale the printout of the Customer Order worksheet:

1. On the PAGE LAYOUT tab, in the Scale to Fit group, click the **Width arrow**, and then click **1 page** on the menu that appears. All of the columns in the worksheet now fit on one page.

2. In the Scale to Fit group, click the **Height arrow**, and then click **1 page**. All of the rows in the worksheet now fit on one page. See Figure 1-39.

| Figure 1-39 | Printout scaled to fit on one page |
| --- | --- |

## Setting the Print Options

**TIP**

To print the gridlines or the column and row headings, click the corresponding Print check box in the Sheet Options group on the PAGE LAYOUT tab.

You can print the contents of a workbook by using the Print screen in Backstage view. The Print screen provides options for choosing where to print, what to print, and how to print. For example, you can specify the number of copies to print, which printer to use, and what to print. You can choose to print only the selected cells, only the active sheets, or all of the worksheets in the workbook that contain data. The printout will include only the data in the worksheet. The other elements in the worksheet, such as the row and column headings and the gridlines around the worksheet cells, will not print by default. The preview shows you exactly how the printed pages will look with the current settings. You should always preview before printing to ensure that the printout looks exactly as you intended and avoid unnecessary reprinting.

Sally asks you to preview and print the Sparrow & Pond workbook now.

**Note:** Check with your instructor first to make sure you should complete the steps for printing the workbook.

### To preview and print the workbook:

▶ **1.** On the ribbon, click the **FILE** tab to display Backstage view.

▶ **2.** Click **Print** in the navigation bar. The Print screen appears with the print options and a preview of the Customer Order worksheet printout. See Figure 1-40.

| Figure 1-40 | Print screen in Backstage view |
| --- | --- |

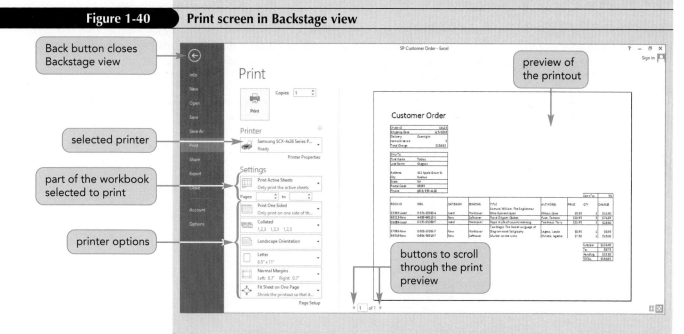

Back button closes Backstage view

selected printer

part of the workbook selected to print

printer options

preview of the printout

buttons to scroll through the print preview

▶ **3.** Click the **Printer** button, and then click the printer to which you want to print, if it is not already selected. By default, Excel will print only the active sheet.

▶ **4.** In the Settings options, click the top button, and then click **Print Entire Workbook** to print all of the sheets in the workbook—in this case, both the Documentation and the Customer Order worksheets. The preview shows the first sheet in the workbook—the Documentation worksheet. Note that this sheet is still in the default portrait orientation.

▶ **5.** Below the preview, click the **Next Page** button ▶ to view the Customer Order worksheet. As you can see, the Customer Order worksheet will print on a single page in landscape orientation.

▶ **6.** If you are instructed to print, click the **Print** button to send the contents of the workbook to the specified printer. If you are not instructed to print, click the **Back** button  in the navigation bar to exit Backstage view.

# Viewing Worksheet Formulas

Most of the time, you will be interested in only the final results of a worksheet, not the formulas used to calculate those results. However, in some cases, you might want to view the formulas used to develop the workbook. This is particularly useful when you encounter unexpected results and you want to examine the underlying formulas, or you want to discuss your formulas with a colleague. You can display the formulas instead of the resulting values in cells.

If you print the worksheet while the formulas are displayed, the printout shows the formulas instead of the values. To make the printout easier to read, you should print the worksheet gridlines as well as the row and column headings so that cell references in the formulas are easy to find in the printed version of the worksheet.

You will look at the Customer Order worksheet with the formulas displayed.

### To display the formulas in cells in the Customer Order worksheet:

▶ **1.** Make sure the Customer Order worksheet is in Page Layout view.

**TIP**

You can also display formulas in a worksheet by clicking the Show Formulas button in the Formula Auditing group on the FORMULAS tab.

▶ **2.** Press the **Ctrl+`** keys (the grave accent symbol ` is usually located above the Tab key). The worksheet changes to display all of the formulas instead of the resulting values. Notice that the columns widen to display all of the formula text in the cells.

▶ **3.** Look at the entry in cell B4. The underlying numeric value of the shipping date (42463) is displayed instead of the formatted date value (4/3/2016). See Figure 1-41.

| Figure 1-41 | Worksheet with formulas displayed |

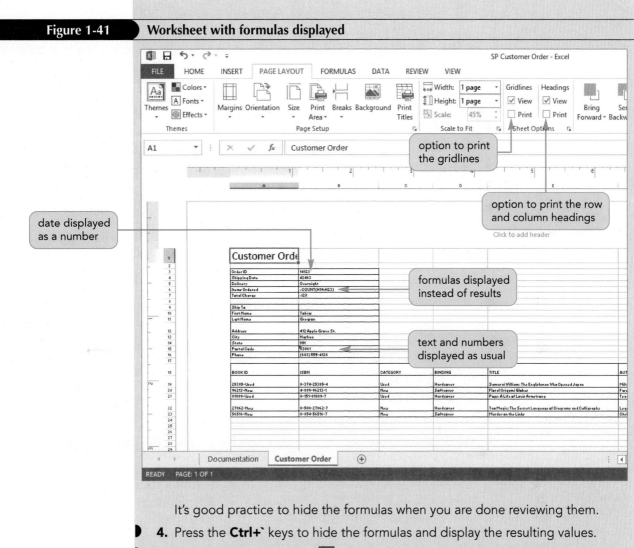

date displayed as a number

option to print the gridlines

option to print the row and column headings

formulas displayed instead of results

text and numbers displayed as usual

It's good practice to hide the formulas when you are done reviewing them.

**4.** Press the **Ctrl+`** keys to hide the formulas and display the resulting values.

**5.** Click the **Normal** button on the status bar to return the workbook to Normal view.

# Saving a Workbook with a New Filename

Whenever you click the Save button on the Quick Access Toolbar or press the Ctrl+S keys, the workbook file is updated to reflect the latest content. If you want to save a copy of the workbook with a new filename or to a different location, you need to use the Save As command. When you save a workbook with a new filename or to a different location, the previous version of the workbook remains stored as well.

You have completed the SP Customer Order workbook. Sally wants to use the workbook as a model for other customer order reports. You will save the workbook with a new filename to avoid overwriting the Tobias Gregson book order. Then you'll clear the information related to Tobias Gregson, leaving the formulas intact. This new, revised workbook will then be ready for a new customer order.

## To save the workbook with a new filename:

1. Press the **Ctrl+S** keys to save the workbook. This ensures that the final copy of the SP Customer Order workbook contains the latest content.

2. On the ribbon, click the **FILE** tab to display Backstage view, and then click **Save As** on the navigation bar. The Save As screen is displayed.

3. Click **Computer**, and then click the **Browse** button. The Save As dialog box opens so you can save the workbook with a new filename or to a new location.

4. Navigate to the location specified by your instructor.

**TIP**

Save the workbook with the new name *before* making your changes to avoid inadvertently saving your edits to the wrong file.

5. In the File name box, type **SP Customer Order Form** as the new filename.

6. Click the **Save** button. The workbook is saved with the new filename and is open in Excel.

7. Select the range **B3:B5**, right-click the selected range to open the shortcut menu, and then click **Clear Contents** to clear the contents of the order ID, shipping date, and delivery type cells.

8. Select the nonadjacent range **B10:B16;A19:H23**, and then press the **Delete** key to clear the contact information for Tobias Gregson and the list of books he ordered from those cells.

9. Select cell **I27**, and then clear the handling fee.

10. Click cell **A3** to make that cell the active cell. The next time someone opens this workbook, cell A3 will still be the active cell.

11. Press the **Ctrl+S** keys to save the workbook.

12. Click the **Close** button ☒ on the title bar (or press the **Ctrl+W** keys). The workbook closes, and the Excel program closes.

Sally is pleased with the workbook you created. With the calculations already in place in the new workbook, she will be able to quickly enter new customer orders and see the calculated book charges without having to recreate the worksheet.

## Session 1.2 Quick Check

**REVIEW**

1. What formula would you enter to add the values in cells B4, B5, and B6? What function would you enter to achieve the same result?

2. What formula would you enter to count the number of numeric values in the range B2:B100?

3. What formula would you enter to find the maximum value of the cells in the range B2:B100?

4. If you insert cells into the range C1:D10 shifting the cells to the right, what is the new location of the data that was previously in cell E5?

5. Cell E11 contains the formula =SUM(E1:E10). How does this formula change if a new row is inserted above row 5?

6. Describe four ways of viewing the content of a workbook in Excel.

7. How are page breaks indicated in Page Break Preview?

8. How do you display the formulas used in a worksheet instead of the formula results?

**ASSESS**

### SAM Projects

Put your skills into practice with SAM Projects! SAM Projects for this tutorial can be found online. If you have a SAM account, go to www.cengage.com/sam2013 to download the most recent Project Instructions and Start Files.

**PRACTICE**

## Review Assignments

**There are no Data Files needed for the Review Assignments.**

Sally wants you to create a workbook to record the recent book purchases made by Sparrow & Pond. The workbook should list the recent acquisitions from private sellers, libraries, and other vendors; include a description of each book; and calculate the total number of books acquired and the total amount spent by Sparrow & Pond. Complete the following:

1. Create a new, blank workbook, and then save the workbook as **Book List** in the location specified by your instructor.
2. Rename the Sheet1 worksheet as **Documentation**, and then enter the data shown in Figure 1-42 in the specified cells.

**Figure 1-42**    **Documentation sheet data**

| Cell | Data |
|------|------|
| A1 | Sparrow & Pond |
| A3 | Author |
| A4 | Date |
| A5 | Purpose |
| B3 | *your name* |
| B4 | *current date* |
| B5 | To record book acquisitions by Sparrow & Pond |

© 2014 Cengage Learning

3. Set the font size of the title text in cell A1 to 26 points.
4. Add a new worksheet after the Documentation sheet, and then rename the sheet as **Books**.
5. In cell A1, enter the text **Book Acquisitions**. Set the font size of this text to 26 points.
6. In cell A2, enter the text **DATE** as the label. In cell B2, enter the date **4/3/2016**.
7. In the range A4:G9, enter the data shown in Figure 1-43.

**Figure 1-43**    **Book list**

| ISBN | STATUS | BINDING | TITLE | AUTHOR | CONDITION | PRICE |
|---|---|---|---|---|---|---|
| 0-670-02103-2 | New | Softcover | Rocket Men: The Epic Story of the First Men on the Moon | Nelson, Craig | Excellent | $12.95 |
| 0-195-09076-4 | Used | Hardcover | Buildings of Colorado | Noel, Thomas J. | Good | $22.50 |
| 0-375-70365-9 | New | Softcover | American Visions: The Epic History of Art in America | Hughes, Robert | Excellent | $22.50 |
| 1-564-77848-7 | New | Softcover | Simple Comforts: 12 Cozy Lap Quilts | Diehl, Kim | Very Good | $9.25 |
| 1-851-70006-4 | Used | Hardcover | Beautiful Stories About Children | Dickens, Charles | Good | $33.50 |

© 2014 Cengage Learning

8. Insert cells into the range A4:A9, shifting the other cells to the right.
9. Enter the label **BOOK ID** in cell A4, type **02103-New** in cell A5, and then type **09076-Used** in cell A6.
10. Use Flash Fill to fill in the remaining book IDs.
11. Set the width of columns A through D to 15 characters each. Set the width of column E to 30 characters. Set the width of column F to 20 characters. Set the width of column G to 15 characters.
12. Set the book titles in the range E4:E9 to wrap to a new line.
13. Autofit the heights of rows 4 through 9.
14. Move the book list in the range A4:H9 to the range A8:H13.
15. In cell G15, enter the text **TOTAL**. In cell H15, enter a function to add the prices in the range H9:H13.
16. In cell A4, enter the text **TOTAL BOOKS**. In cell B4, enter a function to count the number of numeric values in the range H9:H13.
17. In cell A5, enter the text **TOTAL PRICE**. In cell B5, display the value from cell H15.
18. In cell A6, enter the text **AVERAGE PRICE**. In cell B6, enter a formula to calculate the total price paid for the books (listed in cell B5) divided by the number of books purchased (listed in cell B4).
19. Add borders around each cell in the nonadjacent range A4:B6;A8:H13;G15:H15.
20. For the Books worksheet, change the page orientation to landscape and scale the worksheet to print on a single page for both the width and the height. If you are instructed to print, print the entire workbook.
21. Display the formulas in the Books worksheet, and set the gridlines and row/column headings to print. If you are instructed to print, print the entire worksheet.
22. Save and close the workbook.

## Case Problem 1

APPLY

**Data File needed for this Case Problem: Pacific.xlsx**

***American Wheel Tours***   Kevin Bennett is a tours manager at American Wheel Tours, a bicycle touring company located in Philadelphia, Pennsylvania, that specializes in one- and two-week supported tours in destinations across the United States. Kevin wants you to create a workbook that details the itinerary of the company's Pacific Coast tour. The workbook will list the tour itinerary shown in Figure 1-44 and calculate the total number of riding days, total mileage, and average mileage per ride.

| Figure 1-44 | Pacific Tour itinerary |
|---|---|

| DATE | START | FINISH | CAMPSITE | MILES | DESCRIPTION |
|---|---|---|---|---|---|
| 10-Oct-16 | Eugene | Eugene | Richardson Park | | Orientation day. Meet at Richardson Park, located at the Fern Ridge Reservoir. |
| 11-Oct-16 | Eugene | Florence | Honeyman State Park | 66 | Cycle over Low Pass to Honeyman State Park. |
| 12-Oct-16 | Florence | Charleston | Sunset Bay State Park | 56 | Cycle through Oregon Dunes National Recreation Area to Sunset Bay State Park. |
| 13-Oct-16 | Charleston | Port Orford | Humbug Mountain State Park | 60 | Cycle around Bullards Beach State Park and camp at Humbug Mountain State Park. |
| 14-Oct-16 | Port Orford | Brookings | Harris Beach State Park | 52 | Cycle past the mouth of the Rogue River to Harris Beach State Park. |
| 15-Oct-16 | Brookings | Crescent City | Jedediah State Park | 48 | Pass into California and camp at Jedediah State Park. |
| 16-Oct-16 | Crescent City | Eureka | Eureka Fairgrounds | 72 | A long day through Del Norte Coast Redwoods State Park to Eureka. |

© 2014 Cengage Learning

Complete the following:

1. Open the **Pacific** workbook located in the Excel1 ▸ Case1 folder included with your Data Files, and then save the workbook as **Pacific Coast** in the location specified by your instructor.
2. In the Documentation worksheet, enter your name in cell B3 and the date in cell B4.
3. Add a new sheet to the end of the workbook and rename it as **Itinerary**.
4. In cell A1, enter the text **Pacific Coast Tour** and set the font size to 28 points.
5. In the range A3:A8, enter the following labels: **Start Date**, **End Date**, **Total Days**, **Riding Days**, **Total Miles**, and **Miles per Day**.
6. Enter the date **October 10, 2016** in cell B3, and then enter the date **October 16, 2016** in cell B4.
7. In the range D3:D8, enter the labels **Type**, **Surface**, **Difficulty**, **Tour Leader**, **Cost**, and **Deposit**.
8. In the range E3:E8, enter **Van Supported**, **Paved**, **Intermediate**, **Kevin Bennett**, **$1,250**, and **$350**.
9. In the range A11:F18, enter the data shown in Figure 1-44, including the column labels. Leave the mileage value for October 10th blank.
10. In cell B5, enter a formula to calculate the total number of days in the tour by subtracting the starting date (cell B3) from the ending date (cell B4) and adding 1.

11. In cell B6, enter a function to count the total number of riding days based on the numbers in the range E12:E18.

12. In cell B7, enter a function to add the total number of miles in the range E12:E18.

13. In cell B8, enter a formula to calculate the average miles per day by dividing the total miles by the number of riding days.

14. Insert cells in the range A11:A18, shifting the cells to the right. In cell A11, enter **DAY**. In the range A12:A18, enter the numbers 1 through 7 to number each day of the tour.

15. Set the column widths so that column A is 12 characters, columns B through E are 14 characters each, column F is 6 characters, and column G is 50 characters.

16. Wrap text in the range A11:G18 as needed so that any hidden entries are displayed on multiple lines within the cell.

17. Autofit the height of rows 11 through 18.

18. Add borders around the ranges A3:B8, D3:E8, and A11:G18.

19. Format the Itinerary worksheet so that it prints on a single page in landscape orientation. If you are instructed to print, print the entire workbook.

20. Display the formulas in the Itinerary worksheet, and set the gridlines and column/row headings to print. If you are instructed to print, print the worksheet.

21. Return the Itinerary worksheet to Normal view, hide the formulas, set the gridlines and column/row headings so that they won't print, and then save the workbook.

22. Save the workbook as **Pacific Coast Revised** in the location specified by your instructor.

23. Determine what the total mileage and average mileage per day of the tour would be if Kevin adds a 10-mile warm-up ride on October 10th but decreases the length of the October 15th ride to 41 miles. Save the workbook.

## Case Problem 2

**Data File needed for this Case Problem: Tropical.xlsx**

***Tropical Foods***   Tropical Foods is a health food grocery store located in Keizer, Oregon. Monica Li is working on the store's annual financial report. One part of the financial report will be the company's balance sheet for the previous two years. Monica already entered the labels for the balance sheet. You will enter the numeric data and formulas to perform the financial calculations. Complete the following:

1. Open the **Tropical** workbook located in the Excel1 ▸ Case2 folder included with your Data Files, and then save the workbook as **Tropical Foods Balance Sheet** in the location specified by your instructor.

2. In cells B3 and B4 of the Documentation sheet, enter your name and the date. In cell A1, increase the font size of the title to 28 points.

3. Go to the Balance Sheet worksheet. Increase the font size of the title in cell A1 to 28 points, and then increase the font size of the subtitle in cell A2 to 20 points.

4. In the corresponding cells of columns C and D, enter the numbers shown in Figure 1-45 for the company's assets and liabilities.

**Figure 1-45**     **Tropical Foods assets and liabilities**

|  |  | 2015 | 2014 |
|---|---|---|---|
| Assets | Cash | $645,785 | $627,858 |
|  | Accounts Receivable | 431,982 | 405,811 |
|  | Inventories | 417,615 | 395,648 |
|  | Prepaid Expenses | 2,152 | 4,151 |
|  | Other Assets | 31,252 | 26,298 |
|  | Fixed Assets @ Cost | 1,800,000 | 1,750,000 |
|  | Accumulated Depreciation | 82,164 | $77,939 |
| Liabilities | Accounts Payable | $241,191 | $193,644 |
|  | Accrued Expenses | 31,115 | 32,151 |
|  | Current Portion of Debt | 120,000 | 100,000 |
|  | Income Taxes Payable | 144,135 | 126,524 |
|  | Long-Term Debt | 815,000 | 850,000 |
|  | Capital Stock | 1,560,000 | 1,525,000 |
|  | Retain Earnings | 335,181 | 304,508 |

© 2014 Cengage Learning

5. Set the width of column A to 12 characters, column B to 28 characters, columns C and D to 14 characters each, column E to 2 characters, and column F to 10 characters.

6. In cells C8 and D8, enter formulas to calculate the current assets value for 2014 and 2015, which is equal to the sum of the cash, accounts receivable, inventories, and prepaid expenses values.

7. In cells C14 and D14, enter formulas to calculate the net fixed assets value for 2014 and 2015, which is equal to the difference between the fixed assets value and the accumulated depreciation value.

8. In cells C16 and D16, enter formulas to calculate the total assets value for 2014 and 2015, which is equal to the sum of the current assets, other assets, and net fixed assets value.

9. In cells C23 and D23, enter formulas to calculate the sum of the accounts payable, accrued expenses, current portion of debt, and income taxes payable values for 2014 and 2015.

10. In cells C29 and D29, enter formulas to calculate the shareholders' equity value for 2014 and 2015, which is equal to the sum of the capital stock and retained earnings.

11. In cells C31 and D31, enter formulas to calculate the total liabilities & equity value for 2014 and 2015, which is equal to the sum of the current liabilities, long-term debt, and shareholders' equity.

12. In a balance sheet, the total assets should equal the total liabilities & equity. Compare the values in cells C16 and C31, and then compare the values in cells D16 and D31 to confirm that this is the case for the Tropical Foods balance sheet in 2014 and 2015. If the account doesn't balance, check your worksheet for errors in either values or formulas.

13. In cell F4, enter a formula to calculate the percentage change in cash from 2014 to 2015, which is equal to (C4–D4)/D4.

14. Copy the formula in cell F4 and paste it in the nonadjacent range F5:F8;F10;F12:F14;F16; F19:F23;F25;F27:F29;F31 to show the percentage change in all values of the balance sheet.

15. Add borders around the cells in columns B, C, D, and F of the balance sheet, excluding the cells in rows 9, 11, 15, 17, 18, 24, 26, and 30.

16. Set the page layout of the Balance Sheet worksheet to portrait orientation and scaled to print on a single page. If you are instructed to print, print the entire workbook.

17. Display the formulas in the Balance Sheet worksheet, and then set the gridlines and row/column headings to print. If you are instructed to print, print the worksheet.

18. Display the Balance Sheet worksheet in Normal view, hide the formulas, set the gridlines and column/row headings so that they won't print, and then save the workbook.

## CHALLENGE

## Case Problem 3

Data File needed for this Case Problem: Physics.xlsx

*Gladstone Country Day School*   Beatrix Melendez teaches Introduction to Physics at Gladstone Country Day School in Gladstone, Missouri. She wants to record students' quiz scores, and then calculate each student's total and average scores. She also wants to calculate the class average, high score, and low score for each quiz in her records. Beatrix has entered scores from 10 quizzes for 20 students in a worksheet. You will summarize these grades by student and by quiz using the functions listed in Figure 1-46.

**Figure 1-46**    **Excel summary functions**

| Function | Description |
|---|---|
| =AVERAGE (*range*) | Calculates the average of the values from the specified *range* |
| =MEDIAN (*range*) | Calculates the median or midpoint of the values from the specified *range* |
| =MIN (*range*) | Calculates the minimum of the values from the specified *range* |
| =MAX (*range*) | Calculates the maximum of the values from the specified *range* |

© 2014 Cengage Learning

Complete the following:

1. Open the **Physics** workbook located in the Excel1 ▸ Case3 folder included with your Data Files, and then save the workbook as **Physics Grading Sheet** in the location specified by your instructor.

2. In the Documentation sheet, enter your name in cell B3 and the date in cell B4. Increase the font size of the title in cell A1 to 28 points.

3. Go to the Grades worksheet. Increase the font size of cell A1 to 28 points, and then increase the font size of cell A2 to 22 points.

➕ **Explore** 4. In cell M5, enter a formula to calculate the median or midpoint of the quiz scores for Debra Alt. In cell N5, enter a formula to calculate the average of Debra Alt's quiz scores.

5. Copy the formulas in the range M5:N5 to the range M6:N24 to summarize the scores for the remaining students.

➕ **Explore** 6. In cell B26, enter a formula to calculate the minimum class score from the first quiz. In cell B27, enter a formula to calculate the median class score.

➕ **Explore** 7. In cell B28, use the MAX function to calculate the high score from the first quiz.

8. In cell B30, enter a formula to calculate the average score from the first quiz.

9. Copy the formulas in the range B26:B30 to the range C26:K30 to calculate the summary statistics for the rest of the quizzes.

10. Insert 10 new rows above row 4, shifting the student grade table and summary from the range A4:N30 to the range A14:N40. You will enter a summary of all of the students from all of the quizzes at the top of the worksheet.

11. In cell A4, enter the text **Class Size**. In cell B4, enter a formula to calculate the count of scores from the range N15:N34.

12. In the range A6:A9, enter the labels **Overall Scores**, **Lowest Average**, **Median Average**, and **Highest Average**. In cell A11, enter **Class Average**.

13. Using the average scores in the range N15:N34, enter formulas to calculate the overall lowest average score in cell B7, the median of the class averages in cell B8, the overall highest average in cell B9, and the average overall class score in cell B11.

14. Add cell borders around the ranges A4:B4, A7:B9, A11:B11, A14:K34, M14:N34, A36:K38, and A40:K40.

15. Set the page layout of the Grades worksheet to landscape orientation and scaled to print on a single page. If you are instructed to print, print the entire workbook.

16. Display the formulas in the Grades worksheet. Set the gridlines and the row/column headings to print. If you are instructed to print, print the worksheet.

17. Display the Grades worksheet in Normal view, hide the formulas, set the gridlines and column/row headings so that they won't print, and then save the workbook.

18. Determine the effect of raising each student's score on the first quiz by 10 points to curve the results. Report what impact this has on the overall class average from all 10 quizzes.

19. Save the workbook as **Physics Grading Sheet Revised**. If you are instructed to print, print the Grades worksheet.

## Case Problem 4

Data File needed for this Case Problem: Turf.xlsx

*Turf Toughs*    Tim Gables is the owner and operator of Turf Toughs, a lawn and tree removal service located in Chicopee, Massachusetts. He created a workbook to record and analyze the service calls made by his company. So far, the workbook calculates the cost of each service call, the total charges for all of the calls, and the total number of billable hours. Unfortunately, the workbook contains several errors. You will fix these errors and then complete the workbook. Complete the following:

1. Open the **Turf** workbook located in the Excel1 ▸ Case4 folder included with your Data Files, and then save the workbook as **Turf Toughs Service Calls** in the location specified by your instructor.

2. In the Documentation sheet, enter your name in cell B3 and the date in cell B4.

3. Go to the Service Log worksheet. The log lists the contact information and the service calls for each customer.

   Tim wants you to insert a column of IDs for each customer. The customer ID is in the form *last-phone*, where *last* is the customer's last name and *phone* is the last four digits of the customer's phone number.

4. Insert cells in the range A4:A34, shifting the other cells to the right. Type **Cust ID** in cell A4, and then enter **Morris-4380** as the customer ID for Michael Morris. Use Flash Fill to fill in the remaining customer IDs in the column.

5. Add borders around the cells in the range A4:A32.

   ⚙ **Troubleshoot** 6. There is a problem with the all of the customer zip codes. Each zip code should begin with zero. Make the necessary changes to fix this problem.

7. Resize the columns of the worksheet so that all of the column labels in the service calls list are displayed entirely.

   ⚙ **Troubleshoot** 8. The formula in cell L5 is not correctly calculating the number of hours for each service call. Fix the formula so that it multiplies the difference between the starting and ending time by 24.

9. Copy the formula you created for cell L5 to the range L6:L32, replacing the previous calculated values.

10. Calculate the service charge for each service call so that it equals the base fee added to the hourly rate times the number of hours worked.

⚙ **Troubleshoot** 11. Cell N34 contains a formula to calculate the total service charges for all customer visits. Is it calculating the value correctly? If not, edit the formula to fix any errors you find.

12. Above row 4, insert six new rows, shifting the range A4:N34 down to the range A10:N40.

13. In the range A4:A8, enter the labels **From**, **To**, **Total Service Calls**, **Billable Hours**, and **Total Charges**.

14. In cell B4, calculate the starting date of the service calls by entering a formula that finds the minimum value of the dates in the Date column.

15. In cell B5, calculate the ending date of the service calls by entering a formula that finds the maximum value of the dates in the Date column.

16. In cell B6, enter a formula that counts the total number of service calls using the values in the Date column.

17. In cell B7, enter a formula that calculates the sum of hours from the Hours column.

18. In cell B8, enter a formula that references the value of cell N40.

19. Add borders around each cell in the range A4:B8.

20. Set the page layout of the Service Log worksheet so that it prints on a single page in landscape orientation. If you are instructed to print, print the entire workbook.

21. Display the formulas in the Service Log worksheet, scale the worksheet to fit on a single page, and then set the gridlines and row/column headings to print. If you are instructed to print, print the Service Log worksheet.

22. Return the Service Log worksheet to Normal view, hide the formulas, set the gridlines and column/row headings so that they won't print, and then save the workbook.

## OBJECTIVES

**Session 2.1**
- Change fonts, font style, and font color
- Add fill colors and a background image
- Create formulas to calculate sales data
- Apply Currency and Accounting formats and the Percent style
- Format dates and times
- Align, indent, and rotate cell contents
- Merge a group of cells

**Session 2.2**
- Use the AVERAGE function
- Apply cell styles
- Copy and paste formats with the Format Painter
- Find and replace text and formatting
- Change workbook themes
- Highlight cells with conditional formats
- Format a worksheet for printing
- Set the print area, insert page breaks, add print titles, create headers and footers, and set margins

# Formatting Workbook Text and Data

*Designing a Sales Report*

## Case | Big Red Wraps

Sanjit Chandra is a sales manager for Big Red Wraps, a growing restaurant chain that specializes in preparing made-to-order sandwich wraps, seasonal soups, and fresh salads. The first Big Red Wraps opened in Madison, Wisconsin, and has since expanded to 20 restaurants across six states. Four of these restaurants were opened this year. Each spring, the company has a sales conference where the restaurant managers meet to discuss sales concerns and review marketing plans for the upcoming year. Sanjit created a workbook that summarizes the sales data for the previous year and is part of a sales report that will be given to all conference attendees. He wants you to calculate some summary statistics and format the workbook.

**EXCEL**

## STARTING DATA FILES

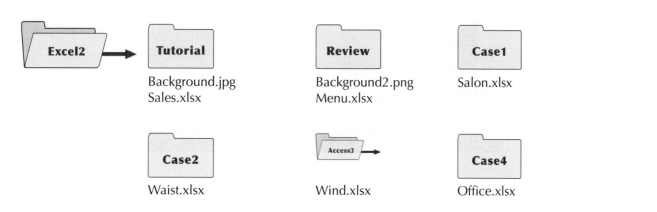

| Excel2 → Tutorial | Review | Case1 |
| --- | --- | --- |
| Background.jpg<br>Sales.xlsx | Background2.png<br>Menu.xlsx | Salon.xlsx |

| Case2 | Access3 → | Case4 |
| --- | --- | --- |
| Waist.xlsx | Wind.xlsx | Office.xlsx |

# Session 2.1 Visual Overview:

You use the Font button to change the font of selected text or numbers.

Every font can be formatted with a **font style**, such as **bold**, *italic*, or <u>underline</u>.

You can format a text string within a cell in Edit mode.

A **font** is a set of characters that employ the same typeface, such as Arial, Times New Roman, and Courier.

You can **merge**, or combine, several cells into one cell. This content is merged and centered across the range A17:A20.

You can rotate content in a cell.

Sales Report - E

| FILE | HOME | INSERT | PAGE LAYOUT | FORMULAS | DATA | REVIEW | VI |

Calibri    11    A    A

B   I   U

Clipboard    Font    Alignment    Number

General

$ - %

A3    fx

| | A | B | C | D | E | F | G |
|---|---|---|---|---|---|---|---|
| 2 | *Big Flavor* , Small Price | | | | | | |
| 3 | | | | | | | |

The Alignment group has buttons for setting the horizontal and vertical alignment, the orientation, indents, and text wrapping of text in a cell, as well as merging cells.

| 4 | Sales Statistics | | | | | |
|---|---|---|---|---|---|---|
| 5 | Category | 2015 | 2014 | Net Change | % Change | |
| 6 | Gross Sales | $ 7,000,000 | $ 8,424,000 | $ (1,424,000) | -16.90% | |
| 7 | Cost of Sales | 3,374,000 | 2,784,000 | 590,000 | 21.19% | |
| 8 | Operating Expenses | 5,032,000 | 4,376,000 | 656,000 | 14.99% | |
| 9 | Net Profit/Loss | $ (1,406,000) | $ 1,264,000 | $ (2,670,000) | -211.23% | |
| 10 | | | | | | |

| 11 | 2015 Monthly Gross Sales | | | | | |
|---|---|---|---|---|---|---|
| 12 | State | Jan | Feb | Mar | Apr | May | Jun |
| 13 | Iowa | 26,000 | 24,000 | 27,000 | 28,000 | 29,000 | 32,( |
| 14 | | | | | | 51,000 | 53,000 | 54,( |
| 15 | | | | | | 47,000 | 47,000 | 51,( |
| 16 | | | | | | 27,000 | 28,000 | 29,8 |

The **Accounting format** lines up numbers within a column by their currency symbol and decimal point; negative numbers are enclosed in parentheses.

| 17 | Kansas | 44,000 | 43,000 | 48,000 | 50,000 | 51,000 | 54,( |
|---|---|---|---|---|---|---|---|
| 18 | | 29,000 | 26,000 | 30,000 | 31,000 | 35,000 | 34,( |
| 19 | | 20,000 | 21,000 | 24,000 | 25,000 | 28,000 | 27,( |
| 20 | | 46,000 | 43,000 | 52,000 | 51,000 | 54,000 | 54,( |
| 21 | Colorado | 38,000 | 35,000 | 43,000 | 42,000 | 44,000 | 44,( |
| 22 | Nebr | 27,000 | 28,( | | | | 37,8 |
| 23 | | 38,000 | 39,000 | 45,000 | 47,000 | 46,000 | 49,( |

The **Percent style** formats numbers as percentages with the % symbol after the number and no decimal places. You can change the number of decimal places that are displayed, as shown here.

Documentation    **Sales Report**    +

READY

# Worksheet with Formatting

eport - Excel    ? ☒ — 🗗 ✕

VIEW    Sign in 👤

🖩 Conditional Formatting ▾    🔻 Insert ▾    Σ ▾    A▾Z▾🝘
🖩 Format as Table ▾    🔻 Delete ▾    ▼ ▾    Sort & Find &
🖩 Cell Styles ▾    🖩 Format ▾    ♦ ▾    Filter ▾ Select ▾

% ’ ←.0 .00 .00 →.0

Number 🔲    Styles    Cells    Editing    ⌃

G    H    I    J    K    L

> The Number group has buttons for formatting numbers in the Accounting format, Percent style, and Comma style, as well as changing the number of decimal places displayed.

> A **fill color** is a background color that can be added to cells to help differentiate parts of a worksheet or highlight data.

| Jun | Jul | Aug | Sep | Oct | Nov |
|---|---|---|---|---|---|
| 32,000 | 33,000 | 34,000 | 30,000 | 32,000 | 30,000 |
| 54,000 | 54,000 | 58,000 | 54,000 | 55,000 | 51,000 |
| 51,000 | 52,000 | 54,000 | 50,000 | 49,000 | 46,000 |
| 29,000 | 32,000 | 30,000 | 30,000 | 28,000 | 27,000 |
| 54,000 | 54,000 | 55,000 | 54,000 | 52,000 | 51,000 |
| 34,000 | 37,000 | 37,000 | 34,000 | 34,000 | 34,000 |
| 27,000 | 27,000 | 29,000 | 24,000 | 26,000 | 24,000 |
| 54,000 | 58,000 | 58,000 | 55,000 | 54,000 | 50,000 |
| 44,000 | 47,000 | 48,000 | 47,000 | 48,000 | 44,000 |
|  |  |  |  |  |  |
| 37,000 | 37,000 | 38,000 | 35,000 | 33,000 | 35,000 |
| 49,000 | 51,000 | 49,000 | 47,000 | 49,000 | 47,000 |

> You can increase or decrease the number of decimal places that are displayed in a value. These values show no decimal places.

> The **Comma style** adds a thousands separator to numbers, adds two decimal places, and lines up values within a column by their decimal points. You can change the number of decimal places that are displayed, as shown here.

⊞ ▣ 🔲 − ▬▬▬▮▬▬▬ + 90%

# Formatting Cell Text

You can add formatting to a workbook by choosing its fonts, styles, colors, and decorative features. Formatting changes only the appearance of data—it does not affect the data itself. In Excel, formatting options are organized into themes. A **theme** is a collection of formatting for text, colors, and graphical effects that are applied throughout a workbook to create a specific look and feel. Each theme has a name. Although the Office theme is the default theme, you can apply other themes or create your own. You can also add formatting to a workbook using fonts and colors that are not part of the current theme.

As you format a workbook, galleries and Live Preview show how a workbook would be affected by a formatting selection. A **gallery** is a menu or grid that shows a visual representation of the options available for the selected button. As you point to options in a gallery, **Live Preview** shows the results of clicking each option. By pointing to different options, you can quickly see different results before selecting the format you want.

**PROSKILLS**

## Written Communication: Formatting Workbooks for Readability and Appeal

Designing a workbook requires the same care as designing any written document or report. A well-formatted workbook is easy to read and establishes a sense of professionalism with readers. Do the following to improve the appearance of your workbooks:

- **Clearly identify each worksheet's purpose.** Include column or row titles and a descriptive sheet name.
- **Include only one or two topics on each worksheet.** Don't crowd individual worksheets with too much information. Place extra topics on separate sheets. Readers should be able to interpret each worksheet with a minimal amount of horizontal and vertical scrolling.
- **Place worksheets with the most important information first in the workbook.** Position worksheets summarizing your findings near the front of the workbook. Position worksheets with detailed and involved analysis near the end as an appendix.
- **Use consistent formatting throughout the workbook.** If negative values appear in red on one worksheet, format them in the same way on all sheets. Also, be consistent in the use of thousands separators, decimal places, and percentages.
- **Pay attention to the format of the printed workbook.** Make sure your printouts are legible with informative headers and footers. Check that the content of the printout is scaled correctly to the page size, and that page breaks divide the information into logical sections.

Excel provides many formatting tools. However, too much formatting can be intrusive, overwhelm data, and make the document difficult to read. Remember that the goal of formatting is not simply to make a "pretty workbook," but also to accentuate important trends and relationships in the data. A well-formatted workbook should seamlessly convey your data to the reader. If the reader is thinking about how your workbook looks, it means he or she is not thinking about your data.

Sanjit has already entered the data and some formulas in a workbook, which is only a rough draft of what he wants to submit to the company. The Documentation sheet describes the workbook's purpose and content. The Sales Report sheet displays a summary of the previous year's sales including a table of monthly gross sales broken down by the 20 franchise stores. In its current form, the data is difficult to read and interpret. Sanjit wants you to format the contents of the workbook to improve its readability and visual appeal.

**To open the workbook:**

▶ **1.** Open the **Sales** workbook located in the Excel2 ▸ Tutorial folder included with your Data Files, and then save the workbook as **Sales Report** in the location specified by your instructor.

▶ **2.** In the Documentation sheet, enter your name in cell B4 and the date in cell B5.

## Applying Fonts and Font Styles

Excel organizes fonts into theme and non-theme fonts. A **theme font** is associated with a particular theme and used for headings and body text in the workbook. These fonts change automatically when you change the theme applied to the workbook. Text formatted with a **non-theme font** retains its appearance no matter what theme is used with the workbook.

Fonts appear in different character styles. **Serif fonts**, such as Times New Roman, have extra strokes at the end of each character that aid in reading passages of text. **Sans serif fonts**, such as Arial, do not include these extra strokes. Other fonts are purely decorative, such as a font used for specialized logos. Every font can be further formatted with a font style such as *italic*, **bold**, or ***bold italic***; with <u>underline</u>; and with special effects such as ~~strikethrough~~ and color. You can also increase or decrease the font size.

**REFERENCE**

### Formatting Cell Content

- To change the font, select the cell or range. On the HOME tab, in the Font group, click the Font arrow, and then click a font.
- To change the font size, select the cell or range. On the HOME tab, in the Font group, click the Font Size arrow, and then click a font size.
- To change a font style, select the cell or range. On the HOME tab, in the Font group, click the Bold, Italic, or Underline button.
- To change a font color, select the cell or range. On the HOME tab, in the Font group, click the Font Color button arrow, and then click a color.
- To format a text selection, double-click the cell to enter Edit mode, and then select the text to format. Change the font, size, style, or color, and then press the Enter key.

Sanjit wants the company name at the top of each worksheet to appear in large, bold letters using the default heading font from the Office theme. He wants the slogan "Big Flavor, Small Price" displayed below the company name to appear in the heading font, but in smaller, italicized letters.

**To format the company name and slogan in the Documentation sheet:**

▶ **1.** In the Documentation sheet, select cell **A1** to make it the active cell. The cell with the company name is selected.

▶ **2.** On the HOME tab, in the Font group, click the **Font button arrow** to display a gallery of fonts available on your computer. Each name is displayed in its corresponding font. When you point to a font in the gallery, Live Preview shows how the text in the selected cell will look with that font. The first two fonts are the theme fonts for headings and body text—Calibri Light and Calibri.

**3.** Point to **Algerian** (or another font) in the All Fonts list. Live Preview shows the effect of the Algerian font on the text in cell A1. See Figure 2-1.

**Figure 2-1**   **Font gallery**

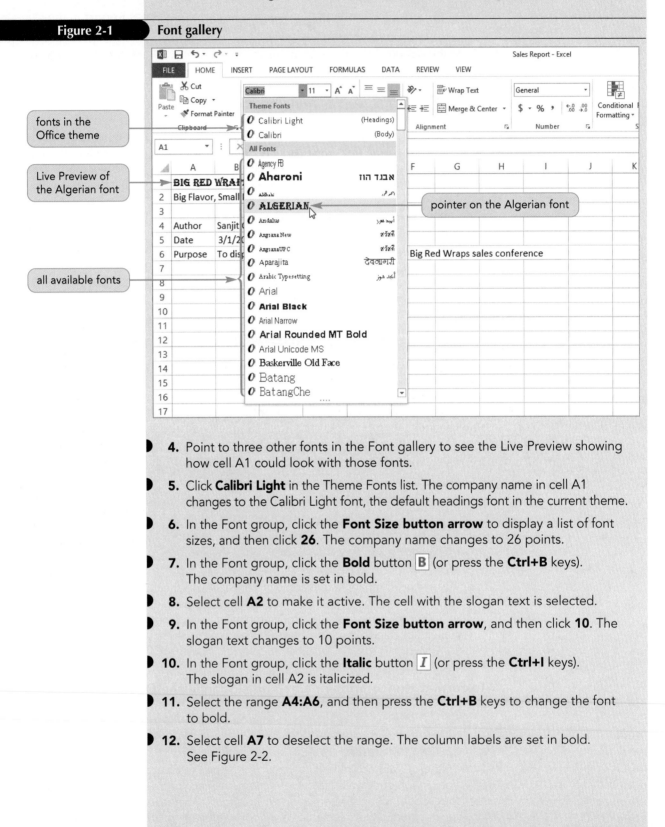

fonts in the Office theme

Live Preview of the Algerian font

all available fonts

pointer on the Algerian font

**4.** Point to three other fonts in the Font gallery to see the Live Preview showing how cell A1 could look with those fonts.

**5.** Click **Calibri Light** in the Theme Fonts list. The company name in cell A1 changes to the Calibri Light font, the default headings font in the current theme.

**6.** In the Font group, click the **Font Size button arrow** to display a list of font sizes, and then click **26**. The company name changes to 26 points.

**7.** In the Font group, click the **Bold** button B (or press the **Ctrl+B** keys). The company name is set in bold.

**8.** Select cell **A2** to make it active. The cell with the slogan text is selected.

**9.** In the Font group, click the **Font Size button arrow**, and then click **10**. The slogan text changes to 10 points.

**10.** In the Font group, click the **Italic** button I (or press the **Ctrl+I** keys). The slogan in cell A2 is italicized.

**11.** Select the range **A4:A6**, and then press the **Ctrl+B** keys to change the font to bold.

**12.** Select cell **A7** to deselect the range. The column labels are set in bold. See Figure 2-2.

**Figure 2-2**  **Formatted cell text**

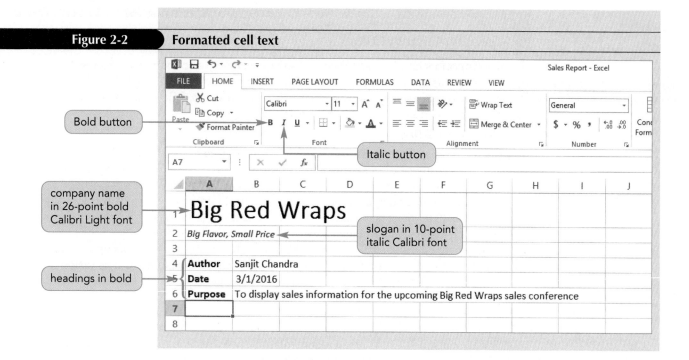

## Applying a Font Color

Color can transform a plain workbook filled with numbers and text into a powerful presentation that captures the user's attention and adds visual emphasis to the points you want to make. By default, Excel displays text in a black font color.

Like fonts, colors are organized into theme and non-theme colors. **Theme colors** are the 12 colors that belong to the workbook's theme. Four colors are designated for text and backgrounds, six colors are used for accents and highlights, and two colors are used for hyperlinks (followed and not followed links). These 12 colors are designed to work well together and to remain readable in all combinations. Each theme color has five variations, or accents, in which a different tint or shading is applied to the theme color.

Ten **standard colors**—dark red, red, orange, yellow, light green, green, light blue, blue, dark blue, and purple—are always available regardless of the workbook's theme. You can open an extended palette of 134 standard colors. You can also create a custom color by specifying a mixture of red, blue, and green color values, making available 16.7 million custom colors—more colors than the human eye can distinguish. Some dialog boxes have an automatic color option that uses your Windows default text and background colors, usually black text on a white background.

INSIGHT

## Creating Custom Colors

Custom colors let you add subtle and striking colors to a formatted workbook. To create custom colors, you use the **RGB Color model** in which each color is expressed with varying intensities of red, green, and blue. RGB color values are often represented as a set of numbers in the format

(*red*, *green*, *blue*)

where *red* is an intensity value assigned to red light, *green* is an intensity value assigned to green light, and *blue* is an intensity value assigned to blue light. The intensities are measured on a scale of 0 to 255—0 indicates no intensity (or the absence of the color) and 255 indicates the highest intensity. So, the RGB color value (255, 255, 0) represents a mixture of high-intensity red (255) and high-intensity green (255) with the absence of blue (0), which creates the color yellow.

To create colors in Excel using the RGB model, click the More Colors option located in a color menu or dialog box to open the Colors dialog box. In the Colors dialog box, click the Custom tab, and then enter the red, green, and blue intensity values. A preview box shows the resulting RGB color.

Sanjit wants the labels in the Documentation sheet to stand out, so you will change the Big Red Wraps company name and slogan to red.

## To change the company name and slogan font color:

1. Select the range **A1:A2**. The company name and slogan are selected.

2. On the HOME tab, in the Font group, click the **Font Color button arrow** to display the gallery of theme and standard colors. (The two colors for hyperlinked text are not shown.)

3. Point to the **Red** color (the second color) in the Standard Colors section. The color name appears in a ScreenTip and you see a Live Preview of the text with the red font color. See Figure 2-3.

**Figure 2-3** | **Font color gallery**

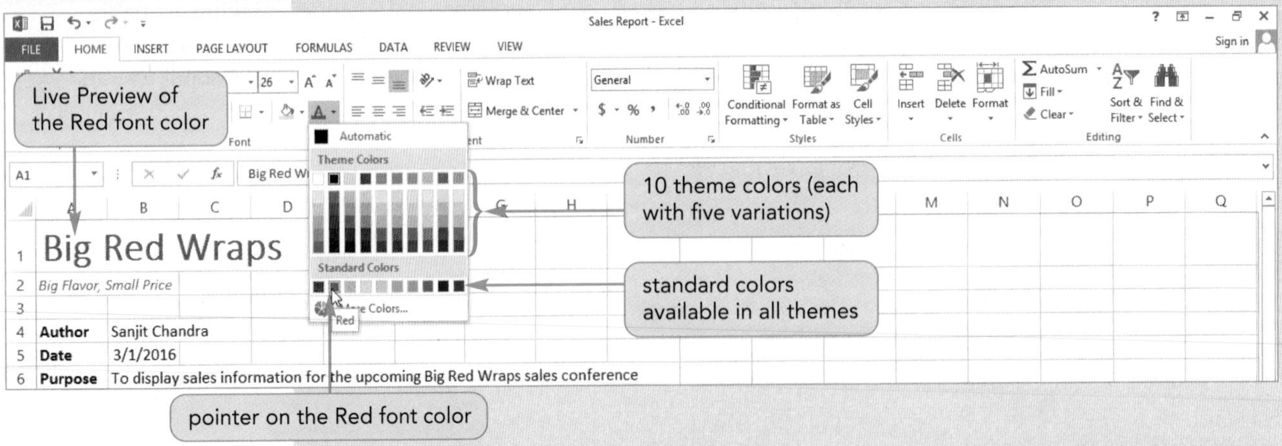

4. Click the **Red** color. The company name and slogan change to red.

## Formatting Text Selections

In Edit mode, you can select and format selections of text within a cell. When the Big Red Wraps slogan is used in marketing materials, "Big Flavor" is set slightly larger than "Small Price." Sanjit wants you to recreate this effect in the workbook by increasing the font size of "Big Flavor" while leaving the rest of the text unchanged. You will use Edit mode to apply a different format to part of the cell text.

### To format part of the company slogan:

1. Double-click cell **A2** to select the cell and enter Edit mode (or click cell **A2** and press the **F2** key). The status bar shows EDIT to indicate that you are working with the cell in Edit mode. The pointer changes to the I-beam pointer.

2. Drag the pointer over the phrase **Big Flavor** to select it. The Mini toolbar appears above the selected text with buttons to change the font, size, style, and color of the selected text in the cell. See Figure 2-4.

**Figure 2-4** | **Mini toolbar in Edit mode**

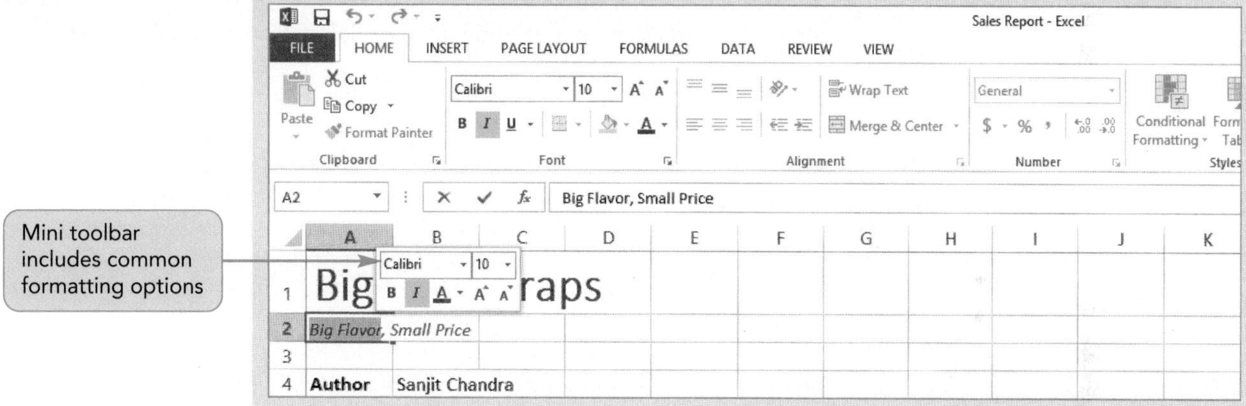

3. On the Mini toolbar, click the **Font Size button arrow**, and then click **14**. The font size of the selected text increases to 14 points.

4. Select cell **A7** to deselect cell A2. See Figure 2-5.

**Figure 2-5** | **Formatted text selection**

# Working with Fill Colors and Backgrounds

Another way to distinguish sections of a worksheet is by formatting the cell background. You can fill the cell background with color or an image. Sanjit wants you to add fill colors and background images to the Documentation worksheet.

**INSIGHT**

### Using Color to Enhance a Workbook

When used wisely, color can enhance any workbook. However, when used improperly, color can distract the user, making the workbook more difficult to read. As you format a workbook, keep in mind the following tips:

- Use colors from the same theme to maintain a consistent look and feel across the worksheets. If the built-in themes do not fit your needs, you can create a custom theme.
- Use colors to differentiate types of cell content and to direct users where to enter data. For example, format a worksheet so that formula results appear in cells without a fill color and users enter data in cells with a light gray fill color.
- Avoid color combinations that are difficult to read.
- Print the workbook on both color and black-and-white printers to ensure that the printed copy is readable in both versions.
- Understand your printer's limitations and features. Colors that look good on your monitor might not look as good when printed.
- Be sensitive to your audience. About 8 percent of all men and 0.5 percent of all women have some type of color blindness and might not be able to see the text when certain color combinations are used. Red-green color blindness is the most common, so avoid using red text on a green background or green text on a red background.

## Changing a Fill Color

**TIP**

You can also change a sheet tab's color. Right-click a sheet tab, point to Tab Color on the shortcut menu, and then click a color.

By default, worksheet cells do not include any background color. But background colors, also known as fill colors, can be helpful for distinguishing different parts of a worksheet or adding visual interest. You add fill colors to selected cells in the worksheet from the Fill Color gallery, which has the same options as the Font Color gallery.

Sanjit wants the labels and text in the Documentation sheet to stand out. You will format the labels in a white font on a red background, and then you'll format the author's name, current date, and purpose of the worksheet in a red font on a white background.

### To change the fill and font colors in the Documentation worksheet:

1. Select the range **A4:A6**.

2. On the HOME tab, in the Font group, click the **Fill Color button arrow** 🎨 ▾, and then click the **Red** color (the second color) in the Standard Colors section.

3. In the Font group, click the **Font Color button arrow** 𝐀 ▾, and then click the **White, Background 1** color in the Theme Colors section. The labels are formatted in white text on a red background.

4. Select the range **B4:B6**, and then format the cells with a red font and a white background.

5. Increase the width of column B to **30** characters, and then wrap the text in the selected range.

6. Select the range **A4:B6**, and then add all borders around each of the selected cells.

7. Click cell **A7** to deselect the range. See Figure 2-6.

| Figure 2-6 | Font and fill colors in the Documentation sheet |
| --- | --- |

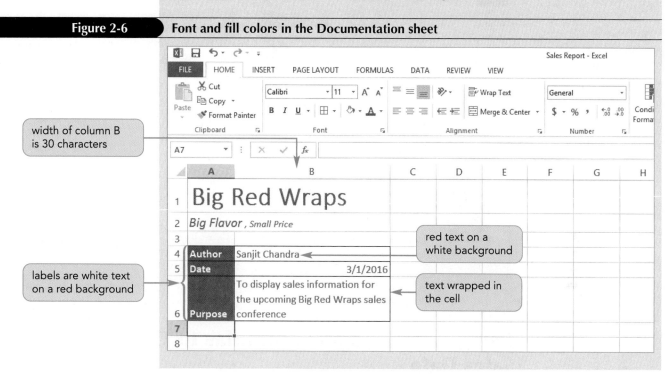

width of column B is 30 characters

red text on a white background

labels are white text on a red background

text wrapped in the cell

## Adding a Background Image

A background image can provide a textured appearance, like that of granite, wood, or fibered paper, to a worksheet. The image is repeated until it fills the entire sheet. The background image does not affect any cell's format or content. Fill colors added to cells appear on top of the image, covering that portion of the image. Background images are visible only on the screen; they do not print.

Sanjit has provided an image that he wants you to use as the background of the Documentation sheet.

### To add a background image to the Documentation sheet:

1. On the ribbon, click the **PAGE LAYOUT** tab to display the page layout options.

2. In the Page Setup group, click the **Background** button. The Insert Pictures dialog box opens with options to select a picture from a file, select Office.com Clip Art, or perform a Bing Image Search.

3. Click the **Browse** button next to the From a file label. The Sheet Background dialog box opens.

4. Navigate to the **Excel2 ▸ Tutorial** folder included with your Data Files, click the **Background** JPEG image file, and then click the **Insert** button. The image is added to the background of the Documentation sheet, and the Background button changes to the Delete Background button, which you can use to remove the background image. See Figure 2-7.

**Figure 2-7**    **Background image in the Documentation sheet**

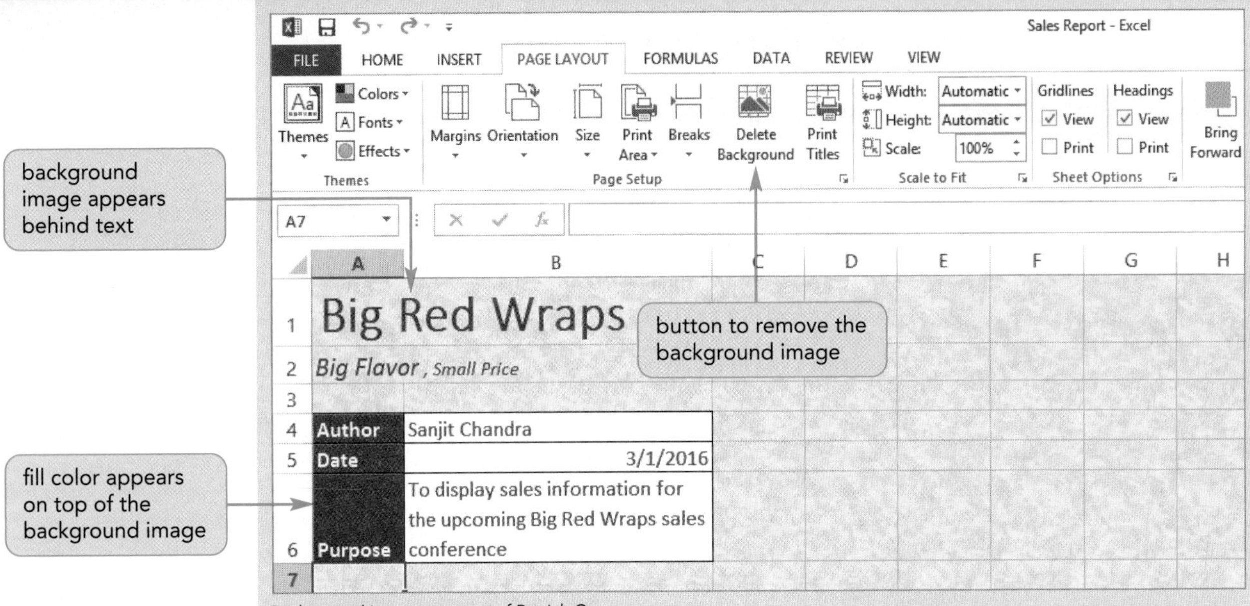

background image appears behind text

button to remove the background image

fill color appears on top of the background image

Background image courtesy of Patrick Carey

# Using Functions and Formulas to Calculate Sales Data

In the Sales Report worksheet, you will format the gross sales from each of the store's 20 restaurants and the summary statistics for those stores. The Sales Report worksheet is divided into two areas. The table at the bottom of the worksheet displays gross sales for the past year for each month by restaurant. The section at the top of the worksheet summarizes the sales data for the past two years. Sanjit collected the following sales data:

- **Gross Sales**—the total amount of sales at all of the restaurants
- **Cost of Sales**—the cost of producing the store's menu items
- **Operating Expenses**—the cost of running the stores including the employment and insurance costs
- **Net Profit/Loss**—the difference between the income from the gross sales and the total cost of sales and operating expenses
- **Units Sold**—the total number of menu items sold by the company during the year
- **Customers Served**—the total number of customers served by the company during the year

Sanjit wants you to calculate these sales statistics for the entire company and per store so he can track how well the stores are performing. First, you will calculate the total gross sales for Big Red Wraps and the company's overall net profit and loss.

### To calculate the company's sales and profit/loss:

1. Click the **Sales Report** sheet tab to make the Sales Report worksheet active.

**2.** Click cell **C6**, type the formula **=SUM(C27:N46)** to calculate the total gross sales from all stores in the previous year, and then press the **Enter** key. Cell C6 displays 9514000, which means that Big Red Wraps' total gross sales for the previous year were more than $9.5 million.

**TIP**

To enter content in a cell, you select the cell, type the specified content, and then press the Enter key.

**3.** In cell **C9**, enter the formula **=C6–(C7+C8)** to calculate the current year's net profit/loss, which is equal to the difference between the gross sales and the sum of the cost of sales and operating expenses. Cell C9 displays 1108000, which means that the company's net profit for 2015 was more than $1.1 million.

**4.** Copy the formula in cell **C9**, and then paste it into cell **D9** to calculate the net profit/loss for 2014. Cell D9 displays 1264000, which means that the company's net profit for that year was more than $1.26 million.

Next, Sanjit asks you to summarize the sales statistics for each store. Sanjit wants the same per-store statistics calculated for the 2015 and 2014 sales data. Per-store sales statistics are calculated by dividing the overall statistics by the number of stores. In this case, you will divide the overall statistics by the value in cell C23, which contains the total number of stores in the Big Red Wraps chain. After you enter the 2015 formulas, you can copy and paste them to calculate the 2014 results.

### To calculate the per-store statistics:

**1.** In cell **C16**, enter the formula **=C6/C23** to calculate the gross sales per store in 2015. The formula returns 475700, which means that the annual gross sales amount for a Big Red Wraps store in 2015 was more than $475,000.

**2.** In cell **C17**, enter the formula **=C7/C23** to calculate the cost of sales per store in 2015. The formula returns the value 168700, which means that the cost of sales for a Big Red Wraps store in 2015 was typically $168,700.

**3.** In cell **C18**, enter the formula **=C8/C23** to calculate the operating expenses per store in 2015. The formula returns the value 251600, which means that operating expenses of a typical store in 2015 were $251,600.

**4.** In cell **C19**, enter the formula **=C9/C23** to calculate the net profit/loss per store in 2015. The formula returns the value 55400, indicating that the net profit/loss of a typical store in 2015 was $55,400.

**5.** In cell **C21**, enter the formula **=C11/C23** to calculate the units sold per store in 2015. The formula returns the value 67200, indicating that a typical store sold 67,200 units during 2015.

**6.** In cell **C22**, enter the formula **=C12/C23** to calculate the customers served per store in 2015. The formula returns the value 7770, indicating that a typical store served 7,770 customers during that year.

**7.** Copy the formulas in the range **C16:C22** and paste them into the range **D16:D22**. The cell references in the formulas change to calculate the sales data for the year 2014.

**8.** Select cell **B24** to deselect the range. See Figure 2-8.

**Figure 2-8**    Sales statistics for the entire company and per store

overall store sales statistics

per-store sales statistics are calculated by dividing the overall statistics by the number of stores

| | A | B | C | D | E | F | G | H | I |
|---|---|---|---|---|---|---|---|---|---|
| 5 | | Category | 2015 | 2014 | Net Change | % Change | | | |
| 6 | | Gross Sales | 9514000 | 8424000 | | | | | |
| 7 | | Cost of Sales | 3374000 | 2784000 | | | | | |
| 8 | | Operating Expenses | 5032000 | 4376000 | | | | | |
| 9 | | Net Profit/Loss | 1108000 | 1264000 | | | | | |
| 10 | | | | | | | | | |
| 11 | | Units Sold | 1344000 | 1104000 | | | | | |
| 12 | | Customers Served | 155400 | 129600 | | | | | |
| 13 | | | | | | | | | |
| 14 | | Sales Statistics per Store | | | | | | | |
| 15 | | Category | 2015 | 2014 | Net Change | % Change | | | |
| 16 | | Gross Sales | 475700 | 526500 | | | | | |
| 17 | | Cost of Sales | 168700 | 174000 | | | | | |
| 18 | | Operating Expenses | 251600 | 273500 | | | | | |
| 19 | | Net Profit/Loss | 55400 | 79000 | | | | | |
| 20 | | | | | | | | | |
| 21 | | Units Sold | 67200 | 69000 | | | | | |
| 22 | | Customers Served | 7770 | 8100 | | | | | |
| 23 | | Stores | 20 | 16 | | | | | |

Documentation    **Sales Report**

number of stores in 2014 and 2015

READY

Sanjit also wants to explore how the company's sales and expenses have changed from 2014 to 2015. To do this, you will calculate the net change in sales from 2014 to 2015 as well as the percent change. The percent change is calculated using the following formula:

$$percent\ change = \frac{2015\ value - 2014\ value}{2014\ value}$$

You will calculate the net and percent changes for all of the sales statistics.

### To calculate the net and percent changes for 2015 and 2014:

1. In cell **E6**, enter the formula **=C6–D6** to calculate the difference between the 2015 and 2014 gross sales. The formula returns 1090000, indicating that gross sales increased by $1.09 million between 2014 and 2015.

Be sure to include the parentheses as shown to calculate the percent change correctly.

2. In cell **F6**, enter the formula **=(C6–D6)/D6** to calculate the percent change in gross sales from 2014 to 2015. The formula returns 0.129392213, indicating a nearly 13% increase in gross sales from 2014 to 2015.

   Next, you'll copy and paste the formulas in cells E6 and F6 to the rest of the sales data to calculate the net change and percent change from 2014 to 2015.

3. Select the range **E6:F6**, and then copy the selected range. The two formulas are copied to the Clipboard.

4. Select the nonadjacent range **E7:F9;E11:F12;E16:F19;E21:F23**, and then paste the formulas from the Clipboard into the selected range. The net and percent changes are calculated for the remaining sales data.

5. Click cell **B24** to deselect the range, and then scroll the worksheet up to display row 5. See Figure 2-9.

| Figure 2-9 | Net and percent changes calculated |
| --- | --- |

column E displays the change in sales values from 2014 to 2015

| | A | B | C | D | E | F | G | H | I | J | K |
| --- | --- | --- | --- | --- | --- | --- | --- | --- | --- | --- | --- |
| 5 | | Category | 2015 | 2014 | Net Change | % Change | | | | | |
| 6 | | Gross Sales | 9514000 | 8424000 | 1090000 | 0.129392213 | | | | | |
| 7 | | Cost of Sales | 3374000 | 2784000 | 590000 | 0.211925287 | | | | | |
| 8 | | Operating Expenses | 5032000 | 4376000 | 656000 | 0.149908592 | | | | | |
| 9 | | Net Profit/Loss | 1108000 | 1264000 | -156000 | -0.12341772 | | | | | |
| 10 | | | | | | | | | | | |
| 11 | | Units Sold | 1344000 | 1104000 | 240000 | 0.217391304 | | | | | |
| 12 | | Customers Served | 155400 | 129600 | 25800 | 0.199074074 | | | | | |
| 13 | | | | | | | | | | | |
| 14 | | Sales Statistics per Store | | | | | | | | | |
| 15 | | Category | 2015 | 2014 | Net Change | % Change | | | | | |
| 16 | | Gross Sales | 475700 | 526500 | -50800 | -0.09648623 | | | | | |
| 17 | | Cost of Sales | 168700 | 174000 | -5300 | -0.03045977 | | | | | |
| 18 | | Operating Expenses | 251600 | 273500 | -21900 | -0.08007313 | | | | | |
| 19 | | Net Profit/Loss | 55400 | 79000 | -23600 | -0.29873418 | | | | | |
| 20 | | | | | | | | | | | |
| 21 | | Units Sold | 67200 | 69000 | -1800 | -0.02608696 | | | | | |
| 22 | | Customers Served | 7770 | 8100 | -330 | -0.04074074 | | | | | |
| 23 | | Stores | 20 | 16 | 4 | 0.25 | | | | | |

Documentation    Sales Report

READY    120%

column F displays the percent change in sales values from 2014 to 2015

percentages are displayed as decimals

The bottom part of the worksheet contains the sales for each restaurant from 2015. You will use the SUM function to calculate the total gross sales for each restaurant during the entire year, the total monthly sales of all 20 restaurants, and the total gross sales of all restaurants and months.

## To calculate different subtotals of the gross sales:

1. Select cell **O26**, type **TOTAL** as the label, and then press the **Enter** key. Cell O27 is now the active cell.

2. On the HOME tab, in the Editing group, click the **AutoSum** button, and then press the **Enter** key to accept the suggested range reference and enter the formula =SUM(C27:N27) in cell O27. The cell displays 355000, indicating gross sales in 2015 for the 411 Elm Drive restaurant were $355,000.

3. Copy the formula in cell **O27**, and then paste that formula into the range **O28:O46** to calculate the total sales for each of the remaining 19 restaurants in the Big Red Wraps chain.

4. Select cell **B47**, type **TOTAL** as the label, and then press the **Tab** key. Cell C47 is now the active cell.

5. Select the range **C47:O47** so that you can calculate the total monthly sales for all of the stores.

6. On the HOME tab, in the Editing group, click the **AutoSum** button, and then press the **Enter** key to calculate the total sales for each month as well as the total sales for all months. For example, cell C47 displays 680000, indicating that monthly sales for January 2015 for all stores were $680,000.

7. Select cell **O48** to deselect the range. See Figure 2-10.

Figure 2-10    **Gross sales summarized by store and month**

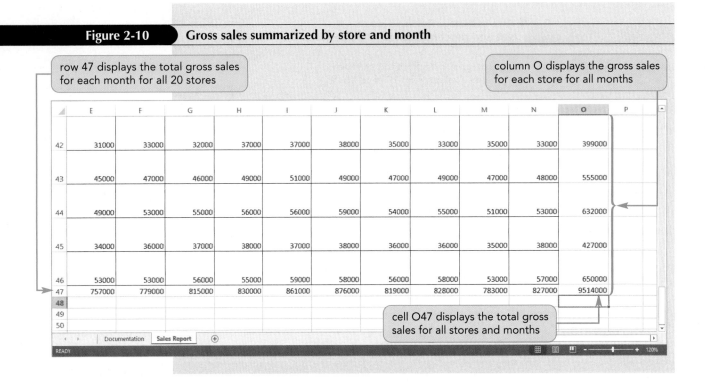

row 47 displays the total gross sales for each month for all 20 stores

column O displays the gross sales for each store for all months

cell O47 displays the total gross sales for all stores and months

# Formatting Numbers

The goal in formatting any workbook is to make the content easier to interpret. For numbers, this can mean adding a comma to separate thousands, setting the number of decimal places, and using percentage and currency symbols to make numbers easier to read and understand. Sanjit asks you to format the numbers in the Sales Report worksheet to improve their readability.

## Applying Number Formats

You can use a number format to display values in a way that makes them easier to read and understand. Changing the number format of the displayed value does not affect the stored value. Numbers are originally formatted in the **General format**, which, for the most part, displays numbers exactly as they are typed. If the number is calculated from a formula or function, the cell displays as many digits after the decimal point as will fit in the cell with the last digit rounded. Calculated values too large to fit into the cell are displayed in scientific notation.

The General format is fine for small numbers, but some values require additional formatting to make the numbers easier to interpret. For example, you might want to:

• Change the number of digits displayed to the right of the decimal point
• Add commas to separate thousands in large numbers
• Apply currency symbols to numbers to identify the monetary unit being used
• Display percentages using the % symbol

**TIP**

To apply the Currency format, click the Number Format button arrow and click Currency, or press the Ctrl+Shift+$ keys.

Excel supports two monetary formats: currency and accounting. Both formats add a thousands separator to the currency values and display two digits to the right of the decimal point. However, the **Currency format** places a currency symbol directly to the left of the first digit of the currency value and displays negative numbers with a negative sign. The **Accounting format** fixes a currency symbol at the left edge of the column, and displays negative numbers within parentheses and zero values with a dash. It also slightly indents the values from the right edge of the cell to allow room for parentheses around negative values. Figure 2-11 compares the two formats.

**Figure 2-11**     **Currency and Accounting number formats**

| Currency Format | Accounting Format |
|---|---|
| $95,000.00 | $            95,000.00 |
| -$3,300.00 | $            (3,300.00) |
| $0.00 | $                       - |
| $1,108.00 | $              1,108.00 |

- negative values displayed with a negative sign
- $ symbols placed to the left of the leading digit
- negative values displayed in parentheses
- zeros displayed with a dash
- $ symbols fixed on the left edge of the cell
- values slightly indented from the right cell edge

## PROSKILLS

### Written Communication: Formatting Monetary Values

Spreadsheets commonly include monetary values. To make these values simpler to read and comprehend, keep in mind the following guidelines when formatting the currency data in a worksheet:

- **Format for your audience.** For general financial reports, round values to the nearest hundred, thousand, or million. Investors are generally more interested in the big picture than in exact values. However, for accounting reports, accuracy is important and often legally required. So, for those reports, be sure to display the exact monetary value.
- **Use thousands separators.** Large strings of numbers can be challenging to read. For monetary values, use a thousands separator to make the amounts easier to comprehend.
- **Apply the Accounting format to columns of monetary values.** The Accounting format makes columns of numbers easier to read than the Currency format. Use the Currency format for individual cells that are not part of long columns of numbers.
- **Use only two currency symbols in a column of monetary values.** Standard accounting format displays one currency symbol with the first monetary value in the column, and optionally displays a second currency symbol with the last value in that column. Use the Accounting format to fix the currency symbols, lining them up within the column.

Following these standard accounting principles will make your financial data easier to read both on the screen and in printouts.

Sanjit wants you to format the gross sales amounts in the Accounting format so that they are easier to read.

### To format the gross sales in the Accounting format:

**1.** Select the range **C6:E6** with the gross sales.

**2.** On the HOME tab, in the Number group, click the **Accounting Number Format** button $. The numbers are formatted in the Accounting format. You cannot see the format because the cells display ##########.

The cells display ########## because the formatted number doesn't fit into the column. One reason for this is that monetary values, by default, show both dollars and cents in the cell. However, you can increase or decrease the number of decimal places displayed in a cell. The displayed value might then be rounded. For example, the stored value 11.7 will appear in the cell as 12 if no decimal places are displayed to the right of the decimal point. Changing the number of decimal places displayed in a cell does not change the value stored in the cell.

Because Sanjit and the other conference attendees are interested only in whole dollar amounts, he wants you to hide the cents values of the gross sales by decreasing the number of decimal places to zero.

### To decrease the number of decimal places displayed in the gross sales:

**1.** Make sure the range **C6:E6** is selected.

**2.** On the HOME tab, in the Number group, click the **Decrease Decimal** button .00→.0 twice. The cents are hidden for gross sales.

**3.** Select cell **C4** to deselect the range. See Figure 2-12.

**Figure 2-12**    Formatted gross sales values

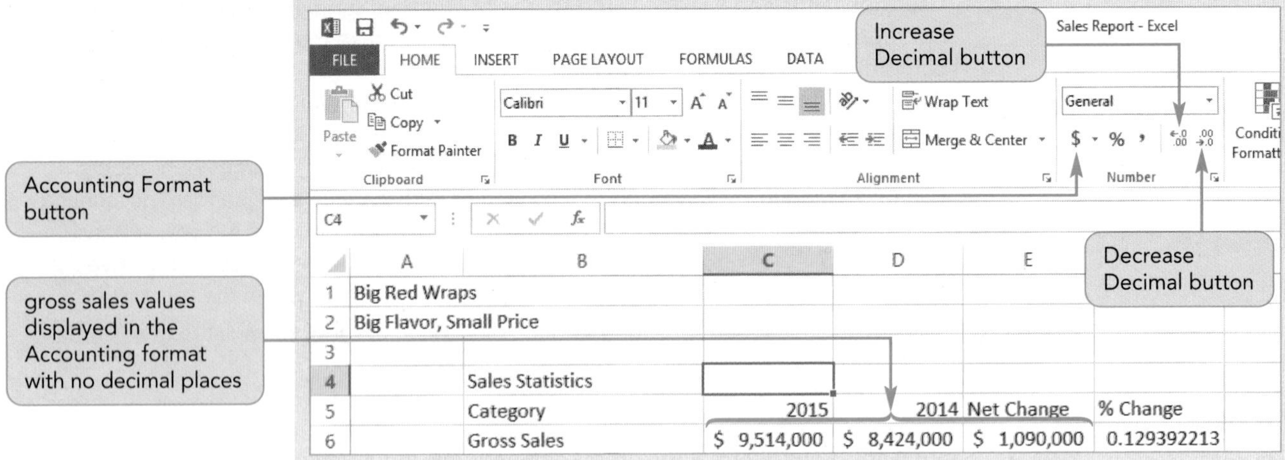

The Comma style is identical to the Accounting format except that it does not fix a currency symbol to the left of the number. The advantage of using the Comma style and the Accounting format together is that the numbers will be aligned in the column.

Sanjit asks you to apply the Comma style to the remaining sales statistics.

### To apply the Comma style to the sales statistics:

▶ 1. Select the nonadjacent range **C7:E9;C11:E12** containing the sales figures for all stores in 2014 and 2015.

▶ 2. On the HOME tab, in the Number group, click the **Comma Style** button. In some instances, the number is now too large to be displayed in the cell.

▶ 3. In the Number group, click the **Decrease Decimal** button twice to remove two decimal places. Digits to the right of the decimal point are hidden for all of the selected cells.

▶ 4. Select cell **C13** to deselect the range. See Figure 2-13.

| Figure 2-13 | Formatted sales values |
|---|---|

numbers with the Accounting format and no decimal places

numbers with the Comma style and no decimal places

numbers aligned within each column

| | | | | | |
|---|---|---|---|---|---|
| 4 | Sales Statistics | | | | |
| 5 | Category | 2015 | 2014 | Net Change | % Change |
| 6 | Gross Sales | $ 9,514,000 | $ 8,424,000 | $ 1,090,000 | 0.129392213 |
| 7 | Cost of Sales | 3,374,000 | 2,784,000 | 590,000 | 0.211925287 |
| 8 | Operating Expenses | 5,032,000 | 4,376,000 | 656,000 | 0.149908592 |
| 9 | Net Profit/Loss | 1,108,000 | 1,264,000 | (156,000) | -0.12341772 |
| 10 | | | | | |
| 11 | Units Sold | 1,344,000 | 1,104,000 | 240,000 | 0.217391304 |
| 12 | Customers Served | 155,400 | 129,600 | 25,800 | 0.199074074 |
| 13 | | | | | |
| 14 | Sales Statistics per Store | | | | |
| 15 | Category | 2015 | 2014 | Net Change | % Change |
| 16 | Gross Sales | 475700 | 526500 | -50800 | -0.09648623 |
| 17 | Cost of Sales | 168700 | 174000 | -5300 | -0.03045977 |
| 18 | Operating Expenses | 251600 | 273500 | -21900 | -0.08007313 |
| 19 | Net Profit/Loss | 55400 | 79000 | -23600 | -0.29873418 |

Documentation | **Sales Report**

READY

The Percent style formats numbers as percentages. When you format values as percentages, the % symbol appears after the number and no digits appear to the right of the decimal point. You can always change how many decimal places are displayed in the cell if that is important to show with your data.

Sanjit wants you to format the percent change from the 2014 to 2015 sales statistics with a percent symbol to make the percent values easier to read.

### To format percentages:

▶ 1. Select the nonadjacent range **F6:F9;F11:F12** containing the percent change values.

▶ 2. On the HOME tab, in the Number group, click the **Percent Style** button (or press the **Ctrl+Shift+%** keys). The values are displayed as percentages.

▶ 3. In the Number group, click the **Increase Decimal** button twice. The displayed number includes two decimal places.

▶ 4. Select cell **F13** to deselect the range. See Figure 2-14.

**Figure 2-14**    **Formatted percent changes**

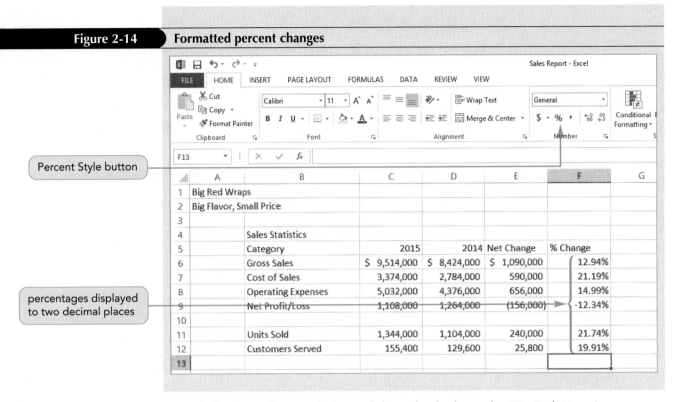

With the data reformatted, the worksheet clearly shows that Big Red Wraps' gross sales increased from 2014 to 2015 by almost 13 percent. However, both the cost of sales and the operating expenses increased by about 21.2 percent and 15 percent, respectively, probably due to the cost of building four new stores. As a result, the company's net profit decreased by $156,000 or about 12.3 percent.

## Formatting Dates and Times

**TIP**

To view the underlying date and time value, apply the General format to the cell or display the formulas instead of the formula results.

Because Excel stores dates and times as numbers and not as text, you can apply different formats without affecting the date and time value. The abbreviated format, *mm/dd/yyyy*, entered in the Documentation sheet is referred to as the **Short Date format**. You can also apply a **Long Date format** that displays the day of the week and the full month name in addition to the day of the month and the year. Other built-in formats include formats for displaying time values in 12- or 24-hour time format.

You will change the date in the Documentation sheet to the Long Date format.

### To format the date in the Long Date format:

1. Go to the **Documentation** sheet, and then select cell **B5**.

2. On the ribbon, make sure the HOME tab is displayed.

3. In the Number group, click the **Number Format button arrow** to display a list of number formats, and then click **Long Date**. The date is displayed with the weekday name, month name, day, and year. Notice that the date in the formula bar did not change because you changed only the display format, not the date value.

# Formatting Worksheet Cells

You can format the appearance of individual cells by modifying the alignment of text within the cell, indenting cell text, or adding borders of different styles and colors.

## Aligning Cell Content

By default, text is aligned with the left and bottom borders of a cell, and numbers are aligned with the right and bottom borders. You might want to change the alignment to make the text and numbers more readable or visually appealing. In general, you should center column titles, left-align other text, and right-align numbers to keep their decimal places lined up within a column. Figure 2-15 describes the buttons you use to set these alignment options, which are located in the Alignment group on the HOME tab.

| Figure 2-15 | Alignment buttons |
| --- | --- |

| Button | Name | Description |
| --- | --- | --- |
| | Top Align | Aligns the cell content with the cell's top edge |
| | Middle Align | Vertically centers the cell content within the cell |
| | Bottom Align | Aligns the cell content with the cell's bottom edge |
| | Align Left | Aligns the cell content with the cell's left edge |
| | Center | Horizontally centers the cell content within the cell |
| | Align Right | Aligns the cell content with the cell's right edge |
| | Decrease Indent | Decreases the size of the indentation used in the cell |
| | Increase Indent | Increases the size of the indentation used in the cell |
| | Orientation | Rotates the cell content to any angle within the cell |
| | Wrap Text | Forces the cell text to wrap within the cell borders |
| | Merge & Center | Merges the selected cells into a single cell |

© 2014 Cengage Learning

The date in the Documentation sheet is right-aligned in the cell because Excel treats dates and times as numbers. Sanjit wants you to left-align the date and center the column titles in the Sales Report worksheet.

### To left-align the date and center the column titles:

▶  **1.** In the Documentation sheet, make sure cell **B5** is still selected.

▶  **2.** On the HOME tab, in the Alignment group, click the **Align Left** button ☰. The date shifts to the left edge of the cell.

▶  **3.** Make the **Sales Report** worksheet the active worksheet.

▶  **4.** Select the range **C5:F5**. The column titles are selected.

▶  **5.** In the Alignment group, click the **Center** button ☰. The column titles are centered in the cells.

## Indenting Cell Content

Sometimes you want a cell's content moved a few spaces from the cell's left edge. This is particularly useful to create subsections in a worksheet or to set off some entries from others. You can increase the indent to shift the contents of a cell away from the left edge of the cell, or you can decrease the indent to shift a cell's contents closer to the left edge of the cell.

Sanjit wants the Cost of Sales and Operating Expenses labels in the sales statistics table offset from the other labels because they represent expenses to the company. You will increase the indent for the expense categories.

**To indent the expense categories:**

▶ 1. Select the range **B7:B8** containing the expense categories.

▶ 2. On the HOME tab, in the Alignment group, click the **Increase Indent** button ▦ twice to indent each label two spaces in its cell.

## Adding Cell Borders

Common accounting practices provide guidelines on when to add borders to cells. In general, a single black border appears above a subtotal, a single bottom border is added below a calculated number, and a double black bottom border appears below the total.

Sanjit wants you to follow these common accounting practices in the Sales Report worksheet. You will add borders below the column titles and below the gross sales values. You will add a top border to the net profit/loss values. Finally, you will add a top and bottom border to the Units Sold and Customers Served rows.

**To add borders to the sales statistics data:**

▶ 1. Select the range **B5:F5** containing the table headings.

▶ 2. On the HOME tab, in the Font group, click the **All Borders button arrow** ▦ ▾, and then click **Bottom Border**. A border is added below the column titles.

▶ 3. Select the range **B6:F6** containing the gross sales amounts.

▶ 4. In the Font group, click the **Bottom Border** button ▦ to add a border below the selected gross sales amounts.

▶ 5. Select the range **B9:F9**, click the **Bottom Border button arrow** ▦ ▾, and then click **Top Border** to add a border above the net profit/loss amounts.

The Units Sold and Customers Served rows do not contain monetary values as the other rows do. You will distinguish these rows by adding a top and bottom border.

▶ 6. Select the range **B11:F12**, click the **Top Border button arrow** ▦ ▾, and then click **Top and Bottom** to add a border above the number of units sold and below the number of customers served.

▶ 7. Select cell **B3** to deselect the range. See Figure 2-16.

**Figure 2-16**    **Worksheet with formatted cells**

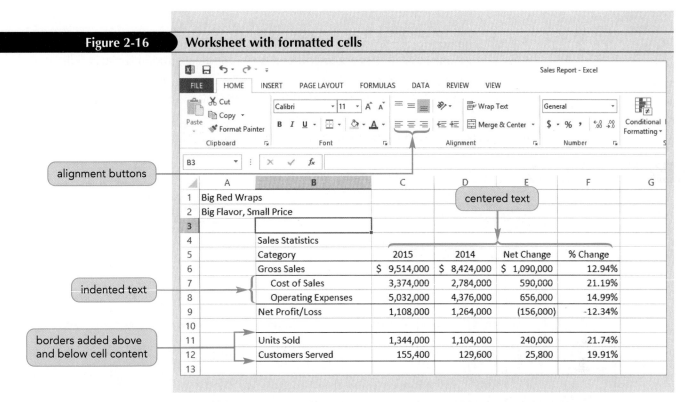

You can apply multiple formats to the same cell to create the look that best fits the data. For example, one cell might be formatted with a number format, alignments, borders, indents, fonts, font sizes, and so on. The monthly sales data needs to be formatted with number styles, alignment, indents, and borders. You'll add these formats now.

### To format the monthly sales table:

**1.** Click the **Name** box to select the cell reference, type **C27:O47**, and then press the **Enter** key to quickly select the range C27:O47 containing the monthly gross sales for each restaurant.

**2.** On the HOME tab, in the Number group, click the **Comma Style** button to add a thousands separator to the values.

**3.** In the Number group, click the **Decrease Decimal** button twice to hide the cents from the sales results.

**4.** In the Alignment group, click the **Top Align** button to align the sales numbers with the top of each cell.

**5.** Select the range **C26:O26** containing the labels for the month abbreviations and the TOTAL column.

**6.** In the Alignment group, click the **Center** button to center the column labels.

**7.** Select the range **B27:B46** containing the store addresses.

**8.** Reduce the font size of the store addresses to **9** points.

**9.** In the Alignment group, click the **Increase Indent** button to indent the store addresses.

**10.** In the Alignment group, click the **Top Align** button to align the addresses at the top of each cell.

**11.** Select the range **B47:O47** containing the monthly totals.

▶ **12.** In the Font group, click the **Top and Bottom Borders button arrow** ⊞ ▾, and then click **All Borders** to add borders around each monthly totals cell.

▶ **13.** Select the range **O26:O46**, which contains the annual totals for each restaurant, and then click the **All Borders** button ⊞ to add borders around each restaurant total.

▶ **14.** Select cell **A24** to deselect the range. See Figure 2-17.

| Figure 2-17 | Formatted monthly gross sales figures |

address text is 9 points

thousands separators displayed

## Merging Cells

You can merge, or combine, several cells into one cell. A merged cell contains two or more cells with a single cell reference. When you merge cells, only the content from the upper-left cell in the range is retained. The cell reference for the merged cell is the upper-left cell reference. So, if you merge cells A1 and A2, the merged cell reference is cell A1. After you merge cells, you can align the content within the merged cell. The Merge & Center button in the Alignment group on the HOME tab includes the following options:

• **Merge & Center**—merges the range into one cell and horizontally centers the content
• **Merge Across**—merges each row in the selected range across the columns in the range
• **Merge Cells**—merges the range into a single cell, but does not horizontally center the cell content
• **Unmerge Cells**—reverses a merge, returning the merged cell to a range of individual cells

The first column of the monthly sales data lists the states in which Big Red Wraps has stores. You will merge the cells for each state name.

### To merge the state name cells:

▶ **1.** Select the range **A27:A33** containing the cells for the Wisconsin stores. You will merge these seven cells into a single cell.

> **2.** On the HOME tab, in the Alignment group, click the **Merge & Center** button. The range A27:A33 merges into one cell with the cell reference A27, and the text is centered and bottom-aligned within the cell.

> **3.** Select the range **A34:A36**, and then click the **Merge & Center** button in the Alignment group to merge and center the Minnesota cells.

> **4.** Select the range **A37:A40**, and then click the **Merge & Center** button to merge and center the Iowa cells.

> **5.** Select cell **A41**, and then center it horizontally to align the Colorado text with the text in the other state cells.

> **6.** Merge and center the range **A42:A43** containing the Nebraska cells.

> **7.** Merge and center the range **A44:A46** containing the Kansas cells. See Figure 2-18. The merged cells make it easier to distinguish restaurants in each state.

**Figure 2-18** | **Merged cells**

| | A | B | C | D | E | F | G |
|---|---|---|---|---|---|---|---|
| 40 | Iowa | 414 Main St.<br>Des Moines, IA 50311<br>(515) 555 - 3134 | 46,000 | 43,000 | 52,000 | 51,000 | 54 |
| 41 | Colorado | 112 Reservoir Ln.<br>Greeley, CO 80631<br>(970) 555 - 2138 | 38,000 | 35,000 | 43,000 | 42,000 | 44 |
| 42 | | 5155 Pocane Dr.<br>Grand Island, NE 68801<br>(402) 555 - 7734 | 27,000 | 28,000 | 31,000 | 33,000 | 32 |
| 43 | Nebraska | 42 East River Rd.<br>Omaha, NE 68111<br>(402) 555 - 9148 | 38,000 | 39,000 | 45,000 | 47,000 | 46 |
| 44 | | 975 Business Dr.<br>Manhattan, KS 66502<br>(785) 555 - 0444 | 46,000 | 45,000 | 49,000 | 53,000 | 55 |
| 45 | | 47 Valley View Ln.<br>Topeka, KS 66604<br>(785) 555 - 6106 | 31,000 | 31,000 | 34,000 | 36,000 | 37 |
| 46 | Kansas | 87210 Causeway Dr.<br>Salina, KS 67401<br>(785) 555 - 8103 | 47,000 | 45,000 | 53,000 | 53,000 | 56 |
| 47 | | TOTAL | 680,000 | 659,000 | 757,000 | 779,000 | 815 |
| 48 | | | | | | | |

merged cell A42 contains the range A42:A43

merged cell A44 contains the range A44:A46

Documentation  **Sales Report**  ⊕

READY

## Rotating Cell Contents

Text and numbers are displayed horizontally within cells. However, you can rotate cell text to any angle to save space or to provide visual interest to a worksheet. The state names at the bottom of the merged cells would look better and take up less room if they were rotated vertically within their cells. Sanjit asks you to rotate the state names.

### To rotate the state names:

> **1.** Select the merged cell **A27**.

> **2.** On the HOME tab, in the Alignment group, click the **Orientation** button to display a list of rotation options, and then click **Rotate Text Up**. The state name rotates 90 degrees counterclockwise.

▶ **3.** In the Alignment group, click the **Middle Align** button ≡ to vertically center the rotated text in the merged cell.

▶ **4.** Select the merged cell range **A34:A44**, and then repeat Steps 2 and 3 to rotate and vertically center the rest of the state names in their cells.

▶ **5.** Select cell **A41** to deselect the range, and then increase the height of row 41 (the Colorado row) to **75** points (**100** pixels) so that the entire state name appears in the cell.

▶ **6.** Reduce the width of column A to **7** characters because the rotated state names take up less space.

▶ **7.** Select cell **A47**. See Figure 2-19.

| Figure 2-19 | Rotated cell content |

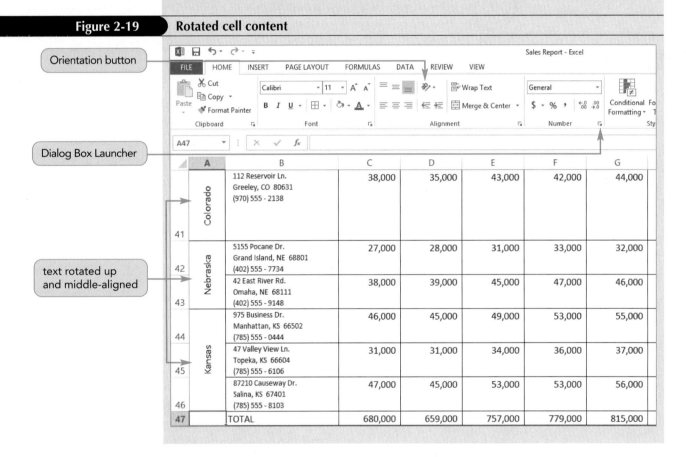

# Exploring the Format Cells Dialog Box

The buttons on the HOME tab provide quick access to the most commonly used formatting choices. For more options, you can use the Format Cells dialog box. You can apply the formats in this dialog box to the selected worksheet cells. The Format Cells dialog box has six tabs, each focusing on a different set of formatting options, as described below:

• **Number**—provides options for formatting the appearance of numbers, including dates and numbers treated as text such as telephone or Social Security numbers
• **Alignment**—provides options for how data is aligned within a cell
• **Font**—provides options for selecting font types, sizes, styles, and other formatting attributes such as underlining and font colors

- **Border**—provides options for adding and removing cell borders as well as selecting a line style and color
- **Fill**—provides options for creating and applying background colors and patterns to cells
- **Protection**—provides options for locking or hiding cells to prevent other users from modifying their contents

Although you have applied many of these formats from the HOME tab, the Format Cells dialog box presents them in a different way and provides more choices. You will use the Font and Fill tabs to format the column titles with a white font on a red background.

### To use the Format Cells dialog box to format the column labels:

1. Select the range **A26:O26** containing the column labels for the table.

2. On the HOME tab, in the Number group, click the **Dialog Box Launcher** located to the right of the group name (refer to Figure 2-19). The Format Cells dialog box opens with the Number tab displayed.

3. Click the **Font** tab to display the font formatting options.

4. Click the **Color** box to display the color palette, and then click the **White, Background 1** theme color. The font is set to white. See Figure 2-20.

| Figure 2-20 | Font tab in the Format Cells dialog box |
|---|---|

5. Click the **Fill** tab to display background options.

6. In the Background Color palette, click the **red** standard color (the second color in the last row). The background is set to red, as you can see in the Sample box.

7. Click the **OK** button. The dialog box closes, and the font and fill options you selected are applied to the column titles.

You will also use the Format Cells dialog box to change the appearance of the row titles. You'll format them to be displayed in a larger white font on a gray background.

## To format the row labels:

▶ **1.** Select the range **A27:A46** containing the rotated state names.

▶ **2.** Right-click the selected range, and then click **Format Cells** on the shortcut menu. The Format Cells dialog box opens with the last tab used displayed— in this case, the Fill tab.

▶ **3.** In the Background Color palette, click the **gray** theme color (the first color in the seventh column). Its preview is shown in the Sample box.

▶ **4.** Click the **Font** tab to display the font formatting options.

▶ **5.** Click the **Color** box, and then click the **White, Background 1** theme color to set the font color to white.

▶ **6.** Scroll down the **Size** box, and then click **16** to set the font size to 16 points.

▶ **7.** Click the **OK** button. The dialog box closes, and the font and fill formats are applied to the state names.

The Border tab in the Format Cells dialog box provides options for changing the border style and color as well as placing the border anywhere around a cell or cells in a selected range. Sanjit wants you to format the borders in the monthly sales data so that the sales result from each state is surrounded by a double border.

## To add a double border to the state results:

▶ **1.** Select the range **A27:O33** containing the monthly sales totals for the Wisconsin restaurants.

▶ **2.** Open the Format Cells dialog box, and then click the **Border** tab to display the border options.

▶ **3.** In the Style box, click the **double line** in the lower-right corner of the box.

▶ **4.** In the Presets section, click the **Outline** option. The double border appears around the outside of the selected cells in the Border preview. See Figure 2-21.

**Figure 2-21**    Border tab in the Format Cells dialog box

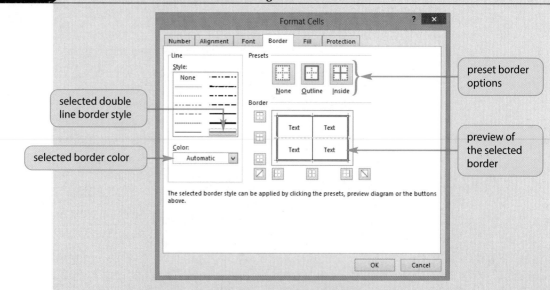

5. Click the **OK** button. The selected border is applied to the Wisconsin monthly sales.

6. Repeat Steps 2 through 5 to apply double borders to the ranges **A34:O36**, **A37:O40**, **A41:O41**, **A42:O43**, and **A44:O46**.

7. Select cell **A48** to deselect the range. See Figure 2-22.

**Figure 2-22**   Worksheet with font, fill, and border formatting

state names in a 16-point white font on a gray background

double borders around state sales rows

| | A | B | C | D | E | F | G |
|---|---|---|---|---|---|---|---|
| | Colorado | 112 Reservoir Ln. Greeley, CO 80631 (970) 555 - 2138 | 38,000 | 35,000 | 43,000 | 42,000 | 44,000 |
| 41 | | | | | | | |
| 42 | Nebraska | 5155 Pocane Dr. Grand Island, NE 68801 (402) 555 - 7734 | 27,000 | 28,000 | 31,000 | 33,000 | 32,000 |
| 43 | | 42 East River Rd. Omaha, NE 68111 (402) 555 - 9148 | 38,000 | 39,000 | 45,000 | 47,000 | 46,000 |
| 44 | Kansas | 975 Business Dr. Manhattan, KS 66502 (785) 555 - 0444 | 46,000 | 45,000 | 49,000 | 53,000 | 55,000 |
| 45 | | 47 Valley View Ln. Topeka, KS 66604 (785) 555 - 6106 | 31,000 | 31,000 | 34,000 | 36,000 | 37,000 |
| 46 | | 87210 Causeway Dr. Salina, KS 67401 (785) 555 - 8103 | 47,000 | 45,000 | 53,000 | 53,000 | 56,000 |
| 47 | | TOTAL | 680,000 | 659,000 | 757,000 | 779,000 | 815,000 |
| 48 | | | | | | | |

Documentation | Sales Report | ⊕

READY

8. Save the Sales Report worksheet.

You have completed much of the formatting that Sanjit wants in the Sales Report worksheet for the Big Red Wraps sales conference. In the next session, you will explore other formatting options.

## Session 2.1 Quick Check

**REVIEW**

1. What is the difference between a serif font and a sans serif font?
2. What is the difference between a theme color and a standard color?
3. A cell containing a number displays ######. Why does this occur and what can you do to fix it?
4. What is the General format?
5. Describe the differences between Currency format and Accounting format.
6. The range A1:C5 is merged into a single cell. What is its cell reference?
7. How do you format text so that it is set vertically within the cell?
8. Where can you access all the formatting options for worksheet cells?

# Session 2.2 Visual Overview:

The PAGE LAYOUT tab has options for setting how the worksheet will print.

The **Format Painter** copies and pastes formatting from one cell or range to another without duplicating any data.

**Print titles** are rows and columns that are included on every page of the printout. In this case, the text in rows 1 and 2 will print on every page.

A **manual page break** is one you set to indicate where a new page of the printout should start and is identified by a solid blue line.

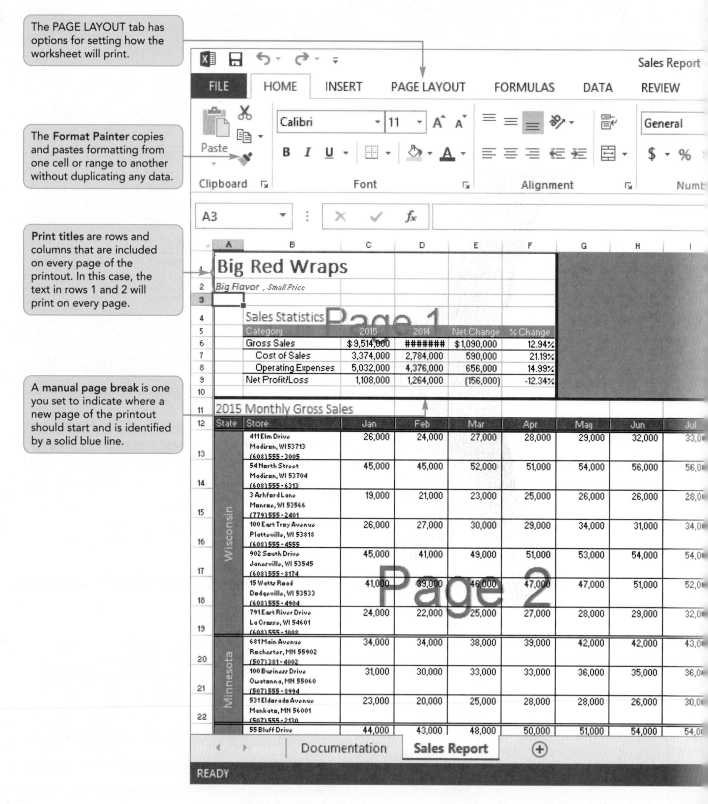

# Worksheet Formatted for Printing

**Report - Excel**    ? 🔼 — 🗗 ✕

.W    VIEW    Sign in 🔘

eral ▾ | 🖼 Conditional Formatting ▾ | 🖽 Insert ▾ | Σ ▾ | A⬇Z |🔍 |
% , ←.0 .00 →.0 | 🖽 Format as Table ▾ | 🖽 Delete ▾ | ⬇ ▾ | Sort & Find & |
| 🖽 Cell Styles ▾ | 🖽 Format ▾ | ◇ ▾ | Filter ▾ Select ▾ |
Number 🔽 | Styles | Cells | Editing ⌃

> The Find and Replace commands, which are available from the Find & Select button, are used to quickly make content and format changes throughout a workbook.

| | I | J | K | L | M | N | O | P | Q | R |

> The **print area** is a range or ranges in a worksheet that you specify to be printed. In Page Break Preview, the print area is not grayed out.

| Jul | Aug | Sep | Oct | Nov | Dec | TOTAL | AVERAGE |
|---|---|---|---|---|---|---|---|
| 33,000 | 34,000 | 30,000 | 32,000 | 30,000 | 30,000 | 355,000 | 29,583 |
| 56,000 | 59,000 | 54,000 | 55,000 | 51,000 | 56,000 | 634,000 | 52,833 |
| 28,000 | 26,000 | 25,000 | 26,000 | 25,000 | 25,000 | 295,000 | 24,583 |
| 34,000 | 36,000 | 31,000 | 31,000 | 31,000 | 35,000 | 375,000 | 31,250 |
| 54,000 | 58,000 | 54,000 | 55,000 | 51,000 | 52,000 | 617,000 | 51,417 |
| 52,000 | 54,000 | 50,000 | 49,000 | 46,000 | 50,000 | 572,000 | 47,667 |
| 32,000 | 30,000 | 30,000 | 28,000 | 27,000 | 30,000 | 332,000 | 27,667 |
| 43,000 | 44,000 | 42,000 | 43,000 | 40,000 | 43,000 | 484,000 | 40,333 |
| 36,000 | 38,000 | 35,000 | 38,000 | 32,000 | 37,000 | 414,000 | 34,500 |
| 30,000 | 28,000 | 26,000 | 26,000 | 26,000 | 26,000 | 312,000 | 26,000 |
| 54,000 | 55,000 | 54,000 | 52,000 | 51,000 | 54,000 | 610,000 | 50,833 |

Page 3

> **Cell styles** contain predefined formatting options that can be applied to cells in the workbook.

> **Cell highlighting** is a conditional format that changes a cell's font color or fill color based on the cell's value.

> An **automatic page break** is set by Excel when the page of the printout is full and is identified by a dotted blue line.

> Page Break Preview shows the location of the print area and all page breaks.

◀ ▶    ⊞ 📄 📖 — ⊞ ——|— + 60%

# Using the Average Function

The **AVERAGE function** calculates the average value from a collection of numbers. The syntax of the Average function is

```
AVERAGE (number1, number2, number3, …)
```

where *number1, number2, number3,* and so forth are either numbers or cell references to the cells or a range where the numbers are stored. For example, the following formula uses the AVERAGE function to calculate the average of 1, 2, 5, and 8, returning the value 4:

```
=AVERAGE(1, 2, 5, 8)
```

However, functions usually reference values entered in a worksheet. So, if the range A1:A4 contains the values 1, 2, 5, and 8, the following formula also returns the value 4:

```
=AVERAGE(A1:A4)
```

The advantage of using cell references is that the values used in the function are visible and can be easily edited.

Sanjit wants to show the average monthly sales for each of the 20 Big Red Wraps stores in addition to the total sales for each store. You will use the AVERAGE function to calculate these values.

### To calculate the average monthly sales for each store:

▶ **1.** If you took a break after the previous session, make sure the Sales Report workbook is open and the Sales Report worksheet is active.

▶ **2.** In cell **P26**, enter the text **AVERAGE** as the label.

▶ **3.** Select cell **P27**. You will enter the AVERAGE function in this cell to calculate the average monthly sales for the store on 411 Elm Drive in Madison, Wisconsin.

▶ **4.** On the HOME tab, in the Editing group, click the **AutoSum button arrow**, and then click **AVERAGE**. The formula =AVERAGE(C27:O27) appears in the cell. The range reference that was included in the function is incorrect. It includes cell O27, which contains the total gross sales for all months. You need to correct the range reference.

▶ **5.** Select **O27** in the function's argument, and then click cell **N27** to replace the cell reference. The range reference now correctly includes only the gross sales for each month.

▶ **6.** Press the **Enter** key to complete the formula. The formula results show 29,583, which is the monthly gross sales from the store on 411 Elm Drive in Madison, Wisconsin.

▶ **7.** Select cell **P27**, and then change the alignment to **Top Align** so that the calculated value is aligned with the top of the cell.

▶ **8.** Copy the formula in cell **P27**, and then paste the copied formula into the range **P28:P47**.

▶ **9.** Select cell **P48** to deselect the range. As shown in Figure 2-23, the average monthly sales from all of the stores are $792,833. Individual stores have average monthly gross sales ranging from about $25,000 up to almost $55,000.

**Figure 2-23**      **AVERAGE function results**

average gross sales for each store per month

| | F | G | H | I | J | K | L | M | N | O | P | Q | R |
|---|---|---|---|---|---|---|---|---|---|---|---|---|---|
| | 42,000 | 44,000 | 44,000 | 47,000 | 48,000 | 47,000 | 48,000 | 44,000 | 46,000 | 526,000 | 43,833 | | |
| 41 | | | | | | | | | | | | | |
| 42 | 33,000 | 32,000 | 37,000 | 37,000 | 38,000 | 35,000 | 33,000 | 35,000 | 33,000 | 399,000 | 33,250 | | |
| 43 | 47,000 | 46,000 | 49,000 | 51,000 | 49,000 | 47,000 | 49,000 | 47,000 | 48,000 | 555,000 | 46,250 | | |
| 44 | 53,000 | 55,000 | 56,000 | 56,000 | 59,000 | 54,000 | 55,000 | 51,000 | 53,000 | 632,000 | 52,667 | | |
| 45 | 36,000 | 37,000 | 38,000 | 37,000 | 38,000 | 36,000 | 36,000 | 35,000 | 38,000 | 427,000 | 35,583 | | |
| 46 | 53,000 | 56,000 | 55,000 | 59,000 | 58,000 | 56,000 | 58,000 | 53,000 | 57,000 | 650,000 | 54,167 | | |
| 47 | 779,000 | 815,000 | 830,000 | 861,000 | 876,000 | 819,000 | 828,000 | 783,000 | 827,000 | 9,514,000 | 792,833 | | |
| 48 | | | | | | | | | | | | | |

Documentation   Sales Report

READY                                                                                                                                            120%

average gross sales for all stores per month

With the last formulas added to the worksheet, Sanjit wants you to continue formatting the workbook.

# Applying Cell Styles

A workbook often contains several cells that store the same type of data. For example, each worksheet might have a cell displaying the sheet title, or a range of financial data might have several cells containing totals and averages. It is good design practice to apply the same format to worksheet cells that contain the same type of data.

One way to ensure that similar data is displayed consistently is with styles. A **style** is a collection of formatting options that include a specified font, font size, font styles, font color, fill color, and borders. The Cell Styles gallery includes a variety of built-in styles that you can use to format titles and headings, different types of data such as totals or calculations, and cells that you want to emphasize. For example, you can use the Heading 1 style to display sheet titles in a bold, blue-gray, 15-point Calibri font with no fill color and a blue bottom border. You can then apply the Heading 1 style to all titles in the workbook. If you later revise the style, the appearance of any cell formatted with that style is updated automatically. This saves you the time and effort of reformatting each cell individually.

You already used built-in styles when you formatted data in the Sales Report worksheet with the Accounting, Comma, and Percent styles. You can also create your own cell styles by clicking New Cell Style at the bottom of the Cell Styles gallery.

*Applying a Cell Style*

- Select the cell or range to which you want to apply a style.
- On the HOME tab, in the Styles group, click the Cell Styles button.
- Point to each style in the Cell Styles gallery to see a Live Preview of that style on the selected cell or range.
- Click the style you want to apply to the selected cell or range.

Sanjit wants you to add more color and visual interest to the Sales Report worksheet. You'll use some of the styles in the Cell Styles gallery to do this.

**To apply cell styles to the Sales Report worksheet:**

▸ **1.** Select cell **B4** containing the text "Sales Statistics."

▸ **2.** On the HOME tab, in the Styles group, click the **Cell Styles** button. The Cell Styles gallery opens.

▸ **3.** Point to the **Heading 1** style in the Titles and Headings section. Live Preview shows cell B4 in a 15-point, bold font with a solid blue bottom border. See Figure 2-24.

**Figure 2-24**   **Cell Styles gallery**

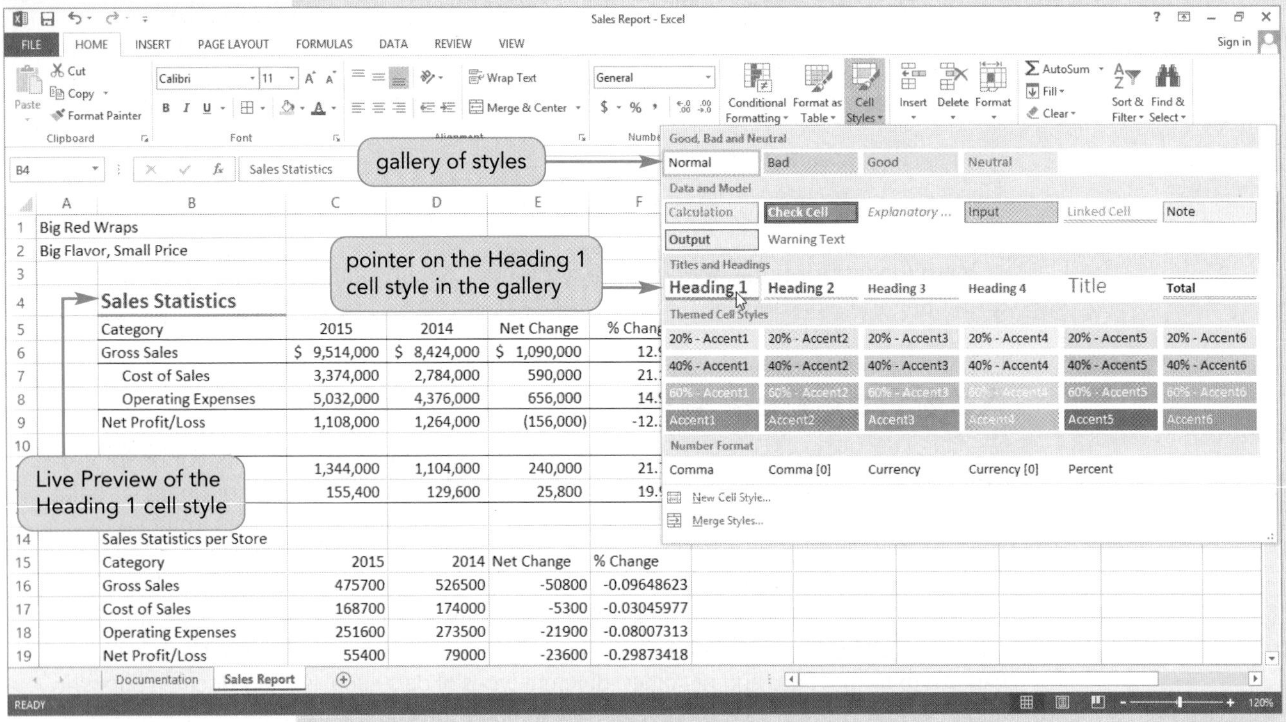

▸ **4.** Move the pointer over different styles in the Cell Styles gallery to see cell B4 with a Live Preview of each style.

▸ **5.** Click the **Title** style. The Title style is applied to cell B4.

▸ **6.** Select the range **B5:F5** containing the column labels for the Sales Statistics data.

▸ **7.** In the Styles group, click the **Cell Styles** button, and then click the **Accent3** style in the Themed Cell Styles section of the Cell Styles gallery.

▸ **8.** Select cell **A25** containing the text "2015 Monthly Gross Sales," and then apply the **Title** cell style to the cell.

▸ **9.** Select cell **A3**. See Figure 2-25.

Figure 2-25    **Cell styles applied to the worksheet**

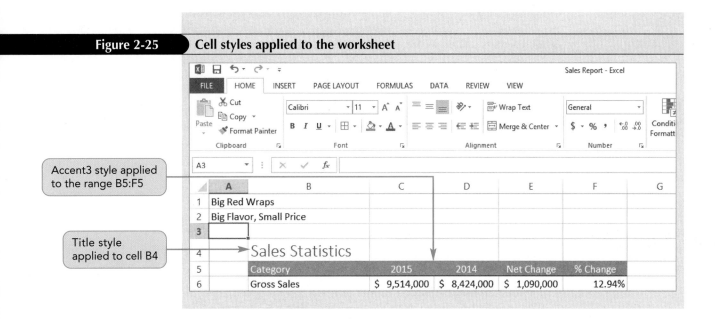

Accent3 style applied
to the range B5:F5

Title style
applied to cell B4

# Copying and Pasting Formats

Large workbooks often use the same formatting on similar data throughout the
workbook, sometimes in widely scattered cells. Rather than repeating the same steps to
format these cells, you can copy the format of one cell or range and paste it to another.

## Copying Formats with the Format Painter

The Format Painter provides a fast and efficient way of copying and pasting formats,
ensuring that a workbook has a consistent look and feel. The Format Painter does not
copy formatting applied to selected text within a cell, and it does not copy data.

Sanjit wants the Sales Report worksheet to use the same formats you applied to the
Big Red Wraps company name and slogan in the Documentation sheet. You will use
the Format Painter to copy and paste the formats.

### To use the Format Painter to copy and paste a format:

1. Go to the **Documentation** worksheet, and then select the range **A1:A2**.

2. On the HOME tab, in the Clipboard group, click the **Format Painter** button.
   The formats from the selected cells are copied to the Clipboard, and a
   flashing border appears around the selected range and the pointer changes
   to ⊕⌗.

3. Return to the **Sales Report** worksheet, and then click cell **A1**. The formatting
   from the Documentation worksheet is removed from the Clipboard and
   applied to the range A1:A2. Notice that the larger font size you applied to
   the text "Big Flavor" was not included in the pasted formats.

4. Double-click cell **A2** to enter Edit mode, select **Big Flavor**, and then increase
   the font size to **14** points. The format for the slogan now matches the slogan
   on the Documentation sheet.

5. Select cell **A3** to exit Edit mode. See Figure 2-26.

**TIP**

To paste the same format
multiple times, double-
click the Format Painter
button to leave the
Format Painter on until
you click the button again
or press the Esc key.

Figure 2-26 **Formats pasted in the Sales Report worksheet**

Format Painter button

format copied from
Documentation sheet

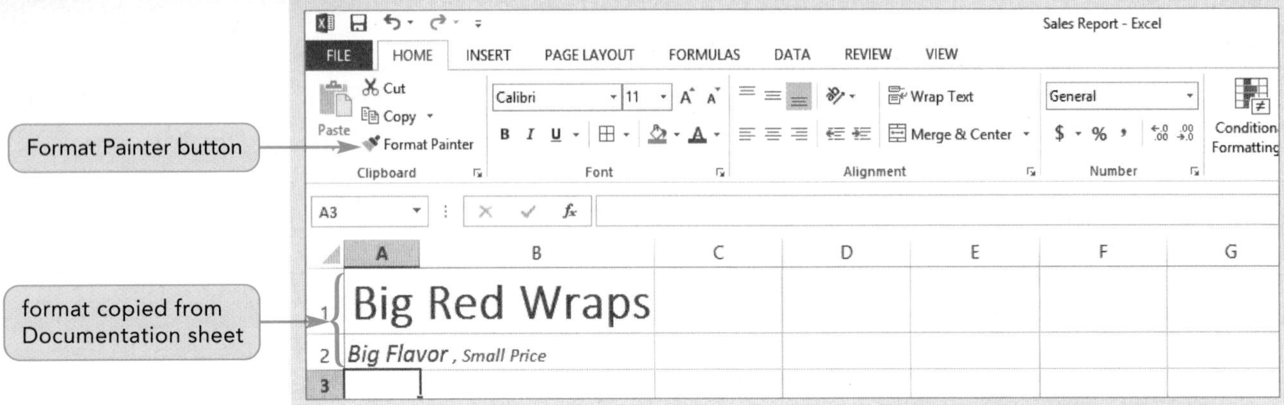

You can use the Format Painter to copy all of the formats within a selected range and then apply those formats to another range that has the same size and shape by clicking the upper-left cell of the range. Sanjit wants you to copy all of the formats you applied to the Sales Statistics data to the sales statistics per store.

**To copy and paste multiple formats:**

1. Select the range **B4:F12** in the Sales Report worksheet.

2. On the HOME tab, in the Clipboard group, click the **Format Painter** button.

3. Click cell **B14**. All of the number formats, cell borders, fonts, and fill colors are pasted into the range B14:F22.

4. Select the range **C23:E23**.

5. On the HOME tab, in the Number group, click the **Comma Style** button, and then click the **Decrease Decimal** button twice to remove the decimal places to the right of the decimal point. The numbers are vertically aligned in their columns.

6. Select cell **F23**.

7. In the Number group, click the **Percent Style** button to change the number to a percentage, and then click the **Increase Decimal** button twice to display two decimal places in the percentage.

8. Click cell **B24**. See Figure 2-27.

**TIP**

If the range in which you paste the formats is bigger than the range you copied, Format Painter will repeat the copied formats to fill the pasted range.

**Figure 2-27**    **Formats pasted from a range**

| | A | B | C | D | E | F | G | H |
|---|---|---|---|---|---|---|---|---|
| 6 | | Gross Sales | $ 9,514,000 | $ 8,424,000 | $ 1,090,000 | 12.94% | | |
| 7 | | Cost of Sales | 3,374,000 | 2,784,000 | 590,000 | 21.19% | | |
| 8 | | Operating Expenses | 5,032,000 | 4,376,000 | 656,000 | 14.99% | | |
| 9 | | Net Profit/Loss | 1,108,000 | 1,264,000 | (156,000) | -12.34% | | |
| 10 | | | | | | | | |
| 11 | | Units Sold | 1,344,000 | 1,104,000 | 240,000 | 21.74% | | |
| 12 | | Customers Served | 155,400 | 129,600 | 25,800 | 19.91% | | |
| 13 | | | | | | | | |
| 14 | | Sales Statistics per Store | | | | | | |
| 15 | | Category | 2015 | 2014 | Net Change | % Change | | |
| 16 | | Gross Sales | $    475,700 | $    526,500 | $    (50,800) | -9.65% | | |
| 17 | | Cost of Sales | 168,700 | 174,000 | (5,300) | -3.05% | | |
| 18 | | Operating Expenses | 251,600 | 273,500 | (21,900) | -8.01% | | |
| 19 | | Net Profit/Loss | 55,400 | 79,000 | (23,600) | -29.87% | | |
| 20 | | | | | | | | |
| 21 | | Units Sold | 67,200 | 69,000 | (1,800) | -2.61% | | |
| 22 | | Customers Served | 7,770 | 8,100 | (330) | -4.07% | | |
| 23 | | Stores | 20 | 16 | 4 | 25.00% | | |
| 24 | | | | | | | | |

copied formats

pasted formats

Documentation    **Sales Report**

READY

## Copying Formats with the Paste Options Button

Another way to copy and paste formats is with the Paste Options button 📋 (Ctrl) ▾, which provides options for pasting only values, only formats, or some combination of values and formats. Each time you paste, the Paste Options button appears in the lower-right corner of the pasted cell or range. You click the Paste Options button to open a list of pasting options, shown in Figure 2-28, such as pasting only the values or only the formatting. You can also click the Transpose button to paste the column data into a row, or to paste the row data into a column.

**Figure 2-28**    **Paste Options button**

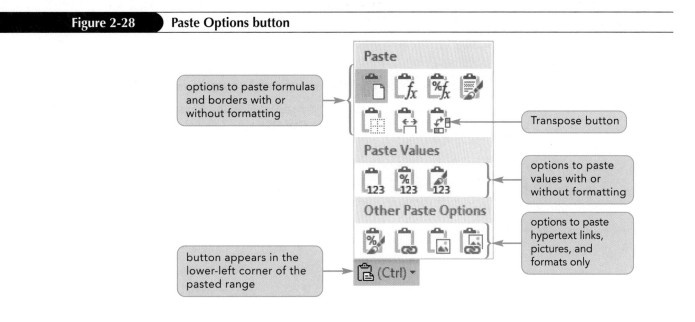

options to paste formulas and borders with or without formatting

Transpose button

options to paste values with or without formatting

options to paste hypertext links, pictures, and formats only

button appears in the lower-left corner of the pasted range

## Copying Formats with Paste Special

The Paste Special command provides another way to control what you paste from the Clipboard. To use Paste Special, select and copy a range, select the range where you want to paste the Clipboard contents, click the Paste button arrow in the Clipboard group on the HOME tab, and then click Paste Special to open the dialog box shown in Figure 2-29.

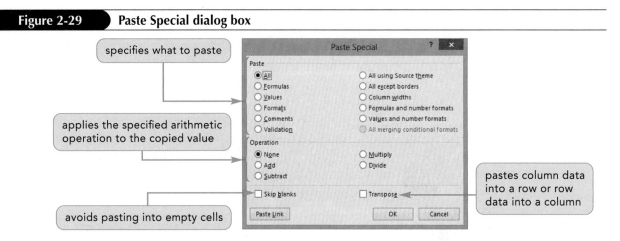

From the Paste Special dialog box, you can control exactly how to paste the copied range.

# Finding and Replacing Text and Formats

The Find and Replace commands let you make content and design changes to a worksheet or the entire workbook quickly. The Find command searches through the current worksheet or workbook for the content or formatting you want to locate, and the Replace command then substitutes it with the new content or formatting you specify.

Sanjit wants you to replace all the street title abbreviations (such as Ave.) in the Sales Report with their full names (such as Avenue). You will use Find and Replace to make these changes.

**To find and replace the street title abbreviations:**

▸ **1.** On the HOME tab, in the Editing group, click the **Find & Select** button, and then click **Replace** (or press the **Ctrl+H** keys). The Find and Replace dialog box opens.

▸ **2.** Type **Ave.** in the Find what box.

▸ **3.** Press the **Tab** key to move the insertion point to the Replace with box, and then type **Avenue**. See Figure 2-30.

**Figure 2-30** Find and Replace dialog box

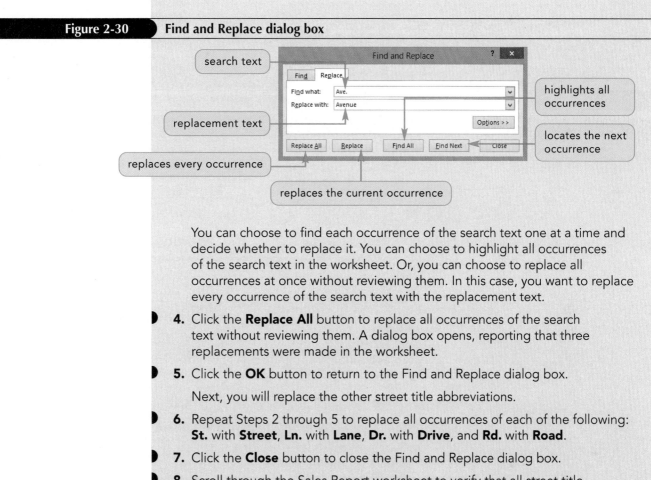

You can choose to find each occurrence of the search text one at a time and decide whether to replace it. You can choose to highlight all occurrences of the search text in the worksheet. Or, you can choose to replace all occurrences at once without reviewing them. In this case, you want to replace every occurrence of the search text with the replacement text.

4. Click the **Replace All** button to replace all occurrences of the search text without reviewing them. A dialog box opens, reporting that three replacements were made in the worksheet.

5. Click the **OK** button to return to the Find and Replace dialog box.

   Next, you will replace the other street title abbreviations.

6. Repeat Steps 2 through 5 to replace all occurrences of each of the following: **St.** with **Street**, **Ln.** with **Lane**, **Dr.** with **Drive**, and **Rd.** with **Road**.

7. Click the **Close** button to close the Find and Replace dialog box.

8. Scroll through the Sales Report worksheet to verify that all street title abbreviations were replaced with their full names.

The Find and Replace dialog box can also be used to replace one format with another or to replace both text and a format simultaneously. Sanjit wants you to replace all occurrences of the white text in the Sales Report worksheet with light yellow text. You'll use the Find and Replace dialog box to make this formatting change.

### To replace white text with yellow text:

1. On the HOME tab, in the Editing group, click the **Find & Select** button, and then click **Replace** (or press the **Ctrl+H** keys). The Find and Replace dialog box opens.

2. Click the **Options** button to expand the dialog box.

3. Click the **Format** button in the Find what row to open the Find Format dialog box, which is similar to the Format Cells dialog box you used earlier to format a range.

4. Click the **Font** tab to make it active, click the **Color** box, and then click the **White, Background 1** theme color.

5. Click the **OK** button to close the dialog box and return to the Find and Replace dialog box.

6. Click the **Format** button in the Replace with row to open the Replace Format dialog box.

7. Click the **Color** box, and then click the **Yellow** standard color.

8. Click the **OK** button to close the dialog box and return to the Find and Replace dialog box. See Figure 2-31.

**Figure 2-31** ▸ **Expanded Find and Replace dialog box**

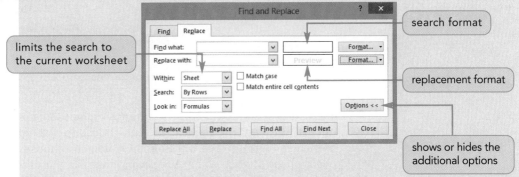

9. Verify that the Within box lists **Sheet** to limit the search to the current worksheet.

10. Click the **Replace All** button to replace all occurrences of white text in the Sales Report worksheet with yellow text. A dialog box appears, reporting that 32 replacements were made.

11. Click the **OK** button to return to the Find and Replace dialog box.

It is a good idea to clear the find and replace formats after you are done so that they won't affect any future searches and replacements. You'll remove the formats from the Find and Replace dialog box.

12. Click the **Format button arrow** in the Find what row, and then click **Clear Find Format**. The search format is removed.

13. Click the **Format button arrow** in the Replace with row, and then click **Clear Replace Format**. The replacement format is removed.

14. Click the **Close** button to return to the worksheet. Notice that every cell in the worksheet that had white text now has yellow text.

# Working with Themes

Recall that a theme is a coordinated selection of fonts, colors, and graphical effects that are applied throughout a workbook to create a specific look and feel. When you switch to a different theme, the theme-related fonts, colors, and effects change throughout the workbook to reflect the new theme. The appearance of non-theme fonts, colors, and effects remains unchanged no matter which theme is applied to the workbook.

Most of the formatting you have applied to the Sales Report workbook is based on the Office theme. Sanjit wants you to change the theme to see how it affects the workbook's appearance.

## To change the workbook's theme:

▶ **1.** Click the **PAGE LAYOUT** tab on the ribbon.

▶ **2.** In the Themes group, click the **Themes** button. The Themes gallery opens. Office—the current theme—is the default.

▶ **3.** Point to the **Organic** theme in the Themes gallery. Live Preview shows how the appearance of the Sales Report worksheet will change if you select the Organic theme. See Figure 2-32.

**Figure 2-32** | **Live Preview of the Organic theme**

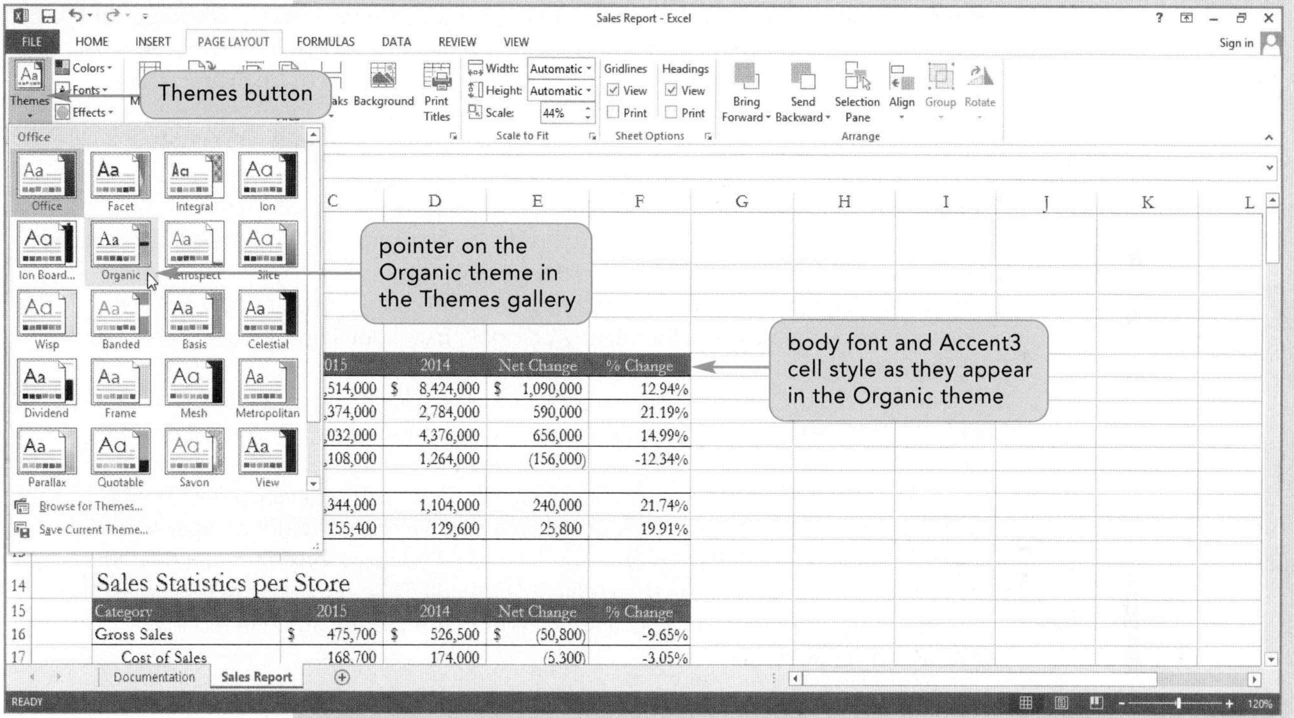

▶ **4.** Point to several other themes in the Themes gallery to see how the worksheet appearance would change.

▶ **5.** Click the **Wisp** theme to apply that theme to the workbook.

Changing the theme made a significant difference in the worksheet's appearance. The most obvious changes to the worksheet are the fill colors and the fonts. Only formatting options directly tied to a theme change when you select a different theme. Any formatting options you selected that were not theme-based remain unaffected by the change. For example, the yellow standard color you just applied to the different column labels is still yellow, even with the Wisp theme applied, because yellow is not a theme color. For the same reason, the red fill color used in the column labels of the monthly sales table remains unchanged under the new theme.

Sanjit informs you that Big Red Wraps requires all documents to be formatted with the Office theme. You will reapply the Office theme to the workbook.

**To reapply the Office theme to the workbook:**

▶ **1.** On the PAGE LAYOUT tab, in the Themes group, click the **Themes** button, and then click the **Office** theme from the gallery of themes.

The workbook now complies with the company's standard formatting.

*Sharing Styles and Themes*

Using a consistent look and feel for all the files you create in Microsoft Office is a simple way to project a professional image. This consistency is especially important when a team is collaborating on a set of documents. When all team members work from a common set of style and design themes, readers will not be distracted by inconsistent or clashing formatting.

To quickly copy the styles from one workbook to another, open the workbook with the styles you want to copy, and then open the workbook in which you want to copy those styles. On the HOME tab, in the Styles group, click the Cell Styles button, and then click Merge Styles. The Merge Styles dialog box opens, listing the currently open workbooks. Select the workbook with the styles you want to copy, and then click the OK button to copy those styles into the current workbook. If you modify any styles, you must copy the styles to the other workbook; Excel does not update styles between workbooks.

Because other Office files, including those created with Word or PowerPoint, use the same file format for themes, you can create one theme to use with all of your Office files. To save a theme, click the Themes button in the Themes group on the PAGE LAYOUT tab, and then click Save Current Theme. The Save Current Theme dialog box opens. Select a save location (in a default Theme folder on your computer or another folder), type a descriptive name in the File name box, and then click the Save button. If you saved the theme file in a default Theme folder, the theme appears in the Themes gallery, and any changes made to the theme are reflected in any Office file that uses that theme.

# Highlighting Cells with Conditional Formats

Conditional formats are often used to help analyze data. A **conditional format** applies formatting to a cell when its value meets a specified condition. For example, a conditional format can be used to format negative numbers in red and positive numbers in black. Conditional formats are dynamic, which means that the formatting can change when the cell's value changes. Each conditional format has a set of rules that define how the formatting should be applied and under what conditions the format will be changed.

*Highlighting Cells with a Conditional Format*

- Select the range in which you want to highlight cells.
- On the HOME tab, in the Styles group, click the Conditional Formatting button, point to Highlight Cells Rules or Top/Bottom Rules, and then click the appropriate rule.
- Select the appropriate options in the dialog box.
- Click the OK button.

Excel has four conditional formats—data bars, highlighting, color scales, and icon sets. In this tutorial, you will apply cell highlighting, which changes the cell's font color or fill color based on the cell's value, as described in Figure 2-33. You can enter a value or a cell reference if you want to compare other cells with the value in a certain cell.

**Figure 2-33**      **Highlight Cells rules**

| Rule | Highlights Cell Values |
|------|------------------------|
| Greater Than | Greater than a specified number |
| Less Than | Less than a specified number |
| Between | Between two specified numbers |
| Equal To | Equal to a specified number |
| Text that Contains | That contain specified text |
| A Date Occurring | That contain a specified date |
| Duplicate Values | That contain duplicate or unique values |

© 2014 Cengage Learning

## Highlighting Cells Based on Their Values

Sanjit wants to highlight important trends and sales values in the Sales Report worksheet. He wants you to use a conditional format to display sales statistics that showed a negative net or percent change in a red font so that they stand out. You will do this by creating a rule to format the cells in ranges E6:F12 and E16:F22 with numbers that are less than 0.

### To highlight negative numbers in red:

1. Select the nonadjacent range **E6:F12;E16:F22** in the Sales Report worksheet.

2. On the ribbon, click the **HOME** tab.

3. In the Styles group, click the **Conditional Formatting** button, and then point to **Highlight Cells Rules** to display a menu of the available rules.

4. Click **Less Than**. The Less Than dialog box opens so you can select the value and formatting to highlight negative values.

5. Type **0** (a zero) in the Format cells that are LESS THAN box, click the **with** arrow, and then click **Red Text**. Live Preview shows that the rule formats any cells in the selected range that have a negative value in a red font. See Figure 2-34.

**Figure 2-34** **Live Preview of the Less Than conditional format**

**Figure 2-34** **Live Preview of the Less Than conditional format**

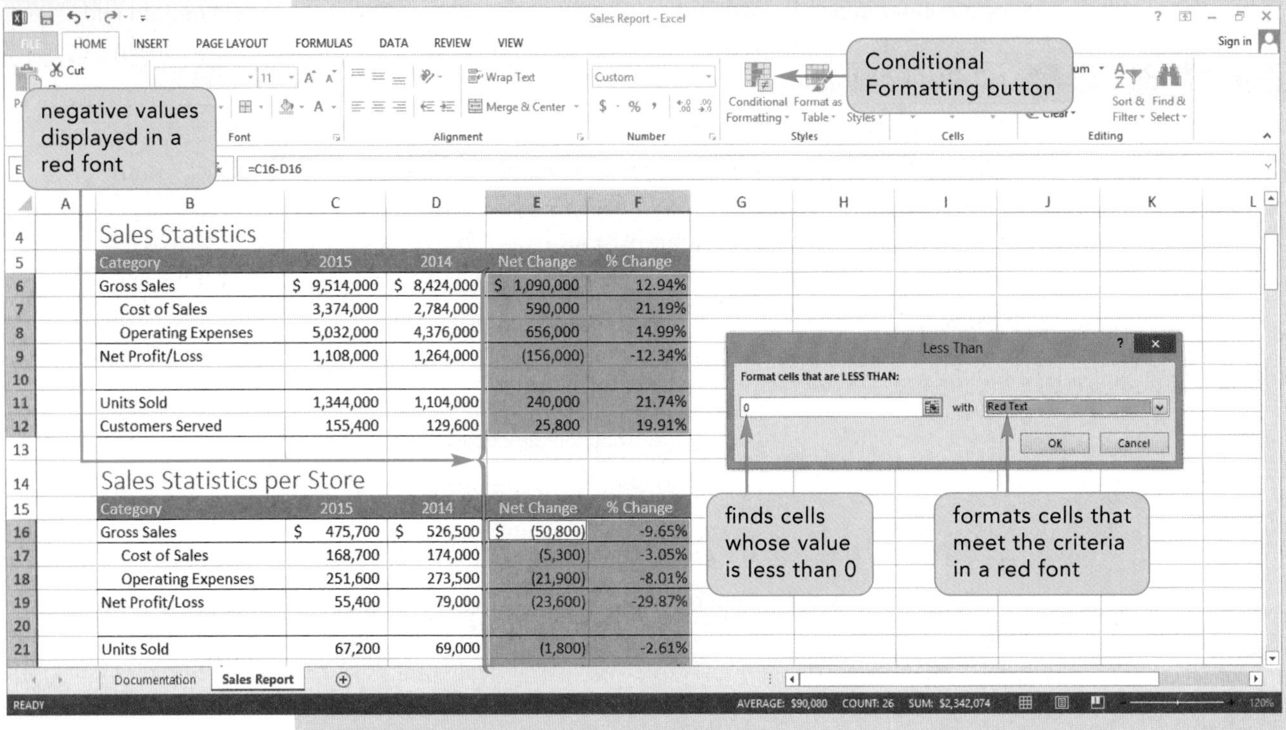

**6.** Click the **OK** button to apply the highlighting rule. You will verify that this format is conditional.

**7.** In cell D8, enter **4,576,000** to change the Operating Expenses value. The now positive values in cells E9 and F9 are formatted in a black font.

**8.** Press the **Ctrl+Z** keys to return the value in cell D8 to 4,376,000. The values in cells E9 and F9 are again negative and in a red font.

The highlighted values show at a glance that Big Red Wraps' gross sales, units sold, and customers served increased from 2014 to 2015, while the company's net profit declined during the same period. The average gross sales per store also declined in 2015. Big Red Wraps opened four new stores in 2015, and Sanjit will argue that the cost of this expansion and low sales from the new stores caused this apparent decline.

## Highlighting Cells with a Top/Bottom Rule

Another way of applying conditional formats is with the Quick Analysis tool. The **Quick Analysis tool**, which appears whenever you select a range of cells, provides access to the most common tools for data analysis and formatting. The FORMATTING category includes buttons for the Greater Than and Top 10% conditional formatting rules. You can highlight cells based on their values in comparison to other cells. For example, you can highlight cells with the 10 highest or lowest values in a selected range, or you can highlight the cells with above-average values in a range.

Sanjit wants you to highlight the five stores in the Big Red Wraps chain that had the highest gross sales in the last fiscal year. You will use a Top/Bottom rule to do this.

### To use a Top/Bottom Rule to highlight the stores with the highest gross sales:

1. Select the range **P27:P46** containing the average monthly gross sales for each of the 20 Big Red Wraps stores. The Quick Analysis button appears in the lower-right corner of the selected range.

2. Click the **Quick Analysis** button, and then point to **Top 10%**. Live Preview colors the cells in the top 10 percent with red font and a red fill. See Figure 2-35.

Figure 2-35 **Quick Analysis tool**

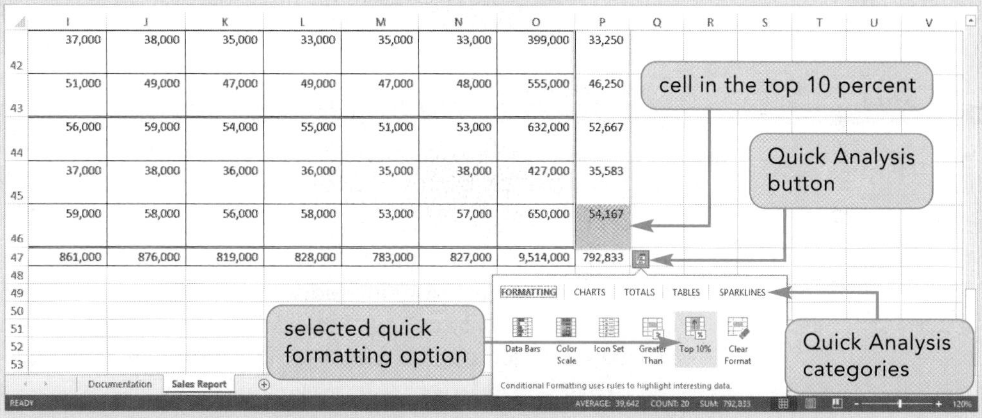

Sanjit wants to see the top five items rather than the cells with values in the top 10 percent, so you won't apply this conditional formatting.

3. Press the **Esc** key to close the Quick Analysis tool. The range P27:P46 remains selected.

4. On the HOME tab, in the Styles group, click the **Conditional Formatting** button, and then point to **Top/Bottom Rules** to display a menu of available rules.

5. Click **Top 10 Items** to open the Top 10 Items dialog box.

6. Click the down arrow on the spin box five times to change the value from 10 to 5. This specifies that the top five values in the selected range will be formatted.

7. Click the **with** arrow, and then click **Green Fill with Dark Green Text** to specify the formatting to apply to the five cells with the top values. Live Preview highlights the top five stores in terms of gross sales. See Figure 2-36.

| Figure 2-36 | Live Preview of the top five selling stores |
| --- | --- |

| | F | G | H | I | J | K | L | M | N | O | P | Q | R |
| --- | --- | --- | --- | --- | --- | --- | --- | --- | --- | --- | --- | --- | --- |
| 41 | 33,000 | 32,000 | 37,000 | 37,000 | 38,000 | 35,000 | 33,000 | 35,000 | 33,000 | 399,000 | 33,250 | | |
| 42 | | | | | | | | | | | | | |
| 43 | 47,000 | 46,000 | 49,000 | | Top 10 Items | ? × | 49,000 | 47,000 | 48,000 | 555,000 | 46,250 | | |
| 44 | | | 56,000 | Format cells that rank in the TOP: | 5 ÷ with Green Fill with Dark Green Text ▼ | | 55,000 | 51,000 | 53,000 | 632,000 | 52,667 | | |
| 45 | 36,000 | 37,000 | 38,000 | OK  Cancel | | | 36,000 | 35,000 | 38,000 | 427,000 | 35,583 | | |
| 46 | 53,000 | 56,000 | 55,000 | 59,000 | 58,000 | 56,000 | 58,000 | 53,000 | 57,000 | 650,000 | 54,167 | | |
| 47 | 779,000 | 815,000 | 830,000 | 861,000 | 876,000 | 819,000 | 828,000 | 783,000 | 827,000 | 9,514,000 | 792,833 | | |
| 48 | | | | | | | | | | | | | |
| 49 | | | | | | | | | | | | | |
| 50 | | | | | | | | | | | | | |
| 51 | | | | | | | | | | | | | |
| 52 | | | | | | | | | | | | | |
| 53 | | | | | | | | | | | | | |

displays the five largest values

formats cells that meet the criteria in a dark green font on a light green background

two of the five top sellers at Big Red Wraps

Documentation   Sales Report

READY    AVERAGE: 39,642    COUNT: 20    SUM: 792,833    120%

▶ 8. Click the **OK** button to accept the conditional formatting.

The Top/Bottom rule highlights the average monthly gross sales for the five top-selling stores: the North Street store in Madison, Wisconsin; the South Drive store in Janesville, Wisconsin; the Main Street store in Des Moines, Iowa; the Business Drive store in Manhattan, Kansas; and the Causeway Drive store in Salina, Kansas.

## Clearing a Conditional Format

You can remove a conditional format at any time without affecting the underlying data by selecting the range containing the conditional format, clicking the Conditional Formatting button, and then clicking the Clear Rules button. A menu opens, providing options to clear the conditional formatting rules from the selected cells or the entire worksheet. You can also click the Quick Analysis button that appears in the lower-right corner of the selected range, and then click the Clear Format button in the FORMATTING category.

## Creating a Conditional Formatting Legend

When you use conditional formatting to highlight cells in a worksheet, the purpose of the formatting is not always immediately apparent. To ensure that everyone knows why certain cells are highlighted, you should include a **legend**, which is a key that identifies each color and its meaning.

You will add a legend to the Sales Report worksheet to document the Top 5 highlighting rule you just created.

### To create a conditional formatting legend:

▶ 1. Select cell **P49**, type **light green**, and then press the **Enter** key. You will use a highlight rule to fill this cell with a dark green font on a light green fill.

▶ 2. Select cell **P49** to make it the active cell.

▶ 3. On the HOME tab, in the Styles group, click the **Conditional Formatting** button, point to **Highlight Cells Rules**, and then click **Text that Contains**. The Text That Contains dialog box opens.

▶ **4.** Verify that **light green** appears in the Format cells that contain the text box. The box shows the text entered in the selected cell.

▶ **5.** Click the **with** arrow, and then click **Green Fill with Dark Green Text** to format cell P49 with the same format used for the top five gross sales.

▶ **6.** Click the **OK** button. Cell P49 remains selected.

▶ **7.** In the Alignment group, click the **Center** button ≡ to center the text in the cell.

▶ **8.** In cell **O49**, enter **Top 5 Stores** to identify the format's purpose, and then select cell **O49**.

▶ **9.** In the Styles group, click the **Cell Styles** button, and then click the **Explanatory Text** style (the third style in the first row of the Data and Model section). The cell style is applied to the selected cell.

▶ **10.** Click cell **O51**. The legend is complete, as shown in Figure 2-37.

| Figure 2-37 | Conditional formatting legend |

legend explains the purpose of the formatting

The conditional formatting makes the top-selling stores stand out.

## Written Communication: Using Conditional Formatting Effectively

Conditional formatting is an excellent way to highlight important trends and data values to clients and colleagues. However, be sure to use it judiciously. Overusing conditional formatting might obscure the very data you want to emphasize. Keep in mind the following tips as you make decisions about what to highlight and how it should be highlighted:

- **Document the conditional formats you use.** If a bold, green font means that a sales number is in the top 10 percent of all sales, include that information in a legend in the worksheet.
- **Don't clutter data with too much highlighting.** Limit highlighting rules to one or two per data set. Highlights are designed to draw attention to points of interest. If you use too many, you will end up highlighting everything—and, therefore, nothing.
- **Use color sparingly in worksheets with highlights.** It is difficult to tell a highlight color from a regular fill color, especially when fill colors are used in every cell.
- **Consider alternatives to conditional formats.** If you want to highlight the top 10 sales regions, it might be more effective to simply sort the data with the best-selling regions at the top of the list.

Remember that the goal of highlighting is to provide a strong visual clue to important data or results. Careful use of conditional formatting helps readers to focus on the important points you want to make rather than distracting them with secondary issues and facts.

PROSKILLS

# Formatting a Worksheet for Printing

You should format any worksheets you plan to print so that they are easy to read and understand. You can do this using the print settings, which enable you to set the page orientation, the print area, page breaks, print titles, and headers and footers. Print settings can be applied to an entire workbook or to individual sheets. Because other people will likely see your printed worksheets, you should format the printed output as carefully as you format the electronic version. Sanjit wants you to format the Sales Report worksheet so he can distribute the printed version at the upcoming sales conference.

## Using Page Break Preview

Page Break Preview shows only those parts of the active sheet that will print and how the content will be split across pages. A dotted blue border indicates a page break, which separates one page from another. As you format the worksheet for printing, you can use this view to control what content appears on each page.

Sanjit wants to know how the Sales Report worksheet would print in portrait orientation and how many pages would be required. You will look at the worksheet in Page Break Preview to find these answers.

**To view the Sales Report worksheet in Page Break Preview:**

▶ **1.** Click the **Page Break Preview** button 🔟 on the status bar. The worksheet switches to Page Break Preview.

▶ **2.** Change the zoom level of the worksheet to **30%** so you can view the entire contents of this large worksheet. See Figure 2-38.

**Figure 2-38** Sales Report worksheet in Page Break Preview

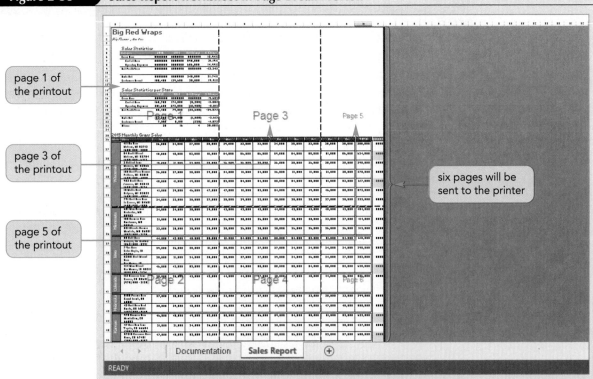

page 1 of the printout

page 3 of the printout

page 5 of the printout

six pages will be sent to the printer

**Trouble?** If you see a different page layout or the worksheet is split onto a different number of pages, don't worry. Each printer is different, so the layout and pages might differ from what is shown in Figure 2-38.

Page Break Preview shows that a printout of the Sales Report worksheet requires six pages in portrait orientation, and that pages 3 and 5 would be mostly blank. Note that each printer is different, so your Page Break Preview might show a different number of pages. With this layout, each page would be difficult to interpret because the data is separated from the descriptive labels. Sanjit wants you to fix the layout so that the contents are easier to read and understand.

## Defining the Print Area

By default, all cells in a worksheet containing text, formulas, or values are printed. If you want to print only part of a worksheet, you can set a print area, which is the region of the worksheet that is sent to the printer. Each worksheet has its own print area. Although you can set the print area in any view, Page Break Preview shades the areas of the worksheet that are not included in the print area, making it simple to confirm what will print.

Sanjit doesn't want the empty cells in the range G1:O24 to print, so you will set the print area to eliminate those cells.

**To set the print area of the Sales Report worksheet:**

▶ 1. Change the zoom level of the worksheet to **80%** to make it easier to select cells and ranges.

▶ 2. Select the nonadjacent range **A1:F24;A25:P49** containing the cells with content.

▶ 3. On the ribbon, click the **PAGE LAYOUT** tab.

▶ 4. In the Page Setup group, click the **Print Area** button, and then click **Set Print Area**. The print area changes to cover only the nonadjacent range A1:F24;A25:P49. The rest of the worksheet content is shaded to indicate that it will not be part of the printout.

▶ 5. Select cell **A1** to deselect the range.

▶ 6. Change the zoom level to **50%** so you can view more of the worksheet. See Figure 2-39.

Figure 2-39 **Print area set for the Sales Report worksheet**

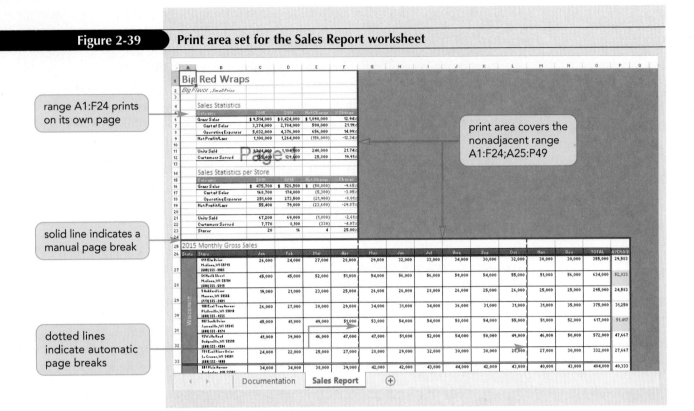

range A1:F24 prints on its own page

print area covers the nonadjacent range A1:F24;A25:P49

solid line indicates a manual page break

dotted lines indicate automatic page breaks

## Inserting Page Breaks

Often, the contents of a worksheet will not fit onto a single printed page. When this happens, Excel prints as much of the content that fits on a single page without resizing, and then inserts automatic page breaks to continue printing the remaining worksheet content on successive pages. The resulting printouts might split worksheet content in awkward places, such as within a table of data.

To split the printout into logical segments, you can insert manual page breaks. Page Break Preview identifies manual page breaks with a solid blue line and automatic page breaks with a dotted blue line. When you specify a print area for a nonadjacent range, as you did for the Sales Report worksheet, you also insert manual page breaks around the adjacent ranges. So a manual page break already appears in the print area you defined (see Figure 2-39). You can remove a page break in Page Break Preview by dragging it out of the print area.

**TIP**

When you remove a page break, Excel will automatically rescale the printout to fit into the allotted pages.

### REFERENCE

### Inserting and Removing Page Breaks

**To insert a page break:**
- Click the first cell below the row where you want to insert a page break, click a column heading, or click a row heading.
- On the PAGE LAYOUT tab, in the Page Setup group, click the Breaks button, and then click Insert Page Break.

**To remove a page break:**
- Select any cell below or to the right of the page break you want to remove.
- On the PAGE LAYOUT tab, in the Page Setup group, click the Breaks button, and then click Remove Page Break.

*or*
- In Page Break Preview, drag the page break line out of the print area.

The Sales Report worksheet has automatic page breaks along columns F and L. You will remove these automatic page breaks from the Sales Report worksheet.

**To remove the automatic page breaks and insert manual page breaks:**

▶ **1.** Point to the dotted blue page break directly to the right of column L until the pointer changes to ↔.

▶ **2.** Drag the page break to the right and out of the print area. The page break is removed from the worksheet.

▶ **3.** Point to the page break located in cell F31 until the pointer changes to ↔, and then drag the page break to the right and out of the print area.

On the PAGE LAYOUT tab, in the Scale to Fit section, notice that the Scale box shows 43%. After removing the two page breaks from the Sales Report printout, Excel scaled the printout from 100% of its actual size to 43% to fit the printout onto two pages.

▶ **4.** Click the **column I** heading to select the entire column. You will add a manual page break between columns H and I to split the monthly gross sales data onto two pages so the printout will be larger and easier to read.

▶ **5.** On the PAGE LAYOUT tab, in the Page Setup group, click the **Breaks** button, and then click **Insert Page Break**. A manual page break is added between columns H and I, forcing the monthly gross sales onto a new page after the June data.

▶ **6.** Select cell **A1** to deselect the column. The printout of the Sales Report worksheet is now limited to three pages. However, the gross sales data in the range A25:O49 is split across pages. See Figure 2-40.

| Figure 2-40 | Manual page break added to the print area |
| --- | --- |

manual page break splits the data onto two pages

## Adding Print Titles

It is a good practice to include descriptive information such as the company name, logo, and worksheet title on each page of a printout in case a page becomes separated from the other pages. You can repeat information, such as the company name, by specifying which rows or columns in the worksheet act as print titles. If a worksheet contains a large table, you can print the table's column headings and row headings on every page of the printout by designating those columns and rows as print titles.

In the Sales Report worksheet, the company name and slogan currently appear on the first page of the printout, but do not appear on subsequent pages. Also, the descriptive row labels for the monthly sales table in column A do not appear on the third page of the printout. You will add print titles to fix these issues.

### To set the print titles:

**TIP**

You can also open the Page Setup dialog box by clicking the Dialog Box Launcher in the Page Setup group on the PAGE LAYOUT tab.

1. On the PAGE LAYOUT tab, in the Page Setup group, click the **Print Titles** button. The Page Setup dialog box opens with the Sheet tab displayed.

2. In the Print titles section, click the **Rows to repeat at top** box, move the pointer over the worksheet, and then select the range **A1:A2**. A flashing border appears around the first two rows of the worksheet to indicate that the contents of the first two rows will be repeated on each page of the printout. The row reference $1:$2 appears in the Rows to repeat at top box.

3. Click the **Columns to repeat at left** box, and then select columns A and B from the worksheet. The column reference $A:$B appears in the Columns to repeat at left box. See Figure 2-41.

**Figure 2-41** **Sheet tab in the Page Setup dialog box**

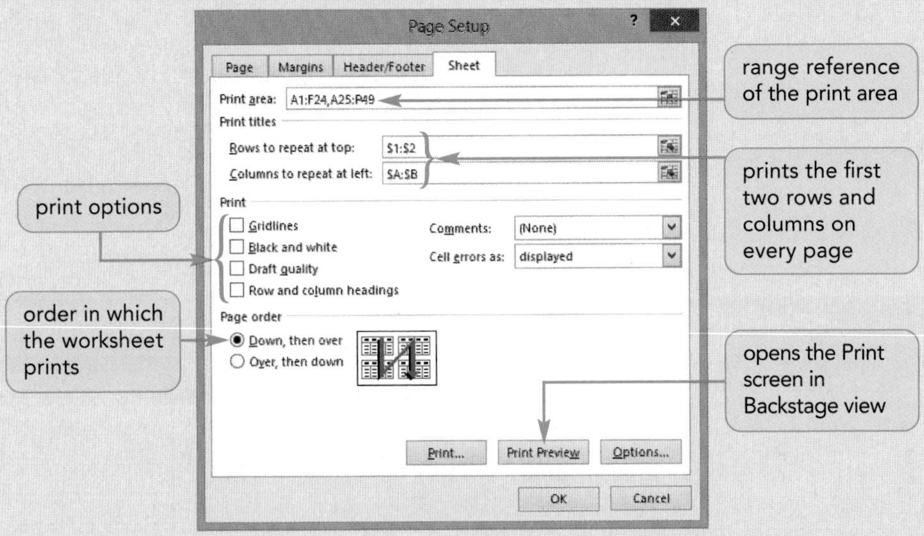

4. Click the **Page** tab in the Page Setup dialog box. You will rescale the worksheet so that it doesn't appear too small in the printout.

5. In the Scaling section, change the Adjust to amount to **65%** of normal size.

6. Click the **Print Preview** button to preview the three pages of printed material on the Print screen in Backstage view.

7. Verify that each of the three pages has the Big Red Wraps title and slogan at the top of the page, and that the state and store names appear in the leftmost columns of pages 2 and 3. See Figure 2-42.

| Figure 2-42 | Print titles on page 3 of the Sales Report worksheet |

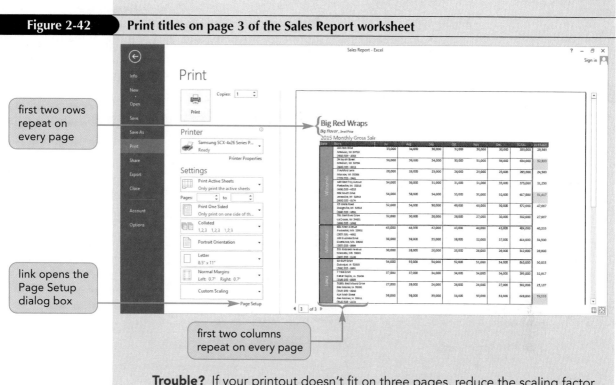

first two rows repeat on every page

link opens the Page Setup dialog box

first two columns repeat on every page

**Trouble?** If your printout doesn't fit on three pages, reduce the scaling factor from 65% to a slightly lower percentage until it does fit on three pages.

## Creating Headers and Footers

You can also use headers and footers to repeat information on each printed page. A **header** appears at the top of each printed page; a **footer** appears at the bottom of each printed page. Headers and footers contain helpful and descriptive text that is usually not found within the worksheet, such as the workbook's author, the current date, or the workbook's filename. If the printout spans multiple pages, you can display the page number and the total number of pages in the printout to help ensure you and others have all the pages.

Each header and footer has three sections—a left section, a center section, and a right section. Within each section, you type the text you want to appear, or you insert elements such as the worksheet name or the current date and time. These header and footer elements are dynamic; if you rename the worksheet, for example, the name is automatically updated in the header or footer. Also, you can create one set of headers and footers for even and odd pages, and you can create another set for the first page in the printout.

Sanjit wants the printout to display the workbook's filename in the header's left section, and the current date in the header's right section. He wants the center footer to display the page number and the total number of pages in the printout, and the right footer to display your name as the workbook's author.

### To create the header and footer:

▶ 1. Click the **Page Setup** link near the bottom of the Print screen to open the Page Setup dialog box.

▶ 2. Click the **Header/Footer** tab to display the header and footer options.

**3.** Click the **Different first page** check box to select it. This lets you create one set of headers and footers for the first page, and one set for the rest of the pages. See Figure 2-43.

**Figure 2-43**    **Header/Footer tab in the Page Setup dialog box**

when selected, displays a different header and footer for even- and odd-numbered pages

displays a different header or footer for the first page

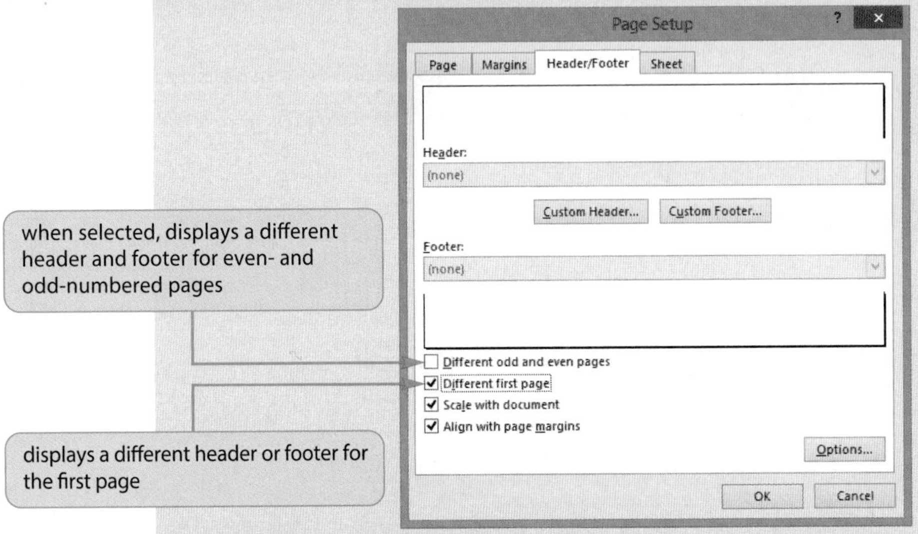

**4.** Click the **Custom Header** button to open the Header dialog box. The dialog box contains two tabs—Header and First Page Header—because you selected the Different first page option.

**TIP**

You can create or edit headers and footers in Page Layout view by clicking in the header/ footer section and using the tools on the DESIGN tab.

**5.** On the Header tab, type **Filename:** in the Left section box, press the **spacebar**, and then click the **Insert File Name** button 📄. The code &[File], which displays the filename of the current workbook, is added to the left section of the header.

**6.** Press the **Tab** key twice to move to the right section of the header, and then click the **Insert Current Date** button 🗓. The code &[Date] is added to the right section of the header. See Figure 2-44.

**Figure 2-44**    **Header dialog box**

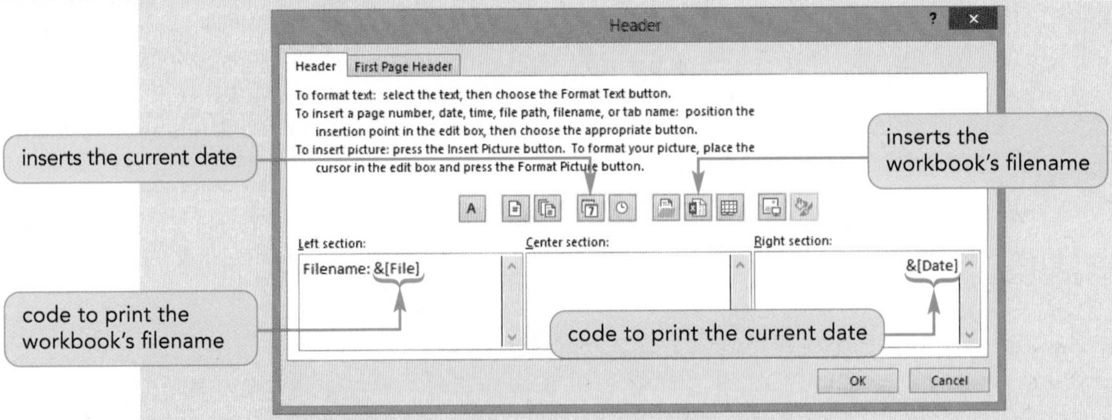

inserts the current date

inserts the workbook's filename

code to print the workbook's filename

code to print the current date

**7.** Click the **OK** button to return to the Header/Footer tab in the Page Setup dialog box. You did not define a header for the first page of the printout, so no header information will be added to that page.

Now you will format the page footer for all pages of the printout.

**8.** Click the **Custom Footer** button to open the Footer dialog box, which is similar to the Header dialog box.

**9.** Click the **Center section** box, type **Page**, press the **spacebar**, and then click the **Insert Page Number** button 📄. The code &[Page], which inserts the current page number, appears after the label "Page."

**10.** Press the **spacebar**, type **of**, press the **spacebar**, and then click the **Insert Number of Pages** button 📑. The code &[Pages], which inserts the total number of pages in the printout, is added to the Center section box. See Figure 2-45.

**Figure 2-45** Footer dialog box

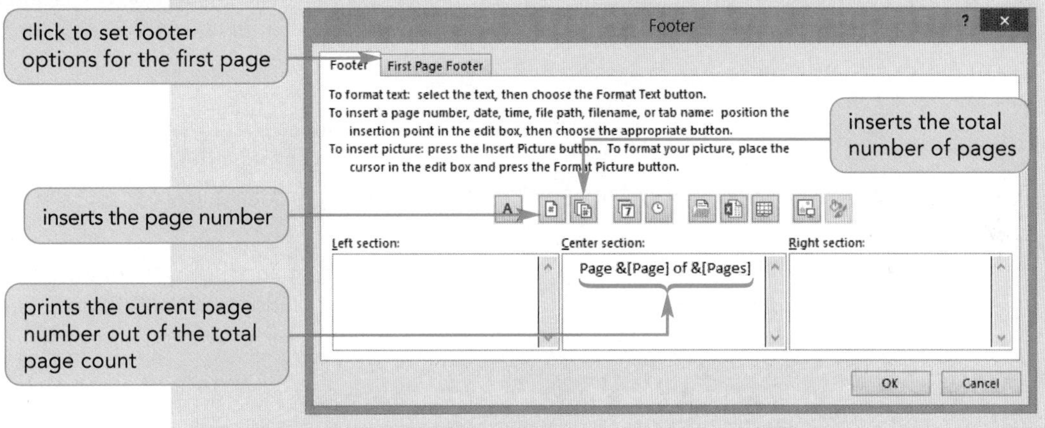

click to set footer options for the first page

inserts the total number of pages

inserts the page number

prints the current page number out of the total page count

**11.** Click the **First Page Footer** tab so you can create the footer for the first page of the printout.

**12.** Click the **Right section** box, type **Prepared by:**, press the **spacebar**, and then type your name.

**13.** Click the **OK** button to return to the Page Setup dialog box.

## Setting the Page Margins

A **margin** is the space between the page content and the edges of the page. By default, Excel sets the page margins to 0.7 inch on the left and right sides, and 0.75 inch on the top and bottom; and it allows for 0.3-inch margins around the header and footer. You can reduce or increase these margins as needed by selecting predefined margin sizes or setting your own.

Sanjit's reports need a wider margin along the left side of the page to accommodate the binding. He asks you to increase the left margin for the printout from 0.7 inch to 1 inch.

### To set the left margin:

**1.** Click the **Margins** tab in the Page Setup dialog box to display options for changing the page margins.

**2.** Double-click the **Left** box to select the setting, and then type **1** to increase the size of the left margin. See Figure 2-46.

**TIP**

To select preset margins, click the Margins button in the Page Setup group on the PAGE LAYOUT tab.

**Figure 2-46** **Margins tab in the Page Setup dialog box**

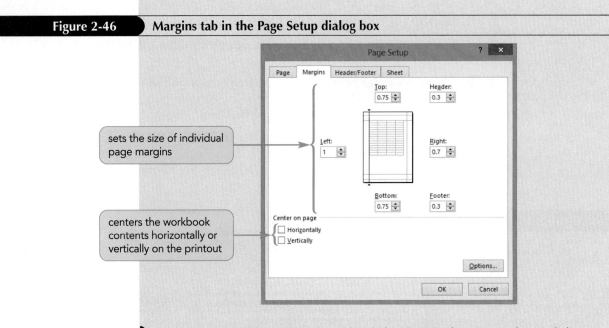

sets the size of individual page margins

centers the workbook contents horizontally or vertically on the printout

▶ **3.** Click the **OK** button to close the dialog box and return to the worksheet.

Sanjit is happy with the appearance of the worksheet and the layout of the printout. You'll save the workbook, and then print the Documentation and Sales Report sheets.

### To save and print the workbook:

▶ **1.** Return the Sales Report worksheet to **Normal** view, and then save the workbook.

▶ **2.** Display the Print screen in Backstage view, and then change the first Settings box to **Print Entire Workbook**. Both the Sales Report worksheet and the Documentation sheet appear in the preview. As you can see, the printout will include a header with the filename and date on every page except the first page, and a footer with your name on the first page and the page number along with the total number of pages on subsequent pages.

▶ **3.** If you are instructed to print, print the entire workbook, and then close it.

### REVIEW

## Session 2.2 Quick Check

1. Describe two methods of applying the same format to different ranges.
2. Red is a standard color. What happens to red text when you change the workbook's theme?
3. What is a conditional format?
4. How would you highlight the top five values in the range A1:C20?
5. How do you insert a manual page break in a worksheet?
6. What is a print area?
7. What are print titles?
8. Describe how to add the workbook filename to the center section of the footer on every page of the printout.

**SAM Projects**

Put your skills into practice with SAM Projects! SAM Projects for this tutorial can be found online. If you have a SAM account, go to www.cengage.com/sam2013 to download the most recent Project Instructions and Start Files.

ASSESS

PRACTICE

## Review Assignments

**Data Files needed for the Review Assignments: Menu.xlsx, Background2.png**

Sanjit has a worksheet that details the sales of individual items from the Big Red Wraps menu. He asks you to format the sales figures and design a layout for the printed sheet as you did for the Sales Report workbook. Complete the following:

1. Open the **Menu** workbook located in the Excel2 ▶ Review folder included with your Data Files, and then save the workbook as **Menu Sales** in the location specified by your instructor.

2. In the Documentation sheet, enter your name in cell B4 and the date in cell B5.

3. Make the following formatting changes to the Documentation sheet:
   a. Set the background image to the **Background2.png** file located in the Excel2 ▶ Review folder.
   b. Format the text in cell A1 in red 26-point bold Calibri Light.
   c. Format the text in cell A2 to red 10-point italic Calibri Light. Change the text string "Big Flavor" to 14 points.
   d. Apply the Accent2 cell style to the range A4:A6.
   e. Change the font color of range B4:B6 to red and change its fill color to white.
   f. Format the date in the Long Date format and left-align the cell contents.

4. Use the Format Painter to copy the formatting in the range A1:A2 in the Documentation sheet and paste it to the same range in the Menu Sales worksheet. (*Hint*: You must increase the size of the text "Big Flavor" manually.)

5. Apply the Title cell style to the titles in cells B4, B12, and A20.

6. Make the following changes to the Units Sold table in the range B5:F10:
   a. In cell C6, calculate the total number of wraps sold by the company (found in the range C22:N31). In cell C7, calculate the total number of soups. In cell C8, calculate the total number of sides. In cell C9, calculate the total number of salads.
   b. In cell C10, calculate the sum of the range C6:C9. Copy the formula to cell D10.
   c. In the range E6:E10, calculate the difference between the 2015 and 2014 values. In the range F6:F10, calculate the percent change from 2014 to 2015.
   d. Apply the Accent2 cell style to the headings in the range B5:F5. Center the headings in the range C5:F5.
   e. Apply the Comma style to the values in the range C6:E10. Do not display any numbers to the right of the decimal point.
   f. Apply the Percent style to the values in the range F6:F10 and show two decimal places.
   g. Add a top border to the values in the range B10:F10.

7. Make the following changes to the range B13:F18:
   a. In cells C18 and D18, calculate the totals of the 2014 and 2015 sales. In the range E14:F18, calculate the change in sales and the percent change.
   b. Copy the format from the range B5:F10 and paste it into the range B13:F18.
   c. Change the format for the values in the ranges C14:E14 and C18:E18 to Accounting format with no decimal places.

8. Make the following changes to the Units Sold per Month table in the range A21:O46:

   a. In the range O22:O45, calculate the total units sold for each menu item. In the range C46:O46, calculate the total items sold per month and overall.

   b. Format the headings in the range A21:O21 with the Accent2 cell style. Center the headings in the range C21:O21.

   c. Format the units sold values in the range C22:O46 with the Comma style and no decimal places.

   d. Change the fill color of the subtotals in the range O22:O45 and C46:N46 to White, Background 1, Darker 15% (the first color in the third row of the theme colors).

   e. Merge each of the menu categories in the range A22:A45 into single cells. Rotate the text of the cells up. Increase the font size to 18 points and middle-align the cell contents.

   f. Format cell A22 with the "Wraps" label in a white font on a Gray-25%, Background 2, Darker 50% fill. Format cell A32 with the "Soups" label in a white font on Blue, Accent 1, Darker 25% fill. Format of cell A37 with the "Sides" label in a white font on a Gold, Accent 4, Darker 25% fill. Format cell A42 with the "Salads" label in a white font on a Green, Accent 6, Darker 25% fill.

   g. Add a thick box border around each category of menu item in the ranges A22:O31, A32:O36, A37:O41, and A42:O45.

9. Create a conditional format for the subtotals in the range O22:O45 highlighting the top five selling items with a yellow fill and dark yellow text.

10. Create a legend for the conditional format. Enter the text **Top 5 Sellers** in cell O48. Add a thick box border around the cell, and then use a conditional format that displays this text in dark yellow text on a yellow fill.

11. Set the following print formats for the Menu Sales worksheet:

    a. Set the print area to the nonadjacent range A1:F19;A20:O48.

    b. Remove any automatic page breaks in the large Units Sold table. Insert a manual page break to separate the June and July sales figures. The printout of the Menu Sales worksheet should fit on three pages.

    c. Scale the printout to 70 percent of normal size.

    d. Define the print titles to repeat the first three rows at the top of the sheet, and the first two columns at the left of the sheet.

    e. Increase the left margin of the printout from 0.7 inch to 1 inch.

    f. Create headers and footers for the printout with a different header for the first page.

    g. For the first page header, print **Prepared by *your name*** in the right section. For every other page, print **Filename: *file*** in the left section and ***date*** in the right section, where *file* is the name of the workbook file and *date* is the current date. (*Hint*: Use the buttons in the Header dialog box to insert the filename and date.)

    h. For every footer, print **Page *page* of *pages*** in the center section, where *page* is the page number and *pages* is the total number of pages in the printout.

12. If you are instructed to print, print the entire workbook in portrait orientation. Verify that the company name and slogan appear on every page of the Menu Sales worksheet printout, and that the menu category and menu item name appear on both pages with the Units Sold table.

13. Save and close the workbook.

## Case Problem 1

**Data File needed for this Case Problem: Salon.xlsx**

*Special Highlights Hair Salon*    Sarah Jones is developing a business plan for a new hair salon, Special Highlights Hair Salon, located in Hatton, North Dakota. As part of the business plan, she needs a projected income statement for the company. You will help her develop and format the income statement. Complete the following:

1. Open the **Salon** workbook located in the Excel2 ▸ Case1 folder included with your Data Files, and then save the workbook as **Salon Income Statement** in the location specified by your instructor.

2. In the Documentation sheet, enter your name in cell B3 and the date in cell B4.

3. Apply the following formatting to the Documentation sheet:
   a. Format cell A1 using the Title cell style.
   b. Format the range A3:A5 using the Accent6 cell style.
   c. In cell B4, format the date value using the long date format, and left-align the cell contents.
   d. In cell B5, format the text string "Special Highlights Hair Salon" in italic.

4. In the Income Statement worksheet, format cell A1 using the Title cell style.

5. Calculate the following items in the Income Statement worksheet:
   a. In cell C7, calculate the Gross Profit, which is equal to the Gross Sales minus the Cost of Sales.
   b. In cell C21, calculate the Total Operating Expenses, which is equal to the sum of the operating expenses.
   c. In cell C22, calculate the Total Operating Profit/Loss, which is equal to the Gross Profit minus the Total Operating Expenses.
   d. In cell C23, calculate the projected Income Taxes, which is equal to 35 percent of the Total Operating Profit/Loss.
   e. In cell C24, calculate the Net Profit/Loss, which is equal to the Total Operating Profit/Loss minus the projected Income Taxes.

6. Set the following formats to the Income Statement worksheet:
   a. Format cells A3 and A26 using the Heading 2 cell style.
   b. Format cells A4 and A9 and the range A27:A38 in bold.
   c. Format cells B5, C7, B10, C21, and C24 using the Accounting format with no decimal places.
   d. Format cells B6, B11:B19, C22, and C23 using the Comma style with no decimal places.
   e. Indent the text in the ranges A5:A6 and A10:A19 two spaces. Indent the text in cell A7 and the range A21:A24 four spaces.
   f. Add a bottom border to cells B6, C7, C21, C22, and C23. Add a double bottom border to cell C24.

7. Merge cells A26:E26 and then left-align the merged cell's contents.

8. Merge the contents of the range B27:E27. Left-align the merged cell's contents and wrap the text within the cell. Increase the height of row 27 to display the entire contents of the cell.

9. Top-align and left-align the range A27:B38.

10. Copy the format from the range A27:B27 to the range A28:B38. Merge columns B through E in each row, left-align the text, and resize the row heights to display the complete contents of the cells.

11. Italicize the text string "National Salon News" in cells B27 and B28.

12. Set the following printing formats to the Income Statement worksheet:

    a. Insert a manual page break directly above row 26 so that the Income Statement prints on two pages.

    b. Set rows 1 and 2 as a print title to print on both pages.

    c. Change the page margins to 1 inch on every side.

    d. On the first page of the printout, print **Prepared by** *your name* in the left section of the header, where *your name* is your name. Print the **current date** in the right section of the header. Do not display header text on any other page.

    e. For every page, add a footer that prints the workbook *filename* in the left section, **Page** *page* in the center section, and the *worksheet name* in the right section.

13. If you are instructed to print, print the entire contents of the workbook in portrait orientation.

14. Save and close the workbook.

## Case Problem 2

**APPLY**

**Data File needed for this Case Problem: Waist.xlsx**

*Waist Trainers*   Alexandra Roulez is a dietician at Waist Trainers, a company in Fort Smith, Arkansas, that specializes in personal improvement, particularly in areas of health and fitness. Alexandra wants to create a meal-planning workbook for her clients who want to lose weight and improve their health. One goal of meal planning is to decrease the percentage of fat in the diet. Alexandra thinks it would be helpful to highlight foods that have a high percentage of fat as well as list their total fat calories. She already created a workbook that contains a few sample food items and lists the number of calories and grams of fat in each item. She wants you to format this workbook. Complete the following:

1. Open the **Waist** workbook located in the Excel2 ▸ Case2 folder included with your Data Files, and then save the workbook as **Waist Trainers Nutrition Table** in the location specified by your instructor.

2. In the Documentation sheet, enter your name in cell B3 and the date in cell B4.

3. Set the following formatting to the Documentation sheet:

    a. In cell A1, apply the Title cell style, increase the font size to 24 points, and then change the font color to a medium orange.

    b. Apply the Accent2 cell style to the range A3:A5.

    c. Wrap the text within the range B3:B5, and then left- and top-align the text in the cells.

    d. Change the format of the date in cell B4 to the long date format.

    e. Add borders around all of the cells in the range A3:B5.

4. Copy the cell format for cell A1 in the Documentation sheet to cell A1 in the Meal Planner worksheet.

5. In cell F4, enter the text **Calories from Fat**. In cell G4, enter the text **Fat Percentage**.

6. In the range F5:F54, calculate the calories from fat for each food item, which is equal to the Grams of Fat multiplied by 9. In the range G5:G54, calculate the fat percentage of each food item, which is equal to the Calories from Fat divided by the Calories.

7. Format cell A3 using the Heading 4 cell style.

8. Format the range A4:G4 using the Accent2 cell style.

9. Format the range D5:F54 with the Comma style and display one decimal place.

10. Format the range G5:G54 with the Percent style and display two decimal places.

11. Merge the cells in the range A5:A8, rotate the text up, and then center-align the cell content both horizontally and vertically. Change the fill color to medium gold, increase the font size to 14 points, and then change the font color to white.

12. Place a thick box border around the beef food items in the range A5:G8.

13. Repeat Steps 11 and 12 for the other six food categories.

14. For good health, the FDA recommends that the fat percentage in a person's diet should not exceed 30 percent of the total calories per day. Create a Conditional Formatting rule for the fat percentages to highlight those food items that exceed the FDA recommendation in dark red text on a light red fill.

15. In cell G2, enter the text **High Fat Food**. Center the text in the cell. Change the format of the cell to dark red text on a light red fill. Add a thick black border around the cell.

16. Set the following print formats for the Meal Planner worksheet:

    a. Change the page orientation to landscape.

    b. Scale the printout so that the width of the worksheet fits on a single page.

    c. If necessary, create manual page breaks directly above row 25 and above row 44. The worksheet should print on three separate pages.

    d. Repeat the first four rows of the worksheet on every printed page.

    e. For every page, add a footer that prints **Prepared by** *your name* in the left section, **Page** *page* in the center section, and the *worksheet name* in the right section.

17. If you are instructed to print, print the entire contents of the workbook.

18. Save and close the workbook.

## CHALLENGE

## Case Problem 3

Data File needed for this Case Problem: Wind.xlsx

***Winds of Change***    Odette Ferris is a researcher at Winds of Change, a privately run wind farm providing supplemental power for communities near Topeka, Kansas. One of Odette's jobs is to record wind speeds from different sectors of the wind farm. She has entered the wind speed data into a workbook as a table with wind speed measures laid out in a grid. Because the numbers are difficult to read and interpret, she wants you to color code the wind speed values using conditional formatting. Complete the following:

1. Open the **Wind** workbook located in the Excel2 ► Case3 folder included with your Data Files, and then save the workbook as **Wind Speed Grid** in the location specified by your instructor.

2. In the Documentation sheet, enter your name in cell B3 and the date in cell B4.

3. In the Wind Speed Grid worksheet, merge the range A1:V1, and then apply the Heading 1 cell style to the merged cell and set the font size to 20 points.

4. Format the range B3:V3 as white text on a black background. Copy this formatting to the grid coordinates in the range A4:A64.

✧ **Explore** 5. Create a conditional format that highlights cells in the range B4:V64 whose value equals 18 with fill color equal to (99, 37, 35). (*Hint*: In the Equal To dialog box, select Custom Format in the with box to open the Format Cells dialog box. On the Fill tab, in the Background Color section, click the More Colors button, and then click the Custom tab to enter the RGB color value.)

✧ **Explore** 6. Repeat Step 5 to continue creating conditional formats that set highlight colors for the wind speed values in the range B4:V64 using the wind speeds and color values shown in Figure 2-47.

Figure 2-47    **Wind speed color values**

| Wind Speed | RGB Color Value |
|---|---|
| 16 m/s | (150, 54, 52) |
| 14 m/s | (218, 150, 148) |
| 12 m/s | (230, 184, 183) |
| 10 m/s | (242, 220, 219) |
| 8 m/s | (242, 242, 242) |
| 6 m/s | (255, 255, 255) |
| 4 m/s | (197, 217, 241) |
| 2 m/s | (141, 180, 226) |
| 0 m/s | (83, 141, 213) |

© 2014 Cengage Learning

7. Reduce the font size of the values in the range B4:V64 to 1 point.

**Explore** 8. Enclose each cell in the range B4:V64 in a light gray border. (*Hint*: Use the Border tab in the Format Cells dialog box.)

9. Use the Format Painter to copy the formats from the range B4:V64 and apply them to the range X3:X12. Increase the font size of the cells in that range to 11 points.

10. Merge the range Y3:Y12, center the contents of the merged cell horizontally and vertically, and then rotate the text down. Format the text in a bold 18-point font.

11. Set the following print formats to the Wind Speed Grid worksheet:

   a  Change the page orientation to landscape.

   b. Set the print area to the range A1:Y64.

   c. Scale the worksheet so that the width and the height of the sheet fit on a single page.

   d. Add a header to the printed page with your name in the left section of the header and the worksheet name in the right section of the header.

12. Save and close the workbook.

## Case Problem 4

**CREATE**

**Data File needed for this Case Problem: Office.xlsx**

**Office Cart**   Robert Trenton is a shipping manager at Office Cart, an online office supply store located in Muncie, Indiana. He wants to use an Excel workbook to track shipping orders. Robert asks you to create and format a worksheet that he can use to enter information for packing slips. Complete the following:

1. Open the **Office** workbook located in the Excel2 ▶ Case4 folder included with your Data Files, and then save the workbook as **Office Cart Packing Slip** in the location specified by your instructor.

2. In the Documentation sheet, enter your name in cell B3 and the date in cell B4.

3. Set the following formats in the Documentation sheet:

   a. Merge cells A1 and B1, and then left-align the contents of the merged cell. Change the font to 28-point white Calibri Light on a dark green background.

   b. Change the font of the range A3:A5 to 14-point white Calibri Light on a dark green background.

   c. Change the format of the date value in cell B4 to the Long Date style, and then left-align the date in the cell.

   d. Italicize the text "Office Cart" in cell B5.

   e. Add a border around each cell in the range A3:B5.

4. Insert a new worksheet at the end of the workbook and name it **Packing Slip**.

5. In the Packing Slip worksheet, select all of the cells in the worksheet. (*Hint*: Click the Select All button at the intersection of the row and column headings, or press the Ctrl+A keys.) Change the font to 10-point dark green Calibri.

6. Add a thick box border around the range A1:D40.

7. For the range A1:D3, change the format to a white Calibri Light font on a dark green background.

8. Set the width of column A to 15 characters. Set the width of column B to 20 characters. Set the width of column C to 30 characters. Set the width of column D to 20 characters.

9. Merge the range A1:B3. Merge the range C1:D3, and then right- and top-align the merged cell. Set the row height of row 1 to 36 points and the heights of rows 2 and 3 to 15 points.

10. In cell A1, enter the following three lines of text, pressing the Alt+Enter keys to start a new line within the cell:
    **Office Cart**
    **14 Trenke Lane**
    **Muncie, IN 47303**
    Format the first line in a 26-point bold font.

11. In cell C1, enter **Packing Slip**, and then format the text in a 26-point bold font using the Headings font of the current theme.

12. In the range A5:A7, enter the following three lines of text in a bold font, and then right-align the text and indent the text one character:
    **Order Date**
    **Order Number**
    **Purchase Order**

13. Format cell B5 in the Long Date format and left-align the cell contents. Insert border lines around each of the cells in the range B5:B7.

14. In the range C5:C7, enter the following three lines of text, and then use the Format Painter to copy the formats from the range A5:B7 to the range C5:D7:
    **Date**
    **Sales Rep**
    **Account Num**

15. In cell B9, enter **Ship To**. In cell D9, enter **Bill To**. Format the text in both cells in bold.

16. In cell A10, enter **Address**, format the text in bold, right-align the text, and then indent it one character.

17. Merge the cells in the range B10:B15, left- and top-align the cell contents, insert a border around the merged cell, and then wrap the text within this cell.

18. In cell C10, enter **Address**. Copy the format from the range A10:B15 to the range C10:D15.

19. Enter the following data in the indicated cells in the worksheet:
    cell A17: **Item**
    cell B17: **Product No.**
    cell C17: **Description**
    cell D17: **Order Quantity**

20. Format the range A17:D17 in bold white Calibri on a dark green background.

21. Format the range A18:D18 with a bottom border and a light green background. Format the range A19:D19 with a bottom border and a white background. Copy the format in the range A18:D19 to the range A20:D27.

22. Apply a Top and Double Bottom Border to the range A28:D28. Merge the contents of the range A28:C28. Enter **Total** in cell A28, bold the text, and right-align the cell contents.

23. In cell D28, enter a formula to calculate the sum of the values in the range D18:D27. Bold the text.

24. In cell A30, enter **Comments** and then bold the text.

25. Merge the range A31:D39, left- and top-align the cell contents, and then add a thick box border around the merged cell.

26. In cell D40, enter **Thank you for your business!** in italic 16-point Calibri, and then right-align the cell contents.

27. Make sure the worksheet is set to portrait orientation, and then add a footer that displays your name in the left section, the filename in the center section, and the current date in the right section. Scale the printout so that it fits onto a single page.

28. Enter the packing slip data shown in Figure 2-48. Save and close the workbook.

**Figure 2-48** Office Cart packing slip form

# Office Cart                                     Packing Slip

14 Trenke Lane
Muncie, IN 47303

| | | | |
|---|---|---|---|
| **Order Date** | Thursday, June 09, 2016 | **Date** | Thursday, June 09, 2016 |
| **Order Number** | OC414-0608 | **Sales Rep** | Helen Richards |
| **Purchase Order** | OC912-1418-3 | **Account Num** | 97 |

**Ship To**  
**Address** c/o Kevin Davidson
Unger and Associates
550 Commerce Drive
Jefferson City, MO 65101

**Bill To**  
**Address** Unger and Associates
550 Commerce Drive
Jefferson City, MO

| Item | Product No. | Description | Order Quantity |
|---|---|---|---|
| 1 | MC10R | Multiuse Copy Paper 10 ream | 5 |
| 2 | SGP10 | Select Gel Pens | 15 |
| 3 | QCLPT4C | QS Laser Print Toner Kit | 2 |
| 4 | OCBE200 | OC Business Envelopes (200 ct) | 3 |
| 5 | OCSL200 | OC Shipping Labels (200 ct) | 5 |
| 6 | | | |
| 7 | | | |
| 8 | | | |
| 9 | | | |
| 10 | | | |
| | | **Total** | 30 |

**Comments**

Please contact shipping manager Robert Trenton (ext. 311) regarding discount shipping rates.

*Thank you for your business!*

# Calculating Data with Formulas and Functions

*Creating a Fitness Tracker*

## OBJECTIVES

**Session 3.1**
- Make a workbook user-friendly
- Translate an equation into an Excel formula
- Understand function syntax
- Enter formulas and functions with the Quick Analysis tool
- Enter functions with the Insert Function dialog box
- Interpret error values
- Change cell references between relative and absolute

**Session 3.2**
- Use the AutoFill tool to enter formulas and data and complete a series
- Display the current date with the TODAY function
- Find the next weekday with the WORKDAY function
- Use the COUNT and COUNTA functions to tally cells
- Use an IF function to return a value based on a condition
- Perform an exact match lookup with the VLOOKUP function
- Perform what-if analysis using trial and error and Goal Seek

## Case | *Fit Fathers Inc.*

Ken Dorsett is a certified fitness professional and founder of Fit Fathers Inc., which is a fitness program he developed to help fathers stay fit and active. From its beginnings in Blue Springs, Missouri, where Ken led daily workouts with three other dads, his program has grown to an enrollment of 318 fathers in five different cities in the northwest corner of the state.

Ken wants to help his members evaluate their fitness goals and track their workouts. He has been working on an Excel workbook that can assess each participant's fitness level and track his workout progress. Ken has developed the basic structure of the workbook, but still needs to enter the formulas to calculate the different statistics and data that are important for his clients. He asks you to enter the appropriate formulas to complete the workbook. To do this, you will use a variety of formulas and functions.

## STARTING DATA FILES

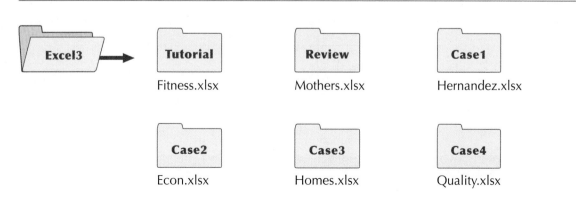

Excel3 → Tutorial
Fitness.xlsx

Review
Mothers.xlsx

Case1
Hernandez.xlsx

Case2
Econ.xlsx

Case3
Homes.xlsx

Case4
Quality.xlsx

Microsoft product screenshots used with permission from Microsoft Corporation.

# Session 3.1 Visual Overview:

Functions are organized by category in the Function Library group. Select a function to open the Function Arguments dialog box.

The Insert Function button opens the Insert Function dialog box from which you can select a function.

The SUM function adds the values in the range.

The AVERAGE function calculates the average value of the range.

The **MEDIAN function** determines the middle value in the range.

The **MAX function** displays the maximum value in the range.

The **MIN function** displays the minimum value in the range.

FILE    HOME    INSERT    PAGE LAYOUT    FORMULAS    DATA    REVIEW    VIE

Fitness Tracker - E

fx Insert Function

Σ AutoSum ▾
Recently Used ▾
Financial ▾

? Logical ▾
Text ▾
Date & Time ▾

Lookup & Reference ▾
Math & Trig ▾
More Functions ▾

Name Manager

Define Na
Use in Fo
Create fr

Function Library

Defined Nan

J17          fx    =MEDIAN(K23:K45)

| | F | G | H | I | J | |
|---|---|---|---|---|---|---|
| 14 | | Exercise Statistics | Jogging | Calisthenics | Strength | |
| 15 | | SUM | 278 | 245 | 347 | |
| 16 | | AVERAGE | 16.4 | 14.4 | 20.4 | |
| 17 | | MEDIAN | 15.0 | 15.0 | 20.0 | |
| 18 | | MAX | 22 | 20 | 30 | |
| 19 | | MIN | 10 | 8 | 12 | |
| 20 | | Jogging (min.) | | | | |
| 21 | | =SUM(I23:I45) | =S | | | |
| 22 | | =AVERAGE(I23:I45) | =AV | Jogging | Calisthenics | Stre |
| | | | | 10 | 10 | |
| | | =MEDIAN(I23:I45) | =M | 10 | 8 | |
| | | =MAX(I23:I45) | =M | 12 | 18 | |
| 26 | | =MIN(I23:I45) | | | | |
| 27 | | | x | 12 | 15 | |
| 28 | | 6 | x | 15 | 10 | |
| 29 | | 7 | | | | |
| 30 | | 8 | x | 15 | 15 | |
| 31 | | 9 | x | 15 | 13 | |
| 32 | | 10 | x | 20 | 15 | |

Documentation    **Fitness Report**    Explanation of Formulas

READY

# Functions and Cell References

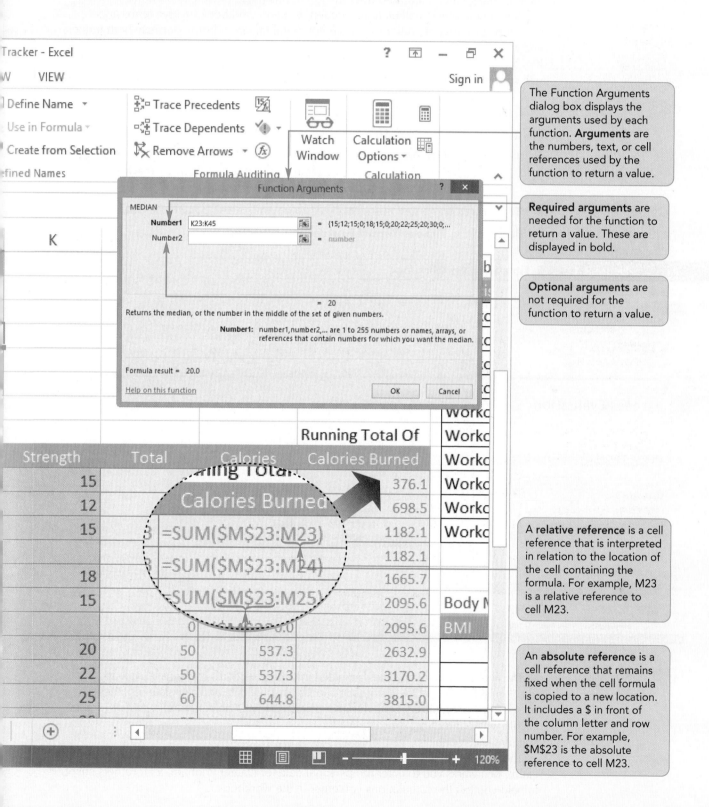

The Function Arguments dialog box displays the arguments used by each function. **Arguments** are the numbers, text, or cell references used by the function to return a value.

**Required arguments** are needed for the function to return a value. These are displayed in bold.

**Optional arguments** are not required for the function to return a value.

A **relative reference** is a cell reference that is interpreted in relation to the location of the cell containing the formula. For example, M23 is a relative reference to cell M23.

An **absolute reference** is a cell reference that remains fixed when the cell formula is copied to a new location. It includes a $ in front of the column letter and row number. For example, $M$23 is the absolute reference to cell M23.

# Making Workbooks User-Friendly

Every workbook should be accessible to its intended users. When a workbook is user-friendly, anyone who needs to enter data in the workbook or interpret its results can understand the workbook's contents, including any jargon or unusual terms, what is being calculated, and how the equations make those calculations.

Many of the fitness calculations needed for Ken's workbook involve terms and equations that are unfamiliar to people not in the fitness industry. Because both trainers and clients will access this workbook, these terms and equations need to be explained. Ken has already included information about the fitness equations in the workbook. You will open the workbook, and examine its layout and structure.

## To open and review the Fitness workbook:

1. Open the **Fitness** workbook located in the Excel3 ► Tutorial folder included with your Data Files, and then save the workbook as **Fitness Tracker** in the location specified by your instructor.

2. In the Documentation sheet, enter your name in cell B3 and the date in cell B4.

3. Go to the **Fitness Report** worksheet. See Figure 3-1.

| Figure 3-1 | Fitness Tracker workbook |
| --- | --- |

The Fitness Report worksheet is divided into three sections. The Fitness Evaluation in columns B through D will store the client's personal data and calculate his fitness status. The Workout Report in columns F through M will contain monthly reports on the client's workout routine and calculate the results from his workouts. The Fitness Tables in columns O through P contain different fitness values that will be used in the calculations.

The Fitness Evaluation contains a section for personal information on a Fit Fathers client. Ken wants you to enter the personal data for Daniel Pridham, a Fit Fathers client, to help you test the calculations you enter in the workbook.

**To enter Daniel's personal data:**

▶ **1.** In cell **C8**, enter **Daniel Pridham** as the client's name.

▶ **2.** In cell **C9**, enter **Sedentary** to describe Daniel's activity level.

▶ **3.** In the range **C10:C14**, enter **45** for his age, **193** for his weight in pounds, **70** for his height in inches, **37** for his waist size in inches, and **15.5** for his neck size in inches.

## Documenting Formulas

Documenting the contents of a workbook helps to avoid errors and confusion. This type of information can make a workbook easier for other people to understand. For workbooks that include many calculations, as the Fitness Tracker workbook does, it is helpful to explain the formulas and terms used in the calculations. Such documentation also can serve as a check that the equations are accurate. Another way to document formulas and terms is to include notes of explanation within the worksheet where the equations are used.

Ken has included explanations of different fitness terms and equations in the Explanation of Formulas worksheet, and explanatory notes in cells B26 and F46 of the Fitness Report worksheet. Before proceeding, he wants you to review the documentation in these worksheets.

**To review the documentation in the Fitness Tracker workbook:**

▶ **1.** Click the **Explanation of Formulas** sheet tab to make it the active sheet.

▶ **2.** Read the sheet contents, reviewing the descriptions of common fitness terms and formulas. As you continue developing the Fitness Tracker workbook, you'll learn about these terms and formulas in more detail.

▶ **3.** Click the **Fitness Report** sheet tab to return to the Fitness Report worksheet.

▶ **4.** Read the explanatory notes in cells B26 and F46.

## Using Constants in Formulas

The first fitness equation Ken wants you to enter is BMI, or body mass index, which estimates the amount of human body fat. The BMI equation is based on the individual's body weight divided by the square of his or her height. The specific formula is

$$BMI = \frac{703w}{h^2}$$

where $w$ is the body weight in pounds and $h$ is the height in inches. BMI values from 18.5 to 24.9 are considered normal; anything higher is considered overweight.

One common skill you need when creating a workbook is to translate an equation like the BMI equation into an Excel formula. Some equations use constants. A **constant** is a value in a formula that doesn't change. In the BMI equation, 703 is a constant because that value never changes when calculating the body mass index.

**INSIGHT**

## Deciding Where to Place a Constant

Should a constant be entered directly into the formula or placed in a separate worksheet cell and referenced in the formula? The answer depends on the constant being used, the purpose of the workbook, and the intended audience. Placing constants in separate cells that you reference in the formulas can help users better understand the worksheet because no values are hidden within the formulas. Also, when a constant is entered in a cell, you can add explanatory text next to each constant to document how it is being used in the formula. On the other hand, you don't want a user to inadvertently change the value of a constant and throw off all the formula results. You will need to evaluate how important it is for other people to immediately see the constant, and whether the constant requires any explanation for other people to understand the formula. For example, Ken wants you to include the 703 constant in the BMI formula rather than in a separate cell because he doesn't feel that clients need to see this constant to understand BMI.

To convert the BMI equation into a formula, you need to replace $w$ and $h$ in the equation with Daniel's actual weight and height. Because Daniel's weight is stored in cell C11 and his height is stored in cell C12, you replace the $w$ in the formula with the C11 cell reference, and replace the $h$ in the formula with the C12 cell reference. The resulting Excel formula is:

```
=703*C11/C12^2
```

Note that the exponent operator ^ is used to square the height value in the denominator of the fraction. Recall that exponentiation raises a value to a power; in this case, the value in cell C12 is raised to the second power, or squared. Following the order of operations, Excel will first square the height value, then multiply the weight value by 703, and finally divide that product by the squared height. You will enter the BMI formula in the Fitness Report worksheet now.

### To enter the BMI formula in the Fitness Report worksheet:

▶ 1. In cell **C19**, enter the formula **=703*C11/C12^2**. The formula multiplies the weight in cell C11 by the constant 703, and then divides the resulting value by the square of the height in cell C12. The calculated BMI value that is displayed in cell C19 is 27.68959184.

   **Trouble?** If your BMI formula results differ from 27.68959184, you probably entered the formula incorrectly. Edit your formula as needed so that the numbers and cell references match those shown in the formula in Step 1.

▶ 2. Select cell **C19**, and then reduce the number of displayed decimals to one. Cell C19 displays 27.7 as the formula results.

The next fitness equation, which calculates the individual's resting basal metabolic rate (BMR), includes four constants. The resting BMR estimates the number of calories a person expends daily (not counting any actual activity). For men, the BMR is calculated with the equation

$$BMR = 6.23w + 12.7h - 6.76a + 66$$

where *w* is the weight in pounds, *h* is the height in inches, and *a* is the age in years. BMR is calculated by multiplying the weight, height, and age by different constants, and then adding the results to another constant. Heavier and taller people require more daily calories to sustain them. As people age, their metabolism slows, resulting in a lower BMR. Daniel's weight, height, and age are stored in cells C11, C12, and C10, respectively, so the BMR equation translates to the following Excel formula:

```
=6.23*C11+12.7*C12-6.76*C10+66
```

You will enter this formula in the Fitness Report worksheet to calculate Daniel's BMR.

### To enter the BMR formula in the Fitness Report worksheet:

▶ 1. In cell **C21**, enter the formula **=6.23*C11+12.7*C12–6.76*C10+66**. Cell C21 displays 1853.19, indicating that Daniel burns about 1853 calories per day before performing any activity.

   **Trouble?** If your BMR formula results differ from 1853.19, you might have entered the formula incorrectly. Edit the formula as needed so that the numbers and cell references match those shown in the formula in Step 1.

▶ 2. Select cell **C21**, and then reduce the number of decimals displayed in the cell to zero. The number of calories per day displayed in cell C21 is 1853.

The 1853 calories per day amount assumes no physical activity. However, even the most sedentary person moves a little bit during the day, which increases the BMR value. The table in the range O7:P12 in the Fitness Report worksheet lists the constant multipliers for different activity levels. For example, the BMR of a sedentary man like Daniel is multiplied by 1.2 (shown in cell P8) to account for daily movements. If Daniel were to increase his activities to a moderate level, the multiplier would increase to 1.55 (as shown in cell P10).

You will enter the formula to calculate Daniel's active BMR based on his sedentary lifestyle. Ken wants you to use the constant value stored in the table rather entering it into the formula because he anticipates that Daniel will increase his activity level under the direction of Fit Fathers, and it is easier to update the amount in a cell rather than editing a formula.

### To calculate Daniel's active BMR:

▶ 1. In cell **C22**, enter the formula **=C21*P8** to multiply Daniel's resting BMR by the sedentary activity level. Based on this calculation, Daniel's active BMR is 2223.828 calories per day.

▶ 2. Select cell **C22**, and then decrease the number of decimal places displayed in the cell to zero. The displayed value changes to 2224. See Figure 3-2.

**Figure 3-2** BMI and BMR calculated values

| C22 | | | $f_x$ | =C21*P8 | | | |
|---|---|---|---|---|---|---|---|

| | A | B | C | D | E | F | G | H |
|---|---|---|---|---|---|---|---|---|
| 6 | | Personal Data | | | | Workout Summary | | |
| 7 | | | | | | Start Date | | |
| 8 | | Name | Daniel Pridham | | | End Date | | |
| 9 | | Activity Level | Sedentary | | | Workouts Scheduled | | |
| 10 | | Age (years) | 45 | | | Workouts Attended | | |
| 11 | | Weight (lb.) | 193 | | | Workouts Missed | | |
| 12 | | Height (in.) | 70 | | | | | |
| 13 | | Waist (in.) | 37 | | | Exercise Statistics | Jogging (min.) | Calisthenics ( |
| 14 | | Neck (in.) | 15.5 | | | SUM | | |
| 15 | | | | | | AVERAGE | | |
| 16 | | | | | | MEDIAN | | |
| 17 | | Fitness Assessment | | | | MINIMUM | | |
| 18 | | | | | | MAXIMUM | | |
| 19 | | BMI | 27.7 | | | | | |
| 20 | | | | | | Workout Routine 5 | | |
| 21 | | Resting BMR (cal./day) | 1853 | | | Day | Attended (x) | Jogging (mi |
| 22 | | Active BMR (cal./day) | 2224 | | | 1 | x | |
| 23 | | | | | | 2 | x | |
| 24 | | | | | | 3 | x | |

client's personal data

estimate of daily metabolism while at rest and active

estimate of body mass index

Documentation | **Fitness Report** | Explanation of Formulas | ⊕

READY

The active BMR shows that Daniel needs about 2224 calories per day to maintain his current weight.

## Identifying Notes, Input Values, and Calculated Values

When worksheets involve notes and many calculations, it is useful to distinguish input values that are used in formulas from calculated values that are returned by formulas. Formatting that clearly differentiates input values from calculated values helps others more easily understand the worksheet. Such formatting also helps prevent anyone from entering a value in a cell that contains a formula.

You can use cell styles to identify cells as containing explanatory text, input values, and calculated values. When you use cell styles or other formatting to identify a cell's purpose, you should include a legend in the worksheet describing the purpose of the formatting.

Ken wants to be sure that whenever he and his staff members update a client's workbook, they can easily see where to enter numbers. You will apply cell styles to distinguish between notes, input cells, and formula cells.

### To apply cell styles to differentiate cells with notes, input values, and calculated values:

1. Select the merged cell **B26**.

2. On the HOME tab, in the Styles group, click the **Cell Styles** button to open the Cell Styles gallery.

3. Click the **Explanatory Text** cell style located in the Data and Model group. Cell B26 is formatted with the Explanatory Text cell style.

4. Format cell **F46** with the **Explanatory Text** cell style.

▶ 5. Format the range **C8:C14** with the **Input** cell style. These cells contain the personal information about Daniel that you entered earlier.

▶ 6. Format the nonadjacent range **C19;C21:C22** containing the calculated BMI and BMR values with the **Calculation** cell style.

▶ 7. Format the range **G22:J44** with the **Input** cell style. These cells store information about Daniel's workout routine, which Ken enters after each workout.

   Next, you'll create a legend to identify which cells are input cells and which cells are calculated cells.

▶ 8. In cell **C2**, enter **Input Values** as the label, format the cell with the **Explanatory Text** cell style, and then right-align the text in the cell.

▶ 9. In cell **C4**, enter **Calculated Values** as the label, and then use the Format Painter to copy the formatting in cell C2 and paste it to cell C4.

▶ 10. Format cell **D2** with the **Input** cell style, and then format cell **D4** with the **Calculation** cell style.

▶ 11. Select cell **C19**. See Figure 3-3.

| Figure 3-3 | Input and calculated values formatted with cell styles |
| --- | --- |

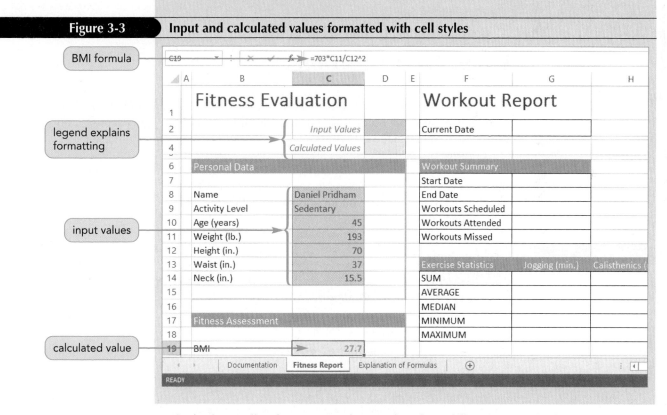

The built-in cell styles are a quick way of marking different types of values in your worksheet. If the formats do not match what you want for your workbook, you can create your own cell styles. However you design your worksheet, your purpose is to make the values easy to interpret.

**PROSKILLS**

### Written Communication: Displaying Significant Digits

Excel stores numbers with up to 15 digits and displays as many digits as will fit into the cell. So even the result of a simple formula such as =10/3 will display 3.33333333333333 if the cell is wide enough.

A number with 15 digits is difficult to read, and calculations rarely need that level of accuracy. Many scientific disciplines, such as chemistry or physics, have rules for specifying exactly how many digits should be displayed with any calculation. These digits are called **significant digits** because they indicate the accuracy of the measured and calculated values. For example, an input value of 19.32 has four significant digits.

The rules are based on several factors and vary from one discipline to another. Generally, a calculated value should display no more digits than are found in any of the input values. For example, because the input value 19.32 has four significant digits, any calculated value based on that input should have no more than four significant digits. Showing more digits would be misleading because it implies a level of accuracy beyond that which was actually measured.

Because Excel displays calculated values with as many digits as can fit into a cell, you need to know the standards for your profession and change the display of your calculated values accordingly.

## Using Excel Functions

Functions provide a quick way to calculate summary data such as the total, average, and median values in a collection of values. Ken recorded the amount of time Daniel spent at each workout doing brisk jogging, calisthenics, and strength exercise. Ken wants you to analyze the results from Daniel's workout routine. You will use Excel functions to summarize these results.

Excel supports an extensive library of functions, organized into the 12 categories shown in Figure 3-4. You can use Excel functions to perform statistical analysis, work with financial data, retrieve information from databases, and generate text strings, among many other tasks.

**Figure 3-4**    **Excel function categories**

| Category | Description |
|---|---|
| Cube | Retrieve data from multidimensional databases involving online analytical processing (OLAP) |
| Database | Retrieve and analyze data stored in databases |
| Date & Time | Analyze or create date and time values and time intervals |
| Engineering | Analyze engineering problems |
| Financial | Analyze information for business and finance |
| Information | Return information about the format, location, or contents of worksheet cells |
| Logical | Return logical (true-false) values |
| Lookup & Reference | Look up and return data matching a set of specified conditions from a range |
| Math & Trig | Perform math and trigonometry calculations |
| Statistical | Provide statistical analyses of data sets |
| Text | Return text values or evaluate text |
| Web | Provide information on web-based connections |

© 2014 Cengage Learning

The Excel Help system provides information on all of the Excel functions.

## Exploring Function Syntax

Before you use functions, you should understand the function syntax. Recall that the syntax of an Excel function follows the general pattern

    FUNCTION(argument1,argument2,...)

where FUNCTION is the name of the function, and argument1, argument2, and so forth are arguments used by the function. An argument can be any type of value including text, numbers, cell references, or even other formulas or functions. Not all functions require arguments.

**TIP**

Optional arguments are always placed last in the argument list.

Some arguments are optional. You can include an optional argument in the function or omit it from the function. Some optional arguments have default values associated with them, so that if you omit the optional argument, Excel will use the default value. These tutorials show optional arguments within square brackets along with the argument's default value (if any), as

    FUNCTION(argument1[, argument2=value2,...])

where argument1 is a required argument, argument2 is optional, and value2 is the default value for argument2. As you work with specific functions, you will learn which arguments are required and which are optional as well as any default values associated with optional arguments.

Figure 3-5 describes some of the more common Math, Trig, and Statistical functions and provides the syntax of those functions.

| Figure 3-5 | Common Math, Trig, and Statistical functions |

| Function | Category | Description |
|---|---|---|
| AVERAGE(number1[, number2, number3, ...]) | Statistical | Calculates the average of a collection of numbers, where number1, number2, and so forth are numbers or cell references; only number1 is required |
| COUNT(value1[, value2, value3, ...]) | Statistical | Counts how many cells in a range contain numbers, where value1, value2, and so forth are text, numbers, or cell references; only value1 is required |
| COUNTA(value1[, value2, value3, ...]) | Statistical | Counts how many cells are not empty in ranges value1, value2, and so forth, or how many numbers are listed within value1, value2, etc. |
| INT(number) | Math & Trig | Displays the integer portion of number |
| MAX(number1[, number2, number3, ...]) | Statistical | Calculates the maximum value of a collection of numbers, where number1, number2, and so forth are either numbers or cell references |
| MEDIAN(number1[, number2, number3, ...]) | Statistical | Calculates the median, or middle, value of a collection of numbers, where number1, number2, and so forth are either numbers or cell references |
| MIN(number1[, number2, number3, ...]) | Statistical | Calculates the minimum value of a collection of numbers, where number1, number2, and so forth are either numbers or cell references |
| RAND() | Math & Trig | Returns a random number between 0 and 1 |
| ROUND(number, num_digits) | Math & Trig | Rounds number to the number of digits specified by num_digits |
| SUM(number1[, number2, number3, ...]) | Math & Trig | Adds a collection of numbers, where number1, number2, and so forth are either numbers or cell references |

© 2014 Cengage Learning

For example, the ROUND function rounds a number to a specified number of decimal places and has the syntax

ROUND(*number*, *num_digits*)

where *number* is the number to be rounded and *num_digits* is the number of decimal places to which you want to round the *number* argument. The following function rounds 2.718282 to two decimal places, resulting in 2.72:

ROUND(2.718282, 2)

However, you usually reference data values stored in worksheet cells rather than entering the numbers directly in the function. For example, the following function rounds the number in cell A10 to three decimal places:

ROUND(A10, 3)

Both arguments in the ROUND function are required. An example of a function that uses optional arguments is the AVERAGE function, which can calculate averages from several ranges or entered values. For example, the function

AVERAGE(A1:A10)

averages the values in the range A1:A10, while the function

AVERAGE(A1:A10, C5:C10, E10)

includes two optional arguments and averages the values from the cells in range A1:A10, range C5:C10, and cell E10.

Functions can be included as part of larger formulas. The following formula calculates the average of the values in the range A1:A100, and then squares that result using the ∧ operator:

=AVERAGE(A1:A100)^2

Functions can also be placed inside another function, or **nested**. If a formula contains several functions, Excel starts with the innermost function and then moves outward. For example, the following formula first calculates the average of the values in the range A1:A100 using the AVERAGE function, and then rounds that value to two decimal places:

=ROUND(AVERAGE(A1:A100),2)

One challenge of nesting functions is to make sure that you include all of the parentheses. You can check this by counting the number of opening parentheses and making sure that number matches the number of closing parentheses. Excel also displays each level of nested parentheses in different colors to make it easier for you to match the opening and closing parentheses in the formula. If the number of parentheses doesn't match, Excel will not accept the formula and will provide a suggestion for how to rewrite the formula so the number of opening and closing parentheses does match.

There are several ways to enter a function. You have already entered a function by typing directly in a cell and using the AutoSum button. Another way to enter a function is with the Quick Analysis tool.

## Entering Functions with the Quick Analysis Tool

The Quick Analysis tool, which you have already used to apply conditional formats that highlight specific data values, can also be used to generate columns and rows of summary statistics that can be used for analyzing data.

Columns F through M in the Fitness Report worksheet will contain the workout report. The range H22:J44 records the number of minutes Daniel spent at each workout jogging, doing calisthenics, and doing strength training. Ken needs to know the total minutes Daniel spent at each exercise to evaluate Daniel's workout effort during the past month. The most efficient way to calculate these totals is with the SUM function. You will use the Quick Analysis tool to enter the SUM function to calculate the total minutes spent at each exercise.

### To calculate the total minutes spent on each exercise:

▶ 1. Select the range **H22:J44** containing the minutes spent on each exercise during each workout. The Quick Analysis button 📖 appears in the lower-right corner of the selected range.

▶ 2. Click the **Quick Analysis** button 📖 (or press the **Ctrl+Q** keys) to display the Quick Analysis tool.

▶ 3. Click the **TOTALS** category to display Quick Analysis tools for calculating totals.

▶ 4. Point to the **Sum** button. Live Preview shows the results of Sum. See Figure 3-6.

| Figure 3-6 | Quick Analysis tool to calculate totals |

▶ 5. Click **Sum** to enter the SUM function for each cell in the selected range. The results show that Daniel spent 278 minutes jogging, 245 minutes doing calisthenics, and 347 minutes doing strength exercises during the previous month's workouts.

The Quick Analysis tool automatically inserts the formulas containing the SUM function at the bottom of the table. Ken wants you to move this information near the top of the worksheet where it can be viewed first.

▶ 6. Select the range **H45:J45**, and then cut the selected range.

▶ 7. Select cell **G14**, and then paste the formulas with the SUM functions. The totals now appear in the range G14:I14.

The Quick Analysis tool can also be used to quickly calculate averages. An average provides an estimate of the most typical value from a data sample. Ken wants to know the average number of minutes that Daniel spent on each exercise during his sessions.

### To calculate the average minutes spent per exercise:

▶ 1. Select the range **H22:J44**, and then click the **Quick Analysis** button 📋 that appears in the lower-right corner of the selected range (or press the **Ctrl+Q** keys).

▶ 2. Click the **TOTALS** category, and then click **Average** to enter the AVERAGE function in the range H45:J45 and calculate the average minutes per exercise type.

▶ 3. Cut the formulas from the range **H45:J45**, and then paste them into the range **G15:I15**.

Excel displays the averages to eight decimal places, which implies a far greater accuracy in measuring the exercise time than could be recorded.

▶ 4. In the range **G15:I15**, decrease the number of decimal places displayed to one. On average, Daniel spent about 16.4 minutes per session jogging, 14.4 minutes on calisthenics, and 20.4 minutes on strength exercises. See Figure 3-7.

| Figure 3-7 | Sums and averages of exercise times |
| --- | --- |

The Quick Analysis tool can be used to summarize values across rows as well as down columns. Ken wants to calculate how long Daniel worked out each day. You will use the Quick Analysis tool to calculate the total exercise minutes per workout.

### To calculate the total workout times per session:

▶ 1. In cell **K21**, enter **Total Minutes** as the heading.

▶ 2. Select the range **H22:J44**, and then open the Quick Analysis tool.

▶ 3. Click the **TOTALS** category, and then click the right scroll button to scroll to the right through the list of calculations.

▶ 4. Click the **Sum** button for the column of summary statistics. SUM functions are entered in the range K22:K44, calculating the sum of the workout minutes per session.

The Quick Analysis tool applies its own style to the formulas it generates. Instead of the bold text, you want the formulas to be formatted with the Calculation style.

▶ 5. Format the range **K22:K44** with the **Calculation** cell style.

6. In cell **J13**, enter **Total Minutes** as the heading.

7. Copy the formulas in the range **I14:I15**, and then paste them into the range **J14:J15** to calculate the sum and average of the total exercise minutes from all of the workouts. As shown in Figure 3-8, Daniel worked out for 870 minutes during the month with an average of 37.8 minutes per workout.

**Figure 3-8** | Total exercise time per workout

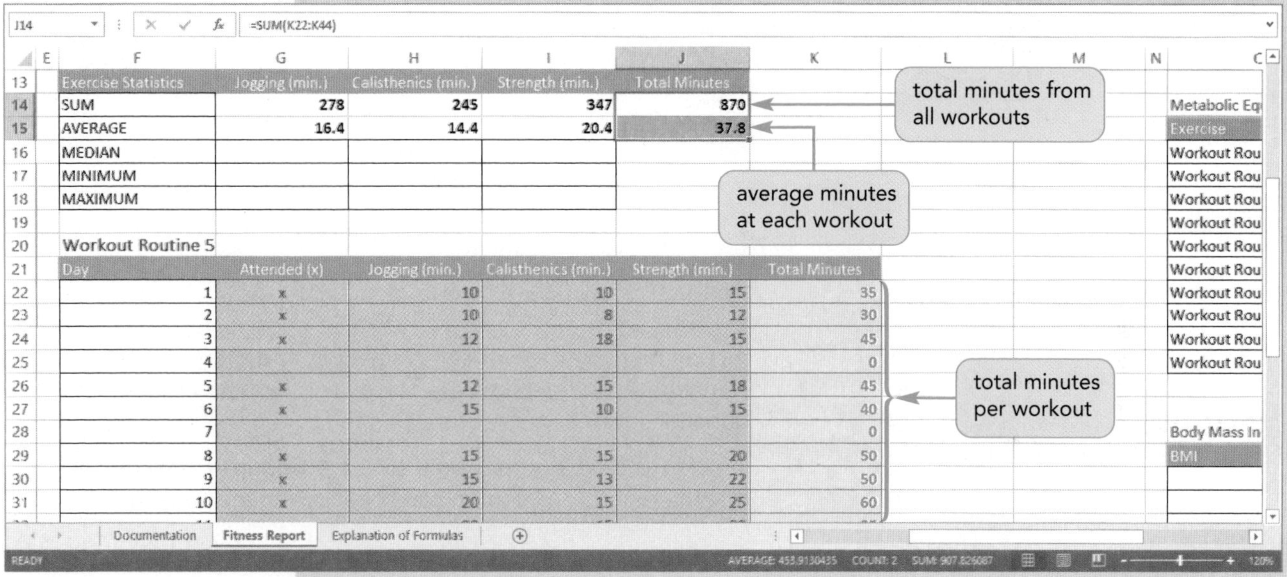

## Entering Functions with the Insert Function Dialog Box

Functions are organized in the Function Library group on the FORMULAS tab. In the Function Library, you can select a function from a function category. You can also open the Insert Function dialog box to search for a particular function based on a description you enter. When you select a function, the Function Arguments dialog box opens, listing all of the arguments associated with that function. Required arguments are in bold type; optional arguments are in normal type.

Ken wants his report to include the median exercise times for the three exercise categories. The **median** provides the middle value from a data sample. You can use the MEDIAN function to determine the middle value in a range of numbers. The Quick Analysis tool doesn't include median, so you will use the Insert Function and Function Arguments dialog boxes to help you correctly insert the MEDIAN function.

### To calculate the median exercise time:

1. Select cell **G16**. This is the cell in which you will enter the MEDIAN function.

2. Click the **Insert Function** button $f_x$ to the left of the formula bar to open the Insert Function dialog box. From the Insert Function dialog box, you can describe the function you want to search for.

3. In the Search for a function box, type **middle value**, and then click the **Go** button. Functions for finding a middle value appear in the Select a function box. The second entry in the list, MEDIAN, is the one you want to use. See Figure 3-9.

**Figure 3-9**   **Insert Function dialog box**

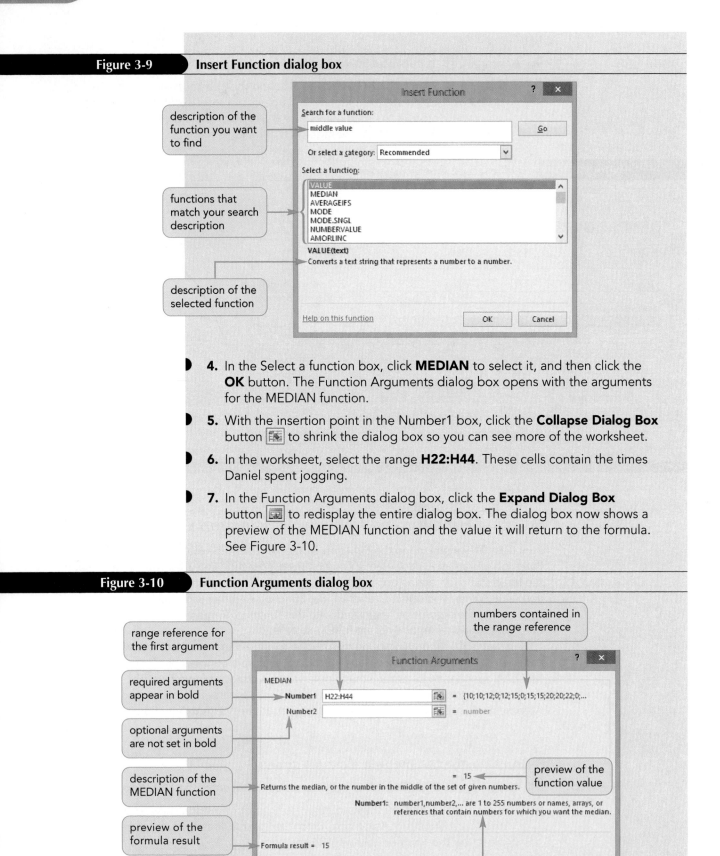

**4.** In the Select a function box, click **MEDIAN** to select it, and then click the **OK** button. The Function Arguments dialog box opens with the arguments for the MEDIAN function.

**5.** With the insertion point in the Number1 box, click the **Collapse Dialog Box** button to shrink the dialog box so you can see more of the worksheet.

**6.** In the worksheet, select the range **H22:H44**. These cells contain the times Daniel spent jogging.

**7.** In the Function Arguments dialog box, click the **Expand Dialog Box** button to redisplay the entire dialog box. The dialog box now shows a preview of the MEDIAN function and the value it will return to the formula. See Figure 3-10.

**Figure 3-10**   **Function Arguments dialog box**

8. Click the **OK** button. The formula =MEDIAN(H22:H44) is entered in cell G16, which displays 15 (the median exercise time for jogging).

9. Copy cell **G16**, and then paste the copied formula into the range **H16:J16** to calculate the median exercise times for calisthenics, strength training, and all exercises. See Figure 3-11.

**Figure 3-11**   Median exercise times

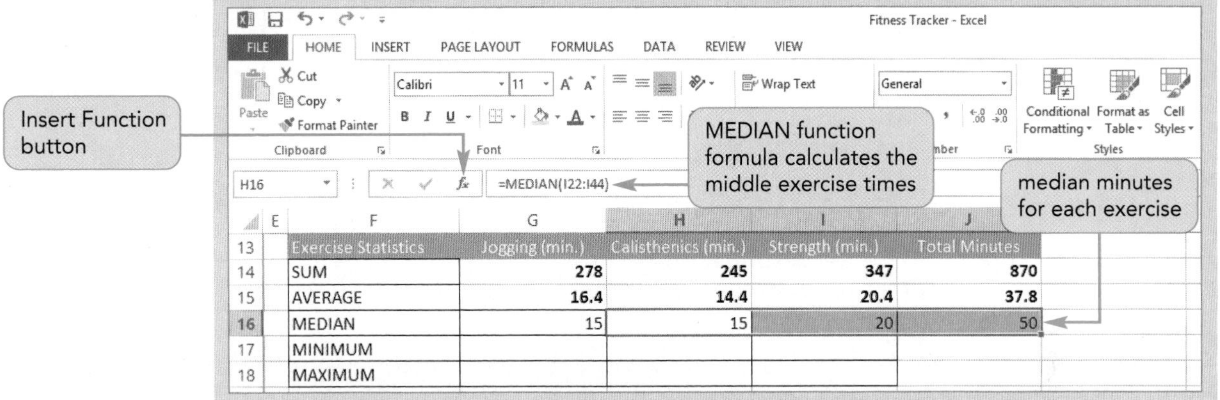

Daniel spent a median time of 15 minutes on calisthenics and 20 minutes on strength training. The median total exercise time was 50 minutes, which is quite a bit higher than the average total exercise time of 37.8 minutes. Why this difference? One reason is that averages are greatly influenced by extremely low or high values. Because Daniel missed several workouts, his exercise time for those days was 0, bringing down the overall average. A median, or middle value, is not as affected by these extreme values, which is why some statisticians advocate medians over averages for analyzing data with widely spaced values.

Ken also wants to know the minimum and maximum minutes Daniel spent exercising during the month. You can access functions by scrolling through the Function Library. You will use this method to enter the functions to calculate the minimum and maximum exercise times.

### To calculate the minimum and maximum minutes of exercise:

1. Select cell **G17**, which is where you will calculate the minimum exercise time.

2. On the ribbon, click the **FORMULAS** tab to display the function categories in the Function Library.

3. Click the **More Functions** button to display the rest of the function categories. Calculations involving maximums and minimums are included with the Statistical functions.

4. Click **Statistical** to display the statistical functions, and then scroll down and point to **MIN**. A ScreenTip appears, displaying the MIN function syntax and a description of the function. See Figure 3-12.

**Figure 3-12**    **MIN function in the Function Library**

functions organized
into categories

syntax of the
selected function

list of statistical
functions

| | | | | |
|---|---|---|---|---|
| 13 | Exercise Statistics | Jogging (min.) | Calisthenics | |
| 14 | SUM | 278 | | |
| 15 | AVERAGE | 16.4 | 14.4 | |
| 16 | MEDIAN | 15 | 15 | 37.8 |
| 17 | MINIMUM | | | 50 |
| 18 | MAXIMUM | | | |
| 19 | | | | |
| 20 | Workout Routine 5 | | | |
| 21 | Day | Attended (x) | Jogging (min.) | Calisthenics |
| 22 | 1 | x | 10 | 15 |
| 23 | 2 | x | 10 | 12 |
| 24 | 3 | x | 12 | 15 |
| 25 | 4 | | | |
| 26 | 5 | x | 12 | 18 |
| 27 | 6 | x | 15 | 15 |
| 28 | 7 | | | |
| 29 | 8 | x | 15 | 20 |

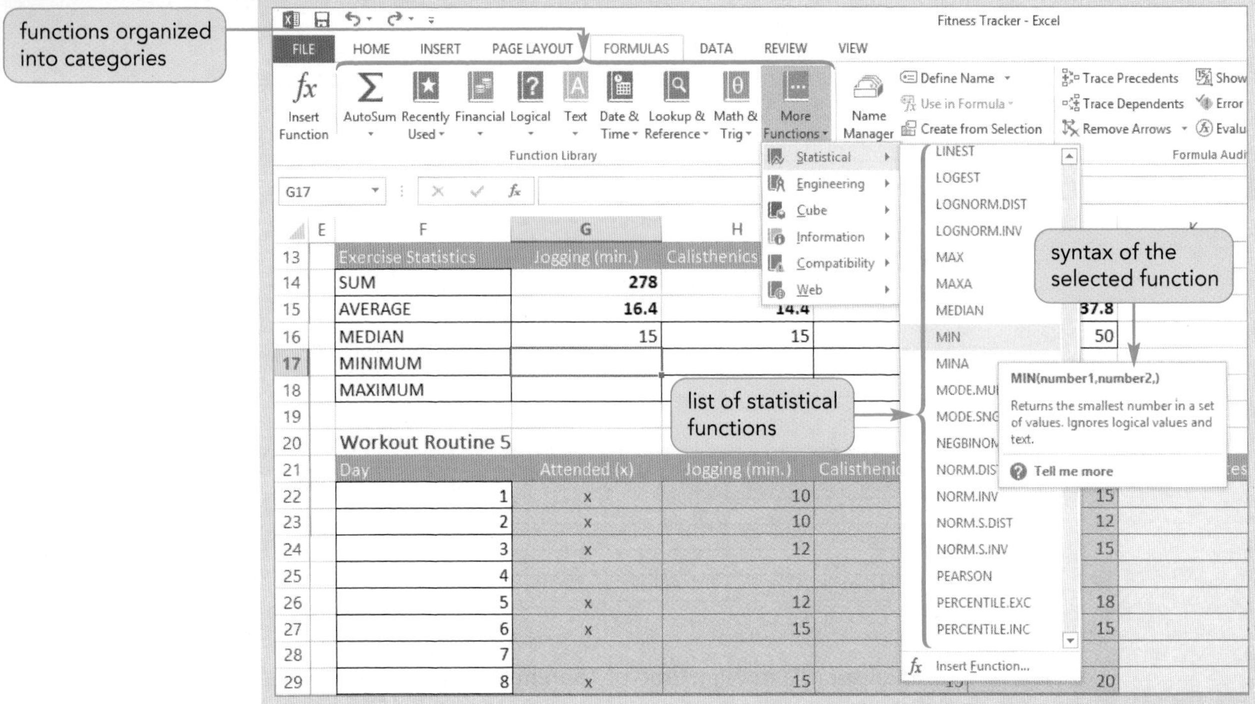

▶  **5.** Click **MIN** to open the Function Arguments dialog box.

▶  **6.** With the insertion point in the Number1 box, select the range **H22:H44** in the worksheet. These cells store the amount of time Daniel spent jogging.

▶  **7.** Click the **OK** button. The dialog box closes, and the formula =MIN(H22:H44) is entered in cell G17, which displays 10, the minimum minutes that Daniel spent jogging during the month.

▶  **8.** Select cell **G18**, click the **More Functions** button in the Function Library group, click **Statistical**, and then scroll down and click **MAX**. The Function Arguments dialog box opens.

▶  **9.** With the insertion point in the Number1 box, select the range **H22:H44** in the worksheet, and then click the **OK** button. The formula =MAX(H22:H44) is entered in cell G18, which displays 22, the maximum minutes that Daniel spent jogging.

▶  **10.** Copy the range **G17:G18**, and then paste the formulas in the range **H17:J18** to calculate the minimum and maximum times for the other exercises and overall.

▶  **11.** Format the range **G14:J18** with the **Calculation** cell style, and then select cell **F19**. See Figure 3-13.

| Figure 3-13 | Summary statistics of the exercise times |
| --- | --- |

## Referencing Function Results in a Formula

The amount of calories burned during exercise is a function of intensity and time. The more intense the exercise or the longer it lasts, the more calories burned. Ken uses the fitness equation

$$\text{Calories} = \frac{METS \times w \times t}{125.7143}$$

to calculate how many calories will be used during exercise, where *METS* is a metabolic factor that measures the intensity of the exercise, *w* is the individual's weight in pounds, *t* is the exercise time in minutes, and 125.7143 is a constant that converts the quantity into calories. Ken listed the METS values for the different workout routines he created in the range O15:P25 of the Fitness Report worksheet. For example, the METS for Workout Routine 5 is 7.0 and the METS for Workout Routine 10 is 16.0. Using the METS information and the weight and exercise times, you can calculate the total calories burned during each workout.

The fitness equation that calculates calories burned during the first workout translates into the formula

```
=P20*C11*K22/125.7143
```

where P20 references the cell with the METS for Workout Routine 5, C11 references the cell that stores Daniel's weight, and K22 references the cell that calculates the total exercise time of the first workout.

You will enter this formula in cell L22, and then copy it to the remaining cells in the column to calculate the calories burned during each workout.

### To calculate the calories burned during Daniel's first workout:

1. In cell **L21**, enter **Calories Burned** as the label.

2. In cell **L22**, enter the formula **=P20*C11*K22/125.7143** to calculate the calories Daniel burned at his first workout. Cell P20 stores the METS value, cell C11 contains Daniel's weight, and cell K22 is the total exercise time for Workout Routine 5 on the first day of the month. Cell L22 displays 376.1306391, which is the number of calories burned at the first workout.

**Trouble?** If your value differs from 376.1306391, edit your formula as needed so it exactly matches the formula shown in Step 2.

3. Select cell **L22**, and then decrease the number of decimal places shown to one. The displayed value is 376.1.

4. Copy the formula in cell **L22**, and then paste the formula to the range **L23:L44** to calculate the calories burned for the rest of the workouts. See Figure 3-14.

**Figure 3-14**  **Formulas incorrectly calculating the calories burned per workout**

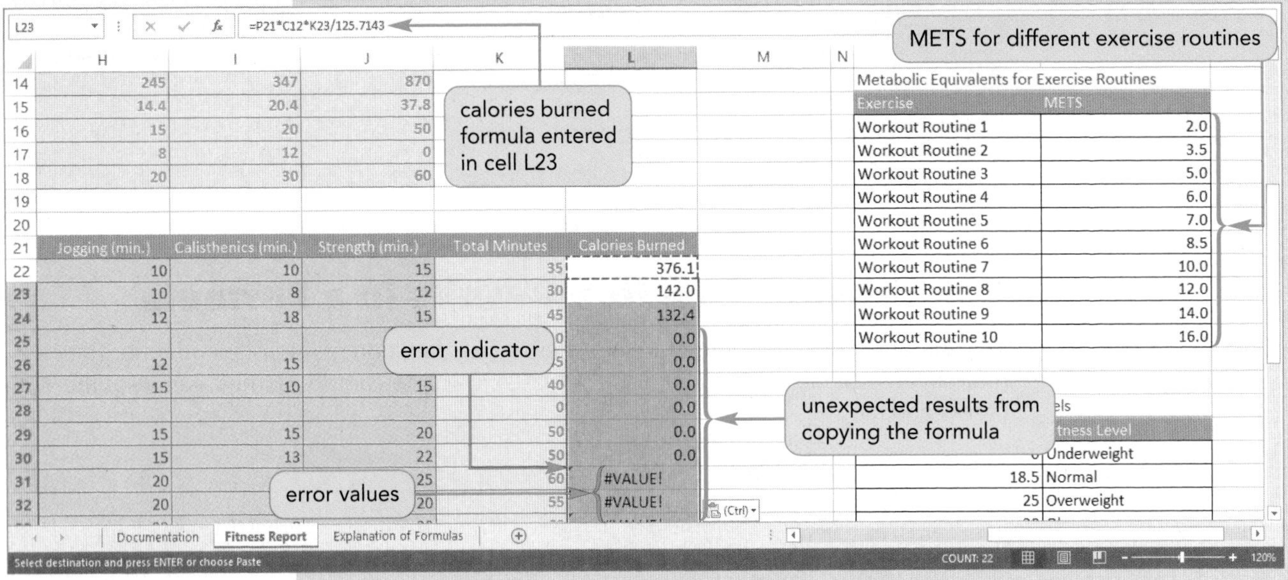

The first few values seem somewhat reasonable, but then several workouts show no calories burned. These are followed by cells displaying #VALUE! rather than a number. Obviously something went wrong when you copied and pasted the formula.

## Interpreting Error Values

The #VALUE! that appears in some of the cells in the Fitness Report worksheet is an error value. An **error value** indicates that some part of a formula is preventing Excel from returning a calculated value. An error value begins with a pound sign (#) followed by an error name that indicates the type of error. Figure 3-15 describes common error values that you might see instead of the results from formulas and functions. For example, the error value #VALUE! indicates that the wrong type of value is used in a function or formula. You will need to examine the formulas in the cells with error values to determine exactly what went wrong.

| Figure 3-15 | Excel error values |
| --- | --- |

| Error Value | Description |
| --- | --- |
| #DIV/0! | The formula or function contains a number divided by 0. |
| #NAME? | Excel doesn't recognize text in the formula or function, such as when the function name is misspelled. |
| #N/A | A value is not available to a function or formula, which can occur when a workbook is initially set up prior to entering actual data values. |
| #NULL! | A formula or function requires two cell ranges to intersect, but they don't. |
| #NUM! | Invalid numbers are used in a formula or function, such as text entered in a function that requires a number. |
| #REF! | A cell reference used in a formula or function is no longer valid, which can occur when the cell used by the function was deleted from the worksheet. |
| #VALUE! | The wrong type of argument is used in a function or formula. This can occur when you reference a text value for an argument that should be strictly numeric. |

© 2014 Cengage Learning

The error value messages are not particularly descriptive or helpful. To help you locate the error, an error indicator appears in the upper-left corner of the cell with the error value. When you point to the error indicator, a ScreenTip appears with more information about the source of the error.

### INSIGHT

#### Deciding When to Correct an Error Value

An error value does not mean that you must correct the cell's formula or function. Some error values appear simply because you have not yet entered any data into the workbook. For example, if you use the AVERAGE function to find the average value of an empty column, the #DIV/0! error value appears because the formula cannot calculate the average of a collection of empty cells. However, as soon as you begin entering data, the #DIV/0! message will disappear.

Ken wants you to figure out why the #VALUE error value appears in some of the cells where you copied the calories burned formula. To figure this out, you will examine the formula in cell L31, which is the first cell that displays the error value instead of the expected number results.

#### To view the formula in cell L31 that results in an error value:

1. Double-click cell **L31**, which displays the #VALUE! error value. In Edit mode, the cell references used in the formula are color coded to match the corresponding cells, making it easier to see which cells are used in the formula.

2. Observe that cell L31 contains the formula =P29*C20*K31/125.7143.

> **3.** Look at the first cell reference in the formula. The first cell reference is to cell P29 containing the text "Fitness Level" instead of cell P20 containing the METS value for Workout Routine 5. The formula is attempting to multiply the text in cell P29, but multiplication can be done only with numbers. This is the problem causing the #VALUE! error value.

> **4.** Look at the second cell reference in the formula. The second cell reference is to cell C20, an empty cell, rather than to cell C11 containing Daniel's weight.

> **5.** Look at the third cell reference in the formula. The third cell reference is to cell K31, which contains the total exercise times for the tenth workout—the correct cell reference.

# Exploring Cell References

Most workbooks include data entered in cells that are then referenced in formulas to perform calculations on that data. The formulas can be simple, such as the formulas you entered to add the total minutes of each workout, or they can be more complex, such as the formulas you entered to calculate the calories burned during each workout. Each of these formulas includes one or more cell references.

## Understanding Relative References

When a formula includes a cell reference, Excel interprets that cell reference as being located relative to the position of the current cell. For example, Excel interprets the following formula entered in cell A1 to mean "add the value of the cell one column to the right of this cell to the value of the cell one column to the right and one row below this cell":

    =B1+B2

This relative interpretation is retained when the formula is copied to a new location. So, if the formula in cell A1 is copied to cell A3 (two rows down in the worksheet), the relative references in the formula also shift two rows down, resulting in the following formula:

    =B3+B4

Figure 3-16 shows another example of how relative references change when a formula is copied to new cell locations. In this figure, the formula =A4 entered in cell D7 displays 10, which is the number entered in cell A4. When pasted to a new location, each of the pasted formulas contains a reference to a cell that is three rows up and three rows to the left of the current cell's location.

**Figure 3-16**     Formulas using relative references

formula references a cell three rows up and three columns to the left of the active cell

when copied to new cells, each formula still references a cell three rows up and three columns to the left

values returned by each formula

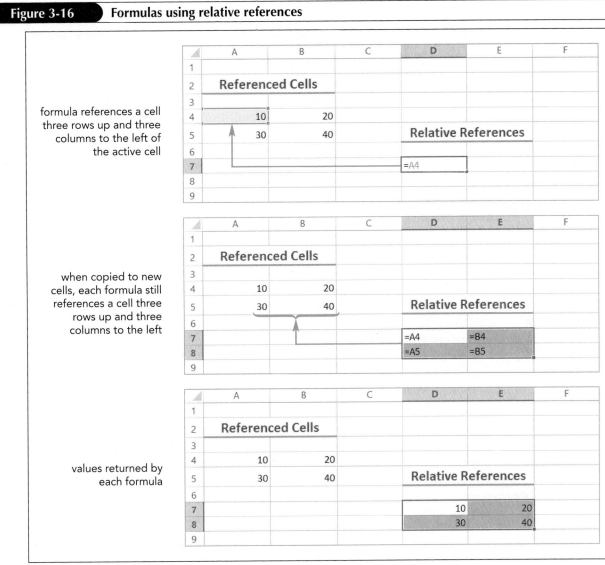

© 2014 Cengage Learning

This explains what happened with the relative references you used to calculate calories burned for each workout. When you entered the following formula in cell L22, cell C11 correctly references the client's weight and the other cells correctly reference the METS for Workout Routine 5 and the total exercise time:

```
=P20*C11*K22/125.7143
```

When you copied the formula down to cell L31, all of the cell references contained in that formula also shifted down nine rows, resulting in the following formula, which accurately references the total exercise time for the corresponding workout but no longer references Daniel's weight or the METS for Workout Routine 5—both of which are necessary for the calculation:

```
=P29*C20*K31/125.7143
```

What you need is a cell reference that remains fixed when the formula is copied to a new location.

## Understanding Absolute References

A fixed reference—one that always references the same cell no matter where it is moved—is called an absolute reference. In Excel, absolute references include a $ (dollar sign) before each column and row designation. For example, B8 is a relative reference to cell B8, and $B$8 is an absolute reference to that cell. When you copy a formula that contains an absolute reference to a new location, that cell reference does not change.

Figure 3-17 shows an example of how copying a formula with an absolute reference results in the same cell reference being pasted in different cells regardless of their position compared to the location of the original copied cell. In this example, the formula =$A$4 will always reference cell A4 no matter where the formula is copied to, because the cell is referenced with the absolute reference $A$4.

| Figure 3-17 | Formulas using absolute references |

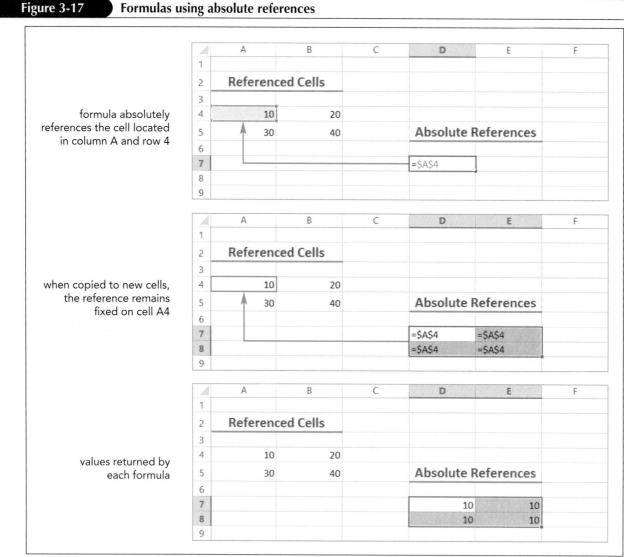

© 2014 Cengage Learning

## Understanding Mixed References

A formula can also include cell references that are mixed. A **mixed reference** contains both relative and absolute references. For example, a mixed reference for cell A2 can be either $A2 or A$2. In the mixed reference $A2, the reference to column A is absolute and the reference to row 2 is relative. In the mixed reference A$2, the column reference is relative and the row reference is absolute. A mixed reference "locks" one part of the cell reference while the other part can change. When you copy and paste a cell with a mixed reference to a new location, the absolute portion of the cell reference remains fixed and the relative portion shifts along with the new location of the pasted cell.

Figure 3-18 shows an example of using mixed references to complete a multiplication table. The first cell in the table, cell B3, contains the formula =$A3*B$2, which multiplies the first column entry (A3) by the first row entry (B2), returning 1. When this formula is copied to another cell, the absolute portions of the cell references remain unchanged and the relative portions of the references change. For example, if the formula is copied to cell E6, the first mixed cell reference changes to $A6 because the column reference is absolute and the row reference is relative, and the second cell reference changes to E$2 because the row reference is absolute and the column reference is relative. The result is that cell E6 contains the formula =$A6*E$2 and returns 16. Other cells in the multiplication table are similarly modified so that each entry returns the multiplication of the intersection of the row and column headings.

**Figure 3-18**    **Formulas using mixed references**

mixed cell reference that fixes the column reference for the first term and the row reference for the second term

when copied to the B3:B7 range, the fixed references remain unchanged and the relative references are shifted

values returned by each formula

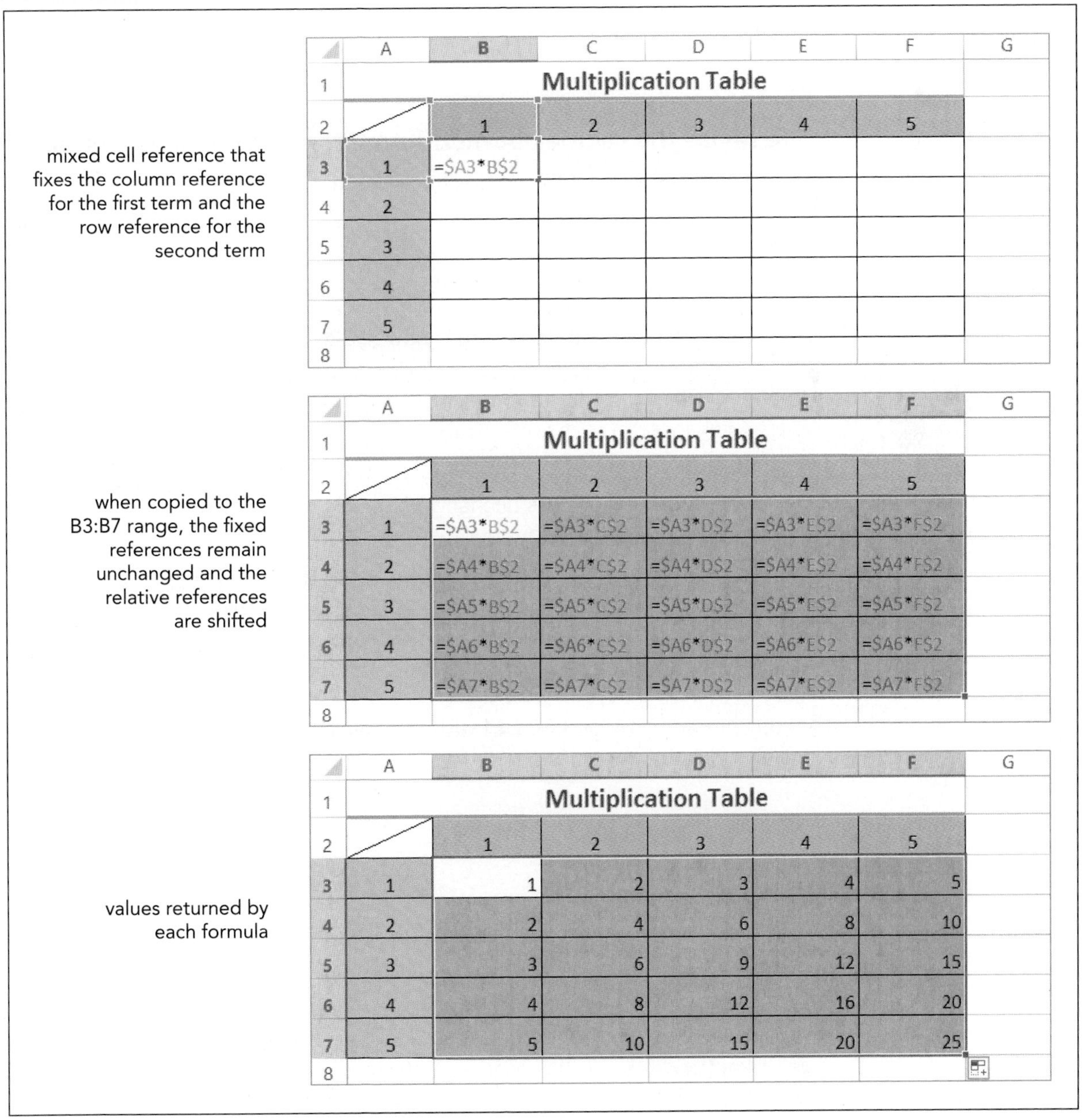

## Changing Cell References in a Formula

You can quickly switch a cell reference from relative to absolute or mixed. Rather than retyping the formula, you can select the cell reference in Edit mode and then press the F4 key. As you press the F4 key, Excel cycles through the different reference types—starting with the relative reference, followed by the absolute reference, then to a mixed reference with the row absolute, and finally to a mixed reference with the column absolute.

Ken wants you to fix the problem with the cell references in the calories burned formulas. You need to revise the formula to use absolute references to Daniel's weight and the METS value that will not change when the formula is copied to new locations. You will leave the relative reference to the total exercise time so that the copied formulas will retrieve the exercise times from the corresponding workouts. The revised formula in cell L22 uses an absolute reference to the METS values in $P$20 and an absolute reference to Daniel's weight in $C$11, as follows:

```
=$P$20*$C$11*K22/125.7143
```

You will edit the calories burned formula in cell L22, and then paste it to the rest of the workouts.

**To revise the calories burned formulas to use absolute references:**

1. Double-click cell **L22** to select it and enter Edit mode.

2. Click immediately to the left of cell reference **P20** in the formula to move the insertion point before the letter P, type **$** to change the column reference to absolute, press the → key to move the insertion point between the letter P and 20, and then type **$** to change the row reference to absolute. The complete absolute reference is now $P$20.

Select only the cell reference you want to change before you press the F4 key.

3. Double-click the cell reference **C11** in the formula to select it, and then press the **F4** key to change it to the absolute reference $C$11. The formula is now =$P$20*$C$11*K22/125.7143.

4. Press the **Enter** key to complete the edit. The 376.1 calories burned displayed in the cell is unchanged because the relative references were accurate in this first formula.

5. Copy cell **L22** and paste it into the range **L23:L44**. The worksheet shows 322.4 calories burned for the second workout and 483.6 calories burned for the third workout. The next row in the list shows 0 calories burned because Daniel did not work out that day. As you can see, the remaining formulas now correctly calculate the calories burned at each workout.

6. Format the range **L22:L44** with the **Calculation** cell style. See Figure 3-19.

**Figure 3-19** Formulas with absolute and relative references

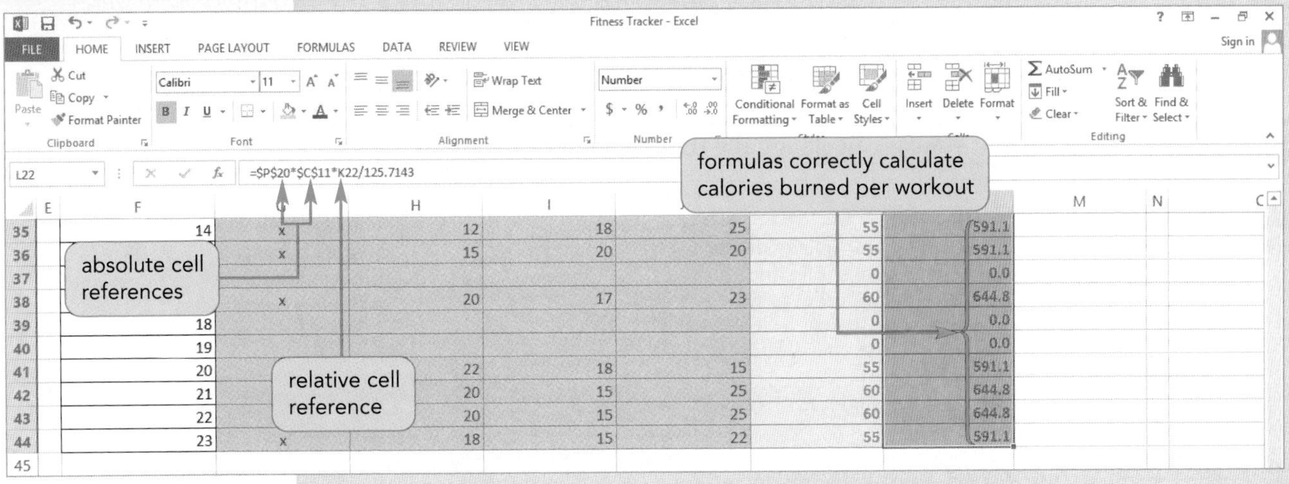

## Planning Which Cell Reference to Use in a Formula

You can include the correct type of cell reference in a formula as you create the formula. This requires a little more thought up front, as you consider how each cell in a formula needs to be referenced before you create the formula. Ken wants you to create a running total of the calories burned during each workout. You can use the SUM function with a combination of absolute and relative cell references to add the values in a range. The formula to calculate the total in the first cell is:

```
=SUM($L$22:L22)
```

In this formula, the starting cell of the range is fixed at cell L22, but the ending cell of the range is relative. When you copy this formula down the column, the starting cell remains absolutely referenced to cell L22, but the ending cell changes to include the current row. For example, when the formula is pasted three rows down, the formula changes to add the numbers in cells L22, L23, L24, and L25, as follows:

```
=SUM($L$22:L25)
```

Continuing in this way, the last cell will contain the sum of all of the calories burned totals using the following formula:

```
=SUM($L$22:L44)
```

Instead of entering the formulas yourself, you can use the Quick Analysis tool to calculate the total calories burned up through the end of each workout session.

### To calculate the running total of calories burned:

1. In cell **M21**, enter **Calories Subtotal** as the label.

2. Select the range **L22:L44** containing the calories burned during each workout, and then click the **Quick Analysis** button ▣ (or press the **Ctrl+Q** keys).

3. Click the **TOTALS** category, and then scroll right to the end of the TOTALS tools.

**4.** Click **Running Total** (the last entry in the list, which is the Running Total of a column). The range M22:M44 displays the total calories burned up through the end of each workout session.

**5.** Format the range **M22:M44** with the **Calculation** cell style. See Figure 3-20.

**Figure 3-20**   Formulas calculating the running total of calories burned

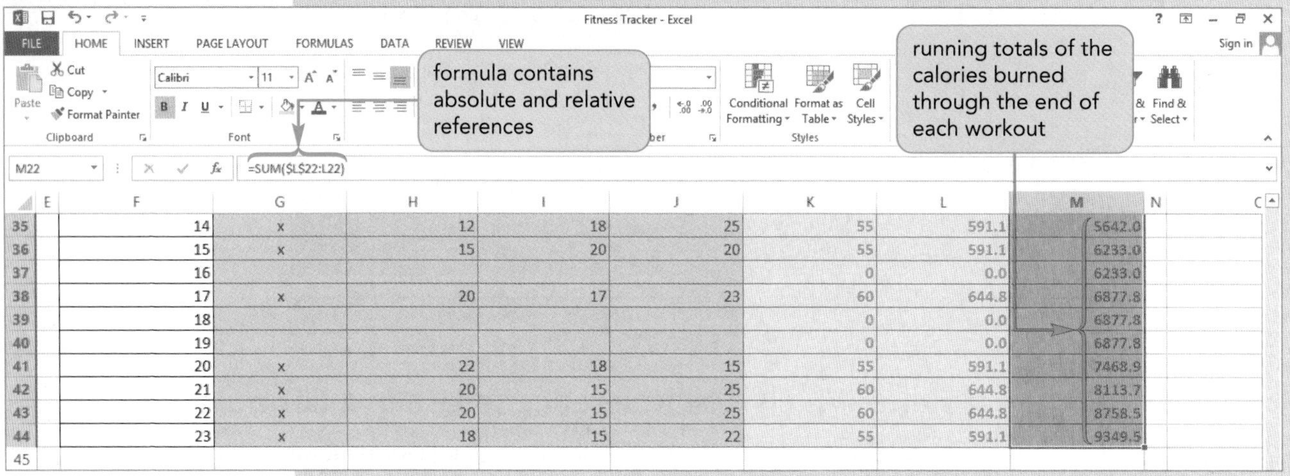

Daniel burned 698.5 calories during the first two workouts and more than 1180 calories after the first three workouts. The formula used to calculate the running totals for the column includes both absolute and relative references. You will review the formulas in column M to see the formulas calculating the running totals.

### To view the formulas for the running totals:

**1.** Select cell **M22**, and then review the formula, which is =SUM($L$22:L22). Notice the absolute and relative references to cell L22.

**2.** Select cell **M23**, and then review the formula, which is =SUM($L$22:L23). Notice that the absolute reference to cell L22 remains unchanged, but the relative reference is now cell L23, expanding the range being added with the SUM function.

**3.** Select each cell in column M and review its formula, noticing that the absolute reference $L$22 always appears as the top cell of the range but the relative reference for the last cell of the range changes.

**4.** Save the workbook.

You can see that the running total is calculated with the SUM function using a combination of absolute and relative cell references. The top of the range used in the SUM function is locked at cell L22, but the bottom of the range is relative, expanding in size as the formula was copied down column M. Entered this way, with absolute and relative cell references, the SUM function calculates partial sums, providing the total calories burned up through the end of each workout session.

**INSIGHT**

## Understanding When to Use Relative, Absolute, and Mixed References

Part of effective workbook design is knowing when to use relative, absolute, and mixed references. Use relative references when you want to apply the same formula with input cells that share a common layout or pattern. Relative references are commonly used when copying a formula that calculates summary statistics across columns or rows of data values. Use absolute references when you want your copied formulas to always refer to the same cell. This usually occurs when a cell contains a constant value, such as a tax rate, that will be referenced in formulas throughout the worksheet. Mixed references are seldom used other than when creating tables of calculated values such as a multiplication table in which the values of the formula or function can be found at the intersection of the rows and columns of the table.

So far, you have entered the fitness formulas and summary statistics in the Fitness Tracker workbook. In the next session, you will explore date and time functions, and then look up values to use in formulas and functions.

**REVIEW**

## Session 3.1 Quick Check

1. What is an optional argument? What does Excel do if you do not include an optional argument?
2. Write the function to return the middle value from the values in the range X1:X10.
3. Write the function to round the value in cell A5 to the fourth decimal place.
4. The range of a set of values is defined as the maximum value minus the minimum value. Write the formula to calculate the range of values in the range Y1:Y10.
5. If cell A11 contains the formula =SUME(A1:A10), what error value will appear in the cell?
6. You need to reference cell Q57 in a formula. What is its relative reference? What is its absolute reference? What are the two mixed references?
7. If cell R10 contains the formula =R1+R2, which is then copied to cell S20, what formula is entered in cell S20?
8. If cell V10 contains the formula = AVERAGE($U1:$U5), which is then copied to cell W20, what formula is entered in cell W20?

# Session 3.2 Visual Overview:

A **lookup table** stores the data you want to retrieve in categories. This is a vertical lookup table that organizes the categories in the first column of the table.

**Compare values** are the categories located in the first column of the lookup table and are used for matching to a lookup value specified by the user.

**Return values** are the data values you want to retrieve from the lookup table and are located in the second and subsequent columns.

A **lookup value** is the category you want to find in a lookup table.

The **VLOOKUP function** returns values from a vertical lookup table by specifying the lookup value to match to a compare value, the location of the lookup table, and the column in the table that contains the return values.

## Basal Metabolic Rate Activity Factors

| Activity Level | BMR Factor |
|----------------|-----------|
| Sedentary | 1.200 |
| Light | 1.375 |
| Moderate | 1.550 |
| High | 1.725 |
| Extreme | 1.900 |

Fitness Tracker - Exc

REVIEW    VIEW

Number

$ · % ·

Number

C2                                          ALSE)*C21

| | B | C | D | E | F | G |
|---|---|---|---|---|---|---|
| 6 | Personal Data | | | | Workout Summary | |
| 7 | | | | | Start Date | 8/1/2016 |
| 8 | Name | Daniel Pridham | | | Ending Date | 8/31/2016 |
| 9 | Activity Level | Light | | | Workouts Scheduled | 23 |
| 10 | Age (years) | 45 | | | Workouts Attended | 17 |
| 11 | Weight (lb.) | 173 | | | Workouts Missed | 6 |
| 12 | Height (in.) | 70 | | | | |
| 13 | Waist (in.) | 37 | | | Exercise Statistics | Jogging (min.) |
| 14 | Neck (in.) | 15.5 | | | SUM | 278 |
| 15 | | | | | AVERAGE | 16.4 |
| 16 | | | | | MEDIAN | 15.0 |
| 17 | Fitness Assessment | | | | MAXIMUM | 22.0 |
| 18 | | | | | MINIMUM | 10.0 |
| 19 | BMI | 24.8 | | | | |
| 20 | | | | | Workout Routine 5 | |
| 21 | Resting BMR (cal./day) | 1729 | | | Day | Attended (x) |
| 22 | Active BMR (cal./d | 2377 | | | 8/1/2016 | x |
| 23 | | | | | 8/2/2016 | x |
| 24 | | | | | 8/3/2016 | x |
| 25 | Notes | | | | 8/4/2016 | |
| 26 | | | | | 8/5/2016 | x |
| 27 | ay) | =6.23*C11+12.7*C12-6.76*C10+ | | | 8/8/2016 | x |
| | d) | =VLOOKUP(C9,O8:P12,2,FALSE) | | | 8/9/2016 | |
| | | | | | 8/10/2016 | x |
| | | | | | 8/11/2016 | x |
| 31 | | | | | 8/12/2016 | x |

tness Report    Explanation of Formulas    ⊕

READY

# Logical and Lookup Functions

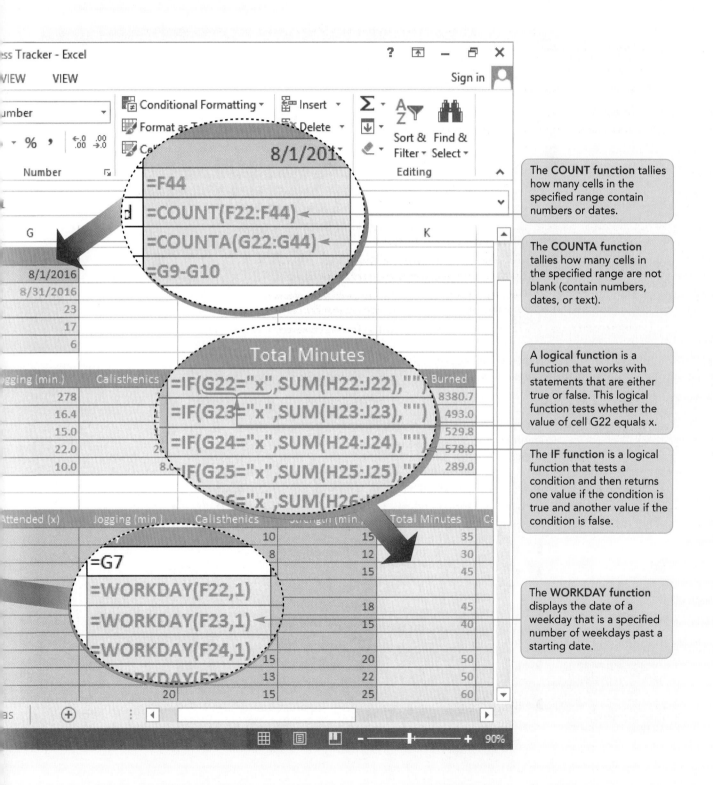

The **COUNT function** tallies how many cells in the specified range contain numbers or dates.

The **COUNTA function** tallies how many cells in the specified range are not blank (contain numbers, dates, or text).

A **logical function** is a function that works with statements that are either true or false. This logical function tests whether the value of cell G22 equals x.

The **IF function** is a logical function that tests a condition and then returns one value if the condition is true and another value if the condition is false.

The **WORKDAY function** displays the date of a weekday that is a specified number of weekdays past a starting date.

# AutoFilling Formulas and Data

**AutoFill** provides a quick way to enter content and formatting in cells based on existing entries in adjacent cells. Ken wants you to include summary statistics for calories burned across all of the scheduled workouts. To add these statistics, you'll use the AutoFill tool.

### Copying Formulas and Formats with AutoFill

- Select the cell or range that contains the formula or formulas you want to copy.
- Drag the fill handle in the direction you want to copy the formula(s), and then release the mouse button.
- To copy only the formats or only the formulas, click the Auto Fill Options button and select the appropriate option.

*or*

- Select the cell or range that contains the formula or formulas you want to copy.
- On the HOME tab, in the Editing group, click the Fill button.
- Select a fill direction and fill type.

*or*

- On the HOME tab, in the Editing group, click Series.
- Enter the desired fill series options, and then click the OK button.

## Using the Fill Handle

After you select a range, a **fill handle** appears in the lower-right corner of the selection. When you drag the fill handle over an adjacent cell or range, AutoFill copies the content and formats from the original cell or range into the adjacent cell or range. This process is often more efficient than the two-step process of copying and pasting.

Ken wants you to calculate the same summary statistics for the calories burned during the workouts as you did for the total minutes of each workout. Because the total minutes formulas use relative references, you can use the fill handle to copy these for the calories burned statistics.

**To copy the calories burned summary statistics and formatting with the fill handle:**

1. In cell **K13**, enter **Calories Burned** as the label.

2. Select the range **J14:J18**, which contains the cells with formulas for calculating the sum, average, median, minimum, and maximum total minutes. A fill handle appears in the lower-right corner of the selected range, directly above and to the left of the Quick Analysis button.

3. Point to the **fill handle**. The pointer changes to ✛.

4. Click and drag the fill handle over the range **K14:K18**. A solid outline appears around the selected range as you move the pointer.

5. Release the mouse button. The selected range is filled in with the formulas and formatting from the range J14:J18, and the Auto Fill Options button appears in the lower-right corner of the selected cells. See Figure 3-21.

> **TIP**
>
> You can also fill a series to the right by selecting both the cells to copy and the cells to be filled in, and then pressing the Ctrl+R keys.

**Figure 3-21**    **Formulas and formatting copied with AutoFill**

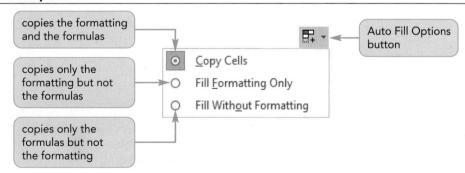

| E | F | G | H | I | J | K | L |
|---|---|---|---|---|---|---|---|
| 12 | | | | | | | |
| 13 | Exercise Statistics | Jogging (min.) | Calisthenics (min.) | Strength (min.) | Total Minutes | Calories Burned | |
| 14 | SUM | 278 | 245 | 347 | 870 | 9349.533028 | |
| 15 | AVERAGE | 16.4 | 14.4 | 20.4 | 37.8 | 406.5 | |
| 16 | MEDIAN | 15 | 15 | 20 | 50 | 537.3294844 | |
| 17 | MINIMUM | 10 | 8 | 12 | 0 | 0 | |
| 18 | MAXIMUM | 22 | 20 | 30 | 60 | 644.7953813 | |
| 19 | | | | | | | |
| 20 | Workout Routine 5 | | | | | | |
| 21 | Day | Attended (x) | Jogging (min.) | Calisthenics (min.) | Stren... | ...al Minutes | Calories Burned   Calories Subtotal |

*formulas and formatting filled into the K14:K18 range*

*Auto Fill Options button*

*fill handle*

▶ **6.** Format the range **K14:K18** to display one decimal place.

Based on the summary statistics, Ken can see that Daniel burned 9349.5 calories during the month, burned an average of 406.5 calories per session, burned a median of 537.3 calories per session, and burned a minimum of 0.0 calories and a maximum of 644.8 calories per session during the month.

## Using the Auto Fill Options Button

By default, AutoFill copies both the content and the formatting of the original range to the selected range. However, sometimes you might want to copy only the content or only the formatting. The Auto Fill Options button that appears after you release the mouse button lets you specify what is copied. As shown in Figure 3-22, clicking this button provides a menu of AutoFill options. The Copy Cells option, which is the default, copies both the content and the formatting. The Fill Formatting Only option copies the formatting into the selected cells but not any content. The Fill Without Formatting option copies the content but not the formatting.

**Figure 3-22**    **Auto Fill Options button**

*copies the formatting and the formulas*

*copies only the formatting but not the formulas*

*copies only the formulas but not the formatting*

- ⦿ Copy Cells
- ○ Fill Formatting Only
- ○ Fill Without Formatting

*Auto Fill Options button*

Because you want to copy the content and the formatting of the summary statistics, you don't need to use the Auto Fill Options button.

## Filling a Series

AutoFill can also be used to create a series of numbers, dates, or text based on a pattern. To create a series of numbers, you enter the initial values in the series in a selected range and then use AutoFill to complete the series.

### Creating a Series with AutoFill

- Enter the first few values of the series into a range.
- Select the range, and then drag the fill handle of the selected range over the cells you want to fill.

*or*

- Enter the first few values of the series into a range.
- Select the entire range into which you want to extend the series.
- On the HOME tab, in the Editing group, click the Fill button, and then click Down, Right, Up, Left, Series, or Justify to set the direction in which you want to extend the series.

Figure 3-23 shows how AutoFill can be used to insert the numbers from 1 to 10 in a selected range. You enter the first few numbers in the range A2:A4 to establish the pattern you want AutoFill to use—consecutive positive numbers in this example. Then, you select the range and drag its fill handle over the cells where you want the pattern continued—in this case, the range A5:A11—and Excel fills in the rest of the series.

**Figure 3-23**    **AutoFill extends a numeric sequence**

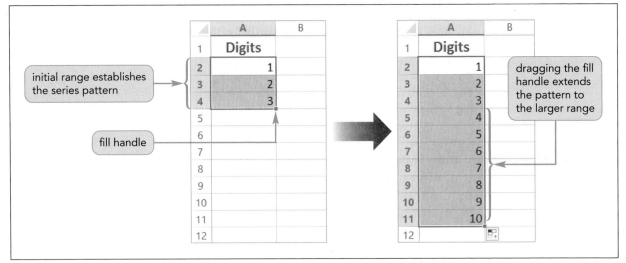

© 2014 Cengage Learning

AutoFill can extend a wide variety of series, including dates and times and patterned text. Figure 3-24 shows some examples of series that AutoFill can generate. In each case, you must provide enough information for AutoFill to identify the pattern. AutoFill can recognize some patterns from only a single entry—such as Jan or January, to create a series of month abbreviations or names, or Mon or Monday, to create a series of the days of the week. A text pattern that includes text and a number such as Region 1, Region 2, and so on can also be automatically extended using AutoFill. You can start the series at any point, such as Weds, June, or Region 10, and AutoFill will complete the next days, months, or text.

**Figure 3-24**    AutoFill extends numbers, dates and times, and patterned text

| Type | Initial Pattern | Extended Series |
|---|---|---|
| Numbers | 1, 2, 3 | 4, 5, 6, .. |
| | 2, 4, 6 | 8, 10, 12, ... |
| Dates and Times | Jan | Feb, Mar, Apr, ... |
| | January | February, March, April, ... |
| | 15-Jan, 15-Feb | 15-Mar, 15-Apr, 15-May, ... |
| | 12/30/2016 | 12/31/2016, 1/1/2017, 1/2/2017, ... |
| | 12/31/2016, 1/31/2017 | 2/29/2017, 3/31/2017, 4/30/2017, ... |
| | Mon | Tue, Wed, Thu, ... |
| | Monday | Tuesday, Wednesday, Thursday, ... |
| | 11:00AM | 12:00PM, 1:00PM, 2:00PM, ... |
| Patterned Text | 1st period | 2nd period, 3rd period, 4th period, ... |
| | Region 1 | Region 2, Region 3, Region 4, ... |
| | Quarter 3 | Quarter 4, Quarter 1, Quarter 2, ... |
| | Qtr3 | Qtr4, Qtr1, Qtr2, ... |

© 2014 Cengage Learning

Ken wants you to fill in the dates of the workouts, replacing the numbers in the range F22:F44. You will use AutoFill to insert the calendar dates starting with 8/1/2016.

### To use AutoFill to enter the calendar dates:

1. In cell **F22**, enter **8/1/2016**. This is the first date you want to use for the series.

2. Select cell **F22** to select the cell with the first date in the series.

3. Drag the fill handle over the range **F23:F44**.

4. Release the mouse button. AutoFill enters the calendar dates ending with 8/23/2016 in cell F44.

**TIP**

You can also fill a series down by selecting both the cells to copy and the cells to be filled in, and then pressing the Ctrl+D keys.

For more complex AutoFill patterns, you can use the Series dialog box to specify a linear or growth series for numbers; a date series for dates that increase by day, weekday, month, or year; or an AutoFill series for patterned text. With numbers, you can also specify the step value (how much each number increases over the previous entry) and a stop value (the endpoint for the entire series).

Ken notices that the workout dates are wrong in the Fitness Report worksheet. Fit Fathers meets only Monday through Friday. He asks you to change the fill pattern to include only weekdays. You will use the Series dialog box to set the fill pattern for the rest of the weekdays in the month.

### To fill the dates of weekdays in August:

1. Make sure the range **F22:F44** is selected. Cell F22 contains the first value for the series that will be entered in the range F23:F44.

2. On the HOME tab, in the Editing group, click the **Fill** button, and then click **Series**. The Series dialog box opens.

3. In the Type section, make sure that the **Date** option button is selected.

▶ **4.** In the Date unit section, click the **Weekday** option button so that the series includes only dates for Mondays through Fridays. See Figure 3-25.

| Figure 3-25 | Series dialog box |
| --- | --- |

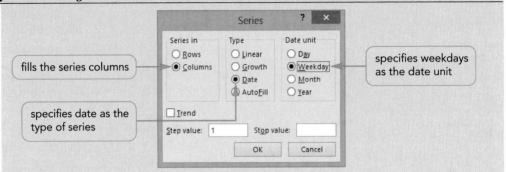

fills the series columns → Columns

specifies weekdays as the date unit

specifies date as the type of series

▶ **5.** Click the **OK** button. The dates of weekdays in August are filled into the selected range ending with 8/31/2016. See Figure 3-26.

| Figure 3-26 | Weekday values filled in |
| --- | --- |

| ◢ | E | F | G | H | I | J | |
| --- | --- | --- | --- | --- | --- | --- | --- |
| 20 | | Workout Routine 5 | | | | | |
| 21 | | Day | Attended (x) | Jogging (min.) | Calisthenics (min.) | Strength (min.) | Tot: |
| 22 | | 8/1/2016 | x | 10 | 10 | 15 | |
| 23 | | 8/2/2016 | x | 10 | 8 | 12 | |
| 24 | | 8/3/2016 | x | 12 | 18 | 15 | |
| 25 | | 8/4/2016 | | | | | |
| 26 | | 8/5/2016 | x | 12 | 15 | 18 | |
| 27 | | 8/8/2016 | x | 15 | 10 | 15 | |
| 28 | | 8/9/2016 | | | | | |
| 29 | | 8/10/2016 | x | 15 | 15 | 20 | |
| 30 | | 8/11/2016 | x | 15 | 13 | 22 | |
| 31 | | 8/12/2016 | x | 20 | 15 | 25 | |
| 32 | | 8/15/2016 | x | 20 | 15 | 20 | |
| 33 | | 8/16/2016 | x | 22 | 8 | 30 | |
| 34 | | 8/17/2016 | | | | | |
| 35 | | 8/18/2016 | x | 12 | 18 | 25 | |
| 36 | | 8/19/2016 | x | 15 | 20 | 20 | |
| 37 | | 8/22/2016 | | | | | |
| 38 | | 8/23/2016 | x | 20 | 17 | 23 | |

only weekdays are entered in the selected range

◁ ▷   Documentation   **Fitness Report**   Explanation of Formulas   ⊕

READY                                                                              AVERAGE: 8

# Working with Date Functions

Excel has several functions that work with dates and times. **Date functions** insert or calculate dates and times. They are particularly useful in business workbooks that involve production schedules and calendar applications. Figure 3-27 describes some of the commonly used Date functions.

| Figure 3-27 | Date functions |
| --- | --- |

| Function | Description |
| --- | --- |
| DATE(year, month, day) | Creates a date value for the date represented by the *year, month*, and *day* arguments |
| DAY(date) | Extracts the day of the month from *date* |
| MONTH(date) | Extracts the month number from *date* where 1=January, 2=February, and so forth |
| YEAR(date) | Extracts the year number from *date* |
| NETWORKDAYS(start, end[, holidays]) | Calculates the number of whole working days between *start* and *end*; to exclude holidays, add the optional *holidays* argument containing a list of holiday dates to skip |
| WEEKDAY(date[, return_type]) | Calculates the weekday from *date*, where 1=Sunday, 2=Monday, and so forth; to choose a different numbering scheme, set *return_type* to 1 (1=Sunday, 2=Monday, ...), 2 (1=Monday, 2=Tuesday, ...), or 3 (0=Monday, 1=Tuesday, ...) |
| WORKDAY(start, days[, holidays]) | Returns the workday after *days* workdays have passed since the *start* date; to exclude holidays, add the optional *holidays* argument containing a list of holiday dates to skip |
| NOW( ) | Returns the current date and time |
| TODAY( ) | Returns the current date |

© 2014 Cengage Learning

## Displaying the Current Date with the TODAY function

Many workbooks include the current date. You can use the **TODAY function** to display the current date in a worksheet. The TODAY function has the following syntax:

=TODAY()

**TIP**

To display the current date and time, which is updated each time the workbook is reopened, use the NOW function.

Note that although the TODAY function doesn't have any arguments, you still must include the parentheses for the function to work. The date displayed by the TODAY function is updated automatically whenever you reopen the workbook or enter a new calculation.

Ken wants the Fitness Report worksheet to show the current date each time it is used or printed. You will use the TODAY function to display the current date in cell G2.

### To display the current date with the TODAY function:

1. Select cell **G2**.

2. On the FORMULAS tab, in the Function Library group, click the **Date & Time** button to display the date and time functions.

3. Click **TODAY**. The Function Arguments dialog box opens and indicates that the TODAY function requires no arguments.

4. Click the **OK** button. The formula =TODAY() is entered in cell G2.

5. Verify that the current date is displayed in the cell.

6. Format the cell using the **Calculation** style.

# Finding the Next Weekday with the WORKDAY function

Instead of using AutoFill to enter a series of dates in a range, you can use the WORKDAY function to fill in the remaining weekdays based on the start date you specify. The WORKDAY function displays the date of the weekday a specific number of weekdays past a starting date. The syntax of the WORKDAY function is

```
=WORKDAY(start, days[, holiday])
```

where *start* is a start date, *days* is the number of weekdays after *start*, and *holiday* is an optional list of dates to skip. If you do not include anything for the optional *holiday* argument, the WORKDAY function does not skip any days. For example, if cell A1 contains the date 11/4/2016, a Friday, the following formula displays the date 11/9/2016, a Wednesday that is three working days after 11/4/2016:

```
=WORKDAY(A1, 3)
```

Ken wants to automate the process of inserting the exercise dates. You will use the WORKDAY function to do this.

### To insert the exercise dates using the WORKDAY function:

▶ 1. In cell **G7**, enter **8/1/2016** to specify the date the workouts will begin, and then format the cell using the **Input** cell style.

▶ 2. In cell **G8**, enter the formula **=F44** to display the date of the last scheduled workout, which is 8/31/2016 in this instance, and then format the cell using the **Calculation** cell style.

▶ 3. In cell **F22**, enter the formula **=G7** to replace the date with a reference to the start date you specified in cell G7. The cell still displays 8/1/2016.

▶ 4. Select cell **F23**, if necessary, and then click the **Insert Function** button $f_x$ next to the formula bar. The Insert Function dialog box opens.

▶ 5. Type **working days** in the Search for a function box, and then click the **Go** button to find all of the functions related to working days.

▶ 6. In the Select a function box, click **WORKDAY** to select the function, and then click the **OK** button. The WORKDAY Function Arguments dialog box opens.

▶ 7. In the Start_date box, type the cell reference **F22** to specify that cell F22 contains the start date you want to use.

▶ 8. In the Days box, type **1** to specify the number of workdays after the date in cell F22 that you want the formula results to show. See Figure 3-28.

**Figure 3-28** Function Arguments dialog box for the WORKDAY function

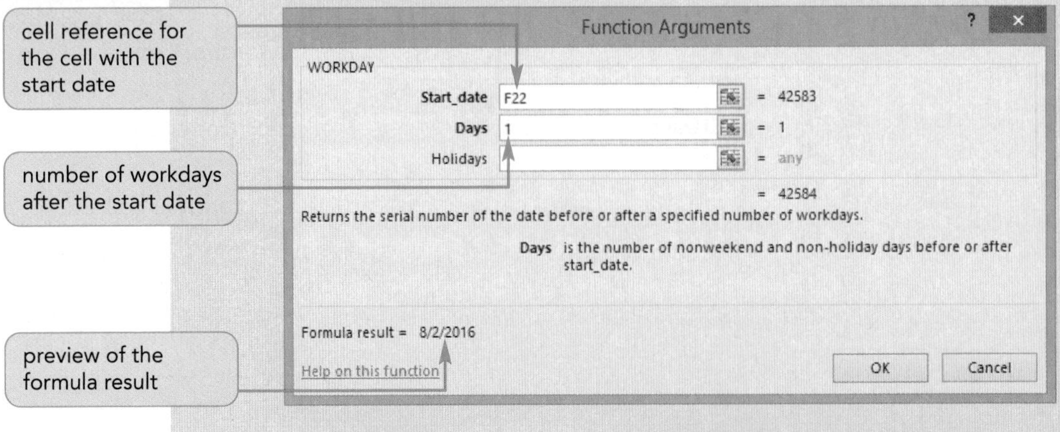

cell reference for the cell with the start date

number of workdays after the start date

preview of the formula result

**9.** Click the **OK** button. Cell F23 contains the formula =WORKDAY(F22, 1) and displays the date 8/2/2016, which is the next workday after 8/1/2016.

You want to use the same formula to calculate the rest of the workout dates. You can use AutoFill to quickly repeat the formula.

**10.** Select cell **F23**, and then drag the fill handle down over the range **F23:F44** to copy the formula and enter the rest of the workdays in the month.

Because the copied formulas use relative references, each cell displays a date that is one workday after the date in the previous cell. The dates should not be different from the dates you entered previously using AutoFill.

**11.** Format the range **F22:F44** with the **Calculation** cell style to show that these dates are calculated by a formula rather than entered manually.

You will test that the formulas in the range F22:F44 are working correctly by entering a different start date.

**12.** In cell **G7**, enter **9/1/2016** as the new start date.

**13.** Review the dates in the range F22:F44, verifying that the workout dates start with 9/2/2016 in cell F23, continue with 9/5/2016 in cell F24, and end with 10/3/2016 in cell F44.

**Trouble?** If the workout dates do not end with 10/3/2016, compare the formula in cell F23 to the formula shown in Step 9, make any edits needed, and then repeat Step 10.

**14.** In cell **G7**, enter **8/1/2016** to return to the original start date.

## INSIGHT

### Selecting the Days in the Work Week

Different countries, regions, and even businesses might have different rules for what constitutes a workday. If you need to create a schedule that doesn't follow the standard U.S. business days (Monday through Friday), you can use the WORKDAY.INTL function to specify the days to use as the work week. The syntax of the WORKDAY.INTL function is:

    =WORKDAY.INTL(start, days[, weekend=1, holidays])

The only difference between the syntax of the WORKDAY.INTL function and the syntax of the WORKDAY function is the optional *weekend* argument, which specifies the days of the week considered to be weekend or nonworking days. If you omit the *weekend* argument, weekends are considered to occur only on Saturday and Sunday. If you include the *weekend* argument, you enter one of the following numbers to specify the two days or the one day to consider as the weekend:

| Weekend | Two-Day Weekend | Weekend | One-Day Weekend |
|---------|-----------------|---------|-----------------|
| 1 | Saturday, Sunday | 11 | Sunday |
| 2 | Sunday, Monday | 12 | Monday |
| 3 | Monday, Tuesday | 13 | Tuesday |
| … | | … | |
| 7 | Friday, Saturday | 17 | Saturday |

For example, a business that is open every day except Sunday would use a *weekend* value of 11 to indicate that only Sunday is considered a nonworking day, and a business that is closed on Monday and Tuesday would use a *weekend* value of 3 to specify a work week of Wednesday through Sunday. For other working week schedules, you can enter text to specify which days are workdays. See Excel Help for more information.

# Counting Cells

Excel has two functions for counting cells—the COUNT function and the COUNTA function. The COUNT function tallies how many cells in a range contain numbers or dates (because they are stored as numeric values). The COUNT function does not count blank cells or cells that contain text. Its syntax is

```
COUNT(value1[, value2, value3, ...])
```

where value1 is the first item or cell reference containing the numbers you want to count. The remaining value arguments are used primarily when you want to count numbers and dates in nonadjacent ranges. For example, the following function counts how many cells in the range A1:A10, the range C1:C5, and cell E5 contain numbers or dates:

```
COUNT(A1:A10, C1:C5, E5)
```

If you want to know how many cells contain entries—whether those entries are numbers, dates, or text—you use the COUNTA function, which tallies the nonblank cells in a range. The following is the syntax of the COUNTA function, which has the same arguments as the COUNT function:

```
COUNTA(value1[, value2, value3, ...])
```

Ken wants the Workout Summary to show the total number of scheduled workouts for the month, the number of attended workouts, and the number of missed workouts. You will use the COUNT function to count the total number of workout dates in the Workout Routine 5 table. Then, you will use the COUNTA function to count the number of workouts actually attended. Each attended workout is marked by an "x" in column G of the Workout Routine 5 table; missing workouts are left blank. Finally, you will enter a formula to calculate the missed workouts.

## To count the scheduled, attended, and missed workouts:

▶ **1.** In cell **G9**, enter the formula **=COUNT(F22:F44)**. Cell G9 displays 23, indicating that Ken scheduled 23 workouts for the month.

▶ **2.** In cell **G10**, enter the formula **=COUNTA(G22:G44)**. Cell G10 displays 17, indicating that Daniel attended 17 of the 23 scheduled workouts.

▶ **3.** In cell **G11**, enter the formula **=G9–G10** to calculate the difference between the number of scheduled workouts and the number of attended workouts. Cell G11 displays 6, which is the number of missed workouts.

▶ **4.** Format the range **G9:G11** with the **Calculation** cell style.

▶ **5.** Select cell **G10**. See Figure 3-29.

**Figure 3-29**     **Completed Workout Summary**

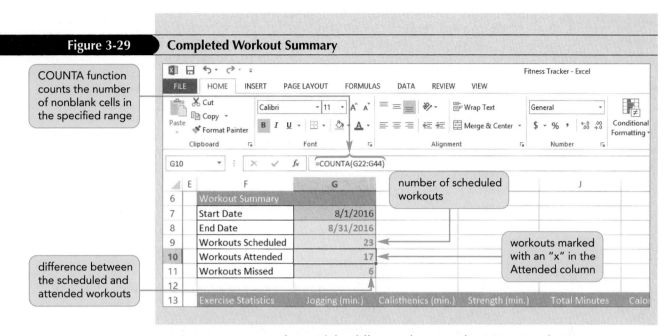

It is important to understand the difference between the COUNT and COUNTA functions. For example, if you had used the COUNT function in cell G10 to tally the number of attended workouts, the result would have been 0 because the range G22:G44 contains no entries with numbers.

Like the COUNT function, many of Excel's statistical functions ignore cells that are blank or contain text. This can create unexpected results with calculated values if you are not careful. Figure 3-30 shows how some of the common summary statistics change when blank cells are used in place of zeroes.

**Figure 3-30**     **Calculations involving blank cells and zeroes**

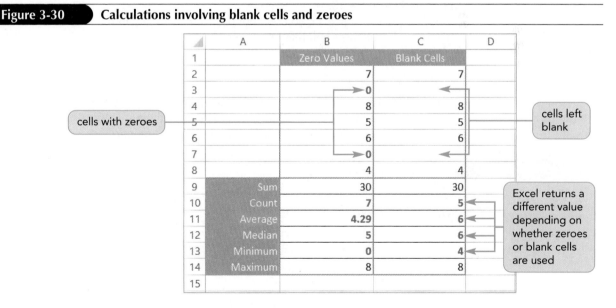

Some of the fitness statistics for total exercise minutes and calories burned include the six workouts that Daniel missed. For example, the minimum exercise minutes and calories burned are both listed as 0 because the calculated values show up as 0 in the worksheet when the workout session was missed. Ken wants the summary statistics based on only the workouts actually attended. One way to exclude missed workouts is to delete the zeroes, leaving blank cells. However, Ken wants the worksheet to be user-friendly and not require anyone to double-check and edit entries for missed workouts. Instead of editing the worksheet, you can use a logical function to automatically replace zeroes with blanks for missed workouts.

# Working with Logical Functions

A logical function returns a different value depending on whether the given condition is true or false, such as whether or not a scheduled workout was attended. In Excel, the condition is expressed as a formula. Consider a condition that includes the expression A5=3. If cell A5 is equal to 3, this expression and condition are true; if cell A5 is not equal to 3, this expression and condition are false. The IF function is one of the many logical functions you can use in Excel.

## Using the IF Function

The IF function is a logical function that returns one value if a condition is true, and returns a different value if that condition is false. The syntax of the IF function is

    IF(*logical_test*, *value_if_true*, *value_if_false*)

where *logical_test* is a condition that is either true or false, *value_if_true* is the value returned by the function if the condition is true, and *value_if_false* is the value returned if the condition is false. The value can be a number, text, a date, or a cell reference. For example, the following formula tests whether the value in cell A1 is equal to the value in cell B1:

    =IF(A1=B1, 100, 50)

If the value in cell A1 equals the value in cell B1, the formula result is 100; otherwise, the formula result is 50.

In many cases, however, you will not use values directly in the IF function. The following formula uses cell references, returning the value of cell C1 if A1 equals B1; otherwise, it returns the value of cell C2:

    =IF(A1=B1, C1, C2)

The = symbol in these formulas is a comparison operator. A **comparison operator** is a symbol that indicates the relationship between two values. Figure 3-31 describes the comparison operators that can be used within a logical function.

| Figure 3-31 | Comparison operators |
| --- | --- |

| Operator | Expression | Description |
| --- | --- | --- |
| = | A1 = B1 | Tests whether the value in cell A1 is equal to the value in cell B1 |
| > | A1 > B1 | Tests whether the value in cell A1 is greater than the value in cell B1 |
| < | A1 < B1 | Tests whether the value in cell A1 is less than the value in cell B1 |
| >= | A1 >= B1 | Tests whether the value in cell A1 is greater than or equal to the value in cell B1 |
| <= | A1 <= B1 | Tests whether the value in cell A1 is less than or equal to the value in cell B1 |
| <> | A1 <> B1 | Tests whether the value in cell A1 is not equal to the value in cell B1 |

© 2014 Cengage Learning

The IF function also works with text. For example, the following formula tests whether the value of cell A1 is equal to "yes":

```
=IF(A1="yes", "done", "restart")
```

If true (the value of cell A1 is equal to "yes"), the formula returns the text "done"; otherwise, it returns the text "restart". Notice that the text in the function is enclosed in quotation marks.

In addition, you can nest other functions inside an IF statement. The following formula first tests whether cell A5 is equal to the maximum of values within the range A1:A100:

```
=IF(A5=MAX(A1:A100), "Maximum", "")
```

**TIP**

For the formula result to show no text, include opening and closing quotation marks with nothing between them.

If it is, the formula returns the text "Maximum"; otherwise, it returns no text.

In the Fitness Report worksheet, you need to rewrite the formulas that calculate the total minutes and total calories from each workout as IF functions that test whether Daniel actually attended the workout. Because every attended workout is marked with an "x" in column G, you can test whether the cell entry in column G is an "x". For example, the following formula in cell K22 is currently being used to calculate the total minutes from the first workout:

```
=SUM(H22:J22)
```

This formula can be revised to the following IF function, which first determines if cell G22 contains an "x" (indicating that the workout was attended), and then uses the SUM function to calculate the total minutes if there is an "x":

```
=IF(G22="x", SUM(H22:J22), "")
```

Otherwise, the formula displays nothing, leaving the cell blank.

You will use relative references in the revised formula so that you can copy it for the other workouts and total columns. You will create the formula with the IF function for the total minutes column now.

### To use an IF function to calculate total minutes for attended workouts:

1. Select cell **K22**, and then press the **Delete** key to clear the original formula from the cell.

2. Click the **Insert Function** button $f_x$ next to the formula bar to open the Insert Function dialog box.

3. Type **if function** in the Search for a function box, and then press the **Enter** key. Functions that match your description appear in the Select a function box.

4. Click **IF** in the Select a function box, and then click the **OK** button to open the Function Arguments dialog box.

5. In the Logical_test box, type **G22="x"** as the expression that tests whether cell G22 is equal to x.

6. Press the **Tab** key to move the insertion point to the Value_if_true box, and then type **SUM(H22:J22)**. If cell G22 does contain an x (the logical test is true), the sum of the values in the range H22:J22 will be displayed in cell K22.

7. Press the **Tab** key to move the insertion point to the Value_if_false box, and then type **""** (opening and closing quotation marks). If cell G22 does not contain an x (the logical test is false), the cell will be left blank. See Figure 3-32.

**Figure 3-32**    **Function Arguments dialog box for the IF function**

statement to evaluate
as true or false

Function Arguments

IF

| Logical_test | G22="x" | = TRUE |
| Value_if_true | SUM(H22:J22) | = 35 |
| Value_if_false | "" | = "" |

calculates the sum if
the statement is true

displays nothing if
the statement is false

= 35

Checks whether a condition is met, and returns one value if TRUE, and another value if FALSE.

**Value_if_false**   is the value that is returned if Logical_test is FALSE. If omitted, FALSE
is returned.

preview of the
formula result

Formula result =   35

Help on this function

OK        Cancel

8. Click the **OK** button. The formula =IF(G22="x", SUM(H22:J22), "") is entered
   into cell K22. The cell displays 35, which is the number of minutes Daniel
   spent exercising at that workout session.

   You will copy the formula with the IF function to calculate the total minutes
   for the rest of the workouts.

9. Select cell **K22**, and then drag the fill handle down over the range **K22:K44**
   to copy the IF formula to the remaining cells in the column. The total number
   of minutes for each workout is recalculated so that the missed workouts in
   cells K25, K28, K34, K37, K39, and K40 are now left blank.

10. Select cell **K22**. The #VALUE! error value appears in columns L and M for
    each of the missed workouts because the current formulas cannot calculate
    calories burned when no total minutes are provided. See Figure 3-33.

**Figure 3-33**    **IF function excludes the total minutes for missed workouts**

IF function tests whether the workout was
attended (marked with an "x") before
calculating the total minutes of exercise

Fitness Tracker - Excel

Total Minutes summary
statistics no longer include
missed workouts

K22    =IF(G22="x",SUM(H22:J22),"")

| | E | F | G | H | I | J | K | L | M | N | C |
|---|---|---|---|---|---|---|---|---|---|---|---|
| 13 | | Exercise Statistics | Jogging (min.) | Calisthenics (min.) | Strength (min.) | Total Minutes | Calories Burned | | | | |
| 14 | | SUM | 278 | 245 | 347 | 870 | #VALUE! | | | | c Eq |
| 15 | | AVERAGE | 16.4 | 14.4 | 20.4 | 51.2 | #VALUE! | | | | |
| 16 | | MEDIAN | 15 | 15 | 20 | 55 | #VALUE! | | | | Rou |
| 17 | | MINIMUM | 10 | 8 | 12 | 30 | #VALUE! | | | | Rou |
| 18 | | MAXIMUM | 22 | 20 | 30 | 60 | #VALUE! | | | | out Rou |
| 19 | | | | | | | | | | | Workout Rou |
| 20 | | Workout Routine 5 | | | | | | | | | Workout Rou |
| 21 | | Day | Attended (x) | Jogging (min.) | Calisthenics (min.) | Strength (min.) | Total Minutes | Calories Burned | Calories Subtotal | | Workout Rou |
| 22 | | 8/1/2016 | x | 10 | 10 | 15 | 35 | 376.1 | 376.1 | | Workout Rou |
| 23 | | 8/2/2016 | x | 10 | 8 | 12 | 30 | 322.4 | 698.5 | | Workout Rou |
| 24 | | 2016 | x | 12 | 18 | 15 | 45 | 483.6 | 1182.1 | | Workout Rou |
| 25 | | 016 | | | | | | #VALUE! | #VALUE! | | Workout Rou |
| 26 | | 016 | x | | 18 | | 45 | 483.6 | #VALUE! | | |
| 27 | | 016 | x | | 15 | | 40 | 429.9 | #VALUE! | | |
| 28 | | 016 | | | | | | #VALUE! | #VALUE! | Body Mass In | |
| 29 | | 2016 | x | 15 | 15 | 20 | 50 | 537.3 | #VALUE! | BMI | |
| 30 | | 8/11/2016 | x | 15 | 13 | 22 | 50 | 537.3 | #VALUE! | | |
| 31 | | 8/12/2016 | x | 20 | 15 | 25 | 60 | 644.8 | #VALUE! | | |

error values appear because
formulas need a total
minutes value to calculate

attended
workouts
marked with
an "x"

missed workouts
displayed as blank cells

Documentation   **Fitness Report**   Explanation of Formulas

READY

Next, you will update the calories burned formulas so that they don't display the #VALUE! error value when a workout is missed. This requires another IF statement similar to the one you used to calculate total minutes. As with the total minutes calculation, any missed workout will display a blank cell for the calories burned in place of a 0. Rather than reentering the complete formula for calories burned, you can edit the existing formula, inserting the IF function.

## To change the calories burned formulas to IF functions:

1. Double-click cell **L22** to enter Edit mode.

2. Press the **Home** key to move the insertion point to the beginning of the formula, and then press the → key to move the insertion point one space to the right, directly after = (the equal sign). You will begin the IF function after the equal sign.

3. Type **IF(G22="x",** to insert the function name and the expression for the logical test.

4. Press the **Ctrl+End** keys to move the insertion point to the end of the formula.

5. Type **, "")** to enter the value if false and complete the IF function. The complete formula is now =IF(G22="x", $P$20*$C$11*K22/125.7143, "").

> Make sure your formula matches the one shown here.

6. Press the **Enter** key to exit Edit mode and make cell L23 active. Cell L22 still displays 376.1 because Ken did not miss the first workout.

   You will use AutoFill to copy the IF function to the rest of the cells in the Calories Burned column.

7. Select cell **L22**, and then drag the fill handle down over the range **L22:L44**. As shown in Figure 3-34, the missed workouts now display blank cells instead of zeroes, and the attended workouts show the same calculated values as earlier.

**Figure 3-34**  **IF function excludes the calories burned for missed workouts**

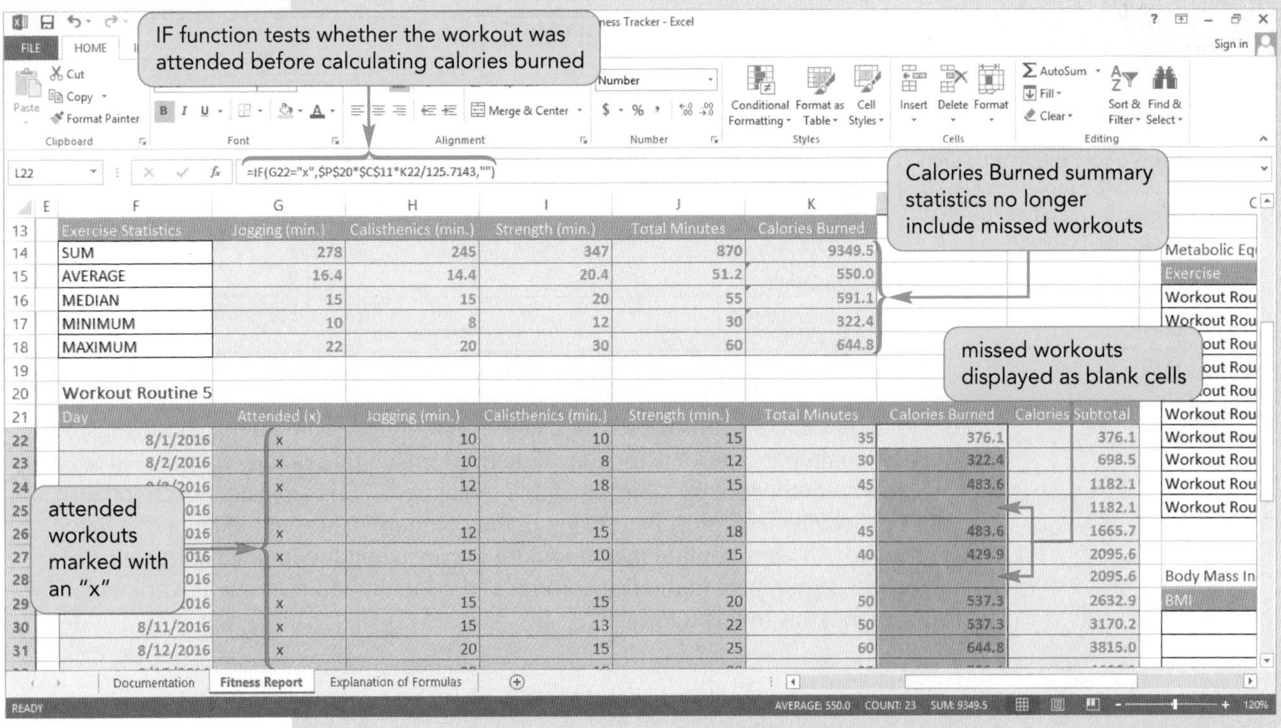

By excluding the missed workouts, Daniel's average exercise time increased from 37.8 minutes to 51.2 minutes, and the average calories burned increased to 550 calories. These averages more closely match the median values because zeroes were removed from the calculations. The minimum values for Total Minutes and Calories Burned now also reflect only attended workouts, changing from 0 (when they were based on a missed workout) to 30 minutes and 322.4 calories, respectively. These measures reflect the true results of the workouts Daniel attended.

# Using a Lookup Function

**Lookup functions** find values in tables of data and insert them in another location in the worksheet such as cells or in formulas. For example, consider the active BMR calculated in cell C22, which adjusts the calculation of Daniel's metabolic rate to account for his activity level. The more active Daniel is, the more calories he can consume without gaining weight. The multiplying factors for each activity level (Sedentary, Light, Moderate, High, or Extreme) are stored in a table in the range O8:P12; you used the value in cell P8 to adjust Daniel's BMR value for his sedentary lifestyle. Instead of including a direct reference to one of the multiplying factors in the table, you can use a function to have Excel choose the multiplying factor that corresponds to the specified activity level.

The table that stores the data you want to retrieve is called a lookup table. A lookup table organizes numbers or text into categories. This particular lookup table organizes the BMR factors by activity levels, as shown in Figure 3-35. Every activity level category in the first column of the lookup table has a corresponding BMR factor in the second column of the table. This table is a vertical lookup table because the categories are arranged vertically. The entries in the first column of a vertical lookup table are referred to as the compare values because they are compared to the category you want to find (called the lookup value). When a match is found, the corresponding value in one of the subsequent columns is returned. For example, to find the return value for the Moderate lookup value, you look down the first column of the lookup table until you find the Moderate entry. Then, you move to the second column to locate the corresponding return value, which is 1.550, in this case.

**Figure 3-35**    **Finding an exact match from a vertical lookup table**

| Lookup Value = "Moderate" | Basal Metabolic Rate Activity Factors | | return the corresponding value from the second column of the table |
| --- | --- | --- | --- |
| go down the first column until the lookup value exactly matches the compare value | Activity Level | BMR Factor | |
| | Sedentary | 1.200 | |
| | Light | 1.375 | |
| | Moderate | 1.550 | |
| | High | 1.725 | |
| | Extreme | 1.900 | Return Value = 1.550 |

© 2014 Cengage Learning

Lookup tables can be constructed for exact match or approximate match lookups. An **exact match lookup** is when the lookup value must match one of the compare values in the first column of the lookup table. The table in Figure 3-35 is an exact match lookup because the activity level must match one of the compare values in the table or a value is not returned. An **approximate match lookup** occurs when the lookup value falls within a range of numbers in the first column of the lookup table. You will work with exact match lookups in this tutorial.

## Finding an Exact Match with the VLOOKUP Function

To retrieve the return value from a vertical lookup table, you use the VLOOKUP function. The syntax of the VLOOKUP function is

```
VLOOKUP(lookup_value, table_array, col_index_num[, range_lookup=TRUE])
```

where *lookup_value* is the compare value to find in the first column of the lookup table, *table_array* is the range reference to the lookup table, and *col_index_num* is the number of the column in the lookup table that contains the return value. Keep in mind that *col_index_num* refers to the number of the column within the lookup table, not the worksheet column. For example, *col_index_num* 2 refers to the second column of the table, *col_index_num* 3 refers to the third column of the table, and so forth. Finally, *range_lookup* is an optional argument that specifies whether the compare values are an exact match or a range of values (for an approximate match). For an exact match, you set the *range_lookup* value to FALSE. For approximate match lookups, you set the *range_lookup* value to TRUE or you can omit it because its default value is TRUE.

For example, the following formula performs an exact match lookup to find the BMR factor for an Extreme activity level based on the values from the lookup table in the range O8:P12 (shown earlier in Figure 3-35):

```
=VLOOKUP("Extreme", O8:P12, 2, FALSE)
```

**TIP**

If the VLOOKUP function cannot find the lookup value, the #N/A error value is displayed in the cell.

The *col_index_num* is 2 because the BMR factors are in the second column of the table. The *range_lookup* is FALSE because this is an exact match. The function looks through the compare values in the first column of the table to locate the "Extreme" entry. When the exact entry is found, the function returns the corresponding value in the second column of the table, which in this case is 1.900.

Daniel's activity level in cell C9 is entered as Sedentary, which has a BMR factor of 1.2. The following active BMR formula you entered earlier calculated that Daniel can consume about 2224 calories per day and maintain his current weight:

```
=P8*C21
```

In this formula, P8 references the Sedentary BMR value in cell P8 and C21 references Daniel's base or resting metabolic rate. To have Excel look up the BMR value, you need to replace the P8 cell reference with a VLOOKUP function, as follows:

```
=VLOOKUP(C9, O8:P12, 2, FALSE)*C21
```

In this formula, C9 contains Daniel's activity level (Sedentary), O8:P12 references the lookup table, 2 specifies the table column to find the BMR factors, and FALSE indicates that this is an exact match lookup. You will enter this formula into the worksheet now.

### To use the VLOOKUP function to calculate Daniel's active BMR:

1. Select cell **C22**, and then press the **Delete** key to clear the formula currently in the cell.

2. On the ribbon, click the **FORMULAS** tab. Because VLOOKUP has several arguments to manage, you will enter the function using the Function Arguments dialog box.

3. In the Function Library group, click **Lookup & Reference** to display a list of functions, and then click **VLOOKUP**. The Function Arguments dialog box opens.

4. With the insertion point in the Lookup_value box, click cell **C9** in the worksheet to enter that cell reference as the location containing the value to look up in the first column of the lookup table.

**5.** Press the **Tab** key to move the insertion point into the Table_array box, and then select the range **O8:P12**, which contains the vertical lookup table in the worksheet.

**6.** Press the **Tab** key to move the insertion point to the Col_index_num box, and then type **2** to return a value from the second column of the lookup table.

**7.** Press the **Tab** key to move the insertion point to the Range_lookup box, and then type **FALSE** to specify an exact match lookup. The dialog box shows the resulting value of the function with these arguments, which in this case is 1.2. See Figure 3-36.

**Figure 3-36**    **Function Arguments dialog box for the VLOOKUP function**

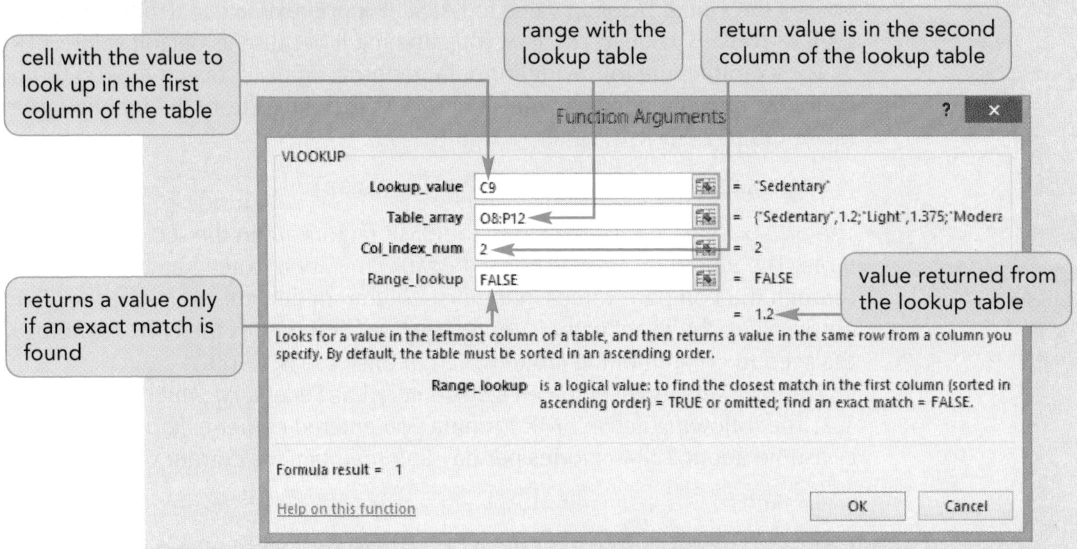

cell with the value to look up in the first column of the table

range with the lookup table

return value is in the second column of the lookup table

returns a value only if an exact match is found

value returned from the lookup table

**8.** Click the **OK** button to close the dialog box.

**9.** Double-click cell **C22** to enter Edit mode, press the **Ctrl+End** keys to move the insertion point to the end of the formula, type **\*C21** to complete the formula, and then press the **Enter** key. The completed formula in cell C22 is =VLOOKUP(C9,O8:P12,2,FALSE)*C21, resulting in an active BMR of 2224 calories per day for a Sedentary activity level.

You will change the activity level to ensure that the formula works correctly.

**10.** In cell **C9**, enter **Moderate** to change the activity level from Sedentary. The active BMR value changes to 2872 because the VLOOKUP function returns a 1.55 BMR factor from the lookup table.

Ken decides that Light is a more accurate description of Daniel's activity level.

**11.** In cell **C9**, enter **Light** as the activity level. At that activity level, the active BMR changes to 2548. With a Light activity level, Daniel can consume about 2548 calories per day and maintain his current weight.

**12.** Select cell **C22** to view the formula. See Figure 3-37.

**TIP**

Exact matches are not case sensitive, so the lookup values Light, light, and LIGHT are considered to be the same.

**Figure 3-37** | **VLOOKUP function calculates the active BMR**

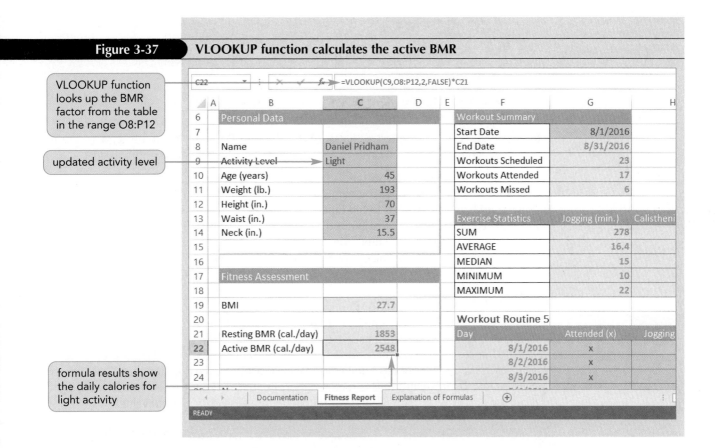

VLOOKUP function looks up the BMR factor from the table in the range O8:P12

updated activity level

formula results show the daily calories for light activity

# Performing What-If Analysis

A **what-if analysis** lets you explore the impact that changing input values has on the calculated values in the workbook. For example, Ken could perform a what-if analysis to determine how many pounds Daniel needs to lose to reach a more healthy weight. Current fitness standards suggest that a body mass index between 18.5 and 24.9 is considered to be within the "normal" classification. Daniel's body mass index is 27.7, which is rated as overweight. So Ken wants to know how many pounds Daniel needs to lose to reduce his body mass index to 24.9.

## Using Trial and Error

One way to perform a what-if analysis is by changing one or more of the input values to see how they affect the calculated results. This **trial-and-error method** requires some guesswork as you estimate which values to change and by how much. In this case, Ken wants you to find out the weight at which Daniel would reach a BMI of 24.9. You'll start by checking the resulting body mass index if Daniel were to lose 10 pounds, reducing his weight to 183 pounds.

### To perform a what-if analysis by trial and error:

▶ **1.** In cell **C11**, change the weight from 193 pounds to **183** pounds. Daniel's body mass index decreases from 27.7 to 26.3, as shown in cell C19. At this weight, he is still considered overweight.

▶ **2.** In cell **C11**, enter **163** pounds. At this weight, Daniel's BMI shown in cell C19 is 23.4. So losing 30 pounds is more than enough to classify Daniel's body weight as normal.

Ken wants to know if Daniel can lose fewer than 30 pounds to reach that classification.

▶ **3.** In cell **C11**, enter **168** pounds. At this weight, Daniel's BMI value is 24.1, which is still within the normal classification, but not exactly equal to 24.9.

If you want to find the exact weight that will result in a body mass index of 24.9, you would have to continue trying different weight values as you close in on the correct weight. This is why the method is called "trial and error." For some calculations, trial and error can be a very time-consuming way to locate the exact input value. A more direct approach to this problem is to use Goal Seek.

## Using Goal Seek

**Goal Seek** automates the trial-and-error process by allowing you to specify a value for a calculated item, which Excel uses to determine the input value needed to reach that goal. In this case, because Ken wants to know how Daniel can reach a body mass index of exactly 24.9 (the upper level of the normal classification), the question that Goal Seek answers is: "What weight value is required to reach that goal?" Goal Seek starts by setting the calculated value and works backward to determine the correct input value.

**REFERENCE**

### Performing What-If Analysis and Goal Seek

**To perform a what-if analysis by trial and error:**
- Change the value of a worksheet cell (the input cell).
- Observe its impact on one or more calculated cells (the result cells).
- Repeat until the desired results are achieved.

**To perform a what-if analysis using Goal Seek:**
- On the DATA tab, in the Data Tools group, click the What-If Analysis button, and then click Goal Seek.
- Select the result cell in the Set cell box, and then specify its value (goal) in the To value box.
- In the By changing cell box, specify the input cell.
- Click the OK button. The value of the input cell changes to set the value of the result cell.

You will use Goal Seek to find the weight that will result in Daniel's BMI reaching exactly 24.9.

### To use Goal Seek to find a weight resulting in a 24.9 BMI:

▶ **1.** On the ribbon, click the **DATA** tab.

▶ **2.** In the Data Tools group, click the **What-If Analysis** button, and then click **Goal Seek**. The Goal Seek dialog box opens.

▶ **3.** Make sure the value in the Set cell box is selected, and then click cell **C19** in the Fitness Report worksheet. The absolute cell reference $C$19 appears in the Set cell box. The set cell is the calculated value you want Goal Seek to change to meet your goal.

4. Press the **Tab** key to move the insertion point to the To value box, and then type **24.9**. This indicates that you want Goal Seek to set this value to 24.9 (the highest body mass index in the normal classification).

5. Press the **Tab** key to move the insertion point to the By changing cell box. There are often various input values you can change to meet a goal. In this case, you want to change the weight value in cell C11.

6. Click cell **C11**. The absolute reference $C$11 appears in the By changing cell box. See Figure 3-38.

**Figure 3-38**    Goal Seek dialog box

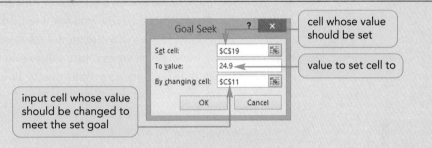

cell whose value should be set

value to set cell to

input cell whose value should be changed to meet the set goal

7. Click the **OK** button. The Goal Seek dialog box closes, and the Goal Seek Status dialog box opens, indicating that Goal Seek found a solution.

8. Click the **OK** button. A weight value of about 173 pounds is displayed in cell C11. Daniel would need to lose roughly 20 pounds, reducing his weight to 173 pounds to reach a weight within the normal classification for BMI. See Figure 3-39.

**Figure 3-39**    Target weight determined by Goal Seek

| | A | B | C | D | E | F | G | H |
|---|---|---|---|---|---|---|---|---|
| 6 | | Personal Data | | | | Workout Summary | | |
| 7 | | | | | | Start Date | 8/1/2016 | |
| 8 | | Name | Daniel Pridham | | | End Date | 8/31/2016 | |
| 9 | | Activity Level | Light | | | Workouts Scheduled | 23 | |
| 10 | | Age (years) | 45 | | | Workouts Attended | 17 | |
| 11 | | Weight (lb.) | 173.5561878 | | | Workouts Missed | 6 | |
| 12 | | Height (in.) | 70 | | | | | |
| 13 | | Waist (in.) | 37 | | | Exercise Statistics | Jogging (min.) | Calistheni |
| 14 | | Neck (in.) | 15.5 | | | SUM | 278 | |
| 15 | | | | | | AVERAGE | 16.4 | |
| 16 | | | | | | MEDIAN | 15 | |
| 17 | | Fitness Assessment | | | | MINIMUM | 10 | |
| 18 | | | | | | MAXIMUM | 22 | |
| 19 | | BMI | 24.9 | | | | | |
| 20 | | | | | | Workout Routine 5 | | |
| 21 | | Resting BMR (cal./day) | 1732 | | | Day | Attended (x) | Jogging |
| 22 | | Active BMR (cal./day) | 2382 | | | 8/1/2016 | x | |
| 23 | | | | | | 8/2/2016 | x | |
| 24 | | | | | | 8/3/2016 | x | |

solution weight

desired BMI

◀ ▶   Documentation   **Fitness Report**   Explanation of Formulas   ⊕

READY

9. Save and close the workbook.

Ken appreciates all of the work you have done in developing the Fitness Tracker workbook. He will use this workbook as a model for all of his other clients at Fit Fathers.

### Session 3.2 Quick Check

1. The first three values in a selected series are 3, 6, and 9. What are the next three values that will be inserted by AutoFill?
2. Write a formula to display the current date.
3. Write a formula to find the date four workdays after the date value stored in cell B10. There are no holidays.
4. Explain the difference between the COUNT function and the COUNTA function.
5. If cell Q3 is greater than cell Q4, you want to display the text "OK"; otherwise, display the text "RETRY". Write the formula that accomplishes this.
6. Jan is entering hundreds of temperature values into an Excel worksheet for a climate research project, and she wants to save time on data entry by leaving freezing point values as blanks rather than typing zeroes. Will this cause complications if she later tries to calculate an average temperature from her data values? Explain why or why not.
7. Provide the formula to perform an exact match lookup with the lookup value from cell G5 using a lookup table located in the range A1:F50. Return the value from the third column of the table.
8. What is the difference between a what-if analysis by trial and error and by Goal Seek?

**ASSESS**

**SAM Projects**

Put your skills into practice with SAM Projects! SAM Projects for this tutorial can be found online. If you have a SAM account, go to www.cengage.com/sam2013 to download the most recent Project Instructions and Start Files.

**PRACTICE**

## Review Assignments

**Data File needed for the Review Assignments: Mothers.xlsx**

Ken and his wife, Sally, are expanding the business, changing its name to Fit Fathers and Mothers Inc., and adding fitness classes for mothers with a special emphasis on pregnant women. The fitness equations for women are different from those for men. Ken and Sally want you to create a workbook similar to the one you created for fathers, but focused on the fitness needs of women. Sally also wants you to calculate the total fat burned in the course of completing the workout schedule. She has already designed much of the workbook's contents, but she needs you to add the formulas and functions. Complete the following:

1. Open the **Mothers** workbook located in the Excel3 ▸ Review folder included with your Data Files, and then save the workbook as **Mothers Fitness** in the location specified by your instructor.

2. In the Documentation sheet, enter your name and the date.

3. Go to the Fitness Analysis worksheet. In the range C8:C15, enter the personal data for **Dorothy Young**. Her activity level is **Moderate**, she is **38** years old, **152** pounds, **64** inches tall, with a **33**-inch waist, **35**-inch hips, and a **14**-inch neck.

4. In cell C20, enter a formula to calculate Dorothy's body mass index based on the equation

   $BMI = 703w/h^2$

   where $w$ is the weight in pounds and $h$ is the height in inches. Display the formula results with one decimal place.

5. In cell C22, enter a formula to calculate the resting metabolism rate for women based on the equation

   $BMR = 4.338w + 4.698h - 4.68a + 655$

   where $w$ is the weight in pounds, $h$ is the height in inches, and $a$ is the age in years. Display the formula results with no decimal places.

6. In cell C23, enter a formula using the VLOOKUP function to calculate the active BMR based on the equation

   Active BMR = *Activity Factor* × *BMR*

   where *Activity Factor* is an exact match lookup for the value in the range O8:Q12 that corresponds to the activity level entered in cell C9, and *BMR* is the value in cell C22. Display the formula results with no decimal places.

7. In cell K22, enter a formula using an IF function to calculate the total minutes for the first workout that displays a blank cell if Dorothy did not attend a workout that day.

8. Use AuotFill to copy the formula you entered in cell K22 to the range K23:K44 to calculate the total minutes for each workout.

9. In cell L22, enter a formula to calculate the calories burned at the first workout based on the equation

   $$\text{Calories} = \frac{METS \times w \times t}{125.7143}$$

   where *METS* is the metabolic factor for the exercise, $w$ is the client's weight, and $t$ is the exercise time. Use the METS value located in cell P19, the weight value located in cell C11, and the time value located in the corresponding cell in column K. Be sure to use an absolute reference for both weight and METS.

10. Edit the formula you entered in cell L22 to be included as part of an IF function that returns a blank cell if Dorothy did not attend the workout that day. Display the formula results with one decimal place.

11. Use AutoFill to copy the formula you entered in cell L22 to the range L23:L44 to calculate the calories burned at each workout.

12. In the range M22:M44, use the Quick Analysis tool to calculate a column running total of the calories burned in the range L22:L44. Display the formula results with two decimal places.

13. Complete the exercise statistics in the range G14:K18 by entering formulas calculating the sum, average, median, maximum, and minimum values of the exercise times, and calories burned values from the workout log. Display the averages and the calories burned statistics with one decimal place.

14. In cell G2, use a function to display the current date whenever the workbook is opened.

15. In cell F22, enter a formula to reference the start date entered in cell G7.

16. In the range F23:F44, use a function to increase the value of the date in the previous row by 1 workday. Format the formula results with the Short Date format.

17. In cell G8, enter a formula to display the ending date entered in cell F44.

18. In cell G9, enter a formula to count the number of days included in the range F22:F44.

19. In cell G10, enter a formula to count the number of attended workouts as indicated in the range G22:G44.

20. In cell G11, enter a formula to calculate the difference between the number of scheduled workouts and the number of attended workouts. Save the workbook.

21. Use Goal Seek to determine the weight Dorothy must attain to reach a body mass index of 22.

22. Save the revised workbook as **Mothers Fitness Goal**, and then close the workbook.

## Case Problem 1

APPLY

Data File needed for this Case Problem: Hernandez.xlsx

*Hernandez Family*    Juan and Olivia Hernandez are a recently married couple in Fort Wayne, Indiana. Juan is currently in graduate school and Olivia is the manager at a local bakery. They want to use Excel to help manage their family budget, but they need help setting up the formulas and functions to project their monthly expenses and help them meet their financial goals. Complete the following:

1. Open the **Hernandez** workbook located in the Excel3 ▶ Case1 folder included with your Data Files, and then save the workbook as **Hernandez Budget** in the location specified by your instructor.

2. In the Documentation sheet, enter your name and the date.

3. Go to the Budget worksheet. In cell B7, calculate the couple's total monthly income.

4. In row 23, use AutoFill to replace the numbers 1 through 12 with the month abbreviations **Jan** through **Dec**.

5. In rows 24 and 25, enter the couple's monthly income by referencing the monthly income estimates in cells B5 and B6. Use an absolute cell reference.

6. In row 26, calculate the couple's monthly income.

7. In row 37, enter formulas to calculate the total estimated expenses for each month.

8. In row 38, calculate each month's net cash flow, which is equal to the total income minus the total expenses.

9. In row 39, calculate the running total of the net cash flow so that Olivia and Juan can see how their net cash flow changes as the year progresses.

10. In the range B10:B19, calculate the average monthly expenses by category based on the values previously entered in rows 27 through 36.

11. In cell B20, calculate the total average monthly expenses.

12. The couple currently has $7,350 in their savings account. Each month the couple will either take money out of their savings account or deposit money. In row 41, calculate the end-of-month balance in their savings account by adding the value in cell E5 to the running total values of the net cash flow in row 39. Use an absolute cell reference for cell E5.

13. In cell E6, enter a formula to display the value of the savings balance at the end of December.

14. Juan and Olivia would like to have $15,000 in their savings account by the end of the year. Olivia is planning to ask for a raise at her job. Use Goal Seek to determine the value of cell B6 that will achieve a final savings balance of $15,000.

15. Save and close the workbook.

**CHALLENGE**

## Case Problem 2

Data File needed for this Case Problem: Econ.xlsx

***Introduction to Economics 102***   Alice Keyes teaches Introduction to Economics 102 at Mountain View Business School in Huntington, West Virginia. She wants to use Excel to track the grades from her class. Alice has already entered the homework, quiz, and final exam scores for all of her students in a workbook, and she has asked you to set up the formulas and functions for her.

You will calculate each student's final average based on his or her homework score, quiz scores, and final exam. Homework counts for 20 percent of the student's final grade. The first two quizzes count for 10 percent each. The second two quizzes count for 15 percent each. The final exam counts for 30 percent of the final grade.

You will also calculate each student's rank in the class. The rank will display which student placed first in terms of his or her overall score, which student placed second, and so forth. Ranks are calculated using the function

```
RANK(number, ref, [order=0])
```

where *number* is the value to be ranked, *ref* is a reference to the cell range containing the values against which the ranking is done, and *order* is an optional argument that specifies whether to rank in descending order or ascending order. The default *order* value is 0 to rank the values in descending order.

Finally, you will create formulas that will look up information on a particular student based on that student's ID so Alice doesn't have to scroll through the complete class roster to find a particular student. Complete the following:

1. Open the **Econ** workbook located in the Excel3 ▸ Case2 folder included with your Data Files, and then save the workbook as **Econ Grades** in the location specified by your instructor.

2. In the Documentation sheet, enter your name and the date.

3. Go to the Grade Book worksheet. In cell B5, count the number of student IDs in the range A22:A57.

✦ **Explore**  4. Cells C15 through H15 contain the weights assigned to each assignment, quiz, or exam. In cell J22, calculate the weighted average of the first student's scores by entering a formula that multiplies each score by its corresponding weight and adds the resulting products.

5. Edit the formula in cell J22, changing the references to the weights in cells C15 through H15 from relative references to absolute references.

6. Use AutoFill to copy the formula from cell J22 into the range J23:J57.

✦ **Explore**  7. In cell K22, use the RANK function to calculate how the first student compares to the other students in the class. Use the weighted average from cell J22 for the *number* argument and the range of weighted averages in the cell range $J$22:$J$57 for the *ref* argument. You do not need to specify a value for the *order* argument.

8. Use AutoFill to copy the formula you entered in cell K22 into the range K23:K57.

9. In the range C16:H18, calculate the class average, minimum, and maximum for each of the six grading components (homework, quizzes, and final exam).

10. In cell B8, enter the student ID **14858**.

⊕ **Explore**  11. Using the VLOOKUP function with an exact match and the student data table in the range A22:K57, retrieve the first name, last name, weighted average, and class rank for student 14858 in the range B9:B12. Use an absolute reference to the lookup table. Note that the first name is found in the third column of the student data table, the last name is found in the second column, the weighted average is found in the tenth column, and the class rank is found in the eleventh column.

12. Brenda Dunford missed the final exam and will be taking a make-up exam. She wants to know what score she would need on the final exam to achieve an overall weighted average of 90. Use Goal Seek to calculate what final exam score Brenda needs to result in a weighted average of 90.

13. Save and close the workbook.

## Case Problem 3

**Data File needed for this Case Problem: Homes.xlsx**

***Homes of Dreams***    Larry Helt is a carpenter and a woodcrafter in Coventry, Rhode Island, who loves to design and build custom dollhouses. He started his business, Homes of Dreams, a few years ago and it has expanded into a very profitable sideline to his ongoing carpentry work. Larry wants to create a shipping form that will calculate the cost for the purchased items, including taxes, shipping, and handling. Larry already designed the worksheet, which includes a table of shipping rates, shipping surcharges, and items sold by Homes of Dreams. He asks you to complete the worksheet. Complete the following:

1. Open the **Homes** workbook located in the Excel3 ▶ Case3 folder included with your Data Files, and then save the workbook as **Homes of Dreams** in the location specified by your instructor.

2. In the Documentation sheet, enter your name and the date.

3. Go to the Order Form worksheet.

4. In cell B21, enter the Item ID **DH007**.

5. In cell C21, enter the VLOOKUP function with an exact match to return the name of the item referenced in cell B21. Reference the lookup table in the range M4:O50 using an absolute cell reference. Return the value from the second column of the table.

6. In cell E21, enter the VLOOKUP function with an exact match to return the price of the item referenced in cell B21. Use an absolute reference to the lookup table in the range M4:O50. Return the value from the third column of the table.

7. In cell F21, enter **1** as the quantity of the item ordered.

8. In cell G21, calculate the price of the item multiplied by the quantity ordered.

⊕ **Explore**  9. Revise your formulas in cells C21, E21, and G21, nesting them within an IF formula. For each cell, test whether the value of cell B21 is not equal to "" (a blank). If it is not, return the value of the VLOOKUP function in cells C21 and E21 and the calculated value in cell G21. Otherwise, those cells should return a blank ("") value.

10. Use AutoFill to copy the formulas in cells C21, E21, and G21 through row 30 in the order items table.

11. In row 22, enter **BD002** as the Item ID and **3** as the quantity of items ordered. Verify that the formulas you created automatically enter the name, price, and charge for the item.

12. In rows 23 through 25, enter **1** order for item **BH003**, **1** order for item **DR002**, and **1** order for item **KR009**.

13. In cell G32, calculate the sum of the item charges from all possible orders.

14. In cell G33, calculate the sales tax on the order, which is equal to the subtotal multiplied by the tax rate (entered in cell J9).

15. In cell C15, enter a function to insert the current date whenever the workbook is opened.

16. In cell C16, enter **3 Day** as the type of delivery for this order.

17. In cell C17, calculate the number of working days it will take to ship the order by inserting a VLOOKUP function using an exact match lookup. Use the delivery type in cell C16 as the lookup value, and use the shipping data in the range I4:K7 as the lookup table. Return the value from the third column of the table.

⊕ **Explore** 18. In cell C18, estimate the date of delivery. Use cell C15 as the start date and cell C17 as the number of working days after the start date.

⊕ **Explore** 19. The shipping and handling fee is based on the delivery method (Standard, 3 Day, 2 Day, or Overnight). In cell G34, calculate the shipping and handling fee for the order using an exact match lookup with the data in the range I4:J7. Use the delivery method specified in cell C16 to find the corresponding shipping and handling fee in the Delivery table.

20. In cell G36, calculate the sum of the merchandise subtotal, sales tax, and shipping and handling fee.

21. Save the workbook, and then delete the item IDs and quantities from the order table.

22. Save the workbook as **Homes of Dreams 2**, calculate the cost of ordering 1 of item BD001 using overnight delivery, and then save the workbook.

23. Save the workbook as **Homes of Dreams 3**, and then delete the item IDs and quantities from the order table. Calculate the cost of ordering 1 of item KR001, 2 of item BH004, and 1 of item DR001 using standard delivery. Save and close the workbook.

TROUBLESHOOT

## Case Problem 4

### Data File needed for this Case Problem: Quality.xlsx

***Karleton Manufacturing***   Carmen Garza is a quality control manager at Karleton Manufacturing, a manufacturing plant located in Trotwood, Ohio. One project that Carmen oversees is the manufacture of tin cans for a major food company. The can widths must be consistent. To compensate for the fact that metal working tools tend to wear down during the day, the pressure behind the tools is increased as the blades become worn. Quality control technicians monitor the process to check that it remains "in control" creating cans whose widths are neither too narrow nor too wide. Carmen has recorded the widths of four cans from 39 batches in an Excel workbook that she wants to use to determine whether the process is "in control." One standard for determining whether a process is "in control" is whether the average value from a process batch falls within the lower and upper control limits. The workbook itself is in need of quality control as some of the formulas are not calculating correctly. You will fix these and then enter the remainder of the formulas needed in the worksheet. Complete the following:

1. Open the **Quality** workbook located in the Excel3 ▸ Case4 folder included with your Data Files, and then save the workbook as **Quality Control Analysis** in the location specified by your instructor.

2. In the Documentation sheet, enter your name and the date.

3. In the Quality Control worksheet, use AutoFill with the value in cell A7 and fill the series of batch numbers from B-1 to B-39 into the range A7:A45.

⚙ **Troubleshoot** 4. In the Quality Control worksheet, cells M3 and M4 display the #NAME? error value instead of the averages. Make the necessary changes to correct the formulas.

⚙ **Troubleshoot** 5. The formulas in the range H7:H45 are supposed to calculate the range of values (maximum minus minimum) within each batch. However, the formula results display 6.2 for every batch. Make the necessary changes in the formulas to fix the problem.

⚙ **Troubleshoot** 6. The formulas in the range I7:I45 are supposed to calculate the average width of the four cans tested in each batch. Unfortunately, the formulas' results don't equal the average widths. Make the necessary changes in the formulas to fix the problem.

7. In cell J7, calculate the lower control limit for the first batch based on the equation

$LCL = XBAR - A2 \times RBAR$

where $LCL$ is the lower and upper control limits, $XBAR$ is the average value from all batches, $RBAR$ is the average range from all batches, and $A2$ is a correction factor that depends on the sample size of the batch. In this case, use the $XBAR$ value from cell M3 and the $RBAR$ value from cell M4. Determine the $A2$ value using an exact match lookup with the sample size in cell G7 as the reference value, and the second column from the table in the range O7:P30 as the return value.

8. AutoFill the lower control limit formula from cell J7 into the rest of the LCL column in the Control Limits table. Check to make sure your formulas were properly copied and that they still reference the correct cells.

9. In cell K7, calculate the upper control limit for the first batch based on the equation

$$UCL = XBAR + A2 \times RBAR$$

where $UCL$ is the upper control limit. Copy your formula into the rest of the UCL column in the Control Limits table.

10. In cell L7, indicate whether the B-1 batch process is "in control low" by testing whether the batch's average is less than its LCL value. If it is, display "NO"; otherwise, display a blank cell.

11. In cell M7, indicate whether the B-1 batch process is "in control high" by testing whether the batch's average is greater than its UCL value. If it is, display "NO"; otherwise, display a blank cell.

12. Fill the in control low and in control high formulas for the rest of the batches.

13. Add conditional formatting to the range L7:M45 so that cells displaying "NO" are formatted in dark red text on a light red background.

⚙ **Troubleshoot** 14. The computer program that recorded the width values entered a missing width value as a 0 instead of leaving the cells blank. This affects the calculations about sample size and which batches are in control. Fix this in the data set and any formulas so that the worksheet accurately indicates which batches are not in control on the low side or not in control on the high side.

15. Save and close the workbook.

TUTORIAL 4

# Analyzing and Charting Financial Data

*Presenting Data for a Business Plan*

EXCEL

<br>

## OBJECTIVES

**Session 4.1**
- Use the PMT function to calculate a loan payment
- Create an embedded pie chart
- Apply styles to a chart
- Add data labels to a pie chart
- Format a chart legend
- Create a clustered column chart
- Create a stacked column chart

**Session 4.2**
- Create a line chart
- Create a combination chart
- Format chart elements
- Modify the chart's data source
- Add sparklines to a worksheet
- Format cells with data bars
- Insert a watermark

## Case | *Levitt Winery*

Bob and Carol Levitt want to establish a new winery in Northern Michigan near the town of Traverse City. After many years of working as a winemaker for other wineries, Bob is eager to strike out on his own. Carol will handle the business and finances side of the business, building on her experience managing other companies.

To establish Levitt Winery, Bob and Carol need to borrow money to supplement their personal funds. Bob and Carol are in the process of applying for a business loan. They plan to use this money to help cover the startup costs for their winery. As part of the business loan application, Bob and Carol need to develop a 10-year business plan. They have analyzed the market and made reasonable projections for future production, expenses, and revenue. This information is compiled in an Excel workbook.

Because they are providing a lot of detailed information, Bob and Carol want to include charts in their Excel workbook to make this information easy to read and interpret. Before you create the financial charts that Bob and Carol need for their workbook, you will complete the contents of this worksheet by calculating the cost of the business loan they will need to get started.

## STARTING DATA FILES

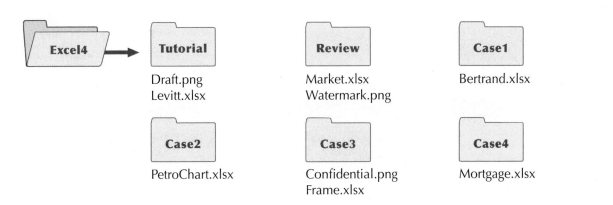

| Excel4 → | Tutorial | Review | Case1 |
|---|---|---|---|
| | Draft.png<br>Levitt.xlsx | Market.xlsx<br>Watermark.png | Bertrand.xlsx |

| Case2 | Case3 | Case4 |
|---|---|---|
| PetroChart.xlsx | Confidential.png<br>Frame.xlsx | Mortgage.xlsx |

Microsoft product screenshots used with permission from Microsoft Corporation.

# Session 4.1 Visual Overview:

A **chart**, or **graph**, is a visual representation of a set of data values. Charts show trends or relationships that may not be readily apparent from numbers alone.

An **embedded chart** is an object in a worksheet.

The **chart area** contains the chart and all of the other chart elements.

A **data label** is text associated with an individual data marker, such as the percentage value next to a pie slice.

Each chart has a **data source**, which is the range that contains the data displayed in the chart. The data source for the pie chart is the range B29:C34.

The **category values** are the groups or categories that the data series values belong to. These category values show the different wines produced.

Levitt Winery - Excel

FILE    HOME    INSERT    PAGE LAYOUT    FORMULAS    DATA    REVIEW    VIEW

Add Chart Element ▾   Quick Layout ▾   Change Colors ▾

Chart Layouts          Chart Styles

Chart 1          ✕ ✓ fx

**CHART ELEMENTS**
- ✓ Chart Title
- ✓ Data Labels
- ✓ Legend

## Production Goal

9.0%
31.5%
16.9%
11.2%
13.5%
18.0%

■ Chardonnay
■ White Riesling
■ Pinot Grigio
■ Pinot Noir
■ Cabernet Franc
■ Ruby Cabernet

| Wine | Production Goal | 10-Year Production |
|------|-----------------|--------------------|
| Chardonnay | 3,500 | |
| White Riesling | 2,000 | |
| Pinot Grigio | 1,500 | |
| Pinot Noir | 1,250 | |
| Cabernet Franc | 1,875 | |
| Ruby Cabernet | 1,000 | |

## Proposed Bottle Price (Retail)

| Wine | First Label | Second Label |
|------|-------------|--------------|
| Chardonnay | $20 | $16 |
| White Riesling | $16 | $11 |
| Pinot Grigio | $18 | $12 |
| Pinot Noir | $27 | $21 |
| Cabernet Franc | $22 | $17 |
| Ruby Cabernet | $15 | $13 |

Projected Re...

$2,000,000
$1,500,000
$1,000,000
$500,000
$-

Year 1  Year 2  Year 3  Y

■ Total Rev

Breakdown c

$1,000,000
$800,000
$600,000
$400,000
$200,000
$-

Year 1  Year 2  Year 3  Y

■ Grapes  ■ Labor  ■ Mainter

◀ ▶ ... Overview | Estimated Production | Projected Ca ... ⊕

READY

A **data series** contains the actual values that are plotted or displayed on the chart. This data series shows the total cases that will be produced for each wine.

The **vertical axis**, or **value axis**, displays the values from the data series.

# Chart Elements

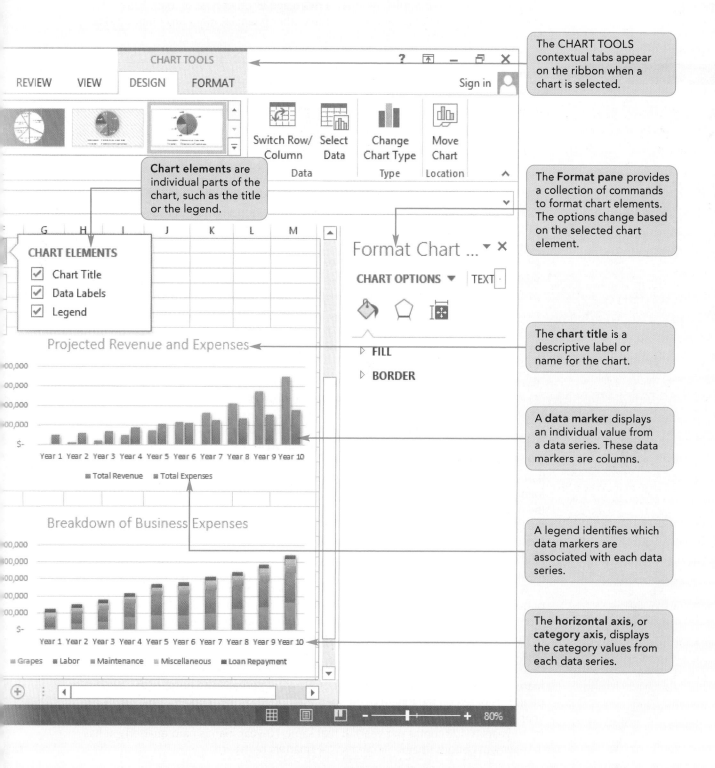

The CHART TOOLS contextual tabs appear on the ribbon when a chart is selected.

Chart elements are individual parts of the chart, such as the title or the legend.

The Format pane provides a collection of commands to format chart elements. The options change based on the selected chart element.

The chart title is a descriptive label or name for the chart.

A data marker displays an individual value from a data series. These data markers are columns.

A legend identifies which data markers are associated with each data series.

The horizontal axis, or category axis, displays the category values from each data series.

**CHART ELEMENTS**
- ☑ Chart Title
- ☑ Data Labels
- ☑ Legend

Projected Revenue and Expenses

Year 1 Year 2 Year 3 Year 4 Year 5 Year 6 Year 7 Year 8 Year 9 Year 10

■ Total Revenue   ■ Total Expenses

Breakdown of Business Expenses

Year 1 Year 2 Year 3 Year 4 Year 5 Year 6 Year 7 Year 8 Year 9 Year 10

■ Grapes  ■ Labor  ■ Maintenance  ■ Miscellaneous  ■ Loan Repayment

# Introduction to Financial Functions

Excel provides a wide range of financial functions related to loans and investments. One of these is the **PMT function**, which can be used to calculate the payment schedule required to completely repay a mortgage or other type of loan. Figure 4-1 describes the PMT function and some of the other financial functions often used to develop budgets and financial projections.

| Figure 4-1 | Financial functions for loans and investments |
| --- | --- |

| Function | Description |
| --- | --- |
| FV(rate, nper, pmt [,pv=0] [,type=0]) | Calculates the future value of an investment, where rate is the interest rate per period, nper is the total number of periods, pmt is the payment in each period, pv is the present value of the investment, and type indicates whether payments should be made at the end of the period (0) or the beginning of the period (1) |
| PMT(rate, nper, pv [,fv=0] [,type=0]) | Calculates the payments required each period on a loan or an investment, where fv is the future value of the investment |
| IPMT(rate, per, nper, pv [,fv=0] [,type=0]) | Calculates the amount of a loan payment devoted to paying the loan interest, where per is the number of the payment period |
| PPMT(rate, per, nper, pv [,fv=0] [,type=0]) | Calculates the amount of a loan payment devoted to paying off the principal of a loan |
| PV(rate, nper, pmt [,fv=0] [,type=0]) | Calculates the present value of a loan or an investment based on periodic, constant payments |
| NPER(rate, pmt, pv [,fv=0] [,type=0]) | Calculates the number of periods required to pay off a loan or an investment |
| RATE(nper, pmt, pv [,fv=0] [,type=0]) | Calculates the interest rate of a loan or an investment based on periodic, constant payments |

© 2014 Cengage Learning

Before you can use the PMT function, you need to understand some of the concepts and definitions associated with loans. The cost of a loan to the borrower is largely based on three factors—the principal, the interest, and the time required to repay the loan. **Principal** is the amount of money being loaned. **Interest** is the amount added to the principal by the lender. You can think of interest as a kind of "user fee" because the borrower is paying for the right to use the lender's money for an interval of time. Generally, interest is expressed at an annual percentage rate, or APR. For example, an 8 percent APR means that the annual interest rate on the loan is 8 percent of the amount owed to the lender.

An annual interest rate is divided by the number of payments per year (often monthly or quarterly). So, if the 8 percent annual interest rate is paid monthly, the resulting monthly interest rate is 1/12 of 8 percent, which is about 0.67 percent per month. If payments are made quarterly, then the interest rate per quarter would be 1/4 of 8 percent, which is 2 percent per quarter.

The third factor in calculating the cost of a loan is the time required to repay the loan, which is specified as the number of payment periods. The number of payment periods is based on the length of the loan multiplied by the number of payments per year. For example, a 10-year loan that is paid monthly has 120 payment periods (that is, 10 years × 12 months per year). If that same 10-year loan is paid quarterly, it has 40 payment periods (that is, 10 years × 4 quarters per year).

## Using the PMT Function

To calculate the costs associated with a loan, such as the one that Bob and Carol need to start their winery, you must have the following information:

- The annual interest rate
- The number of payment periods per year
- The length of the loan in terms of the total number of payment periods
- The amount being borrowed
- When loan payments are due

The PMT function uses this information to calculate the payment required in each period to pay back the loan. The syntax of the PMT function is

```
PMT(rate, nper, pv [, fv=0] [, type=0])
```

where `rate` is the interest rate for each payment period, `nper` is the total number of payment periods required to repay the loan, and `pv` is the present value of the loan or the amount that needs to be borrowed. The PMT function has two optional arguments—`fv` and `type`. The `fv` argument is the future value of the loan. Because the intent with most loans is to repay them completely, the future value is equal to 0 by default. The `type` argument specifies when the interest is charged on the loan, either at the end of the payment period (`type=0`), which is the default, or at the beginning of the payment period (`type=1`).

For example, you can use the PMT function to calculate the monthly payments required to repay a car loan of $10,000 over a 5-year period at an annual interest rate of 9 percent. The `rate` or interest rate per period argument is equal to 9 percent divided by 12 monthly payments, which is 0.75 percent per month. The `nper` or total number of payments argument is equal to 12 × 5 (12 monthly payments over 5 years), which is 60. The `pv` or present value of the loan is 10,000. In this case, because the loan will be repaid completely and payments will be made at the end of the month, you can accept the default values for the `fv` and `type` arguments. The resulting PMT function

```
PMT(0.09/12, 5*12, 10000)
```

returns the value −207.58, or a monthly loan payment of $207.58. The PMT function results in a negative value because that value represents an expense to the borrower. Essentially, the loan is money you subtract from your funds to repay the loan.

Rather than entering the argument values directly in the PMT function, you should include the loan terms in worksheet cells that are referenced in the function. This makes it clear what values are being used in the loan calculation. It also makes it easier to perform a what-if analysis exploring other loan options.

Bob and Carol want to borrow $310,000 for their winery at an 8 percent annual interest rate. They plan to repay the loan in 10 years with monthly payments. You will enter these loan terms in the Overview worksheet.

### To enter the loan information in the Overview worksheet:

1. Open the **Levitt** workbook located in the Excel4 ▸ Tutorial folder included with your Data Files, and then save the workbook as **Levitt Winery**.
2. In the Documentation sheet, enter your name in cell B4 and the date in cell B5.
3. Go to the **Overview** worksheet. The Overview worksheet provides a summary of Bob and Carol's business plan, including their loan request and business forecasts.
4. In cell **C5**, enter **310,000** as the loan amount.
5. In cell **C6**, enter **8%** as the annual interest rate.

**6.** In cell **C7**, enter **12** as the number of payments per year. Twelve payments indicate monthly payments.

**7.** In cell **C8**, enter the formula **=C6/C7** to calculate the interest rate per period. In this case, the 8 percent interest rate is divided by 12 payments per year, calculating the monthly interest rate of 0.67 percent.

**8.** In cell **C9**, enter **10** as the number of years in the loan.

**9.** In cell **C10**, enter **=C7*C9** to multiply the number of payments per year by the number of years in the loan, calculating the total number of payments on the loan, which is 120.

The Overview worksheet includes all the data you need to calculate the monthly payment required to repay the $310,000 loan in 10 years at an 8 percent annual interest rate paid monthly. Next, you will use the PMT function to calculate the monthly payment needed to repay the loan.

**To use the PMT function to calculate Bob and Carol's monthly payment:**

**1.** Select cell **C12** to make it the active cell. You will enter the PMT function in this cell.

**2.** On the ribbon, click the **FORMULAS** tab to display the function library.

**3.** In the Function Library group, click the **Financial** button, and then scroll down and click **PMT** in the list of financial functions. The Function Arguments dialog box opens.

**TIP**

Be sure to enter the interest rate per month (not per year) for the Rate argument for any loan or investment that has monthly payments.

**4.** With the insertion point in the Rate box, click cell **C8** in the worksheet to enter the reference to the cell with the interest rate per month.

**5.** Click in the **Nper** box, and then click cell **C10** in the worksheet to enter the reference to the cell with the total number of monthly payments required to repay the loan.

**6.** Click in the **Pv** box, and then click cell **C5** in the worksheet to enter the reference to the cell with the present value of the loan. See Figure 4-2.

**Figure 4-2**    **Function Arguments dialog box for the PMT function**

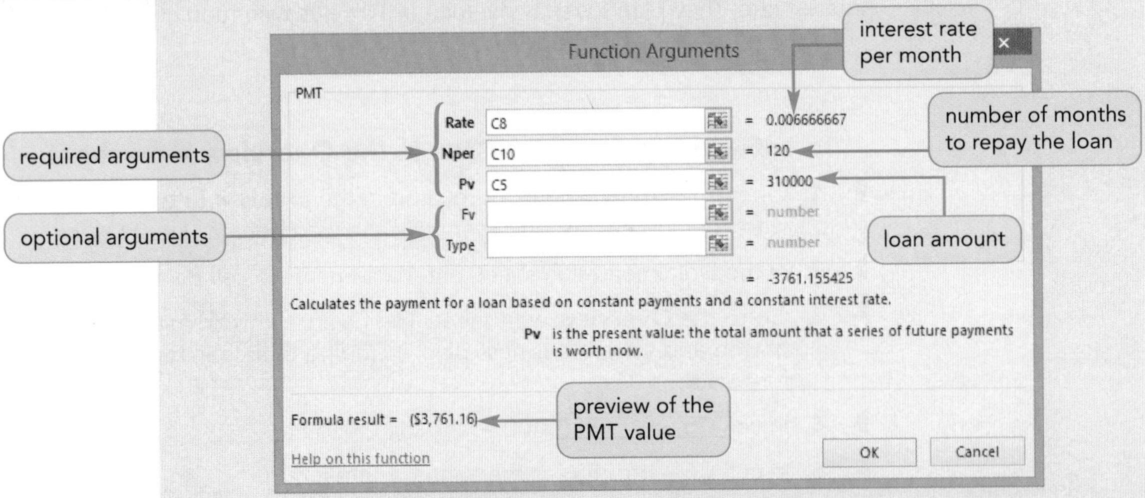

▶ **7.** Click the **OK** button. The monthly payment amount ($3,761.16) appears in cell C12. The number is displayed in parentheses to indicate a negative amount, specifying the amount to be paid.

▶ **8.** In cell **C13**, enter the formula **=C7*C12** to multiply the number of payments per year by the monthly payment amount, calculating the total payments for the entire year. The annual payments would be ($45,133.87), shown as a negative number to indicate money being paid out.

▶ **9.** Select cell **C12**. See Figure 4-3.

| Figure 4-3 | Monthly and annual costs of the business loan |

Carol wants to see the financial impact of taking out a smaller loan.

▶ **10.** In cell **C5**, change the loan amount to **250,000**. With a loan of that size, the monthly payment drops to $3,033 and the annual total decreases to $36,398.

Although the lower loan amount will save money, Bob feels that the winery cannot get off the ground with less than a $310,000 loan.

▶ **11.** In cell **C5**, return the loan amount to **310,000**.

Based on your analysis, the Levitts would spend about $45,000 a year repaying the $310,000 business loan. Carol and Bob want this information included in the Projected Cash Flow worksheet, which estimates Levitt Winery's annual revenue, expenses, and cash flow for the first 10 years. You will enter that amount as an expense for each year, completing the projected cash flow calculations.

## To enter the loan repayment amount in the Projected Cash Flow worksheet:

▶ 1. Go to the **Projected Cash Flow** worksheet and review the estimated annual revenue, expenses, and cash flow for the next decade.

▶ 2. In cell **C17**, enter **45,000** as the projected yearly amount of the loan repayment. Because the projected cash flow is a rough estimate of the projected income and expenses, it is not necessary to include the exact dollar-and-cents cost of the loan.

▶ 3. Copy the annual loan payment in cell **C17** into the range **D17:L17** to enter the projected annual loan payment in each year of the cash flow projections. See Figure 4-4.

| Figure 4-4 | Completed Projected Cash Flow worksheet |
|---|---|

yearly loan payments

| | A | B | C | D | E | F | G | H | I | J | K | L |
|---|---|---|---|---|---|---|---|---|---|---|---|---|
| 12 | | *Expenses* | | | | | | | | | | |
| 13 | | Grapes | $ 35,000 | $ 70,000 | $ 100,000 | $ 150,000 | $ 175,000 | $ 175,000 | $ 200,000 | $ 250,000 | $ 275,000 | $ 325,000 |
| 14 | | Labor | 100,000 | 120,000 | 140,000 | 170,000 | 240,000 | 250,000 | 275,000 | 275,000 | 300,000 | 350,000 |
| 15 | | Maintenance | 20,000 | 35,000 | 50,000 | 50,000 | 50,000 | 50,000 | 60,000 | 70,000 | 80,000 | 90,000 |
| 16 | | Miscellaneous | 50,000 | 35,000 | 25,000 | 25,000 | 35,000 | 50,000 | 50,000 | 50,000 | 75,000 | 75,000 |
| 17 | | Loan Repayment | 45,000 | 45,000 | 45,000 | 45,000 | 45,000 | 45,000 | 45,000 | 45,000 | 45,000 | 45,000 |
| 18 | | Total Expenses | $ 250,000 | $ 305,000 | $ 360,000 | $ 440,000 | $ 545,000 | $ 570,000 | $ 630,000 | $ 690,000 | $ 775,000 | $ 885,000 |
| 19 | | | | | | | | | | | | |
| 20 | | Gross Income | $ (250,000) | $ (245,000) | $ (240,000) | $ (175,000) | $ (170,0(... | | | 0,000 | $ 600,000 | $ 865,000 |
| 21 | | Loss Carry Forward | (250,000) | (495,000) | (735,000) | (910,000) | (1,080,00... | | | 00,000) | - | - |
| 22 | | Income Tax @35% | - | - | - | - | - | - | - | - | (210,000) | (302,750) |
| 23 | | Net Income | $ (250,000) | $ (245,000) | $ (240,000) | $ (175,000) | $ (170,000) | 20,000 | 200,000 | 360,000 | $ 390,000 | $ 562,250 |
| 24 | | | | | | | | | | | | |
| 25 | | Capital Purchases | $ (310,000) | $ (50,000) | $ (50,000) | $ (50,000) | $ (50,0( | | | 0,000) | $ (75,000) | $ (85,000) |
| 26 | | Depreciation | 30,000 | 75,000 | 72,000 | 70,000 | 65,00... | | | 0,000 | 25,000 | 25,000 |
| 27 | | Cash Flow | $ (530,000) | $ (220,000) | $ (218,000) | $ (155,000) | $ (155,000) | $ 35,000 | $ 210,000 | $ 340,000 | $ 340,000 | $ 502,250 |
| 28 | | | | | | | | | | | | |
| 29 | | | | | | | | | | | | |
| 30 | | | | | | | | | | | | |

Documentation | Overview | Estimated Production | **Projected Cash Flow** | Yearly Gross Income ...

READY                    AVERAGE: 45,000   COUNT: 10   SUM: 450,000              120%

total expenses projected over the next 10 years

net income projected over the next 10 years

end-of-the-year cash receipts projected over the next 10 years

After including the projected annual loan payments, the Projected Cash Flow worksheet shows that the winery's projected net income at the end of the tenth year would be about $560,000, assuming all of the other projections are accurate. Based on these figures, the winery should have about $500,000 in cash at that time as well.

**INSIGHT**

### Using Functions to Manage Personal Finances

Excel has many financial functions to manage personal finances. The following list can help you determine which function to use for the most common personal finance calculations:

- To determine how much an investment will be worth after a series of monthly payments at some future time, use the FV (future value) function.
- To determine how much you have to spend each month to repay a loan or mortgage within a set period of time, use the PMT (payment) function.
- To determine how much of your monthly loan payment is used to pay the interest, use the IPMT (interest payment) function.
- To determine how much of your monthly loan payment is used for repaying the principal, use the PPMT (principal payment) function.
- To determine the largest loan or mortgage you can afford given a set monthly payment, use the PV (present value) function.
- To determine how long it will take to pay off a loan with constant monthly payments, use the NPER (number of periods) function.

For most loan and investment calculations, you need to enter the annual interest rate divided by the number of times the interest is compounded during the year. If interest is compounded monthly, divide the annual interest rate by 12; if interest is compounded quarterly, divide the annual rate by 4. You must also convert the length of the loan or investment to the number of payments per year. If you will make payments monthly, multiply the number of years of the loan or investment by 12.

Now that you have completed the cash flow projections for the winery, you can begin displaying this information in charts.

# Creating a Chart

Charts show trends or relationships in data that are easier to see than by looking at the actual numbers. Creating a chart is a several-step process that involves selecting the data to display in the chart, choosing the chart type, moving the chart to a specific location in the workbook, sizing the chart so that it matches the layout of the worksheet, and formatting the chart's appearance. When creating a chart, remember that your goal is to convey important information that would be more difficult to interpret from columns of data in a worksheet.

**REFERENCE**

### Creating a Chart

- Select the range containing the data you want to chart.
- On the INSERT tab, in the Charts group, click the Recommended Chart button or a chart type button, and then click the chart you want to create (or click the Quick Analysis button, click the CHARTS category, and then click the chart you want to create).
- On the CHART TOOLS DESIGN tab, in the Location group, click the Move Chart button, select whether to embed the chart in a worksheet or place it in a chart sheet, and then click the OK button.

## Selecting a Chart's Data Source

The data displayed in a chart comes from the chart's data source. A data source includes one or more data series and a series of category values. A data series contains the actual values that are plotted on the chart, whereas the category values provide descriptive labels for each data series or data value. Category values are usually located in the first column or first row of the data source. The data series are usually placed in subsequent columns or rows. However, you can select category and data values from anywhere within a workbook.

Bob and Carol want a chart to display information about the winery's estimated production in 10 years. The data source for this chart is located in the range B28:C34 of the Overview worksheet. You will select this range now as the data source for the chart.

### To select the data source for a chart showing the projected production:

▶ **1.** Go to the **Overview** worksheet. The production projections are included in this worksheet.

▶ **2.** Select the range **B28:C34** containing the production estimates as the data source for the chart. See Figure 4-5.

| Figure 4-5 | Selected chart data source |
| --- | --- |

This data source includes two columns. The category values are located in the first column, and the one and only data series is located in the second column. When the selected range is taller than it is wide, Excel assumes that the category values and data series are laid out in columns. Conversely, a data source that is wider than it is tall is assumed to have the category values and data series laid out in rows. Note that the first row in this selected data source contains labels that identify the category values (Wine) and the data series (Production Goal).

Now that you've selected the data source for the chart, you want to consider the type of chart to create.

## Exploring Chart Types and Subtypes

Excel provides 53 types of charts organized into the 10 categories described in Figure 4-6. Each category includes variations of the same chart type, which are called **chart subtypes**. You can also design your own custom chart types to meet the specific needs of your reports and projects.

**Figure 4-6**    Excel chart types

| Chart Type | Description |
| --- | --- |
| Column | Compares values from different categories. Values are indicated by the height of the columns. |
| Line | Compares values from different categories. Values are indicated by the height of the lines. Often used to show trends and changes over time. |
| Pie | Compares relative values of different categories to the whole. Values are indicated by the areas of the pie slices. |
| Bar | Compares values from different categories. Values are indicated by the length of the bars. |
| Area | Compares values from different categories. Similar to the line chart except that areas under the lines contain a fill color. |
| X Y (Scatter) | Shows the patterns or relationship between two or more sets of values. Often used in scientific studies and statistical analyses. |
| Stock | Displays stock market data, including the high, low, opening, and closing prices of a stock. |
| Surface | Compares three sets of values in a three-dimensional chart. |
| Radar | Compares a collection of values from several different data sets. |
| Combo | Combines two or more chart types to make the data easy to visualize, especially when the data is widely varied. |

© 2014 Cengage Learning

For example, Figure 4-7 presents the same labor cost data displayed as a line chart, a bar chart, and column charts. The column charts are shown with both a 2-D subtype that has two-dimensional or flat columns and a 3-D subtype that gives the illusion of three-dimensional columns. The various charts and chart subtypes are better suited for different data. You should choose the one that makes the data easiest to interpret.

**Figure 4-7**    **Chart types and subtypes**

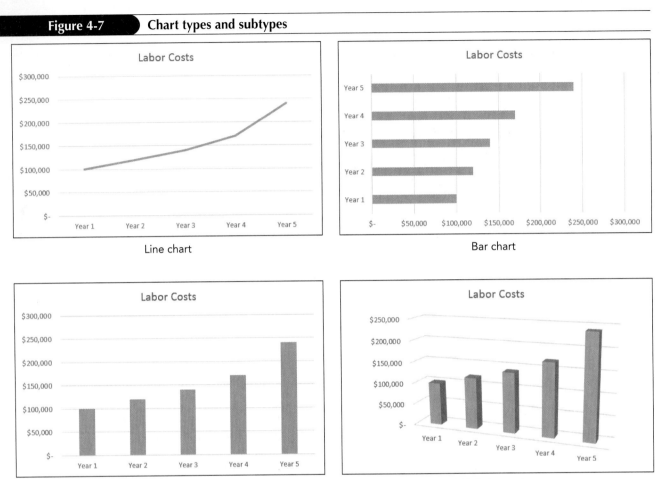

Line chart

Bar chart

2-D Column chart

3-D Column chart

TIP

Most charts should include only the category labels and data values and not row or column totals because Excel will treat those totals as another category to be graphed.

The first chart you will create is a pie chart. A **pie chart** is a chart in the shape of a circle divided into slices like a pie. Each slice represents a single value from a data series. Larger data values are represented with bigger pie slices. The relative sizes of the slices let you visually compare the data values and see how much each contributes to the whole. Pie charts are most effective with six or fewer slices, and when each slice is large enough to view easily.

## Inserting a Pie Chart with the Quick Analysis Tool

After you select an adjacent range to use as a chart's data source, the Quick Analysis tool appears. It includes a category for creating charts. The CHART category lists recommended chart types, which are the charts that are most appropriate for the data source you selected.

For the wine production data, a pie chart provides the best way to compare the production levels for the six wines Levitt Winery plans to produce. You will use the Quick Analysis tool to create a pie chart of the projected wine production data that you selected.

**To create a pie chart with the Quick Analysis tool:**

1. Make sure the range **B28:C34** is selected.

TIP

You can also insert a chart by selecting a chart type in the Charts group on the INSERT tab.

2. Click the **Quick Analysis** button 📊 in the lower-right corner of the selected range (or press the **Ctrl+Q** keys) to open the Quick Analysis tool.

3. Click the **CHARTS** category. The chart types you will most likely want to use with the selected data source are listed. See Figure 4-8.

| Figure 4-8 | CHARTS category of the Quick Analysis tool |

chart types recommended based on the selected data source

displays other chart types that can be used with the data

4. Click **Pie**. A pie chart appears in the Overview worksheet. Each slice is a different size based on its value in the data series. The biggest slice represents the 3500 cases of Chardonnay that the Levitts estimate they will produce. The smallest slice of the pie represents 1000 cases of Ruby Cabernet. See Figure 4-9.

| Figure 4-9 | Pie chart in the Overview worksheet |

CHART TOOLS contextual tabs appear when a chart is selected

Chart Elements button

Chart Styles button

Chart Filters button

embedded pie chart

When you create or select a chart, two CHART TOOLS contextual tabs appear on the ribbon. The DESIGN tab provides commands to specify the chart's overall design. The FORMAT tab supplies the tools needed to format the graphic shapes found in the chart, such as the chart's border or the slices from a pie chart. When you select a worksheet cell or another object that is not a chart, the CHART TOOLS contextual tabs disappear until you reselect the chart.

Three buttons appear to the right of the selected chart. The Chart Elements button + is used for adding, removing, or changing elements displayed in the chart. The Chart Styles button ✎ sets the style and color scheme of the chart. The Chart Filters button ▽ enables you to edit the data points and names displayed on the chart.

## Moving and Resizing a Chart

Excel charts are either placed in their own chart sheets or embedded in a worksheet. When you create a chart, it is embedded in the worksheet that contains the data source. For example, the chart shown in Figure 4-9 is embedded in the Overview worksheet. The advantage of an embedded chart is that you can display the chart alongside its data source and any text that describes the chart's meaning and purpose. Because an embedded chart covers worksheet cells, you might have to move or resize the chart so that important information is not hidden.

Before you can move or resize a chart, it must be selected. When a chart is selected, a **selection box** appears around the selected chart that is used to move or resize the chart. **Sizing handles** appear along the edges of the selection box and are used to change the chart's width and height.

Bob and Carol want the wine production chart to appear above its data source in the Overview worksheet. You will move and resize the chart to fit this location.

**To move and resize the wine production pie chart:**

1. Move the pointer over an empty area of the selected chart until the pointer changes to ⌖ and "Chart Area" appears in a ScreenTip.

2. Hold down the **Alt** key, drag the chart up and to the left until its upper-left corner snaps to the upper-left corner of cell B16, and then release the mouse button and the **Alt** key. The upper-left corner of the chart is aligned with the upper-left corner of cell B16.

   **Trouble?** If the pie chart resizes or does not move to the new location, you probably didn't drag the chart from an empty part of the chart area. Press the Ctrl+Z keys to undo your last action, and then repeat Steps 1 and 2, being sure to drag the pie chart from the chart area.

   The chart moves to a new location, but it still covers some data and needs to be resized.

3. Move the pointer over the sizing handle in the lower-right corner of the selection box until the pointer changes to ⬉.

4. Hold down the **Alt** key, drag the sizing handle up to the lower-right corner of cell D27, and then release the mouse button and the **Alt** key. The chart resizes to cover the range B16:D27 and remains selected. See Figure 4-10.

Figure 4-10    Moved and resized chart

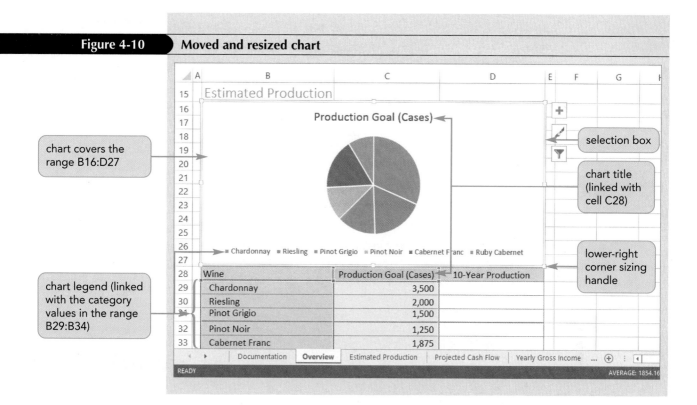

chart covers the range B16:D27

selection box

chart title (linked with cell C28)

lower-right corner sizing handle

chart legend (linked with the category values in the range B29:B34)

# Working with Chart Elements

Every chart contains elements that can be formatted, added to the chart, or removed from the chart. For example, a pie chart has three elements—the chart title, the chart legend identifying each pie slice, and data labels that can be displayed next to each slice providing the data value or percentage associated with that slice. The Chart Elements button that appears next to a selected chart lists the elements associated with that chart. You can use this button to add, remove, and format individual elements. When you add or remove a chart element, the other elements resize to fit in the space. Live Preview shows how changing an element will affect the chart's appearance.

Carol doesn't want the pie chart to include a title because the text in cell B15 and the data in the range B28:D34 sufficiently explain the chart's purpose. However, she does want to display the data values next to the pie slices. You will remove the chart title element and add the data labels element.

**TIP**

To add and remove chart elements, you can also use the Add Chart Element button in the Chart Layouts group on the CHART TOOLS DESIGN tab.

## To remove the pie chart title and add data labels to the slices:

1. Click the **pie chart** to select it. The selection box appears around the chart.

2. To the right of the selected chart, click the **Chart Elements** button [+]. A menu of chart elements that are available for the pie chart opens. As the checkmarks indicate, only the chart title and the chart legend are displayed in the pie chart.

3. Click the **Chart Title** check box to deselect it. The chart title is removed from the pie chart and the chart elements resize to fill the space.

4. Point to the **Data Labels** check box. Live Preview shows how the chart will look when the data labels showing the production goal for each wine are added to the pie slices.

5. Click the **Data Labels** check box to select it. The data labels are added to the chart. See Figure 4-11.

Figure 4-11　Chart elements

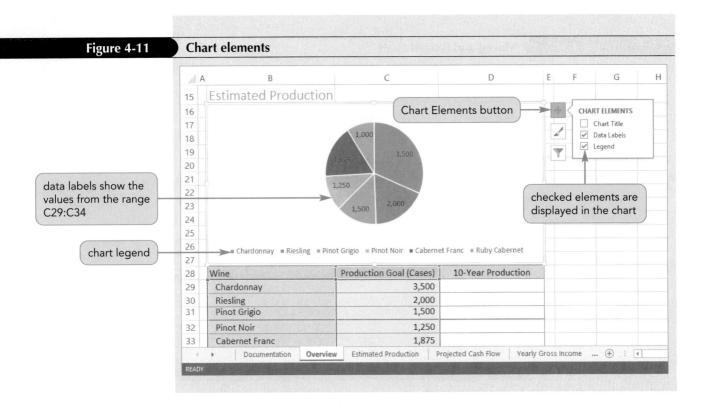

## Choosing a Chart Style

When you create a chart, the chart is formatted with a style. Recall that a style is a collection of formats that are saved with a name and can then be applied at one time. In the pie chart you just created, the format of the chart title, the location of the legend, and the colors of the pie slices are all part of the default pie chart style. You can quickly change the appearance of a chart by selecting a different style from the Chart Styles gallery. Live Preview shows how a chart style will affect the chart.

Carol wants the pie slices to have a raised, three-dimensional look. You will explore different chart styles to find a style that best fulfills her request.

**To choose a different chart style for the wine production pie chart:**

1. Click the **Chart Styles** button ✎ next to the selected pie chart. The Chart Styles gallery opens.

2. Point to different styles in the gallery. Live Preview shows the impact of each chart style on the pie chart's appearance.

3. Scroll to the bottom of the gallery, and then click the **Style 12** chart style. The chart style is applied to the pie chart. See Figure 4-12.

**Figure 4-12**    Chart Styles gallery

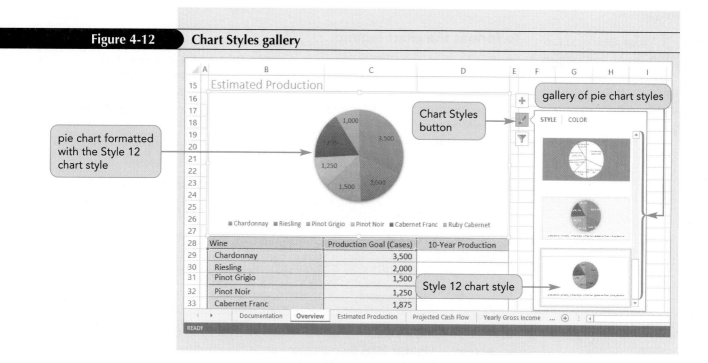

## Formatting the Pie Chart Legend

You can fine-tune a chart style by formatting individual chart elements. From the Chart Elements button, you can open a submenu for each element that includes formatting options, such as the element's location within the chart. You can also open a Format pane, which has more options for formatting the selected chart element.

The default location for the pie chart legend is alongside the chart's bottom edge. Carol thinks the chart would look better if the legend were aligned with the right edge of the chart.

### To reposition the pie chart legend:

1. Click the **Chart Elements** button ➕ next to the selected pie chart.

2. Point to **Legend** in the CHART ELEMENTS menu to display a right arrow icon, and then click the **right arrow** icon ▶. A submenu opens with formatting options available for the selected chart element. For a chart legend, the submenu offers placement options.

3. Point to **Left** to see a Live Preview of that formatting. The legend is aligned along the left side of the chart area, and the pie moves to the right to occupy the remaining space.

4. Click **Right** to place the legend along the right side of the chart area. The pie shifts to the left to make room for the legend.

The Chart Elements button also provides access to the Format pane, which has more design options. Carol wants you to add a drop shadow to the legend similar to the pie chart's drop shadow, change the fill color to a light gold, and add a light gray border. You'll use the Format pane to make these changes.

**TIP**

You can also open the Format pane by double-clicking any chart element.

## To format the chart legend:

1. On the CHART ELEMENTS menu, click the **right arrow** icon next to the Legend entry to display a submenu, and then click **More Options**. The Format pane opens on the right side of the workbook window. The pane's title, "Format Legend," indicates that the options relate to formatting the chart legend.
2. Click the **Fill & Line** button near the top of the Format pane to display options for setting the fill color and border style of the legend.
3. Click **FILL** to display fill options, and then click the **Solid fill** option button to apply a solid fill color to the legend. Color and Transparency options appear below the fill color options.
4. Click the **Fill Color** button, and then click the **Gold, Accent 4, Lighter 60%** theme color located in the third row and eighth column of the color palette to add a light gold fill color to the legend.
5. Click **BORDER** to display the border options, and then click the **Solid line** option button. Additional border options appear below the border options.
6. Click the **Outline color** button, and then click the **Gray - 50%, Accent 3, Lighter 80%** theme color located in the second row and seventh column of the color palette to add a light gray border around the legend.
7. At the top of the Format Legend pane, click the **Effects** button to display options for special visual effects.
8. Click **Shadow** to display the shadow options, and then next to the Presets label, click the **Shadow** button to display a gallery of shadow effects.
9. Click the **Offset Diagonal Button Right** button in the first row and first column to apply the drop shadow effect to the legend. See Figure 4-13.

**Figure 4-13** **Formatted chart legend**

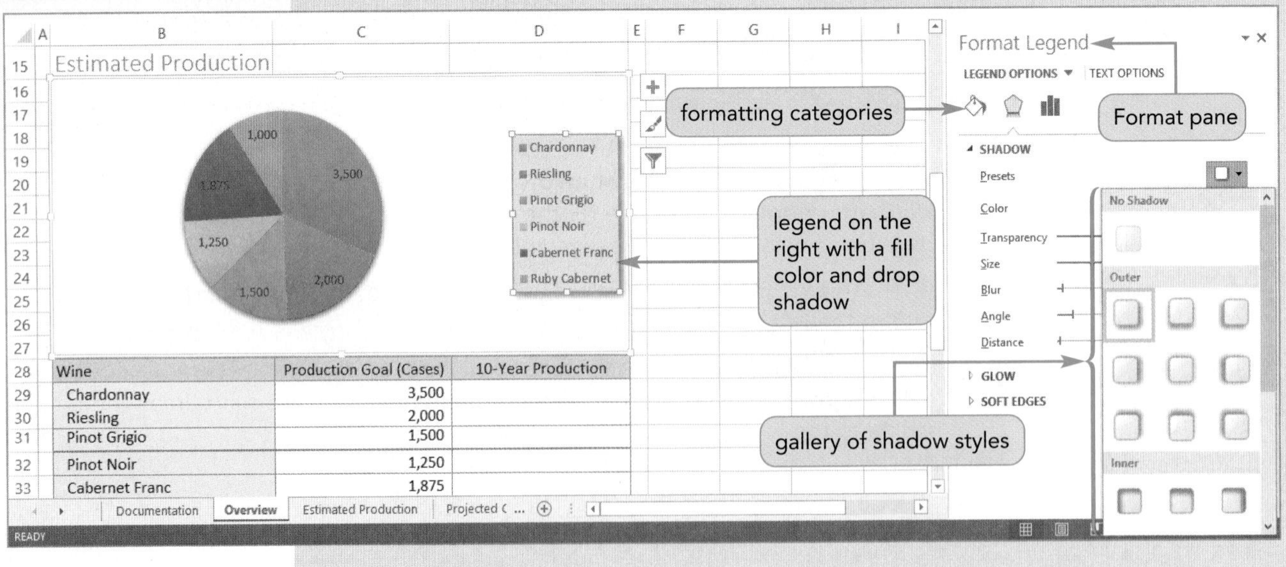

# Formatting Pie Chart Data Labels

You can modify the content and appearance of data labels, selecting what the labels contain as well as where the labels are positioned. By default, data labels are placed where they will keep the chart nicely proportioned, but you can specify a different location. For pie chart labels, you can move the labels to the center of the pie slices or place them outside of the slices. Another option is to set the labels as data callouts, with each label placed within a text bubble and connected to the slice with a callout line. Likewise, you can change the text and number styles used in the data labels as well. These options are all available in the Format pane. You can also drag and drop individual data labels, placing them anywhere within the chart. When a data label is placed far from its pie slice, a **leader line** is added to connect the data label to its pie slice.

The pie chart data labels display the production goal values for the different wines, but this information also appears on the worksheet directly below the chart. The Levitts want to include data labels that add new information to the chart—in this case, the percentage that each wine varietal adds to the whole. You will make this change.

**TIP**

You can also format chart elements using the formatting buttons on the HOME tab or on the CHART TOOLS FORMAT tab.

### To display percentages in the wine production pie chart:

1. At the top of the Format pane, click the **Legend Options** arrow to display a menu of chart elements, and then click **Series "Production Goal (Cases)" Data Labels** to display the formatting options for data labels. The title of the Format pane changes to "Format Data Labels" and includes formatting options for data labels. Selection boxes appear around every data label in the pie chart.

2. Click the **Label Options** button 📊 near the top of the pane to display the options for the label contents and position. Data labels can contain series names, category names, values, and percentages.

3. Click the **Percentage** check box to display the percentage associated with each data label in the pie chart next to its value.

4. Click the **Value** check box to deselect it, removing the data series values from the data labels. The pie chart shows that Chardonnay accounts for 31.5 percent of the estimated wine production.

5. Click the **Outside End** option button to move the labels outside of the pie slices. The labels are easier to read in this location.

   The percentages are displayed with no decimal places, but Carol wants them to show one decimal place to provide a bit more accuracy in the chart.

6. Scroll down the Format pane, and then click **NUMBER** to show the formatting options for numbers.

7. Scroll down the Format pane, click the **Category** box to display the number formats, and then click **Percentage**. The percentages in the data labels include two decimal places.

8. In the Decimal places box, replace the value 2 with **1**, and then press the **Enter** key. The percentages display one decimal place. See Figure 4-14.

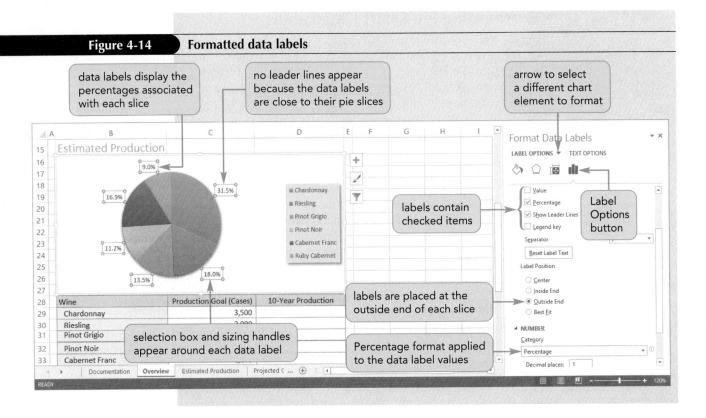

**Figure 4-14**    **Formatted data labels**

data labels display the percentages associated with each slice

no leader lines appear because the data labels are close to their pie slices

arrow to select a different chart element to format

labels contain checked items

Label Options button

labels are placed at the outside end of each slice

selection box and sizing handles appear around each data label

Percentage format applied to the data label values

## Setting the Pie Slice Colors

A pie slice is an example of a data marker that represents a single data value from a data series. You can format the appearance of individual data markers to make them stand out from the others. Pie slice colors should be as distinct as possible to avoid confusion. Depending on the printer quality or the monitor resolution, it might be difficult to distinguish between similarly colored slices. If data labels are displayed within the slice, you also need enough contrast between the slice color and the data label color to make the text readable.

The Levitts are concerned that the blue color of the Cabernet Franc slice will appear too dark when printed, and they want you to change it to a light shade of green.

**To change the color of the Cabernet Franc pie slice:**

1. Click any pie slice to select all of the slices in the pie chart.

2. Click the **Cabernet Franc** slice, which is the darker blue slice that represents 16.9 percent of the pie. Only that slice is selected, as you can see from the handles that appear at each corner of the slice.

3. Click the **HOME** tab, click the **Fill Color button arrow** ![Fill Color] in the Font group, and then click the **Green, Accent 6, Lighter 40%** theme color in the fourth row and last column of the gallery. The Cabernet Franc pie slice changes to a light green and the chart legend automatically updates to reflect that change.

You can also change the colors of all the pie slices by clicking the Chart Styles button ![Chart Styles] next to the selected chart, clicking the COLOR heading, and then selecting a color scheme.

INSIGHT

## Exploding a Pie Chart

Pie slices do not need to be fixed within the pie. An **exploded pie chart** moves one slice away from the others as if someone were taking the piece away from the pie. Exploded pie charts are useful for emphasizing one category above all of the others. For example, to emphasize the fact that Levitt Winery will be producing more Chardonnay than any other wine, you could explode that single slice, moving it away from the other slices.

To explode a pie slice, first click the pie to select all of the slices, and then click the single slide you want to move. Make sure that a selection box appears around only that slice. Drag the slice away from the pie to offset it from the others. You can explode multiple slices by selecting each slice in turn and dragging them away. To explode all of the slices, select the entire pie and drag the pointer away from the pie's center. Each slice will be exploded and separated from the others. Although you can explode more than one slice, the resulting pie chart is rarely effective as a visual aid to the reader.

## Formatting the Chart Area

The chart's background, which is called the chart area, can also be formatted using fill colors, border styles, and special effects such as drop shadows and blurred edges. The chart area fill color used in the pie chart is white, which blends in with the worksheet background. Carol wants you to change the fill color to a light gold to match the worksheet's color scheme, and to make the chart stand out better.

### To change the chart area of the pie chart to light gold:

**TIP**

You can select any chart element using the Chart Elements box in the Current Selection group on the CHART TOOLS FORMAT tab.

1. Click a blank area within the chart, not containing either a pie slice or the chart legend. The chart area is selected, which you can verify because the Format pane title changes to "Format Chart Area."

2. On the HOME tab, in the Font group, click the **Fill Color button arrow** , and then click the **Gold, Accent 4, Lighter 80%** theme color in the second row and eighth column. The chart area fill color is now light gold. See Figure 4-15.

| Figure 4-15 | Chart area fill color |

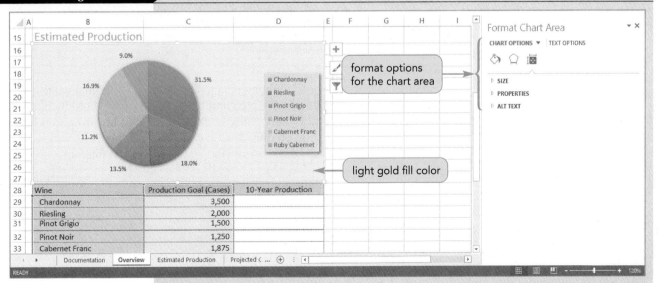

You are done formatting the pie chart, so you will close the Format pane to keep the window uncluttered.

▶ **3.** Click the **Close** button ☒ on the title bar of the Format pane. The pane closes, leaving more space for viewing the worksheet contents.

# Performing What-If Analyses with Charts

A chart is linked to its data source. For the wine production pie chart, the chart title is linked to the text of cell C28, the size of the pie slices is based on the production goals in the range C29:C34, and the category names are linked to the category values in the range B29:B34. Any changes to these cells affect the chart's content and appearance. This makes charts a powerful tool for data exploration and what-if analysis. Excel uses **chart animation** to slow down the effect of changing data source values, making it easier to see how changing one value affects the chart.

Bob and Carol want to see how the pie chart would change if they were to alter some of their production goals. You will edit the data source to see how the changes affect the chart.

### To apply a what-if analysis to the pie chart:

▶ **1.** In cell **C29,** enter **5500** to increase the production goal for Chardonnay by 2000 cases. The pie slice associated with Chardonnay becomes larger, slowly changing from 31.5 percent to 41.9 percent because of the chart animation. The size of the remaining slices and their percentages are reduced to compensate.

▶ **2.** In cell **C29**, restore the value to **3,500**. The pie slices return to their initial sizes and the percentages return to their initial values.

▶ **3.** In cell **C30**, change the production goal for Riesling from 2,000 to **4,000**. The orange slice representing Riesling is now the largest slice in the pie, comprising 30.5 percent of the projected production.

▶ **4.** In cell **C30**, restore the value to **2,000**.

Bob points out that the legend entry "Riesling" should be changed to "White Riesling" to distinguish it from other Riesling varietals.

▶ **5.** In cells **B30** and **B39**, change the text to **White Riesling**. The chart legend automatically updates to show the revised wine name.

Another type of what-if analysis is to limit the data to a subset of the original values in a process called **filtering**. For example, the pie chart shows the estimated production for all six varietals of wine that Levitt Winery will produce. Sometimes, however, Carol and Bob might want to see information on only the red wines or only the white wines. Rather than creating a new chart that includes only those wines, you can filter an existing chart.

Levitt Winery plans to produce three white wines—Chardonnay, White Riesling, and Pinot Grigio. Carol and Bob want to see the different percentages of white wine. You will use the Chart Filters button to limit the pie chart to those three wines.

### To filter the pie chart to show only white wines:

▶ **1.** Click the pie chart to select it.

▶ **2.** Click the **Chart Filters** button ▼ next to the chart to open a menu listing the categories in the chart. In this case, the categories are the different types of wines.

▶ **3.** Click the **Pinot Noir**, **Cabernet Franc**, and **Ruby Cabernet** check boxes to deselect them, leaving only the Chardonnay, White Riesling, and Pinot Grigio check boxes selected.

▶ **4.** At the bottom of the Chart Filters menu, click the **Apply** button. Excel filters the chart, showing only the white wines. After filtering the data, the chart shows that 50 percent of the white wines produced will be Chardonnay. See Figure 4-16.

| Figure 4-16 | Filtered pie chart |

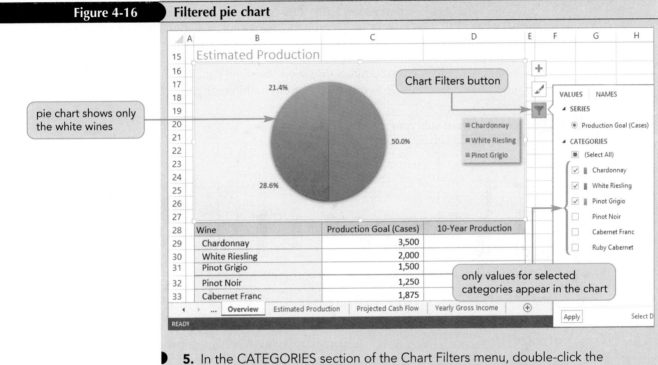

▶ **5.** In the CATEGORIES section of the Chart Filters menu, double-click the **Select All** check box to reselect all six wines.

▶ **6.** Click the **Apply** button to update the chart's appearance.

▶ **7.** Press the **Esc** key to close the menu, leaving the chart selected.

The pie chart that displays the winery's projected level of production for different wines is complete. Next, you'll use column charts to examine the winery's financial projections for the next 10 years.

## Creating a Column Chart

A **column chart** displays data values as columns with the height of each column based on the data value. A column chart turned on its side is called a **bar chart**, with the length of the bar determined by the data value. It is better to use column and bar charts than pie charts when the number of categories is large or the data values are close in value. For example, Figure 4-17 displays the same data as a pie chart and a column chart. As you can see, it's difficult to determine which pie slice is biggest and by how much. It is much simpler to see the differences in a column or bar chart.

**Figure 4-17**    **Data displayed as a pie chart and a column chart**

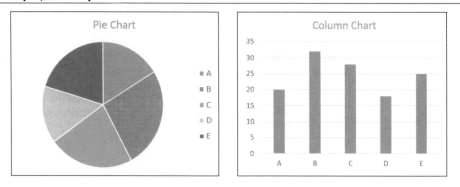

## Comparing Column Chart Subtypes

Unlike pie charts, which can show only one data series, column and bar charts can display multiple data series. For example, you can plot three data series (such as the wine production of Chardonnay, White Riesling, and Cabernet Franc) against one category (such as Years). Figure 4-18 shows the same data charted on the three column chart subtypes available to display data from multiple series.

**Figure 4-18**    **Column chart subtypes**

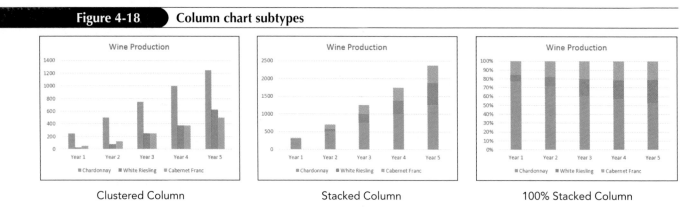

Clustered Column                         Stacked Column                         100% Stacked Column

The **clustered column chart** displays the data series in separate columns side-by-side so that you can compare the relative heights of the columns in the three series. The clustered column chart in Figure 4-18 compares the number of cases of each wine produced in Year 1 through Year 5. Note that the winery produces mostly Chardonnay with the other varietals increasing in volume in the later years.

The **stacked column chart** places the data series values within combined columns showing how much is contributed by each series. The stacked column chart in Figure 4-18 gives information on the total number of wine cases produced each year, and how each year's production is split among the three wine varietals.

Finally, the **100% stacked column chart** makes the same comparison as the stacked column chart except that the stacked sections are expressed as percentages. As you can see from the 100% stacked column chart in Figure 4-18, Chardonnay accounts for about 75 percent of the wine produced in Year 1, and that percentage steadily declines to about 50 percent in Year 5 as more cases of White Riesling and Cabernet Franc are produced.

The chart subtype you use depends on what you want to highlight with your data.

## Creating a Clustered Column Chart

The process for creating a column chart is the same as for creating a pie chart. First, you select the data source. Then, you select the type of chart you want to create. After the chart is embedded in the worksheet, you can move and resize the chart as well as change the chart's design, layout, and format.

Bob and Carol want to show the projected revenue and expenses for each of the next 10 years. Because this requires comparing the data series values, you will create a clustered column chart.

### To create a column chart for the revenue and expenses data:

▶ **1.** Go to the **Projected Cash Flow** worksheet.

▶ **2.** Select the nonadjacent range **B4:L4;B10:L10;B18:L18** containing the Year categories in row 4, the Total Revenue data series in row 10, and the Total Expenses data series in row 18. Because you selected a nonadjacent range, the Quick Analysis tool is not available.

▶ **3.** On the ribbon, click the **INSERT** tab. The Charts group contains buttons for inserting different types of charts.

**TIP**

You can also open the Insert Chart dialog box to see the chart types recommended for the selected data source.

▶ **4.** In the Charts group, click the **Recommended Charts** button. The Insert Chart dialog box opens with the Recommended Charts tab displayed. The charts show how the selected data would appear in that chart type. See Figure 4-19.

| Figure 4-19 | Clustered column chart being created |
| --- | --- |

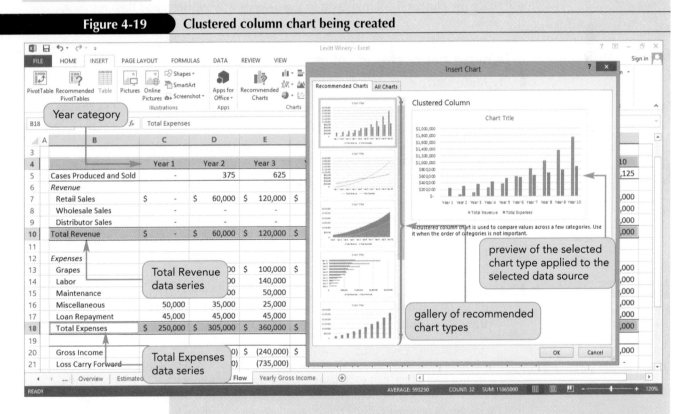

▶ **5.** Make sure the **Clustered Column** chart is selected, and then click the **OK** button. The clustered column chart is embedded in the Projected Cash Flow worksheet.

▶ **6.** Click the **Chart Styles** button next to the selected column chart.

▶ **7.** In the STYLE gallery, scroll down and click the **Style 14** chart style to format the columns with drop shadows.

▶ **8.** Click the **Chart Styles** button to close the STYLE gallery.

### Changing a Chart Type

After creating a chart, you can easily switch the chart to a different chart type without having to recreate the chart from scratch. For example, if the data in a column chart would be more effective presented as a line chart, you can change its chart type rather than creating a new chart. Clicking the Change Chart Type button in the Type group on the CHART TOOLS DESIGN tab opens a dialog box similar to the Insert Chart dialog box, from which you can select a new chart type.

## Moving a Chart to a Different Worksheet

You can move a chart from one worksheet to another, or you can place the chart in its own chart sheet. In a chart sheet, the chart is enlarged to fill the entire workspace. The Move Chart dialog box provides options for moving charts between worksheets and chart sheets. You can also cut and paste a chart between workbooks.

Bob and Carol want all of the charts to be displayed in the Overview worksheet. You will move the clustered column chart to the Overview worksheet, and then resize it.

### To move the clustered column chart to the Overview worksheet:

1. Make sure the clustered column chart is selected.

2. On the CHART TOOLS DESIGN tab, in the Location group, click the **Move Chart** button. The Move Chart dialog box opens.

3. Click the **Object in** arrow to display a list of the worksheets in the active workbook, and then click **Overview**.

4. Click the **OK** button. The embedded chart moves from the Projected Cash Flow worksheet to the Overview worksheet, and remains selected.

5. Hold down the **Alt** key as you drag the chart so that its upper-left corner is aligned with the upper-left corner of cell F16, and then release the mouse button and the **Alt** key to snap the upper-left corner of the chart to the worksheet.

6. Hold down the **Alt** key as you drag the lower-right sizing handle of the clustered column chart to the lower-right corner of cell **M29**, and then release the mouse button and the **Alt** key. The chart now covers the range F16:M29.

The revenue and expenses chart shows that the winery will produce little revenue during its first few years as it establishes itself and its customer base. It is only during Year 6 that the revenue will outpace the expenses. After that, Bob and Carol hope that the winery's revenue will increase rapidly while expenses grow at a more moderate pace.

## Changing and Formatting a Chart Title

When a chart has a single data series, the name of the data series is used for the chart title. When a chart has more than one data series, the "Chart Title" placeholder appears as the temporary title of the chart. You can then replace the placeholder text with a more descriptive title.

The clustered column chart includes the Chart Title placeholder. Bob and Carol want you to replace this with a more descriptive title.

**To change the title of the column chart:**

▶ **1.** At the top of the column chart, click **Chart Title** to select the placeholder text.

▶ **2.** Type **Projected Revenue and Expenses** as the new title, and then press the **Enter** key. The new title is entered into the chart, and the chart title element remains selected.

▶ **3.** Click the **HOME** tab, and then use the buttons in the Font group to remove the bold from the chart title, change the font to **Calibri Light**, and change the font color to the **Blue, Accent 1** theme color. See Figure 4-20.

| Figure 4-20 | Column chart |
| --- | --- |

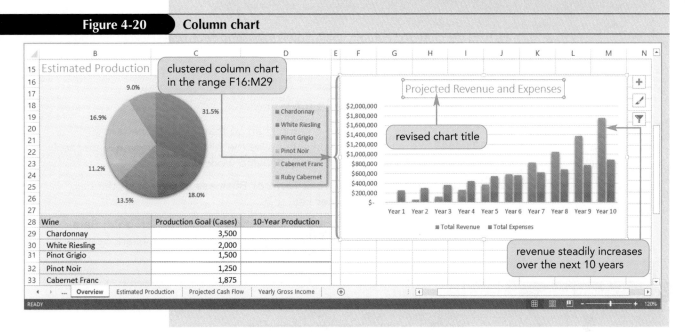

## Creating a Stacked Column Chart

The next chart that the Levitts want added to the Overview worksheet is a chart that projects the expenses incurred by the winery over the next 10 years broken down by category. Because this chart looks at how different parts of the whole vary across time, it would be better to display that information in a stacked column chart. You will create this chart based on the data located in the Projected Cash Flow worksheet.

**To create a stacked column chart:**

▶ **1.** Go to the **Projected Cash Flow** worksheet, and then select the nonadjacent range **B4:L4;B13:L17** containing the year categories and five data series for different types of expenses.

▶ **2.** Click the **INSERT** tab, and then click the **Insert Column Chart** button in the Charts group. A list of column chart subtypes appears.

▶ **3.** Click the **Stacked Column** icon (the second icon in the 2-D Column section). The stacked column chart is embedded in the Projected Cash Flow worksheet.

**4.** With the chart still selected, click the **Chart Styles** button ✎, and then apply the **Style 11** chart style located at the bottom of the style gallery.

You'll place this stacked column chart on the Overview worksheet.

**5.** On the CHART TOOLS DESIGN tab, in the Location group, click the **Move Chart** button to open the Move Chart dialog box.

**6.** Click the **Object in** arrow, and then click the **Overview** worksheet.

**7.** Click the **OK** button. The stacked column chart is moved to the Overview worksheet.

As with the clustered column chart, you'll move and resize the stacked column chart and add a descriptive chart title.

### To edit the stacked column chart:

TIP

To retain the chart's proportions as you resize it, hold down the Shift key as you drag the sizing handle.

**1.** Move and resize the stacked column chart so that it covers the range **F31:M43** in the Overview worksheet. Use the Alt key to help you align the chart's location and size with the underlying worksheet grid.

**2.** Select the chart title, type **Breakdown of Business Expenses** as the new title, and then press the **Enter** key.

**3.** With the chart title still selected, change the font style to **non-bold**; **Blue, Accent 1**; **Calibri Light** font to match the clustered column chart. See Figure 4-21.

**Figure 4-21    Stacked column chart**

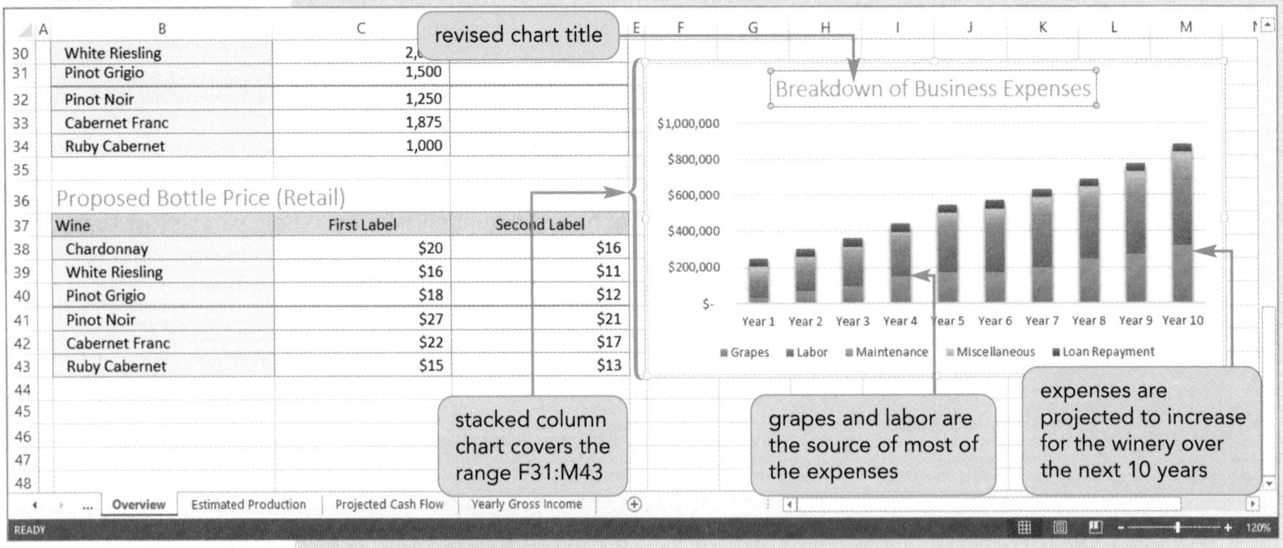

**4.** Save the workbook.

The chart clearly shows that the winery's main expenses over the next 10 years will come from the purchase of grapes and labor costs. General maintenance, miscellaneous, and the business loan repayment constitute a smaller portion of the company's projected expenses. The overall yearly expense of running the winery is expected to increase from about $250,000 in Year 1 to almost $900,000 by Year 10.

*Written Communication: Communicating Effectively with Charts*

Studies show that people more easily interpret information when it is presented as a graphic rather than in a table. As a result, charts can help communicate the real story underlying the facts and figures you present to colleagues and clients. A well-designed chart can illuminate the bigger picture that might be hidden by viewing only the numbers. However, poorly designed charts can mislead readers and make it more difficult to interpret data.

To create effective and useful charts, keep in mind the following tips as you design charts:

- **Keep it simple.** Do not clutter a chart with too many graphical elements. Focus attention on the data rather than on decorative elements that do not inform.
- **Focus on the message.** Design the chart to highlight the points you want to convey to readers.
- **Limit the number of data series.** Most charts should display no more than four or five data series. Pie charts should have no more than six slices.
- **Choose colors carefully.** Display different data series in contrasting colors to make it easier to distinguish one series from another. Modify the default colors as needed to make them distinct on the screen and in the printed copy.
- **Limit your chart to a few text styles.** Use a maximum of two or three different text styles in the same chart. Having too many text styles in one chart can distract attention from the data.

The goal of written communication is always to inform the reader in the simplest, most accurate, and most direct way possible. When creating worksheets and charts, everything in the workbook should be directed toward that end.

So far, you have determined monthly payments by using the PMT function, and created and formatted a pie chart and two column charts. In the next session, you'll continue your work on the winery's business plan by creating line charts, combination charts, sparklines, and data bars.

*Session 4.1 Quick Check*

1. You want to take out a loan for $130,000. The annual interest on the loan is 5 percent with payments due monthly. You plan to repay the loan in 15 years. Write the formula to calculate the monthly payment required to completely repay the loan under those conditions.
2. What function do you use to determine how many payment periods are required to repay a loan?
3. What three chart elements are included in a pie chart?
4. A data series contains values grouped into 10 categories. Would this data be better displayed as a pie chart or a column chart? Explain why.
5. A research firm wants to create a chart that displays the total population growth of a county over a 10-year period broken down by five ethnicities. Which chart type best displays this information? Explain why.
6. If the research firm wants to display the changing ethnic profile of the county over time as a percentage of the county population, which chart type should it use? Explain why.
7. If the research firm is interested in comparing the numeric sizes of different ethnic groups over time, which chart should it use? Explain why.
8. If the research firm wants to display the ethnic profile of the county only for the current year, which chart should it use? Explain why.
9. How does chart animation help you perform a what-if analysis?

# Session 4.2 Visual Overview:

The SPARKLINE TOOLS DESIGN contextual tab provides commands to format sparklines.

A **sparkline** is a chart that is displayed within a cell. You can create line, column, and win/loss sparklines.

Line sparklines can contain data markers to identify the high and low points, negative points, first and last points, and all points.

These column sparklines have been ungrouped and formatted individually.

A **data bar** is a conditional format that adds a horizontal bar to the background of a cell proportional in length to the cell's value.

Levitt Winery - Excel

FILE    HOME    INSERT    PAGE LAYOUT    FORMULAS    DATA    REVIEW    VIEW

Edit Data    Line    Column    Win/Loss

Sparkline    Type

☐ High Point    ☐ First Point
☐ Low Point    ☐ Last Point
☐ Negative Points    ☐ Markers

Show

D29    ✗    ✓    fx

| | Wine | Production Goal (Cases) | 10-Year Production |
|---|---|---|---|
| 28 | Wine | Production Goal (Cases) | 10-Year Production |
| 29 | Chardonnay | 3,500 | |
| 30 | White Riesling | 2,000 | |
| 31 | Pinot Grigio | 1,500 | |
| 32 | Pinot Noir | 1,250 | |
| 33 | Cabernet Franc | 1,875 | |
| 34 | Ruby Cabernet | 1,000 | |

| | Wine | First Label | Second Label | |
|---|---|---|---|---|
| 36 | Wine | First Label | Second Label | |
| 37 | Chardonnay | $20 | $16 | |
| 38 | White Riesling | $16 | $11 | |
| 39 | Pinot Grigio | $18 | $12 | |
| 40 | Pinot Noir | $27 | $21 | |
| 41 | Cabernet Franc | $22 | $17 | |
| 42 | Ruby Cabernet | $15 | $13 | |

11.2%    13.5%    18.0%

Pinot Noir
Cabernet Franc
Ruby Cabernet

Net Income
$700,0
$600,0
$500,0
$400,0
$300,0
$200,0
$100,0

$(100,0
$(200,0
$(300,0

$600,000
$400,000
$200,000
$-
$(200,000)
$(400,000)
$(600,000)

Documentation    Overview    Estimated Production    Projected Ca ...

READY

# Charts, Sparklines, and Data Bars

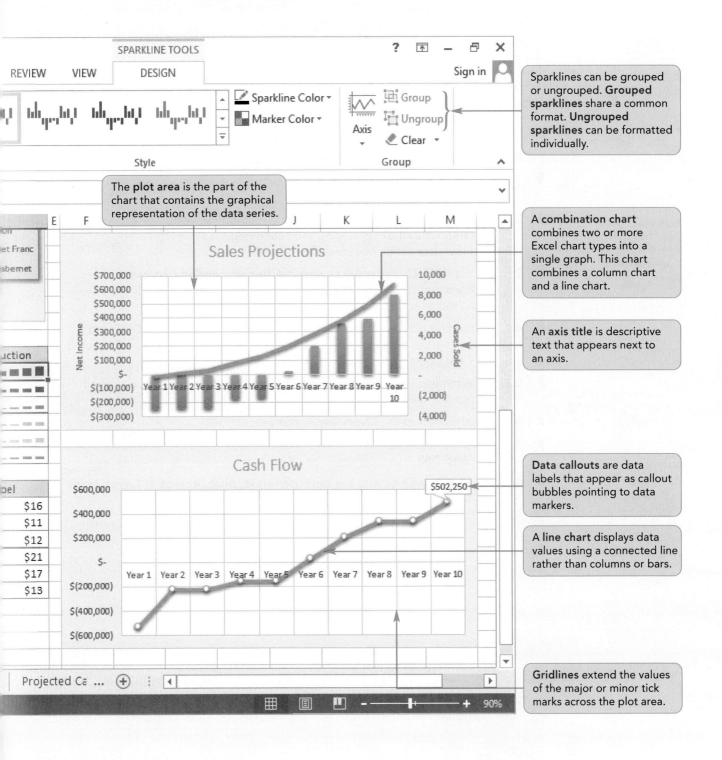

Sparklines can be grouped or ungrouped. **Grouped sparklines** share a common format. **Ungrouped sparklines** can be formatted individually.

The **plot area** is the part of the chart that contains the graphical representation of the data series.

A **combination chart** combines two or more Excel chart types into a single graph. This chart combines a column chart and a line chart.

An **axis title** is descriptive text that appears next to an axis.

**Data callouts** are data labels that appear as callout bubbles pointing to data markers.

A **line chart** displays data values using a connected line rather than columns or bars.

**Gridlines** extend the values of the major or minor tick marks across the plot area.

# Creating a Line Chart

Line charts are typically used when the data consists of values drawn from categories that follow a sequential order at evenly spaced intervals, such as historical data that is recorded monthly, quarterly, or yearly. Like column charts, a line chart can be used with one or more data series. When multiple data series are included, the data values are plotted on different lines with varying line colors.

Bob and Carol want to use a line chart to show the winery's potential cash flow over the next decade. Cash flow measures the amount of cash flowing into and out of a business annually; it is one measure of a business's financial health and ability to make its payments. Because the cash flow values are the only data series, only one line will appear on the chart. You will create the line chart now.

## To create the projected cash flow line chart:

1. If you took a break at the end of the previous session, make sure the Levitt Winery workbook is open.

2. Go to the **Projected Cash Flow** worksheet, and then select the nonadjacent range **B4:L4;B27:L27** containing the Year categories from row 4 and the Cash Flow data series from row 27.

3. Click the **INSERT** tab, and then click the **Recommended Charts** button in the Charts group. The Insert Chart dialog box opens, showing different ways to chart the selected data.

4. Click the second chart listed (the Line chart), and then click the **OK** button. The line chart of the year-end cash flow values is embedded in the Projected Cash Flow worksheet.

5. Format the line chart with the **Style 15** chart style to give the line a raised 3-D appearance.

6. Move the chart to the **Overview** worksheet.

7. Move and resize the line chart in the Overview worksheet so that it covers the range **B45:D58**.

8. Format the chart title with the same **non-bold**; **Blue, Accent 1**; **Calibri Light** font you applied to the two column charts. See Figure 4-22.

> When charting table values, do not include the summary totals because they will be treated as another category.

**Figure 4-22**    **Line chart of the projected cash flow**

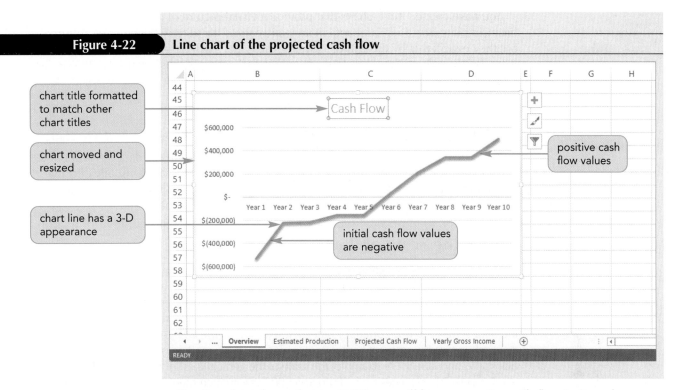

chart title formatted to match other chart titles

chart moved and resized

chart line has a 3-D appearance

positive cash flow values

initial cash flow values are negative

The line chart shows that Levitt Winery will have a negative cash flow in its early years and that the annual cash flow will increase throughout the decade, showing a positive cash flow starting in its sixth year.

## INSIGHT

### Line Charts and Scatter Charts

Line charts can sometimes be confused with XY (Scatter) charts; but they are very different chart types. A line chart is more like a column chart that uses lines instead of columns. In a line chart, the data series are plotted against category values. These categories are assumed to have some sequential order. If the categories represent dates or times, they must be evenly spaced in time. For example, the Cash Flow line chart plotted the cash flow values against categories that ranged sequentially from Year 1 to Year 10.

A scatter chart has no category values. Instead, one series of data values is plotted against another. For example, if you were analyzing the relationship between height and weight among high school students, you would use a scatter chart because both weight and height are data values. On the other hand, if you charted height measures against weight categories (Underweight, Normal, Overweight), a line chart would be more appropriate.

Scatter charts are more often used in statistical analysis and scientific studies in which the researcher is attempting to find a relationship between one variable and another. For that purpose, Excel includes several statistical tools to augment scatter charts, such as trendlines that provide the best fitting line or curve to the data. You can add a trendline by right-clicking the data series in the chart, and then clicking Add Trendline on the shortcut menu. From the Format Trendline pane that opens you can select different types of trendlines, including exponential and logarithmic lines as well as linear (straight) lines.

You have created three charts that provide a visual picture of the Levitt Winery business plan. Bob and Carol anticipate lean years as the winery becomes established; but they expect that by the end of 10 years, the winery will be profitable and stable. Next, you'll look at other tools to fine-tune the formatting of these charts. You'll start by looking at the scale applied to the chart values.

# Working with Axes and Gridlines

A chart's vertical and horizontal axes are based on the values in the data series and the category values. In many cases, the axes display the data in the most visually effective and informative way. Sometimes, however, you will want to modify the axes' scale, add gridlines, and make other changes to better highlight the chart data.

## Editing the Scale of the Vertical Axis

The range of values, or **scale**, of an axis is based on the values in the data source. The default scale usually ranges from 0 (if the data source has no negative values) to the maximum value. If the scale includes negative values, it ranges from the minimum value to the maximum value. The vertical, or value, axis shows the range of values in the data series; the horizontal, or category, axis shows the category values.

Excel divides the scale into regular intervals, which are marked on the axis with **tick marks** and labels. For example, the scale of the vertical axis for the Projected Revenue and Expenses chart ranges from $0 up to $2,000,000 in increments of $200,000. Having more tick marks at smaller intervals could make the chart difficult to read because the tick mark labels might start to overlap. Likewise, having fewer tick marks at larger intervals could make the chart less informative. **Major tick marks** identify the main units on the chart axis while **minor tick marks** identify the smaller intervals between the major tick marks.

Some charts involve multiple data series that have vastly different values. In those instances, you can create dual axis charts. You can plot one data series against a **primary axis**, which usually appears along the left side of the chart, and the other against a **secondary axis**, which is usually placed on the right side of the chart. The two axes can be based on entirely different scales.

By default, no titles appear next to the value and category axes. This is fine when the axis labels are self-explanatory. Otherwise, you can add descriptive axis titles. In general, you should avoid cluttering a chart with extra elements such as axis titles when that information is easily understood from other parts of the chart.

The Levitts think that the value axis scale for the Projected Revenue and Expenses chart is too crowded, and they want tick marks placed at intervals of $250,000 ranging from $0 to $1,750,000. You will modify the scale of the value axis.

### To change the scale of the vertical axis:

▶ 1. Double-click the vertical axis of the Projected Revenue and Expenses chart to open the Format pane.

The Format Axis pane has options to modify the value axis. The Bounds section provides the minimum and maximum boundaries of the axis, which in this case are set from 0.0 to 2.0E6 (which stands for 2,000,000). Note that minimum and maximum values are set to Auto, which means that Excel automatically set these boundaries based on the data values.

TIP

To return a scale value to Auto, click the Reset button next to the value in the Format pane.

▶ 2. In the Bounds section of the AXIS OPTIONS, click in the **Maximum** box, delete the current value, type **1750000** as the new value, and then press the **Enter** key. Excel changes the maximum value of the vertical axis to $1,750,000.

The Units section provides the intervals between the major tick marks and between minor tick marks. These intervals are also set automatically by Excel.

3. In the Units section, click in the **Major** box, delete the current value, type **250000** as the new interval between major tick marks, and then press the **Enter** key. The scale of the value axis has been changed. See Figure 4-23.

**Figure 4-23**    **Formatted value axis**

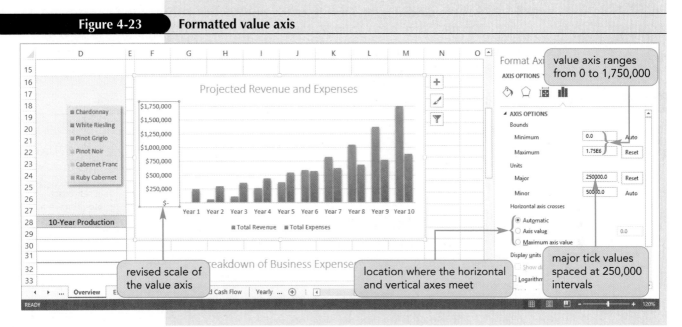

The revised axis scale makes the values easier to read and interpret.

## INSIGHT

### Displaying Unit Labels

When a chart involves large numbers, the axis labels can take up a lot of the available chart area and be difficult to read. You can simplify the chart's appearance by displaying units of measure more appropriate to the data values. For example, you can display the value 20 to represent 20,000 or 20,000,000. This is particularly useful when space is at a premium, such as in an embedded chart confined to a small area of the worksheet.

To display a units label, you double-click the axis to open the Format pane displaying options to format the axis. Select the units type from the Display units box. You can choose unit labels to represent values measured in the hundreds up to the trillions. Excel will modify the numbers on the selected axis and add a label so that readers will know what the axis values represent.

## Adding Gridlines

Gridlines are horizontal and vertical lines that help you compare data and category values. Depending on the chart style, gridlines may or may not appear in a chart, though you can add or remove them separately. Gridlines are placed at the major tick marks on the axes, or you can set them to appear at the minor tick marks.

The chart style used for the two column charts and the line chart includes horizontal gridlines. Carol and Bob want you to add vertical gridlines to help further separate one set of year values from another. You'll add major vertical gridlines to the Projected Revenue and Expenses chart.

**To add vertical gridlines to the Projected Revenue and Expenses chart:**

▶ **1.** With the Projected Revenue and Expenses chart still selected, click the **Chart Elements** button ⊞ next to the selected column chart. The menu of chart elements appears.

▶ **2.** Point to **Gridlines**, and then click the **right arrow** that appears to open a submenu of gridline options.

▶ **3.** Click the **Primary Major Vertical** check box to add vertical gridlines at the major tick marks on the chart. See Figure 4-24.

Figure 4-24     **Vertical gridlines added to the column chart**

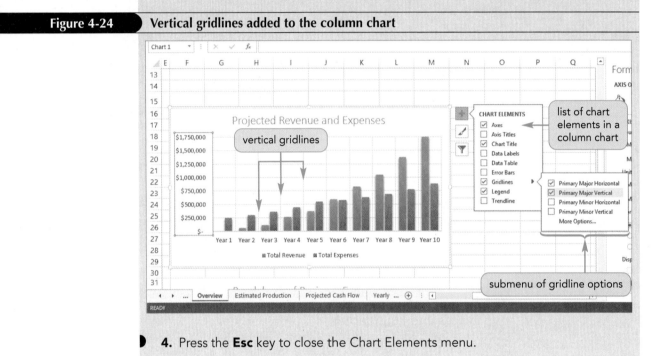

▶ **4.** Press the **Esc** key to close the Chart Elements menu.

## Working with Column Widths

Category values do not have the scale options used with data values. However, you can set the spacing between one column and another in your column charts. You can also define the width of the columns. As with the vertical axis, the default spacing and width are set automatically by Excel. A column chart with several categories will naturally make those columns thinner and more tightly packed.

The Levitts think that the columns in the Projected Revenue and Expenses chart are spaced too closely, making it difficult to distinguish one year's values from another. They want you to increase the gap between the columns.

**To format the chart columns:**

▶ **1.** Make sure the Projected Revenue and Expenses chart is still selected and the Format pane is still open.

▶ **2.** In the Format pane, click the **AXIS OPTIONS arrow**, and then click **Series "Total Revenue"** from the list of chart elements. The Format pane title changes to "Format Data Series" and all of the columns that show total revenue values are selected.

3. In the Format pane, click **SERIES OPTIONS** to display the list of options, if necessary. Series Overlap sets the amount of overlap between columns of different data series. Gap Width sets the amount of space between one group of columns and the next.

4. Drag the **Gap Width** slider until **150%** appears in the Gap Width box. The gap between groups of columns increases and the individual column widths decrease to make room for the larger gap. See Figure 4-25.

| Figure 4-25 | Gap width between columns |
| --- | --- |

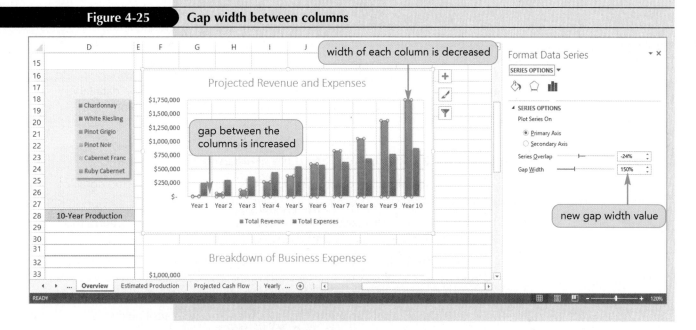

## Formatting Data Markers

Each value from a data series is represented by a data marker. In pie charts, the data markers are the individual pie slices. In column charts, the columns are the data markers. In a line chart, the data markers are the points connected by the line. Depending on the line chart style, these data marker points can be displayed or hidden.

In the Cash Flow line chart, the data marker points are hidden and only the line connecting them is visible. Carol wants you to display these data markers and change their fill color to white so that they stand out, making the chart easier to understand.

### To display and format the line chart data markers:

1. Scroll down the worksheet to display the Cash Flow line chart, and then double-click the line to change the Format pane to the Format Data Series pane.

2. Click the **Fill & Line** button ⬧. You can choose to display the format options for lines or data markers.

3. Click **MARKER**, if necessary, and then click **MARKER OPTIONS** to display a list of options for the line chart data markers. Currently, the None option button is selected to hide the data markers.

4. Click the **Automatic** option button to automatically display the markers. The data markers are now visible in the line chart, but they have a blue fill color. You will change this fill color to white.

▶ **5.** Click **FILL**, if necessary, to expand the fill options.

▶ **6.** Click the **Solid fill** option button, click the **Fill Color** button, and then click the **White, Background 1** theme color. The fill color for the data markers in the line chart changes to white.

▶ **7.** Press the **Esc** key to deselect the data markers in the line chart.

In many charts, you will want to highlight an important data point. Data labels provide a way to identify the different values in a chart. Whether you include data labels depends on the chart, the complexity of the data and presentation, and the chart's purpose. You can include data labels for every data marker, or you can include data labels for individual data points.

Carol and Bob want to highlight that at the end of the tenth year, the winery should have an annual cash flow that exceeds $500,000. They want you to add a data label that displays the value of the last data marker in the chart at that data point.

### To add a data label to the last data marker in the line chart:

▶ **1.** Click the line in the line chart to select the entire data series, including all of the data markers.

▶ **2.** Click the last data marker to select it. Selection handles appear around this data marker, but not any of the others.

▶ **3.** Click the **Chart Elements** button ⊞ next to the line chart, and then click the **Data Labels** check box to insert a checkmark. The data label appears above only the selected data marker.

▶ **4.** Click the **Data Labels arrow** to display a menu of data label positions and options, and then click **Data Callout**. The data label is changed to a data callout box that includes both the category value and the data value, displaying "Year 10, $502,250." You will modify this callout to display only the data value.

▶ **5.** Double-click the data callout to select it. The Format pane is titled "Format Data Labels."

▶ **6.** Click the **Label Options** button 📊, and then click **LABEL OPTIONS**, if necessary, to display those options.

▶ **7.** Click the **Category Name** check box to deselect it.

▶ **8.** Press the **Esc** key to deselect the data label. The data callout now displays only $502,250. See Figure 4-26.

| Figure 4-26 | Formatted data markers and data label |
| --- | --- |

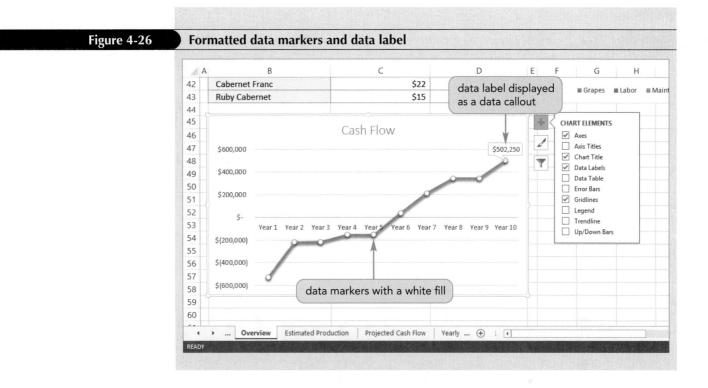

## Formatting the Plot Area

The chart area covers the entire background of the chart, whereas the plot area includes only that portion of the chart in which the data markers, such as the columns in a column chart, have been placed or plotted. You can format the plot area by changing its fill and borders, and by adding visual effects. Changes to the plot area are often made in conjunction with the chart area.

Carol and Bob want you to format the chart area and plot area of the Projected Revenue and Expenses chart. You'll set the chart area fill color to a light gold to match the pie chart, and the plot area fill color to white.

### To change the fill colors of the chart and plot areas:

1. Scroll the worksheet up and select the Projected Revenue and Expenses chart.

2. On the ribbon, click the **CHART TOOLS FORMAT** tab.

3. In the Current Selection group, click the **Chart Elements** arrow to display a list of chart elements in the current chart, and then click **Chart Area**. The chart area is selected in the chart.

4. In the Shape Styles group, click the **Shape Fill** button, and then click the **Gold, Accent 4, Lighter 80%** theme color in the second row and eighth column. The entire background of the chart changes to light gold.

5. In the Current Selection group, click the **Chart Elements** arrow, and then click **Plot Area** to select that chart element.

6. Change the fill color of the plot area to **white**. See Figure 4-27.

**Figure 4-27**        **Final Projected Revenue and Expenses chart**

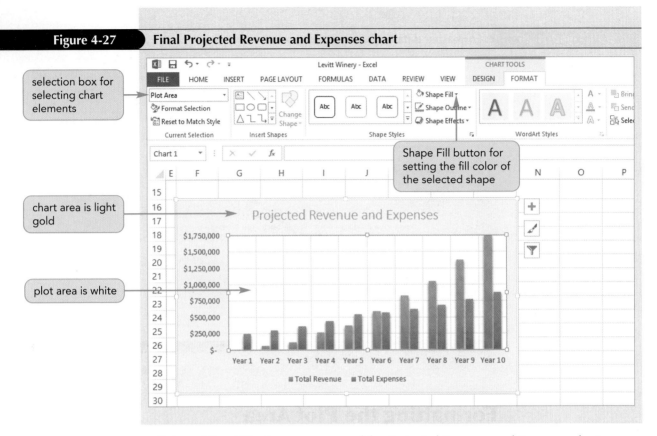

selection box for selecting chart elements

Shape Fill button for setting the fill color of the selected shape

chart area is light gold

plot area is white

Bob and Carol like the appearance of the Projected Revenue and Expenses chart, and they want the same general design applied to the Breakdown of Business Expenses column chart and the Cash Flow line chart. You will add vertical gridlines to each chart, and then change the chart area fill color to light gold and the plot area fill color to white.

**To format the Breakdown of Business Expenses column chart and the Cash Flow line chart:**

1. Select the **Breakdown of Business Expenses** column chart.

2. Select the **chart area**, and then set the fill color of the chart area to the **Gold, Accent 4, Lighter 80%** theme color.

3. Select the **plot area**, and then change the fill color to **white**.

    Next, you'll add vertical gridlines to the chart. You can also use the CHART TOOLS DESIGN tab to add chart elements such as gridlines.

4. On the ribbon, click the **CHART TOOLS DESIGN** tab.

5. In the Chart Layouts group, click the **Add Chart Element** button, scroll down the chart elements, point to **Gridlines**, and then click **Primary Major Vertical** on the submenu. Vertical gridlines are added to the chart. See Figure 4-28.

**Figure 4-28**    **Final Breakdown of Business Expenses chart**

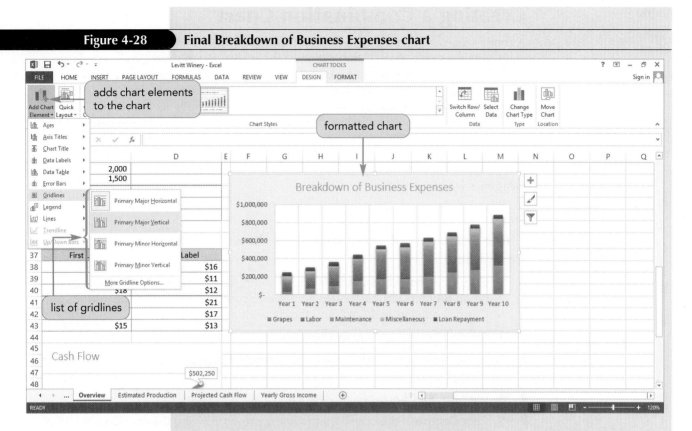

6. Scroll down the worksheet, select the **Cash Flow** line chart, and then repeat Steps 2 through 5 to set the chart area fill color to light gold, set the plot area fill color to white, and add major gridlines to the chart's primary axis.

The Breakdown of Business Expenses column chart and the Cash Flow line chart are now formatted with the same design.

**INSIGHT**

## Overlaying Chart Elements

An embedded chart takes up less space than a chart sheet. However, it can be challenging to fit all of the chart elements into that smaller space. One solution is to overlay one element on top of another. The most commonly overlaid elements are the chart title and the chart legend. To overlay the chart title, click the Chart Title arrow from the list of Chart Elements and select Centered Overlay from the list of position options. Excel will place the chart title on top of the plot area, freeing up more space for other chart elements. Chart legends can also be overlaid by opening the Format pane for the legend and deselecting the Show the legend without overlapping the chart check box in the LEGEND OPTIONS section. Other chart elements can be overlaid by dragging them to new locations in the chart area and then resizing the plot area to recover the empty space.

Don't overuse the technique of overlaying chart elements. Too much overlaying of chart elements can make your chart difficult to read.

# Creating a Combination Chart

A combination chart combines two chart types, such as a column chart and a line chart, within a single chart. Combination charts enable you to show two sets of data using the chart type that is best for each data set. Combination charts can have data series with vastly different values. In those instances, you can create dual axis charts, using primary and secondary axes.

Bob and Carol want to include a chart that projects the net income and cases sold by Levitt Winery over the next 10 years. Because these two data series are measuring different things (dollars and wine cases), the chart might be better understood if the Net Income data series was displayed as a column chart and the Cases Produced and Sold data series was displayed as a line chart.

## To create a combination chart that shows net income and sales data:

1. Go to the **Projected Cash Flow** worksheet, and then select the nonadjacent range **B4:L5;B23:L23** containing the Year category values, the data series for Cases Produced and Sold, and the data series for Net Income.

2. On the ribbon, click the **INSERT** tab.

3. In the Charts group, click the **Recommended Charts** button. The Insert Chart dialog box opens.

4. Click the **All Charts** tab to view a list of all chart types and subtypes.

5. Click **Combo** in the list of chart types, and then click the **Custom Combination** icon (the fourth subtype). At the bottom of the dialog box, you choose the chart type for each data series and whether that data series is plotted on the primary or secondary axis.

6. For the Cases Produced and Sold data series, click the **Chart Type** arrow, and then click **Line**.

7. Click the **Secondary Axis** check box to display the values for that series on a secondary axis.

8. For the Net Income data series, click the **Chart Type** arrow, and then click **Clustered Column**. See Figure 4-29.

**Figure 4-29** ) **Combo chart type**

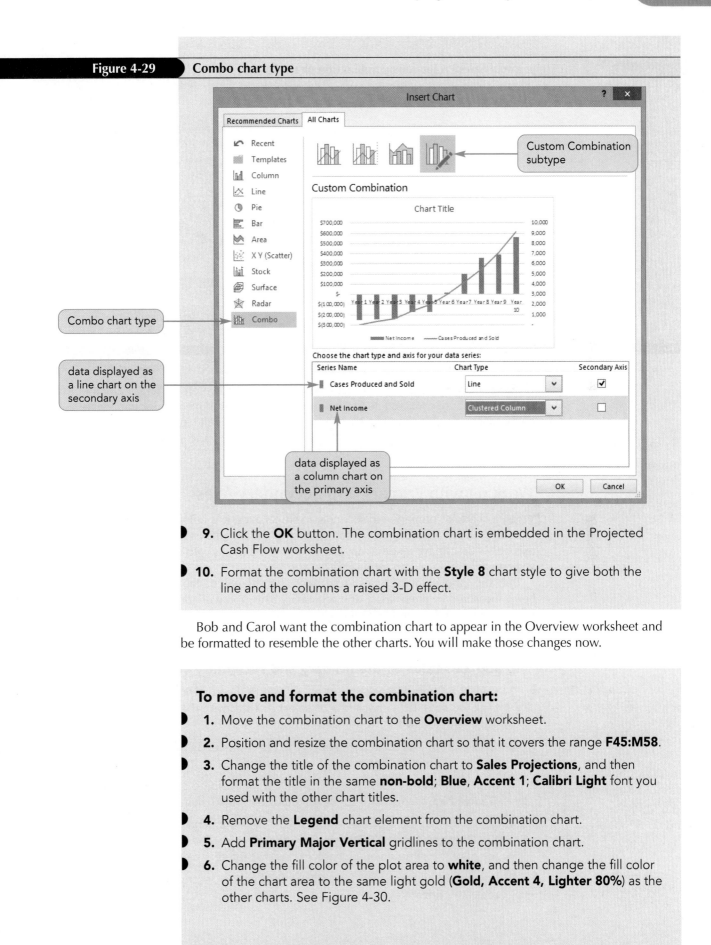

9. Click the **OK** button. The combination chart is embedded in the Projected Cash Flow worksheet.

10. Format the combination chart with the **Style 8** chart style to give both the line and the columns a raised 3-D effect.

Bob and Carol want the combination chart to appear in the Overview worksheet and be formatted to resemble the other charts. You will make those changes now.

### To move and format the combination chart:

1. Move the combination chart to the **Overview** worksheet.

2. Position and resize the combination chart so that it covers the range **F45:M58**.

3. Change the title of the combination chart to **Sales Projections**, and then format the title in the same **non-bold**; **Blue, Accent 1**; **Calibri Light** font you used with the other chart titles.

4. Remove the **Legend** chart element from the combination chart.

5. Add **Primary Major Vertical** gridlines to the combination chart.

6. Change the fill color of the plot area to **white**, and then change the fill color of the chart area to the same light gold (**Gold, Accent 4, Lighter 80%**) as the other charts. See Figure 4-30.

| Figure 4-30 | Initial Sales Projections combination chart |
| --- | --- |

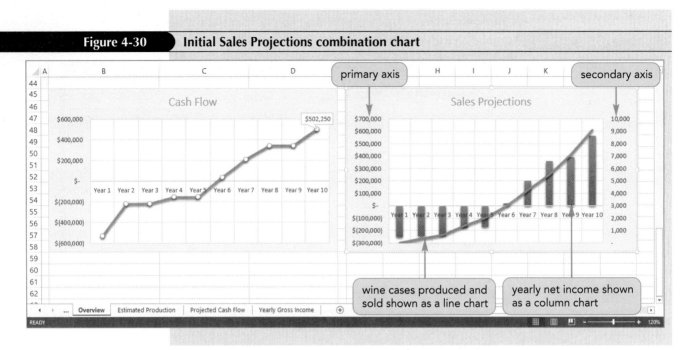

The primary axis scale for the net income values is shown on the left side of the chart; the secondary axis scale for the number of cases produced and sold appears on the right side. The chart clearly shows that the winery will have a negative income for the first five years, while the number of cases produced and sold will start at 0 and increase steadily to more than 9,000 cases by Year 10.

## Working with Primary and Secondary Axes

When a chart has primary and secondary vertical axes, it is helpful to identify exactly what each axis is measuring. You can do this by adding an axis title to the chart. An axis title is descriptive text that appears next to the axis. As with other chart elements, you can add, remove, and format axis titles.

Bob and Carol want the Sales Projections chart to include labels describing what is being measured by the primary and secondary axes. You will add descriptive axis titles to the primary and secondary vertical axes.

### To add axis titles to the primary and secondary vertical axes:

1. Click the **Chart Elements** button + next to the combination chart, and then click the **Axis Title** check box to select it. Titles with the placeholders "Axis Title" are added to the primary and secondary axes.

2. Click the left axis title to select it, type **Net Income** as the descriptive title, and then press the **Enter** key.

3. With the left axis title selected, change the font color to the **Orange, Accent 2, Darker 25%** theme color to match the color of the columns in the chart.

4. Select the numbers on the left axis scale, and then change the font color to the **Orange, Accent 2, Darker 25%** theme color. The left axis title and scale are now the same color as the columns that reference that axis.

5. Select the right axis title, type **Cases Sold** as the descriptive title, and then press the **Enter** key.

**6.** With the right axis title still selected, change the font color to the **Blue, Accent 1, Darker 25%** theme color to match the color of the line in the chart.

**7.** Change the orientation of the right axis title to **Rotate Text Down**. The text is easier to read in this orientation.

**8.** Select the numbers on the right axis scale, and then change the font color to the **Blue, Accent 1, Darker 25%** theme color. The right axis title and scale are now the same color as the line that references that axis.

Excel added the "Axis Title" placeholder to the horizontal category values axis. You can remove this title, freeing up more space for other chart elements.

**9.** Click the horizontal axis title to select it, and then press the **Delete** key to remove it from the chart. See Figure 4-31.

| Figure 4-31 | Combination chart with axis titles |
| --- | --- |

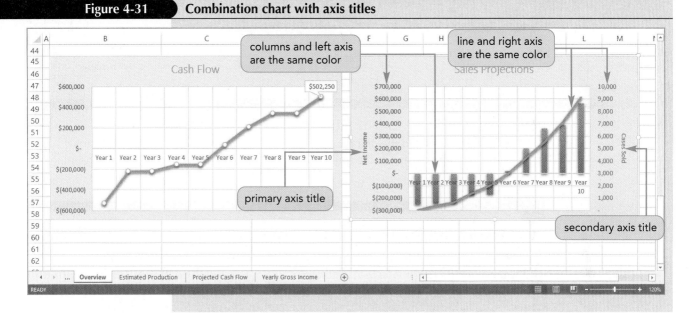

The Levitts are concerned that the line chart portion of the graph makes it look as if the number of cases produced and sold was negative for the first five years. This is because the secondary axis scale, which is automatically generated by Excel, goes from a minimum of 0 to a maximum of 10,000. You will change the scale so that the 0 tick mark for Cases Sold better aligns with the $0 for Net Income.

**To modify the secondary axis scale:**

**1.** Double-click the secondary axis scale to select it and open the Format pane.

**2.** Verify that the **AXIS OPTIONS** list of commands is displayed.

**3.** Click the **Minimum** box, change the value from 0.0 to **–4000**, and then press the **Enter** key. The secondary axis scale is modified. The Cases Sold scale is now better aligned with the Net Income scale, providing a more realistic picture of the data.

▶ **4.** Close the Format pane, and then press the **Esc** key to deselect the secondary axis. See Figure 4-32.

| Figure 4-32 | Final combination chart |

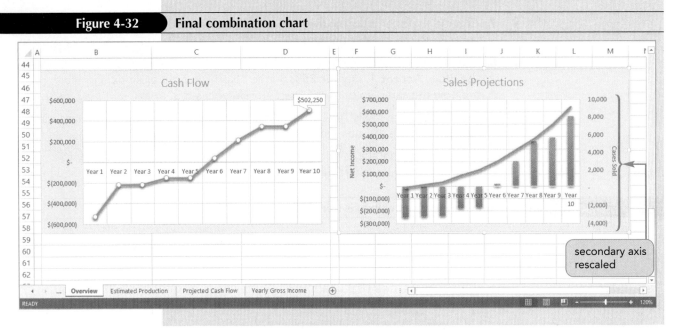

You have completed the charts portion of the Overview worksheet. These charts provide a good overview of the financial picture of the winery that Bob and Carol plan to open.

### INSIGHT

#### Copying and Pasting a Chart Format

You will often want to use the same design over and over again for the charts in your worksheet. Rather than repeating the same commands, you can copy the formatting from one chart to another. To copy a chart format, first select the chart with the existing design that you want to replicate, and then click the Copy button in the Clipboard group on the HOME tab (or press the Ctrl+C keys). Next, select the chart that you want to format, click the Paste button arrow in the Clipboard group, and then click Paste Special to open the Paste Special dialog box. In the Paste Special dialog box, select the Formats option button, and then click the OK button. All of the copied formats from the original chart—including fill colors, font styles, axis scales, and chart types—are then pasted into the new chart. Be aware that the pasted formats will overwrite any formats previously used in the new chart.

## Editing a Chart Data Source

Excel automates most of the process of creating and formatting a chart. However, sometimes the rendered chart does not appear the way you expected. One situation where this happens is when the selected cells contain numbers you want to treat as categories, but Excel treats them as a data series. When this happens, you can modify the data source to specify exactly which ranges should be treated as category values and which ranges should be treated as data values.

## Modifying a Chart's Data Source

- Click the chart to select it.
- On the CHART TOOLS DESIGN tab, in the Data group, click the Select Data button.
- In the Legend Entries (Series) section of the Select Data Source dialog box, click the Add button to add another data series to the chart, or click the Remove button to remove a data series from the chart.
- Click the Edit button in the Horizontal (Category) Axis Labels section to select the category values for the chart.

The Yearly Gross Income worksheet contains a table that projects the winery's gross income for 2015 through 2024. Carol wants to see a simple line chart of this data.

### To create the line chart:

1. Go to the **Yearly Gross Income** worksheet, and then select the range **B4:C14**.

2. On the ribbon, click the **INSERT** tab.

3. In the Charts group, click the **Insert Line Chart** button [icon].

4. In the 2-D Line charts section, click the **Line with Markers** subtype (the first subtype in the second row). The 2-D line chart is created. See Figure 4-33.

**Figure 4-33    Line chart with Year treated as a data series**

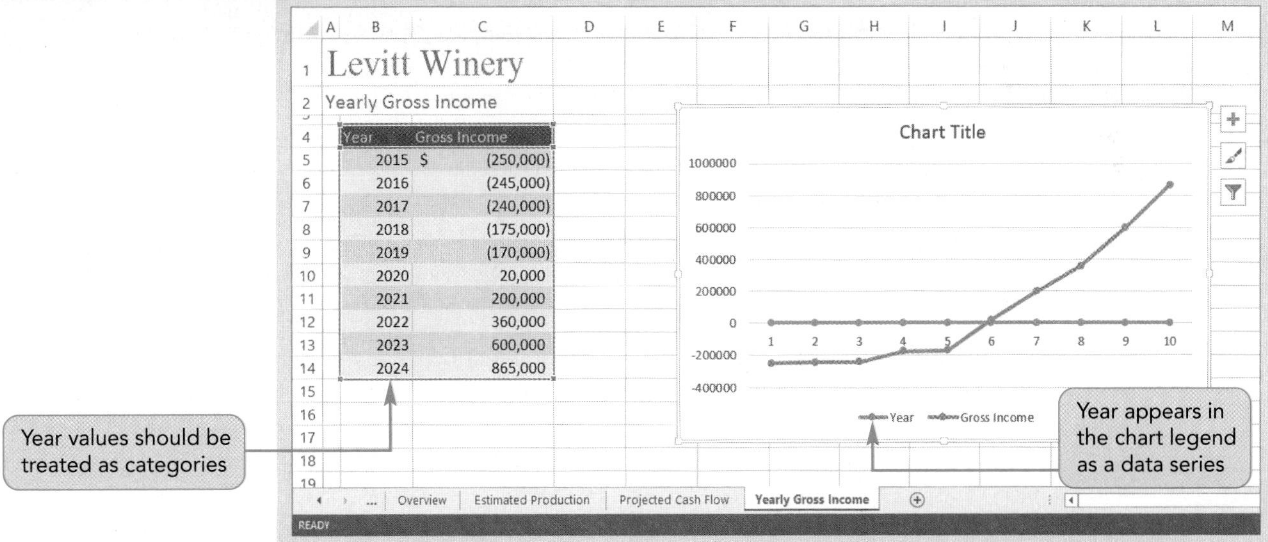

Year values should be treated as categories

Year appears in the chart legend as a data series

The line chart is incorrect because the Year values from the range B5:B14 are treated as another data series rather than category values. The line chart actually doesn't even have category values; the values are charted sequentially from the first value to the tenth. You can correct this problem from the Select Data dialog box by identifying the data series and category values to use in the chart.

## To edit the chart's data source:

> **1.** On the CHART TOOLS DESIGN tab, in the Data group, click the **Select Data** button. The Select Data Source dialog box opens. Note that Year is selected as a legend entry and the category values are simply the numbers 1 through 10. See Figure 4-34.

**Figure 4-34**    **Select Data Source dialog box**

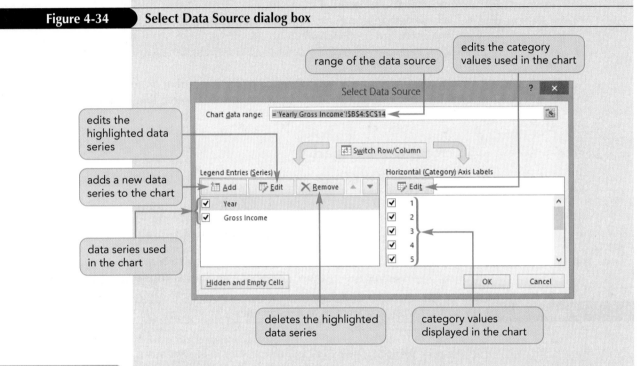

range of the data source

edits the category values used in the chart

edits the highlighted data series

adds a new data series to the chart

data series used in the chart

deletes the highlighted data series

category values displayed in the chart

**TIP**

You can organize your data series in rows rather than columns by clicking the Switch Row/Column button in the Select Data Source dialog box.

> **2.** With Year selected (highlighted in gray) in the list of legend entries, click the **Remove** button. Year is removed from the line chart.

> **3.** Click the **Edit** button for the Horizontal (Category) Axis Labels. You'll specify that Year should be used as the category values.

> **4.** Select the range **B5:B14** containing the Year values, and then click the **OK** button. The values 2015 through 2024 now appear in the list of category values.

> **5.** Click the **OK** button to close the Select Data Source dialog box. The line chart now displays Year as the category values and Gross Income as the only data series. See Figure 4-35.

**Figure 4-35**    **Revised Gross Income line chart**

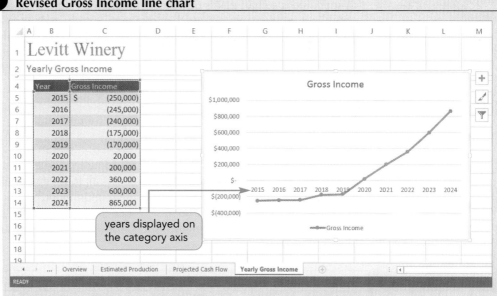

years displayed on the category axis

The Select Data Source dialog box is also useful when you want to add more data series to a chart. For example, if Bob and Carol wanted to include other financial estimates in an existing chart, they could add the data series to the existing chart rather than creating a new chart. To add a data series to a chart, select the chart, click the Select Data button in the Data group on the CHART TOOLS DESIGN tab to open the Select Data Source dialog box, click the Add button, and then select the range for the data series.

**PROSKILLS**

## Decision Making: Choosing the Right Chart

Excel supports a wide variety of charts and chart styles. To decide which type of chart to use, you must evaluate your data and determine the ultimate purpose or goal of the chart. Consider how your data will appear in each type of chart before making a final decision.

- In general, pie charts should be used only when the number of categories is small and the relative sizes of the different slices can be easily distinguished. If you have several categories, use a column or bar chart.
- Line charts are best for categories that follow a sequential order. Be aware, however, that the time intervals must be a constant length if used in a line chart. Line charts will distort data that occurs at irregular time intervals, making it appear that the data values occurred at regular intervals when they did not.
- Pie, column, bar, and line charts assume that numbers are plotted against categories. In science and engineering applications, you will often want to plot two numeric values against one another. For that data, use **XY scatter charts**, which show the patterns or relationship between two or more sets of values. XY scatter charts are also useful for data recorded at irregular time intervals.
- If you still can't find the right chart to meet your needs, you can create a custom chart based on the built-in chart types. Third-party vendors also sell software to allow Excel to create chart types that are not built into the software.

Choosing the right chart and chart style can make your presentation more effective and informative.

# Creating Sparklines

A sparkline is a chart that is displayed entirely within a worksheet cell. Because sparklines are compact in size, they don't include chart elements such as legends, titles, or gridlines. The goal of a sparkline is to convey the maximum amount of information within a very small space. As a result, sparklines are useful when you don't want charts to overwhelm the rest of your worksheet or take up valuable page space.

You can create the following three types of sparklines:

- A line sparkline for highlighting trends
- A column sparkline for column charts
- A win/loss sparkline for highlighting positive and negative values

Figure 4-36 shows examples of each sparkline type. The line sparklines show the sales history from each department and across all four departments of a computer manufacturer. The sparklines provide enough information for you to examine the sales trend within and across departments. Notice that although total sales rose steadily during the year, some departments, such as Printers, showed a sales decline midway through the year.

**Figure 4-36**    Types of sparklines

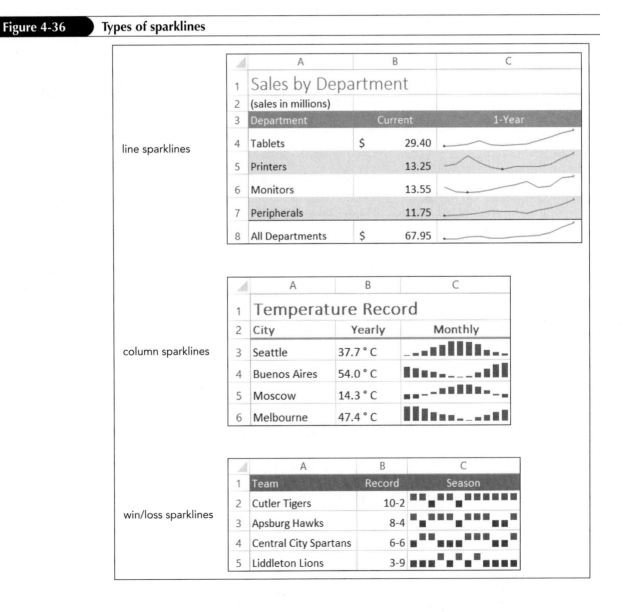

The column sparklines present a record of monthly temperature averages for four cities. Temperatures above 0 degrees Celsius are presented in blue columns; temperatures below 0 degrees Celsius are presented in red columns that extend downward. The height of each column is related to the magnitude of the value it represents.

Finally, the win/loss sparklines reveal a snapshot of the season results for four sports teams. Wins are displayed in blue; losses are in red. From the sparklines, you can quickly see that the Cutler Tigers finished their 10–2 season with six straight wins and the Liddleton Lions finished their 3–9 season with four straight losses.

To create a set of sparklines, you first select the data you want to graph, and then select the location range where you want the sparklines to appear. Note that the cells in which you insert the sparklines do not need to be blank. Sparklines are added as part of the cell background and do not replace any cell content.

## REFERENCE

### Creating and Editing Sparklines

- On the INSERT tab, in the Sparklines group, click the Line, Column, or Win/Loss button.
- In the Data Range box, enter the range for the data source of the sparkline.
- In the Location Range box, enter the range into which to place the sparkline.
- Click the OK button.
- To edit a sparkline's appearance, click the SPARKLINE TOOLS DESIGN tab.
- In the Show group, click the appropriate check boxes to specify which markers to display on the sparkline.
- In the Group group, click the Axis button, and then click Show Axis to add an axis to the sparkline.

The Levitts' business plan involves rolling out the different wine types gradually, starting with Chardonnay and Cabernet Franc and then adding more varietals over the first five years. They won't start producing all six wines until Year 6. They want you to add a column sparkline to the Overview worksheet that displays this 10-year production plan.

### To insert column sparklines showing the 10-year production plan in the Overview worksheet:

1. Go to the **Overview** worksheet, and then select the range **D29:D34**. This is the location range into which you will insert the sparklines.

2. On the INSERT tab, in the Sparklines group, click the **Column** button. The Create Sparklines dialog box opens. The location range is already entered because you selected it before opening the dialog box.

3. With the insertion point in the Data Range box, click the **Estimated Production** sheet tab, and then select the data in the range **C6:L11**. This is the range that contains the data you want to chart in the sparklines.

4. Click the **OK** button. The Create Sparklines dialog box closes and the column sparklines are added to the location range in the Overview worksheet. See Figure 4-37.

**Figure 4-37**  Column sparklines of annual wine production

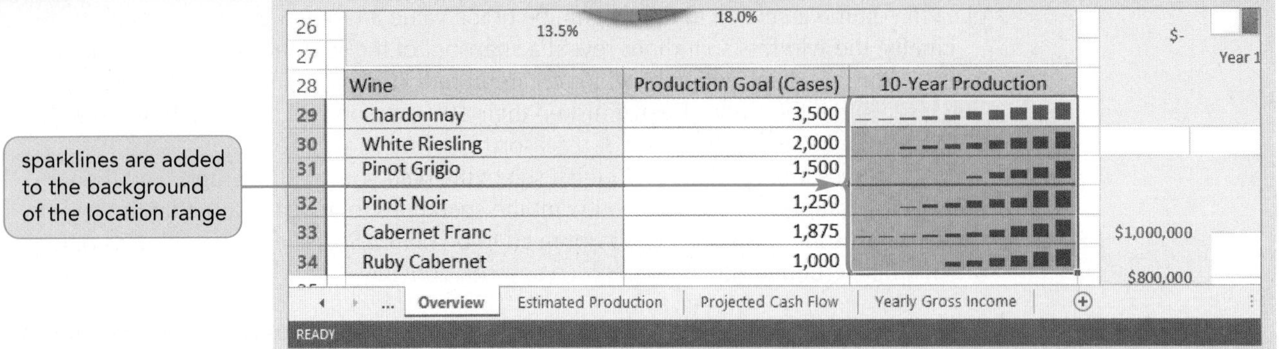

sparklines are added to the background of the location range

The column sparklines make it clear how the wines are placed into production at different times—Chardonnay and Cabernet Franc first, and Pinot Grigio in Year 6. Each wine, once it is introduced, is steadily produced in greater quantities as the decade progresses.

## Formatting the Sparkline Axis

Because of their compact size, you have few formatting options with sparklines. One thing you can change is the scale of the vertical axis. The vertical axis will range from the minimum value to the maximum value. By default, this range is defined differently for each cell to maximize the available space. But this can be misleading. For example, the column sparklines in Figure 4-37 seem to show that Levitt Winery will be producing the same amount of each wine by the end of Year 10 because the heights of the last columns are all the same. You can change the vertical axis scale to be the same for the related sparklines.

Carol and Bob want to use the same vertical axis range for each sparkline showing the 10-year production. You will set the scale of the vertical axis to range from 0 cases to 3500 cases.

**To set the scale of the vertical axis of the column sparklines:**

1. If necessary, select the range **D29:D34**. Because you have selected the sparklines, the SPARKLINE TOOLS DESIGN tab appears on the ribbon.

2. On the SPARKLINE TOOLS DESIGN tab, in the Group group, click the **Axis** button, and then click **Custom Value** in the Vertical Axis Maximum Value Options section. The Sparkline Vertical Axis Setting dialog box opens.

3. Replace the value in the box with **3500**, and then click the **OK** button. You do not have to set the vertical axis minimum value because Excel assumes this to be 0 for all of the column sparklines. The column sparklines are now based on the same vertical scale, and the height of each column is based on the number of cases produced per year.

## Working with Sparkline Groups

The sparklines in the location range are part of a single group. Clicking any cell in the location range selects all of the sparklines in the group. Any formatting you apply to one sparkline affects all of the sparklines in the group, as you saw when you set the range of the vertical axis. This ensures that the sparklines for related data are formatted consistently. To format each sparkline differently, you must first ungroup them.

Carol and Bob think that the column sparklines would look better if they used the same colors as the pie chart for the different wines. You will first ungroup the sparklines so you can format them separately, and then you will apply a different fill color to each sparkline.

### To ungroup and format the column sparklines:

▶ 1. Make sure the range **D29:D34** is still selected.

▶ 2. On the DESIGN tab, in the Group group, click the **Ungroup** button. The sparklines are ungrouped, and selecting any one of the sparklines will no longer select the entire group.

▶ 3. Click cell **D30** to select it and its sparkline.

▶ 4. On the DESIGN tab, in the Style group, click the **Sparkline Color** button, and then click the **Orange, Accent 2, Darker 25%** theme color in the sixth row and fifth column. The fill color of the column sparkline changes to a medium orange.

▶ 5. Click cell **D31**, click the **Sparkline Color** button, and then click the **Gray-50%, Accent 3** theme color.

▶ 6. Set the color of the sparkline in cell **D32** to **Gold, Accent 4**, set the color of the sparkline in cell **D33** to **Green, Accent 6, Lighter 60%**, and then set the color of the sparkline in cell D34 to **Green, Accent 6**.

▶ 7. Select cell **B35** to deselect the sparklines. See Figure 4-38.

**Figure 4-38**  **Formatted sparklines**

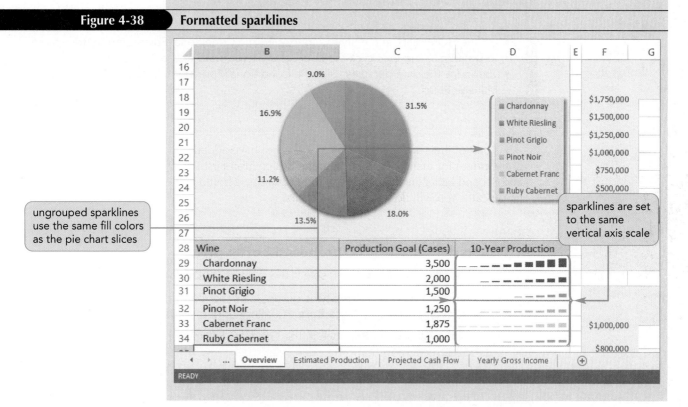

To regroup sparklines, you select all of the cells in the location range containing the sparklines, and then click the Group button in the Group group on the SPARKLINE TOOLS DESIGN tab. Be aware that regrouping sparklines causes them to share a common format, so you will lose any formatting applied to individual sparklines.

The Sparkline Color button applied a single color to the entire sparkline. You can also apply colors to individual markers within a sparkline by clicking the Marker Color button. Using this button, you can set a distinct color for negative values, maximum values, minimum values, first values, and last values. This is useful with line sparklines that track data across a time range in which you might want to identify the maximum value within that range or the minimum value.

# Creating Data Bars

A data bar is a conditional format that adds a horizontal bar to the background of a cell containing a number. When applied to a range of cells, the data bars have the same appearance as a bar chart, with each cell containing one bar. The lengths of data bars are based on the value of each cell in the selected range. Cells with larger values have longer bars; cells with smaller values have shorter bars. Data bars are dynamic, which means that if one cell's value changes, the lengths of the data bars in the selected range are automatically updated.

Data bars differ from sparklines in that the bars are always placed in the cells containing the value they represent, and each cell represents only a single bar from the bar chart. By contrast, a column sparkline can be inserted anywhere within the workbook and can represent data from several rows or columns. However, like sparklines, data bars can be used to create compact graphs that can be easily integrated alongside the text and values stored in worksheet cells.

**REFERENCE**

### Creating Data Bars

- Select the range containing the data you want to chart.
- On the HOME tab, in the Styles group, click the Conditional Formatting button, point to Data Bars, and then click the data bar style you want to use.
- To modify the data bar rules, click the Conditional Formatting button, and then click Manage Rules.

As part of their business plan, Bob and Carol have added a table with the proposed bottle prices for their six wines under the designation First Label (highest quality) and Second Label (average quality). They want these bottle prices to be displayed graphically. You will do this using data bars.

### To add data bars to the proposed bottle prices:

1. In the Overview worksheet, select the range **C38:D43**.

2. On the HOME tab, in the Styles group, click the **Conditional Formatting** button, and then click **Data Bars**. A gallery of data bar styles opens.

3. Click the **Blue Data Bar** style in the Gradient Fill section. Blue data bars are added to each of the bottle price cells.

4. Select cell **B44** to deselect the range. See Figure 4-39.

**Figure 4-39**     **Data bars added to the Overview worksheet**

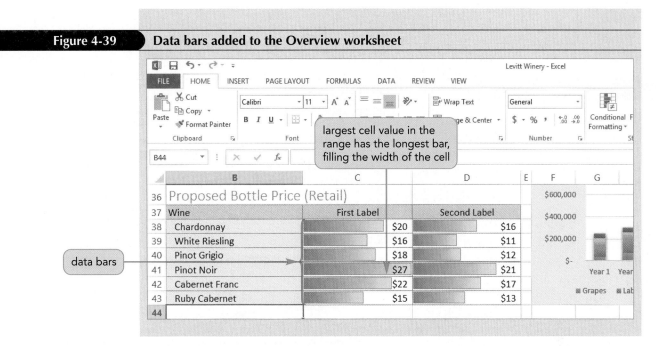

The data bars make it easy to visually compare the proposed prices of the different wines. Pinot Noir will be the most expensive wine sold by the Levitts; White Riesling and Ruby Cabernet will be the least expensive.

## Modifying a Data Bar Rule

The lengths of the data bars are determined based on the values in the selected range. The cell with the largest value contains a data bar that extends across the entire width of the cell, and the lengths of the other bars in the selected range are determined relative to that bar. In some cases, this will result in the longest data bar overlapping its cell's data value, making it difficult to read. You can modify the length of the data bars by altering the rules of the conditional format.

The first label price for Pinot Noir in cell C41 contains the largest value ($27) in the range C38:D43 and has the longest data bar. The data bar for the second label price for Ruby Cabernet ($13) fills only half the cell width by comparison. The Levitts don't want data bars to overlap the cell values. You will change the data bar rule that sets the maximum length of the data bars to 35 so that the longest bar no longer fills the entire cell.

**TIP**

When data bars are used with negative values, the data bars originate from the center of the cell—negative bars extend to the left, and positive bars extend to the right.

### To modify the data bar rule:

‣ 1. Select the range **C38:D43** containing the data bars.

‣ 2. On the HOME tab, in the Styles group, click the **Conditional Formatting** button, and then click **Manage Rules**. The Conditional Formatting Rules Manager dialog box opens, displaying all the rules applied to any conditional format in the workbook.

‣ 3. Make sure **Current Selection** appears in the Show formatting rules for box. You'll edit the rule applied to the current selection—the data bars in the Sectors worksheet.

‣ 4. Click the **Edit Rule** button. The Edit Formatting Rule dialog box opens. You want to modify this rule so that the maximum value for the data bar is set to 35. All data bar lengths will then be defined relative to this value.

‣ 5. In the Type row, click the **Maximum** arrow, and then click **Number**.

▶ **6.** Press the **Tab** key to move the insertion point to the Maximum box in the Value row, and then type **35**. See Figure 4-40.

| Figure 4-40 | Edit Formatting Rule dialog box |

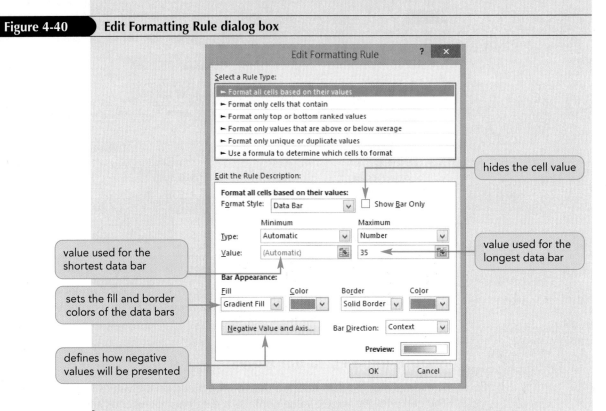

▶ **7.** Click the **OK** button in each dialog box, and then select cell **B44**. The lengths of the data bars are reduced so that the longest bar covers about three-fourths of the cell width. See Figure 4-41.

| Figure 4-41 | Revised data bars |

The data bars provide a good visual of the wine prices.

**INSIGHT**

### Edward Tufte and Chart Design Theory

Any serious study of charts will include the works of Edward Tufte, who pioneered the field of information design. One of Tufte's most important works is *The Visual Display of Quantitative Information*, in which he laid out several principles for the design of charts and graphics.

Tufte was concerned with what he termed as "chart junk," in which a proliferation of chart elements—chosen because they look "nice"—confuse and distract the reader. One measure of chart junk is Tufte's data-ink ratio, which is the amount of "ink" used to display quantitative information compared to the total ink required by the chart. Tufte advocated limiting the use of non-data ink. Non-data ink is any part of the chart that does not convey information about the data. One way of measuring the data-ink ratio is to determine how much of the chart you can erase without affecting the user's ability to interpret the chart. Tufte would argue for high data-ink ratios with a minimum of extraneous elements and graphics.

To this end, Tufte helped develop sparklines, which convey information with a high data-ink ratio within a compact space. Tufte believed that charts that can be viewed and comprehended at a glance have a greater impact on the reader than large and cluttered graphs, no matter how attractive they might be.

## Inserting a Watermark

**TIP**

Fill colors hide a watermark. So if a sheet has a watermark, don't use a fill color for the worksheet background.

Many businesses distinguish works in progress from final versions by including the word "Draft" as a watermark on each page. A **watermark** is text or an image that appears in the background behind other content. You insert a watermark into the header or footer of a worksheet. Even though the watermark is inserted into the header or footer, a large watermark will overflow those sections and appear on the entire sheet. Generally, watermarks are given a "washed-out" appearance and are placed behind text or charts on the sheet so that they don't obscure any of the other content on the sheet. Because the watermark is included in the header/footer section, it is visible in Page Layout view and Page Break Preview but not in Normal view.

Because the current business plan for Levitt Winery will change as Bob and Carol continue to explore their financial options and the status of the wine market, they want to include a watermark with the word "Draft" on the Overview worksheet.

#### To insert a watermark into the worksheet:

1. On the ribbon, click the **PAGE LAYOUT** tab.

2. In the Page Setup group, click the **Dialog Box Launcher** to open the Page Setup dialog box.

3. Click the **Header/Footer** tab to display options for the header or footer of the current worksheet.

4. Click the **Custom Header** button to open the Header dialog box.

5. Click the **Center section** box. You want to insert the watermark in the center section of the header.

6. Click the **Insert Picture** button 🖾 to open the Insert Pictures dialog box.

7. Click the **From a file**, navigate to the **Excel4 ▸ Tutorial** folder included with your Data Files, click the **Draft.png** file, and then click the **Insert** button. Code for the inserted picture is added to the center section of the header. See Figure 4-42.

**Figure 4-42**    Inserting a watermark graphic image

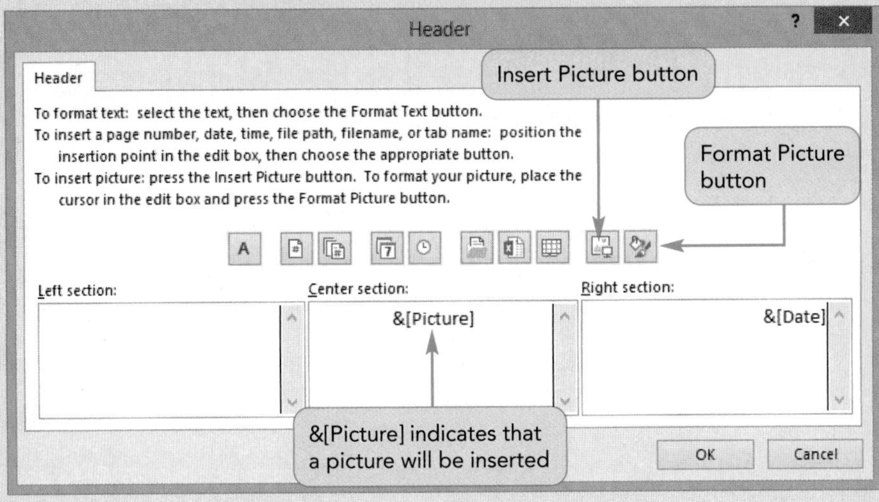

Generally, watermarks are lighter or washed out so that they don't obscure or distract from the sheet content. You can format the appearance of the watermark from the Header dialog box.

## To format the appearance of the watermark:

1. In the Header dialog box, click the **Format Picture** button to open the Format Picture dialog box.

2. Click the **Picture** tab, click the **Color** box, and then click **Washout** from the color options.

3. Click the **OK** button in each dialog box to return to the Page Setup dialog box.

4. Click the **Print Preview** button to preview the printed worksheet in Backstage view. As shown in Figure 4-43, the Draft graphic image appears in the background, faded out so as to not obscure the sheet contents.

| Figure 4-43 | Print preview of the worksheet with the watermark |

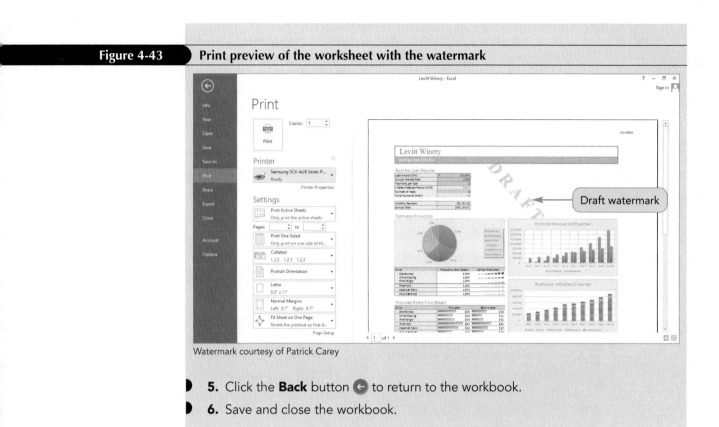

Draft watermark

Watermark courtesy of Patrick Carey

**5.** Click the **Back** button ⊝ to return to the workbook.

**6.** Save and close the workbook.

The Levitts are pleased with the charts and graphics you have created. They provide useful visuals for anyone who is studying the Levitts' proposal.

## Session 4.2 Quick Check

REVIEW

1. What is the difference between a line chart and a scatter chart?
2. A researcher wants to plot weight versus blood pressure. Should the researcher use a line chart or a scatter chart? Explain why.
3. What are major tick marks, minor tick marks, and gridlines?
4. How do you change the scale of a chart axis?
5. What is the difference between the chart area and the plot area?
6. What are sparklines? Describe the three types of sparklines.
7. What are data bars? How do data bars differ from sparklines?
8. What is a watermark?

**ASSESS**

### SAM Projects

Put your skills into practice with SAM Projects! SAM Projects for this tutorial can be found online. If you have a SAM account, go to www.cengage.com/sam2013 to download the most recent Project Instructions and Start Files.

**PRACTICE**

## Review Assignments

**Data Files needed for the Review Assignments: Market.xlsx, Watermark.png**

Another part of Carol and Bob Levitt's business plan for the new Levitt Winery is to analyze current market conditions. The Levitts have created a workbook that explores customer preferences and sales of wine in the United States. The workbook also explores the current wineries in Michigan against which the Levitt Winery will be competing. Bob and Carol asked you to complete their workbook by presenting this data in graphic form using Excel charts. Complete the following:

1. Open the **Market** workbook located in the Excel4 ▸ Review folder included with your Data Files, and then save the workbook as **Market Analysis** in the location specified by your instructor.

2. In the Documentation sheet, enter your name in cell B3 and the date in cell B4.

3. In the Loan Analysis sheet, enter the data values and formulas required to calculate the monthly payment on a business loan of **$225,000** at **8.2** percent annual interest to be repaid in **15** years.

4. In the Market Summary worksheet, use the data in the range E21:F27 showing the types of grapes cultivated by Michigan wineries to create a pie chart comparing production rates. Embed the pie chart in the Market Summary worksheet covering the range B5:G18.

5. Format the pie chart by removing the chart title, applying the Style 11 chart style, and aligning the legend with the right edge of the chart area.

6. In the Michigan Wineries worksheet, create a line chart based on the data in the nonadjacent range B4:B16;F4:F16 showing the increase in the number of wineries in Michigan over the past 12 years. Embed the line chart in the Market Summary worksheet covering the range I5:O16.

7. Format the line chart by making the following changes:
   a. Format the chart with the Style 14 chart style.
   b. Change the chart title to **Michigan Wineries**.
   c. Change the fill color of the chart area to light blue and the plot area to white.
   d. Add primary major vertical gridlines to the plot area.
   e. Change the scale of the primary axis to range from **50** to **140** in steps of **10** units.

8. In the Michigan Wineries worksheet, create a clustered column chart using the data in the range B4:E16 showing the growth of Michigan wineries by region. Embed the chart in the Market Summary worksheet over the range I18:O28.

9. Format the column chart by making the following changes:
   a. Format the chart with the Style 13 chart style.
   b. Change the chart title to **Michigan Wineries** and reduce its font size to 14 points.
   c. Set the fill color of the chart area to light blue and the plot area to white.
   d. Add primary major vertical gridlines to the plot area.

10. In the U.S. Wine Sales worksheet, create a stacked column chart using the data in the range B3:E15 showing the breakout of the wine market into table wines, dessert wines, and sparkling wines or champagne. Embed the stacked column chart in the range B30:G43 of the Market Summary worksheet.

11. Format the stacked column chart by making the following changes:

   a. Format the chart with the Style 6 chart style.

   b. Change the chart title to **U.S. Wine Sales** and set its font size to 14 points.

   c. Add a primary vertical axis title with the text **Millions of Cases** and remove the primary horizontal axis title.

   d. Add primary major vertical gridlines.

   e. Set the fill color of the chart area to light blue and the plot area to white.

12. In the U.S. Wine Consumption worksheet, create a combination chart based on the data in the range B3:D15 showing how much wine Americans consume annually. Display the Gallons (millions) data series as a clustered column chart on the primary axis, and then display the Gallons (per Capita) data series as a line chart on the secondary axis.

13. Move the combination chart to the Market Summary worksheet; embed it over the range I30:O43.

14. Format the combination chart by making the following changes:

   a. Format the chart with the Style 4 chart style.

   b. Change the chart title to **U.S. Wine Consumption** and set its font size to 14 points.

   c. Add the primary axis title **Gallons (millions)** and the secondary axis title **Gallons (per Capita)**. Change the font color of the axis titles and scales to match the column and line markers.

   d. Remove the horizontal axis title and chart legend.

   e. Change the rotation of the secondary axis title to Rotate Text Down.

   f. Change the primary axis scale to range from **650** to **950** in intervals of **50**. Change the scale of the secondary axis to range from **2.2** to **3.0** in steps of **0.1** units.

   g. Change the fill color of the chart area to light blue and the plot area to white.

   h. Add primary major vertical gridlines to the chart.

15. Insert column sparklines in the range G21:G27 of the Market Summary worksheet based on the data in the range C5:N11 of the Michigan Grapes worksheet to show whether the number of wineries growing their own grapes has increased over the past 12 years.

16. Set the axis of the sparklines so that the column heights range from **0** to a maximum of **26** for each sparkline. Ungroup the sparklines and set the color of each to match the color of the corresponding grape in the pie chart.

17. Because the Levitts plan to grow their own grapes rather than purchasing them from out-of-state vendors, they are interested in knowing how many wineries in Michigan also grow their own grapes. The results of their survey are shown in the range B20:C22 in the Market Summary worksheet. Add data bars to the values in the range C20:C22 using the blue gradient fill. Define a rule that sets the maximum length of the data bars in those cells to a value of **100**.

18. Insert the **Watermark.png** graphic file located in the Excel4 ▶ Review folder as a washed-out watermark in the center section of the header of the Market Summary worksheet.

19. Save the workbook, and then close it.

## Case Problem 1

APPLY

Data File needed for this Case Problem: Bertrand.xlsx

*Bertrand Family Budget*   Andrew and Maria Bertrand of Santa Fe, New Mexico, are hoping to purchase their first home and they are using Excel to help manage their family budget. The couple needs to estimate the monthly payments required for a $275,000 mortgage. They want to track their income and expenses using tables, charts, data bars, and sparklines. You will help them do all of these tasks. Complete the following:

1. Open the **Bertrand** workbook located in the Excel4 ▶ Case1 folder included with your Data Files, and then save the workbook as **Bertrand Budget** in the location specified by your instructor.

2. In the Documentation sheet, enter your name in cell B3 and the date in cell B4.

3. In the Budget worksheet, in the range O4:O6, enter the parameters of a **$275,000** loan that is repaid at an annual interest rate of **4.35** percent over **30** years.

4. In the range O8:O9, calculate the total number of months to repay the loan and the interest rate per month.

5. In cell O11, use the PMT function to calculate the monthly payment. Multiply the PMT function by –1 so that the result appears as a positive currency value rather than a negative value.

6. In the range D25:O25, enter the value of the monthly mortgage payment by creating an absolute reference to the value in cell O11.

7. In the range D18:O18, calculate the total income per month. In the range D27:O27, calculate the total expenses incurred each month. In the range D28:O28, calculate the couple's net income (total income minus total expenses) each month.

8. In the range C4:C11, calculate the average monthly value of each expense category.

9. Add green gradient data bars to the values in the range C4:C11. Set the maximum length of the data bars to a value of **2500**.

Explore   10. Insert line sparklines in the range D4:D11 using the expense values in the range D19:O26. On the SPARKLINE TOOLS DESIGN tab, in the Show group, click the High Point check box to mark the high point of each sparkline.

11. Create a clustered column chart of the income, expenses, and net income for each month of the year based on the data in the nonadjacent range D15:O15;D18:O18;D27:O28. Place the chart within the range E2:K13.

12. Format the clustered column chart by making the following changes:

   a. Format the chart with the Style 8 chart style.

   b. Change the chart title to **Income and Expenses** and format it in a Calibri, non-bold 12-point font.

   c. Change the vertical scale of the chart to range from **–1000** to **6500** in steps of **1000**.

   d. Change the series overlap of the columns to **0%** and the gap width to **200%**.

13. Save the workbook.

14. Perform a what-if analysis by changing the length of the loan from 30 years to **15** years. Determine the monthly payments under this new mortgage plan, and then analyze its impact on the couple's projected income and expenses.

15. Save the workbook as **Bertrand Budget 2**, and then close it.

## Case Problem 2

**Data File needed for this Case Problem: PetroChart.xlsx**

*PetroChart Reports*   William Rawlings runs a blog called *PetroChart Reports* that deals with the energy market with special emphasis on crude oil production and consumption. William likes to augment his writing with informative charts and graphics. He has an Excel workbook with some historic data on the crude oil market. He has asked you to create charts from that data that he can use in an article that reviews the history of oil production and consumption, and their impact on the size of the proven world oil reserves. Complete the following:

1. Open the **PetroChart** workbook located in the Excel4 ▸ Case2 folder included with your Data Files, and then save the workbook as **PetroChart Reports**.

2. In the Documentation sheet, enter your name in cell B3 and the date in cell B4.

3. In the World Oil Production worksheet, create a line chart of world oil production from 1980 to 2010 using the data from the range A6:G37. Move the chart to the Summary worksheet covering the range B4:H19.

4. Format the chart with the Style 9 chart style, and then change the chart title to **Oil Production Historic Trends**.

5. Change the line color for the North America data series to white, which is easier to read against the black backdrop.

⊕ **Explore** 6. Revise the vertical axis scale so that the display unit is expressed in terms of thousands (most oil production reports are quoted in terms of thousands of barrels per day). Change the text of the display unit from Thousands to **Thousands of Barrels per Day**.

7. In the World Oil Production worksheet, create a pie chart that displays the relative size of the oil production values for different regions in 2010 based on the data in the nonadjacent range B6:G6;B37:G37. Move the pie chart to the Summary worksheet covering the range J4:P19.

8. Make the following changes to the pie chart:

   a. Format the chart with the Style 7 chart style.

   b. Change the chart title to **2010 Oil Production** and reduce its font size to 14 points.

   c. Move the chart legend to the left edge of the chart area.

   d. Add data labels outside of the pie slices showing the percentage associated with each region.

   e. Change the color of the pie slice for the North America region to white.

9. In the World Oil Consumption worksheet, create a line chart that shows how oil consumption changed from 1980 to 2010 based on the data in the range A6:G37. Move the chart to the Summary worksheet covering the range B21:H36.

10. Change the chart title to **Oil Consumption Historic Trends**.

⊕ **Explore** 11. Copy the Oil Production Historic Trends line chart. Use Paste Special to paste the format of that chart into the Oil Consumption Historic Trends line chart.

12. In the World Oil Consumption worksheet, create a pie chart showing the 2010 regional breakdown of oil consumption based on the data in the range B6:G6;B37:G37. Move the chart to the Summary worksheet covering the range J21:P36.

⊕ **Explore** 13. Change the chart title to **2010 Oil Consumption**. Use Paste Special to copy the 2010 Oil Production pie chart and paste its format into the 2010 Oil Consumption pie chart.

14. There was a fear that with increased oil production and consumption from 1980 to 2010, there would be decreasing amounts of proven reserves. Was this the case? In the Proven Reserves worksheet, create a combination chart based on the data in the range A5:D36. Display the Oil Production and Oil Consumption data series as line charts on the primary axis. Display the Proven Reserves data series as an area chart on the secondary axis. Move the chart to the Summary worksheet covering the range E38:M53.

15. Make the following changes to the combination chart:

   a. Format the chart with the Style 6 chart style.

   b. Change the chart title to **Historic Trends in Proven Oil Reserves**; reduce the font size to 12 points.

   c. Change the primary axis scale to range from **50,000** to **90,000** in steps of **5,000**.

   d. Change the line color of the Oil Production data series to white.

16. Save the workbook, and then close it.

## Case Problem 3

Data Files needed for this Case Problem: Frame.xlsx, Confidential.png

*Frame Financial*  Jeri Carbone is the owner of Frame Financial, a small financial consulting firm in Marion, Iowa. Among her many tasks is to maintain Excel workbooks with information on companies and their stock market activity. One of her workbooks contains information on Harriman Scientific, a company traded on the stock exchange. She wants you to complete the workbook by adding charts that describe the company's financial status and stock charts to display recent values of the company's stock. The stock chart should display the stock's daily opening, high, low, and closing values, and the number of shares traded for each day of the past few weeks. The volume of shares traded should be expressed in terms of millions of shares. Complete the following:

1. Open the **Frame** workbook located in the Excel4 ▸ Case3 folder included with your Data Files, and then save the workbook as **Frame Financial** in the location specified by your instructor.

2. In the Documentation sheet, enter your name in cell B3 and the date in cell B4.

3. Insert the **Confidential.png** graphics file located in the Excel4 ▸ Case3 folder as a washed-out watermark in the center section of the header of the Documentation worksheet.

4. In the Overview worksheet, create a 3-D pie chart describing the company's shareholders based on the data source values in the range K4:L6.

5. Remove the chart title and chart legend, and then resize the chart so that it is contained within the range M3:O7.

6. Change the fill colors of the ranges K4:L4, K5:L5, and K6:L6 to match their corresponding pie slice colors. Change the font color in those ranges to white.

7. Add pink gradient-colored data bars to the values in the range L10:O14. Edit the data bar rules so that the maximum data bar length corresponds to a value of **15,000**, and the bar direction goes from right to left.

8. In the Income Statement worksheet, create a 3-D clustered column chart of the company's net revenue and operating expenses using the data values in the nonadjacent range B4:F4;B6:F6;B12:F12. Move the chart to the Overview worksheet.

⊕ **Explore** 9. On the CHART TOOLS FORMAT tab, use the Size group to set the height of the chart to 2.44″ and the width to 3.51″. Move the chart so that its upper-left corner is aligned with the upper-left corner of cell B17.

10. Format the chart with the Style 11 chart style, change the chart title to **Revenue and Expenses**, and then reduce the font size of the chart title to 11 points.

11. In the Balance Sheet worksheet, create a 3-D clustered column chart of the company's assets and liabilities using the data in the range B4:F4;B18:F18;B26:F26. Move the chart to the Overview worksheet. Set its size to 2.44″ high by 3.51″ wide and place the chart so that it is directly to the right of the Revenue and Expenses chart.

⊕ **Explore** 12. Change the chart title to **Assets and Liabilities**. Copy and paste the format used with the Revenue and Expenses chart into this chart.

13. In the Cash Flow Statement worksheet, create a 2-D line chart of the data in the range C4:F4;C28:F28. Move the chart to the Overview worksheet. Resize the chart to 2.44″ high by 3.51″ wide and place the chart directly to the right of the Assets and Liabilities chart.

14. In the line chart, apply the Style 15 chart style, change the chart title to **Net Cash Flow**, and then reduce the font size of the chart title to 11 points.

15. In the Income Statement, Balance Sheet, and Cash Flow Statement worksheets, add line sparklines in the Trend column based on the financial values for 2012 through 2015.

⊕ **Explore** 16. In the Stock Values worksheet, select the range A4:F34, and then insert a Volume-Open-High-Low-Close stock chart.

⊕ **Explore** 17. Move the chart to a new chart sheet named **Stock History**.

18. Make the following changes to the stock chart:

   a. Change the chart title to **Recent Stock History** and increase the font size to 24 points.

   b. Set the font size of the horizontal and vertical axes to 12 points.

   c. Add Axis titles to the chart. Set the primary vertical axis title to **Volume of Shares Traded**, the secondary vertical axis title to **Stock Value**, and the horizontal axis title to **Date**.

   d. Set the font size of the axis titles to 16 points and rotate the text of the secondary axis title down.

   e. Remove the chart legend.

   f. Change the scale of the primary vertical axis to range from **200,000** to **2,000,000**, and then change the display unit of the primary vertical axis to Thousands.

   g. Change the scale of the secondary vertical axis to range from **10** to **35**.

   h. Add primary major horizontal and vertical gridlines, and remove any secondary gridlines.

   i. Set the gap width of the columns in the stock chart to **20%**.

19. Save the workbook, and then close it.

**TROUBLESHOOT**

## Case Problem 4

Data File needed for this Case Problem: Mortgage.xlsx

***The Mortgage White Paper***    Kyle Lewis of Rockford, Illinois, runs a newsletter and blog called *The Mortgage White Paper* containing valuable financial information for investors, entrepreneurs, and homeowners. Kyle's emphasis is on tracking the world of home mortgages and home equity loans. Kyle's assistant has been creating an Excel workbook with an updated listing of the 15-year and 30-year interest rates on home loans. Now, his assistant reports that the formulas and charts in the workbook aren't working correctly. Kyle has asked you to fix the problems and finish the workbook. Complete the following:

1. Open the **Mortgage** workbook located in the Excel4 ▸ Case4 folder included with your Data Files, and then save the workbook as **Mortgage Report**.

2. In the Documentation sheet, enter your name in cell B3 and the date in cell B4.

3. In the Mortgage Calculator worksheet, calculate the monthly payments required to repay loans of different amounts, which are listed in the range A9:A24. The annual interest rate and length of the loan in years are provided in the range B5:C6 for 15-year and 30-year fixed loans.

⚙ **Troubleshoot** 4. The formulas used to calculate the monthly payments are displaying error values. Kyle is sure that the value in cell B9 is correct, but something happened when the formula was copied to the range B9:C24. Make the necessary changes so that the formula results are shown instead of the error values.

⚙ **Troubleshoot** 5. The line chart that displays the monthly payments for the 15-year and 30-year fixed rate loans is showing the loan amounts plotted as a third data series rather than as category values. Find the problem and fix it.

6. Format the line chart with the chart style and design you think is most appropriate for the data. Make sure the finished chart is easy to read and interpret.

⚙ **Troubleshoot** 7. In the Mortgage Trends worksheet, the data bars that were added to the Mortgage Application Index values in the range D7:D56 all have the same length. Fix the data bars so that reasonable bar lengths are displayed in the cells.

8. Create a combination chart that displays the 15-year and 30-year fixed rates in a line chart on the primary axis, and the Mortgage Application Index in an area chart on the secondary axis. Move and resize the chart to cover the range F6:M22.

9. Make the following changes to the chart:

   a. Format the chart with the Style 1 chart style.

   b. Change the chart title to **Interest Rates vs. Mortgage Applications** and reduce the font size of the title text to 14 points.

   c. Move the legend to the bottom of the chart area.

   d. Add the axis title **Interest Rate** to the primary vertical axis, and then add the axis title **Application Index** to the secondary vertical axis.

   e. Rotate the text of the secondary vertical axis title down.

   f. Change the scale of the primary vertical axis to range from 2 percent to 4.5 percent in increments of 0.5 percent, and then change the scale of the secondary vertical axis to range from 500 to 1000 in increments of 50.

   g. Add primary major vertical gridlines to the plot area.

   h. Set the fill color of the plot area to white and the fill color of the chart area to Brown, Accent 3, Lighter 80%.

10. Save the workbook.

11. Return to the Mortgage Calculator worksheet. One of Kyle's clients wants to take out a $200,000 mortgage but can afford only an $850 monthly payment. Use Goal Seek to determine how low the 30-year fixed rate needs to be to meet that goal.

12. Save the workbook as **Mortgage Report 2**, and then close it.

# ✔ Decision Making

## Creating a Budget Worksheet to Make Financial Decisions

Decision making is the process of choosing between alternative courses of action, usually in response to a problem that needs to be solved. Having an understanding of decision-making processes will lead to better decisions and greater confidence in carrying out those decisions. This is especially important when making financial decisions.

### Gather Relevant Information

Begin by collecting data and information related to the decision you need to make. This information can include data expressed as currency or numbers, as well as data that cannot be measured numerically. For example, when creating a budget, numerical data includes your income and expenses, current savings, future savings and purchases, and so on. Other data might include the amount of savings you need in order to feel comfortable before making a large purchase, such as buying a car or paying tuition.

### Evaluate the Gathered Information and Develop Alternatives

Evaluate the data you collected and determine possible alternatives. Excel workbooks are well suited to evaluating numerical data. You can also use workbooks to evaluate potential outcomes based on other data by assigning numerical weights to them. For example, you can enter your monthly income and fixed expenses into a worksheet along with variable expenses to determine your cash flow. You can then consider this information along with your current savings to determine how much money to contribute to savings or earmark for a purchase. Based on these results, you can develop alternatives for how to distribute your available money among variable expenses (such as entertainment), savings, and a large purchase.

### Select the Best Alternative

Carefully evaluate the alternatives you developed based on your analysis. Before making a decision, be sure to take into account all factors. Consider such questions as:

- Does this alternative make sense for the long term? For example, does this budget allow you to achieve all your financial goals?
- Can you realistically carry out this alternative? For example, does this budget provide enough for necessities such as food and housing as well as for luxuries such as entertainment?
- Will this alternative be acceptable even if its outcome is not perfect or some unconsidered factors emerge? For example, will this budget cover unforeseen expenses such as car repairs or an unexpected trip?
- How comfortable are you with this decision? For example, does this budget relieve or add stress about managing your finances?

After analyzing all the factors, one alternative should begin to emerge as the best alternative. If it doesn't, you might need to develop additional alternatives.

# Prepare an Action Plan

After making a decision, you need to plan how to implement that decision. Consider what steps you need to take to achieve the final outcome. For example, do you need to open a bank account or change services to reduce expenses (such as switching to a less expensive cell phone plan)? Determine a reasonable time table. When do you want to start? How long will each task take? What tasks must be completed before others start? Can tasks be performed at the same time? Develop milestones to track the success of your plan. For example, one milestone might be to increase your savings by 10 percent in three months. Finally, identify what resources you need to be successful. For example, do you need to talk to a financial advisor at your bank?

# Take Action and Monitor the Results

After you develop the action plan, the actual plan begins. For example, you can open bank accounts, change telephone services, and so forth as outlined in your action plan. Be sure to check off completed tasks and assess how well those actions produce the desired outcome. For example, is the budget achieving the financial goals you set? If so, then continue to follow the established plan. If not, you may need to modify the action plan or reevaluate your decision.

## PROSKILLS

### Develop a Budget Worksheet

Excel is valuable to a wide audience of users: from accountants of Fortune 500 companies to homeowners managing their budgets. An Excel workbook can be a complex document, recording data from thousands of financial transactions, or it can track a few monthly household expenses. Anyone who has to balance a budget, track expenses, or project future income can use the financial tools in Excel to help them make good financial decisions about their financing and future expenditures.

In this exercise, you will use Excel to create a sample budget workbook that will contain information of your choice, using the Excel skills and features presented in Tutorials 1 through 4. Use the following steps as a guide to completing your workbook.

**Note:** Please be sure **not** to include any personal information of a sensitive nature in any workbooks you create to be submitted to your instructor for this exercise. Later, you can update the workbooks with such information for your personal use.

1. Gather the data related to your monthly cash inflows and outflows. For example, how much do you take home in your paychecks each month? What other sources of income do you have? What expenses do you have—rent, utilities, gas, insurance, groceries, entertainment, car payments, and so on?
2. Create a new workbook for the sample financial data. Use the first worksheet as a documentation sheet that includes your name, the date on which you start creating the workbook, and a brief description of the workbook's purpose.
3. Plan the structure of the second worksheet, which will contain the budget. Include a section to enter values that remain consistent from month to month, such as monthly income and expenses. As you develop the budget worksheet, reference these cells in formulas that require those values. Later, you can update any of these values and see the changes immediately reflected throughout the budget.
4. In the budget worksheet, enter realistic monthly earnings for each month of the year. Use formulas to calculate the total earnings each month, the average monthly earnings, and the total earnings for the entire year.
5. In the budget worksheet, enter realistic personal expenses for each month. Divide the expenses into at least three categories, providing subtotals for each category and a grand total of all the monthly expenses. Calculate the average monthly expenses and total expenses for the year.
6. Calculate the monthly net cash flow (the value of total income minus total expenses).

7. Use the cash flow values to track the savings throughout the year. Use a realistic amount for savings at the beginning of the year. Use the monthly net cash flow values to add or subtract from this value. Project the end-of-year balance in the savings account under your proposed budget.

8. Format the worksheet's contents using appropriate text and number formats. Add colors and borders to make the content easier to read and interpret. Use cell styles and themes to provide your worksheet with a uniform appearance.

9. Use conditional formatting to automatically highlight negative net cash flow months.

10. Insert a pie chart that compares the monthly expenses for the categories.

11. Insert a column chart that charts all of the monthly expenses regardless of the category.

12. Insert a line chart or sparkline that shows the change in the savings balance throughout the 12 months of the year.

13. Insert new rows at the top of the worksheet and enter titles that describe the worksheet's contents.

14. Examine your assumptions. How likely are certain events to occur? Perform several what-if analyses on your budget, providing the impact of (a) reducing income with expenses remaining constant; (b) increasing expenses with income remaining constant; (c) reducing income and expenses; and (d) increasing income and expenses. Discuss the different scenarios you explored. How much cushion does your projected income give you if expenses increase? What are some things you can do in your budget to accommodate this scenario?

15. Think of a major purchase you might want to make—for example, a car or a house. Determine the amount of the purchase and the current annual interest rate charged by your local bank. Provide a reasonable length of time to repay the loan, such as five years for a car loan or 20 to 30 years for a home loan. Use the PMT function to determine how much you would have to spend each month on the payments for your purchase. You can do these calculations in a separate worksheet.

16. Add the loan information to your monthly budget and evaluate the purchase of this item on your budget. Is it affordable? Examine other possible loans you might pursue and evaluate their impact on your budget. Come up with the most realistic way of paying off the loan while still maintaining a reasonable monthly cash flow and a cushion against unexpected expenses. If the payment exceeds your budget, reduce the estimated price of the item you're thinking of purchasing until you determine the monthly payment you can afford under the conditions of the loan.

17. After settling on a budget and the terms of a loan that you can afford, develop an action plan for putting your budget into place. What are some potential pitfalls that will prohibit you from following through on your proposed budget? How can you increase the likelihood that you will follow the budget? Be specific, and write down a list of goals and benchmarks that you'll use to monitor your progress in following your financial plan.

18. With the worksheet set up and your budget in place, you can take action and monitor your results. You will want to update your worksheet each month as income or expense items change to be sure you remain on track to meet your goals. You will also want to confirm that you made a good decision. If not, evaluate your budget and determine what new action you need to take to get yourself back on track.

19. Format the worksheets for your printer. Include headers and footers that display the workbook filename, the workbook's author, and the date on which the report is printed. If the report extends across several pages, repeat appropriate print titles on all of the pages, and include page numbers and the total number of pages on every printed page.

20. Save and close the workbook.

# Creating a Database

*Tracking Patient, Visit, and Billing Data*

**ACCESS**

## OBJECTIVES

**Session 1.1**
- Learn basic database concepts and terms
- Start and exit Access
- Explore the Microsoft Access window and Backstage view
- Create a blank database
- Create and save a table in Datasheet view
- Enter field names and records in a table datasheet
- Open a table using the Navigation Pane

**Session 1.2**
- Open an Access database
- Copy and paste records from another Access database
- Navigate a table datasheet
- Create and navigate a simple query
- Create and navigate a simple form
- Create, preview, navigate, and print a simple report
- Use Help in Access
- Learn how to compact, back up, and restore a database

## Case | *Chatham Community Health Services*

Chatham Community Health Services, a nonprofit health clinic located in Hartford, Connecticut, provides a range of medical services to patients of all ages. The clinic specializes in the areas of pulmonology, cardiac care, and chronic disease management. Cindi Rodriguez, the office manager for Chatham Community Health Services, oversees a small staff and is responsible for maintaining the medical records of the clinic's patients.

In order to best manage the clinic, Cindi and her staff rely on electronic medical records for patient information, billing, inventory control, purchasing, and accounts payable. Several months ago, the clinic upgraded to **Microsoft Access 2013** (or simply **Access**), a computer program used to enter, maintain, and retrieve related data in a format known as a database. Cindi and her staff want to use Access to store information about patients, billing, vendors, and products. She asks for your help in creating the necessary Access database.

## STARTING DATA FILES

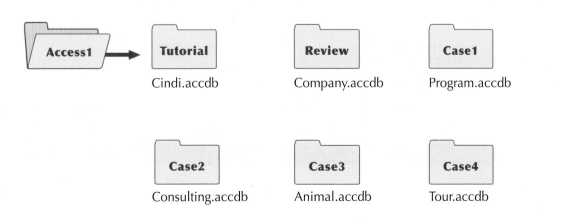

Access1 → Tutorial
Cindi.accdb

Review
Company.accdb

Case1
Program.accdb

Case2
Consulting.accdb

Case3
Animal.accdb

Case4
Tour.accdb

# Session 1.1 Visual Overview:

The **Quick Access Toolbar** provides one-click access to commonly used commands, such as Save.

The **Shutter Bar Open/Close Button** allows you to close and open the Navigation Pane; you might want to close the pane so that you have more room on the screen to view the object's contents.

| | | | | | | TABLE TOOLS |
|---|---|---|---|---|---|---|
| FILE | HOME | CREATE | EXTERNAL DATA | DATABASE TOOLS | FIELDS | TABL |

View

AB Short Text

12 Number

Currency

Date & Time
Yes/No
More Fields

Delete

Name & Caption
Default Value
Field Size

Modify Lookups

Views          Add & Delete          Properties

All Access Obje...

Search...

**Tables**

Table1

**Table1**

ID    Click to Add

＊    (New)

Access assigns the default name "Table1" to the first new table you create. When you save the table, you can give it a more meaningful name.

By default, Access creates the **ID field** as the primary key field for all new tables.

The **Click to Add column** provides another way for you to add new fields to a table.

The **Add & Delete group** contains options for adding different types of fields, including Short Text and Number, to a table.

The **FIELDS tab** provides options for adding, removing, and formatting the fields in a table.

The **Navigation Pane** lists all the objects (tables, reports, and so on) in the database, and it is the main control center for opening and working with database objects.

**Datasheet view** shows the table's contents as a datasheet.

Record: 14  ◄  1 of 1  ►  ►I ►  No Filter  Search

Datasheet View

# The Access Window

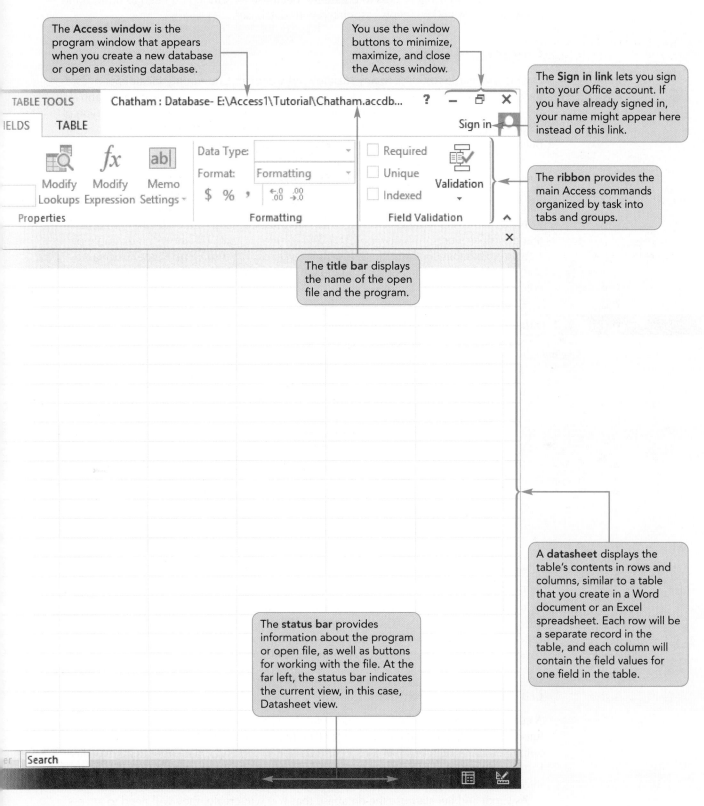

The **Access window** is the program window that appears when you create a new database or open an existing database.

You use the window buttons to minimize, maximize, and close the Access window.

The **Sign in link** lets you sign into your Office account. If you have already signed in, your name might appear here instead of this link.

The **ribbon** provides the main Access commands organized by task into tabs and groups.

The **title bar** displays the name of the open file and the program.

A **datasheet** displays the table's contents in rows and columns, similar to a table that you create in a Word document or an Excel spreadsheet. Each row will be a separate record in the table, and each column will contain the field values for one field in the table.

The **status bar** provides information about the program or open file, as well as buttons for working with the file. At the far left, the status bar indicates the current view, in this case, Datasheet view.

Within the window image:

TABLE TOOLS

IELDS    TABLE

Chatham : Database- E:\Access1\Tutorial\Chatham.accdb...    ?    —    □    ×

Sign in

Modify Lookups    Modify Expression    Memo Settings ▾

Data Type:    ▾

Format:    Formatting    ▾

$  %  ,    ←.0  .00
          .00  →.0

Required
Unique
Indexed

Validation

Properties    Formatting    Field Validation

Search

# Introduction to Database Concepts

Before you begin using Access to create the database for Cindi, you need to understand a few key terms and concepts associated with databases.

## Organizing Data

Data is a valuable resource to any business. At Chatham Community Health Services, for example, important data includes patients' names and addresses, visit dates, and billing information. Organizing, storing, maintaining, retrieving, and sorting this type of data are critical activities that enable a business to find and use information effectively. Before storing data on a computer, however, you must organize the data.

Your first step in organizing data is to identify the individual fields. A **field** is a single characteristic or attribute of a person, place, object, event, or idea. For example, some of the many fields that Chatham Community Health Services tracks are patient ID, first name, last name, address, phone number, visit date, reason for visit, and invoice amount.

Next, you group related fields together into tables. A **table** is a collection of fields that describes a person, place, object, event, or idea. Figure 1-1 shows an example of a Patient table that contains the following four fields: PatientID, FirstName, LastName, and Phone. Each field is a column in the table, with the field name displayed as the column heading.

| Figure 1-1 | Data organization for a table of patients |
|---|---|

| PatientID | FirstName | LastName | Phone |
|---|---|---|---|
| 22501 | Edward | Darcy | 860-305-3985 |
| 22504 | Lilian | Aguilar | 860-374-5724 |
| 22510 | Thomas | Booker | 860-661-2539 |
| 22512 | Lisa | Chang | 860-226-6034 |
| 22529 | Robert | Goldberg | 860-552-2873 |
| 22537 | Amrita | Mehta | 860-552-0375 |

© 2014 Cengage Learning

The specific content of a field is called the **field value**. In Figure 1-1, the first set of field values for PatientID, FirstName, LastName, and Phone are, respectively: 22501; Edward; Darcy; and 860-305-3985. This set of field values is called a **record**. In the Patient table, the data for each patient is stored as a separate record. Figure 1-1 shows six records; each row of field values in the table is a record.

## Databases and Relationships

A collection of related tables is called a **database**, or a **relational database**. In this tutorial, you will create the database for Chatham Community Health Services, and within that database, you'll create a table named Visit to store data about patient visits. Later on, you'll create two more tables, named Patient and Billing, to store related information about patients and their invoices.

As Cindi and her staff use the database that you will create, they will need to access information about patients and their visits. To obtain this information, you must have a way to connect records in the Patient table to records in the Visit table. You connect the records in the separate tables through a **common field** that appears in both tables.

In the sample database shown in Figure 1-2, each record in the Patient table has a field named PatientID, which is also a field in the Visit table. For example, Robert Goldberg is the fifth patient in the Patient table and has a PatientID field value of 22529. This same PatientID field value, 22529, appears in two records in the Visit table. Therefore, Robert Goldberg is the patient who made these two visits.

| **Figure 1-2** | **Database relationship between tables for patients and visits** |
|---|---|

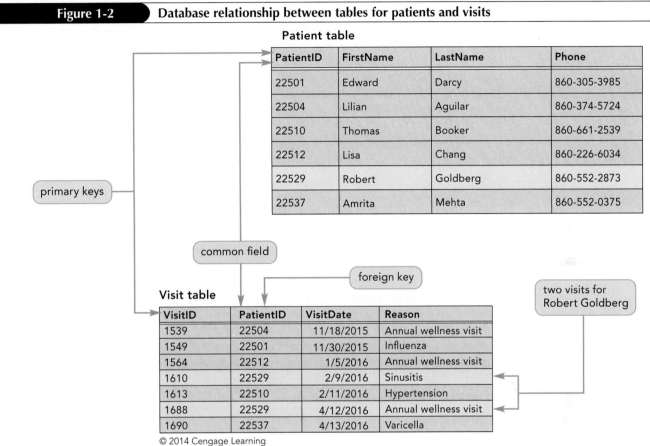

**Patient table**

| PatientID | FirstName | LastName | Phone |
|---|---|---|---|
| 22501 | Edward | Darcy | 860-305-3985 |
| 22504 | Lilian | Aguilar | 860-374-5724 |
| 22510 | Thomas | Booker | 860-661-2539 |
| 22512 | Lisa | Chang | 860-226-6034 |
| 22529 | Robert | Goldberg | 860-552-2873 |
| 22537 | Amrita | Mehta | 860-552-0375 |

primary keys

common field

foreign key

two visits for Robert Goldberg

**Visit table**

| VisitID | PatientID | VisitDate | Reason |
|---|---|---|---|
| 1539 | 22504 | 11/18/2015 | Annual wellness visit |
| 1549 | 22501 | 11/30/2015 | Influenza |
| 1564 | 22512 | 1/5/2016 | Annual wellness visit |
| 1610 | 22529 | 2/9/2016 | Sinusitis |
| 1613 | 22510 | 2/11/2016 | Hypertension |
| 1688 | 22529 | 4/12/2016 | Annual wellness visit |
| 1690 | 22537 | 4/13/2016 | Varicella |

© 2014 Cengage Learning

Each PatientID value in the Patient table must be unique so that you can distinguish one patient from another. These unique PatientID values also identify each patient's specific visits in the Visit table. The PatientID field is referred to as the primary key of the Patient table. A **primary key** is a field, or a collection of fields, whose values uniquely identify each record in a table. No two records can contain the same value for the primary key field. In the Visit table, the VisitID field is the primary key because Chatham Community Health Services assigns each visit a unique identification number.

When you include the primary key from one table as a field in a second table to form a relationship between the two tables, it is called a **foreign key** in the second table, as shown in Figure 1-2. For example, PatientID is the primary key in the Patient table and a foreign key in the Visit table. The PatientID field must have the same characteristics in both tables. Although the primary key PatientID contains unique values in the Patient table, the same field as a foreign key in the Visit table does not necessarily contain unique values. The PatientID value 22529, for example, appears two times in the Visit table because Robert Goldberg made two visits to the clinic. Each foreign key value, however, must match one of the field values for the primary key in the other table. In the example shown in Figure 1-2, each PatientID value in the Visit table must match a PatientID value in the Patient table. The two tables are related, enabling users to connect the facts about patients with the facts about their visits to the clinic.

**INSIGHT**

### Storing Data in Separate Tables

When you create a database, you must create separate tables that contain only fields that are directly related to each other. For example, in the Chatham database, the patient and visit data should not be stored in the same table because doing so would make the data difficult to update and prone to errors. Consider the patient Robert Goldberg and his visits to the clinic, and assume that he has many more than just two visits. If all the patient and visit data were stored in the same table, so that each record (row) contained all the information about each visit and the patient, the patient data would appear multiple times in the table. This causes problems when the data changes. For example, if Robert Goldberg's phone number changed, you would have to update the multiple occurrences of the phone number throughout the table. Not only would this be time-consuming, it would increase the likelihood of errors or inconsistent data.

## Relational Database Management Systems

To manage its databases, a company uses a database management system. A **database management system (DBMS)** is a software program that lets you create databases and then manipulate the data they contain. Most of today's database management systems, including Access, are called relational database management systems. In a **relational database management system**, data is organized as a collection of tables. As stated earlier, a relationship between two tables in a relational DBMS is formed through a common field.

A relational DBMS controls the storage of databases and facilitates the creation, manipulation, and reporting of data, as illustrated in Figure 1-3.

| Figure 1-3 | Relational database management system |
| --- | --- |

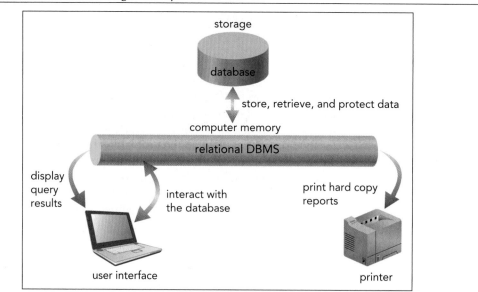

© 2014 Cengage Learning

Specifically, a relational DBMS provides the following functions:

- It allows you to create database structures containing fields, tables, and table relationships.
- It lets you easily add new records, change field values in existing records, and delete records.
- It contains a built-in query language, which lets you obtain immediate answers to the questions (or queries) you ask about your data.
- It contains a built-in report generator, which lets you produce professional-looking, formatted reports from your data.
- It protects databases through security, control, and recovery facilities.

An organization such as Chatham Community Health Services benefits from a relational DBMS because it allows users working in different groups to share the same data. More than one user can enter data into a database, and more than one user can retrieve and analyze data that other users have entered. For example, the database for Chatham Community Health Services will contain only one copy of the Visit table, and all employees will use it to access visit information.

Finally, unlike other software programs, such as spreadsheet programs, a DBMS can handle massive amounts of data and can be used to create relationships among multiple tables. Each Access database, for example, can be up to two gigabytes in size, can contain up to 32,768 objects (tables, reports, and so on), and can have up to 255 people using the database at the same time. For instructional purposes, the databases you will create and work with throughout this text contain a relatively small number of records compared to databases you would encounter outside the classroom, which would likely contain tables with very large numbers of records.

# Starting Access and Creating a Database

Now that you've learned some database terms and concepts, you're ready to start Access and create the Chatham database for Cindi.

**To start Access:**

▶ **1.** Display the Windows Start screen, if necessary.

   **Using Windows 7?** To complete Step 1, click the Start button on the taskbar.

▶ **2.** Click the **Access 2013** tile. Access starts and displays the Recent screen in Backstage view. See Figure 1-4.

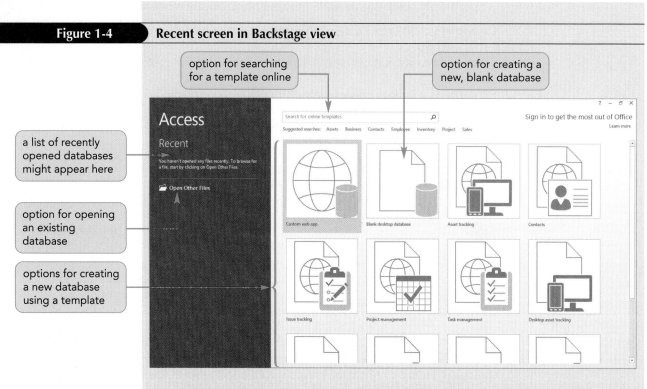

**Trouble?** If you don't see the Access 2013 tile on your Start screen, type Access to display the Apps screen with the Access 2013 tile highlighted, and then click the tile.

**Using Windows 7?** To complete Step 2, point to All Programs on the Start menu, click Microsoft Office 2013, and then click Access 2013.

When you start Access, the first screen that appears is Backstage view, which is the starting place for your work in Access. **Backstage view** contains commands that allow you to manage Access files and options. The Recent screen in Backstage view provides options for you to create a new database or open an existing database. To create a new database that does not contain any data or objects, you use the Blank desktop database option. If the database you need to create contains objects that match those found in common databases, such as databases that store data about contacts or tasks, you can use one of the templates provided with Access. A **template** is a predesigned database that includes professionally designed tables, reports, and other database objects that can make it quick and easy for you to create a database. You can also search for a template online using the Search box.

In this case, the templates provided do not match Cindi's needs for the clinic's database, so you need to create a new, blank database from scratch.

### To create the new Chatham database:

1. Make sure you have the Access starting Data Files on your computer.

   **Trouble?** If you don't have the starting Data Files, you need to get them before you can proceed. Your instructor will either give you the Data Files or ask you to obtain them from a specified location (such as a network drive). If you have any questions about the Data Files, see your instructor or technical support person for assistance.

Be sure to type **Chatham** or you'll create a database named Database1.

**2.** Click the **Blank desktop database** option (see Figure1-4). The Blank desktop database screen opens.

**3.** In the File Name box, type **Chatham** to replace the selected database name provided by Access, Database1. Next you need to specify the location for the file.

**4.** Click the **Browse** button to the right of the File Name box. The File New Database dialog box opens.

**5.** Navigate to the drive and folder where you are storing your files, as specified by your instructor.

**6.** Make sure the "Save as type" box displays "Microsoft Access 2007 – 2013 Databases."

**Trouble?** If your computer is set up to show filename extensions, you will see the Access filename extension ".accdb" in the File name box.

**TIP**

If you don't type the filename extension, Access adds it automatically.

**7.** Click the **OK** button. You return to the Blank desktop database screen, and the File Name box now shows the name Chatham.accdb. The filename extension ".accdb" identifies the file as an Access 2007 - 2013 database.

**8.** Click the **Create** button. Access creates the new database, saves it to the specified location, and then opens an empty table named Table1.

**Trouble?** If you see only ribbon tab names and no buttons, click the HOME tab to expand the ribbon, and then in the bottom-right corner of the ribbon, click the Pin the ribbon button.

Refer back to the Session 1.1 Visual Overview and spend some time becoming familiar with the components of the Access window.

## INSIGHT

### Understanding the Database File Type

Access 2013 uses the .accdb file extension, which is the same file extension used for databases created with Microsoft Access 2007 and 2010. To ensure compatibility between these earlier versions and the Access 2013 software, new databases created using Access 2013 have the same file extension and file format as Access 2007 and Access 2010 databases. This is why the File New Database dialog box provides the Microsoft Access 2007 - 2013 Databases option in the "Save as type" box. In addition, the notation "(Access 2007 - 2013 file format)" appears in the title bar next to the name of an open database in Access 2013, confirming that database files with the .accdb extension can be used in Access 2007, Access 2010, and Access 2013.

## Working in Touch Mode

**TIP**

On a touch device, you tap instead of click.

If you are working on a touch device, such as a tablet, you can switch to Touch Mode in Access to make it easier for you to tap buttons on the ribbon and perform other touch actions. Your screens will not match those shown in the book exactly, but this will not cause any problems.

**Note:** The following steps assume that you are using a mouse. If you are instead using a touch device, please read these steps but don't complete them, so that you remain working in Touch Mode.

### To switch to Touch Mode:

1. On the Quick Access Toolbar, click the **Customize Quick Access Toolbar** button ⏷. A menu opens listing buttons you can add to the Quick Access Toolbar as well as other options for customizing the toolbar.

   **Trouble?** If the Touch/Mouse Mode command on the menu has a checkmark next to it, press the Esc key to close the menu, and then skip to Step 3.

2. Click **Touch/Mouse Mode**. The Quick Access Toolbar now contains the Touch/Mouse Mode button 🖐, which you can use to switch between Mouse Mode, the default display, and Touch Mode.

3. On the Quick Access Toolbar, click the **Touch/Mouse Mode** button 🖐. A menu opens with two commands: Mouse, which shows the ribbon in the standard display and is optimized for use with the mouse; and Touch, which provides more space between the buttons and commands on the ribbon and is optimized for use with touch devices. The icon next to Mouse is shaded red to indicate that it is selected.

   **Trouble?** If the icon next to Touch is shaded red, press the Esc key to close the menu and skip to Step 5.

4. Click **Touch**. The display switches to Touch Mode with more space between the commands and buttons on the ribbon. See Figure 1-5.

| Figure 1-5 | Ribbon displayed in Touch Mode |
| --- | --- |

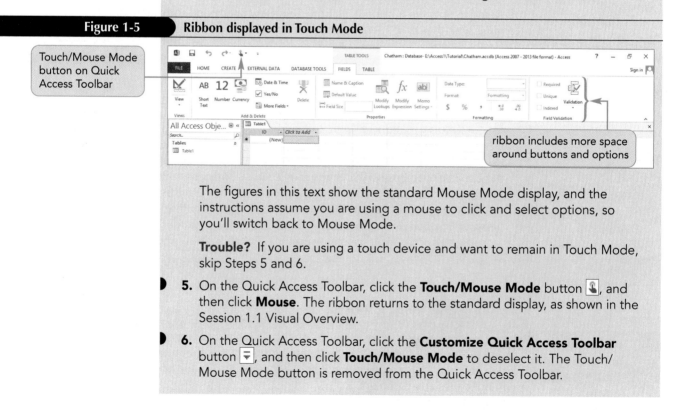

Touch/Mouse Mode button on Quick Access Toolbar

ribbon includes more space around buttons and options

The figures in this text show the standard Mouse Mode display, and the instructions assume you are using a mouse to click and select options, so you'll switch back to Mouse Mode.

**Trouble?** If you are using a touch device and want to remain in Touch Mode, skip Steps 5 and 6.

5. On the Quick Access Toolbar, click the **Touch/Mouse Mode** button 🖐, and then click **Mouse**. The ribbon returns to the standard display, as shown in the Session 1.1 Visual Overview.

6. On the Quick Access Toolbar, click the **Customize Quick Access Toolbar** button ⏷, and then click **Touch/Mouse Mode** to deselect it. The Touch/Mouse Mode button is removed from the Quick Access Toolbar.

# Creating a Table in Datasheet View

Tables contain all the data in a database and are the fundamental objects for your work in Access. There are different ways to create a table in Access, including entering the fields and records for the table directly in Datasheet view.

**REFERENCE**

## Creating a Table in Datasheet View

- On the ribbon, click the CREATE tab.
- In the Tables group, click the Table button.
- Rename the default ID primary key field and change its data type, if necessary; or accept the default ID field with the AutoNumber data type.
- In the Add & Delete group on the FIELDS tab, click the button for the type of field you want to add to the table (for example, click the Short Text button), and then type the field name; or, in the table datasheet, click the Click to Add column heading, click the type of field you want to add from the list that opens, and then press the Tab or Enter key to move to the next column in the datasheet. Repeat this step to add all the necessary fields to the table.
- In the first row below the field names, enter the value for each field in the first record, pressing the Tab or Enter key to move from one field to the next.
- After entering the value for the last field in the first record, press the Tab or Enter key to move to the next row, and then enter the values for the next record. Continue this process until you have entered all the records for the table.
- On the Quick Access Toolbar, click the Save button, enter a name for the table, and then click the OK button.

For Chatham Community Health Services, Cindi needs to track information about each patient visit at the clinic. She asks you to create the Visit table according to the plan shown in Figure 1-6.

**Figure 1-6**    **Plan for the Visit table**

| Field | Purpose |
| --- | --- |
| VisitID | Unique number assigned to each visit; will serve as the table's primary key |
| PatientID | Unique number assigned to each patient; common field that will be a foreign key to connect to the Patient table |
| VisitDate | Date on which the patient visited the clinic |
| Reason | Reason/diagnosis for the patient visit |
| WalkIn | Whether the patient visit was a walk-in or a scheduled appointment |

© 2014 Cengage Learning

As shown in Cindi's plan, she wants to store data about visits in five fields, including fields to contain the date of each visit, the reason for the visit, and if the visit was a walk-in or scheduled appointment. These are the most important aspects of a visit and, therefore, must be tracked. Also, notice that the VisitID field will be the primary key for the table; each visit at Chatham Community Health Services has a unique number assigned to it, so this field is the logical choice for the primary key. Finally, the PatientID field is needed in the Visit table as a foreign key to connect the information about visits to patients. The data about patients and their bills will be stored in separate tables, which you will create later.

Notice the name of each field in Figure 1-6. You need to name each field, table, and other object in an Access database.

## Decision Making: Naming Fields in Access Tables

One of the most important tasks in creating a table is deciding what names to specify for the table's fields. Keep the following guidelines in mind when you assign field names:

- A field name can consist of up to 64 characters, including letters, numbers, spaces, and special characters, except for the period (.), exclamation mark (!), grave accent ('), and square brackets ([ ]).
- A field name cannot begin with a space.
- Capitalize the first letter of each word in a field name that combines multiple words, for example VisitDate.
- Use concise field names that are easy to remember and reference, and that won't take up a lot of space in the table datasheet.
- Use standard abbreviations, such as Num for Number, Amt for Amount, and Qty for Quantity, and use them consistently throughout the database. For example, if you use Num for Number in one field name, do not use the number sign (#) for Number in another.
- Give fields descriptive names so that you can easily identify them when you view or edit records.
- Although Access supports the use of spaces in field names (and in other object names), experienced database developers avoid using spaces because they can cause errors when the objects are involved in programming tasks.

By spending time obtaining and analyzing information about the fields in a table, and understanding the rules for naming Access fields, you can create a well-designed table that will be easy for others to use.

## Renaming the Default Primary Key Field

As noted earlier, Access provides the ID field as the default primary key for a new table you create in Datasheet view. Recall that a primary key is a field, or a collection of fields, whose values uniquely identify each record in a table. However, according to Cindi's plan, the VisitID field should be the primary key for the Visit table. You'll begin by renaming the default ID field to create the VisitID field.

### To rename the ID field to the VisitID field:

1. Right-click the **ID** column heading to open the shortcut menu, and then click **Rename Field**. The column heading ID is selected, so that whatever text you type next will replace it.

2. Type **VisitID** and then click the row below the heading. The column heading changes to VisitID, and the insertion point moves to the row below the heading. See Figure 1-7.

   **Trouble?** If you make a mistake while typing the field name, use the Backspace key to delete characters to the left of the insertion point or the Delete key to delete characters to the right of the insertion point. Then type the correct text. To correct a field name by replacing it entirely, press the Esc key, and then type the correct text.

| Figure 1-7 | ID field renamed to VisitID |
|---|---|

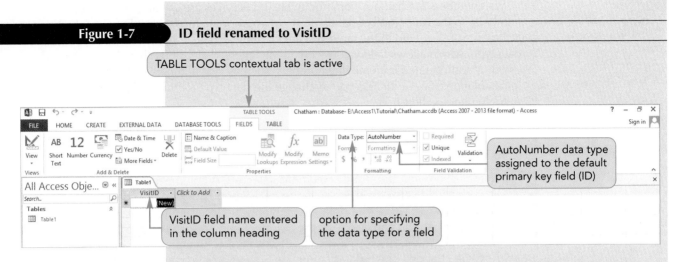

TABLE TOOLS contextual tab is active

AutoNumber data type assigned to the default primary key field (ID)

VisitID field name entered in the column heading

option for specifying the data type for a field

The **insertion point** is a flashing cursor that shows where text you type will be inserted. In this case, it is hidden within the selected field value (New).

Notice that the TABLE TOOLS tab is active on the ribbon. This is an example of a **contextual tab**, which is a tab that appears and provides options for working with a specific object that is selected—in this case, the table you are creating. As you work with other objects in the database, other contextual tabs will appear with commands and options related to each selected object.

## INSIGHT

### Buttons and Labels on the Ribbon

Depending on the size of the monitor you are using and your screen resolution settings, you might see more or fewer buttons on the ribbon, and you might not see labels next to certain buttons. The screenshots in these tutorials were created using a screen resolution setting of 1366 x 768 with the program window maximized. If you are using a smaller monitor or a lower screen resolution, some buttons will appear only as icons, with no labels next to them, because there is not enough room on the ribbon to display the labels.

You have renamed the default primary key field, ID, to VisitID. However, the VisitID field still retains the characteristics of the ID field, including its data type. Your next task is to change the data type of this field.

## Changing the Data Type of the Default Primary Key Field

Notice the Formatting group on the FIELDS tab. One of the options available in this group is the Data Type option (see Figure 1-7). Each field in an Access table must be assigned a data type. The **data type** determines what field values you can enter for the field. In this case, the AutoNumber data type is displayed. Access assigns the AutoNumber data type to the default ID primary key field because the **AutoNumber** data type automatically inserts a unique number in this field for every record, beginning with the number 1 for the first record, the number 2 for the second record, and so on. Therefore, a field using the AutoNumber data type can serve as the primary key for any table you create.

Visit numbers at Chatham Community Health Services are specific, four-digit numbers, so the AutoNumber data type is not appropriate for the VisitID field, which is the primary key field in the table you are creating. A better choice is the **Short Text** data type, which allows field values containing letters, digits, and other characters, and which is appropriate for identifying numbers, such as visit numbers, that are never used in calculations. So, Cindi asks you to change the data type for the VisitID field from AutoNumber to Short Text.

### To change the data type for the VisitID field:

▶ 1. Make sure that the VisitID column is selected. A column is selected when you click a field value, in which case the background color of the column heading changes to orange (the default color) and the insertion point appears in the field value. You can also click the column heading to select a column, in which case the background color of both the column heading and the field value changes (the default colors are gray and blue, respectively).

▶ 2. In the Formatting group on the FIELDS tab, click the **Data Type arrow**, and then click **Short Text**. The VisitID field is now a Short Text field. See Figure 1-8.

| Figure 1-8 | Short Text data type assigned to the VisitID field |
| --- | --- |

Note the Unique check box in the Field Validation group. This check box is selected because the VisitID field assumed the characteristics of the default primary key field, ID, including the fact that each value in the field must be unique. Because this check box is selected, no two records in the Visit table will be allowed to have the same value in the VisitID field.

With the VisitID field created and established as the primary key, you can now enter the rest of the fields in the Visit table.

## Adding New Fields

When you create a table in Datasheet view, you can use the options in the Add & Delete group on the FIELDS tab to add fields to your table. You can also use the Click to Add column in the table datasheet to add new fields. (See Figure 1-8.) You'll use both methods to add the four remaining fields to the Visit table. The next field you need to add is the PatientID field. Similar to the VisitID field, the PatientID field will contain numbers that will not be used in calculations, so it should be a Short Text field.

## To add the rest of the fields to the Visit table:

1. In the Add & Delete group on the FIELDS tab, click the **Short Text** button. Access adds a new field named "Field1" to the right of the VisitID field. See Figure 1-9.

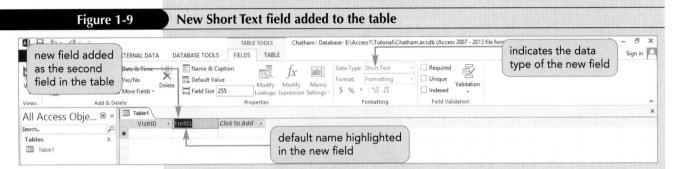

The text "Field1" is selected, so you can simply type the new field name to replace it.

2. Type **PatientID**. The second field is added to the table. Next, you'll add the VisitDate field. Because this field will contain date values, you'll add a field with the **Date/Time** data type, which allows field values in a variety of date and time formats.

3. In the Add & Delete group, click the **Date & Time** button. Access adds a third field to the table, this time with the Date/Time data type.

4. Type **VisitDate** to replace the highlighted name "Field1." The fourth field in the Visit table is the Reason field, which will contain brief descriptions of the reason for the visit to the clinic. You'll add another Short Text field—this time using the Click to Add column.

5. Click the **Click to Add** column heading. Access displays a list of available data types from which you can choose the data type for the new field you're adding.

6. Click **Short Text** in the list. Access adds a fourth field to the table.

7. Type **Reason** to replace the highlighted name "Field1," and then press the **Enter** key. The Click to Add column becomes active and displays the list of field data types.

   The fifth and final field in the Visit table is the WalkIn field, which will indicate whether or not the visit was a walk-in (that is, the patient did not have a scheduled appointment). The **Yes/No** data type is suitable for this field because it is used to define fields that store values representing one of two options—true/false, yes/no, or on/off.

**TIP**

You can also type the first letter of a data type to select it and close the Click to Add list.

8. Click **Yes/No** in the list, and then type **WalkIn** to replace the highlighted name "Field1."

   **Trouble?** If you pressed the Tab or Enter key after typing the WalkIn field name, press the Esc key to close the Click to Add list.

9. Click in the row below the VisitID column heading. All five fields are now entered for the Visit table. See Figure 1-10.

| Figure 1-10 | Table with all fields entered |

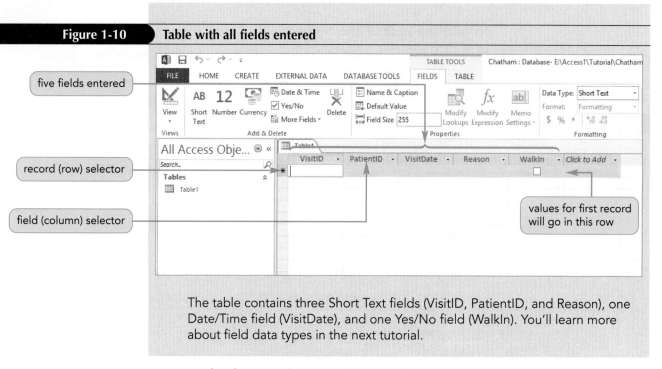

The table contains three Short Text fields (VisitID, PatientID, and Reason), one Date/Time field (VisitDate), and one Yes/No field (WalkIn). You'll learn more about field data types in the next tutorial.

As noted earlier, Datasheet view shows a table's contents in rows (records) and columns (fields). Each column is headed by a field name inside a field selector, and each row has a record selector to its left (see Figure 1-10). Clicking a **field selector** or a **record selector** selects that entire column or row (respectively), which you then can manipulate. A field selector is also called a **column selector**, and a record selector is also called a **row selector**.

## Entering Records

With the fields in place for the table, you can now enter the field values for each record. Cindi requests that you enter eight records in the Visit table, as shown in Figure 1-11.

| Figure 1-11 | Visit table records |

| VisitID | PatientID | VisitDate | Reason | WalkIn |
|---------|-----------|-----------|--------|--------|
| 1550 | 22549 | 12/1/2015 | Influenza | Yes |
| 1527 | 22522 | 11/9/2015 | Allergies - environmental | Yes |
| 1555 | 22520 | 12/7/2015 | Annual wellness visit | No |
| 1542 | 22537 | 11/24/2015 | Influenza | Yes |
| 1530 | 22510 | 11/10/2015 | Seborrheic dermatitis | No |
| 1564 | 22512 | 1/5/2016 | Annual wellness visit | No |
| 1575 | 22513 | 1/13/2016 | Broken leg | Yes |
| 1538 | 22500 | 11/17/2015 | Migraine | Yes |

© 2014 Cengage Learning

To enter records in a table datasheet, you type the field values below the column headings for the fields. The first record you enter will go in the first row (see Figure 1-10).

## To enter the first record for the Visit table:

Be sure to type the numbers "0" and "1" and not the letters "O" and "I" in the field value.

**1.** In the first row for the VisitID field, type **1550** (the VisitID field value for the first record), and then press the **Tab** key. Access adds the field value and moves the insertion point to the right, into the PatientID column. See Figure 1-12.

**Figure 1-12**    First field value entered

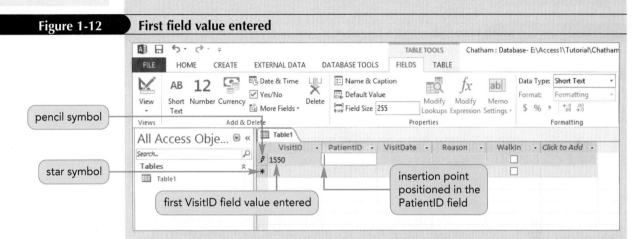

**Trouble?** If you make a mistake when typing a value, use the Backspace key to delete characters to the left of the insertion point or the Delete key to delete characters to the right of the insertion point. Then type the correct value. To correct a value by replacing it entirely, press the Esc key, and then type the correct value.

Notice the pencil symbol that appears in the row selector for the new record. The **pencil symbol** indicates that the record is being edited. Also notice the star symbol that appears in the row selector for the second row. The **star symbol** identifies the second row as the next row available for a new record.

**2.** Type **22549** (the PatientID field value for the first record), and then press the **Tab** key. Access enters the field value and moves the insertion point to the VisitDate column.

**3.** Type **12/1/15** (the VisitDate field value for the first record), and then press the **Tab** key. Access displays the year as "2015" even though you entered only the final two digits of the year. This is because the VisitDate field has the Date/Time data type, which automatically formats dates with four-digit years.

**Trouble?** Depending on your Windows date setting, your VisitDate field values might be displayed in a different format. This difference will not cause any problems.

**4.** Type **Influenza** (the Reason field value for the first record), and then press the **Tab** key to move to the WalkIn column.

Recall that the WalkIn field is a Yes/No field. Notice the check box displayed in the WalkIn column. By default, the value for any Yes/No field is "No"; therefore, the check box is initially empty. For Yes/No fields with check boxes, you press the Tab key to leave the check box unchecked, or you press the spacebar to insert a checkmark in the check box. The record you are entering in the table is for a walk-in visit, so you need to insert a checkmark in the check box to indicate "Yes."

5. Press the **spacebar** to insert a checkmark, and then press the **Tab** key. The first record is entered into the table, and the insertion point is positioned in the VisitID field for the second record. The pencil symbol is removed from the first row because the record in that row is no longer being edited. The table is now ready for you to enter the second record. See Figure 1-13.

| Figure 1-13 | Datasheet with first record entered |
| --- | --- |

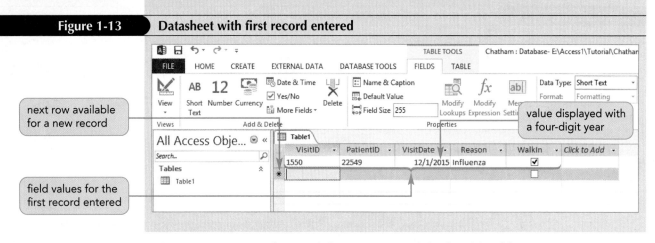

Now you can enter the remaining seven records in the Visit table.

### To enter the remaining records in the Visit table:

1. Referring to Figure 1-11, enter the values for records 2 through 8, pressing the **Tab** key to move from field to field and to the next row for a new record. Keep in mind that you do not have to type all four digits of the year in the VisitDate field values; you can enter only the final two digits and Access will display all four. Also, for any WalkIn field values of "No," be sure to press the Tab key to leave the check box empty.

   **Trouble?** If you enter a value in the wrong field by mistake, such as entering a Reason field value in the VisitDate field, a menu might open with options for addressing the problem. If this happens, click the "Enter new value" option in the menu. You'll return to the field with the incorrect value highlighted, which you can then replace by typing the correct value.

   Notice that not all of the Reason field values are fully displayed. To see more of the table datasheet and the full field values, you'll close the Navigation Pane and resize the Reason column.

2. At the top of the Navigation Pane, click the **Shutter Bar Open/Close Button** ⟪. The Navigation Pane closes, and only the complete table datasheet is displayed.

3. Place the pointer on the vertical line to the right of the Reason field name until the pointer changes to a ↔ shape, and then double-click the vertical line. All the Reason field values are now fully displayed. See Figure 1-14.

**Figure 1-14**    **Datasheet with eight records entered**

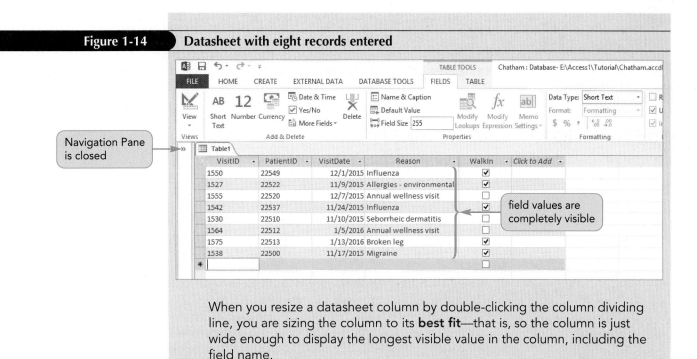

**Navigation Pane is closed**

**field values are completely visible**

When you resize a datasheet column by double-clicking the column dividing line, you are sizing the column to its **best fit**—that is, so the column is just wide enough to display the longest visible value in the column, including the field name.

Carefully compare your VisitID and PatientID values with those in the figure, and correct any errors before continuing.

4. Compare your table to the one in Figure 1-14. If any of the field values in your table do not match those shown in the figure, you can correct a field value by clicking to position the insertion point in the value, and then using the Backspace key or Delete key to delete incorrect text. Then type the correct text and press the Enter key. To correct a value in the WalkIn field, simply click the check box to add or remove the checkmark as appropriate. Also, be sure the spelling and capitalization of field names in your table match those shown in the figure exactly, and that there are no spaces between words. To correct a field name, double-click it to select it, and then type the correct name; or use the Rename Field option on the shortcut menu to rename a field with the correct name.

## Saving a Table

The records you enter are immediately stored in the database as soon as you enter them; however, the table's design—the field names and characteristics of the fields themselves, plus any layout changes to the datasheet—are not saved until you save the table. When you save a new table for the first time, you should give it a name that best identifies the information it contains. Like a field name, a table name can contain up to 64 characters, including spaces.

**REFERENCE**

*Saving a Table*

- Make sure the table you want to save is open.
- On the Quick Access Toolbar, click the Save button. The Save As dialog box opens.
- In the Table Name box, type the name for the table.
- Click the OK button.

According to Cindi's plan, you need to save the table with the name "Visit."

### To save and name the Visit table:

1. On the Quick Access Toolbar, click the **Save** button 🖫. The Save As dialog box opens.

2. With the default name Table1 selected in the Table Name box, type **Visit**, and then click the **OK** button. The tab for the table now displays the name "Visit," and the Visit table design is saved in the Chatham database.

Notice that after you saved and named the Visit table, Access sorted and displayed the records in order by the values in the VisitID field because it is the primary key. If you compare your screen to Figure 1-11, which shows the records in the order you entered them, you'll see that the current screen shows the records in order by the VisitID field values.

Cindi asks you to add two more records to the Visit table. When you add a record to an existing table, you must enter the new record in the next row available for a new record; you cannot insert a row between existing records for the new record. In a table with just a few records, such as the Visit table, the next available row is visible on the screen. However, in a table with hundreds of records, you would need to scroll the datasheet to see the next row available. The easiest way to add a new record to a table is to use the New button, which scrolls the datasheet to the next row available so you can enter the new record.

### To enter additional records in the Visit table:

1. If necessary, click the first record's VisitID field value (**1527**) to make it the current record.

2. On the ribbon, click the **HOME** tab.

3. In the Records group, click the **New** button. The insertion point is positioned in the next row available for a new record, which in this case is row 9. See Figure 1-15.

| Figure 1-15 | Entering a new record |
| --- | --- |

HOME tab displayed

option for entering a new record

new record will be entered in row 9

| VisitID | PatientID | VisitDate | Reason | WalkIn | Click to Add |
| --- | --- | --- | --- | --- | --- |
| 1527 | 22522 | 11/9/2015 | Allergies - environmental | ☑ | |
| 1530 | 22510 | 11/10/2015 | Seborrheic dermatitis | ☐ | |
| 1538 | 22500 | 11/17/2015 | Migraine | ☑ | |
| 1542 | 22537 | 11/24/2015 | Influenza | ☑ | |
| 1550 | 22549 | 12/1/2015 | Influenza | ☑ | |
| 1555 | 22520 | 12/7/2015 | Annual wellness visit | ☐ | |
| 1564 | 22512 | 1/5/2016 | Annual wellness visit | ☐ | |
| 1575 | 22513 | 1/13/2016 | Broken leg | ☑ | |
| * | | | | ☐ | |

**4.** With the insertion point in the VisitID field for the new record, type **1548** and then press the **Tab** key.

**5.** Complete the entry of this record by entering each value shown below, pressing the **Tab** key to move from field to field:

PatientID = **22519**

VisitDate = **11/30/2015**

Reason = **Hypertension**

WalkIn = **No (unchecked)**

**6.** Enter the values for the next new record, as follows, and then press the **Tab** key after entering the WalkIn field value:

VisitID = **1560**

PatientID = **22514**

VisitDate = **12/15/2015**

Reason = **Influenza**

WalkIn = **Yes (checked)**

Your datasheet should now look like the one shown in Figure 1-16.

| Figure 1-16 | Datasheet with additional records entered |
| --- | --- |

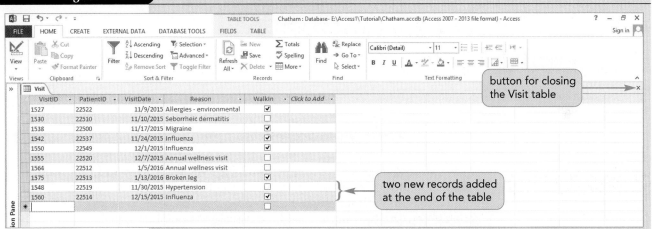

The new records you added appear at the end of the table, and are not sorted in order by the primary key field values. For example, VisitID 1548 should be the fifth record in the table, placed between VisitID 1542 and VisitID 1550. When you add records to a table datasheet, they appear at the end of the table. The records are not displayed in primary key order until you either close and reopen the table or switch between views.

**7.** Click the **Close** button [X] on the object tab (see Figure 1-16 for the location of this button). The Visit table closes, and the main portion of the Access window is now blank because no database object is currently open. The Chatham database file is still open, as indicated by the filename in the Access window title bar.

## Opening a Table

The tables in a database are listed in the Navigation Pane. You open a table, or any Access object, by double-clicking the object name in the Navigation Pane. Next, you'll open the Visit table so you can see the order of all the records you've entered.

**To open the Visit table:**

▶ **1.** On the Navigation Pane, click the **Shutter Bar Open/Close Button** ⟫ to open the pane. Note that the Visit table is listed.

▶ **2.** Double-click **Visit** to open the table in Datasheet view. See Figure 1-17.

| Figure 1-17 | Table with 10 records entered and displayed in primary key order |
|---|---|

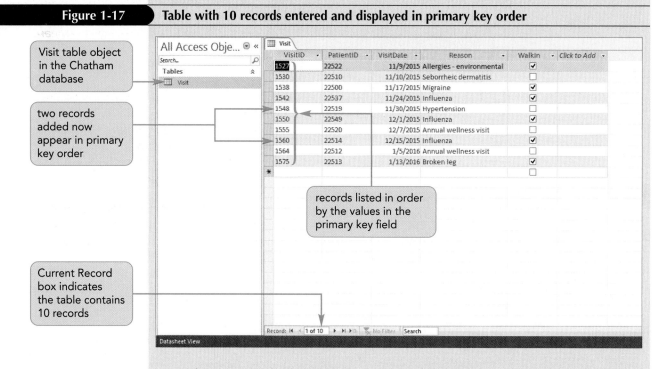

Visit table object in the Chatham database

two records added now appear in primary key order

records listed in order by the values in the primary key field

Current Record box indicates the table contains 10 records

The two records you added, with VisitID field values of 1548 and 1560, now appear in the correct primary key order. The table now contains a total of 10 records, as indicated by the Current Record box at the bottom of the datasheet. The **Current Record box** displays the number of the current record as well as the total number of records in the table.

Each record contains a unique VisitID value because this field is the primary key. Other fields, however, can contain the same value in multiple records; for example, note the three values of "Influenza" in the Reason field.

# Closing a Table and Exiting Access

When you are finished working in an Access table, it's a good idea to close the table so that you do not make unintended changes to the table data. You can close a table by clicking its Close button on the object tab, as you did earlier. Or, if you want to close the Access program as well, you can click the program's Close button. When you do, any open tables are closed, the active database is closed, and you exit the Access program.

## To close the Visit table and exit Access:

**TIP**

To close a database without exiting Access, click the FILE tab to display Backstage view, and then click Close.

1. Click the **Close** button  on the program window title bar. Access closes the Visit table and the Chatham database, and then the Access program closes.

---

### INSIGHT

### Saving a Database

Unlike the Save buttons in other Office programs, the Save button on the Quick Access Toolbar in Access does not save the active document (database). Instead, you use the Save button to save the design of an Access object, such as a table (as you saw earlier), or to save datasheet format changes, such as resizing columns. Access does not have a button or option you can use to save the active database.

Access saves changes to the active database automatically when you change or add a record or close the database. If your database is stored on a removable medium, such as a USB drive, you should never remove the drive while the database file is open. If you do, Access will encounter problems when it tries to save the database, which might damage the database. Make sure you close the database first before removing the drive.

---

Now that you've become familiar with database concepts and Access, and created the Chatham database and the Visit table, Cindi wants you to add more records to the table and work with the data stored in it to create database objects including a query, form, and report. You'll complete these tasks in the next session.

---

### REVIEW

### Session 1.1 Quick Check

1. A(n) _____ is a single characteristic of a person, place, object, event, or idea.
2. You connect the records in two separate tables through a(n) _____ that appears in both tables.
3. The _____, whose values uniquely identify each record in a table, is called a(n) _____ when it is placed in a second table to form a relationship between the two tables.
4. The _____ is the area of the Access window that lists all the objects in a database, and it is the main control center for opening and working with database objects.
5. What is the name of the field that Access creates, by default, as the primary key field for a new table in Datasheet view?
6. Which group on the FIELDS tab contains the options you use to add new fields to a table?
7. What does a pencil symbol at the beginning of a record represent? What does a star symbol represent?
8. Explain how the saving process in Access is different from saving in other Office programs.

# Session 1.2 Visual Overview:

The **CREATE tab** provides options for creating various database objects, including tables, forms, and reports. The options appear on the tab grouped by object type.

The **Forms group** contains options for creating a **form**, which is a database object you use to enter, edit, and view records in a database.

The **Query Wizard button** opens a dialog box with different types of wizards that guide you through the steps to create a query. One of these, the **Simple Query Wizard**, allows you to select records and fields quickly to display in the query results.

You use the options in the Tables group to create a table in Datasheet view or in Design view.

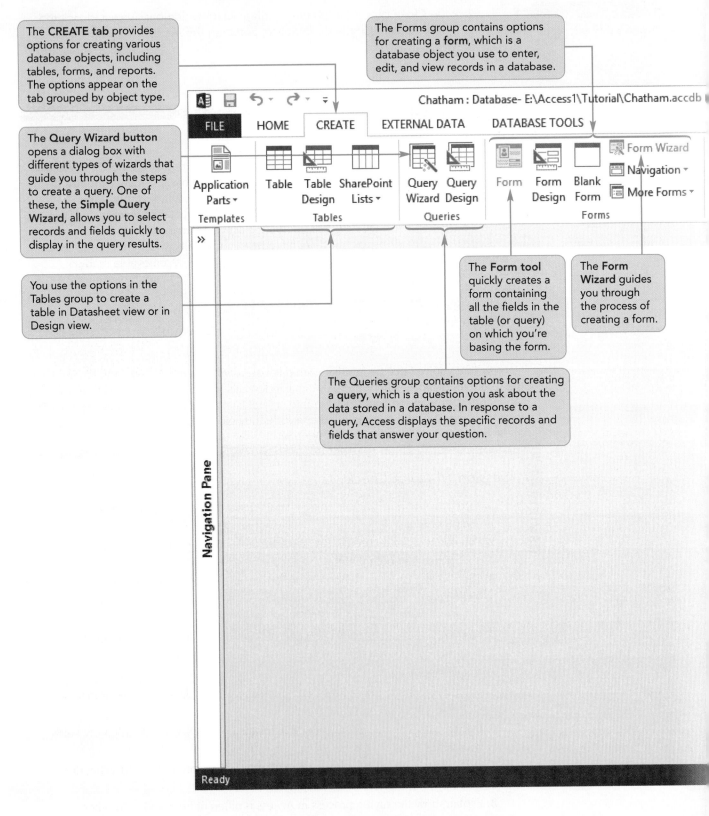

Chatham : Database- E:\Access1\Tutorial\Chatham.accdb

FILE    HOME    CREATE    EXTERNAL DATA    DATABASE TOOLS

Application Parts ▾    Table    Table Design    SharePoint Lists ▾    Query Wizard    Query Design    Form    Form Design    Blank Form    Form Wizard    Navigation ▾    More Forms ▾

Templates    Tables    Queries    Forms

Navigation Pane

Ready

The **Form tool** quickly creates a form containing all the fields in the table (or query) on which you're basing the form.

The **Form Wizard** guides you through the process of creating a form.

The **Queries group** contains options for creating a **query**, which is a question you ask about the data stored in a database. In response to a query, Access displays the specific records and fields that answer your question.

# The CREATE Tab Options

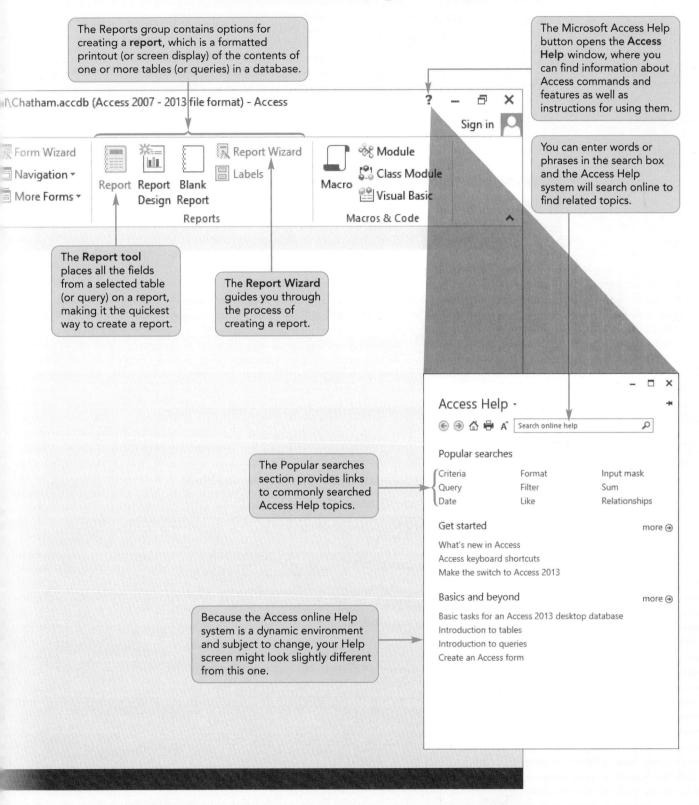

The Reports group contains options for creating a **report**, which is a formatted printout (or screen display) of the contents of one or more tables (or queries) in a database.

The Microsoft Access Help button opens the **Access Help** window, where you can find information about Access commands and features as well as instructions for using them.

I\Chatham.accdb (Access 2007 - 2013 file format) - Access

Sign in

Form Wizard
Navigation ▾
More Forms ▾

Report    Report Design    Blank Report

Report Wizard
Labels

Reports

Macro

Module
Class Module
Visual Basic

Macros & Code

You can enter words or phrases in the search box and the Access Help system will search online to find related topics.

The **Report tool** places all the fields from a selected table (or query) on a report, making it the quickest way to create a report.

The **Report Wizard** guides you through the process of creating a report.

### Access Help ▾

Search online help

Popular searches

| Criteria | Format | Input mask |
| Query | Filter | Sum |
| Date | Like | Relationships |

The Popular searches section provides links to commonly searched Access Help topics.

Get started                                           more ⊕

What's new in Access
Access keyboard shortcuts
Make the switch to Access 2013

Basics and beyond                                     more ⊕

Basic tasks for an Access 2013 desktop database
Introduction to tables
Introduction to queries
Create an Access form

Because the Access online Help system is a dynamic environment and subject to change, your Help screen might look slightly different from this one.

# Copying Records from Another Access Database

When you created the Visit table, you entered records directly into the table datasheet. There are many other ways to enter records in a table, including copying and pasting records from a table into the same database or into a different database. To use this method, however, the two tables must have the same structure—that is, the tables must contain the same fields, with the same design, in the same order.

Cindi has already created a table named Appointment that contains additional records with visit data. The Appointment table is contained in a database named Cindi located in the Access1 ▸ Tutorial folder included with your Data Files. The Appointment table has the same table structure as the Visit table you created.

**REFERENCE**

### Opening a Database

- Start Access and display the Recent screen in Backstage view.
- Click the name of the database you want to open in the list of recently opened databases.

*or*

- Start Access and display the Recent screen in Backstage view.
- In the navigation bar, click Open Other Files to display the Open screen.
- Click Computer, click the Browse button, and then navigate to the drive and folder containing the database file you want to open.
- Click the name of the database file you want to open, and then click the Open button.

Your next task is to copy the records from the Appointment table and paste them into your Visit table. To do so, you need to open the Cindi database.

### To copy the records from the Appointment table:

1. Display the Windows Start screen, if necessary.

   **Using Windows 7?** To complete Step 1, click the Start button on the taskbar.

2. Click the **Access 2013** tile. Access starts and displays the Recent screen in Backstage view.

   **Using Windows 7?** To complete Step 2, click All Programs on the Start menu, click Microsoft Office 2013, and then click Access 2013.

3. Click **Open Other Files** to display the Open screen in Backstage view.

4. On the Open screen, click **Computer**. The right side of the screen now shows folder information for your computer.

   **Trouble?** If you are storing your files on SkyDrive, click SkyDrive, and then log in if necessary.

5. Click the **Browse** button, and then navigate to the drive that contains your Data Files.

6. Navigate to the **Access1 ▸ Tutorial** folder, click the database file named **Cindi**, and then click the **Open** button. The Cindi database opens in the Access program window. Note that the database contains only one object, the Appointment table.

**Trouble?** If a security warning appears below the ribbon indicating that some active content has been disabled, click the Enable Content button next to the warning. Access provides this warning because some databases might contain content that could harm your computer. Because the Cindi database does not contain objects that could be harmful, you can open it safely. If you are accessing the file over a network, you might also see a dialog box asking if you want to make the file a trusted document; click Yes.

**7.** In the Navigation Pane, double-click **Appointment** to open the Appointment table in Datasheet view. The table contains 76 records and the same five fields, with the same characteristics, as the fields in the Visit table. See Figure 1-18.

| Figure 1-18 | Appointment table in the Cindi database |

Cindi wants you to copy all the records in the Appointment table. You can select all the records by clicking the **datasheet selector**, which is the box to the left of the first field name in the table datasheet (see Figure 1-18).

**8.** Click the **datasheet selector** to the left of the VisitID field, as shown in Figure 1-18. Access selects all the records in the table.

**9.** In the Clipboard group on the HOME tab, click the **Copy** button. All the records are copied to the Clipboard.

**10.** Click the **Close 'Appointment'** button ✕ on the object tab. A dialog box opens asking if you want to save the data you copied to the Clipboard. This dialog box opens only when you copy a large amount of data to the Clipboard.

**11.** Click the **Yes** button. The dialog box closes, and then the Appointment table closes.

With the records copied to the Clipboard, you can now paste them into the Visit table. First you need to close the Cindi database while still keeping the Access program open, and then open the Chatham database.

**To close the Cindi database and then paste the records into the Visit table:**

▶ **1.** Click the **FILE** tab to display Backstage view, and then click **Close** in the navigation bar to close the Cindi database. You return to the HOME tab in the Access program window.

▶ **2.** Click the **FILE** tab to return to Backstage view, and then click **Open** in the navigation bar. The Recent section of the Open screen shows a list of the recently opened database files. This list should include the Chatham database.

▶ **3.** In the Recent section of the screen, click **Chatham** to open the Chatham database file.

   **Trouble?** If the Chatham database file is not listed in the Recent section on your computer, click Computer, and then click Browse. In the Open dialog box, navigate to the drive and folder where you are storing your files, and then open the Chatham database file.

   **Trouble?** If the security warning appears below the ribbon, click the Enable Content button, and then, if necessary, click Yes to make the file a trusted document.

▶ **4.** In the Navigation Pane, double-click **Visit** to open the Visit table in Datasheet view.

▶ **5.** On the Navigation Pane, click the **Shutter Bar Open/Close Button** [«] to close the pane.

▶ **6.** Position the pointer on the star symbol in the row selector for row 11 (the next row available for a new record) until the pointer changes to a ➡ shape, and then click to select the row.

▶ **7.** In the Clipboard group on the HOME tab, click the **Paste** button. The pasted records are added to the table, and a dialog box opens asking you to confirm that you want to paste all the records (76 total).

   **Trouble?** If the Paste button isn't active, click the ➡ pointer on the row selector for row 11, making sure the entire row is selected, and then repeat Step 7.

▶ **8.** Click the **Yes** button. The dialog box closes, and the pasted records are highlighted. See Figure 1-19. Notice that the table now contains a total of 86 records—10 records that you entered and 76 records that you copied and pasted.

| Figure 1-19 | Visit table after copying and pasting records |

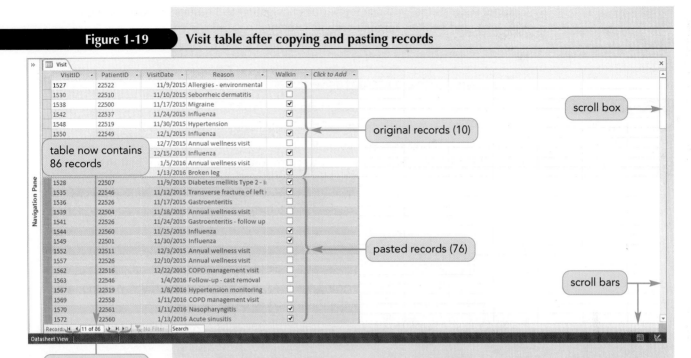

Not all the Reason field values are completely visible, so you need to resize this column to its best fit.

▶ 9. Place the pointer on the vertical line to the right of the Reason field name until the pointer changes to a ✛ shape, and then double-click the vertical line. The Reason field values are now fully displayed.

# Navigating a Datasheet

The Visit table now contains 86 records, but only some of the records are visible on the screen. To view fields or records not currently visible on the screen, you can use the horizontal and vertical scroll bars shown in Figure 1-19 to navigate the data. The **navigation buttons**, shown in Figure 1-19 and also described in Figure 1-20, provide another way to move vertically through the records. The Current Record box appears between the two sets of navigation buttons and displays the number of the current record as well as the total number of records in the table. Figure 1-20 shows which record becomes the current record when you click each navigation button. Note the New (blank) record button, which works in the same way as the New button on the HOME tab you used earlier to enter a new record in the table.

| Figure 1-20 | Navigation buttons |

| Navigation Button | Record Selected | Navigation Button | Record Selected |
| --- | --- | --- | --- |
| I◀ | First record | ▶I | Last record |
| ◀ | Previous record | ▶✱ | New (blank) record |
| ▶ | Next record | | |

© 2014 Cengage Learning

Cindi suggests that you use the various navigation techniques to move through the Visit table and become familiar with its contents.

### To navigate the Visit datasheet:

**TIP**

You can make a field the current field by clicking anywhere within the column for that field.

1. Click the first record's VisitID field value (**1527**). The Current Record box shows that record 1 is the current record.

2. Click the **Next record** navigation button ▶. The second record is now highlighted, which identifies it as the current record. Also, notice that the second record's value for the VisitID field is selected, and the Current Record box displays "2 of 86" to indicate that the second record is the current record.

3. Click the **Last record** navigation button ▶|. The last record in the table, record 86, is now the current record.

4. Drag the scroll box in the vertical scroll bar (see Figure 1-19) up to the top of the bar. Notice that record 86 is still the current record, as indicated in the Current Record box. Dragging the scroll box changes the display of the table datasheet, but does not change the current record.

5. Drag the scroll box in the vertical scroll bar back down until you can see the end of the table and the current record (record 86).

6. Click the **Previous record** navigation button ◀. Record 85 is now the current record.

7. Click the **First record** navigation button |◀. The first record is now the current record and is visible on the screen.

   As you moved through the datasheet, you might have noticed that not all the Reason field values are fully displayed. When you resize a column to its best fit, the column expands to fully display only the field values that are visible on the screen at that time. To make sure all field values are displayed for the entire table, you need to scroll through the datasheet and repeat the resizing process.

8. Drag the scroll box down to display more of the table, until you see other Reason field values that are not fully displayed. Then use the ↔ pointer to resize the field.

9. Repeat Step 8, as necessary, until you reach the bottom of the table and have resized all the Reason field values, and then drag the scroll box back up to display the beginning of the table.

The Visit table now contains all the data about patient visits for Chatham Community Health Services. To better understand how to work with this data, Cindi asks you to create simple objects for the other main types of database objects—queries, forms, and reports.

## Creating a Simple Query

As noted earlier, a query is a question you ask about the data stored in a database. When you create a query, you tell Access which fields you need and what criteria it should use to select the records that will answer your question. Then Access displays only the information you want, so you don't have to navigate through the entire database for the information. In the Visit table, for example, Cindi might create a query to display only those records for visits that occurred in a specific month. Even though a query can display table information in a different way, the information still exists in the table as it was originally entered.

Cindi wants to see a list of all the visit dates and reasons for visits in the Visit table. She doesn't want the list to include all the fields in the table, such as PatientID and WalkIn. To produce this list for Cindi, you'll use the Simple Query Wizard to create a query based on the Visit table.

### To start the Simple Query Wizard:

▶ **1.** On the ribbon, click the **CREATE** tab.

▶ **2.** In the Queries group on the CREATE tab, click the **Query Wizard** button. The New Query dialog box opens.

▶ **3.** Make sure **Simple Query Wizard** is selected, and then click the **OK** button. The first Simple Query Wizard dialog box opens. See Figure 1-21.

---

**Figure 1-21** ▶ **First Simple Query Wizard dialog box**

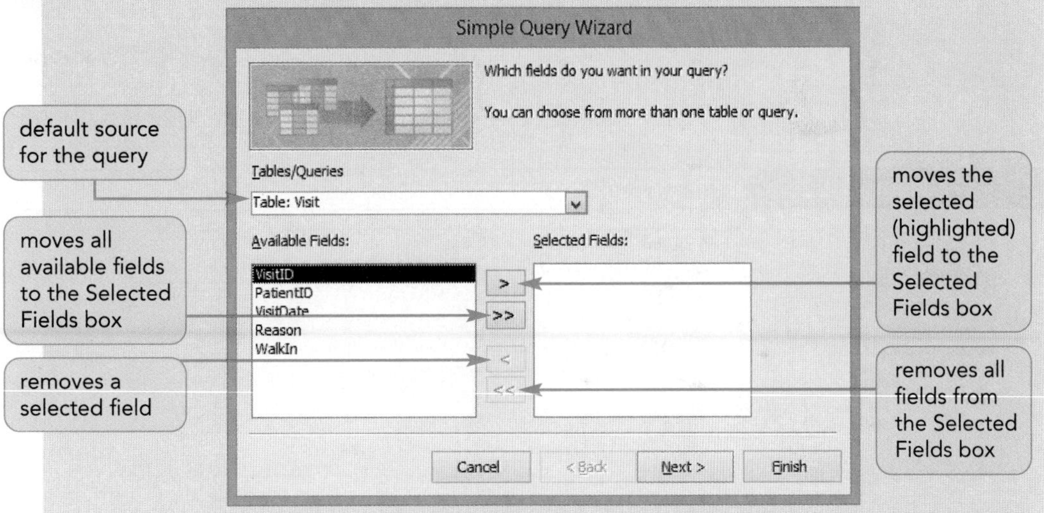

Because the Visit table is the only object in the Chatham database, it is listed in the Tables/Queries box by default. If the database contained more objects, you could click the Tables/Queries arrow and choose another table or a query as the basis for the new query you are creating. The Available Fields box lists all the fields in the Visit table.

You need to select fields from the Available Fields box to include them in the query. To select fields one at a time, click a field and then click the > button. The selected (highlighted) field moves from the Available Fields box on the left to the Selected Fields box on the right. To select all the fields, click the >> button. If you change your mind or make a mistake, you can remove a field by clicking it in the Selected Fields box and then clicking the < button. To remove all fields from the Selected Fields box, click the << button.

Each Simple Query Wizard dialog box contains buttons on the bottom that allow you to move to the previous dialog box (Back button), move to the next dialog box (Next button), or cancel the creation process (Cancel button). You can also finish creating the object (Finish button) and accept the wizard's defaults for the remaining options.

Cindi wants her list to include data from only the following fields: VisitID, VisitDate, and Reason. You need to select these fields to include them in the query.

**TIP**

You can also double-click a field to move it from the Available Fields box to the Selected Fields box.

## To create the query using the Simple Query Wizard:

1. Click **VisitID** in the Available Fields box to select the field (if necessary), and then click the [ > ] button. The VisitID field moves to the Selected Fields box.

2. Repeat Step 1 for the fields **VisitDate** and **Reason**, and then click the **Next** button. The second, and final, Simple Query Wizard dialog box opens and asks you to choose a name (title) for your query. Access suggests the name "Visit Query" because the query you are creating is based on the Visit table. You'll change the suggested name to "VisitList."

3. Click at the end of the suggested name, use the **Backspace** key to delete the word "Query" and the space, and then type **List**. Now you can view the query results.

4. Click the **Finish** button to complete the query. Access displays the query results in Datasheet view, on a new tab named "VisitList." A query datasheet is similar to a table datasheet, showing fields in columns and records in rows—but only for those fields and records you want to see, as determined by the query specifications you select.

5. Place the pointer on the vertical line to the right of the Reason field name until the pointer changes to a ✛ shape, and then double-click the vertical line to resize the Reason field. See Figure 1-22.

| Figure 1-22 | Query results |
|---|---|

only the three selected fields are displayed in the query datasheet

all 86 records are included in the results

| VisitID | VisitDate | Reason |
|---|---|---|
| 1527 | 11/9/2015 | Allergies - environmental |
| 1528 | 11/9/2015 | Diabetes mellitus Type 2 - initial diagnosis |
| 1530 | 11/10/2015 | Seborrheic dermatitis |
| 1535 | 11/12/2015 | Transverse fracture of left ulna |
| 1536 | 11/17/2015 | Gastroenteritis |
| 1538 | 11/17/2015 | Migraine |
| 1539 | 11/18/2015 | Annual wellness visit |
| 1541 | 11/24/2015 | Gastroenteritis - follow up |
| 1542 | 11/24/2015 | Influenza |
| 1544 | 11/25/2015 | Influenza |
| 1548 | 11/30/2015 | Hypertension |
| 1549 | 11/30/2015 | Influenza |
| 1550 | 12/1/2015 | Influenza |
| 1552 | 12/3/2015 | Annual wellness visit |
| 1555 | 12/7/2015 | Annual wellness visit |
| 1557 | 12/10/2015 | Annual wellness visit |
| 1560 | 12/15/2015 | Influenza |
| 1562 | 12/22/2015 | COPD management visit |
| 1563 | 1/4/2016 | Follow-up - cast removal |
| 1564 | 1/5/2016 | Annual wellness visit |
| 1567 | 1/8/2016 | Hypertension monitoring |
| 1569 | 1/11/2016 | COPD management visit |
| 1570 | 1/11/2016 | Nasopharyngitis |
| 1572 | 1/13/2016 | Acute sinusitis |
| 1573 | 1/13/2016 | Cardiac monitoring |

Record: I◄ ◄ 1 of 86 ► ►I ►❏ No Filter Search

Datasheet View

The VisitList query datasheet displays the three selected fields for each record in the Visit table. The fields are shown in the order you selected them in the Simple Query Wizard, from left to right. The records are listed in order by the primary key field, VisitID. Even though the query datasheet displays only the three fields you chose for the query, the Visit table still includes all the fields for all records.

Notice that the navigation buttons are located at the bottom of the window. You navigate a query datasheet in the same way that you navigate a table datasheet.

▶ **6.** Click the **Last record** navigation button ▶|. The last record in the query datasheet is now the current record.

▶ **7.** Click the **Previous record** navigation button ◀. Record 85 in the query datasheet is now the current record.

▶ **8.** Click the **First record** navigation button |◀. The first record is now the current record.

▶ **9.** Click the **Close 'VisitList'** button ✕ on the object tab. A dialog box opens asking if you want to save the changes to the layout of the query. This dialog box opens because you resized the Reason column.

▶ **10.** Click the **Yes** button to save the query layout changes and close the query.

The query results are not stored in the database; however, the query design is stored as part of the database with the name you specified. You can re-create the query results at any time by opening the query again. When you open the query at a later date, the results displayed will reflect up-to-date information to include any new records entered in the Visit table.

Next, Cindi asks you to create a form for the Visit table so that Chatham Community Health Services employees can use the form to enter and work with data in the table easily.

# Creating a Simple Form

As noted earlier, you use a form to enter, edit, and view records in a database. Although you can perform these same functions with tables and queries, forms can present data in many customized and useful ways.

Cindi wants a form for the Visit table that shows all the fields for one record at a time, with fields listed one below another in a column. This type of form will make it easier for her staff to focus on all the data for a particular visit. You'll use the Form tool to create this form quickly and easily.

### To create the form using the Form tool:

▶ **1.** Make sure the Visit table is still open in Datasheet view. The table or other database object you're using as the basis for the form must either be open or selected in the Navigation Pane when you use the Form tool.

**Trouble?** If the Visit table is not open, click the Shutter Bar Open/Close Button ≫ to open the Navigation Pane. Then double-click Visit to open the Visit table in Datasheet view. Click the Shutter Bar Open/Close Button ≪ to close the pane.

▶ **2.** Make sure the CREATE tab is displayed.

▶ **3.** In the Forms group, click the **Form** button. The Form tool creates a simple form showing every field in the Visit table and places it on a tab named "Visit." Access assigns this name because the form is based on the Visit table. See Figure 1-23.

Figure 1-23    **Form created by the Form tool**

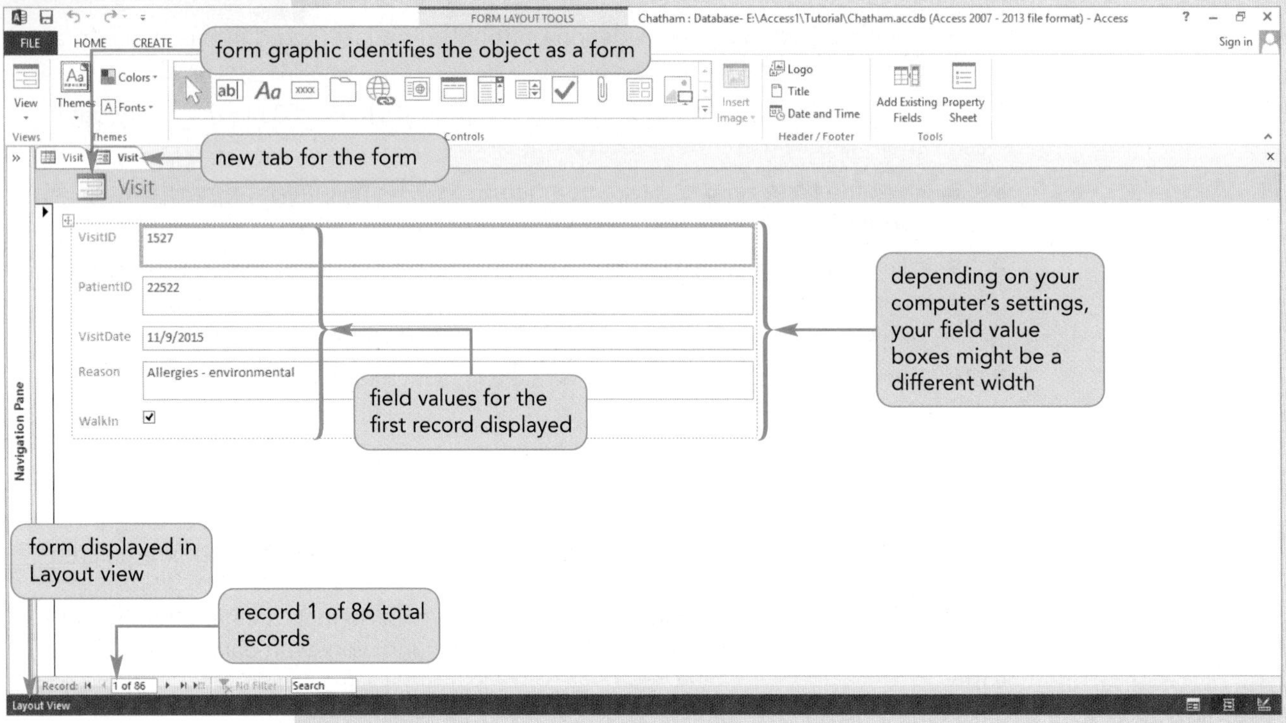

**Trouble?** Depending on the size of your monitor and your screen resolution settings, the fields in your form might appear in multiple columns instead of a single column. This difference will not present any problems.

The form displays one record at a time in the Visit table, providing another view of the data that is stored in the table and allowing you to focus on the values for one record. Access displays the field values for the first record in the table and selects the first field value (VisitID) by placing a border around the value. Each field name appears on a separate line and on the same line as its field value, which appears in a box to the right. Depending on your computer's settings, the field value boxes in your form might be wider or narrower than those shown in the figure. As indicated in the status bar, the form is displayed in Layout view. In **Layout view**, you can make design changes to the form while it is displaying data, so that you can see the effects of the changes you make immediately.

To view, enter, and maintain data using a form, you must know how to move from field to field and from record to record. Notice that the form contains navigation buttons, similar to those available in Datasheet view, which you can use to display different records in the form. You'll use these now to navigate the form; then you'll save and close the form.

### To navigate, save, and close the form:

1. Click the **Next record** navigation button ▶. The form now displays the values for the second record in the Visit table.

2. Click the **Last record** navigation button ▶| to move to the last record in the table. The form displays the information for VisitID 1700.

3. Click the **Previous record** navigation button ◀ to move to record 85.

4. Click the **First record** navigation button |◄| to return to the first record in the Visit table.

   Next, you'll save the form with the name "VisitData" in the Chatham database. Then the form will be available for later use.

5. On the Quick Access Toolbar, click the **Save** button 🖫. The Save As dialog box opens.

6. In the Form Name box, click at the end of the highlighted word "Visit," type **Data**, and then press the **Enter** key. Access saves the form as VisitData in the Chatham database and closes the dialog box. The tab containing the form now displays the name VisitData.

7. Click the **Close 'VisitData'** button ☒ on the object tab to close the form.

**INSIGHT**

### Saving Database Objects

In general, it is best to save a database object—query, form, or report—only if you anticipate using the object frequently or if it is time consuming to create, because all objects use storage space and increase the size of the database file. For example, you most likely would not save a form you created with the Form tool because you can re-create it easily with one mouse click. (However, for the purposes of this text, you usually need to save the objects you create.)

After attending a staff meeting, Cindi returns with another request. She would like to see the information in the Visit table presented in a more readable and professional format. You'll help Cindi by creating a report.

## Creating a Simple Report

As noted earlier, a report is a formatted printout (or screen display) of the contents of one or more tables or queries. You'll use the Report tool to quickly produce a report based on the Visit table for Cindi. The Report tool creates a report based on the selected table or query.

**To create the report using the Report tool:**

1. With the Visit table open in Datasheet view, click the **CREATE** tab on the ribbon.

2. In the Reports group, click the **Report** button. The Report tool creates a simple report showing every field in the Visit table and places it on a tab named "Visit." Again, Access assigns this name because the object you created (the report) is based on the Visit table. See Figure 1-24.

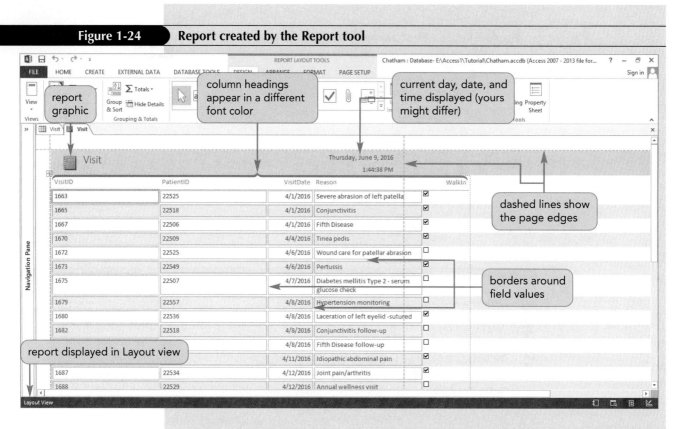

**Figure 1-24**    **Report created by the Report tool**

**Trouble?** The records in your report might appear in a different order from the records shown in Figure 1-24. This difference will not cause any problems.

The report shows each field in a column, with the field values for each record in a row, similar to a table or query datasheet. However, the report offers a more visually appealing format for the data, with the column headings in a different color, borders around each field value, a graphic of a report at the top left, and the current day, date, and time at the top right. Also notice the dashed horizontal and vertical lines on the top and right, respectively; these lines mark the edges of the page and show where text will print on the page.

The report needs some design changes to better display the data. The columns are much wider than necessary for the VisitID and PatientID fields, and the Reason and WalkIn field values and borders are not completely displayed within the page area defined by the dashed lines, which means they would not appear on the same page as the rest of the fields in the printed report. You can resize the columns easily in Layout view.

### To resize the VisitID and PatientID columns:

▶ **1.** Position the pointer on the right border of any field value in the VisitID column until the pointer changes to a ↔ shape.

▶ **2.** Click and drag the mouse to the left; dark outlines surround the field name and each field value to show the column width as you change it. Drag to the left until the column is slightly wider than the VisitID field name.

▶ **3.** Release the mouse button. The VisitID column is now narrower, and the other four columns have shifted to the left. The Reason and WalkIn fields, values, and borders are now completely within the page area. See Figure 1-25.

Figure 1-25    **Report after resizing the VisitID column**

field values and borders are now within the area marked by the dashed lines

column is now narrower

| VisitID | PatientID | | VisitDate | Reason | WalkIn |
|---------|-----------|--|-----------|--------|--------|
| 1663 | 22525 | | 4/1/2016 | Severe abrasion of left patella | ☑ |
| 1665 | 22518 | | 4/1/2016 | Conjunctivitis | ☑ |
| 1667 | 22506 | | 4/1/2016 | Fifth Disease | ☑ |

**4.** Click the first field value for PatientID to establish the field as the current field.

**5.** Position the pointer on the right border of the first value in the PatientID column until the pointer changes to ↔, click and drag to the left until the column is slightly wider than its field name, and then release the mouse button.

**6.** Drag the scroll box on the vertical scroll bar all the way down to the bottom of the report to check its entire layout.

The Report tool displays the number "86" at the bottom left of the report, showing the total number of records in the report and the table on which it is based—the Visit table. The Report tool also displays the page number at the bottom right, but the text "Page 1 of 1" appears cut off through the vertical dashed line. This will cause a problem when you print the report, so you need to move this text to the left.

**7.** Click anywhere on the words **Page 1 of 1**. An orange outline appears around the text, indicating it is selected. See Figure 1-26.

Figure 1-26    **Report page number selected**

| 1640 | 22557 | 3/9/2016 | Hypertension monitoring | ☐ |
| 1642 | 22540 | 3/9/2016 | Onychocryptosis | ☑ |
| 1644 | 22533 | 3/11/2016 | Annual wellness visit | ☐ |
| 1645 | 22531 | 3/14/2016 | UTI | ☑ |
| 1647 | 22535 | 3/18/2016 | Hypertension monitoring | ☐ |
| 1648 | 22550 | 3/18/2016 | Migrane headache follow-up | ☐ |
| 1650 | 22560 | 3/21/2016 | Eczema erythematosum follow-up | ☐ |
| 1652 | 22540 | 3/23/2016 | Onychocryptosis follow-up | ☐ |
| 1653 | 22551 | 3/23/2016 | Elevated blood lipids-monitoring meds | ☐ |
| 1659 | 22531 | 3/28/2016 | UTI follow-up | ☐ |
| 1662 | 22502 | 3/30/2016 | Annual wellness visit | ☐ |
| 86 | | | | |

text to the right of this dashed line would print on its own page

text is selected and can be moved to the left

shows total number of records in the report

Page 1 of 1

With the text selected, you can use the keyboard arrow keys to move it.

**TIP**

You can also use the mouse to drag the selected page number, but the arrow key is more precise.

**8.** Press the ← key repeatedly until the selected box containing the page number is to the left of the vertical dashed line (roughly 35 times). The page number text is now completely within the page area and will print on the same page as the rest of the report.

**9.** Drag the scroll box back up to redisplay the top of the report.

The report is displayed in Layout view, which doesn't show how many pages there are in the report. To see this, you need to switch to Print Preview.

### To view the report in Print Preview:

**1.** In the Views group on the DESIGN tab, click the **View button arrow**, and then click **Print Preview**. The first page of the report is displayed in Print Preview. See Figure 1-27.

**Figure 1-27    First page of the report in Print Preview**

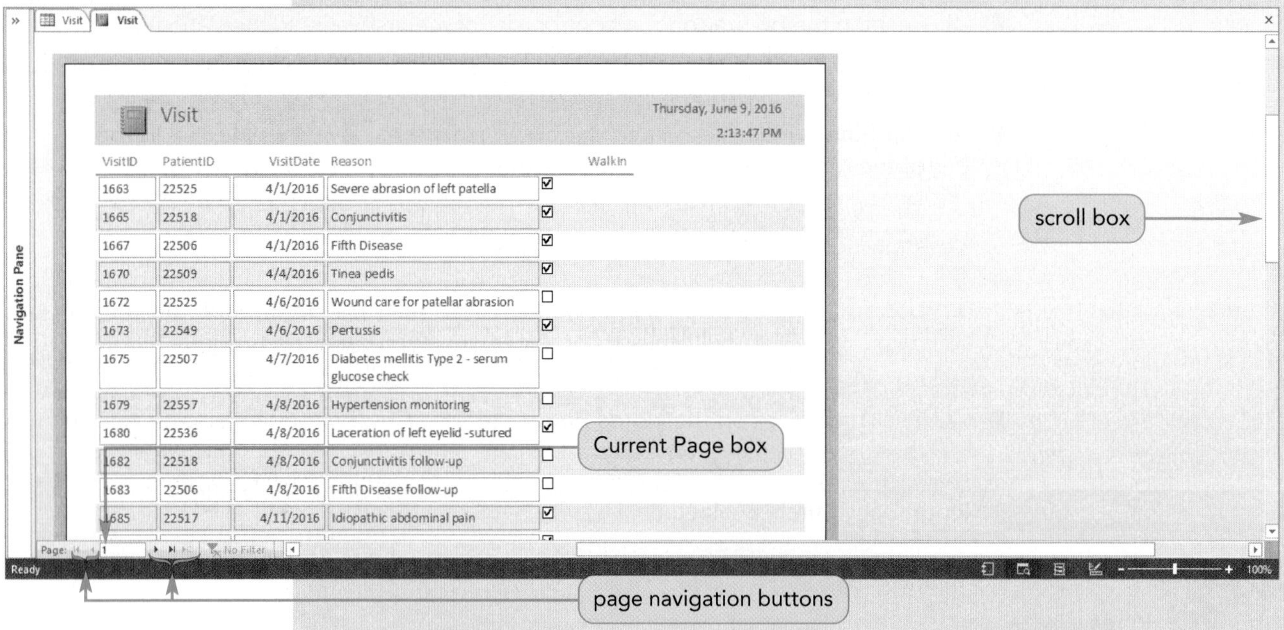

**Print Preview** shows exactly how the report will look when printed. Notice that Print Preview provides page navigation buttons at the bottom of the window, similar to the navigation buttons you've used to move through records in a table, query, and form.

**2.** Click the **Next Page** navigation button ▶. The second page of the report is displayed in Print Preview.

**3.** Click the **Last Page** navigation button ▶| to move to the last page of the report.

**4.** Drag the scroll box in the vertical scroll bar (see Figure 1-27) down until the bottom of the report page is displayed. The notation "Page 3 of 3" appears at the bottom of the page, indicating that you are on page 3 out of a total of 3 pages in the report.

**Trouble?** Depending on the printer you are using, your report might have more or fewer pages, and some of the pages might be blank. If so, don't worry. Different printers format reports in different ways, sometimes affecting the total number of pages and the number of records printed per page.

**5.** Click the **First Page** navigation button ⏮ to return to the first page of the report, and then drag the scroll box in the vertical scroll bar back up so that the top of the report is displayed.

Next you'll save the report as VisitDetails, and then print it.

**6.** On the Quick Access Toolbar, click the **Save** button 🖫. The Save As dialog box opens.

**7.** In the Report Name box, click at the end of the highlighted word "Visit," type **Details,** and then press the **Enter** key. Access saves the report as VisitDetails in the Chatham database and closes the dialog box. The tab containing the report now displays the name "VisitDetails."

## Printing a Report

After creating a report, you might need to print it to distribute it to others who need to view the report's contents. You can print a report without changing any print settings, or display the Print dialog box and select options for printing.

**REFERENCE**

### Printing a Report

- Open the report in any view, or select the report in the Navigation Pane.
- Click the FILE tab to display Backstage view, click Print, and then click Quick Print to print the report with the default print settings.

*or*

- Open the report in any view, or select the report in the Navigation Pane.
- Click the FILE tab, click Print, and then click Print (or, if the report is displayed in Print Preview, click the Print button in the Print group on the PRINT PREVIEW tab). The Print dialog box opens, in which you can select the options you want for printing the report.

Cindi asks you to print the entire report with the default settings, so you'll use the Quick Print option in Backstage view.

**Note:** To complete the following steps, your computer must be connected to a printer. Check with your instructor first to see if you should print the report.

### To print the report and then close it:

**1.** On the ribbon, click the **FILE** tab to display Backstage view.

**2.** In the navigation bar, click **Print**, and then click **Quick Print**. The report prints with the default print settings, and you return to the report in Print Preview.

   **Trouble?** If your report did not print, make sure that your computer is connected to a printer, and that the printer is turned on and ready to print. Then repeat Steps 1 and 2.

**3.** Click the **Close 'VisitDetails'** button ☒ on the object tab to close the report.

**4.** Click the **Close 'Visit'** button ☒ on the object tab to close the Visit table.

   **Trouble?** If you are asked to save changes to the layout of the table, click Yes.

You can also use the Print dialog box to print other database objects, such as table and query datasheets. Most often, these objects are used for viewing and entering data, and reports are used for printing the data in a database.

# Viewing Objects in the Navigation Pane

The Chatham database now contains four objects—the Visit table, the VisitList query, the VisitData form, and the VisitDetails report. When you work with the database file—such as closing it, opening it, or distributing it to others—the file includes all the objects you created and saved in the database. You can view and work with these objects in the Navigation Pane.

### To view the objects in the Chatham database:

1. On the Navigation Pane, click the **Shutter Bar Open/Close Button** ≫ to open the pane. See Figure 1-28.

| Figure 1-28 | Chatham database objects displayed in the Navigation Pane |
| --- | --- |

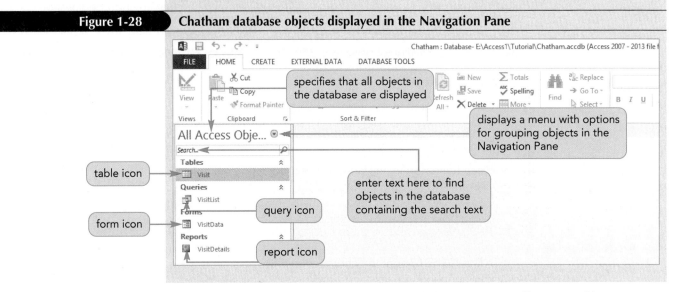

The Navigation Pane currently displays the default category, **All Access Objects**, which lists all the database objects in the pane. Each object type (Tables, Queries, Forms, and Reports) appears in its own group. Each database object (the Visit table, the VisitList query, the VisitData form, and the VisitDetails report) has a unique icon to its left to indicate the type of object. This makes it easy for you to identify the objects and choose which one you want to open and work with.

The arrow on the All Access Objects bar displays a menu with options for various ways to group and display objects in the Navigation Pane. The Search box enables you to enter text for Access to find; for example, you could search for all objects that contain the word "Visit" in their names. Note that Access searches for objects only in the categories and groups currently displayed in the Navigation Pane.

As you continue to build the Chatham database and add more objects to it in later tutorials, you'll use the options in the Navigation Pane to manage those objects.

# Using Microsoft Access Help

The Access program provides a Help system you can use to search for information about specific Access features. You start Help by clicking the Microsoft Access Help button in the top right of the Access window, or by pressing the F1 key. You'll use Help now to learn more about the Navigation Pane.

**To search for information about the Navigation Pane in Help:**

1. Click the **Microsoft Access Help** button [?] on the title bar. The Access Help window opens, as shown earlier in the Session 1.2 Visual Overview.

2. Click in the search box, type **Navigation Pane**, and then press the **Enter** key. The Access Help window displays a list of topics related to the Navigation Pane.

3. Click the topic **Manage database objects in the Navigation Pane**. The Access Help window displays the article you selected. See Figure 1-29.

**Figure 1-29    Article displayed in the Access Help window**

search text entered

selected article is displayed

drag the scroll box to scroll through and read the article

Access Help ▾

Navigation Pane

**Manage database objects in the Navigation Pane**

TIP    Press F11 to display or hide the Navigation Pane.

All the objects in a database are listed in the Navigation Pane, a feature introduced in Access 2007. The Database window of earlier versions is not available.

You can customize the categories and groups of objects in the Navigation Pane. You can also hide objects, groups, or even the entire Navigation Pane. Access provides several categories that you can use right away, and you can also create custom categories and groups.

NOTE    The Navigation Pane is not available when you use an Access app or a web database in a browser. Although you can use the Navigation Pane in an Access app opened in Access, it has a limited feature set: display, sort, and search for database objects.

**In this article**
↓ Overview
↓ Select a category
↓ Display and sort objects

**Trouble?** If the article on managing database objects is not listed in your Help window, choose another article related to the Navigation Pane to read.

4. Scroll through the article to read detailed information about working with the Navigation Pane.

5. When finished, click the **Close** button [X] on the Access Help window to close it.

The Access Help system is an important reference tool for you to use if you need additional information about databases in general, details about specific Access features, or support with problems you might encounter.

# Managing a Database

One of the main tasks involved in working with database software is managing your databases and the data they contain. Some of the activities involved in database management include compacting and repairing a database and backing up and restoring a database. By managing your databases, you can ensure that they operate in the most efficient way, that the data they contain is secure, and that you can work with the data effectively.

## Compacting and Repairing a Database

Whenever you open an Access database and work in it, the size of the database increases. Further, when you delete records or when you delete or replace database objects—such as queries, forms, and reports—the storage space that had been occupied by the deleted or replaced records or objects does not automatically become available for other records or objects. To make the space available, and also to increase the speed of data retrieval, you must compact the database. **Compacting** a database rearranges the data and objects in a database to decrease its file size, thereby making more storage space available and enhancing the performance of the database. Figure 1-30 illustrates the compacting process.

| **Figure 1-30** | **Compacting a database** |
|---|---|

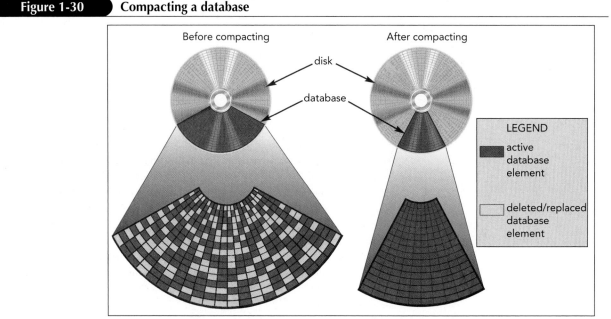

© 2014 Cengage Learning

When you compact a database, Access repairs the database at the same time, if necessary. In some cases, Access detects that a database is damaged when you try to open it and gives you the option to compact and repair it at that time. For example, the data in your database might become damaged, or corrupted, if you exit the Access program suddenly by turning off your computer. If you think your database might be damaged because it is behaving unpredictably, you can use the Compact & Repair Database option to fix it.

**REFERENCE**

*Compacting and Repairing a Database*

- Make sure the database file you want to compact and repair is open.
- Click the FILE tab to display the Info screen in Backstage view.
- Click the Compact & Repair Database button.

Access also allows you to set an option to compact and repair a database file automatically every time you close it. The Compact on Close option is available in the Current Database section of the Access Options dialog box, which you open from

Backstage view by clicking the Options command in the navigation bar. By default, the Compact on Close option is turned off.

Next, you'll compact the Chatham database manually using the Compact & Repair Database option. This will make the database smaller and allow you to work with it more efficiently. After compacting the database, you'll close it.

---

**To compact and repair the Chatham database:**

▶  **1.** On the ribbon, click the **FILE** tab to display the Info screen in Backstage view.

▶  **2.** Click the **Compact & Repair Database** button. Access closes Backstage view and returns to the HOME tab. Although nothing visible happens on the screen, Access compacts the Chatham database, making it smaller, and repairs it at the same time.

▶  **3.** Click the **FILE** tab to return to the Info screen, and then click **Close** in the navigation bar. Access closes the Chatham database.

---

## Backing Up and Restoring a Database

**Backing up** a database is the process of making a copy of the database file to protect your database against loss or damage. The Back Up Database command enables you to back up your database file from within the Access program, while you are working on your database. To use this option, click the FILE tab to display the Info screen in Backstage view, click Save As in the navigation bar, click Back Up Database in the Advanced section of the Save Database As pane, and then click the Save As button. In the Save As dialog box that opens, Access provides a default filename for the backup copy that consists of the same filename as the database you are backing up (for example, "Chatham"), and an underscore character, plus the current date. This filenaming system makes it easy for you to keep track of your database backups and when they were created. To restore a backup database file, you simply copy the backup from the location where it is stored to your hard drive, or whatever device you use to work in Access, and start working with the restored database file. (You will not actually back up the Chatham database in this tutorial unless directed by your instructor to do so.)

---

**INSIGHT**

### *Planning and Performing Database Backups*

Experienced database users make it a habit to back up a database before they work with it for the first time, keeping the original data intact. They also make frequent backups while continuing to work with a database; these backups are generally on flash drives, recordable CDs or DVDs, external or network hard drives, or cloud-based storage (such as SkyDrive). Also, it is recommended to store the backup copy in a different location from the original. For example, if the original database is stored on a flash drive, you should not store the backup copy on the same flash drive. If you lose the drive or the drive is damaged, you would lose both the original database and its backup copy.

If the original database file and the backup copy have the same name, restoring the backup copy might replace the original. If you want to save the original file, rename it before you restore the backup copy. To ensure that the restored database has the most current data, you should update the restored database with any changes made to the original between the time you created the backup copy and the time the original database became damaged or lost.

By properly planning for and performing backups, you can avoid losing data and prevent the time-consuming effort required to rebuild a lost or damaged database.

In the following tutorials, you'll help Cindi complete and maintain the Chatham database, and you'll use it to meet the specific information needs of the clinic's employees.

**PROSKILLS**

## Decision Making: When to Use Access vs. Excel

Using a spreadsheet application like Microsoft Excel to manage lists or tables of information works well when the data is simple, such as a list of contacts or tasks. As soon as the data becomes complex enough to separate into tables that need to be related, you start to see the limitations of using a spreadsheet application. The strength of a database application such as Access is in its ability to easily relate one table of information to another. Consider a table of contacts that includes home addresses, with a separate row for each person living at the same address. When an address changes, it's too easy to make a mistake and not update the home address for each person who lives there. To ensure you have the most accurate data at all times, it's important to have only one instance of each piece of data. By creating separate tables that are related, and keeping only one instance of each piece of data, you'll ensure the integrity of the data. Trying to accomplish this in Excel is a complex process, whereas Access is specifically designed for this functionality.

Another limitation of using Excel instead of Access to manage data has to do with the volume of data. Although a spreadsheet can hold thousands of records, a database can hold millions. A spreadsheet containing thousands of pieces of information is cumbersome to use. Think of large-scale commercial applications such as enrollment at a college or tracking customers for a large company. It's hard to imagine managing such information in an Excel spreadsheet. Instead, you'd use a database. Finally, with an Access database, multiple users can access the information it contains at the same time. Although an Excel spreadsheet can be shared, there can be problems when users try to open and edit the same spreadsheet at the same time.

When you're trying to decide whether to use Excel or Access, ask yourself the following questions.

1. Do you need to store data in separate tables that are related to each other?
2. Do you have a very large amount of data to store?
3. Will more than one person need to access the data at the same time?

If you answer "yes" to any of these questions, an Access database is most likely the appropriate application to use.

**REVIEW**

## Session 1.2 Quick Check

1. To copy the records from a table in one database to another table in a different database, the two tables must have the same _____.
2. A(n) _____ is a question you ask about the data stored in a database.
3. The quickest way to create a form is to use the _____.
4. Which view enables you to see the total number of pages in a report and navigate through the report pages?
5. In the Navigation Pane, each database object has a unique _____ to its left that identifies the object's type.
6. _____ a database rearranges the data and objects in a database to decrease its file size and enhance the speed and performance of the database.
7. _____ a database is the process of making a copy of the database file to protect the database against loss or damage.

## SAM Projects

Put your skills into practice with SAM Projects! SAM Projects for this tutorial can be found online. If you have a SAM account, go to www.cengage.com/sam2013 to download the most recent Project Instructions and Start Files.

**ASSESS**

## Review Assignments

**PRACTICE**

**Data File needed for the Review Assignments: Company.accdb**

For Chatham Community Health Services, Cindi asks you to create a new database to contain information about the vendors that the clinic works with to obtain medical supplies and equipment for the clinic, and the vendors who service and maintain the equipment. Complete the following steps:

1. Create a new, blank database named **Vendor** and save it in the folder where you are storing your files, as specified by your instructor.
2. In Datasheet view for the Table1 table, rename the default ID primary key field to **SupplierID**. Change the data type of the SupplierID field to Short Text.
3. Add the following 10 fields to the new table in the order shown; all of them are Short Text fields *except* InitialContact, which is a Date/Time field: **Company**, **Category**, **Address**, **City**, **State**, **Zip**, **Phone**, **ContactFirst**, **ContactLast**, and **InitialContact**. Resize the columns as necessary so that the complete field names are displayed. Save the table as **Supplier**.
4. Enter the records shown in Figure 1-31 in the Supplier table. For the first record, be sure to enter your first name in the ContactFirst field and your last name in the ContactLast field.

   **Note:** When entering field values that are shown on multiple lines in the figure, do not try to enter the values on multiple lines. The values are shown on multiple lines in the figure for page spacing purposes only.

| Figure 1-31 | Supplier table records |
|---|---|

| SupplierID | Company | Category | Address | City | State | Zip | Phone | ContactFirst | ContactLast | InitialContact |
|---|---|---|---|---|---|---|---|---|---|---|
| ARE318 | Aresco Surgical, Inc. | Supplies | 48 Vienna St | Bridgeport | CT | 06601 | 203-774-3048 | *Student First* | *Student Last* | 9/2/2015 |
| GRE364 | Greinke Labs, Inc. | Supplies | 451 Summit Dr | Tiverton | RI | 02878 | 401-208-9843 | Evan | Brighton | 1/12/2016 |
| DUR368 | Durasurg Equipment, Inc. | Equipment | 74 Jessie St | Roanoke | VA | 24036 | 540-340-3829 | Kristin | Taylor | 12/1/2015 |
| STE472 | Sterile Labs of CT, Inc. | Service | 938 Gormley Ave | North Branford | CT | 06517 | 203-537-5940 | Carmine | San Marcos | 11/3/2015 |
| GSE420 | GSE Medical, Inc. | Equipment | 583 Renovo Dr | Claremont | NH | 03743 | 603-202-4951 | John | Vereen | 9/10/2015 |

© 2014 Cengage Learning

5. Cindi created a database named Company that contains a Business table with supplier data. The Supplier table you created has the same design as the Business table. Copy all the records from the **Business** table in the **Company** database (located in the Access1 ▶ Review folder provided with your Data Files) and then paste them at the end of the Supplier table in the Vendor database.

6. Resize all datasheet columns to their best fit, and then save the Supplier table.

7. Close the Supplier table, and then use the Navigation Pane to reopen it. Note that the records are displayed in primary key order by the values in the SupplierID field.

8. Use the Simple Query Wizard to create a query that includes the Company, Category, ContactFirst, ContactLast, and Phone fields (in that order) from the Supplier table. Name the query **SupplierList**, and then close the query.

9. Use the Form tool to create a form for the Supplier table. Save the form as **SupplierInfo**, and then close it.

10. Use the Report tool to create a report based on the Supplier table. In Layout view, resize all fields except the Company field, so that each field is slightly wider than the longest entry (either the field name itself or an entry in the field). Display the report in Print Preview and verify that all the fields fit across two pages in the report. Save the report as **SupplierDetails**, and then close it.

11. Close the Supplier table, and then compact and repair the Vendor database.

12. Close the Vendor database.

## Case Problem 1

**APPLY**

**Data File needed for this Case Problem: Program.accdb**

*GoGopher!* Amol Mehta, a recent college graduate living in Boulder, Colorado, spent months earning money by running errands and completing basic chores for family members and acquaintances, while looking for full-time employment. As his list of customers needing such services continued to grow, Amol decided to start his own business called GoGopher! The business, which Amol operates completely online from his home, offers customers a variety of services—from grocery shopping and household chores to yard work and pet care—on a subscription basis. Clients become members of GoGopher! by choosing the plan that best suits their needs. Each plan provides a certain number of tasks per month to members, for a specified period of time. Amol wants to use Access to maintain information about the members who have joined GoGopher! and the types of plans offered. He needs your help in creating this database. Complete the following:

1. Create a new, blank database named **Gopher** and save it in the folder where you are storing your files, as specified by your instructor.

2. In Datasheet view for the Table1 table, rename the default primary key ID field to **PlanID**. Change the data type of the PlanID field to Short Text.

3. Add the following three fields to the new table in the order shown: **PlanDescription** (a Short Text field), **PlanCost** (a Currency field), and **FeeWaived** (a Yes/No field). Save the table as **Plan**.

4. Enter the records shown in Figure 1-32 in the Plan table. Note: When entering the PlanCost field values, you do not have to type the dollar signs, commas, or decimal places; Access will enter them automatically.

**Figure 1-32    Plan table records**

| PlanID | PlanDescription | PlanCost | FeeWaived |
|--------|-----------------|----------|-----------|
| 301 | 20 tasks per month for 12 months | $6,000.00 | Yes |
| 311 | 10 tasks per month for 3 months | $750.00 | No |
| 304 | 10 tasks per month for 12 months | $3,000.00 | Yes |
| 303 | 15 tasks per month for 12 months | $4,500.00 | Yes |
| 312 | 8 tasks per month for 3 months | $600.00 | No |

when entering currency values, you do not have to type the dollar signs, commas, or decimal places

© 2014 Cengage Learning

5. Amol created a database named Program that contains a Service table with plan data. The Plan table you created has the same design as the Service table. Copy all the records from the **Service** table in the **Program** database (located in the Access1 ▸ Case1 folder provided with your Data Files) and then paste them at the end of the Plan table in the Gopher database.

6. Resize all datasheet columns to their best fit, and then save the Plan table.

7. Close the Plan table, and then use the Navigation Pane to reopen it. Note that the records are displayed in primary key order by the values in the PlanID field.

8. Use the Simple Query Wizard to create a query that includes the PlanID, PlanDescription, and PlanCost fields from the Plan table. In the second Simple Query Wizard dialog box, select the Detail option. (This option appears because the query includes a Currency field.) Save the query as **PlanData**, and then close the query.

9. Use the Form tool to create a form for the Plan table. Save the form as **PlanInfo**, and then close it.

10. Use the Report tool to create a report based on the Plan table. In Layout view, resize the PlanID field so it is slightly wider than the longest entry, which is the field name in this case. Also, resize the box containing the total amount that appears below the PlanCost column by clicking the box and then dragging its bottom border down so that the amount is fully displayed. (The Report Tool calculated this total automatically.) Display the report in Print Preview; then verify that all the fields are within the page area and all field values are fully displayed. Save the report as **PlanList**, print the report (only if asked by your instructor to do so), and then close it.

11. Close the Plan table, and then compact and repair the Gopher database.

12. Close the Gopher database.

## Case Problem 2

**APPLY**

**Data File needed for this Case Problem: Consulting.accdb**

*O'Brien Educational Services*   After teaching English in a public high school for 15 years, Karen O'Brien decided to channel her experience in education in a new direction and founded O'Brien Educational Services, a small educational consulting company located in South Bend, Indiana. The company offers tutoring services to high school students to help prepare them for standardized tests, such as the SAT and the ACT. The company provides group, private, and semi-private tutoring sessions to best meet the needs of its students. As her business continues to expand, Karen wants to use Access to maintain information about the tutors who work for her, the students who sign up for tutoring, and the contracts they sign. She needs your help in creating this database. Complete the following steps:

1. Create a new, blank database named **OBrien** and save it in the folder where you are storing your files, as specified by your instructor.

2. In Datasheet view for the Table1 table, rename the default primary key ID field to **TutorID**. Change the data type of the TutorID field to Short Text.

3. Add the following five fields to the new table in the order shown; all of them are Short Text fields *except* HireDate, which is a Date/Time field: **FirstName**, **LastName**, **Degree**, **School**, and **HireDate**. Resize the columns, if necessary, so that the complete field names are displayed. Save the table as **Tutor**.

4. Enter the records shown in Figure 1-33 in the Tutor table. For the first record, be sure to enter your first name in the FirstName field and your last name in the LastName field.

**Figure 1-33**    Tutor table records

| TutorID | FirstName | LastName | Degree | School | HireDate |
|---|---|---|---|---|---|
| 31-1200 | *Student First* | *Student Last* | BA | Pierre University | 8/2/2015 |
| 68-8234 | Caitlin | Shea | MS | Towns University | 1/5/2016 |
| 55-1234 | Samuel | Glick | BA | Manoog College | 7/23/2016 |
| 69-2254 | Sachi | Hatanaka | MA | Wyman College | 3/23/2015 |
| 71-1698 | Richard | Keating | Ph.D | Hobert University | 5/3/2015 |

© 2014 Cengage Learning

5. Karen created a database named Consulting that contains an Instructor table with tutor data. The Tutor table you created has the same design as the Instructor table. Copy all the records from the **Instructor** table in the **Consulting** database (located in the Access1 ▸ Case2 folder provided with your Data Files) and then paste them at the end of the Tutor table in the OBrien database.

6. Resize all datasheet columns to their best fit, and then save the Tutor table.

7. Close the Tutor table, and then use the Navigation Pane to reopen it. Note that the records are displayed in primary key order by the values in the TutorID field.

8. Use the Simple Query Wizard to create a query that includes the FirstName, LastName, and HireDate fields from the Tutor table. Save the query as **StartDate**, and then close the query.

9. Use the Form tool to create a form for the Tutor table. Save the form as **TutorInfo**, and then close it.

10. Use the Report tool to create a report based on the Tutor table. In Layout view, resize the TutorID, FirstName, LastName, and Degree fields so they are slightly wider than the longest entry (either the field name itself or an entry in the field). All six fields should fit within the page area after you resize the specified fields. At the bottom of the report, move the text "Page 1 of 1" to the left so it is within the page area. Display the report in Print Preview; then verify that the fields and page number fit within the page area, and that all field values are fully displayed. Save the report as **TutorList**, print the report (only if asked by your instructor to do so), and then close it.

11. Close the Tutor table, and then compact and repair the OBrien database.

12. Close the OBrien database.

## Case Problem 3

Data File needed for this Case Problem: Animal.accdb

***Rosemary Animal Shelter*** Ryan Lang is the director of the Rosemary Animal Shelter in Cobb County, Georgia. The main goals of the shelter, which has several locations in the county, are to rescue dogs and cats and to find people who will adopt them. The shelter was established by Rosemary Hanson, who dedicated her life to rescuing pets and finding good homes for them. Residents of Cobb County generously donate money, food, and equipment in support of the shelter. Some of these patrons also adopt animals from the shelter. Ryan has asked you to create an Access database to manage information about the animals, patrons, and donations. Complete the following steps:

1. Create a new, blank database named **Shelter** and save it in the folder where you are storing your files, as specified by your instructor.

2. In Datasheet view for the Table1 table, rename the default primary key ID field to **PatronID**. Change the data type of the PatronID field to Short Text.

3. Add the following four Short Text fields to the new table in the order shown: **Title**, **FirstName**, **LastName**, and **Phone**. Save the table as **Patron**.

4. Enter the records shown in Figure 1-34 in the Patron table. For the first record, be sure to enter your title in the Title field, your first name in the FirstName field, and your last name in the LastName field.

**Figure 1-34** **Patron table records**

| PatronID | Title | FirstName | LastName | Phone |
|----------|-------|-----------|----------|-------|
| 30405 | *Student Title* | *Student First* | *Student Last* | 770-427-9300 |
| 33287 | Dr. | Ali | Haddad | 770-528-8973 |
| 32189 | Mrs. | Gini | Smith | 770-499-2775 |
| 36028 | Mr. | Michael | Carlucci | 678-283-6334 |
| 30753 | Ms. | Cynthia | Crosby | 678-444-2676 |

© 2014 Cengage Learning

5. Ryan created a database named Animal that contains a Donor table with data about patrons. The Patron table you created has the same design as the Donor table. Copy all the records from the **Donor** table in the **Animal** database (located in the Access1 ▶ Case3 folder provided with your Data Files) and then paste them at the end of the Patron table in the Shelter database.

6. Resize all datasheet columns to their best fit, and then save the Patron table.

7. Close the Patron table, and then use the Navigation Pane to reopen it. Note that the records are displayed in primary key order by the values in the PatronID field.

⊕ **Explore**  8. Use the Simple Query Wizard to create a query that includes all the fields in the Patron table *except* the Title field. (*Hint*: Use the >> and < buttons to select the necessary fields.) Save the query using the name **PatronPhoneList**.

⊕ **Explore**  9. The query results are displayed in order by the PatronID field values. You can specify a different order by sorting the query. Display the HOME tab. Then, click the insertion point anywhere in the LastName column to make it the current field. In the Sort & Filter group on the HOME tab, click the Ascending button. The records are now listed in order by the values in the LastName field. Save and close the query.

⊕ **Explore**  10. Use the Form tool to create a form for the Patron table. In the new form, navigate to record 15 (the record with PatronID 33765), and then print the form *for the current record only*. (*Hint*: You must use the Print dialog box in order to print only the current record. Go to Backstage view, click Print in the navigation bar, and then click Print to open the Print dialog box. Click the Selected Record(s) option button and then click the OK button to print the current record.) Save the form as **PatronInfo**, and then close it.

11. Use the Report tool to create a report based on the Patron table. In Layout view, resize each field so it is slightly wider than the longest entry (either the field name itself or an entry in the field). All five fields should fit within the page area after resizing. At the bottom of the report, move the text "Page 1 of 1" to the left so it is within the page area. Display the report in Print Preview, then verify that the fields and page number fit within the page area and that all field values are fully displayed. Save the report as **PatronList**. Print the report (only if asked by your instructor to do so), and then close it.

12. Close the Patron table, and then compact and repair the Shelter database.

13. Close the Shelter database.

## Case Problem 4

**CHALLENGE**

**Data File needed for this Case Problem: Tour.accdb**

***Stanley EcoTours***   Janice and Bill Stanley live in Pocatello, Idaho, and are the proud owners and operators of Stanley EcoTours. Their passion is to encourage people to visit natural areas around the world in a responsible manner that does not harm the environment. Their advertising has drawn clients from Idaho, Wyoming, Montana, and Canada. As the interest in ecotourism grows, Janice and Bill's business is also expanding to include more tours in Africa and South America. Because of the growth in business that they anticipate, Janice and Bill realize their current recordkeeping system is inadequate. They would like you to build an Access database to manage information about guests, tours, and reservations. Complete the following:

1. Create a new, blank database named **Stanley** and save it in the folder where you are storing your files, as specified by your instructor.

2. In Datasheet view for the Table1 table, rename the default primary key ID field to **GuestID**. Change the data type of the GuestID field to Short Text.

3. Add the following eight Short Text fields to the new table in the order shown: **GuestFirst**, **GuestLast**, **Address**, **City**, **State/Prov**, **PostalCode**, **Country**, and **Phone**. Save the table as **Guest**.

4. Enter the records shown in Figure 1-35 in the Guest table. For the first record, be sure to enter your first name in the GuestFirst field and your last name in the GuestLast field.

**Figure 1-35**    **Guest table records**

| GuestID | GuestFirst | GuestLast | Address | City | State/Prov | PostalCode | Country | Phone |
|---------|-----------|-----------|---------|------|-----------|-----------|---------|-------|
| 401 | *Student First* | *Student Last* | 10 Winter Ave | Boise | ID | 83702 | USA | 208-344-0975 |
| 417 | Isabelle | Rouy | 227 Front Ln | Calgary | AB | T1Y 2N7 | Canada | 403-226-0065 |
| 403 | Brian | Anderson | 5003 Grant Blvd | Great Falls | MT | 59401 | USA | 406-761-4515 |
| 425 | Kelly | Skolnik | 15 Tobin Dr | Red Deer | AB | T4N 3D5 | Canada | 403-755-1597 |
| 420 | Alberto | Lopez | 991 Crestview Dr | Butte | MT | 59701 | USA | 406-782-1183 |

© 2014 Cengage Learning

5. Bill created a database named Tour that contains a Customer table with data about guests. The Guest table you created has the same design as the Customer table. Copy all the records from the **Customer** table in the **Tour** database (located in the Access1 ▸ Case4 folder provided with your Data Files) and then paste them at the end of the Guest table in the Stanley database.

6. Resize all datasheet columns to their best fit, and then save the Guest table.

7. Close the Guest table, and then use the Navigation Pane to reopen it. Note that the records are displayed in primary key order.

8. Use the Simple Query Wizard to create a query that includes the following fields from the Guest table, in the order shown: GuestID, GuestLast, GuestFirst, State/Prov, and Phone. Name the query **GuestData**.

⊕ **Explore** 9. The query results are displayed in order by the GuestID field values. You can specify a different order by sorting the query. Display the HOME tab. Then, click the insertion point anywhere in the State/Prov column to make it the current field. In the Sort & Filter group on the HOME tab, click the Ascending button. The records are now listed in order by the values in the State/Prov field. Save and close the query.

⊕ **Explore** 10. Use the Form tool to create a form for the Guest table. In the new form, navigate to record 10 (the record with GuestID 412), and then print the form *for the current record only*. (*Hint*: You must use the Print dialog box in order to print only the current record. Go to Backstage view, click Print in the navigation bar, and then click Print to open the Print dialog box. Click the Selected Record(s) option button and then click the OK button to print the current record.) Save the form as **GuestInfo**, and then close it.

11. Use the Report tool to create a report based on the Guest table. In Layout view, resize each field so it is slightly wider than the longest entry (either the field name itself or an entry in the field). At the bottom of the report, move the text "Page 1 of 1" to the left so it is within the page area on the report's first page. Display the report in Print Preview and notice that the columns of the report are still spread across two pages, even after resizing the fields. Save the report as **GuestList**.

⊕ **Explore** 12. In the Close Preview group, click the Close Print Preview button to return to the report in Layout view. To make more room on the first page, you'll delete the Address, PostalCode, and Country columns from the report. Click anywhere in the Address column to make it active. Click the ARRANGE tab (one of the REPORT LAYOUT TOOLS contextual tabs), and then click the Select Column button in the Rows & Columns group. Click the HOME tab, and then click the Delete button in the Records group to delete the selected column from the report. Repeat this process to delete the PostalCode and Country columns. The remaining six fields should now all fit on the report's first page.

13. Display the report in Print Preview again, then verify that the fields and page number fit within the page area and that all field values are fully displayed.

14. Save the report, print it (only if asked by your instructor to do so), and then close it.

15. Close the Guest table, and then compact and repair the Stanley database.

16. Close the Stanley database.

# Building a Database and Defining Table Relationships

ACCESS

*Creating the Billing and Patient Tables*

## OBJECTIVES

**Session 2.1**
- Learn the guidelines for designing databases and setting field properties
- Create a table in Design view
- Define fields, set field properties, and specify a table's primary key
- Modify the structure of a table
- Change the order of fields in Design view
- Add new fields in Design view
- Change the Format property for a field in Datasheet view
- Modify field properties in Design view

**Session 2.2**
- Import data from an Excel worksheet
- Create a table by importing an existing table structure
- Add fields to a table with the Data Type gallery
- Delete and rename fields
- Change the data type for a field in Design view
- Set the Default Value property for a field
- Add data to a table by importing a text file
- Define a relationship between two tables

## Case | *Chatham Community Health Services*

The Chatham database currently contains one table, the Visit table. Cindi Rodriguez also wants to track information about the clinic's patients and the invoices sent to them for services provided by Chatham Community Health Services. This information includes such items as each patient's name and address, and the amount and billing date for each invoice.

In this tutorial, you'll create two new tables in the Chatham database—named Billing and Patient—to contain the additional data Cindi wants to track. You will use two different methods for creating the tables, and learn how to modify the fields. After adding records to the tables, you will define the necessary relationships between the tables in the Chatham database to relate the tables, enabling Cindi and her staff to work with the data more efficiently.

## STARTING DATA FILES

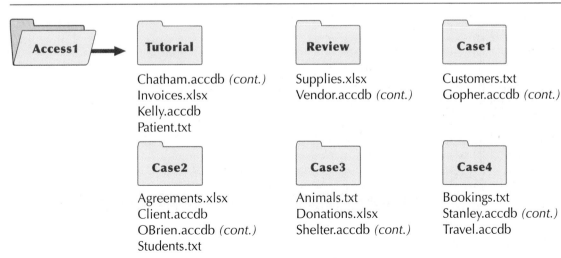

| Access1 → | Tutorial | Review | Case1 |
|---|---|---|---|
| | Chatham.accdb *(cont.)* | Supplies.xlsx | Customers.txt |
| | Invoices.xlsx | Vendor.accdb *(cont.)* | Gopher.accdb *(cont.)* |
| | Kelly.accdb | | |
| | Patient.txt | | |

| | Case2 | Case3 | Case4 |
|---|---|---|---|
| | Agreements.xlsx | Animals.txt | Bookings.txt |
| | Client.accdb | Donations.xlsx | Stanley.accdb *(cont.)* |
| | OBrien.accdb *(cont.)* | Shelter.accdb *(cont.)* | Travel.accdb |
| | Students.txt | | |

# Session 2.1 Visual Overview:

**Design view** allows you to define or modify a table structure or the properties of the fields in a table.

The default name for a new table you create in Design view is Table1. This name appears on the tab for the new table.

The top portion of the Table window in Design view is called the **Table Design grid**. Here, you enter values for the Field Name, Data Type, and Description field properties.

After you assign a data type to a field, the General tab displays additional field properties for that data type. Initially, most field properties are assigned default values.

When defining the fields in a table, you can move from the Table Design grid to the Field Properties pane by pressing the **F6 key**.

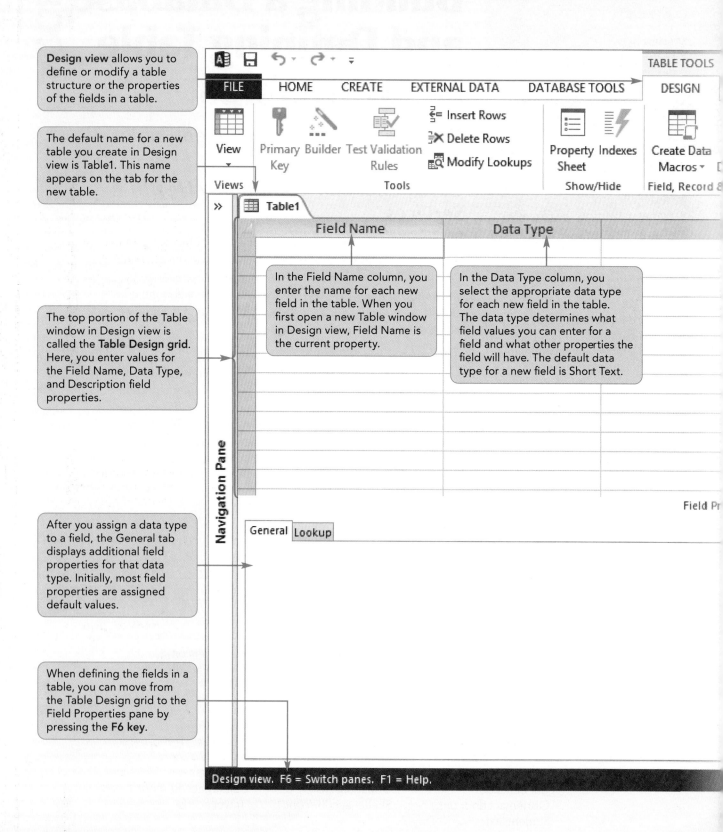

TABLE TOOLS

FILE    HOME    CREATE    EXTERNAL DATA    DATABASE TOOLS    DESIGN

View    Primary Builder Test Validation    Insert Rows    Property Indexes    Create Data
        Key              Rules             Delete Rows      Sheet              Macros
                                           Modify Lookups

Views                    Tools                              Show/Hide          Field, Record &

Navigation Pane

Table1

Field Name    Data Type

In the Field Name column, you enter the name for each new field in the table. When you first open a new Table window in Design view, Field Name is the current property.

In the Data Type column, you select the appropriate data type for each new field in the table. The data type determines what field values you can enter for a field and what other properties the field will have. The default data type for a new field is Short Text.

Field Pr

General    Lookup

Design view.  F6 = Switch panes.  F1 = Help.

# Table Window in Design View

Chatham : Database- E:\Access1\Tutorial\Chatham.accdb (Access...   ?  —  ⧉  ✕

Sign in

OLS

N

Rename/
Delete Macro

Relationships

Object
Dependencies

ata

ord & Table Events        Relationships

Description (Optional)

You can use the **Description property** to enter an optional description for a field to explain its purpose or usage. A field's Description property can be up to 255 characters long, and its value appears on the status bar when you view the table datasheet.

eld Properties

The bottom portion of the Table window in Design view is called the **Field Properties pane**. Here, you select values for all other field properties, most of which are optional.

The purpose or characteristics of the current property (Field Name, in this case) appear in this section of the Field Properties pane.

A field name can be up to 64 characters long, including spaces. Press F1 for help on field names.

You can display more complete Help information about the current property by pressing the **F1 key**.

# Guidelines for Designing Databases

A database management system can be a useful tool, but only if you first carefully design the database so that it meets the needs of its users. In database design, you determine the fields, tables, and relationships needed to satisfy the data and processing requirements. When you design a database, you should follow these guidelines:

- **Identify all the fields needed to produce the required information.** For example, Cindi needs information about patients, visits, and invoices. Figure 2-1 shows the fields that satisfy these information requirements.

| Figure 2-1 | Cindi's data requirements |
| --- | --- |

| | |
| --- | --- |
| VisitID | InvoiceDate |
| PatientID | Reason |
| InvoiceAmt | Phone |
| FirstName | WalkIn |
| LastName | Email |
| Address | VisitDate |
| City | InvoiceNum |
| State | InvoicePaid |
| Zip | BirthDate |

© 2014 Cengage Learning

- **Organize each piece of data into its smallest useful part.** For example, Cindi could store each patient's complete name in one field called PatientName instead of using two fields called FirstName and LastName, as shown in Figure 2-1. However, doing so would make it more difficult to work with the data. If Cindi wanted to view the records in alphabetical order by last name, she wouldn't be able to do so with field values such as "Ben Li" and "Amanda Fox" stored in a PatientName field. She could do so with field values such as "Li" and "Fox" stored separately in a LastName field.
- **Group related fields into tables.** For example, Cindi grouped the fields related to visits into the Visit table, which you created in Tutorial 1. The fields related to invoices are grouped into the Billing table, and the fields related to patients are grouped into the Patient table. Figure 2-2 shows the fields grouped into all three tables for the Chatham database.

| Figure 2-2 | Cindi's fields grouped into tables |
| --- | --- |

| Visit table | Billing table | Patient table |
| --- | --- | --- |
| VisitID | InvoiceNum | PatientID |
| PatientID | VisitID | LastName |
| VisitDate | InvoiceDate | FirstName |
| Reason | InvoiceAmt | BirthDate |
| WalkIn | InvoicePaid | Phone |
| | | Address |
| | | City |
| | | State |
| | | Zip |
| | | Email |

© 2014 Cengage Learning

- **Determine each table's primary key.** Recall that a primary key uniquely identifies each record in a table. For some tables, one of the fields, such as a credit card number, naturally serves the function of a primary key. For other tables, two or more fields might be needed to function as the primary key. In these cases, the primary key is called a **composite key**. For example, a school grade table would use a combination of student number, term, and course code to serve as the primary key. For a third category of tables, no single field or combination of fields can uniquely identify a record in a table. In these cases, you need to add a field whose sole purpose is to serve as the table's primary key. For Cindi's tables, VisitID is the primary key for the Visit table, InvoiceNum is the primary key for the Billing table, and PatientID is the primary key for the Patient table.
- **Include a common field in related tables.** You use the common field to connect one table logically with another table. For example, Cindi's Visit and Patient tables include the PatientID field as a common field. Recall that when you include the primary key from one table as a field in a second table to form a relationship, the field in the second table is called a foreign key; therefore, the PatientID field is a foreign key in the Visit table. With this common field, Cindi can find all visits to the clinic made by a particular patient; she can use the PatientID value for a patient and search the Visit table for all records with that PatientID value. Likewise, she can determine which patient made a particular visit by searching the Patient table to find the one record with the same PatientID value as the corresponding value in the Visit table. Similarly, the VisitID field is a common field, serving as the primary key in the Visit table and a foreign key in the Billing table.
- **Avoid data redundancy.** When you store the same data in more than one place, **data redundancy** occurs. With the exception of common fields to connect tables, you should avoid data redundancy because it wastes storage space and can cause inconsistencies. An inconsistency would exist, for example, if you type a field value one way in one table and a different way in the same table or in a second table. Figure 2-3, which contains portions of potential data stored in the Patient and Visit tables, shows an example of incorrect database design that has data redundancy in the Visit table. In Figure 2-3, the LastName field in the Visit table is redundant, and one value for this field was entered incorrectly, in three different ways.

**Figure 2-3**    Incorrect database design with data redundancy

© 2014 Cengage Learning

- **Determine the properties of each field.** You need to identify the **properties**, or characteristics, of each field so that the DBMS knows how to store, display, and process the field values. These properties include the field's name, data type, maximum number of characters or digits, description, valid values, and other field characteristics. You will learn more about field properties later in this tutorial.

The Billing and Patient tables you need to create will contain the fields shown in Figure 2-2. Before creating these new tables in the Chatham database, you first need to learn some guidelines for setting field properties.

# Guidelines for Setting Field Properties

As just noted, the last step of database design is to determine which values to assign to the properties, such as the name and data type, of each field. When you select or enter a value for a property, you **set** the property. Access has rules for naming fields and objects, assigning data types, and setting other field properties.

## Naming Fields and Objects

You must name each field, table, and other object in an Access database. Access stores these items in the database, using the names you supply. It's best to choose a field or object name that describes the purpose or contents of the field or object so that later you can easily remember what the name represents. For example, the three tables in the Chatham database are named Visit, Billing, and Patient because these names suggest their contents. Note that a table or query name must be unique within a database. A field name must be unique within a table, but it can be used again in another table.

## Assigning Field Data Types

Each field must have a data type, which is either assigned automatically by Access or specifically by the table designer. The data type determines what field values you can enter for the field and what other properties the field will have. For example, the Billing table will include an InvoiceDate field, which will store date values, so you will assign the Date/Time data type to this field. Then Access will allow you to enter and manipulate only dates or times as values in the InvoiceDate field.

Figure 2-4 lists the most commonly used data types in Access, describes the field values allowed for each data type, explains when you should use each data type, and indicates the field size of each data type. You can find more complete information about all available data types in Access Help.

| Figure 2-4 | Common data types |

| Data Type | Description | Field Size |
|---|---|---|
| Short Text | Allows field values containing letters, digits, spaces, and special characters. Use for names, addresses, descriptions, and fields containing digits that are *not used in calculations*. | 0 to 255 characters; default is 255 |
| Long Text | Allows field values containing letters, digits, spaces, and special characters. Use for long comments and explanations. | 1 to 65,535 characters; exact size is determined by entry |
| Number | Allows positive and negative numbers as field values. A number can contain digits, a decimal point, commas, a plus sign, and a minus sign. Use for fields that will be used in calculations, except those involving money. | 1 to 15 digits |
| Date/Time | Allows field values containing valid dates and times from January 1, 100 to December 31, 9999. Dates can be entered in month/day/year format, several other date formats, or a variety of time formats, such as 10:35 PM. You can perform calculations on dates and times, and you can sort them. For example, you can determine the number of days between two dates. | 8 bytes |
| Currency | Allows field values similar to those for the Number data type, but is used for storing monetary values. Unlike calculations with Number data type decimal values, calculations performed with the Currency data type are not subject to round-off error. | Accurate to 15 digits on the left side of the decimal point and to 4 digits on the right side |
| AutoNumber | Consists of integer values created automatically by Access each time you create a new record. You can specify sequential numbering or random numbering, which guarantees a unique field value, so that such a field can serve as a table's primary key. | 9 digits |
| Yes/No | Limits field values to yes and no, on and off, or true and false. Use for fields that indicate the presence or absence of a condition, such as whether an order has been filled or whether an invoice has been paid. | 1 character |
| Hyperlink | Consists of text used as a hyperlink address, which can have up to four parts: the text that appears in a field or control; the path to a file or page; a location within the file or page; and text displayed as a ScreenTip. | Up to 65,535 characters total for the four parts of the hyperlink |

© 2014 Cengage Learning

## Setting Field Sizes

The **Field Size property** defines a field value's maximum storage size for Short Text, Number, and AutoNumber fields only. The other data types have no Field Size property because their storage size is either a fixed, predetermined amount or is determined automatically by the field value itself, as shown in Figure 2-4. A Short Text field has a default field size of 255 characters; you can also set its field size by entering a number from 0 to 255. For example, the FirstName and LastName fields in the Patient table will be Short Text fields with sizes of 20 characters and 25 characters, respectively. These field sizes will accommodate the values that will be entered in each of these fields.

## Decision Making: Specifying the Field Size Property for Number Fields

When you use the Number data type to define a field, you need to decide what the Field Size setting should be for the field. You should set the Field Size property based on the largest value that you expect to store in that field. Access processes smaller data sizes faster, using less memory, so you can optimize your database's performance and its storage space by selecting the correct field size for each field. Field Size property settings for Number fields are as follows:

- **Byte**: Stores whole numbers (numbers with no fractions) from 0 to 255 in one byte
- **Integer**: Stores whole numbers from –32,768 to 32,767 in two bytes
- **Long Integer** (default): Stores whole numbers from –2,147,483,648 to 2,147,483,647 in four bytes
- **Single**: Stores positive and negative numbers to precisely seven decimal places in four bytes
- **Double**: Stores positive and negative numbers to precisely 15 decimal places in eight bytes
- **Replication ID**: Establishes a unique identifier for replication of tables, records, and other objects in databases created using Access 2003 and earlier versions in 16 bytes
- **Decimal**: Stores positive and negative numbers to precisely 28 decimal places in 12 bytes

Choosing an appropriate field size is important to optimize efficiency. For example, it would be wasteful to use the Long Integer field size for a Number field that will store only whole numbers ranging from 0 to 255 because the Long Integer field size uses four bytes of storage space. A better choice would be the Byte field size, which uses one byte of storage space to store the same values. By first gathering and analyzing information about the number values that will be stored in a Number field, you can make the best decision for the field's Field Size property and ensure the most efficient user experience for the database.

## Setting the Caption Property for Fields

The **Caption property** for a field specifies how the field name is displayed in database objects, including table and query datasheets, forms, and reports. If you don't set the Caption property, Access displays the field name as the column heading or label for a field. For example, field names such as InvoiceAmt and InvoiceDate in the Billing table can be difficult to read. Setting the Caption property for these fields to "Invoice Amt" and "Invoice Date" would make it easier for users to read the field names and work with the database.

### Setting the Caption Property vs. Naming Fields

Although Access allows you to include spaces in field names, this practice is not recommended because the spaces cause problems when you try to perform more complex tasks with the data in your database. Setting the Caption property allows you to follow best practices for naming fields, such as not including spaces in field names, while still providing users with more readable field names in datasheets, forms, and reports.

In Tutorial 1, you created the Chatham database file and, within that file, you created the Visit table working in Datasheet view. According to her plan for the Chatham database, Cindi also wants to track information about the invoices the clinic sends to its patients. Next, you'll create the Billing table for Cindi—this time, working in Design view.

# Creating a Table in Design View

Creating a table in Design view involves entering the field names and defining the properties for the fields, specifying a primary key for the table, and then saving the table structure. Cindi documented the design for the new Billing table by listing each field's name and data type; each field's size and description (if applicable); and any other properties to be set for each field. See Figure 2-5.

| Figure 2-5 | Design for the Billing table |
| --- | --- |

| Field Name | Data Type | Field Size | Description | Other |
| --- | --- | --- | --- | --- |
| InvoiceNum | Short Text | 5 | Primary key | Caption = Invoice Num |
| VisitID | Short Text | 4 | Foreign key | Caption = Visit ID |
| InvoiceAmt | Currency | | | Format = Currency |
| | | | | Decimal Places = 2 |
| | | | | Caption = Invoice Amt |
| InvoiceDate | Date/Time | | | Format = mm/dd/yyyy |
| | | | | Caption = Invoice Date |
| InvoicePaid | Yes/No | | | Caption = Invoice Paid |

© 2014 Cengage Learning

You'll use Cindi's design as a guide for creating the Billing table in the Chatham database.

### To begin creating the Billing table:

1. Start Access and open the **Chatham** database you created in Tutorial 1.

   **Trouble?** If the security warning is displayed below the ribbon, click the Enable Content button.

2. If the Navigation Pane is open, click the **Shutter Bar Open/Close Button** « to close it.

3. On the ribbon, click the **CREATE** tab.

4. In the Tables group, click the **Table Design** button. A new table named Table1 opens in Design view. Refer to the Session 2.1 Visual Overview for a complete description of the Table window in Design view.

## Defining Fields

When you first create a table in Design view, the insertion point is located in the first row's Field Name box, ready for you to begin defining the first field in the table. You enter values for the Field Name, Data Type, and Description field properties, and then select values for all other field properties in the Field Properties pane. These other properties will appear when you move to the first row's Data Type box.

**REFERENCE**

### Defining a Field in Design View

- In the Field Name box, type the name for the field, and then press the Tab key.
- Accept the default Short Text data type, or click the arrow and select a different data type for the field. Press the Tab key.
- Enter an optional description for the field, if necessary.
- Use the Field Properties pane to type or select other field properties, as appropriate.

The first field you need to define is the InvoiceNum field. This field will be the primary key for the Billing table. Each invoice at Chatham Community Health Services is assigned a specific five-digit number. Although the InvoiceNum field will contain these number values, the numbers will never be used in calculations; therefore, you'll assign the Short Text data type to this field. Any time a field contains number values that will not be used in calculations—such as phone numbers, zip codes, and so on—you should use the Short Text data type instead of the Number data type.

### To define the InvoiceNum field:

**TIP**

You can also press the Enter key to move from one property to the next in the Table Design grid.

1. Type **InvoiceNum** in the first row's Field Name box, and then press the **Tab** key to advance to the Data Type box. The default data type, Short Text, appears highlighted in the Data Type box, which now also contains an arrow, and the field properties for a Short Text field appear in the Field Properties pane. See Figure 2-6.

**Figure 2-6**    **Table window after entering the first field name**

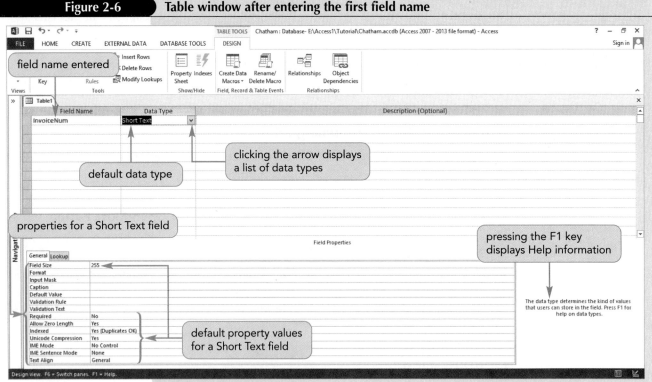

Notice that the right side of the Field Properties pane now provides an explanation for the current property, Data Type.

**Trouble?** If you make a typing error, you can correct it by clicking to position the insertion point, and then using either the Backspace key to delete characters to the left of the insertion point or the Delete key to delete characters to the right of the insertion point. Then type the correct text.

Because the InvoiceNum field values will not be used in calculations, you will accept the default Short Text data type for the field.

2. Press the **Tab** key to accept Short Text as the data type and to advance to the Description (Optional) box.

Next you'll enter the Description property value as "Primary key." The value you enter for the Description property will appear on the status bar when you view the table datasheet. Note that specifying "Primary key" for the Description property does *not* establish the current field as the primary key; you use a button on the ribbon to specify the primary key in Design view, which you will do later in this session.

3. Type **Primary key** in the Description (Optional) box.

   Notice the Field Size property for the field. The default setting of 255 for Short Text fields is displayed. You need to change this number to 5 because all invoice numbers at Chatham Community Health Services contain only five digits.

4. Double-click the number **255** in the Field Size property box to select it, and then type **5**.

   Finally, you need to set the Caption property for the field so that its name appears with a space, as "Invoice Num."

5. Click the **Caption** property box, and then type **Invoice Num**. The definition of the first field is complete. See Figure 2-7.

| Figure 2-7 | InvoiceNum field defined |
|---|---|

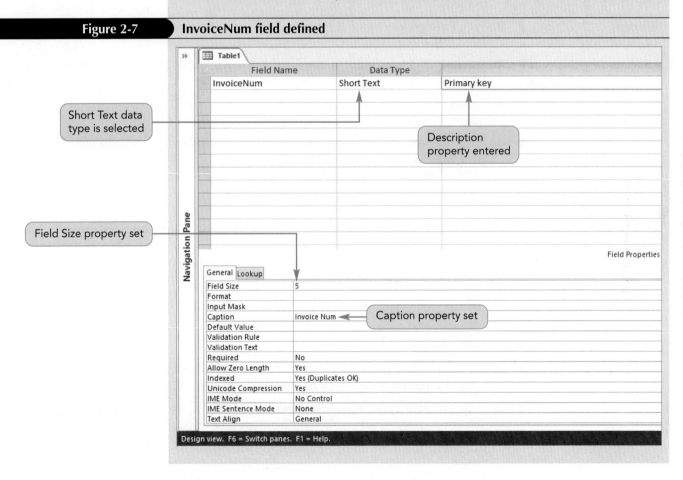

Short Text data type is selected

Description property entered

Field Size property set

Caption property set

Cindi's Billing table design (Figure 2-5) shows VisitID as the second field. Because Cindi and other staff members need to relate information about invoices to the visit data in the Visit table, the Billing table must include the VisitID field, which is the Visit table's primary key. Recall that when you include the primary key from one table as a field in a second table to connect the two tables, the field is a foreign key in the second table. The field must be defined in the same way in both tables—that is, the field properties, including field size and data type, must match exactly.

Next, you will define VisitID as a Short Text field with a field size of 4. Later in this session, you'll change the Field Size property for the VisitID field in the Visit table to 4 so that the field definition is the same in both tables.

### To define the VisitID field:

▶ 1. In the Table Design grid, click the second row's Field Name box, type **VisitID** in the box, and then press the **Tab** key to advance to the Data Type box.

▶ 2. Press the **Tab** key to accept Short Text as the field's data type. Because the VisitID field is a foreign key to the Visit table, you'll enter "Foreign key" in the Description (Optional) box to help users of the database understand the purpose of this field.

▶ 3. Type **Foreign key** in the Description (Optional) box. Next, you'll change the Field Size property to 4.

▶ 4. Press the **F6** key to move to the Field Properties pane. The current entry for the Field Size property, 255, is highlighted.

▶ 5. Type **4** to set the Field Size property. Finally, you need to set the Caption property for this field.

▶ 6. Press the **Tab** key until the insertion point is in the Caption box, and then type **Visit ID** (be sure to include a space between the two words). You have completed the definition of the second field.

**TIP**

The quickest way to move back to the Table Design grid is to use the mouse.

The third field in the Billing table is the InvoiceAmt field, which will display the dollar amount of each invoice the clinic sends to its patients. Cindi wants the values to appear with two decimal places because invoice amounts include cents. She also wants the values to include dollar signs, so that the values will be formatted as currency when they are printed in bills sent to patients. The Currency data type is the appropriate choice for this field.

### To define the InvoiceAmt field:

▶ 1. Click the third row's Field Name box, type **InvoiceAmt** in the box, and then press the **Tab** key to advance to the Data Type box.

▶ 2. Click the **Data Type** arrow, click **Currency** in the list, and then press the **Tab** key to advance to the Description (Optional) box.

According to Cindi's design (Figure 2-5), you do not need to enter a description for this field. If you've assigned a descriptive field name and the field does not fulfill a special function (such as primary key), you usually do not enter a value for the optional Description property. InvoiceAmt is a field that does not require a value for its Description property.

Cindi wants the InvoiceAmt field values to be displayed with two decimal places. The **Decimal Places property** specifies the number of decimal places that are displayed to the right of the decimal point.

**TIP**

You can display the arrow and the list simultaneously by clicking the right side of a box.

3. In the Field Properties pane, click the **Decimal Places** box to position the insertion point there. An arrow appears on the right side of the Decimal Places box. When you position the insertion point or select text in many boxes, Access displays an arrow, which you can click to display a list with options.

4. Click the **Decimal Places** arrow, and then click **2** in the list to specify two decimal places for the InvoiceAmt field values.

5. Press the **Tab** key until the insertion point is in the Caption box, and then type **Invoice Amt**. The definition of the third field is now complete. See Figure 2-8.

**Figure 2-8**    **Table window after defining the first three fields**

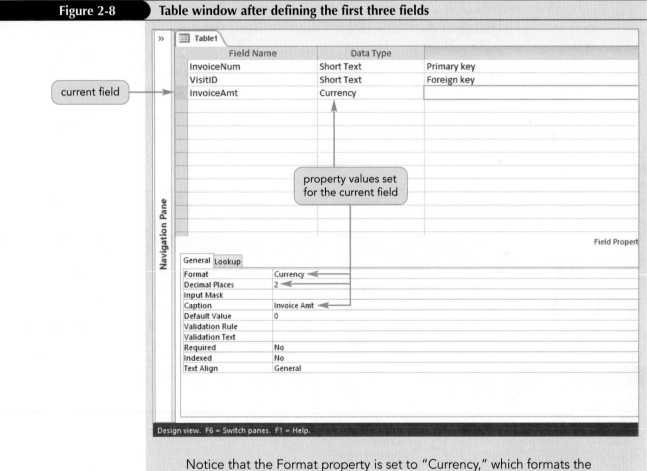

current field

property values set for the current field

Notice that the Format property is set to "Currency," which formats the values with dollar signs.

The fourth field in the Billing table is the InvoiceDate field. This field will contain the dates on which invoices are generated for the clinic's patients. You'll define the InvoiceDate field using the Date/Time data type. Also, according to Cindi's design (Figure 2-5), the date values should be displayed in the format mm/dd/yyyy, which is a two-digit month, a two-digit day, and a four-digit year.

### To define the InvoiceDate field:

1. Click the fourth row's Field Name box, type **InvoiceDate**, and then press the **Tab** key to advance to the Data Type box.

   You can select a value from the Data Type list as you did for the InvoiceAmt field. Alternately, you can type the property value in the box or type just the first character of the property value.

2. Type **d**. The value in the fourth row's Data Type box changes to "date/Time," with the letters "ate/Time" highlighted. See Figure 2-9.

| Figure 2-9 | Selecting a value for the Data Type property |
|---|---|

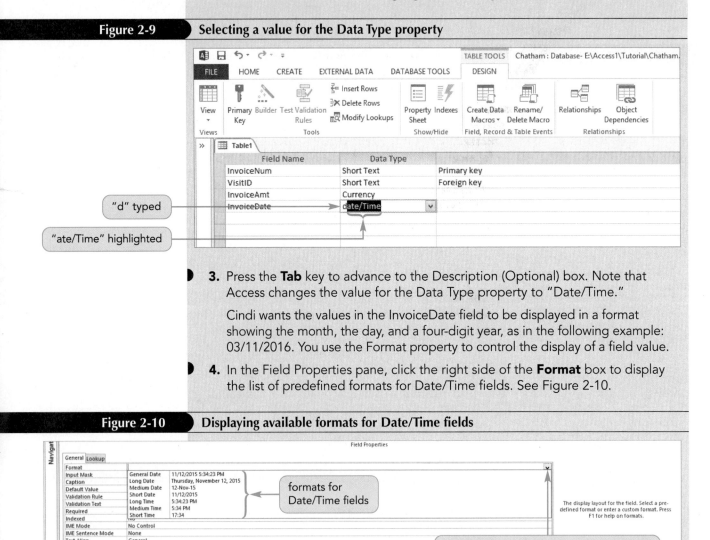

"d" typed

"ate/Time" highlighted

3. Press the **Tab** key to advance to the Description (Optional) box. Note that Access changes the value for the Data Type property to "Date/Time."

   Cindi wants the values in the InvoiceDate field to be displayed in a format showing the month, the day, and a four-digit year, as in the following example: 03/11/2016. You use the Format property to control the display of a field value.

4. In the Field Properties pane, click the right side of the **Format** box to display the list of predefined formats for Date/Time fields. See Figure 2-10.

| Figure 2-10 | Displaying available formats for Date/Time fields |
|---|---|

formats for Date/Time fields

click to display a list of predefined formats

**Trouble?** If you see an arrow instead of a list of predefined formats, click the arrow to display the list.

As noted in the right side of the Field Properties pane, you can either choose a predefined format or enter a custom format. Even though the Short Date format seems to match the format Cindi wants, it displays only one digit for months that contain only one digit. For example, it would display the month of March with only the digit "3"—as in 3/11/2016—instead of displaying the month with two digits, as in 03/11/2016.

Because none of the predefined formats matches the exact layout Cindi wants for the InvoiceDate values, you need to create a custom date format. Figure 2-11 shows some of the symbols available for custom date and time formats.

**Figure 2-11**    **Symbols for some custom date formats**

| Symbol | Description |
|--------|-------------|
| / | date separator |
| d | day of the month in one or two numeric digits, as needed (1 to 31) |
| dd | day of the month in two numeric digits (01 to 31) |
| ddd | first three letters of the weekday (Sun to Sat) |
| dddd | full name of the weekday (Sunday to Saturday) |
| w | day of the week (1 to 7) |
| ww | week of the year (1 to 53) |
| m | month of the year in one or two numeric digits, as needed (1 to 12) |
| mm | month of the year in two numeric digits (01 to 12) |
| mmm | first three letters of the month (Jan to Dec) |
| mmmm | full name of the month (January to December) |
| yy | last two digits of the year (01 to 99) |
| yyyy | full year (0100 to 9999) |

© 2014 Cengage Learning

Cindi wants the dates to be displayed with a two-digit month (mm), a two-digit day (dd), and a four-digit year (yyyy). You'll enter this custom format now.

5. Click the **Format** arrow to close the list of predefined formats, and then type **mm/dd/yyyy** in the Format box.

6. Press the **Tab** key until the insertion point is in the Caption box, and then type **Invoice Date**. See Figure 2-12.

**Figure 2-12** Specifying the custom date format

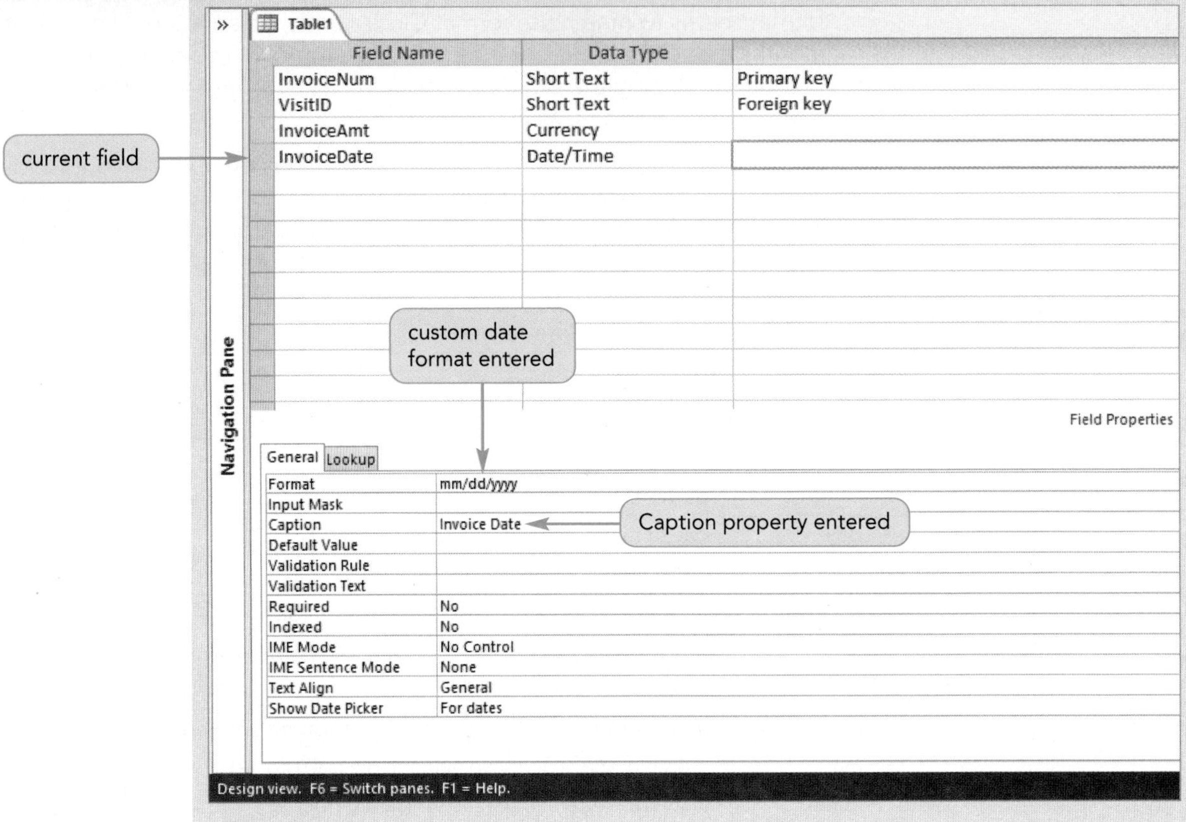

current field → 

| Field Name | Data Type | |
|---|---|---|
| InvoiceNum | Short Text | Primary key |
| VisitID | Short Text | Foreign key |
| InvoiceAmt | Currency | |
| InvoiceDate | Date/Time | |

custom date format entered

Field Properties

General | Lookup

| | |
|---|---|
| Format | mm/dd/yyyy |
| Input Mask | |
| Caption | Invoice Date ← Caption property entered |
| Default Value | |
| Validation Rule | |
| Validation Text | |
| Required | No |
| Indexed | No |
| IME Mode | No Control |
| IME Sentence Mode | None |
| Text Align | General |
| Show Date Picker | For dates |

Design view. F6 = Switch panes. F1 = Help.

The fifth, and final, field to be defined in the Billing table is InvoicePaid. This field will be a Yes/No field to indicate the payment status of each invoice record stored in the Billing table. Recall that the Yes/No data type is used to define fields that store true/false, yes/no, and on/off field values. When you create a Yes/No field in a table, the default Format property is set to Yes/No.

### To define the InvoicePaid field:

**1.** Click the fifth row's Field Name box, type **InvoicePaid**, and then press the **Tab** key to advance to the Data Type box.

**2.** Type **y**. Access completes the data type as "yes/No."

**3.** Press the **Tab** key to select the Yes/No data type and move to the Description (Optional) box. In the Field Properties pane, note that the default format of "Yes/No" is selected, so you do not have to change this property.

**4.** In the Field Properties pane, click the Caption box, and then type **Invoice Paid**.

You've finished defining the fields for the Billing table. Next, you need to specify the primary key for the table.

## Specifying the Primary Key

As you learned earlier, the primary key for a table uniquely identifies each record in the table.

**REFERENCE**

### Specifying a Primary Key in Design View

- Display the table in Design view.
- Click in the row for the field you've chosen to be the primary key to make it the active field. If the primary key will consist of two or more fields, click the row selector for the first field, press and hold down the Ctrl key, and then click the row selector for each additional primary key field.
- In the Tools group on the DESIGN tab, click the Primary Key button.

According to Cindi's design, you need to specify InvoiceNum as the primary key for the Billing table. You can do so while the table is in Design view.

### To specify InvoiceNum as the primary key:

1. Click in the row for the InvoiceNum field to make it the current field.

**TIP**

This button is a toggle; you can click it to remove the key symbol.

2. In the Tools group on the DESIGN tab, click the **Primary Key** button. The Primary Key button in the Tools group is now highlighted, and a key symbol appears in the row selector for the first row, indicating that the InvoiceNum field is the table's primary key. See Figure 2-13.

| Figure 2-13 | InvoiceNum field selected as the primary key |
| --- | --- |

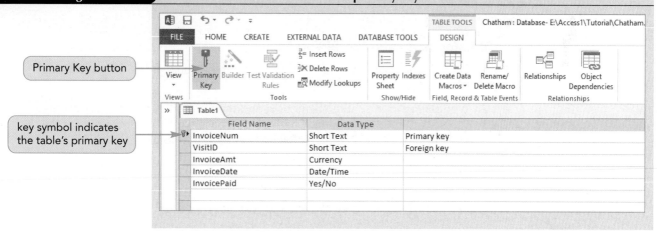

Primary Key button

key symbol indicates the table's primary key

| Field Name | Data Type | |
| --- | --- | --- |
| InvoiceNum | Short Text | Primary key |
| VisitID | Short Text | Foreign key |
| InvoiceAmt | Currency | |
| InvoiceDate | Date/Time | |
| InvoicePaid | Yes/No | |

*Understanding the Importance of the Primary Key*

Although Access does not require a table to have a primary key, including a primary key offers several advantages:

- A primary key uniquely identifies each record in a table.
- Access does not allow duplicate values in the primary key field. For example, if a record already exists in the Visit table with a VisitID value of 1550, Access prevents you from adding another record with this same value in the VisitID field. Preventing duplicate values ensures the uniqueness of the primary key field.
- When a primary key has been specified, Access forces you to enter a value for the primary key field in every record in the table. This is known as **entity integrity**. If you do not enter a value for a field, you have actually given the field a **null value**. You cannot give a null value to the primary key field because entity integrity prevents Access from accepting and processing that record.
- You can enter records in any order, but Access displays them by default in order of the primary key's field values. If you enter records in no specific order, you are ensured that you will later be able to work with them in a more meaningful, primary key sequence.
- Access responds faster to your requests for specific records based on the primary key.

## Saving the Table Structure

The last step in creating a table is to name the table and save the table's structure. When you save a table structure, the table is stored in the database file (in this case, the Chatham database file). Once the table is saved, you can enter data into it. According to Cindi's plan, you need to save the table you've defined as "Billing."

**To name and save the Billing table:**

▶ **1.** On the Quick Access Toolbar, click the **Save** button 🖫. The Save As dialog box opens.

▶ **2.** Type **Billing** in the Table Name box, and then press the **Enter** key. Access saves the Billing table in the Chatham database. Notice that the tab for the table now displays the name "Billing" instead of "Table1."

# Modifying the Structure of an Access Table

Even a well-designed table might need to be modified. Some changes that you can make to a table's structure in Design view include changing the order of fields and adding new fields.

After meeting with her assistant, Kelly Schwarz, and reviewing the structure of the Billing table, Cindi has changes she wants you to make to the table. First, she wants the InvoiceAmt field to be moved so that it appears right before the InvoicePaid field. Then, she wants you to add a new Short Text field named InvoiceItem to the table to include information about what the invoice is for, such as office visits, lab work, and so on. Cindi would like the InvoiceItem field to be inserted between the InvoiceDate and InvoiceAmt fields.

## Moving a Field in Design View

To move a field, you use the mouse to drag it to a new location in the Table Design grid. Although you can move a field in Datasheet view by dragging its column heading to a new location, doing so rearranges only the *display* of the table's fields; the table structure is not changed. To move a field permanently, you must move the field in Design view.

Next, you'll move the InvoiceAmt field so that it is before the InvoicePaid field in the Billing table.

### To move the InvoiceAmt field:

1. Position the pointer on the row selector for the InvoiceAmt field until the pointer changes to a ➡ shape.

2. Click the **row selector** to select the entire InvoiceAmt row.

3. Place the pointer on the row selector for the InvoiceAmt field until the pointer changes to ▷, and then click and drag to the row selector for the InvoicePaid field. Notice that as you drag, the pointer changes to ▷. See Figure 2-14.

| Figure 2-14 | Moving the InvoiceAmt field in the table structure |
|---|---|

4. Release the mouse button. The InvoiceAmt field now appears between the InvoiceDate and InvoicePaid fields in the table structure.

   **Trouble?** If the InvoiceAmt field did not move, repeat Steps 1 through 4, making sure you hold down the mouse button during the drag operation.

## Adding a Field in Design View

To add a new field between existing fields, you must insert a row. You begin by selecting the row below where you want the new field to be inserted.

**REFERENCE**

### Adding a Field Between Two Existing Fields

- In the Table window in Design view, select the row below where you want the new field to be inserted.
- In the Tools group on the DESIGN tab, click the Insert Rows button.
- Define the new field by entering the field name, data type, optional description, and any property specifications.

Next, you need to add the InvoiceItem field to the Billing table structure between the InvoiceAmt and InvoicePaid fields.

### To add the InvoiceItem field to the Billing table:

▶ 1. Click the **InvoicePaid** Field Name box. You need to establish this field as the current field so that the row for the new record will be inserted above this field.

▶ 2. In the Tools group on the DESIGN tab, click the **Insert Rows** button. Access adds a new, blank row between the InvoiceAmt and InvoicePaid fields. The insertion point is positioned in the Field Name box for the new row, ready for you to type the name for the new field. See Figure 2-15.

| Figure 2-15 | Table structure after inserting a row |
| --- | --- |

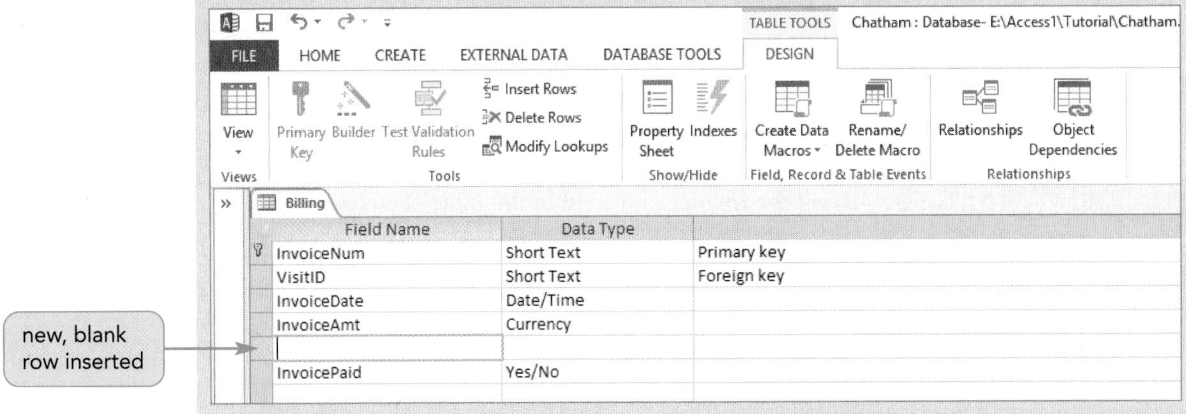

new, blank row inserted

**Trouble?** If you selected the InvoicePaid field's row selector and then inserted the new row, you need to click the new row's Field Name box to position the insertion point in it.

You'll define the InvoiceItem field in the new row of the Billing table. This field will be a Short Text field with a field size of 40, and you need to set the Caption property to include a space between the words in the field name.

▶ 3. Type **InvoiceItem**, press the **Tab** key to move to the Data Type property, and then press the **Tab** key again to accept the default Short Text data type.

▶ 4. Press the **F6** key to move to the Field Size box and to select the default field size, and then type **40**.

▶ 5. Press the **Tab** key until the insertion point is in the Caption box, and then type **Invoice Item**. The definition of the new field is complete. See Figure 2-16.

**Figure 2-16**    **InvoiceItem field added to the Billing table**

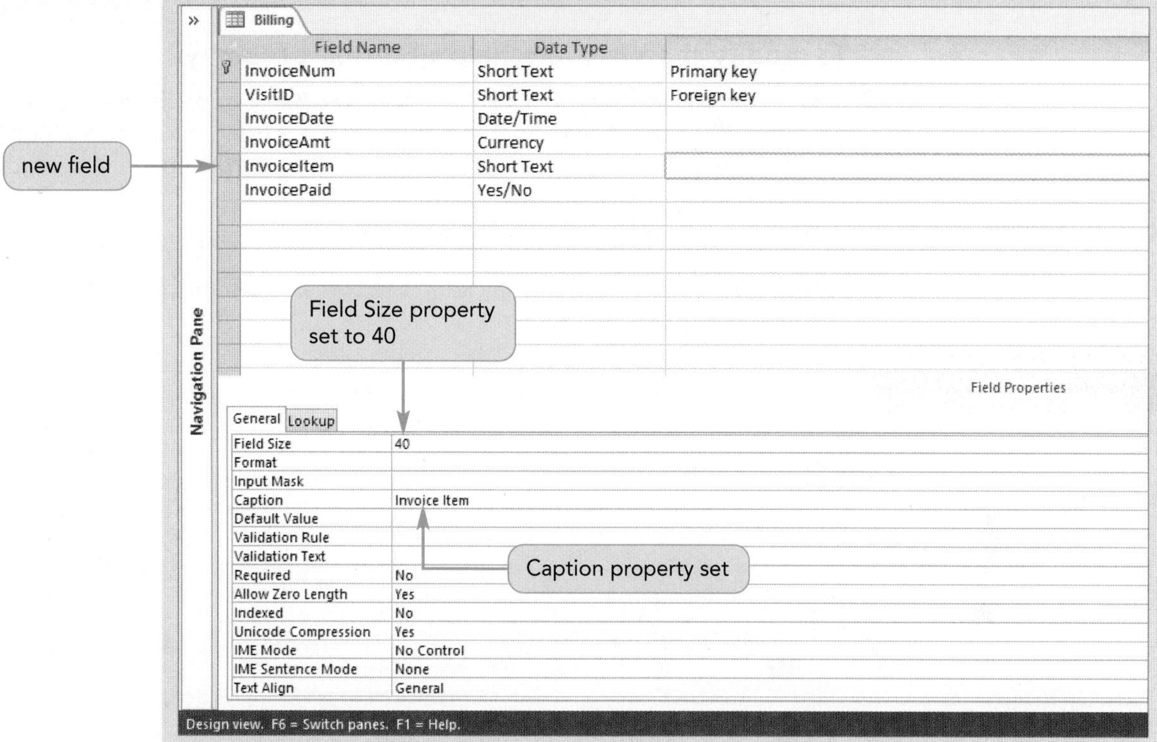

new field

Field Size property set to 40

Caption property set

Field Properties

6. On the Quick Access Toolbar, click the **Save** button 🖫 to save the changes to the Billing table structure.

7. Click the **Close 'Billing'** button ✕ on the object tab to close the Billing table.

# Modifying Field Properties

With the Billing table design complete, you can now go back and modify the properties of the fields in the Visit table you created in Tutorial 1, as necessary. You can make some changes to properties in Datasheet view; for others, you'll work in Design view.

## Changing the Format Property in Datasheet View

The Formatting group on the FIELDS tab in Datasheet view allows you to modify some formatting for certain field types. When you format a field, you change the way data is displayed, but not the actual values stored in the table.

Next, you'll check the properties of the VisitDate field in the Visit table to see if any changes are needed to improve the display of the date values.

## To modify the VisitDate field's Format property:

▸ **1.** On the Navigation Pane, click the **Shutter Bar Open/Close Button** [»] to open the pane. Notice that the Billing table is listed above the Visit table in the Tables section. By default, objects are listed in the pane in alphabetical order.

▸ **2.** Double-click **Visit** to open the Visit table in Datasheet view.

▸ **3.** On the Navigation Pane, click the **Shutter Bar Open/Close Button** [«] to close the pane. See Figure 2-17.

| Figure 2-17 | Visit table datasheet |

Short Text field values are left-aligned

check boxes for Yes/No field are centered

Date/Time field values are right-aligned

Notice that the values in the three Short Text fields—VisitID, PatientID, and Reason—appear left-aligned within their boxes, and the values in the Date/Time field (VisitDate) appear right-aligned. In Access, values for Short Text fields are left-aligned, and values for Number, Date/Time, and Currency fields are right-aligned. The WalkIn field is a Yes/No field, so its values appear in check boxes that are centered within the column.

▸ **4.** On the ribbon, click the **FIELDS** tab.

▸ **5.** Click the first field value in the VisitDate column. The Data Type option shows that this field is a Date/Time field.

By default, Access assigns the General Date format to Date/Time fields. Note the Format option in the Formatting group; this is the same as the Format property in the Field Properties pane in Design view. Even though the Format box is empty, the VisitDate field has the General Date format applied to it. The General Date format includes settings for date or time values, or a combination of date and time values. However, Cindi wants *only date values* to be displayed in the VisitDate field, so she asks you to specify the Short Date format for the field.

▸ **6.** In the Formatting group, click the **Format arrow**, and then click **Short Date**. See Figure 2-18.

**Figure 2-18**    **VisitDate field after modifying the format**

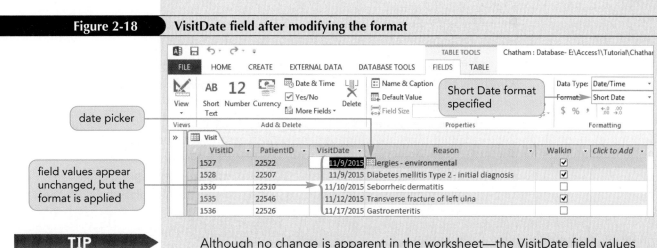

date picker

field values appear
unchanged, but the
format is applied

**TIP**

When working with date
values, you can type dates
directly or click the date
picker shown in Figure 2-18
to select a date from an
interactive calendar.

Although no change is apparent in the worksheet—the VisitDate field values
already appear with the Short Date setting (for example, 11/9/2015), as part
of the default General Date format—the field now has the Short Date format
applied to it. This ensures that only date field values, and not time or
date/time values, are allowed in the field.

## Changing Properties in Design View

Recall that each of the Short Text fields in the Visit table—VisitID, PatientID, and
Reason—still has the default field size of 255, which is too large for the data contained
in these fields. Also, the VisitID and PatientID fields need descriptions to identify them
as the primary and foreign keys, respectively, in the table. Finally, each of these fields
needs a caption either to include a space between the words in the field name or to
make the name more descriptive. You can make all of these property changes more
easily in Design view.

### To modify the Field Size, Description, and Caption field properties:

**TIP**

You can also click the
Design View button in the
far right of the status bar
to switch to Design view.

1. In the Views group on the FIELDS tab, click the **View** button. The table is
   displayed in Design view with the VisitID field selected. You need to enter
   a Description property value for this field, the primary key in the table, and
   change its Field Size property to 4 because each visit number at Chatham
   Community Health Services consists of four digits.

2. Press the **Tab** key until the insertion point is in the Description (Optional) box,
   and then type **Primary key**.

3. Press the **F6** key to move to and select the default setting of 255 for the Field
   Size property, and then type **4**. Next you need to set the Caption property
   for this field.

4. Press the **Tab** key until the insertion point is in the Caption box, and then
   type **Visit ID**.

   Next you need to enter a Description property value for the PatientID field,
   a foreign key in the table, and set its Field Size property to 5 because each
   PatientID number at Chatham Community Health Services consists of five
   digits. You also need to set this field's Caption property.

5. Click the **Description (Optional)** box for the PatientID field, and then type
   **Foreign key**.

▶ **6.** Press the **F6** key, type **5**, press the **Tab** key until the insertion point is in the Caption box, and then type **Patient ID**.

Next you'll set the Caption property for the VisitDate field.

▶ **7.** Click the **VisitDate** Field Name box, click the **Caption** box, and then type **Date of Visit**.

For the Reason field, you will set the Field Size property to 60. This size can accommodate the longer values in the Reason field. You'll also set this field's Caption property to provide a more descriptive name.

▶ **8.** Click the **Reason** Field Name box, press the **F6** key, type **60**, press the **Tab** key until the insertion point is in the Caption box, and then type **Reason/Diagnosis**.

Finally, you'll set the Caption property for the WalkIn field.

▶ **9.** Click the **WalkIn** Field Name box, click the **Caption** box, and then type **Walk-in?** See Figure 2-19.

| Figure 2-19 | Visit table after modifying field properties |
|---|---|

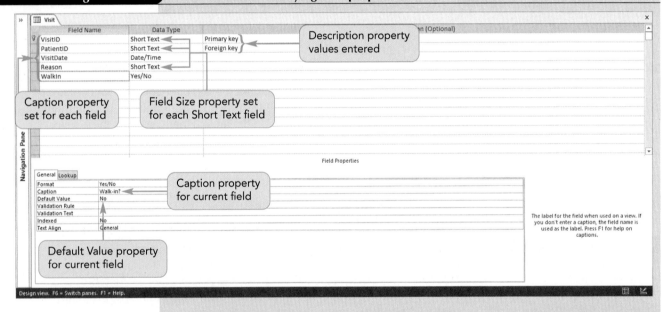

Notice that the WalkIn field's Default Value property is automatically set to "No," which means the check box for this field will be empty for each new record. This is the default for this property for any Yes/No field. You can set the Default Value property for other types of fields to make data entry easier. You'll learn more about setting this property in the next session.

The changes to the Visit table's properties are now complete, so you can save the table and view the results of your changes in Datasheet view.

### To save and view the modified Visit table:

1. On the Quick Access Toolbar, click the **Save** button 🖫 to save the modified table. A dialog box opens informing you that some data may be lost because you decreased the field sizes. Because all of the values in the VisitID, PatientID, and Reason fields contain the same number of or fewer characters than the new Field Size properties you set for each field, you can ignore this message.

2. Click the **Yes** button.

3. In the Views group on the DESIGN tab, click the **View** button to display the Visit table in Datasheet view. Notice that each column (field) heading now displays the text you specified in the Caption property for that field. See Figure 2-20.

| Figure 2-20 | Modified Visit table in Datasheet view |
|---|---|

column headings display Caption property values

| Visit ID | Patient ID | Date of Visit | Reason/Diagnosis | Walk-in? |
|---|---|---|---|---|
| 1527 | 22522 | 11/9/2015 | Allergies - environmental | ☑ |
| 1528 | 22507 | 11/9/2015 | Diabetes mellitis Type 2 - initial diagnosis | ☑ |
| 1530 | 22510 | 11/10/2015 | Seborrheic dermatitis | ☐ |
| 1535 | 22546 | 11/12/2015 | Transverse fracture of left ulna | ☑ |
| 1536 | 22526 | 11/17/2015 | Gastroenteritis | ☐ |
| 1538 | 22500 | 11/17/2015 | Migraine | ☑ |
| 1539 | 22504 | 11/18/2015 | Annual wellness visit | ☐ |
| 1541 | 22526 | 11/24/2015 | Gastroenteritis - follow up | ☐ |
| 1542 | 22537 | 11/24/2015 | Influenza | ☑ |
| 1544 | 22560 | 11/25/2015 | Influenza | ☑ |

4. Click the **Close 'Visit'** button ✕ on the object tab to close the Visit table.

5. If you are not continuing to Session 2.2, click the **FILE** tab, and then click **Close** in the navigation bar to close the Chatham database.

You have created the Billing table and made modifications to its design. In the next session, you'll add records to the Billing table and create the Patient table in the Chatham database.

## Session 2.1 Quick Check

REVIEW

1. What guidelines should you follow when designing a database?
2. What is the purpose of the Data Type property for a field?
3. The _____ property specifies how a field's name is displayed in database objects, including table and query datasheets, forms, and reports.
4. For which three types of fields can you assign a field size?
5. The default Field Size property setting for a Short Text field is _____.
6. In Design view, which key do you press to move from the Table Design grid to the Field Properties pane?
7. List three reasons why you should specify a primary key for an Access table.

# Session 2.2 Visual Overview:

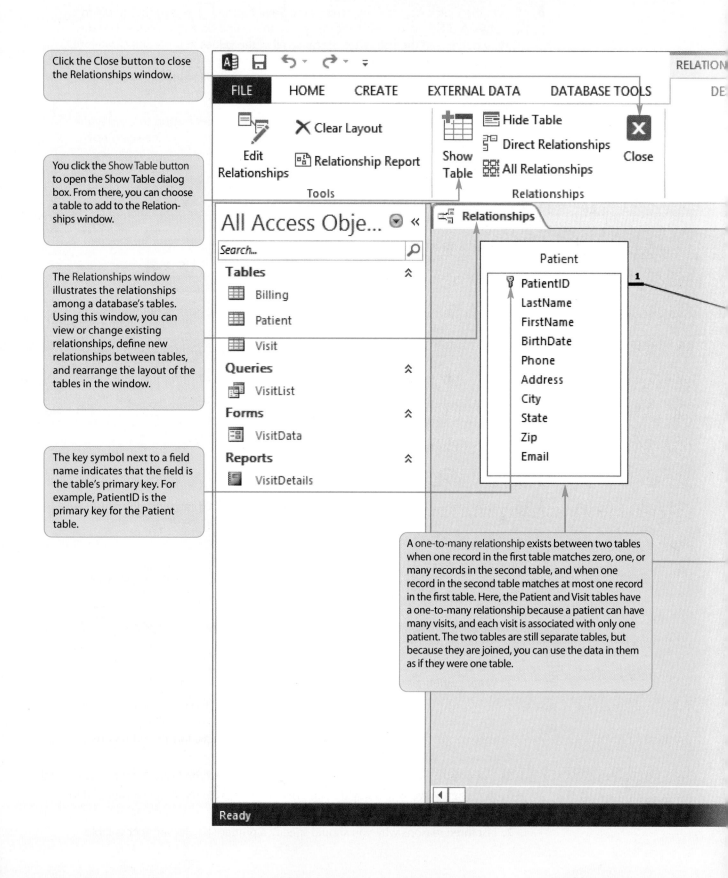

Click the Close button to close the Relationships window.

You click the Show Table button to open the Show Table dialog box. From there, you can choose a table to add to the Relationships window.

The Relationships window illustrates the relationships among a database's tables. Using this window, you can view or change existing relationships, define new relationships between tables, and rearrange the layout of the tables in the window.

The key symbol next to a field name indicates that the field is the table's primary key. For example, PatientID is the primary key for the Patient table.

A one-to-many relationship exists between two tables when one record in the first table matches zero, one, or many records in the second table, and when one record in the second table matches at most one record in the first table. Here, the Patient and Visit tables have a one-to-many relationship because a patient can have many visits, and each visit is associated with only one patient. The two tables are still separate tables, but because they are joined, you can use the data in them as if they were one table.

# Understanding Table Relationships

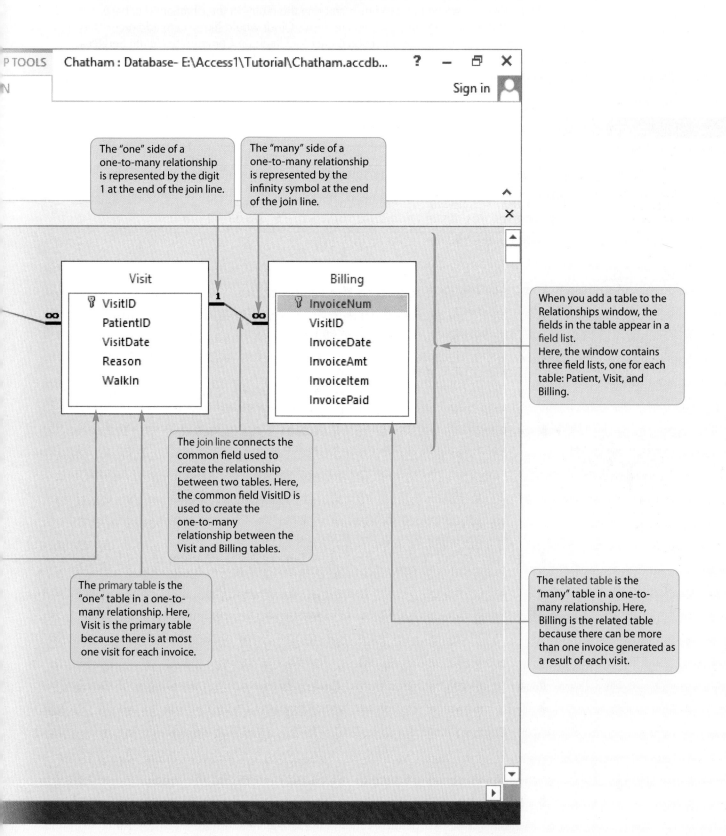

The "one" side of a one-to-many relationship is represented by the digit 1 at the end of the join line.

The "many" side of a one-to-many relationship is represented by the infinity symbol at the end of the join line.

When you add a table to the Relationships window, the fields in the table appear in a field list.
Here, the window contains three field lists, one for each table: Patient, Visit, and Billing.

The join line connects the common field used to create the relationship between two tables. Here, the common field VisitID is used to create the one-to-many relationship between the Visit and Billing tables.

The primary table is the "one" table in a one-to-many relationship. Here, Visit is the primary table because there is at most one visit for each invoice.

The related table is the "many" table in a one-to-many relationship. Here, Billing is the related table because there can be more than one invoice generated as a result of each visit.

Chatham : Database- E:\Access1\Tutorial\Chatham.accdb...

Sign in

**Visit**
- VisitID
- PatientID
- VisitDate
- Reason
- WalkIn

**Billing**
- InvoiceNum
- VisitID
- InvoiceDate
- InvoiceAmt
- InvoiceItem
- InvoicePaid

# Adding Records to a New Table

Before you can begin to define the table relationships illustrated in the Session 2.2 Visual Overview, you need to finish creating the tables in the Chatham database.

The Billing table design is complete. Now, Cindi would like you to add records to the table so it will contain the invoice data for Chatham Community Health Services. As you learned earlier, you add records to a table in Datasheet view by typing the field values in the rows below the column headings for the fields. You'll begin by entering the records shown in Figure 2-21.

**Figure 2-21**    **Records to be added to the Billing table**

| Invoice Num | Visit ID | Invoice Date | Invoice Amt | Invoice Item | Invoice Paid |
|---|---|---|---|---|---|
| 35801 | 1527 | 11/10/2015 | $100.00 | Office visit | Yes |
| 35818 | 1536 | 11/18/2015 | $100.00 | Office visit | Yes |
| 35885 | 1570 | 01/12/2016 | $85.00 | Pharmacy | No |
| 35851 | 1550 | 12/02/2015 | $85.00 | Pharmacy | No |

© 2014 Cengage Learning

## To add the first record to the Billing table:

1. If you took a break after the previous session, make sure the Chatham database is open and the Navigation Pane is open.

2. In the Tables section of the Navigation Pane, double-click **Billing** to open the Billing table in Datasheet view.

3. Close the Navigation Pane, and then use the ✛ pointer to resize columns, as necessary, so that the field names are completely visible.

4. In the Invoice Num column, type **35801**, press the **Tab** key, type **1527** in the Visit ID column, and then press the **Tab** key.

   Next you need to enter the invoice date. Recall that you specified a custom date format, mm/dd/yyyy, for the InvoiceDate field. You do not need to type each digit; for example, you can type just "3" instead of "03" for the month, and you can type "16" instead of "2016" for the year. Access will display the full value according to the custom date format.

5. Type **11/10/15** and then press the **Tab** key. Notice that Access displays the date "11/10/2015" in the Invoice Date column.

   Next you need to enter the invoice amount for the first record. This is a Currency field with the Currency format and two decimal places specified. Because of the field's properties, you do not need to type the dollar sign, comma, or zeroes for the decimal places; Access will display these items automatically for you.

6. Type **100** and then press the **Tab** key. Access displays the value as "$100.00."

7. In the Invoice Item column, type **Office visit** and then press the **Tab** key.

   The last field in the table, InvoicePaid, is a Yes/No field. Recall that the default value for any Yes/No field is "No"; therefore, the check box is initially empty. For the record you are entering in the Billing table, the invoice has been paid, so you need to insert a checkmark in the check box.

8. Press the **spacebar** to insert a checkmark, and then press the **Tab** key. The values for the first record are entered. See Figure 2-22.

Be sure to type the numbers "0" and "1" and *not* the letters "O" and "l" in the field values.

| Figure 2-22 | First record entered in the Billing table |

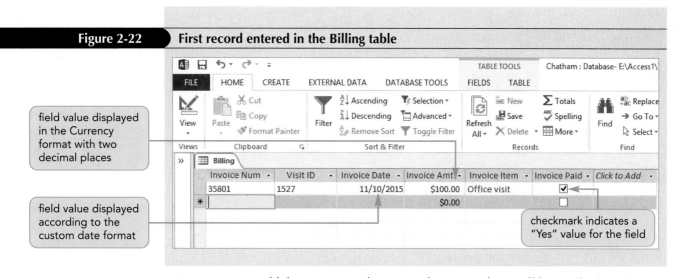

field value displayed in the Currency format with two decimal places

field value displayed according to the custom date format

checkmark indicates a "Yes" value for the field

Now you can add the remaining three records. As you do, you'll learn a keyboard shortcut for inserting the value from the same field in the previous record. A **keyboard shortcut** is a key or combination of keys you press to complete an action more efficiently.

### To add the next three records to the Billing table:

1. Refer to Figure 2-21 and enter the values in the second record's Invoice Num, Visit ID, and Invoice Date columns.

   Notice that the value in the second record's Invoice Amt column is $100.00. This value is the exact same value as in the first record. You can quickly insert the value from the same column in the previous record using the **Ctrl + '** (apostrophe) keyboard shortcut. To use this shortcut, you press and hold down the Ctrl key, press the ' key once, and then release both keys. (The plus sign in the keyboard shortcut indicates you're pressing two keys at once; you do not press the + key.)

2. With the insertion point in the Invoice Amt column, press the **Ctrl + '** keys. Access inserts the value "$100.00" in the Invoice Amt column for the second record.

3. Press the **Tab** key to move to the Invoice Item column. Again, the value you need to enter in this column—Office visit—is the same as the value for this column in the previous record. So, you can use the keyboard shortcut again.

4. With the insertion point in the Invoice Item column, press the **Ctrl + '** keys. Access inserts the value "Office visit" in the Invoice Item column for the second record.

5. Press the **Tab** key to move to the Invoice Paid column, press the **spacebar** to insert a checkmark in the check box, and then press the **Tab** key. The second record is entered in the Billing table.

6. Refer to Figure 2-21 to enter the values for the third and fourth records, using the Ctrl + ' keys to enter the values in the fourth record's Invoice Amt and Invoice Item columns. Also, for both records, the invoices have not been paid. Therefore, be sure to press the Tab key to leave the Invoice Paid column values unchecked (signifying "No"). Your table should look like the one in Figure 2-23.

**Figure 2-23** **Billing table with four records added**

To finish entering records in the Billing table, you'll use a method that allows you to import the data.

# Importing Data from an Excel Worksheet

Often, the data you want to add to an Access table exists in another file, such as a Word document or an Excel workbook. You can bring the data from other files into Access in different ways. For example, you can copy and paste the data from an open file, or you can **import** the data, which is a process that allows you to copy the data from a source without having to open the source file.

Cindi had been using Excel to track invoice data for Chatham Community Health Services and already created a worksheet, named "Invoices," containing this data. You'll import this Excel worksheet into your Billing table to complete the entry of data in the table. To use the import method, the columns in the Excel worksheet must match the names and data types of the fields in the Access table.

## INSIGHT

### Caption Property Values and the Import Process

When you import data from an Excel worksheet into an Access table, any Caption property values set for the fields in the table are not considered in the import process. For example, your Access table could have fields such as InvoiceDate and InvoiceAmt with Caption property values of Invoice Date and Invoice Amt, respectively. If the Excel worksheet you are importing has the column headings Invoice Date and Invoice Amt, you might think that the data matches and you can proceed with the import. However, if the underlying field names in the Access table do not match the Excel worksheet column headings exactly, the import process will fail. It's a good idea to double-check to make sure that the actual Access field names—and not just the column headings displayed in a table datasheet (as specified by the Caption property)—match the Excel worksheet column headings. If there are differences, you can change the column headings in the Excel worksheet to match the Access table field names before you import the data, ensuring that the process will work correctly.

The Invoices worksheet contains the following columns: InvoiceNum, VisitID, InvoiceDate, InvoiceAmt, InvoiceItem, and InvoicePaid. These column headings match the field names in the Billing table exactly, so you can import the data. Before you import data into a table, you need to close the table.

### To import the Invoices worksheet into the Billing table:

▶ **1.** Click the **Close 'Billing'** button ☒ on the object tab to close the Billing table. A dialog box opens asking if you want to save the changes to the table layout. This dialog box opens because you resized the table columns.

▶ **2.** Click the **Yes** button in the dialog box.

▶ **3.** On the ribbon, click the **EXTERNAL DATA** tab.

▶ **4.** In the Import & Link group on the EXTERNAL DATA tab, click the **Excel** button. The Get External Data - Excel Spreadsheet dialog box opens. See Figure 2-24.

| Figure 2-24 | Get External Data - Excel Spreadsheet dialog box |
| --- | --- |

click to find the Excel workbook containing the data you want to import

you might see a different path here

option for adding records to an existing table

**Trouble?** If the Export - Excel Spreadsheet dialog box opens instead of the dialog box shown in Figure 2-24, you probably clicked the Excel button in the Export group. If so, click the Cancel button in the dialog box, and then repeat Step 4, being sure to click the Excel button in the Import & Link group.

The dialog box provides options for importing the entire worksheet as a new table in the current database, adding the data from the worksheet to an existing table, or linking the data in the worksheet to the table. You need to add, or append, the worksheet data to the Billing table.

▶ **5.** Click the **Browse** button. The File Open dialog box opens. The Excel workbook file is named "Invoices" and is located in the Access1 ▶ Tutorial folder provided with your Data Files.

▶ **6.** Navigate to the **Access1 ▶ Tutorial** folder, where your starting Data Files are stored, and then double-click the **Invoices** Excel file. You return to the dialog box.

▶ **7.** Click the **Append a copy of the records to the table** option button. The box to the right of this option becomes active and displays the Billing table name, because it is the first table listed in the Navigation Pane.

**Trouble?** If another table name appears in this box, click the arrow on the box, and then click Billing.

**8.** Click the **OK** button. The first Import Spreadsheet Wizard dialog box opens. See Figure 2-25.

| Figure 2-25 | First Import Spreadsheet Wizard dialog box |

selected check box confirms that the first row contains column headings

data from the worksheet to be imported

The dialog box confirms that the first row of the worksheet you are importing contains column headings. The bottom section of the dialog box displays some of the data contained in the worksheet.

**TIP**

Carefully check the data to make sure it should be imported into the selected table.

**9.** Click the **Next** button. The second, and final, Import Spreadsheet Wizard dialog box opens. Notice that the Import to Table box shows that the data from the spreadsheet will be imported into the Billing table.

**10.** Click the **Finish** button. A dialog box opens asking if you want to save the import steps. If you needed to repeat this same import procedure many times, it would be a good idea to save the steps for the procedure. However, you don't need to save these steps because you'll be importing the data only one time. Once the data is in the Billing table, Cindi will no longer use Excel to track invoice data.

**11.** Click the **Close** button in the dialog box to close it without saving the steps.

The data from the Invoices worksheet has been added to the Billing table. Next, you'll open the table to view the new records.

## To open the Billing table and view the imported data:

**1.** Open the Navigation Pane, and then double-click **Billing** in the Tables section to open the table in Datasheet view.

**2.** Resize the Invoice Item column to its best fit, scrolling the worksheet and resizing, as necessary.

**3.** Press the **Ctrl + Home** keys to scroll to the top of the datasheet. Notice that the table now contains a total of 204 records—four records you entered plus 200 records imported from the Invoices worksheet. The records are displayed in primary key order by the values in the Invoice Num column. See Figure 2-26.

**Figure 2-26**    **Billing table after importing data from Excel**

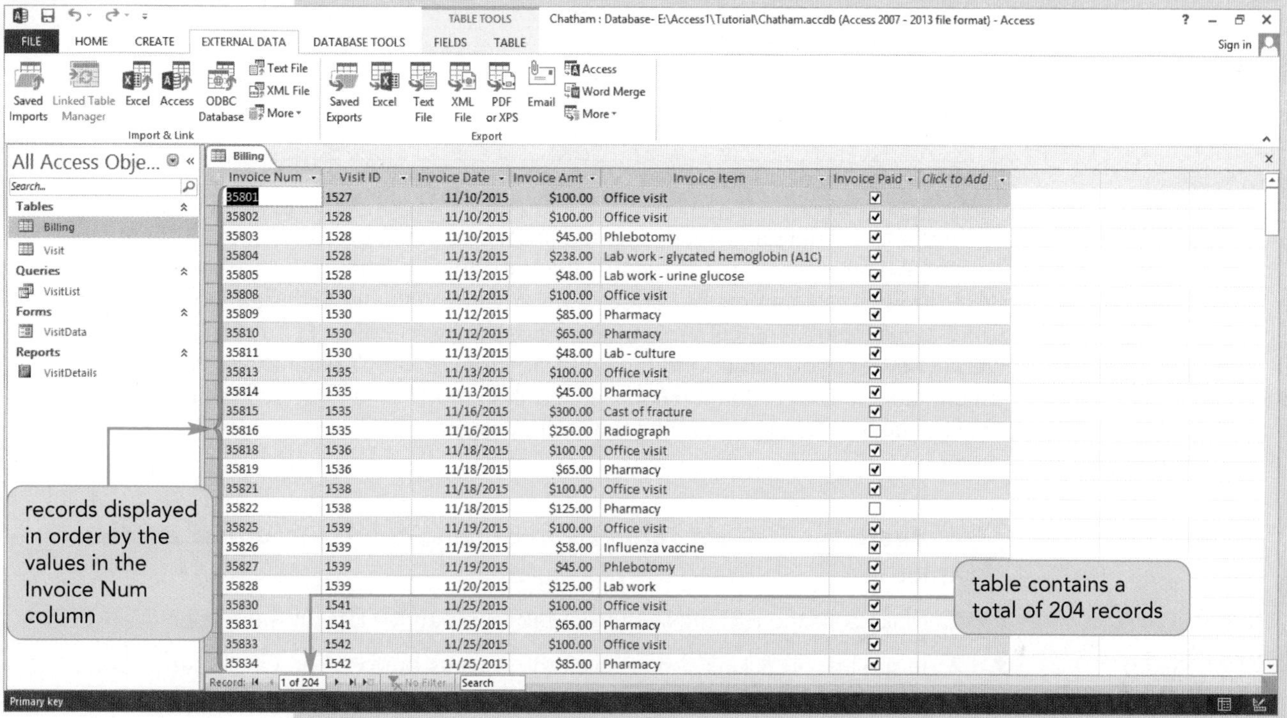

records displayed in order by the values in the Invoice Num column

table contains a total of 204 records

**4.** Save and close the Billing table, and then close the Navigation Pane.

Two of the tables—Visit and Billing—are now complete. According to Cindi's plan for the Chatham database, you need to create a third table, named "Patient," to track data about the clinic's patients. You'll use a different method to create this table.

# Creating a Table by Importing an Existing Table Structure

If another Access database contains a table—or even just the design, or structure, of a table—that you want to include in your database, you can import the table and any records it contains or import only the table structure into your database.

Cindi documented the design for the new Patient table by listing each field's name and data type, as well as any applicable field size, description, and caption property values, as shown in Figure 2-27. Note that each field in the Patient table, except BirthDate, will be a Short Text field, and the PatientID field will be the table's primary key.

Figure 2-27 **Design for the Patient table**

| Field Name | Data Type | Field Size | Description | Caption |
|---|---|---|---|---|
| PatientID | Short Text | 5 | Primary key | Patient ID |
| LastName | Short Text | 25 | | Last Name |
| FirstName | Short Text | 20 | | First Name |
| BirthDate | Date/Time | | | Date of Birth |
| Phone | Short Text | 14 | | |
| Address | Short Text | 35 | | |
| City | Short Text | 25 | | |
| State | Short Text | 2 | | |
| Zip | Short Text | 10 | | |
| Email | Short Text | 50 | | |

© 2014 Cengage Learning

Cindi's assistant Kelly already created an Access database containing a Patient table design. She never entered any records into the table because she wasn't sure if the table design was complete or correct. After reviewing the table design, both Kelly and Cindi agree that it contains some of the fields they want to track, but that some changes are needed. So, you can import the table structure in Kelly's database to create the Patient table in the Chatham database, and then modify the imported table to produce the final table structure according to Cindi's design.

### To create the Patient table by importing the structure of another table:

1. Make sure the EXTERNAL DATA tab is the active tab on the ribbon.

2. In the Import & Link group, click the **Access** button. The Get External Data - Access Database dialog box opens. This dialog box is similar to the one you used earlier when importing the Excel spreadsheet.

3. Click the **Browse** button. The File Open dialog box opens. The Access database file from which you need to import the table structure is named "Kelly" and is located in the Access1 ▸ Tutorial folder provided with your Data Files.

4. Navigate to the **Access1 ▸ Tutorial** folder, where your starting Data Files are stored, and then double-click the **Kelly** database file. You return to the dialog box.

5. Make sure the **Import tables, queries, forms, reports, macros, and modules into the current database** option button is selected, and then click the **OK** button. The Import Objects dialog box opens. The dialog box contains tabs for importing all the different types of Access database objects—tables, queries, forms, and so on. The Tables tab is the current tab.

6. Click the **Options** button in the dialog box to see all the options for importing tables. See Figure 2-28.

**Figure 2-28**    **Import Objects dialog box**

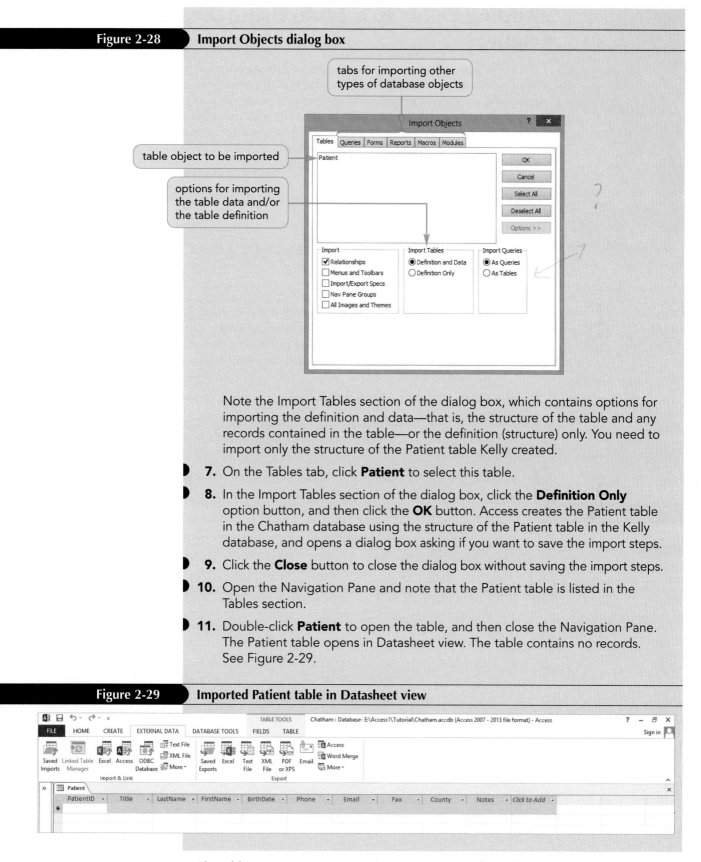

Note the Import Tables section of the dialog box, which contains options for importing the definition and data—that is, the structure of the table and any records contained in the table—or the definition (structure) only. You need to import only the structure of the Patient table Kelly created.

**7.** On the Tables tab, click **Patient** to select this table.

**8.** In the Import Tables section of the dialog box, click the **Definition Only** option button, and then click the **OK** button. Access creates the Patient table in the Chatham database using the structure of the Patient table in the Kelly database, and opens a dialog box asking if you want to save the import steps.

**9.** Click the **Close** button to close the dialog box without saving the import steps.

**10.** Open the Navigation Pane and note that the Patient table is listed in the Tables section.

**11.** Double-click **Patient** to open the table, and then close the Navigation Pane. The Patient table opens in Datasheet view. The table contains no records. See Figure 2-29.

**Figure 2-29**    **Imported Patient table in Datasheet view**

The table structure you imported contains some of the fields Cindi wants, but not all (see Figure 2-27); it also contains some fields Cindi does not want in the Patient table. You can add the missing fields using the Data Type gallery.

# Adding Fields to a Table Using the Data Type Gallery

The **Data Type gallery**, available in the Add & Delete group on the FIELDS tab, allows you to add a group of related fields to a table at the same time, rather than adding each field to the table individually. The group of fields you add is called a **Quick Start selection**. For example, the **Address Quick Start selection** adds a collection of fields related to an address, such as Address, City, State, and so on, to the table at one time. When you use a Quick Start selection, the fields added already have properties set. However, you need to review and possibly modify the properties to ensure the fields match your design needs for the database.

Next, you'll use the Data Type gallery to add the missing fields to the Patient table.

### To add fields to the Patient table using the Data Type gallery:

▶ **1.** On the ribbon, click the **FIELDS** tab.

Note the More Fields button in the Add & Delete group; this button allows you to display the Data Type gallery. Before inserting fields from the Data Type gallery, you need to place the insertion point in the field to the right of where you want to insert the new fields. According to Cindi's design, the Address field should come after the Phone field, so you need to make the next field, Email, the active field.

> Make sure the correct field is active before adding new fields.

▶ **2.** Click the first row in the **Email** field to make it the active field.

▶ **3.** In the Add & Delete group, click the **More Fields** button. The Data Type gallery opens and displays options for different types of fields you can add to your table.

▶ **4.** Scroll the gallery down so the Quick Start section is visible. See Figure 2-30.

| Figure 2-30 | Patient table with the Data Type gallery displayed |
|---|---|

The Quick Start section provides options that will add multiple, related fields to the table at one time. The new fields will be inserted to the left of the current field.

5. In the Quick Start section, click **Address**. Access adds five fields to the table: Address, City, State Province, ZIP Postal, and Country Region. See Figure 2-31.

| Figure 2-31 | Patient table after adding fields from the Data Type gallery |

## Modifying the Imported Table

Refer back to Cindi's design for the Patient table (Figure 2-27). To finalize the table design, you need to modify the imported table by deleting fields, renaming fields, and changing field data types. You'll begin by deleting fields.

### Deleting Fields from a Table Structure

After you've created a table, you might need to delete one or more fields. When you delete a field, you also delete all the values for that field from the table. So, before you delete a field, you should make sure that you want to do so and that you choose the correct field to delete. You can delete fields in either Datasheet view or Design view.

**REFERENCE**

### Deleting a Field from a Table Structure

- In Datasheet view, click anywhere in the column for the field you want to delete.
- In the Add & Delete group on the FIELDS tab, click the Delete button.

or

- In Design view, click the Field Name box for the field you want to delete.
- In the Tools group on the DESIGN tab, click the Delete Rows button.

The Address Quick Start selection added a field named "Country Region" to the Patient table. Cindi doesn't need a field to store country data because all Chatham Community Health Services patients are located in the United States. You'll begin to modify the Patient table structure by deleting the Country Region field.

### To delete the Country Region field from the table in Datasheet view:

▶ 1. Click the first row in the **Country Region** field (if necessary).

▶ 2. In the Add & Delete group on the FIELDS tab, click the **Delete** button. The Country Region field is removed and the first field, PatientID, is now the active field.

You can also delete fields from a table structure in Design view. You'll switch to Design view to delete the other unnecessary fields.

### To delete the fields in Design view:

▶ 1. In the Views group on the FIELDS tab, click the **View** button. The Patient table opens in Design view. See Figure 2-32.

| Figure 2-32 | **Patient table in Design view** |

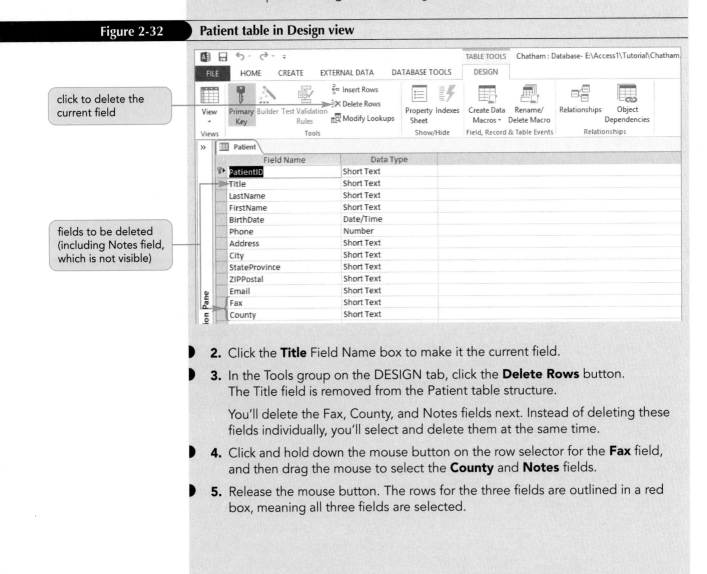

click to delete the current field

fields to be deleted (including Notes field, which is not visible)

▶ 2. Click the **Title** Field Name box to make it the current field.

▶ 3. In the Tools group on the DESIGN tab, click the **Delete Rows** button. The Title field is removed from the Patient table structure.

You'll delete the Fax, County, and Notes fields next. Instead of deleting these fields individually, you'll select and delete them at the same time.

▶ 4. Click and hold down the mouse button on the row selector for the **Fax** field, and then drag the mouse to select the **County** and **Notes** fields.

▶ 5. Release the mouse button. The rows for the three fields are outlined in a red box, meaning all three fields are selected.

**6.** In the Tools group, click the **Delete Rows** button. See Figure 2-33.

Figure 2-33    **Patient table after deleting fields**

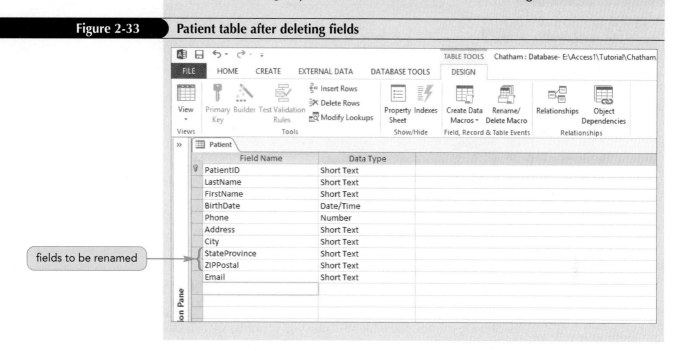

fields to be renamed

## Renaming Fields in Design View

To match Cindi's design for the Patient table, you need to rename the StateProvince and ZIPPostal fields. In Tutorial 1, you renamed the default primary key field (ID) in Datasheet view. You can also rename fields in Design view by simply editing the names in the Table Design grid.

### To rename the fields in Design view:

**1.** Click to position the insertion point to the right of the word **StateProvince** in the eighth row's Field Name box, and then press the **Backspace** key eight times to delete the word "Province." The name of the eighth field is now State.

You can also select an entire field name and then type new text to replace it.

**2.** In the ninth row's Field Name box, drag to select the text **ZIPPostal**, and then type **Zip**. The text you type replaces the original text. See Figure 2-34.

**Figure 2-34** | **Patient table after renaming fields**

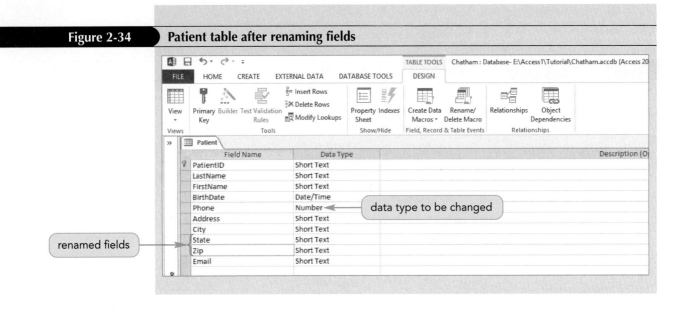

## Changing the Data Type for a Field in Design View

According to Cindi's plan, all of the fields in the Patient table, except BirthDate, should be Short Text fields. The table structure you imported specifies the Number data type for the Phone field; you need to change this to Short Text. In Tutorial 1, you used an option in Datasheet view to change a field's data type. You can also change the data type for a field in Design view.

### To change the data type of the Phone field in Design view:

▶ 1. Click the right side of the **Data Type** box for the Phone field to display the list of data types.

▶ 2. Click **Short Text** in the list. The Phone field is now a Short Text field. Note that, by default, the Field Size property is set to 255. According to Cindi's plan, the Phone field should have a Field Size property of 14. You'll make this change next.

▶ 3. Press the **F6** key to move to and select the default Field Size property, and then type **14**.

Each of the remaining fields you added using the Address Quick Start selection—Address, City, State, and Zip—also has the default field size of 255. You need to change the Field Size property for these fields to match Cindi's design. You'll also delete any Caption property values for these fields because the field names match how Cindi wants them displayed, so captions are unnecessary.

### To change the Field Size and Caption properties for the fields:

▶ **1.** Click the **Address** Field Name box to make it the current field.

▶ **2.** Press the **F6** key to move to and select the default Field Size property, and then type **35**.

Note that the Caption property setting for this field is the same as the field name. This field doesn't need a caption, so you can delete this value.

▶ **3.** Press the **Tab** key until the the word Address is selected in the Caption box, and then press the **Delete** key. The Caption property value is removed.

▶ **4.** Repeat Steps 1 through 3 to change the Field Size property for the City field to **25** and to delete its Caption property value.

▶ **5.** Change the Field Size property for the State field to **2**, and then delete its Caption property value.

▶ **6.** Change the Field Size property for the Zip field to **10**, and then delete its Caption property value.

▶ **7.** On the Quick Access Toolbar, click the **Save** button 🖫 to save your changes to the Patient table.

Finally, Cindi would like you to set the Description property for the Patient ID field and the Caption property for the PatientID, LastName, FirstName, and BirthDate fields. You'll make these changes now.

### To enter the Description and Caption property values:

▶ **1.** Click the **Description (Optional)** box for the PatientID field, and then type **Primary key**.

▶ **2.** In the Field Properties pane, click the **Caption** box.

After you leave the Description (Optional) box, the Property Update Options button 🖅 appears below this box for the PatientID field. When you change a field's property in Design view, you can use this button to update the corresponding property on forms and reports that include the modified field. For example, if the Chatham database included a form that contained the PatientID field, you could choose to **propagate**, or update, the modified Description property in the form by clicking the Property Update Options button, and then choosing the option to make the update everywhere the field is used. The text on the Property Update Options button varies depending on the task; in this case, if you click the button, the option is "Update Status Bar Text everywhere PatientID is used."

Because the Chatham database does not include any forms or reports that are based on the Patient table, you do not need to update the properties, so you can ignore the button for now. In most cases, however, it is a good idea to perform the update.

▶ **3.** In the Caption box for the PatientID field, type **Patient ID**.

▶ **4.** Click the **LastName** Field Name box to make it the current field.

▶ **5.** Click the **Caption** box, and then type **Last Name**.

▶ **6.** Click the **FirstName** Field Name box to make it the current field, click the **Caption** box, and then type **First Name**.

**7.** Click the **BirthDate** Field Name box to make it the current field, click the **Caption** box, and then type **Date of Birth**. See Figure 2-35.

| Figure 2-35 | Patient table after entering description and captions |

**8.** On the Quick Access Toolbar, click the **Save** button 🖫 to save your changes to the Patient table.

**9.** In the Views group on the DESIGN tab, click the **View** button to display the table in Datasheet view.

> **10.** Resize each column to its best fit, and then click in the first row for the **Patient ID** column. See Figure 2-36.

Figure 2-36  **Modified Patient table in Datasheet view**

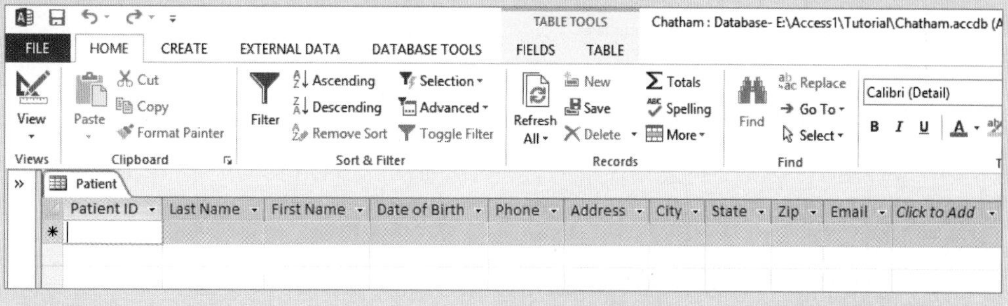

After viewing the Patient table datasheet, both Cindi and Kelly agree that data entry would be made easier if the State field value of "CT" was automatically filled in for each new record added to the table, because all of the clinic's patients live in Connecticut. You can accomplish this by setting the Default Value property for the field.

# Setting the Default Value Property for a Field

The **Default Value property** for a field specifies what value will appear, by default, for the field in each new record you add to a table. Recall the InvoicePaid field in the Billing table; this is a Yes/No field, which automatically includes a Default Value property setting of "No." That's why the check box for the InvoicePaid field is initially empty for a new record in the Billing table.

Because all the patients at Chatham Community Health Services live in Connecticut, you'll specify a default value of "CT" for the State field in the Patient table. With this setting, each new record in the Patient table will have the correct State field value entered automatically.

### To set the Default Value property for the State field:

> **1.** In the Views group on the HOME tab, click the **View** button to display the Patient table in Design view.

> **2.** Click the **State** Field Name box to make it the current field.

> **3.** In the Field Properties pane, click the **Default Value** box, type **CT** and then press the Tab key. See Figure 2-37.

**Figure 2-37** Specifying the Default Value property for the State field

State field is current

Default Value
property entered
and enclosed within
quotation marks

| Field Name | Data Type | Description (Opt |
|---|---|---|
| PatientID | Short Text | Primary key |
| LastName | Short Text | |
| FirstName | Short Text | |
| BirthDate | Date/Time | |
| Phone | Short Text | |
| Address | Short Text | |
| City | Short Text | |
| State | Short Text | |
| Zip | Short Text | |
| Email | Short Text | |

Field Properties

General | Lookup

| | |
|---|---|
| Field Size | 2 |
| Format | |
| Input Mask | |
| Caption | |
| Default Value | "CT" |
| Validation Rule | |
| Validation Text | |
| Required | No |
| Allow Zero Length | No |
| Indexed | No |
| Unicode Compression | Yes |
| IME Mode | No Control |
| IME Sentence Mode | Phrase Predict |
| Text Align | General |

Design view. F6 = Switch panes. F1 = Help.

Note that a text entry in the Default Value property must be enclosed within quotation marks. If you do not type the quotation marks, Access adds them for you. However, for some entries, you would receive an error message indicating invalid syntax if you omitted the quotation marks. In such cases, you have to enter the quotation marks yourself.

4. On the Quick Access Toolbar, click the **Save** button 🖫 to save your changes to the Patient table.

**TIP**

You can change the value in a record from the default value to another value, if necessary.

5. In the Views group on the DESIGN tab, click the **View** button to display the table in Datasheet view. Note that the State field for the first row now displays the default value "CT" as specified by the Default Value property. Each new record entered in the table will automatically have this State field value entered.

With the Patient table design set, you can now enter records in it. You'll begin by entering two records, and then you'll use a different method to add the remaining records.

**Note:** *Be sure to enter your last name and first name where indicated.*

**To add two records to the Patient table:**

▶ **1.** Enter the following values in the columns in the first record; note that you can press Tab to move past the default State field value:

Patient ID = **22500**

Last Name = *[student's last name]*

First Name = *[student's first name]*

Date of Birth = **2/28/1994**

Phone = **860-938-2822**

Address = **501 Perkins Dr**

City = **Hartford**

State = **CT**

Zip = **06120**

Email = **student1@example.edu**

▶ **2.** Enter the following values in the columns in the second record:

Patient ID = **22533**

Last Name = **Rowe**

First Name = **Christina**

Date of Birth = **12/5/1941**

Phone = **860-552-5920**

Address = **27 Tracey Ct**

City = **Windsor**

State = **CT**

Zip = **06095**

Email = **c.rowe@example.com**

▶ **3.** Resize columns to their best fit, as necessary, and then save and close the Patient table.

Before Cindi decided to store data using Access, Kelly managed the clinic's patient data in a different system. She exported that data into a text file and now asks you to import it into the new Patient table. You can import the data contained in this text file to add the remaining records to the Patient table.

# Adding Data to a Table by Importing a Text File

There are many ways to import data into an Access database. So far, you've learned how to add data to an Access table by importing an Excel spreadsheet, and you've created a new table by importing the structure of an existing table. You can also import data contained in text files.

To complete the entry of records in the Patient table, you'll import the data contained in Kelly's text file. The file is named "Patient" and is located in the Access1 ▶ Tutorial folder provided with your Data Files.

## To import the data contained in the Patient text file:

1. On the ribbon, click the **EXTERNAL DATA** tab.

2. In the Import & Link group, click the **Text File** button. The Get External Data - Text File dialog box opens. This dialog box is similar to the one you used earlier when importing the Excel spreadsheet and the Access table structure.

3. Click the **Browse** button. The File Open dialog box opens.

4. Navigate to the Access1 ▸ Tutorial folder, where your starting Data Files are stored, and then double-click the **Patient** file. You return to the dialog box.

5. Click the **Append a copy of the records to the table** option button. The box to the right of this option becomes active. Next, you need to select the table to which you want to add the data.

6. Click the arrow on the box, and then click **Patient**.

7. Click the **OK** button. The first Import Text Wizard dialog box opens. The dialog box indicates that the data to be imported is in a delimited format. A **delimited text file** is one in which fields of data are separated by a character such as a comma or a tab. In this case, the dialog box shows that data is separated by the comma character in the text file.

8. Make sure the **Delimited** option button is selected in the dialog box, and then click the **Next** button. The second Import Text Wizard dialog box opens. See Figure 2-38.

| Figure 2-38 | Second Import Text Wizard dialog box |
| --- | --- |

fields in the text file are separated by commas

preview of the data being imported

This dialog box asks you to confirm the delimiter character that separates the fields in the text file you're importing. Access detects that the comma character is used in the Patient text file and selects this option. The bottom area of the dialog box provides a preview of the data you're importing.

**TIP**

Carefully check the data to make sure it should be imported into the selected table.

9. Make sure the **Comma** option button is selected, and then click the **Next** button. The third, and final, Import Text Wizard dialog box opens. Notice that the Import to Table box shows that the data will be imported into the Patient table.

10. Click the **Finish** button. A dialog box opens asking if you want to save the import steps. You'll only import the patient data once, so you can close the dialog box without saving the import steps.
11. Click the **Close** button in the dialog box to close it without saving the import steps.

Cindi asks you to open the Patient table in Datasheet view so she can see the results of importing the text file.

## To view the Patient table datasheet:

1. Open the Navigation Pane, and then double-click **Patient** to open the Patient table in Datasheet view. The Patient table contains a total of 51 records.
2. Close the Navigation Pane.
3. Resize columns to their best fit, scrolling the table datasheet as necessary, so that all field values are displayed. When finished, scroll back to display the first fields in the table, and then click the first row's Patient ID field. See Figure 2-39.

**Figure 2-39** **Patient table after importing data from the text file**

| Patient ID | Last Name | First Name | Date of Birth | Phone | Address | City | State | Zip | Email | Click to Add |
|---|---|---|---|---|---|---|---|---|---|---|
| 22500 | Student Last | Student First | 2/28/1994 | 860-938-2822 | 501 Perkins Dr | Hartford | CT | 06120 | student1@example.edu | |
| 22501 | Darcy | Edward | 7/15/1986 | 860-305-3985 | 723 Oxford Ave | Bloomfield | CT | 06002 | edarcy@example.org | |
| 22502 | Mendez | Andreas | 3/1/1934 | 860-552-6893 | 57 Wallace Rd | Windsor | CT | 06095 | a.mendez@example.org | |
| 22504 | Aguilar | Lilian | 8/16/1938 | 860-374-5724 | 329 Fairchild Ave | Hartford | CT | 06114 | laguilar@example.com | |
| 22505 | Finnerty | Amber | 5/7/1946 | 860-226-4930 | 37 Noyes Ct | Hartford | CT | 06112 | a.finnerty@example.com | |
| 22506 | Gorski | Drea | 2/19/2005 | 860-305-8394 | 83 Everett Ln | Bloomfield | CT | 06002 | | |
| 22507 | Weiss | Matthew | 6/7/1997 | 860-426-7492 | 38 German St | Hartford | CT | 06106 | matt.weiss@example.org | |
| 22509 | Kervin | Steve | 4/6/1993 | 860-938-0025 | 49 Davenport St | Hartford | CT | 06120 | skervin@example.edu | |
| 22510 | Booker | Thomas | 8/25/1966 | 860-661-2539 | 59 Nicola Ave | Hartford | CT | 06105 | | |
| 22511 | Castro | Daniel | 9/23/1933 | 860-637-0430 | 61 Osmond Way | West Hartford | CT | 06117 | d_castro@example.com | |
| 22512 | Chang | Lisa | 10/5/1955 | 860-226-6034 | 731 Macon Rd | Hartford | CT | 06112 | lchang@example.com | |
| 22513 | Smith | Troy | 1/31/1996 | 860-305-0384 | 16 Ravine Rd | Bloomfield | CT | 06002 | t_smith@example.edu | |
| 22514 | Parker | Ian | 6/3/1953 | 860-938-1873 | 12 Adelbert St | Hartford | CT | 06120 | ian_parker@example.org | |
| 22516 | King | Susan | 12/7/1963 | 860-661-9347 | 48 Fenton St | Hartford | CT | 06105 | susan.king@example.edu | |
| 22517 | O'Brien | Henry | 12/10/1940 | 860-637-9203 | 58 Redmond Dr | West Hartford | CT | 06117 | h.obrien32@example.com | |
| 22518 | Torres | Sera | 4/9/2008 | 860-938-2098 | 27 Reno Dr | Hartford | CT | 06120 | | |
| 22519 | Belanger | Malcolm | 10/17/1950 | 860-637-3927 | 723 Nicola Ave | West Hartford | CT | 06117 | | |
| 22520 | Hallick | Davis | 3/26/1944 | 860-552-4495 | 84 Churchill Pl | Windsor | CT | 06095 | dhallick@example.com | |
| 22521 | Engber | Cathy | 4/7/2006 | 860-305-3048 | 58 Deering Pl | Bloomfield | CT | 06002 | | |
| 22522 | Li | Siyang | 7/25/1986 | 860-305-6548 | 225 Krauss Rd | Bloomfield | CT | 06002 | li.siyang@example.org | |
| 22523 | Fraser | Nancy | 11/8/1977 | 860-552-7392 | 7 Quinn Dr | Windsor | CT | 06095 | | |
| 22525 | Rodriguez | Maria | 2/11/1936 | 860-552-9023 | 624 Noyes St | Windsor | CT | 06095 | m.rodriguez@example.com | |
| 22526 | Swenson | Lucia | 5/1/1943 | 860-226-0293 | 83 Osage Ave | Hartford | CT | 06112 | | |
| 22527 | Lee | Hwan | 8/25/1987 | 860-661 3974 | 153 Agnes Ct | Hartford | CT | 06105 | hwan.lee@example.com | |
| 22529 | Goldberg | Robert | 5/30/1961 | 860-552-2873 | 92 Gaston Ave | Windsor | CT | 06095 | | |

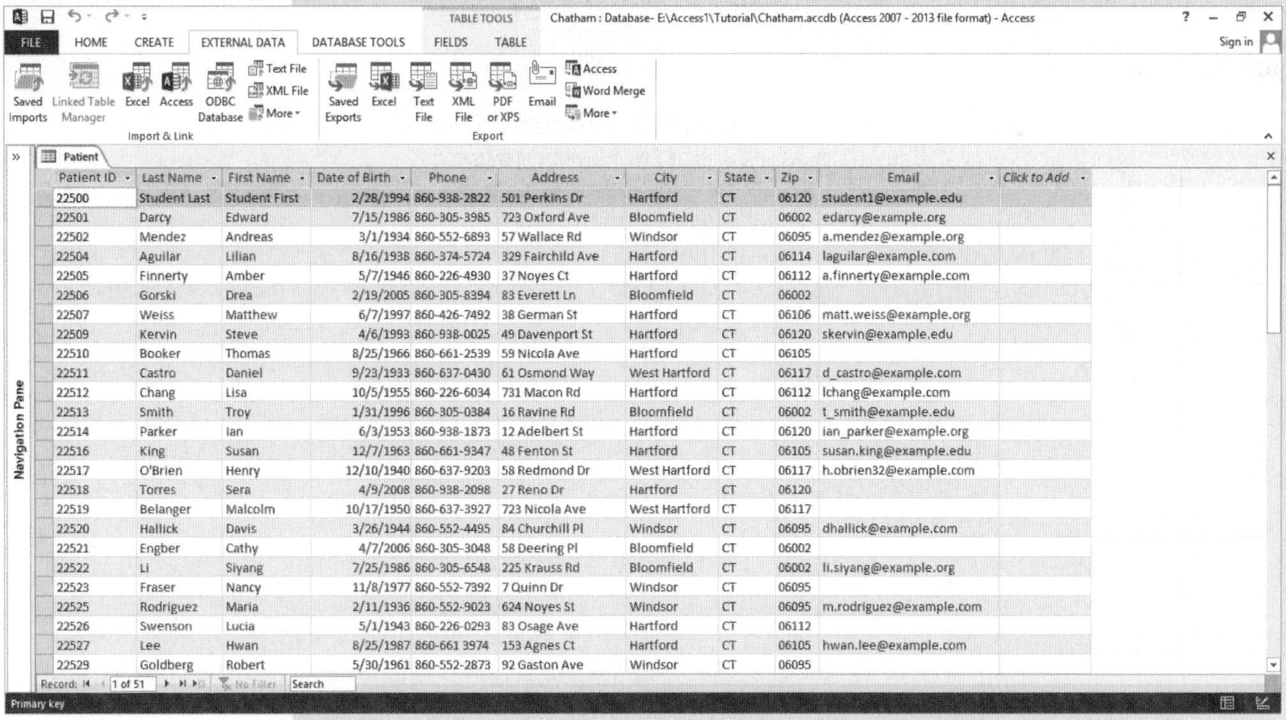

4. Save and close the Patient table, and then open the Navigation Pane.

The Chatham database now contains three tables—Patient, Visit, and Billing—and the tables contain all the necessary records. Your final task is to complete the database design by defining the necessary relationships between its tables.

# Defining Table Relationships

One of the most powerful features of a relational database management system is its ability to define relationships between tables. You use a common field to relate one table to another. The process of relating tables is often called performing a **join**. When you join tables that have a common field, you can extract data from them as if they were one larger table. For example, you can join the Patient and Visit tables by using the PatientID field in both tables as the common field. Then you can use a query, form, or report to extract selected data from each table, even though the data is contained in two separate tables, as shown in Figure 2-40. The PatientVisits query shown in Figure 2-40 includes the PatientID, LastName, and FirstName fields from the Patient table, and the VisitDate and Reason fields from the Visit table. The joining of records is based on the common field of PatientID. The Patient and Visit tables have a type of relationship called a one-to-many relationship.

| Figure 2-40 | One-to-many relationship and sample query |
| --- | --- |

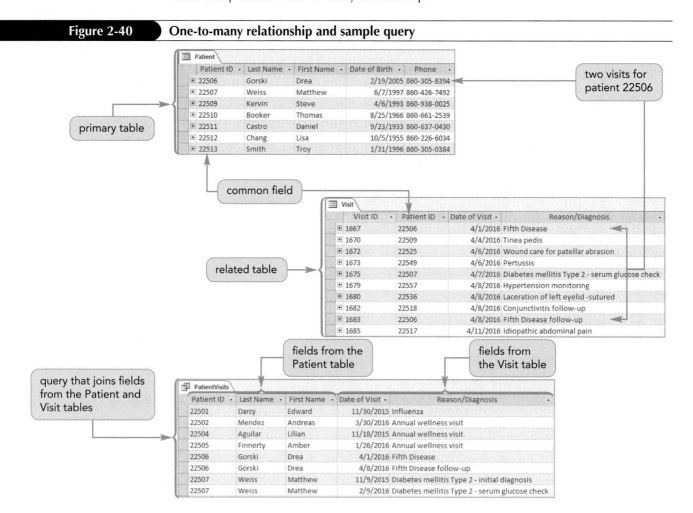

## One-to-Many Relationships

As shown earlier in the Session 2.2 Visual Overview, a one-to-many relationship exists between two tables when one record in the first table matches zero, one, or many records in the second table, and when one record in the second table matches at most one record in the first table. For example, as shown in Figure 2-40, patient 22506 has two visits in the Visit table. Other patients have one or more visits. Every visit has a single matching patient.

Access refers to the two tables that form a relationship as the primary table and the related table. The primary table is the "one" table in a one-to-many relationship; in Figure 2-40, the Patient table is the primary table because there is only one patient for each visit. The related table is the "many" table; in Figure 2-40, the Visit table is the related table because a patient can have zero, one, or many visits.

Because related data is stored in two tables, inconsistencies between the tables can occur. Referring to Figure 2-40, consider the following three scenarios:

- Cindi adds a record to the Visit table for a new patient, Jack Perry, using PatientID 22570. She did not first add the new patient's information to the Patient table, so this visit does not have a matching record in the Patient table. The data is inconsistent, and the visit record is considered to be an **orphaned record**.
- In another situation, Cindi changes the PatientID in the Patient table for Drea Gorski from 22506 to 22601. Because there is no longer a patient with the PatientID 22506 in the Patient table, this change creates two orphaned records in the Visit table, and the database is inconsistent.
- In a third scenario, Cindi deletes the record for Drea Gorski, patient 22506, from the Patient table because this patient moved and no longer receives medical services from Chatham Community Health Services. The database is again inconsistent; two records for patient 22506 in the Visit table have no matching record in the Patient table.

You can avoid these types of problems and avoid having inconsistent data in your database by specifying referential integrity between tables when you define their relationships.

## Referential Integrity

**Referential integrity** is a set of rules that Access enforces to maintain consistency between related tables when you update data in a database. Specifically, the referential integrity rules are as follows:

- When you add a record to a related table, a matching record must already exist in the primary table, thereby preventing the possibility of orphaned records.
- If you attempt to change the value of the primary key in the primary table, Access prevents this change if matching records exist in a related table. However, if you choose the **Cascade Update Related Fields option**, Access permits the change in value to the primary key and changes the appropriate foreign key values in the related table, thereby eliminating the possibility of inconsistent data.
- When you attempt to delete a record in the primary table, Access prevents the deletion if matching records exist in a related table. However, if you choose the **Cascade Delete Related Records option**, Access deletes the record in the primary table and also deletes all records in related tables that have matching foreign key values.

### INSIGHT

#### Understanding the Cascade Delete Related Records Option

Although there are advantages to using the Cascade Delete Related Records option for enforcing referential integrity, its use does present risks as well. You should rarely select the Cascade Delete Related Records option because doing so might cause you to inadvertently delete records you did not intend to delete. It is best to use other methods for deleting records that give you more control over the deletion process.

## Defining a Relationship Between Two Tables

When two tables have a common field, you can define a relationship between them in the Relationships window (see the Session 2.2 Visual Overview). Next, you need to define a one-to-many relationship between the Patient and Visit tables, with Patient as the primary table and Visit as the related table, and with PatientID as the common field (the primary key in the Patient table and a foreign key in the Visit table). You'll also define a one-to-many relationship between the Visit and Billing tables, with Visit as the primary table and Billing as the related table, and with VisitID as the common field (the primary key in the Visit table and a foreign key in the Billing table).

### To define the one-to-many relationship between the Patient and Visit tables:

▶ 1. On the ribbon, click the **DATABASE TOOLS** tab.

▶ 2. In the Relationships group, click the **Relationships** button. The Show Table dialog box opens. See Figure 2-41.

**Figure 2-41**    Show Table dialog box

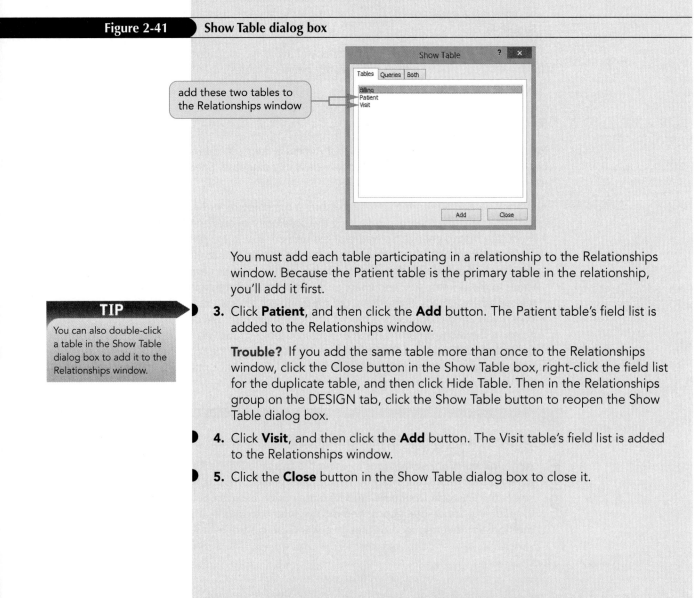

add these two tables to the Relationships window

You must add each table participating in a relationship to the Relationships window. Because the Patient table is the primary table in the relationship, you'll add it first.

**TIP**

You can also double-click a table in the Show Table dialog box to add it to the Relationships window.

▶ 3. Click **Patient**, and then click the **Add** button. The Patient table's field list is added to the Relationships window.

**Trouble?** If you add the same table more than once to the Relationships window, click the Close button in the Show Table box, right-click the field list for the duplicate table, and then click Hide Table. Then in the Relationships group on the DESIGN tab, click the Show Table button to reopen the Show Table dialog box.

▶ 4. Click **Visit**, and then click the **Add** button. The Visit table's field list is added to the Relationships window.

▶ 5. Click the **Close** button in the Show Table dialog box to close it.

So that you can view all the fields and complete field names, you'll resize the Patient table field list.

▶ **6.** Use the 𝕀 pointer to drag the bottom of the Patient table field list to lengthen it until the vertical scroll bar disappears and all the fields are visible.

To form the relationship between the two tables, you drag the common field of PatientID from the primary table to the related table. Then Access opens the Edit Relationships dialog box, in which you select the relationship options for the two tables.

▶ **7.** Click **PatientID** in the Patient field list, and then drag it to **PatientID** in the Visit field list. When you release the mouse button, the Edit Relationships dialog box opens. See Figure 2-42.

**Figure 2-42**  ▶ **Edit Relationships dialog box**

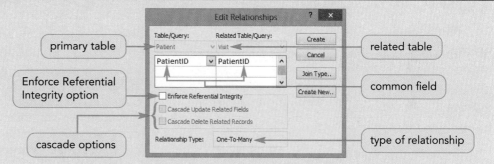

The primary table, related table, common field, and relationship type (One-To-Many) appear in the dialog box. Note that Access correctly identifies the "One" side of the relationship and places the primary table Patient in the Table/Query section of the dialog box; similarly, Access correctly identifies the "Many" side of the relationship and places the related table Visit in the Related Table/Query section of the dialog box.

▶ **8.** Click the **Enforce Referential Integrity** check box.

After you click the Enforce Referential Integrity check box, the two cascade options become available. If you select the Cascade Update Related Fields option, Access will update the appropriate foreign key values in the related table when you change a primary key value in the primary table. You will *not* select the Cascade Delete Related Records option because doing so could cause you to delete records that you do not want to delete; this option is rarely selected.

▶ **9.** Click the **Cascade Update Related Fields** check box.

▶ **10.** Click the **Create** button to define the one-to-many relationship between the two tables and to close the dialog box. The completed relationship appears in the Relationships window, with the join line connecting the common field of PatientID in each table. See Figure 2-43.

**Figure 2-43**    **Defined relationship in the Relationships window**

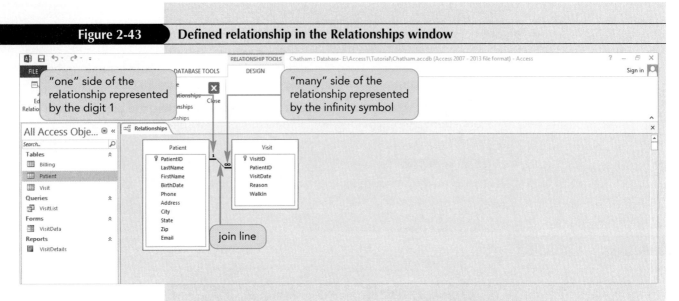

**Trouble?** If a dialog box opens indicating a problem that prevents you from creating the relationship, you most likely made a typing error when entering the two records in the Patient table. If so, click the OK button in the dialog box and then click the Cancel button in the Edit Relationships dialog box. Refer back to the earlier steps instructing you to enter the two records in the Patient table and carefully compare your entries with those shown in the text, especially the PatientID field values. Make any necessary corrections to the data in the Patient table, and then repeat Steps 7 through 10. If you still receive an error message, ask your instructor for assistance.

Now you need to define the one-to-many relationship between the Visit and Billing tables. In this relationship, Visit is the primary ("one") table because there is at most one visit for each invoice. Billing is the related ("many") table because there are zero, one, or many invoices that are generated for each patient visit. For example, some visits require lab work or pharmacy charges, which are invoiced separately.

### To define the relationship between the Visit and Billing tables:

1. In the Relationships group on the DESIGN tab, click the **Show Table** button. The Show Table dialog box opens.

**TIP**

You can also use the mouse to drag a table from the Navigation Pane to add it to the Relationships window.

2. Make sure the **Billing** table is selected on the Tables tab, click the **Add** button, and then click the **Close** button to close the Show Table dialog box. The Billing table's field list appears in the Relationships window to the right of the Visit table's field list.

3. Use the $\text{I}$ pointer to drag the bottom of the Billing table field list to lengthen it until the vertical scroll bar disappears.

   Because the Visit table is the primary table in this relationship, you need to drag the VisitID field from the Visit field list to the Billing field list.

4. Click and drag the **VisitID** field in the Visit field list to the **VisitID** field in the Billing field list. When you release the mouse button, the Edit Relationships dialog box opens.

5. Click the **Enforce Referential Integrity** check box, and then click the **Cascade Update Related Fields** check box.

**6.** Click the **Create** button to define the one-to-many relationship between the two tables and to close the dialog box. The completed relationship appears in the Relationships window. See Figure 2-44.

**Figure 2-44**    **Both relationships defined**

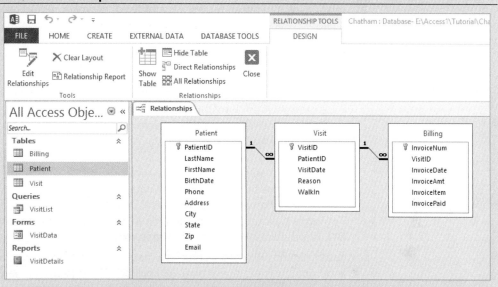

**Trouble?** If a dialog box opens indicating a problem that prevents you from creating the relationship, you most likely made a typing error when entering the two records in the Visit table. If so, click the OK button in the dialog box and then click the Cancel button in the Edit Relationships dialog box. Refer back to the steps in Tutorial 1 instructing you to enter the records in the Visit table and carefully compare your entries with those shown in the text, especially the VisitID field values. Make any necessary corrections to the data in the Visit table, and then repeat Steps 4 through 6. If you still receive an error message, ask your instructor for assistance.

With both relationships defined, you have connected the data among the three tables in the Chatham database.

**7.** On the Quick Access Toolbar, click the **Save** button 🖫 to save the layout in the Relationships window.

**8.** In the Relationships group on the DESIGN tab, click the **Close** button to close the Relationships window.

**9.** Click the **FILE** tab on the ribbon to display Backstage view.

**10.** Click the **Compact & Repair Database** button. Access compacts and repairs the Chatham database.

**11.** Click the **FILE** tab, and then click **Close** to close the Chatham database.

**PROSKILLS**

*Problem Solving: Creating a Larger Database*

When you create a small database that contains only a few tables, and the data and the reports you want to generate from it are fairly simple, you could follow the process outlined in this text: create the tables, populate them, and then define the necessary relationships between tables. This method, however, would not be suitable for creating a larger database. A larger database would most likely have many more tables and different types of relationships that can be quite complex. When creating a large database, a standard process to follow would include these steps:

1. Talk to people who will be using the data, and gather as much documentation as possible to try to understand how the data will be used. Gather sample reports, and ask the users to describe the data they require.
2. Gather some representative sample data, if possible.
3. Plan the tables, fields, data types, other properties, and the relationships between the tables.
4. Create the tables and define the relationships between them.
5. Populate the tables with sample data.
6. Design some queries, forms, and reports that will be needed, and then test them.
7. Modify the database structure, if necessary, based on the results of your tests.
8. Enter the actual data into the database tables.

Testing is critical at every stage of creating a database. Once the database is finalized and implemented, it's not actually finished. The design of a database evolves as new functionality is required and as the data that is gathered changes.

**REVIEW**

*Session 2.2 Quick Check*

1. What is the keyboard shortcut for inserting the value from the same field in the previous record into the current record?
2. _____ data is a process that allows you to copy the data from a source without having to open the source file.
3. The _____ gallery allows you to add a group of related fields to a table at the same time, rather than adding each field to the table individually.
4. What is the effect of deleting a field from a table structure?
5. A(n) _____ text file is one in which fields of data are separated by a character such as a comma or a tab.
6. The _____ is the "one" table in a one-to-many relationship, and the _____ is the "many" table in the relationship.
7. _____ is a set of rules that Access enforces to maintain consistency between related tables when you update data in a database.

ASSESS

## SAM Projects

Put your skills into practice with SAM Projects! SAM Projects for this tutorial can be found online. If you have a SAM account, go to www.cengage.com/sam2013 to download the most recent Project Instructions and Start Files.

PRACTICE

## Review Assignments

**Data Files needed for the Review Assignments: Vendor.accdb** *(cont. from Tutorial 1)* **and Supplies.xlsx**

In addition to tracking information about the vendors Chatham Community Health Services works with, Cindi also wants to track information about their products and services. First, Cindi asks you to modify the necessary properties in the existing Supplier table in the Vendor database; then she wants you to create a new table in the Vendor database to contain product data. Complete the following:

1. Open the **Vendor** database you created in Tutorial 1.
2. Open the **Supplier** table in Design view, and set the field properties as shown in Figure 2-45.

**Figure 2-45**    **Field properties for the Supplier table**

| Field Name | Data Type | Description | Field Size | Other |
|---|---|---|---|---|
| SupplierID | Short Text | Primary key | 6 | Caption = Supplier ID |
| Company | Short Text | | 50 | |
| Category | Short Text | | 15 | |
| Address | Short Text | | 35 | |
| City | Short Text | | 25 | |
| State | Short Text | | 2 | |
| Zip | Short Text | | 10 | |
| Phone | Short Text | | 14 | Caption = Contact Phone |
| ContactFirst | Short Text | | 20 | Caption = Contact First Name |
| ContactLast | Short Text | | 25 | Caption = Contact Last Name |
| InitialContact | Date/Time | | | Format = Short Date |
| | | | | Caption = Initial Contact |

© 2014 Cengage Learning

3. Save the Supplier table. Click the Yes button when a message appears indicating some data might be lost. Switch to Datasheet view and resize columns, as necessary, to their best fit. Then save and close the Supplier table.
4. Create a new table in Design view, using the table design shown in Figure 2-46.

**Figure 2-46**　Design for the Product table

| Field Name | Data Type | Description | Field Size | Other |
|---|---|---|---|---|
| ProductID | Short Text | Primary key | 5 | Caption = Product ID |
| SupplierID | Short Text | Foreign key | 6 | Caption = Supplier ID |
| ProductName | Short Text | | 75 | Caption = Product Name |
| Price | Currency | | | Format = Standard |
| | | | | Decimal Places = 2 |
| TempControl | Yes/No | | | Caption = Temp Controlled? |
| Sterile | Yes/No | | | Caption = Sterile? |
| Units | Number | | Integer | Decimal Places = 0 |
| | | | | Caption = Units/Case |
| | | | | Default Value = [no entry] |

© 2014 Cengage Learning

5. Specify ProductID as the primary key, and then save the table as **Product**.
6. Modify the table structure by adding a new field named **Weight** (data type: **Number**; field size: **Single**; Decimal Places: **2**; Caption: **Weight in Lbs**; Default Value: [no entry]) between the Price and TempControl fields. Then move the **Units** field so that it is positioned between the Price and Weight fields.
7. Enter the records shown in Figure 2-47 in the Product table. Resize all datasheet columns to their best fit. When finished, save and close the Product table.

**Figure 2-47**　Records for the Product table

| Product ID | Supplier ID | Product Name | Price | Units/Case | Weight in Lbs | Temp Controlled? | Sterile? |
|---|---|---|---|---|---|---|---|
| SS582 | DUR368 | Stethoscopes | 65.00 | 1 | 1 | No | No |
| AL487 | COU392 | Alcohol wipes | 15.00 | 1000 | 12 | Yes | Yes |

© 2014 Cengage Learning

8. Use the Import Spreadsheet Wizard to add data to the Product table. The data you need to import is contained in the Supplies workbook, which is an Excel file located in the Access1 ▶ Review folder provided with your Data Files.
   a. Specify the Supplies workbook as the source of the data.
   b. Select the option for appending the data.
   c. Select Product as the table.
   d. In the Import Spreadsheet Wizard dialog boxes, make sure Access confirms that the first row contains column headings, and import to the Product table. Do not save the import steps.
9. Open the **Product** table in Datasheet view and resize columns to their best fit, as necessary. Then save and close the Product table.
10. Define a one-to-many relationship between the primary Supplier table and the related Product table. Resize the table field lists so that all field names are visible. Select the referential integrity option and the cascade updates option for the relationship.
11. Save the changes to the Relationships window and close it, compact and repair the Vendor database, and then close the database.

## Case Problem 1

**Data Files needed for this Case Problem: Gopher.accdb** (*cont. from Tutorial 1*) **and Customers.txt**

*GoGopher!*   Amol Mehta wants to use the Gopher database to track information about members who join his online business, which provides a variety of services on a subscription basis, and the plans in which members are enrolled. He asks you to help maintain this database. Complete the following:

1. Open the **Gopher** database you created in Tutorial 1.
2. Open the **Plan** table in Design view, and change the following field properties:
   a. PlanID: Enter **Primary key** for the description, change the field size to **3**, and enter **Plan ID** for the caption.
   b. PlanDescription: Change the field size to **40** and enter **Plan Description** for the caption.
   c. PlanCost: Change the format to **Standard**, specify **0** decimal places, and enter **Plan Cost** for the caption.
   d. FeeWaived: Enter **Fee Waived** for the caption.
3. Save and close the Plan table. Click the Yes button when a message appears indicating some data might be lost.
4. Create a new table in Design view, using the table design shown in Figure 2-48.

**Figure 2-48**    **Design for the Member table**

| Field Name | Data Type | Description | Field Size | Other |
|---|---|---|---|---|
| MemberID | Short Text | Primary key | 4 | Caption = Member ID |
| PlanID | Short Text | Foreign key | 3 | Caption = Plan ID |
| FirstName | Short Text |  | 20 | Caption = First Name |
| LastName | Short Text |  | 25 | Caption = Last Name |
| Phone | Short Text |  | 14 |  |
| Expiration | Date/Time | Date when membership expires |  | Format = Short Date<br>Caption = Expiration Date |

© 2014 Cengage Learning

5. Specify MemberID as the primary key, and then save the table as **Member**.
6. Use the Address Quick Start selection in the Data Type gallery to add five fields between the LastName and Phone fields.
7. Switch to Design view, and then make the following changes to the Member table design:
   a. Address field: Change the name of this field to **Street**, change the field size to **40**, and delete the entry for the caption.
   b. City field: Change the field size to **25** and delete the entry for the caption.
   c. StateProvince field: Change the name of this field to **State**, change the field size to **2**, delete the entry for the caption, and enter **CO** for the default value.
   d. ZIPPostal field: Change the name of this field to **Zip**, change the field size to **10**, and delete the entry for the caption.
   e. Delete the **CountryRegion** field from the Member table structure.
   f. Add a new field named **DateJoined** (data type: **Date/Time**; format: **Short Date**; Caption: **Date Joined**) between the Phone and Expiration fields.
8. Enter the records shown in Figure 2-49 in the Member table. Be sure to enter your first and last names in the appropriate fields for the first new record. Resize all datasheet columns to their best fit. When finished, save and close the Member table.

| Figure 2-49 | | Records for the Member table |

| Member ID | Plan ID | First Name | Last Name | Street | City | State | Zip | Phone | Date Joined | Expiration Date |
|---|---|---|---|---|---|---|---|---|---|---|
| 1200 | 311 | *Student First* | *Student Last* | 45 Lakeview Dr | Boulder | CO | 80301 | 303-559-1238 | 11/1/2015 | 2/1/2016 |
| 1210 | 312 | Todd | Grant | 6 Rosebriar Rd | Erie | CO | 80516 | 303-674-2140 | 1/20/2016 | 4/20/2016 |

© 2014 Cengage Learning

9. Use the Import Text File Wizard to add data to the Member table. The data you need to import is contained in the Customers text file, which is located in the Access1 ▸ Case1 folder provided with your Data Files.

   a. Specify the Customers text file as the source of the data.

   b. Select the option for appending the data.

   c. Select Member as the table.

   d. In the Import Text File Wizard dialog boxes, choose the options to import delimited data, to use a comma delimiter, and to import the data into the Member table. Do not save the import steps.

10. Open the **Member** table in Datasheet view and resize columns to their best fit, as necessary. Then save and close the Member table.

11. Define a one-to-many relationship between the primary Plan table and the related Member table. Resize the Member table field list so that all field names are visible. Select the referential integrity option and the cascade updates option for this relationship.

12. Save the changes to the Relationships window and close it, compact and repair the Gopher database, and then close the database.

## Case Problem 2

**APPLY**

Data Files needed for this Case Problem: OBrien.accdb *(cont. from Tutorial 1)*, Client.accdb, Students.txt, and Agreements.xlsx

*O'Brien Educational Services*   Karen O'Brien plans to use the OBrien database to maintain information about the students, tutors, and contracts for her educational services company. Karen asks you to help her build the database by updating one table and creating two new tables in the database. Complete the following:

1. Open the **OBrien** database you created in Tutorial 1.

2. Open the **Tutor** table in Design view, and set the field properties as shown in Figure 2-50.

| Figure 2-50 | | Field properties for the Tutor table |

| Field Name | Data Type | Description | Field Size | Other |
|---|---|---|---|---|
| TutorID | Short Text | Primary key | 7 | Caption = Tutor ID |
| FirstName | Short Text | | 20 | Caption = First Name |
| LastName | Short Text | | 25 | Caption = Last Name |
| Degree | Short Text | | 7 | |
| School | Short Text | | 50 | |
| HireDate | Date/Time | | | Format = Short Date |
| | | | | Caption = Hire Date |

© 2014 Cengage Learning

3. Add a new field as the last field in the Tutor table with the field name **Groups**, the **Yes/No** data type, and the caption **Groups Only**.

4. Save the Tutor table. Click the Yes button when a message appears indicating some data might be lost.

5. In the table datasheet, specify that the following tutors conduct group tutoring sessions only: Student First/Student Last (i.e., your name), Amy Hawkins, Lori Burns, Samuel Glick, and Caitlin Shea. Close the Tutor table.

6. Karen created a table named Student in the Client database that is located in the Access1 ▸ Case2 folder provided with your Data Files. Import the structure of the Student table in the Client database into a new table named Student in the OBrien database. Do not save the import steps.

7. Open the **Student** table in Datasheet view, and then add the following two fields to the end of the table: **BirthDate** (Date/Time field) and **Gender** (Short Text field).

8. Use the Phone Quick Start selection in the Data Type gallery to add four fields related to phone numbers between the Zip and BirthDate fields. (*Hint:* Be sure to make the BirthDate field the active field before adding the new fields.)

9. Display the Student table in Design view, delete the BusinessPhone and FaxNumber fields, and then save and close the Student table.

10. Reopen the Student table and modify its design so that it matches the design in Figure 2-51, *including the revised field names and data types.*

    **Note:** You must type the quotation marks around the Default Property value for the State field.

**Figure 2-51     Field properties for the Student table**

| Field Name | Data Type | Description | Field Size | Other |
|---|---|---|---|---|
| StudentID | Short Text | Primary key | 7 | Caption = Student ID |
| LastName | Short Text | | 25 | Caption = Last Name |
| FirstName | Short Text | | 20 | Caption = First Name |
| Address | Short Text | | 35 | |
| City | Short Text | | 25 | |
| State | Short Text | | 2 | Default Value = "IN" |
| Zip | Short Text | | 10 | |
| HomePhone | Short Text | | 14 | |
| CellPhone | Short Text | | 14 | Caption = Cell Phone |
| BirthDate | Date/Time | | | Format = Short Date, Caption = Date of Birth |
| Gender | Short Text | F(emale), M(ale) | 1 | |

© 2014 Cengage Learning

you must type the quotation marks for this Default Value property

11. Move the LastName field so it follows the FirstName field.

12. Save your changes to the table design, and then add the records shown in Figure 2-52 to the Student table.

**Figure 2-52     Records for the Student table**

| Student ID | First Name | Last Name | Address | City | State | Zip | Home Phone | Cell Phone | Date of Birth | Gender |
|---|---|---|---|---|---|---|---|---|---|---|
| TUR8005 | Lynne | Turner | 6 Crowell Ct | South Bend | IN | 46614 | 574-245-2125 | 574-245-8842 | 7/24/2002 | F |
| CHA8034 | Henry | Chang | 1401 Lauren Dr | Oscela | IN | 46561 | 574-607-3045 | 574-674-2410 | 10/5/1999 | M |

© 2014 Cengage Learning

13. Resize the fields to their best fit, and then save and close the Student table.

14. Use the Import Text File Wizard to add data to the Student table. The data you need to import is contained in the Students text file, which is located in the Access1 ▸ Case2 folder provided with your Data Files.

    a. Specify the Students text file as the source of the data.

    b. Select the option for appending the data.

c. Select Student as the table.

d. In the Import Text File Wizard dialog boxes, choose the options to import delimited data, to use a comma delimiter, and to import the data into the Student table. Do not save the import steps.

15. Open the **Student** table in Datasheet view, resize columns in the datasheet to their best fit (as necessary), and then save and close the table.

16. Create a new table in Design view, using the table design shown in Figure 2-53.

**Figure 2-53**   Design for the Contract table

| Field Name | Data Type | Description | Field Size | Other |
|---|---|---|---|---|
| ContractID | Short Text | Primary key | 4 | Caption = Contract ID |
| StudentID | Short Text | Foreign key | 7 | Caption = Student ID |
| TutorID | Short Text | Foreign key | 7 | Caption = Tutor ID |
| SessionType | Short Text | | 15 | Caption = Session Type |
| Length | Number | | Integer | Decimal Places = 0 |
| | | | | Caption = Length (Hrs) |
| | | | | Default Value = [no entry] |
| NumSessions | Number | | Integer | Decimal Places = 0 |
| | | | | Caption = Number of Sessions |
| | | | | Default Value = [no entry] |
| Cost | Currency | | | Format = Currency |
| | | | | Decimal Places = 0 |
| | | | | Default Value = [no entry] |
| Assessment | Yes/No | Pre-assessment exam complete | | Caption = Assessment Complete |

© 2014 Cengage Learning

17. Specify ContractID as the primary key, and then save the table using the name **Contract**.

18. Add a new field to the Contract table, between the TutorID and SessionType fields, with the field name **ContractDate**, the **Date/Time** data type, the description **Date contract is signed**, the **Short Date** format, and the caption **Contract Date**. Save and close the Contract table.

19. Use the Import Spreadsheet Wizard to add data to the Contract table. The data you need to import is contained in the Agreements workbook, which is an Excel file located in the Access1 ▶ Case2 folder provided with your Data Files.

a. Specify the Agreements workbook as the source of the data.

b. Select the option for appending the data to the table.

c. Select Contract as the table.

d. In the Import Spreadsheet Wizard dialog boxes, choose the Agreements worksheet, make sure Access confirms that the first row contains column headings, and import to the Contract table. Do not save the import steps.

20. Open the **Contract** table and add the records shown in Figure 2-54. (*Hint*: Use the New (blank) record button in the navigation buttons to add a new record.)

**Figure 2-54**   Records for the Contract table

| Contract ID | Student ID | Tutor ID | Contract Date | Session Type | Length (Hrs) | Number of Sessions | Cost | Assessment Complete |
|---|---|---|---|---|---|---|---|---|
| 5168 | LUF8037 | 68-8234 | 8/30/2016 | Group | 3 | 12 | $1,440 | Yes |
| 5172 | GOS8029 | 71-1698 | 9/7/2016 | Private | 2 | 6 | $720 | Yes |

© 2014 Cengage Learning

21. Resize columns in the datasheet to their best fit (as necessary), and then save and close the Contract table.

22. Define the one-to-many relationships between the database tables as follows: between the primary Student table and the related Contract table, and between the primary Tutor table and the related Contract table. Resize the table field lists so that all field names are visible. Select the referential integrity option and the cascade updates option for each relationship.

23. Save the changes to the Relationships window and close it, compact and repair the OBrien database, and then close the database.

## CHALLENGE

## Case Problem 3

Data Files needed for this Case Problem: Shelter.accdb *(cont. from Tutorial 1)*, Donations.xlsx, and Animals.txt

***Rosemary Animal Shelter***    Ryan Lang wants to use the Shelter database to maintain information about the patrons, animals, and donations for his not-for-profit agency. Ryan asks you to help him maintain the database by updating one table and creating two new ones. Complete the following:

1. Open the **Shelter** database you created in Tutorial 1.
2. Open the **Patron** table in Design view, and then change the following field properties:
   a. PatronID: Enter **Primary key** for the description, change the field size to **5**, and enter **Patron ID** for the caption.
   b. Title: Change the field size to **4**.
   c. FirstName: Change the field size to **20** and enter **First Name** for the caption.
   d. LastName: Change the field size to **25** and enter **Last Name** for the caption.
   e. Phone: Change the field size to **14.**
3. Save and close the Patron table. Click the Yes button when a message appears indicating some data might be lost.

⊕ **Explore**  4. Use the Import Spreadsheet Wizard to create a table in the Shelter database. As the source of the data, specify the Donations workbook, which is located in the Access1 ▸ Case3 folder provided with your Data Files. Select the option to import the source data into a new table in the database.

⊕ **Explore**  5. Complete the Import Spreadsheet Wizard dialog boxes as follows:
   a. Select Donation as the worksheet you want to import.
   b. Specify that the first row contains column headings.
   c. Accept the field options suggested by the wizard, and do not skip any fields.
   d. Choose DonationID as your own primary key.
   e. Import the data to a table named **Donation**, and do not save the import steps.

6. Open the Donation table in Datasheet view, and then delete the Requires Pickup field.

7. Open the Donation table in Design view, and then modify the table so it matches the design shown in Figure 2-55, including changes to data types, field name, and field position. For the Short Text fields, delete any formats specified in the Format property boxes.

**Figure 2-55**    Design for the Donation table

| Field Name | Data Type | Description | Field Size | Other |
|---|---|---|---|---|
| DonationID | Short Text | Primary key | 4 | Caption = Donation ID |
| PatronID | Short Text | Foreign key | 5 | Caption = Patron ID |
| DonationDate | Date/Time | | | Format = mm/dd/yyyy |
| | | | | Caption = Donation Date |
| Description | Short Text | | 30 | |
| DonationValue | Currency | Dollar amount or estimated value | | Format = Currency |
| | | | | Decimal Places = 2 |
| | | | | Caption = Donation Value |
| | | | | Default Value = [no entry] |

8. Save your changes to the table design, click Yes for the message about lost data, and then switch to Datasheet view.

9. Resize the columns in the Donation datasheet to their best fit.

✛ **Explore**  10. Ryan decides that the values in the Donation Value column would look better without the two decimal places. Make this field the current field in the datasheet. Then, in the Formatting group on the FIELDS tab, use the Decrease Decimals button to remove the two decimal places and the period from these values. Switch back to Design view, and note that the Decimal Places property for the DonationValue field is now set to 0.

11. Save and close the Donation table.

12. Use Design view to create a table using the table design shown in Figure 2-56.

---

**Figure 2-56**     **Design for the Animal table**

| Field Name | Data Type | Description | Field Size | Other |
|---|---|---|---|---|
| AnimalID | Short Text | Primary key | 3 | Caption = Animal ID |
| AnimalName | Short Text | | 15 | Caption = Animal Name |
| Age | Short Text | | 2 | Caption = Age at Arrival |
| Gender | Short Text | | 6 | |
| AnimalType | Short Text | | 5 | Caption = Animal Type |
| Description | Short Text | | 60 | |
| ArrivalDate | Date/Time | | | Format = Short Date |
| | | | | Caption = Arrival Date |
| AdoptionDate | Date/Time | | | Format = Short Date |
| | | | | Caption = Adoption Date |
| Adopted | Yes/No | | | |
| PatronID | Short Text | | 5 | Caption = Patron ID |

© 2014 Cengage Learning

---

13. Specify AnimalID as the primary key, save the table as **Animal**, and then close the table.

14. Use the Import Text File Wizard to add data to the Animal table. The data you need to import is contained in the Animals text file, which is located in the Access1 ▸ Case3 folder provided with your Data Files.

   a. Specify the Animals text file as the source of the data.

   b. Select the option for appending the data.

   c. Select Animal as the table.

   d. In the Import Text File Wizard dialog boxes, choose the options to import delimited data, to use a comma delimiter, and to import the data into the Animal table. Do not save the import steps.

15. Open the Animal table in Datasheet view, and resize all columns to their best fit.

16. Display the Animal table in Design view. Move the PatronID field to make it the second field in the table, and enter the description **Foreign key** for the PatronID field. Then move the Adopted field so it is positioned between the ArrivalDate and AdoptionDate fields. Save the modified Animal table design.

17. Switch to Datasheet view, and then add the records shown in Figure 2-57 to the Animal table. (*Hint*: Use the New (blank) record button in the navigation buttons to add a new record.) Close the table when finished.

---

**Figure 2-57**     **Records for the Animal table**

| Animal ID | Patron ID | Animal Name | Age at Arrival | Gender | Animal Type | Description | Arrival Date | Adopted | Adoption Date |
|---|---|---|---|---|---|---|---|---|---|
| B45 | | Gizmo | 12 | Male | Dog | Hound mix | 3/6/2016 | No | |
| R39 | 38398 | Simba | 3 | Female | Cat | Siamese | 4/12/2016 | Yes | 5/14/2016 |

© 2014 Cengage Learning

18. Define the one-to-many relationships between the database tables as follows: between the primary Patron table and the related Animal table, and between the primary Patron table and the related Donation table. (*Hint:* Place the Patron table as the middle table in the Relationships window to make it easier to join the tables.) Resize the Animal field list so that all field names are visible. Select the referential integrity option and the cascade updates option for each relationship.

19. Save the changes to the Relationships window and close it, compact and repair the Shelter database, and then close the database.

## Case Problem 4

**CHALLENGE**

Data Files needed for this Case Problem: **Stanley.accdb** (*cont. from Tutorial 1*), **Travel.accdb**, and **Bookings.txt**

***Stanley EcoTours***   Janice and Bill Stanley use the Stanley database to track the data about the tours they offer to clients of their ecotourism business. They ask you to help them maintain this database. Complete the following:

1. Open the **Stanley** database you created in Tutorial 1.
2. Open the **Guest** table in Design view and change the following field properties:
   a. GuestID: Enter **Primary key** for the description, change the field size to **3**, and enter **Guest ID** for the caption.
   b. GuestFirst: Change the field size to **20** and enter **Guest First Name** for the caption.
   c. GuestLast: Change the field size to **25** and enter **Guest Last Name** for the caption.
   d. Address: Change the field size to **35**.
   e. City: Change the field size to **25**.
   f. State/Prov: Change the field size to **2**.
   g. PostalCode: Change the field size to **10** and enter **Postal Code** for the caption.
   h. Country: Change the field size to **15**.
   i. Phone: Change the field size to **14**.
3. Save the Guest table, click the Yes button when a message appears indicating some data might be lost, resize the Guest First Name and Guest Last Name columns in Datasheet view to their best fit, and then save and close the table.

⊕ **Explore**  4. In addition to importing the structure of an existing Access table, you can also import both the structure *and* the data contained in a table to create a new table. Import the **Trip** table structure and data from the **Travel** database into a new table in the **Stanley** database as follows:
   a. Start the process for importing an Access table structure.
   b. As the source of the data, specify the Travel database, which is located in the Access1 ▸ Case4 folder provided with your Data Files.
   c. Select the option button to import tables, queries, forms, reports, macros, and modules into the current database.
   d. In the Import Objects dialog box, select the Trip table, click the Options button, and then make sure that the correct option is selected to import the table's data and structure (definition).
   e. Do not save your import steps.

⊕ **Explore**  5. Using a shortcut menu in the Navigation Pane, rename the Trip table as **Tour** to give this name to the new table in the Stanley database.

6. Open the **Tour** table in Design view, delete the VIPDiscount field, and then move the PricePerPerson field so that it appears between the Country and SingleSupplement fields.

7. Change the following properties:
   a. TourID: Enter the description **Primary key**, change the field size to **4**, and enter **Tour ID** for the caption.
   b. TourName: Enter **Tour Name** for the caption.
   c. PricePerPerson: Enter **Price Per Person** for the caption.
   d. SingleSupplement: Enter the description **Additional charge for single accommodation**, and enter **Single Supplement** for the caption.
   e. TourType: Change the field size to **15**, and enter **Tour Type** for the caption.
   f. Nights: Enter **Num of Nights** for the caption.
8. Save the modified table, click the Yes button when a message appears indicating some data might be lost, and then display the table in Datasheet view. Resize all datasheet columns to their best fit, and then save and close the table.
9. In Design view, create a table using the table design shown in Figure 2-58.

**Figure 2-58**     **Design for the Reservation table**

| Field Name | Data Type | Description | Field Size | Other |
|---|---|---|---|---|
| ReservationID | Short Text | Primary key | 3 | Caption = Reservation ID |
| GuestID | Short Text | Foreign key | 3 | Caption = Guest ID |
| TourID | Short Text | Foreign key | 4 | Caption = Tour ID |
| StartDate | Date/Time | | | Caption = Start Date |
| People | Number | Number of people in the party | Integer | Decimal Places = 0 |
| | | | | Default Value = [no entry] |

© 2014 Cengage Learning

10. Specify ReservationID as the primary key, and then save the table as **Reservation**.

⊕ **Explore** 11. Refer back to Figure 2-11 to review the custom date formats. Change the Format property of the StartDate field to a custom format that displays dates in a format similar to 05/25/16. Save and close the Reservation table.

12. Use the Import Text File Wizard to add data to the Reservation table. The data you need to import is contained in the Bookings text file, which is located in the Access1 ▶ Case4 folder provided with your Data Files.
   a. Specify the Bookings text file as the source of the data.
   b. Select the option for appending the data.
   c. Select Reservation as the table.
   d. In the Import Text File Wizard dialog boxes, choose the options to import delimited data, to use a comma delimiter, and to import the data into the Reservation table. Do not save the import steps.
13. Resize columns in the **Reservation** table datasheet to their best fit (as necessary), verify that the date values in the StartDate field are displayed correctly according to the custom format, and then save and close the table.
14. Define the one-to-many relationships between the database tables as follows: between the primary Guest table and the related Reservation table, and between the primary Tour table and the related Reservation table. (*Hint:* Place the Reservation table as the middle table in the Relationships window to make it easier to join the tables.) Resize the Guest and Tour field lists so that all field names are visible. Select the referential integrity option and the cascade updates option for each relationship.
15. Save the changes to the Relationships window and close it, compact and repair the Stanley database, and then close the database.

ACCESS

## OBJECTIVES

**Session 3.1**
- Find, modify, and delete records in a table
- Hide and unhide fields in a datasheet
- Work in the Query window in Design view
- Create, run, and save queries
- Update data using a query datasheet
- Create a query based on multiple tables
- Sort data in a query
- Filter data in a query

**Session 3.2**
- Specify an exact match condition in a query
- Use a comparison operator in a query to match a range of values
- Use the And and Or logical operators in queries
- Change the font size and alternate row color in a datasheet
- Create and format a calculated field in a query
- Perform calculations in a query using aggregate functions and record group calculations
- Change the display of database objects in the Navigation Pane

# Maintaining and Querying a Database

*Updating and Retrieving Information About Patients, Visits, and Invoices*

## Case | *Chatham Community Health Services*

At a recent meeting, Cindi Rodriguez and her staff discussed the importance of maintaining accurate information about the clinic's patients, visits, and invoices, and regularly monitoring the business activities of Chatham Community Health Services. For example, Kelly Schwarz, Cindi's assistant, needs to make sure she has up-to-date contact information, such as phone numbers and email addresses, for all the clinic's patients. The office staff also must monitor billing activity to ensure that invoices are paid on time and in full. Ethan Ward, a staff member who handles marketing and community outreach efforts for the clinic, tracks patient activity to develop new strategies for promoting services provided by the clinic. In addition, Cindi is interested in analyzing other aspects of the business related to patient visits and finances. You can satisfy all these informational needs for Chatham Community Health Services by updating data in the Chatham database and by creating and using queries that retrieve information from the database.

## STARTING DATA FILES

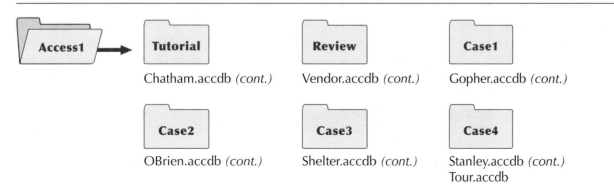

Access1 → Tutorial
Chatham.accdb *(cont.)*

Review
Vendor.accdb *(cont.)*

Case1
Gopher.accdb *(cont.)*

Case2
OBrien.accdb *(cont.)*

Case3
Shelter.accdb *(cont.)*

Case4
Stanley.accdb *(cont.)*
Tour.accdb

# Session 3.1 Visual Overview:

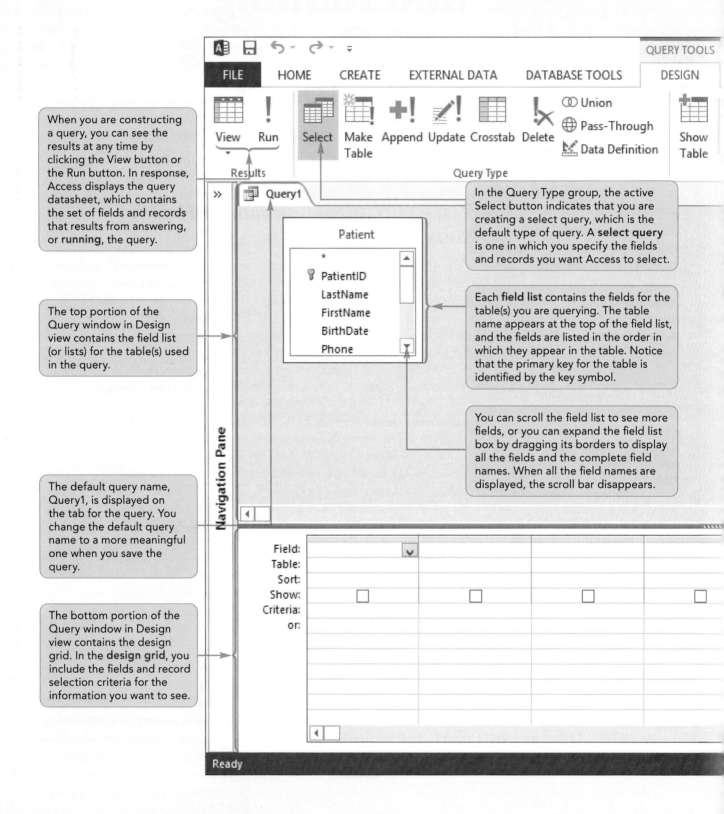

When you are constructing a query, you can see the results at any time by clicking the View button or the Run button. In response, Access displays the query datasheet, which contains the set of fields and records that results from answering, or **running**, the query.

The top portion of the Query window in Design view contains the field list (or lists) for the table(s) used in the query.

The default query name, Query1, is displayed on the tab for the query. You change the default query name to a more meaningful one when you save the query.

The bottom portion of the Query window in Design view contains the design grid. In the **design grid**, you include the fields and record selection criteria for the information you want to see.

In the Query Type group, the active Select button indicates that you are creating a select query, which is the default type of query. A **select query** is one in which you specify the fields and records you want Access to select.

Each **field list** contains the fields for the table(s) you are querying. The table name appears at the top of the field list, and the fields are listed in the order in which they appear in the table. Notice that the primary key for the table is identified by the key symbol.

You can scroll the field list to see more fields, or you can expand the field list box by dragging its borders to display all the fields and the complete field names. When all the field names are displayed, the scroll bar disappears.

# Query Window in Design View

Chatham : Database- E:\Access1\Tutorial\Chatham.accdb (Acces...    ?   —   ⬜   ✕

Sign in

| | | | |
|---|---|---|---|
| ⅀= Insert Rows | ᵘ↑ᵘ Insert Columns | | 🗐 Property Sheet |
| ✗ Delete Rows | ✗ Delete Columns | | XYZ Table Names |
| ⋰ Builder | ᵀ⁰ Return: All ▾ | Σ  🗔? |  |
| | | Totals Parameters | |

Query Setup                          Show/Hide

The ribbon displays the QUERY TOOLS DESIGN tab with options for creating and running queries. Note the Query Type group on the DESIGN tab; it provides buttons you can click to create various types of queries.

In Design view, you specify the data you want to view by constructing a query by example. When you use **query by example (QBE)**, you give Access an example of the information you are requesting. Access then retrieves the information that precisely matches your example.

Each column in the design grid contains specifications about a field you will use in the query. You can choose a single field for your query by double-clicking its name in the field list to place the field in the next available design grid column.

The view buttons on the status bar allow you to change to different views; for example, you can click the Datasheet View button to run the query and display the results in Datasheet view.

# Updating a Database

**Updating**, or **maintaining**, a database is the process of adding, modifying, and deleting records in database tables to keep them current and accurate. After reviewing the data in the Chatham database, Kelly identified some changes that need to be made to the data. She would like you to update the field values in one record in the Patient table, correct an error in one record in the Visit table, and then delete a record in the Visit table.

## Modifying Records

To modify the field values in a record, you must first make the record the current record. Then you position the insertion point in the field value to make minor changes, or select the field value to replace it entirely. In Tutorial 1, you used the mouse with the scroll bars and the navigation buttons to navigate the records in a datasheet. You can also use keyboard shortcuts and the F2 key to navigate a datasheet and to select field values. The **F2 key** is a toggle that you use to switch between navigation mode and editing mode:

- In **navigation mode**, Access selects an entire field value. If you type while you are in navigation mode, your typed entry replaces the highlighted field value.
- In **editing mode**, you can insert or delete characters in a field value based on the location of the insertion point.

Figure 3-1 shows some of the navigation mode and editing mode keyboard shortcuts.

| Figure 3-1 | Navigation mode and editing mode keyboard shortcuts |
| --- | --- |

| Press | To Move the Selection in Navigation Mode | To Move the Insertion Point in Editing Mode |
| --- | --- | --- |
| ← | Left one field value at a time | Left one character at a time |
| → | Right one field value at a time | Right one character at a time |
| Home | Left to the first field value in the record | To the left of the first character in the field value |
| End | Right to the last field value in the record | To the right of the last character in the field value |
| ↑ or ↓ | Up or down one record at a time | Up or down one record at a time and switch to navigation mode |
| Tab or Enter | Right one field value at a time | Right one field value at a time and switch to navigation mode |
| Ctrl + Home | To the first field value in the first record | To the left of the first character in the field value |
| Ctrl + End | To the last field value in the last record | To the right of the last character in the field value |

© 2014 Cengage Learning

The Patient table record Kelly wants you to change is for Patrice Lewis. This patient recently moved to another location in Windsor and also changed her email address, so you need to update the Patient table record with the new street address and email address.

### To open the Patient table in the Chatham database:

▶ **1.** Start Access and open the **Chatham** database you created and worked with in Tutorials 1 and 2.

   **Trouble?** If the security warning is displayed below the ribbon, click the Enable Content button.

▶ **2.** Open the **Patient** table in Datasheet view.

The Patient table contains many fields. Sometimes, when updating data in a table, it can be helpful to remove the display of some fields on the screen.

## Hiding and Unhiding Fields

**TIP**

Hiding a field removes it from the datasheet display *only*; the field and its contents are still part of the table.

When you are viewing a table or query datasheet in Datasheet view, you might want to temporarily remove certain fields from the displayed datasheet, making it easier to focus on the data you're interested in viewing. The **Hide Fields** command allows you to remove the display of one or more fields, and the **Unhide Fields** command allows you to redisplay any hidden fields. Hiding fields can be especially useful in a table with many fields.

To make it easier to modify the patient record, you'll first hide a couple of fields in the Patient table.

### To hide fields in the Patient table and modify the patient record:

▶ **1.** Right-click the **Date of Birth** field name to display the shortcut menu, and then click **Hide Fields** on the shortcut menu. The Date of Birth column is removed from the datasheet display.

▶ **2.** Right-click the **Phone** field name, and then click **Hide Fields** on the shortcut menu. The Phone column is removed from the datasheet display.

   With the fields hidden, you can now update the patient record. The record you need to modify is near the end of the table and has a PatientID field value of 22560.

▶ **3.** Drag the vertical scroll box down until you see the last records in the table.

▶ **4.** Click the PatientID field value **22560**, for Patrice Lewis. The field value is not selected, indicating you are in editing mode.

▶ **5.** Press the **Tab** key to move to the Last Name field value, Lewis. The field value is selected, indicating you are in navigation mode.

▶ **6.** Press the **Tab** key twice to move to the Address field and select its field value, type **83 Highland St**, press the **Tab** key four times to move to the Email field, type **plewis5@example.org**, and then press the **Tab** key. The changes to the record are complete. See Figure 3-2.

| Figure 3-2 | Table after changing field values in a record |

| ⊞ 22555 | Phillips | Aquon | 632 Perkins Dr | Hartford | CT | 06120 | |
| ⊞ 22556 | Grus | Mateo | 18 Norman Rd | Hartford | CT | 06112 | m.grus@example.com |
| ⊞ 22557 | Kirk | Isobel | 48 Grafton St | Bloomfield | CT | 06002 | |
| ⊞ 22558 | Ropiak | Jane | 637 Filbert St | Hartford | CT | 06120 | jropiak@example.edu |
| ⊞ 22559 | Morales | Jose | 251 Lilac St | West Hartford | CT | 06117 | j.morales@example.org |
| ⊞ 22560 | Lewis | Patrice | 83 Highland St | Windsor | CT | 06095 | plewis5@example.org |
| ⊞ 22561 | Shaw | Daniel | 33 Agnes Ct | West Hartford | CT | 06117 | dshaw@example.com |
| * | | | | | CT | | |

field values changed

Record: I◄ ◄ 51 of 51 ► ►I ►* 🏷 No Filter   Search

Primary key

Access saves changes to field values when you move to a new field or another record, or when you close the table. You don't have to click the Save button to save changes to field values or records.

Note that the PatientID field value for the last record in the table is selected, indicating you are in navigation mode.

▶ **7.** Press the **Ctrl+Home** keys to move to the first field value in the first record.

With the changes to the record complete, you can unhide the hidden fields.

▶ **8.** Right-click any field name to display the shortcut menu, and then click **Unhide Fields**. The Unhide Columns dialog box opens. See Figure 3-3.

**Figure 3-3** Unhide Columns dialog box

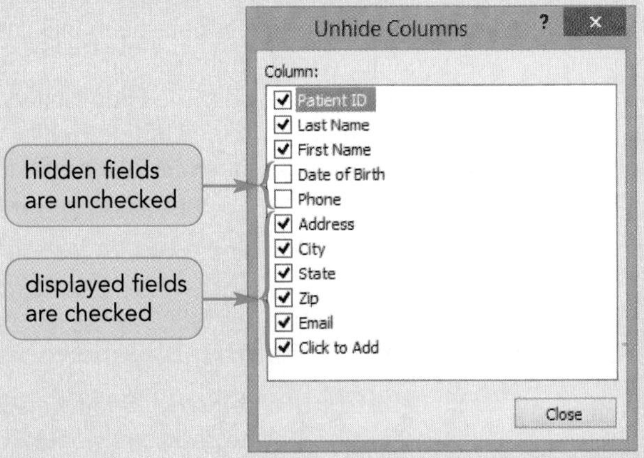

All currently displayed fields are checked in this dialog box, and all hidden fields are unchecked. To redisplay them, you simply click their check boxes to select them.

▶ **9.** In the Unhide Columns dialog box, click the **Date of Birth** check box to select it, click the **Phone** check box to select it, and then click the **Close** button to close the dialog box. The two hidden fields are now displayed in the datasheet.

▶ **10.** Close the Patient table. A dialog box opens asking if you want to save changes to the layout of the Patient table. This box appears because you hid fields and redisplayed them.

In this case, you can click either the Yes button or the No button, because no changes were actually made to the table layout or design.

▶ **11.** Click the **No** button to close the dialog box.

Next you need to correct an error in the Visit table for a visit made by Jane Ropiak, Patient ID 22558. A staff member incorrectly entered "COPD management visit" as the reason for the visit, when the patient actually came to the clinic that day suffering from influenza. Ensuring the accuracy of the data in a database is an important maintenance task.

**To correct the record in the Visit table:**

▶ **1.** Open the **Visit** table in Datasheet view. The record containing the error is for Visit ID 1635.

▶ **2.** Scroll down the Visit table until you locate Visit ID **1635**, and then click at the end of the **Reason** field value for this record. Because the field value is not selected, you are in editing mode.

▶ **3.** Press the **Backspace** key until the current entry for the Reason field is deleted, type **Influenza**, and then press the **Enter** key twice. The record now contains the correct value in the Reason field, and Access saves this change automatically in the Visit table.

The next update Kelly asks you to make is to delete a record in the Visit table. One of the clinic's patients, Robert Goldberg, recently notified Kelly that he received an invoice for an annual wellness visit, but that he had cancelled this scheduled appointment to the clinic. Because this patient visit did not take place, the record for this visit needs to be deleted from the Visit table. Rather than scrolling through the table to locate the record to delete, you can have Access find the data for you.

## Finding Data in a Table

Access provides options you can use to locate specific field values in a table. Instead of scrolling the Visit table datasheet to find the visit that you need to delete—the record for Visit ID 1688—you can use the Find command to find the record. The **Find command** allows you to search a table or query datasheet, or a form, to locate a specific field value or part of a field value. This feature is particularly useful when searching a table that contains a large number of records.

### To search for the record in the Visit table:

**TIP**

You can click any value in the column containing the field you want to search to make the field current.

▶ **1.** Make sure the VisitID field value **1638** is still selected. You need to search the VisitID field to find the record containing the value 1688, so the insertion point is already correctly positioned in the field you want to search.

▶ **2.** Make sure the **HOME** tab is displayed on the ribbon.

▶ **3.** In the Find group, click the **Find** button. The Find and Replace dialog box opens. See Figure 3-4.

**Figure 3-4**    **Find and Replace dialog box**

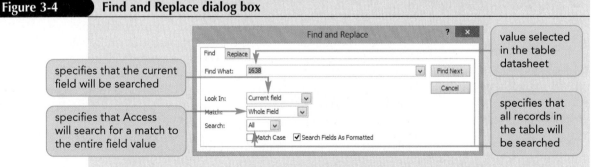

specifies that the current field will be searched

specifies that Access will search for a match to the entire field value

value selected in the table datasheet

specifies that all records in the table will be searched

The field value 1638 appears in the Find What box because this value is selected in the table datasheet. The Look In box indicates that the current field will be searched for the value. The Match box indicates that the Find command will match the whole field value, which is correct for your search. You also can choose to search for only part of a field value, such as when you need to find all Visit IDs that start with a certain value. The Search box indicates that all the records in the table will be searched for the value you want to find. You also can choose to search up or down from the currently selected record.

> **Trouble?** Some of the settings in your dialog box might be different from those shown in Figure 3-4 depending on the last search performed on the computer you're using. If so, change the settings so that they match those in the figure.
>
> ▶ **4.** Make sure the value 1638 is selected in the Find What box, type **1688** to replace the selected value, and then click the **Find Next** button. Access scrolls the datasheet to record 81 and selects the field value you specified.
>
> ▶ **5.** Click the **Cancel** button to close the Find and Replace dialog box.

## Deleting Records

To delete a record, you need to select the record in Datasheet view, and then delete it using the Delete button in the Records group on the HOME tab or the Delete Record option on the shortcut menu.

**REFERENCE**

### Deleting a Record

- With the table open in Datasheet view, click the row selector for the record you want to delete.
- In the Records group on the HOME tab, click the Delete button (or right-click the row selector for the record, and then click Delete Record on the shortcut menu).
- In the dialog box asking you to confirm the deletion, click the Yes button.

Now that you have found the record with Visit ID 1688, you can delete it. To delete a record, you must first select the entire row for the record.

### To delete the record:

▶ **1.** Click the row selector for the record containing the VisitID field value **1688**, which should still be highlighted. The entire row is selected.

▶ **2.** In the Records group on the HOME tab, click the **Delete** button. A dialog box opens and indicates that you cannot delete the record because the Billing table contains records that are related to VisitID 1688. Recall that you defined a one-to-many relationship between the Visit and Billing tables and you enforced referential integrity. When you try to delete a record in the primary table (Visit), Access prevents the deletion if matching records exist in the related table (Billing). This protection helps to maintain the integrity of the data in the database.

> To delete the record in the Visit table, you first must delete the related records in the Billing table.

▶ **3.** Click the **OK** button in the dialog box to close it. Notice the plus sign that appears at the beginning of each record in the Visit table. The **plus sign** indicates that the Visit table is the primary table related to another table—in this case, the Billing table.

▶ **4.** Scroll the datasheet down until you see the rest of the records in the table, so that you have room to view the related records for the visit record.

**5.** Click the **plus sign** next to VisitID 1688. Access displays the one related record from the Billing table for this visit. See Figure 3-5.

| Figure 3-5 | Related record from the Billing table in the subdatasheet |

minus sign appears when
related records are displayed

| | 1683 | 22506 | 4/8/2016 Fifth Disease follow-up | ☐ |
| Reports | ⊞ 1685 | 22517 | 4/11/2016 Idiopathic abdominal pain | ☑ |
| VisitDetails | ⊞ 1687 | 22534 | 4/12/2016 Joint pain/arthritis | ☑ |
| | ⊟ 1688 | 22529 | 4/12/2016 Annual wellness visit | ☐ |

| Invoice Num ▾ | Invoice Date ▾ | Invoice Amt ▾ | Invoice Item | ▾ | Invoice Paid ▾ | Click to Add ▾ |
| 36087 | 04/13/2016 | $100.00 | Office visit | | ☐ | |
| * | | $0.00 | | | ☐ | |

subdatasheet with
related record from
the Billing table

| ⊞ 1690 | 22521 | 4/13/2016 Varicella | ☑ |
| ⊞ 1692 | 22558 | 4/14/2016 COPD management visit | ☐ |
| ⊞ 1695 | 22551 | 4/15/2016 Elevated blood lipids-monitoring meds | ☐ |
| ⊞ 1698 | 22536 | 4/15/2016 Removal of sutures from left eyelid | ☐ |
| ⊞ 1700 | 22509 | 4/18/2016 Tinea pedis follow-up | ☐ |
| | | | ☐ |

plus signs indicate records have
related records in another table

Record: I◄ ◄ 1 of 1 ► ►I ►❋ 🛇 No Filter  Search

Calculating . . .

**TIP**

The plus sign changes to a minus sign for the current record when its related records are displayed.

The related record from the Billing table is displayed in a **subdatasheet**. When you first open a table that is the primary table in a one-to-many relationship, the subdatasheet containing the records from the related table is not displayed. You need to click the plus sign, also called the **expand indicator**, to display the related records in the subdatasheet. When the subdatasheet is open, you can navigate and update it, just as you can using a table datasheet.

You need to delete the record in the Billing table that is related to Visit ID 1688 before you can delete this visit record. The record is for the invoice that was mistakenly sent to the patient, Robert Goldberg, who had cancelled his annual wellness visit at the clinic. You could open the Billing table and find the related record. However, an easier way is to delete the record right in the subdatasheet. The record will be deleted from the Billing table automatically.

**6.** In the Billing table subdatasheet, click the row selector for invoice number **36087**. The entire row is selected.

**7.** In the Records group on the HOME tab, click the **Delete** button. Access opens a dialog box asking you to confirm the deletion of one record. Because the deletion of a record is permanent and cannot be undone, Access prompts you to make sure that you want to delete the record.

**8.** Click the **Yes** button to confirm the deletion and close the dialog box. The record is removed from the Billing table, and the subdatasheet is now empty.

**9.** Click the **minus sign** next to VisitID 1688 to close the subdatasheet.

Now that you have deleted the related record in the Billing table, you can delete the record for Visit ID 1688. You'll use the shortcut menu to do so.

**10.** Right-click the row selector for the record for Visit ID **1688**. Access selects the record and displays the shortcut menu.

Be sure to select the correct record before deleting it.

**11.** Click **Delete Record** on the shortcut menu, and then click the **Yes** button in the dialog box to confirm the deletion. The record is deleted from the Visit table.

**12.** Close the Visit table.

### Process for Deleting Records

When working with more complex databases that are managed by a database administrator, you typically need special permission to delete records from a table. Many companies also follow the practice of archiving records before deleting them so that the information is still available but not part of the active database.

You have finished updating the Chatham database by modifying and deleting records. Next, you'll retrieve specific data from the database to meet various requests for information about Chatham Community Health Services.

# Introduction to Queries

As you learned in Tutorial 1, a query is a question you ask about data stored in a database. For example, Cindi might create a query to find records in the Patient table for only those patients located in a specific city. When you create a query, you tell Access which fields you need and what criteria Access should use to select the records. Access provides powerful query capabilities that allow you to do the following:

- Display selected fields and records from a table
- Sort records
- Perform calculations
- Generate data for forms, reports, and other queries
- Update data in the tables in a database
- Find and display data from two or more tables

Most questions about data are generalized queries in which you specify the fields and records you want Access to select. These common requests for information, such as "Which patients are located in Bloomfield?" or "How many invoices have been paid?" are select queries. The answer to a select query is returned in the form of a datasheet. The result of a query is also referred to as a **recordset** because the query produces a set of records that answers your question.

### Designing Queries vs. Using a Query Wizard

More specialized, technical queries, such as finding duplicate records in a table, are best formulated using a Query Wizard. A **Query Wizard** prompts you for information by asking a series of questions and then creates the appropriate query based on your answers. In Tutorial 1, you used the Simple Query Wizard to display only some of the fields in the Visit table; Access provides other Query Wizards for more complex queries. For common, informational queries, designing your own query is more efficient than using a Query Wizard.

Ethan wants you to create a query to display the patient ID, last name, first name, city, and email address for each record in the Patient table. He needs this information to complete an email campaign advertising a special blood pressure screening being offered to patients of Chatham Community Health Services. You'll open the Query window in Design view to create the query for Ethan.

**To open the Query window in Design view:**

▶ **1.** Close the Navigation Pane so that more of the workspace is displayed.

▶ **2.** On the ribbon, click the **CREATE** tab. Access displays the options for creating different database objects.

▶ **3.** In the Queries group, click the **Query Design** button. The Show Table dialog box opens on the Query window in Design view. See Figure 3-6.

| Figure 3-6 | Show Table dialog box |
| --- | --- |

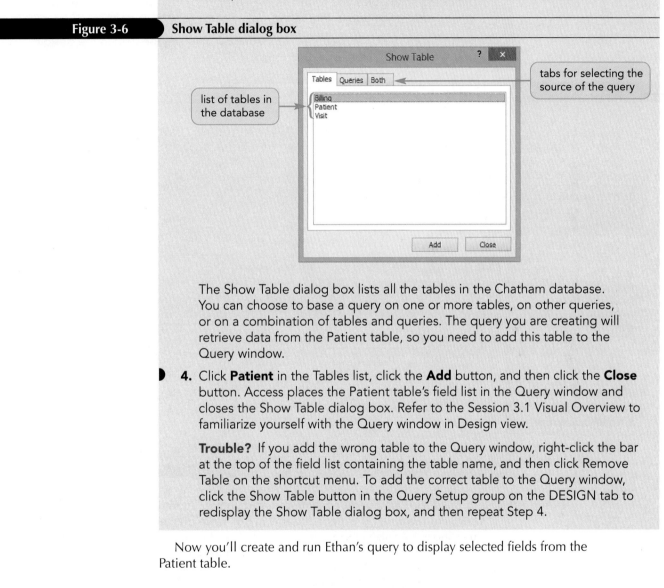

The Show Table dialog box lists all the tables in the Chatham database. You can choose to base a query on one or more tables, on other queries, or on a combination of tables and queries. The query you are creating will retrieve data from the Patient table, so you need to add this table to the Query window.

▶ **4.** Click **Patient** in the Tables list, click the **Add** button, and then click the **Close** button. Access places the Patient table's field list in the Query window and closes the Show Table dialog box. Refer to the Session 3.1 Visual Overview to familiarize yourself with the Query window in Design view.

**Trouble?** If you add the wrong table to the Query window, right-click the bar at the top of the field list containing the table name, and then click Remove Table on the shortcut menu. To add the correct table to the Query window, click the Show Table button in the Query Setup group on the DESIGN tab to redisplay the Show Table dialog box, and then repeat Step 4.

Now you'll create and run Ethan's query to display selected fields from the Patient table.

# Creating and Running a Query

The default table datasheet displays all the fields in the table in the same order as they appear in the table. In contrast, a query datasheet can display selected fields from a table, and the order of the fields can be different from that of the table, enabling those viewing the query results to see only the information they need and in the order they want.

Ethan wants the PatientID, LastName, FirstName, City, and Email fields from the Patient table to appear in the query results. You'll add each of these fields to the design grid. First you'll resize the Patient table field list to display all of the fields.

## To select the fields for the query, and then run the query:

1. Position the pointer on the bottom border of the Patient field list until the pointer changes to a ⫟ shape, and then click and drag the pointer down until the vertical scroll bar in the field list disappears and all fields in the Patient table are displayed in the list.

   Note that it's not necessary to resize the field list in order to create the query, but doing so enables you to see all the fields in the list, making it easier to select fields to include in the query.

2. In the Patient field list, double-click **PatientID** to place the field in the design grid's first column Field box. See Figure 3-7.

| Figure 3-7 | Field added to the design grid |
| --- | --- |

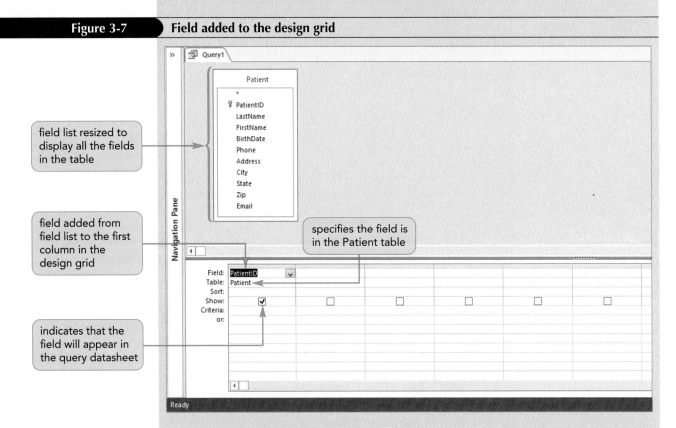

field list resized to display all the fields in the table

field added from field list to the first column in the design grid

specifies the field is in the Patient table

indicates that the field will appear in the query datasheet

In the design grid's first column, the field name PatientID appears in the Field box, the table name Patient appears in the Table box, and the checkmark in the Show check box indicates that the field will be displayed in the datasheet when you run the query. Sometimes you might not want to display a field and its values in the query results. For example, if you are creating a query to list all patients located in Windsor, and you assign the name "WindsorPatients" to the query, you do not need to include the City field value for each record in the query results—the query design only lists patients with the City field value of "Windsor." Even if you choose not to display a field in the query results, you can still use the field as part of the query to select specific records or to specify a particular sequence for the records in the datasheet.

You can also add a field to the design grid using the arrow on the Field box; this arrow appears when you click the right side of an empty Field box.

3. In the design grid, click the right side of the second column's Field box to display a menu listing all the fields in the Patient table, and then click **LastName**. Access adds this field to the second column in the design grid.

4. Use the method you prefer to add the **FirstName**, **City**, and **Email** fields to the design grid in that order.

   **Trouble?** If you accidentally add the wrong field to the design grid, you can remove the field from the grid. Select the field's column by clicking the pointer ↓ on the field selector, which is the thin bar above the Field box, for the field you want to delete, and then press the Delete key (or in the Query Setup group on the DESIGN tab, click the Delete Columns button).

   Having selected the five fields for Ethan's query, you can now run the query.

5. In the Results group on the DESIGN tab, click the **Run** button. Access runs the query and displays the results in Datasheet view. See Figure 3-8.

**Figure 3-8**     **Datasheet displayed after running the query**

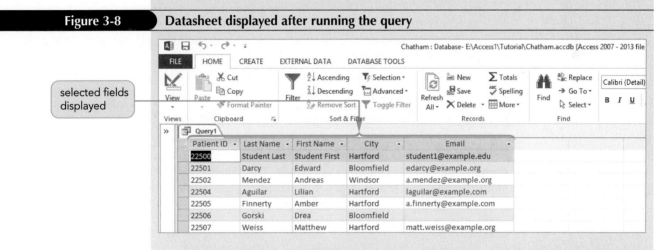

The five fields you added to the design grid appear in the datasheet in the same order as they appear in the design grid. The records are displayed in primary key sequence by PatientID. Access selected all 51 records from the Patient table for display in the query datasheet. Ethan asks you to save the query as "PatientEmail" so that he can easily retrieve the same data again.

6. On the Quick Access Toolbar, click the **Save** button 🖫. The Save As dialog box opens.

7. In the Query Name box, type **PatientEmail** and then press the **Enter** key. Access saves the query with the specified name in the Chatham database and displays the name on the tab for the query.

PROSKILLS

*Decision Making: Comparing Methods for Adding All Fields to the Design Grid*

If the query you are creating includes every field from the specified table, you can use one of the following three methods to transfer all the fields from the field list to the design grid:

- Double-click (or click and drag) each field individually from the field list to the design grid. Use this method if you want the fields in your query to appear in an order that is different from the order in the field list.
- Double-click the asterisk at the top of the field list. Access places the table name followed by a period and an asterisk (as in "Patient.*") in the Field box of the first column in the design grid, which signifies that the order of the fields is the same in the query as it is in the field list. Use this method if you don't need to sort the query or specify conditions based on the fields in the table you added in this way (for example, in a query based on more than one table). The advantage of using this method is that you do not need to change the query if you add or delete fields from the underlying table structure. Such changes are reflected automatically in the query.
- Double-click the field list title bar to highlight all the fields, and then click and drag one of the highlighted fields to the first column in the design grid. Access places each field in a separate column and arranges the fields in the order in which they appear in the field list. Use this method when you need to sort your query or include record selection criteria.

By choosing the most appropriate method to add all the table fields to the query design grid, you can work more efficiently and ensure that the query produces the results you want.

When viewing the query results, Ethan noticed that the record for one of the patients contains information that is not up to date. This patient, Nancy Fraser, had informed the clinic that she was recently married and changed her last name; she also provided a new email address. So Ethan asks you to update the record with the new last name and email address for this patient.

# Updating Data Using a Query

A query datasheet is temporary and its contents are based on the criteria in the query design grid; however, you can still update the data in a table using a query datasheet. In this case, Ethan has changes he wants you to make to a record in the Patient table. Instead of making the changes in the table datasheet, you can make them in the PatientEmail query datasheet because the query is based on the Patient table. The underlying Patient table will be updated with the changes you make.

### To update data using the PatientEmail query datasheet:

1. Locate the record with PatientID 22523, Nancy Fraser (record 21 in the query datasheet).

2. In the Last Name column for this record, double-click **Fraser** to select the name, and then type **Bennett**.

3. Press the **Tab** key three times to move to the Email column, type **n.bennett@example.com** and then press the **Tab** key.

4. Close the PatientEmail query, and then open the Navigation Pane. Note that the PatientEmail query is listed in the Queries section of the Navigation Pane.

Now you'll check the Patient table to verify that the changes you made in the query datasheet are reflected in the Patient table.

▶ **5.** Open the **Patient** table in Datasheet view, and then close the Navigation Pane.

▶ **6.** Locate the record for PatientID 22523 (record 21). Notice that the changes you made in the query datasheet to the Last Name and Email field values were made to the record in the Patient table.

▶ **7.** Close the Patient table.

### Query Datasheet vs. Table Datasheet

Although a query datasheet looks just like a table datasheet and appears in Datasheet view, the contents of a query datasheet are temporary and are based on the criteria you establish in the design grid. Whenever you run a query, the results displayed reflect the current data in the underlying table. In contrast, a table datasheet shows the permanent data in a table. However, you can update data while viewing a query datasheet, just as you can when working in a table datasheet or form.

Kelly also wants to view specific information in the Chatham database. She would like to review the visit data for patients while also viewing certain contact information for them. So, she needs to see data from both the Patient table and the Visit table at the same time.

# Creating a Multitable Query

A multitable query is a query based on more than one table. If you want to create a query that retrieves data from multiple tables, the tables must have a common field. In Tutorial 2, you established a relationship between the Patient (primary) and Visit (related) tables based on the common PatientID field that exists in both tables, so you can now create a query to display data from both tables at the same time. Specifically, Kelly wants to view the values in the City, FirstName, and LastName fields from the Patient table and the VisitDate and Reason fields from the Visit table.

### To create the query using the Patient and Visit tables:

▶ **1.** On the ribbon, click the **CREATE** tab.

▶ **2.** In the Queries group, click the **Query Design** button. Access opens the Show Table dialog box. You need to add the Patient and Visit tables to the Query window.

▶ **3.** Click **Patient** in the Tables list, click the **Add** button, click **Visit**, click the **Add** button, and then click the **Close** button. The Patient and Visit field lists appear in the Query window, and the Show Table dialog box closes.

▶ **4.** Use the ⥮ pointer to resize the Patient and Visit field lists so that all the fields in each list are displayed and the vertical scroll bars disappear.

The one-to-many relationship between the two tables is shown in the Query window in the same way that Access indicates a relationship between two tables in the Relationships window. Note that the join line is thick at both ends; this signifies that you selected the option to enforce referential integrity. If you had not selected this option, the join line would be thin at both ends and neither the "1" nor the infinity symbol would appear, even though the tables have a one-to-many relationship.

You need to place the City, FirstName, and LastName fields (in that order) from the Patient field list into the design grid, and then place the VisitDate and Reason fields from the Visit field list into the design grid. This is the order in which Kelly wants to view the fields in the query results.

5. In the Patient field list, double-click **City** to place this field in the design grid's first column Field box.
6. Repeat Step 5 to add the **FirstName** and **LastName** fields from the Patient table to the second and third columns of the design grid.
7. Repeat Step 5 to add the **VisitDate** and **Reason** fields (in that order) from the Visit table to the fourth and fifth columns of the design grid. The query specifications are complete, so you can now run the query.
8. In the Results group on the DESIGN tab, click the **Run** button. Access runs the query and displays the results in Datasheet view. See Figure 3-9.

**Figure 3-9** **Datasheet for query based on the Patient and Visit tables**

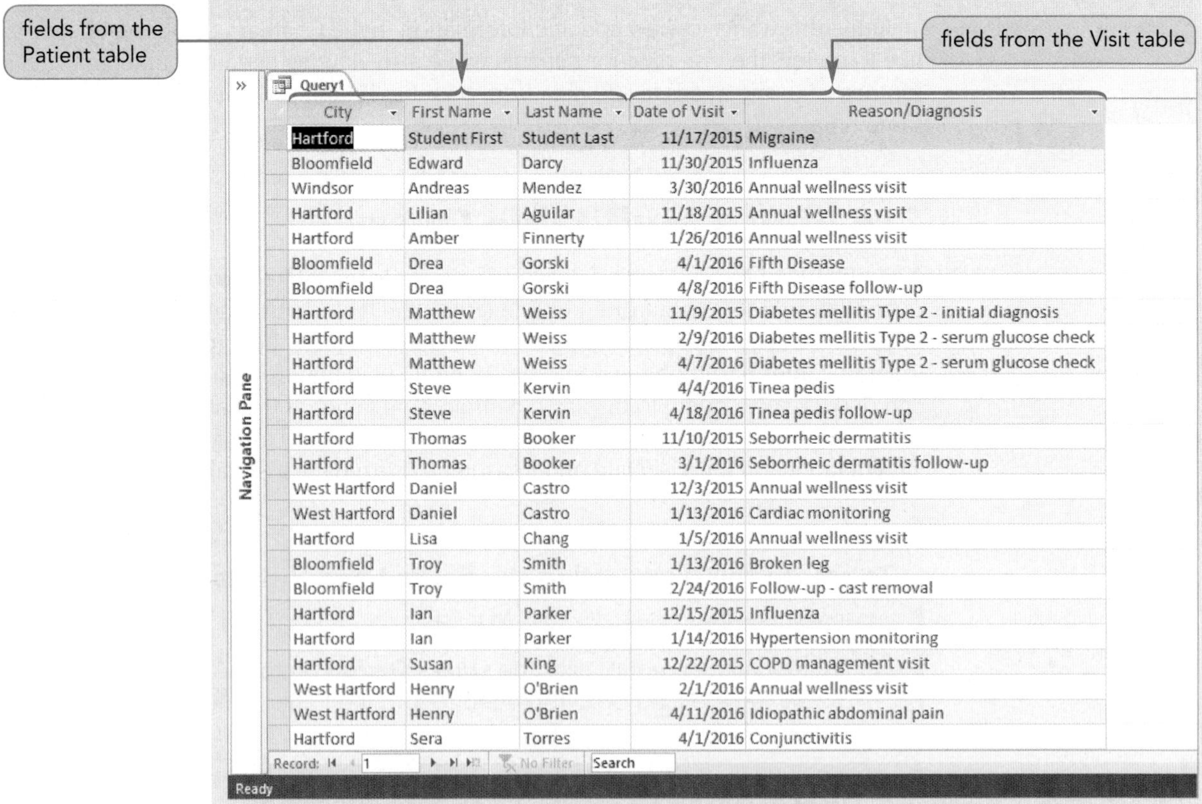


| City | First Name | Last Name | Date of Visit | Reason/Diagnosis |
|---|---|---|---|---|
| Hartford | Student First | Student Last | 11/17/2015 | Migraine |
| Bloomfield | Edward | Darcy | 11/30/2015 | Influenza |
| Windsor | Andreas | Mendez | 3/30/2016 | Annual wellness visit |
| Hartford | Lilian | Aguilar | 11/18/2015 | Annual wellness visit |
| Hartford | Amber | Finnerty | 1/26/2016 | Annual wellness visit |
| Bloomfield | Drea | Gorski | 4/1/2016 | Fifth Disease |
| Bloomfield | Drea | Gorski | 4/8/2016 | Fifth Disease follow-up |
| Hartford | Matthew | Weiss | 11/9/2015 | Diabetes mellitis Type 2 - initial diagnosis |
| Hartford | Matthew | Weiss | 2/9/2016 | Diabetes mellitis Type 2 - serum glucose check |
| Hartford | Matthew | Weiss | 4/7/2016 | Diabetes mellitis Type 2 - serum glucose check |
| Hartford | Steve | Kervin | 4/4/2016 | Tinea pedis |
| Hartford | Steve | Kervin | 4/18/2016 | Tinea pedis follow-up |
| Hartford | Thomas | Booker | 11/10/2015 | Seborrheic dermatitis |
| Hartford | Thomas | Booker | 3/1/2016 | Seborrheic dermatitis follow-up |
| West Hartford | Daniel | Castro | 12/3/2015 | Annual wellness visit |
| West Hartford | Daniel | Castro | 1/13/2016 | Cardiac monitoring |
| Hartford | Lisa | Chang | 1/5/2016 | Annual wellness visit |
| Bloomfield | Troy | Smith | 1/13/2016 | Broken leg |
| Bloomfield | Troy | Smith | 2/24/2016 | Follow-up - cast removal |
| Hartford | Ian | Parker | 12/15/2015 | Influenza |
| Hartford | Ian | Parker | 1/14/2016 | Hypertension monitoring |
| Hartford | Susan | King | 12/22/2015 | COPD management visit |
| West Hartford | Henry | O'Brien | 2/1/2016 | Annual wellness visit |
| West Hartford | Henry | O'Brien | 4/11/2016 | Idiopathic abdominal pain |
| Hartford | Sera | Torres | 4/1/2016 | Conjunctivitis |

Only the five selected fields from the Patient and Visit tables appear in the datasheet. The records are displayed in order according to the values in the PatientID field because it is the primary key field in the primary table, even though this field is not included in the query datasheet.

Kelly plans on frequently tracking the data retrieved by the query, so she asks you to save it as "PatientVisits."

▶ **9.** On the Quick Access Toolbar, click the **Save** button 🔲. The Save As dialog box opens.

▶ **10.** In the Query Name box, type **PatientVisits** and then press the **Enter** key. Access saves the query and displays its name on the object tab.

Kelly decides she wants the records displayed in alphabetical order by city. Because the query displays data in order by the field values in the PatientID field, which is the primary key for the Patient table, you need to sort the records by the City field to display the data in the order Kelly wants.

# Sorting Data in a Query

**Sorting** is the process of rearranging records in a specified order or sequence. Sometimes you might need to sort data before displaying or printing it to meet a specific request. For example, Kelly might want to review visit information arranged by the VisitDate field because she needs to know which months are the busiest for Chatham Community Health Services in terms of patient visits. Cindi might want to view billing information arranged by the InvoiceAmt field because she monitors the finances of the clinic.

When you sort data in a query, you do not change the sequence of the records in the underlying tables. Only the records in the query datasheet are rearranged according to your specifications.

To sort records, you must select the **sort field**, which is the field used to determine the order of records in the datasheet. In this case, Kelly wants the data sorted alphabetically by city, so you need to specify City as the sort field. Sort fields can be Short Text, Number, Date/Time, Currency, AutoNumber, or Yes/No fields, but not Long Text, Hyperlink, or Attachment fields. You sort records in either ascending (increasing) or descending (decreasing) order. Figure 3-10 shows the results of each type of sort for these data types.

| Figure 3-10 | Sorting results for different data types |

| Data Type | Ascending Sort Results | Descending Sort Results |
| --- | --- | --- |
| Short Text | A to Z (alphabetical) | Z to A (reverse alphabetical) |
| Number | lowest to highest numeric value | highest to lowest numeric value |
| Date/Time | oldest to most recent date | most recent to oldest date |
| Currency | lowest to highest numeric value | highest to lowest numeric value |
| AutoNumber | lowest to highest numeric value | highest to lowest numeric value |
| Yes/No | yes (checkmark in check box) then no values | no then yes values |

© 2014 Cengage Learning

Access provides several methods for sorting data in a table or query datasheet and in a form. One of the easiest ways is to use the AutoFilter feature for a field.

## Using an AutoFilter to Sort Data

As you've probably noticed when working in Datasheet view for a table or query, each column heading has an arrow to the right of the field name. This arrow gives you access to the **AutoFilter** feature, which enables you to quickly sort and display field values in various ways. When you click this arrow, a menu opens with options for sorting and displaying field values. The first two options on the menu enable you to sort the values in the current field in ascending or descending order. Unless you save the datasheet or form after you've sorted the records, the rearrangement of records is temporary.

Next, you'll use an AutoFilter to sort the PatientVisits query results by the City field.

### To sort the records using an AutoFilter:

1. Click the **arrow** on the City column heading to display the AutoFilter menu. See Figure 3-11.

| Figure 3-11 | Using AutoFilter to sort records in the datasheet |
| --- | --- |

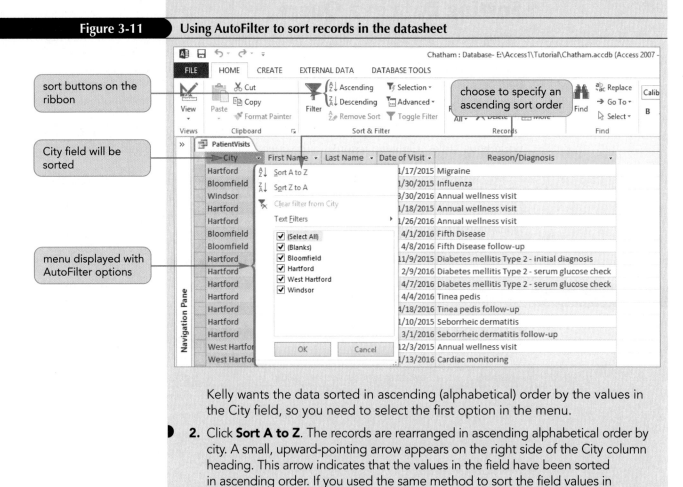

Kelly wants the data sorted in ascending (alphabetical) order by the values in the City field, so you need to select the first option in the menu.

2. Click **Sort A to Z**. The records are rearranged in ascending alphabetical order by city. A small, upward-pointing arrow appears on the right side of the City column heading. This arrow indicates that the values in the field have been sorted in ascending order. If you used the same method to sort the field values in descending order, a small downward-pointing arrow would appear there instead.

After viewing the query results, Kelly decides that she would also like to see the records arranged by the values in the VisitDate field, so that the data is presented in chronological order. She still wants the records to be arranged by the City field values as well. To produce the results Kelly wants, you need to sort using two fields.

# Sorting on Multiple Fields in Design View

Sort fields can be unique or nonunique. A sort field is **unique** if the value in the sort field for each record is different. The PatientID field in the Patient table is an example of a unique sort field because each patient record has a different value in this primary key field. A sort field is **nonunique** if more than one record can have the same value for the sort field. For example, the City field in the Patient table is a nonunique sort field because more than one record can have the same City value.

When the sort field is nonunique, records with the same sort field value are grouped together, but they are not sorted in a specific order within the group. To arrange these grouped records in a specific order, you can specify a **secondary sort field**, which is a second field that determines the order of records that are already sorted by the **primary sort field** (the first sort field specified).

Access lets you select up to 10 different sort fields. When you use the buttons on the ribbon to sort by more than one field, the sort fields must be in adjacent columns in the datasheet. (Note that you cannot use an AutoFilter to sort on more than one field. This method works for a single field only.) You can specify only one type of sort—either ascending or descending—for the selected columns in the datasheet. You highlight the adjacent columns, and Access sorts first by the first column and then by each remaining highlighted column in order from left to right.

Kelly wants the records sorted first by the City field values, as they currently are, and then by the VisitDate values. The two fields are in the correct left-to-right order in the query datasheet, but they are not adjacent, so you cannot use the Ascending and Descending buttons on the ribbon to sort them. You could move the City field to the left of the VisitDate field in the query datasheet, but both columns would have to be sorted with the same sort order. This is not what Kelly wants—she wants the City field values sorted in ascending order so that they are in the correct alphabetical order, for ease of reference; and she wants the VisitDate field values to be sorted in descending order, so that she can focus on the most recent patient visits first. To sort the City and VisitDate fields with different sort orders, you must specify the sort fields in Design view.

In the Query window in Design view, Access first uses the sort field that is leftmost in the design grid. Therefore, you must arrange the fields you want to sort from left to right in the design grid, with the primary sort field being the leftmost. In Design view, multiple sort fields do not have to be adjacent to each other, as they do in Datasheet view; however, they must be in the correct left-to-right order.

**TIP**

The primary sort field is *not* the same as a table's primary key. A table has at most one primary key, which must be unique, whereas any field in a table can serve as a primary sort field.

**REFERENCE**

### Sorting a Query Datasheet

- In the query datasheet, click the arrow on the column heading for the field you want to sort.
- In the menu that opens, click Sort A to Z for an ascending sort, or click Sort Z to A for a descending sort.

*or*

- In the query datasheet, select the column or adjacent columns on which you want to sort.
- In the Sort & Filter group on the HOME tab, click the Ascending button or the Descending button.

*or*

- In Design view, position the fields serving as sort fields from left to right.
- Click the right side of the Sort box for each field you want to sort, and then click Ascending or Descending for the sort order.

To achieve the results Kelly wants, you need to modify the query in Design view to specify the sort order for the two fields.

## To select the two sort fields in Design view:

**TIP**

In Design view, the sort fields do not have to be adjacent, and fields that are not sorted can appear between the sort fields.

1. In the Views group on the HOME tab, click the **View** button to open the query in Design view. The fields are currently in the correct left-to-right order in the design grid, so you only need to specify the sort order for the two fields.

   First, you need to specify an ascending sort order for the City field. Even though the records are already sorted by the values in this field, you need to modify the query so that this sort order, and the sort order you will specify for the VisitDate field, are part of the query's design. Any time the query is run, the records will be sorted according to these specifications.

2. Click the right side of the **City Sort** box to display the arrow and the sort options, and then click **Ascending**. You've selected an ascending sort order for the City field, which will be the primary sort field. The City field is a Short Text field, and an ascending sort order will display the field values in alphabetical order.

3. Click the right side of the **VisitDate Sort** box, click **Descending**, and then click in one of the empty text boxes below the VisitDate field to deselect the setting. You've selected a descending sort order for the VisitDate field, which will be the secondary sort field because it appears to the right of the primary sort field (City) in the design grid. The VisitDate field is a Date/Time field, and a descending sort order will display the field values with the most recent dates first. See Figure 3-12.

| Figure 3-12 | Selecting two sort fields in Design view |
| --- | --- |

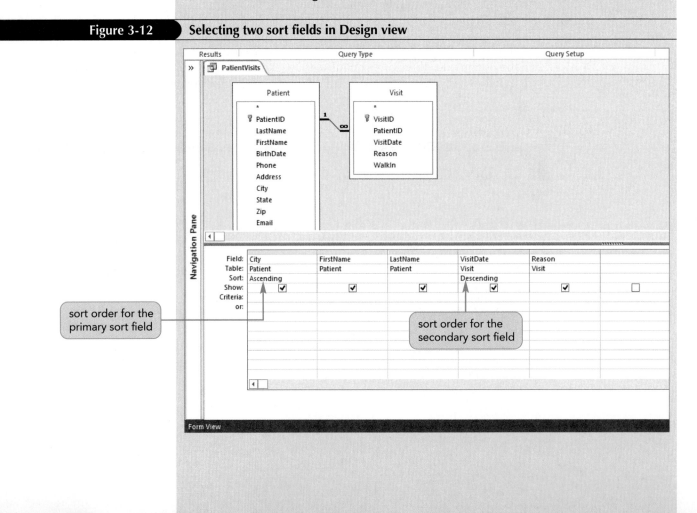

You have finished your query changes, so now you can run the query and then save the modified query with the same name.

**4.** In the Results group on the DESIGN tab, click the **Run** button. Access runs the query and displays the query datasheet. The records appear in ascending order based on the values in the City field. Within groups of records with the same City field value, the records appear in descending order by the values of the VisitDate field. See Figure 3-13.

**Figure 3-13**    **Datasheet sorted on two fields**

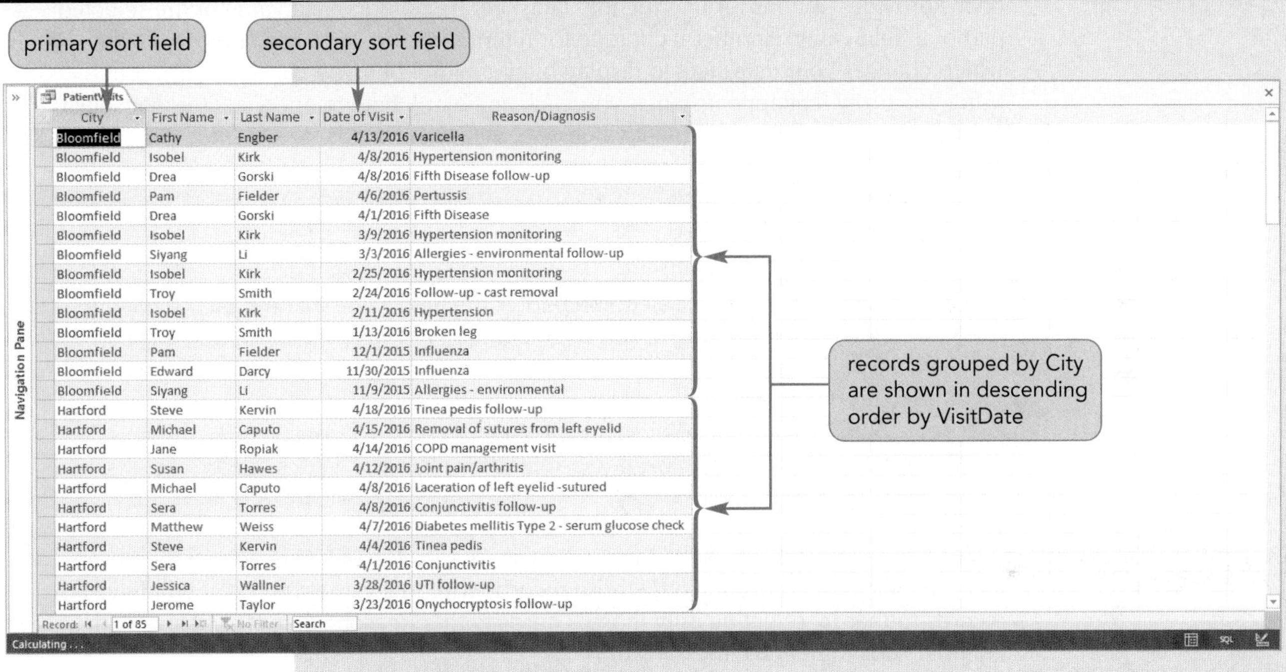

primary sort field

secondary sort field

records grouped by City are shown in descending order by VisitDate

When you save the query, all of your design changes—including the selection of the sort fields—are saved with the query. The next time Kelly runs the query, the records will appear sorted by the primary and secondary sort fields.

**5.** On the Quick Access Toolbar, click the **Save** button to save the revised PatientVisits query.

Kelly knows that Chatham Community Health Services has seen an increase in the number of patients from Windsor. She would like to focus briefly on the information for patients in that city only. Also, she is interested in knowing how many patients from Windsor have had annual wellness exams. She is concerned that, although more patients are coming to the clinic from this city, not enough of them are scheduling wellness visits. Selecting only the records with a City field value of "Windsor" and a Reason field value beginning with "Annual" is a temporary change that Kelly wants in the datasheet, so you do not need to switch to Design view and change the query. Instead, you can apply a filter.

# Filtering Data

A **filter** is a set of restrictions you place on the records in an open datasheet or form to *temporarily* isolate a subset of the records. A filter lets you view different subsets of displayed records so that you can focus on only the data you need. Unless you save a query or form with a filter applied, an applied filter is not available the next time you run the query or open the form.

The simplest technique for filtering records is Filter By Selection. **Filter By Selection** lets you select all or part of a field value in a datasheet or form, and then display only those records that contain the selected value in the field. You can also use the AutoFilter feature to filter records. When you click the arrow on a column heading, the menu that opens provides options for filtering the datasheet based on a field value or the selected part of a field value. Another technique for filtering records is to use **Filter By Form**, which changes your datasheet to display blank fields. Then you can select a value using the arrow that appears when you click any blank field to apply a filter that selects only those records containing that value.

### Using Filter By Selection

- In the datasheet or form, select the part of the field value that will be the basis for the filter; or, if the filter will be based on the entire field value, click anywhere within the field value.
- Make sure the HOME tab is displayed.
- In the Sort & Filter group, click the Selection button.
- Click the type of filter you want to apply.

For Kelly's request, you need to select a City field value of Windsor, and then use Filter By Selection to display only those records with this value. Then you will filter the records further by selecting only those records with a Reason value that begins with "Annual" (for Annual wellness visit).

### To display the records using Filter By Selection:

1. In the query datasheet, locate the first occurrence of a City field containing the value **Windsor**, and then click anywhere within that field value.

2. In the Sort & Filter group on the HOME tab, click the **Selection** button. A menu opens with options for the type of filter to apply. See Figure 3-14.

**Figure 3-14** | **Using Filter By Selection**

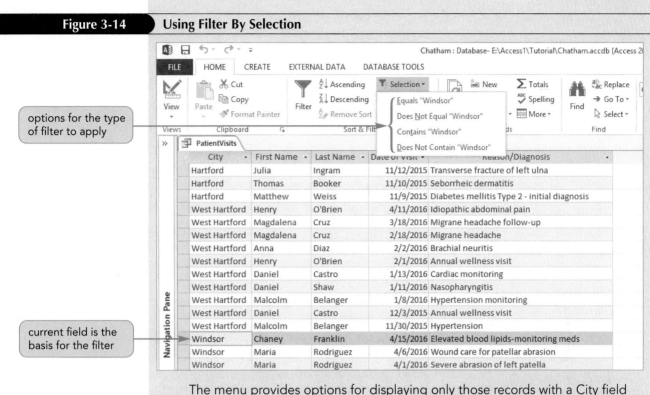

options for the type of filter to apply

current field is the basis for the filter

The menu provides options for displaying only those records with a City field value that equals the selected value (in this case, Windsor); does not equal the value; contains the value somewhere within the field; or does not contain the value somewhere within the field. You want to display all the records whose City field value equals Windsor.

▶ **3.** In the Selection menu, click **Equals "Windsor"**. Access displays the filtered results. Only the 24 records that have a City field value of Windsor appear in the datasheet. See Figure 3-15.

**Figure 3-15** | **Datasheet after applying the filter**

| City | First Name | Last Name | Date of Visit | Reason/Diagnosis |
|---|---|---|---|---|
| Windsor | Chaney | Franklin | 4/15/2016 | Elevated blood lipids-monitoring meds |
| Windsor | Maria | Rodriguez | 4/6/2016 | Wound care for patellar abrasion |
| Windsor | Maria | Rodriguez | 4/1/2016 | Severe abrasion of left patella |
| Windsor | Andreas | Mendez | 3/30/2016 | Annual wellness visit |
| Windsor | Chaney | Franklin | 3/23/2016 | Elevated blood lipids-monitoring meds |
| Windsor | Patrice | Lewis | 3/21/2016 | Eczema erythematosum follow-up |
| Windsor | Alex | Delgado | 3/18/2016 | Hypertension monitoring |
| Windsor | Christina | Rowe | 3/11/2016 | Annual wellness visit |
| Windsor | Patrice | Lewis | 3/7/2016 | Eczema erythematosum |
| Windsor | Chaney | Franklin | 2/24/2016 | Elevated blood lipids-monitoring meds |
| Windsor | Davis | Hallick | 2/22/2016 | Follow-up - gastric reflux |
| Windsor | Robert | Goldberg | 2/9/2016 | Sinusitis |
| Windsor | Davis | Hallick | 2/8/2016 | Gastric reflux |
| Windsor | Alex | Delgado | 2/8/2016 | Hypertension monitoring |
| Windsor | Christina | Rowe | 1/28/2016 | Nasopharyngitis |
| Windsor | Max | Sutherland | 1/26/2016 | Acute viral rhinopharyngitis |
| Windsor | Nancy | Bennett | 1/25/2016 | Nasopharyngitis |
| Windsor | Alex | Delgado | 1/25/2016 | Hypertension |
| Windsor | Patrice | Lewis | 1/22/2016 | Acute sinusitis follow-up |
| Windsor | Ashley | Garrett | 1/15/2016 | Annual wellness visit |
| Windsor | Patrice | Lewis | 1/13/2016 | Acute sinusitis |
| Windsor | Davis | Hallick | 12/7/2015 | Annual wellness visit |
| Windsor | Patrice | Lewis | 11/25/2015 | Influenza |
| Windsor | Amrita | Mehta | 11/24/2015 | Influenza |

Record: 1 of 24    Filtered    Search

click to display more options for filtering the field

indicate that a filter has been applied to the datasheet

datasheet displays only records with a City value of Windsor

The button labeled "Filtered" to the right of the navigation buttons and the notation "FILTERED" on the status bar both indicate that a filter has been applied to the datasheet. Also, notice that the Toggle Filter button in the Sort & Filter group on the HOME tab is active; you can click this button or the Filtered button next to the navigation buttons to toggle between the filtered and unfiltered displays of the query datasheet. The City column heading also has a filter icon on it; you can click this icon to display additional options for filtering the field.

Next, Kelly wants to view only those records with a Reason field value beginning with the word "Annual" so she can view the records for annual wellness visits. You need to apply an additional filter to the datasheet.

4. In any Reason field value beginning with the word "Annual," select only the word **Annual**.

5. In the Sort & Filter group, click the **Selection** button. The same four filter types are available for this selection as when you filtered the City field.

6. On the Selection menu, click **Begins With "Annual"**. The second filter is applied to the query datasheet, which now shows only the four records for customers located in Windsor who have had annual wellness visits at the clinic.

Now you can redisplay all the query records by clicking the Toggle Filter button, which you use to switch between the filtered and unfiltered displays.

**TIP**

The ScreenTip for this button is Remove Filter.

7. In the Sort & Filter group, click the **Toggle Filter** button. Access removes the filter and redisplays all 85 records in the query datasheet.

8. Close the PatientVisits query. Access asks if you want to save your changes to the design of the query—in this case, the filtered display, which is still available through the Toggle Filter button. Kelly does not want the query saved with the filter because she doesn't need to view the filtered information on a regular basis.

9. Click the **No** button to close the query without saving the changes.

10. If you are not continuing to Session 3.2, click the **FILE** tab, and then click **Close** in the navigation bar to close the Chatham database.

REVIEW

## Session 3.1 Quick Check

1. In Datasheet view, what is the difference between navigation mode and editing mode?
2. What command can you use in Datasheet view to remove the display of one or more fields from the datasheet?
3. What is a select query?
4. Describe the field list and the design grid in the Query window in Design view.
5. How are a table datasheet and a query datasheet similar? How are they different?
6. For a Date/Time field, how do the records appear when sorted in ascending order?
7. When you define multiple sort fields in Design view, describe how the sort fields must be positioned in the design grid.
8. A(n) _____ is a set of restrictions you place on the records in an open datasheet or form to isolate a subset of records temporarily.

# Session 3.2 Visual Overview:

When creating queries in Design view, you can enter criteria so that Access will display only selected records in the query results.

| Field: | PatientID | LastName | FirstName | BirthDate | City |
|---|---|---|---|---|---|
| Table: | Patient | Patient | Patient | Patient | Patient |
| Sort: | | | | | |
| Show: | ✔ | ✔ | ✔ | ✔ | ✔ |
| Criteria: | | | | | "Bloomfield" |
| or: | | | | | |

To define a condition for a field, you place the condition in the field's Criteria box in the design grid.

To tell Access which records you want to select, you must specify a condition as part of the query. A **condition** is a criterion, or rule, that determines which records are selected.

| Field: | InvoiceNum | InvoiceDate | InvoiceAmt | |
|---|---|---|---|---|
| Table: | Billing | Billing | Billing | |
| Sort: | | | | |
| Show: | ✔ | ✔ | ✔ | ☐ |
| Criteria: | | | >250 | |
| or: | | | | |

A condition usually consists of an operator, often a comparison operator, and a value. A **comparison operator** asks Access to compare the value in a field to the condition value and to select all the records for which the condition is true.

| Field: | VisitID | PatientID | VisitDate | Reason |
|---|---|---|---|---|
| Table: | Visit | Visit | Visit | Visit |
| Sort: | | | | |
| Show: | ✔ | ✔ | ✔ | ✔ |
| Criteria: | | | Between #12/1/2015# And #12/31/2015# | |
| or: | | | | |

Most comparison operators (such as Between...And...) ask Access to select records that match a range of values for the condition—in this case, all records with dates that fall within the range shown.

# Selection Criteria in Queries

The results of a query containing selection criteria include only the records that meet the specified criteria.

### BloomfieldPatients

| Patient ID | Last Name | First Name | Date of Birth | City |
|---|---|---|---|---|
| 22501 | Darcy | Edward | 7/15/1986 | Bloomfield |
| 22506 | Gorski | Drea | 2/19/2005 | Bloomfield |
| 22513 | Smith | Troy | 1/31/1956 | Bloomfield |
| 22521 | Engber | Cathy | 4/7/2000 | Bloomfield |
| 22522 | Li | Siyang | 7/25/1986 | Bloomfield |
| 22549 | Fielder | Pam | 12/6/1978 | Bloomfield |
| 22557 | Kirk | Isobel | 11/18/1965 | Bloomfield |
| * | | | | |

The results of this query show only patients from Bloomfield because the condition "Bloomfield" in the City field's Criteria box specifies that Access should select records only with City field values of Bloomfield. This type of condition is called an **exact match** because the value in the specified field must match the condition exactly in order for the record to be included in the query results.

### LargeInvoiceAmts

| Invoice Num | Invoice Date | Invoice Amt |
|---|---|---|
| 35815 | 11/16/2015 | $300.00 |
| 35900 | 01/20/2016 | $300.00 |
| 36002 | 03/15/2016 | $450.00 |
| 36074 | 04/12/2016 | $450.00 |
| * | | $0.00 |

The results of this query show only those invoices with amounts greater than $250 because the condition >250, which uses the greater than comparison operator, specifies that Access should select records only with InvoiceAmt field values over $250.

### DecemberVisits

| Visit ID | Patient ID | Date of Visit | Reason/Diagnosis |
|---|---|---|---|
| 1550 | 22549 | 12/1/2015 | Influenza |
| 1552 | 22511 | 12/3/2015 | Annual wellness visit |
| 1555 | 22520 | 12/7/2015 | Annual wellness visit |
| 1557 | 22526 | 12/10/2015 | Annual wellness visit |
| 1560 | 22514 | 12/15/2015 | Influenza |
| 1562 | 22516 | 12/22/2015 | COPD management visit |
| * | | | |

The results of this query show only those patient visits that took place in December 2015 because the condition in the VisitDate's Criteria box specifies that Access should select records only with a visit date between 12/1/2015 and 12/31/2015.

# Defining Record Selection Criteria for Queries

Cindi wants to display patient and visit information for all patients who live in Bloomfield. She is considering having the clinic hold a health fair in Bloomfield, with a special emphasis on hypertension, so she is interested in knowing more about the patients from this city. For this request, you could create a query to select the correct fields and all records in the Patient and Visit tables, select a City field value of Bloomfield in the query datasheet, and then click the Selection button and choose the appropriate filter option to display the information for only those patients in Bloomfield. However, a faster way of displaying the data Cindi needs is to create a query that displays the selected fields and only those records in the Patient and Visit tables that satisfy a condition.

Just as you can display selected fields from a database in a query datasheet, you can display selected records. To tell Access which records you want to select, you must specify a condition as part of the query, as illustrated in the Session 3.2 Visual Overview. A condition usually includes one of the comparison operators shown in Figure 3-16.

**Figure 3-16**    **Access comparison operators**

| Operator | Meaning | Example |
|---|---|---|
| = | equal to (optional; default operator) | ="Hall" |
| <> | not equal to | <>"Hall" |
| < | less than | <#1/1/99# |
| <= | less than or equal to | <=100 |
| > | greater than | >"C400" |
| >= | greater than or equal to | >=18.75 |
| Between ... And ... | between two values (inclusive) | Between 50 And 325 |
| In () | in a list of values | In ("Hall", "Seeger") |
| Like | matches a pattern that includes wildcards | Like "706*" |

© 2014 Cengage Learning

## Specifying an Exact Match

For Cindi's request, you need to create a query that will display only those records in the Patient table with the value Bloomfield in the City field. This type of condition is an exact match because the value in the specified field must match the condition exactly in order for the record to be included in the query results. You'll create the query in Design view.

### To create the query in Design view:

1. If you took a break after the previous session, make sure that the Chatham database is open and the Navigation Pane is closed.
2. On the ribbon, click the **CREATE** tab.
3. In the Queries group, click the **Query Design** button. The Show Table dialog box opens. You need to add the Patient and Visit tables to the Query window.
4. Click **Patient** in the Tables list, click the **Add** button, click **Visit**, click the **Add** button, and then click the **Close** button.

▶ **5.** Use the ⬍ pointer to resize both field lists so that all the fields are displayed and the vertical scroll bars disappear.

▶ **6.** Add the following fields from the Patient table to the design grid in the order shown: **LastName**, **FirstName**, **Phone**, **Address**, **City**, and **Email**.

Cindi also wants information from the Visit table included in the query results.

▶ **7.** Add the following fields from the Visit table to the design grid in the order shown: **VisitID**, **VisitDate**, and **Reason**. See Figure 3-17.

| Figure 3-17 | Design grid after adding fields from both tables |
| --- | --- |

| Field: | LastName | FirstName | Phone | Address | City | Email | VisitID | VisitDate | Reason | | | |
| --- | --- | --- | --- | --- | --- | --- | --- | --- | --- | --- | --- | --- |
| Table: | Patient | Patient | Patient | Patient | Patient | Patient | Visit | Visit | Visit | | | |
| Sort: | | | | | | | | | | | | |
| Show: | ✓ | ✓ | ✓ | ✓ | ✓ | ✓ | ✓ | ✓ | ✓ | ☐ | | ☐ |
| Criteria: | | | | | | | | | | | | |
| or: | | | | | | | | | | | | |

enter condition here

The field lists for the Patient and Visit tables appear in the top portion of the window, and the join line indicating a one-to-many relationship connects the two tables. The fields you selected appear in the design grid.

To display the information Cindi wants, you need to enter the condition for the City field in its Criteria box (see Figure 3-17). Cindi wants to display only those records with a City field value of Bloomfield.

### To enter the exact match condition, and then save and run the query:

▶ **1.** Click the **City Criteria** box, type **Bloomfield**, and then press the **Enter** key. The condition changes to "Bloomfield".

Access automatically enclosed the condition you typed in quotation marks. You must enclose text values in quotation marks when using them as selection criteria. If you omit the quotation marks, however, Access will include them automatically in most cases. Some words—including "in" and "select"—are special keywords in Access that are reserved for functions and commands. If you want to enter one of these keywords as the condition, you must type the quotation marks around the text or Access will display an error message and will not allow the condition to be entered.

▶ **2.** On the Quick Access Toolbar, click the **Save** button 🖫 to open the Save As dialog box.

▶ **3.** In the Query Name box, type **BloomfieldPatients** and then press the **Enter** key. Access saves the query with the specified name and displays the name on the object tab.

▶ **4.** In the Results group on the DESIGN tab, click the **Run** button. Access runs the query and displays the selected field values for only those records with a City field value of Bloomfield. A total of 14 records is selected and displayed in the datasheet. See Figure 3-18.

Figure 3-18 **Datasheet displaying selected fields and records**

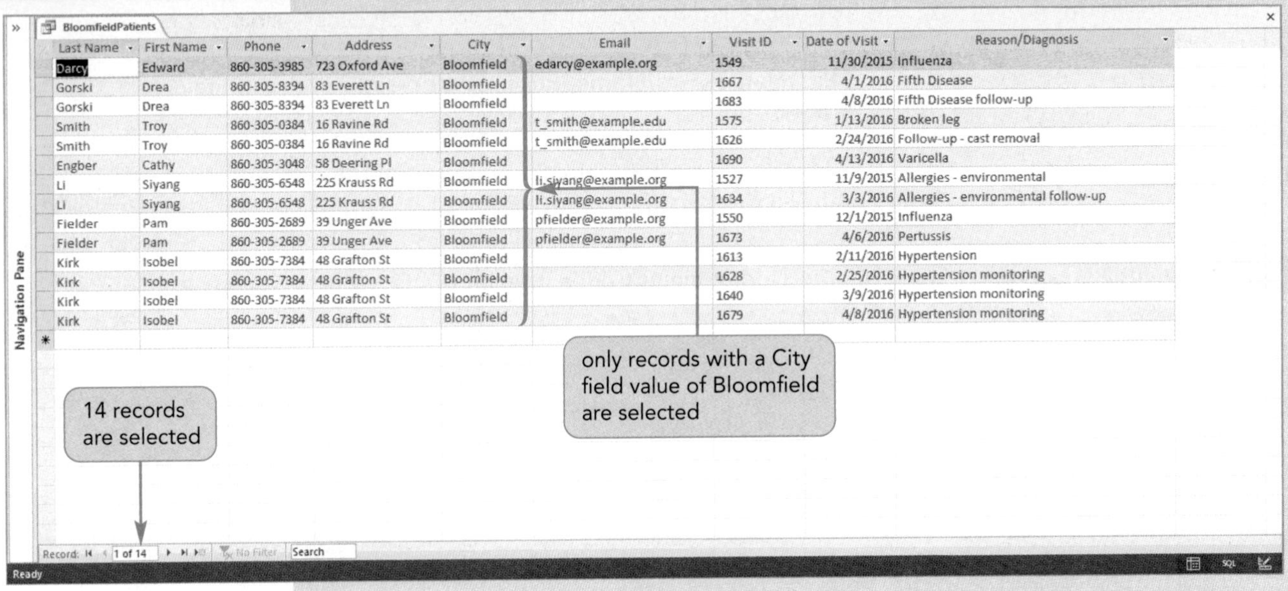

only records with a City field value of Bloomfield are selected

14 records are selected

Cindi realizes that it's not necessary to include the City field values in the query results. The name of the query, BloomfieldPatients, indicates that the query design includes all patients who live in Bloomfield, so the City field values are unnecessary and repetitive. Also, she decides that she would prefer the query datasheet to show the fields from the Visit table first, followed by the Patient table fields. You need to modify the query to produce the results Cindi wants.

## Modifying a Query

After you create a query and view the results, you might need to make changes to the query if the results are not what you expected or require. First, Cindi asks you to modify the BloomfieldPatients query so that it does not display the City field values in the query results.

### To remove the display of the City field values:

▶ **1.** In the Views group on the HOME tab, click the **View** button. The BloomfieldPatients query opens in Design view.

You need to keep the City field as part of the query design because it contains the defined condition for the query. You only need to remove the display of the field's values from the query results.

▶ **2.** Click the **City Show** check box to remove the checkmark. The query will still find only those records with the value Bloomfield in the City field, but the query results will not display these field values.

Next, you need to change the order of the fields in the query so that the visit information is listed first.

## To move the Visit table fields to precede the Patient table fields:

**1.** Position the pointer on the VisitID field selector until the pointer changes to a ↓ shape, and then click to select the field. See Figure 3-19.

Figure 3-19     Selected VisitID field

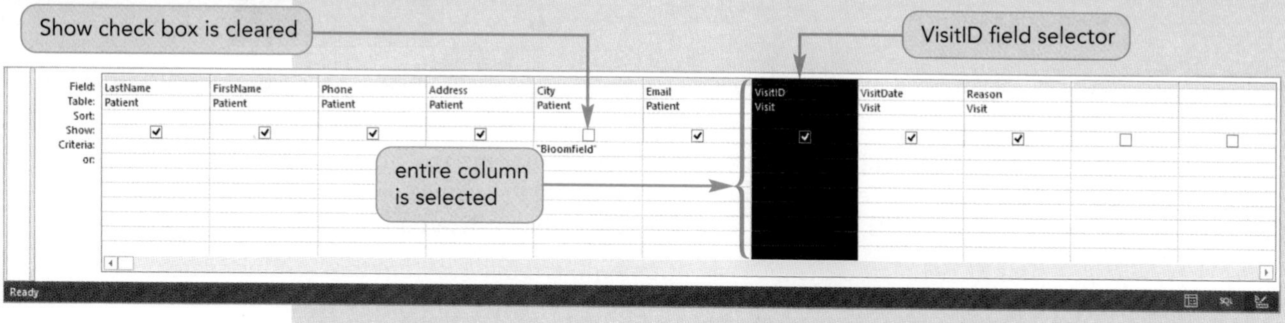

**2.** Position the pointer on the VisitID field selector, and then click and hold down the mouse button; notice that the pointer changes to and a black vertical line appears to the left of the selected field. This line represents the selected field when you drag the mouse to move it.

**3.** Drag to the left until the vertical line representing the selected field is positioned to the left of the LastName field. See Figure 3-20.

Figure 3-20     Dragging the field in the design grid

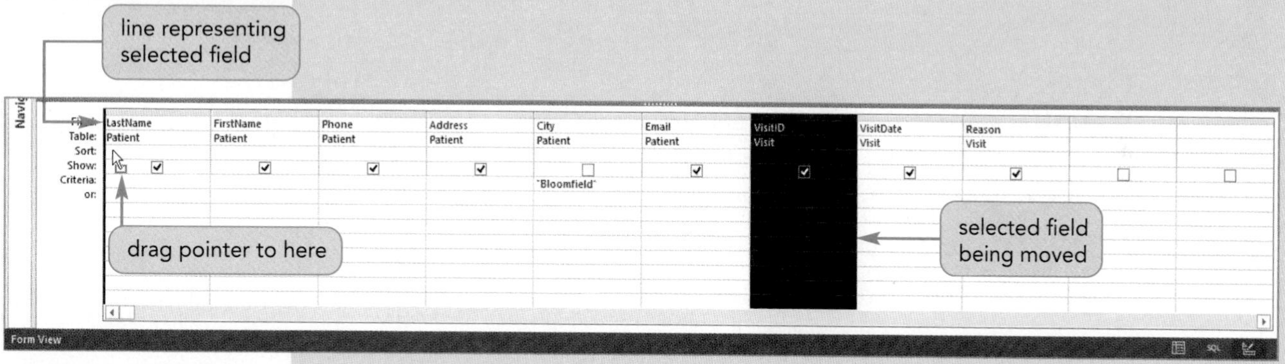

**TIP**

Instead of moving a field by dragging, you can also delete the field and then add it back to the design grid in the location you want.

**4.** Release the mouse button. The VisitID field moves to the left of the LastName field.

You can also select and move multiple fields at once. You need to select and move the VisitDate and Reason fields so that they follow the VisitID field in the query design. To select multiple fields, you click and drag the mouse over the field selectors for the fields you want.

**5.** Click and hold the pointer ↓ on the VisitDate field selector, drag the pointer to the right to select the Reason field, and then release the mouse button. Both fields are now selected. See Figure 3-21.

**Figure 3-21**    **Multiple fields selected to be moved**

| Field: | VisitID | LastName | FirstName | Phone | Address | City | Email | VisitDate | Reason | | |
|---|---|---|---|---|---|---|---|---|---|---|---|
| Table: | Visit | Patient | Patient | Patient | Patient | Patient | Patient | Visit | Visit | | |
| Sort: | | | | | | | | | | | |
| Show: | ✓ | ✓ | ✓ | ✓ | ✓ | ☐ | ✓ | ✓ | ✓ | ☐ | ☐ |
| Criteria: | | | | | | "Bloomfield" | | | | | |
| or: | | | | | | | | | | | |

Ready

**6.** Position the pointer ⊳ anywhere near the top of the two selected fields, and then click and drag to the left until the vertical line representing the selected fields is positioned to the left of the LastName field.

**7.** Release the mouse button. The three fields from the Visit table are now the first three fields in the query design.

You have finished making the modifications to the query Cindi requested, so you can now run the query.

**8.** In the Results group on the DESIGN tab, click the **Run** button. Access displays the results of the modified query. See Figure 3-22.

**Figure 3-22**    **Results of the modified query**

| Visit ID | Date of Visit | Reason/Diagnosis | Last Name | First Name | Phone | Address | Email |
|---|---|---|---|---|---|---|---|
| 1549 | 11/30/2015 | Influenza | Darcy | Edward | 860-305-3985 | 723 Oxford Ave | edarcy@example.org |
| 1667 | 4/1/2016 | Fifth Disease | Gorski | Drea | 860-305-8394 | 83 Everett Ln | |
| 1683 | 4/8/2016 | Fifth Disease follow-up | Gorski | Drea | 860-305-8394 | 83 Everett Ln | |
| 1575 | 1/13/2016 | Broken leg | Smith | Troy | 860-305-0384 | 16 Ravine Rd | t_smith@example.edu |
| 1626 | 2/24/2016 | Follow-up - cast removal | Smith | Troy | 860-305-0384 | 16 Ravine Rd | t_smith@example.edu |
| 1690 | 4/13/2016 | Varicella | Engber | Cathy | 860-305-3048 | 58 Deering Pl | |
| 1527 | 11/9/2015 | Allergies - environmental | Li | Siyang | 860-305-6548 | 225 Krauss Rd | li.siyang@example.org |
| 1634 | 3/3/2016 | Allergies - environmental follow-up | Li | Siyang | 860-305-6548 | 225 Krauss Rd | li.siyang@example.org |
| 1550 | 12/1/2015 | Influenza | Fielder | Pam | 860-305-2689 | 39 Unger Ave | pfielder@example.org |
| 1673 | 4/6/2016 | Pertussis | Fielder | Pam | 860-305-2689 | 39 Unger Ave | pfielder@example.org |
| 1613 | 2/11/2016 | Hypertension | Kirk | Isobel | 860-305-7384 | 48 Grafton St | |
| 1628 | 2/25/2016 | Hypertension monitoring | Kirk | Isobel | 860-305-7384 | 48 Grafton St | |
| 1640 | 3/9/2016 | Hypertension monitoring | Kirk | Isobel | 860-305-7384 | 48 Grafton St | |
| 1679 | 4/8/2016 | Hypertension monitoring | Kirk | Isobel | 860-305-7384 | 48 Grafton St | |

fields from the Visit table are now listed first in the query datasheet

City field values are no longer displayed

Record: 1 of 14    No Filter    Search

Ready

Note that the City field values are no longer displayed in the query results.

**9.** Save and close the BloomfieldPatients query.

After viewing the query results, Cindi decides that she would like to see the same fields, but only for those records with a VisitDate field value before 1/1/2016. She is interested to know which patients of Chatham Community Health Services in all cities have not been to the clinic recently, so that her staff can follow up with these patients by sending them reminder notes or emails. To create the query that will produce the results Cindi wants, you need to use a comparison operator to match a range of values—in this case, any VisitDate value less than 1/1/2016.

# Using a Comparison Operator to Match a Range of Values

After you create and save a query, you can double-click the query name in the Navigation Pane to run the query again. You can then click the View button to change its design. You can also use an existing query as the basis for creating another query. Because the design of the query you need to create next is similar to the BloomfieldPatients query, you will copy, paste, and rename this query to create the new query. Using this approach keeps the BloomfieldPatients query intact.

## To create the new query by copying the BloomfieldPatients query:

1. Open the Navigation Pane. Note that the BloomfieldPatients query is listed in the Queries section.

   You need to use the shortcut menu to copy the BloomfieldPatients query and paste it in the Navigation Pane; then you'll give the copied query a different name.

2. In the Queries section of the Navigation Pane, right-click **BloomfieldPatients** to select it and display the shortcut menu.

3. Click **Copy** on the shortcut menu.

4. Right-click the empty area near the bottom of the Navigation Pane, and then click **Paste** on the shortcut menu. The Paste As dialog box opens with the text "Copy Of BloomfieldPatients" in the Query Name box. Because Cindi wants the new query to show data for patients who have not visited the clinic recently, you'll name the new query "EarlierVisits."

5. In the Query Name box, type **EarlierVisits** and then press the **Enter** key. The new query appears in the Queries section of the Navigation Pane.

6. Double-click the **EarlierVisits** query to open, or run, the query. The design of this query is currently the same as the original BloomfieldPatients query.

7. Close the Navigation Pane.

Next, you need to open the query in Design view and modify its design to produce the results Cindi wants—to display only those records with VisitDate field values that are earlier than, or less than, 1/1/2016.

## To modify the design of the new query:

1. In the Views group on the HOME tab, click the **View** button to display the query in Design view.

2. Click the **VisitDate Criteria** box, type **<1/1/2016** and then press the **Tab** key. See Figure 3-23.

**Figure 3-23**  **Criteria entered for the VisitDate field**

| Field: | VisitID | VisitDate | Reason | LastName | FirstName | Phone | Address | Email | City | | | |
|---|---|---|---|---|---|---|---|---|---|---|---|---|
| Table: | Visit | Visit | Visit | Patient | Patient | Patient | Patient | Patient | Patient | | | |
| Sort: | | | | | | | | | | | | |
| Show: | ✔ | ✔ | ✔ | ✔ | ✔ | ✔ | ✔ | ✔ | ☐ | ☐ | ☐ | ☐ |
| Criteria: | | <#1/1/2016# | | | | | | | "Bloomfield" | | | |
| or: | | | | | | | | | | | | |

new condition entered

original condition needs to be deleted

Form View

Note that Access automatically encloses the date criteria with number signs. The condition specifies that a record will be selected only if its VisitDate field value is less than (earlier than) 1/1/2016. Before you run the query, you need to delete the condition for the City field. Recall that the City field is part of the query, but its values are not displayed in the query results. When you modified the query to remove the City field values from the query results, Access moved the field to the end of the design grid. You need to delete the City field's condition, specify that the City field values should be included in the query results, and then move the field back to its original position following the Address field.

▶ **3.** Press the **Tab** key six times until the condition for the City field is highlighted, and then press the **Delete** key. The condition for the City field is removed.

▶ **4.** Click the **Show** check box for the City field to insert a checkmark so that the field values will be displayed in the query results.

▶ **5.** Use the pointer to select the City field, drag the selected field to the left of the Email field, and then click in an empty box to deselect the City field. See Figure 3-24.

| Figure 3-24 | Design grid after moving the City field |

City field moved back to its original location

Show check box is selected

condition removed from City Criteria box

▶ **6.** In the Results group on the DESIGN tab, click the **Run** button. Access runs the query and displays the selected fields for only those records with a VisitDate field value less than 1/1/2016. The query displays a total of 18 records. See Figure 3-25.

| Figure 3-25 | Running the modified query |

only records with a VisitDate field value less than 1/1/2016 are selected

18 records are selected

**7.** Save and close the EarlierVisits query.

Cindi continues to analyze patient visits to Chatham Community Health Services. She is especially concerned about being proactive and reaching out to older patients well in advance of flu season. With this in mind, she would like to see a list of all patients who are age 60 or older and who have visited the clinic suffering from influenza. She wants to track these patients in particular so that her staff can contact them early for flu shots. To produce this list, you need to create a query containing two conditions—one for the patient's date of birth and another for the reason/diagnosis for each patient visit.

# Defining Multiple Selection Criteria for Queries

Multiple conditions require you to use **logical operators** to combine two or more conditions. When you want a record selected only if two or more conditions are met, you need to use the **And logical operator**. In this case, Cindi wants to see only those records with a BirthDate field value less than or equal to 12/31/1956 *and* a Reason field value of "Influenza." If you place conditions in separate fields in the *same* Criteria row of the design grid, all conditions in that row must be met in order for a record to be included in the query results. However, if you place conditions in *different* Criteria rows, a record will be selected if at least one of the conditions is met. If none of the conditions are met, Access does not select the record. When you place conditions in different Criteria rows, you are using the **Or logical operator**. Figure 3-26 illustrates the difference between the And and Or logical operators.

**Figure 3-26**    Logical operators And and Or for multiple selection criteria

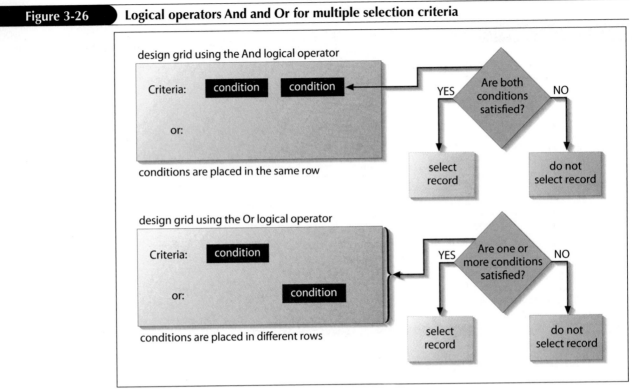

© 2014 Cengage Learning

## The And Logical Operator

To create the query for Cindi, you need to use the And logical operator to show only the records for patients who were born on or before 12/31/1956 *and* who have visited the clinic because of influenza. You'll create a new query based on both the Patient and Visit tables to produce the necessary results. In the query design, both conditions you specify will appear in the same Criteria row; therefore, the query will select records only if both conditions are met.

### To create a new query using the And logical operator:

1. On the ribbon, click the **CREATE** tab.

2. In the Queries group, click the **Query Design** button.

3. Add the **Patient** and **Visit** tables to the Query window, and then close the Show Table dialog box. Resize both field lists to display all the field names.

4. Add the following fields from the Patient field list to the design grid in the order shown: **FirstName**, **LastName**, **BirthDate**, **Phone**, and **City**.

5. Add the **VisitDate** and **Reason** fields from the Visit table to the design grid.

   Now you need to enter the two conditions for the query.

6. Click the **BirthDate Criteria** box, and then type **<=12/31/1956**.

7. Press the **Tab** key four times to move to the **Reason Criteria** box, type **Influenza**, and then press the **Tab** key. See Figure 3-27.

**Figure 3-27** ▶ **Query to find older patients who have had influenza**

| Field: | FirstName | LastName | BirthDate | Phone | City | VisitDate | Reason |
|---|---|---|---|---|---|---|---|
| Table: | Patient | Patient | Patient | Patient | Patient | Visit | Visit |
| Sort: | | | | | | | |
| Show: | ✓ | ✓ | ✓ | ✓ | ✓ | ✓ | ✓ |
| Criteria: | | | <=#12/31/1956# | | | | "Influenza" |
| or: | | | | | | | |

**And logical operator with conditions entered in the same row**

Ready

▶ **8.** Run the query. Access displays only those records that meet both conditions: a BirthDate field value less than or equal to 12/31/1956 *and* a Reason field value of Influenza. Two records are selected for two different patients. See Figure 3-28.

**Figure 3-28** ▶ **Results of query using the And logical operator**

Chatham : Database- E:\Access1\Tutorial\Chatham.accdb (Access 2007 - 2013 file format) - Access

| First Name | Last Name | Date of Birth | Phone | City | Date of Visit | Reason/Diagnosis |
|---|---|---|---|---|---|---|
| Ian | Parker | 6/3/1953 | 860-938-1873 | Hartford | 12/15/2015 | Influenza |
| Jane | Ropiak | 2/7/1950 | 860-938-7830 | Hartford | 3/3/2016 | Influenza |

▶ **9.** On the Quick Access Toolbar, click the **Save** button, and then save the query as **OlderAndFluPatients**.

▶ **10.** Close the query.

Cindi meets with staff member Ethan to discuss the issue of influenza and keeping patients informed about receiving flu shots at the clinic. After viewing the results of the OlderAndFluPatients query, Ethan suggests that the clinic should reach out to all elderly patients regarding flu shots, because this segment of the population is particularly susceptible to the flu. In addition, he thinks they should contact any patient who has visited the clinic suffering from influenza to keep these patients informed about flu shots well in advance of flu season. To help with their planning, Cindi and Ethan have asked you to produce a list of all patients who were born on or before 12/31/1956 or who visited the clinic because of influenza. To create this query, you need to use the Or logical operator.

## The Or Logical Operator

To create the query that Cindi and Ethan requested, your query must select a record when either one of two conditions is satisfied or when both conditions are satisfied. That is, a record is selected if the BirthDate field value is less than or equal to 12/31/1956 *or* if the Reason field value is Influenza *or* if both conditions are met. You will enter the condition for the BirthDate field in the Criteria row and the condition for the Reason field in the "or" criteria row, thereby using the Or logical operator.

To display the information Cindi and Ethan want to view, you'll create a new query based on the existing OlderAndFluPatients query, since it already contains the necessary fields. Then you'll specify the conditions using the Or logical operator.

### To create a new query using the Or logical operator:

1. Open the Navigation Pane. You'll use the shortcut menu to copy and paste the OlderAndFluPatients query to create the new query.

2. In the Queries section of the Navigation Pane, right-click **OlderAndFluPatients** to select it and display the shortcut menu.

3. Click **Copy** on the shortcut menu.

4. Right-click the empty area near the bottom of the Navigation Pane, and then click **Paste** on the shortcut menu. The Paste As dialog box opens with the text "Copy Of OlderAndFluPatients" in the Query Name box. Because Cindi wants the new query to show data for all older patients or patients who have visited the clinic due to influenza, you'll name the new query "OlderOrFluPatients."

5. In the Query Name box, type **OlderOrFluPatients** and then press the **Enter** key. The new query appears in the Queries section of the Navigation Pane.

6. In the Navigation Pane, right-click the **OlderOrFluPatients** query to select it and display the shortcut menu, and then click **Design View** on the shortcut menu to open the query in Design view.

7. Close the Navigation Pane.

   The query already contains all the fields Cindi and Ethan want to view, as well as the first condition—a BirthDate field value less than or equal to 12/31/1956. Because you want records selected if either the condition for the BirthDate field or the condition for the Reason field is satisfied, you must delete the existing condition for the Reason field in the Criteria row and then enter this same condition in the "or" row of the design grid for the Reason field.

8. In the design grid, click at the end of the **Reason Criteria** box and then press the **Backspace** key until the condition "Influenza" is deleted.

9. Press the ↓ key to move to the "or" row for the Reason field, type **Influenza**, and then press the **Tab** key. See Figure 3-29.

| Figure 3-29 | Query window with the Or logical operator |

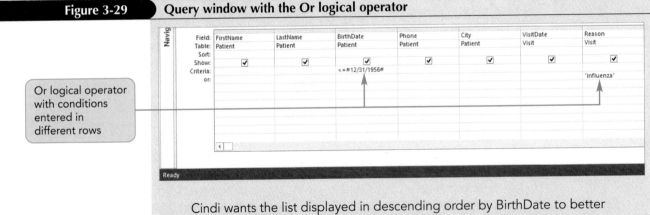

Or logical operator with conditions entered in different rows

Cindi wants the list displayed in descending order by BirthDate to better analyze the data.

▶ **10.** Click the right side of the **BirthDate Sort** box, and then click **Descending**.

▶ **11.** Run the query. Access displays only those records that meet either condition: a BirthDate field value less than or equal to 12/31/1956 *or* a Reason field value of Influenza. Access also selects records that meet both conditions. The query displays a total of 38 records. The records in the query datasheet appear in descending order based on the values in the BirthDate field. See Figure 3-30.

| Figure 3-30 | Results of query using the Or logical operator |

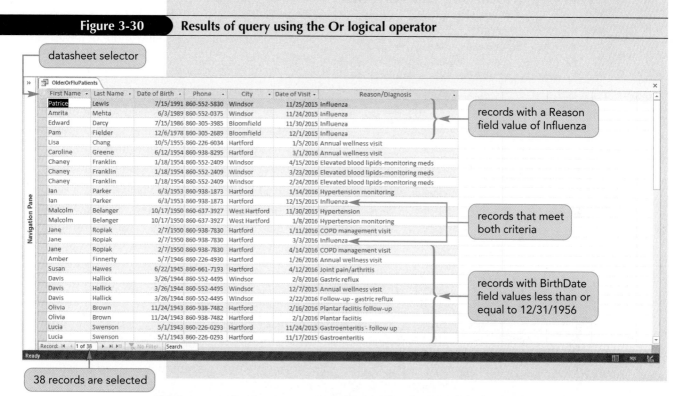

Cindi would like to spend some time reviewing the results of the OlderOrFluPatients query. To make this task easier, she asks you to change how the datasheet is displayed.

## INSIGHT

### Understanding the Results of Using And vs. Or

When you use the And logical operator to define multiple selection criteria in a query, you *narrow* the results produced by the query because a record must meet more than one condition to be included in the results. For example, the OlderAndFluPatients query you created resulted in only 2 records. When you use the Or logical operator, you *broaden* the results produced by the query because a record must meet only one of the conditions to be included in the results. For example, the OlderOrFluPatients query you created resulted in 38 records. This is an important distinction to keep in mind when you include multiple selection criteria in queries, so that the queries you create will produce the results you want.

# Changing a Datasheet's Appearance

You can make many formatting changes to a datasheet to improve its appearance or readability. Many of these modifications are familiar types of changes you can also make in Word documents or Excel spreadsheets, such as modifying the font type, size, color, and the alignment of text. You can also apply different colors to the rows and columns in a datasheet to enhance its appearance.

## Modifying the Font Size

Depending on the size of the monitor you are using or the screen resolution, you might need to increase or decrease the size of the font in a datasheet to view more or fewer columns of data. Cindi asks you to change the font size in the query datasheet from the default 11 points to 14 points so that she can read the text more easily.

**To change the font size in the datasheet:**

1. In the Text Formatting group on the HOME tab, click the **Font Size** arrow, and then click **14**. The font size for the entire datasheet increases to 14 points.

   Next, you need to resize the columns to their best fit, so that all field values are displayed. Instead of resizing each column individually, you'll use the datasheet selector to select all the columns and resize them at the same time.

2. Click the **datasheet selector**, which is the box to the left of the First Name column heading (see Figure 3-30). All the columns in the datasheet are highlighted, indicating they are selected.

3. Position the pointer ↔ on the vertical line on the right of any column in the datasheet, and then double-click the vertical line. All the columns visible on the screen are resized to their best fit. Scroll down and repeat the resizing, as necessary, to make sure that all field values are fully displayed.

   **Trouble?** If all the columns are not visible on your screen, you need to scroll the datasheet to the right to make sure all field values for all columns are fully displayed. If you need to resize any columns, click a field value first to deselect the columns before resizing an individual column.

4. Click any value in the First Name column to make it the current field and to deselect the columns in the datasheet.

## Changing the Alternate Row Color in a Datasheet

**TIP**

When choosing a row color, be sure not to select a color that is too dark because it might obscure the data rather than enhance it.

Access uses themes to format the objects in a database. A **theme** is a predefined set of formats including colors, fonts, and other effects that enhance an object's appearance and usability. When you create a database, Access applies the Office theme to objects as you create them. By default, the Office theme formats every other row in a datasheet with a gray background color to distinguish one row from another, making it easier to view and read the contents of a datasheet. The gray alternate row color provides a subtle difference compared to the rows that have the default white color. You can change the alternate row color in a datasheet to something more noticeable using the Alternate Row Color button in the Text Formatting group on the HOME tab. Cindi suggests that you change the alternate row color in the datasheet to see the effect of using this feature.

## To change the alternate row color in the datasheet:

1. In the Text Formatting group on the HOME tab, click the **Alternate Row Color** button arrow to display the gallery of color choices. See Figure 3-31.

Figure 3-31 Gallery of color choices for alternate row color

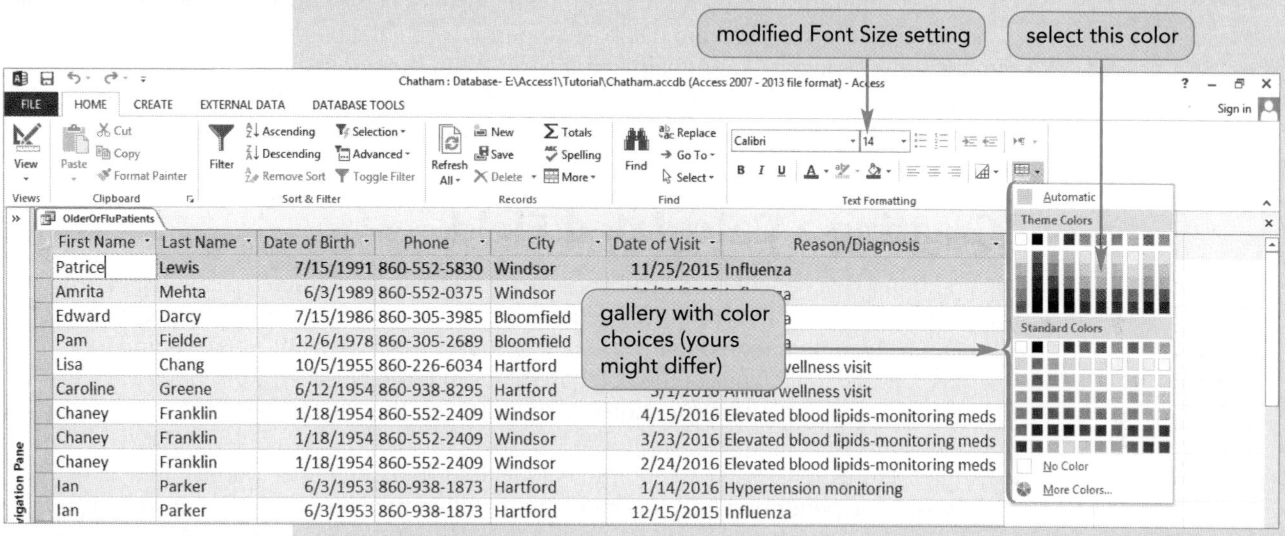

**TIP**

The name of the color appears in a ScreenTip when you point to a color in the gallery.

The Theme Colors section provides colors from the default Office theme, so that your datasheet's color scheme matches the one in use for the database. The Standard Colors section provides many standard color choices. You might also see a Recent Colors section, with colors that you have recently used in a datasheet. At the bottom of the gallery, you could also choose the No Color option, which sets each row's background color to white; or the More Colors option, which creates a custom color. You'll use one of the theme colors.

2. In the Theme Colors section, click the color box for **Orange, Accent 2, Lighter 60%** (third row, sixth color box). The alternate row color is applied to the query datasheet. See Figure 3-32.

Figure 3-32 Datasheet formatted with alternate row color

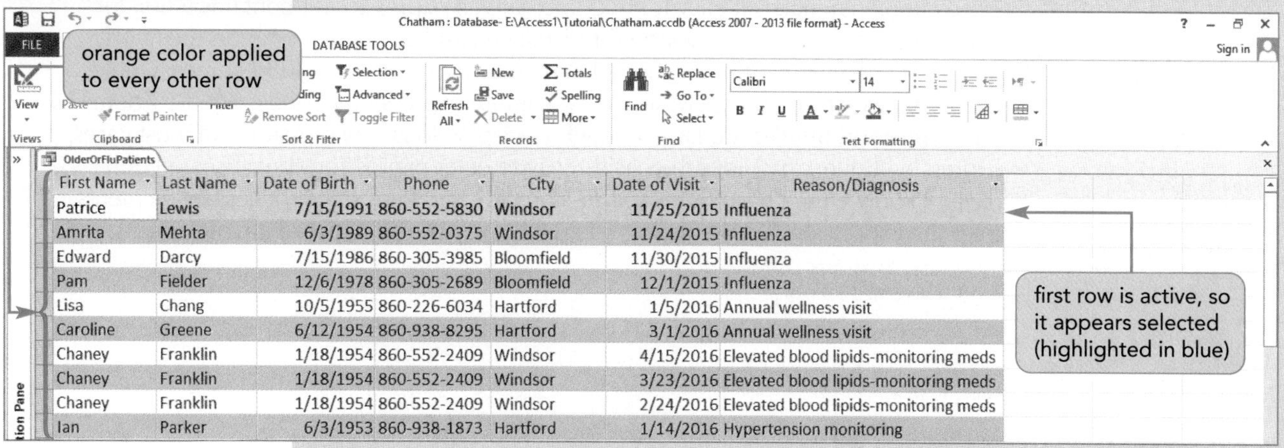

Every other row in the datasheet uses the selected theme color. Cindi likes how the datasheet looks with this color scheme, so she asks you to save the query.

**3.** Save and close the OlderOrFluPatients query. The query is saved with both the increased font size and the orange alternate row color.

Next, Cindi turns her attention to some financial aspects of operating the clinic. She wants to use the Chatham database to perform calculations. She is considering imposing a 2% late fee on unpaid invoices and wants to know exactly what the late fee charges would be, should she decide to institute such a policy in the future. To produce the information for Cindi, you need to create a calculated field.

# Creating a Calculated Field

In addition to using queries to retrieve, sort, and filter data in a database, you can use a query to perform calculations. To perform a calculation, you define an **expression** containing a combination of database fields, constants, and operators. For numeric expressions, the data types of the database fields must be Number, Currency, or Date/Time; the constants are numbers such as .02 (for the 2% late fee); and the operators can be arithmetic operators (+ − * /) or other specialized operators. In complex expressions, you can enclose calculations in parentheses to indicate which one should be performed first; any calculation within parentheses is completed before calculations outside the parentheses. In expressions without parentheses, Access performs basic calculations using the following order of precedence: multiplication and division before addition and subtraction. When operators have equal precedence, Access calculates them in order from left to right.

To perform a calculation in a query, you add a calculated field to the query. A **calculated field** is a field that displays the results of an expression. A calculated field that you create with an expression appears in a query datasheet or in a form or report; however, it does not exist in a database. When you run a query that contains a calculated field, Access evaluates the expression defined by the calculated field and displays the resulting value in the query datasheet, form, or report.

To enter an expression for a calculated field, you can type it directly in a Field box in the design grid. Alternately, you can open the Zoom box or Expression Builder and use either one to enter the expression. The **Zoom box** is a dialog box that you can use to enter text, expressions, or other values. To use the Zoom box, however, you must know all the parts of the expression you want to create. **Expression Builder** is an Access tool that makes it easy for you to create an expression; it contains a box for entering the expression, an option for displaying and choosing common operators, and one or more lists of expression elements, such as table and field names. Unlike a Field box, which is too narrow to show an entire expression at one time, the Zoom box and Expression Builder are large enough to display longer expressions. In most cases, Expression Builder provides the easiest way to enter expressions because you don't have to know all the parts of the expression; you can choose the necessary elements from the Expression Builder dialog box, which also helps to prevent typing errors.

### Using Expression Builder

- Create and save the query in which you want to include a calculated field.
- Open the query in Design view.
- In the design grid, click the Field box in which you want to create an expression.
- In the Query Setup group on the DESIGN tab, click the Builder button.
- Use the expression elements and common operators to build the expression, or type the expression directly in the expression box.
- Click the OK button.

To produce the information Cindi wants, you need to create a new query based on the Billing and Visit tables and, in the query, create a calculated field that will multiply each InvoiceAmt field value by .02 to calculate the proposed 2% late fee.

### To create the new query and the calculated field:

1. On the ribbon, click the **CREATE** tab.

2. In the Queries group, click the **Query Design** button. The Show Table dialog box opens.

   Cindi wants to see data from both the Visit and Billing tables, so you need to add these two tables to the Query window.

3. Add the **Visit** and **Billing** tables to the Query window, and then close the Show Table dialog box. The field lists appear in the Query window, and the one-to-many relationship between the Visit (primary) and Billing (related) tables is displayed.

4. Resize the two field lists so that all field names are visible.

5. Add the following fields to the design grid in the order given: **VisitID**, **PatientID**, and **VisitDate** from the Visit table; and **InvoiceItem**, **InvoicePaid**, and **InvoiceAmt** from the Billing table.

   Cindi is interested in viewing data only for unpaid invoices because a late fee would apply only to them, so you need to enter the necessary condition for the InvoicePaid field. Recall that InvoicePaid is a Yes/No field. The condition you need to enter is the word "No" in the Criteria box for this field, so that Access will retrieve the records for unpaid invoices only.

6. In the **InvoicePaid Criteria** box, type **No**. As soon as you type the letter "N," a menu appears with options for entering various functions for the criteria. You don't need to enter a function, so you can close this menu.

7. Press the **Esc** key to close the menu.

8. Press the **Tab** key. The query name you'll use will indicate that the data is for unpaid invoices, so you don't need to include the InvoicePaid values in the query results.

9. Click the **InvoicePaid Show** check box to remove the checkmark.

10. Save the query with the name **UnpaidInvoiceLateFee**.

> You must close the menu or you'll enter a function, which will cause an error.

Now you can use Expression Builder to create the calculated field for the InvoiceAmt field.

### To create the calculated field:

▶ 1. Click the blank Field box to the right of the InvoiceAmt field. This field will contain the expression.

▶ 2. In the Query Setup group on the DESIGN tab, click the **Builder** button. The Expression Builder dialog box opens.

**TIP**

You must first save and name a query in order for its fields to be listed in the Expression Categories section.

The insertion point is positioned in the large box at the top of the dialog box, ready for you to enter the expression. The Expression Categories section of the dialog box lists the fields from the query so you can include them in the expression. The Expression Elements section contains options for including other elements in the expression, including functions, constants, and operators. If the expression you're entering is a simple one, you can type it in the box; if it's more complex, you can use the options in the Expression Elements section to help you build the expression.

The expression for the calculated field will multiply the InvoiceAmt field values by the numeric constant .02 (which represents a 2% late fee).

▶ 3. In the Expression Categories section of the dialog box, double-click **InvoiceAmt**. The field name is added to the expression box, within brackets and with a space following it. In an expression, all field names must be enclosed in brackets.

Next you need to enter the multiplication operator, which is the asterisk (*), followed by the constant.

▶ 4. Type **\*** (an asterisk) and then type **.02**. You have finished entering the expression. See Figure 3-33.

| Figure 3-33 | Completed expression for the calculated field |
|---|---|

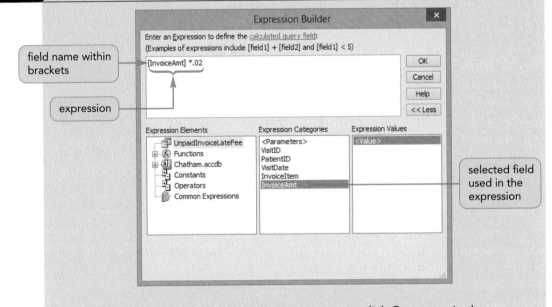

If you're not sure which operator to use, you can click Operators in the Expression Elements section to display a list of available operators in the center section of the dialog box.

**5.** Click the **OK** button. Access closes the Expression Builder dialog box and adds the expression to the design grid in the Field box for the calculated field.

When you create a calculated field, Access uses the default column name "Expr1" for the field. You need to specify a more meaningful column name so it will appear in the query results. You'll enter the name "LateFee," which better describes the field's contents.

**6.** Click to the left of the text "Expr1:" at the beginning of the expression, and then press the **Delete** key five times to delete the text **Expr1**. *Do not delete the colon*; it is needed to separate the calculated field name from the expression.

**7.** Type **LateFee**. Next, you'll set this field's Caption property so that the field name will appear as "Late Fee" in the query datasheet.

**8.** In the Show/Hide group on the DESIGN tab, click the **Property Sheet** button. The Property Sheet for the current field, LateFee, opens on the right side of the window. See Figure 3-34.

| Figure 3-34 | Property Sheet for the calculated field |
| --- | --- |

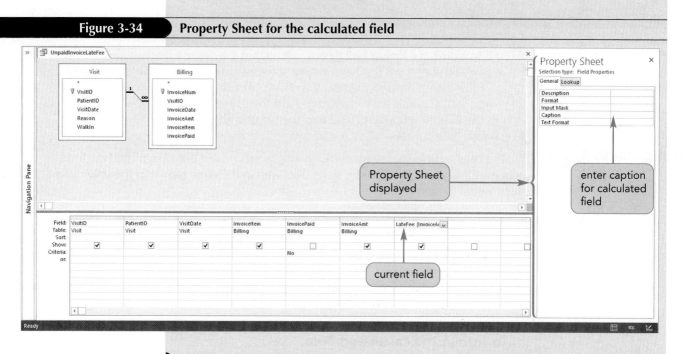

**9.** Click in the Caption box of the Property Sheet, type **Late Fee** and then close the Property Sheet.

**10.** Run the query. Access displays the query datasheet, which contains the specified fields and the calculated field with the caption "Late Fee." See Figure 3-35.

Figure 3-35 **Datasheet displaying the calculated field**

| Visit ID | Patient ID | Date of Visit | Invoice Item | Invoice Amt | Late Fee |
|---|---|---|---|---|---|
| 1535 | 22546 | 11/12/2015 | Radiograph | $250.00 | 5 |
| 1538 | 22500 | 11/17/2015 | Pharmacy | $125.00 | 2.5 |
| 1548 | 22519 | 11/30/2015 | Office visit | $100.00 | 2 |
| 1550 | 22549 | 12/1/2015 | Pharmacy | $85.00 | 1.7 |
| 1550 | 22549 | 12/1/2015 | Radiograph | $250.00 | 5 |
| 1555 | 22520 | 12/7/2015 | Office visit | $100.00 | 2 |
| 1555 | 22520 | 12/7/2015 | Pharmacy | $72.00 | 1.44 |
| 1557 | 22526 | 12/10/2015 | Phlebotomy | $45.00 | 0.9 |
| 1557 | 22526 | 12/10/2015 | Lab work | $32.00 | 0.64 |
| 1562 | 22516 | 12/22/2015 | Office visit | $100.00 | 2 |
| 1562 | 22516 | 12/22/2015 | Respiratory therapy | $150.00 | 3 |
| 1563 | 22546 | 1/4/2016 | Cast removal | $75.00 | 1.5 |
| 1570 | 22561 | 1/11/2016 | Pharmacy | $85.00 | 1.7 |
| 1570 | 22561 | 1/11/2016 | Phlebotomy | $45.00 | 0.9 |
| 1570 | 22561 | 1/11/2016 | Pharmacy | $68.00 | 1.36 |
| 1570 | 22561 | 1/11/2016 | Lab work | $125.00 | 2.5 |
| 1572 | 22560 | 1/13/2016 | Office visit | $100.00 | 2 |
| 1575 | 22513 | 1/13/2016 | Radiograph | $250.00 | 5 |
| 1575 | 22513 | 1/13/2016 | Bone setting and cast | $300.00 | 6 |
| 1576 | 22514 | 1/14/2016 | Office visit | $100.00 | 2 |
| 1580 | 22552 | 1/15/2016 | Pharmacy | $68.00 | 1.36 |
| 1585 | 22555 | 1/25/2016 | Office visit | $100.00 | 2 |
| 1585 | 22555 | 1/25/2016 | Pharmacy | $85.00 | 1.7 |
| 1585 | 22555 | 1/25/2016 | Lab work - culture | $125.00 | 2.5 |
| 1586 | 22523 | 1/25/2016 | Office visit | $100.00 | 2 |

Record: 1 of 76

specified caption for the calculated field

calculated field values

**Trouble?** If a dialog box opens noting that the expression contains invalid syntax, you might not have included the required colon in the expression. Click the OK button to close the dialog box, resize the column in the design grid that contains the calculated field to its best fit, change your expression to LateFee: [InvoiceAmt]*0.02 and then repeat Step 10.

The LateFee field values are currently displayed without dollar signs and decimal places. Cindi wants these values to be displayed in the same format as the InvoiceAmt field values for consistency.

## Formatting a Calculated Field

You can specify a particular format for a calculated field, just as you can for any field, by modifying its properties. Next, you'll change the format of the LateFee calculated field so that all values appear in the Currency format.

**To format the calculated field:**

1. Switch to Design view.

2. In the design grid, click in the **LateFee** calculated field to make it the current field, if necessary.

3. In the Show/Hide group on the DESIGN tab, click the **Property Sheet** button to open the Property Sheet for the calculated field.

   You need to change the Format property to Currency, which displays values with a dollar sign and two decimal places.

4. In the Property Sheet, click the right side of the **Format** box to display the list of formats, and then click **Currency**.

5. Close the Property Sheet for the calculated field, and then run the query. The amounts in the LateFee calculated field are now displayed with dollar signs and two decimal places.

▶ **6.** Save and close the UnpaidInvoiceLateFee query.

**PROSKILLS**

*Problem Solving: Creating a Calculated Field vs. Using the Calculated Field Data Type*

You can also create a calculated field using the Calculated Field data type, which lets you store the result of an expression as a field in a table. However, database experts caution users against storing calculations in a table for several reasons. First, storing calculated data in a table consumes valuable space and increases the size of the database. The preferred approach is to use a calculated field in a query; with this approach, the result of the calculation is not stored in the database—it is produced only when you run the query—and it is always current. Second, the Calculated Field data type provides limited options for creating a calculation, whereas a calculated field in a query provides more functions and options for creating expressions. Third, including a field in a table using the Calculated Field data type limits your options if you need to upgrade the database at some point to a more robust DBMS, such as Oracle or SQL Server, that doesn't support this data type; you would need to redesign your database to eliminate this data type. Finally, most database experts agree that including a field in a table whose value is dependent on other fields in the table violates database design principles. To avoid such problems, it's best to create a query that includes a calculated field to perform the calculation you want, instead of creating a field in a table that uses the Calculated Field data type.

To better analyze costs at Chatham Community Health Services, Cindi wants to view more detailed information about patient invoices. Specifically, she would like to know the minimum, average, and maximum invoice amounts. She asks you to determine these statistics from data in the Billing table.

# Using Aggregate Functions

You can calculate statistical information, such as totals and averages, on the records displayed in a table datasheet or selected by a query. To do this, you use the Access aggregate functions. **Aggregate functions** perform arithmetic operations on selected records in a database. Figure 3-36 lists the most frequently used aggregate functions.

**Figure 3-36** **Frequently used aggregate functions**

| Aggregate Function | Determines | Data Types Supported |
|---|---|---|
| Average | Average of the field values for the selected records | AutoNumber, Currency, Date/Time, Number |
| Count | Number of records selected | AutoNumber, Currency, Date/Time, Long Text, Number, OLE Object, Short Text, Yes/No |
| Maximum | Highest field value for the selected records | AutoNumber, Currency, Date/Time, Number, Short Text |
| Minimum | Lowest field value for the selected records | AutoNumber, Currency, Date/Time, Number, Short Text |
| Sum | Total of the field values for the selected records | AutoNumber, Currency, Date/Time, Number |

© 2014 Cengage Learning

# Working with Aggregate Functions Using the Total Row

If you want to quickly perform a calculation using an aggregate function in a table or query datasheet, you can use the Totals button in the Records group on the HOME tab. When you click this button, a row labeled "Total" appears at the bottom of the datasheet. You can then choose one of the aggregate functions for a field in the datasheet, and the results of the calculation will be displayed in the Total row for that field.

Cindi wants to know the total amount of all invoices for the clinic. You can quickly display this amount using the Sum function in the Total row in the Billing table datasheet.

## To display the total amount of all invoices in the Billing table:

▶ 1. Open the Navigation Pane, open the **Billing** table in Datasheet view, and then close the Navigation Pane.

▶ 2. Make sure the HOME tab is displayed.

▶ 3. In the Records group, click the **Totals** button. Access adds a row with the label "Total" to the bottom of the datasheet.

▶ 4. Scroll to the bottom of the datasheet to view the last records in the datasheet and the Total row. You want to display the sum of all the values in the Invoice Amt column.

▶ 5. In the Total row, click the **Invoice Amt** column. An arrow appears on the left side of the field.

▶ 6. Click the **arrow** to display the menu of aggregate functions. The functions displayed depend on the data type of the current field; in this case, the menu provides functions for a Currency field. See Figure 3-37.

| Figure 3-37 | Using aggregate functions in the Total row |
| --- | --- |

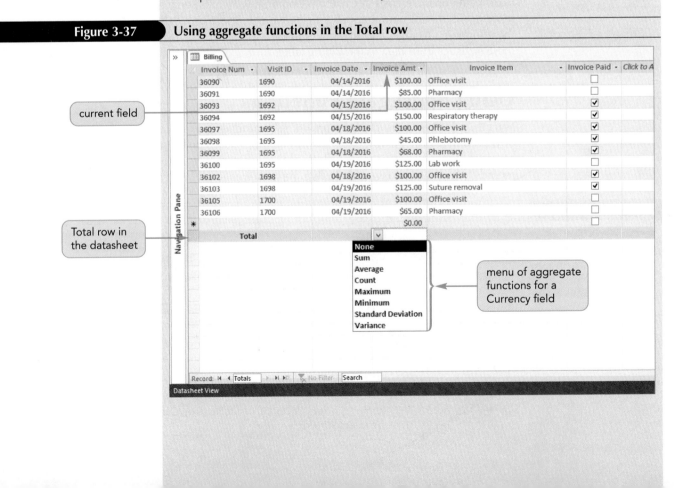

> **7.** Click **Sum** in the menu. Access adds all the values in the Invoice Amt column and displays the total $20,603.00 in the Total row for the column.
>
> Cindi doesn't want to change the Billing table to always display this total. You can remove the Total row by clicking the Totals button again; this button works as a toggle to switch between the display of the Total row with the results of any calculations in the row, and the display of the datasheet without this row.
>
> **8.** In the Records group, click the **Totals** button. Access removes the Total row from the datasheet.
>
> **9.** Close the Billing table without saving the changes.

Cindi wants to know the minimum, average, and maximum invoice amounts for Chatham Community Health Services. To produce this information for Cindi, you need to use aggregate functions in a query.

## Creating Queries with Aggregate Functions

Aggregate functions operate on the records that meet a query's selection criteria. You specify an aggregate function for a specific field, and the appropriate operation applies to that field's values for the selected records.

To display the minimum, average, and maximum of all the invoice amounts in the Billing table, you will use the Minimum, Average, and Maximum aggregate functions for the InvoiceAmt field.

---

### To calculate the minimum of all invoice amounts:

> **1.** Create a new query in Design view, add the **Billing** table to the Query window, and then close the Show Table dialog box. Resize the Billing field list to display all fields.
>
> To perform the three calculations on the InvoiceAmt field, you need to add the field to the design grid three times.
>
> **2.** In the Billing field list, double-click **InvoiceAmt** three times to add three copies of the field to the design grid.
>
> You need to select an aggregate function for each InvoiceAmt field. When you click the Totals button in the Show/Hide group on the DESIGN tab, a row labeled "Total" is added to the design grid. The Total row provides a list of the aggregate functions that you can select.
>
> **3.** In the Show/Hide group on the DESIGN tab, click the **Totals** button. A new row labeled "Total" appears between the Table and Sort rows in the design grid. The default entry for each field in the Total row is the Group By operator, which you will learn about later in this tutorial. See Figure 3-38.

| Figure 3-38 | Total row inserted in the design grid |
|---|---|

In the Total row, you specify the aggregate function you want to use for a field.

▶ **4.** Click the right side of the first column's **Total** box, and then click **Min**. This field will calculate the minimum amount of all the InvoiceAmt field values.

When you run the query, Access automatically will assign a datasheet column name of "MinOfInvoiceAmt" for this field. You can change the datasheet column name to a more descriptive or readable name by entering the name you want in the Field box. However, you must also keep the InvoiceAmt field name in the Field box because it identifies the field to use in the calculation. The Field box will contain the datasheet column name you specify followed by the field name (InvoiceAmt) with a colon separating the two names.

Be sure to type the colon following the name or the query will not work correctly.

▶ **5.** In the first column's Field box, click to the left of InvoiceAmt, and then type **MinimumInvoiceAmt:** (including the colon).

▶ **6.** Using the ✛ pointer, double-click the column dividing line between the first two columns so that you can see the complete field name, MinimumInvoiceAmt:InvoiceAmt.

Next, you need to set the Caption property for this field so that the field name appears with spaces between words in the query datatsheet.

▶ **7.** In the Show/Hide group on the DESIGN tab, click the **Property Sheet** button to open the Property Sheet for the current field.

▶ **8.** In the Caption box, type **Minimum Invoice Amt** and then close the Property Sheet.

You'll follow the same process to complete the query by calculating the average and maximum invoice amounts.

### To calculate the average and maximum of all invoice amounts:

▶ **1.** Click the right side of the second column's **Total** box, and then click **Avg**. This field will calculate the average of all the InvoiceAmt field values.

▶ **2.** In the second column's Field box, click to the left of InvoiceAmt, and then type **AverageInvoiceAmt:**.

▶ **3.** Resize the second column to fully display the field name, AverageInvoiceAmt:InvoiceAmt.

**4.** Open the Property Sheet for the current field, and then set its Caption property to **Average Invoice Amt**. Leave the Property Sheet open.

**5.** Click the right side of the third column's **Total** box, and then click **Max**. This field will calculate the maximum amount of all the InvoiceAmt field values.

**6.** In the third column's Field box, click to the left of InvoiceAmt, and then type **MaximumInvoiceAmt:**.

**7.** Resize the third column to fully display the field name, MaximumInvoiceAmt:InvoiceAmt.

**8.** In the Property Sheet for the current field, set the Caption property to **Maximum Invoice Amt** and then close the Property Sheet. See Figure 3-39.

| Figure 3-39 | Query with aggregate functions entered |
| --- | --- |

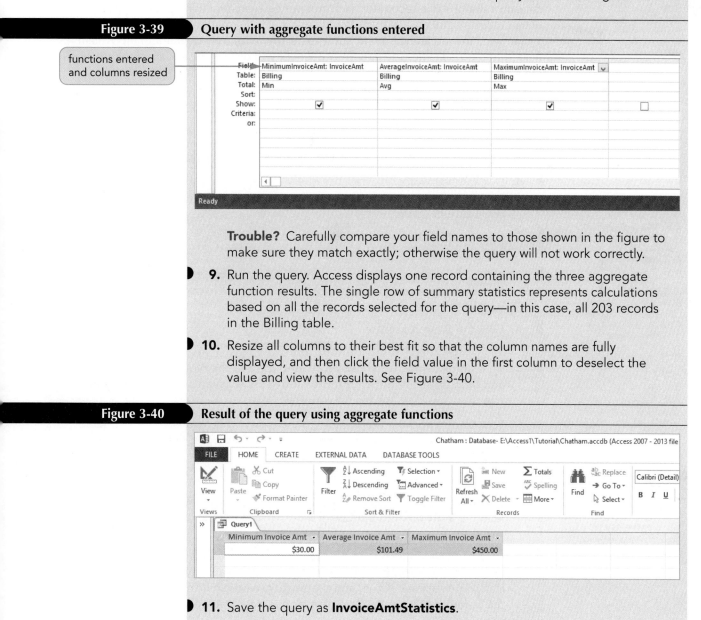

functions entered and columns resized

**Trouble?** Carefully compare your field names to those shown in the figure to make sure they match exactly; otherwise the query will not work correctly.

**9.** Run the query. Access displays one record containing the three aggregate function results. The single row of summary statistics represents calculations based on all the records selected for the query—in this case, all 203 records in the Billing table.

**10.** Resize all columns to their best fit so that the column names are fully displayed, and then click the field value in the first column to deselect the value and view the results. See Figure 3-40.

| Figure 3-40 | Result of the query using aggregate functions |
| --- | --- |

**11.** Save the query as **InvoiceAmtStatistics**.

Cindi would like to view the same invoice amount statistics (minimum, average, and maximum) as they relate to both scheduled appointments and walk-in visits to the clinic.

## Using Record Group Calculations

In addition to calculating statistical information on all or selected records in selected tables, you can calculate statistics for groups of records. For example, you can determine the number of patients in each city or the average invoice amount by city.

To create a query for Cindi's latest request, you can modify the current query by adding the WalkIn field and assigning the Group By operator to it. The **Group By operator** divides the selected records into groups based on the values in the specified field. Those records with the same value for the field are grouped together, and the datasheet displays one record for each group. Aggregate functions, which appear in the other columns of the design grid, provide statistical information for each group.

You need to modify the current query to add the Group By operator to the WalkIn field from the Visit table. The Group By operator will display the statistical information grouped by the values of the WalkIn field for all the records in the query datasheet. To create the new query, you will save the InvoiceAmtStatistics query with a new name, keeping the original query intact, and then modify the new query.

### To create a new query with the Group By operator:

1. Display the InvoiceAmtStatistics query in Design view. Because the query is open, you can use Backstage view to save it with a new name, keeping the original query intact.

2. Click the **FILE** tab to display Backstage view, and then click **Save As** in the navigation bar. The Save As screen opens.

3. In the File Types section on the left, click **Save Object As**. The right side of the screen changes to display options for saving the current database object as a new object.

4. Click the **Save As** button. The Save As dialog box opens, indicating that you are saving a copy of the InvoiceAmtStatistics query.

5. Type **InvoiceAmtStatisticsByWalkIn** to replace the highlighted name, and then press the **Enter** key. The new query is saved with the name you specified and displayed in Design view.

   You need to add the WalkIn field to the query. This field is in the Visit table. To include another table in an existing query, you open the Show Table dialog box.

> **TIP**
>
> You could also open the Navigation Pane and drag the Visit table from the pane to the Query window.

6. In the Query Setup group on the DESIGN tab, click the **Show Table** button to open the Show Table dialog box.

7. Add the **Visit** table to the Query window, close the Show Table dialog box, and then resize the Visit field list.

8. Drag the **WalkIn** field from the Visit field list to the first column in the design grid. When you release the mouse button, the WalkIn field appears in the design grid's first column, and the existing fields shift to the right. Group By, the default option in the Total row, appears for the WalkIn field.

9. Run the query. Access displays 2 records—one for each WalkIn group, Yes and No. Each record contains the WalkIn field value for the group and the three aggregate function values. The summary statistics represent calculations based on the 203 records in the Billing table. See Figure 3-41.

| Figure 3-41 | Aggregate functions grouped by WalkIn |
|---|---|

record groups

aggregate function results

Cindi notes that the invoice amounts for walk-in visits are higher than those for scheduled appointments.

▶ **10.** Save and close the query.

▶ **11.** Open the Navigation Pane.

You have created and saved many queries in the Chatham database. The Navigation Pane provides options for opening and managing the queries you've created, as well as the other objects in the database, such as tables, forms, and reports.

# Working with the Navigation Pane

As noted earlier, the Navigation Pane is the main area for working with the objects in a database. As you continue to create objects in your database, you might want to display and work with them in different ways. The Navigation Pane provides options for grouping database objects in various ways to suit your needs. For example, you might want to view only the queries created for a certain table or all the query objects in the database.

The Navigation Pane divides database objects into categories, and each category contains groups. The groups contain one or more objects. The default category is **Object Type**, which arranges objects by type—tables, queries, forms, and reports. The default group is **All Access Objects**, which displays all objects in the database. You can also choose to display only one type of object, such as tables.

The default group name, All Access Objects, appears at the top of the Navigation Pane. Currently, each object type—Tables, Queries, Forms, and Reports—is displayed as a heading, and the objects related to each type are listed below the heading. To group objects differently, you can select another category by using the Navigation Pane menu. You'll try this next.

**TIP**

You can hide the display of a group's objects by clicking the button to the right of the group name; click the button again to expand the group and display its objects.

## To group objects differently in the Navigation Pane:

▶ **1.** At the top of the Navigation Pane, click the **All Access Objects** button ⊙. A menu is displayed for choosing different categories and groups. See Figure 3-42.

Figure 3-42    **Navigation Pane menu**

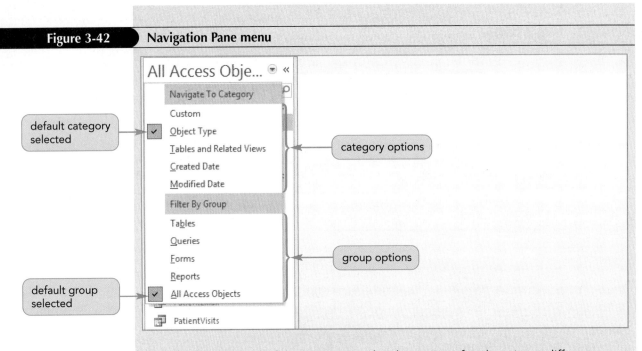

The top section of the menu provides the options for choosing a different category. The Object Type category has a checkmark next to it, signifying that it is the currently selected category. The lower section of the menu provides options for choosing a different group; these options might change depending on the selected category.

2. In the top section of the menu, click **Tables and Related Views**. The Navigation Pane is now grouped into categories of tables, and each table in the database—Visit, Billing, and Patient—is its own group. All database objects related to a table are listed below the table's name. See Figure 3-43.

**Figure 3-43**          Database objects grouped by table in the Navigation Pane

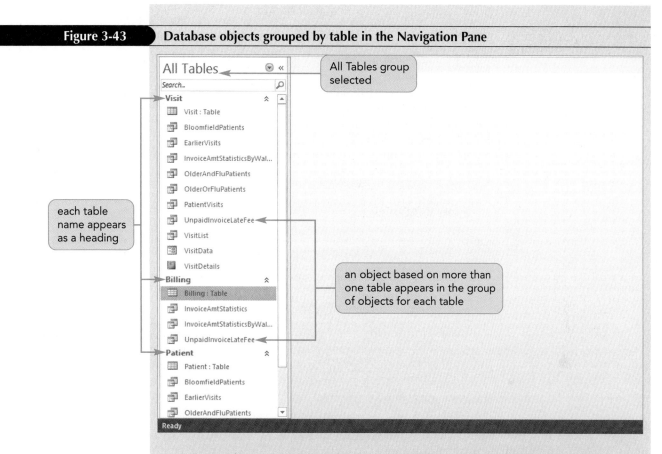

Some objects appear more than once. When an object is based on more than one table, that object appears in the group for each table. For example, the UnpaidInvoiceLateFee query is based on both the Visit and Billing tables, so it is listed in the group for both tables.

You can also choose to display the objects for only one table to better focus on that table.

▶  **3.** At the top of the Navigation Pane, click the **All Tables** button ⊙ to display the Navigation Pane menu, and then click **Patient**. The Navigation Pane now shows only the objects related to the Patient table—the table itself plus the six queries you created that include fields from the Patient table.

▶  **4.** At the top of the Navigation Pane, click the **Patient** button ⊙, and then click **Object Type** to return to the default display of the Navigation Pane.

▶  **5.** Compact and repair the Chatham database, and then close the database.

**Trouble?** If a dialog box opens and warns that this action will cause Microsoft Access to empty the Clipboard, click the Yes button to continue.

The default All Access Objects category is a predefined category. You can also create custom categories to group objects in the way that best suits how you want to manage your database objects. As you continue to build a database and the list of objects grows, creating a custom category can help you to work more efficiently with the objects in the database.

The queries you've created and saved will help Cindi, Kelly, Ethan, and other staff members to monitor and analyze the business activity of Chatham Community Health Services and its patients. Now any staff member can run the queries at any time, modify them as needed, or use them as the basis for designing new queries to meet additional information requirements.

## Session 3.2 Quick Check

**REVIEW**

1. A(n) _____ is a criterion, or rule, that determines which records are selected for a query datasheet.
2. In the design grid, where do you place the conditions for two different fields when you use the And logical operator, and where do you place them when you use the Or logical operator?
3. To perform a calculation in a query, you define a(n) _____ containing a combination of database fields, constants, and operators.
4. Which Access tool do you use to create an expression for a calculated field in a query?
5. What is an aggregate function?
6. The _____ operator divides selected records into groups based on the values in a field.
7. What is the default category for the display of objects in the Navigation Pane?

ASSESS

## SAM Projects

Put your skills into practice with SAM Projects! SAM Projects for this tutorial can be found online. If you have a SAM account, go to www.cengage.com/sam2013 to download the most recent Project Instructions and Start Files.

PRACTICE

## Review Assignments

**Data File needed for the Review Assignments: Vendor.accdb** *(cont. from Tutorial 2)*

Cindi asks you to update some information in the Vendor database and also to retrieve specific information from the database. Complete the following:

1. Open the **Vendor** database you created and worked with in Tutorials 1 and 2, and then click the Enable Content button next to the security warning, if necessary.

2. Open the **Supplier** table in Datasheet view, and then change the following field values for the record with the Supplier ID GRE364: Address to **1550 W Main St**, Contact Phone to **401-625-2745**, Contact First Name to **Andrew**, and Contact Last Name to **Kline**. Close the table.

3. Create a query based on the Supplier table. Include the following fields in the query, in the order shown: Company, Category, ContactFirst, ContactLast, Phone, and InitialContact. Sort the query in ascending order based on the Category field values. Save the query as **ContactList**, and then run the query.

4. Use the ContactList query datasheet to update the Supplier table by changing the Phone field value for Aresco Surgical, Inc. to **203-335-0054**.

5. Change the size of the font in the ContactList query datasheet to 12 points. Resize columns, as necessary, so that all field values and column headings are visible.

6. Change the alternate row color in the ContactList query datasheet to the Theme Color named Green, Accent 6, Lighter 60%, and then save and close the query.

7. Create a query based on the Supplier and Product tables. Select the Company, Category, and State fields from the Supplier table, and the ProductName, Price, Units, and Weight fields from the Product table. Sort the query results in descending order based on price. Select only those records with a State field value of CT, but do not display the State field values in the query results. Save the query as **CTSuppliers**, run the query, and then close it.

8. Create a query that lists all products that cost more than $200 and are sterile. Display the following fields from the Product table in the query results: ProductID, ProductName, Price, Units, and TempControl. (*Hint:* The Sterile field is a Yes/No field that should not appear in the query results.) Save the query as **HighPriceAndSterile**, run the query, and then close it.

9. Create a query that lists information about suppliers who sell equipment or products that require temperature control. Include the Company, Category, ContactFirst, and ContactLast fields from the Supplier table; and the ProductName, Price, TempControl, and Sterile fields from the Product table. Save the query as **EquipmentOrTempControl**, run the query, and then close it.

10. Create a query that lists only those products that cost $1000 or more, along with a 5% discount amount based on the price of the product. Include the Company field from the Supplier table and the following fields from the Product table in the query: ProductID, ProductName, and Price. Save the query as **HighPriceWithDiscount**. Display the discount in a calculated field named **DiscountAmt** that determines a 5% discount based on the Price field values. Set the Caption property **Discount Amt** for the calculated field. Display the query results in descending order by Price. Save and run the query.

11. Modify the format of the DiscountAmt field in the HighPriceWithDiscount query so that it uses the Standard format and two decimal places. Run the query, resize all columns in the datasheet to their best fit, and then save and close the query.

12. Create a query that calculates the lowest, highest, and average prices for all products using the field names **LowestPrice**, **HighestPrice**, and **AveragePrice**, respectively. Set the Caption property for each field to include a space between the two words in the field name. Run the query, resize all columns in the datasheet to their best fit, save the query as **PriceStatistics**, and then close it.

13. In the Navigation Pane, copy the PriceStatistics query, and then rename the copied query as **PriceStatisticsBySupplier**.

14. Modify the PriceStatisticsBySupplier query so that the records are grouped by the Company field in the Supplier table. The Company field should appear first in the query datasheet. Save and run the query, and then close it.

15. Compact and repair the Vendor database, and then close it.

## Case Problem 1

**APPLY**

**Data File needed for this Case Problem: Gopher.accdb** *(cont. from Tutorial 2)*

*GoGopher!*  Amol Mehta needs to modify a few records in the Gopher database and analyze the data for members enrolled in his company's various plans. To help Amol, you'll update the Gopher database and create queries to answer his questions. Complete the following:

1. Open the **Gopher** database you created and worked with in Tutorials 1 and 2, and then click the Enable Content button next to the security warning, if necessary.

2. In the **Member** table, find the record for MemberID 1251, and then change the Street value to **75 Hemlock Ln** and the Phone to **303-553-1847**.

3. In the **Member** table, find the record for MemberID 1228, and then delete the record. Close the Member table.

4. Create a query that lists members who did not have to pay a fee when they joined. In the query results, display the FirstName, LastName, and DateJoined fields from the Member table, and the PlanCost field from the Plan table. Sort the records in descending order by the date joined. Select records only for members whose fees were waived. (*Hint:* The FeeWaived field is a Yes/No field that should not appear in the query results.) Save the query as **NoFees**, and then run the query.

5. Use the NoFees query datasheet to update the Member table by changing the Last Name value for Kara Murray to **Seaburg**.

6. Use the NoFees query datasheet to display the total Plan Cost for the selected members. Save and close the query.

7. Create a query that lists the MemberID, FirstName, LastName, DateJoined, PlanDescription, and PlanCost fields for members who joined GoGopher! between April 1, 2016 and April 30, 2016. Save the query as **AprilMembers**, run the query, and then close it.

8. Create a query that lists all members who live in Louisville and whose memberships expire on or after 1/1/2017. Display the following fields from the Member table in the query results: MemberID, FirstName, LastName, Phone, and Expiration. (*Hint:* The City field values should not appear in the query results.) Sort the query results in ascending order by last name. Save the query as **LouisvilleAndExpiration**, run the query, and then close it.

9. Copy and paste the LouisvilleAndExpiration query to create a new query named **LouisvilleOrExpiration**. Modify the new query so that it lists all members who live in Louisville or whose memberships expire on or after 1/1/2017. Display the City field values in the query results following the Phone field values, and sort the query results in ascending order by city (this should be the only sort in the query). Save and run the query.

10. Change the size of the font in the LouisvilleOrExpiration query datasheet to 14 points. Resize columns, as necessary, so that all field values and column headings are visible.

11. Change the alternate row color in the LouisvilleOrExpiration query datasheet to the Theme Color named Blue, Accent 1, Lighter 80%, and then save and close the query.

12. Create a query that calculates the lowest, highest, and average cost for all plans using the field names **LowestCost**, **HighestCost**, and **AverageCost**, respectively. Set the Caption property for each field to include a space between the two words in the field name. Run the query, resize all columns in the datasheet to their best fit, save the query as **CostStatistics**, and then close it.

13. Copy and paste the CostStatistics query to create a new query named **CostStatisticsByCity**.

14. Modify the CostStatisticsByCity query to display the same statistics grouped by City, with City appearing as the first field. (*Hint:* Add the Member table to the query.) Run the query, and then save and close it.

15. Compact and repair the Gopher database, and then close it.

## Case Problem 2

**CREATE**

**Data File needed for this Case Problem: OBrien.accdb (cont. from Tutorial 2)**

*O'Brien Educational Services*   After reviewing the OBrien database, Karen O'Brien wants to modify some records and then view specific information about the students, tutors, and contracts for her educational services company. She asks you to update and query the OBrien database to perform these tasks. Complete the following:

1. Open the **OBrien** database you created and worked with in Tutorials 1 and 2, and then click the Enable Content button next to the security warning, if necessary.

2. In the **Tutor** table, change the following information for the record with TutorID 79-0678: Degree is **BA** and Hire Date is **9/15/2015**. Close the table.

3. In the **Student** table, find the record with the StudentID MCS8051, and then delete the related record in the subdatasheet for this student. Delete the record for StudentID MCS8051, and then close the Student table.

4. Create a query based on the Student table that includes the LastName, FirstName, and CellPhone fields, in that order. Save the query as **StudentCellList**, and then run the query.

5. In the results of the StudentCellList query, change the cell phone number for Haley Gosnold to **574-252-1973**. Close the query.

6. Create a query based on the Tutor and Contract tables. Display the LastName field from the Tutor table, and the StudentID, ContractDate, SessionType, Length, and Cost fields, in that order, from the Contract table. Sort first in ascending order by the tutor's last name, and then in ascending order by the StudentID. Save the query as **SessionsByTutor**, run the query, and the close it.

7. Copy and paste the SessionsByTutor query to create a new query named **GroupSessions**. Modify the new query so that it displays the same information for records with a Group session type only. Do not display the SessionType field values in the query results. Save and run the query, and then close it.

8. Create and save a query that produces the results shown in Figure 3-44. Close the query when you are finished.

**Figure 3-44**  **SouthBendPrivate query results**

show only records for students from South Bend who are taking private sessions

sort by Last Name

format with a font size of 12 and the Gold, Accent 4, Lighter 60% alternate row Theme Color

| SouthBendPrivate | | | |
|---|---|---|---|
| Student ID | Last Name | First Name | Contract Date |
| MAH8053 | Mahlau | Albert | 7/16/2016 |
| OAT8010 | Oates | Kyle | 1/26/2016 |
| PAP8024 | Pappas | Zach | 7/10/2016 |
| SPE8022 | Spence | Ross | 2/1/2016 |
| TUR8005 | Turner | Lynne | 9/15/2016 |
| VAR8027 | Vargas | Vera | 9/20/2016 |
| VAR8027 | Vargas | Vera | 4/3/2016 |

9. Create and save a query that produces the results shown in Figure 3-45. Close the query when you are finished.

**Figure 3-45**  **OscelaOrSemi query results**

show only records for students from Oscela or students taking semi-private sessions

sort in descending order by Contract Date

| OscelaOrSemi | | | | |
|---|---|---|---|---|
| Student ID | First Name | Last Name | Contract Date | Cost |
| DRO8048 | Emma | Drouin | 9/15/2016 | $720 |
| NAS8012 | Andre | Nastasia | 9/12/2016 | $800 |
| GUS8002 | Michael | Gustafson | 9/10/2016 | $900 |
| RIV8011 | Marco | Rivera | 8/10/2016 | $1,080 |
| DEN8042 | David | DeNardo | 8/1/2016 | $800 |
| CAR8059 | Carol | Carlson | 7/15/2016 | $1,200 |
| YEN8035 | Lila | Yen | 6/22/2016 | $1,440 |
| MAS8056 | Kimberly | Mase | 5/8/2016 | $960 |
| STI8038 | Lily | Stiefel | 3/15/2016 | $720 |
| BIE8000 | Joshua | Biega | 3/14/2016 | $1,800 |
| HIN8040 | Erica | Hinkle | 3/1/2016 | $960 |
| NAS8012 | Andre | Nastasia | 2/1/2016 | $960 |
| GUS8002 | Michael | Gustafson | 1/28/2016 | $720 |
| MUE8041 | Bart | Mueller | 1/15/2016 | $1,440 |
| YEN8035 | Lila | Yen | 1/7/2016 | $1,280 |
| HEC8018 | Eric | Hecht | 12/17/2015 | $900 |
| WOO8071 | Jon | Woodburn | 12/15/2015 | $1,800 |
| NUN8084 | Rodrigo | Nunez | 9/30/2015 | $800 |
| Total | | | | $19,280 |

Total row shows the sum of the Cost values

10. Create and save a query to display statistics for the Cost field, as shown in Figure 3-46. Close the query when you are finished.

**Figure 3-46**  **CostStatistics query results**

set captions to include spaces between words

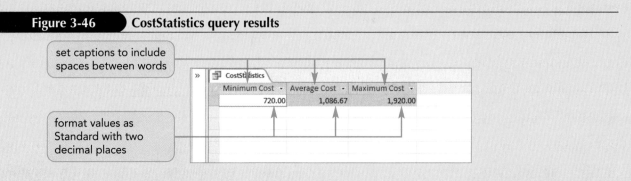

| CostStatistics | | |
|---|---|---|
| Minimum Cost | Average Cost | Maximum Cost |
| 720.00 | 1,086.67 | 1,920.00 |

format values as Standard with two decimal places

11. Copy and paste the CostStatistics query to create a new query named **CostStatisticsByCity**.

12. Modify the CostStatisticsByCity query to display the same statistics grouped by City, with City appearing as the first field. (*Hint:* Add the Student table to the query.) Run the query, and then save and close it.

13. Compact and repair the OBrien database, and then close it.

## Case Problem 3

CHALLENGE

Data File needed for this Case Problem: Shelter.accdb *(cont. from Tutorial 2)*

***Rosemary Animal Shelter***   Ryan Lang needs to modify some records in the Shelter database, and then he wants to find specific information about the animals, patrons, and donations for his not-for-profit agency. Ryan asks you to help him update the database and create queries to find the information he needs. Complete the following:

1. Open the **Shelter** database you created and worked with in Tutorials 1 and 2, and then click the Enable Content button next to the security warning, if necessary.

⊕ **Explore**  2. In the **Patron** table, delete the record with PatronID 36064. (*Hint:* Delete the related record in the Donation subdatasheet first, which you need to display using the Insert Subdatasheet dialog box.) Close the Patron table without saving changes to the table layout.

3. Create a query based on the Animal table that includes the AnimalID, AnimalName, AnimalType, Gender, and ArrivalDate fields, in that order. Save the query as **AnimalsByType**, and then run it.

4. Modify the AnimalsByType query design so that it sorts records in ascending order first by AnimalType and then by Gender. Save and run the query.

5. In the AnimalsByType query datasheet, find the record for the animal with Animal ID D23, and then change the arrival date for this animal to **5/19/2016**. Close the query.

6. Create a query that displays the PatronID, FirstName, and LastName fields from the Patron table, and the Description and DonationValue fields from the Donation table for all donations over $150. Sort the query in ascending order by donation value. Save the query as **LargeDonations**, run the query, and then close it.

7. Copy and paste the LargeDonations query to create a new query named **LargeCashDonations**.

⊕ **Explore**  8. Modify the LargeCashDonations query to display only those records with donations valuing more than $150 in cash. Do not include the Description field values in the query results. Use the query datasheet to calculate the average cash donation. Save and close the query.

9. Create a query that displays the PatronID, FirstName, and LastName fields from the Patron table, and the AnimalName, AnimalType, Age, Gender, and Adopted fields from the Animal table. Specify that the results show records for only those animals that have been adopted. Do not display the Adopted field values in the query results. Save the query as **CatAdoptions**, and then run the query.

10. Filter the results of the CatAdoptions query datasheet to display records for cats only.

⊕ **Explore**  11. Format the datasheet of the CatAdoptions query so that it does not display gridlines, uses an alternate row Standard Color of Purple 2, and displays a font size of 12. (*Hint:* Use the Gridlines button in the Text Formatting group on the HOME tab to select the appropriate gridlines option.) Resize the columns to display the complete field names and values, if necessary. Save and close the query.

✦ **Explore** 12. Create a query that displays the PatronID, FirstName, and LastName fields from the Patron table, and the Description, DonationDate, and DonationValue fields from the Donation table. Specify that the query include records for noncash donations only or for donations made in the month of June 2016. Sort the records first in ascending order by the patron's last name, and then in descending order by the donation value. Save the query as **NonCashOrJuneDonations**, run the query, and then close it.

13. Copy and paste the NonCashOrJuneDonations query to create a new query named **DonationsAfterStorageCharge**.

✦ **Explore** 14. Modify the DonationsAfterStorageCharge query so that it displays records for noncash donations made on all dates. Create a calculated field named **NetDonation** that displays the results of subtracting $3.50 from the DonationValue field values to account for the cost of storing each noncash donated item. Set the Caption property **Net Donation** for the calculated field. Display the results in ascending order by donation value. Run the query, and then modify it to format both the DonationValue field and the calculated field as Currency with two decimal places. Run the query again and resize the columns in the datasheet to their best fit, as necessary. Save and close the query.

✦ **Explore** 15. Create a query based on the **Donation** table that displays the sum, average, and count of the DonationValue field for all donations. Then complete the following:

a. Specify field names of **TotalDonations**, **AverageDonation**, and **NumberofDonations**. Then specify captions to include spaces between words.

b. Save the query as **DonationStatistics**, and then run it. Resize the query datasheet columns to their best fit.

c. Modify the field properties so that the values in the Total Donations and Average Donation columns display two decimal places and the Standard format. Run the query again, and then save and close the query.

d. Copy and paste the DonationStatistics query to create a new query named **DonationStatisticsByDescription**.

e. Modify the DonationStatisticsByDescription query to display the sum, average, and count of the DonationValue field for all donations grouped by Description, with Description appearing as the first field. Sort the records in descending order by Total Donations. Save, run, and then close the query.

16. Compact and repair the Shelter database, and then close it.

## Case Problem 4

**Data File needed for this Case Problem: Stanley.accdb *(cont. from Tutorial 2)* and Tour.accdb**

***Stanley EcoTours*** Janice and Bill Stanley need your help to maintain and analyze data about the clients, reservations, and tours for their ecotourism business. Additionally, you'll troubleshoot some problems in another database containing tour information. Complete the following:

1. Open the **Stanley** database you created and worked with in Tutorials 1 and 2, and then click the Enable Content button next to the security warning, if necessary.

2. In the **Guest** table, change the phone number for Paul Barry to **406-497-1068**, and then close the table.

3. Create a query based on the Tour table that includes the TourName, Location, Country, PricePerPerson, and TourType fields, in that order. Sort in ascending order based on the PricePerPerson field values. Save the query as **ToursByPrice**, and then run the query.

4. Use the ToursByPrice query datasheet to display the total Price Per Person for the tours. Save and close the query.

5. Create a query that displays the GuestLast, City, and State/Prov fields from the Guest table, and the ReservationID, StartDate, and People fields from the Reservation table. Save the query as **GuestTourDates**, and then run the query. Change the alternate row color in the query datasheet to the Theme Color Green, Accent 6, Lighter 40%. In Datasheet view, use an AutoFilter to sort the query results from oldest to newest Start Date. Save and close the query.

6. Create a query that displays the GuestFirst, GuestLast, City, ReservationID, TourID, and StartDate fields for all guests from Montana (MT). Do not include the State/Prov field in the query results. Sort the query in ascending order by the guest's last name. Save the query as **MontanaGuests** and then run it. Close the query.

7. Create a query that displays data from all three tables in the database, as follows: the GuestLast, City, State/Prov, and Country fields from the Guest table; the StartDate field from the Reservation table; and the TourName, Location, and TourType fields from the Tour table. Specify that the query select only those records for guests from Canada or guests who are taking Jeep tours. Sort the query in ascending order by Location. Save the query as **CanadaOrJeep**, and then run the query. Resize datasheet columns to their best fit, as necessary, and then save and close the query.

8. Copy and paste the CanadaOrJeep query to create a new query named **IdahoAndJuly**.

9. Modify the IdahoAndJuly query to select all guests from Idaho who are taking a tour starting sometime in the month of July 2016. Do not include the State/Prov field values or the Country field values in the query results. Run the query. Resize datasheet columns to their best fit, as necessary, and then save and close the query.

10. Create a query that displays the ReservationID, StartDate, and People fields from the Reservation table, and the TourName, Location, Country, PricePerPerson, and SingleSupplement fields from the Tour table for all reservations with a People field value of 1. Save the query as **SingleReservations**. Add a field to the query named **TotalCost** that displays the results of adding the SingleSupplement field values to the PricePerPerson field values. Set the Caption property **Total Cost** for the calculated field. Display the results in descending order by TotalCost. Do not include the People field values in the query results. Run the query. Modify the query by formatting the TotalCost field to show 0 decimal places. Run the query, resize datasheet columns to their best fit, as necessary, and then save and close the query.

11. Create a query based on the Tour table that determines the minimum, average, and maximum price per person for all tours. Then complete the following:
    a. Specify field names of **LowestPrice**, **AveragePrice**, and **HighestPrice**.
    b. Set the Caption property for each field to include a space between the two words in the field name.
    c. Save the query as **PriceStatistics**, and then run the query.
    d. In Design view, specify the Standard format and two decimal places for each column.
    e. Run the query, resize all the datasheet columns to their best fit, save your changes, and then close the query.
    f. Create a copy of the PriceStatistics query named **PriceStatisticsByTourType**.
    g. Modify the PriceStatisticsByTourType query to display the price statistics grouped by TourType, with TourType appearing as the first field. Save your changes and then run and close the query.

12. Compact and repair the Stanley database, and then close it.

⚙ **Troubleshoot** 13. Open the **Tour** database located in the Access1 ▶ Case4 folder provided with your Data Files, and then click the Enable Content button next to the security warning, if necessary. Run the BookingByDateAndState query in the Tour database. The query is not producing the desired results. Fix the query so that the data from the Booking table is listed first, the data is sorted only by StartDate in ascending order, and the results do not display country values. Save and close the corrected query.

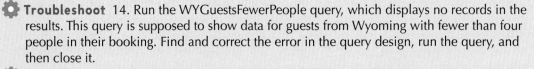 **Troubleshoot**  14. Run the WYGuestsFewerPeople query, which displays no records in the results. This query is supposed to show data for guests from Wyoming with fewer than four people in their booking. Find and correct the error in the query design, run the query, and then close it.

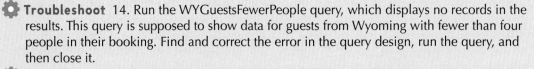 **Troubleshoot**  15. Run the CanadaOrSeptStart query. This query should display the records for all guests who are from Canada or whose booking start date is on or after 9/1/2016. Find and correct the errors in the query design, run the query, and then close it. Compact and repair the Tour database, and then close it.

TUTORIAL **4**

# Creating Forms and Reports

*Using Forms and Reports to Display Patient and Visit Data*

**ACCESS**

## OBJECTIVES

**Session 4.1**
- Create a form using the Form Wizard
- Apply a theme to a form
- Add a picture to a form
- Change the color of text on a form
- Find and maintain data using a form
- Preview and print selected form records
- Create a form with a main form and a subform

**Session 4.2**
- Create a report using the Report Wizard
- Apply a theme to a report
- Change the alignment of field values on a report
- Move and resize fields in a report
- Insert a picture in a report
- Change the color of text on a report
- Apply conditional formatting in a report
- Preview and print a report

## Case | *Chatham Community Health Services*

Cindi Rodriguez wants to continue enhancing the Chatham database to make it easier for her staff to enter, locate, and maintain data. In particular, she wants the database to include a form based on the Patient table to make it easier for staff members to enter and change data about the clinic's patients. She also wants the database to include a form that shows data from both the Patient and Visit tables at the same time. This form will show the visit information for each patient along with the corresponding patient data, providing a complete picture of Chatham Community Health Services patients and their visits to the clinic.

In addition, Ethan Ward would like the database to include a formatted report of patient and visit data so that he and other staff members will have printed output when completing patient analyses and planning strategies for community outreach efforts. He wants the information to be formatted in a professional manner, to make the report appealing and easy to use.

## STARTING DATA FILES

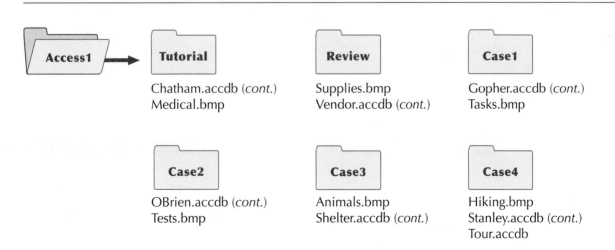

**Access1** → **Tutorial**

Chatham.accdb (*cont.*)
Medical.bmp

**Review**

Supplies.bmp
Vendor.accdb (*cont.*)

**Case1**

Gopher.accdb (*cont.*)
Tasks.bmp

**Case2**

OBrien.accdb (*cont.*)
Tests.bmp

**Case3**

Animals.bmp
Shelter.accdb (*cont.*)

**Case4**

Hiking.bmp
Stanley.accdb (*cont.*)
Tour.accdb

# Session 4.1 Visual Overview:

The form object's name is displayed on the tab for the form.

The form title appears at the top of the form. By default, the form object name is used as the form title, but you can edit the title to display the text you want, as done here—a space was added between the two words for readability.

With the Columnar form layout, the field captions appear in a column on the left side of the form. If captions had not been specified for the fields, the field names would appear here instead.

The navigation buttons allow you to display the first, last, next, or previous record in the form, enter a specific record number and move to that record, and create a new record.

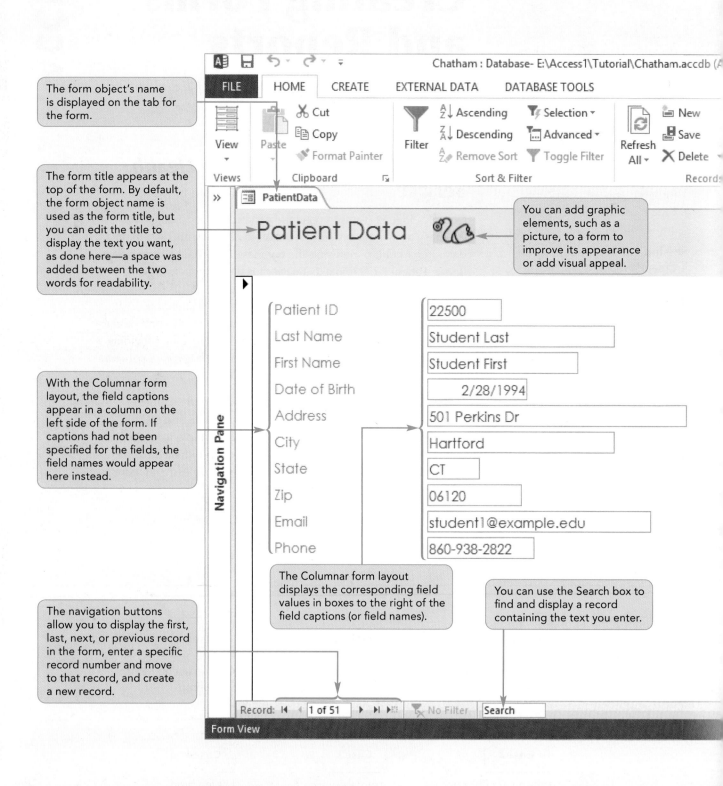

Chatham : Database- E:\Access1\Tutorial\Chatham.accdb (A

FILE   HOME   CREATE   EXTERNAL DATA   DATABASE TOOLS

View   Paste   Cut   Copy   Format Painter
Views   Clipboard

Filter   Ascending   Descending   Remove Sort   Selection   Advanced   Toggle Filter
Sort & Filter

Refresh All   New   Save   Delete
Record

PatientData

Patient Data

You can add graphic elements, such as a picture, to a form to improve its appearance or add visual appeal.

| Patient ID | 22500 |
| Last Name | Student Last |
| First Name | Student First |
| Date of Birth | 2/28/1994 |
| Address | 501 Perkins Dr |
| City | Hartford |
| State | CT |
| Zip | 06120 |
| Email | student1@example.edu |
| Phone | 860-938-2822 |

The Columnar form layout displays the corresponding field values in boxes to the right of the field captions (or field names).

You can use the Search box to find and display a record containing the text you enter.

Record: 1 of 51   No Filter   Search

Form View

# Form Displayed in Form View

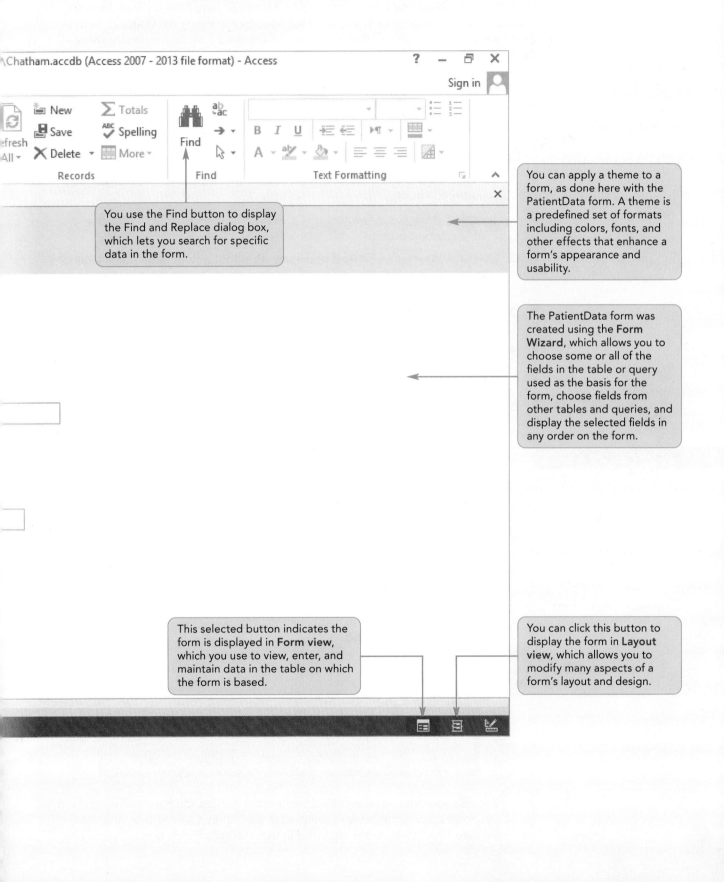

You use the Find button to display the Find and Replace dialog box, which lets you search for specific data in the form.

You can apply a theme to a form, as done here with the PatientData form. A theme is a predefined set of formats including colors, fonts, and other effects that enhance a form's appearance and usability.

The PatientData form was created using the **Form Wizard**, which allows you to choose some or all of the fields in the table or query used as the basis for the form, choose fields from other tables and queries, and display the selected fields in any order on the form.

This selected button indicates the form is displayed in **Form view**, which you use to view, enter, and maintain data in the table on which the form is based.

You can click this button to display the form in **Layout view**, which allows you to modify many aspects of a form's layout and design.

# Creating a Form Using the Form Wizard

As you learned in Tutorial 1, a form is an object you use to enter, edit, and view records in a database. You can design your own forms or have Access create them for you automatically. In Tutorial 1, you used the Form tool to create the VisitData form in the Chatham database. Recall that the Form tool creates a form automatically, using all the fields in the selected table or query.

Cindi asks you to create a new form that her staff can use to view and maintain data in the Patient table. To create the form for the Patient table, you'll use the Form Wizard, which guides you through the process.

## To open the Chatham database and start the Form Wizard:

▶ **1.** Start Access and open the **Chatham** database you created and worked with in Tutorials 1 through 3.

   **Trouble?** If the security warning is displayed below the ribbon, click the Enable Content button.

▶ **2.** Open the Navigation Pane, if necessary. To create a form based on a table or query, you can select the table or query in the Navigation Pane first, or you can select it using the Form Wizard.

▶ **3.** In the Tables section of the Navigation Pane, click **Patient** to select the Patient table as the basis for the new form.

▶ **4.** On the ribbon, click the **CREATE** tab. The Forms group on the CREATE tab provides options for creating various types of forms and designing your own forms.

▶ **5.** In the Forms group, click the **Form Wizard** button. The first Form Wizard dialog box opens. See Figure 4-1.

| Figure 4-1 | First Form Wizard dialog box |
|---|---|

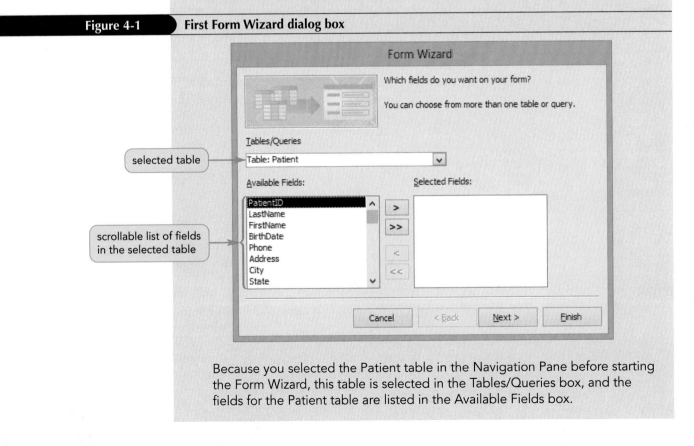

Because you selected the Patient table in the Navigation Pane before starting the Form Wizard, this table is selected in the Tables/Queries box, and the fields for the Patient table are listed in the Available Fields box.

# Modifying a Form's Design in Layout View

After you create a form, you might need to modify its design in Layout view to improve its appearance or to make the form easier to use. In Layout view, you see the form as it appears in Form view, but you can still modify the form's design; in Form view, you cannot make any design changes. Because you can see the form and its data while you are modifying the form, Layout view makes it easy for you to see the results of any design changes you make. You can continue to make changes, undo modifications, and rework the design in Layout view to achieve the look you want for the form.

The first modification you'll make to the PatientData form is to change its appearance by applying a theme.

## Applying a Theme to a Form

By default, a form you create is formatted with the Office theme, which determines the color and font used on the form. Access, like other Microsoft Office programs, provides many built-in themes, including the Office theme, making it easy for you to create objects with a unified look. You can also create a customized theme if none of the built-in themes suit your needs. To change a form's appearance, you can easily apply a new theme to it.

**REFERENCE**

**Applying a Theme to a Form**

- Display the form in Layout view.
- In the Themes group on the DESIGN tab, click the Themes button.
- In the displayed gallery, click the theme you want to apply to all objects; or, right-click the theme to display the shortcut menu, and then choose to apply the theme to the current object only or to all matching objects.

Cindi would like to see if the PatientData form's appearance can be improved with a different theme. To apply a theme, you first need to switch to Layout view.

**To apply a theme to the PatientData form:**

1. Make sure the HOME tab is displayed.

2. In the Views group, click the **View** button. The form is displayed in Layout view. See Figure 4-4.

**Figure 4-4**    **Form displayed in Layout view**

Themes button

FILE    HOME    CREATE    EXTERNAL DATA    DATABASE TOOLS    DESIGN    ARRANGE    FORMAT    FORM LAYOUT TOOLS    Chatham : Database- E:\

View    Themes    Colors ▾    Fonts ▾

Views    Themes    Controls    Insert Image ▾

PatientData

PatientData

DESIGN tab displays options for changing the form's appearance

| Patient ID | 22500 |
| Last Name | Student Last |
| First Name | Student First |
| Date of Birth | 2/28/1994 |
| Address | 501 Perkins Dr |
| City | Hartford |
| State | CT |
| Zip | 06120 |
| Email | student1@example.edu |
| Phone | 860-938-2822 |

orange outline indicates the selected object

Navigation Pane

Record: I◄ ◄ 1 of 51 ► ►I ►  No Filter  Search

Layout View

**Trouble?** If the Field List or Property Sheet opens on the right side of your window, close it before continuing.

You can use Layout view to modify an existing form. In Layout view, an orange outline identifies the currently selected object on the form. In this case, the field value for the PatientID field, 22500, is selected. You need to apply a theme to the PatientData form.

**3.** In the Themes group on the DESIGN tab, click the **Themes** button. A gallery opens showing the available themes for the form. See Figure 4-5.

**Figure 4-5**    Themes gallery displayed

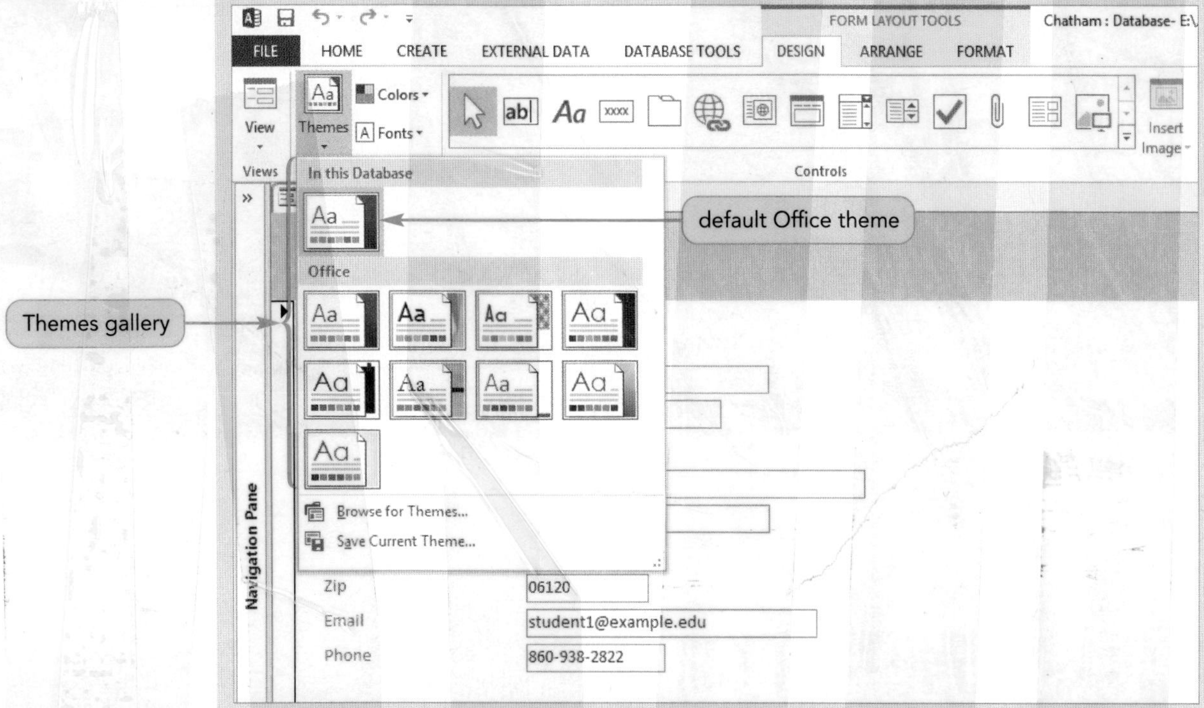

The Office theme, which is shown in the "In this Database" section and is also the first theme listed in the section containing other themes, is the default theme currently applied in the database. Each theme provides a design scheme for the colors and fonts used in the database objects. You can point to each theme in the gallery to see its name in a ScreenTip. Also, when you point to a theme, the Live Preview feature shows the effect of applying the theme to the open object.

**TIP**

Themes other than the Office theme are listed in alphabetical order in the gallery.

4. In the gallery, point to each of the themes to see how they would format the PatientData form. Notice the changes in color and font type of the text, for example.

   **Trouble?** If you click a theme by mistake, repeat Step 3 to redisplay the gallery, and then continue to Step 5.

   Cindi likes the Slice theme because of its bright blue color in the title area at the top and its larger font size, which makes the text in the form easier to read. She asks you to apply this theme to the form.

5. Right-click the **Slice** theme. A shortcut menu opens with options for applying the theme. See Figure 4-6.

**Figure 4-6**    **Shortcut menu for applying the theme**

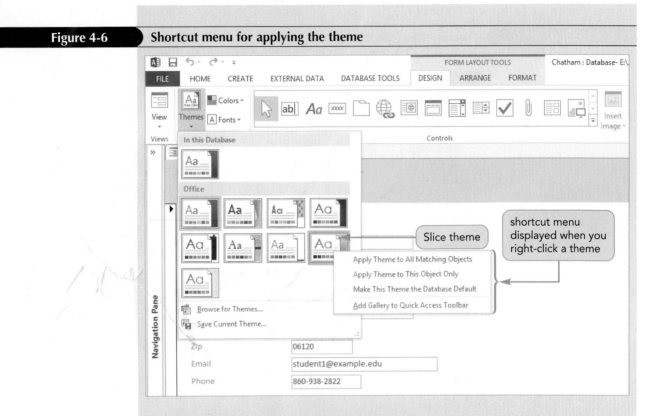

The menu provides options for applying the theme to all matching objects—for example, all the forms in the database—or to the current object only. You can also choose to make the theme the default theme in the database, which means any new objects you create will be formatted with the selected theme. Because Cindi is not sure if all forms in the Chatham database will look better with the Slice theme, she asks you to apply it only to the PatientData form.

Choose this option to avoid applying the theme to other forms in the database.

▶ **6.** On the shortcut menu, click **Apply Theme to This Object Only**.

The gallery closes, and Access formats the form's colors and fonts with the Slice theme.

**Trouble?** If you choose the wrong option by mistake, you might have applied the selected theme to other forms and/or reports in the database. Repeat Steps 3 through 6 to apply the Slice theme to the PatientData form. You can also follow the same process to reapply the default Office theme to the other forms and reports in the Chatham database, as directed by your instructor.

## Working with Themes

Themes provide a quick and easy way for you to format the objects in a database with a consistent look, which is a good design principle to follow. In general, all objects of a type in a database—for example, all forms—should have a consistent design. However, keep in mind that when you select a theme in the Themes gallery and choose the option to apply the theme to all matching objects or to make the theme the default for the database, Access might apply it to *all* the existing forms and reports in the database as well as to new forms and reports you create. Although this ensures a consistent design, this approach can cause problems. For example, if you have already created a form or report and its design is suitable, applying a theme that includes a larger font size could cause the text in labels and field value boxes to be cut off or to extend into other objects on the form or report. The colors applied by the theme could also interfere with elements on existing forms and reports. To handle these unintended results, you would have to spend time checking the existing forms and reports and fixing any problems introduced by applying the theme. A better approach is to select the option "Apply Theme to This Object Only," available on the shortcut menu for a theme in the Themes gallery, for each existing form and report. If the newly applied theme causes problems for any individual form or report, you can then reapply the original theme to return the object to its original design.

Next, Cindi asks you to add a picture to the form for visual interest. The picture, which is included on various flyers and other patient correspondence for Chatham Community Health Services, is a small graphic of a stethoscope. You'll add this picture to the form.

## Adding a Picture to a Form

A picture is one of many controls you can add and modify on a form. A **control** is an item on a form, report, or other database object that you can manipulate to modify the object's appearance. The controls you can add and modify in Layout view for a form are available in the Controls group and the Header/Footer group on the DESIGN tab. The picture you need to add is contained in a file named Medical.bmp, which is located in the Access1 ▸ Tutorial folder provided with your Data Files.

### To add the picture to the form:

1. Make sure the form is still displayed in Layout view and that the DESIGN tab is active.

2. In the Header/Footer group, click the **Logo** button. The Insert Picture dialog box opens.

3. Navigate to the **Access1 ▸ Tutorial** folder provided with your Data Files, click the **Medical** file, and then click the **OK** button. The picture appears as a selected object on top of the form's title. See Figure 4-7.

| Figure 4-7 | Form with picture added |

picture appears on the form title and is selected

move picture to here

control layout containing the picture

A solid orange outline surrounds the picture, indicating it is selected. The picture is placed in a **control layout**, which is a set of controls grouped together in a form or report so that you can manipulate the set as a single control. The dotted bright blue outline indicates the control layout (see Figure 4-7). The easiest way to move the picture off the form title is to first remove it from the control layout. Doing so allows you to move the picture independently.

4. Right-click the selected picture to display the shortcut menu, point to **Layout**, and then click **Remove Layout**. The picture is removed from the control layout. Now you can move the picture to the right of the form title.

5. Position the pointer ⁺↖ on the picture, and then click and drag the picture to the right to move it to the right of the form title.

**TIP**

You can resize a selected image by dragging one of its corners.

6. When the pointer is roughly one-half inch to the right of the form's title, release the mouse button. The picture is positioned to the right of the form title.

7. Click in a blank area on the main form (to the right of the field values) to deselect the picture. See Figure 4-8.

**Trouble?** Don't be concerned if your picture is not in the exact location as the one shown in Figure 4-8. Just make sure the picture is not blocking any part of the form title and that it appears to the right of the form title and within the blue shaded area at the top of the form. Also, if your picture is too large or too small, you can resize it by first selecting it and then dragging a corner of the orange outline in the appropriate direction to increase or decrease the picture size.

**Figure 4-8**   **Form with theme applied and picture repositioned**

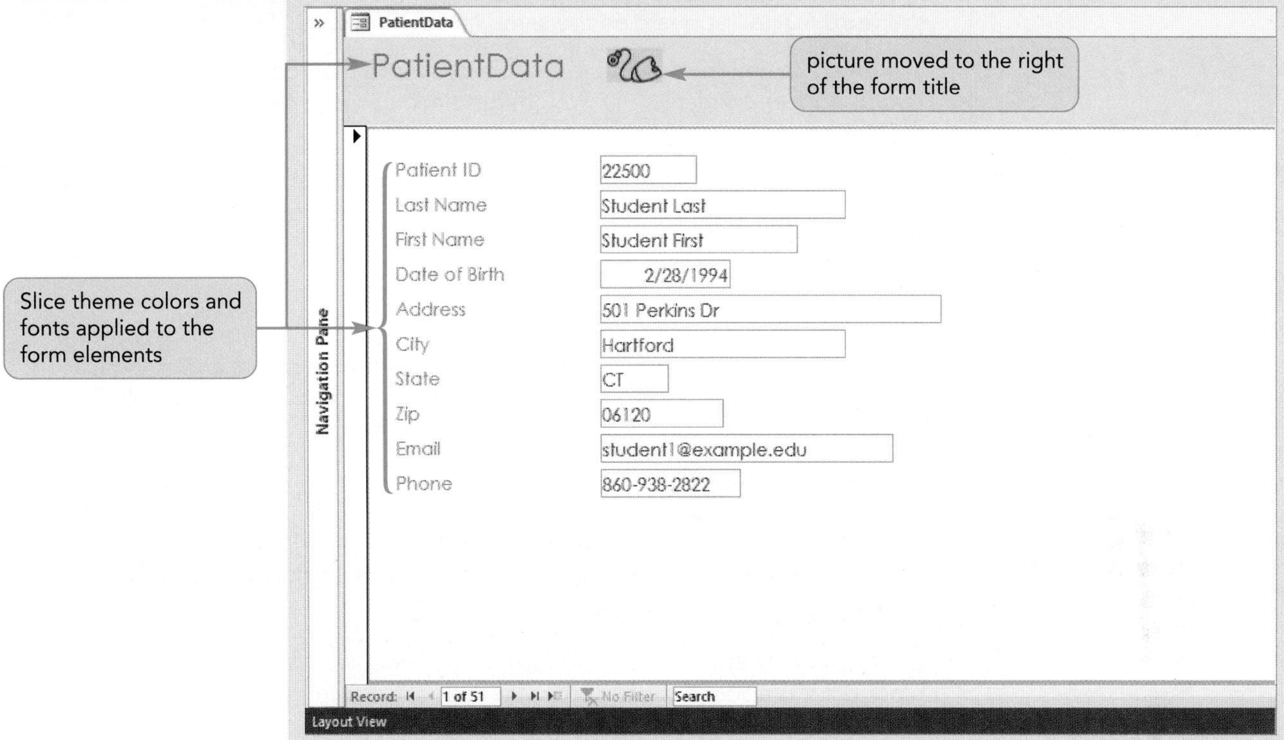

**PatientData**

picture moved to the right of the form title

Slice theme colors and fonts applied to the form elements

| | |
|---|---|
| Patient ID | 22500 |
| Last Name | Student Last |
| First Name | Student First |
| Date of Birth | 2/28/1994 |
| Address | 501 Perkins Dr |
| City | Hartford |
| State | CT |
| Zip | 06120 |
| Email | student1@example.edu |
| Phone | 860-938-2822 |

Record: ◄ ◄ 1 of 51 ► ►I ►☐   No Filter   Search

Layout View

Next, Cindi asks you to change the color of the form title to a darker color so that it will coordinate better with the picture next to the title and stand out more on the form.

## Changing the Color of the Form Title

The Font group on the FORMAT tab provides many options you can use to change the appearance of text on a form. For example, you can bold, italicize, and underline text; change the font, font color, and font size; and change the alignment of text. Before you change the color of the "PatientData" title on the form, you'll change the title to two words so it is easier to read.

### To change the form title's text and color:

1. Click the **PatientData** form title. An orange box surrounds the title, indicating it is selected.

2. Click between the letters "t" and "D" to position the insertion point, and then press the **spacebar**. The title on the form is now "Patient Data" but the added space caused the words to appear on two lines. You can fix this by resizing the box containing the title.

**TIP**

Changing the form's title does not affect the form object name; it is still PatientData, as shown on the object tab.

**3.** Position the pointer on the right vertical line of the box containing the form title until the pointer changes to ↔, and then click and drag to the right until the word "Data" appears on the same line as the word "Patient."

> **Trouble?** You might need to repeat Step 3 more than once in order for the text to appear correctly. Also, you might have to move the picture further to the right to make room for the title.

**4.** Click in the main form area again to deselect the title and check the results, and then click **Patient Data** to reselect the title. The orange outline appears around the words of the title.

**5.** On the ribbon, click the **FORMAT** tab.

**6.** In the Font group, click the **Font Color button arrow** [A ▾] to display the gallery of available colors. The gallery provides theme colors and standard colors, as well as an option for creating a custom color. The theme colors available depend on the theme applied to the form—in this case, the colors are related to the Slice theme. The current color of the title text—Black, Text 1, Lighter 50%—is outlined in the gallery, indicating it is selected.

**7.** In the Theme Colors palette, point to the second color box in the fourth row of boxes. The ScreenTip indicates this is the Black, Text 1, Lighter 25% color.

**8.** Click the **Black, Text 1, Lighter 25%** color box.

**9.** Click in a blank area of the main form to deselect the title text. The darker black color is applied to the form title text, coordinating it with the picture on the form. See Figure 4-9.

| Figure 4-9 | Form title with new color applied |
|---|---|

form title in a darker black font and edited with a space between words

You have made a couple of changes to the form, and should save it now.

**10.** On the Quick Access Toolbar, click the **Save** button [💾] to save the modified form.

**11.** In the bottom right section of the status bar, click the **Form View** button [▦] to display the form in Form view. Refer back to the Session 4.1 Visual Overview; your form should match the PatientData form shown there.

Cindi is pleased with the modified appearance of the form. Later, she plans to revise the existing VisitData form and make the same changes to it, so that it matches the appearance of the PatientData form.

**PROSKILLS**

### Written Communication: Understanding the Importance of Form Design

Similar to any document, a form must convey written information clearly and effectively. When you create a form, it's important to consider how the form will be used, so that its design will accommodate the needs of people using the form to view, enter, and maintain data. For example, if a form in a database mimics a paper form that users will enter data from, the form in the database should have the same fields in the same order as those on the paper form. This will enable users to easily tab from one field to the next in the database form to enter the necessary information from the paper form. Also, it's important to include a meaningful title on the form to identify its purpose and to enhance the appearance of the form. A form that is visually appealing makes working with the database more user-friendly and can improve the readability of the form, thereby helping to prevent errors in data entry. Also, be sure to use a consistent design for the forms in your database whenever possible. Users will expect to see similar elements—titles, pictures, fonts, and so on—in each form contained in a database. A mix of form styles and elements among the forms in a database could lead to problems when working with the forms. Finally, make sure the text on your form does not contain any spelling or grammatical errors. By producing a well-designed and well-written form, you can help to ensure that users will be able to work with the form in a productive and efficient manner.

## Navigating a Form

Cindi wants to use the PatientData form to view some data in the Patient table. As you saw earlier, you use Layout view to modify the appearance of a form. To view, navigate, and change data using a form, you need to display the form in Form view. As you learned in Tutorial 1, you navigate a form in the same way that you navigate a table datasheet. Also, the navigation mode and editing mode keyboard shortcuts you used with datasheets in Tutorial 3 are the same when navigating a form.

The PatientData form is already displayed in Form view, so you can use it to navigate through the fields and records of the Patient table.

### To navigate the PatientData form:

1. If necessary, click in the Patient ID field value box to make it current.

2. Press the **Tab** key twice to move to the First Name field value box, and then press the **End** key to move to the Phone field value box.

3. Press the **Home** key to move back to the Patient ID field value box. The first record in the Patient table still appears in the form.

4. Press the **Ctrl+End** keys to move to the Phone field value box for record 51, which is the last record in the table. The record number for the current record appears in the Current Record box between the navigation buttons at the bottom of the form.

5. Click the **Previous record** navigation button ◀ to move to the Phone field value box in record 50.

6. Press the ↑ key twice to move to the Zip field value box in record 50.

7. Click to position the insertion point between the numbers "8" and "3" in the Address field value to switch to editing mode, press the **Home** key to move the insertion point to the beginning of the field value, and then press the **End** key to move the insertion point to the end of the field value.

> **8.** Click the **First record** navigation button ⏮ to move to the Address field value box in the first record. The entire field value is highlighted because you switched from editing mode to navigation mode.

> **9.** Click the **Next record** navigation button ▶ to move to the Address field value box in record 2, the next record.

Next, Cindi asks you to find the record for a patient named Sam. The paper form containing all the original contact information for this patient was damaged. Other than the patient's first name, Cindi knows only the street the patient lives on. Now she wants to use the form to view the complete data for this patient so she can contact the patient and make any necessary corrections.

# Finding Data Using a Form

As you learned in Tutorial 3, the Find command lets you search for data in a datasheet so you can display only those records you want to view. You can also use the Find command to search for data in a form. You choose a field to serve as the basis for the search by making that field the current field, and then you enter the value you want Access to match in the Find and Replace dialog box.

**REFERENCE**

*Finding Data in a Form or Datasheet*

- Open the form or datasheet, and then make the field you want to search the current field.
- In the Find group on the HOME tab, click the Find button to open the Find and Replace dialog box.
- In the Find What box, type the field value you want to find.
- Complete the remaining options, as necessary, to specify the type of search to conduct.
- Click the Find Next button to begin the search.
- Click the Find Next button to continue searching for the next match.
- Click the Cancel button to stop the search operation.

You need to find the record for the patient Cindi wants to contact. In addition to the patient's first name (Sam), Cindi knows the name of the street on which this patient lives—Bunnell Place—so you'll search for the record using the Address field.

**To find the record using the PatientData form:**

> **1.** Make sure the **Address** field value is still selected for the current record. This is the field you need to search.

   You can search for a record that contains part of the address anywhere in the Address field value. Performing a partial search such as this is often easier than matching the entire field value and is useful when you don't know or can't remember the entire field value.

> **2.** In the Find group on the HOME tab, click the **Find** button. The Find and Replace dialog box opens. The Look In box shows that the current field (in this case, Address) will be searched. You'll search for records that contain the word "bunnell" in the address.

3. In the Find What box, type **bunnell**. Note that you do not have to enter the word as "Bunnell" with a capital letter "B" because the Match Case option is not selected in the Find and Replace dialog box. Access will find any record containing the word "bunnell" with any combination of uppercase and lowercase letters.

4. Click the **Match** arrow to display the list of matching options, and then click **Any Part of Field**. Access will find any record that contains the word "bunnell" in any part of the Address field. See Figure 4-10.

| Figure 4-10 | Completed Find and Replace dialog box |
| --- | --- |

search value entered

specifies that Access will search the current field

specifies that Access will search for the value in any part of the current field

5. Click the **Find Next** button. The PatientData form now displays record 37, which is the record for Sam Boucher (PatientID 22543). The word "Bunnell" is selected in the Address field value box because you searched for this word. Cindi calls the patient and confirms that all the information is correct.

The search value you enter can be an exact value or it can include wildcard characters. A **wildcard character** is a placeholder you use when you know only part of a value or when you want to start or end with a specific character or match a certain pattern. Figure 4-11 shows the wildcard characters you can use when finding data.

| Figure 4-11 | Wildcard characters |
| --- | --- |

| Wildcard Character | Purpose | Example |
| --- | --- | --- |
| * | Match any number of characters. It can be used as the first and/or last character in the character string. | th* finds the, that, this, therefore, and so on |
| ? | Match any single alphabetic character. | a?t finds act, aft, ant, apt, and art |
| [] | Match any single character within the brackets. | a[fr]t finds aft and art but not act, ant, or apt |
| ! | Match any character not within brackets. | a[!fr]t finds act, ant, and apt but not aft or art |
| - | Match any one of a range of characters. The range must be in ascending order (a to z, not z to a). | a[d-p]t finds aft, ant, and apt but not act or art |
| # | Match any single numeric character. | #72 finds 072, 172, 272, 372, and so on |

© 2014 Cengage Learning

Next, to see how a wildcard works, you'll view the records for any patients with phone numbers that contain the exchange 226 as part of the phone number. The exchange consists of the three digits that follow the area code in the phone number. You could search for any record containing the digits 226 in any part of the Phone field, but this search would also find records with the digits 226 in any part of the phone number. To find only those records with the digits 226 as the exchange, you'll use the * wildcard character.

---

### To find the records using the * wildcard character:

▶ **1.** Make sure the Find and Replace dialog box is still open.

▶ **2.** Click anywhere in the PatientData form to make it active, and then press the **Tab** key until you reach the Phone field value box. This is the field you want to search.

▶ **3.** Click the title bar of the Find and Replace dialog box to make it active, and then drag the Find and Replace dialog box to the right so you can see the Phone field on the form, if necessary. The Look In box setting is still Current field, which is now the Phone field; this is the field that will be searched.

▶ **4.** Double-click **bunnell** in the Find What box to select the entire value, and then type **860-226***.

▶ **5.** Click the **Match** arrow, and then click **Whole Field**. Because you're using a wildcard character in the search value, you want Access to search the whole field.

   With the settings you've entered, Access will find records in which any field value in the Phone field begins with the area code 860 followed by a hyphen and the exchange 226.

▶ **6.** Click the **Find Next** button. Access displays record 46, which is the first record found for a customer with the exchange 226. Notice that the search process started from the point of the previously displayed record in the form, which was record 37.

▶ **7.** Click the **Find Next** button. Access displays record 5, which is the next record found for a customer with the exchange 226. Notice that the search process cycles back through the beginning of the records in the underlying table.

▶ **8.** Click the **Find Next** button. Access displays record 11, the third record found.

▶ **9.** Click the **Find Next** button. Access displays record 23, the fourth record found.

▶ **10.** Click the **Find Next** button. Access displays record 34.

▶ **11.** Click the **Find Next** button. Access displays record 37 for Sam Boucher; this is the patient record that was active when you started the search process.

▶ **12.** Click the **Find Next** button. Access displays a dialog box informing you that the search is finished.

▶ **13.** Click the **OK** button to close the dialog box.

▶ **14.** Click the **Cancel** button to close the Find and Replace dialog box.

---

Cindi has identified some patient updates she wants you to make. You'll use the PatientData form to update the data in the Patient table.

## Maintaining Table Data Using a Form

Maintaining data using a form is often easier than using a datasheet because you can focus on all the changes for a single record at one time. In Form view, you can edit the field values for a record, delete a record from the underlying table, or add a new record to the table. You already know how to navigate a form and find specific records. Now you'll use the PatientData form to make the changes Cindi wants to the Patient table.

First, you'll update the record for Felipe Ramos. This patient recently moved from Hartford to West Hartford and provided an email address, so you need to update the necessary fields for this patient. In addition to using the Find and Replace dialog box to locate a specific record, you can use the Search box to the right of the navigation buttons. You'll use the Search box to search for the patient's last name, Ramos, and display the patient record in the form.

### To change the record using the PatientData form:

1. To the right of the navigation buttons, click the **Search** box and then type **Ramos**. As soon as you start to type, Access begins searching through all fields in the records to match your entry. Record 33 (Felipe Ramos) is now current.

   You need to update this record with the new information for this patient.

**TIP**

Note that the pencil symbol appears in the upper-left corner of the form, indicating that the form is in editing mode.

2. Select the current entry in the Address field value box, and then type **145 Jackson Dr** to replace it.

3. Click at the beginning of the City field value box, type **West** and then press the **spacebar**. The City field value is now West Hartford.

4. Press the **Tab** key twice to move to and select the Zip field value, and then type **06117**.

5. Press the **Tab** key to move to the Email field value box, and then type **f.ramos@example.org** for the new email address.

6. Click to place the insertion point at the end of the value in the Phone field value box, press the **Backspace** key to delete everything except the area code and first dash, and then type **637-8841**. The Phone field value is now 860-637-8841. The updates to the record are complete. See Figure 4-12.

**Figure 4-12**     Patient record after changing field values

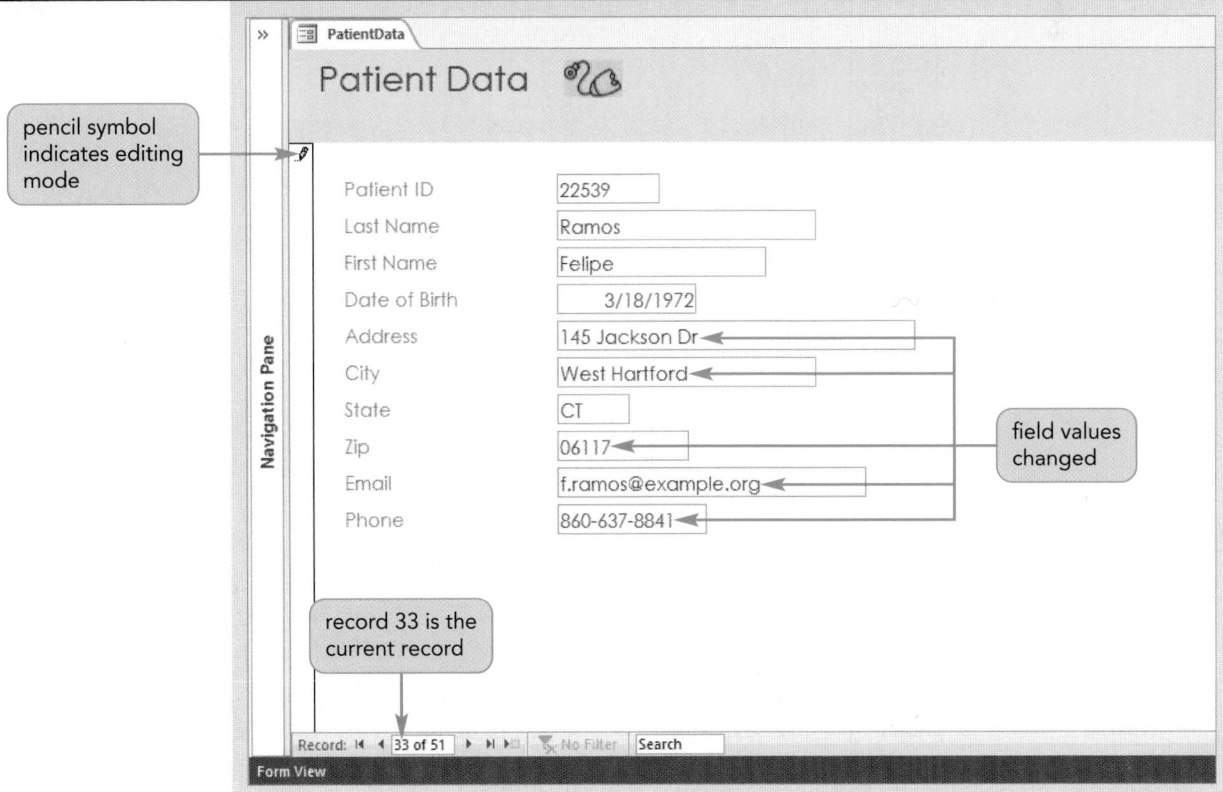

Next, Cindi asks you to add a record for a new patient. This person signed up to be a patient of the clinic at a recent health fair held by Chatham Community Health Services, but has not yet visited the clinic. You'll use the PatientData form to add the new record.

### To add the new record using the PatientData form:

1. In the Records group on the HOME tab, click the **New** button. Record 52, the next available new record, becomes the current record. All field value boxes are empty (except the State field, which displays the default value of CT) and the insertion point is positioned in the Patient ID field value box.

2. Refer to Figure 4-13 and enter the value shown for each field. Press the **Tab** key to move from field to field.

**Figure 4-13**    Completed form for the new record

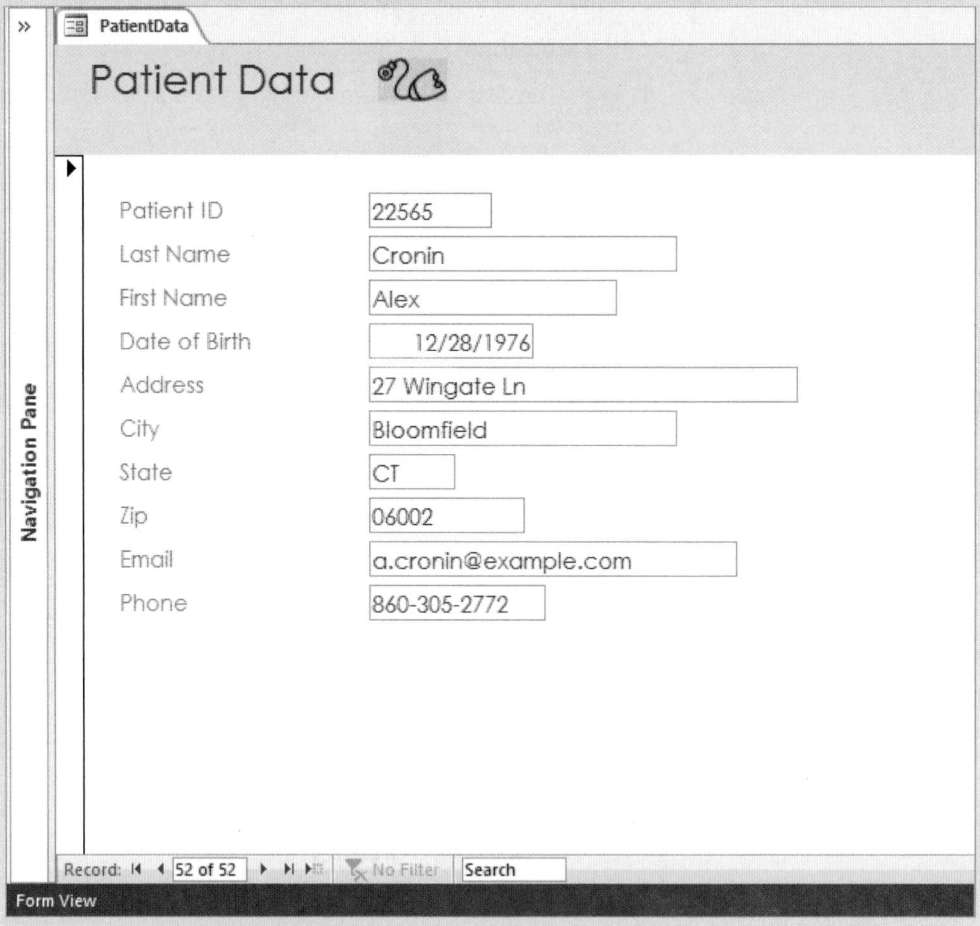

**Trouble?** Compare your screen with Figure 4-13. If any field value is incorrect, correct it now, using the methods described earlier for editing field values.

3. After entering the Phone field value, press the **Tab** key. Record 53, the next available new record, becomes the current record, and the record for PatientID 22565 is saved in the Patient table.

Cindi would like a printed copy of the PatientData form to show to her staff members. She asks you to print one form record.

# Previewing and Printing Selected Form Records

Access prints as many form records as can fit on a printed page. If only part of a form record fits on the bottom of a page, the remainder of the record prints on the next page. Access allows you to print all pages or a range of pages. In addition, you can print the currently selected form record.

Cindi asks you to use the PatientData form to print the first record in the Patient table. Before you do, you'll preview the form record to see how it will look when printed.

### To preview the form and print the data for record 1:

▶ 1. Click the **First record** navigation button 🔢 to display record 1 in the form. This is the record in which you have entered your first and last names.

▶ 2. Click the **FILE** tab to display Backstage view, click **Print** in the navigation bar, and then click **Print Preview**. The Print Preview window opens, showing the form records for the Patient table. Notice that each record appears in its own form, and that shading is used to distinguish one record from another. See Figure 4-14.

| Figure 4-14 | Form records displayed in Print Preview |
|---|---|

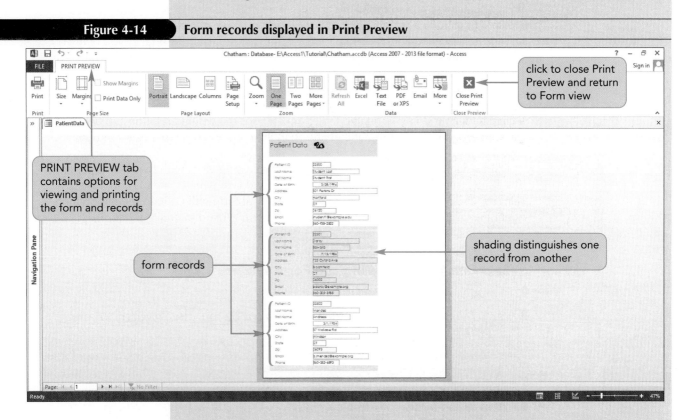

To print one selected record on a page by itself, you need to close Print Preview and then use the Print dialog box.

▶ 3. In the Close Preview group on the PRINT PREVIEW tab, click the **Close Print Preview** button. You return to Form view with the first record still displayed.

▶ 4. Click the **FILE** tab to display Backstage view again, click **Print** in the navigation bar, and then click **Print**. The Print dialog box opens.

▶ **5.** Click the **Selected Record(s)** option button to print the current form record (record 1).

**Trouble?** Check with your instructor to be sure you should print the form; then continue to the next step. If you should not print the form, click the Cancel button, and then skip to Step 7.

▶ **6.** Click the **OK** button to close the dialog box and print the selected record.

▶ **7.** Close the PatientData form.

After reviewing the printed PatientData form with her staff, Cindi realizes that it would be helpful for staff members to also have a form showing information about both patients and their visits.

# Creating a Form with a Main Form and a Subform

Cindi would like you to create a form so that she can view the data for each patient and the patient's visits to the clinic at the same time. The type of form you need to create will include a main form and a subform. To create a form based on two tables, you must first define a relationship between the two tables. In Tutorial 2, you defined a one-to-many relationship between the Patient (primary) and Visit (related) tables, so you can now create a form based on both tables.

When you create a form containing data from two tables that have a one-to-many relationship, you actually create a **main form** for data from the primary table and a **subform** for data from the related table. Access uses the defined relationship between the tables to join them automatically through the common field that exists in both tables.

Cindi and her staff will use the form when discussing visits with the clinic's patients. The main form will contain the patient ID, first and last names, date of birth, phone number, and email address for each patient. The subform will contain the information about the visits for each patient. You'll use the Form Wizard to create the form.

**To create the form using the Form Wizard:**

▶ **1.** On the ribbon, click the **CREATE** tab.

▶ **2.** In the Forms group, click the **Form Wizard** button. The first Form Wizard dialog box opens.

When creating a form based on two tables, you first choose the primary table and select the fields you want to include in the main form; then you choose the related table and select fields from it for the subform.

▶ **3.** If necessary, click the **Tables/Queries** arrow, and then click **Table: Patient**.

Cindi wants the form to include only the PatientID, FirstName, LastName, BirthDate, Phone, and Email fields from the Patient table.

▶ **4.** Click **PatientID** in the Available Fields box (if necessary), and then click the ☐ > ☐ button to move the field to the Selected Fields box.

▶ **5.** Repeat Step 4 for the **FirstName**, **LastName**, **BirthDate**, **Phone**, and **Email** fields.

The PatientID field will appear in the main form, so you do not have to include it in the subform. Otherwise, Cindi wants the subform to include all the fields from the Visit table.

**6.** Click the **Tables/Queries** arrow, and then click **Table: Visit**. The fields from the Visit table appear in the Available Fields box. The quickest way to add the fields you want to include is to move all the fields to the Selected Fields box, and then remove the only field you don't want to include (PatientID).

**7.** Click the >> button to move all the fields in the Visit table to the Selected Fields box.

**8.** Click **Visit.PatientID** in the Selected Fields box, and then click the < button to move the field back to the Available Fields box.

**9.** Click the **Next** button. The next Form Wizard dialog box opens. See Figure 4-15.

**TIP**

The table name (Visit) is included in the PatientID field name to distinguish it from the same field in the Patient table.

**Figure 4-15**    **Choosing a format for the main form and subform**

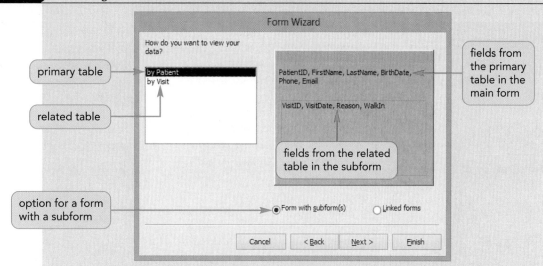

primary table

related table

option for a form with a subform

fields from the primary table in the main form

fields from the related table in the subform

In this dialog box, the section on the left shows the order in which you will view the selected data: first by data from the primary Patient table, and then by data from the related Visit table. The form will be displayed as shown on the right side of the dialog box, with the fields from the Patient table at the top in the main form, and the fields from the Visit table at the bottom in the subform. The selected "Form with subform(s)" option button specifies a main form with a subform. The Linked forms option creates a form structure in which only the main form fields are displayed. A button with the subform's name on it appears on the main form; you can click this button to display the associated subform records.

The default options shown in Figure 4-15 are correct for creating a form with Patient data in the main form and Visit data in the subform.

**To finish creating the form:**

**1.** Click the **Next** button. The next Form Wizard dialog box opens, in which you choose the subform layout.

The Tabular layout displays subform fields as a table, whereas the Datasheet layout displays subform fields as a table datasheet. The layout choice is a matter of personal preference. You'll use the Datasheet layout.

▶ **2.** Click the **Datasheet** option button to select it (if necessary), and then click the **Next** button. The next Form Wizard dialog box opens, in which you choose titles for the main form and the subform.

You'll use the title "PatientVisits" for the main form and the title "VisitSubform" for the subform. These titles will also be the names for the form objects.

▶ **3.** In the Form box, click to position the insertion point to the right of the last letter, and then type **Visits**. The main form name is now PatientVisits.

▶ **4.** In the Subform box, delete the space between the two words so that the subform name appears as **VisitSubform**.

▶ **5.** Click the **Finish** button. The completed form opens in Form view. See Figure 4-16.

| Figure 4-16 | Main form with subform in Form view |
| --- | --- |

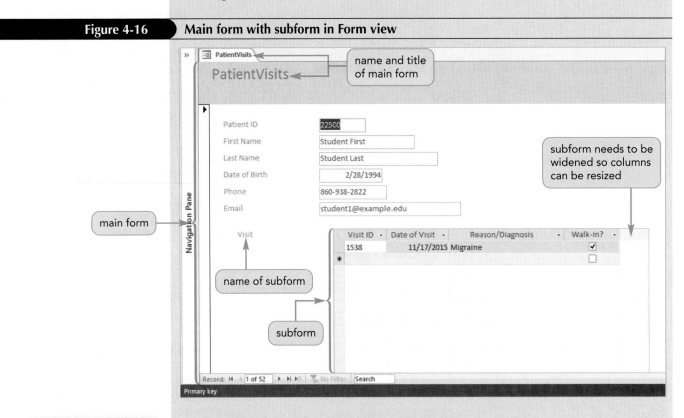

**TIP**

The PatientVisits form is formatted with the default Office theme because you applied the Slice theme only to the PatientData form.

In the main form, Access displays the fields from the first record in the Patient table in a columnar format. The records in the main form appear in primary key order by PatientID. PatientID 22500 has one related record in the Visit table; this record, for VisitID 1538, is shown in the subform, which uses the datasheet format. The main form name, "PatientVisits," appears on the object tab and as the form title. The name of the subform appears to the left of the subform. Note that only the word "Visit" and not the complete name "VisitSubform" appears on the form. Access displays only the table name for the subform itself, but displays the complete name of the object, "VisitSubform," when you view and work with objects in the Navigation Pane.

The subform designation is necessary in a list of database objects so that you can distinguish the Visit subform from other objects, such as the Visit table, but the subform designation is not needed in the PatientVisits form. Only the table name is required to identify the table containing the records in the subform.

Next, you need to make some changes to the form. First, you'll edit the form title to add a space between the words so that it appears as "Patient Visits." Then, you'll resize the subform. Cindi is concerned that the subform is not wide enough to allow for all the columns to be resized and fully display their field values, especially the Reason/Diagnosis column. To make these changes, you need to switch to Layout view.

### To modify the PatientVisits form in Layout view:

1. In the Views group on the HOME tab, click the **View** button to switch to Layout view.

2. Click **PatientVisits** in the blue-gray area at the top of the form. The form title is selected.

3. Click between the letters "t" and "V" to place the insertion point, and then press the **spacebar**. The title on the form is now "Patient Visits."

4. Click in a blank area of the form to the right of the field value boxes to deselect the title. Next, you'll increase the width of the subform.

5. Click the subform. An orange outline surrounds the subform, indicating it is selected.

6. Position the pointer on the right vertical line of the selected subform until the pointer changes to a ↔ shape, and then click and drag to the right approximately two inches. The subform is now wider. See Figure 4-17.

Figure 4-17    Modified form in Layout view

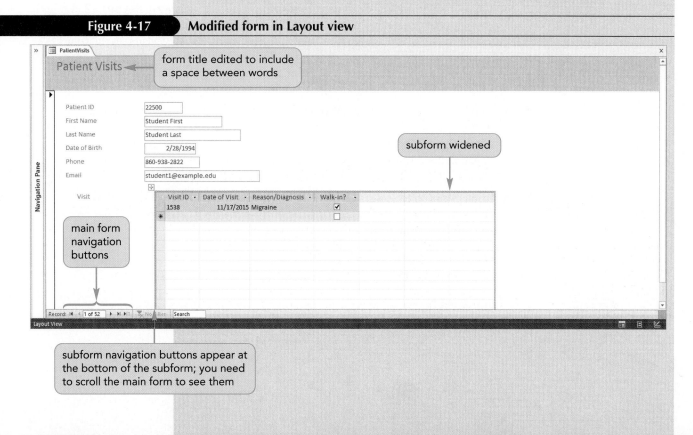

The wider subform will enable you to resize the Reason/Diagnosis column, as necessary, to fully display its field values.

▶ 7. On the Quick Access Toolbar, click the **Save** button 🖫 to save both the main form and the subform.

▶ 8. In the Views group on the DESIGN tab, click the **View** button to display the PatientVisits form in Form view.

**Trouble?** If the fields in the main form are partially out of view, use the vertical scroll bar to scroll to the top of the form and display the fields.

The form includes two sets of navigation buttons. You use the set of navigation buttons at the bottom of the Form window to select records from the primary table in the main form (see Figure 4-17). The second set of navigation buttons is currently not visible; you need to scroll down the main form to see these buttons, which appear at the bottom of the subform. You use the subform navigation buttons to select records from the related table in the subform.

You'll use the navigation buttons to view different records.

### To navigate to different main form and subform records:

▶ 1. In the main form, click the **Next record** navigation button ▶ six times. Record 7 of 52 total records in the Patient table (for Matthew Weiss) becomes the current record in the main form. The subform shows that this patient made three visits to the clinic. Note that the field values in the Reason/Diagnosis column are not fully displayed.

▶ 2. Double-click the pointer ⬌ on the right vertical line of the Reason/Diagnosis column in the subform to resize this field to its best fit and display the complete field values.

> **TIP**
>
> As you move through the form/subform, notice that some field values in the subform are not completely visible. You can resize any subform field to its best fit to fully display the field values.

▶ 3. In the main form, click the **Last record** navigation button ▶|. Record 52 in the Patient table (for Alex Cronin) becomes the current record in the main form. The subform shows that this patient currently has no visits; recall that you just entered this record using the PatientData form. Cindi could use the subform to enter the information for this patient's visits to the clinic, and that information will be updated in the Visit table.

▶ 4. In the main form, click the **Previous record** navigation button ◀. Record 51 in the Patient table (for Daniel Shaw) becomes the current record in the main form. The subform shows that this patient has made one visit to the clinic. If you know the number of the record you want to view, you can enter the number in the Current Record box to move to that record.

▶ 5. In the main form, select **51** in the Current Record box, type **47**, and then press the **Enter** key. Record 47 in the Patient table (for Isobel Kirk) becomes the current record in the main form. The subform shows that this patient made four visits to the clinic.

▶ **6.** In the subform, resize the Reason/Diagnosis column to its best fit to fully display its field values, if necessary.

▶ **7.** If necessary, use the vertical scroll bar for the main form to scroll down and view the bottom of the subform. Note the navigation buttons for the subform.

▶ **8.** In the subform, click the **Last record** navigation button ▶|. Record 4 in the Visit table, for Visit ID 1679, becomes the current record in the subform.

▶ **9.** Save and close the PatientVisits form.

▶ **10.** If you are not continuing to Session 4.2, click the **FILE** tab, and then click **Close** in the navigation bar to close the Chatham database.

Both the PatientData form and the PatientVisits form you created will enable Cindi and her staff to view, enter, and maintain data easily in the Patient and Visit tables in the Chatham database.

## Session 4.1 Quick Check

REVIEW

1. Describe the difference between creating a form using the Form tool and creating a form using the Form Wizard.
2. What is a theme and how do you apply one to an existing form?
3. A(n) _____ is an item on a form, report, or other database object that you can manipulate to modify the object's appearance.
4. Which table record is displayed in a form when you press the Ctrl+End keys while you are in navigation mode?
5. Which wildcard character matches any single alphabetic character?
6. To print only the current record displayed in a form, you need to select the _____ option button in the Print dialog box.
7. In a form that contains a main form and a subform, what data is displayed in the main form and what data is displayed in the subform?

# Session 4.2 Visual Overview:

The report object's name is displayed on the tab for the report.

The report title appears at the top of the report. By default, the report object name is used as the report title, but you can edit the title to display the text you want, as done here, with spaces added between words for readability.

Fields from the primary Patient table appear first in the report.

Fields from the related Visit table appear below the fields from the primary table.

For a **grouped report**, the data from a record in the primary table (the Patient table in this report) appears as a group, followed on subsequent lines of the report by the joined records from the related table (the Visit table in this report).

The navigation buttons allow you to display the first, last, next, or previous page in the report, or to enter a specific page number and move to that page.

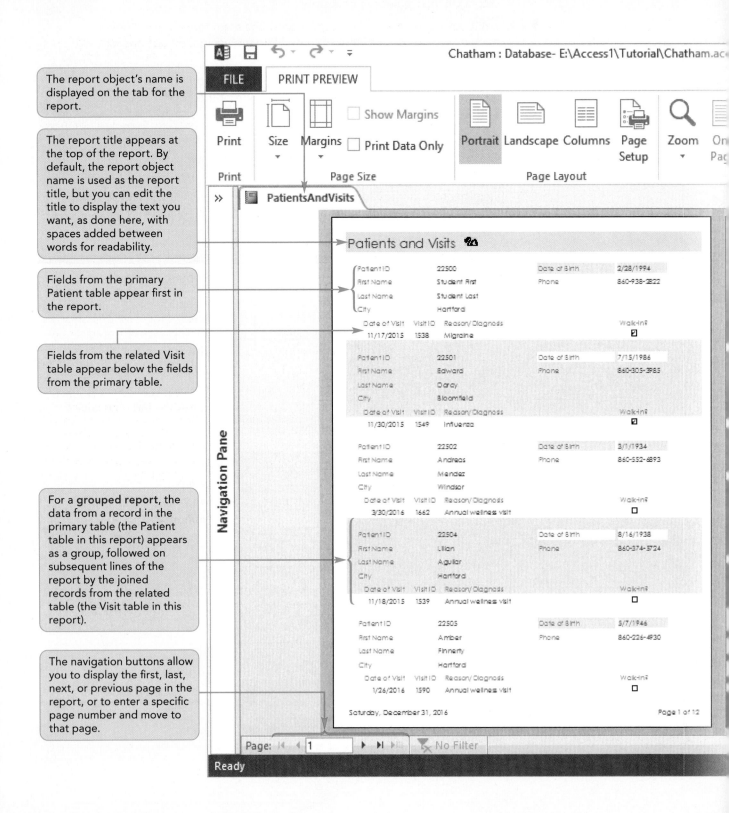

# Report Displayed in Print Preview

Click this button to close Print Preview and return to the report in the previously displayed view.

tham.accdb (Access 2007 - 2013 file format) - Access    ?  —  ☐  ✕

Sign in

| Zoom | One Page | Two Pages | More Pages ▾ | Refresh All | Excel | Text File | PDF or XPS | Email | More ▾ | Close Print Preview |
|---|---|---|---|---|---|---|---|---|---|---|

Zoom                                    Data                              Close Preview

The PatientsAndVisits report was created using the **Report Wizard**, which asks you a series of questions and then creates a report based on your answers. This report is based on data in both the Patient and Visit tables, which are joined in a one-to-many relationship through the common PatientID field.

| PatientID | 22506 | Date of Birth | 2/19/2005 |
| First Name | Drea | Phone | 860-305-8394 |
| Last Name | Gorski | | |
| City | Bloomfield | | |

| Date of Visit | Visit ID | Reason/Diagnosis | Walk-in? |
| 4/1/2016 | 1667 | Fifth Disease | ☑ |
| 4/8/2016 | 1683 | Fifth Disease follow-up | ☐ |

This report uses **portrait orientation**, where the page is taller than it is wide; you can also format a report in **landscape orientation**, where the page is wider than it is tall.

| PatientID | 22507 | Date of Birth | 6/7/1997 |
| First Name | Matthew | Phone | 860-426-7492 |
| Last Name | Weiss | | |
| City | Hartford | | |

| Date of Visit | Visit ID | Reason/Diagnosis | Walk-in? |
| 11/9/2015 | 1528 | Diabetes mellitis Type 2 - initial diagnosis | ☑ |
| 2/9/2016 | 1607 | Diabetes mellitis Type 2 - serum glucose check | ☐ |
| 4/7/2016 | 1675 | Diabetes mellitis Type 2 - serum glucose check | ☐ |

The set of field values for each record in the related table is called a **detail record**. These three detail records are the Visit table records related to the Patient table record for Matthew Weiss.

| PatientID | 22509 | Date of Birth | 4/6/1993 |
| First Name | Steve | Phone | 860-938-0025 |
| Last Name | Kervin | | |
| City | Hartford | | |

| Date of Visit | Visit ID | Reason/Diagnosis | Walk-in? |
| 4/4/2016 | 1670 | Tinea pedis | ☑ |
| 4/18/2016 | 1700 | Tinea pedis follow-up | ☐ |

Shading is used to distinguish one Patient record from another, and one Visit record from another.

| PatientID | 22510 | Date of Birth | 8/25/1966 |
| First Name | Thomas | Phone | 860-661-2539 |
| Last Name | Booker | | |
| City | Hartford | | |

| Date of Visit | Visit ID | Reason/Diagnosis | Walk-in? |
| 11/10/2015 | 1530 | Seborrheic dermatitis | ☐ |
| 3/1/2016 | 1631 | Seborrheic dermatitis follow-up | ☐ |

Saturday, December 31, 2016                                    Page 2 of 12

47%

# Creating a Report Using the Report Wizard

As you learned in Tutorial 1, a report is a formatted printout or screen display of the contents of one or more tables or queries in a database. In Access, you can create your own reports or use the Report Wizard to create them for you. Whether you use the Report Wizard or design your own report, you can change a report's design after you create it.

**INSIGHT**

*Creating a Report Based on a Query*

You can create a report based on one or more tables or queries. When you use a query as the basis for a report, you can use criteria and other query features to retrieve only the information you want to display in the report. Experienced Access users often create a query just so they can create a report based on that query. When thinking about the type of report you want to create, consider creating a query first and basing the report on the query, to produce the exact results you want to see in the report.

Ethan Ward, who handles marketing and outreach efforts for Chatham Community Health Services, wants you to create a report that includes data from both the Patient and Visit tables, as shown in the Session 4.2 Visual Overview. Like the PatientVisits form you created earlier, which includes a main form and a subform, the report will be based on both tables, which are joined in a one-to-many relationship through the common PatientID field. You'll use the Report Wizard to create the report for Ethan.

**To start the Report Wizard and select the fields to include in the report:**

1. If you took a break after the previous session, make sure that the Chatham database is open and the Navigation Pane is closed.

2. On the ribbon, click the **CREATE** tab.

3. In the Reports group, click the **Report Wizard** button. The first Report Wizard dialog box opens.

   As was the case when you created the form with a subform, initially you can choose only one table or query to be the data source for the report. Then you can include data from other tables or queries. You will select the primary Patient table first.

4. Click the **Tables/Queries** arrow, scroll up the list (if necessary), and then click **Table: Patient**.

   You select fields in the order you want them to appear on the report. Ethan wants the PatientID, FirstName, LastName, City, BirthDate, and Phone fields from the Patient table to appear on the report, in that order.

5. Click **PatientID** in the Available Fields box (if necessary), and then click the ⟩ button. The field moves to the Selected Fields box.

6. Repeat Step 5 to add the **FirstName**, **LastName**, **City**, **BirthDate**, and **Phone** fields to the report.

7. Click the **Tables/Queries** arrow, and then click **Table: Visit**. The fields from the Visit table appear in the Available Fields box.

The PatientID field will appear on the report with the patient data, so you do not need to include it in the detail records for each visit. Otherwise, Ethan wants all the fields from the Visit table to be included in the report.

▶ **8.** Click the >> button to move all the fields from the Available Fields box to the Selected Fields box.

▶ **9.** Click **Visit.PatientID** in the Selected Fields box, click the < button to move the field back to the Available Fields box, and then click the **Next** button. The second Report Wizard dialog box opens. See Figure 4-18.

**Figure 4-18** **Choosing a grouped or ungrouped report**

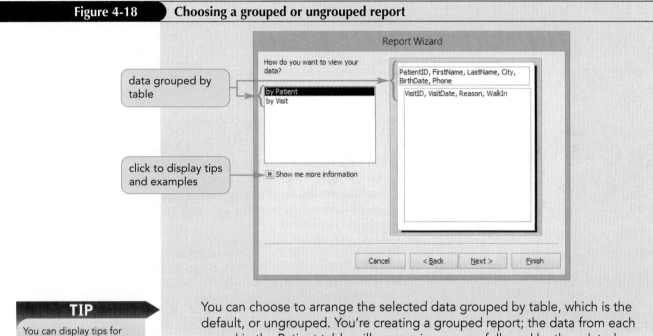

data grouped by table

click to display tips and examples

You can choose to arrange the selected data grouped by table, which is the default, or ungrouped. You're creating a grouped report; the data from each record in the Patient table will appear in a group, followed by the related records for that patient from the Visit table.

The default options shown on your screen are correct for the report Ethan wants, so you can continue responding to the Report Wizard questions.

### To finish creating the report using the Report Wizard:

▶ **1.** Click the **Next** button. The next Report Wizard dialog box opens, in which you choose additional grouping levels.

Currently the report contains only one grouping level, which is for the patient's data. Grouping levels are useful for reports with multiple levels, such as those containing monthly, quarterly, and annual totals, or for those containing city and country groups. Ethan's report requires no further grouping levels, so you can accept the default options.

▶ **2.** Click the **Next** button. The next Report Wizard dialog box opens, in which you choose the sort order for the detail records. See Figure 4-19.

| Figure 4-19 | Choosing the sort order for detail records |
|---|---|

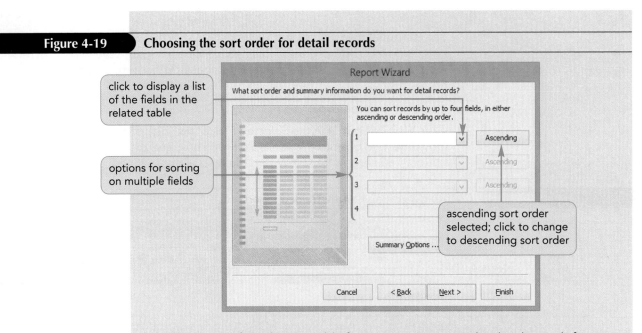

click to display a list of the fields in the related table

options for sorting on multiple fields

ascending sort order selected; click to change to descending sort order

The records from the Visit table for a patient represent the detail records for Ethan's report. He wants these records to appear in ascending order by the value in the VisitDate field, so that the visits will be shown in chronological order. The Ascending option is already selected by default. To change to descending order, you click this same button, which acts as a toggle between the two sort orders. Also, you can sort on multiple fields, as you can with queries.

▶ **3.** Click the **arrow** on the first box, click **VisitDate**, and then click the **Next** button. The next Report Wizard dialog box opens, in which you choose a layout and page orientation for the report. See Figure 4-20.

| Figure 4-20 | Choosing the report layout |
|---|---|

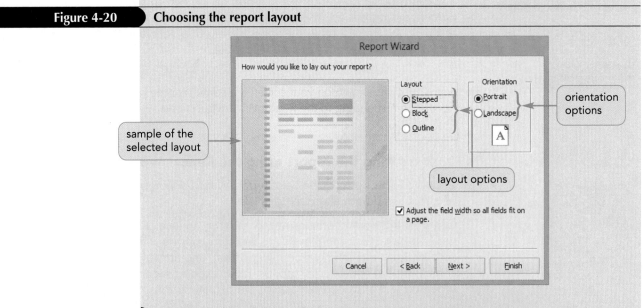

sample of the selected layout

orientation options

layout options

▶ **4.** Click each layout option and examine each sample that appears.

You'll use the Outline layout for Ethan's report. Also, most of the fields in both the Patient and Visit tables contain relatively short field values, so you'll keep the portrait page orientation. This should provide enough space across the page to display all the field values; you will confirm this when viewing the report created by the wizard.

▶ **5.** In the Layout section, click the **Outline** option button, and then click the **Next** button. The final Report Wizard dialog box opens, in which you choose a report title, which also serves as the name for the report object in the database.

Ethan wants the report title "Patients and Visits" at the top of the report. Because the name you enter in this dialog box is also the name of the report object, you'll enter the report name as one word and edit the title on the report later.

▶ **6.** In the box for the title, enter **PatientsAndVisits** and then click the **Finish** button. The Report Wizard creates the report based on your answers, saves it as an object in the Chatham database, and opens the report in Print Preview.

To view the entire page, you need to change the Zoom setting.

▶ **7.** In the Zoom group on the PRINT PREVIEW tab, click the **Zoom button arrow**, and then click **Fit to Window**. The first page of the report is displayed in Print Preview.

▶ **8.** At the bottom of the window, click the **Next Page** navigation button ▶ to display the second page of the report.

When a report is displayed in Print Preview, you can use the pointer to toggle between a full-page display and a close-up display of the report.

▶ **9.** Click the pointer ⊕ at the center of the report. The display changes to show a close-up view of the report. See Figure 4-21.

**Figure 4-21**    **Close-up view of the report**

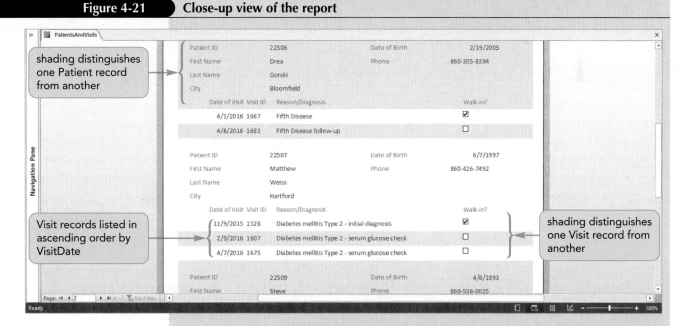

Shading is used to distinguish both one Patient record from another and, within a group of each patient's Visit records, one Visit record from another.

**Trouble?** Depending on your computer settings, the shading and colors used in your report might look different. This difference should not cause any problems.

The detail records for the Visit table fields appear in ascending order based on the values in the VisitDate field. Because the VisitDate field is used as the basis for sorting records, it appears as the first field in this section, even though you selected the fields in the order in which they appear in the Visit table.

▶ **10.** Use the vertical scroll bar to scroll to the bottom of the second page, checking the text in the report as you scroll. Notice the current date and page number at the bottom of the page; the Report Wizard included these elements as part of the report's design.

 **Trouble?** Depending on your computer's settings, the text of the page number might not be completely within the page border. If so, you'll see blank pages every other page as you complete Steps 11 and 12. You'll fix this problem shortly.

▶ **11.** Click the pointer 🔍 on the report to zoom back out, and then click the **Next Page** navigation button ▶ to move to page 3 of the report.

▶ **12.** Continue to move through the pages of the report, and then click the **First Page** navigation button ◀ to return to the first page.

## INSIGHT

### Changing a Report's Page Orientation and Margins

When you display a report in Print Preview, you can easily change the report layout using options on the PRINT PREVIEW tab (refer to the Session 4.2 Visual Overview). For example, sometimes fields with longer values cause the report content to overflow onto the next page. You can fix this problem by clicking the Landscape button in the Page Layout group on the PRINT PREVIEW tab to switch the report orientation to landscape, where the page is wider than it is tall. Landscape orientation allows more space for content to fit across the width of the report page. You can also use the Margins button in the Page Size group to change the margins of the report, choosing from commonly used margin formats or creating your own custom margins. Simply click the Margins button arrow to display the menu of available margin options and select the one that works best for your report.

Earlier, when meeting with Cindi, Ethan viewed and worked with the PatientData form. He likes how the form looks with the Slice theme applied, and would like his report formatted with the same theme. You need to switch to Layout view to make this change. You'll also make other modifications to improve the report's design.

# Modifying a Report's Design in Layout View

Similar to Layout view for forms, Layout view for reports enables you to make modifications to the report's design. Many of the same options—such as those for applying a theme and changing the color of text—are provided in Layout view for reports.

## Applying a Theme to a Report

The same themes available for forms are also available for reports. You can choose to apply a theme to the current report object only, or to all reports in the database. In this case, you'll apply the Slice theme only to the PatientsAndVisits report because Ethan isn't certain if it is the appropriate theme for other reports in the Chatham database.

**To apply the Slice theme to the report:**

1. On the status bar, click the **Layout View** button ▤. The report is displayed in Layout view.

2. In the Themes group on the DESIGN tab, click the **Themes** button. The "In this Database" section at the top of the gallery shows both the default Office theme and the Slice theme. The Slice theme is included here because you applied it earlier to the PatientData form.

3. At the top of the gallery, right-click the **Slice** theme to display the shortcut menu, and then click **Apply Theme to This Object Only**. The gallery closes and the theme is applied to the report.

   The larger font used by the Slice theme has caused the report title text to be cut off on the right. You'll fix this problem and edit the title text as well.

4. Click the **PatientsAndVisits** title at the top of the report to select it.

5. Place the pointer on the right vertical line of the orange outline surrounding the title, and then click and drag the ↔ pointer to the right until the title is fully displayed.

   **Trouble?** You might need to repeat Step 5 more than once in order for the text to appear correctly.

6. Click between the letters "s" and "A" in the title, press the **spacebar**, change the capital letter "A" to **a**, place the insertion point between the letters "d" and "V," and then press the **spacebar**. The title is now "Patients and Visits."

7. Click to the right of the report title in the shaded area to deselect the title.

Ethan views the report and notices some other formatting changes he would like you to make. First, he doesn't like how the BirthDate field values are aligned compared to the Phone field values. You'll fix this next.

## Changing the Alignment of Field Values

The FORMAT tab in Layout view, one of the REPORT LAYOUT TOOLS contextual tabs, provides options for you to easily modify the format of various report objects. For example, you can change the alignment of the text in a field value. Recall that Date/Time fields, like BirthDate, automatically right-align their field values, whereas Short Text fields, like Phone, automatically left-align their field values. Ethan asks you to change the alignment of the BirthDate field so its values appear left-aligned, which will improve the format of the report.

**To change the alignment of the BirthDate field values:**

1. On the ribbon, click the **FORMAT** tab. The ribbon changes to display groups and options for formatting the report. The options for modifying the format of a report are the same as those available for forms.

2. In the report, click the first **BirthDate field value box**, which contains the date 2/28/1994. The field value box is outlined in orange, indicating it is selected. Note that the other BirthDate field value boxes are outlined in a lighter orange, indicating they are selected as well. Any changes you make will be applied to all BirthDate field values throughout the report.

> **3.** In the Font group on the FORMAT tab, click the **Align Left** button. The text in the BirthDate field value boxes is now left-aligned, and the birth dates are aligned with the phone numbers. See Figure 4-22.

**Figure 4-22** **Report after applying a theme and changing field alignment**

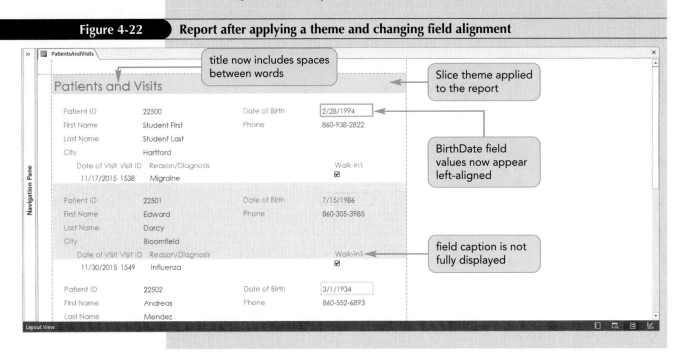

## Moving and Resizing Fields on a Report

Working in Layout view, you can resize and reposition fields and field value boxes to improve the appearance of a report or to address the problem of some field values not being completely displayed. In the PatientsAndVisits report, you need to move and resize the WalkIn field label so that the complete caption, Walk-in?, is displayed. Ethan also thinks the report would look better with more room between the VisitDate and VisitID fields, so you'll move the VisitDate field label and associated field value box to the left.

You can select one or more objects on a report and then drag them to a new location; or, for more precise control over the move, you can use the arrow keyboard keys to move selected objects. Ethan asks you to move the WalkIn field's label to the left so it appears centered over its check box, and also to make the label larger.

### To move and resize the WalkIn field label:

> **1.** In the report, click the first occurrence of the **Walk-in?** field label. All instances of the label are selected throughout the report.

> **2.** Press the ← key repeatedly until the label is centered (roughly) over its check box.

> **3.** Place the pointer on the right vertical line of the orange outline surrounding the label, and then click and drag the ↔ pointer to the right until the label text is fully displayed.

Next, you need to move the VisitDate field label (Date of Visit) and field value box to the left, to provide more space between the VisitDate field and the VisitID field in the report. You can select both objects and modify them at the same time.

## To move the VisitDate field label and field value box:

1. In the report, click the first occurrence of the **Date of Visit** field label, press and hold the **Shift** key, and then click the first occurrence of the field value box, which contains the date 11/17/2015. Both the field label and its associated field value box are selected and can be moved. See Figure 4-23.

**Figure 4-23** | Report after moving and resizing field label

## Patients and Visits

| | | | |
|---|---|---|---|
| Patient ID | 22500 | Date of Birth | 2/28/1994 |
| First Name | Student First | Phone | 860-938-2822 |
| Last Name | Student Last | | |
| City | Hartford | | |

| Date of Visit | Visit ID | Reason/Diagnosis | Walk-in? |
|---|---|---|---|
| 11/17/2015 | 1538 | Migraine | ☑ |

VisitDate field label and field value box selected and ready to be moved

| | | | |
|---|---|---|---|
| Patient ID | 22501 | Date of Birth | 7/15/1986 |
| First Name | Edward | Phone | 860-305-3985 |
| Last Name | Darcy | | |
| City | Bloomfield | | |

| Date of Visit | Visit ID | Reason/Diagnosis | Walk-in? |
|---|---|---|---|
| 11/30/2015 | 1549 | Influenza | ☑ |

all WalkIn field labels moved and resized throughout the report

| | | | |
|---|---|---|---|
| Patient ID | 22502 | Date of Birth | 3/1/1934 |
| First Name | Andreas | Phone | 860-552-6893 |
| Last Name | Mendez | | |

2. Press the ← key four times to move the field label and field value box to the left.

   **Trouble?** Once you press the left arrow key, the report might jump to display the end of the report. Just continue to press the left arrow key to move the label and value. Then scroll the window back up to display the beginning of the report.

   Ethan is pleased with the changes to the report format, but he is concerned that the larger font size of the theme might have caused other text in the report to be cut off—especially some of the Reason/Diagnosis field values, which are lengthy. You need to check the report for such problems. First, you'll save the design changes you've made.

3. On the Quick Access Toolbar, click the **Save** button 🖫 to save the modified report.

4. At the top of the report, click to the right of the report title in the shaded area to deselect the VisitDate field label and field value box.

5. Scroll through the report, checking the field labels and field values as you go to make sure all text is fully displayed. When finished, scroll back up to display the top of the report.

Next, Ethan asks you to enhance the report's appearance by inserting the same picture on the PatientsAndVisits report as you included on the PatientData form, and to change the color of the report title to the same darker color used on the form.

## Changing the Title Font Color and Inserting a Picture in a Report

You can change the color of text on a report to enhance its appearance. You can also add a picture to a report for visual interest or to identify a particular section of the report. Because Ethan plans to print the report, he asks you to change the report title color to the darker black you applied earlier to the PatientData form and to include the Medical picture to the right of the report title.

**To change the color of the report title and insert the picture:**

Make sure the title is selected so the picture is inserted in the correct location.

1. At the top of the report, click the title **Patients and Visits** to select it.

2. Make sure the **FORMAT** tab is still active on the ribbon.

3. In the Font group, click the **Font Color button arrow** [A ▾], and then click the **Black, Text 1, Lighter 25%** color box (fourth row, second box in the Theme Colors palette). The color is applied to the report title.

   Now you'll insert the picture to the right of the report title text.

4. On the ribbon, click the **DESIGN** tab. The options provided on this tab for reports are the same as those you worked with for forms.

5. In the Header/Footer group, click the **Logo** button.

6. Navigate to the **Access1 ▸ Tutorial** folder provided with your Data Files, and then double-click the **Medical** file. The picture is inserted in the top-left corner of the report, partially covering the report title.

7. Position the pointer on the selected picture, and then click and drag it to the right of the report title.

8. Click in a blank area of the shaded bar to deselect the picture. See Figure 4-24.

**Figure 4-24** **Report after changing the title font color and inserting the picture**

font color of the title is now a darker black

picture added and moved to the right of the title

**Trouble?** Don't be concerned if the picture in your report is not in the exact same location as the one shown in the figure. Just make sure it is to the right of the title text and within the shaded area.

Ethan is pleased with the report's appearance and shows it to Cindi. She also approves of the report's contents and design, but has one final suggestion for the report. She'd like to draw attention to patient records for children and teenagers by formatting their birth dates with a bold, red font. Chatham Community Health Services is planning a special event specifically geared to children and teenagers regarding healthy diets, so this format will make it easier to find these patient records in the report. Because Cindi doesn't want all the birth dates to appear in this font, you need to use conditional formatting.

# Using Conditional Formatting in a Report

**Conditional formatting** in a report (or form) is special formatting applied to certain field values depending on one or more conditions—similar to criteria you establish for queries. If a field value meets the condition or conditions you specify, the formatting is applied to the value.

Cindi would like the PatientsAndVisits report to show any birth date that is greater than 1/1/1997 in a bold, dark red font. This formatting will help to highlight the patient records for children and teenagers. Cindi plans to review this report in a planning meeting for the upcoming special event.

## To apply conditional formatting to the BirthDate field in the report:

1. Make sure the report is still displayed in Layout view, and then click the **FORMAT** tab on the ribbon.

   To apply conditional formatting to a field, you must first make it the active field by clicking any field value in the field's column.

2. Click the first BirthDate field value, **2/28/1994**, for PatientID 22500. An orange outline appears around the field value box, and a lighter orange outline appears around each BirthDate field value box throughout the entire report. The conditional formatting you specify will affect all the values for the field.

3. In the Control Formatting group on the FORMAT tab, click the **Conditional Formatting** button. The Conditional Formatting Rules Manager dialog box opens. Because you selected a BirthDate field value box, the name of this field is displayed in the "Show formatting rules for" box. Currently, there are no conditional formatting rules set for the selected field. You need to create a new rule.

4. Click the **New Rule** button. The New Formatting Rule dialog box opens. See Figure 4-25.

**Figure 4-25**     New Formatting Rule dialog box

specify the condition in these boxes

a preview of the conditional format will appear here

use these options to specify the formatting

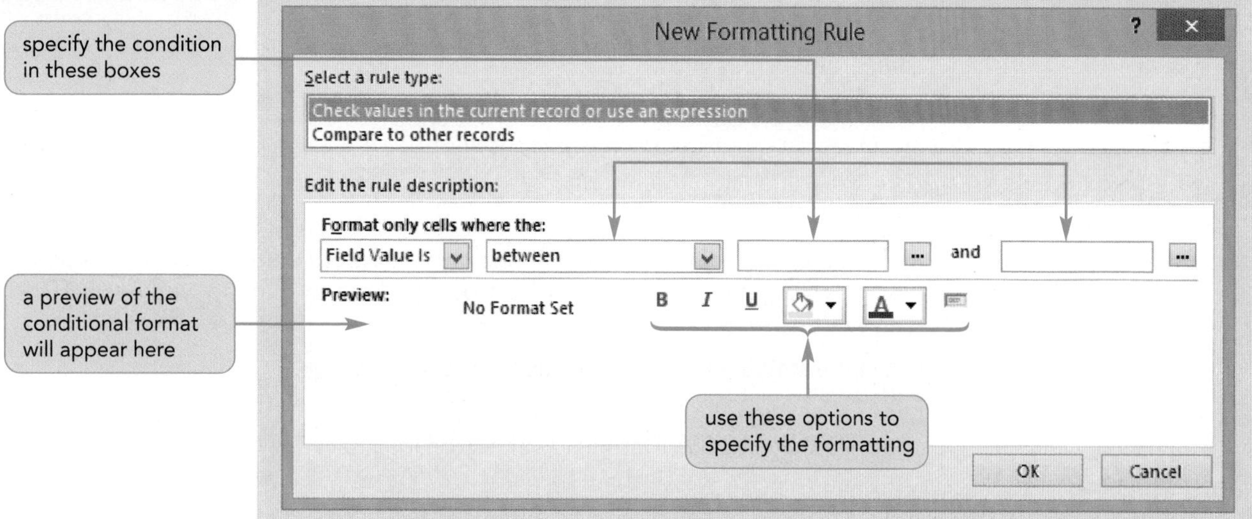

The default setting for "Select a rule type" specifies that Access will check field values and determine if they meet the condition. This is the setting you want. You need to enter the condition in the "Edit the rule description" section of the dialog box. The setting "Field Value Is" means that the conditional format you specify will be applied only when the value for the selected field, BirthDate, meets the condition.

▶ **5.** Click the **arrow** for the box containing the word "between," and then click **greater than**. Cindi wants only those birth dates greater than 1/1/1997 to be formatted.

▶ **6.** Click in the next box, and then type **1/1/1997**.

▶ **7.** In the Preview section, click the **Font color button arrow** ![A ▾] and then click the **Dark Red** color box (first color box in the last row of Standard Colors).

▶ **8.** In the Preview section, click the **Bold** button ![B]. The specifications for the conditional formatting are complete. See Figure 4-26.

| Figure 4-26 | Conditional formatting set for the BirthDate field |
| --- | --- |

condition specifies that the selected field value must be greater than 1/1/1997

preview shows the bold, dark red font that will be applied to field values that meet the condition

Bold button selected

dark red font color selected

▶ **9.** Click the **OK** button. The new rule you specified appears in the Rule section of the dialog box as Value > 1/1/1997; the Format section on the right shows the conditional formatting (dark red, bold font) that will be applied based on this rule.

▶ **10.** Click the **OK** button. The conditional format is applied to the BirthDate field values. To get a better view of the report and the formatting, you'll switch to Print Preview.

▶ **11.** On the status bar, click the **Print Preview** button ![📄].

▶ **12.** Move to page 2 of the report. Notice that the conditional formatting is applied only to BirthDate field values greater than 1/1/1997. See Figure 4-27.

| Figure 4-27 | Viewing the finished report in Print Preview |

conditional formatting applied to BirthDate field values greater than 1/1/1997

conditional formatting not applied to BirthDate field values less than 1/1/1997

## Problem Solving: Understanding the Importance of Previewing Reports

When you create a report, it is a good idea to display the report in Print Preview occasionally as you develop it. Doing so will give you a chance to find any formatting problems or other issues so that you can make any necessary corrections before printing the report. It is particularly important to preview a report after you've made changes to its design to ensure that the changes you made have not created new problems with the report's format. Before printing any report, you should preview it so you can determine where the pages will break and make any necessary adjustments. Following this problem-solving approach will not only ensure that the final report looks exactly the way you want it to, but will also save you time and help to avoid wasting paper if you print the report.

The report is now complete. You'll print just the first page of the report so that Cindi and Ethan can view the final results and share the report design with other staff members before printing the entire report. (*Note:* Ask your instructor if you should complete the following printing steps.)

### To print page 1 of the report:

1. In the Print group on the PRINT PREVIEW tab, click the **Print** button. The Print dialog box opens.

2. In the Print Range section, click the **Pages** option button. The insertion point now appears in the From box so that you can specify the range of pages to print.

3. Type **1** in the From box, press the **Tab** key to move to the To box, and then type **1**. These settings specify that only page 1 of the report will be printed.

4. Click the **OK** button. The Print dialog box closes, and the first page of the report is printed.

5. Save and close the PatientsAndVisits report.

You've created many different objects in the Chatham database. Before you close it, you'll open the Navigation Pane to view all the objects in the database.

### To view the Chatham database objects in the Navigation Pane:

▶ **1.** Open the Navigation Pane and scroll down, if necessary, to display the bottom of the pane.

The Navigation Pane displays the objects grouped by type: tables, queries, forms, and reports. Notice the PatientVisits form. This is the form you created containing a main form based on the Patient table and a subform based on the Visit table. The VisitSubform object is also listed; you can open it separately from the main form. See Figure 4-28.

**Figure 4-28**   Chatham database objects in the Navigation Pane

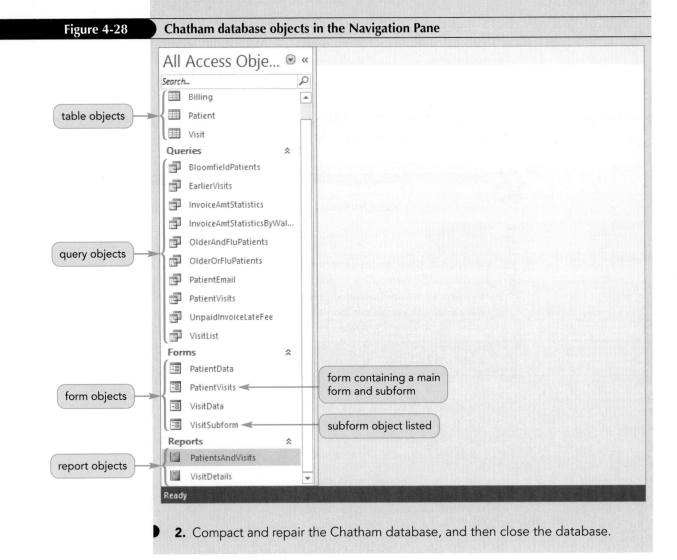

▶ **2.** Compact and repair the Chatham database, and then close the database.

Cindi is satisfied that the forms you created—the PatientData form and the PatientVisits form—will make it easier to enter, view, and update data in the Chatham database. The PatientsAndVisits report presents important information about the clinic's patients in an attractive and professional format, which will help Ethan and other staff members in their community outreach efforts.

**REVIEW**

### Session 4.2 Quick Check

1. In a(n) _____ report, the data from a record in the primary table appears together, followed on subsequent lines by the joined records from the related table.

2. When you create a report based on two tables that are joined in a one-to-many relationship, the field values for the records from the related table are called the _____ records.

3. Identify three types of modifications you can make to a report in Layout view.

4. Describe the process for moving a control to another location on a report in Layout view.

5. When working in Layout view for a report, which key do you press and hold down so that you can click to select multiple controls (field labels, field value boxes, and so on)?

6. _____ in a report (or form) is special formatting applied to certain field values depending on one or more conditions.

**ASSESS**

## SAM Projects

Put your skills into practice with SAM Projects! SAM Projects for this tutorial can be found online. If you have a SAM account, go to www.cengage.com/sam2013 to download the most recent Project Instructions and Start Files.

**PRACTICE**

## Review Assignments

**Data Files needed for the Review Assignments: Vendor.accdb** *(cont. from Tutorial 3)* **and Supplies.bmp**

Cindi asks you to enhance the Vendor database with forms and reports. Complete the following steps:

1. Open the **Vendor** database you created and worked with in Tutorials 1 through 3, and then click the Enable Content button next to the security warning, if necessary.
2. Use the Form Wizard to create a form based on the Product table. Select all fields for the form and the Columnar layout; specify the title **ProductData** for the form.
3. Apply the Facet theme to the ProductData form *only*.
4. Insert the Supplies picture, which is located in the Access1 ▸ Review folder provided with your Data Files, in the ProductData form. Remove the picture from the control layout, and then move the picture to the right of the form title.
5. Drag a bottom corner of the image to increase its size until the items in the picture are all clearly visible. Continue to resize and reposition the image until it is in the location you want, making sure to keep it within the shaded area of the title and to the right of the title.
6. Edit the form title so that it appears as "Product Data" (two words), and change the font color of the form title to the Blue-Gray, Text 2, Darker 25% theme color.
7. Resize the Weight in Lbs field value box so it is the same width (approximately) as the Units/Case field value box above it.
8. Change the alignment of the Price, Units/Case, and Weight in Lbs fields so that their values appear left-aligned in the field value boxes.
9. Save your changes to the form design.
10. Use the ProductData form to update the Product table as follows:
    a. Use the Find command to search for the word "test" anywhere in the ProductName field, and then display the record for the mononucleosis test (ProductID MO269). Change the Price in this record to **49.50**.
    b. Add a new record with the following field values:
    Product ID: **EG400**
    Supplier ID: **SAN481**
    Product Name: **Non-Latex exam gloves**
    Price: **4.75**
    Units/Case: **80**
    Weight in Lbs: **2**
    Temp Controlled?: **no**
    Sterile?: **no**
    c. Save and close the form.
11. Use the Form Wizard to create a form containing a main form and a subform. Select all fields from the Supplier table for the main form, and select ProductID, ProductName, Price, TempControl, and Sterile—in that order—from the Product table for the subform. Use the Datasheet layout. Specify the title **SuppliersAndProducts** for the main form and **ProductSubform** for the subform.

12. Change the form title text to **Suppliers and Products**.

13. Resize the subform to the right, increasing its width by approximately three inches, and then resize all columns in the subform to their best fit, working left to right. Navigate through each record in the main form to make sure all the field values in the subform are completely displayed, resizing subform columns and the subform itself, as necessary. Save and close the SuppliersAndProducts form.

14. Use the Report Wizard to create a report based on the primary Supplier table and the related Product table. Select the SupplierID, Company, City, Category, ContactFirst, ContactLast, and Phone fields—in that order—from the Supplier table, and the ProductID, ProductName, Price, and Units fields from the Product table. Do not specify any additional grouping levels, and sort the detail records in ascending order by ProductID. Choose the Outline layout and Portrait orientation. Specify the title **ProductsBySupplier** for the report.

15. Change the report title text to **Products by Supplier**.

16. Apply the Facet theme to the ProductsBySupplier report *only*.

17. Resize and reposition the following objects in the report in Layout view, and then scroll through the report to make sure all field labels and field values are fully displayed:

    a. Resize the report title so that the text of the title, Products by Supplier, is fully displayed.

    b. Move the ProductName label and field value box to the right a bit (be sure not to move them too far so that the longest product name will still be completely visible).

    c. Resize the Product ID field label on its right side, increasing its width slightly so the label is fully displayed.

    d. Move the Units/Case label and field value box to the right a bit; then resize the label on its left side, increasing its width slightly so the label is fully displayed.

    e. Select the field value boxes *only* (not the field labels) for the following four fields: SupplierID, Company, City, and Category. Then move the four field value boxes to the left until their left edges align (roughly) with the "S" in "Supplier" in the report title.

    f. Resize the Company field value box on its right side, increasing its width slightly so that all company names are fully displayed.

18. Change the color of the report title text to the Blue-Gray, Text 2, Darker 25% theme color.

19. Insert the Supplies picture, which is located in the Access1 ▶ Review folder provided with your Data Files, in the report. Move the picture to the right of the report title. Drag a bottom corner of the image to increase its size until the items in the picture are all clearly visible. Continue to resize and reposition the image until it is in the location you want, making sure to keep it within the shaded area of the title and to the right of the title.

20. Apply conditional formatting so that the Category field values equal to Service appear as dark red and bold.

21. Preview each page of the report, verifying that all the fields fit on the page. If necessary, return to Layout view and make changes so the report prints within the margins of the page and so that all field names and values are completely displayed.

22. Save the report, print its first page (only if asked by your instructor to do so), and then close the report.

23. Compact and repair the Vendor database, and then close it.

## Case Problem 1

**Data Files needed for this Case Problem: Gopher.accdb *(cont. from Tutorial 3)* and Tasks.bmp**

*GoGopher!*    Amol Mehta uses the Gopher database to track and view information about the services his company offers. He asks you to create the necessary forms and a report to help him work with this data more efficiently. Complete the following:

1. Open the **Gopher** database you created and worked with in Tutorials 1 through 3, and then click the Enable Content button next to the security warning, if necessary.

APPLY

2. Use the Form Wizard to create a form based on the Member table. Select all the fields for the form and the Columnar layout. Specify the title **MemberData** for the form.

3. Apply the Wisp theme to the MemberData form *only*.

4. Edit the form title so that it appears as "Member Data" (two words); resize the title so that both words fit on the same line; and then change the font color of the form title to the Dark Red, Accent 1, Darker 25% theme color.

5. Use the Find command to display the record for Marco Krukonis, and then change the Street field value for this record to **75 Woodfield Ave**.

6. Use the MemberData form to add a new record to the Member table with the following field values:

   Member ID: **1261**

   Plan ID: **306**

   First Name: **Taylor**

   Last Name: **Byrne**

   Street: **318 Coolidge Dr**

   City: **Jamestown**

   State: **CO**

   Zip: **80455**

   Phone: **303-751-3152**

   Date Joined: **10/1/2016**

   Expiration Date: **4/1/2017**

7. Save and close the MemberData form.

8. Use the Form Wizard to create a form containing a main form and a subform. Select all the fields from the Plan table for the main form, and select the MemberID, FirstName, LastName, Expiration, and Phone fields from the Member table for the subform. Use the Datasheet layout. Specify the title **MembersByPlan** for the main form and the title **MemberSubform** for the subform.

9. Change the form title text for the main form to **Members by Plan**.

10. Resize all columns in the subform to their best fit, working from left to right; then move through all the records in the main form and check to make sure that all subform field values are fully displayed, resizing the columns as necessary.

11. Save and close the MembersByPlan form.

12. Use the Report Wizard to create a report based on the primary Plan table and the related Member table. Select all the fields from the Plan table, and then select the MemberID, FirstName, LastName, City, Phone, DateJoined, and Expiration fields from the Member table. Do not select any additional grouping levels, and sort the detail records in ascending order by MemberID. Choose the Outline layout and Landscape orientation. Specify the title **MemberPlans** for the report.

13. Apply the Wisp theme to the MemberPlans report *only*.

14. Resize the report title so that the text is fully displayed; edit the report title so that it appears as "Member Plans" (two words); and change the font color of the title to the Dark Red, Accent 1, Darker 25% theme color.

15. Change the alignment of the Plan Cost field so that its values appear left-aligned in the field value boxes.

16. Resize and reposition the following objects in the report in Layout view, and then scroll through the report to make sure all field labels and field values are fully displayed:

    a. Move the FirstName label and field value box to the right a bit (be sure not to move them too far so that the longest first name will still be completely visible).

    b. Resize the MemberID field label on its right side, increasing its width until the label is fully displayed.

    c. Move the Phone label and field value box to the left; then move the DateJoined label and field value box to the left.

    d. Resize the Expiration Date label on its left side, increasing its width until the label is fully displayed.

e. Scroll to the bottom of the report; note that the page number might not be completely within the page border (the dotted vertical line). If necessary, select and move the box containing the text "Page 1 of 1" until the entire text is positioned to the left of the dotted vertical line marking the right page border.

17. Insert the Tasks picture, which is located in the Access1 ▸ Case1 folder provided with your Data Files, in the report. Move the picture to the right of the report title. Drag a bottom corner of the image to increase its size slightly. Continue to resize and reposition the image until it is in the location you want, making sure to keep it within the shaded area of the title and to the right of the title.

18. Apply conditional formatting so that any Expiration field value less than 9/1/2016 appears as bold and with the Red color applied.

19. Preview the entire report to confirm that it is formatted correctly. If necessary, return to Layout view and make changes so that all field labels and field values are completely displayed.

20. Save the report, print its first page (only if asked by your instructor to do so), and then close the report.

21. Compact and repair the Gopher database, and then close it.

## Case Problem 2

**CREATE**

**Data Files needed for this Case Problem: OBrien.accdb** *(cont. from Tutorial 3)* **and Tests.bmp**

*O'Brien Educational Services*    Karen O'Brien is using the OBrien database to track and analyze the business activity of her educational consulting company. To make her work easier, you'll create a form and report in the OBrien database. Complete the following:

1. Open the **OBrien** database you created and worked with in Tutorials 1 through 3, and then click the Enable Content button next to the security warning, if necessary.

2. Create the form shown in Figure 4-29.

| Figure 4-29 | Completed ContractsByTutor form |
| --- | --- |

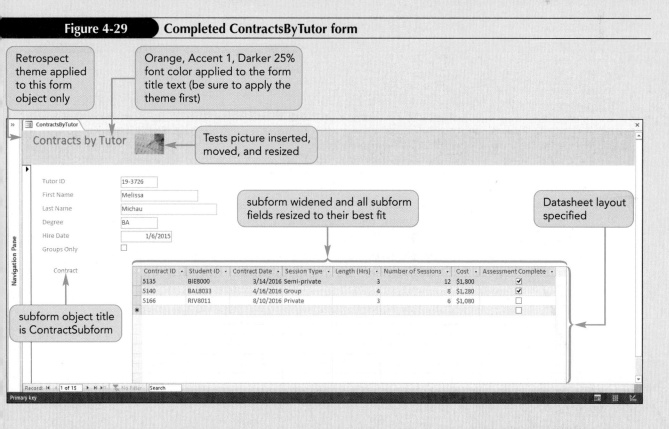

3. Using the form you just created, navigate to the second record in the subform for the third main record, and then change the Assessment Complete field value to **yes**.

4. Use the Find command to move to the record for Samuel Glick, and then change the value in the Groups Only field to **no**.

5. Use the appropriate wildcard character to find all records with a Hire Date field value that begins with the month of March (3). Change the Hire Date field value for Alameda Sarracino (Tutor ID 51-7070) to **3/27/2016**. Save and close the form.

6. Create the report shown in Figure 4-30.

**Figure 4-30**　　　**Completed TutorsAndContracts report**

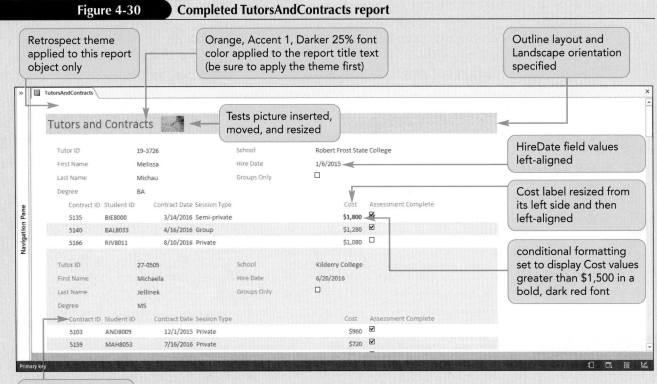

Retrospect theme applied to this report object only

Orange, Accent 1, Darker 25% font color applied to the report title text (be sure to apply the theme first)

Outline layout and Landscape orientation specified

Tests picture inserted, moved, and resized

HireDate field values left-aligned

Cost label resized from its left side and then left-aligned

conditional formatting set to display Cost values greater than $1,500 in a bold, dark red font

detail records sorted by ContractID in ascending order

7. Scroll to the bottom of the report; note that the page number might not be completely within the page border (the dotted vertical line). If necessary, select and move the box containing the text "Page 1 of 1" until the entire text is positioned to the left of the dotted vertical line marking the right page border.

8. Preview each page of the report, verifying that all the fields fit on the page. If necessary, return to Layout view and make changes so the report prints within the margins of the page and so that all field names and values are completely displayed.

9. Save the report, print its first page (only if asked by your instructor to do so), and then close the report.

10. Compact and repair the OBrien database, and then close it.

## Case Problem 3

**CHALLENGE**

Data Files needed for this Case Problem: Shelter.accdb *(cont. from Tutorial 3)* and Animals.bmp

***Rosemary Animal Shelter***    Ryan Lang uses the Shelter database to track, maintain, and analyze data about his shelter's patrons, donations, and animals. You'll help Ryan by creating a form and a report based on this data. Complete the following:

1. Open the **Shelter** database you created and worked with in Tutorials 1 through 3, and then click the Enable Content button next to the security warning, if necessary.

2. Use the Form Wizard to create a form based on the Animal table. Select all the fields for the form and the Columnar layout. Specify the title **AnimalInfo** for the form.

3. Apply the Ion theme to the AnimalInfo form *only*.

4. Edit the form title so that it appears as "Animal Info" (two words), and change the font color of the form title to the Green, Accent 4, Darker 25% theme color.

   **Explore** 5. Use the appropriate button in the Font group on the FORMAT tab to underline the form title. Save the form.

6. Use the AnimalInfo form to update the Animal table as follows:

   a. Use the Find command to search for records that contain "beagle" anywhere in the Description field. Display the record for the dog named Gus (AnimalID R98), and then change the Age field value for this record to **3**.

   b. Add a new record with the following values:

   Animal ID: **T80**
   Patron ID: [leave blank]
   Animal Name: **Tessie**
   Age at Arrival: **1**
   Gender: **Female**
   Animal Type: **Dog**
   Description: **Terrier mix**
   Arrival Date: **4/9/16**
   Adopted: **no**
   Adoption Date: [leave blank]

   **Explore** c. Find the record with AnimalID S35 (for Roggie), and then delete the record. (*Hint:* After displaying the record in the form, you need to select it by clicking the right-pointing triangle in the bar to the left of the field labels. Then use the appropriate button in the Records group on the HOME tab to delete the record. When asked to confirm the deletion, click the Yes button.) Close the form.

7. Use the Form Wizard to create a form containing a main form and a subform. Select all the fields from the Patron table for the main form, and select all fields except PatronID from the Donation table for the subform. Use the Datasheet layout. Specify the name **PatronsAndDonations** for the main form and the title **DonationSubform** for the subform.

8. Apply the Ion theme to the PatronsAndDonations form *only*.

9. Edit the form title so that it appears as "Patrons and Donations." Resize the form title so that the text fits on one line. Change the font color of the title to the Green, Accent 4, Darker 25% theme color.

10. Insert the Animals picture, which is located in the Access1 ▶ Case3 folder provided with your Data Files, in the PatronsAndDonations form. Remove the picture from the control layout, and then move the picture to the right of the form title. Resize the picture so it is approximately double the original size.

    **Explore** 11. Use the appropriate button in the Font group on the FORMAT tab to apply the theme color Green, Accent 4, Lighter 80% as a background color for all the field value boxes in the main form. Then use the appropriate button in the Control Formatting group to change the outline of all the main form field value boxes to have a line thickness of 1 pt. (*Hint:* Select all the field value boxes before making these changes.)

12. Resize the subform to the right, and then resize all columns in the subform to their best fit. Navigate through the records in the main form to make sure all the field values in the subform are completely displayed, resizing subform columns as necessary. Save and close the form.

13. Use the Report Wizard to create a report based on the primary Patron table and the related Donation table. Select all the fields from the Patron table, and select all fields except PatronID from the Donation table. Sort the detail records in *descending* order by DonationValue. Choose the Outline layout and Portrait orientation. Specify the name **PatronsAndDonations** for the report.

14. Apply the Ion theme to the PatronsAndDonations report *only*.

15. Resize the report title so that the text is fully displayed; edit the report title so that it appears as "Patrons and Donations"; and change the font color of the title to the Green, Accent 4, Darker 25% theme color.

16. Move the Donation Value field label and its field value box to the left a bit. Then resize the Donation ID field label on the right to fully display the label. Move the Description field label and its field value box to the right a bit, to provide more space between the Donation Date and Description fields. Finally, resize the Phone field label from its left side to reduce the width of the label box, moving the word "Phone" closer to the phone numbers. Save the report.

17. Insert the Animals picture, which is located in the Access1 ▶ Case3 folder provided with your Data Files, in the PatronsAndDonations report. Move the picture to the right of the report title. Resize the picture so it is approximately double the original size.

✪ **Explore** 18. Use the appropriate button in the Background group on the FORMAT tab to apply the theme color Green, Accent 4, Lighter 60% as the alternate row color for the fields from the Patron table; then apply the theme color Green, Accent 4, Lighter 80% as the alternate row color for the fields from the Donation table. (*Hint:* You must first select an entire row with no background color for the appropriate fields before applying each alternate row color.) Scroll through the report to find a patron record with multiple donations so you can verify the effect of applying the alternate row color to the Donation fields.

19. Apply conditional formatting so that any DonationValue greater than or equal to 250 is formatted as bold and with the Brown font color.

✪ **Explore** 20. Preview the report so you can see two pages at once. (*Hint:* Use a button on the PRINT PREVIEW tab.) Check the report to confirm that it is formatted correctly and all field labels and field values are fully displayed. Save the report, print its first page (only if asked by your instructor to do so), and then close the report.

21. Compact and repair the Shelter database, and then close it.

## Case Problem 4

**TROUBLESHOOT**

**Data Files needed for this Case Problem: Stanley.accdb** (*cont. from Tutorial 3*), **Hiking.bmp, and Tour.accdb**

*Stanley EcoTours*   Janice and Bill Stanley use the Stanley database to maintain and analyze data about the clients, reservations, and tours for their ecotourism business. You'll help them by creating a form and a report in the Stanley database. Additionally, you'll troubleshoot some problems in another database containing tour information. Complete the following:

1. Open the **Stanley** database you created and worked with in Tutorials 1 through 3, and then click the Enable Content button next to the security warning, if necessary.

2. Use the Form Wizard to create a form containing a main form and a subform. Select all the fields from the Guest table for the main form, and select all the fields except GuestID from the Reservation table for the subform. Use the Datasheet layout. Specify the title **GuestReservations** for the main form and the title **ReservationSubform** for the subform.

3. Apply the Organic theme to the GuestReservations form *only*.

4. Edit the form title so that it appears with a space between the two words. Change the font color of the title to the Blue-Gray, Accent 3, Darker 25% theme color.

5. Insert the Hiking picture, which is located in the Access1 ▸ Case4 folder provided with your Data Files, in the GuestReservations form. Remove the picture from the control layout, and then move the picture to the right of the form title. Resize the picture so it is approximately double the original size.

6. Resize all columns in the subform to their best fit so that the subform column titles are fully displayed. Save the form.

7. Use the Find command to search for records that contain "AB" in the State/Prov field. Display the record for Isabelle Rouy (GuestID 417), and then change the Address field value for this record to **15 Brookside Dr**. Close the form.

8. Use the Report Wizard to create a report based on the primary Guest table and the related Reservation table. Select all the fields from the Guest table, and then select all the fields except GuestID from the Reservation table. Do not select any additional grouping levels, and sort the detail records in ascending order by ReservationID. Choose the Outline layout and Portrait orientation. Specify the title **GuestsAndReservations** for the report.

9. Apply the Organic theme to the GuestsAndReservations report *only*.

10. Edit the report title so that it appears as "Guests and Reservations"; then change the font color of the title to the Blue-Gray, Accent 3, Darker 25% theme color.

11. Move the Phone field label to the left, and then resize it from its right side to make the label box smaller. Then move the Phone field value box to the left, and then resize it on its right side to make the box bigger and fully display the field value.

12. Insert the Hiking picture, which is located in the Access1 ▸ Case4 folder provided with your Data Files, in the GuestsAndReservations report. Move the picture to the right of the report title. Resize the picture so it is approximately double the original size.

13. Apply conditional formatting so that any People field value greater than or equal to 5 appears as bold and with the Red color applied.

14. Preview the entire report to confirm that it is formatted correctly. If necessary, return to Layout view and make changes so that all field labels and field values are completely displayed.

15. Save the report, print its first page (only if asked by your instructor to do so), and then close the report.

16. Compact and repair the Stanley database, and then close it.

⚙ **Troubleshoot** 17. Open the Tour database located in the Access1 ▸ Case4 folder provided with your Data Files. Open the CustomerData form in the Tour database. The form is not formatted correctly; it should be formatted with the Ion Boardroom theme and the theme color Plum, Accent 1, Darker 25% applied to the title. There are other problems with the form title's format as well. Additionally, some of the field labels are not properly formatted with regard to spacing between words. Identify and fix the problems with the form's format. (*Hint:* To fix the spacing between words in the necessary field labels, use the same procedure you use to fix the spacing between words in the form title text.) Save and close the corrected form.

⚙ **Troubleshoot** 18. Open the CustomerBookings form, which is also not formatted correctly. Modify the form so that it matches the corrected format of the CustomerData form and has a consistent design, including the correctly placed image (Hiking.bmp). Fix the formatting problems with the subform as well, and then save and close the corrected form with subform.

⚙ **Troubleshoot** 19. Open the CustomersAndBookings report. This report should have a consistent format in terms of theme, color, and so on as the two forms. Additionally, some of the field labels are not properly formatted with regard to spacing between words. (*Hint:* To fix the spacing between words in the necessary field labels, use the same procedure you use to fix the spacing between words in the report title text.) Find and fix these formatting errors. The report also has several problems with field labels and field value boxes, where the labels and values are not fully displayed. Locate and correct all of these problems, being sure to scroll through the entire report. Also, the conditional formatting applied to the People field is supposed to use a bold Red font. Edit the rule to correct the conditional formatting. Save the corrected report, and then preview it to identify and correct any remaining formatting problems. Compact and repair the Tour database, and then close it.

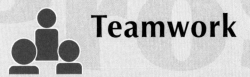

# Teamwork

## Working with a Team to Create a Database

Teamwork is the collaborative effort of individuals working together to achieve a goal. Most organizations rely on teams to complete work tasks, regardless of whether those teams are formal and ongoing or informally organized to achieve a specific goal. Some teams might even be virtual, such as teams that use telecommunications technologies and social networks to complete tasks from different corporate or geographical locations.

When an organization decides to use a database to manage information, the database is rarely planned, created, and maintained by a single individual. In most cases, a team of individuals is assigned to work on different stages of database development. For example, a team might research the needs of the organization, the best database management system to use to meet those needs, and the skills required of the team members to create, update, and maintain the database. Then another team might take over the task of actually creating the database and its objects, inputting the data, and installing the database on the organization's network. Finally, yet another team might conduct training sessions to teach users how to use the database to extract the data they require to perform their jobs.

Regardless of the type of database being created, the roles that individual team members play when working on a team are similar to what you might expect in any situation that requires a collaborative effort.

## The Roles of Team Members

If a team is to be successful, individual members must see the value in their respective contributions and what the team as a whole gets out of each member's contribution. This means two important requirements must be met: task performance and social satisfaction. Task performance usually is handled by one or more members who are task specialists. Task specialists spend a lot of time and effort ensuring that the team achieves its goals. They initiate ideas, give opinions, gather information, sort details, and provide motivation to keep the team on track.

Social satisfaction is handled by individuals who strengthen the team's social bonds through encouragement, empathy, conflict resolution, compromise, and tension reduction. Have you ever been on a team where the tension was high, and someone stepped in to tell a joke or tried to soften the blow of criticism? That person held the role of managing social satisfaction.

Both the task specialist and social satisfaction specialist are important roles on teams. These are not the only roles, however. Other roles include team leaders, work coordinators, idea people, and critics. The roles of individual team members are not always mutually exclusive. For example, the task specialist might also be the team leader, and the idea person might also fill the social satisfaction role. As you begin working with your team in this exercise, watch how these roles are filled and how they change as your team completes its work. Perhaps you'll want to discuss upfront which role each member is comfortable filling to see how complementary your collective skill sets turn out to be. What if your team lacks a role? Then you'll need to figure out, as a team, how to move forward so you can complete your work successfully. The following are tips that everyone should respect as work on a team begins:

- Remember that everyone brings something of value to the team.
- Respect and support each other as you work toward the common goal.
- When criticism or questions arise, try to see things from the other person's perspective.
- If someone needs assistance, find ways to encourage or support that person so the team is not affected.
- Deal with negative or unproductive attitudes immediately so they don't damage team energy and attitude.
- Get outside help if the team becomes stuck and can't move forward.
- Provide periodic positive encouragement or rewards for contributions.

# The Importance of Technology in Teamwork

Many teams now depend on technology to accomplish work tasks. For example, corporate intranets and networks, email and voice mail, texting and instant messaging, teleconferencing and software collaboration tools, social networks, and cell phones can support teamwork. Each time you work in a group, decide at the outset how the team will use different technologies to communicate and document work activities. Determine how the team will organize and combine deliverable documents or presentation materials. Use whatever technology tools make the most sense for your team, your task, and your skills.

PROSKILLS

## Create a Database

Many organizations use Access to manage business data, but Access can also be a valuable tool to track personal data. For example, you might create an Access database to store information about items in a personal collection, such as CDs, DVDs, or books; items related to a hobby, such as coin or stamp collecting, travel, or family history; or items related to sports teams, theater clubs, or other organizations to which you might belong. In this exercise, you'll work with your team members to create a database that will contain information of your choice, using the Access skills and features presented in Tutorials 1 through 4. As a group, you'll choose something the team is interested in tracking, such as members and activities of a college service organization or recruiters and job opportunities at your school.

### Using Templates

Access includes templates for creating databases. A **database template** is a database containing predefined tables, queries, forms, and reports. Using a database template can save you time and effort when creating a database. For example, if the database objects available in one of the database templates are suitable for the data you want to store, you can use the template to quickly create a database with the objects already created for you. You can then modify them, as necessary, to suit your needs. Before you begin to create a database with your team members, review the following steps for using a database template.

### To create a database using a database template:

1. Make sure the New screen is displayed in Backstage view.
2. Click one of the available Desktop templates, or use the box at the top of the screen to search for templates online. (Note that templates without the word "Desktop" in their names require Sharepoint, so do not choose one of those.)
3. Specify the name for your database and a location in which to save the database file.
4. Click the Create button.
5. Use the resulting database objects to enter, modify, or delete data or database objects.

### Work in a Team to Create a Database

Working with your team members, you can decide to use a database template for this exercise if the template fits the data you want to track. Note, however, that you still need to create the additional database objects indicated in the following steps—tables, queries, forms, and reports—to complete the exercise successfully.

**Note:** Please be sure *not* to include any personal information of a sensitive nature in the database you create to be submitted to your instructor for this exercise. Later on, you can update the data in your database with such information for your own personal use.

1. Meet with your team to determine what data you want to track in your new Access database. Determine how many tables you need and what data will go into each table. Be sure that the data you choose to track lends itself to at least three groupings of related data, that at least twenty items are available to track within each group, and that you'll be able to track multiple types of data. Sketch the layout of the columns (fields) and rows (records) for each table.

Also discuss the field properties for each field, so that team members can document the characteristics needed for each field as they collect data. Consider using a standard form to help each person as he or she collects the necessary data.

Next, assign data gathering and documentation tasks to each team member and set a deadline for finishing this initial task. Consider using Excel workbooks for this task, as you can use them to import the data later when working in Access. When all the data for the fields is collected, meet again as a team to examine the data collected and determine the structure of the database you will create. Finally, assign each team member specific tasks for creating the database objects discussed in the following steps.

2. Create a new Access database to contain the data your team wants to track.

3. Create two or three tables in the database that can be joined through one-to-many relationships.

4. Using the preliminary design work done by team members, define the properties for each field in each table. Make sure to include a mix of data types for the fields (for example, do not include only Short Text fields in each table).

5. As a team, discuss and specify a primary key for each table.

6. Define the necessary one-to-many relationships between the tables in the database with referential integrity enforced.

7. Enter 20 to 30 records in each table. If appropriate, your team can import the data for a table from another source, such as an Excel workbook or a text file.

8. Create 5 to 10 queries based on single tables and multiple tables. Be sure that some of the queries include some or all of the following: exact match conditions, comparison operators, and logical operators.

9. For some of the queries, use various sorting and filtering techniques to display the query results in various ways. Save these queries with the sort and/or filter applied.

10. If possible, and depending on the data your team is tracking, create at least one calculated field in one of the queries.

11. If possible, and depending on the data your team is tracking, use aggregate functions to produce summary statistics based on the data in at least one of the tables.

12. Create at least one form for each table in the database. Enhance each form's appearance with pictures, themes, title colors, and so on.

13. Create at least one form with a main form and subform based on related tables in the database. Enhance the form's appearance as appropriate.

14. Create at least one report based on each table in the database. Enhance each report's appearance with pictures, themes, color, and so on.

15. Apply conditional formatting to the values in at least one of the reports.

16. Submit your team's completed database to your instructor as requested. Include printouts of any database objects, such as reports, if required. Also, provide written documentation that describes the role of each team member and his or her contributions to the team. This documentation should include descriptions of any challenges the team faced while completing this exercise and how the team members worked together to overcome those challenges.

TUTORIAL **1**

## OBJECTIVES

**Session 1.1**
- Plan and create a new presentation
- Create a title slide and slides with lists
- Edit and format text
- Move and copy text
- Convert a list to a SmartArt diagram
- Duplicate, rearrange, and delete slides
- Close a presentation

**Session 1.2**
- Open an existing presentation
- Change the theme and theme variant
- Insert and crop photos
- Modify photo compression options
- Resize and move objects
- Create speaker notes
- Check the spelling
- Run a slide show
- Print slides, handouts, speaker notes, and the outline

# Creating a Presentation

*Presenting Information About Community Supported Agriculture*

## Case | *Valley Falls CSA*

Isaac DeSoto graduated from Claflin University in Orangeburg, South Carolina, with a degree in Agriculture Production Technology. He began his career working for the South Carolina Department of Agriculture. Recently, he bought a large farm near Spartanburg, South Carolina, and started a community-supported agriculture program, or CSA. In a CSA, people buy shares each season and, in return, receive weekly portions of produce from the farm. Isaac also created a partnership with other local farmers and founded Valley Falls CSA. Isaac wants to use a PowerPoint presentation to attract new co-op members.

**Microsoft PowerPoint 2013** (or simply **PowerPoint**) is a computer program you use to create a collection of slides that can contain text, charts, pictures, sounds, movies, multimedia, and so on. In this tutorial, you'll use PowerPoint to create a presentation that Isaac can use to explain what Valley Falls CSA is and what it has to offer to potential members and the community. After Isaac reviews it, you'll add graphics and speaker notes to the presentation. Finally, you'll check the spelling, run the slide show to evaluate it, and print the file.

## STARTING DATA FILES

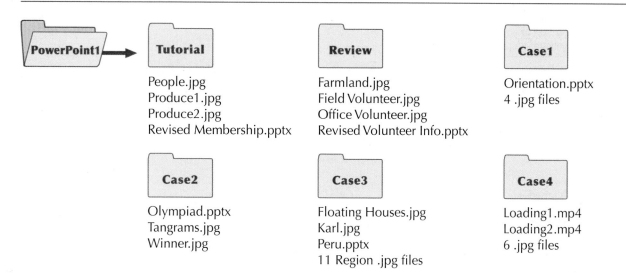

**PowerPoint1** →

**Tutorial**
People.jpg
Produce1.jpg
Produce2.jpg
Revised Membership.pptx

**Review**
Farmland.jpg
Field Volunteer.jpg
Office Volunteer.jpg
Revised Volunteer Info.pptx

**Case1**
Orientation.pptx
4 .jpg files

**Case2**
Olympiad.pptx
Tangrams.jpg
Winner.jpg

**Case3**
Floating Houses.jpg
Karl.jpg
Peru.pptx
11 Region .jpg files

**Case4**
Loading1.mp4
Loading2.mp4
6 .jpg files

# Session 1.1 Visual Overview:

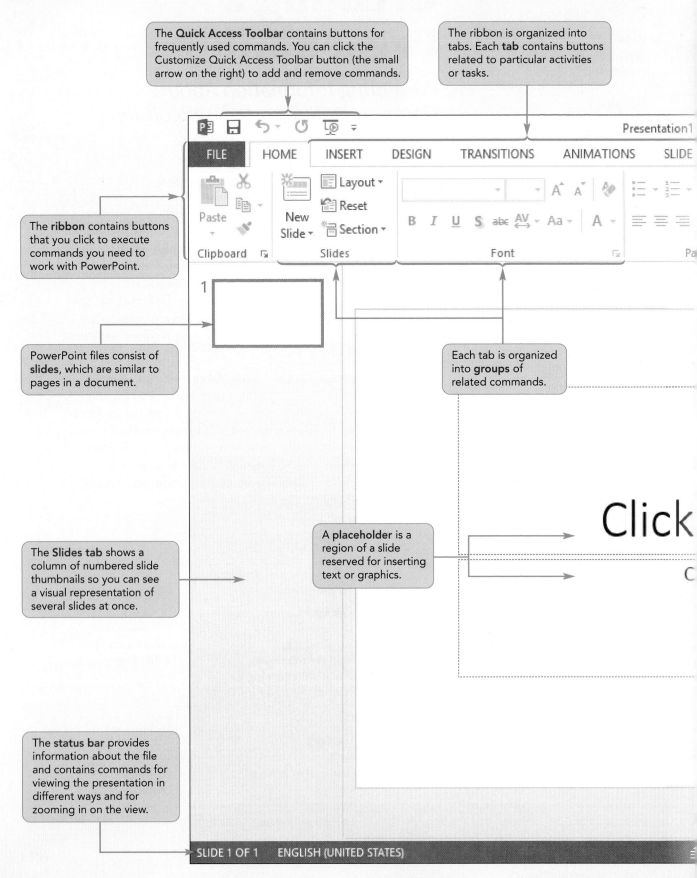

The **Quick Access Toolbar** contains buttons for frequently used commands. You can click the Customize Quick Access Toolbar button (the small arrow on the right) to add and remove commands.

The ribbon is organized into tabs. Each **tab** contains buttons related to particular activities or tasks.

The **ribbon** contains buttons that you click to execute commands you need to work with PowerPoint.

PowerPoint files consist of **slides**, which are similar to pages in a document.

Each tab is organized into **groups** of related commands.

The **Slides tab** shows a column of numbered slide thumbnails so you can see a visual representation of several slides at once.

A **placeholder** is a region of a slide reserved for inserting text or graphics.

The **status bar** provides information about the file and contains commands for viewing the presentation in different ways and for zooming in on the view.

# The PowerPoint Window

The title bar contains the filename of the current presentation. A temporary filename "Presentation" followed by a number appears until you save the file.

You click the Ribbon Display Options button to select commands to display and hide the ribbon.

You use the window buttons to minimize, maximize, and close the PowerPoint window.

The **Sign in link** lets you sign into your Office account. If you have already signed in, your name might appear here instead of this link.

You click the Help button to open the PowerPoint Help window, where you can type key words in the Search box to find information about topics related to those words.

The **Slide pane** shows the current slide as it will appear during your slide show.

The Zoom controls magnify or shrink the display of content in the PowerPoint window. Clicking the Zoom Out (the minus sign) or Zoom In (the plus sign) buttons or dragging the slider changes the zoom percentage.

View buttons allow you to switch to different views of the presentation.

You click the Fit slide to current window button to resize the slide in the Slide pane to fit in the window.

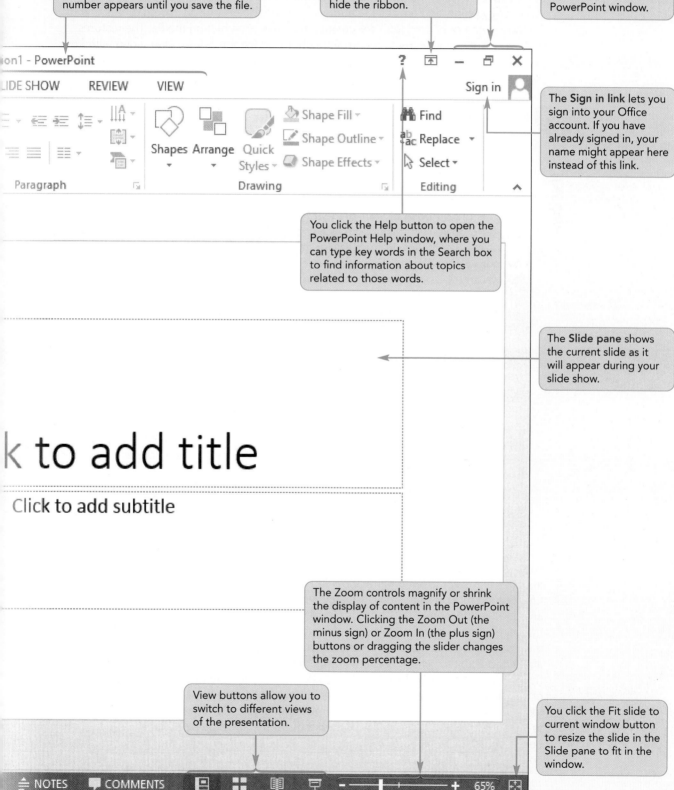

# Planning a Presentation

A **presentation** is a talk (lecture) or prepared file in which the person speaking or the person who prepared the file—the presenter—wants to communicate with an audience to explain new concepts or ideas, sell a product or service, entertain, train the audience in a new skill or technique, or any of a wide variety of other topics.

Most people find it helpful to use **presentation media**—visual and audio aids to support key points and engage the audience's attention. Microsoft PowerPoint is one of the most commonly used tools for creating effective presentation media. The features of PowerPoint make it easy to incorporate photos, diagrams, music, and video with key points of a presentation. Before you create a presentation, you should spend some time planning its content.

**PROSKILLS**

## Verbal Communication: Planning a Presentation

Answering a few key questions will help you create a presentation using appropriate presentation media that successfully delivers its message or motivates the audience to take an action.

- **What is the purpose of your presentation?** In other words, what action or response do you want your audience to have? For example, do you want them to buy something, follow instructions, or make a decision?
- **Who is your audience?** Think about the needs and interests of your audience as well as any decisions they'll make as a result of what you have to say. What you choose to say to your audience must be relevant to their needs, interests, and decisions or it will be forgotten.
- **What are the main points of your presentation?** Identify the information that is directly relevant to your audience.
- **What presentation media will help your audience absorb the information and remember it later?** Do you need lists, photos, charts, or tables?
- **What is the format for your presentation?** Will you deliver the presentation orally or will you create a presentation file that your audience members will view on their own, without you present?
- **How much time do you have for the presentation?** Keep that in mind as you prepare the presentation content so that you have enough time to present all of your key points.
- **Will your audience benefit from handouts? Handouts** are printed documents you give to your audience before, during, or after your presentation.

The purpose of Isaac's presentation is to sell shares in the new CSA. His audience will be members of the local community who are interested in the benefits of belonging to a CSA and want to learn more about it. His key points are that being a member of a CSA is good for consumers because they will be eating fresher, more nutritious food, and good for the community because local farms are supported and there is less of an impact on the environment. He also plans to explain pricing and how members get their produce so that audience members have enough information to make a decision about becoming a member. Isaac will use PowerPoint to display lists and graphics to help make his message clear. He plans to deliver his presentation orally to small groups of people in a classroom-sized room, and his presentation will be 15 to 20 minutes long. For handouts, he plans to have membership applications available to distribute to anyone who is interested, but he will not distribute anything before his presentation because he wants the audience's full attention to be on him and the details are not complex enough that the audience will need a sheet to refer to as he is speaking.

Once you know what you want to say or communicate, you can prepare the presentation media to help communicate your ideas.

# Starting PowerPoint and Creating a New Presentation

Microsoft PowerPoint 2013 is a tool you can use to create and display visual and audio aids on slides to help clarify the points you want to make in your presentation or to create a presentation that people view on their own without you being present.

When PowerPoint starts, the Recent screen in Backstage view is displayed. **Backstage view** contains commands that allow you to manage your presentation files and PowerPoint options. When you first start PowerPoint, the only actions available to you in Backstage view are to open an existing PowerPoint file or create a new file. You'll start PowerPoint now.

### To start PowerPoint:

1. Display the Windows Start screen, if necessary.

   **Using Windows 7?** To complete Step 1, click the Start button on the taskbar.

2. Click the **PowerPoint 2013** tile. PowerPoint starts and displays the Recent screen in Backstage view. See Figure 1-1. In the orange bar on the left is a list of recently opened presentations, and on the right are options for creating new presentations.

**Figure 1-1**    Recent screen in Backstage view

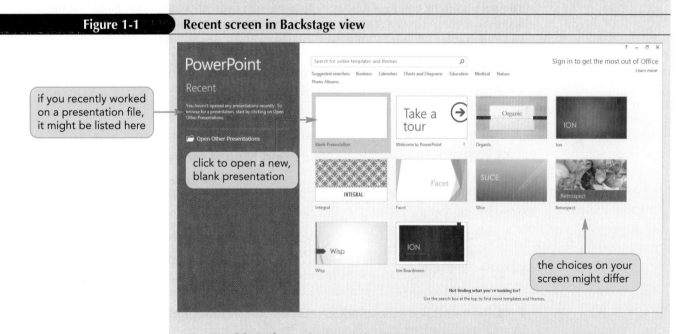

if you recently worked on a presentation file, it might be listed here

click to open a new, blank presentation

the choices on your screen might differ

   **Trouble?** If you don't see the PowerPoint 2013 tile, type PowerPoint to display the Apps screen with the PowerPoint 2013 tile highlighted, and then click the tile.

   **Using Windows 7?** To complete Step 2, point to All Programs on the Start menu, click Microsoft Office 2013, and then click PowerPoint 2013.

3. Click **Blank Presentation**. Backstage view closes and a new presentation window appears. The temporary filename "Presentation1" appears in the title bar. There is only one slide in the new presentation—Slide 1.

**Trouble?** If you do not see the area on the ribbon that contains buttons and you see only the ribbon tab names, click the HOME tab to expand the ribbon and display the commands, and then in the bottom-right corner of the ribbon, click the Pin the ribbon button 📌 that appears.

**Trouble?** If the window is not maximized, click the Maximize button 🔲 in the upper-right corner.

When you create a new presentation, it is displayed in Normal view. **Normal view** displays slides one at a time in the Slide pane, allowing you to see how the text and graphics look on each slide, and displays **thumbnails**—miniature images—of all the slides in the presentation in the Slides tab on the left. The HOME tab on the ribbon is orange to indicate that it is selected when you first open or create a presentation. The Session 1.1 Visual Overview identifies elements of the PowerPoint window.

## Working in Touch Mode

In Office 2013, you can work with a mouse or, if you have a touch screen, you can work in Touch Mode. In **Touch Mode** the ribbon increases in height so that there is more space around each button on the ribbon, making it easier to use your finger to tap the specific button you need. Also, in the main part of the PowerPoint window, the instructions telling you to "Click" are replaced with instructions to "Tap." Note that the figures in this text show the screen with Mouse Mode on. You'll switch to Touch Mode and then back to Mouse Mode now.

**Note:** The following steps assume that you are using a mouse. If you are instead using a touch device, please read these steps but don't complete them, so that you remain working in Touch Mode.

### To switch between Touch Mode and Mouse Mode:

▶ **1.** On the Quick Access Toolbar, click the **Customize Quick Access Toolbar** button ⛁. A menu opens. The Touch/Mouse Mode command near the bottom of the menu does not have a checkmark next to it.

 **Trouble?** If the Touch/Mouse Mode command has a checkmark next to it, press the Esc key to close the menu, and then skip Step 2.

▶ **2.** On the menu, click **Touch/Mouse Mode**. The menu closes and the Touch/Mouse Mode button appears on the Quick Access Toolbar.

▶ **3.** On the Quick Access Toolbar, click the **Touch/Mouse Mode** button 👆. A menu opens listing Mouse and Touch, and the icon next to Mouse is shaded orange to indicate it is selected.

 **Trouble?** If the icon next to Touch is shaded orange, press the Esc key to close the menu and skip Step 4.

▶ **4.** On the menu, click **Touch**. The menu closes and the ribbon increases in height so that there is more space around each button on the ribbon. Notice that the instructions in the main part of the PowerPoint window changed by replacing the instruction to "Click" with the instruction to "Tap." See Figure 1-2. Now you'll change back to Mouse Mode.

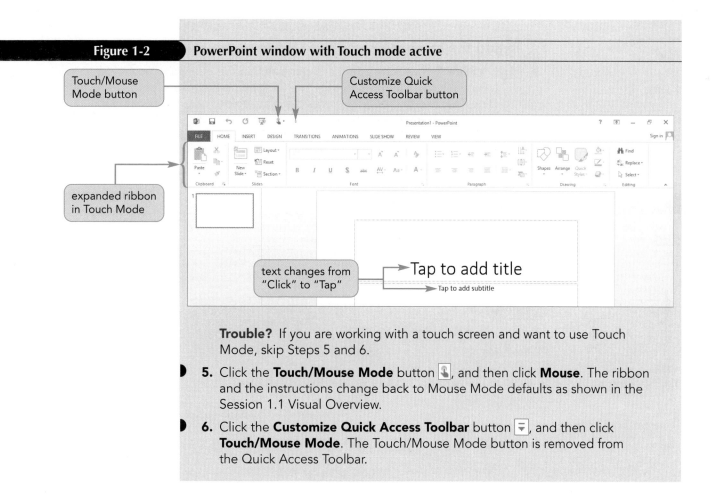

**Figure 1-2**  PowerPoint window with Touch mode active

Touch/Mouse Mode button

Customize Quick Access Toolbar button

expanded ribbon in Touch Mode

text changes from "Click" to "Tap"

Tap to add title

Tap to add subtitle

**Trouble?** If you are working with a touch screen and want to use Touch Mode, skip Steps 5 and 6.

▶ 5. Click the **Touch/Mouse Mode** button, and then click **Mouse**. The ribbon and the instructions change back to Mouse Mode defaults as shown in the Session 1.1 Visual Overview.

▶ 6. Click the **Customize Quick Access Toolbar** button, and then click **Touch/Mouse Mode**. The Touch/Mouse Mode button is removed from the Quick Access Toolbar.

# Creating a Title Slide

The **title slide** is the first slide in a presentation. It generally contains the title of the presentation plus any other identifying information you want to include, such as a company's slogan, the presenter's name, or a company name. The **font**—a set of characters with the same design—used in the title and subtitle may be the same or may be different fonts that complement each other.

The title slide contains two objects called text placeholders. A placeholder is a region of a slide reserved for inserting text or graphics. A **text placeholder** is a placeholder designed to contain text. Text placeholders usually display text that describes the purpose of the placeholder and instructs you to click so that you can start typing in the placeholder. The larger text placeholder on the title slide is designed to hold the presentation title, and the smaller text placeholder is designed to contain a subtitle. Once you enter text into a text placeholder, it is no longer a placeholder and becomes an object called a **text box**.

When you click in the placeholder, the **insertion point**, which indicates where text will appear when you start typing, appears as a blinking line in the center of the placeholder. In addition, a contextual tab, the DRAWING TOOLS FORMAT tab, appears on the ribbon. A **contextual tab** appears only in context—that is, when a particular type of object is selected or active—and contains commands for modifying that object.

You'll add a title and subtitle for Isaac's presentation now. Isaac wants the title slide to contain the company name and slogan.

### To add the company name and slogan to the title slide:

▶ **1.** On **Slide 1**, move the pointer to position it in the title text placeholder (where it says "Click to add title") so that the pointer changes to $\mathrm{I}$, and then click. The insertion point replaces the placeholder text; the border around the text placeholder changes to a dotted line, and the DRAWING TOOLS FORMAT contextual tab appears as the rightmost tab on the ribbon. Note that in the Font group on the HOME tab, the Font box identifies the title font as Calibri Light. See Figure 1-3.

| Figure 1-3 | Title text placeholder after clicking in it |
| --- | --- |

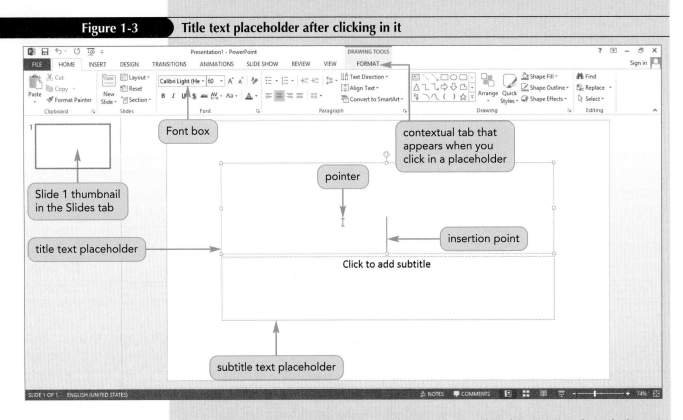

**Trouble?** The insertion point might appear as a thin, blue rectangle with the Mini toolbar above and to the right of it. Ignore this and continue with Step 2.

▶ **2.** Type **Valley Farms CSA**. The placeholder is now a text box.

▶ **3.** Click a blank area of the slide. The border of the text box disappears, and the DRAWING TOOLS FORMAT tab no longer appears on the ribbon.

▶ **4.** Click in the **subtitle text placeholder** (where it says "Click to add subtitle"), and then type **Freshest, most delicious food!**. Notice in the Font group that the subtitle font is Calibri, a font which works well with the Calibri Light font used in the title text.

▶ **5.** Click a blank area of the slide.

## Saving and Editing a Presentation

Once you have created a presentation, you should name and save the presentation file. You can save the file on a hard drive or a network drive, on an external drive such as a USB drive, or to your account on SkyDrive, Microsoft's free online storage area.

## To save the presentation for the first time:

▶ **1.** On the Quick Access Toolbar, point to the **Save** button 🖫. The button becomes shaded and its ScreenTip appears. A **ScreenTip** identifies the names of buttons; sometimes they also display a key combination you can press instead of clicking the button and information about how to use the button. In this case, the ScreenTip displays the word "Save" and the key combination for the Save command, Ctrl+S.

▶ **2.** Click the **Save** button 🖫. The Save As screen in Backstage view appears. See Figure 1-4. Because a presentation is open, more commands are available in Backstage view than when you started PowerPoint. The **navigation bar** on the left contains commands for working with the file and program options.

| Figure 1-4 | Save As screen in Backstage view |
| --- | --- |

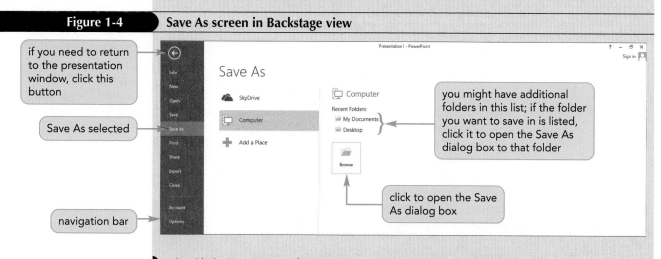

if you need to return to the presentation window, click this button

Save As selected

navigation bar

you might have additional folders in this list; if the folder you want to save in is listed, click it to open the Save As dialog box to that folder

click to open the Save As dialog box

▶ **3.** Click **Computer**, if necessary, and then click the **Browse** button. The Save As dialog box opens, similar to the one shown in Figure 1-5.

| Figure 1-5 | Save As dialog box |
| --- | --- |

the current folder on your screen might differ

suggested filename

your user name will appear here

**Trouble?** If you are saving your files to your SkyDrive account, click SkyDrive on the Save As screen, log in to your account if necessary, and then click the Browse button.

▶ **4.** Navigate to the drive and folder where you are storing your Data Files, and then click in the **File name** box. The suggested filename, Valley Falls CSA, is selected.

▶ **5.** Type **Membership Info**. The text you type replaces the selected text in the File name box.

▶ **6.** Click the **Save** button. The file is saved, the dialog box and Backstage view close, and the presentation window appears again with the new filename in the title bar.

Once you have created a presentation, you can make changes to it. For example, if you need to change text in a text box, you can easily edit it. The Backspace key deletes characters to the left of the insertion point, and the Delete key deletes characters to the right of the insertion point.

If you mistype or misspell a word, you might not need to correct it because the **AutoCorrect** feature automatically corrects many commonly mistyped and misspelled words after you press the spacebar or the Enter key. For instance, if you type "cna" and then press the spacebar, PowerPoint corrects the word to "can." If you want AutoCorrect to stop making a particular change, you can display the AutoCorrect Options menu, and then click Stop making the change. (The exact wording will differ depending on the change made.)

After you make changes to a presentation, you will need to save the file again so that the changes are stored. Because you have already saved the presentation with a permanent filename, using the Save command does not open the Save As dialog box; it simply saves the changes you made to the file.

**To edit the text on Slide 1 and save your changes:**

▶ **1.** On Slide 1, click the **title**, and then use the ← and → keys as needed to position the insertion point to the right of the word "Farms."

▶ **2.** Press the **Backspace** key three times. The three characters to the left of the insertion point, "rms," are deleted.

▶ **3.** Type **lls** to change the second word to "Falls."

▶ **4.** Click to the left of the word "Freshest" in the subtitle text box to position the insertion point in front of that word, type **Teh**, and then press the **spacebar**. PowerPoint corrects the word you typed to "The."

▶ **5.** Move the pointer on top of the word **The**. A small, very faint rectangle appears below the first letter of the word. This indicates that an AutoCorrection has been made.

▶ **6.** Move the pointer on top of the AutoCorrection indicator box so that it changes to the AutoCorrect Options button ⌷ ▾, and then click the **AutoCorrect Options button** ⌷ ▾. A menu opens, as shown in Figure 1-6. You can change the word back to what you originally typed, instruct PowerPoint to stop making this type of correction in this file, or open the AutoCorrect dialog box.

**Trouble?** If you can't see the AutoCorrection indicator box, point to the letter T, and then slowly move the pointer down until it is on top of the box and changes it to the AutoCorrect Options button.

| Figure 1-6 | AutoCorrect Options button menu |

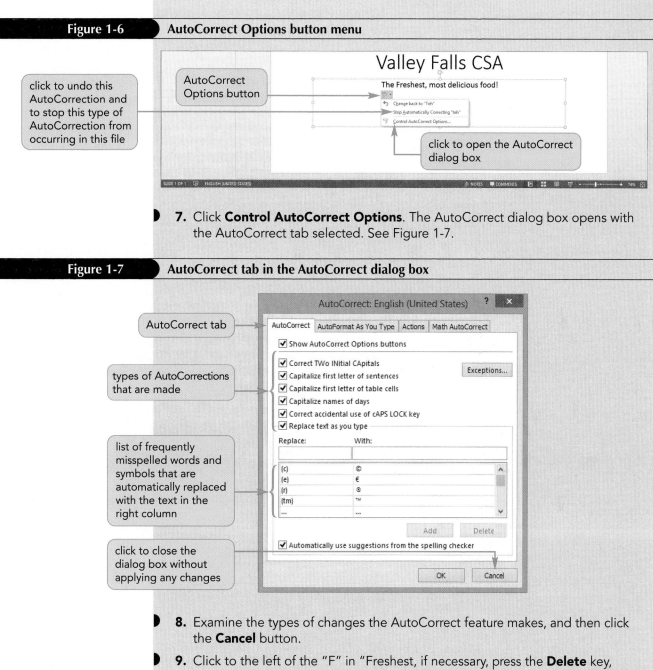

click to undo this AutoCorrection and to stop this type of AutoCorrection from occurring in this file

AutoCorrect Options button

click to open the AutoCorrect dialog box

**7.** Click **Control AutoCorrect Options**. The AutoCorrect dialog box opens with the AutoCorrect tab selected. See Figure 1-7.

| Figure 1-7 | AutoCorrect tab in the AutoCorrect dialog box |

AutoCorrect tab

types of AutoCorrections that are made

list of frequently misspelled words and symbols that are automatically replaced with the text in the right column

click to close the dialog box without applying any changes

**8.** Examine the types of changes the AutoCorrect feature makes, and then click the **Cancel** button.

**9.** Click to the left of the "F" in "Freshest, if necessary, press the **Delete** key, and then type **f**. The subtitle now is "The freshest, most delicious food!" Now that you have modified the presentation, you need to save your changes.

**10.** On the Quick Access Toolbar, click the **Save** button 🔲. The changes you made are saved to the file you named Membership Info.

## Adding New Slides

Now that you've created the title slide, you need to add more slides. Every slide has a **layout**, which is the arrangement of placeholders on the slide. The title slide uses the Title Slide layout. A commonly used layout is the Title and Content layout, which contains a title text placeholder for the slide title and a content placeholder.

A **content placeholder** is a placeholder designed to hold several types of slide content including text, a table, a chart, a picture, or a video.

To add a new slide, you use the New Slide button in the Slides group on the HOME tab. When you click the top part of the New Slide button, a new slide is inserted with the same layout as the current slide, unless the current slide is the title slide; in that case the new slide has the Title and Content layout. If you want to create a new slide with a different layout, click the bottom part of the New Slide button to open a gallery of layouts, and then click the layout you want to use.

You can change the layout of a slide at any time. To do this, click the Layout button in the Slides group to display the same gallery of layouts that appears in the Add Slide gallery, and then click the slide layout you want to apply to the selected slide.

As you add slides, you can switch from one slide to another by clicking the slide thumbnails in the Slides tab. You need to add several new slides to the file.

### To add new slides and apply different layouts:

▶ **1.** Make sure the HOME tab is displayed on the ribbon.

▶ **2.** In the Slides group, click the **New Slide** button (that is, click the top part of the button). A new slide appears in the Slide pane and its thumbnail appears in the Slides tab below Slide 1. The new slide has the Title and Content layout applied. This layout contains a title text placeholder and a content placeholder. In the Slides tab, an orange border appears around the new Slide 2, indicating that it is the current slide.

▶ **3.** In the Slides group, click the **New Slide** button again. A new Slide 3 is added. Because Slide 2 had the Title and Content layout applied, Slide 3 also has that layout applied.

▶ **4.** In the Slides group, click the **New Slide button arrow** (that is, click the bottom part of the New Slide button). A gallery of the available layouts appears. See Figure 1-8.

| Figure 1-8 | Gallery of layouts on the New Slide button menu |
| --- | --- |

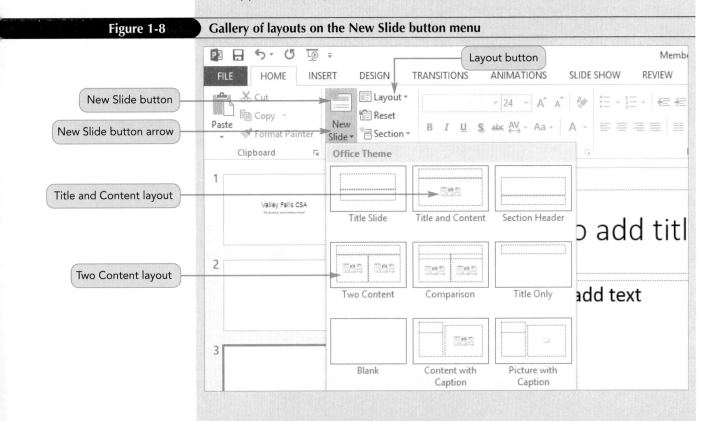

**5.** In the gallery, click the **Two Content** layout. The gallery closes and a new Slide 4 is inserted with the Two Content layout applied. This layout includes three objects: a title text placeholder and two content placeholders.

**6.** In the Slides group, click the **New Slide** button. A new Slide 5 is added to the presentation. Because Slide 4 had the Two Content layout applied, that layout is also applied to the new slide. You need to change the layout of Slide 5.

**7.** In the Slides group, click the **Layout** button. The same gallery of layouts that appeared when you clicked the New Slide button arrow appears. The Two Content layout is selected, as indicated by the orange shading behind it, showing you that this is the layout applied to the current slide, Slide 5.

**8.** Click the **Title and Content** layout. The layout of Slide 5 is changed to Title and Content.

**9.** In the Slides group, click the **New Slide** button three more times to add three more slides with the Title and Content layout. There are now eight slides in the presentation. In the Slides tab, Slides 1 through 3 have scrolled up out of view, and vertical scroll bars are now visible in both the Slides tab and in the Slide pane.

**10.** In the Slides tab, drag the **scroll box** to the top of the vertical scroll bar, and then click the **Slide 2** thumbnail. Slide 2 becomes the current slide—it appears in the Slide pane and is selected in the Slides tab. See Figure 1-9.

| Figure 1-9 | Slide 2 with the Title and Content layout |
|---|---|

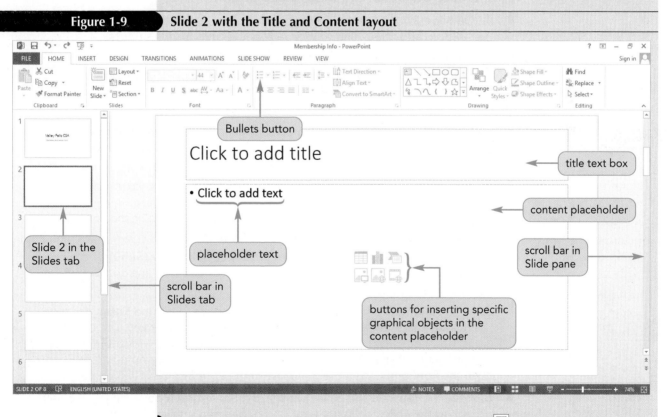

**11.** On the Quick Access Toolbar, click the **Save** button 🖫. The changes you made are saved in the file.

If you accidentally close a presentation without saving changes and need to recover it, you can do so by clicking the FILE tab, clicking Open in the navigation bar, and then clicking the Recover Unsaved Presentations button.

# Creating Lists

One way to help explain the topic or concept you are describing in your presentation is to use lists. For oral presentations, the intent of lists is to enhance the oral presentation, not replace it. In self-running presentations, items in lists might need to be longer and more descriptive. However, keep in mind that PowerPoint is a presentation graphics program intended to help you present information in a visual, graphical manner, not create a written document in an alternate form.

Items in a list can appear at different levels. A **first-level item** is a main item in a list; a **second-level item**—sometimes called a **subitem**—is an item beneath and indented from a first-level item. Usually, the font size—the size of the text—in subitems is smaller than the size used for text in the level above. Text is measured in **points**, which is a unit of measurement. Text in a book is typically printed in 10- or 12-point type; text on a slide needs to be much larger so the audience can easily read it.

## Creating a Bulleted List

A **bulleted list** is a list of items with some type of bullet symbol in front of each item or paragraph. When you create a subitem in the list, a different or smaller symbol is often used. You need to create a bulleted list that describes the requirements of a membership in Valley Farms CSA.

**To create bulleted lists on Slides 2 and 3:**

1. On **Slide 2**, click in the **title text placeholder** (with the placeholder text "Click to add title"), and then type **Membership Requirements**.

2. In the content placeholder, click any area where the pointer is shaped as ⌶; in other words, anywhere except on one of the buttons in the center of the placeholder. The placeholder text "Click to add text" disappears, the insertion point appears, and a light gray bullet symbol appears.

   **Trouble?** The insertion point might appear as a thin, blue rectangle with a rectangle called the Mini toolbar above and to the right of it. Ignore this and continue with Step 3.

3. Type **Purchase**. As soon as you type the first character, the icons in the center of the content placeholder disappear, the bullet symbol darkens, and the content placeholder changes to a text box. On the HOME tab, in the Paragraph group, the Bullets button is shaded orange to indicate that it is selected.

4. Press the **spacebar**, type **full-share ($425) or half-share ($250)**, and then press the **Enter** key. The insertion point moves to a new line and a new, light gray bullet appears on the new line.

5. Type **Volunteer minimum two hours per month**, press the **Enter** key, type **Pick up share once per week**, and then press the **Enter** key. The bulleted list now consists of three first-level items, and the insertion point is next to a light gray bullet on the fourth line in the text box. Notice on the HOME tab, in the Font group, that the point size in the Font Size box is 28 points.

6. Press the **Tab** key. The bullet symbol and the insertion point indent one-half inch to the right, the bullet symbol changes to a smaller size, and the number in the Font Size box changes to 24. See Figure 1-10.

**Figure 1-10**    Subitem created on Slide 2

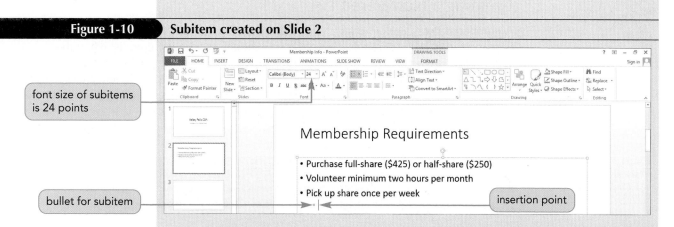

font size of subitems is 24 points

bullet for subitem

insertion point

Membership Requirements

- Purchase full-share ($425) or half-share ($250)
- Volunteer minimum two hours per month
- Pick up share once per week

7. Type **Fridays, 3 p.m. - 5 p.m.** and then press the **Enter** key. When you pressed the spacebar key after typing 5, AutoCorrect changed the dash to an en-dash, a typographical character slightly longer than a hyphen.

8. Type **Saturdays, 7 a.m. - noon**, and then press the **Enter** key. A third subitem is created. You will change it to a first-level item using a key combination. In this book, when you need to press two keys together, the keys will be listed separated by a plus sign. You don't need to press the keys at exactly the same time—press and hold the first key, press and release the second key, and then release the first key.

9. Press the **Shift+Tab** keys. The bullet symbol and the insertion point shift back to the left margin of the text box, the bullet symbol changes back to the larger size, and 28 again appears in the Font Size box because this line is now a first-level bulleted item.

10. Type **Or have it delivered (additional fee)**, press the **Enter** key, and then type **October community celebration**.

11. In the Slides tab, click the **Slide 3** thumbnail to display Slide 3 in the Slide pane, click in the **title text placeholder**, and then type **Members Receive**.

12. In the content placeholder, click the **placeholder text**, type **Share of pre-selected produce**, press the **Enter** key, and then type **Self-selected items**.

If you add more text than will fit in the text box with the default font sizes and line spacing, **AutoFit** adjusts these features to make the text fit. When AutoFit is activated, the AutoFit Options button appears below the text box. You can click this button and then select from among several options, including turning off AutoFit for this text box and splitting the text between two slides. Although AutoFit can be helpful, be aware that it also allows you to crowd text on a slide, making the slide less effective.

PROSKILLS

### Written Communication: How Much Text Should I Include?

Text can help audiences retain the information you are presenting by allowing them to read the main points while hearing you discuss them. But be wary of adding so much text to your slides that your audience can ignore you and just read the slides. Try to follow the 7x7 rule—no more than seven items per slide, with no more than seven words per item. A variation of this rule is 6x6, and some presenters even prefer 4x4. If you create a self-running presentation (a presentation file others will view on their own) you will usually need to add more text than you would if you were presenting the material in person.

## Creating a Numbered List

A **numbered list** is similar to a bulleted list except that numbers appear in front of each item instead of bullet symbols. Generally you should use a numbered list when the order of the items is important—for example, if you are presenting a list of step-by-step instructions that need to be followed in sequence in order to complete a task successfully. You need to create a numbered list on Slide 5 to explain how members can order items in addition to their regular CSA share.

**To create a numbered list on Slide 5:**

▶ 1. In the Slides tab, click the **Slide 5** thumbnail to display Slide 5 in the Slide pane, and then type **Placing Your Order for Additional Items** as the title text.

▶ 2. In the content placeholder, click the **placeholder text**.

▶ 3. On the HOME tab, in the Paragraph group, click the **Numbering** button 📋. The Numbering button is selected, the Bullets button is deselected, and in the content placeholder, the bullet symbol is replaced with the number 1 followed by a period.

   **Trouble?** If a menu containing a gallery of numbering styles appears, you clicked the Numbering button arrow on the right side of the button. Click the Numbering button arrow again to close the menu, and then click the left part of the Numbering button.

▶ 4. Type **Place online by Wednesday**, and then press the **Enter** key. As soon as you start typing, the number 1 darkens to black. After you press the Enter key, the insertion point moves to the next line, next to the light gray number 2.

▶ 5. Type **Verify payment information**, and then press the **Enter** key. The number 3 appears on the next line.

▶ 6. In the Paragraph group, click the **Increase List Level** button 📋. The third line is indented to be a subitem under the second item, and the number 3 that had appeared changes to a number 1 in a smaller size than the first-level items. Clicking the Increase List Level button is an alternative to pressing the Tab key to create a subitem.

▶ 7. Type **Credit card**, press the **Enter** key, type **Debit from checking account**, press the **Enter** key.

▶ 8. In the Paragraph group, click the **Decrease List Level** button 📋. The fifth line is now a first-level item and the number 3 appears next to it. Clicking the Decrease List Level button is an alternative to pressing the Shift+Tab keys to promote a subitem.

▶ 9. Type **Submit**. The list now consists of three first-level numbered items and two subitems under number 2.

▶ 10. In the second item, click before the word "Verify," and then press the **Enter** key. A blank line is inserted above the second item.

▶ 11. Press the ↑ key. A light-gray number 2 appears in the blank line. The item on the third line in the list is still numbered 2.

▶ 12. Type **Specify pickup or delivery**. As soon as you start typing, the new number 2 darkens in the second line and the third item in the list is numbered 3. Compare your screen to Figure 1-11.

| Figure 1-11 | Numbered list on Slide 5 |

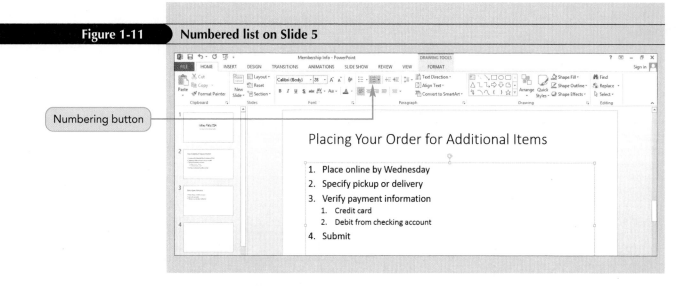

Numbering button

## Creating an Unnumbered List

An **unnumbered list** is a list that does not have bullets or numbers preceding each item. Unnumbered lists are useful in slides when you want to present information on multiple lines without actually itemizing the information. For example, contact information for the presenter, including his or her email address, street address, city, and so on would be clearer if it were in an unnumbered list.

As you have seen, items in a list have a little extra space between each item to visually separate bulleted items. Sometimes, you don't want the extra space between lines. If you press the Shift+Enter keys instead of just the Enter key, a new line is created, but it is still considered to be part of the item above it. Therefore, there is no extra space between the lines. Note that this also means that if you do this in a bulleted or numbered list, the new line will not have a bullet or number next to it because it is not a new item.

You need to create a slide that defines CSA. Also, Isaac asks you to create a slide containing contact information.

**To create unnumbered lists on Slides 4 and 7:**

1. In the Slides tab, click the **Slide 4** thumbnail to display Slide 4 in the Slide pane. Slide 4 has the Two Content layout applied.

2. Type **What Is a CSA?** as the title text, and then in the left content placeholder, click the **placeholder text**.

3. On the HOME tab, in the Paragraph group, click the **Bullets** button . The button is no longer selected, and the bullet symbol disappears from the content placeholder.

4. Type **Community**, press the **Enter** key, type **Supported**, press the **Enter** key, and then type **Agriculture**. Compare your screen to Figure 1-12.

Figure 1-12 **Unnumbered list on Slide 4**

neither the Bullets or Numbering button is selected

no bullet symbol or number appears

5. Display **Slide 7** in the Slide pane, type **For More Information** in the title text placeholder, and then in the content placeholder, click the **placeholder text**.

6. In the Paragraph group, click the **Bullets** button to remove the bullets, type **Valley Falls CSA**, and then press the **Enter** key. A new line is created, but there is extra space above the insertion point. This is not how addresses usually appear.

7. Press the **Backspace** key to delete the new line and move the insertion point back to the end of the first line, and then press the **Shift+Enter** keys. The insertion point moves to the next line and, this time, there is no extra space above it.

8. Type **300 County Fair Road**, press the **Shift+Enter** keys, and then type **Spartanburg, SC 29301**. You need to insert the phone number on the next line, the general email address for the group on the line after that, and the website address on the last line. The extra space above these lines will set this information apart from the address and make it easier to read.

9. Press the **Enter** key to create a new line with extra space above it, type **(864) 555-FOOD**, press the **Enter** key, type **csainfo@valleyfallscsa.example.org**, and then press the **Enter** key. The insertion point moves to a new line with extra space above it, and the email address you typed changes color to blue and is underlined.

When you type text that PowerPoint recognizes as an email or website address and then press the spacebar or Enter key, it automatically formats it as a link that can be clicked during a slide show, and changes its color and adds the underline to indicate this. You can only click links during a slide show.

10. Type **www.valleyfallscsa.example.org**, and then press the **spacebar**. The text is formatted as a link. Isaac plans to click the link during his presentation to show the audience the website, so he wants it to stay formatted as a link. However, there is no need to have the email address formatted as a link because no one will click it during the presentation.

11. Right-click **csainfo@valleyfallscsa.example.org**. A shortcut menu opens.

12. On the shortcut menu, click **Remove Hyperlink**. The email address is no longer formatted as a hyperlink. Compare your screen to Figure 1-13.

**Figure 1-13** **List on Slide 7**

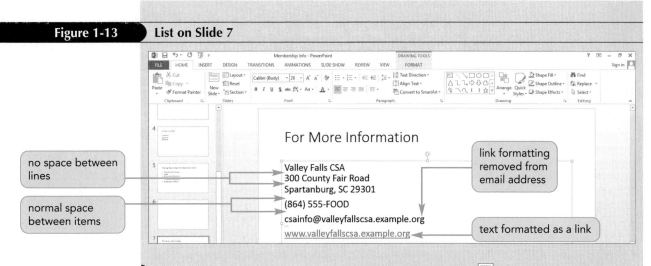

> **13.** On the Quick Access Toolbar, click the **Save** button 🖫 to save the changes.

# Formatting Text

Slides in a presentation should have a cohesive look and feel. For example, the slide titles and the text in content placeholders should be in complementary fonts. However, there are times when you need to change the format of text. For instance, you might want to make specific words bold to make them stand out more.

To apply a format to text, either the text or the text box must be selected. If you want to apply the same formatting to all the text in a text box, you can click the border of the text box. When you do this, the dotted line border changes to a solid line to indicate that the contents of the entire text box are selected.

The commands in the Font group on the HOME tab are used to apply formatting to text. Some of these commands are also available on the Mini toolbar, which appears when you select text with the mouse. The **Mini toolbar** contains commonly used buttons for formatting text. If the Mini toolbar appears, you can use the buttons on it instead of those in the Font group.

Some of the commands in the Font group use the Microsoft Office **Live Preview** feature, which previews the change on the slide so you can instantly see what the text will look like if you apply that format.

Isaac wants the contact information on Slide 7 to be larger. He also wants the first letter of each item in the unnumbered list on Slide 4 ("What Is a CSA?") formatted so they are more prominent.

### To format the text on Slides 4 and 7:

> **1.** On **Slide 7** ("For More Information"), position the pointer on the text box border so that it changes to ⛬, and then click the border of the text box containing the contact information. The border changes to a solid line to indicate that the entire text box is selected.

> **2.** On the HOME tab, in the Font group, click the **Increase Font Size** button A͘ twice. All the text in the text box increases in size with each click.

> **3.** Display **Slide 4** ("What Is a CSA?") in the Slide pane.

**4.** In the unnumbered list, click to the left of "Community," press and hold the **Shift** key, press the → key, and then release the **Shift** key. The letter "C" is selected. See Figure 1-14.

Figure 1-14    **Text selected to be formatted**

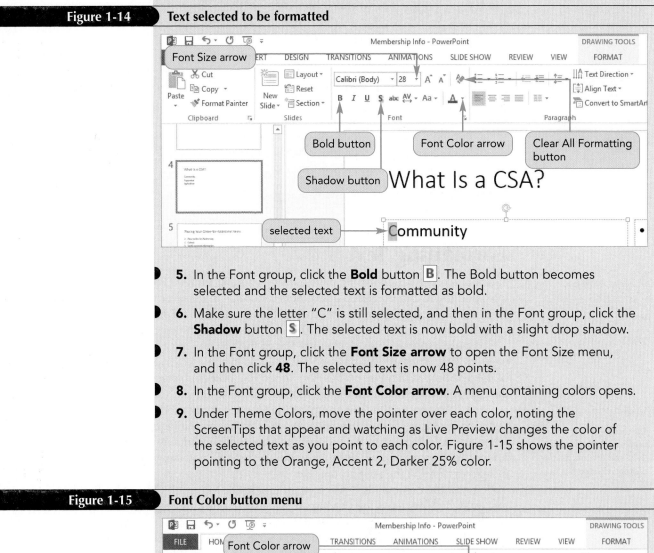

**5.** In the Font group, click the **Bold** button B. The Bold button becomes selected and the selected text is formatted as bold.

**6.** Make sure the letter "C" is still selected, and then in the Font group, click the **Shadow** button S. The selected text is now bold with a slight drop shadow.

**7.** In the Font group, click the **Font Size arrow** to open the Font Size menu, and then click **48**. The selected text is now 48 points.

**8.** In the Font group, click the **Font Color arrow**. A menu containing colors opens.

**9.** Under Theme Colors, move the pointer over each color, noting the ScreenTips that appear and watching as Live Preview changes the color of the selected text as you point to each color. Figure 1-15 shows the pointer pointing to the Orange, Accent 2, Darker 25% color.

**Figure 1-15**    **Font Color button menu**

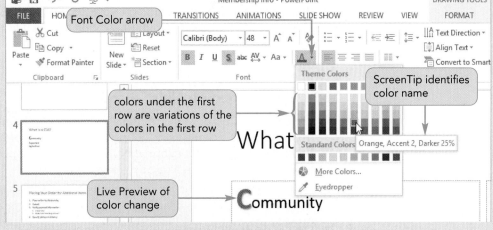

**10.** Using the ScreenTips, locate the **Orange, Accent 2, Darker 25%** color and then click it. The selected text changes to the orange color you clicked.

Now you need to format the first letters in the other words in the list to match the letter "C." You can repeat the steps you did when you formatted the letter "C," or you use the Format Painter to copy all the formatting of the letter "C" to the other letters you need to format.

Also, Isaac wants the text in the unnumbered list to be as large as possible. Because the first letters of each word are larger than the rest of the letters, the easiest way to do this is to select all of the text, and then use the Increase Font Size button. All of the letters will increase in size by four points with each click.

### To use the Format Painter to copy and apply formatting on Slide 4:

▶ **1.** Make sure the letter "C" is still selected.

▶ **2.** On the HOME tab, in the Clipboard group, click the **Format Painter** button, and then move the pointer back to the Slide pane. The button is selected, and the pointer changes to 🖌︎[.

▶ **3.** Position the pointer before the letter "S" in "Supported," press and hold the mouse button, drag over the letter **S**, and then release the mouse button. The formatting you applied to the letter "C" is copied to the letter "S" and the Mini toolbar appears. See Figure 1-16. The Mini toolbar appears whenever you drag over text to select it.

| Figure 1-16 | The Mini toolbar |

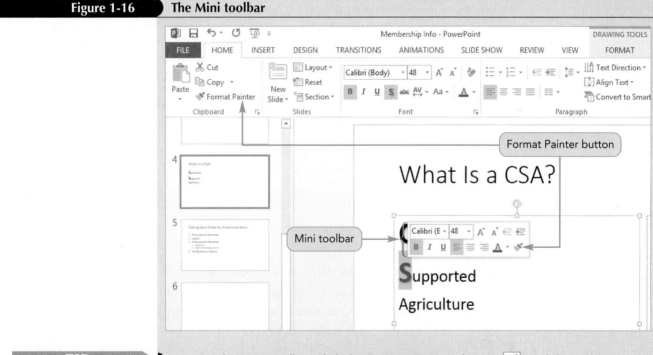

▶ **4.** On the Mini toolbar, click the **Format Painter** button 🖌︎, and then drag across the letter **A** in Agriculture.

▶ **5.** Click the border of the text box to select the entire text box, and then in the Font group, click the **Increase Font Size** button A˄ five times. In the Font group, the Font Size button indicates that the text is 48+ points. This means that in the selected text box, the text that is the smallest is 48 points and there is some text that is a larger point size.

▶ **6.** On the Quick Access Toolbar, click the **Save** button 🖫 to save the changes.

*Undoing and Redoing Actions*

If you make a mistake or change your mind about an action as you are working, you can reverse the action by clicking the Undo button on the Quick Access Toolbar. You can undo up to the most recent 20 actions by continuing to click the Undo button, or by clicking the Undo button arrow and then selecting as many actions in the list as you want. You can also Redo an action that you undid by clicking the Redo button on the Quick Access Toolbar.

When there are no actions that can be redone, the Redo button changes to the Repeat button. You can use the Repeat button to repeat an action, such as formatting text as bold. If the Repeat button is light gray, this means it is unavailable because there is no action to repeat (or to redo).

# Moving and Copying Text

You can move or copy text and objects in a presentation using the Clipboard. The **Clipboard** is a temporary storage area available to all Windows programs on which text or objects are stored when you cut or copy them. To **cut** text or objects—that is, remove the selected text or objects from one location so that you can place it somewhere else— you select the text or object, and then use the Cut button in the Clipboard group on the HOME tab to remove the selected text or object and place it on the Clipboard. To **copy** selected text or objects, you use the Copy button in the Clipboard group on the HOME tab, which leaves the original text or object on the slide and places a copy of it on the Clipboard. You can then **paste** the text or object stored on the Clipboard anywhere in the presentation, or, in fact, in any file in any Windows program.

You can paste an item on the Clipboard as many times and in as many locations as you like. However, the Clipboard can hold only the most recently cut or copied item. As soon as you cut or copy another item, it replaces the previously cut or copied item on the Clipboard.

Note that cutting text or an object is different from using the Delete or Backspace key to delete it. Deleted text and objects are not placed on the Clipboard; this means they cannot be pasted.

Isaac wants a few changes made to Slides 5 and 3. You'll use the Clipboard as you make these edits.

**To copy and paste text using the Clipboard:**

1. Display **Slide 5** ("Placing Your Order for Additional Items") in the Slide pane, and then double-click the word **Order** in the title text. The word "Order" is selected.

2. On the HOME tab, in the Clipboard group, click the **Copy** button. The selected word is copied to the Clipboard.

3. In the last item in the numbered list, click after the word "Submit," and then press the **spacebar**.

4. In the Clipboard group, click the **Paste** button. The text is pasted and picks up the formatting of its destination; that is, the pasted text is the 28-point Calibri font, the same font and size as the rest of the first-level items in the list, instead of 44-point Calibri Light as in the title. The Paste Options button ![Ctrl] appears below the pasted text.

5. Click the **Paste Options** button ![Ctrl]. A menu opens with four buttons on it. See Figure 1-17.

**Figure 1-17**    Buttons on the Paste Options button menu when text is on the Clipboard

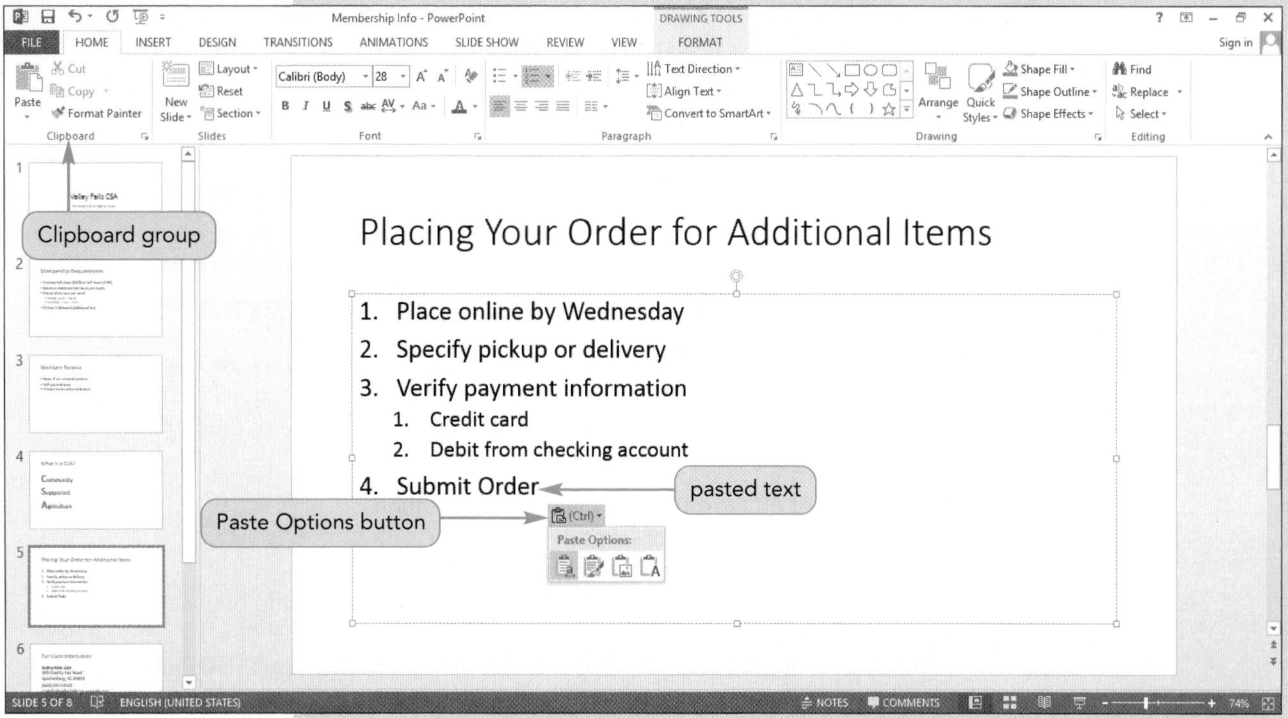

6. Point to each button on the menu, reading the ScreenTips and watching to see how the pasted text changes in appearance. The first button is the Use Destination Theme button [icon], and this is the default choice when you paste text.

7. Click a blank area of the slide to close the menu without making a selection, click to the left of "Order" in the last item in the numbered list, press the **Delete** key, and then type **o**. The word "order" in in the numbered list is now all lowercase.

8. Display **Slide 2** ("Membership Requirements") in the Slide pane. The last bulleted item ("October community celebration") belongs on Slide 3.

9. In the last bulleted item, position the pointer on top of the bullet symbol so that the pointer changes to ⊕, and then click. The entire bulleted item is selected.

10. In the Clipboard group, click the **Cut** button. The last bulleted item is removed from the slide and placed on the Clipboard.

11. Display **Slide 3** ("Members Receive") in the Slide pane, click after the second bulleted item, and then press the **Enter** key to create a third line.

12. In the Clipboard group, click the **Paste** button. The bulleted item you cut is pasted as the third bulleted item on Slide 3 using the default Paste option of Use Destination Theme. The insertion point appears next to a fourth bulleted item.

13. Press the **Backspace** key twice. The extra line is deleted.

**INSIGHT**

### Using the Office Clipboard

The **Office Clipboard** is a special Clipboard available only to Microsoft Office applications. Once you activate the Office Clipboard, you can store up to 24 items on it and then select the item or items you want to paste. To activate the Office Clipboard, click the HOME tab. In the Clipboard group, click the Dialog Box Launcher (the small square in the lower-right corner of the Clipboard group) to open the Clipboard task pane to the left of the Slide pane.

# Converting a List to a SmartArt Diagram

A **diagram** visually depicts information or ideas and shows how they are connected. **SmartArt** is a feature that allows you to create diagrams easily and quickly. In addition to shapes, SmartArt diagrams usually include text to help describe or label the shapes. You can create the following types of diagrams using SmartArt:

- **List**—Shows a list of items in a graphical representation
- **Process**—Shows a sequence of steps in a process
- **Cycle**—Shows a process that is a continuous cycle
- **Hierarchy** (including organization charts)—Shows the relationship between individuals or units
- **Relationship** (including Venn diagrams, radial diagrams, and target diagrams)— Shows the relationship between two or more elements
- **Matrix**—Shows information in a grid
- **Pyramid**—Shows foundation-based relationships
- **Picture**—Provides a location for a picture or pictures that you insert

There is also an Office.com category of SmartArt, which, if you are connected to the Internet, displays additional SmartArt diagrams available in various categories on Office.com, a Microsoft website that contains tools for use with Office programs.

A quick way to create a SmartArt diagram is to convert an existing list. When you select an existing list and then click the Convert to SmartArt Graphic button in the Paragraph group on the HOME tab, a gallery of SmartArt layouts appears. For SmartArt, a **layout** is the arrangement of the shapes in the diagram. Each first-level item in the list is converted to a shape in the SmartArt diagram. If the list contains subitems, you might need to experiment with different layouts to find one that best suits the information in your list.

**REFERENCE**

### Converting a Bulleted List into a SmartArt Diagram

- Click anywhere in the bulleted list.
- In the Paragraph group on the HOME tab, click the Convert to SmartArt Graphic button, and then click More SmartArt Graphics.
- In the Choose a SmartArt Graphic dialog box, select the desired SmartArt type in the list on the left.
- In the center pane, click the SmartArt diagram you want to use.
- Click the OK button.

Isaac wants the numbered list on Slide 5 converted into a SmartArt diagram.

### To convert the list on Slide 5 into a SmartArt diagram:

1. Display **Slide 5** ("Placing Your Order for Additional Items") in the Slide pane, and then click anywhere on the numbered list to make the text box border appear.

2. On the HOME tab, in the Paragraph group, click the **Convert to SmartArt Graphic** button. A gallery of SmartArt layouts appears.

3. Point to the first layout. The ScreenTip identifies this layout as the Vertical Bullet List layout, and Live Preview shows you what the numbered list will look like with that layout applied. See Figure 1-18. Notice that the subitems are not included in a shape in this diagram.

| Figure 1-18 | Live Preview of the Vertical Bullet List SmartArt Layout |
|---|---|

4. Point to several other layouts in the gallery, observing the Live Preview of each one. In some of the layouts, the subitems are included in a shape.

5. At the bottom of the gallery, click **More SmartArt Graphics**. The Choose a SmartArt Graphic dialog box opens. See Figure 1-19. You can click a type in the left pane to filter the middle pane to show only that type of layout.

**Figure 1-19** **Choose a SmartArt Graphic dialog box**

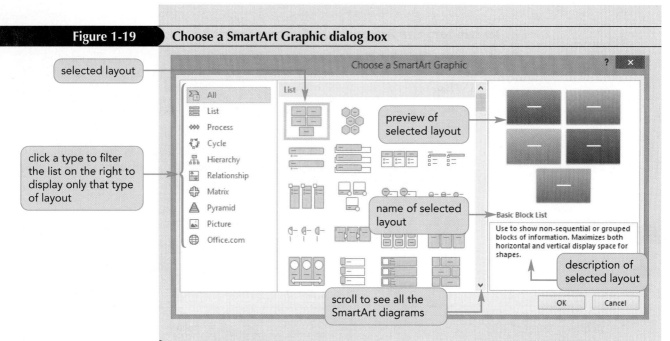

6. In the left pane, click **Process**, and then in the middle pane, click the **Continuous Block Process** layout, using the ScreenTips to identify it (it's the first layout in the third row). The right pane changes to show a description of that layout.

7. Click the **OK** button. The dialog box closes, and each of the first level items in the list appears in the square shapes in the diagram. The items also appear as a bulleted list in the Text pane, which is open to the left of the diagram. The SMARTART TOOLS contextual tabs appear on the ribbon. See Figure 1-20.

In this layout, the subitems below "Verify payment information" are included in the third square; they are not placed in their own shapes in the diagram. Isaac decides the information in the subitems does not need to be on the slide because people will see those options on the website when they log in.

**Trouble?** If you do not see the Text pane, click the Text pane button 🖾 on the left border of the selected SmartArt diagram.

| **Figure 1-20** | **SmartArt diagram with the Continuous Block Process layout** |
|---|---|

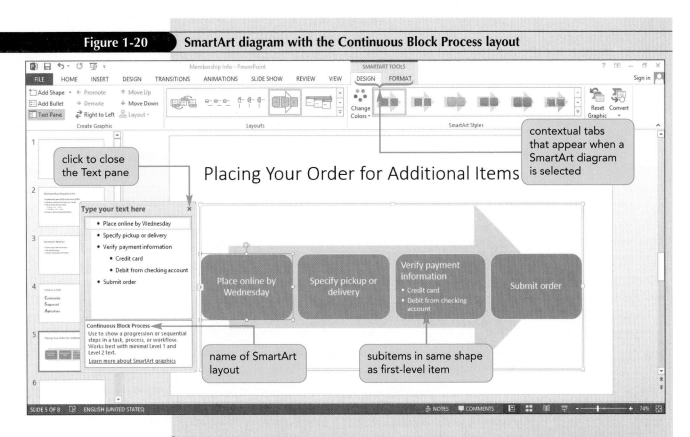

8. In the "Verify payment information shape," select **Debit from checking account**, and then press the **Delete** key. The text is deleted from the shape and from the Text pane.

9. In the Text pane, click after the word "card," press the **Backspace** key as many times as necessary to delete all of the bullet text, and then press the **Backspace** key once more. The bullet changes to a first-level bullet and a new square shape is inserted in the diagram.

10. Press the **Backspace** key one more time. The empty bullet and the blank line are deleted in the Text pane, and the newly added shape is removed from the diagram. The "Verify payment information" square now contains only the first-level item. Notice that AutoFit increased the size of the text in all the boxes so that the text still fills the boxes and is as large as possible.

11. Click a blank area of the slide to deselect the diagram, and then on the Quick Access Toolbar, click the **Save** button 🖫 to save your changes.

# Manipulating Slides

You can manipulate the slides in a presentation to suit your needs. For instance, if you need to create a slide that is similar to another slide, you can duplicate the existing slide and then modify the copy. If you decide that slides need to be rearranged, you can reorder them. And if you no longer want to include a slide in your presentation, you can delete it.

To duplicate, rearrange, or delete slides, you select the slides in the Slides tab in Normal view or switch to Slide Sorter view. In **Slide Sorter view** all the slides in the presentation are displayed as thumbnails in the window; the Slides tab does not appear. You already know that to select a single slide you click its thumbnail. You can also select more than one slide at a time. To select sequential slides, click the first slide, press and hold the Shift key, and then click the last slide you want to select. To select nonsequential slides, click the first slide, press and hold the Ctrl key, and then click any other slides you want to select.

Isaac wants to show the slide that explains what the letters "CSA" stand for at the end of the presentation. You will duplicate that slide instead of recreating it.

### To duplicate Slide 4:

▶ **1.** In the Slides tab, click the **Slide 4** ("What Is a CSA?") thumbnail to display Slide 4 in the Slide pane.

▶ **2.** On the HOME tab, in the Slides group, click the **New Slide button arrow**, and then click **Duplicate Selected Slides**. Slide 4 is duplicated and the copy is inserted as a new Slide 5 in the Slides tab. Slide 5 is now the current slide. If more than one slide were selected, they would all be duplicated. The duplicate slide doesn't need the title; Isaac just wants to reinforce the term.

▶ **3.** Click in the title "What Is a CSA?", click the text box border to select the text box, and then press the **Delete** key. The title and the title text box are deleted and the title text placeholder reappears.

You could delete the title text placeholder, but it is not necessary. When you display the presentation to an audience as a slide show, any unused placeholders will not appear.

Next you need to rearrange the slides. You need to move the duplicate of the "What Is a CSA?" slide so it is the last slide in the presentation because Isaac wants to leave it displayed after the presentation is over. He hopes this visual will reinforce for the audience that CSAs are good for the entire community. Isaac also wants the "Members Receive" slide moved so it appears before the "Membership Requirements" slide, and he wants the original "What Is a CSA?" slide to be the second slide in the presentation.

### To move slides in the presentation:

▶ **1.** In the Slides tab, scroll up, if necessary, so that you can see Slides 2 and 3, and then drag the **Slide 3** ("Members Receive") thumbnail above the Slide 2 ("Membership Requirements") thumbnail. As you drag, the Slide 3 thumbnail follows the pointer and Slide 2 moves down. The "Members Receive" slide is now Slide 2 and "Membership Requirements" is now Slide 3. You'll move the other two slides in Slide Sorter view.

**TIP**

You can also use the buttons in the Presentation Views group on the VIEW tab to switch views.

▶ **2.** On the status bar, click the **Slide Sorter** button ⊞. The view switches to Slide Sorter view. Slide 2 has an orange border, indicating that it is selected.

▶ **3.** On the status bar, click the **Zoom Out** button ▬ as many times as necessary until you can see all nine slides in the presentation. See Figure 1-21.

**Figure 1-21**     Slide Sorter view

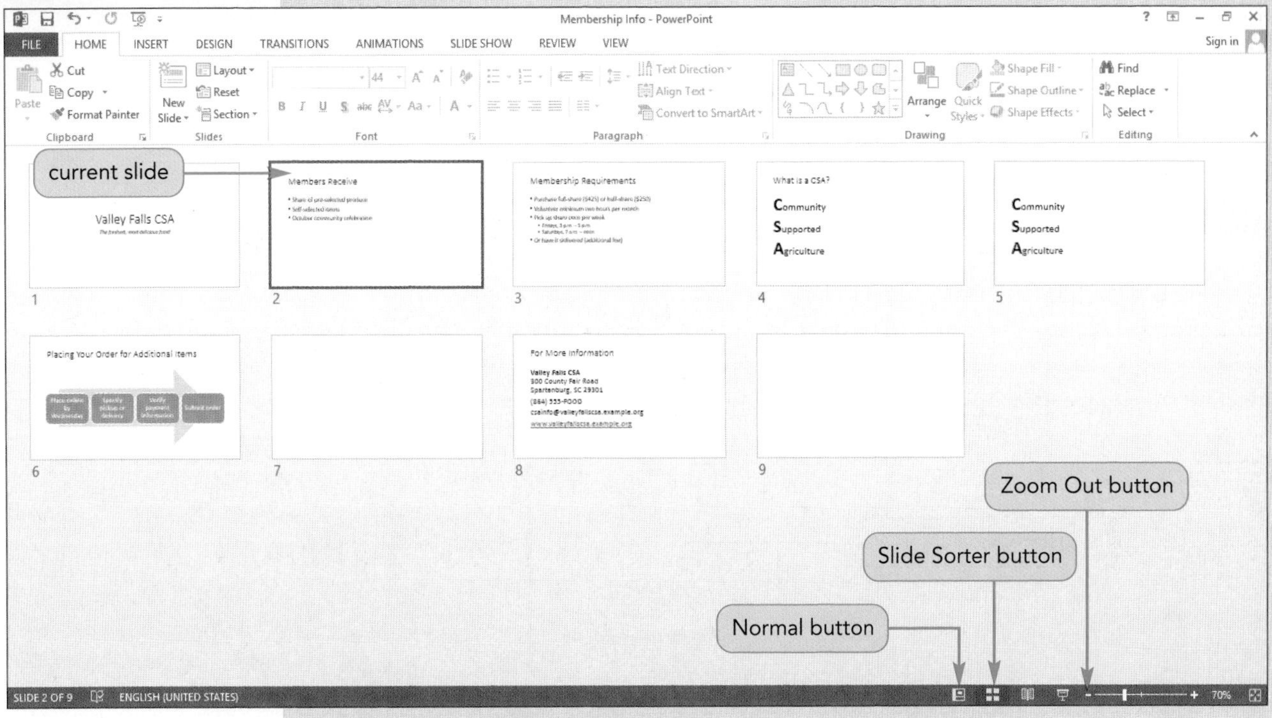

4. Drag the **Slide 4** ("What Is a CSA?") thumbnail between Slides 1 and 2. As you drag, the other slides move out of the way. The slide is repositioned and the slides are renumbered so that the "What Is a CSA?" slide is now Slide 2.

5. Drag the **Slide 5** (the CSA slide without a title) thumbnail so it becomes the last slide in the presentation (Slide 9).

Now you need to delete the two blank slides. To delete a slide, you need to right-click its thumbnail to display a shortcut menu.

### To delete slides:

1. Click **Slide 6** (a blank slide), press and hold the **Shift** key, and then click **Slide 8** (the other blank slide), and then release the **Shift** key. The two slides you clicked are selected, as well as the slide between them. You want to delete only the two blank slides.

2. Click a blank area of the window to deselect the slides, click **Slide 6**, press and hold the **Ctrl** key, click **Slide 8**, and then release the **Ctrl** key. Only the two slides you clicked are selected.

3. Right-click either selected slide. A shortcut menu appears. See Figure 1-22.

**Figure 1-22** **Shortcut menu for selected slides**

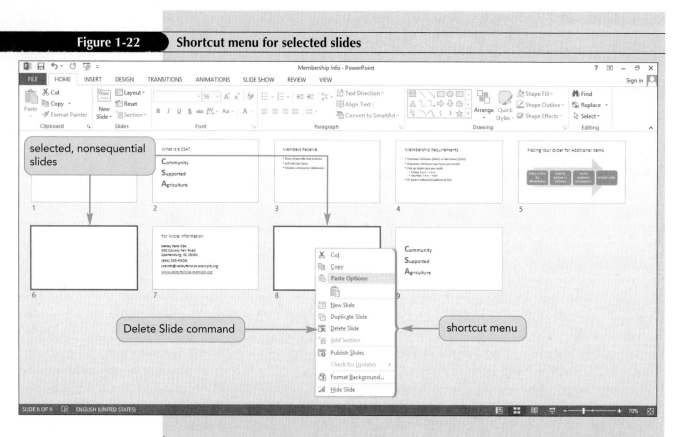

4. On the shortcut menu, click **Delete Slide**. The shortcut menu closes and the two selected slides are deleted. The presentation now contains seven slides.

**TIP**

You can also double-click a slide thumbnail in Slide Sorter view to display that slide in the Slide pane in Normal view.

5. On the status bar, click the **Normal** button 🔲. The presentation appears in Normal view.

6. On the Quick Access Toolbar, click the **Save** button 🔲 to save the changes to the presentation.

# Closing a Presentation

When you are finished working with a presentation, you can close it and leave PowerPoint open. To do this, you click the FILE tab to open Backstage view, and then click the Close command. If you click the Close button ☒ in the upper-right corner of the PowerPoint window and only one presentation is open, you will not only close the presentation, you will exit PowerPoint as well.

You're finished working with the Membership Info file for now, so you will close it. First you will add your name to the title slide.

**To close the Membership Info presentation:**

1. Display **Slide 1** (the title slide) in the Slide pane, click the **subtitle**, position the insertion point after "food!," press the **Enter** key, and then type your full name.

2. On the ribbon, click the **FILE** tab. Backstage view appears with the Info screen displayed. See Figure 1-23. The Info screen contains information about the current presentation, including the name, drive, and folder of the current presentation.

**Figure 1-23** · **Info screen in Backstage view**

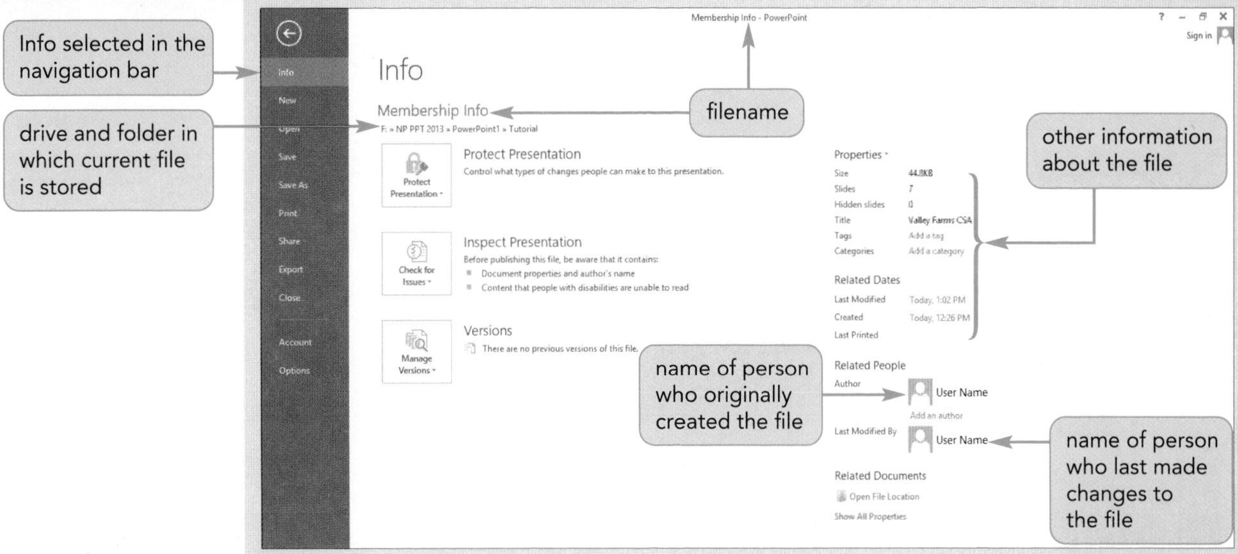

Info selected in the navigation bar

drive and folder in which current file is stored

filename

other information about the file

name of person who originally created the file

name of person who last made changes to the file

> **3.** In the navigation bar, click **Close**. Backstage view closes and a dialog box opens asking if you want to save your changes.

> **4.** In the dialog box, click the **Save** button. The dialog box and the presentation close, and the empty presentation window appears.

> **Trouble?** If you want to take a break, you can exit PowerPoint by clicking the Close button ⊠ in the upper-right corner of the PowerPoint window.

You've created a presentation that includes slides to which you added bulleted, numbered, and unnumbered lists. You also edited and formatted text, converted a list to a SmartArt diagram, and duplicated, rearranged, and deleted slides. You are ready to give the presentation draft to Isaac to review.

## Session 1.1 Quick Check

REVIEW

1. Define "presentation."
2. How do you display Backstage view?
3. What is the main area of the PowerPoint window called?
4. What is a layout?
5. In addition to a title text placeholder, what other placeholder do most layouts contain?
6. What is the term for an object that contains text?
7. What is the difference between the Clipboard and the Office Clipboard?
8. How do you convert a list to a SmartArt diagram?

# Session 1.2 Visual Overview:

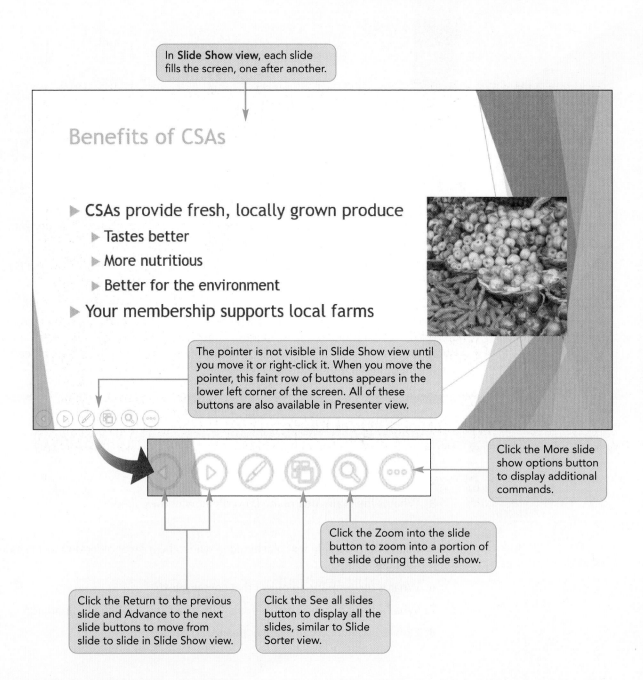

In **Slide Show view**, each slide fills the screen, one after another.

The pointer is not visible in Slide Show view until you move it or right-click it. When you move the pointer, this faint row of buttons appears in the lower left corner of the screen. All of these buttons are also available in Presenter view.

Click the More slide show options button to display additional commands.

Click the Zoom into the slide button to zoom into a portion of the slide during the slide show.

Click the Return to the previous slide and Advance to the next slide buttons to move from slide to slide in Slide Show view.

Click the See all slides button to display all the slides, similar to Slide Sorter view.

# Slide Show and Presenter Views

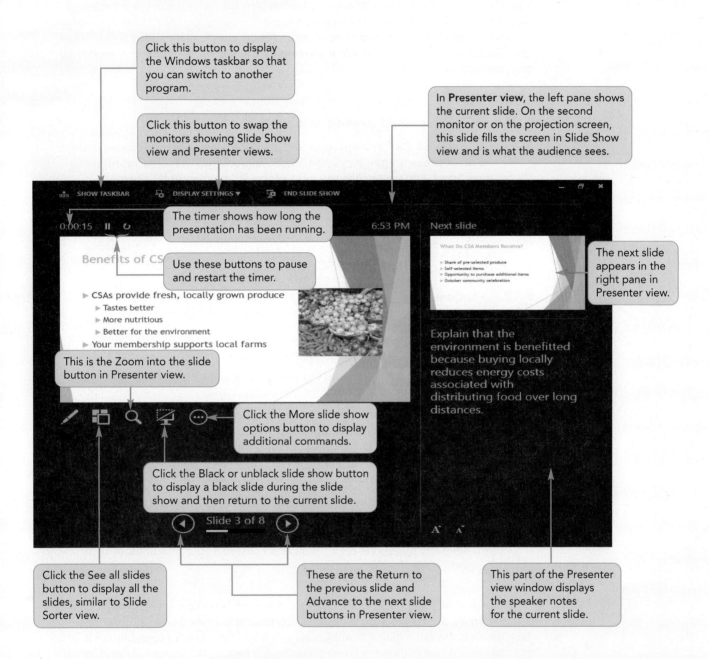

Click this button to display the Windows taskbar so that you can switch to another program.

Click this button to swap the monitors showing Slide Show view and Presenter views.

In **Presenter view**, the left pane shows the current slide. On the second monitor or on the projection screen, this slide fills the screen in Slide Show view and is what the audience sees.

The timer shows how long the presentation has been running.

Use these buttons to pause and restart the timer.

The next slide appears in the right pane in Presenter view.

This is the Zoom into the slide button in Presenter view.

Click the More slide show options button to display additional commands.

Click the Black or unblack slide show button to display a black slide during the slide show and then return to the current slide.

Click the See all slides button to display all the slides, similar to Slide Sorter view.

These are the Return to the previous slide and Advance to the next slide buttons in Presenter view.

This part of the Presenter view window displays the speaker notes for the current slide.

# Opening a Presentation and Saving It with a New Name

If you have closed a presentation, you can always reopen it to modify it. To do this, you can double-click the file in a Windows Explorer window, or you can open Backstage view in PowerPoint and use the Open command.

Isaac reviewed the presentation you created in Session 1.1. He added a slide listing the benefits of CSAs and made a few additional changes. You will continue modifying this presentation.

### To open the revised presentation:

▶ 1. Click the **FILE** tab on the ribbon to display Backstage view. Because there is no open presentation, the Open screen is displayed. Recent Presentations is selected, and you might see a list of the 25 most recently opened presentations on the right.

**Trouble?** If PowerPoint is not running, start PowerPoint, and then in the navigation bar on the Recent screen, click the Open Other Presentations link.

**Trouble?** If another presentation is open, click Open in the navigation bar in Backstage view.

▶ 2. Click **Computer**. The list of recently opened files is replaced with a list of recently accessed folders on your computer and a Browse button.

**Trouble?** If you are storing your files on your SkyDrive, click SkyDrive, and then log in if necessary.

▶ 3. Click the **Browse** button. The Open dialog box appears. It is similar to the Save As dialog box.

▶ 4. Navigate to the drive that contains your Data Files, navigate to the **PowerPoint1 ▸ Tutorial** folder, click **Revised Membership** to select it, and then click the **Open** button. The Open dialog box closes and the Revised Membership presentation opens in the PowerPoint window, with Slide 1 displayed in the Slide pane.

**Trouble?** If you don't have the starting Data Files, you need to get them before you can proceed. Your instructor will either give you the Data Files or ask you to obtain them from a specified location (such as a network drive). If you have any questions about the Data Files, see your instructor or technical support person for assistance.

If you want to edit a presentation without changing the original, you need to create a copy of it. To do this, you use the Save As command to open the Save As dialog box, which is the same dialog box you saw when you saved your presentation for the first time. When you save a presentation with a new name, a copy of the original presentation is created, the original presentation is closed, and the newly named copy remains open in the PowerPoint window.

### To save the Revised Membership presentation with a new name:

▶ 1. Click the **FILE** tab, and then in the navigation bar, click **Save As**. The Save As screen in Backstage view appears.

▶ 2. Click **Computer**, if necessary. On the right under Computer is a list of recently accessed folders with the folder containing the current file at the top.

3. If the folder in which you are saving your Data Files is listed on the right, click it; if the folder in which you are saving your files is not listed, click the **Browse** button. The Save As dialog box opens.

4. If necessary, navigate to the drive and folder where you are storing your Data Files.

5. In the File name box, change the filename to **CSA New Member**, and then click the **Save** button. The Save As dialog box closes, a copy of the file is saved with the new name CSA New Member, and the CSA New Member presentation appears in the PowerPoint window.

# Changing the Theme and the Theme Variant

A **theme** is a coordinated set of colors, fonts, backgrounds, and effects. All presentations have a theme. If you don't choose one, the default Office theme is applied; that is the theme currently applied to the CSA New Member presentation.

You saw the Office theme set of colors when you changed the color of the text on the "What Is a CSA?" slide. You have also seen the Office theme fonts in use on the slides. In the Office theme, the font of the slide titles is Calibri Light and the font of the text in content text boxes is Calibri. In themes, the font used for slide titles is the Headings font, and the font used for the content text boxes is the Body font.

In PowerPoint, each theme has several variants with different coordinating colors and sometimes slightly different backgrounds. A theme and its variants are called a **theme family**. PowerPoint comes with several installed themes, and many more themes are available online at Office.com. In addition, you can use a custom theme stored on your computer or network.

You can select a different installed theme when you create a new presentation by clicking one of the themes on the New or Recent screen in Backstage view instead of clicking Blank Presentation, and then clicking one of the variants. If you want to change the theme of an open presentation, you can choose an installed theme on the DESIGN tab or you can apply a custom theme stored on your computer or network. When you change the theme, the colors, fonts, and slide backgrounds change to those used in the new theme.

Isaac wants the theme of the CSA New Member presentation changed to one that has more color in the background. First you'll display Slide 2 in the Slide pane so you can see the effect a different theme has on the text formatted with a theme color.

**To examine the current theme and then change the theme and theme variant:**

1. Display **Slide 2** ("What Is a CSA?") in the Slide pane, and then, in the unnumbered list select the orange letter **C**.

2. On the HOME tab, in the Font group, click the **Font Color arrow**. Look at the colors under Theme Colors and note the second to last color is selected in the column containing shades of orange. Notice also the row of Standard Colors below the theme colors.

3. In the Font group, click the **Font arrow**. A menu of fonts installed on the computer opens. At the top under Theme Fonts, Calibri (Body) is selected because the letter C that you selected is in a content text box. See Figure 1-24.

**Figure 1-24**   **Theme fonts on the Font box menu**

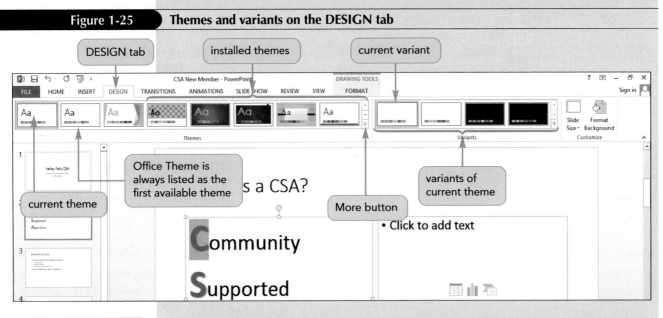

4. On the ribbon, click the **DESIGN** tab. The Font menu closes and the installed themes appear in the Themes gallery on the DESIGN tab. See Figure 1-25. The current theme is the first theme listed in the Themes group on the DESIGN tab. The next theme is the Office theme, which, in this case, is also the current theme.

**Figure 1-25**   **Themes and variants on the DESIGN tab**

**TIP**

To apply a theme from a presentation stored on your computer or network, click the Themes More button, and then click Browse for Themes.

To see all of the installed themes, you need to scroll through the gallery by clicking the up and down scroll buttons on the right end of the gallery or clicking the More button to expand the gallery to see all of the themes at once. The **More button** appears on all galleries that contain additional items or commands that don't fit in the group on the ribbon.

5. In the Themes group, click the **More** button. The gallery of themes opens. See Figure 1-26. When the gallery is open, the theme applied to the current presentation appears in the first row. In the next row, the first theme is the Office theme, and then the rest of the installed themes appear. Some of these themes appear on the Recent and New screens in Backstage view.

**Figure 1-26** | **Theme gallery expanded**

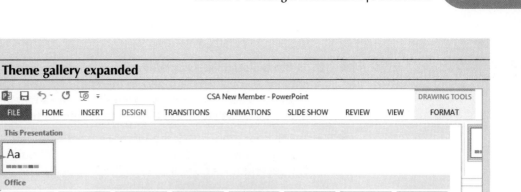

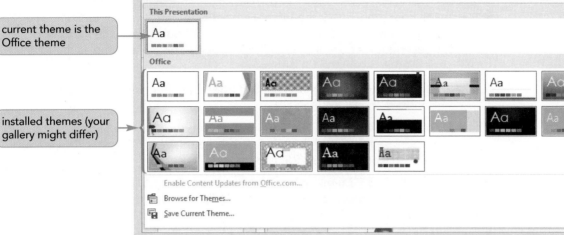

current theme is the Office theme

installed themes (your gallery might differ)

6. Point to several of the themes in the gallery to display their ScreenTips and to see a Live Preview of the theme applied to the current slide, and then click the **Facet** theme. The gallery closes and the Facet theme is applied to all the slides with the default variant (the first variant in the Variants group).

   The title text on each slide changes from black to green, the letters that you had colored orange on Slide 2 are dark green, the bullet symbols change from black circles to green triangles, and in the Slides tab, you can see on the Slide 6 thumbnail that the SmartArt shapes are now green as well.

7. In the Variants group, point to the other three variants to see a Live Preview of each of them. Isaac likes the default green variant best, so you will not change it.

8. Click the **HOME** tab, and then in the Font group, click the **Font Color arrow**. The selected color—the color of the selected letter "C"—is now a shade of green in the Theme Colors of the Facet theme. Notice also that the row of Standard Colors is the same as it was when the Office theme was applied.

9. In the Font group, click the **Font arrow**. You can see that the Theme Fonts are now Trebuchet MS for both Headings (slide titles) and the Body (content text boxes).

10. Press the **Esc** key. The Font menu closes.

After you apply a new theme, you should examine your slides to make sure that they look the way you expect them to. The font sizes used in the Facet theme are considerably smaller than those used in the Office theme. You know that Isaac wants the slides to be legible and clearly visible from a distance, so you will increase the font sizes on some of the slides. The title slide and Slide 2 are fine, but you need to examine the rest of the slides.

### To examine the slides with the new theme and adjust font sizes:

1. Display **Slide 3** ("Benefits of CSAs") in the Slide pane, and then in the bulleted list, click the first bulleted item. (This is the new slide that Isaac added.) In the Font group, the font size is 18 points, quite a bit smaller than the font size of first-level bulleted items in the Office theme, which is 28 points. You can see that the font size of the subitems is also fairly small.

▶ **2.** In the bulleted list, click the text box border to select the entire text box. In the Font group, 16+ appears in the Font Size box. The smallest font size used in the selected text box—the font size of the subitems—is 16, and the plus sign indicates that there is text in the selected text box larger than 16 points.

▶ **3.** In the Font group, click the **Increase Font Size** button $\boxed{A^{\bullet}}$ three times. The font size of the first-level bullets changes to 28 points, and the font size of the second-level bullets changes to 24 points. This is the same as the font sizes used in lists in the Office theme.

   **Trouble?** If the DRAWING TOOLS FORMAT tab becomes selected on the ribbon, click the HOME tab.

▶ **4.** Display **Slide 4** ("What Do CSA Members Receive?") in the Slide pane, and then increase the size of the text in the bulleted list to 28 points. There are misspelled words on this slide and on Slide 5; ignore them for now.

▶ **5.** Display **Slide 5** ("Membership Requirements") in the Slide pane, and then increase the font size of the text in the bulleted list so that the font size of the first-level items is 28 points and of the subitems is 24 points.

▶ **6.** Display **Slides 6, 7, 8,** and then **Slide 1** in the Slide pane. These remaining slides look fine.

▶ **7.** On the Quick Access Toolbar, click the **Save** button $\boxed{\square}$. The changes to the presentation are saved.

**INSIGHT**

### Understanding the Difference Between Themes and Templates

As explained earlier, a theme is a coordinated set of colors, fonts, backgrounds, and effects. A **template**, like any presentation, has a theme applied, but it also contains text, graphics, and placeholders to help direct you in creating content for a presentation. You can create and save your own custom templates or find everything from calendars to marketing templates among the thousands of templates available on Office.com. To find a template on Office.com, display the Recent or New screen in Backstage view, type key words in the Search box or click one of the category links below the Search box to display templates related to the search terms or category. If you create a new presentation based on a template, you can make any changes you want to the slides.

   If a template is stored on your computer, you can apply the theme used in the template to an existing presentation. However, if you want to apply the theme used in a template on Office.com to an existing presentation, you need to download and save the template to your computer first, and then you can apply it to an existing presentation.

# Working with Photos

Most people are exposed to multimedia daily and expect to have information conveyed visually as well as verbally. In many cases, graphics are more effective than words for communicating an important point. For example, if a sales force has reached its sales goals for the year, including a photo in your presentation of a person reaching the top of a mountain can convey a sense of exhilaration to your audience.

## Inserting Photos Stored on Your Computer or Network

Content placeholders contain buttons that you can use to insert things other than a list, including photos stored on your hard drive, a network drive, a USB drive, an SD card from a digital camera, or any other medium to which you have access. You can also use the Picture button in the Images group on the INSERT tab to add photos to slides.

Isaac has photos showing produce from his farm that he wants inserted on two of the slides in the presentation. He also wants a photo of people volunteering on the farm to appear on the last slide in the presentation.

### To insert photos stored on your computer or network on slides:

▶ 1. Display **Slide 2** ("What Is a CSA?") in the Slide pane, and then in the content placeholder on the right, click the **Pictures** button. The Insert Picture dialog box appears. This dialog box is similar to the Open dialog box.

▶ 2. Navigate to the **PowerPoint1 ▶ Tutorial** folder included with your Data Files, click **Produce1**, and then click the **Insert** button. The dialog box closes, and a picture of produce in bins appears in the placeholder and is selected. The contextual PICTURE TOOLS FORMAT tab appears on the ribbon to the right of the VIEW tab and is the active tab. See Figure 1-27.

| Figure 1-27 | Picture inserted on Slide 2 |

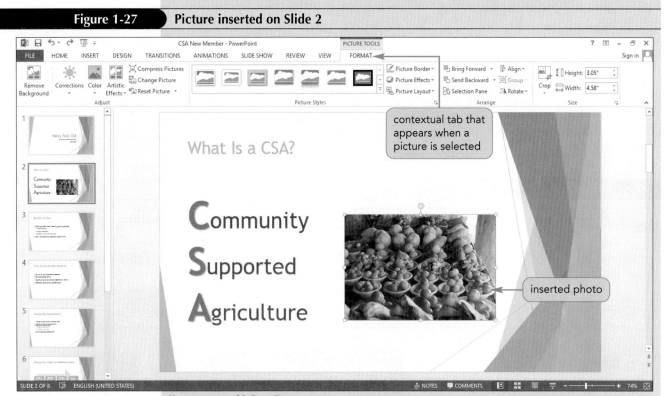

Photo courtesy of S. Scott Zimmerman

▶ 3. Display **Slide 3** ("Benefits of CSAs") in the Slide pane. This slide uses the Title and Content layout and does not have a second content placeholder. You can change the layout to include a second content placeholder or you can use a command on the ribbon to insert a photo.

▶ 4. Click the **INSERT** tab, and then in the Images group, click the **Pictures** button. The Insert Picture dialog box opens.

> **5.** In the PowerPoint1 ▸ Tutorial folder, click **Produce2**, and then click the **Insert** button. The dialog box closes and the picture is added to the center of the slide, covering much of the bulleted list. You will fix this later.
>
> **6.** Display **Slide 8** (the copy of the "What Is a CSA?" slide), and then click the **INSERT** tab on the ribbon.
>
> **7.** In the Images group, click the **Pictures** button, click **People** in the PowerPoint1 ▸ Tutorial folder, and then click the **Insert** button. The picture replaces the content placeholder on the slide.

## Cropping Photos

Sometimes you want to display only part of a photo. For example, if you insert a photo of a party scene that includes a bouquet of colorful balloons, you might want to show only the balloons. To do this, you can **crop** the photo—cut out the parts you don't want to include. In PowerPoint, you can crop it manually to any size you want, crop it to a preset ratio, or crop it to a shape.

On Slide 2, Isaac wants you to crop the photo to a diamond shape to make it more interesting, and to crop the photo on Slide 3 to make the dimensions of the final photo smaller without making the images in the photo smaller.

### To crop the photos on Slides 2 and 3:

> **1.** Display **Slide 3** ("Benefits of CSAs") in the Slide pane, click the photo to select it, and then click the **PICTURE TOOLS FORMAT** tab, if necessary.
>
> **2.** In the Size group, click the **Crop** button. The Crop button is selected, and crop handles appear around the edges of the photo just inside the sizing handles. See Figure 1-28.

**Figure 1-28**    **Photo with crop handles**

Photo courtesy of S. Scott Zimmerman

**3.** Position the pointer directly on top of the **left-middle crop handle** so that it changes to ◂|, press and hold the mouse button, and then drag the crop handle to the right approximately two inches.

**4.** Drag the crop handles on the bottom and right of the photo to match the cropped photo shown in Figure 1-29.

| Figure 1-29 | Cropped photo |
| --- | --- |

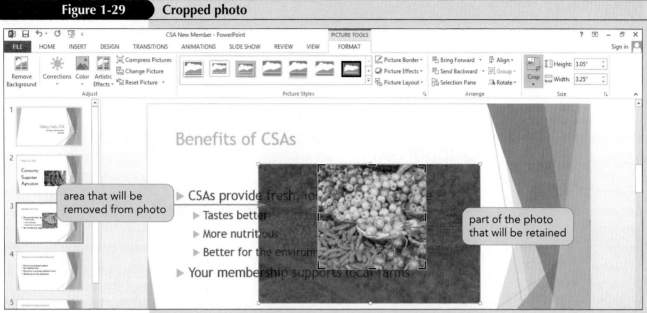

Photo courtesy of S. Scott Zimmerman

**5.** Click the **Crop** button again. The Crop feature is turned off, but the photo is still selected and the FORMAT tab is still the active tab. The photo is still on top of the bulleted list, but you'll fix this later.

**6.** Display **Slide 2** ("What Is a CSA?") in the Slide pane, click the photo to select it, and then click the **FORMAT** tab, if necessary.

**7.** In the Size group, click the **Crop button arrow**. The Crop button menu opens. See Figure 1-30.

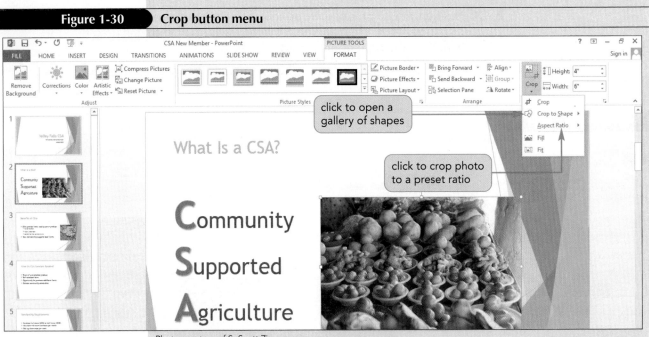

**Figure 1-30**    **Crop button menu**

Photo courtesy of S. Scott Zimmerman

▶ **8.** Point to **Crop to Shape** to open a gallery of shapes, and then under Basic Shapes, click the **Diamond** shape. The photo is cropped to a diamond shape. Notice that the rectangular selection border of the original photo is still showing.

▶ **9.** In the Size group, click the **Crop** button. You can now see the cropped portions of the original, rectangle photo that are shaded gray.

▶ **10.** Click a blank area of the slide. The picture is no longer selected and the HOME tab is the active tab on the ribbon.

## Modifying Photo Compression Options

When you save a presentation that contains photos, PowerPoint automatically compresses the photos to a resolution of 220 pixels per inch (ppi). (For comparison, photos printed in magazines are typically 300 ppi.) Compressing photos reduces the size of the presentation file, but it also reduces the quality of the photos. See Figure 1-31 for a description of the compression options available. If an option in the dialog box is gray, the photo is a lower resolution than that setting. Note that many monitors and projectors are capable of displaying resolutions only a little higher (98 ppi) than the resolution designated for email (96 ppi).

| Figure 1-31 | Photo compression settings |

| Compression Setting | Description |
| --- | --- |
| 220 ppi | Photos are compressed to 220 pixels per inch; use when you need to maintain the quality of the photograph when the slides are printed. This is the default setting for PowerPoint presentations. (Note that although this setting compresses the photos minimally, they are still compressed, and if photograph quality is the most important concern, do not compress photos at all.) |
| 150 ppi | Photos are compressed to 150 pixels per inch; use when the presentation will be viewed on a monitor or screen projector. |
| 96 ppi | Photos are compressed to 96 pixels per inch; use for presentations that need to be emailed or uploaded to a Web page or when it is important to keep the overall file size small. |
| Document resolution | Photos are compressed to the resolution specified on the Advanced tab in the PowerPoint Options dialog box. The default setting is 220 ppi. |
| No compression | Photos are not compressed at all; used when it is critical that photos remain at their original resolution. |

© 2014 Cengage Learning

You can change the compression setting for each photo that you insert or you can change the settings for all the photos in the presentation. If you cropped photos, you also can discard the cropped areas of the photo to make the presentation file size smaller. (Note that when you crop to a shape, the cropped portions are not discarded.) If you insert additional photos or crop a photo after you apply the new compression settings to all the slides, you will need to apply the new settings to the new photos.

**REFERENCE**

### Modifying Photo Compression Settings and Removing Cropped Areas

- After all photos have been added to the presentation file, click any photo in the presentation to select it.
- Click the PICTURE TOOLS FORMAT tab. In the Adjust group, click the Compress Pictures button.
- Click the option button next to the resolution you want to use.
- To apply the new compression settings to all the photos in the presentation, click the Apply only to this picture check box to deselect it.
- To keep cropped areas of photos, click the Delete cropped area of pictures check box to deselect it.
- Click the OK button.

You will adjust the compression settings to make the file size of the presentation as small as possible so that Isaac can easily send it or post it for others without worrying about file size limitations on the receiving server.

### To modify photo compression settings and remove cropped areas from photos:

▶ 1. On **Slide 2** ("What Is a CSA?"), click the photo, and then click the **PICTURE TOOLS FORMAT** tab, if necessary.

▶ 2. In the Adjust group, click the **Compress Pictures** button. The Compress Pictures dialog box opens. See Figure 1-32. Under Target output, the Use document resolution option button is selected.

Figure 1-32 **Compress Pictures dialog box**

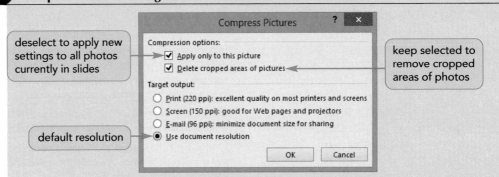

deselect to apply new settings to all photos currently in slides

keep selected to remove cropped areas of photos

default resolution

3. Click the **E-mail (96 ppi)** option button. This setting compresses the photos to the smallest possible size. At the top of the dialog box under Compression options, the Delete cropped area of pictures check box is already selected. This option is not applied to cropped photos until you open this dialog box and then click the OK button to apply it. Because you want the presentation file size to be as small as possible, you do want cropped portions of photos to be deleted, so you'll leave this selected. The Apply only to this picture check box is also selected; however, you want the settings applied to all the photos in the file.

4. Click the **Apply only to this picture** check box to deselect it.

5. Click the **OK** button.

    The dialog box closes and the compression settings are applied to all the photos in the presentation. You can confirm that the cropped areas of photos were removed by examining the photo on Slide 3. (The photo on Slide 2 was cropped to a shape, so the cropped areas on it were not removed.)

6. Display **Slide 3** ("Benefits of CSAs") in the Slide pane, click the photo to select it, click the **FORMAT** tab, if necessary, and then in the Size group, click the **Crop** button. The Crop handles appear around the photo, but the portions of the photo that you cropped out no longer appear.

7. Click the **Crop** button again to deselect it, and then save the changes to the presentation.

Be sure you are satisfied with the way you cropped the photo on Slide 3 before you delete the cropped areas.

INSIGHT

*Keeping Photos Uncompressed*

Suppose you are a photographer and want to create a presentation to show your photos. In that case, you would want to display them at their original, uncompressed resolution. To do this, you need to change a setting in the PowerPoint Options dialog box before you add photos to slides. Click the FILE tab to open Backstage view, click Options in the navigation bar to open the PowerPoint Options dialog box, click Advanced in the navigation bar, and then locate the Image Size and Quality section. To keep images at their original resolution, click the Do not compress images in file check box to select it. Note that you can also change the default compression setting for photos in this dialog box; you can increase the compression or choose to automatically discard cropped portions of photos. Note that these changes affect only the current presentation.

# Resizing and Moving Objects

You can resize and move any object to best fit the space available on a slide. One way to resize an object is to drag a sizing handle. **Sizing handles** are the small squares that appear in the corners and in the middle of the sides of the border of a selected object. When you use this method, you can adjust the size of the object so it best fits the space visually. If you need to size an object to exact dimensions, you can modify the measurements in the Size group on the FORMAT tab that appears when you select the object.

You can also drag an object to reposition it anywhere on the slide. If more than one object is on a slide, **smart guides**, dashed red lines, appear as you drag to indicate the center and the top and bottom borders of the objects. Smart guides can help you position objects so they are aligned and spaced evenly.

In addition to using the smart guides, it can be helpful to display rulers and gridlines in the window. The rulers appear along the top and left sides of the Slide pane. Gridlines are one-inch squares made up of dots one-sixth of an inch apart. As you drag an object, it snaps to the grid, even if it is not visible.

## Resizing and Moving Pictures

Pictures and other objects that cause the PICTURE TOOLS FORMAT tab to appear when selected have their aspect ratios locked by default. The **aspect ratio** is the ratio of the object's height to its width. When the aspect ratio is locked, if you resize the photo by dragging a corner sizing handle or if you change one dimension in the Size group on the PICTURE TOOLS FORMAT tab, the other dimension will change by the same percentage. However, if you drag one of the sizing handles in the middle of an object's border, you will override the locked aspect ratio setting and resize the object only in the direction you drag. Generally you do not want to do this with photos because the images will become distorted.

You need to resize and move the cropped photo on Slide 3 so it is not obscuring the text. You also want to resize and move the photos you inserted on Slides 2 and 8 so the slides are more attractive. You'll display the rulers and gridlines to help you as you do this.

### To move and resize the photos:

1. Click the **VIEW** tab, and then in the Show group, click the **Ruler** and the **Gridlines** check boxes. Rulers appear along the top and left sides of the Slide pane, and the gridlines appear in the Slide pane.

2. On **Slide 3** ("Benefits of CSAs"), select the photo, if necessary, and then position the pointer on the photo anywhere except on a sizing handle so that the pointer changes to ⁺⁏⁖.

3. Press and hold the mouse button, drag the photo down and to the right so that the right edge of the photo is approximately one inch from the right side of the slide and a smart guide appears indicating that the top of the photo and the top of the bulleted list text box are aligned, as shown in Figure 1-33.

**TIP**

If you don't want objects you are moving to snap to the grid, press and hold the Alt key while you are dragging.

| Figure 1-33 | Repositioning photo on Slide 3 using smart guides and gridlines |

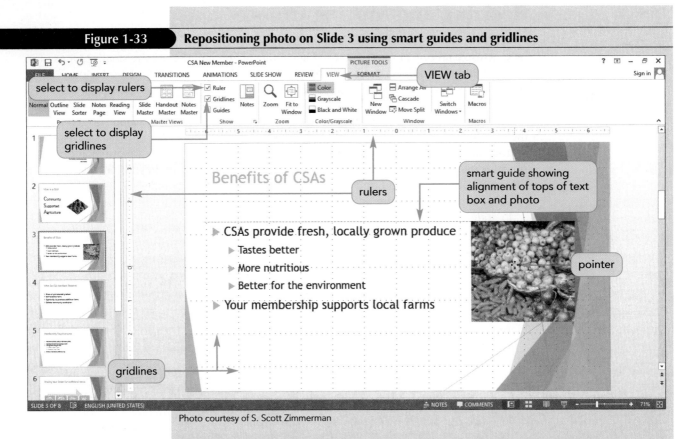

Photo courtesy of S. Scott Zimmerman

> **4.** Release the mouse button. The photo is repositioned to the right of the bulleted list.

> **5.** Display **Slide 2** ("What Is a CSA?") in the Slide pane, click the photo to select it, and then click the **PICTURE TOOLS FORMAT** tab if necessary. Instead of the border and sizing handles being on the diamond border, a rectangular border appears representing the original, uncropped photo's borders. (Remember that cropped portions of photos that are cropped to a shape are not removed.)

> **6.** In the Size group, click in the **Height** box to select the current measurement, type **4**, and then press the **Enter** key. The measurement in the Width box in the Size group changes proportionately, and the new measurements are applied to the photo.

> **7.** Drag the photo up and to the left until a horizontal smart guide appears indicating the alignment of the middle of the text box and the middle of the photo, and a vertical smart guide appears on the left side of the photo indicating the alignment of the left edge of the photo and the right edge of the bulleted list text box, as shown in Figure 1-34.

**Figure 1-34**    Moving resized photo on Slide 2

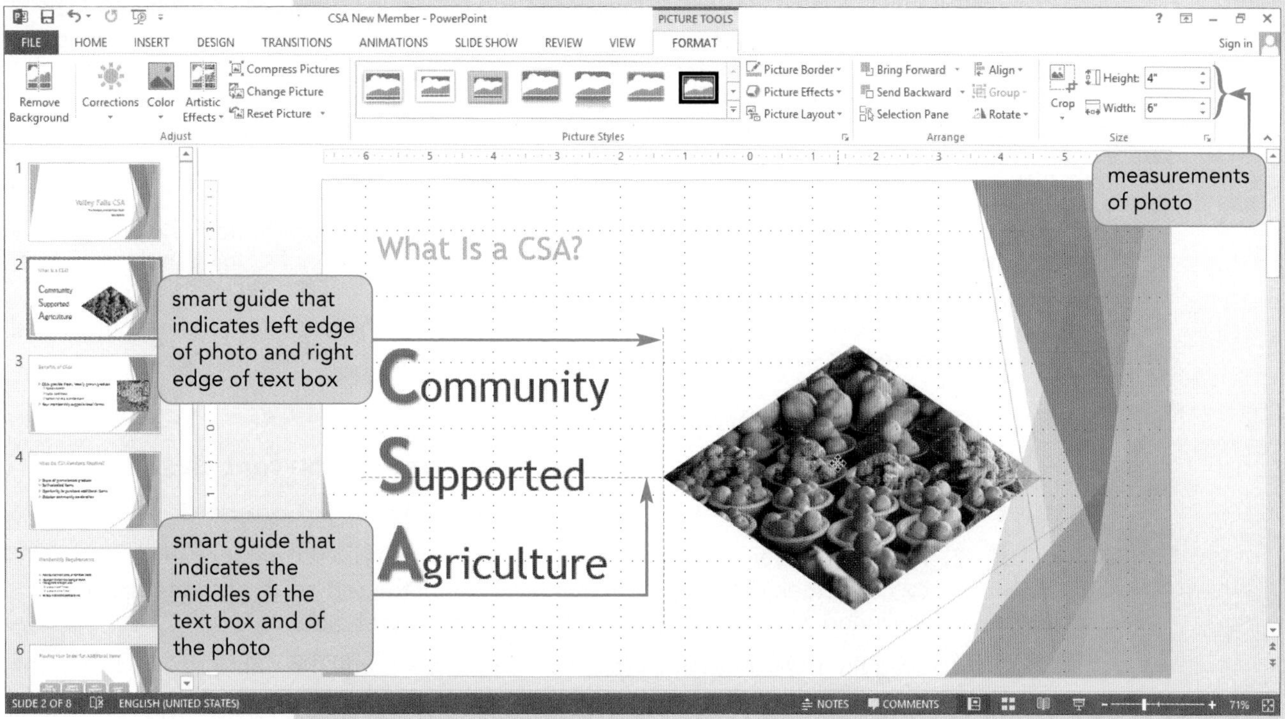

Photo courtesy of S. Scott Zimmerman

8. Display **Slide 8** (the last slide in the presentation) in the Slide pane, click the photo to select it, position the pointer on the top-middle sizing handle to that it changes to ⬍, press and hold the mouse button, and then drag the sizing handle approximately two inches up. The photo is two inches taller, but the image is distorted.

9. On the Quick Access Toolbar, click the **Undo** button ↻. You need to resize the photo by dragging a corner sizing handle to maintain the aspect ratio.

10. Click the **FORMAT** tab, and note the measurements in the Size group. The photo is 3.05 inches high and 4.58 inches wide.

11. Position the pointer on the bottom-right corner sizing handle so that it changes to ⤡, press and hold the mouse button, and then drag the sizing handle down. Even though you are dragging in only one direction, because you are dragging a corner sizing handle, both the width and height are changing proportionately.

12. When the photo is approximately four inches high and six inches wide, release the mouse button. Note that the measurements in the Height and Width boxes changed to reflect the picture's new size.

13. Drag the photo up until the top of the photo aligns with the 2-inch mark on the ruler on the left and the right edge of the photo is aligned with the 6-inch mark on the ruler at the top of the Slide pane. You are done using the ruler and gridlines so you can turn these features off.

14. Click the **VIEW** tab, and then click the **Ruler** and **Gridlines** check boxes to deselect them.

## Resizing and Moving Text Boxes

The themes and layouts installed with PowerPoint are designed by professionals, so much of the time it's a good idea to use the layouts as provided to be assured of a cohesive look among the slides. However, occasionally there will be a compelling reason to adjust the layout of objects on a slide, by either resizing or repositioning them.

Text boxes and other objects that cause the DRAWING TOOLS FORMAT tab to appear when selected do not have their aspect ratios locked by default. This means that when you resize an object by dragging a corner sizing handle or changing one dimension in the Size group, the other dimension is not affected.

Like any other object on a slide, you can reposition text boxes. To do this, you must position the pointer on the text box border, anywhere except on a sizing handle, to drag it to its new location.

To improve the appearance of Slide 8, you will resize the text box containing the unnumbered list so it vertically fills the slide.

### To resize the text box on Slide 8 and increase the font size:

▶ **1.** On Slide 8, click the unnumbered list to display the text box border.

▶ **2.** Position the pointer on the top-middle sizing handle so that it changes to $\updownarrow$, and then drag the sizing handle up until the top edge of the text box is aligned with the top edge of the title text placeholder.

▶ **3.** Drag the right-middle sizing handle to the right until the right edge of the text box is touching the left edge of the photo.

▶ **4.** Click the **HOME** tab, and then in the Font group, click the **Increase Font Size** button $\boxed{A^{^\cdot}}$ three times. Even though the title text placeholder will not appear during a slide show, you will delete it so that it is easier to see how the final slide will look.

▶ **5.** Click the title text placeholder border, and then press the **Delete** key. See Figure 1-35 and adjust the position of the photo if necessary.

**Figure 1-35**     **Slide 8 with resized text box**

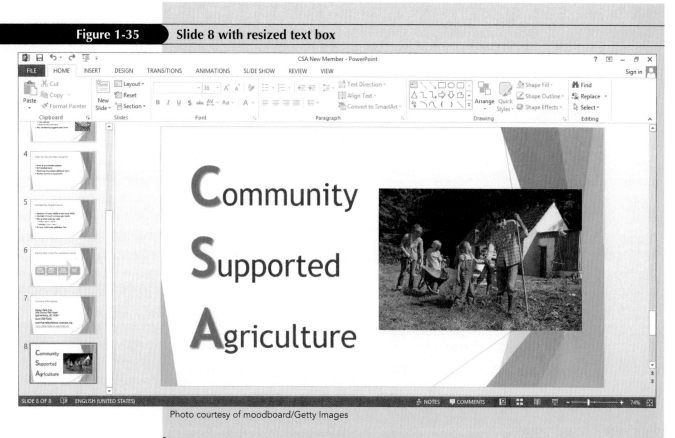

Photo courtesy of moodboard/Getty Images

▶  **6.** Save the changes to the presentation.

## Adding Speaker Notes

**Speaker notes**, or simply **notes**, are information you add about slide content to help you remember to bring up specific points during the presentation. Speaker notes should not contain all the information you plan to say during your presentation, but they can be a useful tool for reminding you about facts and details related to the content on specific slides. You add notes in the **Notes pane**, which you can display below the Slide pane in Normal view, or you can switch to **Notes Page view**, in which an image of the slide appears in the top half of the presentation window and the notes for that slide appear in the bottom half.

### To add notes to Slides 3 and 7:

▶  **1.** Display **Slide 7** ("For More Information") in the Slide pane, and then, on the status bar, click the **NOTES** button. The Notes pane appears below the Slide pane with "Click to add notes" as placeholder text. See Figure 1-36.

**Figure 1-36**    Notes pane below the Slide pane

Photo courtesy of moodboard/Getty Images

> **2.** Click in the **Notes** pane. The placeholder text disappears and the insertion point is in the Notes pane.

> **3.** Type **Tell audience that all the contact info is in the handouts. Use the link to show the audience the website**.

> **4.** Display **Slide 3** ("Benefits of CSAs") in the Slide pane, click in the **Notes** pane, and then type **Explain that the environment is benefitted because buying locally reduces costs associated with distributing food over long distances**.

> **5.** Click the **VIEW** tab on the ribbon, and then in the Presentation Views group, click the **Notes Page** button. Slide 3 is displayed in Notes Page view. See Figure 1-37.

**Figure 1-37**    Slide 3 in Notes Page view

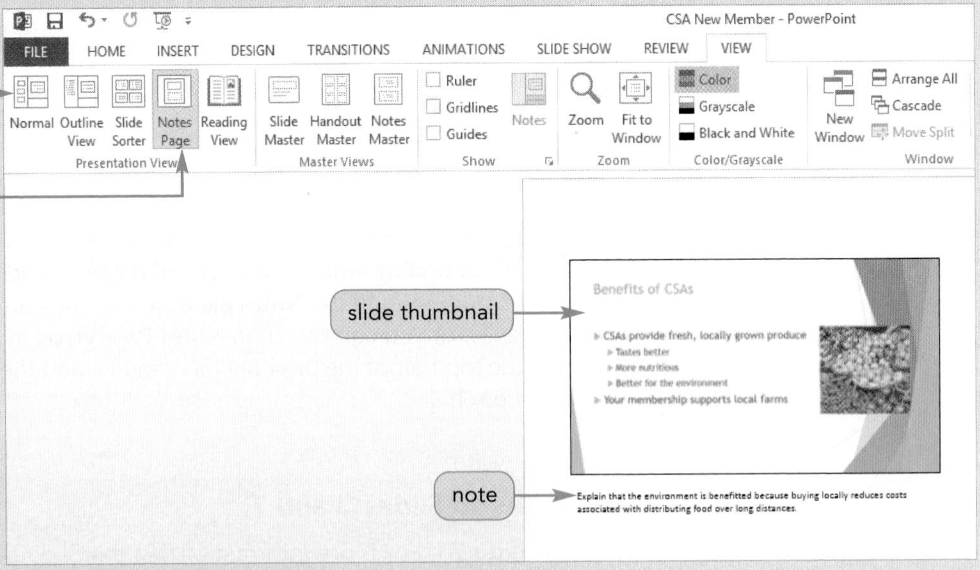

Photo courtesy of S. Scott Zimmerman

**TIP**

Use the Zoom in button on the status bar to magnify the text to make it easier to edit the note.

> **6.** In the note, click after "reduces," press the **spacebar**, and then type **energy**.

> **7.** In the Presentation Views group, click the **Normal** button to return to Normal view. The Notes pane stays displayed until you close it again.

> **8.** On the status bar, click the **NOTES** button to close the Notes pane, and then save the changes to the presentation.

# Checking Spelling

You should always check the spelling and grammar in your presentation before you finalize it. To make this task easier, you can use PowerPoint's spelling checker. You can quickly tell if there are words on slides that are not in the built-in dictionary by looking at the Spelling button at the left end of the status bar. If there are no words flagged as possibly misspelled, the button is ▢; if there are flagged words, the button changes to ▢. To indicate that a word might be misspelled, a wavy red line appears under it.

To correct misspelled words, you can right-click a flagged word to see a list of suggested spellings on the shortcut menu, or you can check the spelling of all the words in the presentation. To check the spelling of all the words in the presentation, you click the Spelling button in the Proofing group on the REVIEW tab. This opens the Spelling task pane to the right of the Slide pane and starts the spell check from the current slide. A **task pane** is a pane that opens to the right or left of the Slide pane and contains commands and options related to the task you are doing. When a possible misspelled word is found, suggestions are displayed for the correct spelling. Synonyms for the selected correct spelling are also listed.

### To check the spelling of words in the presentation:

▶ **1.** Display **Slide 4** ("What Do CSA Members Receive?") in the Slide pane, and then right-click the misspelled word **Oportunity**. A shortcut menu opens listing spelling options. See Figure 1-38.

| Figure 1-38 | Shortcut menu for a misspelled word |

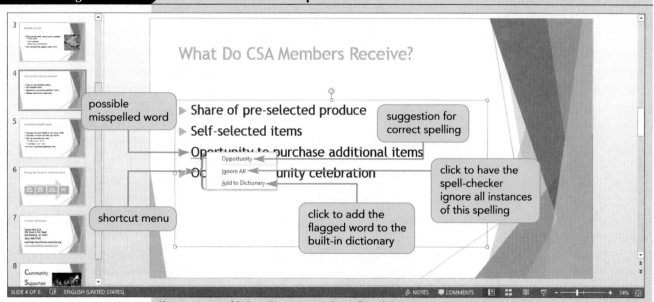

Photos courtesy of S. Scott Zimmerman and moodboard/Getty Images

▶ **2.** On the shortcut menu, click **Opportunity**. The menu closes and the spelling is corrected.

**TIP**

You can also click the Spelling button on the status bar to start the spell check.

▶ **3.** Click the **REVIEW** tab, and then in the Proofing group, click the **Spelling** button. The Spelling task pane opens to the right of the Slide pane, and the next slide that contains a possible misspelled word, Slide 5 ("Membership Requirements"), appears in the Slide pane with the flagged word, "minmum," highlighted. See Figure 1-39. In the Spelling task pane, the first suggested correct spelling is selected. The selected correct spelling also appears at the bottom of the task pane with synonyms for the word listed below it and a speaker icon next to it.

Figure 1-39    **Spelling task pane displaying a misspelled word**

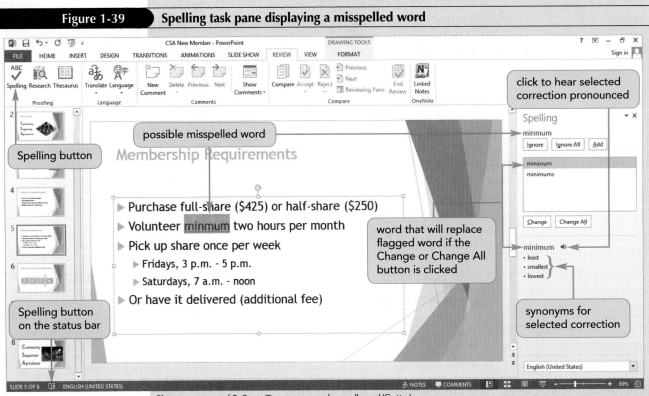

Photos courtesy of S. Scott Zimmerman and moodboard/Getty Images

▶ **4.** In the Spelling task pane, click the **speaker** icon 🔊. A male voice says the word "minimum."

▶ **5.** In the list of suggested corrections, click **minimums**. The word at the bottom of the task pane changes to "minimums," and the synonyms change also.

▶ **6.** In the list of suggested corrections, click **minimum**, and then click the **Change** button. The word is corrected and the next slide containing a possible misspelled word, Slide 1, appears in the Slide pane with the flagged word, "DeSoto," highlighted and listed in the Spelling task pane. This is Isaac's last name so you want the spell checker to ignore this.

    **Trouble?** If the spell checker finds any other misspelled words, correct them.

▶ **7.** In the task pane, click the **Ignore All** button. Because that was the last flagged word in the presentation, the Spelling task pane closes and a dialog box opens telling you that the spell check is complete.

▶ **8.** Click the **OK** button. The dialog box closes. The last flagged word, DeSoto, is still selected on Slide 1.

▶ **9.** Click a blank area of the slide to deselect the text, and then save the changes to your presentation.

# Running a Slide Show

After you have created and proofed your presentation, you should view it as a slide show to see how it will appear to your audience. There are several ways to do this—Slide Show view, Presenter view, and Reading view.

## Using Slide Show View and Presenter View

You can use Slide Show view if your computer has only one monitor and you don't have access to a screen projector. If your computer is connected to a second monitor or a screen projector, Slide Show view is the way an audience will see your slides. Refer to the Session 1.2 Visual Overview for more information about Slide Show view.

Isaac asks you to review the slide show in Slide Show view to make sure the slides look good.

### To use Slide Show view:

**TIP**

To start the slide show from the current slide, click the Slide Show button on the status bar.

1. On the Quick Access Toolbar, click the **Start From Beginning** button. Slide 1 appears on the screen in Slide Show view. Now you need to advance the slide show.

2. Press the **spacebar**. Slide 2 ("What Is a CSA?") appears on the screen.

3. Click the mouse button. The next slide, Slide 3 ("Benefits of CSAs"), appears on the screen.

4. Press the **Backspace** key. The previous slide, Slide 2, appears again.

5. Type **7**, and then press the **Enter** key. Slide 7 ("For More Information") appears on the screen.

6. Move the mouse to display the pointer, and then position the pointer on the website address **www.valleyfoodscsa.example.org**. The pointer changes to 🖑 to indicate that this is a link, and the ScreenTip that appears shows the full website address including "http://". If this were a real website, you could click the link to open your Web browser and display the website to your audience. Because you moved the pointer, a very faint row of buttons appears in the lower-left corner. See Figure 1-40.

**Figure 1-40**     **Link and buttons in Slide Show view**

(864) 555-FOOD

csainfo@valleyfallscsa.example.org

www.valleyfallscsa.example.org

pointer on a link in Slide Show view

http://www.valleyfallscsa.example.org/

ScreenTip identifying the link

row of buttons that appears when you move the pointer

7. Move the pointer again, if necessary, to display the row of buttons that appears in the lower left corner of the screen, and then click the **Return to the previous slide** button ◁ four times to return to Slide 3 ("Benefits of CSAs").

**Trouble?** If you can't see the buttons on the toolbar, move the pointer to the lower left corner so it is on top of the first button to darken that button, and then move the pointer to the right to see the rest of the buttons.

8. Display the faint row of buttons again, and then click the **Zoom into the slide** button. The pointer changes to ⊕ and three-quarters of the slide is darkened. See Figure 1-41.

**Figure 1-41** **Zoom feature activated in Slide Show view**

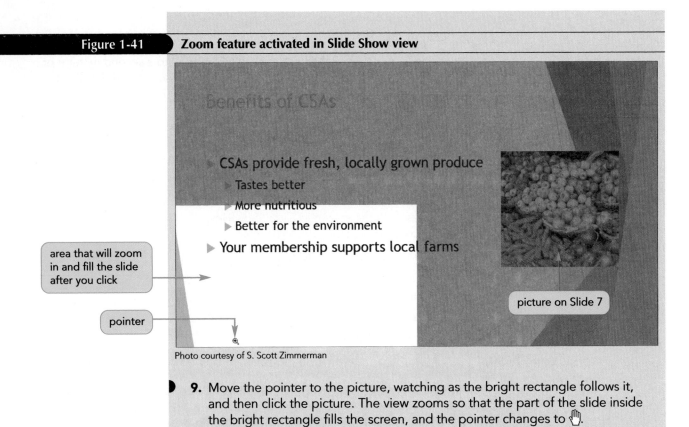

Photo courtesy of S. Scott Zimmerman

**9.** Move the pointer to the picture, watching as the bright rectangle follows it, and then click the picture. The view zooms so that the part of the slide inside the bright rectangle fills the screen, and the pointer changes to ☝.

**10.** Press and hold the mouse button to change the pointer to ✋, and then drag down and to the right to pull another part of the zoomed in slide into view.

**11.** Press the **Esc** key to zoom back out to see the whole slide.

Presenter view provides additional tools for running a slide show. In addition to seeing the current slide, you can also see the next slide, speaker notes, and a timer showing you how long the slide show has been running. Refer to the Session 1.2 Visual Overview for more information about Presenter view. Because of the additional tools available in Presenter view, you should consider using it if your computer is connected to a second monitor or projector. If, for some reason, you don't want to use Presenter view in that circumstance, you can switch to Slide Show view.

If your computer is connected to a projector or second monitor, and you start a slide show in Slide Show view, Presenter view starts on the computer and Slide Show view appears on the second monitor or projection screen. If you want to practice using Presenter view when your computer is not connected to a second monitor or projector, you can switch to Presenter view from Slide Show view.

Isaac wants you to switch to Presenter view and familiarize yourself with the tools available there.

**To use Presenter view to review the slide show:**

**1.** Move the pointer to display the row of buttons in the lower left corner of the screen, click the **More slide show options** button ⊙ to open a menu of commands, and then click **Show Presenter View**. The screen changes to show the presentation in Presenter view.

**2.** Below the current slide, click the **See all slides** button ▦. The screen changes to show thumbnails of all the slides in the presentation, similar to Slide Sorter view.

3. Click the **Slide 4** thumbnail. Presenter view reappears, displaying Slide 4 ("What Do CSA Members Receive?") as the current slide.

4. Click anywhere on the current slide, Slide 4. The slide show advances to display Slide 5.

5. At the bottom of the screen, click the **Advance to the next slide** button ◉. Slide 6 ("Placing Your Order for Additional Items") appears.

6. Press the **spacebar** twice. The slide show advances again to display Slides 7 and then 8.

7. Press the **spacebar** again. A black slide appears. As noted on the slide, the black screen indicates the end of the slide show.

8. Press the **spacebar** once more. Presentation view closes and you return to Normal view.

PROSKILLS

*Decision Making: Displaying a Blank Slide During a Presentation*

Sometimes during a presentation, the audience has questions about the material and you want to pause the slide show to respond to their questions. Or you might want to refocus the audience's attention on you instead of on the visuals on the screen. In these cases, you can display a blank slide (either black or white). When you do this, the audience, with nothing else to look at, will shift all of their attention to you. Some presenters plan to use blank slides and insert them at specific points during their slide shows. Planning to use a blank slide can help you keep your presentation focused and remind you that the purpose of the PowerPoint slides is to provide visual aids to enhance your presentation; the slides themselves are not the presentation.

If you did not create blank slides in your presentation file, but during your presentation you feel you need to display a blank slide, you can easily do this in Slide Show or Presenter view by pressing the B key to display a blank black slide or the W key to display a blank white slide. You can also click the Menu button in the row of buttons or right-click the screen to open a menu, point to Screen on the menu, and then click Black or White. To remove the black or white slide and redisplay the slide that had been on the screen before you displayed the blank slide, press any key on the keyboard or click anywhere on the screen. In Presenter view, you can also use the Black or unblack slide show button 🗗 to toggle a black slide on or off.

An alternative to redisplaying the slide that had been displayed prior to the blank slide is to click the Advance to the next slide button ◉. This can be more effective than redisplaying the slide that was onscreen before the blank slide because, after you have grabbed the audience's attention and prepared them to move on, you won't lose their focus by displaying a slide they have already seen.

## Using Reading View

Reading view displays the slides so that they almost fill the screen, similar to Slide Show view; however, in Reading view, a status bar appears identifying the number of the current slide and providing buttons to advance the slide show. You can also resize the window in Reading view to allow you to work in another window on the desktop.

**To use Reading view to review the presentation:**

1. Display **Slide 2** ("What Is a CSA?"), in the Slide pane, and then on the status bar, click the **Reading View** button 📖. The presentation changes to Reading view with Slide 2 displayed. See Figure 1-42.

**Figure 1-42** Slide 2 in Reading view

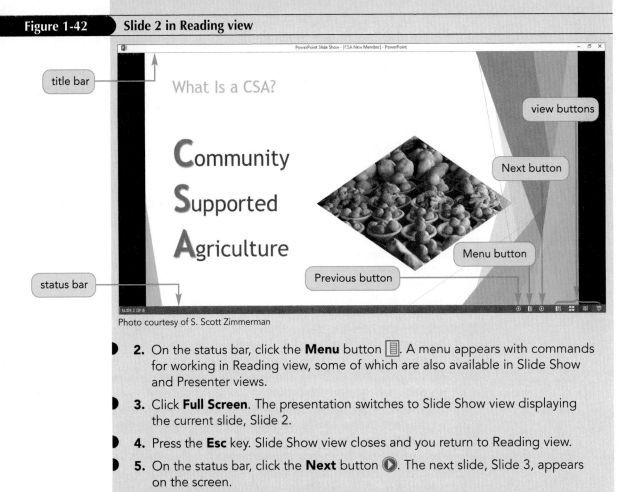

Photo courtesy of S. Scott Zimmerman

2. On the status bar, click the **Menu** button 📃. A menu appears with commands for working in Reading view, some of which are also available in Slide Show and Presenter views.

3. Click **Full Screen**. The presentation switches to Slide Show view displaying the current slide, Slide 2.

4. Press the **Esc** key. Slide Show view closes and you return to Reading view.

5. On the status bar, click the **Next** button 🔘. The next slide, Slide 3, appears on the screen.

6. On the status bar, click the **Normal** button 🔲 to return to Normal view with Slide 1 displayed in the Slide pane.

# Printing a Presentation

Before you deliver your presentation, you might want to print it. PowerPoint provides several printing options. For example, you can print the slides in color, grayscale (white and shades of gray), or pure black and white, and you can print one, some, or all of the slides in several formats.

You use the Print screen in Backstage view to set print options such as specifying a printer and color options.

First, you will replace Isaac's name on Slide 1 with your name.

## To choose a printer and color options:

▶ **1.** Display **Slide 1** in the Slide pane, and then replace Isaac's name in the subtitle with your name.

▶ **2.** Click the **FILE** tab to display Backstage view, and then click **Print** in the navigation bar. Backstage view changes to display the Print screen. The Print screen contains options for printing your presentation, and a preview of the first slide as it will print with the current options. See Figure 1-43.

| Figure 1-43 | Print screen in Backstage view |
|---|---|

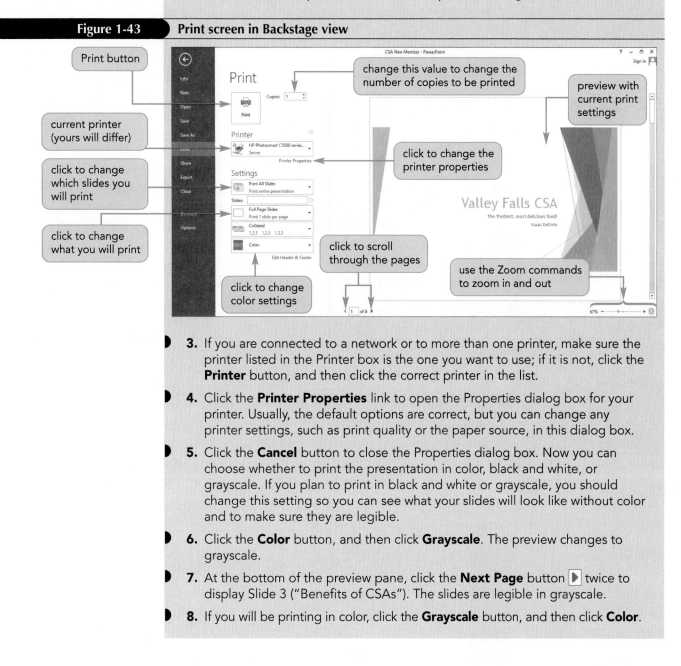

▶ **3.** If you are connected to a network or to more than one printer, make sure the printer listed in the Printer box is the one you want to use; if it is not, click the **Printer** button, and then click the correct printer in the list.

▶ **4.** Click the **Printer Properties** link to open the Properties dialog box for your printer. Usually, the default options are correct, but you can change any printer settings, such as print quality or the paper source, in this dialog box.

▶ **5.** Click the **Cancel** button to close the Properties dialog box. Now you can choose whether to print the presentation in color, black and white, or grayscale. If you plan to print in black and white or grayscale, you should change this setting so you can see what your slides will look like without color and to make sure they are legible.

▶ **6.** Click the **Color** button, and then click **Grayscale**. The preview changes to grayscale.

▶ **7.** At the bottom of the preview pane, click the **Next Page** button ▶ twice to display Slide 3 ("Benefits of CSAs"). The slides are legible in grayscale.

▶ **8.** If you will be printing in color, click the **Grayscale** button, and then click **Color**.

In the Settings section on the Print screen, you can click the Full Page Slides button to choose from among several choices for printing the presentation, as described below:

- **Full Page Slides**—Prints each slide full size on a separate piece of paper.
- **Notes Pages**—Prints each slide as a notes page.
- **Outline**—Prints the text of the presentation as an outline.
- **Handouts**—Prints the presentation with one or more slides on each piece of paper. When printing four, six, or nine slides, you can choose whether to order the slides from left to right in rows (horizontally) or from top to bottom in columns (vertically).

Isaac wants you to print the title slide as a full page slide so that he can use it as a cover page for his handouts.

### To print the title slide as a full page slide:

1. At the bottom of the preview pane, click the **Previous Page** button ◀ three times to display Slide 1 (the title slide) as the preview.
2. If the second button in the Settings section is not labeled "Full Page Slides," click it, and then click **Full Page Slides**. Note that below the preview of Slide 1, it indicates that you are viewing Slide 1 of eight slides to print.
3. In the Settings section, click the **Print All Slides** button. Note on the menu that opens that you can print all the slides, selected slides, the current slide, or a custom range. You want to print just the title slide as a full page slide.
4. Click **Print Current Slide**. Slide 1 appears in the preview pane, and at the bottom, it now indicates that you will print only one slide.
5. Click the **Print** button. Backstage view closes and Slide 1 prints.

Next, Isaac wants you to print the slides as a handout, with all eight slides on a single sheet of paper.

### To print the slides as a handout:

1. Click the **FILE** tab, and then click **Print** in the navigation bar.
2. In the Settings section, click the **Full Page Slides** button. A menu opens listing the various ways you can print the slides. See Figure 1-44.

**Figure 1-44**    **Print screen in Backstage view with print options menu open**

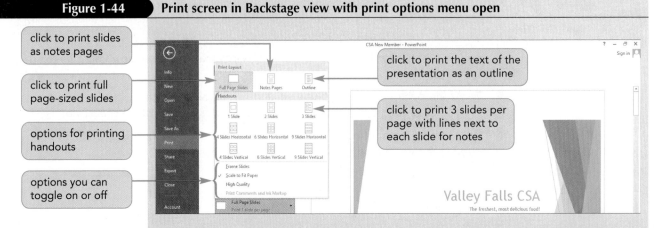

3. In the Handouts section, click **9 Slides Horizontal**. The preview changes to show Slide 1 in the upper-left corner. You need to specify that all eight slides will print.

▶ **4.** Click the **Print Current Slide** button, and then click **Print All Slides**. All eight slides appear in the preview pane, arranged in order horizontally, that is, in three rows from left to right. Notice that the current date appears in the top-right corner and a page number appears in the bottom-right corner.

▶ **5.** At the top of the Print section, click the **Print** button. Backstage view closes and the handout prints.

Recall that you created speaker notes on Slides 3 and 7. Isaac would like you to print these slides as notes pages.

### To print the nonsequential slides containing speaker notes:

▶ **1.** Open the Print screen in Backstage view again, and then click the **9 Slides Horizontal** button. The menu opens. "9 Slides Horizontal" appeared on the button because that was the last printing option you chose.

▶ **2.** In the Print Layout section of the menu, click **Notes Pages**. The menu closes and the preview displays Slide 1 as a Notes Page.

▶ **3.** In the Settings section, click in the **Slides** box, type **3,7** and then click a blank area of the Print screen.

▶ **4.** Scroll through the preview to confirm that Slides 3 and 7 will print, and then click the **Print** button. Backstage view closes and Slides 3 and 7 print as notes pages.

Finally, Isaac would like you to print the outline of the presentation. Recall that Slide 8 is designed to be a visual Isaac can leave displayed at the end of the presentation, so you don't need to include it in the outline.

### To print Slides 1 through 7 as an outline on a single page:

▶ **1.** Open the Print tab in Backstage view, click the **Notes Pages** button, and then in the Print Layout section, click **Outline**. The text on Slides 3 and 7 appears as an outline in the preview pane.

▶ **2.** Click in the **Slides** box, type **1-7**, and then click a blank area of the Print screen. See Figure 1-45.

| **Figure 1-45** | **Print screen in Backstage view with Slides 1-7 previewed as an outline** |
| --- | --- |

text of Slides 1-7 as an outline

▶ **3.** At the top of the Print section, click the **Print** button. Backstage view closes and the text of Slides 1-7 prints on one sheet of paper.

# Exiting PowerPoint

When you are finished working with your presentation, you can exit PowerPoint. If there is only one presentation open, you click the Close button ☒ in the upper-right corner of the program window to exit the program. If more than one presentation is open, clicking this button will only close the current presentation; to exit PowerPoint, you would need to click the Close button in each of the open presentation's windows.

### To exit PowerPoint:

▶ **1.** In the upper-right corner of the program window, click the **Close** button ☒. A dialog box opens asking if you want to save your changes. This is because you did not save the file after you replaced Isaac's name with your own.

▶ **2.** In the dialog box, click the **Save** button. The dialog box closes, the changes are saved, and PowerPoint exits.

In this session, you opened an existing presentation and saved it with a new name, changed the theme, added and cropped photos and adjusted the photo compression, and resized and moved objects. You have also added speaker notes and checked the spelling. Finally, you printed the presentation in several forms and exited PowerPoint. Your work will help Isaac give an effective presentation to potential customers of Valley Farms CSA.

**REVIEW**

*Session 1.2 Quick Check*

1. Explain what a theme is and what changes with each variant.
2. Describe what happens when you crop photos.
3. Describe sizing handles.
4. Describe smart guides.
5. Why is it important to maintain the aspect ratio of photos?
6. What is the difference between Slide Show view and Presenter view?
7. List the four formats for printing a presentation.

ASSESS

PRACTICE

## Review Assignments

Data Files needed for the Review Assignments: Farmland.jpg, Field Volunteer.jpg, Office Volunteer.jpg, Revised Volunteer Info.pptx

Chris Kopache is the Volunteer Coordinator for Valley Falls CSA. He needs to create a presentation for CSA members to explain the various ways they can volunteer. He will give the presentation to small groups. He doesn't want to overwhelm people, but he wants them to have enough information about each type of job so that they can choose one that best suits their abilities. He asks you to begin creating the presentation.

1. Start PowerPoint and create a new, blank presentation. On the title slide, type **Information for Volunteers** as the title, and then type your name as the subtitle. Save the presentation as **Volunteer Info** to the drive and folder where you are storing your files.
2. Edit the title by adding **Valley Falls CSA** before the word "Volunteers."
3. Add a new Slide 2 with the Title and Content layout, type **Jobs for Volunteers** as the slide title, and then in the content placeholder type the following:
   - **Field work**
   - **Work in store**
   - **Deliver shares**
   - **Office work**
     - **Must be familiar with Excel and Word**
     - **Only 3 positions available**
4. Create a new Slide 3 with the Title and Content layout. Add **Expectations** as the slide title, and then type the following as a numbered list on the slide:
   1. **Submit job preferences with membership application**
   2. **Volunteer minimum two hours per month**
   3. **Submit shift changes one week in advance**
   4. **Contact Chris Kopache**
5. Create a new Slide 4 using the Two Content layout. Add **Questions?** as the slide title.
6. Use the Cut and Paste commands to move the last bulleted item on Slide 3 ("Contact Chris Kopache") to the left content placeholder on Slide 4.
7. On Slide 4, remove the bullet symbol from the text you pasted, and then add the following as the next two items in the unnumbered list:
   **Email: c_kopache@example.org**
   **Cell: 803-555-8723**
8. Click after "Kopache" in the first item in the list, and then create a new line below it without creating a new item in the list and so that there is no extra space above the new line. On the new line, type **Volunteer Coordinator**.
9. Remove the hyperlink formatting from the email address.

10. Create a new Slide 5 using the Title and Content layout. Delete the title text placeholder. In the content placeholder, type **Thank You!** as a single item in an unnumbered list. Increase the size of the text "Thank You!" to 96 points, and then change the color of this text to Blue, Accent 1.

11. On Slide 3 ("Expectations"), change the numbered list to a SmartArt graphic. Use the Vertical Curved List layout, which is a List type of diagram.

12. Save your changes, and then close the presentation.

13. Open the file **Revised Volunteer Info**, located in the PowerPoint1 ▸ Review folder included with your Data Files, add your name as the subtitle on the title slide, and then save it as **New CSA Volunteers** to the drive and location where you are storing your files.

14. Change the theme to Wisp and keep the default variant. On Slide 2, change the size of the text in the bulleted list so that the size of the text of the first-level items is 28 points.

15. On Slide 1 (the title slide), insert the photo **Farmland**, located in the PowerPoint1 ▸ Review folder included with your Data Files. Resize the photo, maintaining the aspect ratio, so that it is the same width as the slide, and then reposition the photo so that the top of the photo aligns with the top of the slide. Crop the photo from the bottom, up to the base of the trees on the right, leaving approximately one-quarter inch between the bottom of the photo and the slide title.

16. Change the layout of Slide 4 ("Volunteer in the Fields") to Title and Content, and then duplicate Slide 4. In the title of Slide 5 (the duplicate slide), replace "Fields" with **Office**.

17. On Slide 4, insert the photo **Field Volunteer**, located in the PowerPoint1 ▸ Review folder. Resize the photo so it is 4.9 inches high, maintaining the aspect ratio, and reposition it so it is approximately centered in the space below the slide title.

18. On Slide 5, insert the photo **Office Volunteer**. Crop the top portion of the photo so that there is approximately one-half inch of wall above the top of the paintings in the photo. Resize the cropped photo so it is 5.1 inches high, maintaining the aspect ratio, and then reposition the photo as you did for the photo on Slide 4.

19. Move Slide 5 ("Volunteer in the Office") so it becomes Slide 7.

20. On Slide 9 ("Questions?"), crop the photo to the Oval shape. Increase the size of the text in the unnumbered list to 24 points, and then resize the text box to make it wide enough so that the line containing the email address fits on one line.

21. Compress all the photos in the slides to 96 ppi and delete cropped areas of pictures.

22. Display Slide 3 ("Description of Volunteer Jobs") in the Slide pane and review the information on this slide. Chris wants to include this information as notes on Slides 4 through 7 instead of displaying it as a bulleted list. He has already added the notes to Slides 5 and 6. Display Slide 4 ("Volunteer in the Fields") in the Slide pane, display the Notes pane, and then add **Field workers pull weeds and participate in harvesting produce.** in the Notes pane. Then display Slide 7 ("Volunteer in the Office") in the Slide pane, and add **Office workers use Excel to maintain volunteer schedules and use Word to publish the newsletter.** as a note on this slide.

23. Delete Slide 3 ("Description of Volunteer Jobs") and the last slide (the blank slide).

24. Correct the two spelling errors on Slide 2 and the error on Slide 7, and ignore all instances of Chris's last name. If you made any additional spelling errors, correct them as well. Save the changes to the presentation.

25. Review the slide show in Slide Show, Presenter, and Reading views.

26. View the slides in grayscale, and then print the following: the title slide as a full page-sized slide in color or in grayscale depending on your printer; Slides 1–9 as a handout on a single piece of paper with the slides in order horizontally; Slides 3 and 6 as notes pages, and Slides 1–8 as an outline. Close the presentation when you are finished.

APPLY

## Case Problem 1

**Data Files needed for this Case Problem: Apartment.jpg, Center.jpg, Couple.jpg, Orientation.pptx, Room.jpg**

*Wind Lake Assisted Living Center*  Sylvia Prater is director of human resources at Wind Lake Assisted Living Center in Muskego, Wisconsin. She is in charge of hiring employees and training them. She decided to create a presentation that she will give to new employees as part of their orientation. She asks you to help her create PowerPoint slides that she will use while she gives her presentation. Complete the following steps:

1. Open the presentation named **Orientation**, located in the PowerPoint1 ▸ Case1 folder included with your Data Files, and then save it as **Employee Orientation** to the drive and folder where you are storing your files.

2. Insert a new slide using the Title Slide layout. Move this new slide so it is Slide 1. Type **Employee Orientation** as the presentation title on the title slide. In the subtitle text placeholder, type your name.

3. Create a new Slide 2 with the Title and Content layout. Type **What Is Assisted Living?** as the slide title, and **Residence for people who need some assistance with daily living activities**. as the only item in the content placeholder. Change this to an unnumbered list.

4. Apply the View theme, and then apply its third variant. (If the View theme is not listed in the Themes gallery, choose any other theme and variant that uses a white or mostly white background, places the slide titles at the top of the slides, uses bullet symbols for first-level bulleted items, and positions the content in the bulleted lists starting at the top of the content text box, not the middle.)

5. On Slide 2 ("What Is Assisted Living?"), increase the size of the text of the in the text box below the slide titles to 28 points. On Slide 3 ("What Do We Provide?") increase the size of the text in the bulleted list so it is 24 points. On Slide 4 ("Our Employees") and Slide 7 ("Our Residents"), increase the size of the text in the bulleted list so that the first-level items are 28 points.

6. On Slide 2, insert the photo **Center**, located in the PowerPoint1 ▸ Case1 folder. Crop the top part of the photo off so that there is about one inch of sky above the building. Position the photo so the bottom of the photo aligns with the bottom of the slide and the left edge of the photo aligns with the right edge of the gray bar on the left. Resize the photo, maintaining the aspect ratio, so that it stretches from the gray bar on the left to the orange bar on the right. (If you used a different theme, center the photo horizontally in the space at the bottom of the slide.)

7. On Slide 3 ("What Do We Provide?"), add the speaker note **Personal care, such as bathing, grooming, and dressing, is provided by certified personal care attendants**.

8. On Slide 6 ("Living Quarters"), change the layout to the Comparison layout, which includes two content placeholders and a small text placeholder above each content placeholder. In the large content placeholder on the left, insert the photo **Room**, and in the large content placeholder on the right, insert the photo **Apartment**. Resize the Room photo so it is approximately the same height as the Apartment photo, maintaining the aspect ratio, and then reposition it, if needed, so that it is center-aligned with the caption placeholder above it and top-aligned with the Room photo on the left.

9. On Slide 5 ("Our Facility"), cut the first bulleted item, and then paste it in on Slide 6 in the small text placeholder on the left. If a blank line is added below the pasted text, delete it. On Slide 5, cut the remaining bulleted item, and then paste it on Slide 6 in the small text placeholder on the right, deleting the blank line if necessary.

10. On Slide 7 ("Our Residents"), add **Age** as the third bulleted item in the list, and then add **Minimum 60 years** and **Average 78 years** as subitems under the "Age" first-level item. Change the layout to Two Content.

11. On Slide 7, in the content placeholder, insert the photo **Couple**, located in the PowerPoint1 ▸ Case1 folder. Crop off the part of the photo to the right of the man, resize the photo so it is 5 inches high, maintaining the aspect ratio, and then reposition it as needed so that the top of the photo and the top of the content text box are aligned.

12. Compress all the photos in the presentation to 96 ppi and delete cropped portions of photos.

13. On Slide 8 ("New Employee To Do List"), change the list to a numbered list, and then add the following as a new item 2:

    **2. Attend certification seminars**
       **1. First aid**
       **2. CPR**

14. On Slide 8, convert the numbered list to a SmartArt diagram using the Vertical Block List layout, which is a List type of diagram. In the Text pane, click before "Confidentiality agreement," and then press the Tab key to make it a subitem under "Fill out paperwork." Change "W-4 and other personnel forms" to a second subitem under "Fill out paperwork."

15. Delete Slide 5 ("Our Facility"). Move Slide 4 ("Our Employees") so it becomes Slide 6.

16. Check the spelling in the presentation, and then read the text in the presentation carefully. On Slide 3 ("What Do We Provide?"), change the incorrect word "sight" to **site**.

17. Save the changes to the presentation, view the slide show in Presenter view, and then print the title slide as a full page slide, print Slides 2–7 as a handout using the 6 Slides Horizontal arrangement, and print Slide 3 as a notes page.

## Case Problem 2

**TROUBLESHOOT**

**Data Files needed for this Case Problem: Olympiad.pptx, Tangrams.jpg, Winner.jpg**

*Chandler, AZ School District* Manuel Resendez is the Director of Science Curriculum Development for the Chandler, Arizona school district. One of his responsibilities is to organize an annual district-wide Math and Science Olympiad, during which school children in grades 4 through 6 can demonstrate their skills in math and science. To make sure that the teachers, coaches, parents, and volunteers at the Olympiad understand the purpose of the event and the activities the students will be doing, he plans to visit each school and give a presentation to those involved. He created a PowerPoint presentation with text describing the event, and he asks you to finish it by inserting photos from the previous year's event. Complete the following steps:

1. Open the file named **Olympiad**, located in the PowerPoint1 ▸ Case2 folder included with your Data Files, and then save it as **Math-Science Olympiad** to the drive and folder where you are storing your files. Add your name as the subtitle on Slide 1.

2. Apply the Frame theme. Change the variant to the third variant.

⚙ **Troubleshoot** 3. Evaluate the problem that the theme change caused on the title slide and fix it.

4. On Slide 3, in the first item in the bulleted list, move "9:00 a.m. to 8:00 p.m." to a new line below the first line starting with "When" without creating a new bulleted item. Do the same with "180 S. Arizona Ave." in the second item.

5. Move Slide 4 ("Rules") so it becomes Slide 10.

6. On Slide 10 ("Rules"), change the bulleted list to a numbered list. Add as a new item 4 **Only event administrators allowed on the contest floor**. Change the size of the text in the numbered list to 28 points.

7. Change the layout of Slide 9 ("Tangrams") to Two Content, and then insert the photo **Tangrams**, located in the PowerPoint1 ▶ Case2 folder, in the content placeholder. Increase the size of the picture, maintaining the aspect ratio, and reposition it so it better fills the space on the right.

8. Change the layout of Slide 11 ("Awards") to Two Content, and then insert the photo **Winner**, located in the PowerPoint1 ▶ Case2 folder, in the content placeholder.

⚙ **Troubleshoot** 9. One of the slides contains information that should be explained orally rather than presented as a list. Review the presentation to identify this slide and change that information to a speaker note on that slide. Make any other adjustments necessary to make this an effective slide.

⚙ **Troubleshoot** 10. Review the presentation to identify the slide that contains information that is repeated in the presentation and delete that slide.

⚙ **Troubleshoot** 11. Consider how changing the theme in Step 2 affected the readability of the lists on the slides. Make the appropriate changes to the slides.

12. Compress all the photos in the presentation to 96 ppi, check the spelling in the presentation, and then save the changes. (*Hint*: If the E-mail (96 ppi) option in the Compress Pictures dialog box is gray and not available, close the dialog box, select a different picture, and try again.)

13. View the slide show in Presenter view, zooming in on the pictures of the different events.

14. Print the title slide as a full page slide in grayscale. Print Slides 1–3 and Slides 5–10 as an outline by typing **1-3, 5-10** in the Slides box.

## Case Problem 3

**Data Files needed for this Case Problem: Floating Houses.jpg, Karl.jpg, Peru.pptx, Region1.jpg – Region8 Right.jpg**

*Karl Benson Photography* Karl Benson is a photographer who specializes in scenic photos. He also teaches a course for beginner photographers. Karl recently returned from a trip to Peru. On his trip, he was very interested to learn that Peru has eight distinct regions with different geography and climates. Karl asks you to create a presentation that contains some of the photos he took on his trip. He will not be giving an oral presentation using this file. Instead, he wants his students to view the slides on their own, so he prepared a file with text describing the photos and the regions in Peru. Slides 2 through 10 of the final presentation are shown in Figure 1-46. Refer to Figure 1-46 as you complete the following steps:

**Figure 1-46**    **Slides 2-11 of Peruvian Regions presentation**

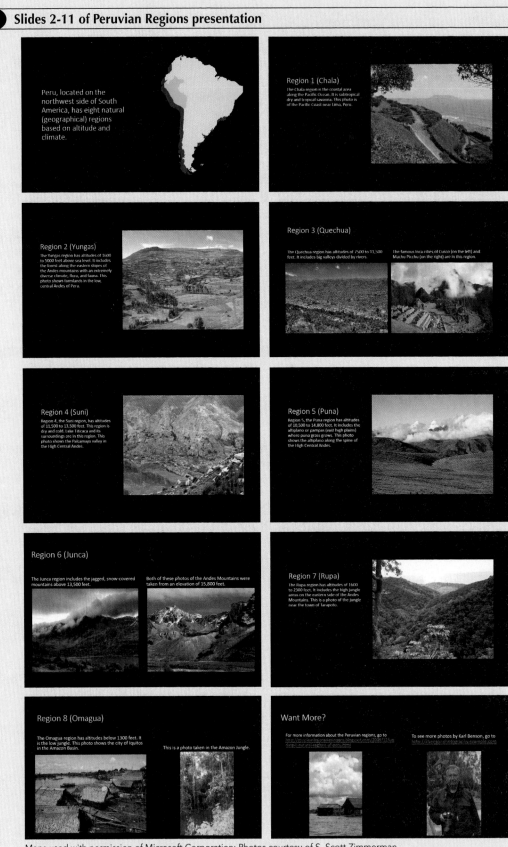

Maps used with permission of Microsoft Corporation; Photos courtesy of S. Scott Zimmerman

1. Open the file named **Peru**, located in the PowerPoint1 ▸ Case3 folder included with your Data Files, and then save it as **Peruvian Regions** to the drive and folder where you are storing your files.

2. Add a new slide with the Title Slide layout, and move it so it is Slide 1. Type **The Eight Regions of Peru** as the title and your name as the subtitle.

3. Change the variant of the Office theme to the third variant.

4. On Slide 2, drag the map of Peru on top of the map of South America as in Figure 1-46. (Use the left edges of the maps as a guide.) Resize the title text box to 4" x 5", change the font size of the text in the title text box to 32 points, and then position it on the left side of the slide, approximately centered vertically.

5. Change the layout of Slides 3 through 7 to Picture with Caption. On all five slides, change the font size of the captions in the text boxes below the titles from 16 points to 18 points.

6. Use the Region numbers on the slides to reorder Slides 3 through 10 in order by Region, starting with Region 1 on Slide 3 and ending with Region 8 on Slide 10.

7. On Slides 3 through 10, insert the photos provided in the PowerPoint1 ▸ Case3 folder that correspond to the region numbers described on each slide. Refer to Figure 1-46 as needed.

8. On Slide 11 ("Want More?"), insert the **Floating Houses** photo, located in the PowerPoint1 ▸ Case3 folder, in the content placeholder on the left and the **Karl** photo, located in the PowerPoint1 ▸ Case3 folder, in the content placeholder on the right.

9. Karl needs to post this presentation to a website that has file size limitations, so he needs the presentation file size to be as small as possible, even though he realizes that compressing the photos will reduce their quality. Compress all the photos in the presentation to 96 ppi.

10. Save the changes to the presentation, and then view the presentation in Reading view.

## Case Problem 4

CHALLENGE

Data Files needed for this Case Problem: Cargo.jpg, Corpus Christi.jpg, Freight.jpg, Loading1.mp4, Loading2.mp4, Submit.jpg, URL.jpg, Woman.jpg

*Corpus Christi Freight Transport, Inc.* Quentin Hershey is a customer relations representative for Corpus Christi Freight Transport, Inc., a large shipping company headquartered in Corpus Christi, Texas, and with offices in Argentina and Sydney. He wants you to help him create a PowerPoint presentation to explain features of the company and the services it offers. Quentin wants to give the presentation to organizations that require shipping services to U.S. waterways and to foreign ports. Complete the following steps:

✪ **Explore** 1. Create a new presentation using the Striped black border presentation template from Office.com. (*Hint*: Use **striped black border** as the search term. If you get no results, type **white** as the search term, and then choose a template with a simple theme.)

2. Replace the title text on the title slide with **Corpus Christi Freight Transport, Inc**. and replace the subtitle text with your name. Save the presentation as **Freight Transport** to the drive and folder where you are storing your files.

3. Delete all the slides except the title slide.

4. Add a new Slide 2 with the Two Content layout. Type **Who We Are** as the title, and then type the following as a bulleted list in the left content placeholder:
   • **International shipping company**
   • **Licensed by Federal Maritime Commission**
   • **Bonded as international freight transporter**
   • **Registered as cosmetic freight forwarder**

5. On Slide 2, in the right content placeholder, insert the photo **Freight**, located in the PowerPoint1 ▸ Case4 folder included with your Data Files. Resize it, maintaining the aspect ratio, so it is 4.8 inches high, and then reposition it as needed so that the middle of the photo and the middle of the bulleted list text box are aligned.

6. Add a new Slide 3 with the Title and Content layout. Type **Online Scheduling** as the title, and then type the following as a bulleted list in the content placeholder:

- **Register at www.freight.example.com**
- **Enter type and amount**
- **Submit information**
- **Receive confirmation within 24 hours**

7. On Slide 3, remove the link formatting from the website address in the first bulleted item.

8. On Slide 3, convert the bulleted list to a SmartArt diagram with the Vertical Picture List layout, which is a List type of diagram.

**Explore** 9. Change the colors of the diagram to Colored Fill – Accent 3 by using the Change Colors button in the SmartArt Styles group on the SMARTART TOOLS DESIGN tab.

**Explore** 10. Insert the following pictures, located in the PowerPoint1 ▸ Case4 folder, in the picture placeholders in the SmartArt diagram, in order from top to bottom: **URL, Cargo, Submit,** and **Woman**.

11. Add a new Slide 4 with the Two Content layout. Type **U.S. Office** as the title. In the content placeholder on the left, type the following as an unnumbered list without extra space between the lines:

**Corpus Christi Freight**

**2405 Shoreline Road**

**Corpus Christi, TX 78401**

12. On Slide 4, add the phone number **(361) 555-1254** and the website address **www.freight.example.com** as new items in the unnumbered list. Press the spacebar after typing the website address to format it as a link.

13. On Slide 4, add the photo **Corpus Christi**, located in the PowerPoint1 ▸ Case4 folder, to the content placeholder on the right. Resize it so it is 3.9 inches high, maintaining the aspect ratio, and then position it so the top edge aligns with the top edge of the text box on the left and there is approximately one inch of space between the right side of the photo and the right edge of the slide.

14. Compress all the photos in the presentation to 96 ppi, and then save the changes.

15. Add a new Slide 5 with the Comparison layout. Type **How Are Containers Loaded?** as the title, type **First a container is selected** in the small text placeholder on the left, and then type **Then it is transported to the ship and loaded** in the small text placeholder on the right. Move this slide so it becomes Slide 4.

**Explore** 16. On Slide 4 ("How Are Containers Loaded?"), insert the video **Loading1**, located in the PowerPoint1 ▸ Case4 folder, in the left content placeholder, and insert the video **Loading2**, located in the same folder, in the right content placeholder. (The video objects might be filled with black when they are inserted.)

**Explore** 17. Open the Info tab in Backstage view. Use the Compress Media command to compress the videos to the lowest quality possible. Use the Back button at the top of the navigation bar in Backstage view to return to Normal view.

18. Run the slide show in Slide Show view. When Slide 4 ("How Are Containers Loaded?") appears, point to each video to make a Play button appear, and then click the Play button to play each video. Note that there is no sound in the videos. (*Hint*: Point to the video as it plays to display the play bar again.)

# Adding Media and Special Effects

*Using Media in a Presentation for a Norwegian Tourism Company*

## Case | *Essential Norway Tours*

Inger Halvorsen was born and raised in Myrdal, Norway, not far from the Flåm Railway that travels through the beautiful mountains of central Norway. She attended college in the United States and graduated with a degree in geography. She then returned to her home country and started a travel agency, Essential Norway Tours, in Oslo. She hired a photographer to take photos and video of scenes from one of her tours from Hønefoss to Myrdal on the Bergen Train, from Myrdal to Flåm on the Flåm Train, and by boat through Aurlandsfjord and Nærøfjords, two of the most beautiful fjords in Norway. She wants to include the photos and video in a presentation that she wants you to give to U.S. travel agents and others who might be interested in booking trips through her agency.

In this tutorial, you will modify a presentation to highlight the beautiful scenery visitors will enjoy when they go on an Essential Norway tour. You will add formatting and special effects to photos and shapes, add transitions and animations to slides, and add and modify video.

## STARTING DATA FILES

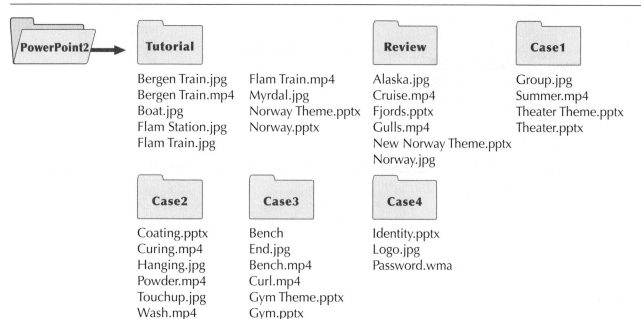

PowerPoint2 → 

**Tutorial**
Bergen Train.jpg
Bergen Train.mp4
Boat.jpg
Flam Station.jpg
Flam Train.jpg
Flam Train.mp4
Myrdal.jpg
Norway Theme.pptx
Norway.pptx

**Review**
Alaska.jpg
Cruise.mp4
Fjords.pptx
Gulls.mp4
New Norway Theme.pptx
Norway.jpg

**Case1**
Group.jpg
Summer.mp4
Theater Theme.pptx
Theater.pptx

**Case2**
Coating.pptx
Curing.mp4
Hanging.jpg
Powder.mp4
Touchup.jpg
Wash.mp4
Welding.jpg

**Case3**
Bench
End.jpg
Bench.mp4
Curl.mp4
Gym Theme.pptx
Gym.pptx
Military.mp4

**Case4**
Identity.pptx
Logo.jpg
Password.wma

# Session 2.1 Visual Overview:

Use the Shape Fill button to change the **fill**, the formatting of the area inside the shape.

To change the color, weight (thickness), or style (solid line, dashed line, and so on) of a shape's border, use the Shape Outline button.

The DRAWING TOOLS FORMAT tab appears when a drawing or a text box—including the slide's title and content placeholders—is selected.

The Shape Height box contains the height measurement of the selected shape, and the Shape Width box contains the width measurement.

To insert a shape, click a shape in the Shapes gallery.

Click the Shape Effects button to add special effects, such as a shadow, reflection, glow, soft edges, beveled edges, or a 3D rotation, to a shape.

You can drag a **rotate handle** to rotate an object, or you can click the Rotate button to open a menu of Rotate and Flip commands.

Use the Shape Styles gallery to apply a **style**, which is a combination of several formats, to a shape.

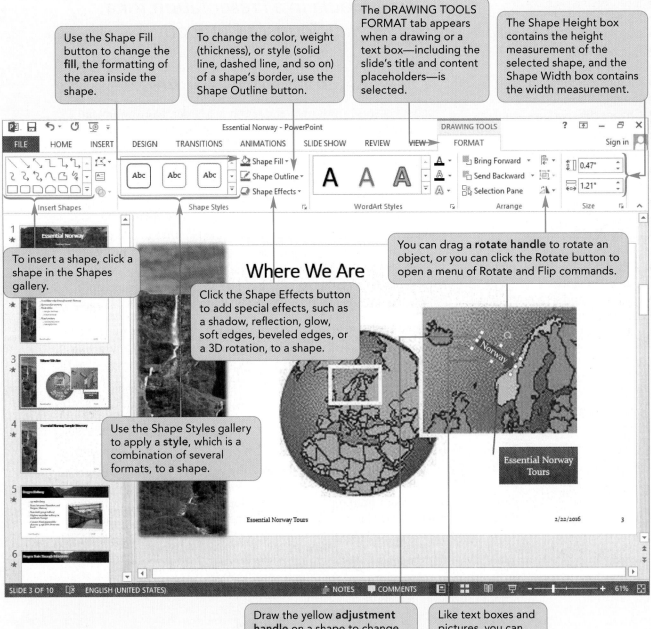

Draw the yellow **adjustment handle** on a shape to change its proportions without changing the size of the shape.

Like text boxes and pictures, you can drag a sizing handle to resize shapes.

# Formatting Graphics

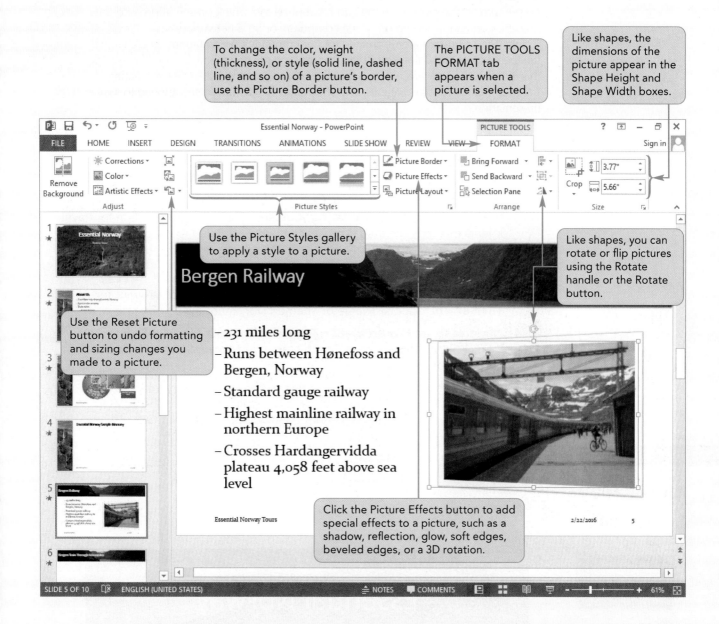

To change the color, weight (thickness), or style (solid line, dashed line, and so on) of a picture's border, use the Picture Border button.

The PICTURE TOOLS FORMAT tab appears when a picture is selected.

Like shapes, the dimensions of the picture appear in the Shape Height and Shape Width boxes.

Use the Picture Styles gallery to apply a style to a picture.

Like shapes, you can rotate or flip pictures using the Rotate handle or the Rotate button.

Use the Reset Picture button to undo formatting and sizing changes you made to a picture.

Click the Picture Effects button to add special effects to a picture, such as a shadow, reflection, glow, soft edges, beveled edges, or a 3D rotation.

### Bergen Railway

- 231 miles long
- Runs between Hønefoss and Bergen, Norway
- Standard gauge railway
- Highest mainline railway in northern Europe
- Crosses Hardangervidda plateau 4,058 feet above sea level

Essential Norway Tours

# Applying a Theme Used in Another Presentation

As you learned earlier, an installed theme can be applied by clicking one in the Themes group on the DESIGN tab. An installed theme is actually a special type of file that is stored with PowerPoint program files. You can also apply themes that are applied to any other presentation stored on your computer. For example, many companies want to promote their brand through their presentations, so they hire presentation design professionals to create custom themes that can be applied to all company presentations. The custom theme can be applied to a blank presentation, and this presentation can be stored on users' computers or on a network drive.

Inger had a custom theme created for her company's presentations. She changed the theme fonts and colors, modified layouts, and created a new layout. She applied this theme to a blank presentation that she sent to you. Inger also began creating her presentation for travel agents, and she wants the custom theme applied to that presentation.

## To apply a theme from another presentation:

▶ **1.** Open the presentation **Norway**, located in the **PowerPoint2 ▸ Tutorial** folder included with your Data Files, and then save it as **Essential Norway** in the location where you are saving your files. This is the presentation for travel agents that Inger created. The Office theme is applied to it. You need to apply Inger's custom theme to it.

▶ **2.** On the ribbon, click the **DESIGN** tab.

▶ **3.** In the Themes group, click the **More** button, and then click **Browse for Themes**. The Choose Theme or Themed Document dialog box opens.

▶ **4.** Navigate to the **PowerPoint2 ▸ Tutorial** folder, click **Norway Theme**, and then click the **Apply** button. The custom theme is applied to the Essential Norway presentation.

▶ **5.** In the Themes group, point to the first theme in the gallery, which is the current theme. Its ScreenTip identifies it as the Norway Theme. See Figure 2-1. Notice that this custom theme does not have any variants.

**Figure 2-1**    **Custom Norway Theme applied**

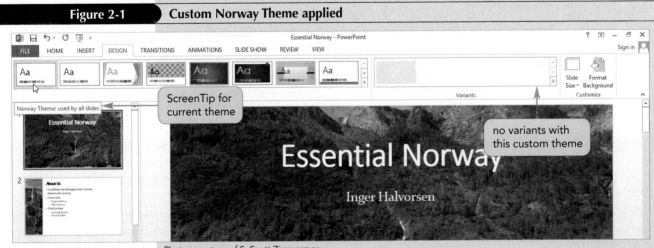

Photos courtesy of S. Scott Zimmerman

6. Click the **HOME** tab, and then on Slide 1 (the title slide), click the title text.

7. In the Font group, click the **Font** arrow. Notice that the theme fonts for the Norway theme are Calibri Light and Constantia. This is different from the Office theme, which uses Calibri for the body text.

8. In the Slides group, click the **Layout** button. The Layout gallery appears. The custom layouts that Inger created are listed in the gallery, as shown in Figure 2-2.

| Figure 2-2 | Custom layouts in the Norway Theme |
| --- | --- |

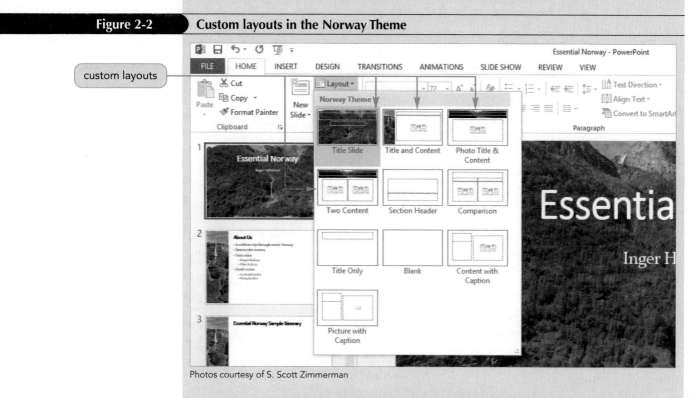

Photos courtesy of S. Scott Zimmerman

Notice the customized Title Slide layout has a photo as a slide background, the Title and Content customized layout has a photo along the left edge of the slide of water running down a cliff, and the customized Two Content layout includes a photo under the slide title. Inger also provided an additional custom layout called Photo Title & Content, which is for a slide with a title and one content placeholder.

9. Press the **Esc** key to close the Layout gallery.

When you applied the custom theme from the Norway Theme presentation, the title slide and the slides with the Title and Content layout and Two Content layout were changed to use the customized versions of these layouts. Slides 4 and 6 have the Two Content layout applied and contain information about the Bergen and Flåm railways. Slides 5 and 7 have the Title and Content layout applied. Currently they only contain a title, but later you will add videos related to the Bergen and Flåm trains to these slides. Inger wants you to change the layout of these two slides to the new Photo Title & Content layout so they better match the slides with the Two Content layouts.

> **To apply a custom layout to Slides 5 and 7:**
>
> ▶ **1.** Display **Slide 5** ("Bergen Train Through Mountains") in the Slide pane.
>
> ▶ **2.** In the Slides group, click the **Layout** button. The Layout gallery appears.
>
> ▶ **3.** Click the **Photo Title & Content** layout. The custom layout is applied to Slide 5.
>
> ▶ **4.** Apply the **Photo Title & Content** layout to Slide 7 ("Flåm Train in Station").
>
> ▶ **5.** Save your changes.

**INSIGHT**

*Saving a Presentation as a Theme*

If you need to use a custom theme frequently, you can save a presentation file as an Office Theme file. A theme file is a different file type than a presentation file. You can then store this file so that it appears in the Themes gallery on the DESIGN tab. To save a custom theme, click the FILE tab, click Save As in the navigation bar, and then click the Browse button to open the Save As dialog box. To change the file type to Office Theme, click the Save as type arrow, and then click Office Theme. This changes the current folder in the Save As dialog box to the Document Themes folder, which is a folder created on the hard drive when Office is installed and where the installed themes are stored. If you save a custom theme to the Document Themes folder, that theme will be listed in its own row above the installed themes in the Themes gallery. (You need to click the More button in the Themes gallery to see this row.) You can also change the folder location and save the custom theme to any location on your computer or network or to a folder on your SkyDrive. If you do this, the theme will not appear in the Themes gallery, but you can still access it using the Browse for Themes command on the Themes gallery menu.

# Inserting Online Pictures

In addition to adding pictures stored on your computer or network to slides, you can also add pictures stored on websites. To do this, you click the Online Pictures button in a content placeholder or in the Images group on the INSERT tab. When you do this, the Insert Pictures window opens, in which you can choose to search for an image on Office.com or use the Bing search engine to search for images across the Internet. The images stored on Office.com are often called clip art, which are images stored in collections so that you can easily locate and use them.

After selecting where you want to search (Office.com or the Internet using the Bing search engine), click in the Search box next to your choice, and then type keywords. **Keywords** are words or phrases that describe an image. When you use the Bing search engine, you get the same results that you would get if you were to type keywords in the Search box on the Bing home page in your browser.

Images stored on Office.com have keywords directly associated with them. For example, a photo of a train might have the keywords "train" and "engine" associated with it. If the photo is a train going over a bridge, additional keywords might be "bridge" and "trestle." The more keywords you use, the narrower (more specific) your search results will be; conversely, to broaden your search, use fewer keywords.

Inger wants you to add a new Slide 3 to the presentation and then insert a map of Norway. You'll search for an image of this on Office.com.

### To insert a picture of a map from Office.com:

▶ **1.** Display **Slide 2** ("About Us") in the Slide pane, and then in the Slides group, click the **New Slide** button. A new Slide 3 is inserted with the same layout as Slide 2, Title and Content.

▶ **2.** Type **Where We Are** as the slide title.

▶ **3.** In the content placeholder, click the **Online Pictures** button ⬚. The Insert Pictures window opens with the insertion point in the Office.com Clip Art search box. See Figure 2-3.

---

**Figure 2-3**    **Insert Pictures window**

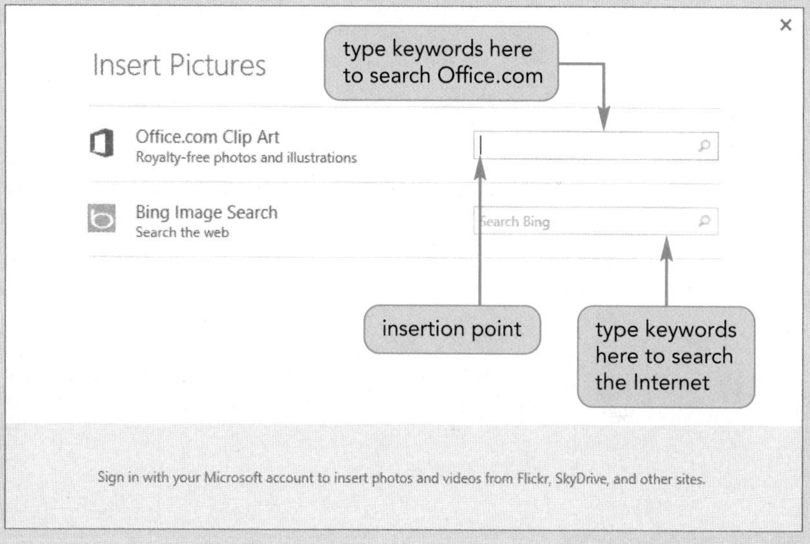

▶ **4.** In the **Office.com Clip Art** search box, type **Norway map**, and then click the **Search** button ⬚. After a moment, images that match your keywords appear in the window.

▶ **5.** Click the drawing of a globe with Scandinavia pulled out in a detail map. The keywords associated with the selected image and the image's measurements in pixels are in the bottom-left corner of the window, as shown in Figure 2-4.

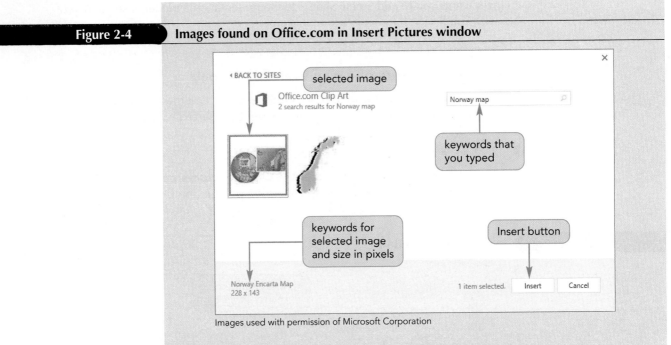

6. Click the **Insert** button. The globe image is added to the slide in place of the content placeholder.

7. Resize the image, maintaining the aspect ratio, so that it is about five inches high, and then reposition it as necessary to roughly center it in the white space below the slide title.

8. Click a blank area of the slide to deselect the image, and then save your changes.

## PROSKILLS

### Written Communication: Respecting Intellectual Property

Make sure you understand and abide by copyright laws. If you use someone else's photograph, illustration, video, music, diagram, or chart, or if you use someone else's data to create your own visuals, give proper credit. Students can, for educational purposes only, use copyrighted material on a one-time basis without getting permission from the copyright holder. On the other hand, if you work for a business or nonprofit organization, much stricter copyright laws apply. You must obtain explicit permission from the copyright owner, and in some cases pay a fee to that person or company. You may use all the images on Office.com in your presentations as long as you are not creating the presentation for commercial purposes. If you need to use an image for a commercial purpose, you need to check to see who owns the image. To do this, go to Office.com, search for the image there, point to the image you want to use, and then click View Details. The image appears on a new webpage with information about the image listed on the right. At the top of this list of information, the name of the copyright holder appears, such as Fotalia or iStockphoto. Contact the copyright holder directly for permission to use the image. If there is no copyright holder listed, the image is owned by Microsoft and you cannot use it for commercial purposes. If you use the Bing search engine when you insert an online picture, you should go to the website from which you are copying the photo and determine if you need to get permission to use the image.

# Inserting Shapes

You can add many shapes to a slide, including lines, rectangles, stars, and more. To draw a shape, click the Shapes button in the Illustrations group on the INSERT tab, click a shape in the gallery, and then click and drag to draw the shape in the size you want. Like any object, a shape can be resized after you insert it.

You've already had a little experience with one shape—a text box, which is a shape specifically designed to contain text. You can add additional text boxes to slides using the Text Box shape. You can also add text to any shape you place on a slide.

Inger wants you to add a few labels to the map image. First, she wants you to add a label to identify Norway in the detail map of Scandinavia.

### To insert and position an arrow shape with text on Slide 3:

1. With **Slide 3** ("Where We Are") in the Slide pane, click the **INSERT** tab, and then in the Illustrations group, click the **Shapes** button. The Shapes gallery opens. See Figure 2-5. The gallery is organized into nine categories of shapes, plus the Recently Used Shapes group at the top.

| Figure 2-5 | Shapes gallery |
| --- | --- |

Image used with permission of Microsoft Corporation; Photos courtesy of S. Scott Zimmerman

**2.** Under Block Arrows, click the **Left Arrow** shape ⇦. The gallery closes and the pointer changes to ╋.

**3.** On the slide, click above the top-left corner of the pop-out, detail map, and then drag to the right to create an arrow approximately 1¼-inches long and ½-inch high.

> A blue, left-pointing arrow appears. (Don't worry about the exact placement or size of the arrow; you will move it later.) Note that the DRAWING TOOLS FORMAT tab is the active tab on the ribbon.

**4.** With the shape selected, type **Norway**. The text you type appears in the arrow. It might not all fit on one line and it may be too tall to fit inside the arrow.

**5.** If necessary, drag the right-middle sizing handle on the end of the arrow to the right to lengthen the arrow until the word "Norway" fits on one line.

**6.** If necessary, drag the bottom-middle sizing handle down until the arrow is tall enough to display all of the text. Now you need to position the arrow shape on the map. When you drag a shape with text, it is similar to dragging a text box, which means you need to drag a border of the shape or a part of the shape that does not contain text.

**7.** Position the pointer on the arrow shape so that the pointer changes to ✥, and then drag the arrow shape on top of the map so that it points to the right-lower side of the yellow area in the detail map of Scandinavia. See Figure 2-6.

Make sure you drag the pointer, not just click it. Otherwise the inserted shape will be tiny.

| Figure 2-6 | Arrow shape with text on Slide 3 |

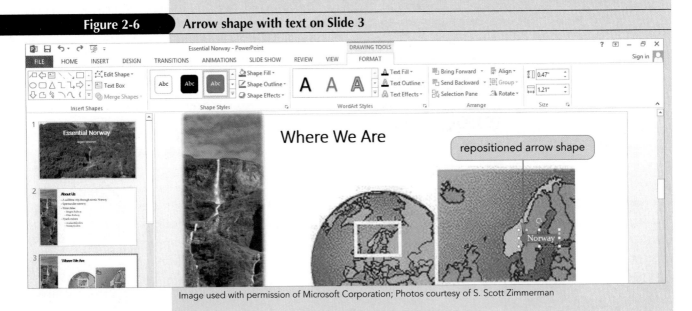

Image used with permission of Microsoft Corporation; Photos courtesy of S. Scott Zimmerman

Next, Inger wants you to add a shape to point to the part of Norway that she is featuring in the presentation. You'll use a callout shape for this.

**To insert and position a callout shape with text on Slide 3:**

1. On the ribbon, click the **INSERT** tab.

2. In the Illustrations group, click the **Shapes** button. The Shapes gallery opens.

3. Under Callouts, click the **Line Callout 1** shape ⌐.

4. Below the detail map, drag to create a box approximately two inches wide and one inch high, and then type **Essential Norway Tours**.

5. Resize the square part of the callout shape, if necessary, so that the text "Essential Norway" fits on one line.

6. Save your changes.

**TIP**

You can also insert a shape using the Shapes gallery in the Drawing group on the HOME tab.

# Formatting Objects

Recall that both shapes and pictures, such as photos and clip art, are treated as objects in PowerPoint. The PICTURE TOOLS and DRAWING TOOLS FORMAT tabs contain tools for formatting these objects. For both shapes and pictures, you can use these tools to apply borders or outlines, special effects such as drop shadows and reflections, and styles. You can also resize and rotate or flip these objects. Some formatting tools are available only to one or the other type of object. For example, the Remove Background tool is available only to pictures, and the Fill command is available only to shapes. Refer to the Session 2.1 Visual Overview for more information about the commands on the FORMAT tabs.

## Formatting Shapes

You can modify the fill of a shape by filling it with a color, a gradient (shading in which one color blends into another or varies from one shade to another), a textured pattern, or a picture. When you add a shape to a slide, the default fill is the Accent 1 color from the set of theme colors, and the default outline is a darker shade of that color.

The default blue of the arrow shape blends into the blue color of the image, so you'll change it.

**To change the fill of the arrow and the style of the callout:**

1. Click the **Norway** arrow, and then click the **DRAWING TOOLS FORMAT** tab, if necessary.

2. In the Shape Styles group, click the **Shape Fill button arrow**. The Shape Fill menu opens. See Figure 2-7. You can fill a shape with a color, a picture, a gradient, or a texture, or you can remove the fill by clicking No Fill.

**Figure 2-7**    Shape Fill button menu

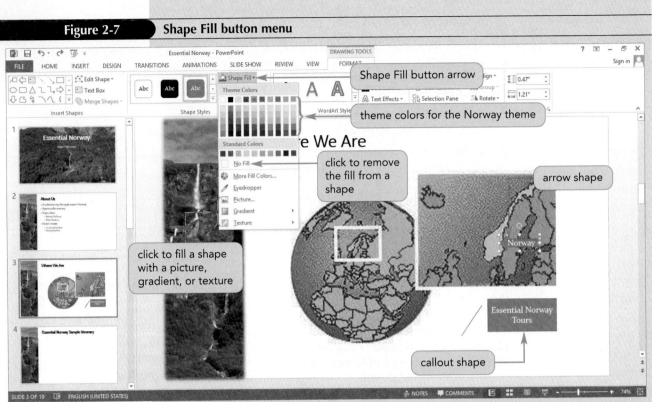

Image used with permission of Microsoft Corporation; Photos courtesy of S. Scott Zimmerman

▶ **3.** Under Theme Colors, click **Red, Accent 2**. The shape fill of the selected arrow changes to the red color. Next, you'll apply a style to the callout shape.

▶ **4.** Click the callout shape, and then in the Shape Styles group, click the **More** button. The Shape Styles gallery opens.

▶ **5.** Click the **Moderate Effect – Red, Accent 2** style. The style, which fills the shape with gradient shades of red and changes the shape outline to the Red, Accent 2 color, is applied to the callout shape.

On some shapes, you can drag the yellow adjustment handle to change the shape's proportions. For instance, if you dragged the adjustment handle on the arrow shape, you would change the size of the arrow head relative to the size of the arrow. The callout shape has two adjustment handles, one on either end of the line that extends out from the part of the shape that contains text. You can drag these adjustment handles to more clearly identify what the callout is pointing to.

You need to position the callout shape and adjust the line so that the line is pointing to the area of Norway highlighted in the presentation.

**To move and adjust the callout shape and change its outline weight:**

▶ **1.** Drag the callout shape so that the right edge is aligned with the right side of the map image and there is approximately one-quarter inch space between the callout and the bottom of the detail portion of the map.

▶ **2.** Drag the yellow adjustment handle on the left end of the callout line so that it points to the lower-left portion of Norway on the map. The callout line is hard to see on top of the map, so you will make the shape's outline thicker by changing its weight.

▶ **3.** In the Shape Styles group, click the **Shape Outline button arrow**, point to **Weight**, and then click **3 pt**. Compare your screen to Figure 2-8 and make any adjustments necessary to match the figure.

**Figure 2-8**    **Formatted and positioned callout shape**

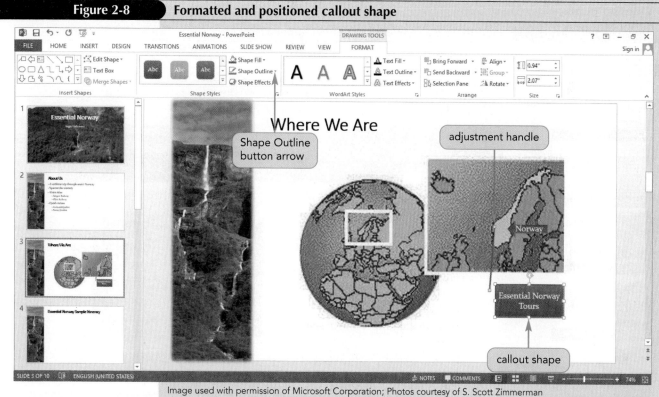

Image used with permission of Microsoft Corporation; Photos courtesy of S. Scott Zimmerman

## Formatting Pictures

You can format photos as well as shapes. To format photos, you use the tools on the PICTURE TOOLS FORMAT tab.

Inger wants you to format the pictures on Slides 5 and 7 by adding a frame and a 3-D effect. To create the frame, you could apply a thick outline, or you can apply one of the styles that includes a frame.

## To format the photos on Slides 5 and 7:

**TIP**

Click the Reset Picture button in the Adjust group on the PICTURE TOOLS FORMAT tab to remove formatting from a picture or resize the picture to its original size.

1. Display **Slide 5** ("Bergen Railway") in the Slide pane, click the photo of the train, and then click the **PICTURE TOOLS FORMAT** tab.

2. In the Picture Styles group, click the **Beveled Matte, White** style. This style applies a 15-point white border with a slight beveled edge and a slight shadow to the photo. Now you need to add a 3-D rotation to the picture.

3. In the Picture Styles group, click the **Picture Effects** button, and then point to **3-D Rotation**. A gallery of 3-D rotation options opens.

4. Under Perspective, click the **Perspective Left** option. The picture rotates slightly to the left. See Figure 2-9. You need to apply the same formatting to the photo on Slide 7. You can repeat the same formatting steps or you can copy the formatting.

**Figure 2-9**  Picture with a style and 3-D effect applied

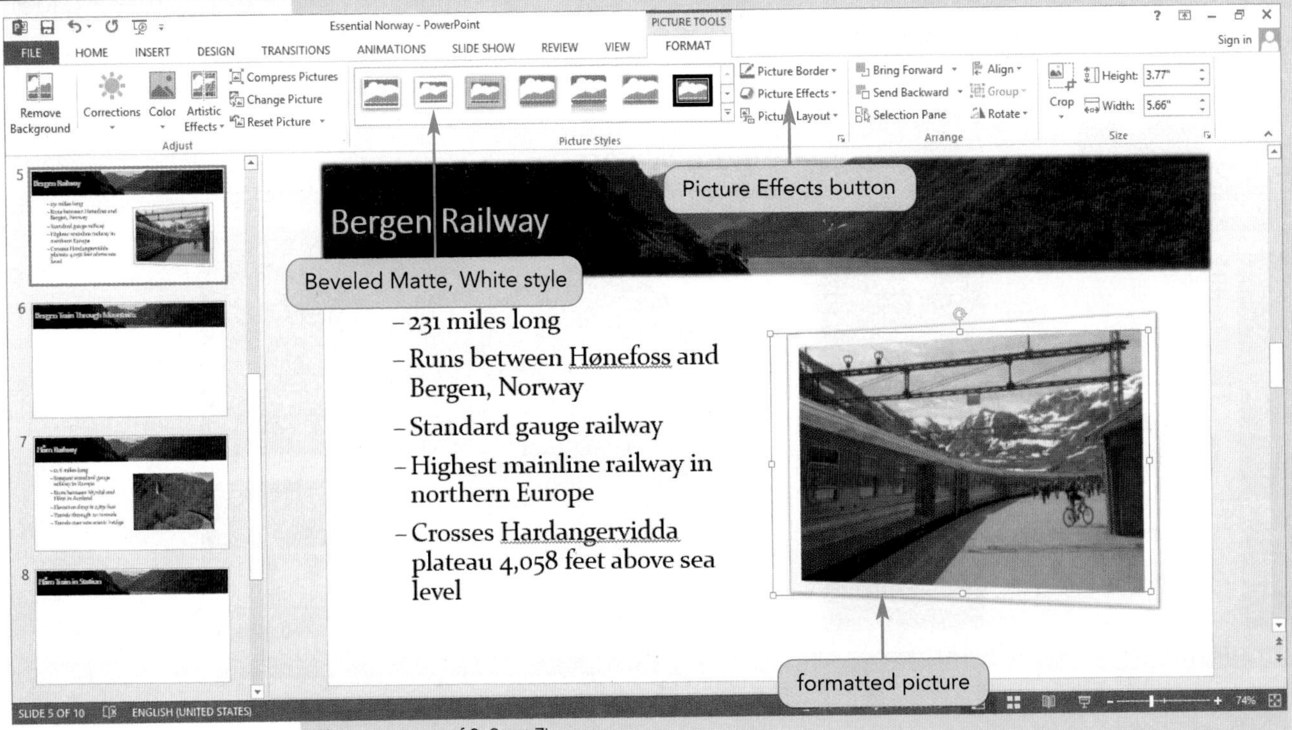

Photos courtesy of S. Scott Zimmerman

5. With the photo on Slide 5 still selected, click the **HOME** tab.

6. In the Clipboard group, click the **Format Painter** button, and then move the pointer to the Slide pane. The pointer changes to ⬚ 🖌.

7. In the Slides tab, click the **Slide 7** thumbnail, and then in the Slide pane, click the photo next to the bulleted list. The style and 3-D rotation formatting is copied from the photo on Slide 5 and applied to the photo on Slide 7.

8. Save your changes.

# Rotating and Flipping Objects

You can rotate and flip any object on a slide. To flip an object, you use the Flip commands on the Rotate button menu in the Arrange group on the DRAWING TOOLS FORMAT tab. To rotate an object, you can use the Rotate commands on the Rotate button menu to rotate objects in 90-degree increments. You can also drag the Rotate handle that appears above the top-middle sizing handle when the object is selected to rotate it to any position that you want, using the center of the object as a pivot point.

The Norway arrow would look better if it were pointing to the west coast of the country on the map. To correctly position the Norway arrow, you first need to flip it.

## To flip the arrow shape on Slide 3:

1. Display **Slide 3** ("Where We Are") in the Slide pane, and then click the **Norway** arrow.

**TIP**

You can also click the Arrange button in the Drawing group on the HOME tab to access the Rotate and Flip commands.

2. Position the pointer on the Rotate handle ⟳ so that the pointer changes to ⟳, and then drag the Rotate handle ⟳ until the Norway arrow is pointing to the right. The arrow is pointing in the correct direction, but the text is upside-down.

3. Undo the rotation, and then click the **DRAWING TOOLS FORMAT** tab.

4. In the Arrange group, click the **Rotate** button. The Rotate menu opens. See Figure 2-10.

| Figure 2-10 | Rotate button menu |

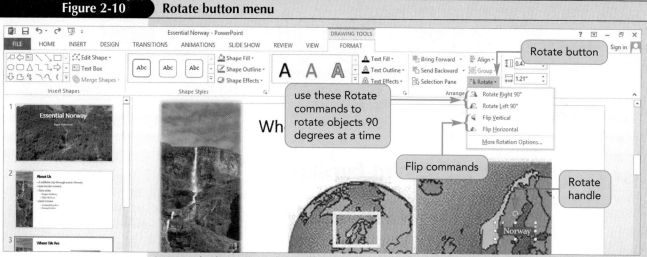

Image used with permission of Microsoft Corporation; Photos courtesy of S. Scott Zimmerman

5. Click **Flip Horizontal**. The arrow flips horizontally and is now pointing right. Unlike when you rotated the arrow so that it pointed right, the text is still right-side up.

Now you need to rotate and reposition the Norway arrow so that it is pointing to the west coast of Norway on the map.

**To rotate the arrow shape and reposition it:**

▶ **1.** Position the pointer on the Rotate handle 🔄 so that the pointer changes to ↻.

▶ **2.** Drag the Rotate handle 🔄 to the right to rotate the arrow so that it points down and to the right at approximately a 45-degree angle.

▶ **3.** Drag the Norway arrow so it is pointing down to approximately the center of Norway's west coast.

▶ **4.** Click a blank area of the slide to deselect the shape, compare your screen to Figure 2-11, and then make any adjustments needed to match the figure.

**Figure 2-11** ▶ **Arrow flipped, rotated, and repositioned on Slide 3**

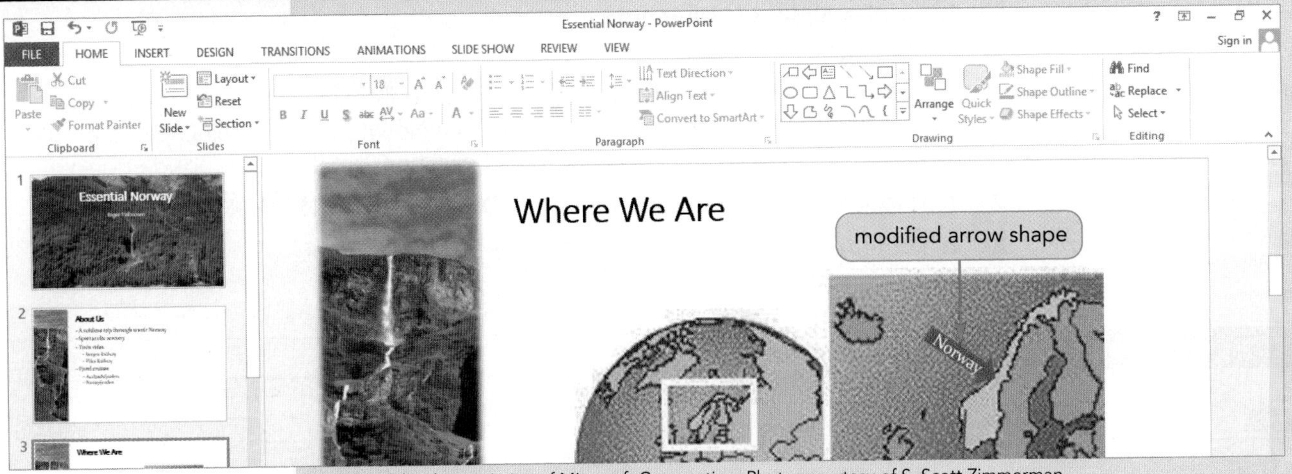

Image used with permission of Microsoft Corporation; Photos courtesy of S. Scott Zimmerman

▶ **5.** Save your changes.

# Creating and Formatting Tables

A **table** is information arranged in horizontal rows and vertical columns. The area where a row and column intersect is called a **cell**. Each cell contains one piece of information. A table's structure is indicated by borders, which are lines that outline the rows and columns.

## Creating and Adding Data to a Table

Inger wants you to add a table to Slide 4 to list a typical tour itinerary. This table will have three columns—one to describe the activity, one to list the time that the activity starts, and one to list notes.

REFERENCE

### Inserting a Table

- In a content placeholder, click the Insert Table button; or, click the INSERT tab on the ribbon, click the Table button in the Tables group, and then click Insert Table.
- Specify the numbers of columns and rows.
- Click the OK button.

*or*

- On the ribbon, click the INSERT tab, and then in the Tables group, click the Table button to open a grid.
- Click a box in the grid to create a table of that size.

Inger hasn't decided how much data to include in the table, so she asks you to start by creating a table with four rows.

### To add a table to Slide 4:

1. Display **Slide 4** ("Essential Norway Sample Itinerary") in the Slide pane.

2. Click the **INSERT** tab, and then in the Tables group, click the **Table** button. A menu opens with a grid of squares above three commands.

3. Point to the squares on the grid, and without clicking the mouse button, move the pointer down and to the right. As you move the pointer, the label above the grid indicates how large the table will be, and a preview of the table appears on the slide. See Figure 2-12.

| Figure 2-12 | Inserting a 3x4 table on Slide 3 |
| --- | --- |

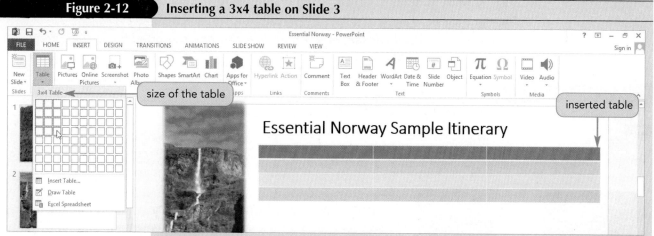

Photos courtesy of S. Scott Zimmerman

4. When the label above the grid indicates 3x4 Table, click to insert a table with three columns and four rows. A selection border appears around the table, and the insertion point is in the first cell in the first row.

Now you're ready to fill the blank cells with the information about the tour. To enter data in a table, you click in the cells in which you want to enter data, and then start typing. You can also use the Tab and arrow keys to move from one cell to another.

### To add data to the table:

▶ **1.** In the first cell in the first row, type **Activity**. The text you typed appears in the first cell.

▶ **2.** Press the **Tab** key. The insertion point moves to the second cell in the first row.

▶ **3.** Type **Time**, press the **Tab** key, type **Notes**, and then press the **Tab** key. The insertion point is in the first cell in the second row.

▶ **4.** In the first cell in the second row, type **Bergen train from Honefoss**, press the **Tab** key, and then type **8:13 a.m.**

▶ **5.** Click in the first cell in the third row, type **Arrive Myrdal for lunch, shopping,** press the **Tab** key, and then type **11:41 a.m.**

▶ **6.** Click in the first cell in the last row, type **Flam train from Myrdal**, press the **Tab** key, and then type **1:11 p.m.**

## Inserting and Deleting Rows and Columns

You can modify the table by adding or deleting rows and columns. You need to add more rows to the table for additional itinerary items. Inger also wants to make the table a little more interesting by adding a new first column in which you will insert pictures related to that part of the itinerary.

### To insert rows in the table:

▶ **1.** Make sure the insertion point is in the last row in the table.

▶ **2.** Click the **TABLE TOOLS LAYOUT** tab, and then in the Rows & Columns group, click the **Insert Below** button. A new row is inserted below the current row. See Figure 2-13.

**Figure 2-13**    **Table with row inserted**

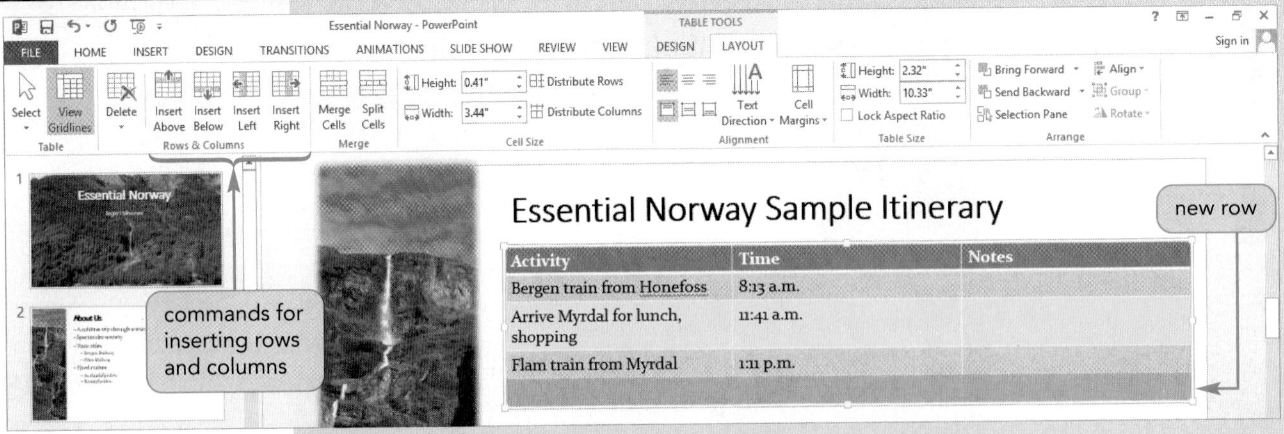

Photos courtesy of S. Scott Zimmerman

**3.** Click in the first cell in the new last row, type **Arrive Flam**, and then press the **Tab** key.

**4.** Type **2:05 p.m.**, and then press the **Tab** key. The insertion point is in the last cell in the last row.

**5.** Press the **Tab** key. A new row is created and the insertion point is in the first cell in the new row.

**6.** Type **Check in at hotel**, press the **Tab** key, and then type **4:30 p.m.** You need to insert a row above the last row.

**7.** In the Rows & Columns group, click the **Insert Above** button. A new row is inserted above the current row.

**8.** Click in the first cell in the new row, type **Fjord cruises from Flam**, press the **Tab** key, and then type **2:20 p.m.**

Inger decided she doesn't want to add notes to the table, so you'll delete the last column. She also decides that the information in the last row in the table about checking into the hotel isn't needed, so you'll delete that row.

### To delete a column and a row in the table:

**1.** Click in any cell in the last column. This is the column you will delete.

**2.** On the TABLE TOOLS LAYOUT tab, in the Rows & Columns group, click the **Delete** button. The Delete button menu opens.

**3.** Click **Delete Columns**. The current column is deleted, and the entire table is selected.

**4.** Click in any cell in the last row. This is the row you want to delete.

**5.** In the Rows & Columns group, click the **Delete** button, and then click **Delete Rows.**

**6.** Click a blank area of the slide to deselect the table. See Figure 2-14.

**Figure 2-14**      **Table after adding and deleting rows and deleting the third column**

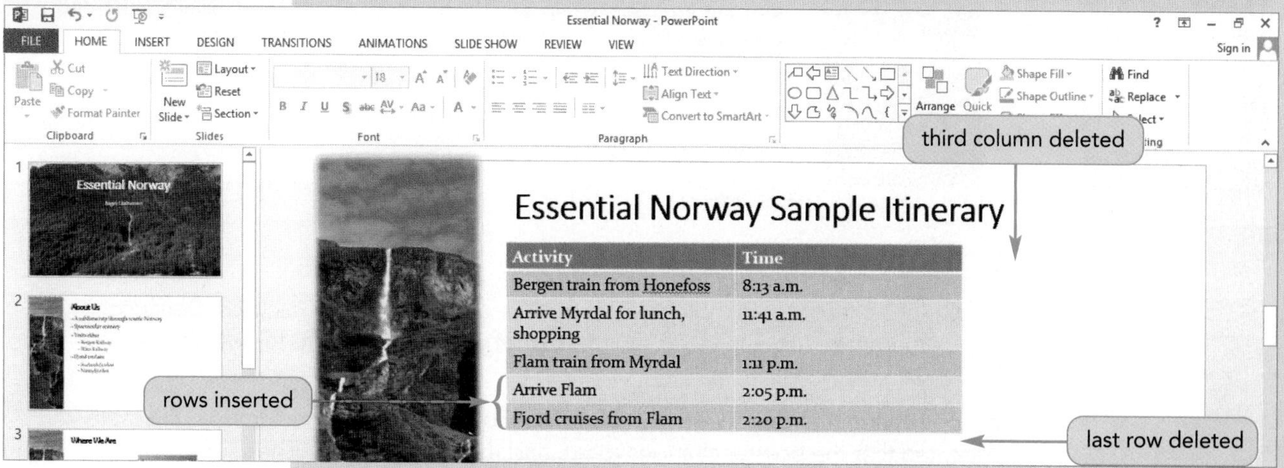

Photos courtesy of S. Scott Zimmerman

## Formatting a Table

After you insert data into a table, you need to think about how the table looks and whether the table will be readable for the audience. As with any text, you can change the font, size, or color, and as with shapes and pictures, you can apply a style to a table. You can also change how the text fits in the table cells by changing the height of rows and the width of columns. You can also customize the formatting of the table by changing the border and fill of table cells.

You need to make the table text larger so that an audience will be able to read it. You will also increase the width of the Activity column so that it is as wide as the widest entry.

### To change the font size and adjust the column size in the table:

▶ **1.** Click any cell in the table. You want to change the size of all the text in the table, so you will select the entire table. Notice that a selection border appears around the table. This border appears any time the table is active.

▶ **2.** Click the **TABLE TOOLS LAYOUT** tab, and then in the Table group, click the **Select** button. The Select button menu appears with options to select the entire table, the current column, or the current row.

▶ **3.** Click **Select Table**. The entire table is selected. Because the selection border appears any time the table is active, the only visual cues you have that it is now selected are that the insertion point is no longer blinking in the cell that you clicked in Step 1 and the Select button is gray and unavailable. See Figure 2-15.

| Figure 2-15 | Table selected on Slide 4 |

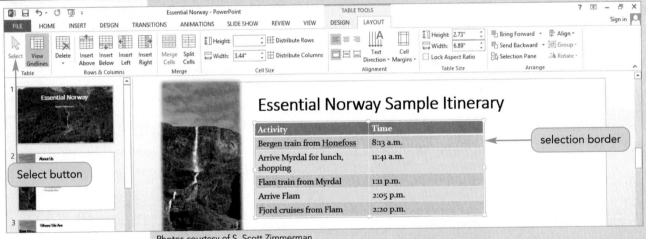

Photos courtesy of S. Scott Zimmerman

▶ **4.** On the ribbon, click the **HOME** tab.

▶ **5.** In the Font group, click the **Font Size** arrow, and then click **28**. Because the entire table is selected, the size of all the text in the table changes to 28 points.

▶ **6.** Position the pointer on the column line between the two columns in the table so that the pointer changes to ↔, and then double-click. The width of the first column expands so that all the text in each cell in the first column fits on one line.

Inger wants you to change the format of the table so it looks more attractive and so that its colors complement the photo in the slide's layout. You will do this by applying a style to the table. When you apply a style to a table, you can specify whether the header and total rows and the first and last columns are formatted differently from the other rows and columns in the table. You can also specify whether to use banded rows or columns; that is, whether to fill alternating rows or columns with different shading.

### To apply a style to the table:

1. Click the **TABLE TOOLS DESIGN** tab on the ribbon, if necessary. In the Table Styles group, the second style, Medium Style 2 – Accent 1, is selected. In the Table Style Options group, the Header Row and Banded Rows check boxes are selected, which means that the header row will be formatted differently than the rest of the rows and that every other row will be filled with shading. See Figure 2-16.

**Figure 2-16**  Default formatting applied to the table

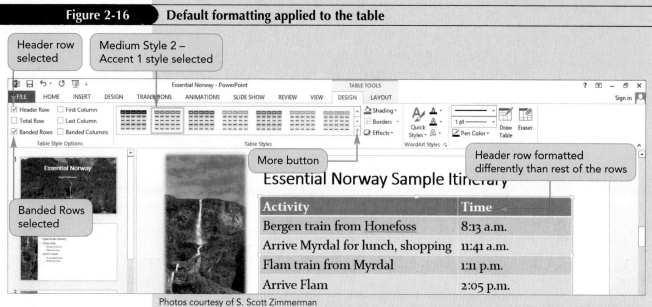

Photos courtesy of S. Scott Zimmerman

2. In the Table Styles group, click the **More** button. The Table Styles gallery opens.

3. Click the **Medium Style 3 – Accent 3** style, and then click a blank area of the slide to deselect the table.

The color in the first row is a little too bright. You can change the fill of table cells in the same manner that you change the fill of shapes.

## To change the fill of cells in the table:

**1.** In the table, click in the first row, and then click the **LAYOUT** tab.

**2.** In the Table group, click the **Select** button, and then click **Select Row**. The first row in the table is selected.

**3.** Click the **TABLE TOOLS DESIGN** tab.

**4.** In the Table Styles group, click the **Shading button arrow**. The Shading menu is similar to the Shape Fill menu you worked with earlier.

**5.** Click **Olive Green, Accent 3, Darker 50%**. The menu closes and the cells in the first row are shaded with olive green.

In addition, the table might be easier to read if the horizontal borders between the rows were visible. You can add these by using the Borders button arrow and the buttons in the Draw Borders group on the TABLE TOOLS DESIGN tab. When you use the Borders button arrow, you can apply borders to all the selected cells at once. The borders will be the style, weight, and color specified by the Pen Style, Pen Weight, and Pen Color buttons in the Draw Borders group.

## To change the borders of the table:

**1.** Position the pointer to the left of the first cell in the second row so that it changes to ➡, press and hold the mouse button, drag down to the left of the last row, and then release the mouse button. You want to apply a horizontal border between the rows below the header row.

**2.** In the Table Styles group, click the **Borders button arrow**. A menu opens listing borders that you can apply to the selected cells.

**3.** Click **Inside Horizontal Border**. A border appears between each row below the header row. As indicated in the Draw Table group, the borders are solid line borders, one point wide, and black. See Figure 2-17. You can change any of these attributes.

**Figure 2-17** **Table with inside horizontal borders added**

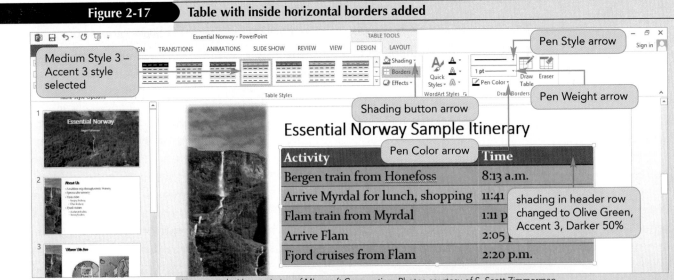

Image used with permission of Microsoft Corporation; Photos courtesy of S. Scott Zimmerman

**4.** In the Draw Borders group, click the **Pen Weight** arrow, and then click **½ pt**. The pointer changes to ⌀. You could drag this pointer along each border to draw them individually. Instead, you will use the Borders button again to apply the new settings to all of the selected cells. Because Inside Horizontal Borders was the last option chosen on the Borders button menu, it is the default option for the Borders button.

**5.** In the Table Styles group, click the **Borders** button. The weight of the borders between each selected row is changed to one-half point.

Inger decides that she wants you to add a picture to each row that is related to that part of the itinerary. Recall that one of the things you can fill a shape with is a picture. You can do the same with cells. First, you'll need to insert a new first column.

### To insert a new column and fill the cells with pictures:

**1.** Click in any cell in the first column, and then click the **LAYOUT** tab.

**2.** In the Rows & Columns group, click the **Insert Left** button. A new column is inserted to the left of the current column.

**3.** Position the pointer on the column line between the new first column and the second column, and then drag left until the column line is approximately below the middle of the "n" in "Essential" in the slide title. The text in each cell in the second column again fits on one line. In the Cell Size group, the measurement in the Width box should be approximately 1.2". See Figure 2-18.

| Figure 2-18 | New column added to table |
| --- | --- |

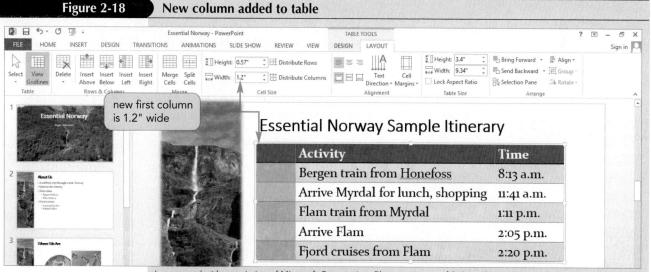

Image used with permission of Microsoft Corporation; Photos courtesy of S. Scott Zimmerman

**4.** Click in the first cell in the second row, and then click the **TABLE TOOLS DESIGN** tab.

**5.** In the Table Styles group, click the **Shading button arrow**, and then click **Picture**. The Insert Pictures window opens. See Figure 2-19.

**Figure 2-19** Insert Pictures window with option for locating a file on your computer

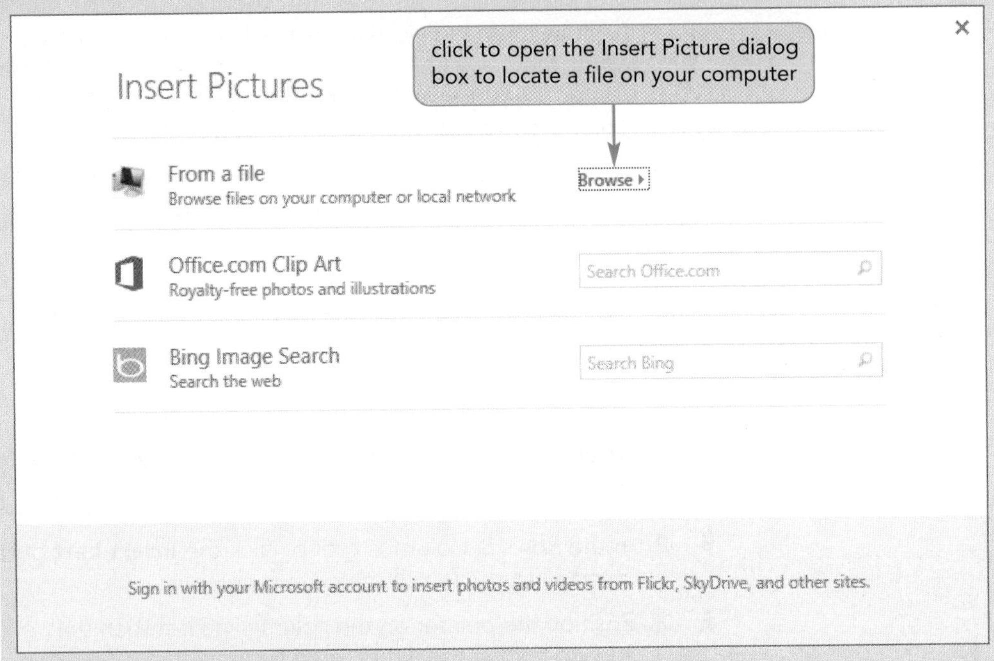

6. Next to From a file, click the **Browse** button. The Insert Picture dialog box opens.

7. Navigate to the **PowerPoint2 ▸ Tutorial** folder, click **Bergen Train**, and then click the **Insert** button. The photo fills the cell.

8. Insert the following photos, all located in the **PowerPoint2 ▸ Tutorial** folder, in the first cells in the next four rows: **Myrdal**, **Flam Train**, **Flam Station**, **Boat**.

The text in the table is large enough, but the photos are too small, and some of them are fairly distorted because they were stretched horizontally to fill the cells. You'll increase the height of the rows below the heading row in the table.

**To increase the row height in the table and adjust cell alignment:**

1. Select all the rows except the heading row.

2. On the ribbon, click the **LAYOUT** tab.

3. In the Cell Size group, click in the **Height** box, delete the selected value, type **1**, and then press the **Enter** key. The height of each selected rows changes to one inch.

Finally, the text in all cells in the table is horizontally left-aligned and vertically aligned at the top of the cells. The headings would look better centered horizontally in the cells, and the text in the other rows would look better vertically aligned in the center of the cells.

You also need to reposition the table on the slide to better fill the space. You move a table the same way you move any other object. The pointer must be positioned on the table border in order to change it to ⌖.

### To adjust the alignment of text in cells and reposition the table:

▶ **1.** Make sure all the rows except the heading row are still selected.

▶ **2.** In the Alignment group, click the **Center Vertically** button ▣. The text in the selected rows is now centered vertically in the cells.

▶ **3.** In the first row, drag across the second and third cells to select them.

▶ **4.** In the Alignment group, click the **Center** button ▤. The headings are now centered horizontally in the cells. Now you will adjust the table's placement on the slide.

▶ **5.** Position the pointer on the table border so that it changes to ⌖, and then drag the table so that its left edge is approximately aligned with the left of the letter "E" in "Essential" in the slide title and vertically centered in the white space below the title. Compare your screen to Figure 2-20.

| Figure 2-20 | Final formatted table |

Image used with permission of Microsoft Corporation; Photos courtesy of S. Scott Zimmerman; Richard Cummins/Getty Images

▶ **6.** Click a blank area of the slide to deselect the table, and then save your changes.

# Inserting Symbols and Characters

The Norwegian alphabet contains three letters that are not in the English alphabet: æ (pronounced like the "a" in "cat"), ø (pronounced like the "u" in "hurt"), and å (pronounced like the "o" in "more"). The city names Flåm and Hønefoss use two of these letters. To insert these letters using a keyboard with only English letters, you can use the Symbol button in the Symbols group on the INSERT tab.

You need to correct the spelling of Flåm and Hønefoss in the table you inserted on Slide 4.

### To insert the special characters:

▶ 1. Display **Slide 4** ("Essential Norway Sample Itinerary") in the Slide pane, if necessary.

▶ 2. In the row below the table header, click after the "H" in "Honefoss," and then press the **Delete** key to delete the "o."

▶ 3. Click the **INSERT** tab, and then in the Symbols group, click the **Symbol** button. The Symbol dialog box opens.

▶ 4. Drag the scroll box to the top of the vertical scroll bar, click the **Subset** arrow, click **Latin-1 Supplement**, and then click the **down scroll arrow** four times. The bottom row contains the letter ø, and the row above it contains the letter å. See Figure 2-21.

| Figure 2-21 | Symbol dialog box |

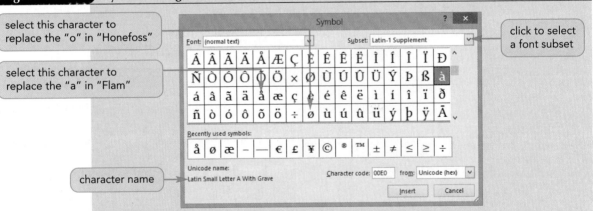

Trouble? If the letters do not appear in the rows mentioned in Step 4, someone might have resized the Symbol dialog box. Refer to Figure 2-21 for help locating the symbols.

▶ 5. In the bottom row, click **ø**. In the bottom-left corner of the Symbol dialog box, the name of the selected character is "Latin Small Letter O With Stroke."

▶ 6. Click the **Insert** button. The letter ø is inserted in the table, and the Cancel button in the dialog box changes to the Close button.

▶ **7.** Click the **Close** button. The cell below the header "Activity" now contains the text "Bergen train from Hønefoss."

▶ **8.** In the third row below the header row, click after the "a" in "Flam," and then press the **Backspace** key to delete the "a."

▶ **9.** In the Symbols group, click the **Symbol** button to open the Symbols dialog box, scroll up one row, and then click **å**, which has the name "Latin Small Letter A With Ring Above."

▶ **10.** Click the **Insert** button, and then click the **Close** button. The cell now contains the text "Flåm train from Myrdal."

▶ **11.** Double-click **Flåm**, click the **HOME** tab, and then, in the Clipboard group, click the **Copy** button.

▶ **12.** In the next row in the table, double-click **Flam**, and then in the Clipboard group, click the **Paste** button.

▶ **13.** In the last row in the table, replace **Flam** with the text **Flåm** on the Clipboard.

▶ **14.** Save your changes.

# Changing the Proofing Language

The spell checker can be very helpful, but when it flags words that are spelled correctly, the wavy red lines can be distracting as you work with the presentation. In the Essential Norway presentation, some of the Norwegian city and fjord names have been flagged as misspelled. This is because the proofing language for the presentation is set to English.

You can change the proofing language for the entire presentation or only for specific words to any language supported by Microsoft Office. If the proofing language you specify is not installed on your computer, PowerPoint will stop flagging the words in that language as misspelled, but it will not be able to determine if the foreign language words are spelled correctly. However, if you open the file on a computer that has the other language installed, you can use the spell checker to check the words in that language.

You will set the proofing language of the Norwegian words to Norwegian to help Inger as she reviews the final presentation.

**To set the proofing language for specific words to Norwegian:**

▶ **1.** Display **Slide 4** ("Essential Norway Sample Itinerary") in the Slide pane, if necessary.

▶ **2.** In the second row of the table, double-click **Hønefoss**. The word is selected.

▶ **3.** On the status bar, click **ENGLISH (UNITED STATES)**. The Language dialog box opens. See Figure 2-22. The default is for the selected text to be marked as English. The spell check icon next to English indicates that this language is installed.

**Figure 2-22**    Language dialog box

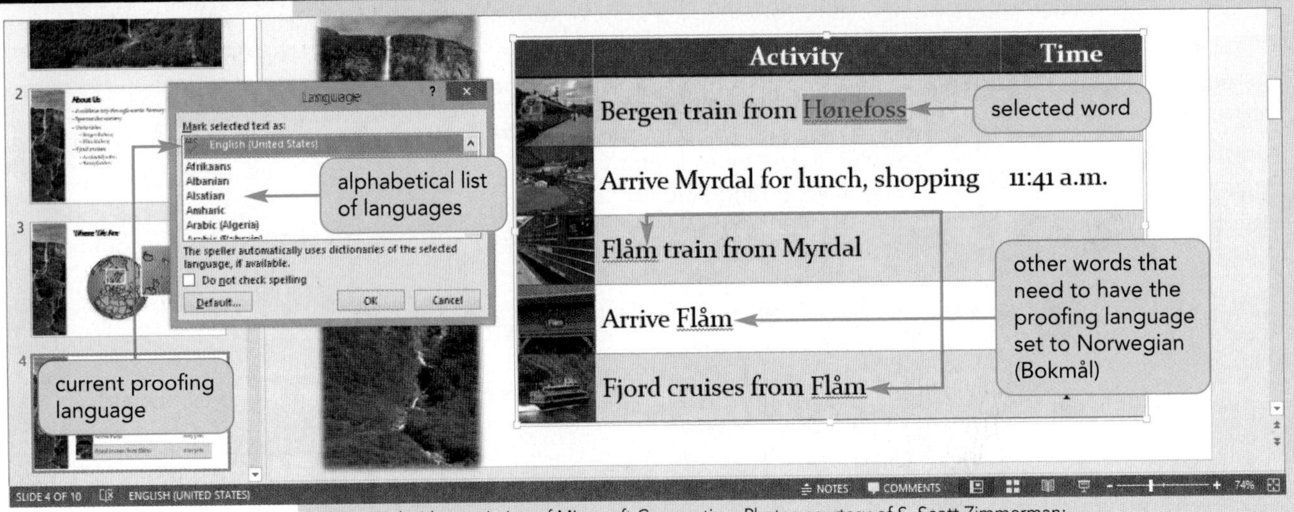

Image used with permission of Microsoft Corporation; Photos courtesy of S. Scott Zimmerman;
Richard Cummins/Getty Images

**Trouble?** If ENGLISH (UNITED STATES) does not appear on the status bar, click the REVIEW tab, click the Language button in the Language group, and then click Set Proofing Language.

4. Scroll down the alphabetical list until you see **Norwegian (Bokmål)**. There is no spell check icon next to this language because Microsoft Office sold in English-speaking countries comes only with English, French, and Spanish languages installed.

**Trouble?** If there is a spell check icon next to Norwegian (Bokmål), then that language is installed on your computer.

5. Click **Norwegian (Bokmål)**, and then click the **OK** button. The wavy red line under the selected word disappears, and next to the Spelling icon on the status bar, the language is now Norwegian (Bokmål).

6. In the fourth row in the table, double-click **Flåm**. Because specifying the Norwegian language as the proofing language was the most recent action, a quicker way to specify it for additional words you select is to use the Repeat button to repeat that action.

7. On the Quick Access Toolbar, click the **Repeat** button ↻. As indicated on the status bar, the language for the selected word is changed to Norwegian.

8. In the fifth and sixth rows of the table, select **Flåm**, and then set the proofing language for both instances to **Norwegian (Bokmål)**.

9. Save your changes.

You have modified a presentation by applying a theme used in another presentation, inserting and formatting online pictures and shapes, and inserting a table and characters that are not on your keyboard. You also changed the proofing language for Norwegian words. In the next session, you will continue modifying the presentation by applying and modifying transitions and animations, adding and modifying videos, and adding footer and header information.

**REVIEW**

## Session 2.1 Quick Check

1. What are keywords?
2. Which contextual tab appears on the ribbon when a shape is selected?
3. What is a style?
4. What is a shape's fill?
5. In a table, what is the intersection of a row and column called?
6. How do you know if an entire table is selected and not just active?
7. How do you insert characters that are not on your keyboard?

# Session 2.2 Visual Overview:

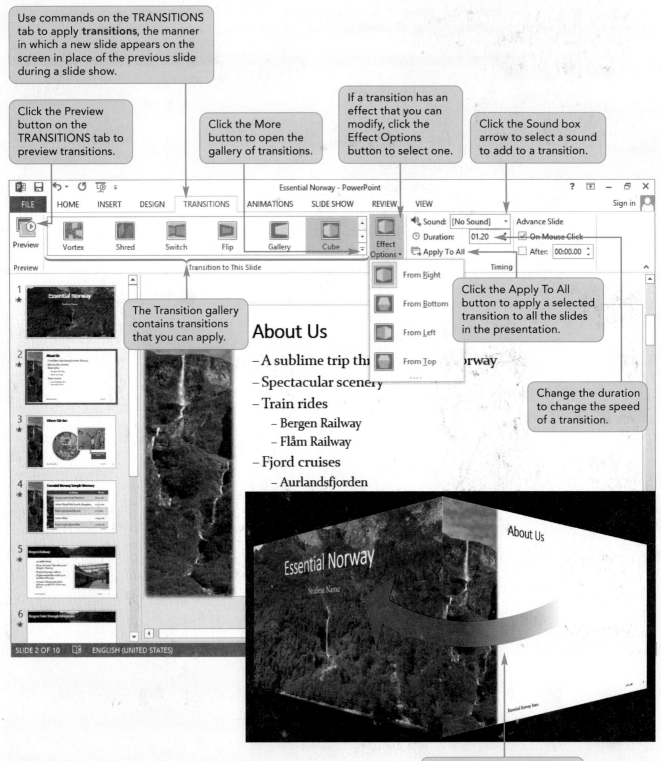

Use commands on the TRANSITIONS tab to apply **transitions**, the manner in which a new slide appears on the screen in place of the previous slide during a slide show.

Click the Preview button on the TRANSITIONS tab to preview transitions.

Click the More button to open the gallery of transitions.

If a transition has an effect that you can modify, click the Effect Options button to select one.

Click the Sound box arrow to select a sound to add to a transition.

The Transition gallery contains transitions that you can apply.

Click the Apply To All button to apply a selected transition to all the slides in the presentation.

Change the duration to change the speed of a transition.

The "About Us" slide is transitioning onto the screen with the Cube transition.

# Using Transitions and Animations

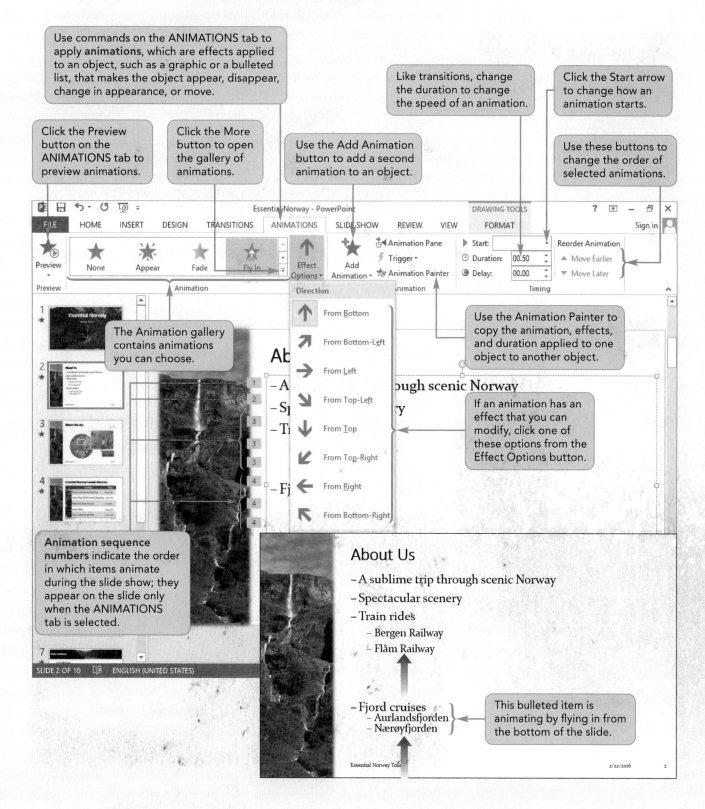

Use commands on the ANIMATIONS tab to apply **animations**, which are effects applied to an object, such as a graphic or a bulleted list, that makes the object appear, disappear, change in appearance, or move.

Like transitions, change the duration to change the speed of an animation.

Click the Start arrow to change how an animation starts.

Click the Preview button on the ANIMATIONS tab to preview animations.

Click the More button to open the gallery of animations.

Use the Add Animation button to add a second animation to an object.

Use these buttons to change the order of selected animations.

The Animation gallery contains animations you can choose.

Use the Animation Painter to copy the animation, effects, and duration applied to one object to another object.

If an animation has an effect that you can modify, click one of these options from the Effect Options button.

**Animation sequence numbers** indicate the order in which items animate during the slide show; they appear on the slide only when the ANIMATIONS tab is selected.

This bulleted item is animating by flying in from the bottom of the slide.

## About Us

- A sublime trip through scenic Norway
- Spectacular scenery
- Train rides
  - Bergen Railway
  - Flåm Railway

- Fjord cruises
  - Aurlandsfjorden
  - Nærøyfjorden

# Applying Transitions

The TRANSITIONS tab contains commands for changing slide transitions. Refer to the Session 2.2 Visual Overview for more information about transitions. Unless you change it, the default is for one slide to disappear and the next slide to immediately appear on the screen. You can modify transitions in Normal or Slide Sorter view.

Transitions are organized into three categories: Subtle, Exciting, and Dynamic Content. Dynamic Content transitions are a combination of the Fade transition for the slide background and a different transition for the slide content. If slides have the same background, it looks like the slide background stays in place and only the slide content moves.

Inconsistent transitions can be distracting and detract from your message, so generally it's a good idea to apply the same transition to all of the slides in the presentation. Depending on the audience and topic, you might choose different effects of the same transition for different slides, such as changing the direction of a Wipe or Push transition. If there is one slide you want to highlight, for instance, the last slide, you can use a different transition for that slide.

**REFERENCE**

### *Adding Transitions*

- In the Slides tab in Normal view or in Slide Sorter view, select the slide(s) to which you want to add a transition, or, if applying to all the slides, select any slide.
- On the ribbon, click the TRANSITIONS tab.
- In the Transition to This Slide group, click the More button to display the gallery of transitions, and then click a transition in the gallery.
- If desired, in the Transition to This Slide group, click the Effect Options button, and then click an effect.
- If desired, in the Timing group, click the Transition Sound arrow to insert a sound effect to accompany each transition.
- If desired, in the Timing group, modify the time in the Duration box to modify the speed of the transition.
- To apply the transition to all the slides in the presentation, in the Timing group, click the Apply to All button.

The Essential Norway presentation contains photos of beautiful vistas. Inger wants a transition between the slides that gives the audience a feel for moving through the open spaces in the photos.

### To apply transitions to the slides:

1. If you took a break after the previous session, make sure the Essential Norway presentation is open, and then display **Slide 2** ("About Us") in the Slide pane.

2. On the ribbon, click the **TRANSITIONS** tab. See Figure 2-23.

**Figure 2-23**    **Commands on the TRANSITIONS tab**

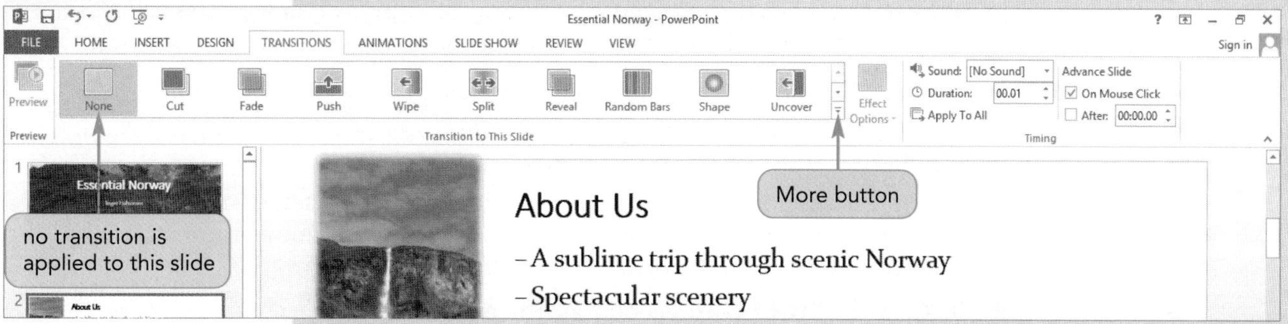

Photos courtesy of S. Scott Zimmerman

> **3.** In the Transition to This Slide group, click **Reveal**. The transition previews in the Slide pane as Slide 1 (the title slide) appears, fades away, and then Slide 2 fades in. The Reveal transition is now highlighted in orange in the gallery. In the Slides tab, a star appears next to the Slide 2 thumbnail. If you missed the preview, you can see it again.

> **4.** In the Preview group, click the **Preview** button. The transition previews in the Slide pane again.

> **5.** In the Transition to This Slide group, click the **More** button. The gallery opens listing all the transitions. See Figure 2-24.

**Figure 2-24**    **Transitions gallery**

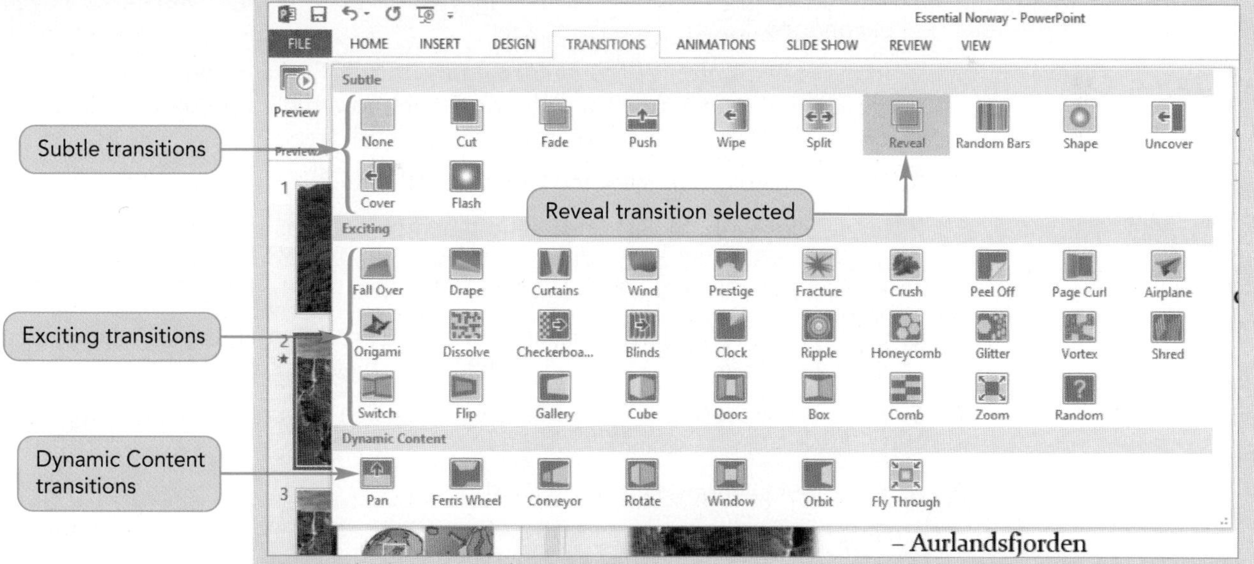

Image used with permission of Microsoft Corporation; Photos courtesy of S. Scott Zimmerman

> **6.** Click **Push**. The preview shows Slide 2 slide up from the bottom and push Slide 1 up and out of view.

Most transitions have effects that you can modify. For example, the Peel Off transition can peel from the bottom left or the bottom right corner, and the Wipe transition can wipe from any direction. You'll modify the transition applied to Slide 2.

**To modify the transition effect for Slide 2:**

▶ **1.** In the Transition to This Slide group, click the **Effect Options** button. The effects that you can modify for the Push transition are listed on the menu.

▶ **2.** Click **From Right**. The Push transition previews again, but this time Slide 2 slides from the right to push Slide 1 left. The available effects change depending on the transition selected.

▶ **3.** In the Transition to This Slide group, click **Shape**. The transition previews with Slide 2 appearing in the center of Slide 1 inside a circle that grows to fill the slide.

▶ **4.** Click the **Effect Options** button. The effects that you can modify for the Shape transition are listed.

▶ **5.** Click **Out**. The preview of the transition with this effect displays Slide 2 in the center of Slide 1 inside a rectangle that grows to fill the slide.

Finally, you can also change the duration of a transition. The duration is how long it takes the transition to finish; in other words, the speed of the transition. To make the transition faster, decrease the duration; to slow the transition down, increase the duration. Inger likes the Shape transition, but she thinks it is a little fast, so you will increase the duration. Then you can apply the modified transition to all the slides.

**To change the duration of the transition and apply it to all the slides:**

▶ **1.** In the Timing group, click the **Duration up** arrow twice to change the duration to 1.5".

▶ **2.** In the Preview group, click the **Preview** button. The transition previews once more, a little more slowly than before. Right now, the transition is applied only to Slide 2. You want to apply it to all the slides.

▶ **3.** In the Timing group, click the **Apply To All** button.

In the Slides tab, the star indicating that a transition is applied to the slide appears next to all of the slides in the presentation. You should view the transitions in Slide Show view to make sure you like the final effect.

▶ **4.** On the Quick Access Toolbar, click the **Start From Beginning** 🔟 button. Slide 1 (the title slide) appears in Slide Show view.

▶ **5.** Press the **spacebar** or the **Enter** key to advance through the slide show. The transitions look fine.

▶ **6.** Save your changes.

> Make sure you click the Apply To All button or the transition is applied only to the currently selected slide or slides.

# Applying Animations

Animations add interest to a slide show and draw attention to the text or object being animated. For example, you can animate a slide title to fly in from the side or spin around like a pinwheel to draw the audience's attention to that title. Refer to the Session 2.2 Visual Overview for more information about animations.

Animation effects are grouped into four types:

• **Entrance**—Text and objects are not shown on the slide until the animation occurs; one of the most commonly used animation types.

- **Emphasis**—Text and objects on the slide change in appearance or move.
- **Exit**—Text and objects leave the screen before the slide show advances to the next slide.
- **Motion Paths**—Text and objects follow a path on a slide.

## Animating Objects

You can animate any object on a slide, including pictures, shapes, and text boxes. To animate an object you click it, and then select an animation in the Animation group on the ANIMATIONS tab.

**REFERENCE**

### Applying Animations

- In the Slide pane in Normal view, select the object you want to animate.
- On the ribbon, click the ANIMATIONS tab.
- In the Animation group, click the More button to display the gallery of animations, and then click an animation in the gallery.
- If desired, in the Animation group, click the Effect Options button, and then click a direction effect; if the object is a text box, click a sequence effect.
- If desired, in the Timing group, modify the time in the Duration box to modify the speed of the animation.
- If desired, in the Timing group, click the Start arrow, and then click a different start timing.

Slide 9 contains two pictures of fjords, one of Aurlandsfjord and one of Nærøyfjord. Inger wants you to add an animation to the title text on this slide.

### To animate the title on Slide 9:

1. Display **Slide 9** ("Views of the Fjords") in the Slide pane, and then click the **ANIMATIONS** tab on the ribbon. The animations in the Animation group are grayed out, indicating they are not available. This is because nothing is selected on the slide.

2. Click the **Views of the Fjords** title text. The animations in the Animation group darken to indicate that they are now available. See Figure 2-25. All of the animations currently visible in the Animation group are entrance animations.

**Figure 2-25**    **Animations available on the ANIMATIONS tab after an object is selected**

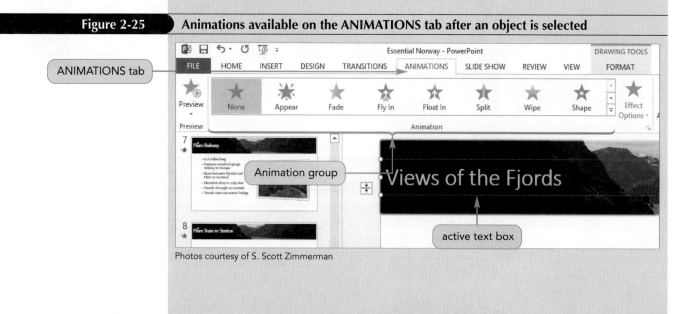

Photos courtesy of S. Scott Zimmerman

3. In the Animation group, click **Fly In**. This entrance animation previews in the Slide pane—the title text disappears and then flies in from the bottom. In the Timing group, the Start box displays On Click, which indicates that this animation will occur when you advance the slide show by clicking the mouse or pressing the spacebar or the Enter key.

   Notice the animation sequence number 1 in the box to the left of the title text box, which indicates that this is the first animation that will occur on the slide. You can preview the animation again if you missed it.

4. In the Preview group, click the **Preview** button. The animation previews again.

5. In the Animation group, click the **More** button. The Animation gallery opens. The animation commands are listed by category, and each category appears in a different color. At the bottom are four commands, each of which opens a dialog box listing all the effects in that category. See Figure 2-26. You will try an emphasis animation.

**Figure 2-26** — **Animations gallery**

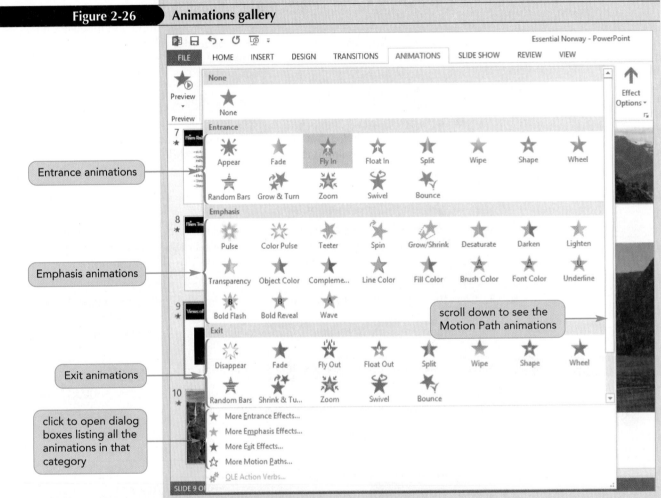

Photos courtesy of S. Scott Zimmerman

6. Under Emphasis, click **Underline**. The Underline animation replaces the Fly In animation, and the slide title is underlined in the preview in the Slide pane. The text did not disappear before the animation started because an emphasis animation causes something to happen to an object already on the slide.

The Underline animation you applied to the slide title is an example of an emphasis animation that is available only to text. You cannot apply that animation to objects such as pictures.

Slide 9 contains photos showing scenic views that customers will see if they book a tour. To focus the audience's attention on one photo at time, you will apply an entrance animation to the photos so that they appear one at a time during the slide show.

### To apply entrance animations to the photos on Slide 9:

1. With **Slide 9** ("Views of the Fjords") in the Slide pane, click the picture on the right.

2. In the Animation group, click the **More** button. Notice that in the Emphasis section, six of the animations, including the Underline animation you just applied to the slide title, are gray, which means they are not available for this object. These six animations are available only for text.

3. In the Entrance section, click **Split**. The picture fades in starting from the left and right edges and fading into the center. In the Timing group, On Click appears in the Start box, indicating that this animation will occur when you advance the slide show. The animation sequence number to the left of the selected picture is 2, which indicates that this is the second animation that will occur on the slide when you advance the slide show.

Like transitions, animations can be modified by changing the effect or the duration (the speed). You need to change the direction from which this animation appears, and you want to slow it down.

### To change the effect and duration of the animation applied to the photo:

1. In the Animation group, click the **Effect Options** button. See Figure 2-27. This menu contains Direction options.

**Figure 2-27**　　**Effect options for the Fly In entrance animation**

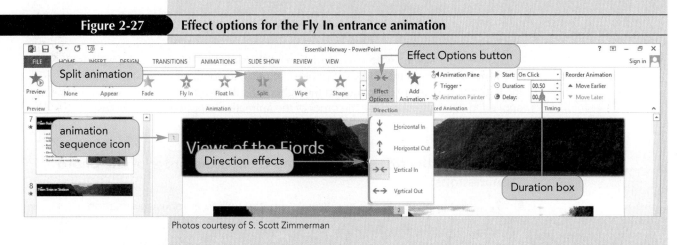

Photos courtesy of S. Scott Zimmerman

2. Click **Vertical Out**. The preview fades the picture in starting from the center and building out to the left and right edges.

3. In the Timing group, click the **Duration up** arrow once. The duration changes from .50 seconds to .75 seconds.

After you have applied and customized the animation for one object, you can use the Animation Painter to copy that animation to other objects. You will copy the Split entrance animation with the Vertical Out effect and a duration of .75 seconds to the other photo on Slide 9.

### To use the Animation Painter to copy the animation on Slide 9:

▶ **1.** Click the photo on the right to select it.

▶ **2.** In the Advanced Animation group, click the **Animation Painter** button, and then move the pointer onto the Slide pane. The pointer changes to ⊾ ⊿.

▶ **3.** Click the photo on the left. The Split animation with the Vertical Out effect and a duration of .75 seconds is copied to the photo on the left.

After you apply animations, you should watch them in Slide Show, Presenter, or Reading view to see what they will look like during a slide show. Remember that On Click appeared in the Start box for each animation that you applied, which means that to see the animation during the slide show, you need to advance the slide show.

### To view the animations on Slide 9 in Slide Show view:

▶ **1.** Make sure **Slide 9** ("Views of the Fjords") is displayed in the Slide pane.

▶ **2.** On the status bar, click the **Slide Show** button 🖳. Slide 9 appears in Slide Show view. Only the photo that is part of the layout and the title appear on the slide.

▶ **3.** Press the **spacebar** to advance the slide show. The first animation, the emphasis animation that underlines the title, occurs.

▶ **4.** Press the **spacebar** again. The photo on the right fades in starting at the center of the photo and building out to the left and right edges.

▶ **5.** Click anywhere on the screen. The photo on the left fades in with the same animation as the photo on the right.

▶ **6.** Press the **Esc** key. Slide 9 appears in Normal view.

Inger doesn't like the emphasis animation on the slide title. It's distracting because the title is not the focus of this slide, the photos are. Also, it would be better if the photo on the left appeared before the photo on the right. To fix this, you can remove the animation applied to the title and change the order of the animations applied to the photos.

### To remove the title animation and change the order of the photo animations:

▶ **1.** Click the title. In the Animation group, the yellow emphasis animation Underline is selected.

▶ **2.** In the Animation group, click the **More** button, and then at the top of the gallery, click **None**. The animation applied to the title is removed, the animation sequence icon no longer appears next to the title text box, and the other two animation sequence icons on the slide are renumbered 1 and 2.

**TIP**

You can also click the animation sequence icon, and then press the Delete key to remove an animation.

Now you need to select the animation applied to the photo on the left and change it so that it occurs first. You can select the object or the animation sequence icon to modify an animation.

**3.** Next to the left photo, click the animation sequence icon **2**. In the Animation group, the green Split entrance animation is selected. See Figure 2-28.

| Figure 2-28 | Animation selected to change its order |
| --- | --- |

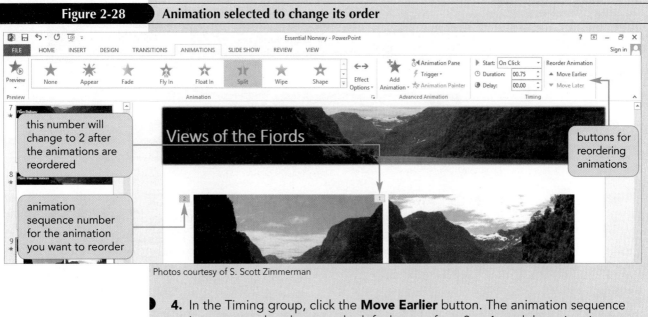

Photos courtesy of S. Scott Zimmerman

**4.** In the Timing group, click the **Move Earlier** button. The animation sequence icon next to the photo on the left changes from 2 to 1, and the animation sequence icon next to the photo on the right changes from 1 to 2.

**5.** In the Preview group, click the **Preview** button. The photo on the left fades in, and then the photo on the right fades in.

## Changing How an Animation Starts

Remember that when you apply an animation, the default is for the object to animate On Click, which means when you advance through the slide show. You can change this so that an animation happens automatically, either at the same time as another animation or when the slide transitions, or after another animation.

Inger wants the photo on the right to appear automatically, without the presenter needing to advance the slide show.

### To change how the animation for the photo on the right starts:

**1.** With **Slide 9** ("Views of the Fjords") displayed in the Slide pane, click the photo on the right. The entrance animation Split is selected in the Animation group, and in the Timing group, On Click appears in the Start box.

**2.** In the Timing group, click the **Start** arrow. The three choices for starting an animation appear. See Figure 2-29.

Figure 2-29     **Options on the Start menu for animations**

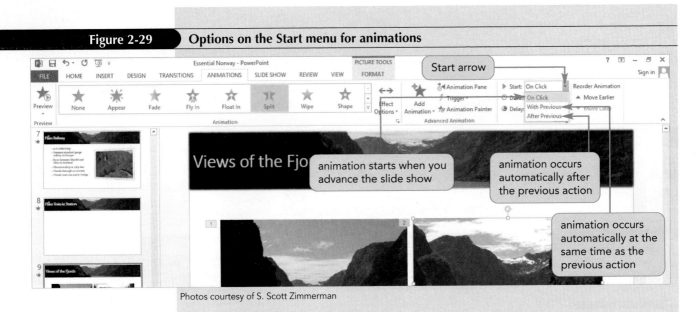

Photos courtesy of S. Scott Zimmerman

> 3. Click **After Previous**. Now this photo will appear automatically after the photo on the left fades in. Notice that the animation sequence number next to this photo changed to 1, the same number as the animation sequence number next to the photo on the left. This is because you will not need to advance the slide show to make this animation happen.

When you preview an animation, it plays automatically on the slide in the Slide pane, even if the timing setting for the animation is On Click. To make sure the timing settings are correct, you need to watch the animation in a slide show.

### To preview and test the animations:

> 1. On the status bar, click the **Slide Show** button 🖵. Slide 9 appears in Slide Show view.

> 2. Press the **spacebar**. The photo on the left fades in, and then the photo on the right fades in.

> 3. Press the **Esc** key to end the slide show.

When you set an animation to occur automatically during the slide show, it happens immediately after the previous action. If that is too soon, you can add a pause before the animation. To do this, you increase the time in the Delay box in the Timing group.

To give the audience time to look at the first photo before the second photo appears on Slide 9, you will add a delay to the animation that is applied to the photo on the right.

### To add a delay to the After Previous animation:

> 1. Click the photo on the right, if necessary. In the Timing group, 00.00 appears in the Delay box.

> 2. In the Timing group, click the **Delay up** arrow four times to change the time to one second. This means that after the photo on the left appears (the previous animation), the photo on the right will appear after a delay of one second. You'll view the slide in Slide Show view again to see the change.

▶ **3.** On the status bar, click the **Slide Show** button 🖵. Slide 9 appears in Slide Show view.

▶ **4.** Press the **spacebar**. The photo on the left fades in, and then after a one-second delay, the photo on the right fades in.

▶ **5.** Press the **Esc** key to end the slide show.

## Animating Lists

If you animate a list, the default is for the first-level items to appear one at a time. In other words, each first-level bulleted item is set to animate On Click. This type of animation focuses your audience's attention on each item, without the distraction of items that you haven't discussed yet.

Inger wants you to add an Entrance animation to the bulleted list on the "About Us" slide. She wants each first-level bulleted item to appear on the slide one at a time so that the audience won't be able to read ahead while you are discussing each point.

### To animate the bulleted lists:

▶ **1.** Display **Slide 2** ("About Us") in the Slide pane, and then click anywhere in the bulleted list to make the text box active.

▶ **2.** On the ANIMATIONS tab, in the Animation group, click **Fly In**. The animation previews in the Slide pane as the bulleted items fly in from the bottom. When the "Train rides" and "Fjord cruises" items fly in, their subitems fly in with them. After the preview is finished, the numbers 1 through 4 appear next to the bulleted items. Notice that the subitems have the same animation sequence number as their first-level items. This means that the start timing for the subitems is set to With Previous or After Previous. See Figure 2-30.

**Figure 2-30**    Fly In entrance animation applied to a bulleted list with subitems

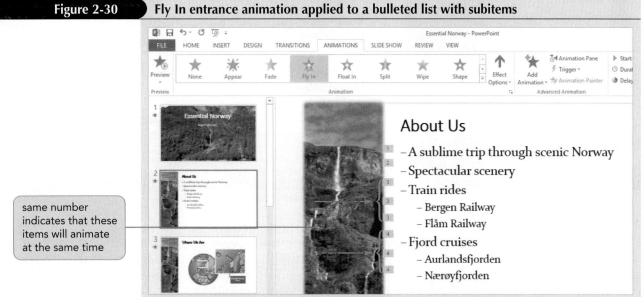

same number indicates that these items will animate at the same time

Image used with permission of Microsoft Corporation; Photos courtesy of S. Scott Zimmerman

▶ **3.** Next to the Train rides bullet item, click the animation sequence icon **3** to select it. In the Timing group, On Click appears in the Start box.

**4.** Next to the subitem "Bergen Railway," click the animation sequence icon **3**. In the Timing group, With Previous appears in the Start box.

If you wanted to change how the items in the list animate during the slide show, you could change the start timing of each item, or you could change the sequence effect. Sequence options appear on the Effect Options menu in addition to the Direction options when an animation is applied to a text box. The default is for the items to appear By Paragraph. This mean each first-level item animates one at a time, with its subitems if there are any, when you advance the slide show. You can change this so that the entire list animates at once as one object, or so that each first-level item animates at the same time but as separate objects.

### To examine the Sequence options for the animated list:

**1.** Click in the bulleted list, and then in the Animation group, click the **Effect Options** button. The Sequence options appear at the bottom of the menu, below the Direction options, and By Paragraph is selected. See Figure 2-31.

**Figure 2-31**    **Animation effect options for a bulleted list**

Image used with permission of Microsoft Corporation; Photos courtesy of S. Scott Zimmerman; Richard Cummins/Getty Images

**2.** Click **As One Object**. The animation preview shows the entire text box fly in. After the preview, only one animation sequence icon appears next to the text box, indicating that the entire text box will animate as a single object. In the Timing group, On Click appears in the Start box.

3. In the Animation group, click the **Effect Options** button, and then under Sequence, click **All At Once**. The animation previews again, but this time each of the first-level items fly in as separate objects, although they all fly in at the same time. After the preview, animation sequence icons, all numbered 1, appear next to each bulleted item, indicating that each item will animate separately but you only need to advance the slide show once.

4. Next to the first bulleted item, click the animation sequence icon. In the Timing group, On Click appears in the Start box.

5. Next to the second bulleted item, click the animation sequence icon. In the Timing group, With Previous appears in the Start box.

6. In the Animation group, click the **Effect Options** button, and then click **By Paragraph**. The sequence effect is changed back to its original setting.

7. Save your changes.

# Adding and Modifying Video

You can add video to slides to play during your presentation. PowerPoint supports various file formats, but the most commonly used are the MPEG-4 format, the Windows Media Audio/Video format, and the Audio Visual Interleave format, which appears in Explorer windows as the Video Clip file type. After you insert a video, you can modify it by changing playback options, changing the length of time the video plays, and applying formats and styles to the video.

## Adding Video to Slides

To insert video stored on your computer or network, click the Insert Video button in a content placeholder, and then in the Insert Video window next to "From a file," click Browse to open the Insert Video dialog box. You can also click the Video button in the Media group on the INSERT tab, and then click Video on My PC to open the same Insert Video dialog box.

## Adding Videos Stored on Your Computer or Network

- In a content placeholder, click the Insert Video button to open the Insert Video window, and then next to "From a file," click Browse to open the Insert Video dialog box; or click the INSERT tab on the ribbon, and then in the Media group, click the Video button, and then click Video on My PC to open the Insert Video dialog box.
- Click the video you want to use, and then click the Insert button.
- If desired, click the VIDEO TOOLS PLAYBACK tab, and then in the Video Options group:
  - Click the Start arrow, and then click Automatically to change how the video starts from On Click.
  - Click the Play Full Screen check box to select it to have the video fill the screen.
  - Click the Rewind after Playing check box to select it to have the poster frame display after the video plays.
  - Click the Volume button, and then click a volume level or click Mute.

Inger has several videos she wants you to add to Slides 6 and 8.

## To add a video to Slide 6 and play it:

1. Display **Slide 6** ("Bergen Train Through Mountains") in the Slide pane, and then in the content placeholder, click the **Insert Video** button ⬚. The Insert Video window opens.

2. Next to "From a file," click **Browse**. The Insert Video dialog box opens.

3. In the **PowerPoint2 ▸ Tutorial** folder, click **Bergen Train**, and then click the **Insert** button. The video is inserted on the slide. The first frame of the video is displayed, and a play bar with controls for playing the video appears below it. See Figure 2-32.

| Figure 2-32 | Video added to Slide 6 |
| --- | --- |

Photos courtesy of S. Scott Zimmerman

**Trouble?** Depending on your computer, the video might appear as a black box on the slide. It should still play.

**Trouble?** This video includes sound, so you might want to adjust your speakers if needed to avoid disturbing others when you complete the next step.

▶ **4.** On the play bar, click the **Play** button ▶. The Play button changes to the Pause button ▮▮ and the video plays. Watch the 14-second video. Next, you'll watch the video in Slide Show view.

▶ **5.** On the status bar, click the **Slide Show** button 🖵. Slide 6 appears in Slide Show view.

▶ **6.** Point to the video. The play bar appears, and the pointer changes to 🖑. You don't need to click the Play button to play the video in Slide Show view; you can click anywhere on the video to play it as long as the pointer is visible. While the video is playing, you can click it again to pause it.

▶ **7.** Click anywhere on the video. The video plays.

**Trouble?** If Slide 7 appeared instead of the video playing, the pointer wasn't visible or you didn't click the video object, so clicking the slide advanced the slide show. Press the Backspace key to return to Slide 6, move the mouse over the video to make the pointer visible, and then click the video.

▶ **8.** Before the video finishes playing, move the pointer to make it visible, and then click the video again. The video pauses.

▶ **9.** Move the pointer to make it visible, if necessary, click the video to finish playing it, and then press the **Esc** key to end the slide show.

As you just saw, you clicked the video to play it during the slide show. When you insert a video, its start timing is set to On Click. This start timing means something different for videos than for animations. For animations, On Click means you can do anything to advance the slide show to cause the animation to start. For videos, On Click means you need to click the video object or the Play button on the play bar. If you click somewhere else on the screen or do anything else to advance the slide show, the video will not play. The start timing setting is on the VIDEO TOOLS PLAYBACK tab.

You'll add the video to Slide 8 and then examine the start timing setting.

### To add a video to Slide 8 and examine the start timing:

▶ **1.** Display **Slide 8** ("Flåm Train in Station") in the Slide pane, and then click the **INSERT** tab on the ribbon.

▶ **2.** In the Media group, click the **Video** button, and then click **Video on My PC**. The Insert Video dialog box opens.

▶ **3.** Click **Flam Train**, and then click the **Insert** button. The video is inserted in the content placeholder.

▶ **4.** On the play bar, click the **Play** button ▶. Watch the 10-second video.

▶ **5.** On the ribbon, click the **VIDEO TOOLS PLAYBACK** tab. In the Video Options group, On Click appears in the Start box. See Figure 2-33.

| Figure 2-33 | Options on the VIDEO TOOLS PLAYBACK tab |
| --- | --- |

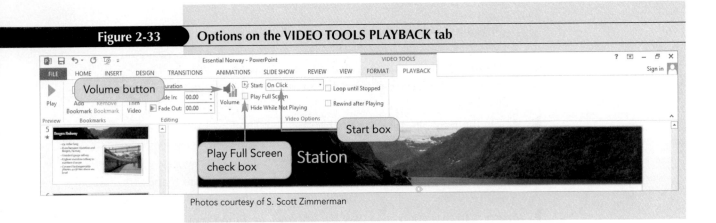

Photos courtesy of S. Scott Zimmerman

## Modifying Video Playback Options

You can change several options for how a video plays. For instance, you can change the start timing so that the video plays automatically when the slide appears during the slide show. The video playback options are listed in Figure 2-34.

| Figure 2-34 | Video playback options |
| --- | --- |

| Video Option | Function |
| --- | --- |
| Volume | Change the volume of the video from high to medium or low or mute it. |
| Start | Change how the video starts, either when the presenter clicks it or the Play button on the play bar or automatically when the slide appears during the slide show. |
| Play Full Screen | The video fills the screen during the slide show. |
| Hide While Not Playing | The video does not appear on the slide when it is not playing; make sure the video is set to play automatically if this option is selected. |
| Loop until Stopped | The video plays until the next slide appears during the slide show. |
| Rewind after Playing | The video rewinds after it plays so that the first frame or the poster frame appears again. |

© 2014 Cengage Learning

Both videos that you inserted have sound. Inger doesn't want you to mute them, but she would like you to lower the volume. You could adjust this while the videos are playing by using the volume control on the play bar, but she wants you to set the default volume lower so that you don't have to worry about it during the presentation. Inger also wants the video on Slide 8 to fill the screen when it plays, and for it to start automatically when the slide appears during the slide show.

### To modify the playback options of the videos:

1. On **Slide 8** ("Flåm Train in Station"), click the video to select it, if necessary, and make sure the PLAYBACK tab is active on the ribbon. First you'll set the volume to low.

2. In the Video Options group, click the **Volume** button, and then click **Low**. Now you will set the video to play full screen.

3. In the Video Options group, click the **Play Full Screen** check box to select it. Finally, you will set this video to play automatically.

4. Click the **Start** arrow, and then click **Automatically**. Now you need to lower the volume of the video on Slide 6.

5. Display **Slide 6** ("Bergen Train Through Mountains") in the Slide pane, click the video, and then click the **PLAYBACK** tab, if necessary. In the Video Options group, On Click appears in the Start box.

6. Set the volume of the video to **Low**. You'll view the videos again in Slide Show view.

7. On the status bar, click the **Slide Show** button 🖵. Slide 6 appears in Slide Show view.

8. Move the mouse to make the pointer visible, and then click the video. The video plays.

9. After the video finishes playing, press the **spacebar** to advance to Slide 7, and then press the **spacebar** again. Slide 8 ("Flåm Train in Station") briefly appears, and then the Flam Train video fills the screen and plays automatically. When the video is finished playing, Slide 8 appears again.

10. Press the **Esc** key to end the slide show.

## Understanding Animation Effects Applied to Videos

**TIP**

The Media animation category appears only when a media object—either video or audio—is selected on a slide.

When you insert a video (or audio) object, an animation is automatically applied to the video so that you can click anywhere on the video to start and pause it when the slide show is run. This animation is the Pause animation in the Media animation category and it is set to On Click. The Pause animation is what makes it possible to start or pause a video during a slide show by clicking anywhere on the video object. (When you click the video to play it, you are actually "unpausing" it.)

When you change the Start setting of a video on the PLAYBACK tab to Automatically, a second animation, the Play animation in the Media animation category, is applied to the video as well as the Pause animation, and the start timing of the Play animation is set to After Previous. If there are no other objects on the slide set to animate before the video, the Play animation has an animation sequence number of zero, which means that it will play immediately after the slide transition.

To see these animations, click the ANIMATIONS tab on the ribbon, and then select a video object on a slide. The Pause and Play animations appear in the Animation gallery in the Media category.

You'll examine the video animations now.

### To examine the Media animation effects for the videos:

1. Display **Slide 6** ("Bergen Train Through Mountains") in the Slide pane. Remember that the video on this slide is set to play On Click.

2. On the ribbon, click the **ANIMATIONS** tab, and then click the video. See Figure 2-35. The animation sequence icon next to the video contains a lightning bolt instead of a number. In the Animation group, Pause is selected, and in the Timing group, On Click appears in the Start box. This animation is applied automatically to all videos when you add them to slides.

**Figure 2-35** Pause animation applied to video

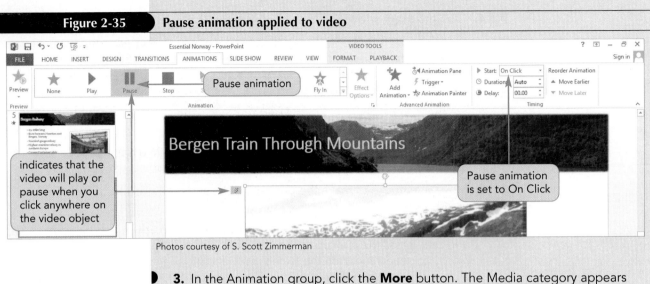

Photos courtesy of S. Scott Zimmerman

3. In the Animation group, click the **More** button. The Media category appears at the top of the Animation gallery because a media object is selected.

4. Press the **Esc** key to close the gallery, display **Slide 8** ("Flåm Train in Station") in the Slide pane, and then click the video. Because you set this video to start automatically, two animation sequence icons appear next to it, one containing a zero and one containing a lightning bolt. In the Animation group, Multiple is selected because two animations are applied to this video.

   When more than one animation is applied to any object, you need to click each animation sequence icon to see which animation is associated with each icon.

5. Click the **lightning bolt** animation sequence icon. In the Animation group, Pause is selected, and in the Timing group, On Click appears in the Start box. This allows you to click the video during a slide show to play or pause it.

6. Click the animation sequence icon **0**. In the Animation group, Play is selected, and in the Timing group, After Previous appears in the Start box. This Play animation was added to this video when you selected Automatically on the PLAYBACK tab. See Figure 2-36.

**Figure 2-36** Play animation settings for video set to play automatically

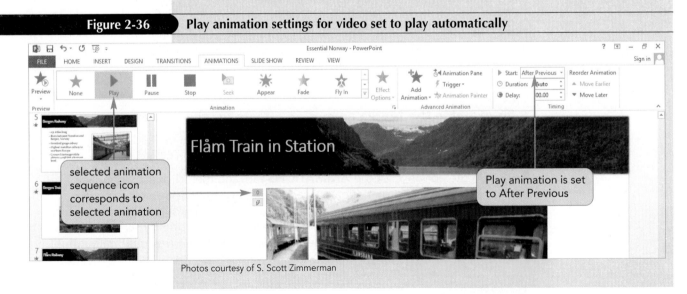

Photos courtesy of S. Scott Zimmerman

## Setting a Poster Frame

The frame that appears when the video is not playing is called the **poster frame**. You can set the poster frame to be any frame in the video or you can set the poster frame to any image stored in a file. The default poster frame for a video is the first frame of the video. You can change this so that any frame from the video or any image stored in a file is the poster frame. The video on Slide 8 is of the Flåm train. To make it clear that this is the Flåm train, you want the poster frame to be the frame in the video in which you can see the train name on the side of the train.

### To set a poster frame for the video on Slide 8:

1. With **Slide 8** ("Flåm Train in Station") displayed in the Slide pane, click the video, and then click the **FORMAT** tab.

2. Point to the **play bar** below the video. A ScreenTip appears identifying the time of the video at that point. See Figure 2-37.

**Figure 2-37**    Setting a poster frame

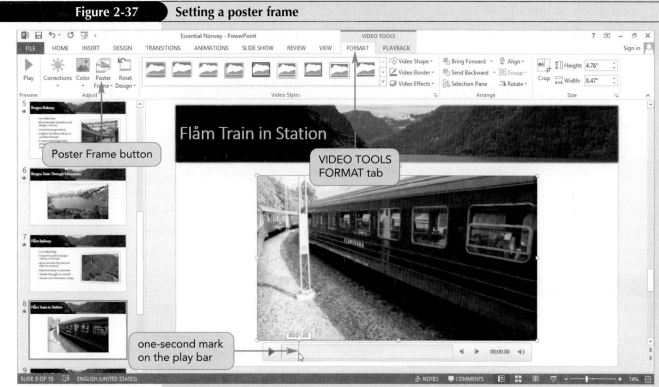

Photos courtesy of S. Scott Zimmerman

**TIP**

If you see a black square when you insert a video, you can override this by setting a poster frame.

3. On the play bar, click at approximately the **one-second mark**. The video advances to the one-second mark, and the frame showing the car with the name of the train, FLÅMSBANA, appears in the video object.

4. In the Adjust group, click the **Poster Frame** button. The Poster Frame menu opens.

5. Click **Current Frame**. The message "Poster Frame Set" appears in the video's play bar, and the frame currently visible in the video object is set as the poster frame.

After you play a video during a slide show, the last frame of the video appears in the video object. You can make the poster frame appear if you set the video to rewind after playing. Inger wants you to do this for the Flåm Train video.

**To set the video on Slide 8 to rewind:**

▶ **1.** On **Slide 8** ("Flåm Train in Station"), click the video, if necessary, and then click the **PLAYBACK** tab.

▶ **2.** In the Video Options group, click the **Rewind after Playing** check box to select it.

▶ **3.** On the play bar, click the **Play** button ▶. The video plays, and then the poster frame appears again.

## Trimming Videos

If a video is too long, or if there are parts you don't want to show during the slide show, you can trim it. To do this, click the Trim Video button in the Editing group on the VIDEO TOOLS PLAYBACK tab, and then, in the Trim Video dialog box, drag the green start slider or the red stop slider to a new position to mark where the video will start and stop.

Although in person the view from the Bergen train is stunning, Inger doesn't think the audience needs to watch 13 seconds of this video, so she wants you to trim it to seven seconds. That should be long enough for her audience to get a feel for what the train ride through the mountains is like.

**To trim the video on Slide 6:**

▶ **1.** Display **Slide 6** ("Bergen Train Through Mountains") in the Slide pane, click the video, and then click the **PLAYBACK** tab, if necessary.

▶ **2.** In the Editing group, click the **Trim Video** button. The Trim Video dialog box opens. See Figure 2-38.

**Figure 2-38**   **Trim Video dialog box**

Photo courtesy of S. Scott Zimmerman

3. Drag the red **Stop** tab to the left until the time in the End Time box is approximately seven seconds, and then click the **OK** button.

4. On the play bar under the video on the right, click the **Play** button ▶. The video plays, but stops after playing for seven seconds.

5. Save your changes.

# Compressing Media

As with pictures, you can compress media files. If you need to send a file via email or you need to upload it, you should compress media files to make the final PowerPoint file smaller. The more you compress files, the smaller the final presentation file will be, but also the lower the quality. For videos, you can compress using the following settings:

- **Presentation Quality**—compresses the videos slightly and maintains the quality of the videos
- **Internet Quality**—compresses the videos to a quality suitable for streaming over the Internet
- **Low Quality**—compresses the videos as small as possible

With all of the settings, any parts of videos that you trimmed off will be deleted, similar to deleting the cropped portions of photos.

After you compress media, you should watch the slides containing the videos using the equipment you will be using when giving your presentation to make sure the reduced quality is acceptable. Usually, if the videos were high quality to start with, the compressed quality will be fine. However, if the original video quality was grainy, the compressed quality might be too low, even for evaluation purposes. If you decide that you don't like the compressed quality, you can undo the compression.

You will compress the media files you inserted. You need to send the presentation to Inger via email, so you will compress the media as much as possible.

### To compress the videos in the presentation:

1. Click the **FILE** tab. Backstage view appears displaying the Info screen. See Figure 2-39.

**Figure 2-39** | **Info screen in Backstage view**

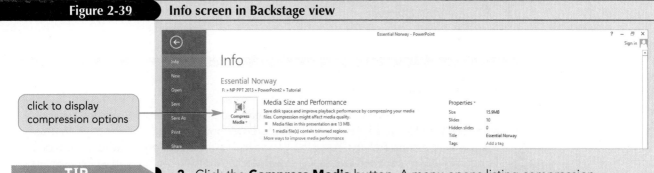

click to display compression options

**TIP**

If you might want to show the presentation using a projector capable of high-quality display, save a copy of the presentation before you compress the media.

2. Click the **Compress Media** button. A menu opens listing compression choices.

> **3.** Click **Low Quality**. The Compress Media dialog box opens listing the two video files in the presentation with a progress bar appearing next to each one in the Status column to show you the progress of the compression. After each file is compressed, the progress bar is replaced by a message indicating that compression for the file is complete and stating how much the video file size was reduced. See Figure 2-40.

**Figure 2-40**    Compress Media dialog box

Compress Media

| Slide | Name | Initial Size (MB) | Status |
|---|---|---|---|
| 6 | Bergen Train | 7.6 | Complete - 6.8 MB Saved |
| 8 | Flam Train | 5.1 | Processing... 39% |

status messages

Cancel button changes to Close button when all video files have been compressed

message about current status

Compression in progress. Processing 'Flam Train'...

progress bar

Cancel

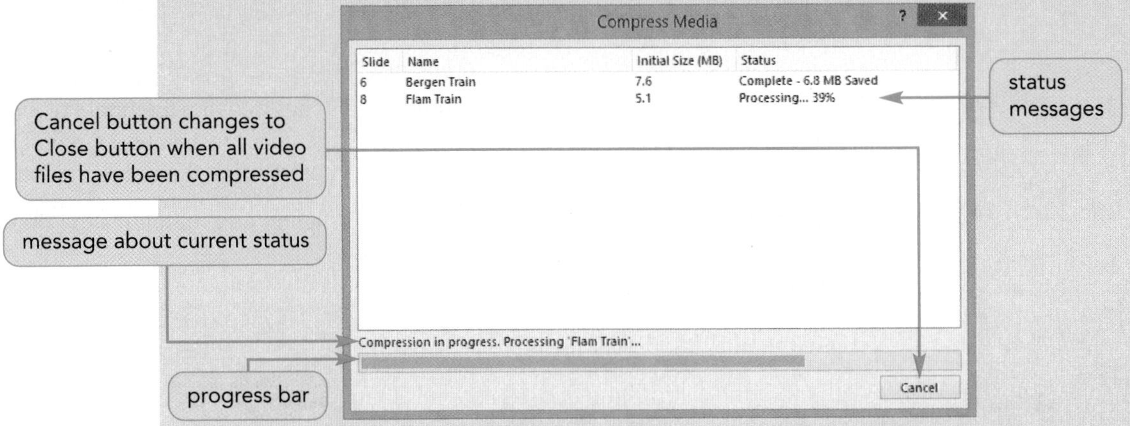

After all the videos have been compressed, a message appears at the bottom of the dialog box stating that the compression is complete and indicating how much the file size of the presentation was reduced.

> **4.** Click the **Close** button. Next to the Compress Media button on the Info screen, the bulleted list states that the presentation's media was compressed to Low Quality and that you can undo the compression if the results are unsatisfactory. Now you need to view the compressed videos.

> **5.** At the top of the navigation bar, click the **Back** button ⊙ to display Slide 6 ("Bergen Train Through Mountains") in the Slide pane.

> **6.** On the status bar, click the **Slide Show** button 🖵 to display the slide in Slide Show view, and then click the video to play it. The quality is lower, but sufficient for Inger to get the general idea after you send it to her via email.

> **7.** Press the **Esc** key to end the slide show.

> **8.** Save your changes.

## INSIGHT

### Optimizing Media

If you insert videos saved in older video formats, such as the Audio Visual Interleave format (whose file type is listed in File Explorer windows as Video Clip and which uses the filename extension ".avi") and the Windows Media Video format (whose file type is listed in File Explorer windows as Windows Media Audio/Video file and which uses the filename extension ".wmv"), the Info screen in Backstage view contains an Optimize Media button as well as the Compress Media button. If you click the Optimize Media button first, any potential problems with the video on the slides, such as problems that might make it difficult to play the video on another computer or would cause the video to stutter during playback, are repaired.

# Adding Footers and Headers

Sometimes it can be helpful to have information on each slide such as the title of the presentation or the company name. This is called a **footer**. It can also be helpful to have the slide number displayed. For example, you might need to distribute handouts that reference slide numbers. And some presentations need the date to appear on each slide, especially if the presentation contains time-sensitive information. You can easily add this information to all the slides. Usually this information is not needed on the title slide, so you can also specify that it not appear on there.

### To add a footer, slide numbers, and the date to slides:

▶ **1.** Click the **INSERT** tab on the ribbon, and then in the Text group, click the **Header & Footer** button. The Header and Footer dialog box opens with the Slide tab selected.

▶ **2.** Click the **Footer** check box to select it, and then click in the **Footer** box. In the Preview box on the right, the left placeholder on the bottom is filled with black to indicate where the footer will appear on slides. See Figure 2-41. Note that the position of the footer, slide number, and date changes in different themes.

**Figure 2-41**     **Slide tab in the Header and Footer dialog box**

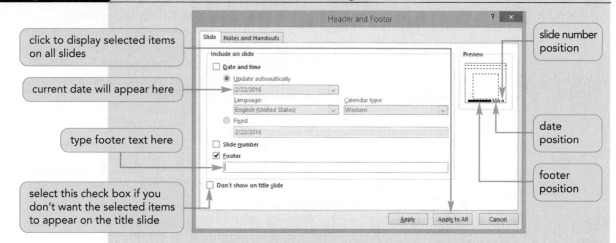

- click to display selected items on all slides
- current date will appear here
- type footer text here
- select this check box if you don't want the selected items to appear on the title slide
- slide number position
- date position
- footer position

▶ **3.** Type **Essential Norway Tours**.

▶ **4.** Click the **Slide number** check box to select it. In the Preview box, the box in the bottom-right is filled with black.

▶ **5.** Click the **Date and time** check box to select it. The options under this check box darken to indicate that you can use them, and in the Preview box, the box in the middle on the bottom is filled with black.

You don't want the date in the presentation to update automatically each time the presentation is opened. You want it to show today's date so people will know that the information is current as of that date.

▶ **6.** Click the **Fixed** option button. Now you want to prevent the footer, slide number, and date from appearing on the title slide.

▶ **7.** Click the **Don't show on title slide** check box to select it, and then click the **Apply to All** button. On Slide 6, the footer, date, and slide number display. See Figure 2-42.

| Figure 2-42 | Footer, date, and slide number on Slide 6 |
| --- | --- |

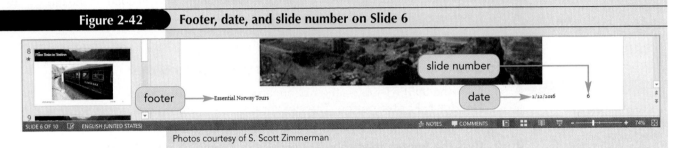

Photos courtesy of S. Scott Zimmerman

In common usage, a footer is any text that appears at the bottom of every page in a document or every slide in a presentation. However, as you saw when you added the footer in the Header and Footer dialog box, in PowerPoint a footer is specifically the text that appears in the Footer box on the Slide tab in that dialog box and in the footer text box on the slides. This text box can appear anywhere on the slide; in some themes the footer appears at the top of slides. This information does not appear on notes pages and handouts. You need to add footers to notes pages and handouts separately.

A **header** is information displayed at the top of every page. Slides do not have headers, but you can add a header to handouts and notes pages. Like a footer, in PowerPoint a header refers only to the text that appears in the Header text box on handouts and notes pages. In addition to headers and footers, you can also display a date and the page number on handouts and notes pages.

## To modify the header and footer on handouts and notes pages:

▶ **1.** On the INSERT tab, in the Text group, click the **Header & Footer** button. The Header and Footer dialog box opens with the Slide tab selected.

▶ **2.** Click the **Notes and Handouts** tab. This tab includes a Page number check box and a header box. The Page number check box is selected, and in the Preview, the lower-right rectangle is bold to indicate that this is where the page number will appear.

▶ **3.** Click the **Header** check box to select it, click in the **Header** box, and then type **Essential Norway Tours**.

▶ **4.** Click the **Footer** check box to select it, click in the **Footer** box, and then type your name.

▶ **5.** Click the **Apply to All** button. To see the effect of modifying the handouts and notes pages, you need to look at the print preview.

▶ **6.** Click the **FILE** tab, and then in the navigation bar, click **Print**.

7. Under Settings, click the **Full Page Slides** button, and then click **Notes Pages**. The preview shows Slide 6 as a notes page. The header and footer you typed appear, along with the page number. See Figure 2-43.

| Figure 2-43 | Header and footer on the Slide 6 notes page |
|---|---|

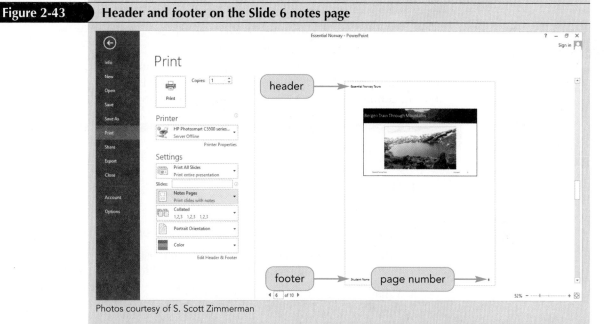

Photos courtesy of S. Scott Zimmerman

8. At the top of the navigation bar, click the **Back** button 🔙 to return to Normal view.

9. Display **Slide 1** (the title slide) in the Slide pane, replace Inger's name in the subtitle text box with your name, and then save the changes to the presentation.

Now that you have finished working on the presentation, you should view the completed presentation as a slide show.

### To view the completed presentation in Slide Show view:

1. On the Quick Access Toolbar, click the **Start From Beginning** button 🖵. Slide 1 appears in Slide Show view.

2. Press the **spacebar**. Slide 2 ("About Us") appears in Slide Show view displaying the photo on the slide layout, the slide background, the slide title, and the footer, date, and slide number.

3. Press the **spacebar** four times to display all the bulleted items, and then press the **spacebar** again to display Slide 3 ("Where We Are").

4. Press the **spacebar** three times to display Slide 4 ("Essential Norway Sample Itinerary"), Slide 5 ("Bergen Railway"), and finally Slide 6 ("Bergen Train Through Mountains").

5. Click the video object. The video plays on the slide.

6. After the video has finished playing, press the **spacebar** to display Slide 7 ("Flåm Railway"), and then press the **spacebar** to display Slide 8 ("Flåm Train in Station"). Slide 8 briefly appears, and then the video of the train fills the screen and plays automatically. After the video finishes playing, Slide 8 appears again in Slide Show view displaying the poster frame you set.

▶ **7.** Press the **spacebar** to display Slide 9 ("Views of the Fjords"), and then press the **spacebar** again. The photo on the left fades in with the Split animation, and then after a one-second delay, the photo on the right fades in.

▶ **8.** Press the **spacebar** to display Slide 10 ("Contact Us"), press the **spacebar** again to display the black slide that appears at the end of a slide show, and then press the **spacebar** once more to return to Normal view.

The final presentation file with transitions, animations, and video is interesting and should enhance the presentation you will give to travel agents in the United States. You can confidently send it to Inger in Norway for a final review.

**REVIEW**

### Session 2.2 Quick Check

1. What is a transition?

2. What are animations?

3. How do you change the speed of a transition or an animation?

4. When you apply an animation to a bulleted list with subitems, how do the first-level items animate? How do the second-level items animate?

5. What does "On Click" mean for a video?

6. What animation is applied to every video that you add to a slide?

7. What is a poster frame?

8. In PowerPoint, what is a footer?

ASSESS

## SAM Projects

PRACTICE

## Review Assignments

**Data Files needed for the Review Assignments: Alaska.jpg, Cruise.mp4, Fjords.pptx, Gulls.mp4, New Norway Theme.pptx, Norway.jpg**

Travel agents often ask Inger Halvorsen questions about fjords. Inger decided to create a PowerPoint presentation that describes fjords. She also revised the custom theme she created for her company so that it uses a different photo in the background on the title slide, and she created two new custom layouts to show three items on a slide. Complete the following:

1. Open the presentation **Fjords.pptx**, located in the PowerPoint2 ▸ Review folder included with your Data Files, add your name as the subtitle, and then save it as **Information about Fjords** to the drive and folder where you are storing your files.

2. Apply the theme from the presentation **New Norway Theme**, located in the PowerPoint2 ▸ Review folder.

3. Change the layout of Slide 5 ("Fjords in Other Countries") to Three Comparison. Type **Chile** in the text placeholder above the picture on the right. Delete "Chile" in the text box above the content placeholder in the middle, and then type **Alaska**. In the empty content placeholder, insert the photo **Alaska**, located in the PowerPoint2 ▸ Review folder. Apply the Compound Frame, Black style and the Reflection effect "Half Reflection, touching" to the three pictures.

4. Change the layout of Slide 6 ("Norwegian Fjords") to Three Content, insert the photo **Norway**, located in the PowerPoint2 ▸ Review folder in the empty content placeholder, and then apply the Compound Frame, Black style to the three photos.

5. On Slide 2 ("What Is a Fjord?"), insert an online picture from Office.com in the content placeholder using **Norway fjord cliff** as the keywords. Apply the Compound Frame, Black style to the picture, and then apply the Perspective Left 3-D Rotation effect.

6. Click the photo you just inserted, and then compress all the photos in the presentation to 96 ppi.

7. On Slide 3 ("Where Are Fjords Located?"), copy the "North America northwest coast" callout, paste it on the same slide, and then flip the pasted copy horizontally. Position the flipped callout so it points to the red circle on the map, and then delete the red circle. Edit the text of the flipped callout by changing "northwest" to **"northeast."**

8. On Slide 3, add a Left Arrow shape. Type **Norway** in the arrow, and then resize the shape so it just fits the text on one line. Rotate the arrow approximately 45 degrees to the right so that it points up to the left, and then position it so that it points to the area of the map indicated by the top of the red triangle. Change the fill color of the arrow to Orange, Accent 6, and then delete the red triangle.

9. On Slide 4 ("Facts About Countries with Fjords"), insert a 3x6 table. In the first row in the table, type **Location, Famous examples, Flag**.

10. In the first cell in the second row, type **Canada--British Columbia**. (When you press the spacebar after typing "British," AutoCorrect changes the two dashes to an em dash, which is a long dash.)

11. Refer to Figure 2-44 to add the rest of the data to the table. Add a row if needed. (*Hint*: To activate AutoCorrect to change the two dashes after "United States" to an em dash, press the Tab key to move the insertion point to the next cell instead of clicking in the next cell.)

**Figure 2-44**    **Data for table on Slide 4 in the Information about Fjords presentation**

| Location | Famous examples | Flag |
| --- | --- | --- |
| Canada—British Columbia | Howe Sound | |
| Chile | Aisen Fjord | |
| Greenland | Ilulissat Icefjord | |
| Iceland | East Fjords | |
| New Zealand | Milford Sound, Doubtful Sound | |
| United States--Alaska | Kenai Fjords | |

© 2014 Cengage Learning

12. In the table, delete the Flag column. Add a new row above the row containing "United States—Alaska." Type **Norway** in the new cell in the Location column, and then type **Geirangerfjord, Naeroyfjord** in the Famous examples column.

13. In the table, in the "Chile" row, replace the "e" in "Aisen" with **é**. Then in the Norway row, in the word "Naeroyfjord," replace the "ae" with **æ** and replace the first "o" with **ø** so the word is spelled "Nærøyfjord." (All three letters are in the Latin-1 Supplement subset.)

14. In the table, set the proofing language for the two words in the Famous examples column in the Norway row to Norwegian (Bokmål), and then set the proofing language for the two words in the Famous examples column in the Greenland row to Greenlandic.

15. Apply the Light Style 3 - Accent 1 table style, and then change the font size of all of the text in the table to 24 points.

16. Insert a new column to the left of the Location column. Use online pictures on Office.com to fill each cell with a picture of the flag of the country listed in the Location column. To locate each flag, type the keywords listed below in the box next to Office.com in the Insert Pictures dialog box. When more than one result appears, click each result and look at the keywords and measurements in the lower-left corner of the dialog box, and then use the result that has a width measurement of 600 pixels.
    - Canada: type **Canada flag country**
    - Chile: type **Chile flag country**
    - Greenland: type **Greenland flag**
    - Iceland: type **Iceland flag country**
    - New Zealand: type **New Zealand flag**
    - Norway: type **Norway flag country**
    - United States: type **United States flag country**

17. In the table, change the width of the first column so it is 0.8 inches wide, and then make the second and third columns just wide enough to hold the widest entry on one line. Reposition the table so the left edge is approximately aligned with the left edge of the title text and so the table is approximately centered vertically in the space below the title.

18. Apply the Uncover transition. Change the Effect Options to From Top, and then change the duration to .50 seconds. Apply this transition to all of the slides.

19. On Slide 2 ("What Is a Fjord?"), animate the bulleted list using the Fade animation. Change the duration of the animation to .75 seconds.

20. On Slide 5 ("Fjords in Other Countries"), apply the Wipe animation using the From Left effect to the "New Zealand" caption. Apply the same animation to the other two text captions.

21. Apply the Wipe animation with the From Left effect to the photo under "New Zealand," and then change the start timing of that animation to After previous. Move the animation applied to the photo earlier so it has the same animation sequence number as the caption above it (it should be a 1). Apply the same animation using the After previous start timing to the photos under "Alaska" and "Chile," and adjust the animation order so that each photo has the same animation sequence number as the caption above it.

22. On Slide 7, add the video **Cruise**, located in the PowerPoint2 ▸ Review folder, in the content placeholder on the left, and set it to play Automatically and Full Screen and to rewind after playing. (This video has no sound.) Set the poster frame to the frame at approximately the 2.30-second mark.

23. Add the video **Gulls**, located in the PowerPoint2 ▸ Review folder, in the content placeholder on the right. This video should play On Click and Full Screen. Set the volume to Low. Leave the poster frame as the first frame of the video.

24. Trim the Gulls video by adjusting the end time so the video is approximately 10 seconds long.

25. Compress the media to Low Quality.

26. Add **Fjords presented by Essential Norway Tours** as the footer on all the slides except the title slide, and display the slide number on all the slides except the title slide. On the Notes and Handouts, add **Essential Norway Tours** as the header and your name as the footer.

27. Save your changes, and then watch the final presentation in Slide Show view.

## Case Problem 1

Data Files needed for this Case Problem: Group.jpg, Summer.mp4, Theater Theme.pptx, Theater.pptx

*Ottawa Children's Theatre Workshop*   Adrielle Schlosser is the director of the Ottawa Children's Theatre Workshop in Ontario, Canada. One of her responsibilities is to inform parents, teachers, and volunteers about the organization. She asked you to help her prepare the PowerPoint presentation, which will include photos, a video, and a table to provide details her audience might be interested in knowing. Complete the following steps:

1. Open the file named **Theater**, located in the PowerPoint2 ▸ Case1 folder included with your Data Files, add your name as the subtitle on Slide 1, and then save it as **Children's Theater** to the drive and folder where you are storing your files.

2. Apply the theme from the presentation **Theater Theme**, located in the PowerPoint2 ▸ Case1 folder.

3. Apply the picture style Moderate Frame, White to the pictures on Slides 2, 3, 4, and 5.

4. On Slide 3 ("Eligibility"), animate the bulleted list using the Float In animation with the Float Down effect, and change the duration to .50 seconds. Animate the bulleted list on Slide 5 ("Performances") using the same animation.

5. On Slide 6 ("Recent Summer Performance"), insert the video **Summer**, located in the PowerPoint2 ▸ Case1 folder. Set the movie to play Automatically and to rewind after playing, and set the volume to Low. Trim the video by changing the end time to approximately the 18.5-second mark. Set the poster frame to the frame at approximately the 13-second mark.

6. Compress the media to Low Quality.

7. On Slide 7 ("Classes"), add a new row above the last row with the following data: **Junior Jazzers**, **$7^{th} – 9^{th}$**, **Rarford Koskosky**, **Tues & Thurs, 4 p.m.** (*Hint*: To activate AutoCorrect to change the "th" after 9 to a superscript, press the Tab key to move to the next cell instead of clicking in the cell.)

8. Change the table style to Medium Style 1 – Accent 1. Select all of the text in the table in the rows below the header row, and then change the font color to Pink, Background 1, Darker 50%. Reposition the table so it is approximately centered vertically in the blank area below the title.

9. On Slide 8, which has the Blank layout applied, draw a rectangle shape so it almost fills the slide but fits inside the purple and pink borders on the slide. (*Hint*: Change the fill color of the rectangle to one of the blue colors in the Theme Colors so that you can more easily see where the rectangle and the purple border lines meet.) After the rectangle is sized to the correct size, fill the shape with the picture **Group**, located in the PowerPoint2 ▶ Case1 folder.

10. On Slide 8, draw another rectangle shape that is one inch high and stretches from the inside of the pink borders on the left and right. Position this rectangle directly below the purple line at the top of the slide. Remove the fill from the shape and remove the outline (that is, change the fill to No Fill and change the outline to No Outline).

11. In the second rectangle, type **See You at the Theater!**. Change the font to Broadway (Headings), and change the font size to 44 points. (If the font color is not White, or if you can't see the text, click the border of the rectangle to select the entire shape, and then change the font color to White.)

12. On Slide 8, animate the text box using the entrance animation Grow & Turn. Set its duration to .50 seconds, set its start timing to After previous, and set a delay of one second.

13. Apply the Drape transition to all the slides using the default Left effect. Then apply the Curtains transition to only Slides 1 and 8. On Slide 8, change the duration of the transition to two seconds.

14. Save your changes, and then watch the slide show in Slide Show view. Remember to wait for the video on Slide 6 ("Recent Summer Performance") to start automatically, and, after the transition to Slide 8, wait for the text box to animate automatically.

## Case Problem 2

**CREATE**

**Data Files needed for this Case Problem: Coating.pptx, Curing.mp4, Hanging.jpg, Powder.mp4, Touchup.jpg, Wash.mp4, Welding.jpg**

*Powder Coating Power Plus*    Yung Hoang owns Powder Coating Power Plus, a company that uses a process called powder coating to paint metal surfaces. Powder coating results in a high-quality painted metal surface because it bonds with the metal instead of sitting on top of it. His company paints items such as exhaust fans, intake vents, pipes, and bike frames. Potential clients want to know the advantages and the process of powder coating, so Yung decided to create a PowerPoint presentation to provide this information and approximate costs. He started with the Project planning overview presentation template from Office.com and added a custom layout. Complete the following steps:

1. Open the presentation **Coating**, located in the PowerPoint2 ▶ Case2 folder included with your Data Files, add your name as the subtitle, and then save the presentation as **Powder Coating** to the drive and folder where you are storing your files.

2. Change the layout of Slides 3 through 8 to the custom layout Two Content Modified.

3. Refer to Figure 2-45 and insert the pictures and video as shown on Slides 3 through 8. All the files are located in the PowerPoint2 ▶ Case2 folder. Note that none of the videos in the presentation have sound.

**Figure 2-45** **Slides 3 – 8 in the Powder Coating presentation**

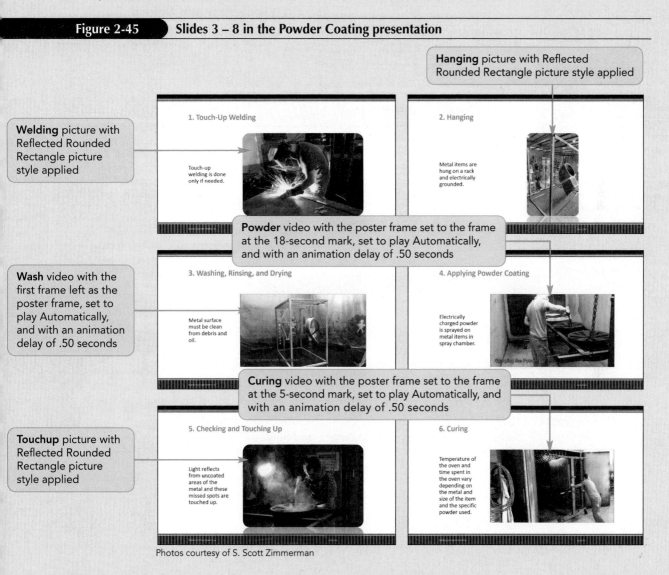

Photos courtesy of S. Scott Zimmerman

4. Compress all the photos to 96 ppi, and compress the media to Low Quality.

5. On Slide 2 ("Why Is Powder Coating Better Than Paint?"), animate the bulleted list to Wipe with the From Top effect.

6. On Slide 9 ("Procedures and Costs"), create the table shown in Figure 2-46, and apply the formatting as described in the figure.

**Figure 2-46**      **Table on Slide 9 in the Power Coating presentation**

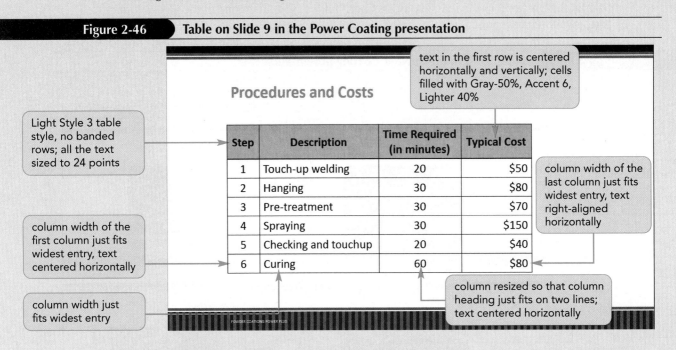

7. Apply the Fade transition to Slides 1 through 3 and Slides 9 and 10. Apply the Conveyor transition to Slides 4 through 8.

8. Add **Powder Coating Power Plus** as a footer on all slides except the title slide, and display the current date to be updated automatically on all slides except the title slide. On the notes and handouts, display the current date to be updated automatically, and add your name as a header.

9. Save your changes, and then view the slide show. The videos on Slide 5 ("3. Washing, Rinsing, and Drying"), Slide 6 ("Applying Powder Coating"), and Slide 8 ("6. Curing") should play automatically one-half second after the slide appears in the slide show.

## Case Problem 3

**APPLY**

Data Files needed for this Case Problem: Bench End.jpg, Bench.mp4, Curl.mp4, Gym Theme.pptx, Gym.pptx, Military.mp4

***St. Louis Fitness Consultants***   St. Louis Fitness Consultants provides consulting and training services to gyms, municipal fitness centers, and large companies. Bianca Kocherhans, a personal trainer and sales consultant who works at St. Louis Fitness, realized that many people want the convenience of having a home gym. She approached the company's owners and was given approval to offer consulting to retail stores that sell fitness equipment and to large companies with employees interested in setting up their own home gym. She prepared a PowerPoint presentation with some information on setting up a home gym and doing a few basic weight-lifting exercises. Complete the following steps:

1. Open the presentation named **Gym**, located in the PowerPoint2 ▶ Case3 folder included with your Data Files, add your name as the subtitle, and then save it as **Home Gym** to the drive and folder where you are storing your files.

2. Apply the theme from the presentation **Gym Theme**, located in the PowerPoint2 ▶ Case3 folder.

3. On Slide 10 ("Bench Press Technique"), change the layout to Comparison Three, insert the picture **Bench End** in the content placeholder, and then type **Ending position** in the text placeholder below this photo. Compress this photo to 96 ppi.

4. Apply the Drop Shadow Rectangle picture style to the three photos on Slide 10.

5. On Slide 3 ("Why a Power Cage?"), add the Line Callout 1 shape to the left of the bottom part of the picture. Type **Safety bar to catch barbell** in the shape. Apply the Moderate Effect – Black, Dark 1 shape style, and then change the outline weight to 3 points. Resize the box part of the callout containing the text so that all the text fits on two lines with "Safety bar to" on the first line.

6. Flip the callout shape horizontally, and then drag the end of the callout line to point to the part of the horizontal safety bar in the photo indicated by the red circle shape. Delete the red circle shape.

7. On Slide 4 ("Typical Costs"), insert a 3x6 table. Keep the default style Medium Style 2 – Accent 1 applied to the table. Enter the data shown in Figure 2-47.

**Figure 2-47**   **Data for table on Slide 4 in the Home Gym presentation**

| Item | Cost per Item | Total Cost |
|---|:---:|:---:|
| Power cage (1) | $650 | $650 |
| Bench (1) | $200 | $200 |
| Barbell (2) | $50 | $100 |
| Barbell plates (12 pairs) | $30 | $360 |
| Dumbbells (9 pairs) | $20 | $180 |

© 2014 Cengage Learning

8. Add a new bottom row to the table. Type **TOTAL** in the first cell in the new row, and then type **$1,490** in the last cell in the new row.

9. Increase the size of all the text in the table to 24 points. Resize the first column so it is just wide enough to fit the widest entry, and then resize the second and third columns so they are 2.5 inches wide.

10. Horizontally center the text in the first row. Horizontally right-align the dollar values in the second and third columns, and then right-align "TOTAL" in its cell in the last row.

11. Add a Gray-50%, Accent 6, Darker 50%, 3-point horizontal border between the last row and the row above it, and then add a 1-point border using the same color to the top and bottom of the table.

12. On Slide 7 ("Executing the Arm Curl"), insert the video **Curl**, on Slide 9 ("Executing the Military Press"), insert the video **Military**, and on Slide 11 ("Executing the Bench Press"), insert the video **Bench**. All three videos are located in the PowerPoint2 ▸ Case3 folder. (None of the videos in this presentation have sound.) For all three videos, keep the first frame as the poster frame.

13. Trim each video as necessary so that only two repetitions of the exercise are shown.

14. Copy the callout you added on Slide 3 ("Why a Power Cage?") to Slide 11 ("Executing the Bench Press"). Reposition the callout to point to the same location on the safety bar that you pointed to on Slide 3.

15. Animate the bulleted list on Slide 3 ("Why a Power Cage?") with the Appear entrance animation, and then animate the callout on Slide 3 with the same animation.

16. Change the start timing of the animation applied to the callout so that it appears at the same time as the "Safe" bulleted item.

17. Compress the media in the presentation.

18. Add **St. Louis Fitness Consultants** as the footer on all of the slides, including the title slide, and display the slide number on all of the slides. Add your name as a header on the notes and handouts.

19. Apply the Gallery transition to all of the slides except the first one using the default effect options From Right.

20. Save your changes, and then view the slide show.

## Case Problem 4

**CHALLENGE**

Data Files needed for this Case Problem: Identity.pptx, Logo.jpg, Password.wma

*KeepMeMine ID*   Dudley Zaunbrecher is a regional sales representative for KeepMeMine ID, an insurance and security company headquartered in Fort Smith, Arkansas that protects, monitors, insures, and recovers personal identity. Dudley travels throughout his region meeting with new customers. He wants to use PowerPoint to give a presentation to explain the seriousness of identity theft and how to create strong passwords, and then wrap up by trying to sign up new clients. He has asked you to help him prepare the presentation. Complete the following steps:

1. Open the presentation **Identity**, located in the PowerPoint2 ▸ Case4 folder included with your Data Files, add your name as the subtitle, and then save the presentation as **Identity Theft** to the drive and folder where you are storing your files.

2. Apply the installed Organic theme, and then change the variant to the fourth variant.

3. On Slide 4 ("What Is a Strong Password?"), insert a picture from <u>Office.com</u>. Use the keyword **password**, and insert the picture of asterisks in a password box.

4. On Slide 4, animate the bulleted list using the Wipe animation with the From Left effect.

5. Slide 5 ("Creating a Strong Password") contains four individual text boxes, not the usual bulleted list in one text box. Click the first bulleted item, press and hold the Shift key, click each of the other three items, and then release the Shift key. Apply the entrance animation Appear to the selected text boxes.

✦ **Explore** 6. On Slide 5, select the four animated text boxes, and then modify the Appear animation so that the letters appear one by one. (*Hint*: Use the Animation group Dialog Box Launcher, and then change the setting in the Animate text box on the Effect tab.) Speed up the effect by changing the delay between letters to 0.1 seconds.

✦ **Explore** 7. On Slide 5, insert the audio clip **Password**, located in the PowerPoint2 ▸ Case4 folder included with your Data Files. Position the sound icon to the right of the slide title so that the centers and right edges of the icon object and the title text object are aligned. Point to the sound icon, and then click the Play button. Listen to the recording and notice how it relates to the bulleted items on the slide.

✦ **Explore** 8. Add bookmarks to the play bar for the sound icon to mark four distinct points in the recording at approximately 9, 15, 19, and 32 seconds to correspond to the four text boxes on the slide. (*Hint*: Click the sound icon, and then click the AUDIO TOOLS PLAYBACK tab. Point to the sound icon, click the Play button, and then click the Add Bookmark button in the Bookmarks group on the PLAYBACK tab at the appropriate times, or click the play bar at the point where you want to add the bookmark.)

✦ **Explore** 9. Set the animation of the bulleted list to play automatically as the recording hits each bookmark. (*Hint*: Select each text box, and then use the Trigger button in the Advanced Animation group on the ANIMATIONS tab.)

10. Display Slide 5 in Slide Show view, point to the sound icon, and then click the Play button. Watch as the text in the text boxes animates automatically, one letter at a time, as each bookmark is reached. End the slide show.

11. On Slide 6 ("We Can Help"), insert the picture **Logo**, located in the PowerPoint2 ▸ Case4 folder.

12. Compress all the pictures to 96 ppi, and then compress the media to the lowest quality.

13. Apply the Switch transition to all the slides in the presentation.

14. Save your changes, and then run the slide show.

# Aa Verbal Communication

## Rehearsing Your Presentation

The best presentations are planned well in advance of their delivery. Once the content has been created, enhanced, and perfected, it is time to prepare you, the presenter. Presenters who try to stand up and "wing it" in front of a crowd usually reveal this amateur approach the moment they start speaking—by looking down at their notes, rambling off topic, or turning their back on the audience frequently to read from the slides displayed on-screen.

To avoid being seen as an amateur, you need to rehearse your presentation. Even the most knowledgeable speakers rehearse to ensure they know how the topic flows, what the main points are, how much time to spend on each slide, and where to place emphasis. Experienced presenters understand that while practice may not make them perfect, it will certainly make them better.

Where you practice isn't that important. You can talk to a mirror, your family, or a group of friends. If you have a video camera, you can record yourself and then review the video. Watching video evidence of your performance often reveals the weaknesses you don't want your audience to see and that your friends or family may be unwilling or unable to identify. Whatever you choose to do, the bottom line is this: If you practice, you will improve.

As you rehearse, you should remember to focus on the following steps:

- Practice speaking fluently.
- Work on your tone of voice.
- Decide how to involve your audience.
- Become aware of your body language.
- Check your appearance.

## Speaking Fluently

Be sure to speak in an easy, smooth manner, and avoid using nonwords and fillers. Nonwords consist of ums, ahs, hms, and other such breaks in speech. Fillers are phrases that don't add any value yet add length to sentences. Both can dilute a speaker's message because they are not essential to the meaning of what's being spoken. At best, they can make you sound unprofessional. At worst, they can distract your audience and make your message incomprehensible.

## Considering Your Tone of Voice

When delivering your presentation, you usually want to speak passionately, with authority, and with a smile. If you aren't excited about your presentation, how will your audience feel? By projecting your voice with energy, passion, and confidence, your audience will automatically pay more attention to you. Smile and look directly at your audience members and make eye contact. If your message is getting across, they will instinctively affirm what you're saying by returning your gaze, nodding their heads, or smiling. There's something compelling about a confident speaker whose presence commands attention. However, be careful not to overdo it. Speaking too loudly or using an overly confident or arrogant tone will turn off an audience and make them stop listening altogether.

## Involving Your Audience

If you involve your audience in your presentation, they will pay closer attention to what you have to say. When an audience member asks a question, be sure to affirm them before answering. For example, you could respond with "That's a great question. What do the rest of you think?" or "Thanks for asking. Here's what my research revealed." An easy way to get the audience to participate is to start with a question and invite responses, or to stop partway through to discuss a particularly important point.

# Being Aware of Your Body Language

Although the content of your presentation plays a role in your message delivery, it's your voice and body language during the presentation that make or break it. Maintain eye contact to send the message that you want to connect and that you can be trusted. Stand up straight to signal confidence. Conversely, avoid slouching, which can convey laziness, lack of energy, or disinterest, and fidgeting or touching your hair, which can signal nervousness. Resist the temptation to glance at your watch; you don't want to send a signal that you'd rather be someplace else. Finally, be aware of your hand movements. The best position for your hands is to place them comfortably by your side, in a relaxed position. As you talk, it's fine to use hand gestures to help make a point, but be careful not to overdo it.

# Evaluating Your Appearance

Just as a professional appearance makes a good impression during a job interview, an audience's first impression of a speaker is also based on appearance. Before a single word is spoken, the audience sizes up the way the presenter looks. You want to make sure you look professional and competent. Make sure your appearance is neat, clean, and well-coordinated, and dress in appropriate clothing.

As you spend time practicing your presentation, you will naturally develop appropriate body language, tone of voice, and a fluent delivery, ensuring a clear connection with your audience and a professional delivery of your presentation's message.

---

**PROSKILLS**

### Create and Deliver a Training Presentation

If you hold a job for any length of time, as part of your employment, you might have to train new employees in their work tasks. For example, if you work in a library, you might have to explain how to process returned books, or if you work in a chemistry stockroom at a college, you might have to describe how to make up solutions for the school's chemistry laboratories. A PowerPoint presentation can be an effective way to start the training process. With a presentation, you can give an overview of the job without needing to repeat yourself to explain detailed aspects. Then you can customize the rest of the training to fit the needs of the specific employee.

In this exercise, you'll create a presentation containing information of your choice, using the PowerPoint skills and features presented in Tutorials 1 and 2, and then you will practice techniques for delivering the presentation.

**Note:** Please be sure not to include any personal information of a sensitive nature in the documents you create to be submitted to your instructor for this exercise. Later on, you can update the documents with such information for your own personal use.

1. Create a new PowerPoint presentation and apply an appropriate theme. Make sure you choose a theme that is relevant to the job you are describing and to your audience. Consider using a template from Office.com.
2. On Slide 1, make the presentation title the same as the title of your job or the job for which you are giving the training. Add your name as a subtitle.
3. Create a new slide for each major category of tasks. For example, task categories for a library job might be "Punching In," "Checking in with Your Supervisor," "Gathering Books from Drop-Off Stations," "Scanning Returned Books into the Computer," "Checking Books for Damage or Marks," "Processing Abused Books," "Processing Late Books," "Sorting Books," "Shelving Books," and "Punching Out."
4. On each slide, create a bulleted list to explain the particular task category or to provide the steps required to perform the task, or consider if a graphic, such as a SmartArt diagram or a table, would better illustrate your point.
5. Where applicable, include clip art, photographs, or a video. For example, you might include a photograph of the punch clock (time clock) used by hourly workers in the library, or a photograph of a book with serious damage relative to one with normal wear.

6. On one or more slides, insert a shape, such as a rectangle, triangle, circle, arrow, or star. For example, you might want to place a small colored star next to a particularly important step in carrying out a task.

7. Apply appropriate formatting to the graphics on the slides.

8. Examine your slides. Are you using too many words? Can any of your bulleted lists be replaced with a graphic?

9. Reevaluate the theme you chose. Do you think it is still appropriate? Does it fit the content of your presentation? If not, apply a different theme.

10. Add appropriate transitions and animations. Remember that the goal is to keep your audience engaged without distracting them.

11. Check the spelling of your presentation, and then proofread it to check for errors that would not be caught by the spell check. Save the final presentation.

12. Rehearse the presentation. Consider your appearance, and decide on the appropriate clothing to wear. Practice in front of a mirror and friends or family, and if you can, create a video of yourself. Notice and fine tune your body language, tone of voice, and fluency to fully engage your audience.

## OBJECTIVES

**Session 1: Integrating Word and Excel**
- Embed an Excel chart in a Word document
- Edit an embedded Excel chart in a Word document
- Link an Excel worksheet to a Word document
- Update a linked Excel worksheet

**Session 2: Integrating Word, Excel, and Access**
- Select a main document and a data source for a mail merge
- Edit a data source
- Insert merge fields into a form letter
- Preview and finish a mail merge
- Export Access query results to Excel

**Session 3: Integrating Word, Excel, Access, and PowerPoint**
- Create PowerPoint slides from a Word outline
- Create an Access query
- Copy Access query results to a PowerPoint slide
- Embed an Excel table in a PowerPoint slide

# Integrating Word, Excel, Access, and PowerPoint

*Creating Documents for a Green Initiative Plan*

## Case | Green Initiative Plan

The city council in Parkerville, Ohio, recently approved a citywide Green Initiative plan. Part of the Green Initiative is to reduce the amount of trash collected at city parks and nature trails by placing recycling containers next to all trash bins. Another part of the Green Initiative is to reduce the amount of mowing at city parks. A committee evaluated the way the parks are used and found that many of the acres needed to be mowed only two or three times during the season—essentially mowing only the ball fields and areas where people picnic every other week.

Kenneth Novak, the supervisor of the Parks and Recreation Department, needs to mail a letter to taxpayers explaining how these new programs support the Green Initiative. He will include an Excel chart to illustrate the reduction in the amount of trash that will be collected once the program starts. Ken also wants to include a table that describes the changes to the number of acres that will be mowed and the new mowing schedule. He also needs to create a PowerPoint file to present at the next city council meeting that describes the plans at the Parks and Recreation Department.

## STARTING DATA FILES

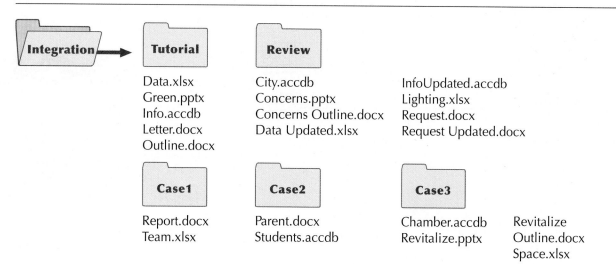

**Integration** → **Tutorial**

Data.xlsx
Green.pptx
Info.accdb
Letter.docx
Outline.docx

**Review**

City.accdb
Concerns.pptx
Concerns Outline.docx
Data Updated.xlsx

InfoUpdated.accdb
Lighting.xlsx
Request.docx
Request Updated.docx

**Case1**

Report.docx
Team.xlsx

**Case2**

Parent.docx
Students.accdb

**Case3**

Chamber.accdb
Revitalize.pptx

Revitalize
Outline.docx
Space.xlsx

# Session 1 Visual Overview:

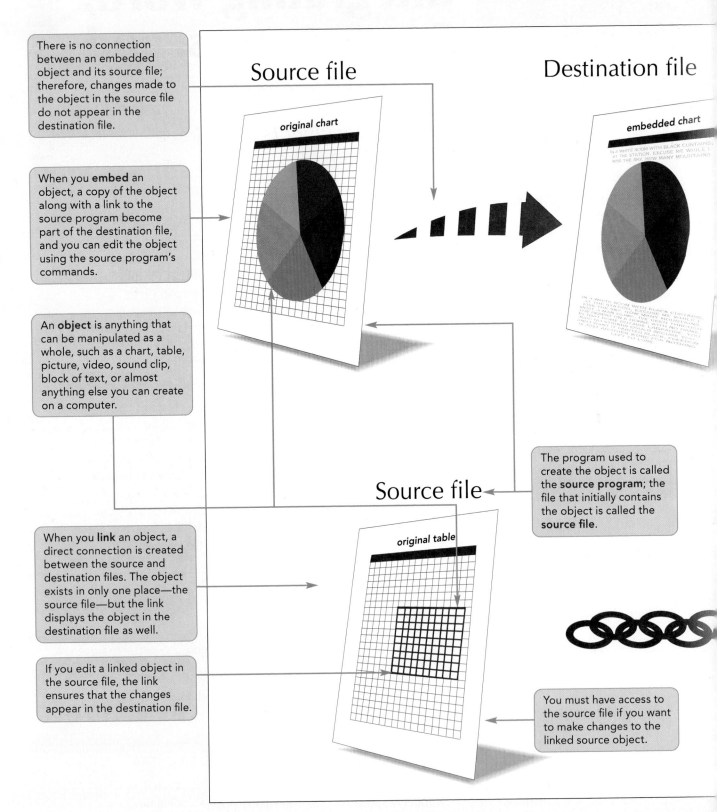

There is no connection between an embedded object and its source file; therefore, changes made to the object in the source file do not appear in the destination file.

When you **embed** an object, a copy of the object along with a link to the source program become part of the destination file, and you can edit the object using the source program's commands.

An **object** is anything that can be manipulated as a whole, such as a chart, table, picture, video, sound clip, block of text, or almost anything else you can create on a computer.

When you **link** an object, a direct connection is created between the source and destination files. The object exists in only one place—the source file—but the link displays the object in the destination file as well.

If you edit a linked object in the source file, the link ensures that the changes appear in the destination file.

The program used to create the object is called the **source program**; the file that initially contains the object is called the **source file**.

You must have access to the source file if you want to make changes to the linked source object.

Source file

Destination file

original chart

embedded chart

Source file

original table

# Embedding and Linking

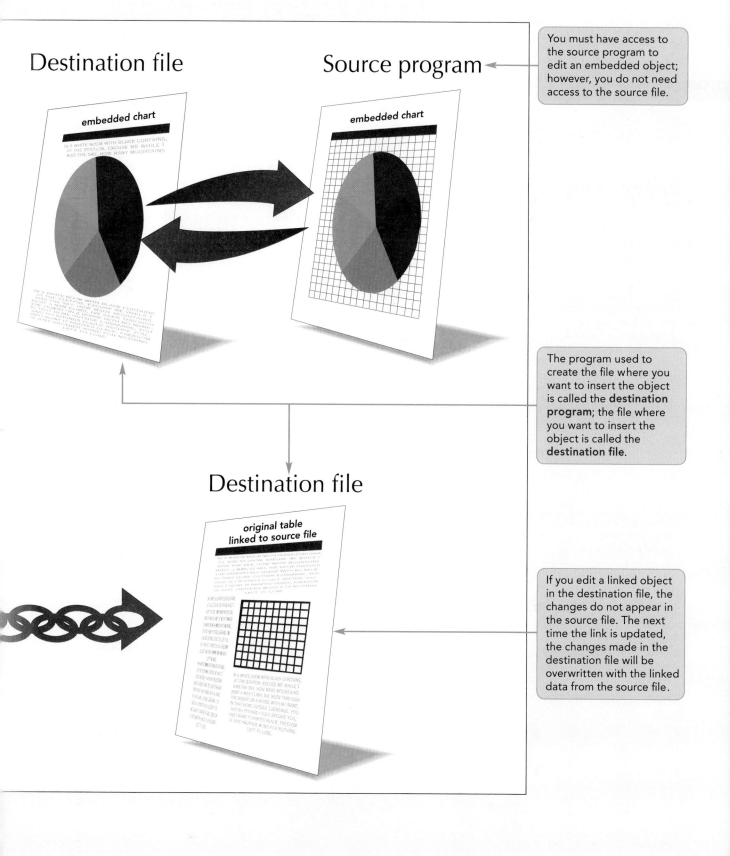

Destination file

Source program

You must have access to the source program to edit an embedded object; however, you do not need access to the source file.

embedded chart

embedded chart

The program used to create the file where you want to insert the object is called the **destination program**; the file where you want to insert the object is called the **destination file**.

Destination file

original table linked to source file

If you edit a linked object in the destination file, the changes do not appear in the source file. The next time the link is updated, the changes made in the destination file will be overwritten with the linked data from the source file.

# Embedding an Excel Chart in a Word Document

Embedding and linking both involve inserting an object into a destination file. The difference between them lies in where their respective objects are stored. Refer to the Session 1 Visual Overview for more information about embedding and linking. The table in Figure 1 further describes embedding and linking, and compares their advantages and disadvantages.

| Figure 1 | Comparing embedding and linking |
|---|---|

|  | Embedding | Linking |
|---|---|---|
| **Description** | Displays and stores an object in the destination file. | Displays an object in the destination file along with the source file's location; stores the object in the source file. |
| **Use if you want to** | Include the object in the destination file, and edit the object using the source program without affecting the source file. | Edit the object in the source file and have the changes appear in the destination file. |
| **Advantages** | The source file and destination file can be stored separately. You can use source program commands to make changes to the object in the destination file. | The destination file size remains fairly small. The source file and the object in the destination file remain identical. |
| **Disadvantages** | The destination file size increases to reflect the addition of the object from the source file. | The source and destination files must be stored together. |

© 2014 Cengage Learning

Ken drafted his letter to taxpayers, and now he wants to include a chart that shows the anticipated reduction in the pounds of trash collected per week at the parks after the recycling program is put into effect. Although you can create an Excel chart directly in a Word document by using the Chart button in the Illustrations group on the INSERT tab, the chart Ken wants to include already exists in an Excel worksheet. So rather than recreate it, you will copy it from the Excel worksheet and embed it in the letter.

You first need to start Word and open the letter, and then start Excel and open the workbook.

## To open the letter in Word and the workbook in Excel:

1. Start Word, and then open the document **Letter**, which is located in the Integration ▸ Tutorial folder included with your Data Files.

   **Trouble?** If you don't have the starting Data Files, you need to get them before you can proceed. Your instructor will either give you the Data Files or ask you to obtain them from a specific location (such as a network drive). If you have any questions about the Data Files, see your instructor or technical support person for assistance.

2. If the window is not maximized, click the **Maximize** button ☐ on the program window title bar.

3. If nonprinting characters are not displayed, click the **Show/Hide ¶** button ¶ in the Paragraph group on the HOME tab. See Figure 2.

**Figure 2** | **Letter from the Parks and Recreation Department to taxpayers**

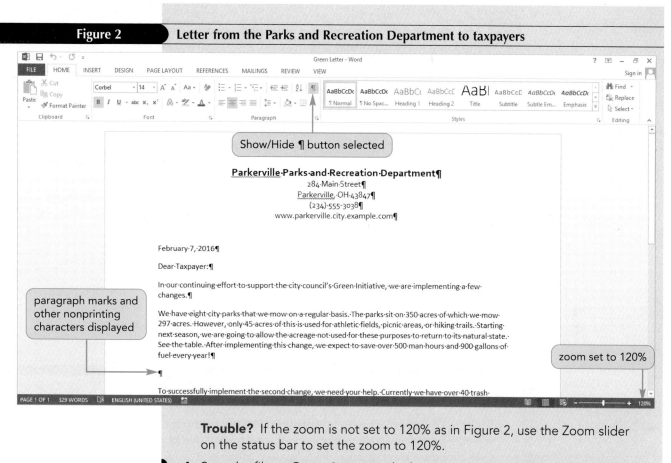

Show/Hide ¶ button selected

paragraph marks and other nonprinting characters displayed

zoom set to 120%

**Trouble?** If the zoom is not set to 120% as in Figure 2, use the Zoom slider on the status bar to set the zoom to 120%.

4. Save the file as **Green Letter** to the location where you are saving your files.

5. Start Excel. Notice that a Microsoft Excel button appears on the taskbar.

6. Open the workbook **Data**, which is located in the Integration ▶ Tutorial folder included with your Data Files. This workbook contains three worksheets. The Recycling Chart worksheet is the active worksheet. See Figure 3.

**Figure 3** | **Recycling Chart worksheet in the Data workbook**

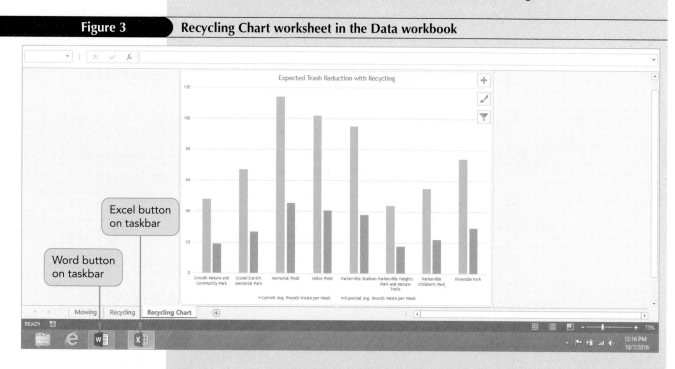

Excel button on taskbar

Word button on taskbar

> **Trouble?** If the Recycling Chart worksheet is not the active worksheet, click the Recycling Chart sheet tab.
>
> **Trouble?** If the window is not maximized, click the Maximize button ▢ on the program window title bar.

▶ **7.** Save the file as **Green Data** to the location where you are saving your files.

To embed the chart in the letter, you'll copy the chart to the Clipboard, and then paste it into the document. When you click the Paste button arrow instead of clicking the Paste button, a menu of buttons appears displaying options for how the item on the Clipboard will be pasted. The options vary depending on what is on the Clipboard. For text and most objects, you can choose whether to keep the source file formatting or use the destination file formatting. For some actions, such as pasting an Excel chart into a Word document, you can also choose whether to embed or link the object, or paste it as a picture. You can point to each button on the Paste button menu to see a Live Preview of the pasted object.

You can also access these paste options after you paste an object. When you paste text or an object into an Office document, the Paste Options button appears just below and to the right of the pasted object. You can click the Paste Options button to display the same options that appear when you click the Paste button arrow.

**REFERENCE**

### Embedding an Excel Chart in a Word Document

- Start the source program (Excel), open the file containing the chart to be embedded, select the chart you want to embed in the destination file (a Word document), and then click the Copy button in the Clipboard group on the HOME tab.
- Start the destination program (Word), open the file that will contain the embedded chart, and then position the insertion point where you want to place the chart.
- In the Clipboard group on the HOME tab in Word, click the Paste button arrow, and then click the Keep Source Formatting & Embed Workbook button or the Use Destination Theme & Embed Workbook button. You can also click the Paste button in the Clipboard group, click the Paste Options button that appears, and then click the Keep Source Formatting & Embed Workbook button or the Use Destination Theme & Embed Workbook button.

You will embed the chart into the letter now.

### To embed the Excel chart in the Word document:

▶ **1.** Click the **CHART TOOLS FORMAT** tab, and then in the Current Selection group, click the **Chart Elements arrow**. See Figure 4.

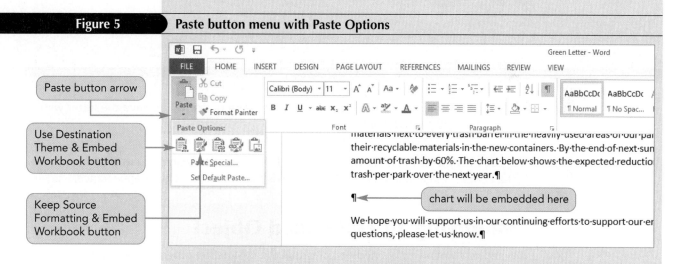

**Figure 4** Chart Elements menu

**Figure 5** Paste button menu with Paste Options

2. On the menu, click **Chart Area**. The entire chart is selected.

3. Click the **HOME** tab, and then in the Clipboard group, click the **Copy** button. The selected chart is copied to the Clipboard.

4. On the taskbar, click the **Microsoft Word** button ⊞ to return to the Green Letter document.

5. Scroll down, and then click the empty paragraph mark above the last paragraph in the body of the letter. This is where you will embed the chart.

6. In the Clipboard group, click the **Paste button arrow**. The Paste menu opens. See Figure 5.

**Trouble?** If the chart appears in the document instead of the Paste menu opening, click the Undo button 🔄 on the Quick Access Toolbar, and then repeat Step 6, taking care to click the arrow below the Paste button icon.

7. On the Paste menu, point to the **Keep Source Formatting & Embed Workbook** button 📋. The chart appears in the document at the insertion point using the fonts and colors of the theme applied to the source file—the Facet theme—instead of the fonts and colors of the destination file theme—the Office theme.

8. On the Paste menu, point to the **Use Destination Theme & Embed Workbook** button 📋. The formatting of the chart changes to match the theme colors used in the letter, including the colors used by the Office theme in the Word document. Because this is the default option, this is how the chart would appear if you clicked the Paste button. Ken wants you to use the document theme for the embedded chart and not the workbook theme.

**9.** Click the **Use Destination Theme & Embed Workbook** button 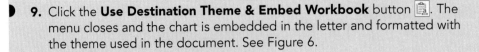. The menu closes and the chart is embedded in the letter and formatted with the theme used in the document. See Figure 6.

**Figure 6** **Excel chart pasted in the Word document**

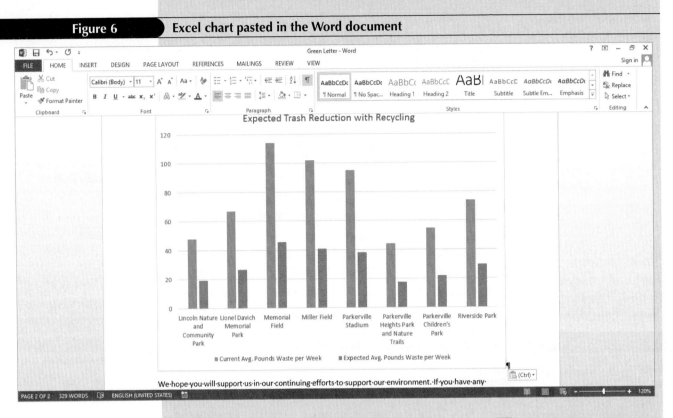

**10.** On the Quick Access Toolbar, click the **Save** button 🔲 to save the letter with the embedded chart.

After reviewing the letter with the embedded chart, Ken wants you to change the chart colors and add a title to the vertical axis to improve the chart's appearance.

# Modifying an Embedded Object

When you edit an embedded object within the destination program, the changes affect only the embedded object; the original object in the source program remains unchanged. When you click an embedded object, the contextual tabs associated with the object appear on the ribbon in the destination program. In the case of a chart, a column of buttons also appears next to the chart on the right, giving you easy access to some of these same commands.

First, you will change the colors of the embedded chart.

### To change the colors of the embedded chart:

**1.** In the letter, click the embedded chart. The selection border and handles appear around the chart object, four buttons appear to the right of the selected chart, and the CHART TOOLS contextual tabs appear on the ribbon. See Figure 7. Now you can modify the chart by changing the chart colors.

**Figure 7** Selected Excel chart in the Word document

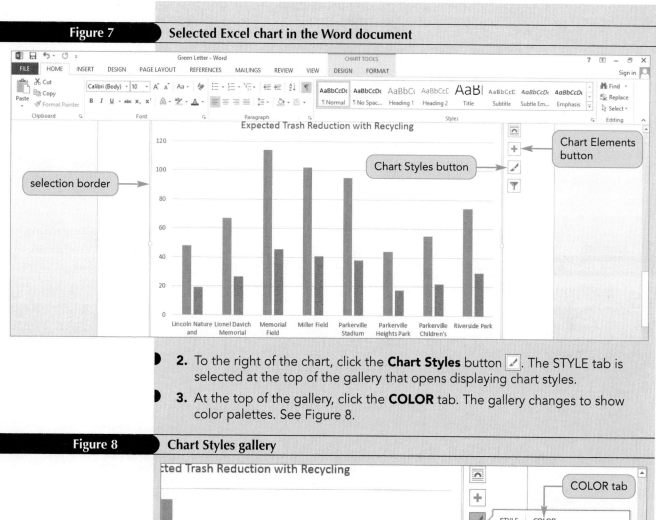

2. To the right of the chart, click the **Chart Styles** button. The STYLE tab is selected at the top of the gallery that opens displaying chart styles.

3. At the top of the gallery, click the **COLOR** tab. The gallery changes to show color palettes. See Figure 8.

**Figure 8** Chart Styles gallery

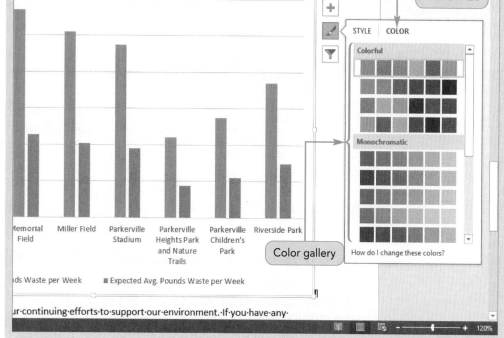

4. Scroll to the bottom of the gallery, and then click **Color 17**. (Use the ScreenTips to find this color palette.) The colors of the columns change so that the Expected Avg. Pounds Waste per Week columns are now green.

Ken also wants you to add a title to the *y*-axis. The horizontal axis doesn't need a title because the labels on each set of columns make it clear what the columns represent.

### To add a title to the vertical axis:

▶ 1. To the right of the chart, click the **Chart Elements** button ➕. A menu of elements in the chart appears with check boxes next to each item. The elements with a checkmark in the check boxes are included on the chart.

▶ 2. Point to **Axis Titles**. A gray arrow appears to the right of Axis Titles.

▶ 3. Click the **arrow** ▶. A submenu opens listing the two axes.

▶ 4. On the submenu, click the **Primary Vertical** check box. A checkmark appears in it and a title is added to the y-axis with the temporary name "Axis Title." See Figure 9.

| Figure 9 | Axis Titles submenu on the CHART ELEMENTS menu |
|---|---|

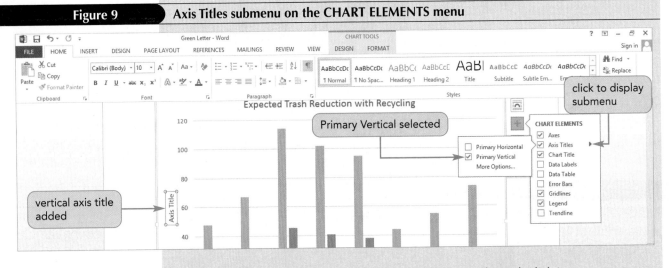

**Trouble?** If the Primary Horizontal check box is selected, click it to remove the checkmark.

▶ 5. In the chart, position the pointer on **Axis Title** so that the pointer changes to Ĩ, and then click. The insertion point appears in the text box.

▶ 6. Press the **Backspace** and **Delete** keys as needed to delete all of the text in the y-axis title, and then type **Average Pounds Trash Per Week**.

▶ 7. Save the changes to the letter.

Your next task is to include the table outlining the mowing plan in Ken's letter. To do this, you will link the table from Excel to Word.

## Linking Excel Worksheet Data to Word

Ken also wants to add a table listing the number of acres that the city currently mows every other week, and the number of acres that will be mowed in the new system. This table is on the Mowing worksheet in the Green Data workbook. Because the table is not complete, Ken wants you to link the data so that when he receives the rest of the data and updates the workbook, the table will be updated in the letter as well.

## REFERENCE

### Linking Excel Worksheet Data to a Word Document

- Start the source program (Excel), open the file containing the data to be linked, select the data you want to link to the destination program, and then click the Copy button in the Clipboard group on the HOME tab.
- Start the destination program (Word), open the file that will contain the linked object, and then position the insertion point where you want to place the data.
- In the Clipboard group on the HOME tab in Word, click the Paste button arrow, and then click the Link & Keep Source Formatting button or the Link & Use Destination Styles button. You can also click the Paste button in the Clipboard group, click the Paste Options button that appears, and then click the Link & Keep Source Formatting button or the Link & Use Destination Styles button.

You'll copy the data from the Excel worksheet, and then link the data to the letter.

### To link the table to the letter:

1. On the taskbar, click the **Microsoft Excel** button [X] to switch back to the Green Data workbook.

2. Click the **Mowing** sheet tab. This worksheet lists the parks and other spaces the Parks and Recreation Department is responsible for, the number of acres currently mowed every two weeks, and the reduced number of acres to be mowed on this schedule. See Figure 10. Note that the proposed number of acres for the last three parks is missing.

**Figure 10**    Mowing worksheet in the Green Data workbook

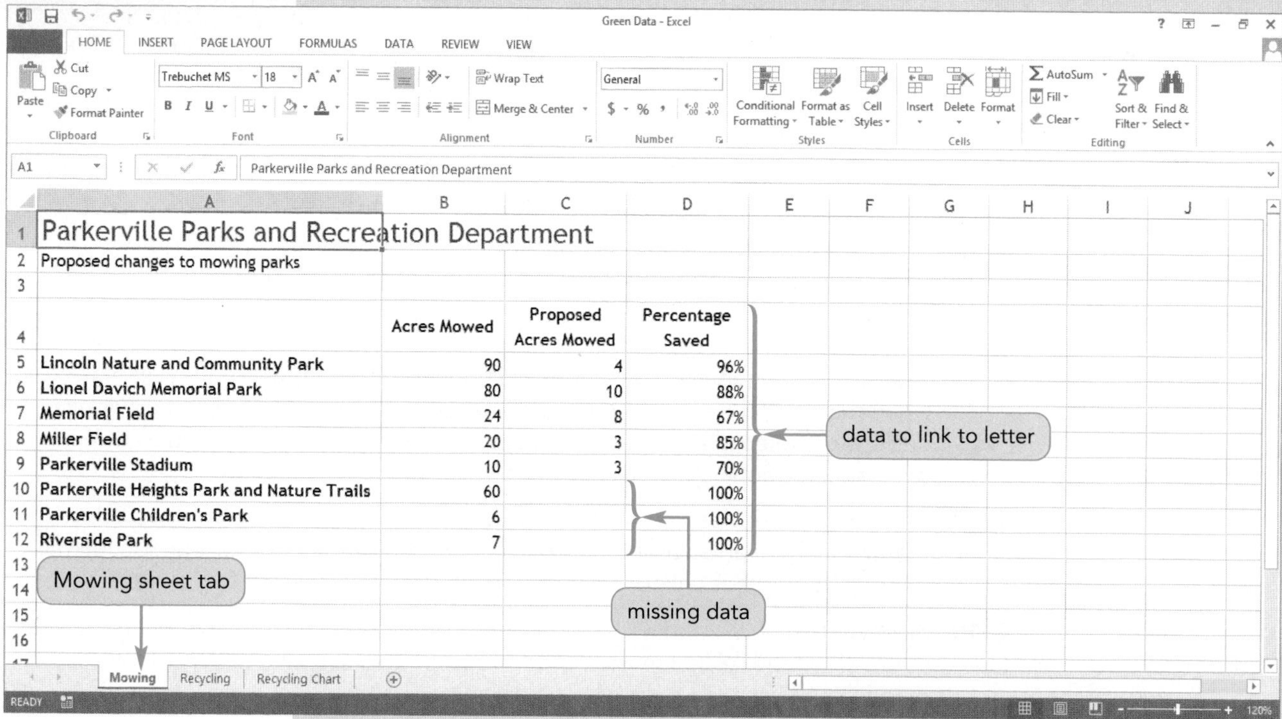

**Trouble?** If the zoom is not set to 120% as in Figure 10, use the Zoom slider on the status bar to adjust it.

▶ **3.** Select the range **A4:D12**.

▶ **4.** On the HOME tab, in the Clipboard group, click the **Copy** button. The selected cells are copied to the Clipboard.

▶ **5.** On the taskbar, click the **Microsoft Word** button ⬛ to return to the letter.

▶ **6.** Scroll up and position the insertion point in the blank paragraph between the second and third paragraphs in the body of the letter. This is where you want the table to appear.

▶ **7.** On the HOME tab, in the Clipboard group, click the **Paste** button. The table is pasted in the document and the Paste Options button 📋 (Ctrl) ▼ appears below the lower-right corner of the table.

▶ **8.** Click the **Paste Options** button 📋 (Ctrl) ▼. A menu of paste options opens. See Figure 11.

**Figure 11**    **Paste Options commands for pasting an Excel table**

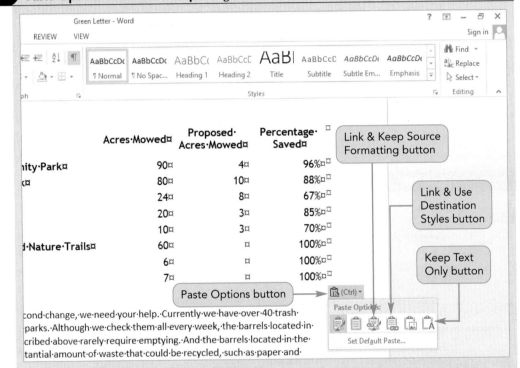

Note that this menu contains one additional option that was not available when the copied item was the chart—Keep Text Only. Keep Text Only would paste the copied data as text without the table structure. You need to select one of the options that will link the copied object.

▶ **9.** Click the **Link & Use Destination Styles** button 📋. The data you copied from Excel is inserted as a table using the default table style of the document theme. The table is linked to the original Excel worksheet.

▶ **10.** Save your work.

## Updating Linked Objects

When objects are linked and information changes in the source file, you can update the linked object in the destination file so that it displays the new information.

Ken learns that under the new program, only 10 acres at Parkerville Heights Park and Nature Trails will be mowed every other week. Ken asks you to update the Excel worksheet and then update the letter.

**To update the data in Excel and update the linked table:**

**1.** In the letter, right-click the table. A shortcut menu opens. See Figure 12.

| Figure 12 | Shortcut menu for a linked table |
|---|---|

click to update the linked data

click to display a submenu containing commands to work with the linked object

**Trouble?** If the Linked Worksheet Object command is not on the shortcut menu, you probably clicked a gridline in the table. Click a blank area of the document, and then repeat Step 1.

**2.** On the shortcut menu, point to **Linked Worksheet Object**, and then click **Edit Link**. The Excel worksheet containing the data you copied becomes active.

**3.** Click cell **C10**, type **10**, and then press the **Enter** key. Now you need to update the linked data.

**4.** Switch to the Word document.

**5.** Right-click anywhere in the table, and then click **Update Link** on the shortcut menu. The number you added to the Excel worksheet for the proposed number of acres to mow at Parkerville Heights Park and Nature Trails, 10, now appears in the Word document because you linked the table from Excel to Word. See Figure 13.

Figure 13          Updated linked data in the table

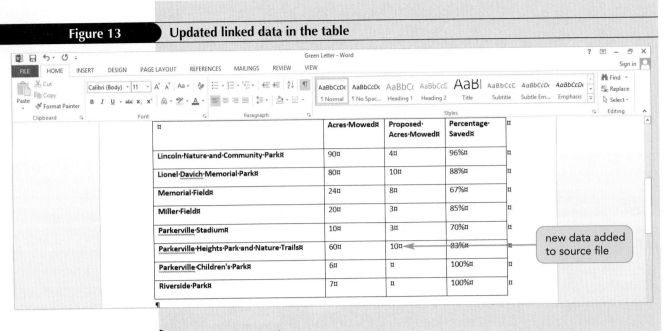

| ¤ | Acres·Mowed¤ | Proposed· Acres·Mowed¤ | Percentage· Saved¤ | ¤ |
|---|---|---|---|---|
| Lincoln·Nature·and·Community·Park¤ | 90¤ | 4¤ | 96%¤ | ¤ |
| Lionel·Davich·Memorial·Park¤ | 80¤ | 10¤ | 88%¤ | ¤ |
| Memorial·Field¤ | 24¤ | 8¤ | 67%¤ | ¤ |
| Miller·Field¤ | 20¤ | 3¤ | 85%¤ | ¤ |
| Parkerville·Stadium¤ | 10¤ | 3¤ | 70%¤ | ¤ |
| Parkerville·Heights·Park·and·Nature·Trails¤ | 60¤ | 10¤ | 83%¤ | ¤ |
| Parkerville·Children's·Park¤ | 6¤ | ¤ | 100%¤ | ¤ |
| Riverside·Park¤ | 7¤ | ¤ | 100%¤ | ¤ |

new data added to source file

**6.** Save your work.

Ken has received the number of acres that will be mowed at Parkerville Children's Park and Riverside Park. But what would happen if you changed the values in the linked Excel workbook when the Word document was closed? Would you still be able to update the information in the letter? To find out, you will enter the rest of the missing data in the Excel workbook with the Word document closed. Then you'll reopen the letter to verify that the changes appear in the linked object.

### To edit the linked table with the Word document closed:

**1.** Click the **FILE** tab to open Backstage view, and then in the navigation bar, click **Close** to close the document without exiting Word.

**2.** Switch to the Excel workbook.

**3.** Enter **3** in cell C11, and then enter **4** in cell C12.

**4.** On the Quick Access Toolbar, click the **Save** button 🖫 to save your changes.

**5.** Switch back to the Word program window, and then click the **FILE** tab. Backstage view opens with the Open screen displayed and Recent Documents selected.

**6.** At the top of the Recent Documents list, click **Green Letter**. A dialog box opens telling you that the document contains links, and asking if you want to update the document with new data. See Figure 14.

Figure 14          Dialog box warning that the document contains links

Microsoft Word

⚠ This document contains links that may refer to other files. Do you want to update this document with the data from the linked files?

Show Help >>

click to include the latest data from the linked source file

| Yes | No |

**Trouble?** If Green Letter does not appear in the Recent Documents list, open the document using the Open dialog box.

**Trouble?** If the warning dialog box does not open, scroll the document to view the linked table, right-click the table, and then click Update Links. Skip Step 7 and compare your screen to Figure 15.

7. Click the **Yes** button, and then scroll the document to view the linked table. The new data appears in the linked table. See Figure 15.

**Figure 15**       Updated values in the linked table

| ¤ | Acres·Mowed¤ | Proposed· Acres·Mowed¤ | Percentage· Saved¤ | ¤ |
|---|---|---|---|---|
| Lincoln·Nature·and·Community·Park¤ | 90¤ | 4¤ | 96%¤ | ¤ |
| Lionel·Davich·Memorial·Park¤ | 80¤ | 10¤ | 88%¤ | ¤ |
| Memorial·Field¤ | 24¤ | 8¤ | 67%¤ | ¤ |
| Miller·Field¤ | 20¤ | 3¤ | 85%¤ | ¤ |
| Parkerville·Stadium¤ | 10¤ | 3¤ | 70%¤ | ¤ |
| Parkerville·Heights·Park·and·Nature·Trails¤ | 60¤ | 10¤ | 83%¤ | ¤ |
| Parkerville·Children's·Park¤ | 6¤ | 3¤ | 50%¤ | ¤ |
| Riverside·Park¤ | 7¤ | 4¤ | 43%¤ | ¤ |

updated data from source file

## INSIGHT

### Working with Links

There might be times when the location of a linked object's source file needs to change. For example, if you send a file containing a linked object to a colleague, you also need to send the source file if you want your colleague to edit the linked object and have the changes appear in both the destination file and the source file. Your colleague likely will not have the same folder structure as you do; therefore, you will need to identify the new location (that is, the file path) of the source file. To do this, you need to open the Links dialog box either by right-clicking the linked object, pointing to Linked *Object* (this command will vary depending on the linked object), and then clicking Links; or by opening the Info screen in Backstage view, and then at the bottom of the Properties list, clicking Edit Links to Files. In the Links dialog box, click the link whose location has changed, click the Change Source button, and then navigate to the new location of the source file.

You can also break a link. This is a good idea if you plan to send the file to someone who will not have access to the linked object's source file. After you break a link, users who open the destination file will not get a message asking if they want to update the links—an impossible task if the users do not have access to the source file. To break a link, select it in the Links dialog box, and then click the Break Link button. After you break a link, any changes you make to the object in the source file will not appear in the destination file.

To finish the document, you need to format the table. You'll apply a style to the table and then view the entire document.

## To finish the document:

1. Click anywhere in the table, and then click the **TABLE TOOLS DESIGN** tab on the ribbon.

2. In the Table Styles group, click the **More** button, scroll down the gallery, and then click the **List Table 3 – Accent 6** style.

3. At the bottom of the letter, replace "Kenneth Novak" with your name.

4. Click the **VIEW** tab, and then in the Zoom group, click the **Multiple Pages** button. The view changes so that you can see both pages of the letter. See Figure 16.

**Figure 16**    **Final version of the letter**

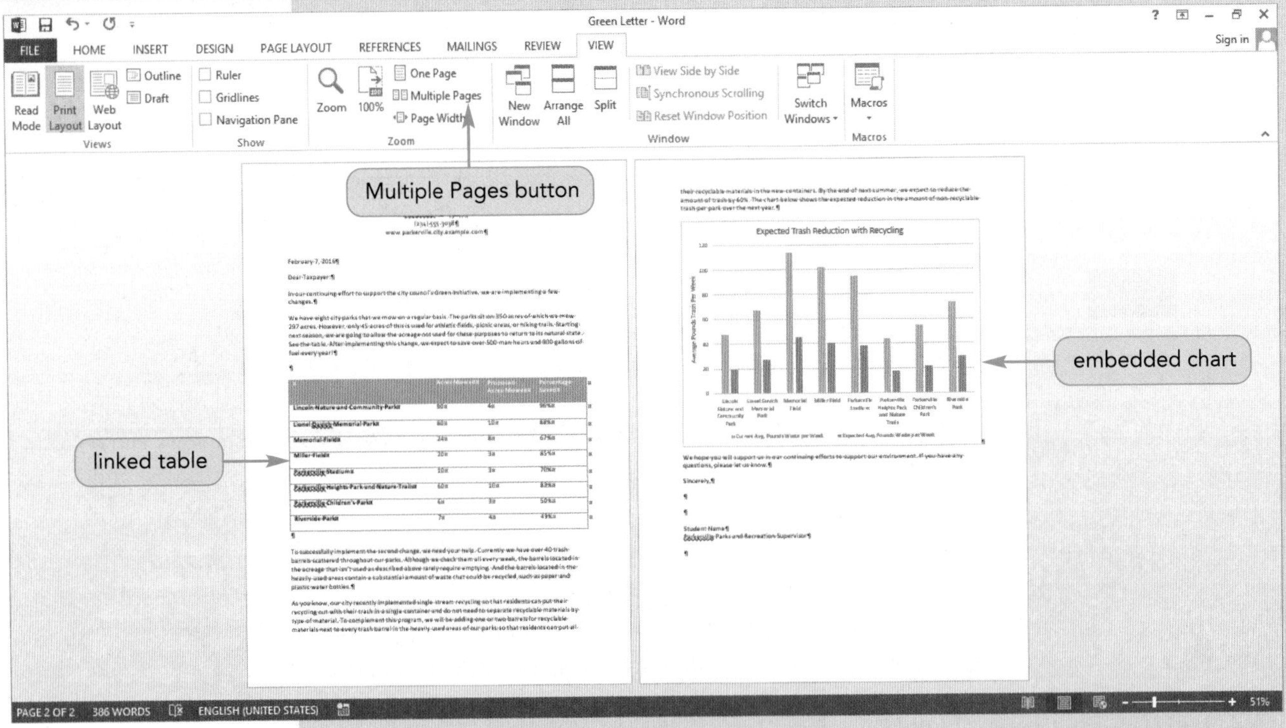

**Trouble?** If you can't see both pages or if they are too small, use the Zoom slider to adjust the zoom until you can see both pages as in Figure 16.

5. Save your changes.

**PROSKILLS**

## Written Communication: Evaluating the Final Document

When you create a document with objects in it, you should view the entire document to make sure that the styles and formatting of the inserted objects match the look and style of the document. For example, if you insert a table and a chart as you did in the document you created in this session, review both objects to make sure their styles and colors complement each other. If they do not, you should make the appropriate formatting changes to one or all of the objects. When you create a document that is longer than one page, make sure that the page breaks are in logical places. For instance, unless a table spans multiple full pages, you should not allow a table to appear on two pages. To view the entire document, use the One Page or Multiple Pages view, or print it.

In this session, you embedded an Excel chart in a Word document and then formatted it in the document. Then you linked Excel data to the same document, updated the table in the Excel workbook, and updated the linked data in the Word document. In the next session, you will merge data stored in an Access table with a Word document to create form letters individually addressed to each person listed in the Access table. You will also export query results from Access to Excel.

**REVIEW**

## Session 1 Quick Check

1. What are source and destination files?
2. What is the difference between embedding an object and linking an object?
3. When an object is embedded, how many copies of the object exist?
4. If an Excel chart is linked to a Word document, which is the source program?
5. If a file contains a linked object and you need to modify the linked object in both the source file and the destination file, in which file should you make the changes?

# Session 2 Visual Overview:

Combining the main document with the data source so that Word replaces the merge fields in the main document with the appropriate information from the data source is called **merging**. A **mail merge** is when you merge a main document with a list of addresses from a data source.

**Parkerville Parks and Recreation Department**

**Merge fields** contain instructions for replacing these field placeholders with the variable information from a data source.

Date

«FirstName» «LastName»
«Street»
«City», «State» «Zip Code»

Dear «FirstName» «LastName»:

The **main document** in a mail merge contains the text and other information (including punctuation, spaces, and graphics) that you want to keep the same in each merged document.

# The Mail Merge Process

The variable information in a main document is contained in a **data source**. The data in the fields in the data source that corresponds to the merge fields will replace those merge fields in the main document.

### Contact Info

| FirstName | LastName | Street | City | State | Zip Code |
|-----------|----------|--------|------|-------|----------|
| Alex | Gonzalez | 201 County Line Rd. | Parkerville | OH | 43847 |
| Sylvia | Ingraham | 35 Pleasant St. | Parkerville | OH | 43847 |
| Aiden | Butterfield | 282 Harrison St. | Parkerville | OH | 43847 |

A data source can be an Access table or query, an Excel table, or a Word table.

# Merging an Access Data Source with a Word Document

Ken plans to use the letter he wrote as a form letter to send to all taxpayers. Ken's letter is the main document, and the Access database containing the names and addresses of the taxpayers is the data source. See the Session 2 Visual Overview for more information on how main documents and data sources can be used to perform a mail merge.

The first step in completing the mail merge is to open the document you want to use as the main document and specify what type of main document it will be, such as a form letter, mailing labels, or envelopes. Then you select recipients from the data source. When you use an Access database as the data source for a mail merge, you select a table or query defined in the database as the actual data source. After you identify the open document as the main document and specify the data source, you insert merge fields into the main document. Finally, you preview the main document, make any needed changes, and then merge the main document and the data source to produce customized form letters.

## Selecting a Main Document and Data Source

The main document is Ken's letter to taxpayers. Your first step in setting up the mail merge is to identify the letter as the main document.

**To select the main document and data source for the mail merge:**

▶ **1.** If you took a break after the previous session, make sure the **Green Letter** document is open in Word, and then change the zoom to **120%**.

▶ **2.** Press the **Ctrl+Home** keys to move the insertion point to the beginning of the document, and then on the ribbon, click the **MAILINGS** tab. The ribbon changes to display commands for working with mailings. Notice that only a few buttons on the ribbon are available. See Figure 17. The other buttons will become available as you set up the mail merge.

| Figure 17 | MAILINGS tab on the ribbon |

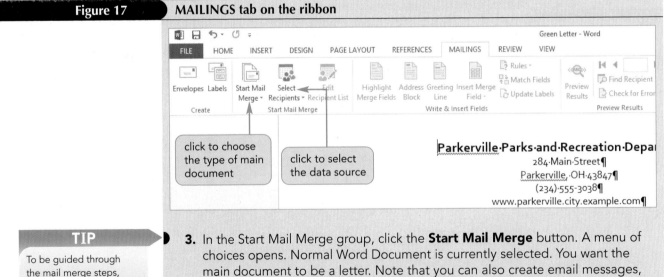

▶ **3.** In the Start Mail Merge group, click the **Start Mail Merge** button. A menu of choices opens. Normal Word Document is currently selected. You want the main document to be a letter. Note that you can also create email messages, envelopes, labels, or a directory, which is a listing of the fields you specify from the data source containing the entire list.

▶ **4.** Click **Letters**. This tells Word that you want the main document to be a letter.

**TIP**

To be guided through the mail merge steps, click the Start Mail Merge button, and then click Step by Step Mail Merge Wizard.

The next step is to select the recipients of the letter. You want to select recipients from the list of taxpayers in an Access database. First you will open the database in Access and save it with a new name.

### To open the database and save it with a new name:

1. Start Access, and then open the **Info** database, which is located in the Integration ▶ Tutorial folder included with your Data Files.

2. On the ribbon, click the **FILE** tab, and then in the navigation bar, click **Save As**. The Save As screen opens in Backstage view.

3. Click the **Save As** button. The Save As dialog box opens.

4. Navigate to the location where you are saving your files, replace the text in the File name box with **TaxpayerInfo**, and then click the **Save** button.

   **Trouble?** If the database opened in Protected View, click the Enable Content button on the yellow bar below the ribbon.

5. In the Navigation Pane, double-click the **Taxpayers** table. The table that opens contains names, addresses, and phone numbers of taxpayers in Parkerville. It also contains a field that indicates whether the taxpayers donated to the Green Initiative, and another field listing the amount if they made a donation.

**TIP**

To start the mail merge from Access, click the EXTERNAL DATA tab on the ribbon. In the Export group, click the More button, and then click Merge it with Microsoft Office Word.

Now you will identify the Taxpayers table as the data source for the mail merge document.

### To select the Access table as the data source:

1. Switch back to the Word document. The MAILINGS tab is active on the ribbon.

2. In the Start Mail Merge group, click the **Select Recipients** button, and then click **Use an Existing List**. The Select Data Source dialog box opens, displaying a list of possible data sources. You need to find the list of taxpayer names and addresses, which is located in the Taxpayers table in the TaxpayerInfo database.

3. Navigate to the location where you are saving your files, click **TaxpayerInfo**, and then click the **Open** button. The Select Table dialog box opens, listing all of the tables and queries in the selected database—in this case, one table and one query. (If the database contained only one table, the Select Table dialog box would not open; instead, the Mail Merge Recipients dialog box would open immediately after you selected the database.) You need to choose a table or query in the selected database as the data source.

4. Click the **Taxpayers** table to select it, and then click the **OK** button. Several buttons, including the Edit Recipient List button, are now available on the MAILINGS tab.

5. In the Start Mail Merge group, click the **Edit Recipient List** button. The Mail Merge Recipients dialog box opens. See Figure 18.

**Figure 18**    Mail Merge Recipients dialog box

to exclude an individual recipient from the merge, click to deselect the recipient's check box

click to open the Sort Records tab in the Filter and Sort dialog box

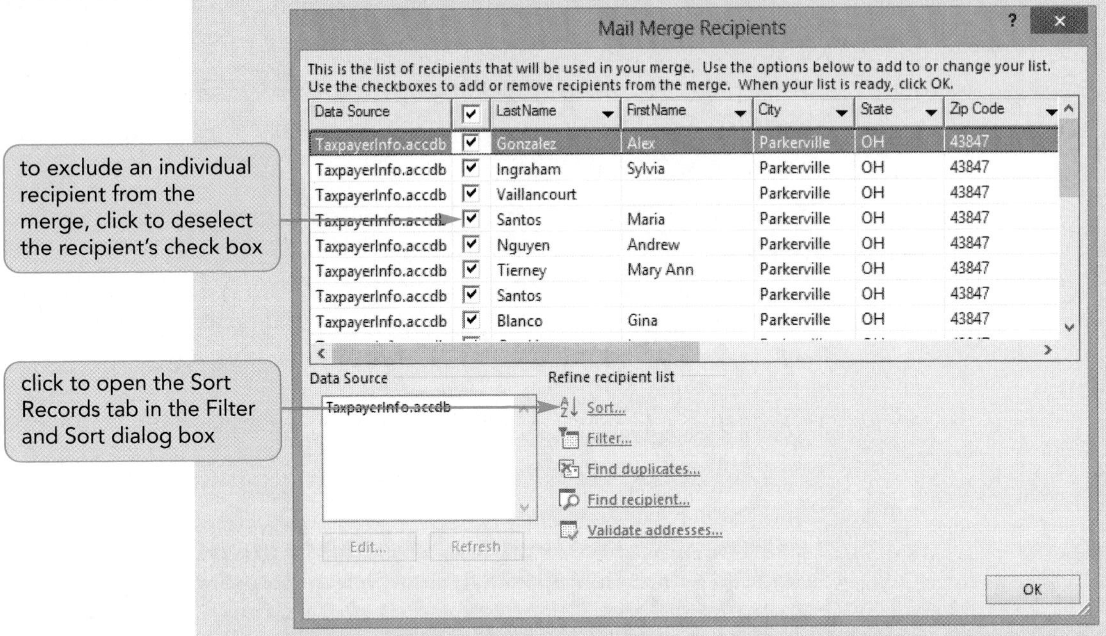

You can use the Mail Merge Recipients dialog box to select the people who will receive the letter. You can sort this list by any field by clicking a column heading. You can also narrow the list by deselecting records individually, or filtering the list to include only records that meet specific criteria. Ken wants to sort the list alphabetically by last name, and then by first name. To sort by two fields, you need to open the Filter and Sort dialog box.

6. In the Refine recipient list section, click the **Sort** link. The Filter and Sort dialog box opens with the Sort Records tab selected. See Figure 19.

**Figure 19**    Sort Records tab in the Filter and Sort dialog box

click to choose the first field on which to sort

click to choose the second field on which to sort

options for changing the sort order

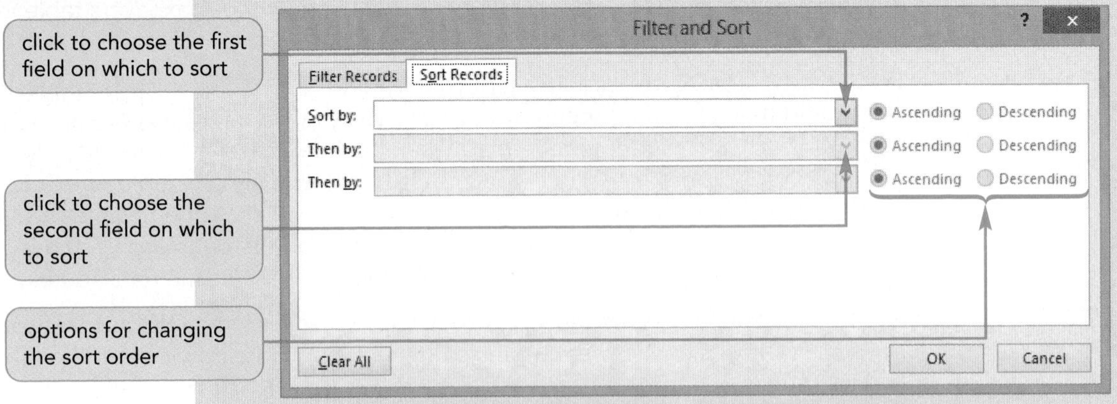

7. Click the **Sort by** arrow, and then click **LastName**. To the right of the Sort by box, the Ascending option button is selected. This means that the list will be sorted in alphabetical order.

8. Click the first **Then by** arrow, and then click **FirstName**. If there are taxpayers with the same last name, those names will be sorted in alphabetical order by the first name.

**9.** Click the **OK** button. The names in the Mail Merge Recipients dialog box are now sorted first by last name and then by first name.

**10.** In the Mail Merge Recipients dialog box, click the **OK** button.

## Inserting the Merge Fields

The variable information in the letter is the inside address and the name in the salutation, so you'll insert merge fields to tell Word what information to pull from the data source. You can use the Insert Merge Field button in the Write & Insert Fields group on the MAILINGS tab to insert individual fields from the data source.

**To insert individual merge fields in the letter:**

**1.** Click at the end of the line containing the date in the letter, and then press the **Enter** key.

**2.** In the Write & Insert Fields group, click the **Insert Merge Field button arrow**. A menu opens listing all of the fields in the data source. See Figure 20.

**Figure 20**   Insert Merge Field menu

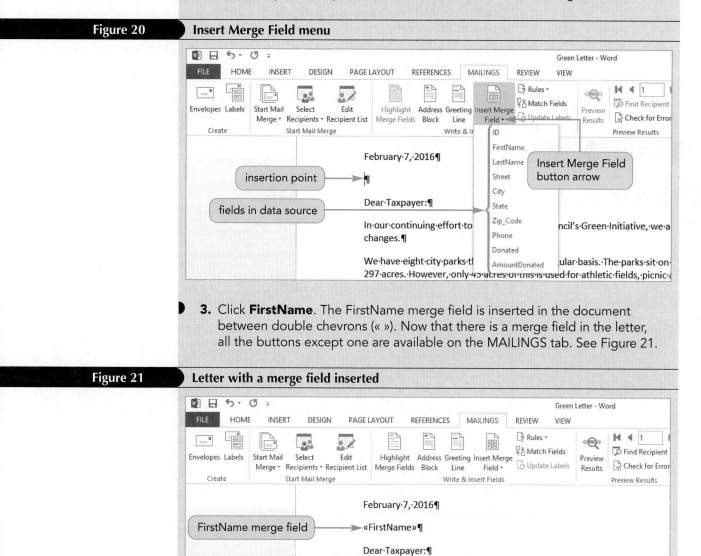

**3.** Click **FirstName**. The FirstName merge field is inserted in the document between double chevrons (« »). Now that there is a merge field in the letter, all the buttons except one are available on the MAILINGS tab. See Figure 21.

**Figure 21**   Letter with a merge field inserted

The first line of the inside address includes the first and last names of the recipient. So you need to type a space and then insert the LastName merge field.

▶  **4.** Press the **spacebar**.

▶  **5.** In the Write & Insert Fields group, click the **Insert Merge Field button arrow**, and then click **LastName**. The FirstName and LastName merge fields, separated by a space, appear in the document.

You could continue adding the rest of the merge fields, remembering to add spaces between words as needed and the comma after the City merge field. However, because an inside address is a common set of fields in a mail merge, a combined merge field—the Address Block merge field—is provided to make it easier for you. First you will delete the merge fields you just added, and then insert the Address Block merge field.

### To insert the Address Block merge field in the main document:

▶  **1.** If necessary, click after the chevrons following the LastName merge field, and then press the **Backspace** key as many times as needed to delete the LastName and FirstName merge fields. The insertion point is in the blank paragraph after the date.

▶  **2.** In the Write & Insert Fields group, click the **Address Block** button. The Insert Address Block dialog box opens, as shown in Figure 22. You use this dialog box to choose the format of the recipient's name, and to specify whether to include the company name and country in the address. The Preview box shows how the address block will look with data from your recipient list.

| Figure 22 | Insert Address Block dialog box |

Notice that the street is missing from the preview. Word tries to match fields in a recipient list with predetermined fields in the Address Block, but sometimes you need to explicitly identify a field. In this case, Word did not find a match for the Address fields.

▶  **3.** In the Correct Problems section of the dialog box, click the **Match Fields** button. The Match Fields dialog box opens, as shown in Figure 23.

**Figure 23**    Match Fields dialog box

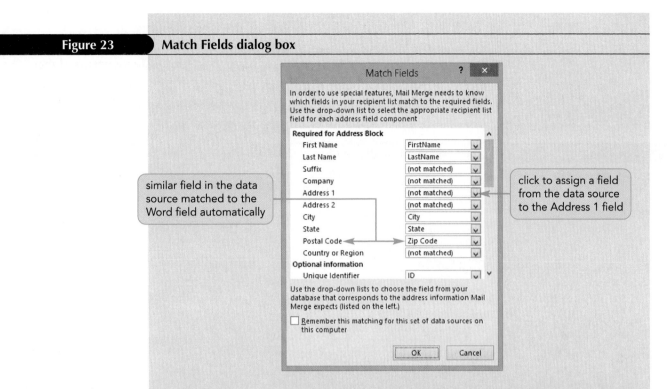

similar field in the data source matched to the Word field automatically

click to assign a field from the data source to the Address 1 field

On the left are the fields Word expects in the Address Block. On the right are the fields in the data source. You want Word to match the Address 1 field in the Address Block with the Street field in the Access table.

4. Click the **Address 1** arrow, and then click **Street**.

5. Click the **OK** button. A dialog box opens warning that if you match a field in your data source with the built-in Unique Identifier field, that field might be available to people who read your document.

The Unique Identifier field picks up the primary key field in the table. If the primary key field in your Access database contained confidential data such as Social Security numbers, you would click the No button, change the Unique Identifier field to "(not matched)," and then close the Match Fields dialog box. However, you are not using the ID field in your letter, so it's fine to click the Yes button.

6. Click the **Yes** button. The Preview area in the Insert Address Block dialog box now displays the street as part of the address.

7. Click the **OK** button to close the Insert Address Block dialog box. The Address block merge field appears in the main document.

   **Trouble?** If the Address block merge field appears between curly braces and includes additional text, such as {ADDRESSBLOCK \f}, Word is displaying field codes. Click the FILE tab, click Options in the navigation bar to open the Word Options dialog box, click Advanced in the navigation bar, scroll down the list on the right, and then, in the Show document content section, click the Show field codes instead of their values check box to deselect it.

Next, you need to insert a greeting line to personalize the salutation. You could use the individual merge fields, but the Greeting Line merge field allows you to insert the entire salutation at once, and it provides a greeting when the first or last name is missing in the data source. You'll use the Greeting Line merge field to add the salutation to appear in the format "Dear John Smith:".

**To insert the Greeting Line merge field:**

1. In the line below the Address Block merge field, delete **Taxpayer:**, and then press the **spacebar**, if necessary, to add a space after the word "Dear."

2. In the Write & Insert Fields group, click the **Greeting Line** button. The Insert Greeting Line dialog box opens, as shown in Figure 24.

**Figure 24** **Insert Greeting Line dialog box**

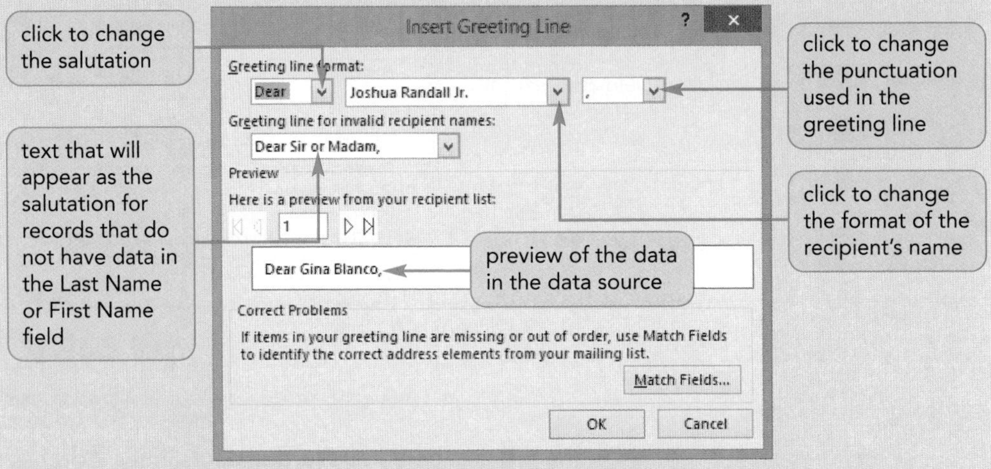

click to change the salutation

Greeting line format:

click to change the punctuation used in the greeting line

text that will appear as the salutation for records that do not have data in the Last Name or First Name field

click to change the format of the recipient's name

preview of the data in the data source

The Greeting line format and the preview at the bottom of the dialog box show that Word will insert "Dear" as the salutation followed by the recipient's full name, and then a comma. You will keep the default format for the name, but the word "Dear" is already in the greeting line, so you will delete it from the Greeting line format in this dialog box. You also need to change the comma after the name to a colon.

3. In the Greeting line format section, click the first arrow (next to "Dear"), and then click **(none)**.

4. In the Greeting line format section, click the third arrow (next to the comma), and then click **:** (the colon). In the Greeting line for invalid recipient names box, the default is "Dear Sir or Madam." The other choice in the list is "To Whom It May Concern." The text in this box will appear in place of the recipient's name if this information is missing in the recipient list. If the name is missing, Kenneth wants the salutation to be "Dear Taxpayer:".

5. In the **Greeting line for invalid recipient names** box, delete the text "Dear Sir or Madam," and then type **Taxpayer:** (including the colon) in the box.

6. Click the **OK** button. Word inserts the Greeting Line merge field in the main document.

## Performing the Mail Merge

With the starting document and merge fields in place, you're ready to perform the mail merge. First, you will preview the merged letter to make sure the merged documents look the way you expect.

## To preview the merged document:

▶ **1.** In the Preview Results group, click the **Preview Results** button, and then examine the merged fields in the document. The first merged form letter appears with Gino Blanco as the first recipient. See Figure 25.

| Figure 25 | Preview of mail merge |

extra space between lines in inside address

Preview Results button

Go to Record box indicates first letter is displayed

February·7,·2016¶

Gina·Blanco¶

201·County·Line·Rd.¶

Parkerville,·OH·43847¶

Dear·Gina·Blanco:¶

Notice that each line in the inside address has space after it. This is not standard formatting for an inside address in a letter. To fix this, you'll turn off the preview and then format the merge field.

▶ **2.** In the Preview Results group, click the **Preview Results** button. The preview turns off and you see the merge fields again.

▶ **3.** Click the **HOME** tab, and then click anywhere in the line containing the Address Block merge field.

▶ **4.** In the Paragraph group, click the **Line and Paragraph Spacing** button $\downarrow\equiv$ ▾, and then click **Remove Space After Paragraph**. The space is removed after the current paragraph. Now you need a blank line between the last line in the inside address and the salutation.

▶ **5.** Move the insertion point to the end of the Address Block line, and then press the **Enter** key. A single blank line (a paragraph with no space after it) is added between the last line of the inside address and the salutation.

▶ **6.** Click the **MAILINGS** tab, and then in the Preview Results group, click the **Preview Results** button. Gina Blanco's information is now properly formatted in the letter.

▶ **7.** In the Preview Results group, click the **Next Record** button ▶ to preview the next recipient's letter. The letter to Sonia Burke appears.

▶ **8.** In the Preview Results group, click in the **Go to Record** box, type **15**, and then press the **Enter** key. The 15th letter appears. In the inside address, there is no first name for this person because there is no entry in the FirstName field in the Access database for this record. This is also why the salutation in this letter is "Dear Taxpayer:".

▶ **9.** In the Preview Results group, click the **Preview Results** button to turn the preview off.

▶ **10.** Save your changes to the main document with the merge fields.

You are ready to complete the mail merge. To do this, you can print the letters, send the letters as email messages, or create a new document that contains a letter addressed to each recipient on a separate page. Ken wants the merged results saved in a new document. The new document you create with the merge results will contain one letter for each contact in the data source. Each letter will be identical except for the merge fields, which will contain the individual names and addresses.

### To complete the mail merge:

▶ **1.** In the Finish group, click the **Finish & Merge** button. A menu opens listing the three ways you can complete the merge. Ken wants you to create a copy of the merged documents.

▶ **2.** Click **Edit Individual Documents**. The Merge to New Document dialog box opens.

▶ **3.** Click the **All** option button, if necessary, and then click the **OK** button. Word opens a new document with the temporary name "Letters" followed by a number. This document contains one letter for each person in the Taxpayers table in the TaxpayerInfo database.

▶ **4.** Scroll through the document to see the merged addresses and salutations. Word replaced each merge field with the appropriate Access data. Notice that the merged document contains 40 pages: Each letter is two pages long, and there are 20 letters in all.

▶ **5.** On the Quick Access Toolbar, click the **Save** button 🖫 to open the Save As dialog box.

▶ **6.** Save the document as **Merged Letters** in the location where you are saving your files, and then close the document. You return to the main document.

▶ **7.** Close the Green Letter document, saving changes if prompted.

**TIP**

If you need to customize any letters, such as deleting the extra space before the last name in the inside addresses where there is no first name, you could do this now.

Ken plans to review the merged letters before he prints and mails them.

**INSIGHT**

### Performing a Mail Merge with an Email Message

You can make the most of your email correspondence by merging your Outlook Contacts with an email message. To do this, you click the Start Mail Merge button, and then click E-mail Messages. To select the recipients, click the Select Recipients button, and then click Select from Outlook Contacts. Using the Mail Merge Recipients dialog box, you can filter the contacts to include only those people to whom you want to send your message. After you compose your message, click the Finish & Merge button, and then click Send E-mail Messages. This opens the Merge to E-mail dialog box in which you can type the subject for your email message. After you click the OK button, Word creates new email messages addressed to each person in your recipients list and places them in your Outlook Outbox, where they are ready to send the next time you send email messages.

# Exporting Query Results from Access to Excel

Access is not included with all versions of Microsoft Office. If you have information in an Access database that you need to share with others who do not have Access installed on their computers, you can export a table or query datasheet to an Excel worksheet or a Word table. When you do this, a new Excel workbook or Word document is automatically created and saved.

**REFERENCE**

### Exporting the Results of an Access Query to Excel or Word

- In the Navigation Pane, click the query to be exported.
- Click the EXTERNAL DATA tab on the ribbon.
- In the Export group, click the Excel button or the More button, and then click Word.
- In the Export – Excel Spreadsheet or Export – RTF File dialog box, click the Browse button to select the folder in which you want to save the file you're exporting, if necessary.
- In the File Name box, enter the name of the Excel or Word file, and then click Save.
- Click the "Open the destination file after the export operation is complete" check box to select it if you want the file to open automatically after it is exported.
- Click the OK button.
- In the Export – Excel Spreadsheet or the Export – RTF File dialog box, click the Close button.

An intern in the mayor's office uses a computer that does not have Access installed. He needs to distribute the list of Green Initiative donors to several other people in the mayor's office. You need to export the list of people who donated to the Green Initiative to an Excel worksheet so that the intern can open the list.

### To export the results of a query to an Excel worksheet:

1. On the taskbar, click the **Access** button, if necessary. The TaxpayerInfo database appears with the Taxpayers table open.

2. In the Navigation Pane, double-click the **Donors** query to open it in Datasheet view. This query contains the list of taxpayers from the Taxpayers table who donated to the Green Initiative.

3. On the ribbon, click the **EXTERNAL DATA** tab.

4. In the Export group, click the **Excel** button. The Export – Excel Spreadsheet dialog box opens. The suggested filename "Donors.xlsx" appears after the default path. The file extension .xlsx indicates that the file will be an Excel file. See Figure 26.

**TIP**

To export a query to a Word document, click the More button in the Export group on the EXERNAL DATA tab, and then click Word.

| Figure 26 | Export – Excel Spreadsheet dialog box |
|-----------|----------------------------------------|

**Export - Excel Spreadsheet**    ?    ✕

Select the destination for the data you want to export

Specify the destination file name and format.

*path and filename of source file appear here*

File name:    C:\Users\UserName\Documents\Donors.xlsx    Browse...

File format:    Excel Workbook (*.xlsx)    ⌄

*click to change the folder where the exported file will be stored*

*select to export the data with the same formatting and layout as the Access query*

Specify export options.

☐ **Export data with formatting and layout.**
Select this option to preserve most formatting and layout information when exporting a table, query, form, or report.

*select to open the exported file automatically*

☐ Open the destination file after the export operation is complete.
Select this option to view the results of the export operation. This option is available only when you export formatted data.

☐ Export only the selected records.
Select this option to export only the selected records. This option is only available when you export formatted data and have records selected.

OK    Cancel

**Trouble?** If you can't see the suggested filename and the file extension because the path is too long, click anywhere in the File name box, and then press and hold the → key until the insertion point moves to the end of the filename.

You need to change the path in the File name box to the path of the folder where you are storing your files.

▶ **5.** Click the **Browse** button. The File Save dialog box opens with the suggested filename in the File name box.

▶ **6.** Navigate to the location where you are storing your files, and then click the **Save** button. The new path and filename appear in the File name box in the Export – Excel Spreadsheet dialog box.

▶ **7.** Under Specify export options, click the **Export data with formatting and layout** check box. With this check box selected, the formatting and layout of the data in the query datasheet will be preserved.

▶ **8.** Click the **Open the destination file after the export operation is complete** check box to select it. Now the new file will open automatically after you close this dialog box.

▶ **9.** Click the **OK** button. Access converts the query results into an Excel worksheet stored in an Excel workbook named Donors, and opens the new workbook.

▶ **10.** Close the Donors workbook.

▶ **11.** On the taskbar, click the **Access** button 🅰. In the Export – Excel Spreadsheet dialog box, the Save Export Steps screen is displayed. You don't need to save the sequence of steps, so you will simply close this dialog box.

▶ **12.** In the dialog box, click the **Close** button.

## Teamwork: Sharing Information

Most organizations rely heavily on teams to complete work tasks, and, consequently, team members rely on each other to complete their assigned projects successfully. For example, you might be responsible for providing data for others to analyze, or for collecting other team members' data and creating a report. When a team works together to complete a project, it is vital that each member of the team complete his or her piece of the project. If even one person fails to do this, the entire project is affected. Learning the different roles team members play, how they complement each other for efficient task completion, and how to lead and motivate a team toward goal achievement can mean the difference between professional success and failure. As you work in different Microsoft Office programs, keep in mind that you might need to share your work with others on your team at school or in a professional environment. Take the time to make sure your work is complete and ready to be shared with others, and that it can be imported or exported, as needed, for use in other programs.

In this session, you merged data in an Access table with a Word document to create a form letter addressed individually to different people. Then you exported the results of a query from Access to a worksheet in a new Excel workbook. In the next session, you will import an outline that Ken created in Word into a PowerPoint presentation to create new slides. Then you will copy an Access query to a slide in the presentation and embed an Excel worksheet in a slide.

## Session 2 Quick Check

1. What is a form letter?
2. What is a data source?
3. What types of files can be a data source?
4. What are merge fields?
5. What happens to the merge fields in a main document when you complete the merge?
6. How can you provide Access data to someone who does not have Access installed on his or her computer?

# Session 3 Visual Overview:

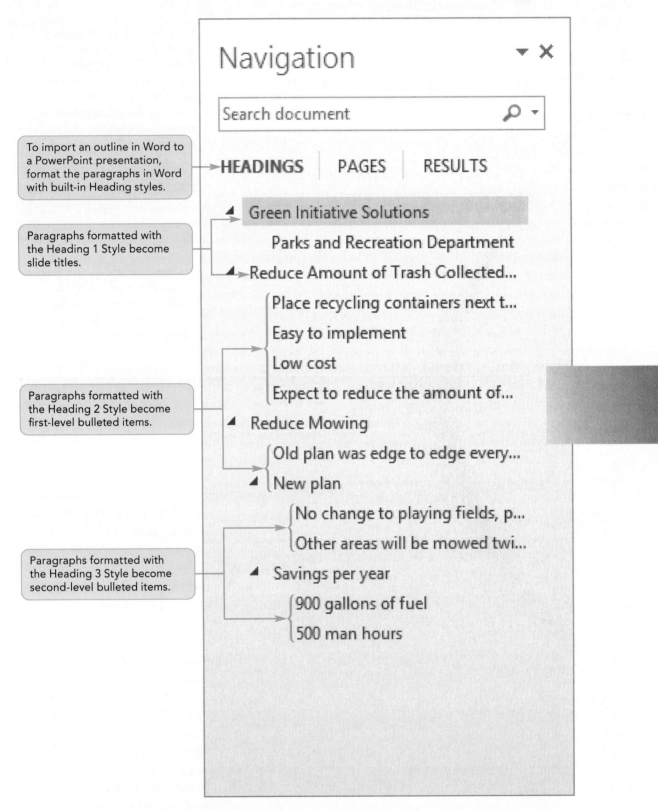

To import an outline in Word to a PowerPoint presentation, format the paragraphs in Word with built-in Heading styles.

Paragraphs formatted with the Heading 1 Style become slide titles.

Paragraphs formatted with the Heading 2 Style become first-level bulleted items.

Paragraphs formatted with the Heading 3 Style become second-level bulleted items.

**An Outline in the Navigation Pane in Word**

# Importing an Outline to PowerPoint

**Green Initiative Solutions**

Parks and Recreation Department

*1*

> New slides and slide titles are created from paragraphs formatted with the Heading 1 style.

**Reduce Amount of Trash Collected at Parks**

Place recycling containers next to every trash barrel

Easy to implement

Low cost

Expect to reduce the amount of non-recyclable trash by 60%

*2*

> First-level bulleted items are created from paragraphs formatted with the Heading 2 style.

**Reduce Mowing**

Old plan was edge to edge every other week

New plan
- No change to playing fields, paths, and picnic areas
- Other areas will be mowed twice a year or as needed

Savings per year
- 900 gallons of fuel
- 500 man hours

*3*

> Second-level bulleted items are created from paragraphs formatted with the Heading 3 style.

## PowerPoint Slides Created from the Word Outline

# Creating PowerPoint Slides from a Word Outline

You need to create the PowerPoint file for Ken to use in his presentation to the city council. He created an outline in Word by using the built-in heading styles; you'll use this Word document to create the PowerPoint slides for Ken. First, you'll examine Ken's outline.

**To examine Ken's outline in Word:**

▶ **1.** If you took a break after the previous session, make sure that Word is open, the **Green Data** workbook is open in Excel, and the **TaxpayerInfo** database is open in Access.

▶ **2.** In Word, open the document **Outline**, which is located in the Integration ▶ Tutorial folder included with your Data Files.

▶ **3.** If the Navigation pane is not open, click the **VIEW** tab on the ribbon, and then in the Show group, click the **Navigation Pane** check box. The document consists only of text formatted with the Heading 1, Heading 2, or Heading 3 styles. See Figure 27.

| Figure 27 | Outline document |
|---|---|

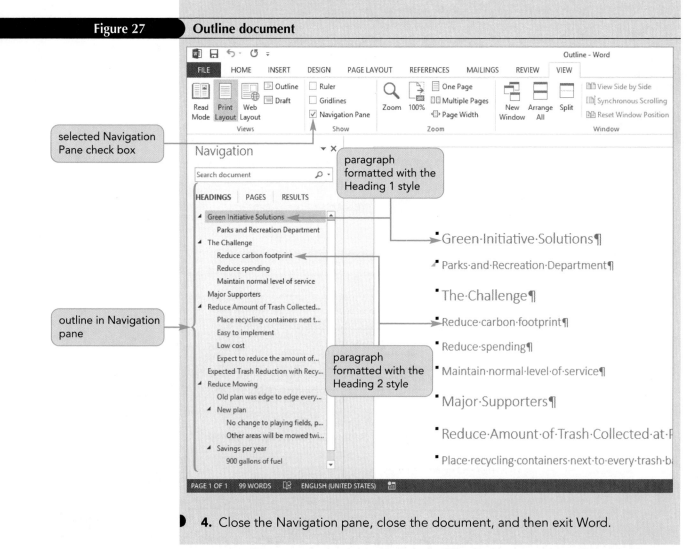

**4.** Close the Navigation pane, close the document, and then exit Word.

To create a PowerPoint presentation from a Word outline, you import it into an existing presentation. To do this, you use the Slides from Outline command on the New Slide button menu.

### To create new PowerPoint slides from the Word outline:

▶ 1. Start PowerPoint, open the presentation **Green**, which is located in the Integration ▸ Tutorial folder included with your Data Files, and then save the presentation as **Green Presentation** in the location where you are saving your files.

▶ 2. On the HOME tab, in the Slides group, click the **New Slide button arrow**, and then click **Slides from Outline**. The Insert Outline dialog box opens.

▶ 3. Navigate to the Integration ▸ Tutorial folder included with your Data Files, click **Outline**, and then click the **Insert** button. The text of the Word outline is inserted to create Slides 2 through 7. Slide 2 contains the same text as the title slide. See Figure 28.

| Figure 28 | Slides inserted from the Word outline |
|---|---|

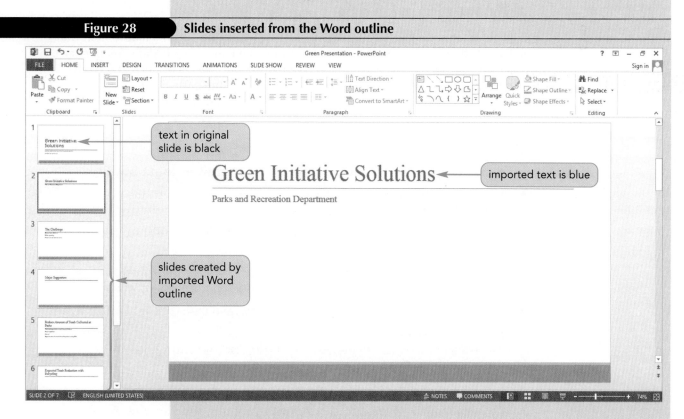

▶ 4. In the Slides tab, right-click the **Slide 2** thumbnail (the slide with the blue "Green Initiative Solutions" title), and then click **Delete Slide**. The slide is deleted.

▶ 5. Display each slide in the Slide pane to see how the Word outline was converted into PowerPoint slides.

The title slide, which was not created from the imported outline, has black text. The text on the slides created from the imported outline is blue. This is because the document containing the outline has the Office theme with the first variant applied. However, the presentation uses the Retrospect theme with the second variant applied. You need to reset the slides, which will reset the position, size, and formatting of the slide placeholders to match the settings in the slide masters.

**To reset the slides to the presentation theme:**

▶ **1.** In the Slides tab, click the **Slide 2** thumbnail ("The Challenge"), press and hold the **Shift** key, and then click the **Slide 6** thumbnail ("Reduce Mowing").

▶ **2.** In the Slides group, click the **Reset** button. The color and font of the text change to the formatting used in the Retrospect theme with the second variant. Notice that this theme does not include bullet symbols for the first-level items in the bulleted lists.

▶ **3.** Save your changes to the presentation.

Next, you need to include a list of donors who gave at least $500. You will add this list by creating an Access query and then copying the results to a slide.

# Copying Access Query Results into a PowerPoint Slide

To thank donors who gave donations of at least $500 to the Green Initiative, Ken wants to include their names and the amounts they donated on Slide 3 ("Major Supporters"). You cannot export Access data directly to a PowerPoint slide as you can to a Word document or an Excel workbook, so you need to copy and paste the data.

First, you need to create a query in the database to extract the name and donation amount for each person who donated at least $500.

**To create a query to list people who donated at least $500:**

▶ **1.** Switch to the TaxpayerInfo database in Access, and then on the ribbon, click the **CREATE** tab.

▶ **2.** In the Queries group, click the **Query Wizard** button. The New Query dialog box opens with Simple Query Wizard selected.

▶ **3.** Click the **OK** button. The dialog box showing the first step in the wizard appears. You want to create this query based on the Taxpayers table.

▶ **4.** If necessary, click the **Tables/Queries** arrow, and then click **Table: Taxpayers**.

▶ **5.** In the Available Fields list, click **FirstName**, and then click the  > button. FirstName is moved to the Selected Fields list, and LastName is selected in the Available Fields list.

▶ **6.** Click the  > button. LastName is moved to the Selected Fields list.

▶ **7.** In the Available Fields list, click **AmountDonated**, and then click the  > button. AmountDonated is added to the Selected Fields list.

▶ **8.** Click the **Next** button twice. The screen in the wizard in which you can name the query appears.

▶ **9.** Delete the text in the **What title do you want for your query?** box, type **BigDonors**, and then click the **Finish** button. The query results are displayed in Datasheet view.

The query results list all of the donors, but Ken wants the results to display only those donors who donated $500 or more. You need to modify the query in Design view to add this condition. Ken also wants the list to be sorted in order from highest to lowest amount, and for the people who gave the same amount to be listed alphabetically.

### To modify the query:

▶ **1.** Click the **HOME** tab, and then in the Views group, click the **View** button. The query is displayed in Design view.

▶ **2.** In the design grid, click in the **AmountDonated Criteria** box, and then type **>=500**. Now you need to specify the primary sort field.

▶ **3.** Click the right side of the **AmountDonated Sort** box to display the arrow and the sort options, and then click **Descending**. Compare your screen to Figure 29. Now you need to run the modified query.

| Figure 29 | Modified BigDonors query |
|---|---|

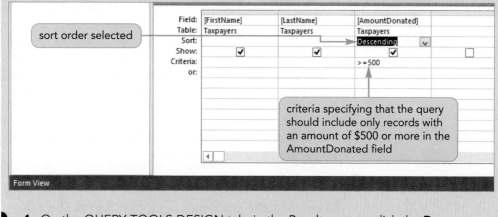

▶ **4.** On the QUERY TOOLS DESIGN tab, in the Results group, click the **Run** button. The modified query lists the three people who donated $500 or more, sorted in descending order by Amount Donated.

▶ **5.** Save the query.

Now you need to copy the query results to Slide 3 in the Green Presentation file.

### To copy the query results to Slide 3:

▶ **1.** In the BigDonors datasheet, click the **datasheet selector**. All of the data in the BigDonors datasheet is selected.

▶ **2.** On the HOME tab, in the Clipboard group, click the **Copy** button. The selected data is copied to the Clipboard.

▶ **3.** Switch to the **Green Presentation** file, and then display **Slide 3** ("Major Supporters") in the Slide pane.

▶ **4.** In the content placeholder, click the placeholder text to position the insertion point.

▶ **5.** In the Clipboard group, click the **Paste button arrow**, and then click the **Keep Text Only** button. The data you copied from the query is pasted as a bulleted item on the slide. (Remember that in the Retrospect theme, the first-level bulleted items do not have bullet symbols.) See Figure 30.

**Figure 30**    **Access data pasted on Slide 3 as plain text**

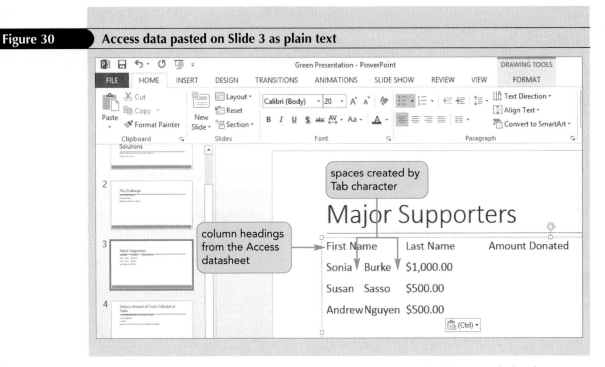

Notice that the column headings from the query were copied along with the data. They are not needed on Slide 3, so you will delete them.

Also, when you pasted the Access data as text, PowerPoint inserted a tab character between each column. You need to replace the tab character between the first names and the last names with a space. Also, the amounts donated should appear as subitems under each name.

### To modify the pasted query results on Slide 3:

**1.** Delete the first item in the list (the line containing the column headings from the Access datasheet). Now you will fix the spacing between the words in each item.

**Trouble?** If there is still a blank line above the line containing Sonia Burke's name, click in the blank line, and then press the Delete key.

**2.** In the first item, click to the left of Burke, press the **Backspace** key to delete the Tab character, and then press the **spacebar**.

**3.** In the first item, click to the left of $1,000.00, press the **Enter** key so that $1,000.00 becomes a new item in the list, and then press the **Tab** key to make it a subitem under Sonia Burke.

**4.** Delete the Tab character between the first and last names in the other two first-level items in the list, and then change the donation amounts to subitems under each name.

**Trouble?** If you are having difficulty positioning the insertion point immediately to the left of "Nguyen," click between "Andrew" and "Nguyen," and then press the ← key or the → key to position the insertion point precisely.

**5.** Click the text box border to select the entire text box, and then click the **Increase Font Size** button A three times to increase the size of the text in the list so that the first-level items are 32 points and the second-level items are 28 points. See Figure 31.

**Figure 31**    Formatted data from the Access query on Slide 3

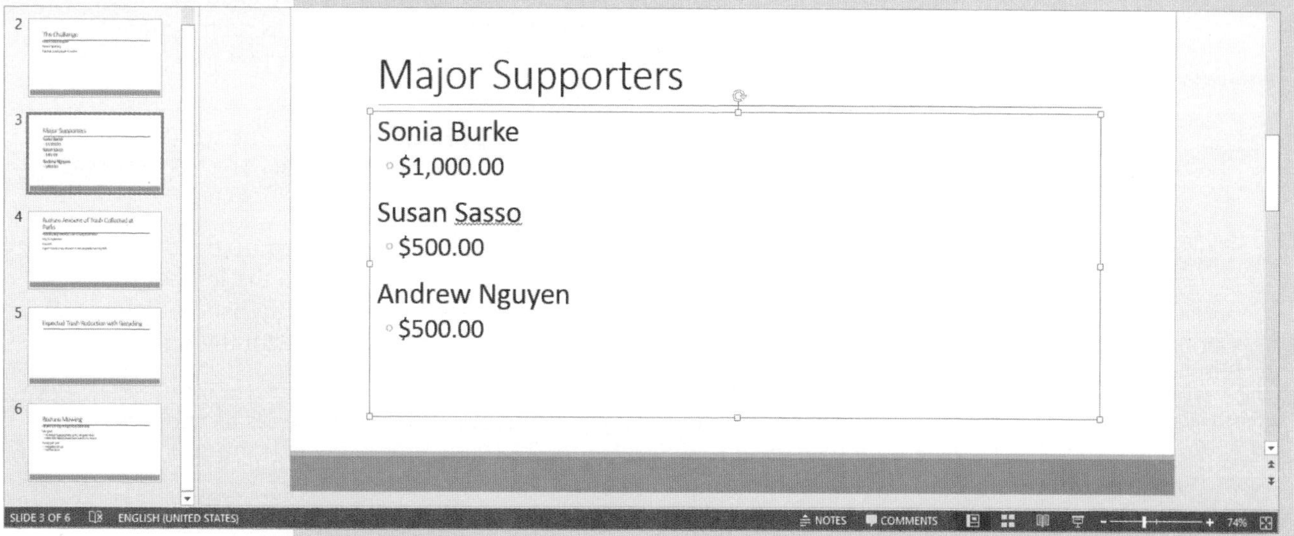

6. Save your changes.

Now that you have inserted the Access query results into Slide 3, you can complete the slide presentation by embedding Excel data on Slide 5.

## Embedding an Excel Table in a PowerPoint Presentation

On Slide 5, Ken wants to include the Excel data that lists the number of acres currently mowed and the proposed number of acres to mow. He also wants to add one more row that displays the total for each of those numbers, as well as the percentage difference between the total number of acres mowed now and the total number of acres that will be mowed under the new plan.

When Excel worksheet data is on the Clipboard, the Paste Options menu in PowerPoint includes options to paste the data as a table formatted with either the source or destination theme styles; embed the workbook; paste the contents of the Clipboard as a picture; or paste the data as unformatted text. Because Ken wants to use Excel functions to modify the worksheet, he wants the Excel data embedded instead of pasting it as a table. Be aware that when you embed Excel worksheet data, you actually embed a copy of the entire workbook. Depending on the size of the workbook, this can significantly increase the size of the presentation file.

When you double-click an Excel worksheet that is embedded on a slide, the window changes so that the ribbon contains Excel tabs and commands.

### To embed the Excel table on Slide 5:

1. Switch to the **Green Data** workbook in Excel, select the range **A4:D12** on the Mowing sheet, and then copy the selected data to the Clipboard.

2. Switch back to the **Green Presentation** PowerPoint file, display **Slide 5** ("Expected Trash Reduction with Recycling") in the Slide pane, and then change the layout to the **Title Only** layout.

3. On the HOME tab, in the Clipboard group, click the **Paste button arrow**. When you copy data in a worksheet, you can paste it on a slide as a table using the destination or source styles (the first two options on the menu), embed the worksheet, paste it as a picture, or paste it as text that is not in a table. You will embed the worksheet.

4. On the Paste Options menu, click the **Embed** button 🔲. The worksheet is embedded in the presentation. Notice that the DRAWING TOOLS FORMAT tab appears on the ribbon.

Make sure you drag the corner sizing handles and not the side sizing handles; otherwise, you will only change the size of the columns in the embedded worksheet.

5. Drag the lower-left corner sizing handle of the embedded object down and to the left until the left edge of the object is aligned with the left edge of the title text box, and then drag the bottom-right corner sizing handle down and to the right until the right edge of the object is aligned with the right edge of the title text box.

The size of the text in the embedded object table increases as you drag the corner sizing handles. See Figure 32.

**Figure 32**    **Resized embedded object on Slide 5**

Expected Trash Reduction with Recycling

| | Acres Mowed | Proposed Acres Mowed | Percentage Saved |
|---|---|---|---|
| Lincoln Nature and Community Park | 90 | 4 | 96% |
| Lionel Davich Memorial Park | 80 | 10 | 88% |
| Memorial Field | 24 | 8 | 67% |
| Miller Field | 20 | 3 | 85% |
| Parkerville Stadium | 10 | 3 | 70% |
| Parkerville Heights Park and Nature Trails | 60 | 10 | 83% |
| Parkerville Children's Park | 6 | 3 | 50% |
| Riverside Park | 7 | 4 | 43% |

Now Ken wants you to insert a row in which Excel's AutoSum function adds the total number of acres mowed currently and the total number that will be mowed under the new plan. He also wants you to add a formula to calculate the percentage difference between these two values.

## To modify the embedded Excel worksheet:

1. Double-click the selected table. The table changes to show that it is the Mowing sheet in the embedded Excel workbook, and all of the tabs on the PowerPoint ribbon are replaced with the Excel tabs. See Figure 33.

| Figure 33 | Excel ribbon active in the Green Presentation |

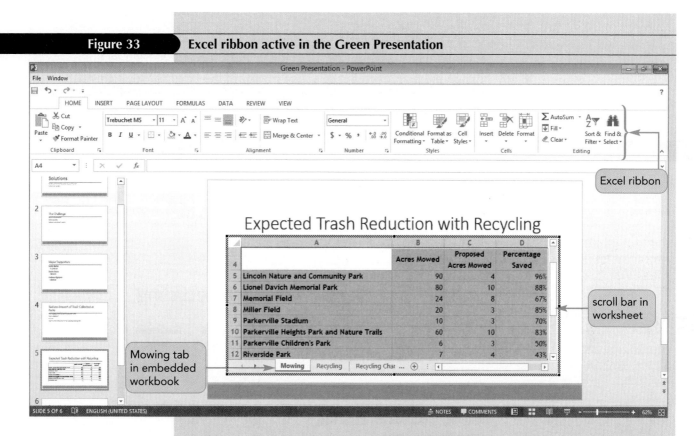

2. In the worksheet, scroll down so that you can see row 13, click in cell **A13**, type **Total**, and then press the → key. Cell B13 is the active cell.

3. On the HOME tab, in the Editing group, click the **AutoSum** button, and then press the **Enter** key. The SUM function is inserted in cell B13 to add the total acres currently mowed.

4. Click cell **C13**, and then insert the **AutoSum** function to calculate the total number of acres that will be mowed under the new plan. Now you need to add a formula to cell D13 to calculate the percentage difference between the total number of acres mowed now and the number of acres that will be mowed under the new plan.

5. Click cell **D13**, type **=(** to begin the formula, click cell **B13**, type **–** (a minus sign), click cell **C13**, type **)/**, click cell **B13**, and then press the **Enter** key. The complete formula in cell D13 is =(B13-C13)/B13. The total percentage difference in the number of acres mowed is displayed in cell D13.

6. Scroll back up so that row 4 is visible again.

7. Drag the bottom-middle sizing handle on the dashed line border down so that it is about two-thirds of the way down the green bar at the bottom of the slide. Now rows 4 through 13 are visible.

8. Click a blank area of the slide.

**Trouble?** If Excel becomes the active window, click the PowerPoint button on the taskbar to display Slide 5 of the Green Presentation file again.

9. Position the pointer on the selection border of the table so that it changes to ⬚, and then drag the object up to approximately center it in the area below the title. See Figure 34.

| Figure 34 | Updated, resized, and repositioned embedded object on Slide 5 |

## Expected Trash Reduction with Recycling

|  | Acres Mowed | Proposed Acres Mowed | Percentage Saved |
|---|---|---|---|
| Lincoln Nature and Community Park | 90 | 4 | 96% |
| Lionel Davich Memorial Park | 80 | 10 | 88% |
| Memorial Field | 24 | 8 | 67% |
| Miller Field | 20 | 3 | 85% |
| Parkerville Stadium | 10 | 3 | 70% |
| Parkerville Heights Park and Nature Trails | 60 | 10 | 83% |
| Parkerville Children's Park | 6 | 3 | 50% |
| Riverside Park | 7 | 4 | 43% |
| Total | 297 | 45 | 85% |

data added to row 13

10. Click a blank area of the slide.

11. On Slide 1, replace Kenneth Novack's name in the subtitle with your name. Save your changes.

12. Close all open programs, saving when prompted.

PROSKILLS

*Decision Making: The Paste Options Button vs. the Paste Special Dialog Box*

The Paste Special dialog box offers additional choices for moving data on the Clipboard to the destination file. For example, if you want to link Excel worksheet data instead of embedding it or pasting it as a table, you must use the Paste Special command; there are no Paste Options for linking Excel worksheet data. The Paste Special dialog box offers additional choices for pasting the data in different formats. For example, if you want to paste an Excel table as text, you can choose to paste it as formatted or unformatted text; and if you want to paste a table or chart as an image, you can choose from a few additional file types. One limitation of the Paste Special dialog box is that you cannot choose to automatically apply the destination file theme and formatting—the source file formatting is carried over with the pasted object. To access the Paste Special dialog box, in the Clipboard group on the HOME tab in the destination program, click the Paste button arrow, and then click Paste Special. In the dialog box, click the Paste option button to display a list of commands to embed or paste the contents of the Clipboard; click the Paste link option button to display a list of commands for linking the contents of the Clipboard to its source program.

How do you know when you need to open the Paste Special dialog box instead of using one of the Paste Options buttons? Start by examining the choices available on the Paste button menu. If none of the buttons yields the results you want, click Paste Special on the menu instead.

The Green Presentation file is complete, and Ken will review it before presenting it to the city council.

## Session 3 Quick Check

REVIEW

1. Describe the slide or slides that PowerPoint would create from a Word outline that has one paragraph formatted with the Heading 1 style, and three paragraphs formatted with the Heading 2 style.
2. After importing a Word outline, how do you change the format of a slide so that it matches the theme used in the presentation?
3. How do you get data in an Access datasheet onto a slide?
4. When you embed Excel worksheet data in a slide, how do you access Excel commands to modify that data?
5. Why would you use the Paste Special dialog box instead of the Paste Options buttons?

ASSESS

### SAM Projects

Put your skills into practice with SAM Projects! SAM Projects for this tutorial can be found online. If you have a SAM account, go to www.cengage.com/sam2013 to download the most recent Project Instructions and Start Files.

PRACTICE

## Review Assignments

**Session 1: Integrating Word and Excel**

**Data Files needed for the Session 1 Review Assignments: Data Updated.xlsx, Request.docx**

Josh Denoff is an intern in the mayor's office. He wrote a follow-up letter for the mayor to send to taxpayers who have not donated to the Green Initiative. Now, Josh needs you to embed an Excel chart in the document to illustrate the cost savings with the new recycling program. He also needs you to link Excel data to the letter that lists the current number of kilowatt hours that ball fields in the parks are lit, and the expected number under a new plan for lighting. He is waiting to hear from the Parks and Recreation Department regarding how many lit ball fields are in each park. To create the letter, complete the following steps:

1. Start Word, open the document **Request**, which is located in the Integration ▸ Review folder included with your Data Files, and then save the document as **Donation Request** in the location where you are saving your files.
2. Start Excel, open the **Data Updated** workbook, which is located in the Integration ▸ Review folder included with your Data Files, and then save the workbook as **Green Updates** in the location where you are saving your files.
3. Copy the chart in the Cost Savings Chart worksheet, and then embed it in the Donation Request document, in the blank paragraph between the second and third paragraphs in the body of the letter, matching the theme and formatting used in the Donation Request document.
4. Change the color palette of the chart to Color 16.
5. Switch to the Green Updates workbook, and then copy the range A4:D13 in the Lights worksheet to the Clipboard.
6. Switch to the Donation Request letter, and then locate the blank paragraph at the top of page 2 or the bottom of page 1 (the exact location changes depending on the printer connected to your computer). Position the insertion point in the blank paragraph, and then link the copied cells using the destination styles.
7. Switch to the Lights worksheet in the Green Updates workbook, and then add the following numbers of lit ball fields to column B, starting with cell B5: **0**, **3**, **2**, **1**, **1**, **0**, **0**, **2**. Save your changes to the workbook, and then close it.
8. Switch back to the Donation Request document, and then update the link.
9. Apply the Grid Table 4 – Accent 1 table style to the table.
10. At the end of the letter, change the name "Paul Winters" to your name. Change the view to Multiple Pages, save the document, and then close it.

**Session 2: Integrating Word, Excel, and Access**

**Data Files needed for the Session 2 Review Assignments: InfoUpdated.accdb, Request Updated.docx**

After the mayor made a few changes, Josh Denoff, the intern in the mayor's office, needs you to merge the letter requesting donations with the list in the database of taxpayers who have not yet donated. In addition, he needs you to export the list from Access to an Excel worksheet so he can send it to the mayor's assistant, who doesn't have Access installed on his computer. To create the documents, complete the following steps:

1. Open the Word document **Request Updated**, which is located in the Integration ▸ Review folder included with your Data Files, and then save it as **Final Letter** in the location where you are saving your files. Replace the name Paul Winters in the closing with your name.

2. Start Access, open the database **InfoUpdated**, which is located in the Integration ▸ Review folder, and then save it as **TaxpayersUpdated** in the location where you are saving your files. Open the NonDonors query and examine the data.

3. Make Final Letter the main document in a mail merge as a letter.

4. Select the NonDonors query in the TaxpayersUpdated database as the recipient list for the mail merge.

5. Sort the recipient list in alphabetical order by the LastName field.

6. Near the top of the first page, replace the text "<Inside Address>" with the Address Block merge field. Match the mail merge Address 1 field with the Street field in the recipient list.

7. In the letter, delete the text "<Salutation>" and replace it with the Greeting Line merge field. Adjust the greeting line options so that the salutation in the letter appears as "Dear Joshua:", and the salutation that appears when the recipient's first name is missing is "Dear Sir or Madam:" (with a colon instead of a comma).

8. Preview the merged letter, fix the spacing in the inside address, and then complete the merge by creating a new document with all of the merged letters in it.

9. Save the new document as **Nondonors Merged** in the location where you are saving your files, and then close the Nondonors Merged document.

10. In the Final Letter main document, turn off the preview of the merged results, and then save your changes. Close the Final Letter document.

11. Switch to the TaxpayersUpdated database, and then export the results of the NonDonors query to an Excel file named **NonDonors List** in the location where you are saving your files. Preserve the formatting and layout, open the file automatically after the export operation is complete, and do not save the export steps. Close the database.

12. Examine the worksheet created in the NonDonors List workbook, and then close the workbook.

**Session 3: Integrating Word, Excel, Access, and PowerPoint**

**Data Files needed for the Session 3 Review Assignments: City.accdb, Concerns.pptx, Concerns Outline.docx, Lighting.xlsx**

Some people have expressed concerns to the mayor about the proposed changes to how parks are lit. The mayor created a presentation outline that he needs imported into a PowerPoint file. Josh Denoff, the intern in the mayor's office, needs you to create the presentation from the outline. To complete the presentation, you need to create a query in an Access database to find the athletic leagues that submit the most requests for field use permits, and then copy the results of this query to a slide in the presentation. You also need to embed the updated Excel data listing the number of kilowatts currently used and the expected reduction in this number. Complete the following steps:

1. Open the Word document **Concerns Outline**, which is located in the Integration ▸ Review folder included with your Data Files. Examine the outline, and then close the document without saving changes.

2. Start PowerPoint, open the presentation **Concerns**, which is located in the Integration ▸ Review folder, and then save it as **Concerns Presentation** in the location where you are saving your files. Add your name as the subtitle.

3. Create new slides by inserting the Concerns Outline document after Slide 1. Reset slides 2–6.

4. Open the Access database **City**, which is located in the Integration ▸ Review folder, and then save it as **CityInfo** in the location where you are saving your files.

5. Open the AthleticLeagues table.

6. Create a new query based on the AthleticLeagues table that lists each league and the number of permits each league requested last year. Name the query **PermitRequests**.

7. Copy the results of the PermitRequests query to the Clipboard, and then paste the contents of the Clipboard as Text Only in the content placeholder on Slide 2 ("Who Uses the Ball Fields?") in the Concerns Presentation file. Delete the column headings, and then replace the large spaces left by Tab characters between each league name and the number of permit requests with a colon and a space.

8. Change the layout of Slide 5 ("Expected Reduction in Kilowatt Hours") to Title Only.

9. Open the Excel workbook **Lighting**, which is located in the Integration ▸ Review folder. The worksheet in this workbook is an updated version of the Lighting worksheet in the Green Updates workbook.

10. Copy the range A4:G13 to the Clipboard, and then embed the Excel data on Slide 5.

11. Make the embedded worksheet active, and then in cell F13, enter the formula =(C13-D13)/C13 to calculate the percentage reduction in the number of kilowatt hours used.

12. In the active embedded worksheet, scroll so you can see rows 4 through 13, and then click a blank area of the slide.

13. Drag the bottom corner sizing handles to resize the worksheet object as large as possible, leaving approximately an inch between the right edge of the object and the right edge of the slide and without overlapping the graphic on the left. Save your changes to the presentation. Close all open programs.

## Case Problem 1

**APPLY**

**Data Files needed for this Case Problem: Report.docx, Team.xlsx**

*Edge Ski Team* Dante Pearson is the program director for the nonprofit Edge Ski Team ski club at Haystack Mountain in Vermont. The team has an enrolled membership of more than 60 families with approximately 90 children ages 7–18 participating in multiple levels of ski racing. The team supports four levels of competitive skiing—Beginners (ages 7–9); Level 1 (ages 10–12); Level 2 (ages 13–16); and Advanced (ages 17–20). The program is controlled by a board of directors and is funded through event fees, club dues, races, and fundraisers such as the annual Ski, Board, and Skate Swap. At the end of each season, Dante writes a short report for the board of directors summarizing the team's racing season. He created the text of the report and wants you to add a chart from an Excel file that shows the total number of skiers at each level, and a table listing the number of skiers who competed at each level in each race. Complete the following steps:

1. Open the Word document **Report**, which is located in the Integration ▸ Case1 folder included with your Data Files, and then save it as **Board Report** in the location where you are saving your files.

2. Open the Excel workbook **Team**, which is located in the Integration ▸ Case1 folder, and then save it as **Team Info** in the location where you are saving your files.

3. Copy the chart on the Demographics Chart worksheet. Switch back to the Board Report document, delete the text "<Pie Chart>" between the two full paragraphs in the body of the report, and then embed the pie chart in that paragraph using the destination theme.

4. Modify the embedded chart so that the legend doesn't show, and change the data labels so they are formatted as callouts. Keep the default chart style.

5. Resize the chart so that it is 3.5 inches high and 6 inches wide, and then use the Center button in the Paragraph group on the HOME tab to center the chart horizontally.

6. Switch to the Team Info workbook, and then copy the range A4:F9 in the Race Qualifiers worksheet. Switch back to the Board Report document, delete the text "<Excel Data>", and then link the copied data in that paragraph using the destination styles.

7. Switch back to the Race Qualifiers worksheet in the Team Info workbook, and then add the number of Advanced skiers for each race as follows, starting in cell E5: **10, 7, 7, 10, 5**. Save your changes, and then close Excel.

8. Switch back to the Board Report document, and then update the link.

9. In the Board Report document, apply the Grid Table 4 – Accent 5 table style to the table.

10. In the last paragraph in the document, type your name. Save the document, and then close Word.

## Case Problem 2

Data Files needed for this Case Problem: Parent.docx, Students.accdb

*Pandion Charter School*   Two years ago, Jennifer Quigley started Pandion Charter School, a small, nonprofit, public charter school for Kindergarten through fourth grade in Hancock, Michigan, that provides highly individualized learning experiences for its students. In the first two years, the school has enrolled 22 students, with the goal of reaching its growth cap of 40 students by its fifth year. City taxes pay for part of the school expenses. For the first three years, the school has access to federal grant money; but after that, it needs to raise money to support the school.

Jennifer needs to send a letter to parents to inform them of the fundraising strategy and to ask for their support. In addition, the school board would like to have three parent representatives on the committee—preferably parents whose children have attended the school since its opening in September 2014. Jennifer wrote the letter and wants you to use mail merge to merge it with an Access table. She also created a query that identifies the parents who have had a child enrolled since the school opened, and wants you to export this data to a Word file. Complete the following steps:

1. Open the Word document **Parent**, which is located in the Integration ▸ Case2 folder included with your Data Files, and then save it as **Parent Letter** in the location where you are saving your files. In the closing, replace Jennifer Quigley with your name.

2. Open the Access database **Students**, which is located in the Integration ▸ Case2 folder, and then save it as **StudentsInfo** in the location where you are saving your files. Open the StudentList table and examine the data. Notice that the First Name and Last Name fields contain the students' first and last names, and the guardians' first and last names are in the Guardian First Name and Guardian Last Name fields.

3. Switch to the Parent Letter document, and then at the top, replace "<Date>" with the current date.

4. Make Parent Letter the main document in the mail merge as a letter.

5. Select the StudentList table in the StudentsInfo database as the recipient list for the mail merge.

⊕ **Explore**  6. There is one guardian with two children enrolled at the school. Edit the recipient list using the Find duplicates command to remove one of the records for that guardian.

7. Near the top of the page, replace the text "<Inside Address>" with the Address Block merge field. Match the mail merge First Name field with the GuardianFirst field in the recipient list, and then match the mail merge Last Name field with the GuardianLast field in the recipient list.

8. In the letter, delete the text "<Salutation>" and replace it with the Greeting Line merge field. Adjust the greeting line options so that the salutation in the letter appears as "Dear Joshua,".

⊕ **Explore**  9. Use a command on the MAILINGS tab to highlight the merge fields.

10. Preview the merged letter, fix the spacing in the inside address, and then complete the merge by creating a new document with all of the merged letters in it.

11. Save the new document as **Merged Parent Letters** in the location where you are saving your files, and then close the Merged Parent Letters document.

12. In the Parent Letter main document, turn off the preview of the merged results, and then save your changes. Close Word.

13. Switch to Access, and then open the RecommendedParents query in Datasheet view. This query lists the first and last names of parents whose children have been enrolled since September 2014.

⊕ **Explore**  14. Export the RecommendedParents query results to a PDF file named **Recommended Parents** in the location where you are saving your files. Automatically open the Recommended Parents file after publishing. Do not save the export steps. (*Hint*: If given a choice, use the Windows 8 Reader app to view the file.)

15. Close the Windows 8 Reader app or whatever program you used to view the PDF file, and then close Access.

## Case Problem 3

**Data Files needed for this Case Problem: Chamber.accdb, Revitalize.pptx, Revitalize Outline.docx, Space.xlsx**

*Wenham Chamber of Commerce* Phyllis Green is the new executive director of the Chamber of Commerce for Wenham, Connecticut, a town with a population of 1800. In the 1950s and 1960s, Main Street was the heart of the community and was filled with local businesses, and townspeople and shop owners greeted each other by name. Today, Main Street is a quiet place with a limited number of stores and meeting places, and there are several empty retail spaces. Phyllis wants to revitalize the Main Street business district as a hub for the community. She has arranged a meeting with the town administrator and local business leaders to discuss her plans. She has created a Word document outlining her plan, and an Excel worksheet listing the locations of currently empty retail space. Phyllis wants you to create a presentation using the Word outline. She also wants you to include data from an Access query and an embedded Excel worksheet. Complete the following steps:

1. Open the PowerPoint presentation **Revitalize**, which is located in the Integration ▶ Case3 folder included with your Data Files, and then save it as **Revitalize Presentation** in the location where you are saving your files. Replace the subtitle on Slide 1 with your name.

2. Create new slides from the **Revitalize Outline** Word document, which is located in the Integration ▶ Case3 folder.

⚙ **Troubleshoot** 3. Scroll through the new slides, delete any duplicate slides, and then fix the formatting of the new slides.

4. Open the Access database **Chamber**, which is located in the Integration ▶ Case3 folder, save it as **ChamberBusinesses** in the location where you are saving your files, and then open the BusinessesInfo table.

5. Create a query named **WestEnd** based on the BusinessesInfo table that lists the names of the businesses that are located on the west end of Main Street. These businesses do not currently have enough parking near them. Sort the query results alphabetically by business name.

6. Copy the query results to the Clipboard. Close Access, saving changes when prompted.

7. In the Revitalize Presentation file, display Slide 8 ("Parking Concerns"), and then paste the data on the Clipboard as Text Only as subitems below the third bulleted item in the content placeholder.

⚙ **Troubleshoot** 8. Evaluate Slide 8 and make adjustments as needed so that the text is more readable. (*Hint*: Consider changing the layout.)

9. Open the Excel file **Space**, which is located in the Integration ▶ Case3 folder.

10. Copy the range A4:D8 to the Clipboard.

11. In the Revitalize Presentation file, create a new Slide 5 using the Title Only layout. Add **Available Retail Space** as the slide title, and then embed the copied Excel data.

12. Edit the embedded worksheet by entering **Total** in cell C9, and then use the SUM function in cell D9 to add the total amount of available square footage downtown. Right-align "Total" in cell C9. Apply the Total cell style to the range C9:D9.

⚙ **Troubleshoot** 13. While the Excel embedded object is still active, adjust the embedded object so that you can see rows 4 through 9 and so that the format of the embedded table matches the theme used in the presentation. (*Hint*: Change the theme of the embedded object from within the embedded program.) Make any other necessary adjustments so that the table looks good on the slide.

14. Save the changes to the presentation. Close PowerPoint and Excel.

## OBJECTIVES

- Learn about Office 365 and Office on Demand
- Determine if you have a Microsoft account
- Understand the SkyDrive app and the SkyDrive desktop application
- Learn how to upload files to and download files from SkyDrive
- Learn how to share files and folders on SkyDrive
- Learn how to access Office Web Apps to create and edit files

# Introduction to Cloud Computing

*Sharing Files and Collaborating with Others Online*

The **cloud** refers to powerful computers called servers connected to the Internet that allow you to store and share files and access data, applications, and resources rather than storing these resources on your own computer. People store files in the cloud so they can access them from any device that has Internet access. Files stored in the cloud are also accessible to others with whom you want to share. **SkyDrive** is free storage provided in the cloud by Microsoft. SkyDrive is like having a personal hard drive in the cloud. You store files on your SkyDrive in folders, similar to the folders on your computer. You can store many types of files on your SkyDrive, including Office documents, photos, and videos. You can also sync files between your SkyDrive and your computer. Software that is stored in the cloud is accessible through a browser from any computer or device that can access the Internet. Examples of software stored in the cloud are **Office Web Apps** (sometimes referred to as **SkyDrive apps** or **Office 365 apps**), which are versions of Microsoft Office applications with basic functionality. Other examples include Google Docs and Zoho.

In this appendix, you will learn about cloud computing. You will also learn how to determine if you have a Microsoft account. Then you will learn about uploading files to and managing files in your storage space in the cloud, and how to use the Office Web Apps and share files with others.

> **Note:** SkyDrive and Office Web Apps are dynamic webpages, and might change over time, including the way they are organized and how commands are performed. The information provided in this appendix, including the information about Office 365 subscriptions, was accurate at the time this book was published.

## STARTING DATA FILES

There are no starting data files for this appendix.

# Overview of Office 365 and Office on Demand

**Office 365** is a subscription to Microsoft cloud services. There are different plans available for home and business users. **Office on Demand** is a benefit of some Office 365 subscription plans. With Office on Demand, you can access Office programs from any computer, even if that computer does not have Office installed. For details on the various subscription plans, go to www.microsoft.com. (Only some of the plans include Office 2013.) Pricing and installation options for each plan differ.

To subscribe to Office 365, you need a Microsoft account. A **Microsoft account** is a free account that you can create that associates your email address and a password with Microsoft cloud services, such as Outlook.com for email, Xbox Live for games, and SkyDrive for file storage.

# Determining If You Have a Microsoft Account

In order to access any of Microsoft's cloud services, you must sign in to your Microsoft account. Even if you think you did not sign up for one, you might already have a Microsoft account. You have a Microsoft account if you have one of the following:

- a subscription to Office 365
- a Hotmail account
- a live.com email account
- a SkyDrive account
- an Xbox account
- a Windows phone
- a Windows 8 user account with a user name that is an email address and that requires a password

If you are not sure if your Windows 8 user account is a Microsoft account, you can check on the PC settings screen. To do this, display the Start screen, display the Charms bar, click the Settings charm, and then click Change PC settings to display the PC settings screen. On the left, click Users to display options for managing Windows 8 user accounts. If you are currently signed in to Windows 8 with a local account, your user name appears as shown in Figure A-1.

| Figure A-1 | Users screen showing a local account signed in |

PC settings

Personalize

Users

Notifications

Search

Share

General

Your account

User Name ← username when signed in with a local account
Local Account

You can use your email address as a Microsoft account to sign in to Windows. You'll be able to access files and photos anywhere, sync settings, and more.

Switch to a Microsoft account

Sign-in options

Create a password

Your account doesn't have a password. A password is required to set up a PIN or a picture password.

If you are currently signed in to Windows 8 with a Microsoft account, your user name will appear as an email address. See Figure A-2. If your Windows 8 user account is a Microsoft account, every time you use your computer, you are signed into your Microsoft account and you have access to SkyDrive and other Microsoft cloud services.

| Figure A-2 | Users screen showing a Microsoft account signed in |
|---|---|

## PC settings

Personalize

**Users**

Notifications

Search

Share

General

Privacy

Devices

### Your account

**User Name**
User_Name@example.com    ← username when signed in with a Microsoft account

You can switch to a local account, but your settings won't sync between the PCs you use.

Switch to a local account

More account settings online

### Sign-in options

Change your password

Create a picture password

Create a PIN

If you do not have a Microsoft account, you will need to create one in order to access SkyDrive and other Microsoft cloud services. When you attempt to access a Microsoft cloud service—for example, when you try to save to SkyDrive from Backstage view in Microsoft Word, Excel, or PowerPoint, or when you try to use an app such as Mail, People, or Messaging—and you are not signed in to a Microsoft account, a screen will appear asking you to sign in or to create a new Microsoft account. Click the Sign up link, and then follow the instructions to create your account.

**INSIGHT**

### How to Determine if You Are Signed In To Your Microsoft Account in an Office Application

If your Windows 8 account is a Microsoft account, when you start Office 2013 applications, you will be signed in to your Microsoft account. Your user name will appear in the upper-right corner, and you will be able to save to your SkyDrive from Backstage view in Word, Excel, and PowerPoint without signing in again. If your Windows 8 account is not a Microsoft account, you might see a Sign in link in the upper-right corner of the Office applications. You can click this to sign in to your Microsoft account. Or, if you try to save to SkyDrive, you will be prompted to sign in, and then your user name will replace the Sign in link in the upper-right corner.

# Understanding the SkyDrive App and the SkyDrive Desktop Application

The **SkyDrive app** comes with Windows 8 and runs like any other app in Windows 8. The SkyDrive tile appears on the Start screen and you click it to run the app. If you are signed in to your Microsoft account, the folders on your SkyDrive appear. If you are not signed in to a Microsoft account, you will be prompted to sign in. Figure A-3 shows one user's SkyDrive in the SkyDrive app. Using the SkyDrive app, you can click a file to open it in the appropriate app or desktop application on your computer. For example, if you click a photo, the Photo app will start and the photo will appear in the Photo app; if you click a Word document, Word will start and the document will open in Word. You can also download files from your SkyDrive to your computer or upload files from your computer to your SkyDrive. You can also create new folders on your SkyDrive or delete folders from it.

| Figure A-3 | Folders and files on SkyDrive in SkyDrive app |

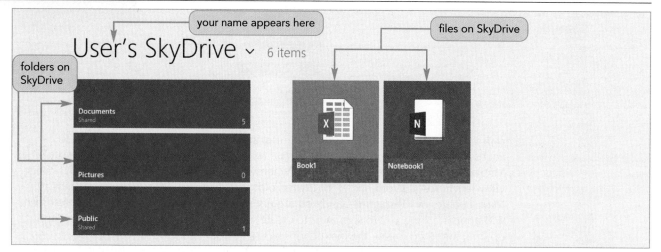

The **SkyDrive desktop application** is available for download from the Windows 8 App Store. (Note that the SkyDrive desktop application is named "Microsoft SkyDrive" in the Windows 8 store.) It runs on the desktop and looks like any other folder in File Explorer. See Figure A-4.

**Figure A-4**    **File Explorer window after installing SkyDrive desktop application**

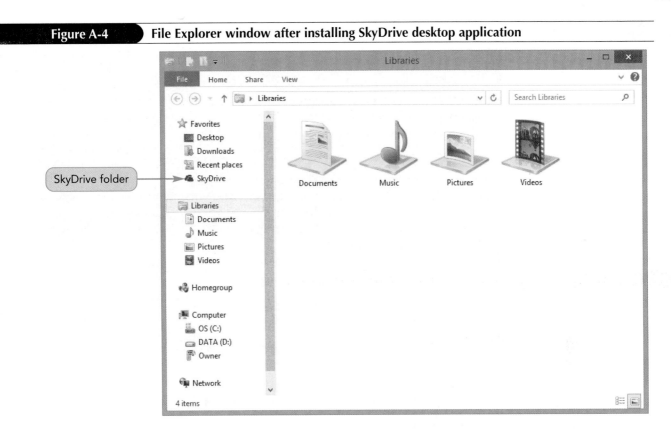

When you install the SkyDrive desktop application, you are asked if you want to sync all the folders on your SkyDrive to your computer. If you do not, you can deselect the folders you do not want to sync. Once the SkyDrive application is installed, any files you place in the SkyDrive folder are automatically uploaded and saved to your SkyDrive. If you edit one of these files on your computer, the edited file is synced with the version on your SkyDrive. If you access the file on your SkyDrive, either through a browser or from another computer, and make changes to it, the changes are automatically synced to the copy on your computer the next time you start your computer.

When you search for SkyDrive from the Start screen, both the SkyDrive app and the SkyDrive desktop application are named "SkyDrive," but the icons are different. Refer to Figure A-5 to see the difference.

**Figure A-5** **SkyDrive app and desktop application on the Apps screen**

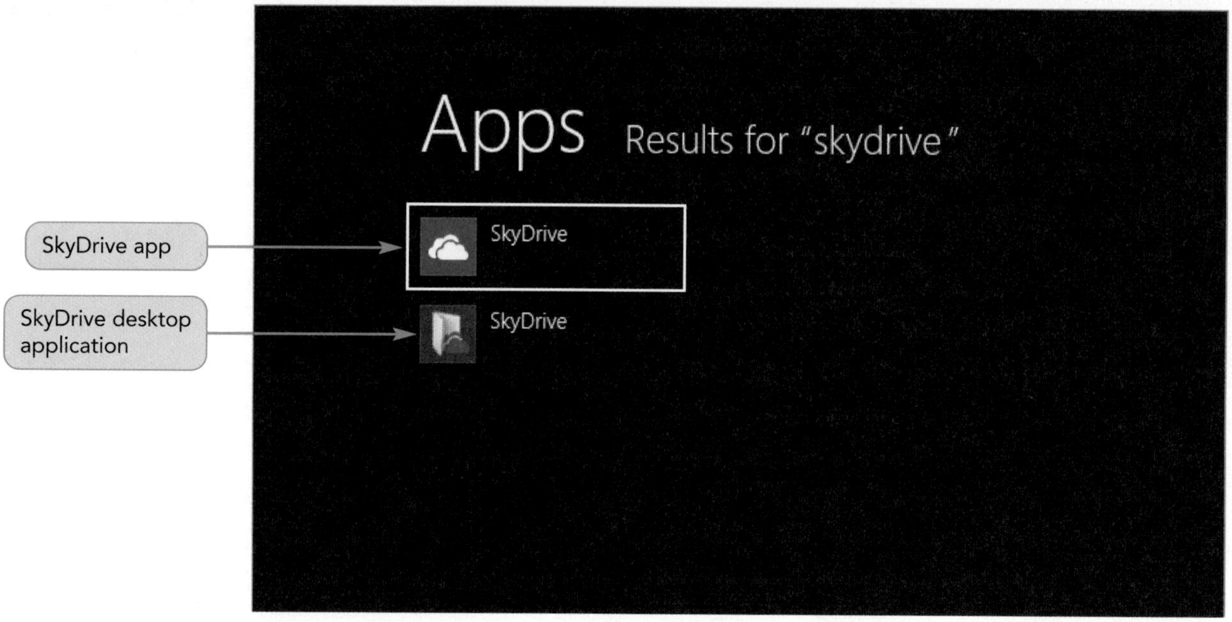

SkyDrive app

SkyDrive desktop application

# Moving Files Between SkyDrive and Your Computer

Once you are signed in to your Microsoft account, you can store files on your SkyDrive. You can do this from within Word, Excel, or PowerPoint, you can use the SkyDrive app or the SkyDrive desktop application, or you can use your browser to go to www.skydrive.com, log in, and then use the commands on the website. Each file that you upload can be a maximum size of 300 GB if you upload it using a browser or 2 GB if you upload it using the SkyDrive desktop application or SkyDrive app.

**TIP**

You cannot save to SkyDrive from Backstage view in Access.

To upload a file from within Word, Excel, or PowerPoint, display the file in the application window, click the FILE tab to display Backstage view, and then click Save As in the navigation bar. On the Save As screen, click SkyDrive. (Note that your Microsoft account user name will appear before SkyDrive; for example, "John Smith's Skydrive.") Then click the Browse button to open the Save As dialog box with the current location as your SkyDrive. Figure A-6 shows the Save As dialog box open on the Save As screen in Backstage view in Word. The folders on the user's SkyDrive are listed in the dialog box. Double-click a folder to make it the current folder, and then save the file to this folder on your SkyDrive in the same manner that you save files to a folder on your computer.

| Figure A-6 | Save As dialog box open on the Save As screen in Word's Backstage view |

To upload files using the SkyDrive app, start the app from the Start screen. Each of the tiles on the screen represents a folder. Click the folder to which you want to upload the file to open that folder, or right-click anywhere on the screen to display the Apps bar at the bottom of the screen, as shown in Figure A-7 and then use the New Folder button to create a new folder. To upload a file, display the Apps bar, and then click the Upload button. This displays the Files screen, which lists all the files in the current folder (usually the Documents folder). You can select a file in this folder or switch to another folder. After you click a file to select it, click the Add to SkyDrive button at the bottom of the screen. To download files, right-click the file on SkyDrive to select it, and then click the Download button on the Apps bar.

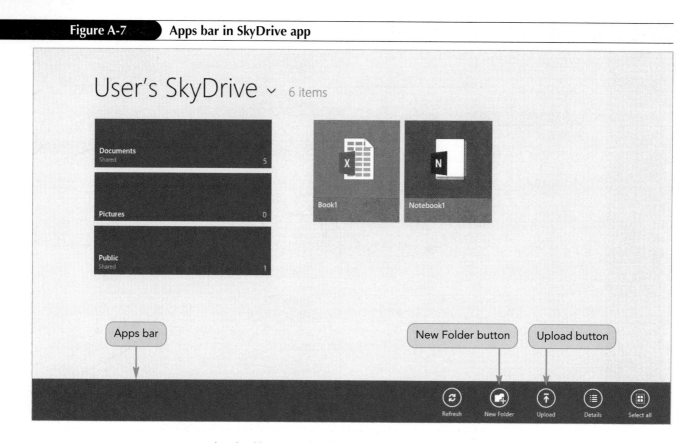

To upload a file using the SkyDrive desktop application, you either save a file to the SkyDrive folder from within an application, or copy or move a file from another folder to the SkyDrive folder. The file will be automatically synced to your SkyDrive. Likewise, to download a file, simply copy it from the SkyDrive folder to any other folder on your computer.

You can also move files between your SkyDrive and your computer by opening a browser window, going to www.skydrive.com, and signing in to your Microsoft account from that webpage. If your SkyDrive is not the current page, click SkyDrive at the top. Figure A-8 shows a typical SkyDrive page. As in the SkyDrive app, each of the tiles in your SkyDrive window represents a folder. To open a folder, click the folder tile. Then you can use the Upload button at the top of the screen to open the Choose File to Upload dialog box, which is very similar to the Save As dialog box. To download a file, point to it to display a check box in the upper-right corner, and then click the check box to display additional commands at the top of the browser including the Download command.

| Figure A-8 | SkyDrive in Internet Explorer browser |
| --- | --- |

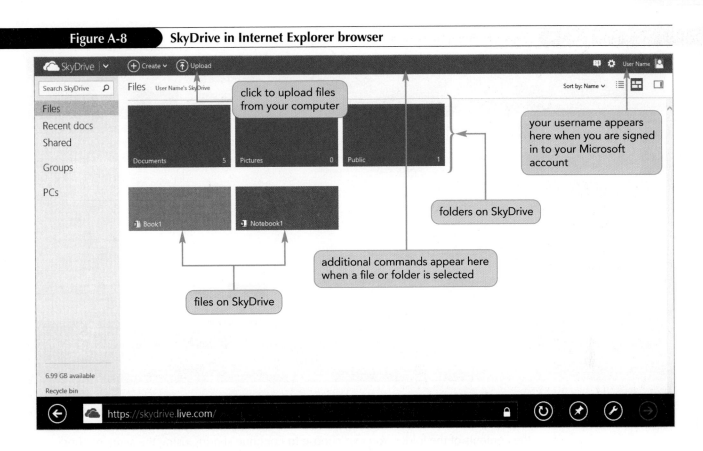

# Sharing Files and Folders on Your SkyDrive

One of the great advantages of working with SkyDrive is that you can share your files with others. Suppose, for example, that you want a colleague to review and edit a presentation you created in PowerPoint. You can upload the PowerPoint file to SkyDrive, and then give your colleague access to the file.

You can choose to share individual files or folders on your SkyDrive. Keep in mind that if you share folders, you are granting permission to whomever you are sharing access to all of the files in that folder.

**TIP**

You can also share a file from within the corresponding Office Web App. To do this, click the FILE tab, and then click Share in the navigation pane.

To share files and folders on your SkyDrive, you need to access your SkyDrive from a browser. To share a single file, point to it to display a check box in the upper-right corner of the file tile, and then click the check box to select the file. When you do this, additional commands appear at the top of the browser screen or window. Click the Sharing command to display a screen similar to the one shown in Figure A-9. You can then send an email to someone, which will include a direct link to the item you are sharing. You can also choose to post the link to one of the social media sites listed, or you can copy the link and paste it anywhere you choose. Finally, you can choose whether the people with whom you are sharing can edit the files or only read them.

| Figure A-9 | SkyDrive after clicking Share command |

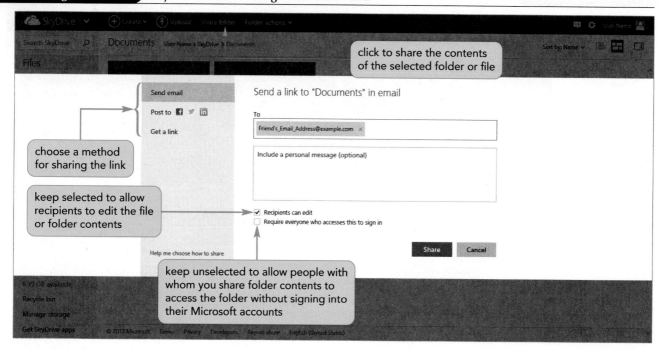

To share a folder, click the folder to open it, and then click the Sharing command at the top of the browser. A warning appears reminding you that you will be sharing all of the contents of the folder. You can choose to continue sharing using the same methods you use to share a file or cancel the sharing request. Note that files stored in the Public folder are viewable by anyone who has the link to them.

Because people with whom you share a file or folder click a direct link to access the file or folder, they do not need to sign in to their Microsoft accounts in order to view or download the files stored in it (unless you require it by selecting that option when you share the file or folder). However, if they want to use the Office Web Apps to edit those files, they do need to sign in to a Microsoft account.

**INSIGHT**

*Viewing Photos and Videos on SkyDrive*

You can use SkyDrive as a photo viewer and video player. When you click a photo or a video stored in a folder on SkyDrive, the screen changes to show the photo or the video much larger on the screen. At the bottom, thumbnails of the other photos and videos in the folder appear. You can click each thumbnail to display that photo or video on the screen, or move the pointer to display scroll arrows on the left or right edges of the screen, and then click these to scroll through the photos and videos in the folder.

# Using Office Web Apps

When you sign in to your SkyDrive using a browser, you also have access to Office Web Apps. The programs included in Office Web Apps are limited versions of Microsoft Word, Excel, PowerPoint, and **OneNote** (an electronic notebook program). You can use the Office Web Apps from any computer that is connected to the Internet, even if Microsoft Office is not installed on that computer. Although the interface for each Office Web App is similar to the interface of the full-featured program on your computer, only a limited number of commands are available for editing documents using the Office Web App. Figure A-10 shows the Word Web App.

**Figure A-10**    **Word Web App**

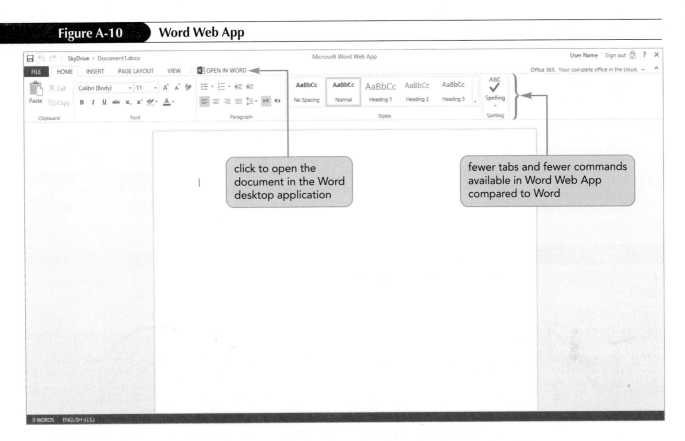

You cannot access Office Web Apps from the SkyDrive App. When you access SkyDrive from the browser, you can choose to open the file in the corresponding Web App, or the corresponding Office desktop application installed on your computer.

To create new files on SkyDrive using an Office Web App, sign in to your SkyDrive in a browser, and then click the Create button at the top of the browser. See Figure A-11. A menu opens allowing you to create a new folder, Word document, Excel workbook, PowerPoint presentation, OneNote notebook, or an Excel survey (an Excel template that allows you to create a survey and collect the responses in an Excel workbook). Select the Office Web App you want to use to open a new file in Edit mode in that Web App.

**Figure A-11**    **Create button menu listing Office Web Apps**

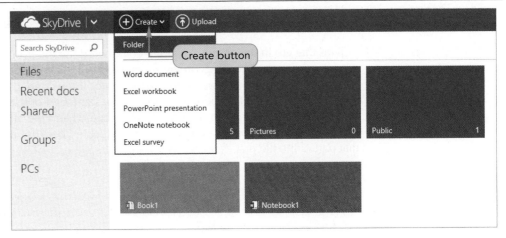

When you work in an Office Web app, you do not need to save your changes. All changes are saved automatically.

## Coauthoring with the Office Web Apps

The ability to work on files at the same time as others is called **coauthoring**. When you coauthor a file using an Office Web App, you and others with whom the file is shared open the file in the appropriate Web App on your own computers. As each new user opens the file, a message appears briefly telling you the Microsoft account username of the person who is now editing the file with you. On the left end of the status bar, a button appears indicating that the file is being coauthored, and the number next to the button indicates the number of people coauthoring. You can click this button to see a list of their Microsoft account usernames. See Figure A-12.

| Figure A-12 | File open in PowerPoint Web App with two people editing it |
|---|---|

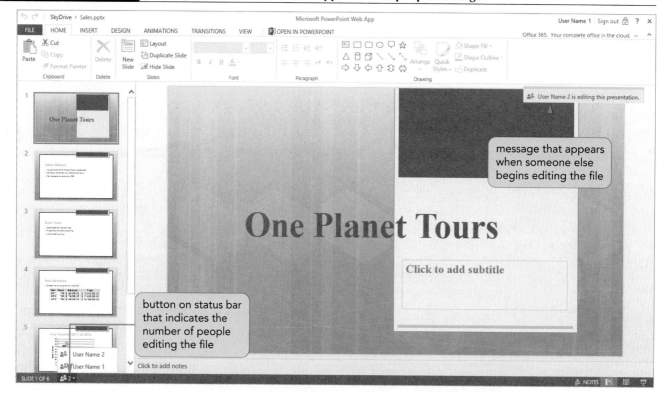

Files that are in the process of being coauthored update every few minutes. The speed of the update depends on the speed of your Internet connection and the size of the file. There can be a delay of up to 10 minutes if the connection is very slow or the files are very large. If two people try to edit the same part of the file at the same time, the edits of the person who started first are accepted and the other user sees a message telling them that his or her edits will not be accepted because another user was editing that part of the file first.

# Capstone Projects

*Word, Excel, Access, and PowerPoint 2013*

This appendix contains eight comprehensive Capstone Projects that cover all the major skills and concepts presented in this text. For each Office 2013 application, this appendix includes two Capstone Projects that students can use to demonstrate how well they understand the Office 2013 software and how proficiently they can apply their Office 2013 skills in an independent project.

The following Capstone Projects are included in this appendix:

- Word Capstone Project 1: Covers material in Word Tutorials 1 and 2
- Word Capstone Project 2: Covers material in Word Tutorials 1–4, with a greater emphasis on Tutorials 3 and 4
- Excel Capstone Project 1: Covers material in Excel Tutorials 1 and 2
- Excel Capstone Project 2: Covers material in Excel Tutorials 1–4, with a greater emphasis on Tutorials 3 and 4
- Access Capstone Project 1: Covers material in Access Tutorials 1 and 2
- Access Capstone Project 2: Covers material in Access Tutorials 1–4, with a greater emphasis on Tutorials 3 and 4
- PowerPoint Capstone Project 1: Covers material in PowerPoint Tutorial 1
- PowerPoint Capstone Project 2: Covers material in PowerPoint Tutorials 1–2, with a greater emphasis on Tutorial 2

Each Capstone Project presents a new case scenario that clarifies the tasks that need to be completed. The scenarios cover a range of disciplines and business types so that students can apply their skills and knowledge in a variety of new and stimulating situations.

## OBJECTIVES

**Word Capstone Project 1**
- Edit and format documents, including one in the MLA style

**Word Capstone Project 2**
- Create tables, SmartArt diagrams, and other graphics

**Excel Capstone Project 1**
- Enter data and formulas, and format a workbook

**Excel Capstone Project 2**
- Enter formulas and functions, and create charts

**Access Capstone Project 1**
- Design tables and define relationships

**Access Capstone Project 2**
- Create and run queries, and create and format a form

**PowerPoint Capstone Project 1**
- Apply layouts and add content to slides

**PowerPoint Capstone Project 2**
- Enhance a presentation with transitions, animations, photos, and videos

## STARTING DATA FILES

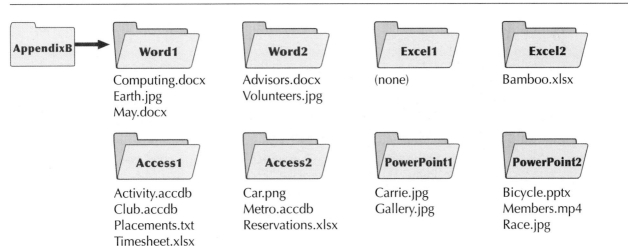

AppendixB → Word1
Computing.docx
Earth.jpg
May.docx

Word2
Advisors.docx
Volunteers.jpg

Excel1
(none)

Excel2
Bamboo.xlsx

Access1
Activity.accdb
Club.accdb
Placements.txt
Timesheet.xlsx

Access2
Car.png
Metro.accdb
Reservations.xlsx

PowerPoint1
Carrie.jpg
Gallery.jpg

PowerPoint2
Bicycle.pptx
Members.mp4
Race.jpg

# Word Project 1: Formatting a Flyer and Revising an Article for EcoLife Magazine

**Data Files needed for this Capstone Project: May.docx, Earth.jpg, Computing.docx**

**TIP**

This Capstone Project maps to the material in Word Tutorials 1 and 2.

Eva Santiago is the editorial director of *EcoLife Magazine*, an online publication devoted to environmental topics such as climate change, energy conservation, and creative recycling. As Eva's assistant, you research, write, and format articles and promotional materials for the magazine. Eva created a flyer advertising the upcoming issue of *EcoLife Magazine* and asked you to format it. She also asked you to write a short article on green computing. You have completed the first draft of the article, but now need to format it according to the MLA Style guidelines, which Eva requires for all articles.

## To format the flyer and magazine article:

1. Open the file **May**, located in the AppendixB ▸ Word1 folder included with your Data Files. Save the document as **May Flyer** in the folder where you are storing your files, as specified by your instructor.

2. Check for and correct spelling and grammar errors.

3. Change the page orientation to Portrait and the margins to Normal.

4. Apply the Frame document theme to the document.

5. Format the paragraphs of text as follows:

   a. Format paragraph 1 ("EcoLife Magazine") in the Title style.

   b. Format paragraph 2 ("Making the world clean and green") in the Heading 1 style.

   c. Format paragraphs 3–6 (starting with "50 ways…" and ending with "…of EcoLife magazine") in 14-point Lucida Bright font and right-align the paragraphs.

6. Format the first paragraph ("EcoLife Magazine") with an outside border, and then add blue shading, using the Turquoise, Accent 1 theme color. Format the paragraph text in white.

7. Format the last paragraph in the document using the same formatting you applied to the first paragraph. Center the last paragraph, and then change the font size to 12 points.

8. Increase the paragraph spacing before the last paragraph in the document to 48 points. Increase the paragraph spacing after the second paragraph to 48 points.

9. Format the second paragraph with the Fill – Turquoise, Accent 1, Shadow text effect.

10. In paragraph 3, make the number "50" bold and apply the Turquoise, Accent 1, Darker 25% font color to the text. Apply the same formatting to the number "10" in paragraph 4, the number "3" in paragraph 5, and the word "All" in paragraph 6.

11. Format the "Read it online at www.ecolife.cengage.com" paragraph in italic. In the web address, replace "ecolife" with your first name and replace "cengage" with your last name.

12. Delete the picture and replace it with the **Earth** photo, located in the AppendixB ▸ Word1 folder included with your Data Files.

13. Resize the new photo so that it is 3.5 inches tall and 4.77 inches wide, and then center the photo. Add the Rotated, White picture style to the photo.

▶ **14.** Save your changes to the flyer and preview it. The flyer should look like Figure B-1. Make any changes as necessary to match the figure, and then save and close the May Flyer document.

| Figure B-1 | May Flyer document |

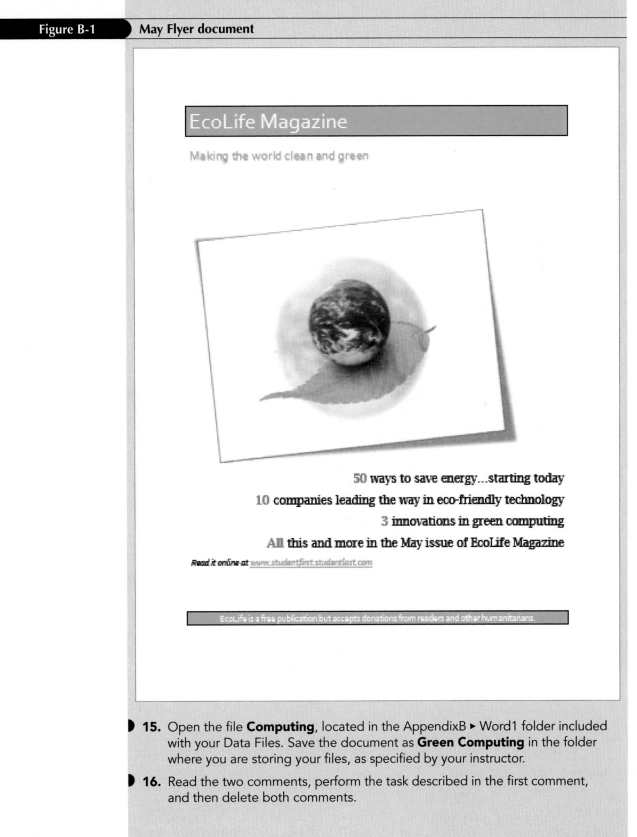

▶ **15.** Open the file **Computing**, located in the AppendixB ▶ Word1 folder included with your Data Files. Save the document as **Green Computing** in the folder where you are storing your files, as specified by your instructor.

▶ **16.** Read the two comments, perform the task described in the first comment, and then delete both comments.

17. Adjust the font size, line spacing, paragraph spacing, and paragraph indents to match the MLA style.

18. Insert your last name and a page number in a header on every page except the first. Right-align the header.

19. Revise the title of the article so that only the first letter of each word is capitalized. Edit the title to make the words "to" and "a" lowercase. Attach a comment to this paragraph that explains your revision.

20. At the end of page 1, format the list of three paragraphs starting with "Reducing power consumption…" and ending with "Replacing the physical with the digital" as a bulleted list with square bullets.

21. On pages 2 and 3, remove the indents from the three heading paragraphs: "Low-Power Hardware," "Energy-Efficient Programs," and "Replacing the Physical with the Digital," if necessary.

22. Select MLA Seventh Edition as the citations and bibliography style.

23. Find the first instance of "CITATION" in the document, and then delete it. Create a new source with the following information:

    Type of Source: **Web site**

    Corporate Author: **Electronics Take Back Coalition**

    Name of the Web Page: **Facts and Figures on E-Waste and Recycling**

    Year Accessed: **2016**

    Month Accessed: **March**

    Day Accessed: **28**

    Medium: **Digital**

24. Insert a space before the citation (if necessary), and then edit the citation to add **6** as the page number.

25. Delete the second instance of "CITATION" and create a new source with the following information:

    Type of Source: **Article in a Periodical**

    Author: **Anne Eisenberg**

    Title: **Bye-Bye Batteries: Radio Waves as a Low-Power Source**

    Periodical Title: **The New York Times**

    Year: **2010**

    Month: **July**

    Day: **17**

    Pages: **BU3**

    Medium: **Print**

26. Insert a space before the citation (if necessary), and then edit the citation to add **BU3** as the page number.

27. At the end of the document, start a new page and insert a bibliography with the heading "Works Cited."

28. Format the bibliography according to MLA standards.

29. Save the Green Computing document and then close it.

# Word Project 2: Designing a Report for WLVX Radio

**TIP**

This Capstone Project maps to the material in Word Tutorials 1–4.

**Data Files needed for this Capstone Project: Advisors.docx, Volunteers.jpg**
Nick Ryan is the assistant director of WLVX, a listener-sponsored radio station in Louisville, Kentucky. He is working on a report to the station's advisory board that summarizes the programming, management, and funding of the station. After developing a draft of the report, he asks you to complete it by adding text, graphics, and a table, and then formatting the report.

## To complete the report:

1. Open the file **Advisors**, located in the AppendixB ▸ Word2 folder included with your Data Files. Save the document as **Advisors Board** in the folder where you are storing your files, as specified by your instructor.

2. Apply the Parallax document theme to the document.

3. On page 1, format the entire first paragraph ("WLVX: The State of the Station") as WordArt, using the Fill - Red, Accent 4, Soft Bevel style.

4. Change the text box width to 7 inches and retain the default height of .87 inches.

5. Apply the Chevron Up transform effect, change the text fill to Blue, Accent 1, Darker 50%, and then add a shadow using the Offset Diagonal Bottom Left style.

6. After the "Summary" heading, change the "T" in "This report" to a drop cap that drops three lines.

7. After the "Mission" heading, create a bulleted list including the four paragraphs of text that start with "To" and use the open-circle style of bullet.

8. Below the "Background" heading, replace the text "[milestones]" with a tabbed list of dates and events, using the following information: **1967, Station founded; 1978, Listenership expands to 175,000; 1986, Station helps launch the Kentucky Bluegrass Festival; 1990, Broadcasting power increases to 52,000 watts; 1997, WLVX wins the Independent Radio Station Award; 2012, Listenership expands to 300,000**. Insert a tab after each date and don't include any punctuation in the list.

9. For the paragraphs you just entered, insert a left tab stop 1.25 inches from the left margin, and then remove the spacing after all the paragraphs in the milestone list except the last paragraph.

10. To the right of the "Background" heading, insert a preformatted text box, using the Austin Quote style.

11. Change the text wrapping setting for the text box to Square, change its height to 1.75 inches and its width to 2 inches, and then position it so that the top edge of the text box aligns with the top edge of the "Background" heading and the right border of the text box is at about the 6.5" mark on the page.

12. Replace the placeholder text with the following text: **The station has always relied on volunteers and listeners who donate their time, money, and other resources to sustain programming.**

13. Promote the "Programming" and "Management" headings to Heading 1 text.

14. Below the "Programming" heading, insert a page break so the paragraph that starts with "The following table..." appears at the top of page 2.

15. In the blank paragraph on page 2, insert a table using the information shown in Figure B-2. Format the header row in bold.

| Figure B-2 | WLVX programming schedule |
| --- | --- |

| Time | Weekday | Weekend |
| --- | --- | --- |
| 6:00 am | News and analysis | Music |
| 12:00 pm | News and analysis | Music |
| 10:00 am | Music | News |
| 3:00 pm | Community forum | Humor |
| 2:00 pm | Arts and literature | Arts and literature |
| 2:30 pm | Announcements | Announcements |
| 4:00 pm | News and analysis | Music |
| 8:30 pm | Music | Music |
| 7:00 pm | Humor | Community talk |
| 11:30 pm | Signoff | Signoff |

© 2014 Cengage Learning

16. Sort the table by the contents of the "Time" column in ascending order.

17. In the appropriate location in the table, insert a new row for an **8:00 pm** program, which is **News updates** on weekdays and on weekends.

18. Delete the "2:30 pm" row from the table.

19. Modify the widths of all columns to accommodate the widest entry in each, and then apply the Grid Table 5 Dark - Accent 1 style to the table.

20. In the blank paragraph following the table, insert the following text: **© WLVX Radio Station**

21. After the "Management" heading, locate the sentence that starts "We are working…" and ends with "…public relations activities." At the end of that sentence, directly after the period, insert a footnote that reads **The marketing plan will be released in September 2016.**

22. Format the entire list of WLVX staff in two columns.

23. At the beginning of the "Funding" heading, insert a section break that starts a new page. Format the new section in landscape orientation. In the blank paragraph after the "Funding" heading, insert a SmartArt graphic that illustrates the four sources of funding for the radio station. Use the Circle Process graphic, and then add a fourth shape to the diagram. From left to right, include the following text in the SmartArt diagram: **Listener Donations, Corporate Underwriting, Government Support**, and **Foundations**. Do not include any punctuation in the SmartArt. Increase the width of the SmartArt graphic to 8 inches, and then change its style to Subtle Effect.

24. At the beginning of the "Volunteer Coordination" heading, insert a section break that starts a new page. Format the new section in portrait orientation.

25. At the beginning of the second paragraph on page 4 (which begins with "WLVX volunteers serve in many ways."), insert the image file named **Volunteers** from the AppendixB ▶ Word2 folder included with your Data Files.

26. Change the height of the photo to 1.35 inches and the width to 2 inches, and then fix the position of the photo in the upper-right side of the page with square text wrapping. Apply the Reflected Rounded Rectangle picture style to the photo.

**27.** Create a footer for all sections in the document that aligns your first and last names at the left margin. Below your name, insert the word "Page" followed by the page number but no other design elements.

**28.** Insert a cover page using the Ion (Light) style. Enter the following information in the content controls on the cover page:

Year: **2016**

Document title: **WLVX: The State of the Station**

Document subtitle: **Report to the Advisory Board**

Author: Your first and last name

**29.** Save and preview the report. Save the document again as a PDF named **Advisors Board** in the location specified by your instructor. Wait for the PDF to open, review it, and then close the program that opened the file. Close the Advisors Board document in Word.

# Excel Project 1: Creating an Invoice for Compassionate Skin Care

**There are no Data Files needed for this Capstone Project**

Leslie Tran is the distribution manager for Compassionate Skin Care, a company based in New Brunswick, New Jersey, that sells skin care products on the web. Their products include 100 percent organic, plant-based ingredients and are manufactured using renewable resources, solar and wind energy, and environmentally friendly practices. Leslie wants to use an Excel workbook to create and track the customer invoices included with every shipment. Leslie asks you to create and format a worksheet she can use for invoices.

> **TIP**
>
> This Capstone Project maps to the material in Excel Tutorials 1 and 2.

### To create and format a customer invoice worksheet:

**1.** Create a new, blank workbook, and then save it as **Customer Invoice** in the folder where you are storing your files, as specified by your instructor.

**2.** Rename the Sheet1 worksheet as **Documentation**, and then enter the data shown in Figure B-3 in the specified cells.

**Figure B-3**     **Documentation worksheet text**

| Cell | Text |
|------|------|
| A1 | Compassionate Skin Care |
| A3 | Author |
| A4 | Date |
| A5 | Purpose |
| B3 | Your name |
| B4 | Current date |
| B5 | To display a customer invoice for Compassionate Skin Care orders |

© 2014 Cengage Learning

▶ **3.** Set the following formats in the Documentation sheet:

    **a.** Increase the width of column A to 10 characters and the width of column B to 60 characters. Merge cells A1 and B1, and then left-align the contents of the merged cell.

    **b.** Set the font of the title text in cell A1 to 26-pt Calibri Light. Change the font color to white and fill the cell with the Orange, Accent 2, Darker 25% theme color.

    **c.** Change the font of the range A3:A5 to 14-point Calibri Light. Change the font color to white and fill the cell with the Orange, Accent 2, Darker 25% theme color.

    **d.** Change the format of the date value in cell B4 to the Long Date style, and then left-align the date in the cell.

    **e.** Italicize the text "Compassionate Skin Care" in cell B5.

    **f.** Add a border around each cell in the range A3:B5.

▶ **4.** Add a new worksheet after the Documentation sheet, and then rename the sheet as **Invoice**.

▶ **5.** In the Invoice worksheet, add a thick box border around the range A1:D30.

▶ **6.** Apply cell styles to ranges in the Invoice worksheet as follows:

    **a.** Range A1:D6: Accent2 cell style

    **b.** Ranges A7:D7, A13:D13, and A30:D30: Accent1 cell style

    **c.** Ranges A8:D12, A31:B34, and D32:D33: 20% - Accent1 cell style

    **d.** Range A14:D29: 20% - Accent2 cell style

    **e.** Cell D34: 40% - Accent1 cell style

▶ **7.** Set the width of column A to 15 characters, column B to 30 characters, column C to 20 characters, and column D to 20 characters.

▶ **8.** Merge the range A1:B2, and then left-align and top-align the merged cell. Merge the range C1:D2, and then right-align and top-align the merged cell. Merge the following ranges: A7:D7, A8:D12, A30:C30, and A31:B34. Middle-align the merged cell in A8. Left-align the following merged cells: A7, A30, and A31.

▶ **9.** Set the height of rows 1 and 2 to 36 points.

▶ **10.** Bold the ranges B4:B6 and D4:D6. Format cell A31 in the 10-pt Calibri font, and then add an outside border to the merged cell. Add a border around each cell in the range D32:D34. Format cell D34 using the 12-pt bold Calibri font.

▶ **11.** In cell A1, change the font to Perpetua, and then enter the following four lines of text:

**Compassionate Skin Care**

**800 W. King Highway**

**New Brunswick, NJ 08902**

**(732) 555-2700**

Format the first line as 16-point bold text.

▶ **12.** In cell C1, enter **INVOICE**, and then format the text in the 36-pt Calibri font.

▶ **13.** Enter text as shown in Figure B-4, and then wrap the text in cell A31.

| Figure B-4 | Invoice worksheet text |

| Cell | Text |
|------|------|
| A4 | Address |
| A6 | Phone |
| C4 | Date |
| C5 | Invoice Number |
| C6 | Order Number |
| A7 | Bill to: |
| A13 | Quantity |
| B13 | Description |
| C13 | Unit Price |
| D13 | Amount |
| A30 | Subtotal |
| A31 | Make all checks payable to Compassionate Skin Care. Contact Customer Service at (732) 555-2700 with questions. |
| | Thank you for your business! |
| C32 | Credit |
| C33 | Shipping |
| C34 | Balance Due |

© 2014 Cengage Learning

14. Format the range C32:C34 using the Blue, Accent 1, Darker 50% font color, and then right-align the cells. In cell C34, increase the font size to 12 points and bold the text.

15. Increase the indent of cell A8 by one character. Right-align the range C4:D6 and the range C13:D13.

16. Format the range A14:D14 with a bottom border and a white background. Format the range A15:D15 with a bottom border. Copy the format in the range A14:D15 to the range A16:D29. Format the range A29:D29 with a double bottom border. Reapply a thick bottom border to the range A30:D30 if necessary.

17. Create conditional formats for the Descriptions in the range B14:B29 that highlight the descriptions "Natural body scrub" and "Natural face scrub" in red text.

18. Create a legend for the conditional formats. In cell A36, enter the text **Discounted price** and add a thick box border around the cell. Use a conditional format that displays this cell value using red text.

19. In cell D14, enter a formula that multiplies the quantity by the unit price. Use the Fill Without Formatting option to copy the formula to the range D15:D29.

20. Format the range C14:D14 and cells D30 and D34 using the Accounting number style. Format the ranges C15:D29 and D32:D33 using the Comma number style.

21. In cell D30, enter the SUM function to calculate the sum of the values in the range D14:D29.

▶ **22.** In cell D33, enter a formula that uses the value in cell D30 to calculate the 10 percent shipping charge.

▶ **23.** In cell D34, enter a formula that adds the subtotal and the shipping charge, and then subtracts the credit amount.

▶ **24.** Make sure the worksheet is set to portrait orientation, and then add a footer that displays your name in the left section, the filename in the center section, and the current date in the right section. Scale the printout so that it fits onto a single page.

▶ **25.** Enter the invoice data shown in Figure B-5. Save and close the workbook.

**Figure B-5**    **Final Invoice worksheet**

## Compassionate Skin Care

### INVOICE

800 W. King Highway
New Brunswick, NJ 08902
(732) 555-2700

| Address | 2414 E. Morrison St. | Date | 4/22/2016 |
| | Asheville, NC 28803 | Invoice Number | 1097 |
| Phone | (828) 555-8283 | Order Number | SC-2512 |

Bill to:

Ms. Janet Wilkinson
2414 E. Morrison St.
Asheville, NC 28803
(828) 555-8283

| Quantity | Description | Unit Price | | Amount |
| --- | --- | --- | --- | --- |
| 2 | Pure & Simple cleanser | $ | 11.00  $ | 22.00 |
| 1 | Pure & Simple moisturizer | | 36.00 | 36.00 |
| 1 | Capri body lotion | | 18.50 | 18.50 |
| 3 | Natural body scrub | | 8.50 | 25.50 |
| | | | | - |
| | | | | - |
| | | | | - |
| | | | | - |
| | | | | - |
| | | | | - |
| | | | | - |
| | | | | - |
| | | | | - |
| | | | | - |
| | | | | - |

| Subtotal | | | $ | 102.00 |

Make all checks payable to Compassionate Skin Care.
Contact Customer Service at (732) 555-2700 with questions.
Thank you for your business!

| Credit | 15.00 |
| --- | --- |
| Shipping | 10.20 |
| **Balance Due**  $ | **97.20** |

Discounted price

# Excel Project 2: Making Financial Calculations and Creating Charts for Banerjee Bamboo

**Data File needed for this Capstone Project: Bamboo.xlsx**

Anya Banerjee is part owner of her family's business, Banerjee Bamboo, which imports bamboo from countries around the world and then processes it into production-grade material for the construction, furniture, and textile industries. The Banerjees want to expand their business by acquiring a loan to purchase new equipment. As part of the loan application, they need to provide information about their market and sales. You will help them complete the financial calculations and create charts to make the information easy to read and interpret.

## To complete the worksheets and create charts:

1. Open the **Bamboo** workbook, which is located in the AppendixB ▶ Excel2 folder provided with your Data Files, and then save the workbook as **Bamboo Expansion** in the location specified by your instructor.

2. In the Documentation sheet, enter your name and the date.

3. In the Loan Analysis worksheet, enter the data values and formulas required to calculate the monthly payment on a business loan of $375,000 at 7.8% annual interest to be repaid in 20 years.

4. In the Production worksheet, replace the numbers 1 through 12 in column B with the years 2005 through 2016. (*Hint*: Use a custom format to display a date such as 1/1/2005 with the year only.)

5. In column F, enter formulas that calculate the total production material sold each year.

6. In the Total Sales worksheet, calculate the total sales for each year.

7. In the range D18:D20, calculate statistics: average sales in cell D18, maximum sales in cell D19, and minimum sales in cell D20.

8. In the Market Summary worksheet, use the data in the range E21:F27 showing the suppliers' countries to create a pie chart comparing production from each country. Embed the pie chart in the Market Summary worksheet covering the range B5:G18.

9. Format the pie chart by removing the chart title, applying the Style 9 chart style, and displaying percentages with the data labels.

10. In the Production worksheet, create a line chart based on the data in the nonadjacent range B4:B16;F4:F16 showing the increase in the production-grade material Banerjee Bamboo sold over the past 12 years. Embed the line chart in the Market Summary worksheet covering the range I5:O16.

11. Format the line chart by making the following changes:

    a. Apply the Style 4 chart style.

    b. Change the chart title to **Production Material Sold**.

    c. Change the fill color of the chart area to the Green, Accent 1, Lighter 80% theme color.

    d. Change the scale of the primary vertical axis to go from 40 to 130 in steps of 10 units.

**12.** In the Production worksheet, create a clustered column chart using the data in the range B4:E16 showing the growth in production-grade material sold by region. Embed the chart in the Market Summary worksheet over the range I18:O28.

**13.** Format the column chart by making the following changes:

    **a.** Apply the Style 5 chart style.

    **b.** Change the chart title to **Production Material Sold**.

    **c.** Set the fill color of the chart area to the Green, Accent 1, Lighter 80% theme color.

**14.** In the Total Sales worksheet, create a stacked column chart using the data in the range B3:E15 showing the breakout of Banerjee Bamboo's market into flooring, furniture, and textiles. Embed the stacked column chart in the range B30:G43 of the Market Summary worksheet.

**15.** Format the stacked column chart by making the following changes:

    **a.** Apply the Style 5 chart style.

    **b.** Change the chart title to **Total Sales**.

    **c.** Add a primary vertical axis title with the text **(MILLIONS)**.

    **d.** Set the fill color of the chart area to the Green, Accent 1, Lighter 80% theme color.

**16.** Insert column sparklines in the range G21:G27 of the Market Summary worksheet based on the data in the range C5:N11 of the Suppliers worksheet to show how the supply of bamboo has changed over the past 12 years.

**17.** Set the axis of the sparklines so that the column heights range from 0 to a maximum of 29 for each sparkline. Ungroup the sparklines and set the color of each to match their color of the corresponding country in the pie chart.

**18.** Add data bars to the values in the range C20:C22 using the blue gradient fill to compare the three types of agreements. Define a rule that sets the maximum length of the data bars in those cells to 130. Be sure to preserve the blue gradient fill and solid border formatting.

**19.** Add a header that displays your name in the left section and the current date in the right section. Add a footer that shows the filename in the left section, the word "Page" followed by the page number in the center section, and the worksheet name in the right section.

**20.** Save the workbook. The Market Summary worksheet should look similar to Figure B-6.

| Figure B-6 | Final Market Summary worksheet |

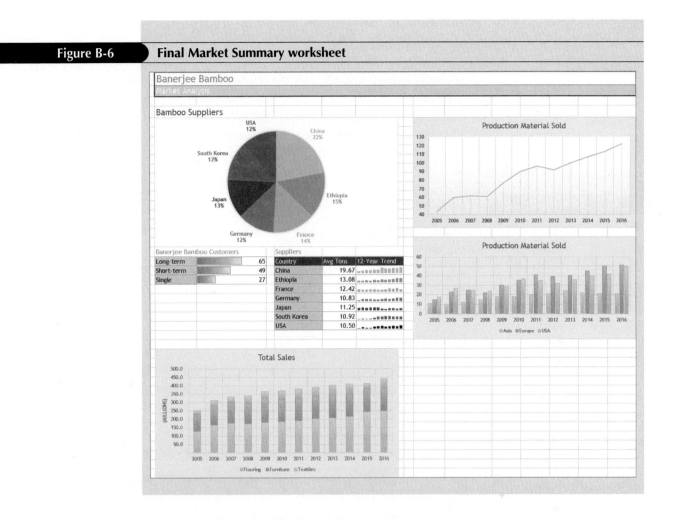

# Access Project 1: Creating a Database for GetInvolved

**Data Files needed for this Capstone Project: Club.accdb, Placements.txt, Activity.accdb, Timesheet.xlsx**

**TIP**

This Capstone Project maps to the material in Access Tutorials 1 and 2.

Tamara Jackson is the assistant director of GetInvolved, an organization in Berkeley, California, that matches youth volunteers to community projects needing help. Volunteers join GetInvolved as members, and then receive training about how to be effective and make a difference as a volunteer. Members select a project that GetInvolved supports, and then donate their time and energy to efforts such as improving the environment, working for animal rights, and helping kids in innovative preschool programs. Tamara wants to use Access to maintain information about community projects, members, and the services they provide. She needs your help creating this database.

## To create the Involved database:

1. Create a new, blank database named **Involved** and save it in the folder where you are storing your files, as specified by your instructor.

2. In Datasheet view for the Table1 table, rename the default primary key ID field to **MemberID**. Change the data type of the MemberID field to Short Text.

▶ **3.** Add the following five fields to the new table in the order shown: **FirstName** (a Short Text field), **LastName** (a Short Text field), **Phone** (a Short Text field), **Email** (a Hyperlink field), and **BirthDate** (a Date/Time field). Save the table as **Member**.

▶ **4.** Enter the records shown in Figure B-7 in the Member table. For the first record, be sure to enter your first name in the FirstName field, your last name in the LastName field, and your first name followed by **@mail.cengage.net** in the Email field.

| Figure B-7 | Records for the Member table |
| --- | --- |

| MemberID | FirstName | LastName | Phone | Email | BirthDate |
| --- | --- | --- | --- | --- | --- |
| 1025 | *Student First* | *Student Last* | 510-213-4587 | studentfirst@mail.cengage.net | 2/14/1999 |
| 1026 | Mark | Jacobson | 510-981-6744 | mjacobson@mobile.cengage.net | 6/2/1995 |
| 1028 | Anita | Salazar | 510-332-2156 | asalazar@mail.cengage.net | 12/23/1993 |
| 1031 | Natalie | Benoit | 510-255-1027 | nbenoit@ca.cengage.net | 8/30/1997 |
| 1032 | Ted | Sherwood | 510-213-0084 | teds@uc.cengage.edu | 3/8/1999 |

© 2014 Cengage Learning

▶ **5.** Tamara created a database named Club that contains a Volunteer table with member data. The Member table you created has the same design as the Volunteer table. Copy all the records from the **Volunteer** table in the **Club** database (located in the AppendixB ▶ Access1 folder provided with your Data Files) and then paste them at the end of the Member table in the Involved database.

▶ **6.** Resize all datasheet columns to their best fit, save the Member table, and then open it in Design view. Change the following field properties:

    **a.** MemberID: Enter **Primary key** for the description, change the field size to **4**, and enter **Member ID** for the caption.

    **b.** FirstName: Change the field size to **20** and enter **First Name** for the caption.

    **c.** LastName: Change the field size to **25** and enter **Last Name** for the caption.

    **d.** Phone: Change the field size to **14**.

    **e.** BirthDate: Change the format to **Short Date** and enter **Birth Date** for the caption.

▶ **7.** Save and close the Member table, accepting the message indicating some data might be lost.

▶ **8.** Create a new table in Design view, using the table design shown in Figure B-8.

| Figure B-8 | Design for the new table |
| --- | --- |

| Field Name | Data Type | Description | Field Size | Caption |
| --- | --- | --- | --- | --- |
| ProjectID | Short Text | Primary key | 5 | Project ID |
| ProjectName | Short Text | | 40 | Project Name |
| ProjectType | Short Text | | 25 | Project Type |

© 2014 Cengage Learning

**9.** Specify ProjectID as the primary key, and then save the table as **Project**.

**10.** In Datasheet view, use the Start and End Dates Quick Start selection in the Data Type gallery to add two fields to the end of the table.

**11.** Use the Address Quick Start selection in the Data Type gallery to add five more fields to the end of the table.

**12.** Switch to Design view, and then make the following changes to the Project table design:

  **a.** Address field: Change the name of this field to **Street**, change the field size to **40**, and delete the entry for the caption.

  **b.** City field: Change the field size to **25** and delete the entry for the caption.

  **c.** StateProvince field: Delete this field because all projects take place in California.

  **d.** ZIPPostal field: Change the name of this field to **Zip**, change the field size to **10**, and delete the entry for the caption.

  **e.** CountryRegion field: Delete this field.

  **f.** Move fields as necessary so they appear in the following order: ProjectID, ProjectName, ProjectType, StartDate, EndDate, Street, City, Zip.

  **g.** Add a new field named **New** (data type: **Yes/No**; description: **Yes = New project, No = Repeat project**) between the ProjectType and StartDate fields.

**13.** Enter the records shown in Figure B-9 in the Project table. When finished, save and close the Project table.

| Figure B-9 | Records for the Project table |
| --- | --- |

| Project ID | Project Name | Project Type | New | Start Date | End Date | Street | City | Zip |
| --- | --- | --- | --- | --- | --- | --- | --- | --- |
| AR101 | Arts in Education | Education | Yes | 3/15/2016 | 6/15/2016 | 2435 Alameda Dr. | Berkeley | 94701 |
| BK302 | Baykeepers | Environment | No | 9/1/2015 | 6/1/2017 | 132 W. 2nd St. | | Berkeley | 94707 |

© 2014 Cengage Learning

**14.** Use the Import Text File Wizard to add data to the Project table. The data you need to import is contained in the Placements text file, which is located in the AppendixB ▶ Access1 folder provided with your Data Files.

  **a.** Specify the Placements text file as the source of the data.

  **b.** Select the option for appending the data.

  **c.** Select Project as the table.

**d.** In the Import Text File Wizard dialog boxes, choose the options to import delimited data, to use a comma delimiter, and to import the data into the Project table. Do not save the import steps.

**15.** Open the **Project** table in Datasheet view and resize columns to their best fit, as necessary. Then save and close the Project table.

**16.** Tamara created a table named Service in the Activity database that is located in the AppendixB ▶ Access1 folder provided with your Data Files. Import the structure of the Service table in the Activity database into a new table named Service in the Involved database. Do not save the import steps.

**17.** Open the **Service** table in Datasheet view, and then add the following two fields to the end of the table: **Activity** (Short Text field) and **Hours** (Number field).

**18.** Modify the design of the Service table so that it matches the design in Figure B-10, *including the revised field names and data types.*

**Figure B-10** ▶ **Design of the Service table**

| Field Name | Data Type | Description | Field Size | Other |
|---|---|---|---|---|
| ServiceID | Short Text | Primary key | 5 | Caption = Service ID |
| MemberID | Short Text | Foreign key | 4 | Caption = Member ID |
| ProjectID | Short Text | Foreign key | 5 | Caption = Project ID |
| ServiceDate | Date/Time | | | Caption = Service Date |
| | | | | Format = Short Date |
| Activity | Short Text | | 30 | |
| Hours | Number | | Double | Format = Standard |
| | | | | Decimal Places = 1 |
| | | | | Default Value = [no entry] |

© 2014 Cengage Learning

**19.** Move the ProjectID field so it follows the ServiceID field.

**20.** Save your changes to the table design, and then add the records shown in Figure B-11 to the Service table.

**Figure B-11** ▶ **Records in the Service table**

| Service ID | Project ID | Member ID | Service Date | Activity | Hours |
|---|---|---|---|---|---|
| 30020 | CC139 | 1025 | 1/15/2016 | Tutoring | 2.0 |
| 30022 | WW285 | 1043 | 1/15/2016 | Animal care | 3.0 |

© 2014 Cengage Learning

**21.** Resize the fields to their best fit, and then save and close the Service table.

**22.** Use the Import Spreadsheet Wizard to add data to the Service table. The data you need to import is contained in the Timesheet workbook, which is an Excel file located in the AppendixB ▶ Access1 folder provided with your Data Files.

**a.** Specify the Timesheet workbook as the source of the data.

**b.** Select the option for appending the data to the table.

    **c.** Select Service as the table.

    **d.** In the Import Spreadsheet Wizard dialog boxes, choose the Service worksheet, make sure Access confirms that the first row contains column headings, and import to the Service table. Do not save the import steps.

**23.** Open the **Service** table, resize columns in the datasheet to their best fit (as necessary), and then save and close the Service table.

**24.** Use the Simple Query Wizard to create a query that includes the FirstName, LastName, and Phone fields from the Member table. Save the query as **MemberPhone**, and then close the query.

**25.** Use the Form tool to create a form for the Project table. Save the form as **ProjectInfo**, and then close it.

**26.** Use the Report tool to create a report based on the Service table. In Layout view, resize the ServiceID, ProjectID, and MemberID fields so they are slightly wider than the longest entry in each field. Display the report in Print Preview; then verify that all the fields are within the page area and all field values are fully displayed. Save the report as **ServiceList**, print the report (only if asked by your instructor to do so), and then close it.

**27.** Define the one-to-many relationships between the database tables as shown in Figure B-12. Select the referential integrity option and the cascade updates option for each relationship.

| Figure B-12 | Relationships in the Involved database |
| --- | --- |

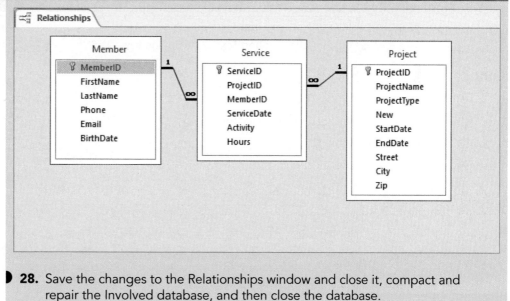

**28.** Save the changes to the Relationships window and close it, compact and repair the Involved database, and then close the database.

# Access Project 2: Creating Tables, Queries, Forms, and Reports for Metro Car Share

**Data Files needed for this Capstone Project: Metro.accdb, Reservations.xlsx, Car.png**

Jake Minn is the general manager of Metro Car Share, a company in Austin, Texas, that provides cars by the hour to Austin residents and visitors. Customers can rent hybrid or electric cars and trucks located in reserved parking spaces throughout the city. If customers become members of Metro Car Share, they can eventually earn rewards and rental discounts. Jake is using Access to maintain information about customers and vehicles. He needs your help to add information about rentals, analyze the data he is maintaining, and then track and view information about the services Metro Car Share offers. To help Jake, you'll create a table in the Metro database, and then create queries to answer his questions. You will also create a form and report to help him work efficiently.

## To add objects to the Metro database:

1. Open the **Metro** database, which is located in the AppendixB ▸ Access2 folder provided with your Data Files, and enable content, if necessary.

2. Create a new table in Design view, using the table design shown in Figure B-13.

**Figure B-13    Design for the Rental table**

| Field Name | Data Type | Description | Field Size | Other |
|---|---|---|---|---|
| RentalID | Short Text | Primary key | 7 | Caption = Rental ID |
| CustomerID | Short Text | Foreign key | 5 | Caption = Customer ID |
| VehicleID | Short Text | Foreign key | 4 | Caption = Vehicle ID |
| RentalDate | Date/Time | | | Caption = Rental Date<br>Format = Short Date |
| PickupTime | Date/Time | | | Caption = Pickup Time<br>Format = Medium Time |
| Hours | Number | | Double | Format = Standard<br>Decimal Places = 1<br>Default Value = [no entry] |

© 2014 Cengage Learning

3. Specify RentalID as the primary key, and then save the table as **Rental**.

4. Add the records shown in Figure B-14 to the Rental table.

**Figure B-14    Records for the Rental table**

| Rental ID | Customer ID | Vehicle ID | Rental Date | Pickup Time | Hours |
|---|---|---|---|---|---|
| 02-3002 | 10042 | AB14 | 2/1/2016 | 7:00 AM | 2.0 |
| 02-3004 | 10023 | FA14 | 2/2/2016 | 12:30 PM | 4.0 |

© 2014 Cengage Learning

5. Save and close the Rental table.

**6.** Jake created an Excel workbook named Reservations that is located in the AppendixB ▸ Access2 folder provided with your Data Files. Use the Import Spreadsheet Wizard to append data to the Rental table using the Reservations workbook as the source of the data. Make sure Access confirms that the first row contains column headings, and do not save the import steps.

**7.** Open the **Rental** table, resize the fields to their best fit, find the record for RentalID 02-3078, and then change the VehicleID value to **AB12** and the PickupTime to **8:00 AM**.

**8.** Find the record for RentalID 02-3045, and then delete the record. Save and close the Rental table.

**9.** Define the one-to-many relationships between the database tables as follows: between the primary Customer table and the related Rental table, and between the primary Vehicle table and the related Rental table. Select the referential integrity option and the cascade updates option for each relationship. Save the changes to the Relationships window and then close it.

**10.** Create a query that lists customers who are not members of Metro CarShare. In the query results, display the FirstName, LastName, and Phone fields from the Customer table, and the RentalDate field from the Rental table. Sort the records first in ascending order by the customer's last name and then in descending order by the rental date. Select records only for customers who are not members. (*Hint:* The Member field is a Yes/No field that should not appear in the query results.) Save the query as **NotMembers**, and then run the query.

**11.** Use the NotMembers query datasheet to update the Customer table by changing the record for Ernesto Bianco. Change the FirstName value to your first name and change the LastName value to your last name. In the query datasheet, also display the total number of times the selected customers have rented a car. (*Hint:* Use the Count aggregate function.) Save and close the query.

**12.** Create a query that lists the CustomerID, FirstName, LastName, RentalDate, and Nickname fields for customers who rented vehicles in March 2016. Save the query as **MarchCustomers**, run the query, and then close it.

**13.** Create a query that lists all customers who are members of Metro Car Share and rented a vehicle after 3/19/16. Display the following fields in the query results: CustomerID, FirstName, LastName, and Phone from the Customer table and RentalDate from the Rental table. (*Hint:* The Member field values should not appear in the query results.) Sort the query results in ascending order by last name. Save the query as **MembersAndSpring**, run the query, and then close it.

**14.** Copy and paste the MembersAndSpring query to create a new query named **MembersOrSpring**. Modify the new query so that it lists all customers who are members or who rented a vehicle after 3/19/16. Display the RentalDate field values in the query results following the CustomerID field values, and sort the query results in ascending order by the rental date. (This should be the only sort in the query.) Save and run the query.

**15.** Change the alternate row color in the MembersOrSpring query datasheet to the Dark Blue, Text 2, Lighter 80% theme color, and then save and close the query.

**16.** Create a query that calculates the total dollar amount of each rental. Display the following fields in the query results: FirstName and LastName from the Customer table, RentalDate and Hours from the Rental table, and Nickname and Rate from the Vehicle table. Move the Hours field so it follows the Nickname field. Create a calculated field named **RentalAmt** that displays the results of multiplying the Hours field values by the Rate field values. Set the Caption property for the calculated field to **Rental Amount**. Sort the query results in ascending order first by the customer's last name and then by the rental amount. Save the query as **RentalTotals**, run it, and then resize the columns in the datasheet to their best fit, as necessary. Format the calculated field as Currency with two decimal places. Save and run the query, and then close it.

**17.** Create a query and display only the field list for the RentalTotals query. (*Hint*: Click the Queries tab in the Show Table dialog box.) Calculate the lowest, highest, and average rental amounts for all customers using the field names **LowestRental**, **HighestRental**, and **AverageRental**, respectively. Set the Caption property for each field to include a space between the two words in the field name. Format each field as Currency with two decimal places. Save the query as **RentalStatistics**, run it, and then resize all columns in the datasheet to their best fit, as necessary. Save and close the query.

**18.** Use the Form Wizard to create a form containing a main form and a subform. Select all the fields from the Customer table for the main form, and select the VehicleID, RentalDate, PickupTime, and Hours fields from the Rental table for the subform. Use the Datasheet layout. Specify the title **CustomerRentals** for the main form and the title **RentalSubform** for the subform.

**19.** Apply the Facet theme to the CustomerRentals form *only*. Edit the form title so that it appears as "Customer Rentals" (two words), and then change the font color of the form title to the Blue-Gray, Text 2 theme color.

**20.** Find and display the record for Claire Hubbard, and then change the Street field value for this record to **1488 W. Beaumont Dr**. Save and close the CustomerRentals form.

**21.** Use the Report Wizard to create a report based on the primary Vehicle table and the related Rental table. Select all the fields from the Vehicle table, and then select the RentalID, RentalDate, and Hours fields from the Rental table. Do not select any additional grouping levels, and sort the detail records in ascending order by RentalDate. Choose the Outline layout and Portrait orientation. Specify the title **VehicleRentals** for the report.

**22.** Apply the Facet theme to the VehicleRentals report *only*. Resize the report title so that the text is fully displayed; edit the report title so that it appears as "Vehicle Rentals" (two words); and change the font color of the title to the Blue-Gray, Text 2 theme color.

**23.** Adjust the alignment, size, and position of the following objects in the report in Layout view, and then scroll through the report to make sure all field labels and field values are fully displayed:

  **a.** Left-align the values in the Rate field value boxes.

  **b.** Move the Rental ID label and field value box to the right a bit to add more space between the Rental Date and Rental ID columns.

  **c.** Resize the Hours label and field value box to better fit their contents, and then move them to the left so they are closer to the Rental ID label and field value box.

**24.** Insert the Car picture, which is located in the AppendixB ▶ Access2 folder provided with your Data Files, in the report. Move the picture to the right of the report title, and then make it slightly larger.

**25.** Apply conditional formatting so that any Hours field value greater than 3.0 appears as bold and red.

**26.** Preview the entire report to confirm that it is formatted correctly. It should look similar to Figure B-15, which shows part of the first page of the report. If necessary, return to Layout view and make changes so that all field labels and field values are completely displayed.

| Figure B-15 | Final VehicleRentals report |
|---|---|

**27.** Save the report, print its first page (only if asked by your instructor to do so), and then close the report.

**28.** Compact and repair the Metro database, and then close it.

# PowerPoint Project 1: Creating a Presentation for the ArtNetwork Gallery

**Data Files needed for this Capstone Project: Carrie.jpg, Gallery.jpg**

**TIP**

This Capstone Project maps to the material in PowerPoint Tutorial 1.

Carrie Waters is the owner of the ArtNetwork Gallery in Lincoln, Nebraska. The gallery exhibits art from local and national artists and works with corporations throughout the country to procure artwork for their buildings and offices. Carrie is a graduate of the University of Nebraska in Lincoln, and occasionally visits classes to encourage students to pursue a career in the visual arts. She wants to create a presentation that briefly describes her gallery and explains how to submit art to be exhibited there. You will create this presentation for Carrie by entering and formatting text, photos, and diagrams.

## To create a presentation:

1. Create a new, blank presentation named **ArtNetwork** and save it in the folder where you are storing your files, as specified by your instructor.

2. On the title slide, enter **ArtNetwork: Contemporary Art Gallery** as the title and your name as the subtitle.

3. Add a new Slide 2 with the Title and Content layout, enter **About ArtNetwork** as the slide title, and then in the content placeholder enter the following text:

   - **Contemporary art**
   - **Historic Eastridge neighborhood**
   - **Specializing in art for corporate settings**
   - **Rotating exhibitions**
   - **Lithographs**
   - **Paintings**
   - **Pastels**
   - **Photography**
   - **Sculpture**

4. Create a new Slide 3 with the Title and Content layout. Add **Artists Seeking Representation** as the slide title, and then enter the following text as a numbered list:

   1. **Create a CD or DVD of your images and send it to the gallery.**
   2. **Include a brief biography and list of achievements.**
   3. **Write "New Artist Submission" on the envelope.**
   4. **Contact Carrie Waters for more information.**

5. Create a new Slide 4 using the Two Content layout. Add **For More Information** as the slide title.

6. Move the last numbered item on Slide 3 ("Contact Carrie Waters for more information") to the left content placeholder on Slide 4.

7. On Slide 4, delete the bullet symbol from the text you moved, and then add the following text as the next two items in the unnumbered list:

   **Email: cwaters@cengage.com**

   **Phone: 402-555-2427**

8. Reduce the font size of the text in the left placeholder to 24 points.

9. Delete the text "for more information." from the left placeholder, including the period. Add a new line with the text **Gallery owner** below the "Contact Carrie Waters" line.

10. Remove the hyperlink formatting from the email address.

11. In the right placeholder, insert the image file named **Carrie**, which is located in the AppendixB ▶ PowerPoint1 folder provided with your Data Files. Reposition the photo so it appears in the middle-right part of the slide.

12. Change the presentation theme to Frame and keep the default variant.

13. Insert a new Slide 3 using the Title and Content layout. Move the "Rotating exhibitions" bullet and its subitems from Slide 2 to the content placeholder on Slide 3. Move the "Rotating exhibitions" text to the title placeholder, and then edit the text so it appears as "Rotating Exhibitions".

14. Convert the bulleted list on Slide 3 to a SmartArt graphic using the Basic Cycle layout.

15. Return to Slide 2 and change its layout to Two Content. In the right content placeholder, insert the image file named **Gallery**, which is located in the AppendixB ▸ PowerPoint1 folder provided with your Data Files.

16. Resize the photo, maintaining the aspect ratio, so that it is 3.5 inches high, and then move it to the middle-right part of the slide.

17. On Slide 4 ("Artists Seeking Representation"), reduce the font size of the title text to 32 points.

18. Duplicate Slide 4 and then revise the new Slide 5 by changing its title to **Submission Steps for Sculptors**. Insert a new Step 3 in the content placeholder and insert the following text: **List places you have exhibited your sculpture.**

19. Move Slide 3 ("Rotating Exhibitions") so it becomes Slide 5.

20. On Slide 6 ("For More Information"), crop the photo so the laptop computer does not appear in the image. Crop the photo again to the Oval shape, and then resize the photo so it is 5 inches high, maintaining the aspect ratio. Move the photo to the middle-right part of the slide.

21. Display the phone number ("402-555-2427") on a separate line after "Phone:", and remove any space before and after the phone number line.

22. Compress all the photos in the slides to 96 ppi and delete cropped areas of pictures.

23. Display the Notes pane, and then add the following note to Slide 5: **These are only some examples of the exhibitions the gallery has hosted.**

24. Check the spelling in the presentation, ignoring all instances of "Eastridge" and the gallery's name. Save the changes to the presentation, and then review the slide show in Slide Show, Presenter, and Reading views. Figure B-16 shows Slides 1–6 in the ArtNetwork presentation.

| Figure B-16 | Final ArtNetwork presentation |

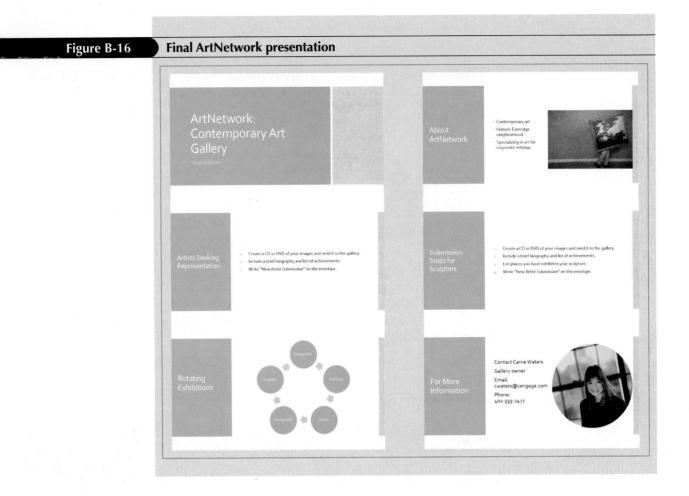

# PowerPoint Project 2: Creating a Multimedia Presentation for the Northern Lakeshore Bicycle Club

**Data Files needed for this Capstone Project: Bicycle.pptx, Race.jpg, Members.mp4**

Dwight Murray is the president of the Northern Lakeshore Bicycle Club in Traverse City, Michigan. During the winter when it's difficult to ride, Dwight travels around the state of Michigan to recruit members of the club. He has started to create a presentation he can show as he travels and asks you to complete it. To do so, you will insert media such as photos, diagrams, and videos, add slide transitions, and animate text and objects.

## To create a multimedia presentation:

1. Open the **Bicycle** presentation, which is located in the AppendixB ▶ PowerPoint2 folder provided with your Data Files, and then save it as **Bicycle Club** in the folder where you are storing your files, as specified by your instructor.

2. On Slide 1, insert your name as the subtitle, and then move the title and subtitle text boxes down so the title text box is in the middle of the slide.

3. On Slide 2, swap the position of the text box and the content placeholder so the text box appears on the right and the content placeholder appears on the left. Remove the bullet from the first line in the right text box ("The Northern Lakeshore Bike Club:").

▶ **4.** In the left content placeholder, insert the image file **Race**, which is located in the AppendixB ▶ PowerPoint2 folder provided with your Data Files. Increase the height of the photo to 4 inches, maintaining the aspect ratio. Align the top of the photo with the top of the text box in the right part of the slide. Apply the Drop Shadow Rectangle picture style to the photo.

▶ **5.** On Slide 3, insert a callout containing the text **Traverse City**. Copy the formatting of the other callouts to the new callout. Move the new callout so it points to Traverse City on the map.

▶ **6.** Add a Right Arrow shape to Slide 3. Type **Club meets here** in the arrow, and then resize the shape so it is about 1 inch tall and the text just fits on one line. Rotate the arrow approximately 45 degrees down and to the right, and then arrange the objects on the slide so that the arrow points to Traverse City but doesn't cover any of the callouts. Change the fill color of the arrow to Red, Accent 2, and change the outline color to black.

▶ **7.** Move Slide 4 so it becomes Slide 5. Change the layout of the new Slide 4 ("National Tours), to Photo Title & Content. Resize all of the photos so they are each 4 inches tall, maintaining the aspect ratio. Arrange the photos as shown in Figure B-17. Insert a text box above the first photo on the left that contains the text **Colorado**. Increase the font size to 24 points, bold the text, and then align the text box with the center of the photo below it.

| Figure B-17 | ▶ Formatting Slide 4 |
| --- | --- |

▶ **8.** Insert three other text boxes with the text **Nevada**, **Utah**, and **Washington** centered above the three other photos. Align the top edges of the text boxes.

▶ **9.** Apply the Tight Reflection, touching effect to the four photos on Slide 4.

▶ **10.** On Slide 5 ("Biking Tips"), insert the following four bulleted items:

- **Ride in a group**
- **Check your equipment**
- **Wear bright colors**
- **Stay hydrated**

▶ **11.** Convert the bulleted list on Slide 5 to a SmartArt diagram using the Basic Matrix layout. Apply the Intense Effect SmartArt style to the diagram.

▶ **12.** On Slide 6 ("Ride Categories"), change the layout to Title and Content. Insert a 2x7 table. In the first row in the table, enter **Ride Level** and **Description**. Refer to Figure B-18 to add the rest of the data to the table. Let PowerPoint convert the hyphen to a longer dash between two numbers.

**Figure B-18** ▶ **Ride categories**

| Ride Level | Description |
|---|---|
| A | Average speed 17 – 19 mph |
| B | Average speed 14 – 16 mph |
| C | Average speed 11 – 14 mph |
| D | Average speed 9 – 11 mph |
| O | Orientation ride |
| M | Mountain trail |

© 2014 Cengage Learning

▶ **13.** Apply the Medium Style 3 - Accent 1 table style, and then change the font size of all of the text in the table to 28 points.

▶ **14.** In the table, change the width of the first column to 3 inches, and then make the second column just wide enough to hold the widest entry on one line. Reposition the table so it is centered in the middle of the slide.

▶ **15.** Delete Slide 7 ("Ride Schedule"), and then compress all the photos in the presentation to 96 ppi.

▶ **16.** Apply the Wipe transition. Change the Effect Options to From Left, and then change the duration to 1.25 seconds. Apply this transition to all of the slides.

▶ **17.** On Slide 2 ("Welcome"), animate the bulleted list using the Float In animation. Change the duration of the animation to 2 seconds.

▶ **18.** On Slide 4 ("National Tours"), apply the Zoom animation to the "Colorado" text box. Apply the same animation to the other three text boxes. Change the start timing of all four animations to After Previous.

▶ **19.** Apply the Zoom animation to all four photos, and then change the start timing of these animations to With Previous. Move the animation applied to the Colorado photo so it appears with the Colorado text box. Move the animations for the other three photos so each photo appears with its corresponding text box.

▶ **20.** On Slide 7, change the layout to Two Content, and then add the video **Members**, located in the AppendixB ▶ PowerPoint2 folder, in the content placeholder on the right. Set the video to play Automatically and to rewind after playing. (This video has no sound.) Apply the Center Shadow Rectangle video style to the video.

▶ **21.** Compress the media to Low Quality.

▶ **22.** Add **Northern Lakeshore Bicycle Club** as the footer on all the slides except the title slide.

▶ **23.** Save the changes to the presentation, and then review the slide show in Slide Show, Presenter, and Reading views. Figure B-19 shows Slides 1–7 in the Bicycle Club presentation.

**Figure B-19**    **Final Bicycle Club presentation**

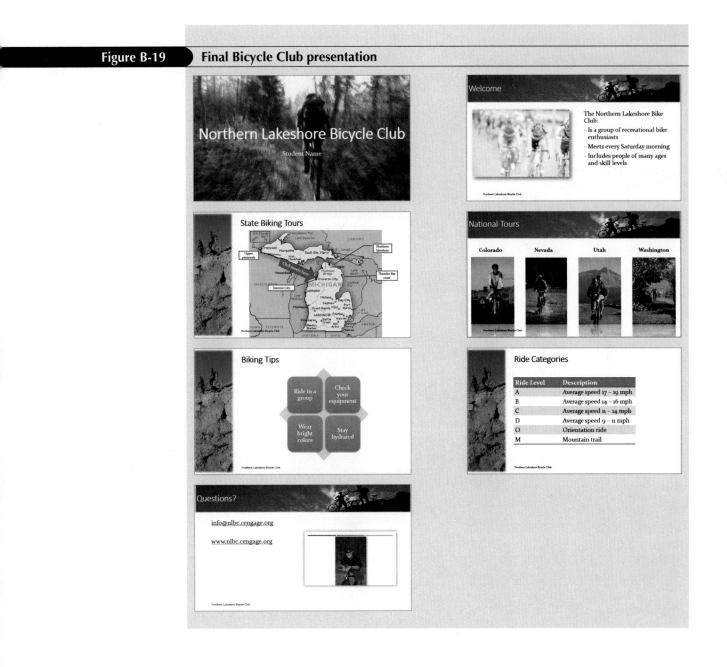

# GLOSSARY/INDEX

**grouped sparklines** A set of sparklines that share a common format. EX 219, EX 240–242

GUI. *See* graphical user interface

## H

**handle** The square, circle, or other shape on the border of a selected object, which you can drag to change the object's shape, size, or position. WD 49

handout, printing, PPT 58–59

**hanging indent** A type of paragraph indent in which all lines except the first line of the paragraph are indented from the left margin. WD 98

**Hanging Indent marker** A moveable icon on the horizontal ruler that looks like the bottom half of an hour glass and that can be dragged left or right to change the indent for all of a paragraph except the first line. WD 98

**hard copy** A printed copy of computer output. ECC 11

hard disk. *See* hard disk drive

**hard disk drive** A magnetic storage device that contains several magnetic oxide-covered metal platters that are usually sealed in a case inside the computer. Also called hard drive or hard disk. ECC 3, FM 6

hard drive. *See* hard disk drive

**hardware** The physical components of a computer. ECC 7
    connecting peripheral devices, ECC 12–13
    input devices, ECC 8–10
    output devices, ECC 10–12
    processing, ECC 7–8

**HDMI (high-definition multimedia interface) port** A port that digitally transmits video and audio. ECC 3

**header (Excel)** Information that appears at the top of each printed page. EX 119–121

**header (PowerPoint)** Information that appears at the top of notes pages or handouts of a presentation. PPT 122–124

**header (Word)** Text, date, or other information that is printed above the top page margin; also, the blank area at the top of a page where such information can be inserted. WD 98, WD 144
    adding, WD 159–160, WD 162–164

HEADER & FOOTER TOOLS DESIGN tab, WD 98, WD 99–100, WD 145, WD 159
    Footer button, WD 160
    Header button, WD 160

Header and Footer dialog box, PPT 121–122

**Header and Footer view** A Word view in which a document's header and footer areas are available

for editing, and the main document is unavailable for editing. WD 145

Header button, WD 159, WD 160

Header dialog box, EX 120

**header row** The top row of a table, containing the headings that identify the type of information in each column. WD 121

heading, Navigation pane, WD 122–126

heading style, WD 87

Help, WD 53–54

**Help and Support** A window that provides articles, video demonstrations, and steps for performing tasks in Windows 8. WIN 27–29
    searching Help pages, WIN 29
    selecting topics from Browse help list, WIN 28–29
    viewing Get started topics, WIN 28

Help button, PPT 3

Help page, searching, WIN 29

**Hide Fields** In Datasheet view, the command that allows you to remove the display of one or more fields. AC 119

**hiding (Excel)** To make a row, column, or worksheet not visible. EX 48

hiding (Access), fields, AC 119–120

hierarchy diagram, PPT 24

highlighting cells, EX 108–113
    based on values, EX 109–110
    with top/bottom rule, EX 110–112

**History list** A feature in Internet Explorer that tracks the webpages you visit over a certain time period, not just during one browsing session. IB 15–16

**hit** Page returned in search results that contain content that matches your search words. Hits are generally organized in order of relevancy. IB 12

**home page** The webpage that appears when the browser starts. The main page of a website is also called the home page. IB 3

**HOME tab** A ribbon tab that provides access to frequently used commands. WIN 20, WIN 21
    Add or Remove Columns button, PPT 111
    Borders button, WD 45
    Bullets button, WD 70–71
    Cell Styles button, EX 108
    Convert to SmartArt Graphic button, PPT 24
    Copy button, PPT 22
    Cut button, PPT 22
    Delete button, AC 122
    Font group, PPT 19–21, WD 30
    Format button, EX 48
    Format Painter button, WD 47

formatting buttons, EX 207
    Line and paragraph Spacing button, WD 20
    Spelling & Grammar button, WD 31
    Text Effects and Typography button, WD 41
    Totals button, AC 163

**horizontal axis (category axis)** The axis that displays the category values from each data series. EX 191

**hot corner** One of the four corners of the Start screen; you point to one to display objects for interacting with Windows. WIN 2

**hyperlink** Text or a graphic on a webpage that, when clicked, connects to and displays another part of the webpage or a different webpage. Also called link. ECC 19, IB 2, IB 3
    clicking, IB 7–8

**hyperlink (Word)** Text or a graphic you can click to jump to another file or to somewhere else in the same file; the two most common types are email hyperlinks and web hyperlinks. WD 12–13

Hyperlink data type, AC 57

hyphenation, WD 152–153

## I

**icon** A small picture that represents an object available on your computer. WIN 3
    Windows and Windows 7 compared, FM 4

**ID field** The default field Access creates to serve as the primary key field for all new tables. AC 11, AC 12–13

**IF function** The logical function that tests a condition and then returns one value if the condition is true and another value if the condition is false. EX 161, EX 172–176

image, background, EX 77–78

Import Objects dialog box, AC 84–85

Import Spreadsheet Wizard dialog box, AC 82

**importing** A process that allows you to copy the data from a source, without having to open the source file, and to add the imported data in an Access table. AC 80
    adding data to tables by importing text files, AC 95–97
    data from Excel worksheet to tables, AC 80–83
    existing table structure, AC 83–85

In () operator, AC 142

Increase Indent button, EX 87

indenting
    bullets, WD 72
    cell content, EX 88
    paragraphs, WD 96–98

information bar message, IB 7

Information function, EX 140

**information management software** Software that keeps track of schedules, appointments, contacts, and "to-do" lists. ECC 25

**inkjet printer** A printer that sprays ink onto paper and produces output whose quality is comparable to that of a laser printer. ECC 11

**inline object** An object that behaves as if it were text; like an individual letter, an inline object has a specific location within a line of text, and its position changes as you add or delete text. Compare to a floating object. WD 186

inline picture, WD 52

**input** The data or instructions you type into the computer. ECC 2

**input device** An instrument, such as a keyboard or a mouse, that you use to enter data and issue commands to the computer. ECC 8–10

Insert Address Block dialog box, INT 24

Insert Chart dialog box, EX 213

Insert Citation button, WD 102

Insert Function button, EX 132

Insert Function dialog box
    entering functions, EX 145–149

Insert Greeting Line dialog box, INT 26

Insert Merge Field button, INT 23

INSERT tab
    Chart button, INT 4, WD 209
    Charts group, EX 200
    Cover Page button, WD 164
    Footer button, WD 159
    Header button, WD 159
    Object button arrow, WD 192, WD 193
    Online Picture button, WD 208
    Online Pictures button, PPT 74
    Page Number button, WD 159
    Picture button, PPT 39
    Pictures button, WD 30
    Recommended Chart button, EX 197
    Shapes button, PPT 77, WD 194, WD 195
    Table button, WD 120, WD 128
    Video button, PPT 111, PPT 112

**insertion point** An object on the screen that indicates where text will appear when you start typing, usually appears as a blinking line. AC 13, PPT 7, WD 2
    moving, WD 14

INT function, EX 141

**Integer** The Field Size property that stores whole numbers from -32,768 to 32,767 in two bytes. AC 58

**intellectual property** All creations of the human mind, such as original ideas and creative works

presented in a form that can be shared or that others can recreate, emulate, or manufacture. On a webpage, intellectual property includes the text, images, and videos on the page, as well as the design of the page itself. IB 21–23, PPT 76
    fair use, IB 21–22
    plagiarism, IB 22–23
    public domain, IB 22

**interest** The amount added to the principal by the lender. EX 192

international date format, EX 23

**Internet** A worldwide collection of computer networks that allows people to communicate and exchange information; the largest network in the world. ECC 19–20, IB 4
    connecting to, IB 4

Internet Explorer app, IB 2, IB 11–16
    History list, IB 15–16
    starting, IB 4–5, IB 11–12
    tabbed browsing, IB 13–15

Internet Explorer button, IB 3

Internet Protocol (IP) addresses, IB 5

**Internet service provider (ISP)** A company that provides Internet access by connecting your computer to one of its servers via a telephone or cable modem. IB 4

invisible web. *See* deep web

**IP address** A unique number consisting of four sets of numbers from 0 to 255, separated by periods (such as 216.35.148.4), that identifies the server or computer connected to the Internet. IB 5

IP addresses. *See* Internet Protocol addresses

IPMT function, EX 192, EX 197

ISP. *See* Internet service provider

## J

**join line** In the Relationships window, the line that connects the common field that joins two tables. AC 77

**joining** To relate tables using a common field. AC 98

JPEG file, WD 224

**justified alignment** A type of alignment in which full lines of text are evenly spaced between both the left and the right margins, and no text is ragged. WD 43, WD 44

## K

K. *See* kilobyte

KB. *See* kilobyte

**Key Tip** Label that appears over each tab and command on the ribbon when you press the Alt key that specifies the key or keys to click to access that tab, button, or command. EX 6

**keyboard** The most frequently used input device; consists of three major parts: the main keyboard, the keypads, and the function keys. ECC 2, ECC 8, ECC 9, WIN 4
    Windows and Windows 7 compared, FM 4

**keyboard shortcut** A key or combination of keys you press to access a feature or perform a command more efficiently. AC 79, EX 6, WIN 25

**keyword (Internet)** Specific word or phrase that describes a topic of interest and can be used to search for information on that topic. IB 2, IB 3

**keyword (PowerPoint)** Word or phrase that you can enter in as search box that describes an image that you want to search for. PPT 74

**kilobyte (KB or K)** 1,024 bytes, or approximately one thousand bytes. ECC 13

**kilobytes per second (Kbps)** The measurement used for the data transfer rate for CD and DVD drives. ECC 16

## L

label, ribbon, AC 13

LAN. *See* local area network

**landscape orientation** The orientation where the page is wider than it is tall. AC 206, EX 53, WD 38

language, proofing, PPT 94–97

**laptop computer** A small, lightweight computer designed for portability. Also called notebook computer. ECC 4, ECC 5

Large icons view button, FM 3

**laser printer** A printer that produces high-quality output quickly and efficiently by transferring a temporary laser image onto paper with toner. ECC 11

**layout** The arrangement of placeholders on the slide; in SmartArt, the arrangement of the shapes in the diagram. PPT 11, PPT 24

**Layout view** The Access view in which you can make design changes to a form or report while it is displaying data so that you can immediately see the effects of changing the design. AC 34, AC 181
    modifying form design, AC 185–193
    modifying report design, AC 212–216

**LCD (liquid crystal display)** A display technology that creates images by manipulating light within a layer of liquid crystal. ECC 10

**leader line** A line that connects a data label to its corresponding data marker. EX 207

**workbook** An Excel file that stores a spreadsheet; contains a collection of worksheets and chart sheets. EX 2
  enhancing with color, EX 76
  existing, opening, EX 4–5
  formatting, EX 70
  opening, EX 71
  printing, EX 51–56
  saving with new name, EX 57–58
  themes, EX 106–108
  user-friendly, EX 134–140

**workbook window** The area of the Excel window that displays the contents of the workbook. EX 3

**WORKDAY function** The function that displays the date of a weekday that is specified number of weekdays past a starting date. EX 161, EX 167, EX 168–169

**works cited list** In the MLA style, term used to refer to a bibliography. WD 93, WD 112

**worksheet** In spreadsheet software, a grid of rows and columns in which content is entered. ECC 23, EX 3
  AutoComplete, EX 20–21
  background images, EX 77–78
  cells. See formatting worksheet cells; worksheet cell
  changing active sheet, EX 8–9
  changing font size, EX 51
  changing views, EX 51–53
  closing, EX 13
  columns. See worksheet column
  deleting, EX 17
  displaying numbers as text, EX 21–22
  effective, EX 14
  entering dates, EX 22–24
  entering numbers, EX 24–25

  entering text, EX 18–21
  formatting cells. See formatting worksheet cells
  formatting for printing. See formatting worksheets for printing
  formulas. See formula
  hiding and unhiding, EX 48
  identifying notes, input values, and calculated values, EX 138–139
  inserting, EX 16
  moving, EX 16
  moving charts between, EX 214
  navigating within, EX 9–11
  new, creating, EX 15–17
  page orientation, EX 53
  planning, EX 13–14
  redoing actions, EX 19
  renaming, EX 16
  rows. See worksheet row
  saving, EX 17
  scaling, EX EX 43
  undoing and actions, EX 19

**worksheet cell**
  borders, EX 50
  editing content, EX 19–20
  formatting. See formatting worksheet cells
  selecting cell ranges, EX 11–13

**worksheet column**
  changing width, EX 25–27
  deleting, EX 44, EX 45
  hiding and unhiding, EX 48
  inserting, EX 43–45
  wrapping text within cells, EX 25–27

**worksheet row**
  changing height, EX 29
  deleting, EX 44, EX 45
  hiding and unhiding, EX 48
  inserting, EX 43–45

World Wide Web. See web

Worldwide Interoperability for Microwave Access. See WiMAX

**wrap** In relation to text, to flow around a graphic. WD 176

Wrap Text button, EX 87

**X**

**XY scatter chart** A chart that shows the pattern or relationship between two or more sets of values. EX 199, EX 237
  line charts compared, EX 221

**Y**

YEAR function, EX 167

Yes/No data type, AC 57
  sorting results, AC 131

**Z**

**Zoom box** A dialog box you can use to enter text, expressions, or other values. AC 154

Zoom button, WIN 2

**Zoom control** Control that increases or decreases the magnification of the worksheet content. EX 3

Zoom In button, PPT 3

Zoom into the slide button, PPT 32, PPT 33

Zoom Out button, PPT 3

**zooming (Word)** Magnifying or shrinking the display of content in the Word window. WD 3

zooming (Windows), Start screen, WIN 10–11

# TASK REFERENCE

| TASK | PAGE # | RECOMMENDED METHOD |
|---|---|---|
| **Absolute reference, create** | EX 154 | Type a $ before both the row and column references |
| **Access Query results, copy to PowerPoint slide** | INT 37 | In query datasheet, click datasheet selector, click HOME tab, in Clipboard group click Copy, on taskbar click PowerPoint button, click in content placeholder, click HOME tab, in Clipboard group click Paste button arrow, click Keep Text Only button |
| **Access Query Results, export from Access database to Excel or Word** | INT 29 | *See* Reference box: Exporting the Results of an Access Query to Excel or Word |
| **Access, start** | AC 7 | Click the Access 2013 tile on the Windows Start screen |
| **Action, reverse last in WordPad** | WIN 21 | Click ▧ on the Quick Access Toolbar |
| **Action, undo or redo** | EX 19 | Click ↺ or ↻ on the Quick Access Toolbar |
| **Aggregate functions, use in a datasheet** | AC 162 | Open the table or query in Datasheet view, in Records group on HOME tab click Totals button, click Total field row, click function |
| **Aggregate functions, use in a query** | AC 163 | Display the query in Design view, click the Totals button in the Show/Hide group on the DESIGN tab |
| **Animation Painter, use** | PPT 106 | Click animated object, click ANIMATIONS tab, in Advanced Animation group, click Animation Painter, click object to animate |
| **Animation, apply** | PPT 103 | *See* Reference box: Applying Animations |
| **Animation, change order** | PPT 106 | Click ANIMATIONS tab, click animation sequence icon, in Timing group click Move Earlier or Move Later |
| **Application, close** | WIN 27 | Press Alt+F4 |
| **Application, start** | WIN 13 | *See* Reference box: Starting an Application |
| **Apps screen, display** | WIN 15 | Right-click a blank area on the Start screen, click All apps |
| **AutoCorrect, change** | PPT 10 | Click ⟥ ▾, click command on menu |
| **AutoSum feature, enter function with** | EX 37 | Click a cell, click Σ AutoSum ▾ in the Editing group on the HOME tab, click a function, verify the range, press Enter |
| **Bibliography, insert** | WD 109 | Create citations in the document, click the desired location for the bibliography, click Bibliography button in Citations & Bibliography group on REFERENCES tab, click a bibliography style |
| **Bold text, enter in WordPad** | WIN 21 | Click **B** in the Font group on the Home tab |
| **Border, add to cells** | EX 50 | Select a range, click ▦ ▾ in the Font group on the HOME tab, click a border |
| **Border, insert around page** | WD 226 | Click DESIGN tab, click the Page Borders button in the Page Background group, click the Page Border tab, click Box |
| **Border, insert around paragraph** | WD 45 | Click in a paragraph, click ▦ ▾ in the Paragraph group on the HOME tab, click a border style |
| **Bulleted or numbered item, demote** | PPT 14, 16 | Click bullet or number, click ⇥ |
| **Bulleted or numbered item, promote** | PPT 15, 16 | Click bullet or number, click ⇤ |
| **Bullets, add to paragraph** | WD 71 | Select paragraphs, click ▤ in the Paragraph group on the HOME tab |
| **Calculated field, add to a query** | AC 157 | *See* Reference box: Using Expression Builder |

| TASK | PAGE # | RECOMMENDED METHOD |
|---|---|---|
| **Cell, change fill color** | EX 76 | Click 🪣 ▾ in the Font group on the HOME tab, click a color |
| **Cell, clear contents of** | EX 58 | Select a cell, press Delete |
| **Cell, delete** | EX 46 | Select a cell, range, column, or row; click Delete button in the Cells group on the HOME tab |
| **Cell, edit** | EX 19 | Double-click a cell, enter changes |
| **Cell, go to** | EX 10 | Click Find & Select button in the Editing group on the HOME tab, click Go To |
| **Cell contents, align within a cell** | EX 87 | Click ≣, ≣, or ≣ in the Alignment group on the HOME tab |
| **Cell contents, change indent of** | EX 88 | Click ▸≣ or ◂≣ in the Alignment group on the HOME tab |
| **Cell contents, rotate** | EX 91 | Click ≫ ▾ in the Alignment group on the HOME tab, click angle |
| **Cells, merge and center** | EX 90 | Select adjacent cells, click ⊞ in the Alignment group on the HOME tab |
| **Charms bar, display** | WIN 11 | Point to the upper-right or lower-right corner of screen |
| **Chart, choose style** | EX 204 | Select the chart, click 🖌, select a chart style |
| **Chart, create** | EX 197 | See Reference box: Creating a Chart |
| **Chart, resize** | EX 202 | Select the chart, drag the sizing handle |
| **Chart element, format** | EX 205 | Double-click the chart element, make changes in the Format pane |
| **Chart type, change** | EX 214 | Select the chart, click the Change Chart Type button in the Type group on the CHART TOOLS DESIGN tab, click a new chart type |
| **Citations, create and edit** | WD 103 | See Reference box: Creating Citations |
| **Clip art, insert** | WD 213 | Click INSERT tab, click the Online Pictures button in the Illustrations group, type keywords in the Office.com Clip Art search box, press Enter, click an image, click the Insert button |
| **Clipboard task pane, open** | WD 76 | In Clipboard group on HOME tab, click the Dialog Box Launcher |
| **Column, change width** | EX 25 | Drag the right border of the column heading left or right |
| **Column, delete from table** | WD 136 | Select the column to delete, click the Delete button on the Mini toolbar, click Delete Columns |
| **Column, insert in table** | WD 135 | Point to the border between two columns, click ⊕ |
| **Column, resize width in a datasheet** | AC 18 | Double-click ↔ on the right border of the column heading |
| **Column, select** | EX 26 | Click the column heading |
| **Columns, format section in** | WD 181 | Click PAGE LAYOUT tab, click Columns button in the Page Setup group, select options, click OK |
| **Comments, display and insert** | WD 67 | See Reference box: Working with Comments |
| **Compressed folder, extract all files and folders from** | FM 27 | Click the compressed folder, click the Compressed Folder Tools Extract tab, click the Extract all button |
| **Compressed folder, open** | FM 27 | Double-click the compressed folder |
| **Conditional format, apply** | EX 108 | See Reference box: Highlighting a Cell with a Conditional Format |
| **Cover page, delete** | WD 164 | Click INSERT tab, click the Cover Page button in the Pages group, click Remove Current Cover Page |
| **Cover page, insert** | WD 164 | Click INSERT tab, click the Cover Page button in the Pages group, click cover page |
| **Data bars, create** | EX 242 | See Reference Box: Creating Data Bars |

| TASK | PAGE # | RECOMMENDED METHOD |
|------|--------|--------------------|
| Data, find | AC 194 | *See* Reference box: Finding Data in a Form or Datasheet |
| Data Type gallery, add fields to a table with | AC 86 | Click the FIELDS tab, click More Fields in the Add & Delete group, click the field or Quick Start selection to add |
| Database, compact and repair | AC 42 | *See* Reference box: Compacting and Repairing a Database |
| Database, create a blank | AC 7 | Start Access, click Blank desktop database, type the database name, select the drive and folder, click OK, click Create |
| Database, open | AC 26 | *See* Reference box: Opening a Database |
| Datasheet view for tables, switch to | AC 75 | In the Views group on the DESIGN tab, click the View button |
| Date, display on slides | PPT 121 | Click INSERT tab, in Text group, click Header & Footer, click Date check box, click Apply to All |
| Date, enter into a cell | EX 23 | Click a cell, type the date, press Enter or Tab |
| Date, insert the current | EX 167 | Enter TODAY() or NOW() function in cell |
| Design view, switch to | AC 73 | In the Views group on the FIELDS tab, click the View button |
| Desktop application, close inactive | WIN 26 | Right-click the application's button on taskbar, click Close window |
| Desktop application, switch to another open | WIN 23 | Click the application's button on taskbar |
| Document, print | WD 25 | Click FILE tab, click Print, click Print button |
| Document, save as a PDF | WD 227 | Click FILE tab, click Export, click the Create PDF/XPS Document button, navigate to the location where you want to save the PDF, click the Publish button |
| Documents library, open | FM 10 | In File Explorer, click ▷ next to Libraries, click ▷ next to Documents |
| Drop cap, insert | WD 200 | Click in paragraph, click the INSERT tab, click the Drop Cap button in the Text group, select options, click OK |
| Endnotes and footnotes, create | WD 150 | *See* Reference box: Inserting a Footnote or an Endnote |
| Envelope, create and save in current document | WD 28 | Click the MAILINGS tab, click the Envelopes button in the Create group, enter return address, if necessary, enter delivery address, click Add to Document |
| Excel chart, embed in Word document | INT 6 | *See* Reference box: Embedding an Excel Chart in a Word Document |
| Excel Table, embed in PowerPoint slide | INT 39 | In worksheet, select cells, click HOME tab, in Clipboard group click Copy, on taskbar click PowerPoint button, click HOME tab, in Clipboard group click Paste button arrow, click Embed |
| Excel worksheet, import data from | AC 81 | Click the EXTERNAL DATA tab, click Excel in the Import & Link group, complete the import dialog boxes |
| Excel worksheet, link to Word document | INT 11 | *See* Reference box: Linking Excel Worksheet Data to a Word Document |
| Excel, start | EX 4 | Click the Excel 2013 title on the Start screen |
| Favorite webpage, delete | IB 19 | Click ☆, click Favorites tab, right-click favorite, click Delete |
| Favorite webpage, save from desktop application | IB 17 | Click ☆, click Favorites tab, click Add to favorites, change name or folder, click Add |
| Field, add to a table | AC 69 | *See* Reference box: Adding a Field Between Two Existing Fields |
| Field, define in a table | AC 59 | *See* Reference box: Defining a Field in Design View |
| Field, delete from a table | AC 87 | *See* Reference box: Deleting a Field from a Table Structure |

| TASK | PAGE # | RECOMMENDED METHOD |
|------|--------|--------------------|
| **Field, move to a new location in a table** | AC 69 | Display the table in Design view, click the field's row selector, drag the field with the pointer |
| **Field property change, update** | AC 91 | Click ⚡, select the option for updating the field property |
| **File Explorer, open** | FM 10 | Click 🗎 on the taskbar |
| **File Explorer, return to a previous location** | FM 14 | Click ⬅ |
| **File list, sort** | FM 14 | Click the column heading button |
| **File, copy** | FM 24 | Right-click the file, click Copy, right-click destination, click Paste |
| **File, delete** | FM 25 | Right-click the file, click Delete |
| **File, move** | FM 21 | Drag the file to the folder |
| **File, open from File Explorer** | FM 15 | Right-click the file, point to Open with, click an application |
| **File, rename** | FM 26 | Right-click the file, click Rename, type the new filename, press Enter |
| **File, save with new name in WordPad** | FM 18 | Click the File tab, click Save as, enter the filename, click Save |
| **Files and folders, compress** | FM 27 | Select the files to compress, click the Share tab, click the Zip button in the Send group |
| **Files, select multiple** | FM 24 | Press and hold the Ctrl key and click the files |
| **Files, view in Large Icons view** | FM 13 | Click the View tab, click 🖿 in the Layout group |
| **Fill handle, use** | EX 162 | *See Reference box: Copying Formulas and Formats with AutoFill* |
| **Filter By Selection, activate** | AC 136 | *See Reference box: Using Filter By Selection* |
| **Find and replace, text or format** | EX 104 | Click Find & Select in the Editing group on the HOME tab, click Replace |
| **Flash Fill, apply** | EX 49 | Type a few entries in a column to establish a pattern, Flash Fill adds the remaining entries |
| **Folder, create** | FM 19 | Click the New folder button in the New group on the Home tab |
| **Font, change color** | EX 73 | Click 🅰 ▾ in the Font group on the HOME tab, click a color |
| **Font, change size** | EX 71 | Click the Font Size arrow in the Font group on the HOME tab, click a point size |
| **Font, change style** | EX 71 | Click **B**, *I*, or U̲ in the Font group on the HOME tab |
| **Font, change typeface** | EX 71 | Click the Font arrow in the Font group on the HOME tab, click a font |
| **Footer, add** | WD 160 | Double-click the bottom margin, type footer text, or select a preformatted footer by clicking the Footer button in the Header & Footer group on the DESIGN tab |
| **Footer, add to slides** | PPT 121 | Click INSERT tab, in Text group, click Header & Footer, click Footer check box, click Footer box, type footer, click Apply to All |
| **Footer, don't show on title slide** | PPT 122 | Click INSERT tab, in Text group, click Header & Footer, click Don't show in title slide check box, click Apply to All |
| **Format Painter, use** | PPT 21 | Select formatted text or object, click HOME tab, in Clipboard group click Format Painter, select object to format |
| **Form Wizard, activate** | AC 182 | Click the CREATE tab, click Form Wizard in the Forms group, choose the table or query for the form, select fields, click Next |

| TASK | PAGE # | RECOMMENDED METHOD |
|---|---|---|
| Formula, enter | EX 32 | Click the cell, type = and then a formula, press Enter or Tab |
| Formulas, display in a worksheet | EX 56 | Press Ctrl+` |
| Function, insert | EX 145 | Click a function category in the Function Library group on the FORMULAS tab, click a function, enter arguments, click OK |
| Goal seek, perform | EX 180 | *See* Reference box: Performing What-if Analysis and Goal Seek |
| Graphic object, resize | WD 50 | Click graphic object, click the FORMAT tab, change the height and width settings in the Size group |
| Graphic object, wrap text around | WD 187 | Click graphic object, click 🖾 next to the graphic object, click a text wrapping option |
| Header and footer, add to notes and handouts | PPT 122 | Click INSERT tab, in Text group, click Header & Footer, click Notes and Handouts, select check boxes for items to display, type information, click Apply to All |
| Header, add | WD 159 | Double-click the top margin, type header text, or select a preformatted header by clicking the Header button in the Header & Footer group on the DESIGN tab |
| Help, search for topic | WIN 29 | On the Help home page, click in the Search box, type word or phrase, press Enter |
| Help, start | WIN 27 | On the Start screen, type help, click Help and Support on the Apps screen |
| Help, use Browse help list | WIN 29 | On the Help home page, click Browse help |
| Help, view Get started topics | WIN 28 | On the Help home page, click Get started link |
| History list, use (desktop application only) | IB 15 | Click ⭐, click History tab, click folder, click webpage |
| Hyperlink, remove | WD 12 | Right-click hyperlink, click Remove Hyperlink |
| Hyphenation, turn on | WD 142 | Click PAGE LAYOUT tab, click the Hyphenation button in the Page Setup group, click Automatic |
| Internet Explorer app, start | IB 4 | On Start screen, click Internet Explorer tile |
| Internet Explorer desktop application, start | IB 11 | On Start screen, click Desktop tile; on taskbar click 🖉 |
| Layout, change | PPT 13 | Click HOME tab, in Slides group click Layout button, click layout |
| Line spacing, change | WD 18 | Select text, click ↕≡ ▾ in the Paragraph group on HOME tab, click a spacing option |
| Linked object, edit | INT 14 | Right-click linked object, point to Linked <Type> Object, click Edit Link, edit linked file |
| Linked object, update | INT 13 | Right-click linked object, click Update Link |
| Link, use | IB 7 | Point to link to see URL in ScreenTip; click link to load page |
| Mail Merge, create merged document | INT 28 | Click MAILINGS tab, in Finish group, click Finish & Merge, click Edit Individual Documents, click All option button, click OK |
| Mail Merge, edit recipient list | INT 22 | Click MAILINGS tab, in Start Mail Merge group, click Edit Recipients, make selections, click OK |
| Mail Merge, insert combined merge fields | INT 24 | Click MAILINGS tab, in Write & Insert Fields group, click Address Block or Greeting Line, make format selections, click OK |
| Mail Merge, insert individual merge fields | INT 23 | Click MAILINGS tab, in Write & Insert Fields group, click Insert Merge Field button arrow, click merge field |

| TASK | PAGE # | RECOMMENDED METHOD |
|------|--------|--------------------|
| **Mail Merge, preview merged document** | INT 27 | Click MAILINGS tab, in Preview Results group, click Preview Results |
| **Mail Merge, select existing Access data source** | INT 21 | Click MAILINGS tab, in Start Mail Merge group, click Select Recipients, click Use an Existing List, navigate to location, click file, click Open, click table or query, click OK |
| **Mail Merge, sort recipient list** | INT 22 | Click MAILINGS tab, in Start Mail Merge group, click Edit Recipients, click Sort link, click Sort by arrow, click field name, click Ascending or Descending option button, click OK |
| **Mail Merge, start** | INT 20 | Click MAILINGS tab, in Start Mail Merge group, click Start Mail Merge, click Letters |
| **Margins, change** | WD 23 | Click PAGE LAYOUT tab, click the Margins button in the Page Setup group on HOME tab, click a margins option |
| **Margins, set** | EX 121 | Click the Margins button in the Page Setup group on the PAGE LAYOUT tab, select a margin size |
| **Media, compress** | PPT 119 | Click FILE tab, on Info screen, click Compress Media, click quality option, click Close |
| **Microsoft Access Help, search** | AC 41 | Click ? on the title bar, enter the search text in the search box, press Enter |
| **Mixed reference, create** | EX 154 | Type $ before either the row or column reference |
| **My Documents folder, open** | FM 10 | In File Explorer, click ▷ next to Libraries, click ▷ next to Documents, click My Documents |
| **Number format, apply** | EX 82 | Click $, %, ❜, or the Number Format arrow in the Number group on the HOME tab |
| **Number, enter as text** | EX 21 | Type ' and then type the number |
| **Numbered list, create** | PPT 16 | Select list, click HOME tab, in Paragraph group click 📋 |
| **Numbering, add to paragraphs** | WD 72 | Select paragraphs, click 📋 in the Paragraph group on HOME tab |
| **Object, delete** | PPT 48 | Click object, press Delete |
| **Object, flip** | PPT 83 | Click object, click DRAWING TOOLS FORMAT tab, in Arrange group click Rotate, click Flip option |
| **Object, move** | PPT 45 | Click object, drag to new position with ✛ |
| **Object, open** | AC 22 | Double-click the object in the Navigation Pane |
| **Object, rotate** | PPT 83 | Click object, drag rotate handle |
| **Object, save** | AC 20 | Click 💾, type the object name, click OK |
| **Online pictures, insert** | PPT 75 | In content placeholder click 🖼, type keywords in Office.com Clip Art box, click 🔍, click image, click Insert |
| **Page break, insert** | WD 108 | Click where you want to insert a page break, click INSERT tab, click the Page Break button in the Pages group |
| **Page break, insert or remove** | EX 116 | *See* Reference box: Inserting and Removing Page Breaks |
| **Page number, insert** | WD 98 | Click INSERT tab, click the Page Number button in the Header & Footer group, select options from menu |
| **Page orientation, change** | WD 38 | Click PAGE LAYOUT tab, click the Orientation button in the Page Setup group, click an orientation |
| **Page tab, close** | IB 14 | On page tab, click ⊗ or ✖ |

| TASK | PAGE # | RECOMMENDED METHOD |
|---|---|---|
| **Page tab, open** | IB 13 | *See* Reference box: Opening Tabs for Browsing |
| **Paragraph spacing, add or remove default** | WD 18 | Click paragraph, click ▦ in the Paragraph group on HOME tab, click options to add or remove space before or after paragraphs |
| **Paragraph spacing, select specific setting** | WD 48 | Click paragraph, click PAGE LAYOUT tab, adjust settings in the Spacing Before and After boxes in Paragraph group |
| **PDF, open in Word** | WD 228 | Click the FILE tab, click Open, navigate to the folder containing the PDF, click the PDF, click the Open button, click the OK button |
| **Photo compression options, change** | PPT 43 | *See* Reference box: Modifying Photo Compression Settings and Removing Cropped Areas |
| **Picture style, apply** | WD 51 | Click a picture, click FORMAT tab, click the More button in the Picture Styles group, click a style |
| **Picture, apply effect** | PPT 82 | Click photo, click PICTURE TOOLS FORMAT tab, in Picture Styles group, click Picture Effects, point to effect type, click effect |
| **Picture, apply style** | PPT 82 | Click photo, click PICTURE TOOLS FORMAT tab, in Picture Styles group click style |
| **Picture, crop** | PPT 40 | Click picture, click PICTURE TOOLS FORMAT tab, in Size group, click Crop, drag Crop handles, click Crop |
| **Picture, crop** | WD 210 | Click a picture, click FORMAT tab, click the Crop button in the Size group, drag picture border to crop, deselect picture |
| **Picture, crop to shape** | WD 210 | Click picture, click FORMAT tab, click Crop button arrow in Size group, point to Crop to Shape, click shape |
| **Picture, insert** | WD 49 | Click INSERT tab, click Pictures button in the Illustrations group, select picture file, click Insert button |
| **Picture, insert from your computer** | PPT 39 | In content placeholder click ▤, navigate to picture file location, click picture file, click Insert |
| **Picture, insert in a form** | AC 189 | In Layout view, click the DESIGN tab, click the Logo button in the Header/Footer group, select the picture file, click OK |
| **Picture, resize** | PPT 46 | Click object, drag a corner sizing handle |
| **Pinned tile, unpin from Start screen** | IB 20 | On Start screen, right-click pinned tile, click Unpin from Start |
| **PowerPoint, exit** | PPT 60 | Click ✖ |
| **Presentation, close** | PPT 30 | Click FILE tab, click Close |
| **Presentation, open** | PPT 34 | Click FILE tab, click Open, click Computer, click Browse, navigate to location of file, click file, click Open |
| **Presentation, print** | PPT 57 | Click FILE tab, click Print, select options, click Print |
| **Presentation, save changes** | PPT 11 | On Quick Access Toolbar, click 🖫 |
| **Presentation, save for the first time** | PPT 9 | On Quick Access Toolbar, click 🖫, on Save As screen click Computer, type filename, navigate to location, click Save |
| **Presentation, save with a new name** | PPT 34 | Click FILE tab, click Save As, on Save As screen click Computer, type filename, navigate to location, click Save |
| **Primary key, specify** | AC 67 | *See* Reference box: Specifying a Primary Key in Design View |
| **Print area, set** | EX 115 | Select range, click the Print Area button in the Page Setup group on PAGE LAYOUT tab, click Set Print Area |
| **Print dialog box, open in WordPad** | WIN 21 | Click the File tab, click Print |

| TASK | PAGE # | RECOMMENDED METHOD |
|---|---|---|
| Print titles, add | EX 117 | Click the Print Titles button in the Page Setup group on the PAGE LAYOUT tab, click Rows to repeat at top, select a range, click OK |
| Proofing language, change for selected word | PPT 95 | Select text, on status bar click ENGLISH (UNITED STATES), click language, click OK |
| Property sheet, open | AC 159 | Make the object current in Design view, click the Property Sheet button in the Show/Hide group on the DESIGN tab |
| Query, define | AC 125 | Click the CREATE tab, click the Query Design button in the Queries group |
| Query, run | AC 127 | Double-click the query in the Navigation Pane or, in the Results group on the DESIGN tab, click the Run button |
| Query results, sort | AC 133 | See Reference box: Sorting a Query Datasheet |
| Quick Start selection, add | AC 86 | Click the FIELDS tab, click More Fields in the Add & Delete group, click the Quick Start selection |
| Range, select adjacent | EX 11 | Click a cell, drag the pointer from the selected cell to the cell in the lower-right corner of the range |
| Range, select nonadjacent | EX 12 | Select a cell or an adjacent range, press the Ctrl key as you select additional cells or adjacent ranges |
| Record, add new | AC 20 | In the Records group on the HOME tab, click the New button |
| Record, delete | AC 122 | See Reference box: Deleting a Record |
| Record, move to first | AC 30 | Click |◀ |
| Record, move to last | AC 30 | Click ▶| |
| Record, move to next | AC 30 | Click ▶ |
| Record, move to previous | AC 30 | Click ◀ |
| Records, print selected in a form | AC 199 | Click the FILE tab, click Print in the navigation bar, click Print, click Selected Record(s), click OK |
| Records, redisplay all after filter | AC 138 | In Sort & Filter group on HOME tab, click the Toggle Filter button |
| Recycle Bin, open | WIN 22 | Double-click the Recycle Bin icon on desktop |
| Relative reference, create | EX 150 | Type the cell reference as it appears in the worksheet |
| Report, print | AC 39 | See Reference box: Printing a Report |
| Report, print specific pages of | AC 219 | In the Print group on the PRINT PREVIEW tab, click Print, click Pages, enter number of pages to print in From and To boxes, click OK |
| Report Wizard, activate | AC 208 | Click the CREATE tab, click Report Wizard button in Reports group, choose the table or query for the report, select fields, click Next |
| Ribbon, expand in File Explorer | FM 13 | Click ⌄ |
| Row, change height | EX 29 | Drag the bottom border of the row heading up or down |
| Row, delete from table | WD 136 | Select the row to delete, click the Delete button on the Mini toolbar, click Delete Rows |
| Row, insert in table | WD 131 | Click a row, click the LAYOUT tab, click the Insert Above or Insert Below button in Rows & Columns group |
| Row, select | EX 26 | Click the row heading |
| Rows, repeat in printout | EX 118 | Click the Print Titles button in the Page Setup group on the PAGE LAYOUT tab, click Rows to repeat at top, select range, click OK |

| TASK | PAGE # | RECOMMENDED METHOD |
|---|---|---|
| Section break, insert in document | WD 153 | Click where you want to insert a section break, click PAGE LAYOUT tab, click Breaks button in the Page Setup group, click a section break type |
| Series, create with AutoFill | EX 162 | Enter the first few entries in a series, drag the fill handle over the adjacent range |
| Settings menu, open | WIN 11 | Display the Charms bar, click Settings |
| Shading, apply to paragraph | WD 45 | Click in paragraph, click [icon] in Paragraph group on HOME tab, click color |
| Shape, apply style | PPT 80 | Click shape, click DRAWING TOOLS FORMAT tab, in Shape Styles group, click style |
| Shape, change fill color | PPT 79 | Click shape, click DRAWING TOOLS FORMAT tab, in Shape Styles group click Shape Fill button arrow, click color |
| Shape, change outline weight | PPT 81 | Click shape, click DRAWING TOOLS FORMAT tab, in Shape Styles group click Shape Outline button arrow, point to Weight, click weight |
| Shape, insert | PPT 77 | Click INSERT tab, in Illustrations group click Shapes, click shape, drag on slide |
| Shortcut menu, open | WIN 15 | Right-click the object |
| Slide number, display on slides | PPT 121 | Click INSERT tab, in Text group, click Header & Footer, click Slide number check box, click Apply to All |
| Slide show, run from current slide | PPT 53 | On the status bar, click [icon] |
| Slide show, run from Slide 1 | PPT 53 | On the Quick Access Toolbar, click [icon] |
| Slide show, run in Presenter view | PPT 54 | In Slide Show view, click (...), click Show Presenter View |
| Slide show, run in Reading view | PPT 56 | On status bar, click [icon] |
| Slide, add | PPT 12 | Click HOME tab, in Slides group click New Slide button arrow, click layout |
| Slide, delete | PPT 29 | Right-click slide thumbnail, click Delete Slide |
| Slide, duplicate | PPT 28 | Click slide thumbnail, click HOME tab, in Slides group click New Slide button arrow, click Duplicate Selected Slides |
| Slide, move | PPT 28 | Drag slide thumbnail to new location |
| Slide, reset | INT 36 | Click slide thumbnail, click HOME tab, in Slides group, click Reset |
| Slides, create from Word outline | INT 35 | Click HOME tab, in Slides group, click New Slide button arrow, click Slides from Outline, navigate to location, click outline file, click Insert |
| SmartArt diagram, convert from list | PPT 24 | See Reference box: Converting a Bulleted List into a SmartArt Diagram |
| SmartArt, create | WD 152 | Click INSERT tab, click the SmartArt button in the Illustrations group, in the left pane of the Choose a SmartArt Graphic dialog box click a category, in the middle pane click a SmartArt style, click OK, replace placeholder text with new text |
| Sort, specify ascending in datasheet | AC 132 | Click a column heading arrow, click Sort A to Z |
| Sort, specify descending in datasheet | AC 132 | Click a column heading arrow, click Sort Z to A |
| Sparklines, create | EX 239 | See Reference box: Creating and Editing Sparklines |
| Speaker notes, add | PPT 49 | On status bar click NOTES, click in Notes pane, type note |

| TASK | PAGE # | RECOMMENDED METHOD |
|---|---|---|
| Spelling and grammar, correct for entire document | WD 36 | Click the REVIEW tab, click the Spelling & Grammar button in the Proofing group |
| Spelling, check entire presentation | PPT 51 | Click REVIEW tab, in Proofing group click Spelling |
| Spelling, correct flagged word | PPT 51 | Right-click flagged word, click correct spelling |
| Start PowerPoint | PPT 5 | On Windows Start screen, click the PowerPoint 2013 tile |
| Start screen, scroll | WIN 9 | Move the pointer, drag the scroll bar |
| Start screen, zoom | WIN 2 | Move the pointer, click ▬ on the Start screen |
| Style, apply | WD 85 | Select text, click a style in the Styles group on HOME tab or click ▼ in the Styles group on HOME tab and click a style |
| Switch List, display | WIN 24 | Point to the upper-left corner of the screen, move the pointer down along left edge of the screen |
| Symbols, insert | PPT 94 | Click INSERT tab, in Symbols group click Symbol, click symbol, click Insert, click Close |
| Tab stop, set | WD 143 | See Reference box: Setting, Moving, and Clearing Tab Stops |
| Table, add or delete rows and columns | PPT 86 | Click in row or column, click TABLE TOOLS LAYOUT tab, in Rows & Columns group, click option |
| Table, change alignment in cells | PPT 93 | Click cell, click TABLE TOOLS LAYOUT tab, in Alignment group, click option |
| Table, change borders | PPT 90 | Click table, click TABLE TOOLS DESIGN tab, in Draw Borders group select options, in Table Styles group click Borders button arrow, click border |
| Table, change cell fill color | PPT 90 | Click table, click TABLE TOOLS DESIGN tab, in Table Styles group click Shading button arrow, click color |
| Table, change column width | PPT 88 | Point to column border, double-click or drag |
| Table, change row height | PPT 92 | Point to row border, double-click or drag |
| Table, change style | PPT 89 | Click table, click TABLE TOOLS FORMAT tab, in Table styles group, click style |
| Table, create in Datasheet view | AC 11 | See Reference box: Creating a Table in Datasheet View |
| Table, fill cell with pictures | PPT 91 | Click cell, click TABLE TOOLS DESIGN tab, in Table Styles group click Shading button arrow, click Picture, navigate to location, click picture file, click Insert |
| Table, insert | WD 124 | Click INSERT tab, click the Table button in the Tables group, move the pointer across the grid to select columns and rows |
| Table, insert on slide | PPT 85 | Click INSERT tab, in Tables group, click Table, click grid |
| Table, open in a database | AC 22 | Double-click the table in the Navigation Pane |
| Table, save in a database | AC 19 | See Reference box: Saving a Table |
| Table, sort | WD 133 | See Reference box: Sorting the Rows of a Table |
| Text box, insert | WD 188 | See Reference box: Inserting a Text Box |
| Text Effects, apply | WD 42 | Select text, click 🄰▾ in the Font group on HOME tab, click a text effect |
| Text file, import data from | AC 96 | Click the EXTERNAL DATA tab, click Text File in the Import & Link group, complete the import dialog boxes |
| Text, change format of | PPT 19 | Select text, click HOME tab, in Font group click appropriate button to apply formatting |
| Text, enter into a cell | EX 18 | Click cell, type entry, press Enter or Tab |

| TASK | PAGE # | RECOMMENDED METHOD |
|------|--------|---------------------|
| **Text, enter multiple lines in a cell** | EX 28 | Type the first line of the entry, press Alt+Enter, type the next line |
| **Text, move or copy** | PPT 22 | Select text, click HOME tab, in Clipboard group click Cut or Copy, click at new location, in Clipboard group click Paste |
| **Text, wrap within a cell** | EX 28 | Select the cell, click ▦ in the Alignment group on the HOME tab |
| **Theme and theme variant, change** | PPT 36 | Click DESIGN tab, in Themes group click theme |
| **Theme, apply from another presentation** | PPT 72 | Click DESIGN tab, in Themes group click More button, click Browse for Themes, navigate to location, click presentation, click Apply |
| **Theme, apply to a form** | AC 185 | *See* Reference box: Applying a Theme to a Form |
| **Theme, change for workbook** | EX 107 | Click the Themes button in the Themes group on the PAGE LAYOUT tab, click a theme |
| **Theme, select new** | WD 89 | Click DESIGN tab, click Themes button in the Document Formatting group, click a theme |
| **Touch Mode, switch to** | PPT 6 | On Quick Access Toolbar, click ▾, click Touch/Mouse mode if not selected, click 👆, click Touch |
| **Touch mode, turn on** | WD 5 | Click ▾ on the Quick Access toolbar, click Touch/Mouse Mode, click Touch |
| **Transition, change** | PPT 100 | *See* Reference box: Adding Transitions |
| **Unnumbered list, create** | PPT 17 | Select list or placeholder, click HOME tab, in Paragraph group click ▤ or ▤ to deselect it |
| **Video, add to slide** | PPT 112 | *See* Reference box: Adding Videos Stored on Your Computer or Network |
| **Video, set a poster frame** | PPT 117 | On play bar, click time to display frame, click VIDEO TOOLS FORMAT tab, in Adjust group click Poster Frame, click Current Frame |
| **Video, trim** | PPT 118 | Click video, click VIDEO TOOLS PLAYBACK tab, in Editing group, click Trim Video, drag sliders, click OK |
| **View, change in File Explorer** | FM 12 | *See* Reference box: Changing the View in File Explorer |
| **Webpage, pin to Start screen from desktop application** | IB 19 | Click ⚙, click Add site to Start Screen, click Add |
| **Webpage, preview and print from desktop application** | IB 24 | Click ⚙, point to Print, click Print preview, click 🖨 |
| **Webpage, save from desktop application** | IB 26 | Click ⚙, point to File, click Save as, navigate to save location, select Save as type, enter filename, click Save |
| **Webpages, move between with app** | IB 8 | Click ◀ or ◁ and ▶ or ▷ |
| **Webpages, move between with desktop application** | IB 12 | Click ◀ or ▶ |
| **Website, visit** | IB 5 | Click in Address bar, type URL, press Enter |
| **Window, close** | WIN 26 | Click ✕ |
| **Window, maximize** | WIN 19 | Click ▢ |
| **Window, minimize** | WIN 19 | Click ▬ |
| **Window, move** | WIN 19 | Drag the title bar |

| TASK | PAGE # | RECOMMENDED METHOD |
|------|--------|--------------------|
| Window, resize | WIN 19 | Drag the edge or the corner of the window |
| Window, restore | WIN 19 | Click ⬒ |
| Windows 8 application, close | WIN 27 | Press Alt+F4 |
| Windows 8 application, snap | WIN 16 | Point to the upper-left corner of the screen, right-click the thumbnail, click Snap left or click Snap right |
| Windows 8 application, start | WIN 13 | Click the application's tile on the Start screen |
| Windows 8 application, switch to another open | WIN 24 | Display the Switch List, click the application's thumbnail |
| Windows 8 application, unsnap | WIN 16 | Drag the separator bar to left or right |
| Windows 8 desktop, display | WIN 2 | Click the Desktop tile on the Start screen |
| Windows 8, start | WIN 8 | Turn on the computer |
| Windows 8, turn off | WIN 30 | Display the Charms bar, click Settings, click Power, click Shut down |
| WordArt, convert text to | WD 204 | Select text, click 🖌, click INSERT tab, click the WordArt button in the Text group, click WordArt style |
| Workbook, close | EX 13 | Click the FILE tab, click Close |
| Workbook, create a new | EX 15 | Click the FILE tab, click New |
| Workbook, open an existing | EX 4 | Click the FILE tab, click Open, select the workbook file |
| Workbook, preview and print | EX 55 | Click the FILE tab, click Print |
| Workbook, save | EX 17 | Click 💾 on the Quick Access Toolbar |
| Worksheet, change orientation | EX 53 | Click the Orientation button in the Page Setup group on the PAGE LAYOUT tab, click Landscape or Portrait |
| Worksheet, change view | EX 52 | Click ▦, ▤, or ▥ on the status bar |
| Worksheet, copy | EX 16 | Hold down Ctrl and drag a sheet tab to a new location |
| Worksheet, delete | EX 17 | Right-click a sheet tab, click Delete |
| Worksheet, insert | EX 16 | Click ⊕ |
| Worksheet, move | EX 16 | Drag the sheet tab to a new location |
| Worksheet, rename | EX 16 | Double-click the sheet tab, type a new name, press Enter |
| Worksheet, scale for printing | EX 54 | Set the width and height in the Scale to Fit group on the PAGE LAYOUT tab |
| Worksheets, move between | EX 8 | Click a sheet tab or click a tab scrolling button and then click a sheet tab |